The Cambridge Handbook of Technology and Employee Behavior

Experts from all areas of industrial-organizational (I-O) psychology describe how increasingly rapid technological change has affected the field. In each chapter, authors reveal how this has altered the meaning of I-O research within a particular subdomain and what steps must be taken to avoid I-O research from becoming obsolete. This handbook presents a forward-looking review of I-O psychology's understanding of both workplace technology and how technology is used in I-O research methods. Using interdisciplinary perspectives to further this understanding and serving as a focal text from which this research will grow, it tackles three main questions facing the field. First, how has technology affected I-O psychological theory and practice to date? Second, given the current trends in both research and practice, could I-O psychological theories be rendered obsolete? Third, what are the highest priorities for both research and practice to ensure I-O psychology remains appropriately engaged with technology moving forward?

RICHARD N. LANDERS is Associate Professor, John P. Campbell Distinguished Professor of Industrial and Organizational Psychology, Department of Psychology, University of Minnesota, USA.

The Cambridge Handbook of Technology and Employee Behavior

Edited by

Richard N. Landers
University of Minnesota

CAMBRIDGE
UNIVERSITY PRESS

University Printing House, Cambridge CB2 8BS, United Kingdom

One Liberty Plaza, 20th Floor, New York, NY 10006, USA

477 Williamstown Road, Port Melbourne, VIC 3207, Australia

314–321, 3rd Floor, Plot 3, Splendor Forum, Jasola District Centre, New Delhi – 110025, India

79 Anson Road, #06–04/06, Singapore 079906

Cambridge University Press is part of the University of Cambridge.

It furthers the University's mission by disseminating knowledge in the pursuit of education, learning, and research at the highest international levels of excellence.

www.cambridge.org
Information on this title: www.cambridge.org/9781108476706
DOI: 10.1017/9781108649636

First published 2019

Printed and bound in Great Britain by Clays Ltd, Elcograf S.p.A.

A catalogue record for this publication is available from the British Library.

Library of Congress Cataloging-in-Publication Data
Names: Landers, Richard N., editor.
Title: The Cambridge handbook of technology and employee behavior / edited by Richard N. Landers, University of Minnesota.
Description: Cambridge, United Kingdom; New York, NY : Cambridge University Press, 2019.
Identifiers: LCCN 2018034519 | ISBN 9781108476706
Subjects: LCSH: Employees – Effect of technological innovations on. | Employees – Effect of automation on. | Organizational behavior. | Psychology, Industrial.
Classification: LCC HD6331 .C2665 2019 | DDC 302.3/5–dc23
LC record available at https://lccn.loc.gov/2018034519

ISBN 978-1-108-47670-6 Hardback
ISBN 978-1-108-70132-7 Paperback

Cambridge University Press has no responsibility for the persistence or accuracy of URLs for external or third-party internet websites referred to in this publication and does not guarantee that any content on such websites is, or will remain, accurate or appropriate.

I dedicate this handbook to my wife, Amy, who has supported me completely in every step of my professional career, all the way from my humble beginnings as a lowly graduate student.

Amy, I would not have seen the success I have today without you, and I am forever thankful that you have been here with me for every step. These will always be our successes, together.

Contents

Notes on Contributors

Editor

RICHARD N. LANDERS is an associate professor of psychology and holds the John P. Campbell Distinguished Associate Professorship of Industrial/Organizational Psychology at the University of Minnesota, Twin Cities. His research program concerns the use of innovative technologies in assessment, employee selection, adult learning, and research methods, with his work appearing in *Journal of Applied Psychology, Industrial and Organizational Psychology, Computers in Human Behavior, Simulation & Gaming,* and *Psychological Methods,* among others. His research and writing have been featured in *Forbes, Business Insider, Science News, Popular Science, Maclean's,* and the *Chronicle of Higher Education,* among others. He currently serves as Associate Editor of the *International Journal of Selection & Assessment, Simulation & Gaming* and the *International Journal of Gaming and Computer-Mediated Simulations.* In 2016, he was awarded a Certificate of Recognition for his research on big data presented to the Society for Industrial and Organizational Psychology and in 2015 was Old Dominion University's nominee for the State Council of Higher Education in Virginia's Outstanding Faculty Award in the "Rising Star" category.

Contributors

SEYMOUR ADLER is a partner in the Talent Advisory practice at Aon. He has served as co-practice leader for the Talent Consulting practice at Aon and as head of the Global Leadership Practice Council. Seymour directs the development and implementation of leadership development, talent assessment, succession, and talent management programs for organizations across a variety of industries. He has partnered with leading US and global organizations in both the private and public sectors to enhance capabilities in leadership assessment and development, and talent and performance management. Seymour was a founder and principal of Assessment Solutions Incorporated, a firm he helped take public in 1997, which was acquired by Aon in 2001. In addition to a forty-year career as a practitioner, Seymour has taught in graduate programs at Purdue University, Stevens Institute of Technology, Tel Aviv University, New York University, and currently is an adjunct professor at Hofstra University's doctoral program in Applied Organizational

Psychology. A graduate of the Doctoral Program in Industrial-Organizational Psychology at New York University, Seymour is a Fellow of the Society of Industrial-Organizational Psychology and the American Psychological Association, has served as President of the Metropolitan New York Association of Applied Psychology, and has contributed extensively to both the scientific and practitioner literatures in Industrial-Organizational Psychology. He is a frequent presenter at SIOP and other professional conferences and is the co-editor of *Technology Enhanced Assessment of Talent* in the SIOP Professional Practice book series.

MICHAEL "BO" ARMSTRONG is a hiring innovation selection and assessment research analyst at Google. Bo graduated with his PhD in Industrial-Organizational Psychology from Old Dominion University in 2018 and with his Bachelor's degree in psychology from Western Kentucky University in 2013. He is a leading authority on the gamification of training and employee assessment, working as a consultant to several companies in the development and validation of game-based assessment products. Bo has published his work on gamification in several outlets, including the *International Journal of Training & Development, Simulation & Gaming, Computers in Human Behavior, Industrial-Organizational Psychology: Perspectives on Science and Practice*, and several handbook chapters. Apart from his paid and pro bono consulting work, Bo has worked as an applied social scientist with the US Department of Defense and as an adjunct psychology instructor at ODU.

WINFRED ARTHUR, JR. is a professor of psychology and management at Texas A&M University. He is a Fellow of the Society for Industrial and Organizational Psychology, the Association of Psychological Science, and the American Psychological Association. He is an associate editor of Human Performance, and currently serves on the editorial boards of *Journal of Applied Psychology, Personnel Psychology, Journal of Business and Psychology, Industrial and Organizational Psychology: Perspectives on Science and Practice*, and *Personnel Assessment and Decisions*. He is also a past associate editor of *Journal of Applied Psychology*. His current research interests are in the areas of personnel psychology with an emphasis in testing, selection, and validation, and individual and team training. He has extensive experience in conceptualizing, developing, and directing projects and research in these areas and has also published extensively in these areas as well.

ELENA M. AUER is an Industrial-Organizational Psychology doctoral student at the University of Minnesota. She graduated from The George Washington University in 2016 where she earned a BA in Psychology and Organizational Sciences with an I-O concentration. She earned a MS in Industrial-Organizational Psychology at Old Dominion University in 2018. Her research interests include the use of innovative technology in employee selection and methodology. She has presented, published, and conducted research on numerous topics including machine learning, big data, natural language processing, automatic interview/resume scoring, gamification, and unproctored internet testing.

LARISSA K. BARBER earned her PhD in Industrial-Organizational Psychology from Saint Louis University in 2010. She is currently an associate professor in the Social/Industrial-Organizational Psychology program at Northern Illinois University. She teaches graduate and undergraduate courses in occupational health psychology, personnel psychology, and organizational research methods (with a focus on work-life balance). She conducts research on the topics of work-life balance, employee stress and well-being, and sleep. In 2015, she received grant funding from the Society of Human Resource Management to support her work on how organizational policies and family-supportive culture affects employees' connectedness to work via technology (workplace telepressure), and subsequently employee recovery and health. Her research has been published in a variety of peer-reviewed outlets, including the *Journal of Applied Psychology, Journal of Occupational Health Psychology, Stress & Health, Applied Psychology: Health and Well-Being, Organizational Research Methods*, and the *Journal of Organizational Behavior*. In 2017, she received an Early Career Achievement Award for exceptional early career contributions to the science of occupational health psychology. She is also an associate editor at *Stress & Health*. Her professional affiliations include the American Psychological Association, Society for Industrial and Organizational Psychology, Society for the Teaching of Psychology, Association for Psychological Science, Midwestern Psychological Association, and the Society for Occupational Health Psychology.

MATT BARNEY is the founder and CEO of LeaderAmp, a funded startup with a mobile platform for assessment, and mobile expert and artificially intelligent coaching. He has held senior and innovative organizational psychological leadership roles for over twenty years at multinationals, most recently as an expat at Infosys, where he led an evidence-based, coaching-centric model for global leader development. In prior roles with AT&T, Motorola, and Sutter Health he authored six books, delivered 178 keynotes in thirteen countries and was awarded five technology patents. He currently has three AI assessment and coaching-related patents pending. He holds a BS in Psychology from the University of Wisconsin-Madison; and an MA and PhD in Industrial-Organizational Psychology from the University of Tulsa.

KELLY A. BASILE is an assistant professor in the Department of Business and Economics at Emmanuel College in Boston, MA. She holds a PhD in Organizational Behavior from the London School of Economics and Political Science. Her research interests focus on the boundary conditions between work and non-work activities, the impact of organizational as well as national culture on these boundaries as the impact of fit between boundary preference and organizational supply of segmenting vs. integrating practices. More recently, she has also studied the development of boundary management strategies in pre-professional (intern) roles, the relationship between employee relations and corporate social responsibility, as well as global leadership. In addition to her academic research experience, Dr. Basile worked in commercial research and consulting for over a decade, and she was involved in the design and implementation of hundreds of qualitative and quantitative research projects across a range of public and private industry sectors. She also holds a Master's in Business Administration from Babson College and a Master's in Social Work from Boston University and is a Fellow of the Higher Education Academy.

TALYA N. BAUER (PhD, Purdue University) teaches and conducts research across the employee lifecycle on recruitment, selection, HR analytics, onboarding, and leadership and has received NSF, NIH, OTREC, SHRM Foundation, and SIOP Foundation grants to support her research. She has worked with dozens of organizations and has been a Visiting Scholar in France, Spain, and at Google Headquarters as well as giving keynote addresses in Australia, Greece, Spain, the UK, and the United States. Her work has been published in multiple outlets including the *Academy of Management Journal, Academy of Management Perspectives, Journal of Applied Psychology, Journal of Management, Organizational Behavior and Human Decision Processes*, and *Personnel Psychology*. She is the area director within the School of Business for the Management & Leadership undergraduate degree option as well as for the Human Resource Management option. She has won awards from PSU, including the Branford Millar Award, Civic Engagement Award, and Teaching with Technology Award. Externally, she was awarded Purdue University's Distinguished Woman Scholar Award, the Academy of Management's HR Division Innovative Teaching Award, as well as SIOP's Distinguished Teaching Award. She has co-authored textbooks including the titles *Organizational Behavior, Principles of Management*, and *Psychology and Work: Introduction to Industrial and Organizational Psychology*. She is the incoming President of SIOP, a 9,000-member organization focused on the practice and study of people at work (www.siop.org). She currently serves as an associate editor for the *Journal of Applied Psychology* (and is the former editor of *Journal of Management*). Her work has been discussed by *BusinessWeek, New York Times, Wall Street Journal, Harvard Business Review, USA Today*, and NPR's *All Things Considered*. She is a Fellow of the SIOP, the American Psychological Association, and the Association for Psychological Science.

T. ALEXANDRA BEAUREGARD is an associate professor in Human Resource Management at Middlesex University Business School, where she co-chairs the Gender and Diversity Research Cluster. Alexandra's research interests are centered on the work-life interface, flexible working arrangements, and diversity management. She has published widely on these topics in academic journals and in practitioner outlets, as well as authoring chapters in a number of edited scholarly books and teaching-oriented texts. As well as presenting her research to academic audiences at international conferences, Alexandra is committed to knowledge exchange and impact. She has carried out commissioned research for both public- and private-sector organizations such as Acas, Avon UK, and LinkedIn, and has delivered a number of invited lectures on the topics of gender equality, diversity management, and flexible working to organizations such as the Chartered Institute of Management Accountants, Citywealth, the Columbia Business School Alumni Association, the Financial Conduct Authority, Forward Ladies, Handelsbanken, KPMG, and Shell. She has also spoken on these topics for mainstream media outlets (e.g., BBC World News, CNN, the Daily Mail, Channel 4 News, BBC Radio FiveLive, Share Radio, City AM). Alexandra serves on the editorial boards of *Work, Employment, and Society, Journal of Organizational Behavior, British Journal of Management, International Journal of Management Reviews, Canadian Journal of Administrative Sciences*, and *Equality, Diversity and Inclusion: An International Journal*. Alexandra also serves in elected leadership roles for the Gender and Diversity Division of the Academy of Management, and the Technology, Work and Family Special Interest Group of the Work and Family Researchers Network.

TARA S. BEHREND is an associate professor of Industrial and Organizational Psychology at The George Washington University, in Washington, DC. Her research group, the Workplaces and Virtual Environments (WAVE) lab, focuses on understanding and resolving barriers to computer-mediated work effectiveness, especially in the areas of training, recruitment, and selection. Her research in this arena has been published widely in technology and psychology outlets. She is also interested in career decision-making, specifically relating to STEM fields; her work in this area has been funded by a research grant from the National Science Foundation. She is a previous Cyber Initiative Fellow at Stanford's Center for Advanced Study in the Behavioral Sciences. She provides consulting for a range of public and private organizations globally, in the areas of training, selection, and workforce development. Her work has been covered in popular press outlets such as *Forbes Magazine* and the *Wall Street Journal*. She is an active member of SIOP, APA, and APS. She holds a PhD in Psychology from North Carolina State University. She is the editor of the *Industrial-Organizational Psychologist*.

MARGARET E. BEIER is an associate professor of Industrial and Organizational Psychology at Rice University in Houston, TX. She received her BA from Colby College, and her MS and PhD degrees from the Georgia Institute of Technology. Margaret's research examines the influence of individual differences in age, gender, abilities, and motivation as related to success in educational and organizational environments. In particular, her work examines the cognitive, attitudinal, and motivational determinants of job and training performance, as well as the influence of these factors on lifelong development and learning. Her work has been funded by the National Science Foundation and widely published in outlets such as *Journal of Applied Psychology*, and the *Journal of Business and Psychology, Educational Psychology, Psychology and Aging*, and *Psychological Bulletin*. She currently serves on the editorial boards of *Journal of Applied Psychology, Psychological Bulletin*, the *Journal of Business and Psychology*, and *Work, Aging, and Retirement*. She is a Fellow of the Society for Industrial and

Organizational Psychologists (SIOP) and a Fellow of the Association for Psychological Science (APS).

BRADFORD S. BELL is an associate professor of Human Resource Studies and Director of Executive Education in the School of Industrial and Labor Relations at Cornell University. He received his BA in Psychology from the University of Maryland at College Park and his MA and PhD in Industrial and Organizational Psychology from Michigan State University. Dr. Bell's research interests include training and development, team development and effectiveness, and virtual work. His research has appeared in a number of journals, including the *Journal of Applied Psychology, Personnel Psychology, Human Resource Management, Academy of Management Learning & Education, International Journal of Human Resource Management, Group and Organization Management*, and the *International Journal of Selection and Assessment*. In addition, Dr. Bell has published numerous chapters that have appeared in edited research volumes. Dr. Bell was awarded the Early Career Achievement Award by the HR Division of the Academy of Management and he is a former editor of *Personnel Psychology*.

BHARATI B. BELWALKAR has earned her Master's degree in I-O Psychology from Florida Institute of Technology and her PhD in the same field from Louisiana Tech University. She has previously worked for the City of Jacksonville and Aon Hewitt specifically in the areas of job analysis, test development, and data analytics. Bharati is currently working for the City of New Orleans in a Personnel Administrator role. During her tenure at the City, she has led the City through its online performance management system and has re-engineered some of the selection and training practices. Other than her applied I-O work, she enjoys research; her interests are personnel selection, workplace diversity, and proactive personality. As a recent graduate and a young practitioner, she cares deeply about issues related to I-O education and training.

FRANK BOSCO is a member of the Department of Management at Virginia Commonwealth University. His research spans the areas of human resource management, organizational behavior, and organizational research methods. Dr. Bosco is especially interested in employee staffing (e.g., employee selection), cognitive ability testing, meta-analysis, big data, open science, and approaches for summarizing entire scientific literatures. His research appears in outlets such as *Journal of Applied Psychology, Journal of Management, Organizational Research Methods, Personnel Psychology*, and *Science*. Dr. Bosco is co-founder of metaBUS.org, a winner of the 2013 National Endowment for the Humanities' Digging into Data Challenge, and currently or previously funded by the National Science Foundation, SHRM Foundation, Social Sciences and Humanities Research Council, Canadian Centre for Advanced Leadership, and the VCU Presidential Research Quest Fund. The project enables researchers and practitioners to make sense of more than 1,000,000 research findings by navigating an easy-to-understand "map" of constructs that conducts instant meta-analyses on virtually any topic in the scientific space.

ANTHONY (TONY) S. BOYCE is a partner with Aon's Assessment Solutions practice. Dr. Boyce has more than twelve years of experience partnering with clients to help them align their human capital practices to enable achievement of their organizations' goals. In his current role, he directs a team of PhDs, data scientists, and other colleagues to develop assessment and leadership strategies, tools, and points-of-view that help organizations identify, develop, and retain top talent. He has worked with a number of Fortune 500 companies (e.g., Anheuser-Busch Inbev, IBM, Kellogg Company, Marriott, McDonald's, Procter & Gamble, Prudential Financial), and federal government agencies (e.g., Federal Reserve, Internal Revenue Service, Transportation Security Administration) providing external and internal consulting services. His work has predominately focused on the development, validation, and implementation of innovative, impactful and legally defensibly selection assessments for a variety of jobs (e.g., executive-level, sales/business development, consulting, professional, and manufacturing). The type of assessments he has been responsible for developing and implementing include work simulations, interviews, job knowledge, biographical data, situational judgment, personality, and various types of traditional and computerized adaptive tests. Dr. Boyce's experience also includes extensive work in competency modeling, job and needs analysis, and ROI analysis. Dr. Boyce received his PhD in Industrial-Organizational Psychology from Michigan State University, the top-ranked school in the USA. He has published several book chapters, research papers in leading journals (e.g., *Journal of Applied Psychology*, *Journal of Management*, *Applied Psychology: An International Review*), and has presented dozens of papers at the annual meetings of the Society for Industrial and Organizational Psychology and the Academy of Management. Dr. Boyce has also received several professional awards, including the prestigious Society for Industrial and Organizational Psychology's M. Scott Myers Award for Applied Research recognizing his leadership in creating the Adaptive Employee Personality Test (ADEPT-15®) and the Distinguished Early Career Contributions Award for Practice.

BRITTANY C. BRADFORD is a doctoral student in Industrial/Organizational Psychology at Rice University, where she studies learning, motivation, and education. She holds a BBA in Finance from Texas Christian University, where she graduated summa cum laude, and studied psychology as a post-baccalaureate student at Portland State University. Her recent research has focused on post-secondary educational interventions and STEM interest and retention.

CHARALAMPOS CHELMIS is an assistant professor in Computer Science at the University at Albany, State University of New York, and director of the UAlbany Intelligent Big Data Analytics, Applications, and Systems (IDIAS) Lab. Dr. Chelmis specializes in Network Science and Big Data analytics with a proven track record on the analysis, modeling, and accurate prediction of process dynamics on large-scale real-world networks. He is guest co-editor of the *Springer Encyclopedia of Social Network Analysis and Mining*, and serves as PC member of international conferences including the World Wide Web Conference, the International AAAI Conference on Web and Social Media, and the IEEE/ACM International

Conference on Advances in Social Networks Analysis and Mining. Dr. Chelmis is also a reviewer of journals including *PLOS ONE, IEEE Transactions on Knowledge and Data Engineering, IEEE Transactions on Computational Social Systems*, and *IEEE Transactions on Information Forensics and Security*. Among other distinctions, Dr. Chelmis, along with Dr. Anand Panangadan and Ajitesh Srivastava, has earned national recognition for developing a novel machine-learning model that delivers accurate six-month forecasts of the spread of the Chikungunya virus in fifty-five different countries and territories in North, Central and South America and the Caribbean as part of the 2015 DARPA Chikungunya Forecasting Challenge. Before joining the University at Albany, Dr. Chelmis was Senior Research Associate with the Department of Electrical Engineering at the Viterbi School of Engineering, University of Southern California. Dr. Chelmis received his PhD and MSc degrees in Computer Science in 2013 and 2010 respectively from the University of Southern California, and BEng in Computer Engineering and Informatics from the University of Patras, Greece.

ANDREW B. COLLMUS is a doctoral student in Industrial-Organizational Psychology at Old Dominion University. He graduated with honors from Colorado State University earning a Bachelor of Science in psychology with an I-O concentration. Since then, Andrew has authored or co-authored eight peer-reviewed publications and ten peer-reviewed presentations at scientific conferences. He and recent ODU Alumnus Mike Litano write a recurring column "Lost in Translation" in SIOP's trade journal, *The Industrial-Organizational Psychologist*. Andrew's research broadly focuses on selection, assessment, machine learning and analytics, and gamification.

IOANA C. CRISTEA is a Postdoctoral Researcher in the Technology Management Program at the University of California, Santa Barbara. Her research focuses on how organizations can leverage their globally distributed workforce to improve collaboration and knowledge sharing with the help of communication technologies and physical space. In her current research projects, she is taking a qualitative approach to study employee presence management and sacrifice in the workplace. Dr. Cristea received her PhD from Aarhus University, Denmark. During her doctoral studies, she was a SCANCOR Visiting Scholar at Stanford University and a Visiting Scholar at Northwestern University. Prior to her PhD, she completed a double Master of Science Degree as a EURECA Scholar at Aarhus University, Denmark, and the Technical University in Munich, Germany.

ARLA DAY is a professor in Industrial/Organizational Psychology at Saint Mary's University, specializing in Occupational Health Psychology, and she is the director of the CN Centre for Occupational Health & Safety, and a founding member of the Centre for Leadership Excellence. She is a Fellow of the Canadian Psychological Association, and she was a Canada Research Chair at Saint Mary's University in I/O psychology for ten years. Arla has been Associate Editor at the *Journal of Occupational Health Psychology* and a Consulting Editor at the *European Journal of Work & Organizational Psychology*. She regularly reviews for a number of scholarly journals, and she is currently a board member of the *Journal of Occupational Health Psychology* and *Work & Stress*. She currently serves as an international advisor on the Stockholm Stress Centre's Advisory Board, and was awarded an Erskine Fellowship from the University of Canterbury in Christchurch, New Zealand, to teach and conduct research on healthy workplaces. Arla served on the American Psychological Association's Psychology in the Workplace Network, which coordinates the state and provincial psychologically healthy workplace awards and programs, and she has chaired the Nova Scotia Psychological Healthy Workplace Program committee since 2005, organizing healthy workplace workshops and honoring excellence in provincial organizations. Arla is the project director for the SSHRC/CIHR-funded EMPOWER Partnership, a collaborative group of researchers and organizations, workplace experts, and stakeholders, whose goals are to provide evidence-based solutions to foster psychologically healthy workplaces by empowering employees facing chronic health and caregiving demands. EMPOWER programs focus on supporting individual employees, strengthening groups, and developing leaders to create overall healthy workplaces. Arla has authored articles, chapters, and books pertaining to healthy workers and workplaces, respect and civility in the workplace, leadership, occupational stress, employee well-being, and work-life balance. Her funded research programs are focused on developing and implementing valid organizational and individual initiatives and training programs. She consults with a number of private and public organizations, focusing on organizational health issues, and she regularly gives workshops and talks on issues related to her expertise.

SUZANNE C. DE JANASZ is currently a visiting professor of Management and Conflict Analysis and Resolution (a joint appointment) at George Mason University in Fairfax, Virginia. Prior to this appointment, Dr. de Janasz was the Gleed Distinguished Chair of Business at Seattle University, and a professor of Leadership and Organization Development at IMD in Lausanne, Switzerland. Her research on mentoring, careers, authenticity, work–family conflict, and leadership appears in such journals as *Harvard Business Review*, *Academy of Management Executive*, *Journal of Organizational Behavior*, *Journal of Vocational Behavior*, *British Journal of Management*, *Career Development International*, and *Journal of Management Education*, and has been featured in domestic and international newspapers, online publications, and radio programs. The latest editions of her co-authored textbooks (*Interpersonal Skills in Organizations*, 6/e; *Negotiation and Dispute Resolution*, 2/e) were released in 2018, and she's currently working on a book that follows from and expands upon her co-authored HBR piece on the mentoring of CEOs.

RACHEL C. DREIBELBIS is an associate on the assessment-solutions team at Aon and a doctoral candidate in Industrial and Organizational Psychology at the University of South Florida (USF). She holds an MA in I-O Psychology from USF and a BS in Psychology from Penn State University. She has experience in assessment development, validation, and employee selection and engagement and has previously worked in the US Department of Defense and the Walt Disney Company. Her research interests span the human-technology interface, and include technology based assessments, cybersecurity-related behaviors at work, and cybersecurity personnel training and performance. Rachel has served as a volunteer consultant for non-profit organizations around the country since July 2014.

NATHANAEL FAST is an associate professor of management and organization at the University of Southern California's Marshall School of Business, and director of the Hierarchy, Networks, and Technology Lab at USC. He completed his PhD in Organizational Behavior at Stanford University. His research focuses on the tools people use to lead, organize, and influence others, both in face-to-face and virtual contexts. His work examines the determinants and consequences of power and status hierarchies in groups and organizations as well as the social psychological mechanisms that lead people, ideas, and practices to become and stay prominent. He also studies the psychology of social networks and the causes and consequences of adopting and using new technologies in the workplace. He co-founded the Psychology of Technology Institute in 2016 and serves on the editorial boards for the *Journal of Personality and Social Psychology, Personality and Social Psychology Bulletin*, and *Organizational Behavior and Human Decision Processes*.

DIANNE P. FORD is a professor in the Faculty of Business Administration at Memorial University of Newfoundland, St. John's, Canada. Her research interests focus at areas that utilize her double major in Organizational Behavior and Management Information Systems. Her topics of research include workplace cyber-aggression, workplace cyber-deviance, sexual harassment, knowledge management, perceived value of knowledge, cross-cultural implications for MIS and knowledge flows, trust, job engagement, and disengagement from knowledge sharing. Dr. Ford is an associate editor for the *Journal of Organizational Computing and Electronic Commerce* and has served as a guest co-editor on a double-special issue on social media and knowledge management for JOCEC. Dr. Ford has served as a co-chair of mini-tracks for Hawaii International Conference for Systems Sciences, Divisional Editor and Divisional co-chair for the Organizational Behaviour Division of Administrative Sciences Association of Canada, and is a member of the editorial board for *International Journal of Knowledge Management*. Dr. Ford's publications may be found in *IEEE: Transactions in Engineering Management, Journal of Knowledge Management, Journal of Managerial Psychology, Knowledge Management Research & Practice, Journal of Applied Social Psychology, Journal of Organizational Computing and Electronic Commerce, International Journal on Knowledge Management, International Journal of Workplace Health Management*, and she has presented her research at Academy of Management Annual Meeting, Hawaii International Conference for Systems Sciences, Americas Conferences for Information Systems, Workplace Health & Safety, Administrative Sciences Association of Canada, and Canadian Psychological Association.

LORI FOSTER is a professor in the Department of Psychology at North Carolina State University (USA), where she leads the 4D Lab devoted to research at the intersection of work, psychology, technology, and development. She also holds an honorary professorship in the Faculty of Commerce at the University of Cape Town (South Africa). She is a University Faculty Scholar at North Carolina State University, and recently completed a two-year (2014–2016) fellowship in Washington with the White House Social and Behavioral Sciences Team, as well as an assignment as Behavioural Sciences Advisor to the United Nations (2016). Prior to her career in academia, Lori worked for Personnel Decisions Research Institutes. She earned her PhD in Industrial-Organizational (I-O) Psychology in 1999. Lori's areas of research and practice expertise include behavioral insights, humanitarian work psychology, workforce development, computer-mediated work behavior, and organizational survey design and analysis. Her current efforts focus on how these areas and other aspects of I-O psychology can be used to enrich and improve work carried out for the purpose of addressing the most pressing economic, social, and environmental challenges facing our world today. Lori has delivered hundreds of papers and talks to audiences in countries spanning six continents. Her printed scholarship has taken the form of refereed journal articles, book chapters, authored, and edited books. Her work has been featured in popular media outlets such as *The Wall Street Journal*, *ARS Technica*, *Fast Company*, *NSF Science 360*, *US News and World Report*, *MSN Money*, *The Chronicle of Higher Education*, *Scientific American*, and National Public Radio. She is co-editor of several recent books: *Using I-O Psychology for the Greater Good* (with Julie Olson-Buchanan and Laura Koppes Bryan), *The Psychology of Workplace Technology* (with Michael Coovert), and *Internationalizing the Curriculum in Organizational Psychology* (with Richard Griffith and Brigitte Armon). She is currently co-editing a new book on *Workforce Readiness* with Fred Oswald and Tara Behrend. Lori has held visiting scholar appointments at universities around the world, including the London Business School, Singapore Management University, and the Universities of Valencia, Barcelona, and Bologna. As a scientist-practitioner, she has more than twenty years of experience as a consultant, applying the science of work to regional, state, national, and international organizations in the private and public sectors. She is a Fellow of the American Psychological Association (APA), the Association for Psychological Science (APS), and the Society for Industrial-Organizational Psychology (SIOP).

MAHYAR GARMSIRI is a candidate for an MSc in Management with a specialization in Organizational Behavior and Human Resources at Memorial University of Newfoundland. He graduated with a Hon. BSc in Psychology, Neuroscience and Behavior from McMaster University, then completed his diploma in Human Resources Management at McMaster's Centre of Continuing Education. After starting his MSc degree, he also worked as a research assistant in a project leader role. Mahyar supervises a team of undergraduate students to conduct experimental studies investigating disability biases in the performance appraisal process and leadership. The need for evidence-based practice drives his passion for research.

KONSTANTINA GEORGIOU is a post-doctoral Fellow at Athens University of Economics and Business, Greece, working on gamification in the employee selection process. She holds a doctoral degree in Organizational Behavior (PhD) from Athens University of Economics and Business. She carried out her bachelor studies (BSc) in Business Administration and her master studies in Human Resource Management at Athens University of Economics and Business. Following the completion of her MSc, she worked as an HR Assistant at the HR Department of Beiersdorf Hellas. She has also worked on various research projects in the field of employee selection. She teaches human resources management and organizational behavior at the undergraduate, postgraduate, and executive training level (e.g., Open Hellenic University, University of Liverpool online, AUEB), and she has significant experience conducting seminars in career counseling and job seeking. She has published her work in international peer-reviewed academic journals (e.g., *International Journal of Selection and Assessment*) while her research has appeared in major scientific conferences (e.g., *Academy of Management, Society for Industrial and Organizational Psychology, European Association of Work and Organizational Psychology*). Her research interests focus mostly on employee recruitment and selection and job search, as well as on the use of serious games in employee selection.

NILOOFAR GHODS is an executive coach and senior leadership consultant at Cisco Systems. She helped establish and currently leads Cisco's coaching practice with the goal to help democratize coaching across the business, making coaching services available to over 10,000 Cisco leaders of all levels. In addition to coaching, she assesses and facilitates team process for Cisco's top 300 senior executives. She is a published expert on the topic of virtual coaching effectiveness. Prior to Cisco, Niloofar consulted for YSC, a global leadership consultancy firm, assessing and coaching the senior executives of Fortune 100 and other multinational organizations. As part of her time at YSC, she lived in South Africa and coached South African leaders on key leadership transitions within a complex political environment. Prior to YSC, Niloofar worked at Dell in their Global Talent Management Team responsible for designing and delivering integrated talent management processes and programs for Dell's 100,000 employees globally. Niloofar has also worked closely with the renowned leadership expert Marshall Goldsmith and the Right Management Consultancy group. Niloofar holds a doctoral degree in both Industrial Organizational and Clinical Psychology from Alliant International University and a BA in Psychology from the University of California at Irvine. Her doctoral research, funded in part by an award by the Foundation of Coaching, evaluated a large-scale distance coaching program. Niloofar is an active affiliate of The Institute of Coaching at Harvard Medical School and member of the Leadership Council of the Society of Consulting Psychology. She is a member of the American Psychological Association, Society of Consulting Psychology and Industrial Organizational Psychology.

CARTER GIBSON has worked as a senior associate at Shaker on projects across a range of applied contexts requiring expertise in test construction, validation, and the identification of high-potential talent. He assists clients in the development and ongoing maintenance of theoretically and empirically based pre-hire selection systems supporting hiring decisions. His specific role on the Shaker Insights Team is to lead ongoing research on topics that matter the most to practitioners, such as completion rates, response distortion on high-stakes testing, and best practicing for norming assessments. Before starting with Shaker, Carter assisted in projects ranging from the creation of theoretical models of leadership for long-duration space exploration for NASA, to identifying strategies for improving ethics training programs for the NIH, as well as working with the FAA to implement a developmental feedback program. His work on understanding the role of networking in organizations was formally recognized as the paper of the year for Career Development International, and has had work appear in many journals, the *Journal of Applied Psychology*, *Psychology of Aesthetics, Creativity, and the Arts*, and the *Journal of Creative Behavior*.

KARL GIUSEFFI is Director of Research Consultants at Talent Plus, Inc. He works effectively to accurately provide clear data insights to complicated questions through quantitative and qualitative processes, ROI studies, benchmarking, and building new structured interviews and online assessments to help client partners select highly talented individuals into various roles. Giuseffi earned his BA in political science and criminal justice from the University of South Dakota. He has an MA in Political Science from the University of Nebraska-Lincoln and will soon earn his PhD upon completing his dissertation.

DARRIN M. GRELLE is currently a managing research scientist in the field of talent assessment. He has been the lead scientist for a large-scale computer adaptive testing program for ten years. He received his PhD in Applied Psychology from the University of Georgia in 2008, completing his dissertation using latent class growth modeling to better understand the performance growth trajectories of entry-level employees. His graduate training focused on psychometrics, and he has since used that training to lead the growth and development of one of the largest cognitive ability testing programs in employment talent assessment. His research interests include innovative cognitive question types and scoring algorithms for computer adaptive testing.

Specializing in Organizational Behavior and Human Resources, AMANDA J. HANCOCK is pursuing a PhD in Management at the Faculty of Business Administration, Memorial University of Newfoundland. Amanda has accumulated ten years of human resources and management experience through positions in the private sector with a development company, and a publicly funded healthcare organization. She was named a Fellow of the School of Graduate Studies upon completion of a Master's in Applied Health Services Research and holds a Bachelor of Commerce from Queen's University. Amanda has presented her research on employee well-being and gender at national and international academic conferences. Through a commitment to high-quality research and knowledge dissemination, she pursues her passion for leadership and diversity every day. She is an active member of the Women to Women Empowering Leadership Committee, and a volunteer member of the Board of Directors for Special Olympics NL and the national charity Fertile Future.

ADRIAN B. HELMS is a graduate of Old Dominion University (ODU) where he received his Bachelor of Science degree in Psychology in 2017. As an undergraduate, he participated in ODU's Undergraduate Research Apprenticeship Program and has worked with Dr. Richard Landers and Dr. Debra Major to cultivate his abilities in research. He is currently fine-tuning his research interests with a focus on STEM major embeddedness of minority groups. His research has been influenced by his Filipino culture. As past president of Old Dominion University's Chapter of Psi Chi, he has pushed for a better understanding of psychology for the betterment of his peers and university.

ROBERT D. HICKMAN is a graduate student at Memorial University, currently enrolled in the MSc in Management program. He also completed his undergrad at Memorial, graduating in 2016 with a Bachelor of Commerce degree. Robert's concentrations are organizational behavior and human resources, with a particular interest in goal setting and employee wellness. He has also presented his research at the ASAC international conference.

N. SHARON HILL is an associate professor of Management at The George Washington University School of Business. She received her PhD in Business and Management from the University of Maryland, College Park. Dr. Hill's research focuses on organizational change and virtual work, with an emphasis on virtual teams. A dominant theme in her research is the critical role that leadership at different levels of the organization plays in facilitating the success of both organizational change and virtual work. Her articles have appeared in multiple journals, including *Organizational Behavior and Human Decision Processes*, *Organization Science, Personnel Psychology, Leadership Quarterly*, and *Research in Personnel and Human Resource Management*.

JULIA E. HOCH holds a PhD in Industrial and Organizational Psychology. She taught courses in human resources management and organizational behavior at Michigan State University and the Technical Universities of Munich and Dresden, among others. Dr. Hoch currently teaches in the Department of Management, David Nazarian College of Business and Economics at California State University, Northridge. Dr. Hoch has published her work in the *Journal of Applied Psychology, Journal of Management, Journal of Business and Psychology, Human Resource Management Review* and others. In addition, she has written over a dozen peer handbook and book chapters and presented her research at various conferences in Europe and in the United States. Her research interests are in globally distributed work, such as virtual teams, team leadership, shared leadership, and diversity issues. She has consulted with companies, such as Avaya, Audi, Bosch, BehrGroup, BMW, Medtronic, Porsche Consulting, Volkswagen, and others. She is on the editorial board of *Human Resource Management Review* and *Research in Human Resource Management*.

MATT C. HOWARD is currently an assistant professor in the Mitchell College of Business at the University of South Alabama, and he received his PhD from the Pennsylvania State University in Industrial/Organizational Psychology. His research interests include, but are not limited to, employee training and development, applications of novel technologies to the workplace, personality, and statistics and methodologies. Matt's authored publications have appeared in *Organizational Research Methods*, *Journal of Organizational Behavior*, *Computers & Education*, *Computers in Human Behavior*, *International Journal of Human-Computer Interaction*, and many other outlets. His personal academic website is MattCHoward.com, which includes more information about this academic and professional pursuits.

A. JAMES ILLINGWORTH is an Industrial-Organizational (I-O) psychologist who works with organizations to implement evidence-based, technology-enabled talent solutions. Prior to his current position at Geode People as Director of Talent Solutions, he worked at PDRI and APTMetrics providing customized talent management consulting services to federal government agencies and Fortune 500 organizations across a wide range of industries and job levels. His areas of expertise include job analysis and competency modeling; assessment development, validation, and implementation; performance management; employee training and development; and the legal compliance and defensibility of personnel selection processes. Dr. Illingworth's research interests focus on the application of emerging technologies to hiring and promotional assessments, including the use of mobile devices, big data, machine learning, artificial intelligence (AI), and virtual/ augmented reality (VR/AR). His research has been published in the *International Journal of Selection & Assessment*, *Industrial & Organizational Psychology: Perspectives on Science & Practice*, *Journal of Business Psychology*, and *Personality & Individual Differences*, as well as a recent book chapter about big data talent assessment in *Big Data at Work: The Data Science Revolution and Organizational Psychology*. He also regularly presents at the annual conference of the Society for Industrial and Organizational Psychology (SIOP), and shares his passion and excitement for the application of technology to talent assessment through invited presentations to organizations and professional groups. Dr. Illingworth received his MS and PhD in I-O Psychology from The University of Akron in 2004.

RICHARD D. JOHNSON is an associate professor of Management, department chair, and director of the Human Resource Information Systems (HRIS) program at the University at Albany, State University of New York. He has published over fifty journal articles and book chapters on topics such as human resource technology, the psychological impacts of computing, training and e-learning, and issues surrounding the digital divide. His research has been published in outlets such as *Information Systems Research*, *Journal of the Association for Information Systems*, *Human Resource Management Review*, and the *International Journal of Human Computer Studies*. Dr. Johnson is a past chair of AIS SIGHCI and is a senior editor at Data Base and AIS Transactions on Human-Computer Interaction. He is also an editor of the books, *Human Resource Information Systems: Basics, Applications and Future Directions* and *The Wiley Blackwell Handbook of the Psychology of the Internet at Work.*

TRACY M. KANTROWITZ is Director, Talent Solutions at PDRI. She has fifteen years of experience developing innovative and award-winning talent management solutions, leading teams of industrial/organizational psychology experts and multidisciplinary product development teams, designing selection programs for organizations, and conducting market and scientific research related to assessment and talent management trends. She has published in leading peer-reviewed journals and presented at national scientific and client conferences, workshops, and educational webinars on topics such as computer adaptive testing, unproctored internet testing, and mobile assessment. Tracy has received multiple distinctions from the Society for Industrial and Organizational Psychology (SIOP), including the M. Scott Myers Award for applied research in the workplace, the Distinguished Early Career Contributions – Practice Award, and Fellow status. Tracy was Program Chair for the SIOP 2018 conference, past chair of the Professional Practice Committee for SIOP, and is an editorial board member of *Industrial-Organizational Psychology: Perspectives on Science and Practice* and *The Industrial-Organizational Psychologist*. Dr. Kantrowitz holds a PhD in Industrial/organizational Psychology from the Georgia Institute of Technology.

JONATHAN KIRSCHNER is the founder and CEO of AIIR Consulting. He is also a member of the AIIR Global Coaching Alliance through his executive coaching work. AIIR Consulting is a global consultancy that creates value for individuals and their organizations through robust, technologically enhanced leadership solutions. In 2009, Jonathan developed the AIIR® coaching method for achieving sustained behavioral change. He developed AIIR Consulting's technology platforms, including the Coaching Zone® and Enterprise Coaching Manager® (ECM), and is the creator of the mobile app Stress Check™, a stress assessment that has been downloaded by over 1.5 million people worldwide. As an executive coach and business psychologist, Jonathan's areas of expertise are helping leaders increase strategic thinking, bolster team effectiveness, harness emotional intelligence for results, increase influence, and better manage stress. He coaches senior leaders from the director level to the CEO, and his experiences span a range of sectors including financial services, technology, pharmaceutical, hospital, manufacturing, retail, chemicals, oil and gas, government, non-profit, and higher education.

CORNELIUS J. KÖNIG is a full professor of Work and Organizational Psychology at the Universität des Saarlandes in Saarbrücken, Germany. He received his PhD in Psychology from the Philipps-Universität Marburg, Germany. Before coming to Saarbrücken, he spent several years at the Universität Zürich. His main research interests are personnel selection, job insecurity and the management of layoffs, time management, and the research–practitioner gap. In the last years, he started to research on the use of latest computer science developments for training and personnel selection. He has published in outlets such as *Academy of Management Review, Journal of Applied Psychology, Personnel Psychology*, and *Computers in Human Behavior*. He is currently also the president of the section for work, organizational, and business psychology within the German Psychological Society.

STEVE W. J. KOZLOWSKI is a professor of Organizational Psychology at Michigan State University. He is a recognized authority in the areas of multilevel theory; team leadership and team effectiveness; and learning, training, and adaptation. The goal of his programmatic research is to generate actionable theory, research-based principles, and deployable tools to develop adaptive individuals, teams, and organizations. His research is, or has been, supported by the Agency for Health Research and Quality (AHRQ), the Air Force Office of Scientific Research (AFOSR), the Army Research Institute for the Behavioral and Social Sciences (ARI), the National Aeronautics and Space Administration (NASA), the National Science Foundation (NSF), and the Office of Naval Research (ONR), among others. His research has generated over \$10 M in funded work. He has produced over 500 articles, books, chapters, reports, and presentations. His work has been cited over 23,000 times (Google Scholar). Dr. Kozlowski is the recipient of the SIOP Distinguished Scientific Contributions Award and the INGRoup McGrath Award for Lifetime Achievement in the Study of Groups. He is Editor for the Oxford Series on Organizational Psychology and Behavior and Editor for the new SIOP/Oxford Organizational Science, Translation, and Practice Series. He is the former Editor-in-Chief and a former associate editor for the *Journal of Applied Psychology*. He is an editorial board member for the Academy of Management Review, the *Journal of Management*, and *Leadership Quarterly*, and has served on the editorial boards of the *Academy of Management Journal, Human Factors*, the *Journal of Applied Psychology*, and *Organizational Behavior and Human Decision Processes*. He is a Fellow of the American Psychological Association, the Association for Psychological Science, the International Association for Applied Psychology, and the Society for Industrial and Organizational Psychology (SIOP). He was President of SIOP (2015–2016) and is the SIOP Research and Science Officer (2017–2020). Dr. Kozlowski received his BA in psychology from the University of Rhode Island, and his MS and PhD degrees in organizational psychology from The Pennsylvania State University.

BENJAMIN KUMPF leads the Innovation Facility of the UN Development Programme (UNDP) in New York. He manages UNDP's Innovation Fund, a pooled funding vehicle created to support and scale innovations that address challenges related to poverty, governance, climate change, and gender equality across the globe. Benjamin advises internal and external clients on innovation and on achieving impact at scale. Benjamin has worked on social change, innovation and development for multiple years in Rwanda, Nepal, India, and Jordan. He has a Master's Degree in Political Science and Psychology from the University of Heidelberg, Germany.

MARKUS LANGER is research associate at the Department of Work and Organizational Psychology at the Universität des Saarlandes in Saarbrücken, Germany. In his research, he is connecting computer science and psychology. Specifically, he is conducting research on novel technologies for human resource management processes such as personnel selection and training. For example, he investigates virtual characters as interviewers; sensor-based recognition of verbal, paraverbal, and nonverbal behavior for personnel selection and training; and acceptance of novel technologies for human resource management purposes. Furthermore, he examines the use of serious games and gamification for human resource management. His work is published in *Computers in Human Behavior* and in the *International Journal of Selection and Assessment.*

PAUL M. LEONARDI is the Duca Family Professor of Technology Management at UC Santa Barbara. He holds appointments in the Technology Management Program and the Department of Communication. He is also the Investment Group of Santa Barbara Founding Director of the Master of Technology Management Program. Leonardi's research, teaching, and consulting focus on helping companies to create and share knowledge more effectively. He is interested in how implementing new technologies and harnessing the power of informal social networks can help companies take advantage of their knowledge assets to create innovative products and services.

YIN LIN is currently a managing research scientist at SHL Talent Measurement Solutions, and a PhD researcher at the University of Kent, United Kingdom. She holds a Master of Science in applied statistics from the University of Oxford, and a Master of Arts in mathematics from the University of Cambridge. Prior to her current roles, she worked as a statistician for the National Foundation for Educational Research in England and Wales. Her current research focuses on multidimensional item response theory, forced-choice response modeling, and computerized adaptive testing.

WOLFGANG MAASS (MAASS) is professor in Business Informatics and professor in Computer Science (co-opted) at Saarland University, scientific director at German Research Center for Artificial Intelligence (DFKI), and adjunct professor at the Department for Biomedical Informatics at Stony Brook School of Medicine, NY. He studied Computer Science at the RWTH Aachen and the Saarland University. His PhD in Computer Science at the Saarland University was funded by the German National Science Foundation (DFG). He was post-doc researcher at the Institute of Technology Management (ITEM) at the University of St. Gallen, Switzerland, where he also received his habilitation by the Department of Management. He was guest researcher at the National Center for Geographic Information and Analysis (NCGIA), UC Santa Barbara, CA, guest professor at the Department of Bioinformatics and Computational Biology at MD Anderson Cancer Center, University of Texas, TX, and at Stony Brook University Health Sciences Center School of Medicine, NY. In his research, he investigates digital transformation of industries applying methods of Artificial Intelligence. Results are mainly published in Information Systems, Computer Science and Computer Linguistic journals and conferences.

STANTON MAK is a doctoral student in the Organizational Psychology Program at Michigan State University. He received his BA in Psychology from University of California, Irvine. His research interests include team leadership and team effectiveness, motivation and performance, and employee training and development.

SEBASTIAN MARIN is a doctoral student at the University of Minnesota studying topics related to Industrial/Organizational Psychology. His research interests include how emerging technology is changing the way we behave in the workplace and how new innovative methods can be used to capture behavioral data. Broadly, he is also interested in research methods, open science, and the philosophy of science.

CHAD J. MARSHALL is a doctoral candidate at the University of South Alabama and currently serves as the Laboratory Demonstration Program Manager for the US Army Aviation and Missile Research, Development, and Engineering Center (AMRDEC) at Redstone Arsenal, Alabama. In this capacity, he serves on agency- and service-level panels focused on personnel, workplace development, and talent management within science and technology laboratories. He has served in numerous roles in both the public and private sectors including previous roles in human resources with responsibilities in training and human resources development. He studied business administration at Columbia College and chemistry and biology at the University of Tennessee at Chattanooga, and holds both a MBA and Bachelor's degree from Columbia College. His research interests include leadership, performance management, and employee development, with a special interest in professionals within the science, technology, engineering, and mathematics (STEM) workforce.

NICHOLAS R. MARTIN is a senior consultant with Aon with over fifteen years of consulting and test-development experience working in and consulting with private and public sector organizations. He consults in the areas of assessment and selection, employee and leadership development, and assessment strategy and implementation. He serves as the leader of the Global Products & Analytics division and is responsible for thought leadership and the design and development of Aon's next generation assessments and assessment and analytical methodologies, as well as the further refinement and development of legacy assessments. He also serves as subject matter expert to internal and external clients and supports the design of assessment interventions for Aon's clients. At Aon, he has worked with numerous Fortune 500 and 100 organizations supporting the design and implementation of innovative and legally sound selection systems that serve to support the entire human-capital lifecycle. Prior to joining Aon, Dr. Martin was a program manager of the USA Hire assessment program which is a government-wide selection testing initiative led by the US Office of Personnel Management. He supported the implementation of selection systems for agencies of all sizes to include enterprise programs for Cabinet-level Federal agencies. He has also worked as an independent consultant supporting selection programs for small and medium-sized companies. Dr. Martin received his PhD in I/O Psychology and an MA in Human Resources Management from The George Washington University. He has published numerous articles in leading, peer-reviewed journals and has presented dozens of papers and symposia at the annual meetings of the Society of Industrial-Organizational Psychology, American Psychological Association, and the International Personnel Assessment Council.

BERTOLT MEYER is a professor of Organizational Psychology at the Institute of Psychology at Chemnitz University of Technology, Germany. He received his PhD in Social and Organizational Psychology from Humbold University Berlin in 2008. His research focuses on social processes at the work place, including diversity, employee well-being, and leadership. He has a strong interest in research methods; some of his studies involve computer-based assessments of social behavior and he has contributed to the development of an R package for detecting faultlines. He is currently an associate editor at Small Group Research.

KRISTIE L. MCALPINE is an assistant professor in the School of Human Resources and Labor Relations at Michigan State University. She earned a PhD degree in Human Resource Studies at the School of Industrial and Labor Relations at Cornell University. Professor McAlpine conducts research in three related areas. Her primary interest is exploring the changing nature of employee work arrangements, specifically the increased flexibility in when and where employees conduct their work (e.g., telecommuting). She examines the effects of flexibility for individuals and teams and pays particular attention to the contextual factors that shape these relationships. In a second area of research, she evaluates how organizations manage diversity and inclusion and how it shapes the quality of employee relationships and experiences. Finally, in a third area of research, she studies how individuals navigate the work-family interface and make decisions about their work and non-work lives in the context of dual career couples.

TARA K. MCCLURE is a Senior Consultant with Aon, working within the Product and Analytics group and leading the Assessment Analytics team for North America. During her time at Aon, she has been responsible for developing, implementing, validating, and maintaining assessment solutions for clients and has also been involved in work to develop and enhance Aon's simulation offerings. She earned her PhD in Industrial/Organizational Psychology from Wayne State University.

JEREMIAH T. MCMILLAN is a doctoral student in industrial/organizational psychology at the University of Georgia. His research interests include the work-family interface, reintegration of military veterans into the civilian workplace, and applied psychometrics and latent modeling techniques. He is currently working on a NIOSH-funded study to examine the role of previous combat exposure and organizational support factors in military veterans' civilian work experiences.

NEIL A. MORELLI is an Industrial-Organizational (I-O) psychologist with special expertise in the areas of executive recruitment, talent assessment, and data analysis. Dr. Morelli is currently Head of Selection Science for The Cole Group, a premier retained search firm serving high-growth technology companies based in the San Francisco Bay Area. He has also held an executive team member position for an early stage technology-enabled assessment company, and has worked as a talent management consultant, where he provided services to Fortune 500 companies in the areas of employee assessment and selection, job analysis, competency modeling, performance management, and litigation support. Dr. Morelli's consulting experience covers a variety of industries such as technology, retail, government, utilities, manufacturing, and financial services, and includes organizations such as Georgia Pacific, Wal-Mart, Bridgestone Tires, and Texas Instruments. Dr. Morelli received his PhD in I-O Psychology from the University of Georgia, and his MS in I-O Psychology from the University of Tennessee at Chattanooga. His research interests include technology-enabled recruitment and assessment and he has published peer-reviewed articles on these topics in *Industrial and Organizational Psychology*, the *International Journal of Selection and Assessment*, and the *Journal of Business and Psychology.*

WENDY MURPHY is an associate professor of Management at Babson College. Her research is at the intersection of careers, mentoring, and work-life issues, with particular attention to nontraditional developmental relationships and learning. Murphy has published her work in a range of journals, including *Academy of Management Learning & Education, Human Resource Management, Gender in Management, Journal of Management*, and the *Journal of Vocational Behavior*, among others. Her book with Dr. Kathy Kram, *Strategic Relationships at Work: Creating Your Circle of Mentors, Sponsors, and Peers for Success in Business and Life*, bridges mentoring scholarship and practice.

IOANNIS NIKOLAOU is associate professor in Organisational Behaviour and director of the MSc in Human Resources Management at Athens University of Economics and Business, Greece. He has studied psychology at the University of Crete and has carried out his postgraduate studies (MSc, PhD) at Manchester School of Management, University of Manchester Institute of Science and Technology (UMIST), UK. He has gained wide working experience as an assistant manager for PricewaterhouseCoopers, Greece and as head of the Training Department of a Greek bank before starting his academic career. He has written two books on organizational psychology in Greek and co-edited with Janneke Oostrom the book *Employee Recruitment, Selection, and Assessment. Contemporary Issues for Theory and Practice*. He has also published in international peer-reviewed academic journals (e.g., *Applied Psychology: An International Review, European Journal of Work and Organizational Psychology, International Journal of Human Resources Management, Personnel Review, International Journal of Selection and Assessment, Personality & Individual Differences, Employee Relations, Stress & Health, Journal of Managerial Psychology*) and is also an editorial board member on a number of journals (e.g., *Journal of Business and Psychology,*

International Journal of Selection & Assessment, Journal of Personnel Psychology, Personnel Assessment and Decisions). His research interests focus mostly on employee recruitment, selection, and assessment, and more recently on the use of social media and serious games/gamification in recruitment/selection. He teaches courses at the undergraduate and post-graduate level, while maintaining active links with the industry through HR consulting projects and executive training. He is a member of the Academy of Management, Society for Industrial and Organizational Psychology, European Association of Work and Organizational Psychology, and the International Association of Applied Psychology (IAAP). He is the co-founder of the European Network of Selection Researchers (ENESER) and has also served as a member of the executive committee of the European Association of Work and Organizational Psychology (2013–2017). Since 2017, he represents Greece in the European Network of Organizational Psychologists (ENOP) and he is also the co-founder of the NGO Job-Pairs, supporting young graduates via mentoring.

As an associate at Shaker International, NICOLE PETERSEN supports the development and validation of Shaker's hallmark pre-hire assessment, the Virtual Job Tryout, for clients in the United States and internationally. As a member of the Build Team, she creates a unique experience for both employers and applicants through the design, build, and implementation of custom employee selection tools, as well as standard solutions. Nicole also supports research initiatives at Shaker including the development of innovative assessment methods. Nicole received her PhD in Industrial-Organizational Psychology from Bowling Green State University. Prior to joining Shaker, she was an assistant professor of Psychology at Radford University. She taught undergraduate and graduate courses in I-O psychology, research methods, and statistics. She also conducted research and provided consulting services on topics broadly within employee selection, performance management, personality assessment, and job attitude measurement.

ROSHNI RAVEENDHRAN is an assistant professor in the leadership and organizational behavior area at the Darden School of Business, University of Virginia. She received her PhD in Business Administration (Management) from the Marshall School of Business at the University of Southern California. Roshni's research focuses on understanding the future of work. In particular, she examines how technological advancements influence organizational actors, workplace practices, and the management of employees. In doing so, she develops insights about how organizations can effectively integrate novel technologies into the workplace to manage their employees. She also explores how organizations can increase the effectiveness of their human resource management practices to address the changing nature of work. Her dissertation on emerging technologies was recognized as a finalists in the INFORMS Best Dissertation Competition in 2017.

DANIEL M. RAVID is a doctoral student in Industrial and Organizational Psychology at The George Washington University, in Washington, DC. His research largely focuses on understanding employee stress and occupational well-being, and in particular the role that technology can play as both an antecedent and intervention tool for stress in the workplace. Daniel is works as a graduate researcher in the Workplace and Virtual Environment (WAVE) lab and is currently working on projects having to do with surveillance outcomes.

MARIANNE SCHMID MAST is full professor of Organizational Behavior at HEC at the University of Lausanne. After having received her PhD in Psychology from the University of Zurich, she pursued her research at Northeastern University in Boston (USA). She held positions as assistant professor in Social Psychology at the University of Fribourg and she was a full professor at the Department of Work and Organizational Psychology at the University of Neuchatel. Her research addresses how individuals in power hierarchies interact, perceive, and communicate (verbally and nonverbally), how first impressions affect interpersonal interactions and evaluations, how people form accurate impressions of others, and how physician communication affects patient outcomes. She uses immersive virtual environment technology to investigate interpersonal behavior and communication, as well as computer-based automatic sensing to analyze nonverbal behavior in social interactions. She is currently an associate editor of the *Journal of Nonverbal Behavior* and on the editorial board of the journal *Leadership Quarterly*. Marianne Schmid Mast is a former member of the Swiss National Research Council and acted as president of the Swiss Psychological Society. In 2018, she has been named one of the 50 most influential living psychologists.

BENJAMIN SIEVERT is a senior research consultant at Talent Plus, Inc. where he works closely with clients to leverage "Big Data" into actionable insights, which drive their businesses forward. In addition, Benjamin studies individuals through quantitative and qualitative processes to help our client partners select and develop highly talented individuals. Prior to joining Talent Plus, Benjamin was a consultant for Black Diamond Financial Group, LLC as well as a graduate assistant at the University of Nebraska-Lincoln. Benjamin received his Master's degree in Political Psychology from the University of Nebraska-Lincoln. He is currently working on his PhD in Political Psychology also at the University of Nebraska-Lincoln.

TILMAN L. SHEETS is Director of Training for the PhD program in I-O Psychology at Louisiana Tech University. Tilman has been at Louisiana Tech for fourteen years and is an associate professor in the Department of Psychology. His research interests are primarily in the areas of organizational metrics and the impact of technology in the workplace. He is currently consulting on projects involving organizational surveys, test development, and employee selection.

KRISTEN M. SHOCKLEY received her PhD in Industrial/Organizational Psychology from the University of South Florida. She is currently an assistant professor of Psychology at the University of Georgia. Her main area of research focuses on understanding the intersection of employees' work and family lives, with an emphasis on dual-earner couples and health impacts. Her work has been published in several books and journals, such as *Journal of Applied Psychology, Academy of*

Management Review, Personnel Psychology, and the *Journal of Management*. She has been recognized for her scholarly work through several national awards, including the Society for Industrial and Organizational Psychology's S. Rains Wallace award for the best dissertation in the field and as a finalist for the Rosabeth Moss Kanter Award for Excellence in Work-Family Research. She currently serves as an associate editor at the *Journal of Business and Psychology* as well as on the editorial board of several journals.

ELIZABETH SHORT graduated from Missouri University of Science and Technology in May of 2017, where she received her Masters of Science degree in Industrial Organizational Psychology along with graduate certificates in Psychometrics and Leadership. As a student, her research examined the use of games to measure performance and individual differences, and she has been involved in two research projects that have incorporated video games and individual difference measures. The first involved looking at technology use and personality differences in virtual team performance. The second study was a continuation of the first that looked at the cross-domain generalizability of goal orientations, organizational citizenship behaviors, and counterproductive workplace behaviors. She has been fortunate enough to present both of these projects at the annual conference of the Society for Industrial Organizational Psychology. Currently, she is still researching how videogames can be used to enhance organizational processes while considering the advancement of her education. She wishes to not only continue her research, but to one day help other students discover their own loves and passion through education.

DIANNA L. STONE received her PhD from Purdue University, and is now a visiting professor at the University at Albany, SUNY, a research professor, University of New Mexico, and an affiliate professor at Virginia Tech. Her research focuses on diversity in organizations, especially issues of race and disabilities, cross-cultural issues, privacy in organizations and electronic human resource management (eHRM) (e.g., articles on e-recruiting, e-selection, and privacy and social media). She has published approximately 105 articles and book chapters, and disseminated results of her research in the *Journal of Applied Psychology, Personnel Psychology, Journal of Management, Organizational Behavior and Human Decision Processes*, the *Academy of Management Review*, and *Human Resources Management Review*. She has authored four books on technology and Human Resources Management including *The Brave New* World of eHRM: *Human Resources Management in the Digital Age* with Hal Gueutal, *Brave New World of eHRM 2.0*, and the *Wiley/Blackwell Handbook of the Psychology of the Internet at Work* with Guido Hertel, Richard Johnson, and Jonathan Passmore. She also authored *The Influence of Culture on Human Resource Processes and Practices"* with Eugene Stone-Romero. Dianna is currently the editor of *Researching Human Resource Management* with James Dulebohn, the associate editor of *Human Resources Management Review,* and served as editor of the *Journal of Managerial Psychology* for five years. She recently won the Scholarly Achievement Award and the Janet Chusmir Sage Service Award in the Gender and Diversity Division of the

Academy of Management, the Lead Editor Award from Emerald Publishing, and the Trailblazer Award. She is a fellow of the Society for Industrial and Organizational Psychology, the Association for Psychological Science, and the American Psychological Association.

STEVEN R. TOADDY earned a PhD in I-O Psychology from North Carolina State University and currently serves as an assistant professor specializing in organizational psychology and statistics/research methods. His primary research and practice interests all relate to the concept of justice and include new conceptions of organizational justice, the future of work, the use of technology in organizations, survey design methodology, and the scholarship of teaching and learning.

DAVID L. TOMCZAK is a doctoral student of Industrial and Organizational Psychology at The George Washington University, in Washington, DC. As a researcher in the Workplaces and Virtual Environments (WAVE) lab, he has led and coauthored projects that study the psychology of technology in the workplace, specifically employee reactions to surveillance and electronic performance monitoring. His research interests also include recruitment, personnel selection, and training. He has applied his knowledge of selection and job analysis in positions with the Johns Hopkins University Applied Physics Laboratory and the United States Postal Service national headquarters. He serves on the board of directors and oversees research projects for YourStory International, a nonprofit organization. He is an active contributor and editorial assistant for *The Industrial-Organizational Psychologist*.

JILLIAN TONET is currently an MSc candidate in Applied (I/O) Psychology at Saint Mary's University, where she has gained expertise in organizational behavior and fostering psychologically healthy workplaces. This year, she was a recipient of the Joseph Armand Bombardier Canada Graduate Scholarship – Master's award through the Social Sciences and Humanities Research Council of Canada (SSHRC). In 2013, Jillian received a Master's degree in Communication Management with a focus in marketing and media at the University of Southern California. Since then, she has been working in a consulting capacity for several organizations aiding in business development, branding and marketing, and strategic planning. Recently, Jillian coordinated the APA's Psychologically Healthy Workplace Awards program for Nova Scotia, with an outstanding finalist moving on to national recognition. Her research interests include technology and worker well-being, recovery, and work-life balance, and applying psychological principles to optimize workspaces through workplace design.

W. JACKELINE TORRES is currently a doctoral student in Industrial and Organizational Psychology at Rice University in Houston, Texas. Her research interests include effective work design across the lifespan, the role of technology in work design, and the influence of work features on performance, motivation, and well-being. Her current projects include investigating cognitive demands-abilities fit on health and work outcomes among older adults, and the person-level factors that influence participation and engagement in autonomous learning activities, such as massive open online courses (MOOCs). She has previously published her research in outlets such as *Industrial and Organizational Psychology: Perspectives on Science and Practice* and *Work, Aging, and Retirement.*

ZACH TRAYLOR is a graduate student in Texas A&M University's industrial/organizational psychology doctoral program. He is a student member of the Society for Industrial and Organizational Psychology. His current research interests are in the domains of personnel psychology (particularly with respect to personnel selection), statistical and research methodologies, and psychometrics.

DONALD M. TRUXILLO is a professor of Psychology at Portland State University in Portland, Oregon. His work examines issues related to personnel selection, applicant reactions, older workers, and occupational health and safety. He has published over 100 peer-reviewed journal articles and book chapters. He is currently on the editorial boards of nine peer-reviewed journals. He served as associate editor for the *Journal of Management* and is currently an associate editor at *Work, Aging and Retirement.* He is a Fellow of the American Psychological Association, Association for Psychological Science, the International Association for Applied Psychology, and the Society for Industrial and Organizational Psychology (SIOP). His research has been supported by grants from the National Science Foundation (NSF), Society for Human Resource Management (SHRM) Foundation, and the National Institute for Occupational Safety and Health (NIOSH). He received three Fulbright Scholarship to work at the University of Trento (Italy) and ISCTE Business School (Lisbon, Portugal). He serves as a doctoral school committee member at the University of Trento, and he has also been a visiting scholar at the University of Zurich (Switzerland), University of Valencia (Spain), ISCTE Business School (Lisbon, Portugal), and University of Palermo (Italy).

KRISTA UGGERSLEV is the Applied Research Chair in Leadership and Talent at the Northern Alberta Institute of Technology. Krista holds PhD and MSc degrees in Industrial and Organizational Psychology from the University of Calgary, and was a tenured associate professor in the Asper School of Business at the University of Manitoba. Krista's research has appeared in the world's top academic journals in applied psychology and business, and has been presented to national and international audiences including NATO. She is a co-founder of the metaBUS project, aimed to transform how we locate and integrate scientific data in the field of applied psychology and management.

EMMANUELLE VAAST is professor of Information Systems at the Desautels Faculty of Management of McGill University. She has long been fascinated by the reproduction and transformation of practices associated with information technology use. More recently, her work has also dealt with the emergence of new forms of organizing and collective engagement associated with social media. Her research has been published, among others, in *MIS Quarterly, Information Systems*

Research, *Organization Science*, *Journal of MIS*, and *Academy of Management Annals*.

DALY VAUGHN, as Director of Assessment Strategy at Shaker International, helps create, define, and oversee the execution of strategic initiatives for Shaker's Design-Build team. In addition, Daly is a trusted advisor to a variety of Fortune 500 companies. He has contributed to the near 100 percent retention rate and continued growth of Shaker's business. Daly specializes in the development of multi-method pre-hire selection tools for high-volume roles, delivering solutions to primarily private-sector clients across diverse industries such as banking, retail, healthcare, and manufacturing. Over the course of his career, Daly has led numerous consulting engagements to design job-relevant game-like simulations, explore innovative item types and approaches, and deliver mobile-enabled tools. In addition to his practical experience in employee selection, Daly conducts research and publishes on topics related to innovative measure development and social media use in a selection context.

NATHAN WEIDNER grew up in the Florissant suburb of St. Louis, Missouri. He attended the University of Missouri Columbia for his undergraduate education. He was pinned and initiated into the Bet Beta Chapter of the Delta Sigma Phi fraternity in fall of 2001. He graduated in 2006 with Bachelor's degrees in Psychology and Sociology. Nathan continued his psychological training in Detroit where he attended Wayne State University. In 2012, he graduated with his PhD in Industrial-Organizational Psychology. In August 2012, he moved to Rolla Missouri where he accepted a position as an assistant professor at the Missouri University of Science and Technology (S&T). Nathan's research program broadly focuses on how technology is being integrated into organizations. He has worked on research projects examining the impacts of social media in organizations, new techniques for mobile assessment, using videogames to predict organizational attitudes and behaviors, as well as examining employee perceptions related to adopting new technologies. Nathan is a passionate teacher and is currently serving as the coordinator for the Master of Science in Industrial-Organizational Psychology program at Missouri S&T. He teaches courses on advanced research methods, leadership, tests and measurement, and industrial-organizational psychology. Nathan has been very happy to share his passion for gaming with some of his students and former professors.

BRETT M. WELLS is the Chief Research Officer at Talent Plus, Inc., and leads a team who is responsible for the creation and continuous improvement of talent selection, development, and analytics solutions and consulting services. Prior to joining Talent Plus, Brett was a consultant within Aon Hewitt's Performance, Reward and Talent practice, the director of New Test Development at Wonderlic, Inc., and senior research associate at the National Safety Council. Over the span of his career, Dr. Wells has had the pleasure to work closely with and consult great organizations on their human capital strategies, including Allstate, AT&T, The Estée Lauder Companies, and Delta Air Lines. Dr. Wells received his PhD in Social and Industrial-Organizational Psychology from Northern Illinois University, served as a post-doctoral research fellow at the Center for the Study of Family Violence and Sexual Assault, and continued his postdoctoral training at University of Illinois at Chicago in psychometrics. He has published a book chapter in *The Oxford Handbook of Social Cognition*, original research articles in top-tier, peer-reviewed scientific journals and has presented over twenty papers at the annual meetings of the Society for Industrial and Organizational Psychology, Society for Personality and Social Psychology and Association for Psychological Science, among others. Dr. Wells also serves on the Scientific Affairs Committee for the Society for Industrial and Organizational Psychology.

FRAN WESTFALL is Director of Solution Consultants at Talent Plus, Inc. She works closely with the Talent Plus Research Consultants to design selection and development processes utilizing technology. Since joining Talent Plus in 2002, Westfall has been directly involved with the development of TalentBank®, an online talent management system providing interviewing functions, Talent Online® Assessments, reporting, as well as employee development capabilities. More recently, she has utilized Tableau software to create data visualizations for Talent Plus clients around selection, development, succession planning, and workforce planning. Westfall serves as the senior technology lead for The Estée Lauder Companies, UCLA, Cancer Treatment Centers of America, Mercy, Delta Air Lines, and The Dorchester Collection.

Preface

Technology, like art, is a soaring exercise of the human imagination.

(Bell, 1973)[1]

Industrial-organizational (I-O) psychology, and the management sciences more broadly, are facing a daunting challenge. New technologies are increasingly permeating every aspect of the employee experience of an organization, yet our theories and research are often ill-equipped to fully understand this change. Nevertheless, we must try, seeking to build relevant knowledge so that we do not step forward in this bright new future completely blinded by its shine.

Within this handbook, I have curated seven types of chapter that speak to this challenge, to better understand the complex relationship between technology in organizations and employees. Specifically, a priori, I defined key concerns in I-O psychology in relation to its technology and designed a book to address them all. With that blueprint laid, I invited authors that I trusted could give a fair but critical treatment within each area and asked them to address three key questions:

(1) First, how have technologies affected I-O theory and practice in this domain to date?
(2) Second, given current trends in both research and practice, could I-O theories be rendered obsolete without adequate attention paid to these technologies in the future? And if so, how can we prevent this?
(3) Third, what are the highest priorities for both research and practice to ensure I-O remains appropriately engaged with technology moving forward?

Each chapter underwent a blind review, and during that process, I asked reviewers to provide their reactions and commentary regarding these three questions, to ensure that all chapters were aligned to similar goals. Ultimately, I believe this produced a compelling and fascinating walk through all the technologies currently relevant to I-O psychology, regardless of the quantity of research already available to understand them. I hope this handbook will stimulate researchers to fill the many gaps identified by these authors.

---

[1] Bell, D. (1973). Technology, nature and society: The vicissitudes of three world views and the confusion of realms. *The American Scholar*, 42, 385–404.

To orient you to the content of this handbook, I will briefly describe each of its seven parts:

Part I Technology in I-O Psychology. This first part is intended to ask the big questions: what is I-O psychology in relation to technology, and what will our future hold? The chapters in this part take a distinctly philosophical tone, but it is one that is very important in defining what I-O psychology will become in this new era.

Part II Technology in Staffing. This part focuses upon recruitment, selection, and assessment applications of technology, running the gamut from the known I-O technologies of internet-based and adaptive testing through the cutting edge, including social media, mobile assessment, games, and other state-of-the-art technologies.

Part III Technology in Training and Development. This part discusses the most cutting edge of training and development research in I-O psychology, including games and gamification, virtual mentoring, virtual coaching, and virtual reality.

Part IV Technology in Leadership and Teams. This part explores how technology changes the relationships between people working in teams, both among each other, and with their leadership, via technologies both mundane (e.g., telephone) and modern (e.g., social media).

Part V Technology in Motivation and Performance. This part describes a wider range of research than the previous parts, but all focusing upon how technology changes the employee's experience of work. This includes such diverse topics as employee privacy, aging workers, the work-family interface, and the impact of technology on work in the developing world.

Part VI Technology in Statistics and Research Methods. Although the research of I-O psychology is changing, so too are the tools used by I-O psychologists to conduct that research. This part describes how technology is changing our approach to research, including new internet technologies, data science, crowdsourcing, wearables, and visualization.

Part VII Interdisciplinary Perspectives on Employees and Technology. This final part of the handbook gives voice to researchers working in disciplines parallel to management science but often uncited by I-O psychologists. This includes a chapter on microblogging from the perspective of an information systems scientist, electronic human resource management from the perspective of human resources researchers, and social evaluation in technological systems from the perspective of social psychologists. I hope this part will encourage I-O psychologists to explore just a few of the domains that are so relevant to our work in I-O technology but so often ignored, to our field's detriment.

I hope you enjoy reading this collection of scholarship as much as I enjoyed putting it together.

Acknowledgments

Something that was not obvious to me before I put together my first book was just how many people are critical to the process who remain mostly or entirely uncredited. This page alone will never be sufficient, but regardless, I wish to express my thanks to several people for their contributions.

First and foremost, I would like to thank Elena Auer, my graduate student and editorial assistant. Elena managed a huge amount of the grunt work for this book project, keeping track of deadlines and harassing chapter authors for materials, taking a massive piece of that headache away from me. I am not sure that the book would have even been completed without her. Elena, thank you so much for your time and effort on this project. I hope it was worth it!

Second, I would like to thank the enormous number of reviewers who provided feedback on the chapters within this book's pages. Across 33 chapters, with two or three reviewers each, this was an enormous review undertaking, yet I believe that the reviews we received improved the quality of the content here dramatically. Thank you all.

Third, I would like to thank series editor Tammy Allen for allowing me to bring the good word of technology unto I-O psychology. I truly believe we are at a turning point for our field, one that could embrace a fruitful and beneficial inter-disciplinary approach to technology, and I hope this handbook will be at the center of it. Thank you for recognizing this need and giving me the opportunity to try.

Finally, I would like to thank my editors at Cambridge for supporting this project, and of course, since I'm an academic, for their flexibility with deadlines!

PART I

Technology in I-O Psychology

1 The Existential Threats to I-O Psychology Highlighted by Rapid Technological Change

Richard N. Landers

For decades, there has been a quiet murmur of existential discontent within industrial-organizational (I-O) psychology. This has taken many forms, such as calls to mind the science-practice gap (Briner & Rousseau, 2011), expressions of concern over the usefulness of I-O psychology's general approach to science (Highhouse & Zickar, 1997), and calls to increase our influence on and efforts to improve the world at large (Maynard & Ferdman, 2009). Despite decades of commentary encouraging actions to address these concerns, little has changed, and this murmur has in recent years become a bit louder and more insistent, in part because the increasingly rapid pace of technological change, the changing nature of work itself, has made these weaknesses more problematic, more destructive, and more obvious. In short, we are poised to plunge headfirst into our own obsolescence.

In this chapter, my first goal is to explain how we reached this point by describing five key threats to I-O psychology that set us up for this dive. My second goal is to describe some troubling outcomes of these threats so far, to more clearly illustrate why these threats must be addressed. To summarize these outcomes, I-O practice has pulled far ahead of academia in terms of technological expertise, yet in an absolute sense, neither practice nor academia are particularly current or competitive in terms of their understanding of or approach to technology. Third, I provide a list of four recommendations that I believe will turn us toward a better path, one which fully embraces an interdisciplinary future for our field.

1.1 A Perfect Storm for Irrelevance

Some of the threats to I-O psychology I will next describe were created by I-O itself, or more specifically, its culture and common practices, whereas other threats reflect market conditions or the realities of the technological world we now find ourselves in. I will describe these threats in an order of increasing compounding; in other words, each reason is made worse by the reasons that came before it, and in combination, they may be lethal.

1.1.1 Threat #1: Developing Theory for Its Own Sake Is Popular but Not Typically Useful

Numerous I-O researchers over the past decade have noted that I-O psychology literature is becoming more oriented toward an unusual and harmful type of theory development (e.g., Campbell & Wilmot, 2018). To illustrate, consider Table 1.1, which contains a list of titles of articles published in the *Journal of Applied Psychology* from 2018 Issue 1 alongside those published in 1988 Issue 1, thirty years earlier. Even a brief study of this table reveals a noticeable priority shift. Whereas 1988 articles develop measures, investigate effects, and compare methods, 2018 articles are more likely to present theories, test models, and propose mediators. Importantly, my listing of these titles is not to somehow shame or minimize the contributions of either set of researchers or their findings; instead, I use this to illustrate just how abstract and theory-oriented much published I-O psychology research has now become in relation to the I-O psychology of yesteryear. If you have been staying current on the I-O literature, this also should not be at all surprising.

So what might be less obvious to I-Os is that this idea, that the *purpose* of research is to propose theory, puts our field not only in contrast to the historical roots of I-O psychology but also to virtually all research literatures on I-O–related technologies created outside our field. In contrast to I-O theory-building research, technology and the way it is typically researched is highly concrete. In the third column of Table 1.1, I have added a list of recent articles from a respected outlet in the field of human-computer interaction (HCI), an interdisciplinary field that falls at the intersection point between psychology and computer science. In that column, you will find much of the same language of 1988 *JAP*, with lots of measuring, evaluating, and exploring, yet relatively few papers concerning theory as an overarching goal. A cynical traditionalist might interpret this to mean that HCI is 30 years behind I-O, whereas a futurist might interpret it to mean that HCI's increasing popularity must be driven by this applied focus. The truth, as usual, is likely somewhere in the middle. At the very least, this difference reflects a real mismatch between the typical goals of technologists and the typical goals of (publishing) I-O psychologists.

1.1.2 Threat #2: Research on Technology as Yet-More-Stimuli is Artificially Limiting

In the classic language of psychology, technologies are stimuli. They are designed by humans to realize an intended purpose, but once they exist and are in use, they are inherently part of the situations in which people find themselves. People make decisions regarding how to interact with those technologies, or they react as those technologies are forced upon them. Unfortunately, psychology has historically considered and defined its stimuli quite poorly (Gibson, 1960). This is most obvious in social psychology, where even today, stimuli are often developed for use in a single study without extensive pilot testing to ensure that those stimuli are

Table 1.1 *Seven most recent studies across three journals*

JAP 2018, Issue 1	JAP 1988, Issue 1	IJHCS 2018, Volumes 112–113
Attention to change: A multilevel theory on the process of emergent continuous organizational change.	Development of a new evacuation method for emergencies: Control of collective behavior by emergent small groups.	Head-tracking interfaces on mobile devices: Evaluation using Fitts' law and a new multi-directional corner task for small displays.
A cross-level investigation of informal field-based learning and performance improvements.	Relation of job stressors to affective, health, and performance outcomes: A comparison of multiple data sources.	Evaluating Fitts' law on vibrating touch-screen to improve visual data accessibility for blind users.
Detecting and differentiating the direction of change and intervention effects in randomized trials.	An investigation of sex discrimination in recruiters' evaluations of actual applicants.	A practical approach to measuring user engagement with the refined user engagement scale (UES) and new UES short form.
Cheating under pressure: A self-protection model of workplace cheating behavior.	Effects of preinterview impressions on questioning strategies in same- and opposite-sex employment interviews.	A study of dynamic information display and decision-making in abstract trust games.
The dark side of subjective value in sequential negotiations: The mediating role of pride and anger.	Importance of specialized cognitive function in the selection of military pilots.	Multilingual phrase sampling for text entry evaluations.
On the relative importance of individual-level characteristics and dyadic interaction effects in negotiations: Variance partitioning evidence from a twins study.	Joint relation of experience and ability with job performance: Test of three hypotheses.	Bodily sensation maps: Exploring a new direction for detecting emotions from user self-reported data.
Leadership and member voice in action teams: Test of a dynamic phase model.	Escalation bias in performance appraisals: An unintended consequence of supervisor participation in hiring decisions.	Designing mobile based computational support for low-literate community health workers.

Note. JAP = Journal of Applied Psychology; IJHCS = International Journal of Human-Computer Studies

in fact valid representations of whatever they are intended to represent. This might be attributed to the focus of the field; psychology is, as evidenced by its own name, primarily the study of people's mental states and not the things happening to those people. But such a simple treatment belies the complexity of the world in which people exist. Lewin (1936) already knew this when he stated, "Every psychological event depends upon the state of the person and at the same time on the environment, although their relative importance is different in different cases" (p. 12). Despite many calls since that time to better integrate both the person and the situation (Ekehammar, 1974), it remains a challenge even today.

When researchers adopt this classic stance, consciously or not, they limit the types of questions that they ask of technology and the approaches they take to studying it. In psychology, such researchers typically default to a stance in which technology takes the form of a well-defined and specific cause, something to either be manipulated by an experimenter or passively recorded in a correlational study, evidenced by research questions like, "Do mobile devices harm measurement?" The reality of technology's relationship with people is more complex, which is recognized explicitly in other fields. For example, in a highly influential article in the field of Management Information Systems, Orlikowski (1992) presented a non-recursive model of workplace technology in which people create and change technology, technology in turn influences organizational policies and norms, and those policies and norms in turn influence how people treat technology; additionally, the technology itself changes how people work, as shown in Figure 1.1. This is a much more flexible and useful approach to studying technology than the simple and uninformative meta-research question "what does technology do to people?" pervasive in psychology and management, the existence of which is in part caused by Threat #1.

Additionally, due to this limited view of technology, specific technologies are often ill defined and misapplied. Grawitch, Winton, Mudigonda, and Buerck (2017) made this argument convincingly and phrased in a way relatable to psychologists: "technology is more than just error" (Grawitch et al., 2017). Importantly, this operationalization of misapplication is not unique to I-O psychology; for example, in media psychology, which is a field that studies the effects of various technologies on human psychology as its primary purpose, researchers still appear to have a significant bias toward investigating psychological concerns instead of technological ones (Reeves, Yeykelis, & Cummings, 2016). In short, because we are trained as psychologists, it is seductive to focus on psychology alone in our research. In the modern world, this approach is often not particularly useful.

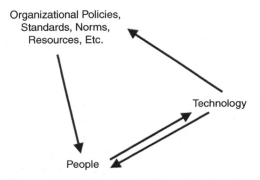

Figure 1.1 *Orlikowski (1992) model of workplace technology*

To remain relevant, we need to be active, integrative, and increasingly inter-disciplinary. In contrast to this charge, psychology's mind-set about technology is generally passive, reactive, and siloed. It encourages researchers to sit back and wait until technologies are implemented, often wreaking some degree of havoc upon the world; only when the dust has settled does it become appropriate to begin sifting through what has happened and try to make sense of it. This is, furthermore, reinforced by Threat #1, because one needs to be a passive observer to develop a theory that is only to be tested with confirmatory hypothesis testing, an approach in stark contrast to the natural sciences, where pushing the boundaries of knowledge through invention and discovery are the raison d'être. When is the last time you recall an academic I-O psychologist inventing something new, trustworthy, and immediately useful to practitioners? Although there are a few examples (e.g., De Corte, Sackett, & Lievens, 2011), they are rare, scattered, and tend to fall on the "industrial" side of I-O. It does not need to be this way.

1.1.3 Threat #3: Both Psychology and Technology Are Moving Targets, but Technology Is Worse

The most common epistemology among modern social scientists is likely post-positivism. Many I-O psychologists are not aware of this philosophy of science underlying their research, so I shall take a moment to explore it. Post-positivism, in brief, asserts that there is some "true" state of the world. In statistical terms, these are populations, and within those populations, various relationships, both causal and correlational, are true. So for example, perhaps in the true world, conscientiousness is indeed an emergent state of a person's brain that affects how they behave. We can never know this "true" world; instead, we must make inferences about it via observation, data collection, and statistical tests. Given certain assumptions, we can state with some degree of confidence that our observations in our own world reflect this true world. If I were to stop there, I would be describing the most common philosophical framework behind most modern *natural* sciences, logical positivism. This approach works quite well when measuring the behavior of atoms, or planets, or biological systems, because these relationships are quite stable. The fundamental forces of the universe (i.e., think $E = MC^2$) will not change over time or because we observe them. In psychology as currently studied, this is not a safe assumption. When I conduct a research study to observe the usefulness of Facebook metadata in predicting human behavior, I have no reason to assume between this study and the next that (1) Facebook will be the same, (2) the population using Facebook will be the same, (3) the capabilities of Facebook will be the same, (4) the data being produced by Facebook will be the same, (5) people will behave the same way on Facebook, and so on. Facebook is a living, reactive system, just as the people who use it are themselves complex biological systems. Thus, logistical positivism is not enough for psychology, because (1) researchers need to interpret what they find through these various lenses to make sense of what they find and (2) even if true scores exist, these scores may change over time between one study and the next. Post-positivism is thus a common refinement of logical positivism that adds these caveats: that we must always reflect upon our own influence, as researchers, on the systems we are researching and also recognize that causal forces from outside the scope of our studies might change the nature of our observations even as we make those observations.

To make this a bit more relatable, realize that post-positivism is the philosophical framework that enables us to conduct meta-analyses of psychological constructs that we explicitly expect to change over time; if we did not believe true scores could move around depending upon when the study was conducted and the assumptions surrounding it at the time, we would expect later meta-analytic estimates to only become more precise, not to fundamentally change. If the true-score relationship between conscientiousness and job performance in 1991 was $\rho=.22$ (Barrick & Mount, 1991), in a logical positivist framework, we would also expect $\rho=.22$ in 2091, although measured more precisely. But I suspect most I-O psychologists do not have such an expectation. Jobs will change, people will change, and that number is going to change with them; it is only a matter of how quickly. Thus, even if you have never articulated what post-positivism involves, you probably have an intuitive understanding of it; it is hard-baked into the very foundations of our field.

Why this is critical is that the study of technology on human behavior relies on post-positivism too, although it takes a somewhat different shape. You, as a researcher, do not have the power to personally change the $\rho=.22$ mentioned above. If the true score is .22 in an organization today, it is very likely to be close to .22 a year or two from now. It may drift over the long term, if the job itself changes, or society changes, or some other "big" thing changes. But it is not something that a researcher, as an individual, can influence. In contrast, modern technologies are constantly being developed, designed, and redesigned by humans according to human needs. Modern technologies are updated continuously with the intent of continuous improvement. Thus, human decisions and behaviors *actively* change true scores between technologies and other variables in ways that are unlikely when examining relationships between psychological constructs alone. If we believe a technology is ineffective in its purpose (i.e., some desirable effect caused by the technology is too weak), we may redesign the technology to increase its effectiveness (i.e., to increase its true score effect). There may be a ceiling to this true effect, given particular design considerations within a particular technology, but there is no clear way to know where either our observed or true scores are in relation to that ceiling.

We have seen the negative effects of assuming technology to be much more stable than it actually is in all areas of I-O psychology where technologies are studied. It is particularly strongly evidenced by the decades-long arguments in our literature regarding assessment center validity (cf., Klimoski & Brickner, 1987; Jackson, Michaelides, Dewberry, & Kim, 2016). The assessment center method, like all selection methods, is a technology, designed by humans to assess other humans' KSAOs. Assessment centers are typically defined by certain common design characteristics, such as the use of multiple raters and exercises (International Taskforce on Assessment Center Guidelines, 2015), but the details vary dramatically – by purpose, by constructs assessed, by methods employed, by exercises selected, by rater populations sampled, and so on. Thus, as a technology, assessment centers are multidimensional. They incorporate and combine multiple distinct technologies, each with their own quirks, effects, and design considerations. For example, leaderless group discussion is an assessment exercise, and therefore a selection method, and therefore a technology. It can be designed well or designed poorly, and these design considerations are also multidimensional. This logic can similarly be applied to *every technology* contained within *any* assessment center, keeping in mind that some assessment centers may not even overlap with others in terms of the specific technologies employed. This is a startling level of interactive complexity, once the true number of dimensions involved are considered accurately. Furthermore, as the assessment center method has developed, the specific design considerations related to each of these issues have changed; an assessment center designed to the guidelines of 2015 might not have even been referred to as an "assessment center" twenty years earlier. To even *investigate* the "validity of assessment centers" as such in this context is an absolute waste of researcher time and effort. Although the futility of this approach has been recognized to an increasing degree in the last few years (e.g., Kuncel & Sackett, 2014), it took decades to get here. In other technology-oriented literatures within I-O psychology, we face this same road ahead again and again.

As we dig deeper into any technology, whether speaking of the technologies that enable co-located work or the technologies that enable online assessment or the technologies that enable chatbots to teach people leadership skills, the effects of human-contributed variance on true scores will only become more complex. The value of evaluating technologies as if they behave similarly to psychological constructs will remain similarly fruitless. For our field to remain relevant in this new technology-driven landscape, we cannot afford to repeat this same path across every technology-focused research stream within I-O psychology (Landers & Behrend, 2017). This also builds on Threat #2 in that we should not *react* continuously for decades to every innovative technology as it becomes popular, a new stimulus that has appeared suitable for study, pretending that each incarnation of it in our research literature is a random sample from some grand population of technologies. This is unreasonable. And building on Threat #1, neither should we pretend that new technological advancements are simply new versions of technologies we have already studied; our default position should not be to scramble for existing theory as a comfortable and familiar crutch (e.g., Chamorro-Premuzic, Winsborough, Sherman, & Hogan, 2016).

1.1.4 Threat #4: I-O Psychologists Are Not Adequately Trained in Technology

Until recently, it appeared that I-O psychologists, especially those in academia, did not consider technology, as distinct concept needing focused training, to be integral to the field. This is evidenced by Tett, Walser, Brown, Simonet, and Tonidandel's (2013) report on the 2011 SIOP Graduate Program survey, which in part assessed the degree to which both "substantive" and "methods" topics were covered in I-O psychology programs. Technology did not even make the list of questions, and among what was asked, the most technology-oriented competency area was "human factors." Perhaps unsurprisingly, zero doctoral programs surveyed included this in their curriculum. The next year, Byrne et al. (2014), writing an article inspired by a Society for Industrial and Organizational Psychology (SIOP) panel discussion centered on Tett et al.'s work, described new competency priorities for graduate training in I-O; the word "technology" does not even appear in their work. It is understandable not to *focus* on technology in an I-O psychology graduate program, but this suggests that even just a few years ago, in terms of training new I-Os, technology was not even on the proverbial radar, despite better understanding of technology appearing among the concerns of both I-O students (Harris & Hollman, 2013) and I-O practitioners (Church, 1998; Silzer & Cober, 2010).

Things have certainly changed in the last five years. In 2015, Guzzo, Fink, King, Tonidandel, and Landis (2015) called for I-O psychology to formally respond to the sudden popularity of big data. To inspire I-Os, they provided several examples of I-O work in the big data space already. Yet all their citations to I-O's work in this area appeared in working papers, unpublished manuscripts, and a single published book, all of which were written or published that same year. Importantly, the term "big data" in its current usage has been around since at least 2008, but the concept of analytics at scale had existed for decades before that (Boyd & Crawford, 2012). From this timeline, it is straightforward to conclude that I-O fell a bit behind modern analytics. In response to Guzzo et al.'s article, Aiken and Hanges (2015) called to integrate some degree of modern data science into the core I-O graduate curriculum, including programming skills and modern predictive modeling, primarily suggesting that I-O students should read more books and consider supplementing their own educations by participating in massive online courses on data science until I-O faculty teach themselves enough to in turn teach seminars on the topic. As they noted, "This is not just something that would be nice to see; this is an imperative, and our graduate training needs to reflect this imperative immediately" (p. 544). The threat of technology to I-O became so plain to SIOP that in 2016, the Executive Board established the Future Scanning Task Force to assess threats to the future existence of both SIOP and I-O psychology in general brought by the changing world of work, and to provide recommendations regarding these threats. Understanding technology emerged as a major theme. In 2018, the Executive Board promoted this Task Force to become an Ad Hoc Committee, meaning it will be likely to continue advising the Executive Board for some time. Additionally, two technology-oriented columns intended to teach I-Os about technology now appear in the *Industrial-Organizational Psychologist*: Poeppelman and Sinar's (2016) "The Modern App" and Landers' (2017) "Crash Course in I-O Technology." The push from within for I-O psychologists to understand technology, regardless of application domain, has never been higher.

Despite this increasing pressure, in terms of both initial and continuing education, I-O psychology is struggling to respond. The sudden demand for a new skillset that most academic I-O psychologists do not have means that there are relatively few people capable of teaching this skillset currently employed to teach graduate students or lead SIOP workshops. This too is changing, although slowly, and Aiken and Hanges' (2015) recommendation to outsource these needs to computer science departments in the interim is unlikely to be successful. Computer scientists have quite dissimilar needs from psychologists in terms of programming expertise, and I-O psychologists are different still. I have chatted with students in I-O graduate programs where this is currently recommended, and, universally, I have heard complaints of perceived relevance and value. I-O psychologists completing programming courses in computer science departments creates the same problem as I-O psychologists completing statistics courses in mathematics departments; it is difficult to understand why what you are learning is useful, and it this kind of contextualization that is presently most critical.

1.1.5 Threat #5: It Is Easier to Bury Our Heads in the Sand

Although this may seem a minor point, it is still worth noting that field momentum is a difficult force to counter. In other words, I-O psychology is a difficult and unwieldy ship to steer. As a field, we are generally decentralized, and SIOP, the European Association of Work and Organizational Psychology (EAWOP), and other national I-O organizations can only do so much. In the case of SIOP, it is a volunteer-run organization, which means that it is in the interests of its leadership to avoid courting controversy. There are no licensure programs or graduate program certification programs to leverage a field-wide shift. Thus, the organization cannot simply tell graduate programs to run themselves differently for the good of the field; instead, committees must be formed, debate the issues, and make recommendations, which the programs can then choose to heed or ignore. This adds significant complexity to decision-making and, more critically, adds a lot of time. I-O psychology, as a field, is about as far from "agile" as is possible, and it is hurting us.

Additionally, finger-pointing is already common. I have heard from numerous I-O academic researchers that this is ultimately the problem of practitioners; academia, after all, can only move so fast. I have also heard from numerous I-O practitioners that the problem is ultimately one of academics; after all, the field has changed, so the training must adapt too. Frankly, neither of these perspectives is productive, as both simply encourage their respective constituencies to "stay the course" on a course that is already off-track. The truth is that I-O psychology, as a field, will live or die together, because these problems are all interconnected (Aguinis, Bradley, & Brodersen, 2014), a so-called "wicked problem" (Behrend & Landers, 2017). The problem with our field's bifurcation is particularly salient in light of Threats #1 – #4. Although practitioners are at the very forefront of exploratory applied research, following and learning about new technologies literally as they change in front of them, it is extremely difficult for any of them to publish in I-O journals given the apparent need to propose novel theory in a confirmatory framework with well-established parameters in every paper.

1.2 Storm Damage So Far

Together, these five threats are interactive; they cause more damage in combination than their individual effects would suggest. This interaction has already manifested itself in at least three ways that promise to become worse if not mitigated soon.

1.2.1 Practitioners Lead the Way in Technology Because Academia Forces Them To

What brought the limitations of academia's approach into greatest relief for me, and really the inspiration for this chapter, come from the results of the first ever SIOP Machine Learning Competition at the SIOP 2018 conference (Putka et al., 2018). In this competition, 17 teams of either academics or practitioners attempted a prediction problem using an authentic turnover dataset provided by a volunteer organization. The dataset was quite large (for I-O research) and complex, with hundreds of variables, systematic missingness, and longitudinal characteristics, among numerous other features. Each team was tasked with creating the predictive model that would hold up the best in a hold-out sample using whatever techniques they had at their disposal. Additionally, teams received feedback on the quality of their models each week for about a month in the form of a leaderboard. Importantly, although academic-practitioner teams were permitted, none formed. At the end of the competition, the top four scoring teams were asked to present on their methods at SIOP. It was revealed that the four winning teams consisted entirely of practitioners.

What is striking about that story, to me, is that academic researchers in both the natural and other social sciences, including the rest of applied psychology, *lead the way*. This is where academics in universities are intended to bring the greatest value, by standing at the forefront of knowledge, unconstrained by organizational politics and the bottom line. Yet, in this competition, the very best minds in machine learning and predictive modeling in I-O psychology were all among practitioners. And perhaps more importantly, very few of the skills used by any of those teams are traditionally taught in I-O psychology programs. Instead, these were all skills picked up in personal professional development, by both the academics and the practitioners, and the practitioners were, as a group, more successful. This suggests that practitioners, or at least academic-practitioner teams, should be leading the charge in our research literature to define best practices and explore the value of all this technology appearing in the employee selection and retention space. So why are there so few such articles? Why are most of the articles we see still building theory of limited practical use?

A troubling truth is that I-O practice, as it is exists right now, is not particularly evidence-based (Briner & Rousseau, 2011). Although this statement prima facie may suggest that practitioners are the problem, the reality is that academia is equally, if not more, to blame. I-O practice does not generally benefit from I-O academia in its current state, because academia is no longer supplying much practical theory. Practitioners instead must create, interpret, and market their own brand of evidence. There is little motivation for practitioners to adopt and employ academic research for which they see little value. There are only two ways I see for academia to compete for attention in this situation. The first is for I-O psychology academic researchers to transition to the role that academic research has traditionally filled in the natural sciences: inventors and testers of new, trusted technologies. The second is to encourage academic-practitioner partnerships in which academics learn from practitioners, translate for a broader audience, test the ideas, and publish their findings collaboratively. We have seen calls for the second approach for a long while; perhaps it is time to try the first approach, as well. For example, outside psychology in academic engineering fields, new inventions routinely appear, and patents are a major source of revenue for such programs. But unlike the creations of industry, inventions created by these academic departments tend to address more fundamental challenges that industry is unlikely to spend its time and resources investigating, given a higher risk of failure. This is because academia typically serves a social good; it creates fundamental advances in our scientific understanding of phenomena that might not be cost effective for a single organization to pioneer yet benefit all (Behrend & Landers, 2017). I-O psychology historically did the same; it is time to return to our roots.

1.2.2 Existing Discussions of I-O Technology Reveal Significant Knowledge Gaps

Arthur and Villado (2008) reminded researchers that characteristics of people (i.e., constructs) and the technologies being used to assess them (i.e., methods) are in fact different things. The existence of such an article, or more specifically, the legitimate need for it then and now, suggests the sort of thinking that might have necessitated it: "because psychological constructs are familiar, anything worth studying is probably a construct." This might be called the psychology scholarship heuristic: because most concepts of interest in psychology have traditionally been constructs, constructs are therefore the most important subject of research. It is a default philosophical orientation. But such an orientation is limiting and harmful for I-O psychology when exploring technology, because it places artificial limits on both research and practice. Two examples from the I-O literature will illuminate the issue.

First, Adler, and Boyce (2016) made a rather forceful statement regarding the data science brand of predictive modeling in which the specific causes of a model's predictive ability are not explainable by humans:

> In our view, surrender to using "black box" solutions – when we don't understand why those solutions work – may in isolated cases be expedient but is simply not a long-term option for building our science … What distinguishes us as advisors to organizations around talent issues is in part our grasp of the conceptual frameworks we can apply to develop those insights and produce those hypotheses a priori in addition, of course, to the discipline and techniques for empirically testing those frameworks and hypotheses. (p. 642)

On its face, this comment seems like a reasonable stance and sound advice. It echoes the old criticisms of "dustbowl empiricism" in the earlier days of I-O psychology, a time that many current I-Os are glad is dead and buried. It suggests, quite reasonably, that prediction without understanding the constructs involved is not worth the effort. However, it also closes us off to possibilities. What it reveals to me, as someone who follows recent developments in computer science research, is a disparity between what Adler and Boyce believe the interpretability of black box solutions are and what computer science researchers believe their interpretability could become. In the computer science research area of neural network modeling, commonly called "deep learning" and what Adler and Boyce are most likely referring to as "black box solutions," there is currently a substantial effort to create approaches and visualizations that will help explain precisely why these models predict outcomes so well, and why they do so better, in general, than any predictive modeling approach we currently commonly employ in I-O psychology. Although these approaches are in their infancy, they are certainly in development.

Additionally, by wholesale discounting "black box solutions," I-O psychology closes itself to the possibility that there may be specific situations or contexts in which understanding why a model predicts well is legitimately a secondary goal. For example, if you could employ a model predicting turnover with an R^2 of .45 using traditional regression-based modeling or an R^2 of .55 using convolutional neural networks, and those predicted scores themselves were correlated .8, would you automatically turn to the .45, simply because it is more explainable? I suggest you probably would not. That inter-algorithmic reliability of .8 is evidence that the sorts of variables being weighted more heavily in the regression are likely the same ones being picked up in the neural network approach, and if the ΔR^2 of .10 is generalizable out-of-sample, the neural network model emerges as a clearly superior choice for practical decision-making. Thus, automatically discounting black box solutions both (1) reveals an ignorance of the research in computer science currently underway to improve interpretation of such solutions, which is likely to become mainstream within the next five years anyway, and (2) forces I-O psychologists to wait until those approaches already exist, rather than working collaboratively with computer scientists or data scientists to ensure they meet the needs of I-O psychology. Once again, this sort of stance puts us as passive consumers of technology rather than active builders of the technologies that would most benefit our field.

A second example comes from Chamorro-Premuzic, Winsborough, Sherman, and Hogan (2016), who attempted to re-brand various technology trends as reincarnations of existing I-O practices: "gamified assessments are the digital equivalent of situational judgment tests, digital interviews represent computerized versions of traditional selection interviews, and professional social networks, such as LinkedIn, are the modern equivalent of a resumé and recommendation letters" (p. 622). Much like Adler and Boyce's (2016) recommendations, there is an intuitive appeal to this approach. They make technologies that seem alien and foreign relatable within the comfortable, warm embrace of existing theory and practice in I-O psychology. However, this has the same effect as in Adler and Boyce's treatment; it limits our possibilities and betrays a lack of expertise in these specific technologies. To illustrate, consider their treatment of gamification, which is never defined except to list "SJT and self-report" as the non-digital I-O equivalent, along with descriptions of the products of three companies they label as gamification: Knack, Pymetrics, and Tinder. As Armstrong, Ferrell, Collmus, and Landers (2016) explain in a response article, the area of game-thinking in assessment is quite broad and dissimilar to traditional I-O assessment methods, encompassing both game-based assessment, in which a full assessee experience is designed, and gamification, in which existing assessments are modified using lessons from the game-design literature. For example, they describe personality surveys in which narrative elements have been added and simulations in which animation and sound effects have been added. None of this is to say that a situational judgment test is not *one example* of gamification, but rather that defining gamification *as* digital situational judgment tests closes off numerous possibilities for I-O psychology to grow along with modern technology. And beyond that, there is no reason to assume that our current theoretical understanding of situational judgment tests is adequate to understand the full spectrum of game-related changes that could be made to situational judgment tests administered via the internet. Situational judgment tests are not constructs that instantiate themselves as different technologies over time, and they vary widely even within the label of "situational judgment test." Once again, this implicit view creates an artificial limit and belies an ignorance of what is possible with the technology, not only as it exists today, but as it will exist in the future.

1.2.3 Published I-O Psychology Is Becoming (Even) Less Useful

One of the core challenges to I-O psychology in recent years has been the migration of I-O psychologists to business schools (Aguinis, Bradley, & Brodersen, 2014). This has happened for several reasons, but most cynically, a primary draw is because business schools can pay much better salaries and may even provide cash bonuses for publication (Luthans, 2017). Realistically, this is not something with which I-O psychology will ever be able to compete. Psychology departments, historically, are situated in either Colleges of Liberal Arts or Colleges of Science. In most universities, faculty are expected to bring funding to their institution by seeking external funding, through grants and contracts, and sharing indirect costs. In short, a funding model has developed for colleges and universities in which college expenses are covered by faculty research (Zusman, 2005), a situation that is increasingly common worldwide (Polster, 2007). Because of the significant tuition currently paid by students seeking Master's degrees in Business Administration (MBA), faculty in business schools typically do not face the same expectation, and there is also a sizable pot of money from which to pay lucrative salaries. Thus, whereas faculty in the rest of the university are expected to supplement their own salaries with external funding that they must themselves apply for, business schools leverage their MBA-driven funding model to lure faculty that are perceived as "the best of the best" from disciplines relevant to business. Increasingly, this includes psychologists, typically I-O and social psychologists.

This pattern is not by itself a problem for I-O psychology. If I-Os in business schools continued to publish I-O psychology research, it would not particularly matter where they were employed at the time. But what has happened instead is that the norms and values of business schools, and particularly of organizational behavior (OB), have changed the type of research that business school I-O psychologists deem valuable and important (Lefkowitz, 2008). Because business schools were historically seen as less "serious" than traditional academic disciplines, their faculties needed to fight for their relevance to universities, and a major outcome of that struggle was the development of the theory fetish described earlier as Threat #1. Over the last two decades, as I-O psychologists have left for business schools but continued to publish in I-O psychology, they have increasingly brought these business schools' values with them into I-O journals. Now, such thinking seems to have infected mainstream academic I-O psychology, field-wide.

Considering that the business school community has known these values to have created an existential problem that they have been grappling with for decades (Pfeffer & Fong, 2002), it is unfortunate that I-O psychology continues to import them freely. The negative effects are significant, yet these values have spread like a cancer, gradually nudging I-O psychology journals to publish a different sort of work than they did before. As more I-O psychology journals fall to this influence, we create a research literature that is "overly abstract, pedantic, and somewhat pretentious" (Campbell & Wilmot, 2018). With such values and such a literature, academics become increasingly siloed within not just I-O psychology but within their own narrowly defined research areas, and practitioners see decreasing value in I-O research to further their own organizational and job-related goals. Academics write papers for an ever-shrinking number of other academics within a tightly defined research area, while practitioners keep their own research proprietary, behind the organizational curtain. At the end of this road, no one learns anything new or useful from anyone else within the I-O community. Realistically, it would probably never get quite so apocalyptic as that, but the field is already too far down this path. We need to stop now and reverse course.

1.3 Recommendations for a Brighter Future

With so much gloom in these pages, it might sound like I am saying that I-O psychology is doomed to failure. To be clear, I do not think that it is. I-O psychology can and does bring substantial value to people in organizations, but we are currently straying far from the path that would most directly bring about a positive vision in the future; our value to people in organizations is high but currently diminishing, and I would like to stop this trend before the situation deteriorates further. If we wish to become undisputed experts in the domain of understanding, predicting, and changing human behavior in organizations –

a righteous and appropriate goal, I would argue – there are many threats ahead. More tangibly, if we do not want Silicon Valley to "disrupt" I-O psychology and render us voiceless, we need to fix it now. To that end, I have developed four key recommendations for the field, two focusing upon academia and two bridging academia and practice.

First, it does I-O psychology no good to be "OB-lite," pursing esoteric business-school-values-inspired theory-building as the primary goal of published academic work, but at half the salaries. I-O psychology will never win that fight, but more importantly, we should not want to win that fight. The value of I-O psychology has traditionally been its ability to walk the tightrope between science and practice, integrating them both into a cohesive whole for the betterment of organizations. Technology has become central to practice, yet our science is not only woefully behind but actively trying to diminish that importance in the name of theory building, and in the name of staying nestled where we are comfortable. To reintegrate, academic I-O psychology must abandon business school values. The origins of our field are as an interdisciplinary applied psychology (Zickar & Highhouse, 2017), and we need to return to this view. It is this approach that made I-O psychology useful in the first place, an attractive recruiting pool for the very business schools that now threaten us. We must not lose that aspect of our identity; we are psychologists first (Adler & Boyce, 2016). Yet we should not be psychologists only. We must recognize that our field is already interdisciplinary in nature; integrating and studying technology, incorporating existing technology research into our own expertise, is merely another extension of this interdisciplinarity. Even business school research has a role to play in an interdisciplinary I-O psychology; it simply should not define I-O psychology. For those I-O psychologists already in business schools, I urge you to heed Zickar and Highhouse's recommendations: seek joint appointments in psychology and forge explicit, documented ties with your institution's psychology department. If you want your PhD students to be able to call themselves I-O psychologists, ensure they complete coursework in I-O psychology and interact with psychologists; do not put the burden solely on yourself to teach them to be an "I-O in a business school environment." It is not the same, and it never will be.

Second, we must repair the problems already emergent within academic I-O psychology. Most critically, journal editors must be more open to non-theoretical contributions. Importantly, this does not imply "atheoretical," nor does it imply that the theory we incorporate must be psychological in nature. For example, simply presenting data, a null hypothesis significance test, and an effect size without any context is not particularly useful in scientific research literature. This is atheoretical; it does not involve theory. However, if a researcher can make a compelling case that the test improves our understanding of some existing theory or leads to an interesting theoretical *question* that has not yet been answered, each of these are valid science. High-quality non-theoretical research contributions will call upon theory but do not seek to build new theory until sufficient information is known to be confident in that label. Individual studies do not need to "create theory" to be useful; instead, they can develop, test, comment, create new questions, or provide context for theory, among other purposes. Journal editors should not discard research simply because it does not present boxes and arrows linking concepts together alongside what two or three reviewers consider to be convincing narration. In the technology space, this is particularly relevant regarding exploratory research, the first scientific poke at what could become new research domains for I-O psychology. In the current publishing environment of our "top tier" journals, exploratory research related to a novel, untested technology is essentially unpublishable. This must change.

Third, we must improve training in technology for both academics and practitioners. For my part, I have tried to contribute one partial solution to this problem by releasing free, open-access course materials in data science intended for social scientists (http://datascience.tntlab.org). This course can be used to teach a one-semester graduate-level course in the statistical programming language R (Culpepper & Aguinis, 2011), starting from zero prior exposure and ending with web apps, natural language processing, and machine learning. Alternatively, it can be used to self-teach, using both the resources I provided and those found in websites providing interactive coding instruction and practice. From the feedback I have received on it, I know that I-O academics, I-O graduate students, and I-O practitioners have all been completing it; it does meet a need. But this is alone is insufficient. New graduate courses, retraining efforts among I-O psychologists working in organizations, data science groups in large consultancies, and other such formal efforts are needed. We cannot rely on grassroots technology evangelism alone; there are simply too many people currently undertrained in technology and lacking the skills they need to compete in the modern I-O environment. Sheets et al. (Chapter 2, this volume) provide specific, concrete steps for program chairs and I-O faculty, graduate students, and professionals to take to help narrow this gap. If all their suggestions were implemented field-wide, by both institutions and individuals, we would be in a much better position than we are now.

Fourth, I-O psychology must allow itself to become truly interdisciplinary. As mentioned before, I-O psychology has always had an interdisciplinary flavor to it. Historically, we have borrowed concepts and ideas from other areas of psychology, such as personality and social psychology, applied them to the context of employee management, and used that to develop advice for practitioners, whether in the form of practical theories, guidelines, or simple recommendations. We even integrated the field of statistics and helped realize its human psychology applications as the field of psychometrics. It is time to expand this effort to explicitly include technology, to formally blend I-O psychology research and practice with fields like computer science, data science, and human-computer interaction. Adler and Boyce (2016) stated, "We are I-O psychologists, not human resource technologists or data scientists" (p. 642). Although a true statement, this does not imply that human resource technology and data science should not be a part of modern I-O psychology. They absolutely must. As Ducey et al. (2015) argued, I-O psychologists should "join business analysts, data scientists, statisticians, mathematicians, and economists in creating the vanguard of expertise as we acclimate to the reality of analytics in the world of big data" (pp. 555–556). Their statement is specific to big data, but the view it implicitly endorses is broader than that. It suggests integrating these other fields into I-O psychology while integrating I-O psychology back into these other fields. This is what we must work toward. We cannot retreat into our siloes if we wish to have any impact on the world of work as it continues to change.

1.4 Conclusion

I-O psychology is at a crossroads. Down one path, we turn toward business school values, building ever-more-complex theories to better understand and explore every minute detail of organizational functioning, a rigorous but not particularly useful science to people trying to enact change within those organizations, staking a claim to exhaustive understanding of psychological constructs as what defines us. In the other direction, we embrace our own foundations as an interdisciplinary and applied psychology, integrating our field with the disciplines surrounding it, contributing to those fields while being augmented by them, forging our own unique identity, building a practical science, working shoulder to shoulder with all those working to understand employee behavior in the modern workplace, regardless of their discipline of origin. I do not know which way I-O will turn, but I hope it is toward this latter, brighter future.

References

Adler, S. & Boyce, A. S. (2016). In defense of practical theory. *Industrial and Organizational Psychology, 9*, 641–645.

Aguinis, H., Bradley, K. J., & Brodersen, A. (2014). Industrial-organizational psychologists in business schools: Brain drain or eye opener? *Industrial and Organizational Psychology, 7*, 284–303.

Aiken, J. R. & Hanges, P. J. (2015). Teach an I-O to fish: Integrating data science into I-O graduate education. *Industrial and Organizational Psychology, 8*, 539–544.

Armstrong, M. B., Ferrell, J. Z., Collmus, A. B., & Landers, R. N. (2016). Correcting misconceptions about gamification of assessment: More than SJTs and badges. *Industrial and Organizational Psychology, 9*, 671–677.

Arthur, W. & Villado, A. J. (2008). The importance of distinguishing between constructs and methods when comparing predictors in personnel selection research and practice. Journal of Applied Psychology, 93, 435–442.

Barrick, M. R. & Mount, M. K. (1991). The big five personality dimensions and job performance: A meta-analysis. *Personnel Psychology, 44*, 1–26.

Behrend, T. S. & Landers, R. N. (2017). The wicked problem of scholarly impact. *Industrial and Organizational Psychology, 10*, 602–605.

Boyd, D. & Crawford, K. (2012). Critical questions for big data: Provocations for a cultural, technological, and scholarly phenomenon. *Information, Communication & Society, 15*, 662–679.

Briner, R. B. & Rousseau, D. M. (2011). Evidence-based I-O psychology: Not there yet. *Industrial and Organizational Psychology, 4*, 3–22.

Byrne, Z. S., Hayes, T. L., McPhail, S. M., Hakel, M. D., Cortina, J. M., & McHenry, J. J. (2014). Educating industrial-organizational psychologists for science and practice: Where do we go from here? *Industrial and Organizational Psychology, 7*, 2–14.

Campbell, J. P. & Wilmot, M. P. (2018). The functioning of theory in industrial, work and organizational psychology. In D. S. Ones, N. Anderson, C. Viswesvaran, and H. K. Sinangil (Eds.), *The SAGE handbook of industrial, work and organizational psychology: Personnel psychology and employee performance* (Vol. 1, pp. 3–37). London, UK: Sage.

Chamorro-Premuzic, T., Winsborough, D., Sherman, R. A., & Hogan, R. (2016). New talent signals: Shiny new objects or a brave new world? *Industrial and Organizational Psychology, 9*, 621–640.

Church, A. H. (1998). From both sides now: A look to the future. *The Industrial-Organizational Psychologist, 35*(4), 91–104.

Culpepper, S. A. & Aguinis, H. (2011). R is for revolution: A cutting-edge, free, open source statistical package. *Organizational Research Methods, 14*, 735–740.

De Corte, W., Sackett, P. R., & Lievens, F. (2011). Designing pareto-optimal selection systems: Formalizing the decisions required for selection system development. *Journal of Applied Psychology, 96*, 907–926.

Ducey, A. J., Guenole, N., Weiner, S. P., Herleman, H. A., Gibby, R. E., & Delany, T. (2015). I-Os in the vanguard of big data analytics and privacy. *Industrial and Organizational Psychology, 8*, 555–563.

Ekehammar, B. (1974). Interactionism in personality from a historical perspective. *Psychological Bulletin, 81*, 1026–1048.

Gibson, J. J. (1960). The concept of the stimulus in psychology. *American Psychologist, 15*, 694–703.

Grawitch, M. J., Winton, S. L., Mudigonda, S. P., & Buerck, J. P. (2017). Technology is more than just error. *Industrial and Organizational Psychology, 10*, 654–701.

Guzzo, R. A., Fink, A. A., King, E., Tonidandel, S., & Landis, R. S. (2015). Big data recommendations for industrial-organizational psychology. *Industrial and Organizational Psychology, 8*, 491–508.

Harris, M. M. & Hollman, K. D. (2013). TIP-TOPICS – The top trends in I-O psychology: A graduate student perspective. *The Industrial-Organizational Psychologist, 50* (4), 120–124.

Highhouse, S. & Zickar, M. J. (1997). Where has all the psychology gone? *The Industrial-Organizational Psychologist, 35*(2), 82–88.

International Taskforce on Assessment Center Guidelines. (2015). Guidelines and ethical considerations for assessment center operations. *Journal of Management, 41*, 1244–1273.

Jackson, D. J. R., Michaelides, G., Dewberry, C., & Kim, Y.-J. (2016). Everything that you have ever been told about assessment center ratings is confounded. *Journal of Applied Psychology, 101*, 976–994.

Klimoski, R. & Brickner, M. (1987). Why do assessment centers work? The puzzle of assessment center validity. *Personnel Psychology*, 40, 243-260.

Kuncel, N. R. & Sackett, P. R. (2014). Resolving the assessment center construct validity problem (as we know it). *Journal of Applied Psychology, 99*, 38–47.

Landers, R. N. (2016). Crash course in I-O technology: An introduction plus a crash course in R. *The Industrial-Organizational Psychologist*. Retrieved from www.siop.org/tip/july16/crash.aspx.

Landers, R. N. & Behrend, T. S. (2017). When are models of technology in psychology most useful? *Industrial and Organizational Psychology, 10*, 668–675.

Lefkowitz, J. (2008). To prosper, organizational psychology should . . . expand the values of organizational psychology to match the quality of its ethics. *Journal of Organizational Behavior, 29*, 439–453.

Lewin, K. (1936). *Principles of topological psychology* (F. Heider & G. M. Heider, Trans.). New York, NY: McGraw-Hill.

Maynard, D. C. & Ferdman, B. M. (2009). The marginalized workforce: How I-O psychology can make a difference. *The Industrial-Organizational Psychologist, 46*(4), 25–29.

Orlikowski, W. J. (1992). The duality of technology: Rethinking the concept of technology in organizations. *Organization Science, 3*, 398–427.

Pfeffer, J. & Fong, C. T. (2002). The end of business schools? Less success than meets the eye. *Academy of Management Learning & Education, 1*, 78–95.

Polster, C. (2007). The nature and implications of the growing importance of research grants to Canadian universities and academics. *Higher Education, 53*, 599–622.

Poeppelman, T. & Sinar, E. (2016). The modern app: 2017 technology trends: Are I-O psychologists prepared? *The Industrial-Organizational Psychologist*. Retrieved from www.siop.org/tip/jan17/ma.aspx.

Putka, D. J., Schwall, A. R., Taylor, B. J., Bateman, T., Beatty, A. S., Jin, J., . . . Walmsley, P. T. (2018). SIOP Select: A SIOP machine learning competition: Learning by doing. Presented at the 2018 annual conference of the Society for Industrial and Organizational Psychology, Chicago, IL.

Reeves, B., Yeyekelis, L., & Cummings, J. J. (2016). The use of media in media psychology. *Media Psychology, 19*, 49–71.

Sheets, T. L., Belwalkar, B. B., Toaddy, S. R., & McClure, T. K. (2019). Filling the I-O/technology void: Technology and training in I-O psychology. In R. N. Landers (Ed.), *Cambridge handbook of technology and employee behavior*. Cambridge, UK: Cambridge University Press.

Silzer, R. F. & Cober, R. (2010). The future of I-O psychology practice: Part I: Future directions for I-O practice identified by leading practitioners. *The Industrial-Organizational Psychologist, 48*(2), 67–79.

Tett, R. P., Walser, B., Brown, C., Simonet, D. V., & Tonidandel, S. (2013). The 2011 SIOP graduate program benchmarking survey: Part 3: Curriculum and competencies. *The Industrial-Organizational Psychologist, 50*(4), 69–90.

Zickar, M. J. & Highhouse, S. (2017). Where has all the psychology gone? (Twenty years later). *Industrial and Organizational Psychology, 10*, 616–621.

Zusman, A. (2005). Challenges facing higher education in the twenty-first century. In P. G. Altbach, R. O. Berdahl, & P. J. Gumport (Eds.), *American higher education in the twenty-first century* (2nd edn., pp. 115–160). Baltimore, MD: The John Hopkins University Press.

2 Filling the I-O/Technology Void

Technology and Training in I-O Psychology

Tilman L. Sheets, Bharati B. Belwalkar, Steven R. Toaddy, and Tara K. McClure

When IBM's Watson won at Jeopardy against the then-champion Brad Rutter in 2011, it became apparent that technology was well on its way to surpassing human capabilities. Just a few decades ago, the idea that a computer system could understand idiomatic expressions, puns, and human components of language was unfathomable. According to Rayz (2017), such notions are no longer a question of *if*, but of *when*. Technology continues to permeate every sphere of modern life, and the workplace is no exception. Over two decades ago, Cascio (1995) recognized the influence of technology and how it would influence the domain of work.

In the time since Leavitt & Whisler's (1958) Harvard Business Review article, *Management in the 1980's*, which outlined their vision of technology's future impact on organizations, management theorists have viewed technology as a pervasive and essential part of most organizations. One would think that this embedded view of technology would lead to a sufficient understanding of technology on the part of those who rely on it. This does not appear to be the case, however; perhaps due to the pace of technological change, most non-technology workers have limited knowledge about the field (Bessen, 2014) which could result in a restricted view of technology's strategic role in their organization.

Given the rate of change in various organizational functions due to technology, there is an increasing need for industrial-organizational psychology (I-O) to understand the influence of technology on jobs and organizations (Cascio, 1995; Craiger, 1997; Turnage, 1990), because, for the organizations, the costs of not doing so could be missed opportunities, obscurity, or even becoming irrelevant in their respective industries (Perez & Soete, 1988). From a local Girl Scout troop's use of social media to announce sales of cookies at a stand on the corner to Google's use of powerful machine-learning algorithms to quickly and dynamically select the best color for a particular graphic on a webpage, many of the changes taking place in the way work is accomplished are inextricably tied to technology. Part of this change involves the incorporation of technology into the language of business. While the technical savvy of most people often does not go beyond the superficial use of apps on their tablets and phones, the information revolution is changing at an exponential rate and market forces are requiring the leadership of organizations to keep up (Bonchek, 2016). The inability to effectively communicate with technology professionals and to understand the value of such communication can result in some costly consequences.

The extent of this problem within the corporate world is in some way demonstrated by the increased availability of training on this topic. For example, Massachusetts Institute of Technology (MIT) offers a course entitled "Essential IT for Non-IT Executives" which is aimed at teaching non-technical senior business managers to better understand technology and communicate with Information Technology (IT) professionals. In addition to understanding and communicating with members of the IT team, I-O professionals need expertise in the use of a growing list of apps/programs to accomplish many of the tasks associated with their jobs.

As a group, I-O professionals seem to suffer from a limited understanding of technology and technology's potential contribution to organizational change. There are few things that an I-O practitioner or researcher would touch in an organization that would not benefit from including the expertise of IT professionals (Fitzgerald et al., 2014). Yet, there appears to be a gap between IT and I-O. For example, I-O relies on organizational data to assess organizational needs and the effectiveness of interventions. Although the use of data is at the core of how I-O approaches organizations from a scientist/practitioner perspective, with few exceptions, most of those in our field would be hard pressed to explain how to access and explore their organization's database on their own. While we are by no means advocating that I-O take over the IT role, we do believe that it is important for the I-O community to become more knowledgeable consumers of technological services within an organizational context and that they are able to effectively communicate with IT professionals. One important step in this direction is to develop technology training for graduate students in I-O. However, there is little in the way of guidance regarding the content of the curriculum needed for training. Along these lines, this chapter will explore the need for technology training for I-O students and for those who have already moved beyond the classroom. We address the need for training by looking at some of the areas in which I-O professionals work: academics, research, and applied practice (Silzer, Cober, & Erickson, 2010).

2.1 Evolution of Technology in Organizations

In the period from 1945 to 1960, workplaces undertook heavy technological adoption due to the Second World War (WWII). After WWII, structure and functioning of organizations through technology were substantially revolutionized. Computer technology slowly moved from just military use to business use. When IBM introduced the first personal computer, businesses had to reassess their practices and work structure (Craiger, 1997). During this period, the most important feature of a more technology-focused organization was an emphasis on teamwork instead of individualized work roles. Systems became more open and groupware computing became an essential tool to many organizations. Organizations changed from isolation to an open-networked system (Craiger, 1997). The use of technology in the workplace continued to steadily increase thereafter.

In the period from 1960 to 1990, workplace/office automation increased dramatically (Turnage, 1990). Office technology altered job tasks of many front-line workers, and computerization largely reduced tasks such as data input. Teleworking communication technologies such as computer conferencing and electronic mail made it easier for employees to work outside the office. Managerial decisions began to be heavily aided by technology support systems and data analytics. Electronic monitoring systems changed the way in which supervisors monitored and evaluated performance, allowing them to use more accurate projections of completed tasks.

As we entered the twenty-first century, the fast-paced changes in our technology-driven world have increased the transformation of business to a more globalized market. Indeed, the assumption that technology will replace many jobs may be erroneous, when in fact there is an ever-increasing need for a higher-skilled workforce (Xue & Larson, 2015). However, the trend that Cascio (1995) identified of companies downsizing because they prefer to pay fewer, smarter people who can handle cutting-edge technology appears to continue (Boniface & Rashmi, 2012). These smart people are valuable due to their ability to use technology to increase productivity. The field of I-O is no exception: I-O has the opportunity to use technology in the way we study and work with organizations. For example, technology has allowed I-O professionals to expand their skillset from more traditional approaches of working with and studying organizations to more advanced technological approaches (e.g., virtual reality, machine learning). Moreover, I-O professionals have an opportunity to use the large amount of information that technology has provided to find new and innovative ways to help companies advance in selection, assessment, training, teamwork, and performance management.

Examining the "dark" and "smart" side of workplace technology, Holland and Bardoel (2016) state that although technological changes have revolutionized the way work is conceptualized, these advances have provided an unprecedented ability to monitor employees inside and outside the workplace. For instance, technology has made a work-from-home option available to employees; it has also made tracking hours and people easier. However, the same technology has blurred the line between working and non-working hours. Additionally, the impact of technology creates challenging legal (Schess, 2013) and ethical (Sandler, 2014) ramifications that are important in understanding work and organizations. All in all, technology has advanced business in very powerful ways, but with all of the positives there come concerning negatives upon which I-O research and practice will need to focus attention.

2.2 I-O and Technology

As far back as 1995, Cascio recognized that in the world of technology-dependent organizations, I-O professionals have an opportunity to contribute substantially. Through job analysis, employee selection, training and development, performance appraisal, compensation, and organizational development, I-O professionals can leverage and have leveraged technology to revolutionize the workplace. More recently, Cascio and Montealegre (2016) examined five technologies that I-O professionals should know in order to better understand technology's impact on the way work is done in organizations: cloud and mobile computing, big data and machine learning, sensors and intelligent manufacturing, advanced robotics and drones, and clean-energy technologies. As is the case with the world of business in general, technology has changed I-O practices and reshaped research agendas in several ways (Harris & Hollman, 2013).

Within the area of recruitment, technology has altered organizational strategy from letting qualified candidates come to them to being more strategic, personalized, and targeted in the search for top talent (Blacksmith & Poeppelman, 2014). Recruiters have gone from placing job postings in newspapers and on websites, using face-to-face networking, and cold-calling candidates to leveraging social media like LinkedIn, Facebook, and Twitter to gain quick and easy access to qualified candidates who are not actively seeking new employment. This has opened up a much wider talent pool and organizations are turning to technological advances such as artificial intelligence, machine learning, big data, and analytics to assist recruiters in sifting through large talent pools to identify top candidates who are the right fit for the job (Fallon, 2016; Maurer, 2017; Zielinski, 2017). For example, artificial-intelligence tools can be used to automate much of the initial communication process with candidates, using natural language processing to ask questions based on job requirements and answer candidate questions about the organization, and keeping candidates apprised of their status in the hiring process (Zielinski, 2017). Organizations also have the ability to collect large amounts of data on job candidates and employees (Guilfoyle et al., 2016). They can then employ analytics and predictive modeling to identify sources that lead to new hires, as well as to identify ideal talent profiles that can be used to seek out both active and passive job seekers (Maurer, 2017). In addition to these trends, we are seeing organizations leverage mobile applications in their recruitment processes, allowing candidates to search and apply for jobs using their smart devices (Noguchi, 2017). Organizations are also making use of gamification to build their brand awareness, attract candidates, and allow candidates to evaluate both candidate-company and candidate-role fit (Armstrong, Landers, & Collmus, 2016; Zielinski, 2015). Because the use of social media has become an important tool for recruitment, organizations run the risk of finding information about candidates that they are not legally permitted to have (Schess, 2013). An employer may not inquire about protected characteristics that allow discrimination, but the use of social media can easily uncover candidate identities and thus information regarding these protected characteristics. Although the jury is still out on how (and whether) organizations should use information about their potential employees gained through social media, I-O professionals are often looked at as subject matter experts in the area of social media, recruitment, and employment law. I-O professionals are required to keep abreast of not only the evolving role of technology in recruitment, but also with technology's potential negative consequences.

Technology has become an integral component within the area of selection. Turnage (1990) stated that the primary concern for I-O professionals has somewhat changed from selecting the right candidate for the job to finding the right job that fits with the right candidate, which requires the workplace to develop an environment that accommodates the abilities of the worker. Traditional paper-and-pencil tests are now being delivered through computers and mobile devices, where candidates can access them anytime, from anywhere (Arthur et al., 2017; Reynolds & Dickter, 2017). Increasingly, assessments are incorporating computer-adaptive testing to protect test content, mitigate cheating, and provide a more accurate assessment of a candidate's ability, and are also incorporating high-fidelity item presentation, including embedded video, audio, and animated graphics (Reynolds & Dickter, 2017). In addition, automated item generation using algorithms to build assessments on the fly is an example of another technology-based tool (Lee & Cho, 2015). We are also seeing alternative item response formats such as hotspots and drag and drop, as well as more free-form responses given advances in natural language processing (Reynolds & Dickter, 2017). In an effort to create an engaging and entertaining candidate experience, more and more organizations are turning toward gamified assessments, serious games, and simulations (Arthur et al., 2017; Zielinski, 2015). While the introduction of virtual games, which integrate points, badges, competition, and role-playing, is fairly recent (Zielinski, 2015), simulations have continued to grow in popularity, as they provide high fidelity representations of actual work tasks and exhibit higher validities compared to other assessment methods (Lievens & Patterson, 2011). As technology continues to develop, high fidelity simulations will become even more realistic through the use of virtual, mixed, and augmented reality (Aguinis, Henle, & Beaty, 2001; Reynolds & Dickter, 2017). Organizations are also beginning to incorporate virtual interviews into the selection process and are working to leverage voice-analysis and emotion-recognition software to help gauge a candidate's emotional reaction and truthfulness during the interview by analyzing things like facial expressions, word choice, speech rate, and vocal tones (Zielinski, 2017). The rise of big data and predictive analytics has also brought about increased interest in mining social-media profiles to obtain information on candidates' background, personality, experience, and attitudes to assist with selection decisions (Guilfoyle et al., 2016). These recent advancements in the selection and assessment area have changed the requirements of I-O psychologists' roles. Apart from understanding the fundamental psychometric principles, they are required to know about the different components of technology used in building, deploying, and maintaining such high-fidelity selection and assessment tools.

Within the area of training and development, technology is redefining workforce learning methods and tools. As Kapadia (2016) points out, training is no longer confined to a classroom and led by an instructor; advanced software, technology tools, and innovative methods are being used to enhance quality of and participation and engagement in training programs. Kapadia identifies the top technology trends within training and development as mobile learning, video-based training, virtual environments and avatars, HTML-5 and responsive design, automation and adaptive learning, and big data. Similar to the selection space, online training is going mobile, allowing learners to access training on demand using their smart devices, and will soon be the most conventional medium to reach the digitally connected workforce (Parsons, 2014). While virtual reality has been used for training within the military and medical fields for some time (Aguinis et al., 2001; Beach, 2016; Davies, 2016a), advances in technology will make this method of training more popular for a wider number of industries and roles (Feloni, 2017). In addition, augmented reality is being used as the primary tool in a type of just-in-time training where workers access training on an as-needed basis through a heads-up display (Shamma, 2017). Through the use of artificial intelligence, organizations are also leveraging virtual training coaches or avatars who engage with learners during the training process (Kapadia, 2016). The development of HTML-5 and responsive design has allowed for the ability to design interactive and engaging learning experiences that are accessible across most platforms, devices and browsers, providing a seamless and uniform user experience (Kapadia, 2016). Adaptive training systems allow organizations to personalize the learning experience by altering the content presented during the training based on learner needs (Kapadia, 2016; Poeppelman, Lobene & Blacksmith, 2015). Big data are impacting the training space as well; as organizations amass large data sets from their digital training offerings, the data can be analyzed to provide insights into the learning process, learner behavior, usage patterns, and effectiveness, which can in turn be used to enhance, develop, and customize training offerings (Kapadia, 2016). Organizations are also using gamification to improve overall training effectiveness and learner motivation during training (Armstrong, et al., 2016; Meister, 2012). Finally, wearable technologies, such as smartwatches and smartglasses, are being incorporated into the learning process to provide access to manuals and tutorials, real-time support resources, and even immediate, inconspicuous feedback during the training process (Pappas, 2015). I-O professionals have been playing a crucial role in building such training programs; they understand adult learning theories and feedback principles and they integrate this knowledge with IT.

Craiger's (1997) observation that I-O professionals need to change their view of performance and appraisal systems because workers are participating in more teamwork due to technological advances remains true today. In addition to teamwork within highly matrixed organizations, there has been a shift from fixed paper-and-pencil or highly static in-house enterprise technology platforms to more dynamic online systems within the area of performance management due in large part to cloud-computing technology (Hunt, 2011). This has not only made the process more efficient, flexible, and easy to use, but has also allowed organizations to collect data on their performance-management processes that can be combined with other organizational data and used to provide talent insights in real time. Technology is helping organizations get better performance data with greater frequency to facilitate performance-management conversations throughout the year, rather than just on a yearly basis. Some organizations have implemented systems to crowdsource performance data in real time, allowing employees to request feedback from supervisors, colleagues, and internal customers after meetings and completed projects (Ewenstein, Hancock, & Komm, 2016). This feedback includes both structured and unstructured formats and weights responses based on how much exposure the feedback provider has to the requestor. Electronic monitoring systems and wearable computing devices such as smartwatches and sensors embedded into identification cards are also able to gather real-time data from employees and their environment which can provide valuable performance information and help employees increase productivity by better understanding how they spend their time (Cascio & Montealegre, 2016). Developments in technology (e.g., the Internet of Things) allow organizations to track how employees are spending their time, as well as to track employee whereabouts within the office (Greenwald, 2017). By analyzing employee email and other messages and scoring them as containing positive or negative sentiment, managers can be alerted to any shifts or changes in tone as indicator of low engagement or intention to leave (2017).

Finally, another technological trend is the amount of new information that is produced every day. International Data Corporation (2017) estimates that the digital universe is doubling in size every two years, and by 2020 will approach 44 trillion gigabytes of data. This dramatic increase in information used by organizational decision-makers and managers for predictive analyses, communication, accounting tasks, work scheduling, and other routinized operations at work has led to the development of innovative approaches in the analysis of data (Guzzo et al., 2015). The use of such big data and analytics has enabled organizations to proactively and actively retain valuable talent by predicting when employees might be looking to make a career change, advising managers on how they can retain them, and providing suggestions for potential next steps in their career path based on what others in similar situations have done (Boudreau, 2014).

These are just a few examples of how technology has permeated the world of I-O and altered the way we manage talent. While technology fell off the Society of Industrial-Organizational Psychology's (SIOP) list of the Top 10 Workplace Trends of 2017, it is reflected in nearly all of the trends that made the list in 2016. For example, capturing the voice of the employee (Trend #7) involves collecting employee feedback through innovations like mobile pulse tools and feedback apps, as well as analyzing both qualitative and passive data (SIOP, 2016). These developments are leading to the demise of the annual organizational survey, allowing organizations to be more flexible and responsive to their workforces (Davies, 2016b). Several of SIOP's 2017 trends are related to data and analytics: the need to integrate data across sources, systems, and processes (Trend #9), people analytics (Trend #4), and leveraging data to make data-driven decisions (Trend #3; SIOP, 2016). Big data are shaping talent management in a number of ways; applicants and employees alike are leaving a digital footprint and organizations are exploring how best to use those data (Blacksmith & Poeppelman, 2015; Davies, 2016b). Given these trends, topics such as data acquisition, data storage, and data retrieval are becoming more commonplace, and exposure to big-data tools (e.g., MongoDB, Hadoop, and Python) and data visualization tools (e.g., Tableau) is beneficial to keeping up with changes in this area.

In conclusion, technology has become an ingrained part of our work life in more ways than we could have imagined just a couple of decades ago. Needless to say, it has also transformed the role that I-O professionals play within organizations. It is, therefore, essential that I-O professionals study technology and prepare for future technological changes.

2.3 Prioritization of Training Needs

While the scope of technology and its role in the work of I-O professionals is somewhat overwhelming, we took a straightforward approach to answer the question of what technology training is needed for I-O psychologists. Our approach was to look at the need for training in technology from the perspective of those who professionally identify with I-O psychology. We used a snowball-sampling approach using social media (viz. Twitter) and by asking friends and associates in our professional networks to survey I-O professionals regarding the importance of training on a variety of technological tools (viz., R, Excel, SPSS, and SAS) and areas of technology (viz., cloud computing, programing languages, internet-specific languages, IoT, and Structured Query Language). Participants were asked to categorize tools and areas and to rank each of them into three different groups: Important, Not Essential, and Not Needed.

Over 52 percent of our survey participants (n = 64) indicated that they *always* interact with technology. Moreover, 50 percent of our participants indicated that they have experience in hiring I-O professionals, implying that they recruit and/or select I-O graduates. Although making up a smaller proportion of our sample (viz. a little over 30 percent), we closely inspected responses from the participants who were both: frequent users of technology and highly involved in hiring I-O professionals on their teams. We figured that their responses would be helpful in understanding what technological skills are frequently in use and required on the job upon entry for I-O professionals.

Results unanimously indicated that Microsoft Excel, SPSS, and R were the most important technological tools. On the other hand, programing languages (e.g., Python, Java), cloud technologies (e.g., Hadoop, Spark), and internet coding (e.g., HTML, PHP) were considered the least essential technologies. We noticed a peculiar response pattern for such technologies as machine learning, artificial intelligence, and SAS, which demonstrated divided opinions among our participants. The survey did not contain questions on additional background information regarding the nature of participant's job, organization, and sector. The results of our survey are listed in Table 2.1 in the order of their rankings.

Given I-O psychology's close relationship with the world of business, it is of little surprise that Microsoft's Excel program was at the top of the list of important technology ("Survey reveals popularity of Excel," 2015). R and SPSS tied for second place on the list of importance. Given the long history of SPSS in many academic programs, it is interesting that has established itself as a competitor. The remaining tools were primarily seen as not essential for training

Table 2.1 *Technology importance survey*

Important	Not Essential
Excel	SQL
SPSS	IoT
R	SAS
	Programing languages
	AI/Machine learning
	Cloud technologies
	Internet programming

I-O professionals. These results provide limited evidence that the three software programs in our *Important* list represent what I-O professionals see as fundamental skills for I-O graduates. Additionally, the results seem to indicate that the primary technological skills in which I-O professionals need expertise involve the manipulation and analysis of data. There is less concern that I-O professionals have training in areas that would increase communication with IT or allow them to better understand technological infrastructure. However, it is of note that none of the tools or areas was ranked as *Not Needed*.

2.4 I-O Academia and Practice

I-O academicians need to have an arsenal of technical skills that allow them to train their students – both those intending to become academicians and those intending to become practitioners. While there may not be any clear distinction between the two in terms of the type of technical expertise needed, the degree of expertise may be different for the two types of I-O professionals. For example, while all I-O professionals might benefit from a general familiarity with the concepts associated with Learning Management Systems (LMS), academicians are much more likely to use an LMS (e.g., Blackboard or Moodle). Conversely, academics may need to understand Tableau at least well enough to introduce it to students, while many practitioners may need to master the software. Additionally, as mentioned earlier, any instance of technical acumen needed by an academic may also be needed by a practitioner, and vice versa. It all boils down to the probability associated with the need to use a particular technical skill or set of skills.

As mentioned earlier, in their review of technology's impact on work and organizations, Casio and Montealegre (2016) identify five categories of technology that are dramatically changing business on a global scale. A basic understanding of each of these areas should be required learning for any budding I-O professional, but a deeper understanding of these technologies would benefit aspiring academicians and researchers by allowing them to understand how the categories of technology are changing work and how research can assist in understanding such change. Additionally, I-O academicians should understand how these technologies are specifically changing the work of I-O professionals (e.g., machine learning as an analytic tool).

Within each of Casio and Montealegre's (2016) broad categories is a long list of specific technologies. For example, while cloud computing involves an understanding of the basic premise of distributed data and network services, there are many different technologies that can be used in the design of a cloud strategy. The degree to which a student should receive training in any specific technology is a judgment call on the part of the faculty providing training. As is the case with most areas of academic training, many topics are introduced and it is up to students to take a deeper dive into a specific topic.

Of particular interest within the long list of emerging technologies is the area of big data and the analytic approaches used to bring meaning to it. While traditional approaches to data analysis remain an important part of I-O training, alternative approaches such as those using big data require a change in how I-O professionals view data and the *sense making* required to understand it (Crane & Self, 2014). Traditional approaches (e.g., GLM) often do not apply, and the skill sets used to manipulate and analyze big data require very different approaches. In addition, and luckily, big-data analytics is becoming easier and more accessible (e.g., Watson Analytics). Indeed, as machine learning improves and makes the analysis of big data more accessible, the need for special expertise related to the analysis of big data will be greatly reduced. However, experts who can understand and make sense of the results will continue to be in demand (Chen, Chiang, & Storey, 2012).

2.5 Training Recommendations: Steps for Program Chairs/ Faculty

The clearest course through which we can promote a broad standard package of technology skills in our field is through curriculum design in graduate programs. These recommendations are aimed at program chairs and at individual faculty; in some cases, small supplements of content within a course will be adequate to address training needs while in other cases broad curricular redesign will be necessary or at least prudent.

In the former category fall the examination of existing core content areas – such as statistics and research methodology – from new perspectives. For instance, modifying or augmenting traditional statistics curricula with R and with Excel content – in addition to SPSS content – will cover some of the important technology skills discussed above. In adding modules regarding tools such as Tableau, educators can serve three purposes simultaneously: helping I-O students understand database architecture and philosophy (in connecting to datasets), practicing essential skills in business communication, and becoming familiar with technology tools with which they will be working on a weekly or daily basis in their careers (in some cases). More challenging but still within the purview of statistics instructors will be coverage of the art of wielding I-O content knowledge to both drive and to give meaning to data-science functions like data mining and machine-learning-algorithm deployment; both before and after the "black box" is developed, I-Os can and should lend their expertise from the theoretical and empirical bases of understanding of human functioning.

A tried and tested method for covering content that program chairs consider important but not within the domains of expertise of core program faculty is, of course, requiring elective or specific courses taught in other disciplines (e.g., management, human resources, marketing, and statistics). As those curricula evolve along similar lines, these same strategies – and perhaps even these same elective courses – will serve some of the training needs; marketing and statistics courses in particular should pick up some of the slack in data-science technologies. However, I-O program chairs should also consider widening the list of acceptable and/or required courses to include those from more IT-focused disciplines.

It is unfair to say that curricula have been static, unresponsive, and slow to evolve previously – faculty update their course content with the most recent empirical and theoretical work – but the pace of change that we observe in the technologies discussed above necessitates a two-part modification of such update strategies. First and most obviously, faculty must be willing to adjust whole chunks of their course content – see as a gateway example how training courses have changed over the past few decades to accommodate the coverage of new training-deployment strategies. This is true both in terms of the specific content covered (think new theories of leadership) but also in terms of the course learning objectives (think of selection-system design following the popularization of nonlinear-effects modeling – the game itself changed). Beyond this simple adaptation, though, lies a second and more subtle skill: not throwing in one's lot with flashes in the pan. These recommendations and this chapter and book in general voice a perspective of change and of embracing the future, but it is possible to embrace the future too enthusiastically – and it is difficult to tell, without the benefit of hindsight, just where that line lies. For a simple (if thus not illustrative) example, consider expertise in database architecture: should program chairs decide that the equivalent of a minor in this topic be necessary for all I-O students, we will likely find ourselves with an inappropriately high level of knowledge in that area. This recommendation is, admittedly, vague and perhaps thus unhelpful, but we advise caution – discretion may be the better part of innovation.

In a similar vein, consider that program chairs are, sadly, not perfect. Ignoring even the vagaries of technology and thus the vicissitudes of curriculum/training-needs matches, it is easier to know what must be done than to do it – because of one's workload or because of the resistance of the herd of cats that we call a core faculty. Additionally, a balance between (a) doing what it says on the box (i.e., teaching to SIOP's standards; giving students the preparation expected and advertised for the program in question), (b) keeping up with all of these changes and covering the necessary additional content, and (c) helping each student prepare for their specific career objectives/trajectory generates some potentially intractable problems. We thus recommend that program faculty clearly communicate that, at least in part, the onus is on each student to take control of their own preparation whilst in graduate school.

Additionally, as per the recommendations of the SIOP Futures Task Force (2017), I-O programs need to take specific steps. They need to increase their focus on work-centric/vocational-training opportunities, develop interdisciplinary I-O curricula, redefine I-O principles in light of technology, and introduce courses on HR technology. Additionally, they need to forge multidisciplinary partnerships with other fields (e.g., business, management, human factors, industrial engineering) by connecting students from other disciplines and introducing coursework or projects that require students from other related disciplines to work together. In summary, graduate schools will need to encourage multidisciplinary thinking among students.

2.6 Training Recommendations: Steps for Graduate Students

In concord with the above discussion of program curricula and individual responsibility, graduate students have several steps that they can take to improve their technology-training outcomes. They can make deliberate choices about elective courses – choosing and even, as necessary, advocating for the acceptance of those that will best serve their professional needs. Students can, to the extent permitted by the courses that they take, steer their particular course projects/papers/exercises to include as much of the correct flavor of a technology focus as possible – for instance, using a course report as a justification to learn and deploy data-visualization software, switching between SPSS and R and Excel to complete statistics assignments, and communicating with data scientists in careers courses. Finally, students can make use of the abundantly available technologies in the categories that Kapadia (2016) discussed – video-based supplemental instruction on all of the above technologies is available free of charge on the internet, wanting only for the time and motivation of a student to make use of it. Of additional benefit, the use of these training technologies in any context can help students understand those technologies' deployment in professional contexts – that is, for example, completing a video-based online course can help the student appreciate viscerally the design and deployment of such courses, tasks in which they may need to engage professionally following graduation.

2.7 Training Recommendations: Steps for Professionals

Graduate school serves as an opportunity for focused self-improvement. The life professional, whether academic or applied or both or neither, does not – or at least does not to such an extent. The loss of available time for learning can be compensated for, in some circumstances, by the gain in proximal motivation to learn, however; professionals can encounter pressing needs to become conversant in a technology, be it necessary for immediate and personal use or for communicating with members of an organization with depth of expertise in an unfamiliar area. Regardless, while courses at the graduate level may be unavailable to most professionals, the same free-of-charge internet-based resources are still available – and additional, intense, expensive short courses in everything from statistical packages to data-science methods to refreshers of recent findings from the field of I-O may be available to more well-funded I-O professionals and not to graduate students. Continued advocacy for one's development is perhaps more necessary for professionals than it is for graduate students, and these tools and opportunities offer routes by which such development can occur.

2.8 Concluding Thoughts

Raymond Kurzweil – American author, inventor, futurist, and engineer working on Google's natural language project – has made the prediction that, by 2029, technology will be capable of human-level intelligence and emotions and that technology will have the ability to improve upon itself (Kurzweil & Kapor, 2009). Although it has its critics (see Kurzweil & Kapor, 2009), Kurzweil's prediction indicates that we are living in the world of rapid technological change. Reflecting on how equipped I-O psychology is to grapple with such rapid change and its impact on I-O training, it is important to assess how well, and if, we are currently training I-O psychologists-to-be in terms of technology and whether our current approach is "enough." SIOP's educational training in I-O psychology guidelines seem to have failed to adequately address this consideration (Coovert & Thompson, 2014; Sheets & Belwalkar, 2017). While their Guidelines for Education and Training in Industrial-Organizational Psychology (SIOP, 2016) sporadically mention technology training, there remains a tremendous need to initiate a dialogue on the importance of including technology in the I-O competency model.

References

Aguinis, H., Henle, C. A., & Beaty Jr., J. C. (2001). Virtual reality technology: A new tool for personnel selection. *International Journal of Selection and Assessment*, *9*, 70–83.

Armstrong, M. B., Landers, R. N., & Collmus, A. B. (2016). Gamifying recruitment, selection, training, and performance management: Game-thinking in human resource management. In H. Gangadharbatla & D. Z. Davis (Eds.), *Emerging research and trends in gamification* (pp. 140–165). Hershey, PA: IGI Global.

Arthur Jr., W., Doverspike, D., Kinney, T. B., & O'Connell, M. (2017). The impact of emerging technologies on selection model and research: Mobile devices and gamification as exemplars. In J. L. Farr & N. T. Tippins (Eds.), *Handbook of employee selection* (2nd edn., pp. 855–873). New York, NY: Routledge.

Beach, D. (October 3, 2016). The impact of technology on employee training. *LinkedIn*. Retrieved from www.linkedin.com/pulse/impact-technology-employee-training-david-beach.

Bessen, J. (2014). Workers Don't Have the Skills They Need – and They Know It. *Harvard Business Review*. Retrieved from https://hbr.org/2014/09/workers-dont-have-the-skills-they-need-and-they-know-it.

Blacksmith, N. & Poeppelman, T. (2014). Three ways social media and technology have changed recruitment. *The Industrial-Organizational Psychologist*, *52*(1), 114–121.

Blacksmith, N. & Poeppelman, T. (2015). A year in review: #SIOP15 technology & social media highlights! *The Industrial-Organizational Psychologist*, *53*(1), 74–82.

Bonchek, M. (2016). How to Create an Exponential Mindset. *Harvard Business Review*. Retrieved from https://hbr.org/2016/07/how-to-create-an-exponential-mindset.

Boniface, M., & Rashmi, M. (2012). Outsourcing: Mass layoffs and displaced workers' experiences. *Management Research Review*, 35, 1029–1045.

Bourdeau, J. (2014). Predict What Employees Will Do Without Freaking Them Out. *Harvard Business Review Blog Network*. Retrieved from hbr.org/2014/09/predict-what-employees-will-do-without-freaking-them-out.

Cascio, W. (November, 1995). Whither industrial and organizational psychology in a changing world of work? *American Psychologist*, *50*(11), 928–939.

Cascio, W. F. & Montealegre, R. (2016). How technology is changing work and organizations. *Annual Review of Organizational Psychology and Organizational Behavior*, *3*, 348–375.

Chen, H., Chiang, R. H. L., & Storey, V. C. (2012). Business intelligence and analytics: From big data to big impact. *MIS Quarterly: Management Information Systems*, *36*(4), 1165–1188.

Coovert, M. D., & Thompson, L. F. (2014). Toward a synergistic relationship between psychology and technology. In M. D. Coovert & L. F. Thompson (Eds.), *The psychology of workplace technology* (pp. 1–17). New York, NY: Routledge.

Craiger, J. (1997). Technology, Organizations, and Work in the 20th century. *Industrial-Organizational Psychologists*. *34*(3), 89–96.

Crane, L. & Self, R. J. (2014). *Big Data Analytics: A Threat or an Opportunity for Knowledge Management?* Paper presented at 9th International Conference on Knowledge Management in Organizations, Santiago, Chile.

Davies, I. (April 1, 2016a). How virtual reality will impact the hiring process. *Forbes*. Retrieved from www.forbes.com/sites/forbestechcouncil/2016/04/01/how-virtual-reality-will-impact-the-hiring-process.

Davies, I. (March 17, 2016b). Three ways technology is transforming talent management in 2016. *Forbes*. Retrieved from www.forbes.com/sites/forbestechcouncil/2016/03/17/three-ways-technology-is-transforming-talent-management-in-2016/.

Ewenstein, B., Hancock, B., & Komm, A. (2016). Ahead of the curve: The future of performance management. *McKinsey Quarterly*. Retrieved from www.mckinsey.com/business-functions/organization/our-insights/ahead-of-the-curve-the-future-of-performance-management.

Fallon, N. (January 11, 2016). Hiring in the digital age: What's next for recruiting? *Business News Daily*. Retrieved from www.businessnewsdaily.com/6975-future-of-recruiting.html.

Feloni, R. (June 1, 2017). Walmart is using virtual reality to train its employees. *Business Insider*. Retrieved from www.businessinsider.com/walmart-using-virtual-reality-employee-training-2017-6.

Fitzgerald, M., Kruschwitz, N., Bonnet, D., & Welch, M. (2014). Embracing Digital Technology: A New Strategic Imperative. *MIT Sloan Management Review*. *55*(2), 1–12.

Greenwald, T. (March 10, 2017). How AI is transforming the workplace. *The Wall Street Journal*. Retrieved from www.wsj.com/articles/how-ai-is-transforming-the-workplace-1489371060.

Guilfoyle, S., Bergman, S. M., Hartwell, C., & Powers, J. (2016). Social media, big data, and employment decisions: Mo' data, mo' problems? In R. N. Landers & G. B. Schmidt (Eds.), *Social media in employee selection and recruitment* (pp. 127–155). Switzerland: Springer International Publishing.

Guzzo, R. A., Fink, A. A., King, E., Tonidandel, S, & Landis, R. S. (2015). Big Data recommendations for Industrial–Organizational Psychology. *Industrial and Organizational Psychology: Perspectives on Science and Practice, 8*(4), 491–508.

Harris, M. M. & Hollman, K. D. (2013). TIP-Topics – The top trends in I-O Psychology: A graduate student perspective. *The Industrial-Organizational Psychologist, 50* (4), 120–124.

Holland, P. & Bardoel, A. (2016). The impact of technology on work in the twenty-first century: Exploring the smart and dark side, *The International Journal of Human Resource Management, 27*(21), 2579–2581.

Hunt, S. T. (2011). Technology is transforming the nature of performance management. *Industrial Organizational Psychology, 4*, 188–189.

International Data Corporation (2017). The Digital Universe of Opportunities: Rich Data and the Increasing Value of the Internet of Things. Retrieved from www.emc.com/leadership/digital-universe/2014iview/executive-summary.htm.

Kapadia, V. (May 20, 2016). The 6 hottest training technologies that you can't overlook. *eLearning Industry*. Retrieved from https://elearningindustry.com/6-training-technologies-cant-overlook.

Kurzweil, R., & Kapor, M. (2009). A wager on the Turing Test. In R. Epstein, G. Roberts, G. Beber (Eds.) *Parsing the Turing Test* (pp. 463–477). Dordrecht: Springer.

Leavitt, H. J. & Whisler, T. L. (1958). Management in the 1980's. *Harvard Business Review, 36*(6), 41–48.

Lee, Y. & Cho, J. (2015). Personalized item generation method for adaptive testing systems. *Multimedia Tools and Applications, 74*(19), 8571–8859.

Lievens, F. & Patterson, F. (2011). The validity and incremental validity of knowledge tests, low-fidelity simulations, and high-fidelity simulations for predicting job performance in advanced-level high-stakes selection. *Journal of Applied Psychology, 96* (5), 927–940.

Maurer, R. (February 23, 2017). 2017 recruiting trends point to technology driving change. *Society of Human Resource Management*. Retrieved from www.shrm.org/resourcesandtools/hr-topics/talent-acquisition/pages/recruiting-trends-2017-technology-change.aspx.

Meister, J. (May 21, 2012). The future of work: How to use gamification for talent management. *Forbes*. Retrieved from www.forbes.com/sites/jeannemeister/2012/05/21/the-future-of-work-how-to-use-gamification-for-talent-management/.

Noguchi, Y. (July 7, 2017). Recruiters use "geofencing" to target potential hires where they live and work. *National Public Radio: All Tech Considered*. Retrieved from www.npr.org/sections/alltechconsidered/2017/07/07/535981386/recruiters-use-geofencing-to-target-potential-hires-where-they-live-and-work.

Pappas, C. (August 25, 2015). 7 ways wearable technology could be used in *corporate training. eLearning Industry*. Retrieved from https://elearningindustry.com/7-ways-wearable-technology-used-corporate-training.

Parsons, D. (2014). The future of mobile learning and implications for education and training. In M. Ally & A. Tsinakos (Eds.), *Perspectives on open and distance learning* (pp.217–229). Vancouver: Commonwealth of Learning and Athabasca University.

Perez, C. & Soete, L. (1988). Catching-up in technology: Entry barriers and windows of opportunity. In G. Dosi, C. Freeman, R. R. Nelson, G. Silverberg, & L. Soete (Eds.), *Technical change and economic theory* (pp. 458–479). London: Francis Pinter.

Poeppelman, T., Lobene, E., & Blacksmith, N. (2015). Personalizing the learning experience through adaptive training. *The Industrial-Organizational Psychologist*, 52 (4), 82–88.

Rayz, J. T. (2017). In pursuit of human-friendly interaction with a computational system: Computational humor. Proceedings from IEEE 15th International Symposium on Applied Machine Intelligence and Informatics. Retrieved from ieeexplore.ieee .org/document/7880297/.

Reynolds, D. H. & Dickter, D. N. (2017). Technology and employee selection: An overview. In J. L. Farr & N. T. Tippins (Eds.), *Handbook of employee selection* (2nd edn, pp. 855–873). New York, NY: Routledge.

Sandler, R. L. (2014). Introduction: Technology and ethics. In R. L. Sandler (Ed.), *Ethics and emerging technologies* (pp. 1–23). United Kingdom: Palgrave Macmillan.

Schess, N. B. (2013). Then and now: How technology has changed the workplace. *Hofstra Labor and Employment Law Journal*, 30(2).

Silzer, R. F., Cober, R. T., & Erickson, A. (2010). Practice Perspectives: Where I-O Worlds Collide: The Nature of I-O Practice. *The Industrial-Organizational Psychologist*, 47(4), 95–103.

Sheets T. L. & Belwalkar, B. B. (2017). ATTN: Training in technology is the need of the hour. *The Industrial-Organizational Psychologist*, 54(4), 86–92.

SIOP Futures Task Force: Findings and Recommendations (2017). Unpublished manuscript, *Society for Industrial and Organizational Psychology*, Bowling Green, Ohio.

SIOP Administrative Office (December 20, 2016). Top 10 workplace trends 2017. The *Society of Industrial-Organizational Psychologists*. Retrieved from www .siop.org/article_view.aspx?article=1610.

Shamma, T. (2017). Google glass didn't disappear. You can find it on the factory floor. *National Public Radio*. Retrieved from www.npr.org/sections/alltechconsidered/ 2017/03/18/514299682.

Survey reveals popularity of Excel-based business intelligence among SMEs. (April 7, 2017). Retrieved from www.cio.co.ke/news/top-stories/survey-reveals-popular ity-of-excel-based-business-intelligence-among-smes.

Turnage, J. (1990). The challenge of new workplace technology for psychology. *American Psychologist*, 45(2), 171–178.

Yi Xue, Y. & Larson, R. (2015). STEM crisis or STEM surplus? Yes and yes. *Monthly Labor Review*. Retrieved from doi.org/10.21916/mlr.2015.14.

Zielinski, D. (February 13, 2017). Recruiting gets smart thanks to artificial intelligence. *Society of Human Resource Management*. Retrieved from www.shrm.org/resource sandtools/hr-topics/technology/pages/recruiting-gets-smart-thanks-to-artificial-intelligence.aspx.

Zielinski, D. (November 1, 2015). The gamification of recruitment. *HR Magazine*. Retrieved from www.shrm.org/hr-today/news/hr-magazine/pages/1115-gamifica tion-recruitment.aspx.

3 The Reciprocal Roles of Artificial Intelligence and Industrial-Organizational Psychology

Matt Barney

3.1 Introduction

Long before Hugo Münsterberg pioneered workplace psychology, our species has dominated the world. This happened because more than any other species, homo sapiens are able to perform cognitive tasks. Our ancestors used our cognition to create increasingly better tools that have allowed our ancestors to survive and reproduce better than most species. These same tools caused the extinction of about 322 species of birds, mammals and reptiles (Viegas, 2014). Our intellectual advantages have allowed us to create language, technology, and complex social organizations. And the evolution of our scientific and tool culture is memetic – each generation has built on the cultural accomplishments of our predecessors.

Given the central role of cognition in our evolutionary success, it is not surprising, post behaviorism, that cognitive constructs have a central focus in psychology, including Industrial-Organizational psychology (I-O). Psychometric general cognitive ability "G" is one of the most studied constructs in the history of I-O. Contemporary cognitive-behavioral models in I-O psychology posit information processing as central to understanding latent constructs that drive workplace behavior. But there are new synthetic forms of proto-cognition that are rapidly advancing. Computer scientists are creating artificial intelligence (AI) that is already outperforming workers in areas as diverse as medical research, legal discovery, and self-driving cars. In the past, technology upended physical and farm labor, such as the automobile overtaking the horse-and-buggy industry. Computers had a similar, transformative force in replacing typewriters and paper-based file systems. In these prior eras, automation largely displaced blue-collar and low-skilled work. What is unique today is that AI is already starting to replace cognitive tasks that once could only be done by lawyers, artists, and scientists.

This chapter outlines a reciprocal relationship between science and practice within AI and I-O. On the one hand, AI is advancing to the point of complementing or supplanting traditional I-O psychological work such as employee assessment and development. On the other, experts in AI have made numerous calls for help in proactively mitigating immediate and long-term risks with AI. New institutes, several funded by Elon Musk such as OpenAI (https://openai.com) and the Future of Life Institute (https://futureoflife.org/), invest in research and teams of not-for-profit research to proactively avoid having AI hurt people. This is important because, in the short run, robotic AI holds the promise of making dangerous work such as bomb disposal dramatically safer. In the medium term, it appears that AI may help solve previously intractable problems like a cure for cancer, reversing climate change, or ameliorating poverty. But ultimately, many computer scientists are expressing serious concerns about AI's profound potential for harm in the future. Some experts are worried about AI making mistakes with dangerous substances (e.g., uranium), or that it may be overly focused on narrow goals where human interests (or lives) get trampled inadvertently because the AI doesn't understand the context of human values. Others are worried about the likely displacement of knowledge workers, traditionally unaffected by automation. Lastly, the most extreme concerns about AI safety are that it will eventually outsmart its creators and decide that humans are not worth keeping around. Some visionaries, like Elon Musk, worry publicly that this ultimate tool will also produce the ultimate extinction – our own.

Given that I-O includes the scientific study of the individuals, teams, and organizations creating AI that have the potential to create both great outcomes and perhaps our own extinction, it is logical that I-O science and practice be part of the effort to improve the work-team effectiveness of these specialists. Ultimately, this chapter argues that AI is useful for I-O and I-O is useful for AI.

3.2 What is AI

Artificial Intelligence involves the creation of machines whose behavior approximates or exceeds what humans are able to perform, not just physically as with machinery, but typically with respect to our cognitive abilities (Russell & Norvig, 2010). Some AI tries to emulate what a person does mentally, such as Neural Networks and Deep Learning algorithms, while others try to meet or beat human levels of performance in an entirely non-human method. AI experts attempt to engineer technologies that are creative, self-improving and that use human language. Experts describe forms of AI that merely simulate cognition as "weak" AI; whereas they envision the potential of AI in the future that actually thinks, possibly even with human-type consciousness, as "strong" AI. AI that approximates human intelligence needs several abilities:

1 *Natural Language Processing* – the system needs the ability to understand and communicate in a human language like English.
2 *Knowledge Representation* – the system must be able to store information about what it knows, sees, or hears, so that it can use these models to achieve future goals.
3 *Automated Reasoning* – the system must be able to use stored data to answer questions, draw new conclusions and/or solve problems.

4 *Learning* – it must be able to adapt to new situations, notice new phenomena and extrapolate patterns. Computer scientists call this ability "machine learning" to denote the engineered nature of the AI distinct from organic, human learning.

5 *Computer Sensing* – it must be able to perceive objects or people that may be relevant to an AI's goals, either through synthetic vision, audition and/or olfactory methods.

6 *Robotics* – some, but not all, types need to be able to manipulate physical objects or interact in physical space with people, animals, and/or objects.

These six broad areas comprise most of AI (Russell & Norvig, 2010, p. 3). Computer science has historically looked toward neurology, psychology and biology for ideas about how to design what humans already are able to do. This has resulted in an interdisciplinary field called cognitive science that integrates evidence from psychology and neuroscience with computer technology. The goal of this interdisciplinary field is to better model psychological phenomena in silicon and to better understand psychology with computational models.

It is useful to notice how similar the aforementioned six types of machine behaviors are to a job task analysis that summarizes the work an employee must perform. Because AI is making rapid advances in all six areas, increasingly AI is taking over job tasks with requirements that once could only be done by a worker.

3.3 Where is AI Especially Relevant to I-O?

AI is transforming the world of work in many ways. First, because AI represents advanced tools that can replace or enhance workers, the very subject of our discipline – progress in AI is likely to disrupt and transform our science and practice. It has already started to disrupt the logistical backend maintenance of hardware and software infrastructure. In 2017, there were 56,000 layoffs in the Indian outsourcing market, for example, whose high-paying software jobs are now being done by a machine (Bhattacharya, 2017).

Second, AI represents a new class of tools that were previously unavailable for science and practice. When embodied in software, AI can be an extremely cost-effective way to save labor in cognitive tasks and supplant the need for manual effort in many cases. Increasingly, AI-based I-O tools allow I-O psychologists an unprecedented ability to scale our science and practice in areas such as this author's work with LeaderAmp, a cloud/mobile system to scale human and AI coaching and assessment. This use of AI allows the masses to receive evidence-based coaching – an intervention traditionally only affordable for the C-Suite.

To organize the current and possible future areas where AI may be especially useful, relevant, or disruptive to I-O science and practice, this chapter will examine different levels of analysis to review possibilities before suggesting specific areas where AI may transform I-O and I-O may transform AI.

3.3.1 Reciprocal I-O and AI Relationships

Computer science has different language and traditions that need to be mapped to psychology to better understand how AI and I-O are related. While the focus of psychological science is on latent human processes and manifest behavior, the computational linguistic counterpart to a psychological construct is a topic. Topics are often conceptualized as a group of like objects such as words, that are related to a higher-level concept.

Computer science has developed a wide variety of analytical techniques to work with topics such as latent dirichlet allocation, correlated topic models, hierarchical dirichlet processes and meaning extraction methods (Teh et al., 2006, Chung & Pennebaker, 2008; Wilson et al., 2016). Some of the most exciting methods are those that are being called "deep learning" that use neural networks, emulated from human neurological models, that comprise one form of machine learning (LeCun, Bengio, & Hinton, 2015). It is in this last area of machine learning where some of the most powerful innovations have the most immediate implications for I-O psychology. Next, each level of analysis will be reviewed for how AI is already disrupting, or may soon transform the workplace.

3.3.1.1 Micro: Replacing Labor

Because AI already outperforms human intelligence in a variety of domains, including game competitions (Bostrom, 2014; Kelion, 2017), it makes particular sense to examine what areas AI is already supplanting micro-level behavior. In 2017, Japan's Fukoku Mutual Life Insurance company laid off 34 claims adjusters who used to make insurance payouts and replaced them with IBM's Watson Explorer AI (McCurry, 2017). Fukoku Mutual Life believes the AI will increase productivity by 30 percent and save 140 M Yen once it has been in place for a year. They also estimate that it will drastically reduce the time needed to compute the payouts for insurance claims, further producing better customer service.

Similarly, Wall Street Investment house BlackRock announced that it downsized 40 human portfolio managers' jobs, replacing them with AI stock-trading algorithms, part of an industry-wide shift (Shen, 2017). *Fortune* reports that by 2025, financial institutions will have 230,000 fewer jobs, 10 percent of their workforce in the area of money management (Shen, 2017).

And the legal profession is also being transformed. In the area of legal discovery, traditionally each lawyer had to manage about 18,000 documents per year, with as many as 200 terabytes of information (McDonald, 2017). They traditionally had to do searches on the documents, like an administrative assistant, which is not a great use of their expensive time. Now, there are a variety of AI algorithms from competing firms, from IBM to Veritone Legal, that can perform discovery tasks more comprehensively and in a vastly shorter period of time than lawyers can (McDonald, 2017).

When organizations have goals to improve safety, quality, scalability, or costs, it now makes sense to consider AI as one more way to consider whether work should be transformed. This is consistent with the I-O approach to strategic work modeling, a strategic form of job analysis that proactively examines what work should be outsourced, or automated, before considering human workplace behavior (Schippmann, 1999). By examining AI in addition to traditional strategic work modeling approaches, a firm can gain strategic advantage by proactively examining historical employee work behavior and revisiting whether having a task done by a person or a machine is best to achieve higher-order goals.

When considering re-designing or eliminating jobs with AI, there are several considerations. There are three major ways in which AI can approach, equal, or overtake human intelligence (Bostrom, 2014). First, they can be orders of magnitude faster than a human intellect, known as speed superintelligence. Second, they can be comprised of a large number of smaller intellects such that the AI's overall performance across several domains outstrips human cognition. For example, even without computers, I-O science as a profession is better than any one I-O psychologist by himself or herself. AI that can work together, similar to how I-O scientists can collaborate and outperform an individual, is what computer scientists call collective superintelligence. Third, AI that is as quick as the human mind, but is vastly more creative or better at problem solving is known as quality superintelligence.

3.3.1.2 Micro: Electronic Performance Support

Another emerging area that is affecting I-O is including AI in computer-based training, decision support, expert systems, and computer-supportive cooperative work. Collectively, these electronic performance support systems (EPSS) are software programs that help employees learn or perform. The simplest forms, like spell checking software, have been helping flag or automatically correct misspellings for many years. One special case of EPSS is knowledge-based systems that are programs that have explicitly modeled problem-solving knowledge that they can use to arrive at solutions to problems. Some of these knowledge-based systems (KBS) are decision support systems that help collect, refine, and analyze data so that the worker can make a better decision. Knowledge-based systems have been used in manufacturing, medicine, finance, and agriculture.

3.3.1.3 Meso: Synthetic Team Members

At the next level of analysis, groups of people are gradually being disrupted by automating some jobs out of existence. Just as downsizing, outsourcing, and switching vendors disrupts the workplace, so does automation, even without the sort of cognitive automation that AI represents. With both ordinary automation and AI, technology can sometimes be seen as taking the place of a worker, thereby becoming a "synthetic" member of the team (Griffith, Deaton, & Steelman, 2003). The US Navy has been using synthetic teammates in training simulations, for example, to help people practice in realistic situations (Griffith et al., 2003). Simulations, or virtual reality worlds have a big advantage in training programs because they give learners a safe place to practice. For example, flight simulators – without AI – have been valuable for training new pilots for many decades. But if synthetic teammates become better than the people doing the tasks, it obviates the need for the worker in the first place. For example, while autopilot has been used for many decades, AI aviation now allows planes to fly without any pilot in any part of the process. In fact, the future of fighter jets is without a human pilot (Revell, 2017).

The rapid and relentless march of AI progress suggests that teams and their leaders will continue to have to lead transformational changes by encouraging learning and development of members so that they are prepared to switch to performing valuable tasks that AI cannot yet perform. Perhaps a leader's ability to persuade individuals and teams to proactively invest in new skills will become paramount to help people cope with these changes. In prior eras, Labor Unions led wildcat strikes and other forms of workplace slowdowns in direct opposition to robots and physical automation taking union workers jobs, and it appears that this same type of labor upset is on the horizon for teams that are downsized by AI.

3.3.1.4 Macro: Decentralized Autonomous Organization

At the organization level, new developments with blockchain technology, a decentralized digital ledger, have created the possibility of "decentralized autonomous organizations" (DAOs; Vigna & Casey, 2015). Also called decentralized autonomous corporations (DACs), they are organizations whose rules are encoded as software programs called smart contracts. The contracts are maintained on a blockchain and triggered only once contract specifications are met, automatically, without the need for a human to make a decision. Examples of DAOs today include Dash, The DAO and digix.io.

Even though the earliest example of a DAO on the Etherium platform was hacked, losing investors $50 million dollars, the presence of blockchain technology, married to AI technology, portends a possible future where at least some decisions traditionally made by senior leaders are done automatically by software (Price, 2016). But perhaps this is only likely if security protocols can become sufficiently strong to avoid these types of early setbacks by greedy hackers. And there is significant concern in the computer science literature about the potential of a quantum computer that is so fast, that it may render useless the most current security systems and even degrade the utility of the blockchain (Hurd, 2017).

3.3.2 Examples of AI at Work

Throughout the history of the workplace, new technologies have taken over job tasks that were previously done by workers, mostly blue collar. A century ago, buggy manufacturers went out of business as cars became ubiquitous. The job of a telephone receptionist is now replaced by a voice recognition and dialog management system. But because AI is a type of technology that replaces or augments human cognition, it is likely to be more transformational. Earlier we've highlighted mostly the constructive transformational outcomes that are already occurring and likely to continue. However, there are also new destructive areas of AI, both in terms of the workplace around bias that is infamously problematic with computer science approaches to deep learning and around advanced AI getting out of control of its inventors. This section will explore both areas in more detail.

In terms of exciting possible solutions to intractable problems, experts estimate that the world population of robots is currently greater than 10 million in areas as diverse as AI for surgery, to rescue, and even as pets (Bostrom, 2014). Crucially, the sorts of tasks that AI is starting to perform once required a PhD, so the development of AI is disrupting new parts of the workplace in ways distinct from prior technological areas. Some concrete examples of current AI that is changing the nature of work include:

Medicine
- IBM and the Baylor College of Medicine's KnIT (Knowledge Integration Toolkit) is a joint effort to create an AI that automatically scans the medical literature for evidence around protein interactions and generates new plausible hypotheses for research (Nagarajan et al., 2015).
- In pharmaceuticals, Atomwise has a system that attempts to generate potential drugs for diseases like Ebola and multiple sclerosis. Similarly, Johnson & Johnson's subsidiary Janssen is working with BenevolentAI to identify likely drug targets (Quartz, 2017).
- Professor Sharon Xioalei Huang has created a cervical cancer screening technique that performs as well or better than expert physicians in interpreting traditional tests such as Pap and Human Papilloma Virus tests, at a lower costs (ScienMag, 2017).

Archeology
- Computer Scientists at Tel Aviv University have modified facial recognition software to piece together 300,000 ancient Jewish manuscripts that were barely preserved in the attic of an ancient Cairo synagogue (*Economist*, 2015).

Law
- TurboPatent uses AI to automate the process of preparing intellectual property documentation. Ultimately TurboPatent's goal is to liberate lawyers and inventors away from tedious work, toward more creative and valuable tasks (Levy, 2017).

Finance
- Increasingly, banks and credit card companies are partially or completely using artificially intelligent systems to determine whether applicants should be approved for a loan or a line of credit (Datta, 2017). A new innovation in personal finance is the advent of "robo-advisors" that give consumers a form of AI for personal financial planning and portfolio management. And investment banks are now using automated stock-trading systems that combine data-mining, marketplace "sentiment analysis" – a form of AI to detect emotions about a stock or

company – and financial news feeds to find arbitrage opportunities (Bostrom, 2014). More than half of all equity shares are traded by algorithmic high-frequency traders, partially accounting for volatility that resulted in the 2010 Flash Crash (Bostrom, 2014).

- Similarly, on the investing side of Finance, robo-advising is on the rise. Companies such as Charles Schwab and Vanguard now have AI systems that will invest on behalf of clients (Barron's, 2017).

Insurance

- Companies such as underwrite.ai use an approach to AI that uses techniques from genomics and particle physics to create dynamic models of credit risk that they claim outperform traditional approaches. One study found that the phrases borrowers use when applying for a loan predict the likelihood of repayment (Netzer, Lemarie, & Herzenstein, 2016), suggesting that natural language assessments may be a good way to improve predictive validity of actuarial models.

Automotive

- Famously, the Tesla Autopilot is already in use today on the Tesla Model S cars, for partial AI-based driving. By the end of 2017, Tesla claimed they would enable completely AI driving in their cars (Etherington, 2017). Uber is reported to have similar automatic driving AI under development.

Linguistics

- Many services, such as Google Translate, now can do a better job translating from one spoken human language to another using new AI-based approaches based on machine learning that is able to analyze the whole sentence at once, as opposed to word-by-word, or segment of a sentence.

Government

- Given their billion-dollar budgets, governments are using AI in a wide range of applications. Military and intelligence specialists are using bomb-disposing robots, as well as robots that spy and AI-powered drones that attack enemies. Operations specialists are using an automated logistics planning and scheduling tool powered by AI known as "DART." Face recognition is now being used in Europe and Australia to automate border crossings (Bostrom, 2014).
- Skopos Labs has a new AI system that can predict which congressional bills will pass. Shockingly, they estimate that only about 4 percent of bills actually become law, suggesting that the defect density of lawmaker's efforts is 96 percent (Hutson, 2017).

Marketing

- Companies such as ladder.io have expert systems that help marketers perform experiments on different lead-generation strategies. And other AI firms like Fusemachines have built AI to bundle prospective customers who are most likely to buy a particular product or service, so that marketing campaigns in the experiments are most likely to pay off.

3.4 Using AI in I-O

While automation has been used in I-O for many years, newer expert systems and other forms of AI are increasingly being employed. Bostrom (2014) argues that AI can be categorized into four broad categories – tools, oracles, genies, and sovereigns. Tools tend to be the simplest, being implements for performing a task. These can include software for performing job analysis, or statistical analyses that speed up what otherwise would be a manual task for an I-O psychologist. The earliest I-O tools also included applicant-selection tools that implemented rules for the sequence of tests in a battery, scoring methods, and automated recommendation for hiring. I-O expert systems such as the Job Analysis Wizard are an example of an I-O tool that improved the speed and comprehensiveness of job analyses and coordination of assessments, training, and job aides across psychologists globally (Barney, Harkey, & Pearlman, 1997). Today's expert systems that include gamified, unobtrusive assessment platforms from firms such as Pymetrics, Revelian, and Arctic Shores provide psychometrics in an engaging game-like user experience that is intended to be hard to fake.

Second, oracles involve a type of AI that only answers questions. Chatbots and knowledge support systems fall into this category. Apple's "Siri" and Amazon's "Alexa" are other examples of oracles where a user can ask a simple question and get an immediate approximate answer, or the oracle can perform a simple task like playing some music. In I-O Psychology, the metabus (http://metabus.org) project can be considered an early example of an I-O Oracle. Metabus is a cloud-based platform that makes it extremely fast to perform ad-hoc meta-analyses "on the fly" in contrast with the large amount of traditional manual effort to screen, collate, and program meta-analyses in the past. A future version of metabus that allows voice command to perform the meta-analyses automatically would be an even closer match to computer scientists' vision of an AI oracle.

Third and next most sophisticated are the genies – AI that carries out high level commands and then waits for the next instruction to be given. One proto-genie for automated psychometric analyses, for example, allows an I-O Psychologist to give the AI an item bank and training sample of raw data and ask it to automatically ensure unidimensionality, calibrate items, and leave the psychologist with an instrument free from differential item functioning (DIF), without having to program any of those analyses manually (Barney, 2016; Barney & Riley, 2018). These types of genies free up the I-O psychologist to think about substantive theoretical, practical, and innovative issues rather than repetitive, mundane analyses. It further reduces the time required for manual psychometric analyses from days or hours, to minutes or seconds.

Lastly, sovereigns represents the most sophisticated type of AI. A sovereign acts autonomously, pursuing short-, medium-, and long-term objectives without any human intervention needed. Autonomous vacuum cleaners, for example, maintain themselves, including automatically recharging their batteries, sensing their environment, emptying their waste, and navigating the areas they need to clean. NASA and the US Department of Defense typically fund autonomous robots such as

Seekur that is designed to autonomously perform tasks for situations where human labor is impossible today (e.g., on other planets). A search for sovereigns in I-O psychology revealed no examples as of 2018.

3.4.1 AI Emerging in I-O

Increasingly, I-O psychologists are starting to use natural language processing for assessment (Barney, 2016; IBM, 2017; Psychobabble, 2017). Companies such as HireVue are also using video-based AI as a replacement for some forms of human interviewing. The video-based AI analyzes keywords, voice intonation, and body language and provides a natural language report for the hiring manager to make the final decision (Feloni, 2017). Unilever claims that this video-based approach has doubled the number of applicants matched to jobs within 90 days of starting the new AI assessment, hired its most diverse class to date and reduced the average time for a candidate to be hired from four months to four weeks (Feloni, 2017). The HireVue example is exciting because it raises the possibility of increasing the number of behavioral observations made in an assessment center while providing real-time feedback to a degree impossible with human raters. But it remains to be seen as to whether this AI-based approach improves upon the validity and/or fairness of our best pre-hire selection systems (e.g., fewer false positives and false negatives, especially for protected groups).

I-O psychologists seem to be quickly using deep-learning forms of AI across the full range of science and practice, from description and prediction of human behavior at work, as with selection and succession uses of AI-based assessments, to interventions. There are several electronic performance support systems (EPSS) that combine assessment and development, sometimes with AI anchored in neo-Kolbergian models of developmental psychology that show distinct linear and non-linear developmental levels of a latent construct (e.g., Barney & Riley, 2018; Dawson & Stein, 2011). This trend is likely to continue to impact I-O psychology, just as it is affecting every profession with knowledge workers. It may portend a day in the future when the job requirements of an I-O psychologist will include the ability to program AI to perform I-O psychology tasks and PhD students will have to take courses in computer science to complete degrees.

3.5 Using I-O in AI

A near-term concern among AI experts is the role AI is having on displacing jobs, especially for the first-time white-collar jobs, as with the Japanese insurance analysts that were noted earlier to be replaced by AI in 2017. In these areas, I-O psychology's longstanding science and practice around vocational interests, job search, person-job fit, and retraining are relevant to smooth these inevitable labor displacements.

Longer term, some experts are very worried about the safety of AI. Imagine North Korea getting super intelligent guidance systems for nuclear devices. Or the development of AI that is smarter than Einstein, but with malevolent values. How can we be sure that super intelligent AI won't hurt us? While these examples might just be speculation, there is reason to worry even with the current forms of AI.

First, even with today's technology, well-intentioned people make plenty of mistakes. Johns Hopkins patient safety experts estimate that human medical errors are the third biggest cause of death in the USA, causing more than 250,000 unnecessary deaths (Makary & Daniel, 2016). Today's error rates are vastly better than they were historically because of efforts over more than a century to improve healthcare quality. In contrast, AI's advances have been very rapid and recent. Healthcare system risks to safety come from many sources, but the vast majority are from the well-meaning caregivers who lack skills, miscommunicate, or are fatigued. While no medical professional would desire to implement AI unless it could improve upon the baseline of practice, including reduce these errors, there are reasons to be concerned about the current state of AI's own error rate.

Current forms of natural language AI have infamously been shown to be highly biased. In part, this may be because the computational neural networks were modeled on human neural models of cognitive functioning that psychologists know are often biased. This bias is also due to the fact that computer scientists don't really understand how neural nets or deep-learning algorithms work. Just as the child of a Klu Klux Klan member may grow up to hold the biased values of his or her parents, it appears that limited, unrepresentative samples used to teach AI can similarly introduce bias. For example, Microsoft's artificially intelligent chat-bot "Tay" was turned into a racist by internet trolls and had to be shut down shortly after its release (*The Guardian*, 2016). The current state-of-the-art methods for teaching deep-learning algorithms is highly sample-specific and does not include psychometric science around proactively avoiding, detecting, or removing bias (e.g., differential item and test functioning).

Second, an experiment by Carnegie Mellon computer scientists has shown important employment consequences of this bias. Google's AI that controls what advertisements are displayed to job candidates was found to be sexist – female candidates with identical credentials were offered lower paying jobs than male candidates (Datta, Tschantz, & Datta, 2015). Some scholars feel strongly that these risks have social-science solutions and should have I-O scientists and practitioners collaborate with computer scientists to solve these problems given our field's long history of working with employment fairness (George et al., 2016). This section of the chapter will review some of the approaches computer scientists are taking to ensure safe and useful AI, followed by an outline of additional places in which I-O psychologists should contribute to improving these challenges in computer science and engineering.

3.5.1 Computer Science Safety

As problematic as sexist AI is to the workplace, another ominous threat that worries computer scientists is the risk of physical harm by AI. AI experts have two categories of methods that attempt to mitigate the risk of unsafe AI (Bostrom,

2014). First are attempts at controlling or constraining the capabilities of AI. Cognitive or physical capability controls include:

- Boxing methods involve software or hardware that confines the AI so that it is only able to access pre-approved channels and cannot access the external world
- Stunting methods impose constraints on the upper limits of cognitive capabilities of the AI
- Tripwires ensures that the system regularly self-diagnoses and, if it finds an error, shuts the system down if dangerous behavior is detected

A second group of approaches to safe AI include ways that directly engineer a motivational system into the AI:

- Direct specification involves programming a motivational system that can include rewards similar to classical or operant conditioning
- Domesticity involves teaching the system to limit its own goal setting and task performances
- Indirect normativity incorporates broad principles that specify rules that the system must follow or values that it should pursue
- Augmentation involves trying to create an AI with human morals, or benevolent motivations, akin to an ethical human

But none of these options is entirely satisfactory. Bostrom (2014) acknowledges that each of these approaches has limitations and weaknesses and it is not known whether these are comprehensive. Given that AI experts have created this initial set of safety strategies, using creative problem solving and moral reasoning, the stage has been set for I-O psychology to contribute our science and practice to mitigate these risks.

3.5.2 I-O Solutions to AI Problems

Most of the concerns around AI safety and utility are fundamentally difficult problems that require innovative solutions. Because I-O psychology is the study of workers, teams and organizations, we are uniquely positioned to help teams and organizations focused on or using AI to better achieve their objectives.

3.5.3 Individual Level

Organizations that focus on AI safety, such as Elon Musk's Open AI (openai.com) or the Future of Life Institute (futureoflife.org), require a diverse set of skills to achieve their goals, but one clear job family is AI researchers themselves. The Department of Labor's O*Net system details the job requirements of "Computer and Information Research Scientists". It lists 15 tasks, 41 work activities (17 detailed), 27 skills, 23 tools, 33 dimensions of knowledge, 35 dimensions of skill, and 52 abilities as needed to perform effectively in the field. Given the AI safety problem, it is surprising that as comprehensive as O*Net is, it fails to list moral reasoning as being central to designing AI, given that one group of strategies computer scientists are facing is to teach deep-learning algorithms ethical decision making.

The O*Net oversight could be because the targeted job family is intentionally broader than just computer scientists specializing in AI. But in principle, if part of the problem to be solved is to teach synthetic machines to have ethical values, it seems logical that the computer scientists themselves need to be sufficiently proficient in moral reasoning. There is a long line of research in measuring and developing moral reasoning that can bolster these attributes in researchers including neo-Kohlbergian approaches (Rest et al., 2000) and moral foundations theory (Haidt, 2001; Graham, et al., 2012). Given I-O's ability to measure and intervene in these crucial workplace areas, our field has a great deal to contribute to the personnel skill sources of risk to safe AI.

Further, there are several predictor variables that the selection literature has identified as antecedents to moral reasoning and moral behavior. One meta-analysis demonstrated that moral identity predicts moral and pro-social behavior and given that AI researchers must engineer morality into machine systems, it appears to be worth considering as part of a pre-hire selection assessment (Hertz & Krettenaur, 2016).

Another obvious I-O domain relevant to selecting and developing computer scientists is their creative problem-solving capabilities (e.g., Harari, Reaves, & Viswesvaran, 2016). There is evidence that individual-difference variables of intelligence and personality are predictive of creativity and therefore may be useful in pre-hire screening of AI team members (Agnoli, Corazza, & Runco, 2016; Batey & Furnham, 2006). Naturally, these pre-hire methods, whether they use AI or more traditional assessments deployed with cloud/mobile technology, will improve the odds of AI organizations effectively hiring individual AI experts with better fit to what the safety aspects of their job requirements ought to be.

At the individual intervention level of analysis, there is science suggesting that creativity training is useful (Scott, Leritz, & Mumford, 2004). Consequently the development of skills in design thinking enabling experimentation and prototyping with rapid feedback on potential solutions (Razzouk & Shute, 2012). Lastly, the selection and development of skills in risk management and the creation of alternative options may be especially valuable as forms of insurance policies that mitigate the downside and leverage the upside potential of AI.

3.5.4 Team Level

The attempts at mitigating AI risks are typically done by multiple authors at research institutes where collaborative, interdisciplinary science and engineering is paramount. Given the multi-facet nature of AI, with its social disruption of entire classes of work (e.g., self-driving trucks taking out the truck-driving workforce) and the need to look at holistic risks, it is sensible that interdisciplinary teams are required. There is increasing agreement in I-O that complex problem solving and collaborative skills span multiple domains and are critical in the twenty-first century workplace (Neubert et al., 2015).

I-O has more than 20 years of research to offer AI teams around the science and practice of teamwork. Past President of SI-OP Eduardo Salas, for example, suggests that mutual performance monitoring, backup behavior, adaptability, shared mental models, mutual trust, and closed loop communications are especially relevant to team performance (Salas, Sims, & Burke, 2005). From the perspective of reducing the team-level variation in achieving goals, we would expect that the systematic use of I-O psychology methods to select, train, and develop teams to coordinate effectively should result in significantly higher levels of performance.

3.5.5 Organization Level

At the organization level, one branch of I-O that already overlaps with computer science, computational organizational theory (COT), is especially relevant. Carnegie Mellon's Kathleen Carley and her colleagues have decades of research in creating computer-based models of organizational processes and structures that can result in stress-resistant organizations (e.g., Lin & Carley, 2003). It would be sensible to simulate organizational designs and processes for AI scientist-practitioners to be as stress resistant as possible. The simulation of different distribution of uncertainty, using COT methods, can be helpful in understanding the team and organizational models that are more consistently likely to produce the results AI teams desire.

Similarly, there is a very large body of research that organizational cultures affect organizational effectiveness (Hartnell, Ou, & Kinicki, 2011). Given that cultures are created and sustained or changed by the behavior of founders and senior leaders, their behavior should also be in focus. In particular, senior leaders are a special threat because there is evidence that power corrupts leaders, suggesting that leaders should have limited decision rights and checks and balances to make sure their weaknesses' impact on others is truncated (Wang & Sun, 2016). For senior leaders to help their teams identify emerging AI threats and opportunities and other risks to the team, they need to be good at scanning the environment, formulating strategy, persuading stakeholders, and engaging in operational risk management (Barney, 2013). In each of these cases, there is a large body of I-O research and practice that ought to be leveraged to realize the goals of safe AI. This is important to proactively prevent powerful AI getting into the hands of unethical or toxic leaders.

3.6 Conclusion

The potential for AI to solve some of humanity's most vexing problems holds unprecedented promise for the utility of the science and technology. At the same time, AI is the latest in a long series of technologies that will transform jobs, teams, and even entire industries. In the near term this should be a net positive. The prospect of advanced robots that rescue people in burning buildings and perform other tasks that are highly unsafe or boring, portends great things in the years ahead for safer workplaces and better customer service. For workers with high levels of intelligence, creativity, and the ingenuity to reinvent themselves, the rise of machine AI can be a renaissance of more creative, enriching work devoid of the pain and drudgery of earlier work eras.

At the same time, AI is starting to disrupt white-collar jobs, especially those held by workers disinclined to re-skill themselves. Conversely, a future where people can manage their own cadre of robot workers to take care of their lives without the need to work is one that could afford more leisure and family time. Perhaps the biggest near-term risk is the use of AI by evil or toxic leaders, especially those who control the power of the state. But the existential risk that many AI specialists increasingly are also worried about is if "strong AI" outsmarts humans, and has no ethics, or considers itself better off without us around. Their greatest fear is that we could be the architects of our own extinction. Fortunately, our science and practice are well suited to help our colleagues in computer science and engineering mitigate the workplace side of these risks, and leverage the exciting upside potential of AI.

References

Agnoli, S., Corazza, G. E., & Runco, M. A. (2016). Estimating creativity with a multiple-measurement approach within scientific and artistic domains. *Creativity Research Journal*, *28*(2), 171–176. doi:10.1080/10400419.2016.1162475.

Barney, M. (2016). System and method for creating a metrological/psychometric instrument. US Patent Pending, Application number 1524912.

Barney, M., Harkey, S., & Pearlman, K. (1997). System and method for analyzing work requirements and linking human resource products to jobs. US Patent #US6070143A.

Barney, M. & Riley, B. (April 20, 2018). Automated Rasch analyses as a foundation for unobtrusive measurement. To appear in M. Barney, The Bleeding Edge of Measurement – Innovations with Artificially Intelligent Psychometrics. Paper accepted for presentation at the 33rd Annual Conference of the Society for Industrial Organizational Psychology, Chicago, IL.

Barron's (June 21, 2017). Vanguard's Robo-advisor setting the standard: Vanguard's robo-advisor platform is dominating its rivals and may be the template the industry needs to follow. Downloaded June 30, 2017, from www.barrons.com/articles/vanguards-robo-advisor-setting-the-standard-1498063278.

Batey, M. & Furnham, A. (2006). Creativity, intelligence and personality: A critical review of the scattered literature. *Genetic, Social and General Psychology Monographs*, *132*(4), 355–429.

Bhattacharya, A. (December 26, 2017). 56,000 layoffs and counting: India's IT bloodbath this year may just be the start. *Quartz India*. Downloaded January 16, 2018, from https://qz.com/1152683/indian-it-layoffs-in-2017-top-56000-led-by-tcs-infosys-cognizant/.

Bostrom, N. (2014). *Superintelligence: Paths, Dangers, Strategies*. Oxford, UK: Oxford University Press.

Chung, C. K. & Pennebaker, J. W. (February 2008). Revealing dimensions of thinking in open-ended self-descriptions: An automated meaning extraction method for natural language. *Journal of Research in Personality, 42*(1), 96-132. doi:10.1016/j.jrp.2007.04.006.

Datta, A. (March 19, 2017). Did artificial intelligence deny you credit? *Time*. Downloaded April 20, 2017, from http://time.com/4705040/artificial-intelligence-credit/.

Datta, A., Tschantz, M. C., & Datta, A. (2015). Automated experiments on ad privacy settings. *Proceedings on Privacy Enhancing Technologies, 1*, 92–112.

Dawson, T. L. & Stein, Z. (2011). Virtuous cycles of learning: Redesigning testing during the digital revolution. Presentation, Ettore Majorana Center for Scientific Culture, Erice (Sicily), Italy, International School on Mind, Brain and Education. doi:10.13140/2.1.2448.5121.

The Economist (October 17, 2015). Professor Dr Robot QC. Schumpeter Column. Downloaded October 24, 2015, from www.economist.com/node/21674779/print.

Etherington, D. (April 28, 2017). Elon Musk teases Tesla electric semi truck, up to 4 new gigafactory locations. *Techcrunch*. Downloaded June 30, 2017, from https://techcrunch.com/2017/04/28/elon-musk-teases-tesla-electric-semi-truck-up-to-4-new-gigafactory-locations/.

Feloni, R. (June 28, 2017). Consumer-goods giant Unilever has been hiring employees using brain games and artificial intelligence – and it's a huge success. *Business Insider*. Downloaded June 29, 2017, from www.businessinsider.com/unilever-artificial-intelligence-hiring-process-2017-6.

George, G., Howard-Grenville, J., Joshi, A., & Tihanyi, L. (December 2016). Understanding and tackling societal grand challenges through management research. *Academy of Management Journal, 59*(6), 1880–1895. doi:10.5465/amj.2016.4007.

Graham, J., Haidt, J., Koleva, S., Motyl, M., Iyer, R., Wojcik, S. P., & Ditto, P. H (November 28, 2012). Moral foundations theory: The pragmatic validity of moral pluralism. *Advances in Experimental Social Psychology, 47*, 55–130.

Griffith, R. L., Deaton, J. E., & Steelman, L. A. (October 2003). I-O psychology and the synthetic team member: The blue pill or the red pill?. *The Industrial-Organizational Psychologist, 41*(2), 55–58.

The Guardian (March 24, 2016). Tay, Microsoft's AI Chatbot, gets a crash course in racism from Twitter. Downloaded May 23, 2017, from www.theguardian.com/technology/2016/mar/24/tay-microsofts-ai-chatbot-gets-a-crash-course-in-racism-from-twitter.

Haidt, Jonathan (October 2001). The emotional dog and its rational tail: A social intuitionist approach to moral judgement. *Psychological Review, 108*(4), 814–834. doi:10.1037/0033-295x.108.4.814.

Hariri, M. B., Reaves, A. C., & Viswesvaran, C. (2016). Creative and innovative performance: A meta-analysis of relationships with task, citizenship and counterproductive job performance dimensions. *European Journal of Work and Organizational Psychology, 25*(4), 495–511. doi:10.1080/1359432X.2015.1134491.

Hartnell, C. A., Ou, A. Y., & Kinicki, A. (2011). Organizational culture and organizational effectiveness: A meta-analytic investigation of the competing values framework's theoretical suppositions. *Journal of Applied Psychology, 96*(4), 677–694.

Hertz, S. G. & Krettenaur, T. (June 2016). Does moral identity effectively predict moral behavior?: A meta-analysis. *Review of General Psychology, 20*(2), 129–140.

Hurd, W. (December 7, 2017). Quantum computing is the next big security risk. *Wired*. Downloaded January 16, 2018, from www.wired.com/story/quantum-computing-is-the-next-big-security-risk/.

Hutson, M. (June 21, 2017). Artificial intelligence can predict which congressional bills will pass. *Science*. doi:10.1126/science.aan7003. Downloaded June 30, 2017, from www.sciencemag.org/news/2017/06/artificial-intelligence-can-predict-which-congressional-bills-will-pass.

Kelion, L. (April 10, 2017). Google's AI seeks further Go glory. *BBC News*. Downloaded April 22, 2017, from www.bbc.com/news/technology-39553291.

IBM (2017). Watson developer cloud: The science behind the personality Insights service. Downloaded April 22, 2017, from www.ibm.com/watson/developercloud/doc/personality-insights/science.html.

LeCun, Y., Bengio, Y., Hinton, G. (May 28, 2015). Deep learning. *Nature*, *521*, 436–444. doi:10.1038/nature14539.

Levy, N. (June 28, 2017). Turbo patent aims to improve the patent process with new artificial intelligence products. *Geekwire*. Downloaded June 28, 2017, from www.geekwire.com/2017/turbopatent-aims-speed-filing-patents-new-artificial-intelligence-products/.

Lin, Z. & Carley, K. M. (2003). Designing stress resistant organizations: Computational theorizing and crisis applications. Springer Science+Business Media. doi:10.1007/978-1-4757-3703-5.

Makary, M. A. & Daniel, M. (May 3, 2016). Medical error – the third leading cause of death in the US. *The BMJ*. doi:10.1136/bmj.i2139.

McCurry, J. (January 5, 2017). Japanese company replaces office workers with artificial intelligence. *The Guardian*. Downloaded January 15, 2018, from www.theguardian.com/technology/2017/jan/05/japanese-company-replaces-office-workers-artificial-intelligence-ai-fukoku-mutual-life-insurance.

McDonald, M. (June 17, 2017). The legal reality of artificial intelligence. Downloaded on January 15, 2018, from www.veritone.com/insights/the-legal-reality-of-artificial-intelligence/.

Nagarajan, M., Wilkins, A. D., Bachman, B. J., Novikov, I. B., Bao, S., Haas, P. J., . . . Lichtarge, O. (August 11–14, 2015). Predicting Future Scientific Discoveries Based on a Networked Analysis of the Past Literature. KDD '15, Sydney, NSW, Australia. doi:10.1145/2783258.2788609.

Netzer, O., Lemaire, A., & Herzenstein, M. (November 6, 2016) When words sweat: Identifying signals for loan default in the text of loan applications. Columbia Business School Research Paper No. 16-83. Retrieved from SSRN https://ssrn.com/abstract=2865327.

Neubert, J. C., Mainert, J., Kretzschmar, A., & Grieff, S. (March, 2015). The assessment of 21st century skills in industrial and organizational psychology: Complex and collaborative problem solving. *Industrial and Organizational Psychology*, *8*(2) 1–31. doi:10.1017/iop.2015.14.

Price, R. (June 17, 2016). Digital currency Ethereum is cratering amid claims of a $50 million hack. *Business Insider*. Retrieved June 30, 2016 from www.businessinsider.com.au/dao-hacked-ethereum-crashing-in-value-tens-of-millions-allegedly-stolen-2016-6.

Psychobabble (2017). Corporate Website. Downloaded June 29, 2017, from http://psychobabble.com/.

Quartz (2017). Artificial intelligence could build new drugs faster than any human team. Downloaded April 21, 2017, from https://qz.com/963484/artificial-intelligence-could-build-new-drugs-faster-than-any-human-team/.

Razzouk, R. & Shute, V. (September 2012). What is design thinking and why is it important? *Review of Educational Research, 82*(3), 330–348.

Rest, J. R., Navaez, D., Thoma, S. J., & Bebeau, M. J. (2000). A neo-Kohlbergian approach to morality research, *Journal of Moral Education, 29*(4), 381–395

Revell, T. (August 21, 2017) Inside the fighter jet of the future where AI is the pilot. *New Scientist*. Downloaded January 16, 2018, from www.newscientist.com/article/2144601-inside-the-fighter-jet-of-the-future-where-ai-is-the-pilot/.

Russell, S. J. & Norvig, P. (2010). *Artificial intelligence: A modern approach*. 3rd edn., Upper Saddle River: Prentice Hall.

Salas, E., Sims, D. E., & Burke, C. S. (2005). Is there a "Big Five" in teamwork? *Small Group Research, 36*, 555–596. doi:10.1177/1046496405277134.

Schippmann, J. S. (1999). *Strategic job modeling: Working at the core of integrated human resources*. Mahwah, NJ: Lawrence Erlbaum.

ScienMag (April 24, 2017). Robot radiology: Low cost A.I. could screen for cervical cancer better than humans. Downloaded April 24, 2017, from https://scienmag.com/robot-radiology-low-cost-a-i-could-screen-for-cervical-cancer-better-than-humans/.

Scott, G., Leritz, L. E., & Mumford, M. D. (2004). The effectiveness of creativity training: A quantitative review. *Creativity Research Journal, 16*(4), 361–388.

Shen, L. (March 30, 2017). Robots are replacing humans at all these Wall Street firms. *Fortune*. Downloaded January 15, 2018, from http://fortune.com/2017/03/30/blackrock-robots-layoffs-artificial-intelligence-ai-hedge-fund/.

Teh, Y. W., Jordan, M., Beal, M. J., & Blie, D. M. (December, 2006). Hierarchical dirichlet processes. *Journal of the American Statistical Association, 101*(476), 1566–1581

Viegas, J. (July 24, 2014). Humans caused 322 animal extinctions in past 500 years. *Seeker*. Downloaded January 16, 2018, from www.seeker.com/humans-caused-322-animal-extinctions-in-past-500-years-1768850883.html.

Vigna, P. & Casey, M. J. (2015). *The age of cryptocurrency: How bitcoin and the blockchain are challenging the global economic order*. New York, NY: St. Martin's Press.

Wang, F. & Sun, X. (2016). Absolute power leads to absolute corruption? Impact of power on corruption depending on the concepts of power one holds. *European Journal of Social Psychology, 46*, 77–89.

Wilson, S. R., Mihalcea, R., Boyd, R. L., & Pennebaker, J. W. (November 5, 2016). Disentangling topic models: A cross-cultural analysis of personal values through words. Proceedings of 2016 EMNLP Workshop on Natural Language Processing and Computational Social Science, 143–152, Austin TX.

PART II

Technology in Staffing

4 The Next Wave of Internet-Based Recruitment

Neil A. Morelli and A. James Illingworth

4.1 The Next Wave of Internet-Based Recruitment

At a macro-level, human capital theory states that workers bring the sum of their skills and characteristics to jobs, which adds value to an organization and differentiates it from the competition (Acemoglu & Autor, 2011). Recruitment is the process of adding human capital to an organization and is pivotal for an organization's success. Simply put, recruitment is "finding and putting the right person in the right job at the right time and place to enable firms to implement strategy and create competitive advantage" (Ployhart, Schmitt, & Tippins, 2017, p. 3). Enabling the recruitment process with the internet has become essential in modern staffing and talent acquisition practice, and is referred to here as internet-based recruitment. To put this trend in perspective, industry analysts estimate that in 2015 approximately $240 billion were spent on recruitment and talent acquisition technologies in the United States alone (Bersin, 2016).

Arguably, the mainstream version of the internet began with Netscape, a point-and-click web browser that non-technical people could use. Netscape was one of many internet technologies released during an era named Web 1.0 (McCullough, 2015). Among the early Web 1.0 users were recruiters, who learned that their reach was expanded more cheaply and quickly than traditional analog methods. This broadened access to candidates ushered in the first digitization of recruitment methods. For example, job lists, career information, and job descriptions could now be posted to websites. Early internet-based recruitment research examined the characteristics of these websites, and how those characteristics affected recruitment outcomes and candidate reactions (Ployhart et al., 2017). In 2004, the era of innovations that built on Web 1.0 use cases and infrastructure was coined as Web 2.0. Most of the internet-based applications, social media, multi-media, and content platforms used today were first introduced at this time (Battelle & O'Reilly, 2004). The more dynamic and robust Web 2.0 systems allowed for a greater exchange of information between recruiters and candidates using two-way, constant communication channels (Llorens & Wilson, 2012). Web 2.0 technologies also empowered "social recruiting" where, instead of posting static job and organizational messages online hoping the right candidates saw them, recruiters could now attract, engage, and influence job applicants and candidates dynamically (Doherty, 2010; Gandini, 2016; Meister & Willyerd, 2010).

In this chapter, we summarize the existing empirical literature on internet-based recruitment with a specific emphasis on the latest research involving Web 2.0 technologies. In their recent review of recruitment and selection research, Ployhart et al. (2017) noted that most internet-based recruitment research was published nearly ten years after Web 1.0 practices and tools became popular. This same pattern is also evident for Web 2.0 technologies. Recruitment studies published in the past few years have focused on social media, multi-media content sharing, blogging, long-form marketing content, podcasts, and internet games – all technologies launched in the mid-2000s. This research is informative, but, as America Online co-founder Steve Case (2016) recently argued, the technology industry is beginning to enter a new era of innovation dubbed the "Third Wave." The Third Wave is best described as a full and complete integration of the internet into all aspects of daily life. The Internet of Things (IoT), or the constellation of technologies and practices that embed internet connectivity into physical items, is one example of this ubiquitous connectivity that stands to disrupt industries such as healthcare, education, food production, and, of course, recruitment.

The initial stages of the Third Wave are already impacting internet-based recruitment. In addition to the automation of traditional recruitment methodologies (Mead, Olson-Buchanan, & Drasgow, 2014), internet recruiting tools now include more sophisticated systems such as artificial intelligence (AI) and machine learning (ML) within job matching tools, conversational recruiting chatbots, recruitment marketing platforms, and virtual job marketplaces and content communities. These advances in technology offer an unprecedented level of personalized and interactive capabilities for attracting, engaging, and influencing job applicants and candidates. Thus, in this chapter we summarize and describe representative examples of the latest research on the use and impact of existing technologies for internet-based recruitment, and also offer examples of new, unstudied internet technologies that could upend current understanding and best practices.

To provide a structural framework for our review, we focus on the Web 2.0 technologies influencing each primary phase of the recruitment process. Previous summaries have included the strategizing and evaluation phases as part of the overall recruitment process (Breaugh, 2008), while others have focused on recruitment activities themselves, such as attracting (i.e., generating viable candidates), sorting and contacting (i.e., maintaining status of viable candidates), and closing (i.e., post-offer closure) (Cappelli, 2001; Dineen & Allen, 2014; Dineen & Soltis, 2011; Ryan & Delany, 2010). For our purposes, we use the sourcing, attracting, sorting, nurturing, and closing labels to define the five main phases of recruitment. Therefore, we provide an overview of the latest internet-based recruitment research organized by each phase and identify how upcoming or current market technologies could create potential gaps in our understanding of these phases. We conclude with a discussion of how these internet technologies are changing the nature of work and how these changes could influence recruitment practice. Table 4.1 summarizes our review of the internet-based recruitment literature, highlighting the technologies and psychological theories associated with each recruitment phase.

Table 4.1 *Recruitment phases and relevant web 2.0 technology and psychological theory*

	Recruiting				
	Sourcing	**Attracting**	**Sorting**	**Nurturing**	**Closing**
	Identifying active and passive job seekers	Enticing job seekers to become job applicants	Narrowing job applicant group to most qualified job candidates	Developing and maintaining relationships with job candidates	Persuading selected candidates to accept a job offer
Web 2.0 Technology					
Pages & Communities					
Social media (e.g., Facebook, LinkedIn, Twitter)	✓	✓	✓		
Professional content communities (e.g., GitHub)	✓	✓	✓		
Job boards (e.g., Monster.com, Indeed.com)	✓	✓			
Job marketplaces (e.g., Glassdoor)	✓	✓			
Employer webpage(s)	✓	✓			
Employer career webpage(s)	✓	✓			
Content					
Games, challenges, and simulations	✓	✓	✓		
Organization information (e.g., virtual reality tour)		✓			
Job information (e.g., video job description)		✓			
Communication Tools					
Automated messaging (e.g., text, email)		✓		✓	
Instant messaging (e.g., text, video-chat)				✓	✓
Video-recorded interviews (e.g., HireVue)			✓		
Organization Recruiting Tools					
Applicant tracking system (ATS)			✓	✓	
Human resource management system (HRMS)			✓	✓	
Artificial Intelligence Tools					
Applicant identification (e.g., Koru)	✓				
Resume evaluation (e.g., Ideal)	✓		✓		
Job matching (e.g., Workey)	✓		✓		
Chatbots (e.g., Mya)		✓		✓	
Psychological Theory					
Differentiation-Consolidation Theory	✓	✓			
Elaboration Likelihood Model	✓	✓			
Expectation-Confirmation Model	✓	✓			
Institutional Theory	✓	✓			
Instrumental-Symbolic Framework	✓	✓			
Organizational Justice Theory				✓	✓
Person-Organization (P-O) Fit	✓	✓		✓	✓
Person-Job (P-J) Fit	✓	✓		✓	✓
Psychological Contract Theory		✓			✓
Self-Determination Theory		✓			
Signaling Theory		✓		✓	
Value Congruence Theory		✓			

4.2 Sourcing and Attracting Job Seekers

The first two recruitment phases, sourcing and attracting, often go hand-in-hand. Sourcing job seekers and attracting them to become job applicants often include similar methods in practice, while the literature has focused on theoretical antecedents of organizational attraction (Barber, 1998; Breaugh, 2013). Therefore, we have chosen to combine our discussion of the first two phases. As a definitional clarification, we use "job seeker" to identify the individuals targeted by recruiters during the sourcing and attracting phases. These individuals can be either active or passive job seekers. We refer to individuals targeted during the sorting phase as "job applicants" as they have expressed interest in an open position. Finally, we refer to individuals targeted during the nurturing and closing phases as "job candidates."

Reviews of the attraction literature have summarized the effects of information quantity and quality on organizational attraction: organizational attraction is increased as more information about the company is provided that balances an image of prestige with a realistic representation of the work (Ryan & Delany, 2010). The internet-based recruitment literature has often focused on the use of digital job boards or employer career sites as the primary method for providing this information. These systems are designed to post available jobs online and passively receive resumes from interested applicants (Breaugh, 2008; Ross & Slovensky, 2012). Thus, much of the research conducted during the Web 1.0 era focused on the technological characteristics of career websites and online recruiter behaviors, without directly tying these characteristics to organizational attraction theories (Viswesvaran & Ones, 2010). As recruitment practices have entered the Web 2.0 era, new trends are emerging that move recruitment beyond just modifying the richness of the organizational information offered via the internet to providing tools that interact with job seekers as consumers and promote employment brands that are attractive to specific job seekers. In the following sections, we discuss how these trends are influencing job seeker sourcing and attraction within the context of employment branding, realistic job previews, and employee referrals.

4.3 Employment Branding

Many organizations show brand awareness by devoting millions of dollars to marketing campaigns designed to influence how their brand affects customer behavior. This brand awareness has also entered the recruitment function and more companies are focusing on how internet-based tools can help influence job seeker behavior. Recruiters are using internet-based tools to help craft and deliver an employment brand via consumer marketing-type recruitment messages (Gandini, 2016; Maurer & Cook, 2011). However, potential job seekers and applicants also use the internet as a two-way communication channel (e.g., Van Hoye & Lievens, 2007), and have resources such as Glassdoor to find previous candidate and employee experiences. Thus, organizations are having to become more transparent and inclusive by personalizing recruitment messages to specific talent audiences and be open to potential job seeker and applicant questions and requests for more detailed information (Ordioni, 2017).

For some time, researchers and practitioners alike have understood that personnel recruitment is marketing (Maurer & Cook, 2011). In the Web 1.0 era, online job board companies were ascendant as they capitalized on the greater reach and attention that could be gathered from an online audience. Audiences were so big in these online forums that recruiters realized marketing strategies were required to reach the right talent pool and compel them to apply for an open position. In these forums, the strength and clarity of an organization's employment brand and reputation became tantamount to creating the impressions that were needed to generate a meaningful talent pipeline (Cappelli, 2001). In a study designed to explain organizational attraction, Lievens and Highhouse (2003) discovered that the traits applicants infer about organizations explained incremental variance in predicting organizational attractiveness more than job or organizational information alone (e.g., opportunities for advancement, employee testimonials). This finding can be explained through a marketing concept called the instrumental – symbolic framework: The instrumental components of a brand represent the product's tangible benefits that offer the consumer ways to avoid pain and maximize pleasure. The symbolic components of a brand represent the non-tangible aspects of the product that make consumers feel a certain way or maintain a certain identity. People often associate these symbolic brand features with human characteristics and find them attractive because these features are similar to how their self-concepts and personalities are expressed. Slaughter et al. (2004) built on this framework to explain applicant attraction by how organizational personality characteristics are ascribed from brand marketing messages. The researchers discovered that organizational personality traits were related to overall organizational attraction, explaining attraction above and beyond just familiarity with the organization. These and other studies have consistently found that an organization's image, reputation, and symbolic brand characteristics affect applicant attraction and offer an organization a competitive advantage if these characteristics can be effectively leveraged for talent sourcing (Ployhart, 2006).

Organizational attraction as a function of employment branding can also be explained from an institutional theory perspective, where organizations that adopt technologies that can surface and communicate more salient brand characteristics are seen as more legitimate by job seekers (DiMaggio & Powell, 1983; Dineen & Allen, 2014). However, while organizations have recognized the importance of establishing and communicating brand characteristics as part of the recruitment process, applicants may vary in their reactions based on their own experiences and values. Vanderstukken, Van den Boreck, and Proost (2016) examined the organizational attraction mechanism using self-determination and value congruence theories (e.g., Deci & Ryan, 2000) and found that job seekers are either attracted or repulsed by the organizational identities inferred from company brand messages depending on how these identities align with their personal values and underlying motivations.

Contemporary internet-based recruitment tools have made it possible to amplify and clarify these brand messages when sourcing and attracting job seekers. For example, organizations have moved beyond sending one-way communications to potential applicants through company career sites, online advertising, and open positions posted on job boards. Third-party social media tools such as Facebook, LinkedIn, and Twitter are now being used to build brand awareness, engage potential applicants, and showcase attractive aspects of the employment brand (Acikgoz & Bergman, 2016). This is especially true when "farming" passive job seekers by building an attractive employment brand on social media tools such as Twitter (Karl & Pelochute, 2013) and "hunting" for passive job seekers through social networks such as LinkedIn (Nikolau, 2014). As opposed to active job seekers, who are proactively looking for open positions, passive job seekers are individuals who are currently employed and not actively looking for a job but may be open to a new opportunity. These individuals are often seen as higher quality by recruiters and are in higher demand (Ployhart et al., 2017). Thus, social media platforms used as recruitment tools are shifting the prevailing recruitment paradigm from "push" (i.e., sending organizational information into the world for job seekers to become applicants) to "pull" (i.e., job seekers are engaged as information consumers on their own terms) (Dineen & Allen, 2014). These new tools and associated methods have shifted control of the recruitment process from recruiters and organizations to job seekers and applicants. As such, recruiters must now use internet-based tools such as social media and networking platforms to "narrow cast" or specifically target particular groups with educational and rapport-building materials and interactions (Dineen & Allen, 2014). This is possible as new internet technologies allow recruiters to access information about job seekers that was previously only available from job applications or personal interactions (Ashuri & Bar-Ilan, 2017).

In a similar vein, new Web 2.0 recruitment applications and social media services have helped establish online, professional "content communities" – forums for user-generated content that can act as a channel for sharing information with job seekers and applicants (Kaplan & Haenlein, 2010). Although professional online communities overall have not been studied extensively, their rapid proliferation in the last several years has prompted researchers to investigate their impact on the recruitment process. A recent study by Chiang and Suan (2015) examined how potential job applicants self-present on LinkedIn and how recruiters form impressions of the job seeker's person-organization (P-O) fit and person-job (P-J) fit based on these presentations. P-O fit refers to the degree to which an individual's personal characteristics, such as their values and interests, are compatible with the organization's values and cultural norms. P-J fit refers to the degree to which an individual's knowledge, skills, abilities, and other characteristics are compatible with the requirements and activities of the job (Kristof-Brown & Guay, 2011). While job and organizational characteristics, as well as recruiter behaviors, are still important predictors of applicant attraction, P-O fit is one of the strongest predictors of recruitment outcomes such as job pursuit intentions, intentions to accept a job offer (whether or not an offer is actually made), and actual job choice/acceptance behaviors (Chapman et al., 2005; Uggerslev, Fassina, & Kraichy, 2012).

Chiang and Suan (2015) discovered that job seeker self-presentation behaviors (i.e., the extent job seekers provide informative, valuable, and persuasive information on their profile) did impact recruiters' fit perceptions and hiring recommendations. Since its founding in 2003 and subsequent launch of public profiles in 2006, LinkedIn has only entrenched itself as the de facto professional online community for potential job candidates to maintain a professional online identity and for recruiters to search and engage relevant talent (Bersin, 2016; Gandini, 2016). Thus, professional online communities that exist on social networks such as LinkedIn are only building more cachet with recruiters over time and allowing active or passive job seekers to present their desired professional personas in a format that is more job-relevant than other social media tools.

Swider, Barrick, and Zimmerman (2015) also recently incorporated decision-making theory with P-O fit to explain how applicants develop fit perceptions during three phases of the recruitment process: attraction, maintenance, and job choice. Specifically, Swider et al. incorporated differentiation-consolidation theory (DCT), which posits that decision makers actively adjust their initially perceived differences between options over time as more information is gathered, and that clearer differences between options leads to more confident decisions. They hypothesized that greater differentiation between job choices, created by differing levels of initial and continued P-O fit perceptions, would be related to job choice decisions. These hypotheses were confirmed as the amount of initial P-O fit differentiation varied significantly across four organizations at the start of the recruitment process and those differences increased over time. These initial differences in P-O fit perceptions and the change in these differences over time significantly related to applicant job choice. In other words, Swider et al.'s study provided a mechanism for how P-O fit perceptions affect applicant decisions both before and during each recruitment phase, and ultimately how recruitment outcomes are realized. As new, internet-based tools offer desirable active or passive job seekers more choices and opportunities, tools that also help organizations differentiate their brand message from competing firms early in the recruitment process (pre-decision) will be the most effective at influencing job choice decisions. For example, internet-based tools that offer two-way forms of communication, even during the attraction phase, can offer organizations a chance to further differentiate themselves from competitors who are also targeting the same talent.

4.4 Realistic Job Previews (RJPs)

An important aspect of attracting job seekers to organizations is providing accurate and realistic information about the job, co-workers, and workplace culture. Current internet technologies allow job seekers to see what it is like to work in a position on a day-to-day basis through online videos, and in some cases, virtual reality (VR) tours and job simulations. Many internet job boards allow videos to be posted in conjunction with text-based job descriptions (Hurtz & Wright, 2012). The immersive potential and fidelity of these job previews is accelerating as the technology continually advances. For instance, Google recently acquired Owlchemy, a startup company that developed a game-like VR job simulation (Cheesman, 2017). The United States Navy is also using VR to engage potential recruits at public events (Raphael, 2017). High-fidelity RJPs like those offered in VR simulations help applicants self-select out of the recruitment process (Phillips, 1998) by providing positive and negative information about the job, showcasing both its assets (e.g., pay, perks, satisfaction level among employees) and liabilities (e.g., challenging nature of the work, dangerous environments, political nature of work environment) (Rynes, 1991; Wanous, 1989).

Additionally, while RJPs have been used to help manage expectations among applicants or new hires, organizations are now attracting potential job applicants using more robust, day-in-the-life videos of employees on the job *before* job seekers formally enter the hiring process (Sullivan, 2014). For example, Home Depot showcases open positions with their "Behind the Apron" videos highlighting "day in the life" snapshots of sales, customer service, and supply chain roles. Video job descriptions posted to the internet have been shown to generate a 60 percent response rate among job seekers compared to a 20 percent response rate for job descriptions that only use text (Staney, 2017). In addition, companies such as Smashfly and Animoto are making it easy for organizations to create, post, and market video job descriptions to target talent audiences. In a study conducted by Kraichy and Chapman (2014), videos of a recruiter answering scripted questions were posted to a company's career website to provide realistic job information in a simulated conversation. The researchers discovered that study participants acting as potential applicants responded to these videos more positively when affective information (i.e., information that induced feelings), rather than cognitive fact-based information, was provided. Video is well suited for distributing this type of affective information.

Not only do online video job descriptions appeal to a wider demographic of potential applicants and work well with mobile devices, they also function similarly to the well-researched findings for face-to-face and video-based RJPs, which have been shown to reduce voluntary turnover by increasing perceived organizational honesty (Earnest, Allen, & Landis, 2011). This finding is important as recent industry surveys have discovered that 84 percent of recent college graduates applying for jobs said the most important factor when applying for a job was "insight into the role" (TalentQ, 2013). Thus, providing high-fidelity job information through internet-based videos and simulations can help job applicants and candidates increase their engagement during the initial phases of the recruitment process, more accurately evaluate perceived job and organization fit, and be more confident about job choices when accepting an offer (Boatman & Erker, 2012).

4.5 Employee Referrals

Another new internet-based recruitment trend has been the increasing use of technology-mediated employee referral programs. As an example, Google's hiring needs during a period of high business growth required over 300,000 referrals. Google's recruiters helped employees comb their own social networks and generated a home-grown candidate database to track and cultivate potential job applicants from this referral effort (Bock, 2015). Vendors also enable smaller businesses to use their employees' referral network. For example, Roikoi is a web and mobile application that gamifies the referral process. LinkedIn has recently released an employee referral tool for their platform and 1-Page is a human resources (HR) technology company that builds employee referral engines for large enterprises. These tools have gained popularity because they decentralize the recruitment function to the individual employee level through visualizing and accessing existing online connections (Dineen & Allen, 2014).

Although the sophistication of these internet-based referral tools has grown in recent years, research has already demonstrated that employee referrals often help recruitment efforts because they set realistic job expectations in the minds of potential applicants (Breaugh, 2008; Hill, 1970; Ullman, 1966). More realistic job expectations lead to lower rates of withdrawal (Zattoli & Wanous, 2000), and positive word-of-mouth explains unique and incremental variance in organizational attraction (Van Hoye et al., 2016). As with internet-based RJPs, effective employee referrals help appropriately set expectations among job seekers, which is critical for driving more job seekers to apply and helping hired candidates to stay with the company. To explain this phenomenon, Eveleth, Baker-Eveleth, and Stone (2015) applied the expectation-confirmation model (ECM; Fan & Suh, 2014) to understand how website utility and perceived usefulness influences job applicant expectations and behaviors. The ECM is based on consumer theory and states that an individual's purchase decisions are influenced when early expectations of the product or service are confirmed. In other words, when initial expectations are confirmed, repurchase decisions are higher. Eveleth et al. discovered that perceived website usability positively influenced website satisfaction and intentions to apply. In their study, a career website's usability was defined by how well it engaged applicants, provided helpful content concerning the job, and offered opportunities for feedback related to expectations. As organizations leverage new recruitment tools to help form job seeker expectations about the organization through amplifying recruitment marketing messages, providing high-fidelity videos and RJPS, and turning employee connections into referral networks, we believe theoretical frameworks such as the ECM will only become more important for explaining both active and passive job seeker attitudes and behaviors.

4.6 Future Questions

For many recruiters, the most coveted candidates are high-performers that are already employed but are open to taking a new position. Although these passive job seekers are hard to reach with Web 1.0 recruitment methods such as job posts, online advertisements, or career sites, they make up a majority of the most in-demand talent. For example, a recent survey of nearly 40,000 developers discovered that 62 percent were not looking for a new job, but were still open to new opportunities, whereas 25 percent were not open to new opportunities and 13 percent were actively looking (Stack Overflow, 2017). Thus, an accelerating trend has been to automate sourcing passive job seekers using "big data" and focusing recruiter efforts on attracting applicants. However, some passive job seeker attraction activities bleed into talent assessment activities. For example, companies such as Entelo can monitor and scrape available online resume or social media data to score job seekers on job-relevant dimensions, such as social interactions, to "proactively" match them to jobs without their opting-in as a formal applicant (Bersin, 2016). New startup companies such as Restless Bandit are developing artificial intelligence systems to "proactively" search online resume repositories to automatically alert organizations to potential applicants. Beamery is a company designed to use machine-learning-based algorithms to automate the relationship-tracking experience for recruiters so the recruitment experience can be treated like customer acquisition (i.e., outbound sourcing, pipeline building, targeted nurturing). These technologies call into question whether or not theories currently used to explain job seeker attraction, such as signaling theory (e.g., Gregory, Meade, & Thompson, 2013), apply to these "above the selection funnel" type tools. In other words, if high-potential candidates are being approached with a pre-matched job opportunity in hand, are meaningful psychological connections between the applicant and organization being lost for the sake of efficiency and automation? Or are these tools skipping the "messy" perception-setting phase of fit and jumping straight to the matches that have the best chance of a job seeker deciding to apply? These are research questions that are still unanswered due to the rapid development and use of these tools in recruiting applicants.

The internet also enables new "guerrilla marketing" tactics designed to both narrowly target high-potential job seekers and communicate an employment brand message. This is another recent trend with little empirical examination. For example, The Lad Bible, an internet entertainment company, hid recruitment messages in its website's source code for technical job seekers who examine it to find. Google has tried embedding games within technical search topics that would reward those who completed them with recruiters' contact information. Uber also famously employed a "code on the road" game where certain users were invited to complete a hacking challenge through the app during an Uber ride (Motroc, 2016). These types of hidden recruitment tactics can send a strong employment brand message to job seekers that find them, specifically target potential applicants with messages that both "buy" (i.e., assess) and "sell" (i.e., communicate an attractive recruitment message), and act as compelling public relations talking points; however, we could find no research examining how these tactics affect applicant attraction or perceived fit. In addition, large organizations such as Unilever, L'Oreal, and the United States Army are turning toward recruitment games to engage talent pools, share a brand message, and "reduce bias" (Gale, 2017a; Wheeler, 2010). Nonetheless, other than vendor-led studies, no empirical research exists to examine whether these games and subtle recruitment messages in fact reduce bias of any kind in hiring outcomes. Stated as a question, what effects, if any, do these new tactics have on the quantity and quality of the messages surrounding the employment brand, organizational identity, perceptions of job-related information, or organizational attraction?

Finally, one of the most drastic technology-related changes affecting the sourcing and attracting recruitment phases is the advent of digital job marketplaces designed to find, attract, qualify, and hire contingent, freelance, or "gig" workers (Bersin, 2016; Kuhn, 2016). Companies and platforms that facilitate this type of recruitment include Upwork, Fiverr, HourlyNerd, Toptal, Pilot, Catalant, and many others. Although these platforms are fairly new, previous research has discovered that contingent workers who are converted to full-time employees perform as well as new hires added through traditional recruitment channels (Dahling et al., 2013).

Thus, recruiters may not only look to contingent workers for performing short-term projects, but may also attract high-quality contingent workers as a pipeline for vetted, full-time employees. A related but less understood issue is how "reputation metrics" in digital job marketplaces act as sourcing signals and influence both job seeker and recruiter impressions and behaviors. In an ethnographic study of free-lance workers on the Upwork job marketplace, Gandini (2016) observed that workers "fetishized" their reputational score on the platform as they believed it was the only element employers look at when assigning a job (i.e., workers believe that those with the highest scores are contacted more often and do not have to compete for jobs). This has raised questions about the fetishizing of an algorithm to match contingent workers with jobs (Gandini, 2016; Rainie & Anderson, 2017). For instance, how do platforms that facilitate anonymous bidding and bi-directional attraction techniques affect organizational attraction and job choice? Or does using a ranking algorithm as an intermediary between job seeker and organization shroud or undermine theoretical explanations of merit-based hiring practices (e.g., perceptions of P-O and P-J fit; Aguinis & Lawal, 2013)? Although we found little published research on these questions from Industrial-Organizational (I-O) psychology journals, other fields, such as marketing science, are attempting to find answers (e.g., Yoganarasimhan, 2013). There is an opportunity for I-O psychologists to supply psychological processes that explain how these types of workers are sourced and attracted for work opportunities using digital marketplaces.

4.7 Sorting Job Applicants

Once job seekers make the decision to apply for a position with an organization, the next phase in the recruitment process is to "sort" applicants based on their qualifications (Gatewood, Feild, & Barrick, 2016). The purpose of this sorting phase is to reduce the larger pool of applicants by "screening out" those who are unqualified for the position. While this phase has traditionally received less attention in the traditional recruitment literature, it has become more important in internet-based recruitment because the internet makes it easier for people to apply for jobs and has exponentially increased the size of the applicant pool for any given job posting (Cappelli, 2001). The growth in the size of applicant pools has also led to an increase in the number of potentially unqualified applicants being considered for a position (Dineen & Noe, 2009), which further emphasizes the need for pre-screening tools that can quickly and accurately winnow down the applicant pool. Therefore, in this section, we only consider internet-based pre-screening tools used "above" the personnel selection funnel to evaluate an applicant's eligibility and basic qualifications, those tools that focus on background characteristics or background predictors as opposed to individual difference constructs or psychological construct-based predictors (Sullivan, 2012; Viswesvaran & Ones, 2010). Other chapters in this handbook provide extensive reviews of technology-based pre-hire assessments (e.g., games, mobile applications, simulations) used for "screening in" job candidates based on their knowledge, skills, abilities, and other personal characteristics (KSAOs) "inside" the selection funnel and are not discussed here.

4.8 Online Resumes

Resumes continue to be the mainstay for how job applicants provide information about their background and work experiences, despite the ability to establish a widely distributed professional presence online through LinkedIn, personal landing pages, and blog posts (Samuel, 2013). During the Web 1.0 era, internet technology simply made it easier for applicants to share digital versions of their text-based resumes with recruiters through email attachments and file uploads. Web 2.0 technology has created new opportunities for alternative online resume formats, such as video resumes and e-portfolios, which allow applicants to provide additional information about their skills, qualifications, and experiences that cannot be easily conveyed in traditional resumes or text-based, online professional profiles.

Video resumes. A video resume is a brief video created by a job applicant to elaborate on information contained in a traditional resume (Apers & Derous, 2017; Hiemstra & Derous, 2015). During the video, applicants may talk about their work experience and performance or use the video as an opportunity to demonstrate their personality, knowledge, skills, or abilities. Intended to complement traditional resumes, video resumes are submitted during the application process or posted to video hosting websites where recruiters can access them. Organizations are interested in using video resumes (BusinessWire, 2007), recruiters are aware of them (Heathfield, 2016), and websites like Spark Hire and VideoResumeNow can create and host them, but video resumes have yet to see widespread adoption for several reasons. First, it is unclear if video resumes are equivalent to traditional resumes, even when both formats contain the same content (e.g., academic qualifications, work experiences). Some researchers find that applicants who submit video resumes are perceived more negatively than those who submit paper resumes, whereas others find no differences in perceptions of applicants across the two formats (e.g., Apers & Derous, 2017; Derous, Taveirne, & Hiemstra, 2012; Waung, Hymes, & Beatty, 2014). Second, video resumes include visual cues about protected characteristics (e.g., ethnicity, sex) that could lead to illegal employment discrimination (Baldas, 2007; Lefkow, 2007). Despite these concerns, however, research suggests the availability of this information has no effect on the recruitment outcomes of protected groups relative to majority group members (Derous et al., 2012; Hiemstra, 2013; Waung et al., 2015). Third, it seems applicants and recruiters like paper resumes better. Both groups tend to rate video resumes more negatively in terms of their fairness, validity, and opportunity to perform (Hiemstra, 2013), except in situations when the labor market is tight and applicants see video resumes as another way to share more information about themselves (Hiemstra et al., 2012). Finally, recruiters think it takes too long to screen video resumes (GlobalHRResearch, 2016), but this may change with recent work to automate the review process. Nguyen and Gatica-Perez (2016) demonstrated computers can extract nonverbal audio-visual cues from video resumes that predict applicant personality and hirability. As innovations in these applications of machine learning and artificial intelligence continue, the review and scoring of video resumes may become completely automated.

e-Portfolios. The e-portfolio is another online resume format made possible by Web 2.0 multi-media capabilities. With origins in the education field (e.g., Bryant & Chittum, 2013; Wills & Rice, 2013), e-portfolios are a digital way for applicants to collect, document, and share professional accomplishments that are reflected in work products or "artifacts" (Flanigan, 2012; Lorenzo & Ittelson, 2005). Through the internet, these portfolios can be displayed on webpages with many different types of multi-media, including audio, video, text, and graphics. On their surface, e-portfolios appear to contain information that would be useful to recruiters for pre-screening applicant qualifications because they expand on information available in a resume (Coker, 2016; Strohmeier, 2010). Unfortunately, surveys of employers and recruiters tend to find most of them have never heard of e-portfolios (ePortfoliohub, 2016; Ward & Moser, 2008; Yu, 2012), but do think e-portfolios would be useful during initial applicant screening (ePortfoliohub, 2016; Straumsheim, 2014). What little research exists suggests e-portfolios are primarily used during the interview process, with some hiring managers using them to make initial screening decisions (Nodoye, Ritzhaupt, & Parker, 2012). Additionally, modifications to the traditional e-portfolio, like including a brief introductory video by the applicant, could increase the use of e-portfolios throughout the different phases of the hiring process, including pre-screening (Hartwick & Mason, 2014).

Although e-portfolios show promise as a job-related way to sort applicants, e-portfolios have not yet reached the maturity level required to be used as a pre-screening tool. Feedback from hiring managers indicates that applicant tracking systems (ATS) are not designed to accept them during the application process, they are burdensome to review because of the time required, and there is no standardization in the presentation and evaluation of their contents (Korn, 2014; Nodoye et al., 2012). Moreover, e-portfolios lend themselves well to fields that produce very tangible outputs; however, aside from art, education, music, computer science, and marketing, very few fields provide its students and professional members with enough artifacts that could be incorporated into an e-portfolio and shared with a recruiter. For these reasons e-portfolios in their current form may continue to operate at the fringes of internet-based recruitment in the near future. But already there are signs the idea behind e-portfolios is becoming more widespread, as professional networking websites such as LinkedIn now allow members to add a wide variety of multi-media (e.g., video, audio, images) and content (e.g., presentations, documents) to their profiles that demonstrate a skill or accomplishment (Chang, 2013; Morgan, 2017).

4.9 Video-Recorded Interviews

One of the most common applicant pre-screening tools is the interview (Barber, 1998). Traditionally, interviews occurred by telephone at the very beginning of the selection funnel to confirm eligibility and willingness to work under certain conditions (e.g., nights, shift work), and then again later in the selection funnel, often in-person, to evaluate applicant KSAOs. But advances in internet communication technology have pushed interviews above the selection funnel in the form of video-recorded interviews. In video-recorded interviews, applicants log onto a website and submit video responses to an employer's interview questions without ever talking to another person; the questions are presented to respondents as text, video, and even animated avatars. Results from surveys of organizations indicate that almost half (47 percent) are using video-recorded interviews for pre-screening (Korn Ferry, 2017), primarily because they are so cost-effective, efficient, standardized, and easily distributed to applicants across geographical boundaries (Aberdeen Group, 2014; Beagrie, 2015). Additionally, video-recorded interviews allow recruiters to obtain more applicant information earlier in the pre-screening process, which further narrows the applicant pool before initiating the manual, resource-intensive aspects of the pre-screening process (Harmsel, 2011).

Enabled by advances in internet technology and a growing trend to incorporate video into every step of the recruitment process (Cooke & Moulton, 2015; Grossman, 2015; Maurer, 2015), the adoption of video-recorded interviews has far outpaced efforts to examine them empirically (Blacksmith & Poeppelman, 2016; Torres & Mejia, 2017). The limited research that has been conducted creates a quandary for organizations. Video-recorded interviews appear to yield reliable and predictive ratings without discriminating against legally protected groups, yet applicants have negative reactions to them. Comparisons of video-recorded interviews and face-to-face interviews have found the two formats are similar in their reliability (Crenshaw, 2006), although video-recorded interviews do have lower mean ratings (Blacksmith, Willford, & Behrend, 2016). There is also some preliminary evidence that video-recorded interviews have predictive validities similar to other hiring assessments. For example, Gorman (2014) found that ratings of video-recorded interviews significantly predicted a wide variety of job-related outcomes (e.g., performance, promotions, absences, accidents, turnover) at levels equivalent to structured, behaviorally-based job interviews. Finally, a laboratory study by Kroll and Ziegler (2016) demonstrated that ratings of video-recorded interviews do not differ by gender or ethnic group membership.

The promising findings associated with video-recorded interviews must be tempered by the fact that applicants respond negatively to them. Of job seekers who have actually completed a video-recorded interview, 43 percent describe it as being more stressful than a face-to-face interview (Lighthouse, 2017). And relative to other technology-mediated interview formats (e.g., video-conference, interactive voice response), applicants have the most negative reactions to video-recorded interviews (Blacksmith et al., 2016). What is it about this type of interview that leads to such strong reactions? Part of the problem is that people feel video-recorded interviews are too impersonal – there is no two-way communication because they are talking to a computer, and the interaction can feel awkward and disorienting since there are no clues about how they are performing. People are also concerned this interview format prevents them from presenting themselves realistically (Guchait et al., 2014). Thus, negative reactions to video-recorded interviews appear to be driven by the additive effects of the interview experience and perceptions that the interview format restricts a person's ability to fully describe job-relevant information.

4.10 Cybervetting

Internet-based recruitment also includes a practice called cybervetting to pre-screen applicants. Cybervetting is the use of online search engines and publicly available social media websites such as Facebook, Twitter, or Instagram to obtain information about job applicants (Berkelaar & Buzzanell, 2014; Mikkelson, 2010). There are two main goals of cybervetting: (1) determine if there is disqualifying information (e.g., evidence of illegal drug use), and (2) verify information reported in job applications and supporting materials (Davison et al., 2012; Kluemper & Rosen, 2009; Peebles, 2012). If cybervetting leads to the discovery of disqualifying or discrepant information, applicants are removed from the hiring process; the assumption is that this information serves as a signal for the way applicants may behave on the job.

Surveys of employers and recruiters confirm that cybervetting continues to grow year-over-year, and the information obtained from these online activities is being considered when making pre-screening recruitment decisions (Society for Human Resource Management, 2016). In a recent survey of 2,186 organizations, 60 percent reported using social media to research job applicants and determine their qualifications, which for 49 percent of those companies led to the discovery of information that prevented applicants from being hired; the most common types of disqualifying information included inappropriate images (46 percent), drinking or using drugs (43 percent), discriminatory comments about protected groups (33 percent), and bad mouthing former employers and co-workers (31 percent) (CareerBuilder, 2016).

The widespread and growing use of cybervetting to evaluate job applicants has raised several concerns. First, the use of social media to inform staffing decisions could reveal information about an applicant's protected characteristics (e.g., ethnicity, gender, age, disability status, religious affiliation) and potentially lead to illegal employment discrimination (Brown & Vaughn, 2011; Davison et al., 2012; Equal Employment Opportunity Commission, 2014). Second, reviewing social media information may expose recruiters to job-irrelevant information that explicitly or implicitly impacts applicant screening decisions. Third, there is a lack of empirical studies to support the standardized, reliable, and valid use of social media to make any type of employment decision (Davison et al., 2016; Roth et al., 2016). Finally, there is very little information available about the effectiveness of social media in pre-screening decisions or best practice recommendations regarding its use (Acikgoz & Bergman, 2016; Berger & Zickar, 2016). These concerns have prompted tremendous growth in research investigating the use of social media during the recruitment and hiring process (e.g., Landers & Schmidt, 2016). However, almost all of this research has focused on the use of social media to assess applicant KSAOs (e.g., Kluemper, Rosen, & Mossholder, 2012; Van Iddekinge et al., 2013).

Very little is known about the use of cybervetting to evaluate an applicant's qualifications or suitability for a position during the pre-screening process. The available research suggests that if applicant social media profiles do contain negative information or evidence of questionable behavior (e.g., heavy alcohol use), applicants are perceived as less qualified and unlikely to be given opportunities to continue in the hiring process (Bohnert & Ross, 2010). Moreover, recruiters who use social media to screen applicants appear to value negative social media information more than those who do not use social media, and tend to focus their attention on negative information much more than positive information (Chang & Madera, 2012). But what about the most important question underlying the reason for cybervetting: Does negative social media content actually predict job performance? Presumably, social media contains indicators of the inappropriate, unsafe, illegal, or unethical behavior applicants may engage in as employees. Unfortunately, this assumption does not appear to be true, at least in terms of counterproductive work behaviors (CWB) such as theft, destruction of property, alcohol use, or unsafe behavior. Becton et al. (2017) found that people with inappropriate content (e.g., offensive language, drugs, alcohol) on their Facebook pages were no more likely to engage in CWBs or experience workplace accidents than those who did not post this content on Facebook. A study by Fama, a company that offers cybervetting services to organizations, also found no relationship between the presence of alcohol-related information on social media and job performance in a sample of 15,000 employees (O'Donnell, 2016). These findings confirm the need for additional research into the use and utility of cybervetting as a pre-screening tool.

4.11 Future Questions

Web 2.0 technologies have significantly expanded the number and variety of ways job applicants can share their qualifications with organizations and recruiters during the sorting phase. As a result, the pool of applicants has continued to expand year-over-year, but so too has the amount of information that must be processed to narrow the applicant pool and determine which applicant progresses to the next phase of the hiring process. One of the most exciting technological advances being leveraged by recruiters to address this issue is artificial intelligence (AI). Recruiters can now choose from a growing array of startup companies offering AI-solutions that sift through resumes and online profiles to identify the most qualified job applicants (Goyal, 2017). This technology has come a long way from the days of simple keyword matching (e.g., Chapman, 1999; Mohamed, Orife,

& Wibowo, 2002). These new tools capitalize on innovations in latent semantic analysis (LSA) and natural language processing (NLP) to extract meaning from the written language used by job seekers and organizations (e.g., Campion et al., 2016; Sadiq et al., 2016), and successfully match applicants to jobs even when different words are used to describe the same concept (Schmitt, Caillou, & Sebag, 2016). This is just the beginning – artificial intelligence is now also able to accurately interpret and score the contents of video resumes (e.g., Nguyen & Gatica-Perez, 2016), as well as the verbal and visual information available in video-recorded interviews (e.g., Alsever, 2017).

But the emergence of AI for sorting applicants is a relatively new trend and has created more questions than answers. While there is preliminary evidence that AI can match applicants to jobs as consistently as human recruiters (e.g., Faliagka et al., 2014), it is still unknown how applicants selected by AI-based systems fare through the remaining recruitment phases or whether they are more likely to be successful employees. Similarly, recruiters are hopeful AI may remove the human limitations and biases associated with the pre-screening process that can lead to employment discrimination for protected groups (e.g., Kuncel et al., 2013), but a number of high profile incidents have demonstrated that AI can unintentionally absorb and reproduce the same biases it is supposed to prevent (e.g., Buranyi, 2017; Miller, 2015). Time will tell whether these types of biases in AI-based recruiting tools can be prevented or mitigated (e.g., Caliskan, Bryson, & Narayanan, 2017; Veale & Binns, 2017). Finally, AI cannot fully eliminate the human element from the applicant sorting process. Job seekers are more aware of AI's role in pre-screening decisions, and preliminary surveys indicate they are not happy about it. The findings from a Pew Research Center study indicated a majority of respondents (67 percent) were worried about the use of hiring algorithms in employment contexts (Smith & Anderson, 2017). This worry was so great that 76 percent would not even apply for a job if an algorithm was used to make the hiring decision, primarily because of concerns that it cannot capture everything about an applicant (41 percent), seemed too impersonal (20 percent), may be susceptible to manipulation by applicants (4 percent), and could potentially be more biased (2 percent). The negative perceptions of this technology should raise alarms for organizations and staffing practitioners given the extensive evidence documenting the undesirable outcomes that can follow when applicants question the appropriateness and fairness of recruitment and personnel selection systems (e.g., Bauer et al., 2011; McCarthy et al., 2017).

Using Web 2.0 technology to automate sorting job applicants has also led to questions about how it can remove information from applicant materials that trigger unconscious decision-making biases (Lustman, 2017). Prompted by concerns about gender and racial inequities and the lack of diversity in the workplace (The Economist, 2015), new internet-based tools are being developed to pre-screen applicants that scrub any indication of an applicant's demographic characteristics (e.g., name, ethnicity, gender, age) (Sullivan, 2015). Applicant tracking systems can hide demographic information and force "blind" or anonymous pre-screening decisions based on merit (i.e., only considering an applicant's qualifications and eligibility) (Smith, 2015). A number of companies such as Blendoor and Talent Sonar now offer tools that remove biasing information from application materials before recruiters review it (Sepp, 2017). To date, this idea has been described as a viable alternative to current pre-screening practices (Grothaus, 2016; Miller, 2016), and companies like Deloitte, HSBC, and KPMG have modified their recruitment processes and human resource management (HRM) systems to implement it (Kottasova, 2015). But other than anecdotes about its effectiveness (e.g., Rice, 2013), little is known about how "blind" pre-screens actually work in practice (Aslund & Skans, 2012; Krause, Rinne, & Zimmermann, 2012). Do they reduce or eliminate adverse impact in recruitment and selection decisions? Are members of minority groups just as likely as majority group members to be contacted by recruiters when job application materials are anonymized? What effect do they have on the quality of the applicant pool and subsequent new hires? These are just a few of the questions that need to be addressed as "blind" pre-screening tools are adopted by organizations and embedded in their applicant tracking systems and career websites.

Finally, an intriguing and relatively unknown application of Web 2.0 technology in the sorting phase involves the verification of applicant qualifications. In many fields, workers acquire "hard" skills that are often reflected in their credentials and certifications, which are then used by recruiters and hiring managers to pre-sort qualified and unqualified candidates. As these workers move from job to job within organizations or seek employment in the "gig" economy, employers need some way to confirm their credentials and certifications are real before time and resources are invested to hire them. One way to do this is to create digital "badges" or credentials, given by an accredited group or organization, which workers can take with them wherever they go (Barabas & Schmidt, 2016; Catalano & Doucet, 2013; Hughes & Coates, 2014; Mozilla, 2013). When applying for jobs online, applicants can share relevant badges or direct recruiters to their professional social media profiles or personal landing pages where badges are also available. Consider a computer programmer who is applying for a job and claims to have programming skills in a certain computer language. Before digital credentials, an employer would only be able to assess the programmer's proficiency in this particular language after the sorting phase. Furthermore, the only evidence of the skills and related certifications in the programming language would be what the applicant reported in an online application, resume, or social media profile. A digital credential would eliminate this problem in every field that requires certification of these types of hard skills. Yet almost nothing is known about the use of digital credentials or their related ecosystems. Employers and licensing groups have been surveyed about their interest in and use of digital credentialing (e.g., Erickson, 2015), but there is no research examining job seeker preferences and reactions or the reliability and validity of the inferences associated with digital credentialing. Most importantly, it is not known how much variance there is in skill proficiency for credential badges. Aside from research to create the digital architecture to protect the integrity of digital badges (e.g., Barabas & Schmidt, 2016), a great deal of work remains to be done before they can be used to verify an applicant's credentials or enhance and potentially shorten the sorting phase of recruitment.

4.12 Nurturing Job Candidates

After applicants are contacted by an organization, recruiters begin the "nurturing" phase of the recruitment process. During this phase, recruiters attempt to maintain the interest of viable, high-quality candidates until a job offer is made or they are eliminated from consideration (Barber, 1998; Breaugh, 2008; Dineen & Soltis, 2011). This phase has traditionally been dominated by a transaction-based perspective (Girard & Fallery, 2011), which assumes the recruitment process ends when an application is submitted because the next steps are often dictated by organizations (Breaugh, 2008; Dineen & Soltis, 2011). However, with developments in internet-based recruitment, a more relationship-based perspective is dominating this phase that focuses on maintaining rapport with candidates and ensuring two-way communication occurs (Dineen & Allen, 2014). As a result, the nurturing phase becomes a continuation of the relationship established during earlier interactions, and it is this relationship that is nurtured until the final employment decision is made (Dineen & Allen, 2014). The success of this phase hinges on the ability of organizations and recruiters to create a positive "candidate experience." Candidates constantly monitor their interactions with organizations and interpret them as signals about what it is like to work there and how they may be treated as an employee. If the interaction seems unfair, either in terms of the procedures followed, information shared, or quality of interpersonal exchanges, candidates re-evaluate their fit perceptions and, depending on their personal situation and previous job search experience, may withdraw from the recruitment process (Dineen & Soltis, 2011).

Previous research indicates a successful candidate experience in the nurturing phase is primarily driven by two factors: organizational processes and recruiter interactions (Ryan & Delany, 2010; Rynes, Reeves, & Darnold, 2014). For organizational processes, candidates respond negatively to any administrative delays after submitting an application (e.g., Breaugh, 2013). Advances in internet technology have led to the development of new end-to-end applicant tracking systems that handle sourcing, advertising management, analytics, online interviewing, interview management, candidate scoring, ongoing candidate relationship management, and onboarding (Bersin, 2016). This technology automates many of the daily administrative tasks for recruiters (Min, 2017; Sullivan, 2017), such as sending status updates and information to candidates, a source of many negative recruitment experiences (e.g., Boswell et al., 2003). With these developments, it is anticipated that process factors will play a much smaller role in future candidate experiences.

Freed of administrative constraints, recruiters now spend more time on "high-touch" activities such as interacting with candidates at a personal level to cultivate a relationship that further enhances the candidate experience (Cappelli, 2001;

Chapman & Webster, 2003). With tools made possible by Web 2.0 technology, recruiters can establish more contact points with candidates and expand opportunities for relationship building through email, text messaging, and video-chat (Ryan & Delany, 2010). This increased contact is important, as research suggests candidate fit perceptions are not static during the recruitment process, but in fact are dynamic, and can change in response to interactions across recruitment phases (Ryan, 2012; Swider et al., 2015; Walker et al., 2013). This means recruiters have to be careful when interacting with candidates using these new tools, since initial fit perceptions from earlier recruitment phases can fluctuate positively or negatively in response to recruiter behavior. Recently, researchers have begun to explore the impact of these new communication technologies on the formation, management, and evolution of relationships formed during the nurturing phase. For example, Walker et al. (2015) demonstrated that if job applicants receive a personal email (i.e., contains detailed information presented in a sensitive manner) after submitting a job application, they perceive the process as being more informationally and interpersonally just. Other research has explored how candidates respond to recruiters later in the nurturing phase, when there is real-time interaction during online interviews conducted through video-conferencing or video-chat services (e.g., Skype, Google Hangout). Initial findings suggest it may be difficult for recruiters to build relationships during technology-mediated interviews because applicants perceive recruiters as less personable, trustworthy, and competent during an online interview than during an in-person interview (Blacksmith et al., 2016; Sears et al., 2013). These findings are problematic because previous research has linked recruiter personability, trustworthiness, and competence to positive candidate reactions to the recruitment process (e.g., Ryan & Delany, 2010). Thus, despite new internet technologies making it easier to maintain relationships with candidates, recruiters must still be aware of how the communication method influences candidate reactions, intentions, and job choice behavior.

Adding internet technology to the candidate nurturing process has also decentralized who communicates with job candidates (Dineen & Soltis, 2011). In the past, recruiters were often the sole contact for candidates. But organizations are now taking advantage of internet communication tools to connect job candidates with other organizational agents to obtain additional information, better evaluate organizational fit, and develop deeper relationships with the organization (Dineen & Allen, 2014). For example, Gnatta is a company that uses the collaboration tool Slack so its employees can talk about their work online in dedicated, text-based channels. When Gnatta identifies its top job candidates, it invites them to join one of their informal Slack channels and talk with employees (Gale, 2017b). Similarly, companies are allowing candidates to email and chat with other organizational representatives (Chaykowski, 2017). Diffusing the relationship-building process beyond the recruiter increases the chances that candidates will feel more connected to the organization and have a better candidate experience.

4.13 Future Questions

A significant change to the nurturing phase is the automation of many recruiter tasks and responsibilities (Min, 2017). Automation has increased so quickly in these areas that it is now being applied to direct interactions with applicants and candidates – interactions that were, until now, primarily the domain of "high-touch" recruiter activities expected by job seekers. For example, artificially intelligent robots ("bots" or "chatbots") are being used as assistants to screen resumes and online professional profiles, contact viable job seekers, respond to frequently asked questions, provide hiring status updates, and conduct preliminary screening interviews (e.g., Brin, 2016; Efron, 2016; Sullivan, 2016). Robots are even making their way into the later stages of recruitment during the nurturing phase, conducting interviews with job candidates (e.g., Apostolides, 2016; Tarling, 2016). But at what point and for how long should robots be the main contact? Where is the balancing point between automation and human interaction to maintain positive and productive relationships with job candidates during the nurturing phase? Conventional wisdom would argue that more frequent and continuous "human" contact is preferred by job candidates during this phase (e.g., Dineen, Noe, & Wang, 2004), but this may not be the case. A recent survey of job seekers indicated that approximately 59 percent were fairly comfortable or extremely comfortable engaging with a chatbot for a preliminary job interview, and 66 percent were open to working with a chatbot to schedule or prepare for job interviews (Cheesman, 2017; Fisher, 2017). Clearly, much more research is needed to understand the proper balance of automation and human interaction that creates positive reactions among candidates and preserves their intention to continue through the hiring process to ultimately accept a job offer. More importantly, work in this area would identify the impact of automation on the ability of recruiters to establish, develop, and maintain relationships with job candidates.

The main benefit of internet technology during the nurturing phase is that job candidates and recruiters can engage in two-way, interactive communication through a variety of messaging tools such as real-time video, email, text, or chat (e.g., Dineen & Allen, 2014; Gale, 2017b; Hess, 2015). While these tools have made it easier for recruiters to stay in touch with their most promising candidates and share timely information and updates, they may also inadvertently undermine candidate perceptions of the organization. Compared to more traditional means of communicating between recruiters and candidates, internet-based messaging tools often involve conversations that are more informal and deviate from common grammatical rules and expectations. What impact do these new communication mediums and their related communication protocols have on the perceptions of recruiters and candidates and the relationships that form between them? Do these communication tools change how recruiters respond to candidates or the way candidates perceive the organization (e.g., Fullwood et al., 2015; Tskhay & Rule, 2014)? These are important questions whose answers could shed light on the effects of using messaging tools to foster and maintain relationships with job candidates.

4.14 Closing Job Candidates

After job candidates have been sourced, attracted, sorted, and nurtured, a job offer is made and the recruiting organization must "close" the candidate by obtaining acceptance of the job offer (Cappelli, 2001; Dineen & Soltis, 2011). This is perhaps the most critical and delicate step of the recruitment process as it represents the payoff for the time and resources invested to get the desired candidate to join the organization. However, at this stage organizations typically engage in more "high-touch contact than high-tech contact" with a late stage candidate who has been offered a job (Ryan & Delany, 2010). Researchers have also suggested that the internet not be used at all during this high-touch phase, but instead recruiters should connect with candidates at a personal level to sell them on the opportunity (Cappelli, 2001). Thus, fewer internet-based tools are specifically built to address or facilitate this recruitment phase.

Once a job offer is made, a number of factors influence a candidate's job choice, including pay and promotion opportunities, timeliness of the offer, inducements with accepting the offer (e.g., signing bonuses or other perks), influences of family and friends, and work-life balance (Ryan & Delany, 2010). In addition, job candidates are influenced by recruiter behaviors such as friendliness. These behaviors are seen as signals of organizational attractiveness, which predict acceptance intentions and job choice behaviors, especially for high-value candidates who have received multiple offers (Chapman & Webster, 2006). Moreover, as Swider et al. (2015) observed, the influence of perceived P-O fit with an organization has an increasingly strong, positive relationship with job choice behaviors as the recruitment process enters the later stages. Thus, internet tools that can directly or indirectly influence or facilitate these decision-making factors in the minds of candidates could help "close" desired candidates for open positions. For instance, research has shown that candidates are more likely to accept earlier job offers (Becker, Connolly, & Slaughter, 2010). Internet-based systems, such as Smashfly, which provide data visualizations and feedback on how long candidates have been in the recruitment process can assist recruiters with making timely job offers. This could have a positive impact on recruitment metrics such as the time to fill an open position and selection ratios, although there is some research that suggests there are no performance differences between candidates who accepted early job offers versus those who accepted late job offers (e.g., Becker et al., 2010).

In addition, organizations who utilize technological collaboration and remote working tools could influence candidates' perceived work-life balance. Some organizations, such as Cisco, are already considering how internet-based tools that help employees work from anywhere are helping recruit and retain internal talent (Larsen, 2017). However, technology-related policies that contribute to an "always on" work culture might negatively influence perceived work-life balance, thereby affecting job choice behaviors. This is an important question for future studies.

4.15 Future Questions

In the final stages of the recruitment process, the desired candidate and the organization will often negotiate terms before signing an employment agreement. These final negotiations and discussions are often conducted through multiple high-level meetings, site visits, and frequent follow-up conversations between the recruiter or hiring manager and the candidate (Boswell et al., 2003). Although these interactions are not often mediated by sophisticated technological tools, little is known about how these tools could influence outcomes in this final recruitment phase. For instance, research has shown that a candidate's perception of fairness about the recruitment process accounts for 19–30 percent of the variance in job offer acceptance decisions (Harold et al., 2016). What is less known is whether internet-based communication tools (e.g., video calling, text, chat) or HRM platforms designed to streamline the onboarding process (e.g., Gusto, Namely, Zenefits, BambooHR) affect this fairness perception. As these internet-based communication systems become more robust, and systems designed to facilitate the recruitment process become more intuitive and responsive, candidate fairness expectations are sure to change in ways that are hard to predict today.

These internet communication systems also have the potential for influencing the negotiation process used to close a job candidate. Wiltermuth and Neale (2011) examined how possessing non-diagnostic information (i.e., information about the other party that is irrelevant in making a decision during a negotiation) can lead to inferior negotiation outcomes. Wiltermuth and Neale discovered that when two parties interacted via electronic communication and possessed non-diagnostic information, the negotiation was more likely to come to an impasse. In the Web 2.0 era, internet-based applications and websites can provide volumes of information about the candidate and the organization in the form of social media content, online reviews, and access to backchannel references via social networks. Thus, the chances of non-diagnostic information entering the job offer negotiation phase are high. However, we are unaware of research specifically examining how internet-based systems and tools used in earlier phases of the recruitment process to source, attract, sort, or nurture candidates could inadvertently add irrelevant information that derails the offer closure phase. This is an opportunity for future research.

4.16 Future Directions

As we surveyed the recruitment literature, we identified several recently published, high-quality literature reviews (e.g., Dineen & Allen, 2014; Dineen & Soltis, 2011; Ployhart et al., 2017) and considered how we might contribute to them. We concluded that technology is changing too rapidly to wait several more years for a "meaningful" amount of new research to be published; instead, we not only wanted to summarize the studies that had been published since the most recent reviews, we also wanted to provide a snapshot of the current internet-based recruitment marketplace. This market is growing and evolving rapidly – both researchers and practitioners must be constantly aware of these changes to make sure their efforts are as effective as possible. In our review of how Web 2.0 internet-based systems, platforms, and tools are impacting the primary phases of personnel recruitment in organizations, we highlighted a number of very specific questions that require the attention of researchers and practitioners in the future. Here we present several future directions related to internet-based recruitment at a much broader level. We focus on larger questions about the impact of this technology in four areas: (1) the rapidly growing contingent workforce, (2) development of psychological contracts among job applicants and candidates, (3) reconceptualization of the recruitment process, and (4) the adoption of technology in recruitment.

4.17 The Contingent Workforce

While it is hard to predict how human work will drive market values in the future, what seems certain, and has been the case for centuries, is that technology will continue to change how work is performed (Forman, King, & Lyytinen, 2014). Beyond the direct influence on how individuals are recruited for open positions, we see technology also impacting the types of positions that will exist and the quality, quantity, and interests of future human talent pools. Although the topic of technological changes to modern work has been discussed for almost two decades (National Academy of Sciences, 1999), we see technological changes to work crystallizing more recently around two key trends: the distribution of work (i.e., remote work) and the democratization of work (i.e., freelance and "gig" work). These trends have profound near-term implications for how future workers will be recruited. For instance, both the distribution and democratization of work using internet systems have created contingent or temporary workers who are hired to perform small data processing or categorization tasks labeled microwork or crowd-sourcing. These internet systems include microwork marketplaces such as Amazon's Mechanical Turk (MTurk) and CrowdFlower (Irani, 2015). Brawley and Pury (2016) examined how the behaviors of a MTurk "Requester," an individual who posts tasks and employs crowdsourcing workers, affect worker satisfaction. They discovered that Requester behaviors that build relationships and provide encouraging feedback were highly associated with strong worker satisfaction, whereas unfair pay and inaccurate time estimates for tasks were associated with low worker satisfaction. These findings demonstrate that microwork may be an extreme version of project-based, short-term contract work common among contingent workers, but that it still functions according to familiar I-O psychology principles such as motivation and leader-subordinate support. Therefore, familiar tactics for recruiting "traditional" workers (e.g., providing relevant, high-fidelity job information; promoting the intrinsically motivating and interesting elements of the work; building relationships with applicants) may also be effective for recruiting individuals for microwork.

However, there are key differences between microwork, contingent work, and traditional work. For instance, traditional work is set within the context of a job that operates within a greater organization that has an organizational identity and brand message. Therefore, the work tasks and job title are "sold" to job seekers along with the organizational brand message. For contingent workers, job tasks are disconnected from an organizational identity, thus changing or nullifying the typical employment brand message inherent to the recruitment process. For example, Uber must continuously recruit high-quality independent contractor drivers who will promote and represent the brand to customers, without formally admitting drivers as members of the organization. Thus, Uber's recruitment marketing messages focus on the intrinsic motivations associated with the type of work or employment relationship (e.g., having autonomy over one's schedule) rather than the organization itself. In a study of temporary and self-employed workers, Felfe et al. (2008) discovered that "commitment to the form of employment" (p. 81), rather than to the organization, explained variance in work-related outcomes, such as job satisfaction and organizational citizenship behavior, above organizational commitment. Although this study did not look at recruitment outcomes, we suggest that organizations that successfully tap into the "commitment to the form of employment" among the growing contingent workforce will also be successful in recruiting the best talent from this population.

4.18 Psychological Contracts

As organizations increasingly use digital job marketplaces to recruit traditional employees and contingent workers, questions arise about how this technology-mediated recruitment process may change the formation of psychological contracts among new hires (e.g., Ryan, 2012). Related to social exchange theory (e.g., Blau, 1964), the psychological contract is the cognitive schema formed by an employee who enters into a working relationship with an organization (Rousseau, 1989). This schema is made up of the obligations each party owes the other. In the employee's case, what work should be performed, when, and for how long; in the organization's case, what type of pay and other rewards are owed for the employee's time and effort. This schema becomes the filter for how employer actions or non-actions are interpreted by the employee. The psychological contract usually takes one of two forms: relational (e.g., relationship-oriented, intangible, long-lasting) and transactional (e.g., economic, materialistic, specific, short-term) (Hansen & Griep, 2017).

Applying psychological contract theory to a work setting involving independent contractors, Lemmon et al. (2016) examined how certain negotiation behaviors formed different psychological contracts, which influenced the contractors' perceived resources required to fulfill the psychological contract. Lemmon et al. hypothesized that forcing negotiation terms on the independent contractor created transitional or transactional psychological contracts, which signaled that limited resources (e.g., goods, status, love) were obligated to the contractor. Fewer perceived resources led to decrements in contractor performance and perceived justice. However, in this study, love (i.e., perceptions of friendship and togetherness) was the only perceived resource that was significantly related to a contractor's performance and justice perceptions. A notable implication from this study is that although contingent or contract workers may be hired for a discrete task or job, treating the relationship with these workers as purely transactional can create unproductive psychological contracts and, in turn, lower performance and trust. Therefore, recruitment messages focused on creating these supportive relationships, as evidenced by positive negotiation behaviors, will potentially be more effective at engaging and leveraging a workforce that is quickly becoming more independent. While this study provides an important early examination of how psychological contract theory informs the relationships and outcomes between new worker categories and organizations, Lemmon et al.'s model received mixed support. We posit that this is an example of how traditional psychological contract theory may function differently in future work contexts. This study also highlights concerns about whether the same rules of the psychological contract apply to the attraction and engagement of contingent workers, especially when the organization may need to convert them to full-time employees. Finally, Lemmon et al.'s study poses new questions focused on the effectiveness of the recruitment function: Should the same recruitment metrics be applied to contingent workers? If not, what other metrics are more suitable for measuring staffing success? We see this as an important topic for future research.

4.19 Reconceptualization of the Recruitment Process

Our review of internet-based recruitment was organized around the five main phases of recruitment: sourcing, attracting, sorting, nurturing, and closing. Similar to the observations of others (Dineen & Allen, 2014; Holm, 2014; Ployhart et al., 2017), however, we noticed this traditional, linear description of the recruitment process, one that involves very specific and discrete phases, stages, or steps, may no longer be accurate or applicable. We consistently found that the lines between phases were not just blurred but were in most cases completely non-existent. This revealed a "process" more akin to a dynamic, inter-connected network, with multiple nodes that are triggered individually or all at once in response to applicants or candidates. For example, the current emphasis on "social recruiting" cuts across every recruitment phase except closing and works within each phase at the same time: organizations create brand awareness on social media websites (sourcing), manipulate the presentation and sharing of information on these sites to promote applicant interest (attracting), scrape applicant social media data and use algorithms to evaluate their qualifications and skills (sorting), and establish relationships with passive job seekers on social media who have not formally entered the recruitment or hiring process (nurturing). The blurring of the lines within and around the recruitment process is also affecting the distinction between recruitment and selection (e.g., Cable & Yu, 2014). For this handbook, staffing topics are treated separately, but repeatedly we encountered instances of technology-enabled assessments that were pushed above the selection funnel and incorporated into the recruitment process (e.g., interviews, non-cognitive/cognitive measures, skill assessments). The best example of this change is the use of online games for recruitment and selection. Primarily developed as assessment tools to evaluate job-related characteristics, online games have quickly been co-opted by recruiters as a means of attracting and sorting applicants, while also nurturing budding relationships with future job candidates. Where recruitment ends and selection begins became increasingly unclear to us.

Finally, it seems the strategic focus of the recruitment process continues to evolve because of the internet. Dineen and Allen (2014) originally described this change as moving from a "push" to a "pull" approach, which acknowledged that job seekers no longer had to wait for recruitment information to be pushed out to them by organizations, but could now actively pull the information they desired from a variety of online sources. Although we found the pull approach still dominates internet-based recruitment, we also discovered an emerging approach that allows organizations to "point" recruitment efforts at very specific applicants in targeted ways. The proliferation of so much online applicant information (e.g., professional profiles, professional communities of interest, blogs, personal landing pages) has fostered the development of internet technologies that companies can use to automatically mine these data, find people that match position requirements, and approach them directly about open positions. Under this "point" approach we see organizations redefining themselves as more active participants in the recruitment process, which is a significant change from their passive role in the "push" and "pull" paradigms.

4.20 Technology Adoption in Recruitment

In the coming years, innovative and cutting-edge internet-based technologies will continue their disruption of the recruitment space. Already, every phase of recruitment has been touched and enhanced by internet technology in some way. The apparent success of these technologies in terms of efficiency, cost savings, applicant quality, and candidate experience, would suggest that recruitment technology is completely risk free; that the incorporation of technology certainly means good recruitment outcomes for both job seekers and organizations. But sometimes internet-based recruitment works (e.g., applicant tracking systems), other times it fails (e.g., recruiting in virtual worlds), and many times, with the lag between adoption and empirical evaluation, there is not enough information available yet to judge its effectiveness or appropriateness (e.g., cybervetting). For instance, consider the results of a study by Badger, Kaminsky and Behrend (2014). This study illustrates the potential dangers of adopting recruitment technology too quickly without sufficient research into its efficacy, but probably more importantly, the contextual factors driving when it is appropriate to adopt technology (e.g., Dineen & Allen, 2014). Noting the trend among organizations to share recruitment information with job applicants online through increasingly diverse and interactive multi-media (e.g., video, animation, virtual environments), Badger et al. asked a simple question: Do these types of interactive media lead to greater acquisition and retention of organizational information? This is an important question because the information included in recruitment materials is what influences applicant interest in and attraction to organizations. Surprisingly, the answer is no. People who learned about an organization in a virtual environment remembered less about the organization than those who read the same information as text on a website. Apparently, participants devoted their cognitive resources to navigating the virtual environment instead of focusing on the information available in the environment. For organizations that have already invested resources to embed this kind of media in their internet recruiting efforts, they may actually be hurting their ability to attract top talent. This is but one example of the potential consequences that can result from implementing recruitment technology without first considering or evaluating its potential impact. So, while the use of internet-based technology has undoubtedly revolutionized the recruitment function, and in many ways redefined what recruitment means and how it is conducted, it is important to continue to empirically evaluate its effectiveness, utility, and fairness. We recognize this is not a new insight (e.g., Dineen & Allen, 2014; Ployhart et al., 2017), but it is important enough that it bears repeating.

4.21 Conclusion

In May of 2017, Walt Mossberg retired his popular technology column, "Personal Technology," which was first published in 1991 as a review of the earliest personal computers. Reflecting back on his career and the historical arc of information technology and the internet, Mossberg (2017) predicts that the computer will continue to "disappear" by fully computerizing and connecting every aspect of our daily lives without much thought by the user. As we close this review of internet-based recruitment practices, we also see certain parallels with how the internet is creating "always on" recruitment practices that continuously generate and gather data during the recruitment process. As computing technology enters the third decade of the twenty-first century, perhaps adding the "internet-based" distinction to recruitment as a field will either be redundant or superfluous. In this hyperconnected future, researchers may return to well-established psychological theories and principles exposited by the literature, but may also face new challenges and opportunities as the passive data collection of our internet-connected lives becomes fertile ground for sourcing, attracting, sorting, nurturing, and closing the workers of the future.

References

Aberdeen Group (2014, November). Can you see me now? What video talent acquisition can do for you [White paper]. Retrieved from https://engage.montagetalent.com/aberdeen-research-white-paper.

Acemoglu, D. & Autor, D. H. (2011). Skills, tasks, and technologies: Implications for employment and earnings. In O. Ashenfelter & D. E. Card (Eds.), *Handbook of labor economics* (vol. 4, pp. 1043–1171). Amsterdam: Elsevier.

Acikgoz, Y. & Bergman, S. M. (2016). Social media and employee recruitment: Chasing the run away bandwagon. In R. N. Landers & G. B. Schmidt (Eds.), *Social media in selection and recruitment* (pp. 175–195). Switzerland: Springer International Publishing.

Aguinis, H. & Lawal, S. O. (2013). eLancing: A review and research agenda for bridging the science-practice gap. *Human Resource Management Review, 23*, 6–17.

Alsever, J. (May 19, 2017). How AI is changing your job hunt. Retrieved from http://fortune.com/2017/05/19/ai-changing-jobs-hiring-recruiting/

Apers, C. & Derous, E. (2017). Are they accurate? Recruiters' personality judgments in paper versus video resumes. *Computers in Human Behavior, 73*, 9–19.

Apostolides, Z. (December 14, 2016). Soon robots could be taking your job interview: Can artificial intelligence solve the problem of unconscious bias in job interviews? Retrieved from www.theguardian.com/careers/2016/dec/14/soon-robots-could-be-taking-your-job-interview.

Ashuri, T. & Bar-Ilan, Y. (2017). Collective action recruitment in a digital age: Applying signaling theory to filtering behaviors. *Communication Theory, 27*, 70–91.

Aslund, O. & Skans, O. N. (2012). Do anonymous job application procedures level the playing field? *Industrial and Labor Relations Review, 65*(1), 82–107.

Badger, J. M., Kaminsky, S. E., & Behrend, T. S. (2014). Media richness and information acquisition in internet recruitment. *Journal of Managerial Psychology, 29*(7), 866–883.

Baldas, T. (June 4, 2007). Employers told to stay away from video resumes: The latest job-searching trend sparks concern over discrimination suits. Retrieved from www.law.com/nationallawjournal/almID/900005482683/employers-told-to-stay-away-from-video-resumes/.

Barabas, C. & Schmidt, P. (August, 2016). Transforming chaos into clarity: The promises and challenges of digital credentialing [White paper]. Retrieved from http://rooseveltinstitute.org/wp-content/uploads/2016/08/The-Promises-and-Challenges-of-Digital-Credentialing.pdf

Barber, A. E. (1998). *Recruiting employees: Individual and organizational perspectives.* Thousand Oaks, CA: Sage Publications.

Battelle, J. & O'Reilly, T. (October 5, 2004). Opening welcome: The state of the internet industry. Session presented at the Web 2.0 Conference, San Francisco, CA.

Bauer, T. N., Truxillo, D. M., Mack, K., & Costa, A. B. (2011). Applicant reactions to technology-based selection: What we know so far. In N. T. Tippins & S. Adler (Eds.), *Technology-enhanced assessment of talent* (pp. 190–223). San Francisco, CA: Jossey-Bass.

Beagrie, S. (January 28, 2015). Video interviewing: The future of recruitment? Retrieved from www.hrmagazine.co.uk/article-details/video-interviewing-the-future-of-recruitment.

Becker, W. J., Connolly, T., & Slaughter, J. E. (2010). The effect of job offer timing on offer acceptance, performance, and turnover. *Personnel Psychology, 63*, 223–241.

Becton, J. B., Walker, H. J., Schwager, P., & Gilstrap, J. B. (April 20, 2017). Is what you see what you get? Investigating the relationship between social media content and counterproductive work behaviors, alcohol consumption, and episodic heavy drinking. *The International Journal of Human Resource Management*, 1–22.

Berger, J. L. & Zickar, M. J. (2016). Theoretical propositions about cybervetting: A common antecedents model. In R. N. Landers & G. B. Schmidt (Eds.), *Social media in employee selection and recruitment: Theory, practice, and current challenges* (pp. 43–57). Switzerland: Springer International Publishing.

Berkelaar, B. L. & Buzzanell, P. M. (2014). Cybervetting, person-environment fit, and personnel selection: Employers' surveillance and sensemaking of job applicants' online information. *Journal of Applied Communication Research*, 42(4), 456–476.

Bersin, J. (October, 2016). HR technology disruptions for 2017: Nine trends reinventing the HR software market. Retrieved from www2.deloitte.com/content/dam/Deloitte/us/Documents/human-capital/us-hc-disruptions.pdf.

Blacksmith, N. & Poeppelman, T. (October, 2014). Video-based technology: The next generation of recruitment and hiring. *The Industrial-Organizational Psychologist*, 52(2), 84–88.

Blacksmith, N., Willford, J. C., & Behrend, T. S. (2016). Technology in the employment interview: A meta-analysis and future research agenda. *Personnel Assessment and Decisions*, 2(1), 12–20.

Blau, P. M. (1964). *Exchange and power in social life*. New York, NY: Wiley.

Boatman, J. & Erker, S. (2012). DDI global selection forecast 2012. Retrieved from www.ddiworld.com/ddi/media/trend-research/globalselectionforecast2012_tr_ddi.pdf

Bock, L. (2015). *Work rules!: Insights from inside Google that will transform how you live and lead*. New York, NY: Twelve.

Bohnert, D. & Ross, W. H. (2010). The influence of social networking web sites on the evaluation of job candidates. *Cyberpsychology, Behavior, and Social Networking*, 13(3), 341–347.

Boswell, W. R., Roehling, M. V., LePine, M. A., & Moynihan, L. M. (2003). Individual job-choice decisions and the impact of job attributes and recruitment practices: A longitudinal field study. *Human Resource Management*, 42(1), 23–37.

Brawley, A. M. & Pury, C. L. S. (2016). Work experiences on MTurk: Job satisfaction, turnover, and information sharing. *Computers in Human Behavior*, 54, 531–546.

Bryant, L. H. & Chittum, J. R. (2013). ePortfolio effectiveness: A(n ill-fated) search for empirical support. *International Journal of ePortfolio*, 3(2), 189–198.

Breaugh, J. A. (2008). Employee recruitment: Current knowledge and important areas for future research. *Human Resource Management Review*, 18, 103–118.

Breaugh, J. A. (2013). Employee recruitment. *Annual Review of Psychology*, 64, 389–416.

Brin, D. (December 16, 2016). Recruiting bots are here to stay: More companies use 'bots' to aid the hiring process. Retrieved from www.shrm.org/resourcesandtools/hr-topics/technology/pages/recruiting-bots-are-here-to-stay.aspx.

Brown, V. R. & Vaughn, E. D. (2011). The writing on the (Facebook) wall: The use of social networking sites in hiring decisions. *Journal of Business Psychology*, 26, 219–225.

Buranyi, S. (August 8, 2017). Rise of the racist robots–how AI is learning all our worst impulses. Retrieved from www.theguardian.com/inequality/2017/aug/08/rise-of-the-racist-robots-how-ai-is-learning-all-our-worst-impulses.

BusinessWire (March 27, 2007). 89% of employers open to viewing video resumes, says Vault: Vault releases first-ever video resume survey. Retrieved from www.busi

nesswire.com/news/home/20070327005962/en/89-Employers-Open-Viewing-Video-Resumes-Vault.

Cable, D. M. & Yu, K. Y. (2014). Rethinking recruitment: A look into the future. In D. M. Cable & K. Y. Yu (Eds.), *The Oxford handbook of recruitment* (pp. 527–531). New York, NY: Oxford University Press.

Caliskan, A., Bryson, J. J., & Narayanan, A. (2017). Semantics derived automatically from language corpora contain human-like biases. *Science, 356*(6334), 183–186.

Campion, M. C., Campion, M. A., Campion, E. D., & Reider, M. H. (2016). Initial investigation into computer scoring of candidate essays for personnel selection. *Journal of Applied Psychology, 101*(7), 958–975.

Cappelli, P. (2001). Making the most of on-line recruiting. *Harvard Business Review, 79*(3), 139–146.

CareerBuilder (April 28, 2016). Number of employers using social media to screen candidates has increased 500 percent over the last decade [Press release]. Retrieved from www.careerbuilder.com/share/aboutus/pressreleasesdetail.aspx?ed=12%2F31%2F2016&id=pr945-4%2F28%2F2016.

Case, S. (2016). *The third wave: An entrepreneur's vision of the future*. New York, NY: Simon & Schuster.

Catalano, F. & Doucet, K. J. (August 2013). Digital badges emerge as part of credentialing's future [White paper]. Retrieved from http://finepointwriting.com/wp-content/uploads/2013/07/White-Paper-Freelance-Writer-Sample.pdf.

Chang, A. (May 1, 2013). LinkedIn now lets you add a visual portfolio to your profile. *Wired*. Retrieved from www.wired.com/2013/05/linkedin-professional-portfolio/.

Chang, W. & Madera, J. M. (2012). Using social network sites for selection purposes: An investigation of hospitality recruiters. *Journal of Human Resources in Hospitality & Tourism, 11*, 183–196.

Chapman, D. S. (1999). Expanding the search for talent: Adopting technology-based strategies for campus recruiting and selection. *Journal of Cooperative Education, 34*(2), 35–41.

Chapman, D. S., Uggerslev, K. L., Carroll, S. A., Piasentin, K. A., & Jones, D. A. (2005). Applicant attraction to organizations and job choice: A meta-analytic review of the correlates of recruiting outcomes. *Journal of Applied Psychology, 90*(5), 928–944.

Chapman, D. S. & Webster, J. (2003). The use of technologies in the recruiting, screening, and selection processes for job candidates. *International Journal of Selection and Assessment, 11*(2), 113–120.

Chapman, D. S. & Webster, J. (2006). Toward an integrated model of applicant reactions and job choice. *International Journal of Human Resource Management, 17*(6), 1032–1057.

Chaykowski, K. (March 14, 2017). This new app lets job seekers secretly chat with employees. *Forbes*. Retrieved from www.forbes.com/sites/kathleenchaykowski/2017/03/14/this-new-app-lets-job-seekers-secretly-chat-with-employees/#3aed2b0f709d.

Cheesman, J. (May 5, 2017). Survey says job seekers are mostly ok engaging with chatbots. Retrieved from www.eremedia.com/ere/survey-job-seeker-chatbots/.

Chiang, J. K. & Suan, H. (2015). Self-presentation and hiring recommendations in online communities: Lessons from LinkedIn. *Computers in Human Behavior, 48*, 516–524.

Coker, D. (August 31, 2016). Say yes to ePortfolio and bid adieu to traditional CVs. Retrieved from www.thehrdigest.com/say-yes-eportfolio-bid-adieu-traditional-cvs/.

Cooke, S. & Moulton, D. (January 1, 2015). The next generation of video technology in talent acquisition. Retrieved from www.bersin.com/Practice/Detail.aspx?id=18217.

Crenshaw, J. L. (2006). *The use of video and audio technology in structured interviews: Effects of psychometric properties, group differences, and candidate perceptions* [Doctoral dissertation]. Retrieved from www.worldcat.org/title/use-of-video-and-audio-technology-in-structured-interviews-effects-on-psychometric-properties-group-differences-and-candidate-perceptions/oclc/615598214?referer=di&ht=edition.

Dahling, J. J., Winik, L., Schoepfer, R., & Chau, S. (2013). Evaluating contingent workers as a recruitment source for full-time positions. *International Journal of Selection and Assessment, 21*(2), 222–225.

Davison, H. K., Maraist, C. C., Hamilton, R. H., & Bing, M. N. (2012). To screen or not to screen? Using the internet for selection decisions. *Employee Rights and Responsibilities Journal, 24*, 1–21.

Davison, H. K., Bing, M. N., Kluemper, D. H., & Roth, P. L. (2016). Social media as a personnel selection and hiring resource: Reservations and recommendations. In R. N. Landers & G. B. Schmidt (Eds.), *Social media in employee selection and recruitment: Theory, practice, and current challenges* (pp. 15–42). Switzerland: Springer International Publishing.

Deci, E. L. & Ryan, R. M. (2000). The "what" and "why" of goal pursuits: Human needs and the self-determination of behavior. *Psychological Inquiry, 11*(4), 227–268.

Derous, E., Taveirne, A., & Hiemstra, A. (April 2012). Resume, resume on the video wall: Who's most hireable of all? Poster presented at the 27th annual conference of the Society for Industrial and Organizational Psychology, San Diego, CA.

DiMaggio, P. J. & Powell, W. W. (1983). The iron cage revisited: Institutional isomorphism and collective rationality in organizational fields. *American Sociological Review, 48*, 147–160.

Dineen, B. R. & Allen, D. G. (2014). Internet recruiting 2.0: Shifting paradigms. In D. M. Cable & K. Y. Yu (Eds.), *The Oxford handbook of recruitment* (pp. 382–401). New York, NY: Oxford University Press.

Dineen, B. R. & Noe, R. A. (2009). Effects of customization on application decisions and applicant pool characteristics in a web-based recruitment context. *Journal of Applied Psychology, 94*(1), 224–234.

Dineen, B. R., Noe, R. A., & Wang, C. (2004). Perceived fairness of web-based applicant screening procedures: Weighing the rules of justice and the role of individual differences. *Human Resource Management, 43*, 127–145.

Dineen, B. R. & Soltis, S. M. (2011). Recruitment: A review of research and emerging directions. In S. Zedeck (Ed.), *APA handbook of industrial and organizational psychology, Volume 2: Selecting and developing members for the organization* (pp. 43–66). Washington, DC: American Psychological Association.

Doherty, R. (2010). Getting social with recruitment. *Strategic HR Review, 9*(6), 11–15.

Earnest, D. R., Allen, D. G., & Landis, R. S. (2011). Mechanisms linking realistic job previews with turnover: A meta-analytic path analysis. *Personnel Psychology, 64*, 865–897.

The Economist (October 29, 2015). No names, no bias? Anonymizing job applications to eliminate discrimination is not easy. Retrieved from www.economist.com/news/business/21677214-anonymising-job-applications-eliminate-discrimination-not-easy-no-names-no-bias.

Efron, L. (2016, July 12). How A.I. is about to disrupt corporate recruiting. *Forbes*. Retrieved from www.forbes.com/sites/louisefron/2016/07/12/how-a-i-is-about-to-disrupt-corporate-recruiting/#529cf8843ba2.

ePortfoliohub (2016). Using ePortfolios for recruitment: Employer's perspectives. Retrieved from http://eportfoliohub.ie/wp-content/uploads/2016/09/Survey-Employer-Report.pdf.

Equal Employment Opportunity Commission (March 12, 2014). Social media is part of today's workplace but its use may raise employment discrimination concerns [Press release]. Retrieved from www.eeoc.gov/eeoc/newsroom/release/3–12-14.cfm.

Erickson, C. C. (2015). Digital credentialing: A qualitative exploratory investigation of hiring director's perceptions [Doctoral dissertation]. Retrieved from http://search.proquest.com/openview/d4dadbab5419874078e87b18e573a9b3/1?pq-origsite=gscholar&cbl=18750&diss=y.

Eveleth, D. M., Baker-Eveleth, L. J., & Stone, R. W. (2015). Potential applicants' expectation-confirmation and intentions. *Computers in Human Behavior*, *44*, 183–190.

Faliagka, E., Iliadis, L., Karydis, I., Rigou, M., Sioutas, S., Tsakalidis, A., & Tzimas, G. (2014). On-line consistent ranking on e-recruitment: Seeking the truth behind a well-formed CV. *Artificial Intelligence Review*, *42*, 515–528.

Fan, L. & Suh, Y. (2014). Why do users switch to a disruptive technology? An empirical study based on expectation-disconfirmation theory. *Information Management*, *51*(2), 240–248.

Felfe, J., Schmook, R., Schyns, B., & Six, B. (2008). Does the form of employment make a difference? Commitment of traditional, temporary, and self-employed workers. *Journal of Vocational Behavior*, *72*(1), 81–94.

Fisher, C. (May 1, 2017). Ready for the robots: Survey says job candidates are mostly okay with AI Apps in the application process. Retrieved from www.allegisglobalsolutions.com/blog/2017/may/ready-for-robots.

Flanigan, E. J. (2012). ePortfolios and technology: Customized for careers. *International Journal of Information and Communication Technology Education*, *8*(4), 29–37.

Forman, C., King, J. L., & Lyytinen, K. (2014). Information, technology, and the changing nature of work. *Information Systems Research*, *25*(4), 789–795.

Fullwood, C., Quinn, S., Chen-Wilson, J., Chadwick, D., & Reynolds, K. (2015). Put on a smiley face: Textspeak and personality perceptions. *Cyberpsychology, Behavior, and Social Networking*, *18*(3), 147–151.

Gale, S. F. (January 17, 2017a). Gaming the system to boost recruiting: Companies like Unilever are employing gamification to eliminate bias in recruiting, but does it really work? Retrieved from www.workforce.com/2017/01/17/gaming-system-boost-recruiting/.

Gale, S. F. (June 1, 2017b). OMG! Ur hired! Could texting make your recruiting process more user-friendly? Retrieved from www.workforce.com/2017/06/01/omg-ur-hired/.

Gandini, A. (2016). *The reputation economy: Understanding knowledge work in digital society*. London, England: Macmillan.

Gatewood, R., Feild, H. S., & Barrick, M. (2016). *Human resource selection* (7th edn.). Mason, OH: South-Western.

Girard, A. & Fallery, B. (2011). e-Recruitment: From transaction-based practices to relationship-based approaches. In T. Bondarouk, H. Ruel, & J. C. Looise (Eds.), *Electronic HRM in theory and practice* (advanced series in management, vol. 8) (pp. 143–158). Bingley, England: Emerald Group.

GlobalHRResearch (August 9, 2016). Candidate screening: Are video resumes a good idea? Retrieved from www.ghrr.com/blog/2016/08/09/candidate-screening-are-video-resumes-a-good-idea/.

Gorman, C. A. (August 2014). Exploring the validity of asynchronous web-based video interviews. Paper presented at the 122nd annual conference of the American Psychological Association, Washington, DC.

Goyal, M. (October 8, 2017). How artificial intelligence is reshaping recruitment and what it means for the future of jobs. Retrieved from https://economictimes.indiatimes.com/jobs/how-artificial-intelligence-is-reshaping-recruitment-and-what-it-means-for-the-future-of-jobs/articleshow/60985946.cms.

Gregory, C. K., Meade, A. W., & Thompson, L. F. (2013). Understanding internet recruitment via signaling theory and the elaboration likelihood model. *Computers in Human Behavior, 29*, 1949–1959.

Grossman, K. W. (February 20, 2015). Three reasons why video-enabled recruiting gives you an unfair advantage. Retrieved from www.aberdeenessentials.com/hcm-essentials/three-reasons-video-enabled-recruiting-gives-unfair-advantage/.

Grothaus, M. (March 14, 2016). How "blind recruitment" works and why you should consider it. Retrieved from www.fastcompany.com/3057631/how-blind-recruitment-works-and-why-you-should-consider.

Guchait, P., Ruetzler, T., Taylor, J., & Toldi, N. (2014). Video interviewing: A potential selection tool for hospitality managers: A study to understand applicant perspective. *International Journal of Hospitality Management, 36*, 90–100.

Hansen, S. D. & Griep, Y. (2017). Psychological contracts. In J. Meyer (Ed.), *Handbook of employee commitment* (pp. 119–134). Northampton, MA: Edward Elgar Publishing.

Harmsel, J. A. (2011). Consequences of using pre-recorded video interviews as a (pre-) selection tool [Master's thesis]. Retrieved from http://essay.utwente.nl/62860/.

Harold, C. M., Holtz, B. C., Griepentrog, B. K., Brewer, L. M., & Marsh, S. M. (2016). Investigating the effects of applicant justice perceptions on job offer acceptance. *Personnel Psychology, 69*, 199–227.

Hartwick, J. M. & Mason, R. W. (2014). Using introductory videos to enhance ePortfolios and to make them useful in the hiring process. *International Journal of ePortfolio, 4*(2), 169–184.

Heathfield, S. M. (September 3, 2016). Do employers want video resumes? Retrieved from www.thebalance.com/video-resumes-1918979.

Hess, C. (December 9, 2015). Is text messaging a viable way to recruit? Retrieved from www.recruiter.com/i/is-text-messaging-a-viable-way-to-recruit/.

Hiemstra, A. M. F. (2013). Fairness in paper and video resume screening [Doctoral dissertation]. Retrieved from https://repub.eur.nl/pub/50432/Hiemstra_PhDThesis_2013.pdf.

Hiemstra, A. M. F. & Derous, E. (2015). Video resumes portrayed: Findings and challenges. In I. Nikolaou & J. K. Oostrom (Eds.), *Employee recruitment, selection, and assessment: Contemporary issues for theory and practice* (pp.45–60). London, England: Psychology Press.

Hiemstra, A. M. F., Derous, E., Serlie, A. W., & Born, M. P. (2012). Fairness perceptions of video resumes among ethnically diverse applicants. *International Journal of Selection and Assessment, 20*(4), 423–433.

Hill, R. E. (1970). New look at employee referrals as a recruitment channel. *Personnel Journal, 49,* 144–148.

Holm, A. B. (2014). E-recruitment: Towards an ubiquitous recruitment process and candidate relationship management. *German Journal of Research in Human Resource Management, 26*(3), 241–259.

Hughes, F. & Coates, C. (2014). Credentialing across the globe: Approaches and applications. In K. A. Goudreau & M. C. Smolenski (Eds.), *Health policy and advanced practice nursing: Impact and implications* (pp. 349–358). New York, NY: Springer.

Hurtz, G. M. & Wright, C. W. (2012). Designing work descriptions to maximize the utility of employee recruitment efforts. In M. A. Wilson, W. Bennett, S. G. Gibson, & G. M. Alliger (Eds.), *The handbook of work analysis: The methods, systems, applications and science of work measurement in organizations* (pp. 347–364). New York, NY: Routledge.

Irani, L. (2015). The cultural work of microwork. *New Media & Society, 17*(5), 720–739.

Kaplan, A. M. & Haenlein, M. (2010). Users of the world, unite! The challenges and opportunities of social media. *Business Horizons, 53,* 59–68.

Karl, K. A. & Pelochute, J. V. (2013). Possibilities and pitfalls of using online social networking in human resource management. In K. Karl & M. Paludi (Eds.), *Psychology for business success* (pp. 119–139). Santa Barbara, CA: Praeger.

Kluemper, D. H. & Rosen, P. A. (2009). Future employment selection methods: Evaluating social networking web sites. *Journal of Managerial Psychology, 24*(6), 567–580.

Kluemper, D. H. Rosen, P. A., & Mossholder, K. W. (2012). Social networking websites, personality ratings, and the organizational context: More than meets the eye? *Journal of Applied Social Psychology, 42*(5), 1143–1172.

Korn, M. (February 5, 2014). Giant resumes fail to impress employers. Retrieved from www.wsj.com/articles/giant-r233sum233s-fail-to-impress-employers-1391647892.

Korn Ferry (2017). The talent forecast: Part 2: Improving talent acquisition through alignment, strategy, technology, and partnerships. Retrieved from http://focus.korn ferry.com/wp-content/uploads/2015/02/Korn-Ferry-Futurestep_The-Talent-Forecast-Part-Two.pdf.

Kottasova, I. (October 26, 2015). Big finance tackles racism by hiring 'nameless' graduates. Retrieved from http://money.cnn.com/2015/10/26/news/blind-hiring-white-sound ing-names/.

Kraichy, D. & Chapman, D. S. (2014). Tailoring web-based recruiting messages: Individual differences in the persuasiveness of affective and cognitive messages. *Journal of Business Psychology, 29,* 253–268.

Krause, A., Rinne, U., & Zimmermann, K. F. (2012). Anonymous job applications of fresh Ph.D. economists. *Economics Letters, 117,* 441–444.

Kristof-Brown, A. & Guay, R. P. (2011). Person-environment fit. In S. Zedeck (Ed.), *APA handbook of industrial and organizational psychology, Volume 3: Maintaining, expanding, and contracting the organization* (pp. 3–50). Washington, DC: American Psychological Association.

Kroll, E. & Ziegler, M. (2016). Discrimination due to ethnicity and gender: How susceptible are video-based job interviews? *International Journal of Selection and Assessment, 24*(2), 161–171.

Kuhn, K. (2016). The rise of the "gig economy" and implications for understanding work and workers. *Industrial and Organizational Psychology, 9*(1), 157–162.

Kuncel, N. R., Klieger, D. M., Connelly, B. S., & Ones, D. S. (2013). Mechanical versus clinical data combination in selection and admissions decisions: A meta-analysis. *Journal of Applied Psychology, 98*(6), 1060–1072.

Landers, R. N. & Schmidt, G. B. (Eds.). (2016). Social media in employee selection and recruitment: Theory, practice, and current challenges. Retrieved from www.springer.com/us/book/9783319299877?wt_mc=ThirdParty.SpringerLink.3 .EPR653.About_eBook.

Larsen, J. (May 19, 2017). At Cisco, we're trying to create our own 'gig economy' for employees [Web log post]. Retrieved from www.eremedia.com/ere/at-cisco-were-trying-to-create-our-own-gig-economy-for-employees.

Lefkow, D. (March 21, 2007). Why you shouldn't be afraid of video resumes. Retrieved from www.eremedia.com/ere/why-you-shouldnt-be-afraid-of-video-resumes/.

Lemmon, G., Wilson, M. S., Posig, M., & Gibowski, B. C. (2016). Psychological contract development, distributive justice, and performance of independent contractors: The role of negotiation behaviors and the fulfillment of resources. *Journal of Leadership & Organizational Studies, 23*(4), 424–439.

Lievens, F. & Highhouse, S. (2003). The relation of instrumental and symbolic attribute to a company's attractiveness as an employer. *Personnel Psychology, 56*, 75–102.

Lighthouse (2017). The candidate experience: Perspectives on video interviews, assessments, and hiring. Retrieved from http://lhra.io/blog/candidate-experience-perspectives-video-interviews-assessments-hiring/.

Llorens, J. J. & Wilson, A. W. (2012). Leveraging web 2.0 technologies in the recruitment of millennial job candidates. In W. Sauser, Jr. & R. Sims (Eds.), *Managing human resources for the millennial generation* (pp. 141–157). Charlotte, NC: Information Age Publishing.

Lorenzo, G. & Ittelson, J. (July 2005). An overview of e-portfolios. Retrieved from www .educause.edu/ir/library/pdf/ELI3001.pdf.

Lustman, L. (May 15, 2017). Blind recruitment: The way to overcome bias in hiring? Retrieved from www.hireright.com/blog/2017/05/blind-recruitment-way-over coming-bias-hiring/?utm_medium=Blog&utm_campaign=Blog&lsmr= Blog&lso=Blog&cid=70132000000h5j8AAA.

Maurer, R. (August 21, 2015). Use of video for recruiting continues to grow [Web log post]. Retrieved from www.shrm.org/resourcesandtools/hr-topics/talent-acquisition/ pages/use-video-recruiting-grow.aspx.

Maurer, S. D. & Cook, D. P. (2011). Using company web sites to e-recruit qualified applicants: A job marketing based review of theory-based research. *Computers in Human Behavior, 27*, 106–117.

McCarthy, J. M., Bauer, T. N., Truxillo, D. M., Anderson, N. R., Costa, A. C., & Ahmed, S. M. (2017). Applicant perspectives during selection: A review addressing "So what?," "What's new?," and "Where to next?" *Journal of Management, 43*(6), 1693–1725.

McCullough, B. (2015, August 7). 20 years on: Why Netscape's IPO was the "big bang" of the internet era [Web log post]. Retrieved from www.internethistorypodcast.com/2015/08/20-years-on-why-netscapes-ipo-was-the-big-bang-of-the-internet-era/.

Mead, A. D., Olson-Buchanan, J. B., & Drasgow, F. (2014). Technology-based selection. In M. D. Coovert & L. F. Thompson (Eds.), *The psychology of workplace technology* (pp. 21–42). New York, NY: Routledge.

Meister, J. C. & Willyerd, K. (2010). *The 2020 workplace: How innovative companies attract, develop, and keep tomorrow's employees today*. New York, NY: Harper Collins.

Mikkelson, K. (2010). Cybervetting and monitoring employees' online activities: Assessing the legal risks for employers. *The Public Lawyer, 18*(2), 1–6.

Miller, C. C. (2015, July 9). When algorithms discriminate. Retrieved from www.nytimes.com/2015/07/10/upshot/when-algorithms-discriminate.html.

Miller, C. C. (February 25, 2016). Is blind hiring the best hiring? Retrieved from www.nytimes.com/2016/02/28/magazine/is-blind-hiring-the-best-hiring.html.

Min, J. (April 3, 2017). Enhancing recruitment through AI: Recruiters can put forward more of a human face when screening, feedback and testing tasks are automated. Retrieved from www.hrreporter.com/hr-technology/33021-enhancing-recruitment-through-ai/.

Mohamed, A. A., Orife, J. N., & Wibowo, K. (2002). The legality of key word search as a personnel selection tool. *Employee Relations, 24*(5), 516–522.

Morgan, H. (March 3, 2017). Convert your LinkedIn profile into an online portfolio. Retrieved from www.linkedin.com/pulse/convert-your-linkedin-profile-online-portfolio-hannah-morgan.

Mossberg, W. (May 25, 2017). Mossberg: The disappearing computer. Retrieved from www.recode.net/2017/5/25/15689094/mossberg-final-column.

Motroc, G. (April 12, 2016). Code on the road: Uber, Google, Marriott and US army are gamifying recruitment. Retrieved from https://jaxenter.com/code-on-the-road-uber-google-and-us-army-are-gamifying-recruitment-125529.html.

Mozilla (August 2013). Expanding education and workforce opportunities through digital badges. Retrieved from http://10mbetterfutures.org/wp-content/uploads/2013/11/Expanding-Workforce-and-Education-Opportunities-through-digital-badges.pdf.

National Academy of Sciences (1999). *The changing nature of work: Implications for occupational analysis*. Washington, DC: National Academy Press.

Nikolau, I. (2014). Social networking web sites in job search and employee recruitment. *International Journal of Selection and Assessment, 22*(2), 179–189.

Nguyen, L. S. & Gatica-Perez, D. (2016). Hirability in the wild: Analysis of online conversational video resumes. *IEEE Transactions On Multimedia, 18*(7), 1422–1437.

Nodoye, A., Ritzhaupt, A. D., & Parker, M. A. (2012). Use of eportfolios in K-12 teacher hiring in North Carolina: Perspectives of school principals. *International Journal of Education Policy & Leadership, 7*(4), 1–10.

O'Donnell, J. T. (November 15, 2016). Posting a picture of you drinking a beer no longer hurts your career, but this could. Retrieved from www.inc.com/jt-odonnell/posting-a-picture-of-you-drinking-a-beer-no-longer-hurts-your-career-but-this-co.html.

Ordioni, J. (March 21, 2017). Recruiting, employment branding, and everyone you know [Web log post]. Retrieved from www.eremedia.com/ere/recruiting-employment-branding-and-everyone-you-know/.

Peebles, K. A. (2012). Negligent hiring and the information age: How state legislatures can save employers from inevitable liability. *William & Mary Law Review*, *53*(4), 1398–1431.

Phillips, J. M. (1998). Effects of realistic job previews on multiple organizational outcomes: A meta-analysis. *Academy of Management Journal*, *41*(6), 673–690.

Ployhart, R. E. (2006). Staffing in the 21st century: New challenges and strategic opportunities. *Journal of Management*, *32*(6), 868–897.

Ployhart, R. E., Schmitt, N., & Tippins, N. T. (2017). Solving the supreme problem: 100 years of selection and recruitment at the Journal of Applied Psychology. *Journal of Applied Psychology*, *102*(3), 291–304.

Rainie, L. & Anderson, J. (February 8, 2017). Code-dependent: Pros and cons of the algorithm age. Retrieved from www.pewinternet.org/2017/02/08/code-depen dent-pros-and-cons-of-the-algorithm-age/.

Raphael, T. (May 24, 2017). More virtual reality recruiting: This week it's the U.S. Navy in New York, New Jersey [Web log post]. Retrieved from www.eremedia.com/ere/ more-virtual-reality-recruiting-this-week-its-the-u-s-navy-in-new-york-new-jer sey/.

Rice, C. (October 14, 2013). How blind auditions help orchestras to eliminate gender bias. *The Guardian*. Retrieved from www.theguardian.com/women-in-leadership/ 2013/oct/14/blind-auditions-orchestras-gender-bias.

Roth, P. L., Bobko, P., Van Iddekinge, C. H., & Thatcher, J. B. (2016). Social media in employee-selection-related decisions: A research agenda for uncharted territory. *Journal of Management*, *42*(1), 269–298.

Ross, W. & Slovensky, R. (2012). Using the internet to attract and evaluate job candidates. In Z. Yan (Ed.), *Encyclopedia of cyber behavior* (pp. 537–549). Hershey, PA: IGI Global.

Rousseau, D. M. (1989). Psychological and implied contracts in organizations. *Employee Responsibilities and Rights Journal*, *2*(2), 121–139.

Ryan, A. M. (2012). Applicant-organization relationship and employee-organization rela- tionship: What is the connection? In L. Shore, J. A. Coyle-Shapiro, & L. E. Tetrick (Eds.), *The employee-organization relationship: Applications for the 21st century* (pp. 363–389). New York, NY: Taylor and Francis.

Ryan, A. M. & Delany, T. (2010). Attracting job candidates to organizations. In A. M. Ryan, J. L. Farr, & N. T. Tippins (Eds.), *Handbook of employee selection* (2nd edn., pp. 127–150). New York, NY: Taylor and Francis.

Rynes, S. L. (1991). Recruitment, job choice, and post-hire consequences: A call for new research directions. In M. Dunnette, L. Hough, & H. Triandis (Eds.), *Handbook of industrial and organizational psychology* (vol. 2, pp. 399–444). Palo Alto, CA: Consulting Psychologists Press.

Rynes, S. L., Reeves, C. J., & Darnold, T. C. (2014). The history of recruitment research. In D. Cable & K. Yu (Eds.), *The Oxford handbook of recruitment* (pp. 335–760). Oxford, England: Oxford University Press.

Sadiq, S., Ayub, J., Narsayya, G., Ayyas, M., & Tahir, K. (2016). Intelligent hiring with resume parser and ranking using natural language processing and machine learning. *International Journal of Innovative Research in Computer and Communication Engineering*, *4*(4), 7437–7444.

Samuel, A. (2013, August 5). Do you need a resume in the LinkedIn era? Retrieved from https://hbr.org/2013/08/do-you-need-a-resume-in-the-li.

Schmitt, T., Caillou, P., & Sebag, M. (September 2016). Matching jobs and resumes: A deep collaborative filtering task. Presented at the 2nd annual Global Conference on Artificial Intelligence, Berlin, Germany.

Sears, G. J., Zhang, H., Wiesner, W. H., Hackett, R. D., & Yuan, Y. (2013). A comparative assessment of videoconference and face-to-face employment interviews. *Management Decision, 51*(8), 1733–1752.

Sepp, M. (October 20, 2017). 7 tools that can help you recruit more diverse candidates. Retrieved from http://recruitingdaily.com/7-tools

Slaughter, J. E., Zickar, M. J., Highhouse, S., & Mohr, D. C. (2004). Personality trait inferences: Development of a measure and assessment of construct validity. *Journal of Applied Psychology, 89*(1), 85–103.

Smith, J. (May 31, 2015). Why companies are using 'blind auditions' to hire top talent. Retrieved from www.businessinsider.com/companies-are-using-blind-auditions-to-hire-top-talent-2015–5.

Smith, A. & Anderson, M. (October 2017). Automation in everyday life. Retrieved from www.pewinternet.org/2017/10/04/americans-attitudes-toward-hiring-algorithms/.

Society for Human Resource Management (January 2016). SHRM survey findings: Using social media for talent acquisition-recruitment and screening [White paper]. Retrieved from www.shrm.org/hr-today/trends-and-forecasting/research-and-sur veys/Documents/SHRM-Social-Media-Recruiting-Screening-2015.pdf.

Stack Overflow (2017). Developer survey results 2017 [Web log post]. Retrieved from https://insights.stackoverflow.com/survey/2017#overview.

Staney, W. (Speaker). (2017). Recruiting top talent using unconventional strategies [Online video]. Available from https://youtu.be/1fLOkw2IOHE.

Straumsheim, C. (January 27, 2014). Promising portfolios [Web log post]. Retrieved from www.insidehighered.com/news/2014/01/27/aacu-conference-shows-plenty-uses-e-portfolios-also-pitfalls-hype.

Strohmeier, S. (2010). Electronic portfolios in recruiting? A conceptual analysis of usage. *Journal of Electronic Commerce Research, 11*(4), 268–280.

Sullivan, J. (April 9, 2012). Leading-edge candidate screening, interviewing, and assessment practices [Web log post]. Retrieved from www.eremedia.com/ere/leading-edge-candidate-screening-interviewing-and-assessment-practices/.

Sullivan, J. (May 15, 2014). The 8 great benefits of going to video job descriptions [Web log post]. Retrieved from www.eremedia.com/tlnt/the-8-great-benefits-of-going-to-video-job-descriptions/.

Sullivan, J. (November 16, 2015). Recruiting trends for 2016 and their supporting best practices, part 1 of 2. Retrieved from www.eremedia.com/ere/recruiting-trends-for-2016-and-their-supporting-best-practices-part-1-of-2/.

Sullivan, J. (April 18, 2016). Add a chatbot–and take 'the human' out of answering recruiting questions [Web log post]. Retrieved from www.eremedia.com/ere/add-a-chatbot-and-take-the-human-out-of-answering-recruiting-questions/.

Sullivan, J. (May 8, 2017). The future of recruiting is an internal talent consulting group, as technology handles daily recruiting tasks [Web log post]. Retrieved from www.eremedia.com/ere/the-future-of-recruiting-is-an-internal-talent-consulting-group-as-technology-handles-daily-recruiting-tasks/.

Swider, B. W., Barrick, M. R., & Zimmerman, R. D. (2015). Searching for the right fit: Development of applicant person-organization fit perceptions during the recruitment process. *Journal of Applied Psychology, 100*(3), 880–893.

TalentQ (2013). Through the eyes of a graduate: What do graduates think of the recruitment process? What do graduates want? What puts them off? Retrieved from www .talentqgroup.com/media/98030/graduate-survey-report-2013.pdf.

Tarling, S. (November 17, 2016). Robots muscle in on the job interview: Automation may avoid human error but it could discourage recruits. Retrieved from www.ft.com/ content/b71f0afa-9c36-11e6-8324-be63473ce146.

Torres, E. N. & Mejia, C. (2017). Asynchronous video interviews in the hospitality industry: Considerations for virtual employee selection. *International Journal of Hospitality Management, 61*, 4–13.

Tskhay, K. O. & Rule, N. O. (2014). Perceptions of personality in text-based media and OSN: A meta-analysis. *Journal of Research in Personality, 49*, 25–30.

Uggerslev, K. L., Fassina, N. E., & Kraichy, D. (2012). Recruiting through the stages: A meta-analytic test of predictors of applicant attraction at different stages of the recruiting process. *Personnel Psychology, 65*, 597–660.

Ullman, J. C. (1966). Employee referrals: Prime tool for recruiting workers. *Personnel, 43*, 30–35.

Van Hoye, G. & Lievens, F. (2007). Investigating web-based recruitment sources: Employee testimonials versus word-of-mouse. *International Journal of Selection and Assessment, 15*(4), 372–382.

Van Hoye, G., Weijters, B., Lievens, F., & Stockman, S. (2016). Social influences in recruitment: When is word-of-mouth most effective? *International Journal of Selection and Assessment, 24*(1), 42–53.

Van Iddekinge, C. H., Lanivich, S. E., Roth, P. L., & Junco, E. (2013). Social media for selection? Validity and adverse impact potential of a Facebook-based assessment. *Journal of Management, 42*(7), 1811–1835.

Vanderstukken, A., Van den Boreck, A., & Proost, K. (2016). For love or for money: Intrinsic and extrinsic value congruence in recruitment. *International Journal of Selection and Assessment, 24*(1), 34–41.

Veale, M. & Binns, R. (2017). Fairer machine learning in the real world: Mitigating discrimination without collecting sensitive data. *Big Data & Society, 4*(2), 1–17.

Viswesvaran, C. & Ones, D. S. (2010). Employee selection in times of change. In G. P. Hodgkinson & J. K. Ford (Eds.), *International review of industrial and organizational psychology* (vol. 25, pp. 169–226). Madden, MA: Wiley-Blackwell.

Walker, H. J., Bauer, T. N., Cole, M. S., Bernerth, J. B., Field, H. S., & Short, J. C. (2013). Is this how I will be treated? Reducing uncertainty through recruitment interactions. *Academy of Management Journal, 56*(5), 1325–1347.

Walker, H. J., Helmuth, C. A., Field, H. S., & Bauer, T. N. (2015). Watch what you say: Job applicants' justice perceptions from initial organizational correspondence. *Human Resource Management, 54*(6), 999–1011.

Wanous, J. P. (1989). Installing a realistic job preview: Ten tough choices. *Personnel Psychology, 42*, 117–134.

Ward, C. & Moser, C. (2008). E-portfolios as a hiring tool: Do employers really care? *Educause Quarterly, 31*(4), 13–14.

Waung, M., Hymes, R. W., & Beatty, J. E. (2014). The effects of video and paper resumes on assessments of personality, applied social skills, mental capability, and resume outcomes. *Basic and Applied Social Psychology, 36*, 238–251.

Waung, M., Hymes, R. W., Beatty, J. E., & McAuslan, P. (2015). Self-promotion statements in video resumes: Frequency, intensity, and gender effects on job applicant evaluation. *International Journal of Selection and Assessment, 23*(4), 345–360.

Wheeler, K. (2010, December 22). Serious recruiting games: 6 tips for using games and simulations for recruiting success [Web log post]. Retrieved from www.eremedia .com/ere/6-tips-on-using-games-and-simulations-for-recruiting-success/.

Wills, K. & Rice, R. (Eds.) (2013). *ePortfolio performance support systems: Constructing, presenting, and assessing portfolios*. Fort Collins, CO: The WAC Clearinghouse.

Wiltermuth, S. S. & Neale, M. A. (2011). Too much information: The perils of nondiagnositc information in negotiations. *Journal of Applied Psychology, 96*(1), 192–201.

Yoganarasimhan, H. (2013). The value of reputation in an online freelance marketplace. *Marketing Science, 32*(6), 1526–1548.

Yu, T. (2012). E-portfolio, a valuable job search tool for college students. *Campus-Wide Information Systems, 29*(1), 70–76.

Zattoli, M. A. & Wanous, J. P. (2000). Recruitment source research: Current status and future directions. *Human Resource Management Review, 10*(4), 353–382.

5 Applicant Reactions in Employee Recruitment and Selection

The Role of Technology

Ioannis Nikolaou, Konstantina Georgiou, Talya N. Bauer, and Donald M. Truxillo

Employee recruitment and selection has been one of the most active research and practice fields in work/organizational psychology and human resources management. Numerous psychology and management graduates work in recruitment and selection related jobs. New recruitment and selection methods appear, although traditional or "settled" research questions still remain and attract increased attention (Ryan & Ployhart, 2014). Many of these new methods are largely affected by or merely exist due to changes in technology. Also, applicant reactions research has become an important topic of study within the broader area of employee selection and assessment. It has been a fruitful and highly productive stream of research since the mid-1980s, when the first highly influential empirical study on this topic was published by Harris and Fink (1987). Ryan and Ployhart (2000) defined applicant reactions as the "attitudes, affect or cognitions an individual might have about the hiring process" (p. 566). McCarthy et al. (2017) describe applicant reactions, as " ... how job candidates perceive and respond to selection tools (e.g., personality tests, work samples, situational judgment tests) on the basis of their application experience. They include perceptions of fairness and justice, feelings of anxiety, and levels of motivation, among others" (p. 1695).

Technology has had a major impact on employee recruitment and selection practices, although research has not followed with the same speed. The interplay between technology and employee recruitment and selection has also had an impact on applicant reactions research and practice. We believe that in the future, employee recruitment, selection, and applicant reactions research and practice must continue to evolve and take on a different focus and shape, considering the changing nature of staffing practices in the twenty-first century and the impact of technology.

The current chapter will focus on two main issues: we will first review the literature on applicant reactions since the most recent reviews on the topic from Gilliland and Steiner (2012) and Hausknecht (2013). We will briefly review and present the most important theoretical frameworks pertaining to applicant reactions

Note: Special thanks to Ms Evdokia Tsoni, Athens University of Economics and Business, for assisting us with reference collection

research, and recent empirical studies not covered in these reviews. In the second part of this chapter, we will focus on the role that technology plays on employee recruitment and selection. We will cover the most relevant and recent research, along with the most important practical applications and trends relevant to this topic. Finally, in the third and last section of this chapter, we will focus on the future of the interplay between technology and applicant reactions research and practice, in an attempt to propose new avenues for research and practice in the field.

5.1 Applicant Reactions Theory and Frameworks

A number of different theoretical approaches have been developed in the field of applicant reactions. Probably the first theoretical approach in applicant reactions research was introduced by Peter Herriot (1989). The *social psychological* theories focus on the perceptual processes that underlie these reactions and the two-way interaction occurring between applicants and the organizations during the selection process. Herriot (2004) later extended his approach by exploring the role of applicants' personal-social identities and how these are associated with organizational identities, referring to applicants' perceived characteristics of an organization's culture. A congruence (or incongruence) between those two will have an impact on applicants' perceptions of both the selection methods employed and the organization. Building on Herriot's work, a number of researchers, such as Ployhart and his colleagues (Ployhart & Harold, 2004; Ployhart & Ryan, 1997) explored the role of applicants' self-concept and attribution theory on the behavioral outcomes of applicant reactions.

Soon after Herriot (1989), Schuler (1993) explored the notion of "*social validity.*" He described a four-factor model influencing the acceptability of the selection process to candidates, that is, the information provided to candidates regarding the position and the organization, the degree of the candidates' active involvement in the selection process, the transparency of the process so that they can understand its objective and its relevance to organizational requirements, and finally the provision of acceptable feedback in terms of content and form. Although this model has not been studied extensively, it is obvious that it has a significant impact on the way of thinking of other theorists in fairness reactions. Moreover, it is notable that Schuler's social validity model can be further explored in relation to technology, since many of the concepts covered in his four-component model, entail a strong technological aspect. For example, candidates now receive information about job openings in an automated way, via job boards' mailings or via companies' websites, which they also visit to gather information about potential openings.

However, the most influential theoretical approach in the field of applicant reactions has been Gilliland's (1993) *organizational justice* framework (Truxillo et al., 2017). In Gilliland's model, selection practices, policies, and decisions influence perceptions of organizational justice and subsequently create perceptions of fairness and also influence pre-hire and post-hire outcomes. Gilliland also put increased emphasis on the role of procedural as opposed to distributive organizational justice. He developed ten procedural rules, grouped into three categories: *formal characteristics* (job relatedness, opportunity to perform, reconsideration opportunity, and consistency), *explanation* (feedback, selection information, and honesty), and *interpersonal treatment* (interpersonal effectiveness, two-way communication, and propriety of questions). This model was further refined by Bauer et al. (2001) who confirmed and expanded the model while creating the Selection Procedural Justice Scale (SPJS), a psychometrically sound measure to tap the justice rules. Steiner and Gilliland (1996) also added that a selection method may be considered as more acceptable by candidates when it is widely used, and they developed a model of eight procedural justice dimensions, which formed the basis of considerable research on applicant reactions, especially in cross-cultural settings (Anderson, Ahmed, & Costa, 2012; Hoang et al., 2012; Nikolaou & Judge, 2007). Gilliland's model, and especially the procedural rules, has many applications in relation to technology. For example, technology and especially on-line assessment have enabled companies to provide immediate feedback and explanations to candidates, but at the same time create distance between the applicant and the organization, thus having implications for interpersonal treatment. Similarly, new selection methods, such as digital interviews, as we will discuss later in the chapter, eliminate personal contact between the two parties, with a direct impact on candidates' reactions (Sears et al., 2013).

Another widely used theoretical approach in applicant reactions research has been the *test-taking motivation* model developed by Arvey, Strickland, Drauden, and Martin (1990). Their approach deals with job applicants' motivation during the selection process and how this affects their own performance but also the measures' validity. They developed the Test Attitude Scale, which measures nine different dimensions, with test motivation being the most important since it was accounting for the majority of the variance in the scale (Gilliland & Steiner, 2012). *Test anxiety* has also been studied as a potential cause on applicants' perceptions of the different selection methods. The meta-analysis by Hausknecht, Day, and Thomas (2004) has indicated a negative relationship between test anxiety and test performance, although McCarthy et al. (2013) more recently identified a positive relation between test anxiety and job performance for one occupational group of their study (product technicians). It is clear then that we need more research on this topic in the future. The *self-serving bias* mechanism, defined as the extent to which preservation of a positive self-image has an impact on applicants' perceptions of the different selection methods, has also been studied in the area of test-taking motivation. In other words, rejected or poorly performing applicants, in an attempt to maintain a positive self-image, attribute their poor test performance to beliefs that the method is not valid or irrelevant.

Another recent approach that seems to relate with the role of technology in applicant reactions research is the *invasion of privacy* model developed by Bauer et al. (2006). The authors focused on the negative consequences of invading applicants' personal lives, through the use of selection methods, such as drug, integrity, and maybe personality testing. Gilliland and Steiner (2012) suggest however, that the invasion of privacy model can be incorporated into the organizational justice perspective, since it is associated with justice perceptions, such as job relatedness and opportunity to perform. This is another interesting area for future research, where technology seems to play a critical role, with many of the new methods (e.g., social networking websites) to raise important invasion of privacy concerns.

Gilliland and Steiner (2012), providing an interesting theoretical integration of the main theoretical approaches, emphasized three main domains in applicant reactions research: *self-interest, group-values motives,* and *deontic outrage.* Self-interest deals with the conscious or unconscious attempt people make to maximize the likelihood of favorable outcomes, leading thus to positive reactions, if treated fairly on an individual level. The group values motives, although not very popular among researchers, is based on the assumption applicants often make that as employees, if they get the job, they will be treated in a similar way as they have been treated during the selection process. Finally, deontic outrage deals with the impact of mistreatment of third parties, not the applicants themselves. As Gilliland and Steiner (2012) illustrate: " . . . when we see or hear about other applicants being treated poorly, do we form negative impressions (about the company) that shape our own reactions and decision making?" (p. 648). We believe that recent technological developments, and more specifically the use of social networking websites (SNWs) and similar technological platforms (e.g., Glassdoor) by applicants and companies, might strengthen the importance of this approach in applicant reactions research.

5.1.1 Predictors of Applicant Reactions

In the current section, we will focus on the most important predictors of applicant reactions according to the most recent reviews on the topic (e.g., Gilliland & Steiner, 2012; Hausknecht, 2013).

An integral part of applicant reactions research has traditionally been on how applicants perceive the different selection methods. Numerous studies have explored if applicants' perceptions in different countries converge or diverge in relation to their perceptions of the selection procedures and the characteristics of the selection methods that seem to lead to positive or negative applicant reactions. Almost all of these studies adopted the Gilliland and Steiner framework of organizational justice and most of them replicated across countries the initial study conducted by Steiner and Gilliland (1996) and Moscoso and Salgado (2004).

The issue of which procedures are preferred by applicants was one of the questions that Hausknecht and colleagues (2004) addressed in their meta-analysis. Individuals were asked to rate the favorability (job relatedness or fairness) of different selection procedures. Interviews, work samples, resumes, and references were rated most favorably, cognitive ability testing, personality testing, and biodata as moderately favorable. Personal contacts, honesty tests, and graphology were rated as the least favorable selection procedures.

In an effort to update this meta-analysis and also to determine whether there are cross-cultural differences in preferences, Anderson, Salgado, and Hülsheger

(2010) conducted a meta-analysis of thirty-eight samples from seventeen different countries. Additionally, they measured preferences according to the eight dimensions relating to Gilliland's justice rules: overall favorability, scientific evidence, employers' right to use, opportunity to perform, interpersonal warmth, face validity, widely used, and respectful of privacy. Their findings supported the *reaction generalizability* hypothesis, that is, the fact that candidates seem to have very similar reactions toward the different selection methods, across very different countries, similar to what Hausknecht and colleagues found. The most preferred methods were work samples and resumes. Favorably evaluated were cognitive ability tests, references, and personality tests. The least preferred were honesty tests, personal contacts, and graphology. Moreover, there were no differences across countries in these preferences. Their major advantage is that, via these methods, the applicants have the opportunity to meet in person with the assessors, as opposed to other methods, which might be more valid (e.g., cognitive tests) or more widely used (e.g., resumes) (Nikolaou & Judge, 2007).

Overall, the aforementioned findings suggest that applicants tend to prefer the valid selection procedures (Truxillo, Bauer, & Garcia, 2017). Unfortunately, though, organizations are not always able to use the most preferred procedures in the selection process. This could be for reasons such as cost or validity, or other practical constraints, such as time (Konig et al., 2010). For example, an organization would likely not be able to interview everyone in a large pool of applicants. The role of technology can be very useful here, with digital interviewing for example, providing a useful platform for interaction between a company and its applicants. Also, organizations and HR professionals may want to consider ways to make some of the less preferable methods more favorably evaluated by applicants, for example, by providing explanations about the selection procedures.

The role of providing explanations to applicants has been studied in the applicant reactions literature. In a meta-analysis conducted by Truxillo, Bodner, Bertolino, Bauer, and Yonce (2009) the authors made the distinction between "structure" and "social fairness," with the former emphasizing the job-related and procedural characteristics of the selection method, whereas the latter focuses on issues such as the interpersonal sensitivity and the justification provided before or after the selection decisions are made. The meta-analytic evidence demonstrated the existence of positive associations between explanations and most applicant reactions outcomes (perceived fairness, organizational perceptions, test performance, test-taking motivation).

Personality has also been studied as a potential predictor of applicant reactions, but the small number of studies today has only shown minimal effect sizes. Truxillo, Bauer, Campion, and Paronto (2006) explored the relationship between the five-factor model of personality and applicants' post-test fairness perceptions, perceptions of themselves, and perceptions of the hiring organization using a sample of actual law enforcement applicants and their reactions to a written test (*N*=120). Personality accounted for significant variance in self-perceptions and perceptions of the hiring organization beyond that accounted for by fairness perceptions. Neuroticism and agreeableness were the most consistent predictors of applicant perceptions. Nikolaou and Judge (2007) found only weak associations between core self-evaluations and fairness reactions across different popular selection methods. Honkaniemi, Feldt, Metsapelto, and Tolvanen (2013) explored in their study the role of personality types in a real-life selection setting; they showed that personality types explained applicants' fairness perceptions, when controlling for gender, but they were not associated with the face validity perceptions or predictive validity perceptions. Apart from personality, other individual characteristics, such as emotional intelligence and positive/negative affect, might also play a role on applicant reactions. For example, applicants high on empathy, a construct often associated with emotional intelligence, might be better equipped to understand why companies prefer certain selection methods over others. Similarly, how applicants perceive the company's recruitment and selection procedure is likely to have an impact on their affectivity and mood; for example, how recruiters treat candidates, if they respond and/or provide feedback might influence candidates' perceptions of the company and its recruitment and selection procedures. This is a promising line of research requiring longitudinal designs or diary studies among applicants across different stages of the selection process. In conclusion, the evidence seems to show that individual characteristics and especially personality has a weak, albeit real, effect on applicants' perceptions of the selection process, although there is only a small number of studies today exploring this topic.

Another issue which has not yet attracted a great deal of interest in applicant reactions research, but has the potential to be considered an important predictor of applicant reactions is trust and trustworthiness. Klotz, Da Motta Veiga, Buckley, and Gavin (2013) claimed that trustworthiness is important in the pre-entry period, where applicants have limited access to information about their future employer. The role of organizational reputation has been shown to influence job applicants' initial perceptions of organizational trustworthiness, but the extent to which aspects of candidates' trustworthiness has an impact, especially at the early stages of the recruitment process, remains unclear. Klotz et al. (2013) emphasize the role that internet job sites and SNWs play on influencing organizations' initial perceptions of applicants' trustworthiness. Walker et al. (2013) explored how job seekers react to recruitment activities following the application submission process. They drew from three management theories (signaling, uncertainty reduction, and uncertainty management theories) to develop a conceptual model exploring the relationships between recruitment interactions of the job applicants with the recruiter/company and organizational attraction. They demonstrated that justice perceptions influence organizational attraction via positive relational certainty (i.e., reducing the uncertainty applicants feel regarding relations at work following organizational entry). They also provided additional evidence of the relational certainty mechanism, through which justice signals influence organizational attraction and also demonstrated that this relationship is dynamic, suggesting that organizations should pay increased attention to their communication process and policies during the recruitment and selection process as they do matter to applicants a great deal. Summing up, trust and trustworthiness seem to be an important topic in applicant reactions research, especially in relation to technology.

5.1.2 Outcomes of Applicant Reactions

The most interesting and useful aspect of applicant reactions' research, especially from a practitioner's perspective, is the impact reactions might have on applicants' subsequent attitudes, behaviors, personal beliefs, and/or even the selection results and outcomes themselves. Truxillo and Bauer (2011) and more recently McCarthy et al. (2017) summarized the empirical literature on the relationship between applicant reactions and a number of different outcomes. Similarly to Gilliland and Steiner (2012), they suggested that applicant perceptions seem to have a much stronger association with applicants' attitudes, as opposed to their actual behaviors. However, in the most recent review of the topic, McCarthy et al. (2017) have been more positive about the impact that applicant reactions might have on actual work-related outcomes such as job performance.

Earlier research has shown that the impact of applicant reactions on applicants' attitudes is quite considerable, especially in pre-hire conditions. However, this relationship is far weaker, when the hiring outcome is known, suggesting the existence of a strong self-serving bias in applicant reactions (Gilliland & Steiner, 2012). In the pre-hire condition, researchers have explored a number of attitudes, such as satisfaction with the selection process, organizational attractiveness, organizational commitment, intentions to recommend the organization, to accept a job offer, to purchase the organization's products and services, and intentions to pursue legal actions. On the other hand, limited research has explored the relationship between applicant reactions during the selection process and their post-hire attitudes, if selected, such as job satisfaction and organizational commitment, calling for further research on this matter (Hausknecht et al., 2004).

Similarly, the impact of applicant reactions on their actual behaviors is also worth exploring. This is another fundamental issue on applicant reactions research, if we assume that applicant reactions have a significant impact on organizational life. However, this is yet another area of limited research in this field, especially in the post-hire condition. In one of the few studies exploring this topic, McCarthy et al. (2013) conducted large-scale research with four studies, six selection methods (personality tests, job knowledge tests, cognitive ability tests, work samples, situational judgment tests, and a selection inventory), five candidate reactions (anxiety, motivation, belief in tests, self-efficacy, and procedural justice), two contexts (industry and education), two study designs (predictive and concurrent), four occupational areas (medical, sales, customer service, and technological), across three continents (North America, South America, and Europe). In summary, they showed that applicant reactions were related to test scores, and test scores were related to job performance. Further, there was some evidence that reactions affected performance indirectly through their influence on test scores. However, they found no evidence on the predictive validity of applicant reactions on actual job performance. In another recent study, Schinkel, van Vianen, and van Dierendonck (2013) demonstrated that successful applicants reported both highest well-being and organizational attractiveness when they perceived the selection outcome as fair. On the other hand, rejected applicants reported higher well-being when they thought the outcome was unfair.

Selection outcome and procedural fairness interacted with organizational attractiveness, with higher procedural fairness leading to higher attractiveness for rejected applicants. These outcomes demonstrate that the impact of applicant reactions on actual behavior and performance is probably minimal, although more studies are required on this topic, especially with real-life applicants, but their effect on employee attitudes, even in the post-hire condition, remain considerable.

However, the effect of applicant reactions on work-related outcomes and behaviors might be stronger and more apparent in promotional contexts with internal applicants. The case for internal applicants is crucial for organizations, since in most cases, companies wish to retain the rejected applicants; therefore, the practical importance of applicant reactions in this field is strong. Nevertheless, research on this topic has attracted limited attention. Ford, Truxillo, and Bauer (2009) were among the first to raise this issue, urging applicant reaction researchers to actively study this area of research. Truxillo et al. (2017) referred to this issue as one of the greatest missed opportunities in the field of applicant reactions. McCarthy, Hrabluik, and Jelley (2009) examined anxiety, motivation and justice perceptions as predictors of promotional exam performance and intentions to recommend the exam to others. Their results demonstrated that justice perceptions predicted recommendation intentions and that candidate reactions predicted exam performance. García-Izquierdo, Moscoso, and Ramos-Villagrasa (2012) also showed that employees who perceived organizational promotion methods as transparent reported a high level of perceived procedural justice, which was strongly related with job satisfaction. Future research on this topic should explore the impact of applicant reactions on employees' work-related outcomes and behaviors, such as leader-member exchange, citizenship behavior, counterproductive work behavior, job performance, withdrawal cognitions, and intentions to leave an organization.

Another important outcome of applicant reactions concerns the impact of the selection process on applicants' self-perceptions, and especially on their self-efficacy and self-esteem levels. Earlier research has shown that the selection process can have a detrimental impact on applicants' self-concept and self-esteem (Hausknecht et al., 2004). However, this relationship seems to be moderated by the hiring outcome. Thus, job relatedness of the selection process positively influences successful applicants' self-efficacy levels (Gilliland, 1994). Rejected applicants tend to attribute their failure to other, external factors, rather than themselves, in order to retain a positive self-image of themselves and also increased psychological well-being, as recently demonstrated by Schinkel et al. (2013).

5.1.3 The Role of the Internet and Technology in Human Resources, Recruitment and Selection

Technological advances have changed the way people live and work. Day-to-day life processes have been automated in most aspects allowing humans to do things with a click (e.g., on-line shopping, e-banking, e-learning). Individuals can work from home through, for example, teleconferencing and portable computing devices, as well as be constantly connected to workplace (e.g., email, chatting). As a result, technological evolution has made the workforce more flexible, efficient, and powerful. However, shaping the nature of the work requires jobs and HR processes to be transformed. Technology has changed not only the nature of work and work relationships, but also the way organizations gather, store, utilize, and diffuse information about prospective and current employees (Stone et al., 2015). In other words, continuous innovations in technology have altered how organizations attract, select, motivate, and retain their staff, having thus, a profound and increasing impact on recruitment and selection as well as other organizational processes, such as performance management, training, and rewards.

Innovations in technology, such as computing, were first employed by HRM into large organizations in the USA and Europe back in the1960s (Parry, Stefan, & Holm, 2014). The use of technology in HRM has significantly increased since then and so has research on how organizations could leverage technological resources to make the staffing process faster, more flexible, and more efficient (Ployhart, Schmitt, & Tippins, 2017). The internet, one of the greatest technological innovations, has influenced the nature of HR processes, leading to the emergence of a new term, electronic human resource management (e-HRM). E-HRM is defined as "the administrative support of the HR function in organizations by using internet technology" (Voermans & van Veldhoven, 2007, p. 887) or "a way of implementing HRM strategies, policies, and practices in organizations through the conscious and direct support of and/or with the full use of channels based on web-technologies" (Ruël & Bondarouk, 2004, p. 368). In other words, e-HRM supports the implementation of HR practices and enables organizations to achieve their HR goals. The main goals of the HR are first, to attract and recruit high quality candidates; second, to choose and hire the best candidate among applicants; third, to empower staff through training and development; fourth, to manage employees' performance; and fifth, to motivate and retain the talented workforce (Stone et al., 2015).

To facilitate the recruitment process, organizations now use web-based technologies, such as corporate websites and job boards to create a large and diverse pool of applicants, while various forms of technology enable recruiters to choose the best applicant. For example, on-line tests, video conferencing interviews, and gamified assessment methods, support organizations to assess candidates' knowledge, skills, abilities, and other qualifications (KSAOs) in order to fill a vacancy overcoming the barriers of distance and time. Videoconferencing and virtual simulations can also be used to develop the knowledge and skills of employees by delivering training material and enabling on-line communication (Stone et al., 2015). Moreover, technology has an impact on performance management. Organizations might use technology to monitor, record, and report the performance of employees, as well as to provide feedback to them by summarizing ratings from multiples sources (e.g., Cardy & Miller, 2005; Spinks, Wells, & Meche, 1999). Finally, organizations might use various forms of technology in order to design, automate, and administer compensation and reward systems improving thus the compensation processes while reducing dramatically time and cost (e.g., Dulebohn & Marler, 2005; Gherson & Jackson, 2001).

Focusing on hiring and staffing, the main reasons organizations use web-based technologies in the recruitment and selection process are flexibility, speed, and cost effectiveness (Jones, Brasher, & Huff, 2002). Technology has enabled HR professionals to save cost and time by conducting interviews through videoconference in remote parts of the globe, and screening candidates and resumes through applicant tracking systems (Chapman, Uggerslev, & Webster, 2003). Recruiters do not have to reduce their options to local applicants in case of skills shortages. On the contrary, organizations may locate highly skilled and prospective employees regardless of their geographic location using electronic technology (Toldi, 2011).

Moreover, the internet has increased the applicants pool since vacancies can be posted on various job boards, and corporate and social networking websites, increasing the chances of finding the best candidate. On the other hand, the easy access to information via the internet, has led to a vast number of applications that organizations have to handle, screen, and respond to in a short period of time. Talent management systems can electronically support candidates' attraction, applications filtering, and applicants' communication, facilitating the recruitment process and promoting a positive organizational image (Laumer, Eckhardt, & Weitzel, 2012). As a result, the automation of recruiting processes, such as incoming applications management and resume screening, has increased organizations' efficiency in hiring and their responsiveness to applicants, improving their organizational image.

Although several factors lead to the increased use of electronic technologies in recruitment and selection, issues such as adverse impact, cheating, and absence of personal contact should be taken into consideration while implementing technology-based tools (Chapman et al., 2003). The internet might provide easy access to information that previously was hard or impossible to find and enable people to communicate synchronously or asynchronously across time and space (Cascio & Montealegre, 2016). Nevertheless, it should not be the sole solution to HR professionals. A mix of traditional (e.g., face-to-face) and web-based technologies should be considered as appropriate to make the most of the hiring process.

5.1.4 Technology in Recruitment

The first step in the hiring process is recruitment. "Recruitment involves searching for and obtaining qualified applicants for the organization when filling job openings" (Jackson & Schuler, 2003, p. 252). Through recruiting activities, such as job postings and career fairs, organizations seek to attract and connect with talented candidates in order to fill a vacancy. Continuous changes in the external environment (e.g., globalization, economic and demographic shifts, technological advances) called for new efficient recruitment practices capable of locating candidates with a diverse set of skills, knowledge, and interests, across the word (Ployhart et al., 2017). The emergence of the internet, as a revolutionary technology in the 1990s, altered traditional recruitment methods, paving the way for electronic recruiting (e-recruiting) (Ployhart et al., 2017). As a result, the need for fast and effective recruiting turned HR professionals to internet technologies in order to increase the applicant pool, as well as to save money and time by automating many of the recruiting activities.

E-recruiting describes the process of using technology in recruitment activities (Stone et al., 2013). More explicitly, internet recruitment is defined "as any method of attracting applicants to apply for a job that relies heavily on the Internet," e.g., job boards, corporate web sites and job aggregators (Lievens & Harris, 2003, p. 133). Nowadays, the majority of organizations use the internet for recruitment purposes, thus replacing the traditional recruitments methods, such as job-ads, career offices, and employment agencies, with job boards, company websites, and applicant tracking systems (Ployhart et al., 2017).

Recruiters choose to attract applicants via on-line recruiting activities for the following reasons. First, individuals have altered the way they are searching for a job. Job seekers, especially of younger age, have become very familiar with the web and increasingly use it to quickly reach the information they seek, while looking for employment. They can also easily locate independent information about a company from various sources, e.g., other websites, blogs, and electronic bulletin boards (Van Hoye & Lievens, 2007). Consequently, organizations and governments have changed their recruiting processes augmenting the use of e-recruitment (e.g., Cappelli, 2001; Llorens & Kellough, 2007; Young & Foot, 2005). For example, even back in 2006 (Cober & Brown, 2006) 50 percent of new employees hired in the USA was from online sources. More recently, the numbers have been even higher with more than 80 percent of US employers recruiting via social media (SHRM, 2016). Second, the internet gives employers an opportunity to reach more candidates in remote parts of the world with technical and computing skills, target the applicants they need, as well as easily and quickly attract and respond to applicants (e.g., Cappelli, 2001; Galanaki, 2002), while saving a significant cost per hire (approx. 87 percent) (Maurer & Liu, 2007). Third, organizations might provide a wealth of information to applicants about themselves and their job positions in a more dynamic way, either on corporate websites or job boards (e.g., Lievens & Harris, 2003). Moreover, web-based recruitment enables them to oversee information that is placed on their corporate website (Selden & Orenstein, 2011), as well as assess the information that job seekers put on-line (e.g., social media). Finally, via the internet, and specifically social media platforms, recruiters can reach passive candidates, those who are not actively searching for a job but who are open to new opportunities and seem to fit to the job (Nikolaou, 2014).

Internet-based recruitment or e-recruitment includes, among others, job boards, social network websites, gamified applications, and virtual career fairs. *Job boards or job search websites*, defined as third-party recruitment websites providing media for connecting job seekers to organizations facilitating job hunting, were early introduced into the recruitment process (e.g., Lievens & Harris, 2003; Lin, 2010). At the end of 1990s, job seekers were extensively using job boards, such as Monster.com or CareerBuilder.com to upload their resumes on-line and/or submit it to prospective employers (Nikolaou, 2014). Instead of seeking job ads in news-papers for example, people who are looking for employment might visit a job board and access a dynamic and constantly growing database of job openings for free. On the other hand, employers or recruiters can use job boards to post job ads, usually for a fee, and look for prospective employees. The large database of resumes that is created from candidates submitting their curriculum vitae (CV) on-line, enables organizations to decrease the recruiting cycle time (Lin, 2010). Job boards have several advantages for both employers and job seekers, such as cost and time savings, easy access regardless of distance and time, and increased pools of jobs/applicants (e.g., Pearce & Tuten, 2001; Perry et al., 2003; Tomlinson, 2002). However, they leave aside candidates who either do not have access to the Internet or do not possess computing skills (e.g., older people).

Another web-based recruitment tool that is heavily used by both recruiters and job seekers is *social media or social networking websites* (SNWs) (Stopfer & Gosling, 2013). SNWs use technology to build digital platforms that enable individuals and organizations to create and share information, altering dramatically the way persons interact and communicate (e.g., Derks & Bakker, 2013; McFarland & Ployhart, 2015). Examples of well-known SNWs are Facebook, LinkedIn, Twitter, and YouTube. Being the most visited sites on the internet after the major search engines (Lory, 2010), it is not surprising that the use of SNWs to collect information about candidates has grown rapidly. SNWs do not "ask" users to interact in the traditional way (face to face) nor to create a traditional resume (paper-and-pencil). On the contrary, users interact via digital media (chat, email, video calls, etc.) and show their skills, knowledge, experiences, and pictures in a more dynamic way (McFarland & Ployhart, 2015; Zide, Elman & Shahani-Denning, 2014). Among SNWs, LinkedIn and Facebook are most commonly used as recruitment tools. The vast majority of HR professionals who participated in a SHRM survey reported that they use LinkedIn to reach passive prospective employees, as well as Facebook (58 percent) and Twitter (42 percent) (Karl & Peluchette, 2013). In particular, LinkedIn and Facebook are likely to be used by employers in order to gather additional information about applicants, decide to call them for an interview (Caers & Castelyns, 2011), or make organization fit infer-ences (Roulin & Bangerter, 2013). The emergence of SNWs has altered the traditional relationship between employers and prospective employees. Candidates used to reach prospective employers expressing their interest through job ads. Nowadays, recruiters are likely to use SNWs reaching even those who are not actively looking for work (passive candidates). LinkedIn especially, is more effective and widely used in attracting passive candidates, a process often called as "poaching" (Nikolaou, 2014). Moreover, both candidates and employers could closely monitor the information presented to each other in the past (McFarland & Ployhart, 2015). However, SNWs and their public nature give access to much more information about the company (e.g., working conditions, relationships, culture) and applicants (e.g., interests, interpersonal interactions), which employers and candidates respectively may have little control over. Finally, the use of SNWs can make the recruitment efforts wider, faster, and easier. Employers might advertise their vacancies via SNWs spreading the word through digital word of mouth, expanding their means of attracting and reaching candidates (McFarland & Ployhart, 2015). As a result, they can easily and quickly attract vast quantities of candidates, including qualified passive candidates. They can also make background checks on these candidates. In addition, candidates might search for a job more broadly using SNWs in addition to traditional channels, such as the press, corporate websites, and career fairs (Nikolaou, 2014). Overall, the SNWs might have not replaced the traditional resume entirely yet but they do complement the traditional recruiting methods to help recruiters make better and more informed decisions (Zide et al., 2014).

Technological characteristics, such as interactivity, might improve the way messages are transferred (e.g., Cable & Yu, 2006; Walker et al., 2009), enhancing the effectiveness of internet recruitment. Organizations employ technological components, such as animations, videos, blogs, and virtual reality into the recruitment process making it more vivid, interactive, and personal (Badger, Kaminsky & Behrend, 2014; Stone et al., 2015). For example, some organizations have begun to use virtual environments to conduct job fairs. A *virtual career fair* is an online meeting place where potential candidates can meet and find information about prospective employers via chat rooms, webinars, interactive interview games, etc. (Leece, 2005). In other words, attendants can virtually experience the life in an organization as well as having interactive conversations with the organization's staff members. A technological platform, which was quite extensively used until recently to hold a virtual job fair is Second Life, a computer-based simulated virtual environment that permits people from all over the world to virtually meet and interact in "real" time experiencing a visit to a parallel world full of opportunities (Zelenskaya & Singh, 2011). Organizations such as GM, IBM, eBay, T-Mobile, and the US Army have used Second Life, giving the opportunity to users to visit simulated worlds, managing to reach more and diverse people across the globe, reduce recruiting costs, as well as build their image (Kaplan & Haenlein, 2009; Zelenskaya & Singh, 2011). Similarly, in virtual job fairs, Second Life permits employers to effectively reach a new pool of prospective employees in a more personal and professional way (Zelenskaya & Singh, 2011), while participants indicated that a virtual career fair is useful and can complement university career services (Leece, 2005). However, use of Second Life has been dramatically reduced in recent years, probably because of the emergence of new tools, such as the SNWs. Research supports that media influence message comprehension on the part of applicants while face-to-face communication and audiovisual materials enable them to learn more about the organization and have a more accurate view than web sites and email (Allen, Scotter, & Otondo, 2004; Cable & Yu, 2006). Recruiters have begun to consider the use of interactive media, such as videos and virtual career fairs, in the recruitment process in order to increase recruitment effectiveness.

Advances in technology have also paved the way for *gamification* and, in particular, *internet based gamified applications* in the recruitment process. Gamification is defined as the use of game elements in non-game contexts to evoke game-like experiences and behaviors (Chow & Chapman, 2013; Hamari, Koivisto & Sarsa, 2014). Serious games and gamified applications may be employed to inform potential applicants about the vacancies into an organization and attract a wide audience of prospective employees and are often used to enhance the process of employee recruitment (Armstrong, Landers, & Collmus, 2016). Although no empirical research has established the validity and effectiveness of gamifying the recruitment process, organizations have started to gamify elements of the recruitment process reporting positive results (Chow & Chapman, 2013). For example, employers hope to attract new applicants by gamifying the employee referral system and specifically, by awarding points to employees using an application to recruit new candidates (Armstrong et al., 2016). In addition, gamified applications might help candidates evaluate their knowledge about the work while getting a realistic preview of a working day in the recruiting organization (Laumer et al., 2012). For example, organizations might create gamified competitions where candidates interact and compete with each other on simulated working settings, having thus a realistic job preview of the work and skills required (Armstrong et al., 2016). Moreover, the use of game-like elements and interaction in the recruitment process might enhance fun, playfulness, engagement, and motivation (Laumer et al., 2012), especially for younger applicants who have grown up using computers and playing video games. Along these lines, gamifying the recruitment processes might reach, engage, and motivate a wider range of prospective employees. Organizations might use game-like applications to diffuse information about job openings to a large pool of candidates, since the fun aspect of serious games "enables their fluidity and propels them across social media outlets, such as Facebook, LinkedIn, Twitter, etc." (Chow & Chapman, 2013, p. 93). Summing up, gamified applications might be used in the recruitment process in order to increase enjoyment among job seekers while giving information about available positions/work and helping them to decide whether to make an application or not (Laumer et al., 2012).

Overall, findings about e-recruitment effectiveness are mixed. On the one hand, internet recruitment might generate a larger pool of candidates (Chapman et al., 2003; Galanaki, 2002), with higher levels of motivation and persistence (McManus & Ferguson, 2003) than traditional recruitment processes. On the other hand, studies did not find that e-recruiting generates a higher quality pool of applicants but ill-suited candidates as well (Chapman et al., 2003; Galanaki, 2002; McManus & Ferguson, 2003). Moreover, research has found that using websites, organizations might attract more candidates, but the administrative and transaction costs of handling the augmented pool of applicants are in fact increased (Stone, Lukaszewski & Isenhour, 2005). Furthermore, e-recruitment efforts might not enable organizations reach diverse job applicants, since they are accessible only to people with computing skills and internet access, although nowadays the percentage of people with internet access has dramatically increased. As a result, e-recruiting might not be efficient in some ethnic minorities but in young and technology savvy candidates (Stone et al., 2015). However, the two-way communication online technologies that enhance interaction might be more effective in generating a higher quality and diverse workforce as they enable applicants to interact with organizational members making questions and gathering information, instead of one-way processes that are likely to be quite impersonal, passive and distant (Schneider, Goffin, & Daljeet, 2015). To sum up, internet technologies might be more effective in employee recruitment if organizations treat potential applicants as individuals who need employment information and not candidates that have to be filtered (Cober, Brown, & Levy, 2004).

5.1.5 Technology in Employee Selection

As soon as the recruitment efforts have been completed and the applicant pool has been generated, the selection process begins. The selection process consists of methods used to assess whether the knowledge, skills, abilities, and other characteristics (KSAOs) of applicants meet the requirements for effective performance in a position. Changes in business and technology have affected these methods too. Instead of having candidates complete paper-and-pencil application forms and tests or go through face-to-face interviews, recruiters employ various forms of technology, such as digital interviews, games, and on-line testing, to help them decide who the best candidate is. The use of technology to perform job analysis, collect candidates' data, and assess their KSAOs in order to make hiring decisions is called *e-selection* (Stone et al., 2015). Many large organizations use modern technology for selection purposes as well as in assessment centers, including phone or virtual interactions, online simulations or computers on site (e.g., Stone et al., 2015). Also, many small companies provide technologically based testing and assessment services (Tippins, 2015). The automation of selection processes, such as scheduling, storing candidates' information, screening applications, interviewing and recording, scoring, generating reports and feedback, and assessing selection process effectiveness, make e-selection more time effective and cost effective than traditional selection methods (Stone & Dulebohn, 2013; Tippins, 2015). Moreover, the use of technology in selection makes the assessment of some KSAOs easier, such as the time elapsed to respond to a question or detect a stimulus, while it ensures accurate content delivery and response recording via audiovisual material (Tippins, 2015). Finally, web screening and background check may differ from traditional filtering, since the internet provides more information that is likely to be less censored too (Davison, Maraist, & Bing, 2011). On the other hand, the focus on saving money and time might distract organizations from the primary purpose of selection, that is, choosing among the best applicants, while the use of technology might enhance adverse impact, cheating, and privacy intrusion (e.g., Harris, Hoye, & Lievens, 2003; Kehoe, Dickter, Russell, & Sacco, 2005).

Some examples of how technology is currently used in the selection process are on-line tests, digital interviews, serious games, and SNWs. *On-line testing, or internet-based testing and assessment* refers to "the use of the Internet or intranet (an organization's private network) for administering tests and inventories in the context of assessment and selection" (Lievens & Harris, 2003, p. 144). On-line tests give employers the opportunity to use less resources (e.g., facilities, proctors), and to assess many candidates in a short period of time since candidates can be in any location with access to the internet and can take the test at any convenient time (Makransky & Glas, 2011). Another advantage of on-line testing is the presentation of items in different formats using audio and video material and, as a result, the measurement of different aspects of candidates' behavior (Lievens & Harris, 2003). Last but not least, savings in money and time might occur due to the ease of administration. In particular, both questions and answers are in electronic form making thus paper copies unnecessary, content is easily altered and mistakes checked, while scores on tests and feedback are instantly generated (Lievens & Harris, 2003). Examples of internet testing include web-based cognitive ability tests (Baron & Austin, 2000), webcam tests such as multimedia or video-based situational judgment tests (Richman-Hirsch, Olson-Buchanan, & Drasgow, 2000) and virtual reality tests (Aguinas, Henle, & Beaty Jr, 2001). Findings of research about the measurement equivalence between web-based and paper-and-pencil cognitive ability tests are mixed (e.g., Ployhart et al., 2003; Potosky & Bobko, 2004). However, internet tests, and specifically those without supervision (unproc-tored), are widely used from organizations and recruitment/headhunting companies to evaluate candidates (Tippins et al., 2006). A major concern about unproctored tests is the likelihood of cheating. To ensure that the individual who took the test is the candidate, organizations might verify the scores by repeating the test under supervision at a later stage (Ployhart et al., 2017; Stone et al., 2013), or use encryption technology and webcams (Lievens & Harris, 2003). Many organiza-tions employ webcam tests in employee selection to make tests more realistic by presenting stimuli and collecting responses using audio or video. Research, although scarce, provides support of using webcam tests to predict work and academic performance beyond traditional selection methods, such as cognitive ability tests (Oostrom, Born, & van der Molen, 2013). Overall, on-line testing might have several benefits in terms of administration, scoring, and recording, as well as accuracy if test-taking settings are somehow supervised.

Another application of technology is *digital interviewing*. In order to reduce face-to-face interview costs (e.g., supervisors, accommodation, and travel costs), organizations have begun conducting interviews using videoconferencing. Instead of asking candidates to join a face-to-face interview on site, organizations can create an online live interview environment using technological applications, such as Skype. Employers may interact live with candidates via audio and video and conduct the interview, as in traditional settings, albeit remotely. However, it is likely to conduct an interview in a non-live environment too. Web-based interview platforms (e.g., HireVue) enable organizations to conduct an interview "on demand" (Guchait et al., 2014). In particular, the interview is conducted in a non-live environment without the "live" presence of an interviewer. Interview questions are recorded and presented to candidates via video and audio material. The candidates respond to interview questions via webcam while their answers are recorded. Video interviews are likely to be used in the initial steps of the selection process in order to assess minimum job requirements and reduce the applicant pool. Managers might interview several applicants at the same time without being present, while multiple assessors might view the interview afterwards in order to collectively reach an agreement (Guchait et al., 2014). Many companies specializing in big data analytics in selection attempt to measure many indicators of the applicant during the digital interviews, such as the number of times they blinked, seconds between responses, body temperature changes and word speed, and essentially put all of that information into a big regression equation and see what it predicts. Although this work is not reflected in the published empirical research yet, it is a potentially fruitful and promising line of future research. On the other hand, candidates have the opportunity to apply to international job positions, thus saving money and time (Guchait et al., 2014). Moreover, the type of technology used (e.g., video or telephone) might influence the effectiveness of the interviewing process. Telephone interviews are likely to result in higher ratings about candidates' ability and likeability than traditional interviews, while video interviews are not (Straus, Miles, & Levesque, 2001). Overall, video interviews have several advantages in applicants' screening process but a candidate's familiarity with webcams and computing access is necessary.

Another example of how technology is used in the selection process is *serious games*. Serious games might be used in employee selection assessing the KSAOs that candidates should have in order to be hired. The use of game elements in the selection process might reduce faking, since desirable behaviors may be less obvious while playing a game, and as a result, improve the quality of information about applicants and prediction of job performance (Armstrong et al., 2016). There are different types of game-based assessments that were developed for practice and are currently in use (e.g., Arctic Shores, cut-e, Owiwi). Using mobile or computing devices, candidates are exposed to a gamified environment or virtual world with questions that candidates have to answer. Virtual worlds may be similar to real work settings and avatars may represent employees. The purpose of using virtual worlds and simulated avatars is to elicit job relevant behaviors in situations similar to those taking place in a working environment (Laumer et al., 2012). Moreover, the use of game elements in the selection process might promote fun, transparency, challenge, and interaction. Games enable players to interact and compete with each other (Tippins, 2015). However, hardly any research has established the effectiveness of serious games in employee selection. Preliminary findings provide support that game elements can be applied to situational judgment tests to effectively assess candidates' soft skills, eliciting positive applicant reactions (Georgiou, Nikolaou, & Gouras, 2017). However, more research is needed to establish the validity of game-based assessments above and beyond what traditional selection methods evaluate.

Social Networking Websites (SNWs) can also be used in the selection process helping recruiters making inferences about candidates' KSAOs. The prevalence of SNWs and specifically, the large number of people with SNW profiles and the vast amount of information they share, led organizations to use social media in employee selection screening job applicants. Recruiters are likely to evaluate candidates' personality characteristics, such as the Five-Factor Model of Personality based on the information included on applicants' SNWs (Gueutal,

Kluemper & Rosen, 2009). Although more reliable inferences about candidates' qualifications may be drawn using SNWs due to anonymity and consequently, more sincere posts, recruiters should be careful to base their selection decisions only on job-related information (McFarland & Ployhart, 2015). It is likely that employers hire or reject a candidate if the information included on the SNWs is perceived as positive or negative (Madera, 2012). Along these lines, SNWs, such as Facebook, which do not provide job-related information, have been described as inappropriate for employee selection in contrast to LinkedIn (Roth et al., 2016). Stoughton, Thompson, and Meade (2015) explored the use of SNWs in employee selection and more specifically in relation to applicant reactions. In their first study, they explored whether perceptions of privacy influence procedural justice and selection system perceptions. In addition, they tested whether employers' use of SNWs for screening purposes affects applicants' perceptions of organizational attractiveness in a realistic hiring scenario. Finally, they explored the moderating influence of agreeableness on applicant reactions to SNW screening. Participants in this study were undergraduate psychology students, and the researchers only focused on Facebook and not on other work-oriented SNWs, such as LinkedIn. The results demonstrated that pre-employment SNW screening increases applicants' perceptions of invasion of privacy, decreases perceptions of organizational justice, and lowers organizational attraction. Perceptions of privacy partially mediated the relationship between screening and justice perceptions. Also, justice perceptions partially mediated the relationship between perceptions of invasion of privacy and organizational attraction. Finally, agreeableness moderated the effect of SNW screening on procedural justice perceptions with participants low in agreeableness demonstrating very negative reactions when informed that their SNW profiles had been screened. In their second study, Stoughton et al. (2015) used a non-student (but also non-applicant) sample to explore further their previous hypotheses on a simulated selection scenario. They explored the impact invasion of privacy might have on litigation intentions and also the role of the hiring decision on the relationship between SNW screening and procedural justice. Their results showed that applicants' perceptions of organizational justice lowered organizational attraction and increased litigation intentions. Also, the hiring decision of the organization had no effect on applicant perceptions of procedural justice. This was an interesting finding demonstrating that SNW screening practices affect privacy outcomes (e.g., organizational attractiveness, intentions to litigate) irrespective of the hiring decision.

Two more studies (Black et al., 2012; Sanchez et al., 2012) have explored the interaction between SNWs and applicant reactions. Black et al. (2012) presented a conceptual model, extending earlier research on privacy models, and considering a number of factors that may affect applicant reactions to the use of SNWs. They propose a number of research questions for researchers to explore in the future. In their model, they suggested that informational, procedural, social, cultural, and individual factors may influence applicants' beliefs and attitudes and subsequently lead to behavioral intentions, such as job acceptance and litigation. Sanchez et al. (2012) in an empirical/experimental study with undergraduate students, explored the impact of checking applicants' SNW profiles in a simulated selection process. Controlling for age, gender, and time spent on SNWs, they found no differences from SNW screening on the following applicant reaction measures: perceptions of SNW checks, organizational attractiveness, job pursuit intentions, procedural justice, and informational justice. SNW screening resulted in lower organizational attraction and decreased job pursuit intentions over those not subjected to social networking presence checks, compared to the other selection methods (personality test, skills inventory).

In summary, SNWs have some potential, with relatively low costs for the organization (Jacobs, 2009). They may produce additional information in order to filter candidates (Madera, 2012), thus increasing the effectiveness of selection processes. However, concerns over legality, discrimination, privacy intrusion, and predictive validity remain (Ryan & Ployhart, 2014), calling for further research in this field (Roth et al., 2016).

Another application of technology is *Interactive Voice Response* (IVR) systems. Organizations have begun using IVR systems in employee selection, enabling them to manage application blanks and inventories via audio devices or telephones, in order to gather candidates' data for the purpose of initial screening (Stone & Dulebohn, 2013). These systems might contribute to gathering demographic data that governments need but these data/questions may be irrelevant to job positions and not in accordance with legal standards (Stone & Dulebohn, 2013). It is a similar case with the use of big data in employee selection. On the one hand, the use of big data in employee selection enables organizations to base their hiring decisions on a large volume of information about candidates (e.g., information from social media). On the other hand, the use of these nontraditional, personal and job irrelevant predictors might face legal issues (Ployhart et al., 2017).

Overall there are several advantages to employing technology in the selection process. Web-based technologies might make the employee selection procedures faster, easier, and more vivid and fun, while expanding the number of applicants by eliminating barriers of distance, cost, and time. However, technology applications raise important worries about legal issues, adverse impact, and cheating that need to be addressed.

5.2 Future Research in Technology and Applicant Reactions

Ryan and Ployhart (2014), in the most recent review of recruitment and selection research published in the *Annual Review of Psychology*, have discussed the role of applicant reactions in staffing research, especially in relation to negative word of mouth, consumer behavior, and organizational image/reputation. This is especially the case for new selection approaches, not widely employed yet and therefore still relatively unfamiliar to job seekers, such as digital interviewing, serious games, and social media.

Since the early 2000s, when one of the first papers on internet recruitment and selection appeared in the *International Journal of Selection and Assessment*

(Bartram, 2000), many things have changed in the field bringing a dramatic impact on both research and practice in staffing. Many of the issues raised then – such as security, confidentiality, authentication, control of assessment conditions, equality of access – remain important, but many others have also surfaced, most of them as a result of the advent and increased use of Web 2.0 technologies, such as blogging, micro-blogging (e.g., Twitter) and more recently of SNWs (e.g., Facebook, LinkedIn). The main characteristic of these technological developments, as applied to recruitment, selection, and applicant reactions, is the high degree of interaction allowed between parties, namely, companies, interviewers, job applicants themselves, and/or potential intermediaries, such as third-party vendors that are strongly involved in online assessment these days.

One of the theoretical approaches we could use in order to explore the impact of the internet on applicant reactions is the *deontic outrage,* which, as mentioned earlier, deals with the impact of mistreatment to third parties, not the applicants themselves. This approach might be very useful today, in the era of SNWs, when the selection process is not an isolated and "behind closed doors" process, as it used to be in the past. More than 41 million people per month now use Glassdoor, a website providing for free "company reviews, CEO approval ratings, salary reports, interview reviews and questions, office photos and more" (Glassdoor. com, 2017). Word of mouth can have a powerful impact on organizational attraction, as demonstrated by a number of studies (e.g., Van Hoye, 2014), but much less is known about the individual characteristics of people most likely to spread and receive word of mouth, what organizations can do to stimulate word of mouth, what mechanisms explain the effects of word of mouth, and the conditions under which word of mouth is less or more influential (Van Hoye, 2014). Also, despite its independent nature, only a few studies have considered negative word of mouth (Van Hoye, 2014). In particular, the latter is associated with applicant reactions and could also be part of the deontic outrage approach. Applicants sharing their negative experiences with an employer in SNWs and other websites, such as glassdoor.com, are quite likely to generate a negative word of mouth and create a respective image of potential employers. Thus, this information might affect candidates' job search activities and/or create negative word of mouth between potential job seekers, even without immediate experience of the organization's recruitment and selection process. Taking this even further, it is also possible that such negative word of mouth might ultimately influence the valuation of a company, thus affecting its bottom line.

Future research on this area could explore the interplay between candidates' preconceptions of an employer, as influenced by other applicants' reactions/perceptions, and the impact those have on current applicants' attitudinal, emotional, and behavioral intentions. For instance, are candidates discouraged by information they collect from the internet or social media to apply for positions in companies that do not treat applicants/employees well? Or where the working conditions or salaries are poorly evaluated from current or past employees? How is this information assessed and evaluated by candidates when they make a decision to apply or when they are invited to participate in an interview?

Obviously, another major area of research is how applicants perceive the new recruitment and selection methods, in comparison to the existing methods. We know, for example, that the face-to-face interview has traditionally been the most positively perceived selection method. Is this the case for equivalent methods, such as videoconferencing (e.g., Skype) or digital interviewing? Sears et al. (2013) examined the influence of videoconferencing (VC) technology on applicant reactions and interviewer judgments in the employment interview using media richness and procedural justice theories in a laboratory study. According to media richness theory, VC interviews lack in communication resulting in negative applicants' reactions, especially across the main procedural justice dimensions. They demonstrated that applicants perceived VC interviews as less job-related than personal interviews and also as offering less of a chance to perform. Applicants also rated interviews less favorably in VC interviews compared to face-to-face interviews. Finally, applicants in VC interviews received lower ratings of affect (likeability) and lower interview scores, and were less likely to be recommended for the position. Similar questions are raised in the comparison between traditional paper-and-pencil psychometric testing and on-line (proctored or unproctored) testing. Only limited research has explored these issues. Moreover, no research has explored how applicants perceive new methods, such as serious games and gamification (with the exception of Nikolaou & Georgiou, 2017),

More research is also needed in the field of big data and SNWs. Everyone seems to be talking about big data nowadays, but there is significant lack of research on it in the recruitment and selection context. However, as mentioned earlier, there are many staffing professionals and specialized companies already working in this space, especially in digital interviewing and games-based assessment. As mentioned by Roth et al. (2016), the use of SNWs demonstrates a relatively rare moment in staffing research, where a new and un-researched assessment method arrives on the scene raising the need for new research on this topic. Many of the existing studies focus on privacy issues regarding the use of SNWs in recruitment and selection. It is clear, however, that more studies are needed on this issue, since privacy concerns are strongly connected with applicants' reactions. Anderson's (2011) perceived job discrimination model could be used here as a guide. For example, how applicants perceive discrimination via SNWs and they make a decision to turn against the employer in a discriminatory case initiation?

As evidenced by the Stoughton et al. (2015) study, the use of undergraduate students, instead of actual job applicants, is a common theme in applicant reactions research. In the future, researchers should seek to explore the moderating effect of the type of SNW, for example Facebook as opposed to LinkedIn. These two SNWs have different identities and characteristics, with the former used mainly for personal purposes and the latter used almost exclusively as a professional SNW. Therefore, we would expect them to be received differently by job applicants, who will also react differently when future employers use those as a screening tool, even without their previous permission. Also, future research needs to explore the impact of applicants' impression management on creating and maintaining

SNWs. Since more companies use SNWs for screening purposes, active job seekers are now more aware of these tactics; therefore, it is quite likely that they will actively seek to improve or even amend their SNWs profiles accordingly in order to increase the chance of attracting recruiters' interest.

Another area of future research is the existence of cross-cultural differences in the use of SNWs amongst employers and job seekers. Employers use SNWs as a recruiting tool and also for screening job applicants' information, and job seekers use SNWs as another way of looking for a job and contacting potential employers. Nikolaou (2014) conducted two studies in Greece, exploring the use of SNWs among employees-job seekers and recruiters/human resource (HR) professionals in one of the very few studies conducted in a non-English country. His results demonstrated that job boards (e.g., CareerBuilder.com or Monster.com) are perceived as more effective job searching tools, among active job seekers. However, it was interesting to note that the association between SNWs usage and effectiveness is stronger for "passive" candidates, demonstrating the important role of SNWs for "poaching," that is, the process of attracting "passive" candidates, a major advantage of the use of SNWs for HR professionals. Roulin (2014) also proposed that the use of SNWs as a screening tool by employers may vary from one country to another, potentially leading to different applicant reactions. Also, in many countries (e.g., Germany) the use of personal SNWs in recruitment and selection is prohibited by law. Future studies should explore the evolution of employers' strategies and applicant reactions to the use of SNWs across different countries. More studies should also explore the intersection of SNWs with other established job search methods, such as job boards and the traditional personal networking and how the use of SNWs in employee screening interacts with the existing and well-established recruitment and selection methods.

Selection researchers should come closer to technology researchers in identifying factors influencing applicant reactions and intentions toward new technology in selection methods. For example, the Technology Acceptance Model (TAM) (Davis, 1989) can be a useful theory in this area. TAM explores how perceived usefulness and perceived ease of use influences an individual's behavioral intention to use a system or a piece of technology. Kashi and Zheng (2013), in one of the few applicant reactions study to explore this issue, examined applicant reactions to online recruitment in Iran. Their results demonstrated that perceived usefulness influences applicants' behavioral intentions to apply for a job online (based on TAM), and that impression of the organizational website appeared to create interest in the organization, which in turn encouraged applicants to apply for jobs.

Summing up, the future of applicant reactions research should take into account the changing business context and how this is affected by technology. How will new and emerging recruitment and selection technologies affect candidates' perceptions? How will the legal context and the use (or abuse) of personal information influence staffing practices?

5.3 Practical Implications

The impact of applicant reactions on candidates' attitudinal, emotional, and behavioral intentions and their association with organizational attractiveness and, potentially, other important personal and organizational outcomes, demonstrate their importance for organizations and HR departments. HR professionals need to take the impact of applicant and fairness reactions in the selection process more seriously into consideration. This is especially the case today due to the increased use of technology in hiring and staffing decisions.

The recruitment and selection process is no longer an isolated and "behind closed doors" process. Applicants today are very often looking for more than just the mailing address of potential employers. They have, for example, the means to search for inside information about a company, to connect with recruiters and interviewers, to read employees' and candidates' experiences and share their own experiences with potential past, current, or potential employers. The impact these actions can have on a company's recruitment and organizational image can often be dramatic. Moreover, companies also need to adapt their recruitment and attraction policies in order to attract high-caliber candidates, who might only use technological platforms such as SNWs in order to look for job opportunities. These candidates are very often the ones who can have a major impact into small communities (e.g., colleges and student clubs) and are often keen to share their experiences with others through SNWs. This is especially the case in specific sectors of the economy, such as the technology sector or in start-up companies, where people are accustomed to the extensive use of technological platforms, such as the SNWs. Therefore, HR professionals should pay increased attention on how they deal with applicants in these sectors and the impact of their actions among job seekers.

Another important practical implication is associated with the actions companies themselves should take in order to manage applicant reactions. Following Van Hoye's (2014) perspective, organizations could take the role of observer, moderator, mediator, or participant in managing applicant reactions. As an observer, they should be aware of what is being said about them, by whom, to whom, and through which media, both for themselves and for competitors. As a moderator, companies could, for example, actively disseminate information extracted from employee or applicant surveys on the effective use of recruitment/selection tools. As a mediator, they should more actively manage and/or even take control of applicant reactions, if possible. For example, most companies are now actively managing their Twitter and Facebook accounts, dealing with both customers' and applicants' issues and/or complaints, a very effective tool, since applicant reactions are mostly subjective in nature. Finally, as a participant, Van Hoye (2014) proposes that recruiters could "create" their own word of mouth by participating actively in social interactions with applicants and potential applicants. Similarly, with regard to applicant reactions, recruiters should explain the rationale behind the selection methods employed and the selection decision made by providing feedback and explanations for the selection process, especially to rejected applicants.

5.4 Conclusion

The area of recruitment and selection has now reached an increased level of maturity (Ryan & Ployhart, 2014). Similarly, applicant reactions research has now progressed well throughout the years, but there are still many things to be done in the future. The focus of our chapter has been to review the most recent research and emphasize a number of issues we consider important in future applicant reactions research in relation to technology and their interplay and impact on applicant reactions, both from a research and a practical perspective.

References

Aguinis, H., Henle, C. A., & Beaty Jr, J. C. (2001). Virtual reality technology: A new tool for personnel selection. *International Journal of Selection and Assessment, 9*(1–2), 70–83.

Allen, D. G., Scotter, J. R., & Otondo, R. F. (2004). Recruitment communication media: Impact on prehire outcomes. *Personnel Psychology, 57*(1), 143–171.

Anderson, N. (2011). Perceived Job Discrimination: Toward a model of applicant propensity to case initiation in selection. *International Journal of Selection and Assessment, 19*(3), 229–244.

Anderson, N., Ahmed, S., & Costa, A. C. (2012). Applicant Reactions in Saudi Arabia: Organizational attractiveness and core-self evaluation. *International Journal of Selection and Assessment, 20*(2), 197–208.

Anderson, N., Salgado, J. F., & Hülsheger, U. R. (2010). Applicant Reactions in Selection: Comprehensive meta-analysis into reaction generalization versus situational specificity. *International Journal of Selection and Assessment, 18*(3), 291–304.

Armstrong, M. B., Landers, R. N., & Collmus, A. B. (2016). Gamifying recruitment, selection, training, and performance management: Game-thinking in human resource management. In H. Gangadharbatla & D. Z. Davis (Eds.), *Emerging research and trends in gamification* (pp. 140–165). Hershey, PA: IGI Global.

Arvey, R. D., Strickland, W., Drauden, G., & Martin, C. (1990). Motivational components of test taking. *Personnel Psychology, 43*(4), 695–716.

Badger, J., Kaminsky, S., & Behrend, T. (2014). Media richness and information acquisition in internet recruitment. *Journal of Managerial Psychology, 29*(7), 866–883.

Baron, H., & Austin, J. (2000). Measuring ability via the internet: Opportunities and issues. Paper presented at the Annual Conference of the Society for Industrial and Organizational Psychology, New Orleans, LA.

Bartram, D. (2000). Internet recruitment and selection: Kissing frogs to find princes. *International Journal of Selection and Assessment, 8*(4), 261–274.

Bauer, T., Truxillo, D., Sanchez, R., Craig, J., Ferrara, P., & Campion, M. (2001). Applicant reactions to selection: Development of the selection procedural justice scale (SPJS). *Personnel Psychology, 54*(2), 387–419.

Bauer, T. N., Truxillo, D. M., Tucker, J. S., Weathers, V., Bertolino, M., Erdogan, B., & Campion, M. A. (2006). Selection in the Information Age: The impact of privacy concerns and computer experience on applicant reactions. *Journal of Management, 32*(5), 601–621.

Black, S. L., Johnson, A. F., Takach, S. E., & Stone, D. L. (August 2012). Factors affecting applicants' reactions to the collection of data in social network websites. Presented at the Academy of Management Annual Conference, Philadelphia, PA.

Cable, D. M. & Yu, K. Y. T. (2006). Managing job seekers' organizational image beliefs: The role of media richness and media credibility. *Journal of Applied Psychology, 91*(4), 828.

Caers, R. & Castelyns, V. (2011). LinkedIn and Facebook in Belgium: The influences and biases of social network sites in recruitment and selection procedures. *Social Science Computer Review, 29*(4), 437–448.

Cappelli, P. (2001). Making the most of online recruitment. *Harvard Business Review, 79,* 139–146.

Cardy, R. & Miller, J. (2005). *eHR and performance management: A consideration of positive potential and the dark side.* In H. Gueutal, D. L. Stone & E. Salas, The brave new world of eHR: Human resources management in the digital age (pp. 138–165), Chichester: Wiley.

Cascio, W. F. & Montealegre, R. (2016). How technology is changing work and organizations. *Annual Review of Organizational Psychology and Organizational Behavior, 3,* 349–375.

Chapman, D. S., Uggerslev, K. L., & Webster, J. (2003). Applicant reactions to face-to-face and technology-mediated interviews: A field investigation. *Journal of Applied Psychology, 88*(5), 944.

Chow, S. & Chapman, D. (2013). Gamifying the employee recruitment process. Paper presented at the Proceedings of the First International Conference on Gameful Design, Research, and Applications.

Cober, R. & Brown, D. (2006). Direct employers association recruiting trends survey. Booz Allen Hamilton, Washington, DC.

Cober, R. T., Brown, D. J., & Levy, P. E. (2004). Form, content, and function: An evaluative methodology for corporate employment web sites. *Human Resource Management, 43*(2–3), 201–218.

Davis, F. (1989). Perceived usefulness, perceived ease of use, and user acceptance of information technology. *MIS Quarterly,* 13(3), 319–340.

Davison, H. K., Maraist, C., & Bing, M. N. (2011). Friend or foe? The promise and pitfalls of using social networking sites for HR decisions. *Journal of Business and Psychology, 26*(2), 153–159.

Derks, D. & Bakker, A. (2013). *The psychology of digital media at work.* London: Routledge.

Dulebohn, J. H. & Marler, J. H. (2005). e-Compensation: The potential to transform practice. In H. Gueutal, D. L. Stone, & E. Salas, *The brave new world of eHR: Human resources management in the digital age* (pp. 166–189), Chichester: Wiley.

Ford, D. K., Truxillo, D. M., & Bauer, T. N. (2009). Rejected but still there: Shifting the focus in applicant reactions to the promotional context. *International Journal of Selection and Assessment, 17*(4), 402–416.

García-Izquierdo, A. L., Moscoso, S., & Ramos-Villagrasa, P. J. (2012). Reactions to the fairness of promotion methods: Procedural justice and job satisfaction. *International Journal of Selection and Assessment, 20*(4), 394–403.

Galanaki, E. (2002). The decision to recruit online: A descriptive study. *Career Development International, 7*(4), 243–251.

Georgiou, K., Nikolaou, I., & Gouras, A. (2017). Serious gaming in employee selection process. In I. Nikolaou (2017): Alliance for Organizational Psychology Invited Symposium-The Impact of Technology on Recruitment and Selection: An International Perspective. 32nd Annual Conference of the Society for Industrial and Organizational Psychology, Orlando, USA.

Gherson, D. & Jackson, A. (2001). Web-based compensation planning. In A. J. Walker (Ed.), *Web-based human resources* (pp. 83–95). New York, NY: McGr.aw-Hill

Gilliland, S. W. (1993). The perceived fairness of selection systems: An organizational justice perspective. *Academy of Management Review, 18*(4), 694.

Gilliland, S. W. (1994). Effects of procedural and distributive justice on reactions to a selection system. *Journal of Applied Psychology, 79*, 691–701.

Gilliland, S. W., & Steiner, D. D. (2012). Applicant Reactions to Testing and Selection. In N. Schmitt (Ed.), *The Oxford Handbook of Personnel Assessment and Selection* (pp. 629–666). Oxford: Oxford University Press.

Glassdoor (2017). Site Stats. Retrieved from www.glassdoor.com/press/facts/.

Guchait, P., Ruetzler, T., Taylor, J., & Toldi, N. (2014). Video interviewing: A potential selection tool for hospitality managers: A study to understand applicant perspective. *International Journal of Hospitality Management, 36*, 90–100.

Gueutal, H. G., Kluemper, D. H., & Rosen, P. A. (2009). Future employment selection methods: Evaluating social networking web sites. *Journal of Managerial Psychology, 24*(6), 567–580.

Hamari, J., Koivisto, J., & Sarsa, H. (2014). Does gamification work? A literature review of empirical studies on gamification. Paper presented at the System Sciences (HICSS), 2014 47th Hawaii International Conference.

Harris, M. & Fink, L. (1987). A field study of applicant reactions to employment opportunities: Does the recruiter make a difference? *Personnel Psychology, 40*(4), 765–784.

Harris, M. M., Hoye, G. V., & Lievens, F. (2003). Privacy and attitudes towards internet-based selection systems: A cross-cultural comparison. *International Journal of Selection and Assessment, 11*(2–3), 230–236.

Hausknecht, J. P. (2013). Applicant Reactions. In K. Y. T. Yu & D. M. Cable (Eds.), *The Oxford Handbook of Recruitment* (pp. 35–46). Oxford: Oxford University Press.

Hausknecht, J. P., Day, D. V., & Thomas, S. C. (2004). Applicant reactions to selection procedures: An updated model and meta-analysis. *Personnel Psychology, 57*(3), 639–683.

Herriot, P. (1989). Selection as a social process. In M. Smith & I. T. Robertson (Eds.), *Advances in selection and assessment* (pp. 171–187). Chichester: Wiley.

Herriot, P. (2004). Social Identities and Applicant Reactions. *International Journal of Selection and Assessment, 12*(1–2), 75–83.

Hoang, T. G., Truxillo, D. M., Erdogan, B., & Bauer, T. N. (2012). Cross-cultural examination of applicant reactions to selection methods: United States and Vietnam. *International Journal of Selection and Assessment, 20*(2), 209–219.

Honkaniemi, L., Feldt, T., Metsapelto, R. L., & Tolvanen, A. (2013). Personality types and applicant reactions in real-life selection. *International Journal of Selection and Assessment, 21*(1), 32–45.

Jackson, S. & Schuler, R. (2003). *Managing human resources through strategic partnerships* (8th edn.). Mason, OH: Thompson South-Western.

Jacobs, D. (2009). Surviving the social explosion. *Landscape Management, 48*(12), 10–13.

Jones, J. W., Brasher, E. E., & Huff, J. W. (2002). Innovations in integrity-based personnel selection: Building a technology-friendly assessment. *International Journal of Selection and Assessment, 10*(1–2), 87–97.

Kaplan, A. M. & Haenlein, M. (2009). The fairyland of Second Life: Virtual social worlds and how to use them. *Business Horizons, 52*(6), 563–572.

Karl, K. & Peluchette, J. (2013). Possibilities and pitfalls of using online social networking in human resources management. *Psychology for Business Success, 4*, 119–138.

Kashi, K. & Zheng, C. (2013). Extending technology acceptance model to the e-recruitment context in Iran. *International Journal of Selection and Assessment, 21*(1), 121–129.

Kehoe, J. F., Dickter, D. N., Russell, D. P., & Sacco, J. M. (2005). E-selection. In H. G. Gueutal & D. L. Stone (Eds.), *The brave new world of eHR: Human resources management in the digital age* (pp. 54–103). San Francisco, CA: Jossey-Bass.

Klotz, A. C., da Motta Veiga, S. P., Buckley, M. R., & Gavin, M. B. (2013). The role of trustworthiness in recruitment and selection: A review and guide for future research. *Journal of Organizational Behavior, 34*(1), 104–119.

Konig, C. J., Klehe, U. C., Berchtold, M., & Kleinmann, M. (2010). Reasons for Being Selective When Choosing Personnel Selection Procedures. *International Journal of Selection and Assessment, 18*(1), 17–27.

Laumer, S., Eckhardt, A., & Weitzel, T. (2012). Online gaming to find a new job: Examining job seekers' intention to use serious games as a self-assessment tool. *German Journal of Human Resource Management, 26*(3), 218–240.

Leece, R. (2005). A virtual careers fair. *Australian Journal of Career Development, 14*(2), 34–39.

Lievens, F. & Harris, M. M. (2003). Research on internet recruiting and testing: Current status and future directions. *International Review of Industrial and Organizational Psychology, 18*, 131–166.

Lin, H. F. (2010). Applicability of the extended theory of planned behavior in predicting job seeker intentions to use job-search websites. *International Journal of Selection and Assessment, 18*(1), 64–74.

Llorens, J. J. & Kellough, J. E. (2007). A revolution in public personnel administration: The growth of web-based recruitment and selection processes in the federal service. *Public Personnel Management, 36*(3), 207–221.

Lory, B. E. (2010). Using Facebook to assess candidates during the recruiting process: Ethical implications. *NACE Journal, 71*(1), 37–40.

Madera, J. M. (2012). Using social networking websites as a selection tool: The role of selection process fairness and job pursuit intentions. *International Journal of Hospitality Management, 31*(4), 1276–1282.

Makransky, G. & Glas, C. A. (2011). Unproctored internet test verification: Using adaptive confirmation testing. *Organizational Research Methods, 14*(4), 608–630.

Maurer, S. D. & Liu, Y. (2007). Developing effective e-recruiting websites: Insights for managers from marketers. *Business Horizons, 50*(4), 305–314.

McCarthy, J. M., Bauer, T. N., Truxillo, D. M., Anderson, N. R., Costa, A. C., & Ahmed, S. M. (2017). Applicant perspectives during selection: A review addressing "So What?," "What's New?," and "Where to Next?." *Journal of Management, 43*(6), 1693–1725.

McCarthy, J., Hrabluik, C., & Jelley, R. B. (2009). Progression through the ranks: Assessing employee reactions to high-stakes employment testing. *Personnel Psychology, 62 (4),*793–832.

McCarthy, J. M., Van Iddekinge, C. H., Lievens, F., Kung, M. C., Sinar, E. F., & Campion, M. A. (2013). Do candidate reactions relate to job performance or affect criterion-related validity? A multistudy investigation of relations among reactions, selection test scores, and job performance. *Journal of Applied Psychology, 98*(5), 701–719.

McFarland, L. A., & Ployhart, R. E. (2015). Social media: A contextual framework to guide research and practice. *Journal of Applied Psychology, 100*(6), 1653–1677.

McManus, M. A., & Ferguson, M. W. (2003). Biodata, personality, and demographic differences of recruits from three sources. *International Journal of Selection and Assessment, 11*(2–3), 175–183.

Moscoso, S. & Salgado, J. F. (2004). Fairness reactions to personnel selection techniques in Spain and Portugal. *International Journal of Selection and Assessment, 12*(1–2), 187–196.

Nikolaou, I. (2014). Social networking web sites in job search and employee recruitment. *International Journal of Selection and Assessment, 22*(2), 179–189.

Nikolaou, I. & Georgiou, K. (2017). Serious gaming and applicants' reactions: The role of openness to experience. In M. Armstrong, D. R. Sanchez & K. N. Bauer (2017), Gaming and Gamification IGNITE: Current Trends in Research and Application. 32nd Annual Conference of the Society for Industrial and Organizational Psychology, Orlando, USA

Nikolaou, I. & Judge, T. A. (2007). Fairness reactions to personnel selection techniques in Greece: The role of core self-evaluations. *International Journal of Selection and Assessment, 15*(2), 206–219.

Oostrom, J. K., Born, M. P., & van der Molen, H. T. (2013). Webcam tests in personnel selection. In D. Derks & A. Bakker (Eds.), *The psychology of digital media at work* (pp. 166–180), London: Routledge.

Parry, E., Stefan, S., & Holm, A. (2014). Institutional context and e-recruitment practices of Danish organizations. *Employee Relations, 36*(4), 432–455.

Pearce, C. G. & Tuten, T. L. (2001). Internet recruiting in the banking industry. *Business Communication Quarterly, 64*(1), 9–18.

Perry, E. L., Simpson, P. A., NicDomhnaill, O. M., & Siegel, D. M. (2003). Is there a technology age gap? Associations among age, skills, and employment outcomes. *International Journal of Selection and Assessment, 11*(2–3), 141–149.

Ployhart, R. E. & Harold, C. M. (2004). The applicant attribution-reaction theory (AART): An integrative theory of applicant attributional processing. *International Journal of Selection and Assessment, 12*(1–2), 84–98.

Ployhart, R. E. & Ryan, A. M. (1997). Toward an explanation of applicant reactions: An examination of organizational justice and attribution frameworks. *Organizational Behaviour and Human Decision Processes, 72*(3), 308–335.

Ployhart, R. E., Schmitt, N., & Tippins, N. T. (2017). Solving the supreme problem: 100 years of selection and recruitment. *Journal of Applied Psychology, 102*(3), 291–304.

Ployhart, R. E., Weekley, J. A., Holtz, B. C., & Kemp, C. (2003). Web-based and paper-and-pencil testing of applicants in a proctored setting: Are personality, biodata, and situational judgment tests comparable? *Personnel Psychology, 56*(3), 733–752.

Potosky, D. & Bobko, P. (2004). Selection testing via the internet: Practical considerations and exploratory empirical findings. *Personnel Psychology, 57*(4), 1003–1034.

Richman-Hirsch, W. L., Olson-Buchanan, J. B., & Drasgow, F. (2000). Examining the impact of administration medium on examinee perceptions and attitudes. *Journal of Applied Psychology, 85*(6), 880.

Roth, P. L., Bobko, P., Van Iddekinge, C. H., & Thatcher, J. B. (2016). Social media in employee-selection-related decisions: A research agenda for uncharted territory. *Journal of Management, 42*(1), 269–298.

Roulin, N. (2014). The Influence of employers' use of social networking websites in selection, online self-promotion, and personality on the likelihood of faux pas postings. *International Journal of Selection and Assessment, 22*(1), 80–87.

Roulin, N. & Bangerter, A. (2013). Social networking websites in personnel selection. *Journal of Personnel Psychology, 12*(3), 143–151.

Ruël, H. & Bondarouk, T. (2004). e-HRM: Innovation or irritation. *ECIS 2004 Proceedings*, 110.

Ryan, A. M. & Ployhart, R. E. (2000). Applicants' perceptions of selection procedures and decisions: A critical review and agenda for the future. *Journal of Management, 26* (3), 565–606.

Ryan, A. M. & Ployhart, R. E. (2014). A century of selection. *Annual Review of Psychology, 65*(1), 693–717.

Sears, J., Zhang, H., Wiesner, H. W., Hackett, D. R., & Yuan, Y. (2013). A comparative assessment of videoconference and face-to-face employment interviews. *Management Decision, 51*(8), 1733–1752.

Sanchez, R. J., Roberts, K., Freeman, M., & Clayton, A. C. (2012, August). Do they care? Applicant reactions to on-line social networking presence checks. Paper presented at the Academy of Management Annual Conference, Boston, MA.

Schinkel, S., van Vianen, A., & van Dierendonck, D. (2013). Selection fairness and outcomes: A field study of interactive effects on applicant reactions. *International Journal of Selection and Assessment, 21*(1), 22–31.

Schneider, T. J., Goffin, R. D., & Daljeet, K. N. (2015). "Give us your social networking site passwords": Implications for personnel selection and personality. *Personality and Individual Differences, 73*, 78–83.

Schuler, H. (1993). Social validity of selection situations: A concept and some empirical results. In H. Schuler, J. L. Farr, & M. Smith (Eds.), *Personnel selection and assessment: Individual and Organizational Perspectives* (pp. 11–26). Hillsdale, NJ: Lawrence Erlbaum.

Selden, S. & Orenstein, J. (2011). Government e-recruiting web sites: The influence of e-recruitment content and usability on recruiting and hiring outcomes in US state governments. *International Journal of Selection and Assessment, 19*(1), 31–40.

Society for Human Resources Management-SHRM (2016). Using Social Media for Talent Acquisition – Recruitment and Screening. Retrieved from www.shrm.org/hr-today/trends-and-forecasting/research-and-surveys/pages/social-media-recruiting-screening-2015.aspx.

Spinks, N., Wells, B., & Meche, M. (1999). Appraising the appraisals: Computerized performance appraisal systems. *Career Development International, 4*(2), 94–100.

Steiner, D. D. & Gilliland, S. W. (1996). Fairness reactions to personnel selection techniques in France and the United States. *Journal of Applied Psychology, 81*(2), 134–141.

Stone, D. L., Deadrick, D. L., Lukaszewski, K. M., & Johnson, R. (2015). The influence of technology on the future of human resource management. *Human Resource Management Review, 25*(2), 216–231.

Stone, D. L. & Dulebohn, J. H. (2013). Emerging issues in theory and research on electronic human resource management (eHRM). *Human Resource Management Review, 23*(1), 1–5.

Stone, D. L., Lukaszewski, K. M., & Isenhour, L. C. (2005). E-recruiting: Online strategies for attracting talent. In H. Gueutal, D. L. Stone & E. Salas, The brave new world of eHR: Human resources management in the digital age (pp. 22–53), Chichester: Wiley.

Stone, D. L., Lukaszewski, K. M., Stone-Romero, E. F., & Johnson, T. L. (2013). Factors affecting the effectiveness and acceptance of electronic selection systems. *Human Resource Management Review, 23*(1), 50–70.

Stopfer, J. M. & Gosling, S. D. (2013). Online social networks in the work context. In D. Derks & A. Bakker (Eds.), *The psychology of digital media at work* (pp. 39–59), London: Routledge.

Stoughton, J. W., Thompson, L., & Meade, A. (2015). Examining applicant reactions to the use of social networking websites in pre-employment screening. *Journal of Business and Psychology, 30*(1), 73–88.

Straus, S. G., Miles, J. A., & Levesque, L. L. (2001). The effects of videoconference, telephone, and face-to-face media on interviewer and applicant judgments in employment interviews. *Journal of Management, 27*(3), 363–381.

Tippins, N. T. (2015). Technology and assessment in selection. *Annual Review of Organizational Psychology and Organizational Behavior, 2*(1), 551–582.

Tippins, N. T., Beaty, J., Drasgow, F., Gibson, W. M., Pearlman, K., Segall, D. O., & Shepherd, W. (2006). Unproctored internet testing in employment settings. *Personnel Psychology, 59*(1), 189–225.

Toldi, N. L. (2011). Job applicants favor video interviewing in the candidate-selection process. *Employment Relations Today, 38*(3), 19–27.

Tomlinson, A. (2002). Energy firm sharpens recruiting, saves money with in-house job board. *Canadian HR Reporter, 15*(20), 7–8.

Truxillo, D. M. & Bauer, T. N. (2011). Applicant Reactions to Organizations and Selection Systems. In S. Zedeck (Ed.), *APA Handbook of Industrial and Organizational Psychology.* (pp. 379–398). Washington, DC: American Psychological Association.

Truxillo, D. M., Bauer, T. N., Campion, M. A., & Paronto, M. E. (2006). A field study of the role of Big Five personality in applicant perceptions of selection fairness, self, and the hiring organization. *International Journal of Selection & Assessment, 14*(3), 269–277.

Truxillo, D. M., Bauer, T. N., & Garcia, A. M. (2017). Applicant Reactions to Hiring Procedures. In H. W. Goldstein, E. D. Pulakos, J. Passmore, & C. Semedo (Eds.) The Wiley Blackwell Handbook of the Psychology of Recruitment, Selection and Employee Retention (pp. 53–70). New York, NY: John Wiley & Sons.

Truxillo, D. M., Bauer, T. N., McCarthy, J. M., Anderson, N., & Ahmed, S. M. (2017). Applicant Perspectives on Employee Selection Systems. In D. Ones, N. Anderson, C. Viswesvaran, & H. Sinangil (Eds.), *Handbook of Industrial, Work and Organizational (IWO) Psychology* (2nd edn., pp. 508–532), London: Sage.

Truxillo, D. M., Bodner, T. E., Bertolino, M., Bauer, T. N., & Yonce, C. A. (2009). Effects of explanations on applicant reactions: A meta-analytic review. *International Journal of Selection and Assessment*, *17*(4), 346–361.

Van Hoye, G. (2014). Word-of-mouth as a recruitment source: An integrative model. In K. Y. T. Yu & D. M. Cable (Eds.), *The Oxford Handbook of Recruitment* (pp. 251–268). New York, NY: Oxford University Press.

Van Hoye, G. & Lievens, F. (2007). Investigating Web-Based Recruitment Sources: Employee testimonials vs word-of-mouse. *International Journal of Selection and Assessment*, *15*(4), 372–382.

Voermans, M. & van Veldhoven, M. (2007). Attitude towards e-HRM: An empirical study at Philips. *Personnel Review*, *36*(6), 887–902.

Walker, H. J., Bauer, T., Cole, M., Bernerth, J., Feild, H., & Short, J. (2013). Is this how I will be treated? Reducing uncertainty through recruitment interactions. *Academy of Management Journal*, *56*(5), 1325–1347.

Walker, H. J., Feild, H. S., Giles, W. F., Armenakis, A. A., & Bernerth, J. B. (2009). Displaying employee testimonials on recruitment web sites: Effects of communication media, employee race, and job seeker race on organizational attraction and information credibility. *Journal of Applied Psychology*, *94*(5), 1354–1364.

Young, J. & Foot, K. (2005). Corporate e-cruiting: The construction of work in Fortune 500 recruiting web sites. *Journal of Computer-Mediated Communication*, *11*(1), 44–71.

Zelenskaya, K. & Singh, N. (2011). Exploring virtual recruiting from employers' perspective using "Second Life." *Journal of Human Resources in Hospitality & Tourism*, *10*(2), 117–128.

Zide, J., Elman, B., & Shahani-Denning, C. (2014). LinkedIn and recruitment: How profiles differ across occupations. *Employee Relations*, *36*(5), 583–604.

6 Applying Adaptive Approaches to Talent Management Practices

Tracy M. Kantrowitz, Darrin M. Grelle, and Yin Lin

Technology has evolved to provide an increasingly tailored experience to users. Shopping websites provide ideas for future purchases based on browsing history, music programs suggest songs you might like, and fitness trackers use activity information to suggest activities to meet users' goals. Similarly, the intersection of technology and big data has also brought about a new era in talent management. The abundance of data and new techniques to harness the power of those data are leading to advances in the efficacy and precision of data-driven talent management practices. Whether it is employee assessment, training, or surveys, adaptive techniques are being applied to improve measurement, efficiency, and the user experience. Methods of data collection are becoming increasingly sophisticated as organizations incorporate adaptive approaches to measurement tools. In addition to data sources that are actively sought out and collected, organizations are increasingly using existing information sources that do not necessarily require candidate and/or employee effort, including application and system of record (e.g., human resources information systems data), in order to evolve evidence-based talent programs like selection, training, and engagement. Regardless of whether the data are proactively collected or "scraped" through available sources, adaptive methods are being applied to a variety of talent management areas. Through the use of sophisticated algorithms and backed by large amounts of data, adaptive techniques take into account existing information regarding employees' skills, training needs, or other previously collected data to tailor a subsequent measurement opportunity or intervention (Kantrowitz, Dawson, & Fetzer, 2011).

In this chapter, we describe the use of computer adaptive approaches to measurement of behavior across the employee life cycle. We start by tracing changes in the assessment landscape that precipitated the rise of computer adaptive assessment. Next, we discuss applications of computer adaptive approaches to assessment, survey, and training, with a particular focus on specific types of assessment. We conclude with a description of new frontiers in adaptive assessment and how technology and evolving expectations will continually drive demands for new methods of measuring employee aptitude and behavior.

6.1 Changes in the Talent Management Landscape

The changing landscape of assessment in organizations can be attributed to multiple factors, including changes in economic conditions, enhanced technology, and organizations' desire to make talent management tools more accessible, available, and easy to use. One area where this shift has been particularly apparent is pre-employment testing. Global economic trends have forced organizations to slot testing earlier in the hiring process to help reduce more time- and resource-intensive phases of hiring such as interviewing. As a result, unproctored (unsupervised) internet testing (UIT) emerged in the late 1990s as a mode of administration that brought multiple advantages to organizations, including decreased time-to-fill and recruitment costs (Beaty et al., 2009; Tippins, 2009). In more recent years, testing has evolved from UIT to mobile internet-based assessment (MIT; King et al., 2015). MIT presents great opportunities (e.g., potentially larger and more diverse candidate pools) as consumer data indicates that mobile device purchases exceed PC purchases (Gartner, 2015). Yet, MIT also brings new challenges to the integrity of assessment programs, namely the increasingly variable environments in which candidates may complete assessments, the equivalence of test scores when compared to traditional computer based administration, and candidate reactions to mobile assessment. Most recently, the use of data "scraping" (e.g., leveraging existing data sources such as job application or social media data) to glean predictive information about job candidates has emerged as a new way to determine candidates' fit for jobs.

Alongside the growing standards of test consumers, the expectations of test takers are also evolving as part of the candidate-driven assessment market (Sullivan, 2014). Competition for top candidates between organizations, the need to retain candidates in the hiring pipeline, and an organization's desire to put forth a positive candidate experience to enhance its employment brand have precipitated the candidate-driven market. Candidates now expect a brief, informative, and engaging assessment experience. The candidate-driven market has also changed the psychological contract between candidate and hiring organization. In order to avoid perceptions that job applications land in a "black hole," organizations aim to increase transparency in recruitment procedures through enhanced communication such as informing candidates about procedures and expected level of effort so the candidate can decide whether to pursue subsequent phases of the application process. The growing expectations of test consumers and test takers have spurred test providers to innovate and evolve their methods.

Another area of talent management that has adapted is the employee survey. As organizations aim to retain top talent, more efforts are invested in measuring employee attitudes and perceptions to gauge satisfaction and engagement. The notion of "survey fatigue" arose out of the substantial time invested in providing feedback for opinion, preferences, engagement, satisfaction, pulse, 360 rating, performance appraisal, professional development, and exit surveys. Employees become frustrated and lack interest in filling out multiple, lengthy surveys. Survey fatigue can impact response rates and data quality. Companies reacted by moving toward exceedingly short but frequent surveys, in order to capture timely information for feedback and planning.

Training is another area of talent management that has evolved. In the past, training delivery has ranged from actively providing one-on-one instruction with skilled trainers, to passively pointing new employees to stacks of technical manuals and user guides. In the last decade or so, traditional training methods are gradually being replaced by technology-assisted delivery methods. According to the Training Magazine 2016 annual report, 30.5 percent of training and development is now delivered online or through other computer assisted methods. Human trainers can deliver training live to trainees via the internet, and new employees can be granted access to repositories of content they can access at will. Moreover, live human trainers can be expensive, and therefore many organizations opt for pre-configured training modules that employees can take at their convenience. This, of course, assumes that all trainees come in with the same amount of knowledge, are equally motivated, and are equally capable of learning and retaining new material. Because this is generally not the case (Ackerman, 1987), adaptive training programs can deliver vital information to employees in a manner more efficient than static training modules.

To sum up, as the landscape of employment testing, employee survey, and on-the-job training continues to grow and change, it is clear that the methods for designing talent management initiatives need to evolve. That is, they need to account for the changing expectations, new technologies, and innovations that can allow organizations to build increasingly successful talent practices. Not long ago, it was the case that the skills and capabilities needed to transform traditional talent management processes were limited to those of large organizations employing those with very specialized skills and access to large amounts of data. While certain areas of adaptive technology are in their infancy (e.g., adaptive surveys), others like adaptive testing have become more widespread as a result of several factors, including changes in the training of industrial-organizational (I-O) psychologists and the types of specialized statistical analysis skills needed to design adaptive tests, general knowledge about the advantages of adaptive tests even by non-technical users, greater accessibility to data sources (e.g., Amazon's Mechanical Turk), and the availability of adaptive tests from a number of commercial providers.

6.2 Applications of Adaptive Approaches to Talent Management Initiatives

Computer adaptive approaches have successfully been applied to assessment, survey, and training to achieve desirable results against many criteria – including validity/reliability, user experience, and efficiency. In this section, we provide several examples of adaptive approaches to measurement and adaptive methods that tailor the talent assessment or intervention to each participant's particular needs.

6.2.1 Computer Adaptive Testing (CAT)

CAT represents a major methodological and technological advancement in measurement, and has rapidly become the norm for assessment of constructs with objective right/wrong answers, helping to support organizational needs for UIT while increasing the integrity and security of selection processes. CAT adapts to each candidate by dynamically selecting subsequent questions based on a candidate's responses to previous test questions. This candidate-centric assessment tailoring of CAT is made possible through the application of item response theory (IRT), the design of sophisticated automated test assembly (ATA) algorithms, the development of an extensive item pool, and the harvesting of a large amount of data to calibrate and set up the assessment up-front. In essence, CAT has the effect of creating a unique testing experience for each candidate, thereby greatly increasing the security of the assessment and reducing the opportunities for cheating due to pre-knowledge of the test questions. CAT also presents a number of other advantages to recruiters and hiring managers, including reduced testing time and increased reliability (compared to static/fixed form test equivalents). These key advantages make CAT a more appropriate alternative to UIT programs than traditional or static assessments.

CAT-based testing programs have existed for decades in educational and certification testing (Fetzer, 2009), but have only been adopted for the purpose of pre-employment testing in the past ten years. Prior research in educational settings has established the predictive capabilities of CAT (Smittle, 1993). Substantial progress has been made in the development and validation of specific types of CATs designed to measure knowledge, skills, abilities, and other characteristics that are predictive of employee performance. The increasing need for UIT for selection has spurred the development of CAT-based versions of assessments traditionally used in selection processes. Simultaneously, increases in the availability of personal technology and access to the internet have made UIT viable and promoted the possibility of CAT in personnel selection. Although CAT requires sophisticated algorithms and large item banks to operate, the computing power necessary to deliver a CAT program is now wide-spread and the skills needed to design and administer CAT have become more common through changes in the training of I-O psychologists who commonly develop these. That is, training in item response theory methods have become more common in graduate training, which provides the basis for CAT. And, while access to large samples (i.e., 400+) of test takers who could provide data on hundreds of provisional test questions or the purpose of item calibration was a limiting factor for the development of CAT, greater accessibility through task-based workers (e.g., Amazon Mechanical Turk) has opened up the feasibility of CAT development for organizations of all sizes. Furthermore, it is also no longer entirely necessary to have dedicated testing centers or particularly sophisticated computers to maintain an internet based testing program, be it CAT or static (Gutierrez, Grelle, & Borneman, 2009).

In the pre-employment testing realm, selection processes often incorporate assessments of cognitive ability, personality, and knowledge. Many of these assessments (particularly cognitive ability and knowledge tests) were restricted for use in proctored testing environments due to test security concerns. Attention has been given to the vulnerabilities of traditional online static tests in which the same test questions are presented in the same order to all candidates (Maynes, 2010). Static tests are prone to cheating since those less-than-honorably intentioned candidates can obtain all the items after completing the test only once if they have the opportunity, capability, and motivation to do so (Tippins, 2009). Once the security of a static test has been compromised, often the entire test becomes invalid and has to be removed from the process. CAT is one method that reduces many of the risks associated with UIT, but it isn't a silver bullet. Similar to challenges presented with any UIT, when a CAT is administered unproctored it is impossible to know whether the candidate or one of his or her smarter friends took the test. Depending on the level of risk the organization is willing to assume, other strategies should be employed to further reduce the risks associated with UIT, including UIT followed up by brief on-site testing and identity verification. While we believe CAT has been perhaps the single most promising technological innovation in pre-employment testing in recent history, careful guidelines for implementation should be followed (cf. Beaty et al., 2009). Specifically, suggestions like using verification testing, limiting the access of the assessment through technology, implementing warnings against cheating, and monitoring scores over time help increase the integrity of the testing program.

A research agenda for CAT was proposed by Kantrowitz, Dawson, and Fetzer (2011). Questions regarding the criterion-related validity, item exposure, candidate reactions, and implementation challenges related to CAT were proposed as key areas of inquiry to bear out the advantages of this approach to testing. Since then, a substantial amount of research activity has informed the usefulness, validity, and operational considerations related to CAT. For example, Gutierrez (2011) investigated test taker reactions to CAT when test takers were informed about the adaptive nature of the assessment. Test takers did not react negatively when informed that test questions were tailored to their specific abilities and may have differed from questions presented to others. The validity of CAT-based assessments has also been a topic of substantial research (e.g., Schneider et al., 2009; Grelle, Gutierrez, & Fetzer, 2011), indicating that the validity of CAT-based personality and ability tests to be on par with traditional fixed-form assessment. In addition, research has investigated the item exposure of CAT-based assessments (Moclaire et al., 2012) in terms of balancing the need for large item banks with practical considerations for developing and refreshing item banks. They offered suggestions for minimizing item exposure by using an alternative item presentation algorithm that uses a broader range of items than the item with the most ideal parameters. Research on CAT continues to grow as its use has taken hold in employment testing. While CAT programs require substantial resources and expertise to develop and maintain, CAT is now largely seen as compulsory for supporting UIT.

6.2.2 Adaptive Survey Techniques

To overcome the challenge of survey fatigue, adaptive survey techniques have been developed to make surveys more efficient and less tedious. New approaches have originated in market research but have application to employee survey. Conjoint analysis is a survey-based statistical technique used in market research that helps determine how people value different attributes that make up an individual product or service. It allows for the evaluation of various stimuli, in order to evaluate the trade-offs between different options, attributes, or characteristics. For instance, a conjoint survey may present respondents with different elements of a recruitment and selection process, and, through a series of paired comparisons, ask respondents to indicate which have the most potential to drive a job offer acceptance. Adaptive conjoint analysis (ACA) arose as an innovation in conjoint analysis, and asks respondents to evaluate attribute levels directly, and then to assess the importance of level differences, and finally to make paired comparisons between profile descriptions. ACA is adaptive in two ways. First, it asks for attribute importances and can frame this question in terms of the difference between the most and least valued levels as expressed by that respondent. Second, the paired comparisons are utility balanced based on the respondent's previously expressed values. This balancing avoids pairs in which one alternative is much better than the other, thereby engaging the respondent in more challenging questions. For example, this process may be used to assess features of several different types of mobile phones. First, several brands of mobile phones are presented and respondents are asked to rate the overall desirability of each. Then, aspects of mobile phones would be presented and rated based on specific features, like amount of storage or screen size. Then, for the highly rated mobile phone brands rated initially, two brands are pitted against each other and respondents are asked to rate which brand would be selected if all other options (e.g., amount of storage, screen size) were the same. Each feature can also be rated in terms of the strength of preference for amount of storage size between two options for storage. Thus, ACA helps us out distinguishing features and details based on initial ratings provided about various features. While this approach works quite well, most notably for market and product research, its application to employee survey is untested but starting to become clear. For instance, elements of a company culture could be rated this way to help determine which culture factors are most important to influence to increase employee engagement and retention.

In market research, ACA revolutionized conjoint analysis replacing fixed static surveys. Most recently, ACBC (adaptive choice-based conjoint analysis; Sawtooth Software Inc. 2009) is a new approach to preference modeling that leverages the best aspects of CBC (choice-based conjoint) and ACA (adaptive conjoint analysis). An adaptive choice survey is an interactive experience, customized to the preferences and opinions of each individual. ACBC surveys more closely approximate the decision-making processes that influence real-world choices. Respondents begin ACBC surveys by completing a build-your-own (BYO) task identifying the level of each attribute that they prefer. The ACBC software composes a series of attribute combinations clustering around each respondent's BYO choices. During a first screener section, informants decide whether each of these concepts is a possibility or not. Probe questions determine whether attribute levels consistently included in or excluded from each informant's screener section choices reflect "Unacceptable" or "Must Have" simplifying heuristics. Finally, concepts identified as possibilities during the screener section are carried forward to a choice tournament. The winning concept in each choice tournament set advances to the next choice set until a winner is determined.

Innovations in survey technology to adapt the survey experience have occurred predominantly in the market research area. The opportunity to leverage these advances for the purposes of the many types of surveys that organizations use is clear and necessary. Before the opportunity presented by adaptive survey techniques can be realized, I-O psychologists (those often closest to the design and analysis of surveys in organizations) need to acquaint themselves with the techniques, methodologies, and analytical procedures needed to design, analyze, and interpret these types of surveys. There is a tremendous learning opportunity for those interested to become familiar with the history and uses of adaptive survey techniques from researchers in market research.

6.2.3 Training & Development

According to the Training Magazine 2016 Annual Report, US companies spend about $70.65 billion on employee training and development. The amount has remained relatively flat over the past five years. The report notes the trend, however, that how that money is spent has changed over the years. While the majority of training is still delivered in person in classroom settings, technology assisted training methods are on the rise. Moving training from the classroom to the internet offers organizations substantial savings in travel and training space, and opens up possibilities that are not available in classroom settings (e.g., simulations and serious games). Computer based training also opens up possibilities for computer adaptive training.

While the focus of this chapter is on computer adaptive technologies in organizational contexts, it can be argued that the most adaptive training programs are one-to-one tutoring. In education research, a phenomenon called the "2-sigma problem" (Bloom, 1984) describes how students who underwent one-on-one tutoring outperformed students participating in regular classroom instruction by two standard deviations. A human tutor is aware of the trainee's progress, the trainee's weaknesses, and, with experience, the best methods to ensure the trainee retains the material. Therefore, an effective adaptive training program seeks to replicate these attributes via computer algorithm (Goldberg et al., 2012). Indeed, much of the basis for computer adaptive training programs is rooted in educational psychology theory (Corno, 2008).

There are two levels at which adaptive training programs can be developed; micro- and macroadaptations (Snow, 1997). Macroadaptations are week-to-week or day-to-day adjustments in curriculum that include which lessons are taught or which exercises are given. These adjustments can be made based on how the learner has progressed through lessons and the success of each exercise. Similar to how an item information curve peaks at the point where examinee ability is equal to item difficulty (a concept described by item response theory which shows the increase in knowledge about a candidate through the administration of a question), exercises are most effective at specific points of topic mastery: an exercise will be useless if the learner has either mastered the topic or does not yet possess enough knowledge to progress through the exercise (Vogel-Walcutt et al., 2016). Macroadaptations may lend themselves to organizations in which new topics are frequently introduced or become obsolete. The overall structure of the program can stay in place while lessons and exercises are added and removed as necessary.

Microadaptations are minute-to-minute, hour-to-hour adjustments that occur within a lesson or exercise or set of lessons. If a learner understands the material, then the content may become more challenging or the lesson might just end sooner, allowing the learner to progress to other lessons. If the learner does not understand the material, content may become easier or the material could be presented multiple times in different modes. Exercises themselves generally operate the same way as standard computer adaptive tests do, and the outcomes of those exercises may dictate macroadaptations in curriculum. Using IRT to drive microadaptations for learners enhances learning and training efficiency (Chen, Lee, & Chen, 2005).

As mentioned earlier, the human tutor is a model for developing a successful computer adaptive training program. In a comprehensive review of experiments comparing human tutors to technology based instruction, VanLehn (2011) evaluated several hypotheses for why tutoring is superior to classroom instruction and how those attributes would be incorporated into technology based instruction. While many hypotheses could not explain the differences, the hypothesis that human tutors aid trainees by providing feedback to aid in problem solving is a likely explanation for the differences. While many technology based instruction programs provide feedback to a trainee based on the end result, providing feedback when a trainee begins to deviate from expected behavior can be much more effective in ensuring training transfer (Liu & Yu, 2011).

Military psychology, ergonomics, and computer science researchers have far outpaced organizational researchers in adaptive training and development (e.g., Daniels et al., 2015). The US Army has spent millions of dollars on adaptive technology based instruction systems in an effort to reduce costs. By creating macroadaptive training programs with automated content authoring, the Army hopes to reduce training costs and the time and skill required to develop training courses, and increase training transfer (Johnston et al., 2015).

Advancements have been made in this area in other fields, and now is the time for organizational research to catch up. Developing the tools and metrics to evaluate the effectiveness and return on investment of computer adaptive training programs is an area ripe for opportunity. This is a particularly promising new frontier for organizations as they seek more nimble and tailored employee systems to upskill employees on critical developmental and training areas. Training practitioners would be well-served by acquainting themselves with advancements made in education to drive important changes in organizational training systems.

6.3 Recent Innovations in CAT

In this section, we discuss recent advances in the application of adaptive approaches to assessment, specifically in the areas of cognitive and non-cognitive assessment. We describe psychometric advances that have given rise to practical benefits to organizations that use assessment as part of their selection and/or development initiatives.

6.3.1 Cognitive Assessment

As with the smartphone, the first CAT was groundbreaking, but since the updates in computing that allowed CAT to be administered online, change in cognitive CAT has been steady and incremental. While there have been some major breakthroughs in the past ten years that the increased computing power of the average personal computer has allowed, most advancement in CAT for cognitive ability assessment has focused on one of the following: item selection algorithms, theta estimation algorithms, item exposure controls, cheating detection, classification accuracy, or item calibration. While many innovations have been introduced to cognitive ability testing generally (simulations, mobile-based, text analysis, and games), most CAT are still dichotomously scored multiple choice questions. The innovations discussed here deal primarily with improving this type of test.

It is well understood that CAT is much more efficient and accurate as compared to traditional fixed item tests (Weiss & Kingsbury, 1984). Most of the accuracy and efficiency comes from how questions are selected for examinees. In IRT, the most information is gained on an examinee's ability when the difficulty of a question is equal to the ability of the candidate. There are many different algorithms available that are used to identify the best next question for each examinee, and they range in complexity and the amount of information upon which they draw. Some methods use the current ability estimate of the examinee and draw the question from the question bank whose difficulty is closest to that estimate. Others use information from all of the questions administered so far and calculate which question in the bank will provide the most information based on all of the questions' parameters (Veerkamp & Berger, 1997). Still others that are used in a specific class of CAT – computerized classification tests (CCT) and cognitive diagnostic models (CDM) – use probability based algorithms that select the questions that are most likely to classify an examinee as pass or fail. CCT and CDM are unique in that the goal is not to generate an accurate score along a continuum, but to accurately classify an examinee as pass or fail with the fewest number of questions possible (e.g., van Buuren & Eggen, 2017). Many of the more advanced item selection algorithms are computationally complex and were not practical for operational CAT until computers gained the bandwidth to implement them without disrupting the examinee's experience.

Research shows that the computationally advanced item selection algorithms increase the accuracy and efficiency of CAT (van der Linden & Pashley, 2000), but the best performing questions are administered much more frequently even when question banks are large (Weiss, 1982). Because item overexposure can be a security risk (not to mention a poor use of resources), item exposure controls have been developed to make better use of an entire question bank. Naturally, any adjustment to which question is selected for an examinee is going to cause a reduction in accuracy and efficiency, so the ideal item exposure control would maximize question bank usage and test accuracy (Georgiadou, Triantafillou, & Economides, 2007). Much of the advancement in item exposure controls is the ability to simulate data to determine which item selection/item exposure control algorithm combination is ideal for a specific question bank and target population (Han, 2012). It is incumbent on CAT researchers to operationalize what has been gleaned from simulation research to translate it to CAT administered under real-world operational conditions, as one of the chief benefits of CAT (improved test security) becomes tenuous if CAT disproportionately exposes a small number of items. Given the advances in simulation techniques, anyone building a CAT should be able optimize test administration settings for that test's unique item pool without the need for extensive trialing with live candidates.

Cognitive ability tests, regardless of mode of administration, are administered with some kind of time constraint. As soon as a timer is introduced, a cognitive ability test is no longer a pure test of ability (Lu & Sirecy, 2007). Timers can introduce unique problems with CAT as the time required to answer questions is correlated with the difficulty of the question (van der Linden, 2009). Recent research on CAT and response time has attempted to integrate response time into different parts of CAT. Some have incorporated response time into item selection algorithms such that shorter items are selected if a candidate is running out of time (Veldkamp, 2016). Other models add a speed parameter to their ability estimation algorithms in an attempt to disentangle speed from ability (van der Linden, 2009). A great deal of research is still being conducted here due to the collinearity between cognitive ability and cognitive processing speed, as well as the complex relationship between question difficulty and response times (De Boeck, 2017). As the dominant use of CAT in organizations is to facilitate unproctored cognitive ability testing and because cognitive ability remains one of the single best predictors of organizationally relevant outcomes (Schmidt & Hunter, 1998), it is critical to advance methods for ideally accounting for speed in CAT scoring. While work continues in the area, practitioners have been using a handful of effective techniques to deal with speed. Practitioners either do extensive trialing to identify the ideal point where most candidates can complete a test without the timer being too liberal or encourage speededness and use it as a predictor of performance in its own right. The advances in speed modeling hold promise to improve both of the current approaches materially.

CAT is based on IRT, and therefore it is subject to the assumptions of IRT. One of these assumptions is that all of the questions on a test are measuring a single unidimensional trait (Embretson & Reise, 2000). Operationally, this means that cognitive CAT tend to measure single facets of cognitive ability (e.g., deductive reasoning, spatial ability). It is well known from decades of research on cognitive ability that various facets of cognitive ability are highly correlated and all load on a single general factor (Carroll, 1993). Multidimensional IRT (MIRT) can take advantage of the intercorrelation among cognitive facets to measure multiple facets more efficiently than administering sequential tests of individual cognitive facets (Reckase, 2009). Naturally, MIRT can also be applied to CAT opening up numerous possibilities for comprehensive assessment of cognitive ability (Segall, 1996).

As with standard cognitive CAT discussed above, multidimensional adaptive tests (MAT) also have multiple options for item selection algorithms, item exposure control, and ability estimation. There is also the need to choose a baseline model for the constructs being measured. MIRT is analogous to confirmatory factor analysis in classical test theory in that a model is hypothesized on how questions load on factors and how those factors correlate. There are three primary MIRT models (see Seo & Weiss, 2015, for a review): a correlated factors model, a second-order factor model, and the bifactor model. In the correlated factors model, questions load on single factors (e.g., numerical ability), and the factors are permitted to correlate. The second-order factor model is the MIRT representation of the Cattel-Horn-Carrol (McGrew, 1997) model of human intelligence. In this model, questions load on single factors, and the factors load onto a general factor. In this model, all covariance among the factors is explained by the general factor. The bifactor model is unique in that questions load onto the individual factors and onto a general factor. This model treats the individual factors and the general factor as independent. This means the variance captured by the general factor is variance in general cognitive ability not explained by the individual facets measured in the test (Reckase, 2009).

The choice of MIRT model has many implications for the resulting MAT. The model influences the ability estimation methods, item selection algorithms, and exposure controls. The choice of model also determines how the resulting scores can be interpreted. MAT has grown in use in educational testing, but is relatively new to organizational research. We were unable to locate any criterion-related validity studies using the bifactor model, so it is unclear whether the unique treatment of variance in the general factor has incremental validity in the prediction of job performance as compared to more traditional measures of specific and general cognitive ability. This nascent area of research has many possibilities for applications in organizations. At a minimum, it holds great promise for the administration of multiple types of cognitive ability assessments (e.g., numerical and verbal reasoning) given the correlated nature of most abilities. The approach that shows most promise is MAT as the combination of computing speed and increasingly efficient score estimation algorithms increase the feasibility.

6.3.2 Non-Cognitive Assessment

6.3.2.1 Practical Challenges of Traditional Non-Cognitive Assessments

Just like cognitive ability, non-cognitive constructs can have a significant impact on outcomes in the workplace and beyond (Ozer & Benet-Martinez, 2006; Roberts et al., 2007) and have been a focus of ongoing innovation. Moreover, non-cognitive constructs can form part of a person's identity and are less prone to change, and thus they potentially have a long-lasting impact throughout the entire employee life cycle. Therefore, in order to build a holistic picture of an individual, workplace assessments often go beyond the "hard" cognitive assessments to also cover other important "soft" non-cognitive constructs. The assessment of non-cognitive constructs, however, faces two main challenges.

The typical question format in a non-cognitive assessment consists of a statement followed by a rating scale (e.g., the Likert scale). It is easy for respondents to present themselves as they would like to be seen when answering rating scale questions, and rating scale assessments are therefore at risk of faking, especially in pre-employment testing and other high-stake situations (Birkeland et al., 2006). The faking risk intensifies further if the assessment is static (i.e., the same questions are presented to every respondent), making question memorization possible and increasing the risk of successful collusion. The first challenge of non-cognitive assessments is, therefore, the threat to the integrity of the measurement due to the transparency and subjective nature of these question formats.

Unlike cognitive assessments, which typically focus on one single scale (with some innovative exceptions – see previous section), most non-cognitive assessments attempt to measure a collection of traits (scales) pertaining to a psychological model (framework). For example, personality assessments often contain scales mapping into the Five Factor Model (FFM) of Openness, Conscientiousness, Extroversion, Agreeableness, and Neuroticism (e.g., Costa & McCrae, 1992). In the case of workplace personality assessments, the FFM tends to be too broad for practical use. For workplace application purposes, a larger number of traits are often needed to provide a more in-depth picture of the person. In order to accurately and simultaneously measure such a large number of scales, non-cognitive assessments often need a lot of information. The demand for comprehensive measurement leads to long and repetitive assessments where respondents must answer all questions, even when some questions only give additional insight to some respondents and can be safely omitted for others without impacting on measurement accuracy. These traditional challenges have undermined the practical utility of non-cognitive assessments. In order to realize their full potential, several alternative assessment methods have emerged and flourished in the last decade.

6.3.2.2 Recent Innovations on Non-Cognitive Assessments

In order to reduce the effect of impression management and faking, researchers have turned their attention to alternative response formats, the forerunner being the forced-choice (FC) response format. The FC format presents several items simultaneously in a question block, and asks the respondent to choose between them. This format has many different presentations, varying by:

• The number of items within each question block (e.g., pairs, triplets, quads);

- The number of scales involved in each question block (i.e., "unidimensional" if all the items in a block are mapped to the same scale, "multidimensional" if items in the same block are mapped to more than one scale);
- The response collected (e.g., a binary choice between two options, a sliding scale of strength of preference between two options).

Example – multidimensional triplet – ranking

Scale[1]	Item[2]	Please select one statement that is most true or typical of you, and another statement that is least like you[3]
Extroversion	I like to socialize	Least
Openness	I like to explore new ideas	
Agreeableness	I cooperate with others	Most

1. The FC block is *multidimensional* because multiple scales are present in the same block. This information is not displayed to the candidate.
2. There are three items in a block, making it a *triplet* format.
3. A ranking response is collected, showing the order of the items in terms of the candidate's preferences.

By collecting a choice rather than a rating, the possibility to fake a good rating on every single item is removed. Moreover, items within the same question block are often balanced carefully to be similarly desirable, therefore making it even harder to fake by choosing an obvious "correct answer." As a result, the effect of faking on the final assessment scores is reduced (Christiansen, Burns, & Montgomery, 2005; Jackson, Wroblewski, & Ashton, 2000). In addition, the FC format also reduces response biases and enhances differentiation between scales (Brown, Inceoglu, & Lin, 2017; Cheung & Chan, 2002), thus further improving the accuracy of the final assessment scores.

Despite its recent popularity, the FC format had historical concerns arising from its classical scoring method, which assigned the same total score to every individual (i.e., the score is ipsative – each person can assign a rank to each item in a forced choice block, but the sum for each person will be identical), thus hindering the comparison between people (e.g., Johnson, Wood, & Blinkhorn, 1988). The ipsativity debate, however, is settling following the development of new item response theory (IRT) models that can score FC responses properly (Brown & Maydeu-Olivares, 2011, 2013; Brown, 2016). The IRT models not only remove ipsativity in the final assessment scores, but also open up the possibility of creating adaptive FC assessments (FC-CAT). Commercially available assessments are now offered that leverage these new IRT models to overcome the challenge of ipsativity.

In a non-cognitive CAT, the computer based automatic test assembly (ATA) algorithm chooses relevant follow-up questions for a respondent, based on the answers they provided to earlier questions. This process is conceptually similar to how a human interviewer would ask more targeted questions as an interview progresses. While the idea is centuries-old, modern CAT requires not only the theoretical models for mimicking the human judgment process of choosing targeted questions, but also the computational technology for delivering the assessment in a timely fashion on a large scale. Both theory and technology are coming to a maturity point in the twenty-first century for non-cognitive CAT, and the last decade saw the birth of several FC-CATs in the I/O space (e.g., Houston et al., 2006; Boyce et al., 2015; SHL, 2009, 2016; Dragsow et al., 2012). These CATs have been shown to reduce faking good (e.g., Kantrowitz & Robie, 2011), reduce the assessment administration time compared to traditional static assessment (e.g., Stark & Chernyshenko, 2011), and achieve high levels of validity and reliability (e.g., Boyce et al., 2015).

To summarize, compared to traditional personality assessments, FC-CATs deliver more robust, fake-resistant information for personnel decision making, and often requiring only half the time due to the efficiency of CAT (Stark & Chernyshenko, 2007; Stark et al., 2012). Moreover, the adaptive format also adds test security (i.e., different people get different questions) and makes the assessment experience more relevant to the respondents (i.e., the questions are tailored to each respondent). While FC-CAT personality assessments were considered a powerful cutting-edge novelty just ten years ago, they have now become more commonplace.

6.3.2.3 The Future of Adaptive Non-Cognitive Assessments

Far from reaching maturity, adaptive non-cognitive assessments continue to be an active field of research, with development and innovation being made in content, method, and applications. These developments have made their way into cutting-edge assessment programs used by industry and in the military. We next review areas in which advancements are occurring in each of these domains.

In terms of content, development efforts are expanding beyond personality constructs, thereby not only answering the question of "how" people tend to behave, but also capturing other important questions such as "why" people behave like they do and "what" would make a difference and lead to better outcomes in the workplace. The resulting multi-angled view collected through various non-cognitive assessments will likely lead to better personnel decisions.

In terms of method, because non-cognitive constructs (e.g., motivation) do not always function in the same way as personality constructs, different item types may be needed to measure them properly. The development of novel item types to measure alternative constructs will likely lead to new IRT models and the accompanying CAT algorithms for administering such items. Another area of method innovation concerns the production efficiency of CAT. Adaptive assessments are typically tailored to the requirements of a well-defined assessment scenario and contain many unique features, thus making the development work less generalizable and less re-usable across different assessment situations.

In terms of application, adaptive non-cognitive assessments are still predominantly used in selection scenarios given the benefits of CAT for higher-stakes testing applications. While selection is likely to continue as a major application area, their utility in other phases of the employment cycle should not be overlooked. For example, performance review is one of the more obvious areas where non-cognitive CAT may readily apply, significantly cutting down on the rating time needed to obtain robust ratings from multiple sources.

Ultimately, adaptive non-cognitive assessments will join forces with adaptive cognitive assessments, ensuring not only that the right person is placed in the right role, but also helping create the right environment to motivate and engage them so as to achieve the best potential and productivity over time. Cognitive and non-cognitive assessments have long been used as core elements of talent assessment systems. The innovations occurring in each of these domains have the potential to improve the accuracy of the resulting scores and to improve the test taking experience.

6.3.3 Next Frontiers of Innovation in Adaptive Measurement

Beyond the innovations we described, the challenges facing talent management professionals related to identification, retention, management, and development of top talent demand researchers and product developers think outside the box of the traditional assessment format. One possible expansion is to consider alternative data collection methods beyond the single-sitting assessment format, for example, by scattering responding across different times to lighten the load and to get access to short-term fluctuation or longitudinal trend data. Another possible expansion is to incorporate information from other data types in addition to traditional self-report assessments. In the increasingly digital future, electronic data trails contain more information that can be harvested to adaptively drive decision-making processes, and it is an area where assessment and non-assessment data are equally usable, and CAT, machine learning, and big data methodologies merge to create more powerful tools than we have today.

While an adaptive approach has been used extensively in assessment, relatively less attention has been placed on leveraging adaptive methods for survey and training, though the opportunity for achieving tangible benefits through its use is high. In both areas, adaptive methods have been used extensively in other domains. Conjoint survey concepts represent an area in which organizational researchers and practitioners can learn from market research to identify specific aspects of employee satisfaction, engagement, and performance that drive employees to be better performers, more engaged, and to remain with the organization. Adaptive training is another area in which organizational practitioners can learn from what has been implemented in educational training, to make training more effective, efficient, and tailored to the individual's needs.

As computing power increases, the feasibility of adaptive programs grows. Organizations can use algorithms and delivery methods that were once too computationally complex for the average computer. Advances continue to grow in fields outside industrial/organizational psychology. Brilliant work is being done in cognitive psychology, neuropsychology, educational measurement, and military assessment and training that researchers in workplace psychology should be incorporating into their work. It is time to take advantage of the tools available to us to propel research in adaptive technology forward.

References

Ackerman, P. L. (1987). Individual differences in skill learning: An integration of psychometric and information processing perspectives. *Psychological Bulletin, 102*(1), 3–27. doi:10.1037/0033–2909.102.1.3.

Beaty, J. C., Dawson, C. R., Fallaw, S. S., & Kantrowitz, T.M. (2009). Recovering the scientist–practitioner model: How I-Os should respond to unproctored Internet testing. *Industrial and Organizational Psychology: Perspectives on Science and Practice, 2*, 58–63.

Birkeland, S. A., Manson, T. M., Kisamore, J. L., Brannick, M. T., & Smith, M. A. (2006). A meta-analytic investigation of job applicant faking on personality measures. *International Journal of Selection and Assessment, 14*(4), 317–335. doi:10.1111/j. 1468–2389.2006.00354.x.

Bloom, B. S. (1984). The 2 sigma problem: The search for methods of group instruction as effective as one-to-one tutoring. *Educational Researcher, 13*(6), 4–16. doi:10.2307/ 1175554.

Boyce, A. S., Conway, J. S., Caputo, P. M., & Huber, C. R. (2015). Development of the adaptive employee personality test (ADEPT-15TM). Paper Presented at the 2015 Conference of the International Personnel Assessment Council, Atlanta, GA.

Brown, A. (2016). Item response models for forced-choice questionnaires: A common framework. *Psychometrika, 81*(1), 135–160. doi:10.1007/s11336-014–9434-9.

Brown, A., Inceoglu, I., & Lin, Y. (2017). Preventing rater biases in 360-degree feedback by forcing choice. *Organizational Research Methods, 20*(1), 121–148. doi:10.1177/ 1094428116668036.

Brown, A. & Maydeu-Olivares, A. (2011). Item response modeling of forced-choice questionnaires. *Educational & Psychological Measurement, 71*(3), 460–502. doi:10.1177/0013164410375112.

Brown, A. & Maydeu-Olivares, A. (2013). How IRT can solve problems of ipsative data in forced-choice questionnaires. *Psychological Methods, 18*(1), 36–52. doi:10.1037/ a0030641.

Carroll, J. B. (1993). *Human cognitive abilities: A survey of factor-analytic studies.* New York, NY: Cambridge University Press.

Chen, C., Lee, H., & Chen, Y. (2005). Personalized e-learning system using item response theory. *Computers & Education, 44*(3), 237–255.

Cheung, M. W. L., & Chan, W. (2002). Reducing uniform response bias with ipsative measurement in multiple-group confirmatory factor analysis. *Structural Equation Modeling: A Multidisciplinary Journal, 9*(1), 55–77. doi:10.1207/ S15328007SEM0901_4.

Christiansen, N. D., Burns, G. N., & Montgomery, G. E. (2005). Reconsidering forced-choice item formats for applicant personality assessment. *Human Performance, 18*(3), 267–307. doi:10.1207/s15327043hup1803_4.

Corno, L. (2008). On teaching adaptively. *Educational Psychologist, 43*(3), 161–173. doi:10.1080/00461520802178466.

Costa, P. T., Jr., & McCrae, R. R. (1992). *Revised NEO personality inventory (NEO–PI–R) and NEO five-factor inventory (NEO–FFI) professional manual.* Odessa, FL: Psychological Assessment Resources.

Daniels, J. A., Spero, R. A., Leonard, J. M., & Schimmel, C. J. (2015). A content analysis of military psychology: 2002–2014. *Military Pschology, 27*(6), 366–375.

De Boeck, P. (2017). Interwovenness of response time and response accuracy in cognitive tests. Paper Presented at the 82nd International Meeting of the Psychometric Society, Zurich, Switzerland.

Drasgow, F., Stark, S., Chernyshenko, O. S., Nye, C. D., Hulin, C. L., & White, L. A. (2012). *Development of the tailored adaptive personality assessment system (TAPAS) to support army selection and classification decisions* (tech. rep. no. 1311). Arlington, VA: U.S. Army Research Institute for the Behavioral and Social Sciences.

Embretson, S., & Reise, S. (2000). *Item response theory for psychologists.* Mahwah, NJ: Lawrence Erlbaum Associates.

Fetzer, M. (2009, April). Validity and utility of computer adaptive testing in personnel selection. Symposium presented at the annual meeting for the Society for Industrial and Organizational Psychology. New Orleans, LA.

Gartner (2015). www.gartner.com/newsroom/id/3088221. Retrieved on December 20, 2015.

Georgiadou, E., Triantafillou, E., & Economides, A. A. (2007). A review of item exposure control strategies for computerized adaptive testing developed from 1983 to 2005. *The Journal of Technology, Learning, and Assessment, 5*(8), 3–38.

Goldberg, B., Brawner, K., Sottilare, R., Tarr, R., Billings, D. R., & Malone, N. (2012). Use of evidence-based strategies to enhance the extensibility of adaptive tutoring technologies. Interservice/Industry Training, Simulation, and Education Conference (I/ITSEC), Orlando, FL.

Grelle, D., Gutierrez, S. L., & Fetzer, M. (2010, June). Validity of CAT in Personnel Selection. Presented at the Annual Meeting of the International Association of Computer Adaptive Testing, Arnhem, Netherlands.

Gutierrez, S. L. (2011, October). Perceptions of fairness and opportunity to perform on CAT in personnel selection. Paper presented at the annual meeting of the International Associated of Computer Adaptive Testing, Pacific Grove, CA.

Gutierrez, S., Grelle, D., & Borneman, M. (2009, April). Computer Adaptive Measures of Cognitive Ability: Validity and Utility. Presented at the Annual Meeting of the Society of Industrial Organizational Psychologists, New Orleans, LA.

Han, K. T. (2012). SimulCAT: Windows software for simulating computerized adaptive test administration. *Applied Psychological Measurement, 36*(1), 64–66.

Houston, J. S., Borman, W. C., Farmer, W. L., & Bearden, R. M. (2006). Development of the navy computer adaptive personality scales (NCAPS). (No. NPRST-TR-06–2). Millington, TN: Navy Personnel Research, Studies, and Technology Division, Bureau of Naval Personnel (NPRST/PERS-1).

Jackson, D. N., Wroblewski, V. R., & Ashton, M. C. (2000). The impact of faking on employment tests: Does forced choice offer a solution? *Human Performance, 13* (4), 371–388.

Johnson, C. E., Wood, R., & Blinkhorn, S. F. (1988). Spuriouser and spuriouser: The use of ipsative personality tests. *Journal of Occupational Psychology, 61*(2), 153–162.

Johnston, J. H., Goodwin, G., Moss, J., Sottilare, R., Ososky, S., Cruz, D. & Graesser, A. (2015). Effectiveness evaluation tools and methods for adaptive training and education in support of the US army learning model: Research outline. Retrieved from www.dtic.mil/get-tr-doc/pdf?AD=ADA621295.

Kantrowitz, T. M., Fetzer, M. S., & Dawson, C. R. (2011). Computer adaptive testing (CAT): A faster, smarter, and more secure approach to pre-employment testing. *Journal of Business and Psychology, 26*, 227–232.

Kantrowitz, T. M. & Robie, C. (2011). Estimates of faking on computer adaptive and static personality assessments. In T. Kantrowitz (Chair) *Innovations in Mitigating Faking on Personality Assessments.* Paper presented at the annual meeting of the Society for Industrial and Organizational Psychology, Chicago, IL.

King, D., Ryan, A. M., Kantrowitz, T. M., Grelle, D., & Dainis, A. (2015). Mobile internet testing: An analysis of equivalence, individual differences, and reactions. *International Journal of Selection and Assessment, 23*, 382–394.

Liu, M. T. & Yu, P. T. (2011). Aberrant learning achievement detection based on person-fit statistics in personalized e-learning systems. *Educational Technology & Society, 14*(1), 107–120.

Lu, Y. & Sireci, S. G. (2007). Validity issues in test speededness. *Educational Measurement: Issues and Practice, 26*(4), 29–37. doi:10.1111/j.1745-3992.2007.00106.x.

Maynes, D. (2010). Research in test security: The latest research in test security data analysis. Symposium presented at the 11th annual conference of the Association of Test Publishers, Orlando, FL.

McGrew, K. S. (1997). Analysis of the major intelligence batteries according to a proposed comprehensive Gf–Gc framework. In D. P. Flanagan, J. L. Genshaft & P. L. Harrison (Eds.), *Contemporary intellectual assessment: Theories, tests, and issues* (pp. 151–179). New York, NY: Guilford.

Moclaire, C., Middleton, E., Fox, B., Foster, C., & Prettyman, T. (2012). Balancing security and efficiency in limited-size computer adaptive test libraries. Poster presented at the annual meeting of the Society for Industrial and Organizational Psychology, San Diego, CA.

Ozer, D. J. & Benet-Martínez, V. (2006). Personality and the prediction of consequential outcomes. *Annual Review of Psychology, 57*, 401–421. doi:10.1146/annurev. psych.57.102904.190127.

Reckase, M. D. (2009). *Multidimensional item response theory.* New York, NY: Springer.

Roberts, B. W., Kuncel, N. R., Shiner, R., Caspi, A., & Goldberg, L. R. (2007). The power of personality: The comparative validity of personality traits, socioeconomic status, and cognitive ability for predicting important life outcomes. *Perspectives on Psychological Science (Wiley-Blackwell), 2*(4), 313–345. doi:10.1111/j.1745–6916.2007.00047.x.

Sawtooth Software, Inc. ACBC technical paper [Sawtooth Software technical paper series]. Sequim (WA): Sawtooth Software, Inc., 2009 [online]. Retrieved August 15, 2017, from www.sawtoothsoftware.com/download/techpap/acbctech. Pdf.

Schmidt, F., & Hunter, J. (1998). The validity and utility of selection methods in personnel psychology: Practical and theoretical implications of 85 years of research findings. *Psychological Bulletin, 124*, 262–274.

Schneider, R. J., McLellan, R. A., Kantrowitz, T. M., Houston, J. S., & Borman, W. C. (2009). Criterion-related validity of an innovative CAT-based personality measure. Proceedings from the GMAC Conference on Computerized Adaptive Testing.

Segall, D. O. (1996). Multidimensional adaptive testing. *Psychometrika, 61*(2), 331–354. doi:10.1007/BF02294343.

Seo, D. G. & Weiss, D. J. (2015). Best design for multidimensional computerized adaptive testing with the bifactor model. *Educational and Psychological Measurement, 75* (6), 954–978. doi:10.1177/0013164415575147.

SHL. (2009–2014). Global personality inventory – adaptive: Technical manual. Surrey, UK: SHL.

SHL. (2016). *Apta™ architecture technical manual*. Surrey, UK: SHL.

Smittle, P. (1993). Computer adaptive testing: A new era. *Journal of Development Education, 17*, 8–10.

Snow, R. E. (1997). Individual differences. In R. D. Tennyson, F. Schott, N. M. Seel, & S. Dijkstra (Eds.), *Instructional design: International perspectives* (vol. 1, pp. 215–242). Mahwah, NJ: Lawrence Erlbaum Associates.

Stark, S. & Chernyshenko, O. S. (2007). Adaptive testing with the multi-unidimensional pairwise preference model. Proceedings of the 2007 GMAC Conference on Computerized Adaptive Testing, Minneapolis, MN.

Stark, S. & Chernyshenko, O. S. (2011). Computerized adaptive testing with the Zinnes and Griggs pairwise preference ideal point model. *International Journal of Testing, 11* (3), 231–247. doi:10.1080/15305058.2011.561459.

Stark, S., Chernyshenko, O. S., Drasgow, F., & White, L. A. (2012). Adaptive testing with multidimensional pairwise preference items: Improving the efficiency of personality and other noncognitive assessments. *Organizational Research Methods, 15* (3), 463–487. doi:10.1177/1094428112444611.

Stark, S., Chernyshenko, O. S., Drasgow, F., Nye, C. D., White, L. A., Heffner, T., & Farmer, W. L. (2014). From ABLE to TAPAS: A new generation of personality tests to support military selection and classification decisions. *Military Psychology, 26*(3), 153–164. doi:10.1037/mil0000044.

Sullivan, J. (2014). The power has shifted to the candidate, so current recruiting practices will stop working. Retrieved December 20, 2015, from www.eremedia.com/ere/the-power-has-shifted-to-the-candidate-so-current-recruiting-practices-will-stop-working

Tippins, N. T. (2009). Internet alternatives to traditional proctored testing: Where are we now? *Industrial and Organizational Psychology: Perspectives on Science and Practice, 2*, 2–10.

Training. (2016). 2016 training industry report. Retrieved from https://trainingmag.com/trgmag-article/2o16-training-industry-report.

van Buuren, N., & Eggen, T. J. H. M. (2017). Latent-class-based item selection for computerized adaptive progress tests. *Journal of Computerized Adaptive Testing, 5*(2), 22–43. Retrieved from http://iacat.org/jcat/index.php/jcat/article/view/62/29.

van der Linden, W. J. (2009). Conceptual issues in response-time modeling. *Journal of Educational Measurement, 46*(3), 247–272. doi:10.1111/j.1745–3984.2009.00080.x.

van der Linden, W. J., & Pashley, P. J. (2000). Item selection and ability estimation in adaptive testing. In W. J. van der Linden, & G. A. W. Glas (Eds.), Computerized adaptive testing: Theory and practice (pp. 1–25). Dordrecht: Springer Netherlands. doi:10.1007/0–306-47531–6_1.

VanLehn, K. (2011). The relative effectiveness of human tutoring, intelligent tutoring systems, and other tutoring systems. *Educational Psychologist, 46*(4), 197–221. doi:10.1080/00461520.2011.611369.

Veerkamp, W. J. J. & Berger, M. P. F. (1997). Some new item selection criteria for adaptive testing. *Journal of Educational and Behavioral Statistics, 22*(2), 203–226. doi:10.2307/1165378.

Veldkamp, B. P. (2016). On the issue of item selection in computerized adaptive testing with response times. *Journal of Educational Measurement, 53*(2), 212–228. doi:10.1111/jedm.12110.

Vogel-Walcutt, J., Ross, K. G., Phillips, J. K., & Stensrud, B. (2016). Improving the efficiency and effectiveness of adaptive training: Using developmental models as a framework and foundation for human-centred instructional design. *Theoretical Issues in Ergonomics Science, 17*(2), 127–148. doi:10.1080/1463922X.2015.1111460.

Weiss, D. J. (1982). Improving measurement quality and efficiency with adaptive testing. *Applied Psychological Measurement, 6*(4), 473–492. doi:10.1177/014662168200600408.

Weiss, D. J. & Kingsbury, G. G. (1984). Application of computerized adaptive testing to educational problems. *Journal of Educational Measurement, 21*(4), 361–375. doi:10.1111/j.1745–3984.1984.tb01040.x.

7 Playing with a Purpose

The Role of Games and Gamification in Modern Assessment Practices

Nathan Weidner and Elizabeth Short

Employee assessment and selection methods such as interviews (Macan 2009), assessment centers (Thornton & Gibbons, 2009), cognitive tests (Ones, Dilchert, & Viswesveran, 2012), as well as self-report measures including biodata (Breaugh, 2009) and personality measures (Barrick & Mount, 2012), have been used to effectively evaluate and hire job applicants for decades now. Recent advances in these methods have primarily focused on updating and adapting these methods due to the modern proliferation of technology. This has included advances such as expanding our understanding of the use of video interviews (Sears et al., 2013), exploring the potential of virtual assessment centers (Howland, et al., 2015), and adapting self-report and cognitive assessment tools for use on mobile devices (Arthur et al., 2014; Illingworth, et al., 2015).

Another major trend shaping modern organizational practices is gamification (Carador, Northcraft, & Whicker, 2017). Gamification is a method in which game-like elements are incorporated into more traditional processes. The incorporation of story elements (Collmus & Landers, 2015), leaderboards (Landers, Bauer, & Callan, 2015), badges (Hamari, 2017), and even simple tools like progress bars (Yan et al., 2011) are just a few examples of gamification elements which have begun to be incorporated into practices such as training and assessment. Research on gamification as a process generally supports that it enhances user engagement and results in higher levels of performance although the theoretical mechanisms by which different elements of gamification improve performance are still being explored (e.g., Landers, Bauer, & Callan, 2017; Mekler et al., 2017; Sailer et al., 2017). Gamified assessment methods, in particular, may be able to help reduce test anxiety in order to improve validity of measurement (Cassady & Johnson, 2002; Mavridis & Tsiatsos, 2016) as well as increase the intrinsic motivation of test takers (Dickey, 2007) which could reduce survey fatigue during longer assessments. Ideally, this could allow for longer and more in-depth assessments of candidates to improve the reliability and validity of assessment practices overall. The present chapter will seek to further describe current research in gamifying assessment practices as well as to explore the potential benefits and drawback of including gamification elements as part of an employee selection system.

Additionally, the proliferation of handheld mobile internet devices as well as the ever-increasing capabilities of traditional computing devices has resulted in the development of entirely new methods for employee assessment and selection.

In particular, assessment games are a new method of employee assessment in which gameplay behaviors are used to evaluate applicants. Games that are developed for purposes other than enjoyment are commonly known as 'serious games' (Connolly et al., 2014). While defining serious games has been a matter of some debate (Boyle, 2014; Fetzer, 2015), they are generally recognized as, "Games that do not have entertainment, enjoyment, or fun as their primary purpose." (Michael & Chen, 2005: p. 21). It is important to note that this definition does not exclude these games from being fun, but instead articulates that it is not the primary purpose of their design. Serious games have been widely adopted across a variety of organizational contexts for use in recruiting, training, and assessment processes (Fetzer, 2015). While relatively new, assessment games may be particularly appealing to younger digital natives who have grown up in a media-rich world (Prensky, 2001). Early research on assessment games has suggested that they show promise in being able to address some of the limitations of current assessment methods (see Landers, 2015). Additionally, many assessment games are optimized for administration on mobile devices which are predicted to be a growing trend in modern assessment practices (Lawrence & Kinney, 2017). The present chapter will also review recent research and applications of serious games for assessment purposes, in particular as they relate to employee selection practices.

7.1 Overview of Assessment Games and Gamified Assessments

Many assessment games and gamified assessment practices are already commonly in use across a variety of industries. For example, computer games have been used by educators for assessment and training in a wide variety of fields since the late 1960s due to their consistently being associated with increased student engagement and learning (Tobias & Fletcher, 2011). Many of these educational games have been developed specifically for use as assessment tools (Connolly et al., 2014; Rufo-Tepper, 2015), and evaluate characteristics relevant for organizations (Greco, Baldissin, & Nonino, 2013; Klein & Fleck, 1990). Although primarily used for educational purposes, these games involve assessing knowledge, skills, abilities, and other characteristics (KSAOs) that are desired by many employers and may transfer well to employee assessment and selection practices.

Much of our current knowledge of gamification comes from research in education (Wiggins, 2016) and is often applied to organizational training programs (Landers, 2014; Landers & Armstrong, 2017). Researchers and practitioners have, however, begun to apply similar gamification principles to update other organizational practices such as job design (Liu, Huang, & Zhang, 2018) and assessment practices (Armstrong et al., 2016). For example, while simulations have had a long history of use in personnel selection (Thornton & Gibbons, 2009), many modern simulations have become gamified (Grossman, Heyne, & Salas, 2015). Similarly, incorporating more interactive multi-media elements into situational judgment tests has been found to enhance the user experience

(Richman-Hirsch, Olson-Buchannan, & Drasgow, 2000). Researchers and practitioners have just begun to scratch the surface of what gamification can do to improve assessments (Armstrong et al., 2016).

Alternatively, some commercial games have been developed to replicate simulations used for training and assessment due to their entertaining and engaging nature (e.g., flight simulators). Due to the ever-increasing popularity of commercial video games as a form of recreation, some researchers have sought to examine how gameplay behaviors and performance metrics from casually played commercial games may be related to desirable KSAOs (e.g., Baniqued et al., 2013). Some companies are even developing assessment games specifically designed for employee recruitment and selection (e.g., Arctic Shores; Knack; Revelian). Collectively, these games may provide organizations with a variety of new assessment tools that can be used to enhance employee selection processes.

7.2 Educational and Business Games

One area that has widely adopted the use of games for assessment purposes is the education industry (Connolly et al., 2014; Tobias & Fletcher, 2011). While educational assessment games often target specific content areas such as math or physics, a growing number of them target more basic learning skills such as data literacy and visualization (Chin, Blair, & Schwartz, 2016), design skills (Conlin, et al., 2015), feedback seeking behaviors (Cutumisu et al., 2015), and generic problem solving skills (Shute et al., 2016) all of which may be relevant for performance in organizations as well. Organizational practitioners may seek to use educational games such as these as a baseline tool to help evaluate many of these KSAOs for selection purposes.

Business simulation games (BSGs) may be of particular interest to organizational practitioners and researchers. Greco, Baldissin, and Nonino (2013) define BSGs as games designed for the purpose of training business skills or the evaluation of players' performance in displaying those skills. In general, research has supported the use of BSGs as effective tools to train business skills (Rachman-Moore & Kenett, 2006). Research linking BSG performance to subsequent career success, however, has been mixed (Norris & Snyder 1982; Wolfe 1985). Longitudinal studies (Wolfe & Roberts 1986; 1993) did find some correlations between scores on business simulation games and subsequent career success such as salary ($r = .28$) and number of promotions ($r = .32$) five years after graduation. As BSGs are designed to accurately replicate real business challenges and market conditions, it makes sense that they would be valid predictors of subsequent performance in organizations.

Current generation BSGs (e.g., CESIM, n.d.) are highly automated and allow for detailed tracking of progress throughout the simulation. Although research into the internal validity of BSGs for learning relevant knowledge and skills has continued to be of importance (Wolfe, 2016), research on the external validity of BSGs has not kept pace with the rate of technological enhancements that have been incorporated (Anderson & Lawton, 2009). At present, the full extent to which behaviors and performance in BSGs are capable of being used to predict future workplace performance is unknown. Future research should continue to examine the usefulness of BSGs for the assessment of a variety of relevant KSAOs such as domain specific knowledge, teamwork skills, cognitive abilities, and in particular for the assessment of leadership potential amongst MBA students (Avolio, Waldman, & Einstein, 1988).

7.3 Gamification of Workplace Simulations

Educators have also been quick to adopt gamification elements to enhance classroom education (Wiggins, 2016). Many of these same elements have transitioned to organizational training programs as well (Landers, 2014; Landers & Armstrong, 2017). Recently, researchers have begun to examine the application of gamification to other aspects of organizations through the process of game-thinking (Armstrong, Landers, Collmus, 2015). This approach has led to the incorporation of gamification elements into other organizational practices such as job design (Liu, Huang, & Zhang, 2018), recruitment (Collmus, Armstrong, & Landers, 2016), and assessments (Armstrong et al., 2016). Some of the most notable examples of this have been incorporated into modern simulations.

Job simulations have had a long history of use in assessment practices (Lievens & De Soete, 2012). Simulations are often categorized into either high-fidelity simulations such as those found in assessment centers or low-fidelity simulations commonly known as situational judgment tests (SJTs) (Motowidlo, Dunnette, & Carter, 1990). The fidelity of a simulation has been found to relate positively to its predictive validity with assessment centers demonstrating incremental validity over situational judgment tests (Lievens & Patterson, 2011). SJTs may however be much more cost effective than assessment centers due to the reduced cost of staff and assessors (Motowidlo, et al., 1990). Video based (or medium fidelity) simulations in which participants react to video-recorded scenarios have been found to be valid predictors of performance (Cucina, et al., 2015) and generally receive favorable reactions from applicants (Bruk-Lee et al., 2016). These media-rich simulations are one avenue that organizations have commonly used to incorporate gamified elements into already existing selection practices. PDRI's (n.d.) Learning Agility Simulation (Kubisak et al., 2014) is an example of a gamified simulation assessment designed to evaluate a candidate's ability and willingness to learn from experience through three stages measuring observation, connection, and assessment. Initial results indicated that the gamified simulation held strong relationships with both inductive ($r = .43$) and verbal ($r = .50$) reasoning skills (Kubisak et al., 2014).

Similarly, many industries commonly use high-fidelity simulations for training purposes such as heavy machinery (ThoroughTec; Industrial Training International), disaster management (ETC), aviation (Virtual Aviation), and even surgery (OssoVR). While many of these simulations are serious in nature, they often have been gamified by incorporating many game-based elements such as leaderboards and real-time feedback in order to make them more enjoyable and immersive. Adapting these gamified simulators for use in personnel assessment and selection could have a variety of benefits for organizations. By their very nature, these simulators are designed to collect high amounts of very precise data to evaluate physical skills such as hand-eye coordination (Gallagher et al., 2005). Similar to BSGs as described above, these simulators could serve as an effective tool for assessment of candidates in a wide variety of occupations.

Games such as Job Simulator (2016) offer a lighthearted whimsical take on a virtual-reality-based simulation of a variety of workplace activities. While Job Simulator was developed for entertainment purposes, it highlights the multitude of ways that the increasing proliferation of virtual reality technology could help to shape future job assessments. Future performance assessments could utilize platforms such as this to evaluate not only decision-making strategies, but process knowledge and judgment. When combined with their Mixed Reality Tech (Owlchemy Labs, 2016), this could create highly adaptable simulations that could be monitored by assessors from afar. Having a high fidelity and immersive assessment available virtually could potentially cut both the time and costs of assessments. As the presence of home-based virtual reality systems begins to grow (Merel, 2017), this may offer a more detailed form of work assessment that could be administered online and unproctored.

7.4 Further Applications of Gamification to Assessment

The process of gamification, holds great promise for improving organizational assessment practices in general (Armstrong et al., 2016; Armstrong, Landers, & Collmus, 2015). Many gamification elements such as progress bars are relatively cheap to incorporate into current assessment practices and if used properly may enhance employee motivation during assessment with little to no additional cost (Yan et al., 2011). Other elements, such as offering badges that can be displayed on social media sites upon the completion of an assessment, may increase motivation to complete the assessment (Collmus et al., 2016) thus attracting more applicants. Other features such as including narrative elements are less understood and are just beginning to be explored (Collmus & Landers, 2015). Technological advances, such as computer adaptive testing and ecological momentary assessment (Gibbons, 2017), can potentially allow assessment designers to further enhance assessments with gamification principles by incorporating branching story lines, automatically adjusting levels of difficulty, and allowing for more timely assessment across different contexts. It is safe to say that current researchers have only just begun to scratch the surface of what gamification elements can be incorporated into assessments.

That isn't to say that all gamification elements should be incorporated into assessment practices, but rather that researchers are just beginning to explore the various impacts of doing so. Practitioners and researchers alike should approach gamification of assessments with an open mind and a careful touch. Progress bars, for example, are one of the simpler elements of gamification that are commonly applied to assessments. Progress bars provide a simple visual form of feedback to participants that helps them to gauge how much time and effort remain in an assessment relative to what they have already completed. Progress bars have been theorized to increase engagement and completion rates in surveys and assessments by helping people to more easily visualize their end goal of completion (Cheema & Bagchi, 2011). However, the practical impact of including progress bars in assessments has been found to rely heavily on user expectations prior to beginning the assessment. Research has demonstrated that progress bars can result in increased satisfaction (Downes-Le Guin et al., 2012) and completion rates (Conrad et al., 2010; Yan et al., 2010) provided that the progress indicated is consistent with or even quicker than the users' expectations. Conversely, if a progress bar indicates slower progress than an individual had expected when beginning the assessment, they may actually be more likely to quit mid-assessment. Therefore, it is important to appropriately indicate the expected length of an assessment before including a progress bar. It serves to show that even though progress bars are a fairly simple element of gamification, even they may cause unintended consequences if incorporated into assessment practices without due consideration.

7.5 Using Emergent Gameplay to Predict Behaviors

An alternative approach to using gamified forms of assessments could be to use data from recreational gameplay behavior to evaluate KSAOs of interest. There is a growing body of research that has found relationships between emergent gameplay behaviors and various personality (See Table 7.1) and cognitive (See Table 7.2) dimensions. These studies often examine gameplay from mass-marketed commercial and casual games that are widely available and played by millions of people worldwide (Casual Games Association, n.d.). The potential for using emergent gameplay from videogames to predict organizational behavior is a research area that is still relatively undeveloped. Modern gaming platforms often track player achievements ranging from specific in-game accomplishments to broad level player rankings such as Microsoft's GamerScore (n.d.). These data points are often easily accessed through publicly available rankings and may related to a wide variety of workplace relevant KSAOs.

Many studies have found promising links for in-game behaviors transferring to other environments. These studies have ranged from early studies looking at motor functions (Griffith et al., 1983) to more recent examinations of cognitive abilities and skills (Gnambs & Appel, 2017). For instance, games such as World of Warcraft (WoW; n.d.) have been a tool used by researchers to better understand human behavior for a variety of social sciences (Bainbridge 2012; Morrison & Fontenla, 2013), and it was even used by the Center for Disease Control to model human behavior during an epidemic (Sydell, 2005). Commercial games such as WoW

Table 7.1 *Personality and non-cognitive relationships with gameplay behaviors*

Construct	r	In-game behaviors	Source
Extraversion			
	.34	Socializer game style	Zeigler-Hill, 2015
	.27	Daredevil game style	Zeigler-Hill, 2015
	.28	Helping behaviors	Worth & Book, 2014
	.23	Social behaviors	Worth & Book, 2014
	.19	Conqueror game style	Zeigler-Hill, 2015
Conscientiousness			
	.24	Working behaviors	Worth & Book, 2014
	.16	Mastermind game style	Zeigler-Hill, 2015
	−.21	Aggressive behaviors toward others	Worth & Book, 2014
Agreeableness			
	.35	As the director, offering money	Baumert et al., 2013
	.22	Helping behaviors	Worth & Book, 2014
	.16	Participating in world events	Yee et al., 2011
	.16	Socializer game style	Zeigler-Hill, 2015
	−.17	Aggressive behaviors toward others	Worth & Book, 2014
Openness			
	.37	Immersion/roleplay behaviors	Worth & Book, 2014
	.35	Seeker game style	Zeigler-Hill, 2015
	.34	Helping behaviors	Worth & Book, 2014
	.22	Working behaviors	Worth & Book, 2014
	.16	Mastermind game style	Zeigler-Hill, 2015
	−.16	Conqueror game style	Zeigler-Hill, 2015
	−.17	Team tasks (5 M)	Yee et al., 2011
Neuroticism/ emotionality			
	.22	Working behaviors	Worth & Book, 2014
	.21	Achiever game style	Zeigler-Hill, 2015
	.19	Seeker game style	Zeigler-Hill, 2015
	−.16	Conqueror game style	Zeigler-Hill, 2015
	−.23	Daredevil game style	Zeigler-Hill, 2015
Honesty/humility			
	.21	Helping behaviors	Worth & Book, 2014
	.16	Immersion/roleplay behavior	Worth & Book, 2014
	−.45	Aggressive behaviors toward others	Worth & Book, 2014
Persistence (low performers)			
	.47	Unsolved challenges	Ventura & Shute, 2013
	.42	Obtaining trophies	Ventura & Shute, 2013
	.30	Learning from material	Ventura & Shute, 2013

Table 7.1 (*cont.*)

Construct	*r*	In-game behaviors	Source
Persistence (high performers)			
	.31	Obtaining trophies	Ventura & Shute, 2013
Values			
Cooperativeness	.53	Monetary offers made	Baumert et al., 2013
Justice – Observer	.32	Monetary offers made	Baumert et al., 2013
Justice – Beneficiary	.32	Monetary offers made	Baumert et al., 2013
Social Responsibility	.31	Monetary offers made	Baumert et al., 2013
Moral Identity	.26	Monetary offers made	Baumert et al., 2013
Individualistic	−.39	Monetary offers made	Baumert et al., 2013

Note: All included correlations were significant (p < .05). Due to space limitations, only correlations (r > .15) are reported.

have identified many personality traits as well as cognitive skills and abilities that may transfer from the game to the workplace (Graham & Gosling, 2013; Rubenfire, 2014; Worth & Book, 2015; Yee et al., 2011). Tracking performance and emergent behavioral data from commercial games such as this (Lewis & Wardrip-Fruin, 2010) may provide a useful avenue for further developing and understanding game-based assessment tools.

7.6 Personality and Non-Cognitive Measures

Personality is one of the most commonly used methods of candidate assessment for personnel selection. Models of personality such as the Big Five (Costa & McCrae, 1992; Goldberg, 1993) and the expanded HEXACO model (Ashton & Lee, 2001, 2007) have been found to be important predictors of job performance as well as a variety of career outcomes (Barrick & Mount, 1991; Hurtz & Donovan, 2000; Judge et al., 1999; Oh et al., 2014). Traditional measures of personality still typically rely on self-report and often utilize Likert-scale type responses despite some noted limitations to these methods (Spector, 2012). Game-based assessments may prove to be a tool that is capable of addressing some of these limitations for a variety of non-cognitive predictors (see Table 7.1).

In order to understand how to properly utilize game-based assessments, it is important to first understand which gameplay behaviors will be indicative of desired KSAOs. Research has consistently found that socio-demographic and personality variables relate to general gaming preferences (Bean et al., 2016; Braun et al., 2016; Nagygyörgy et al., 2013), as well as preferences for specific genres of games (Apperley, 2006; Braun et al., 2016). For example, Braun et al. (2016) found that conscientiousness was associated with a preference for

Table 7.2 *Cognitive abilities as measured by emergent gameplay performance*

Construct	r	In-game behaviors	Source
Fluid intelligence			
	.64	Visualization games	Quiroga et al., (2015)
	.62	Analytical games	Quiroga et al., (2015)
	.46	Performance/score	Buford & O'Leary, (2015)
	.45	Computational games	Quiroga et al., (2015)
	.42	Memory games	Quiroga et al., (2015)
Crystallized intelligence			
	.49	Performance/score	Buford & O'Leary, (2015)
	.47	Computational games	Quiroga et al., (2015)
	.44	Memory games	Quiroga et al., (2015)
	.40	Analytical games	Quiroga et al., (2015)
	.34	Visualization games	Quiroga et al., (2015)
Inductive reasoning			
	.45	Demonstrate knowledge	Kubisak et al. (2014)
	.38	Connecting patterns	Kubisak et al. (2014)
	.15	Assess their own performance	Kubisak et al. (2014)
Verbal Reasoning			
	.44	Demonstrate knowledge	Kubisak et al. (2014)
	.40	Connecting patterns	Kubisak et al. (2014)
	.28	Assess their own performance	Kubisak et al. (2014)
Visual perception			
	.66	Visualization games	Quiroga et al. (2015)
	.65	Analytical games	Quiroga et al. (2015)
	.48	Computational games	Quiroga et al. (2015)
	.32	Memory games	Quiroga et al. (2015)
Memory & learning			
	.44	Computational games	Quiroga et al. (2015)
	.37	Memory games	Quiroga et al. (2015)
	.30	Analytical games	Quiroga et al. (2015)
	.29	Visualization game	Quiroga et al. (2015)
Cognitive speed			
	.55	Analytical games	Quiroga et al. (2015)
	.46	Computational gamed	Quiroga et al. (2015)
	.44	Memory games	Quiroga et al. (2015)
	.41	Visualization games	Quiroga et al. (2015)

Note: All correlations presented are significant ($p < .05$). See cited studies for more game specific details.

simulation games while extraversion was associated with a preference for action games. Additionally, different motives for playing casual games have been documented across game genres (Hainey et al., 2011; Kahn et al., 2015). This has led to several different taxonomies of gamer types based on motivations for play (Kahn et al., 2015). These have included such classifications as Bartle's player types (Bartle, 1996), Yee's MMORPG User Motivations (Yee, 2006a, 2006b), and, more recently, the BrainHex Model (Bateman & Nacke, 2010).

The BrainHex typology (Nacke, Bateman, & Mandryk, 2014) is particularly interesting as it was designed to gauge seven basic dimensions of gaming style preferences that are directly linked to different neurobiological drivers of behavior (see Bateman & Nacke 2010 for a review). Preferences for the different gameplay motives as measured by the BrainHex model have been linked to both Myers-Briggs personality types (Nacke, Bateman, & Mandryk, 2014) as well as to HEXACO personality traits (Zeigler-Hill & Monica, 2015). These findings suggest it is theoretically possible to use gameplay style and game design to make the assessments more attractive to desired candidates thus improving recruitment efforts. For example, an assessment tool which emphasized social connections with other players (Zeigler-Hill & Monica, 2015) as part of an action game play style (Braun et al., 2016) would likely attract more extraverted applicants.

Other studies have examined the relationships between personality and more specific in-game behaviors using games such as WoW. Worth and Book (2014) found that WoW in-game helping behaviors such as giving gold and healing others was related to openness ($r = .34$), while task completion behaviors such as earning gold and gathering resources were related to conscientiousness ($r = .24$). Many in-game behaviors from commercial games can be tracked through publicly posted achievements (Lewis & Wardrip-Fruin, 2010). Using this method, Yee et al. (2011) found small, but statistically significant relationships between each of the big five personality traits and various in-game achievements. For example, participants who were high in extraversion had more team-related achievements such as completions of five-man team dungeons ($r = .12$), while agreeableness was inversely related to competitive and hostile practices, such as killing other players ($r = -.08$), and other player versus player (PVP) activities ($r = -.12$) (Yee et al., 2011). Organizations could theoretically seek to use information such as this to evaluate applicants' personality based on casual gameplay behaviors. It has even been suggested that applicants could include in-game accomplishments on resumes as a way to demonstrate their possession of particular KSAOs (see Rubenfire, 2014).

Not only large-scale commercial games such as WoW can be used in this manner. Baumert, Schlösser, and Schmitt (2014) examined the relationship between personality dimensions and a simple economic simulation game revolving around making an offer to share resources with another hypothetical player or not. They found that even simple in-game choices such as this had moderate relationships to a variety of personality measures including HEXACO Honesty/humility ($r = .16$) and Agreeableness ($r = .35$). Additionally, these in-game choices related to self-reported voluntary services ($r = .16$) which are similar to OCBs (Finkelstein & Penner, 2004; Lavelle, 2010). Baumert et al. (2014) further found that choosing to share was related to cooperative values orientation ($r = .53$) and inversely with individualistic value orientation ($r = -.39$). Collectively, these findings suggest that gameplay behaviors may be an effective method by which organizations could covertly assess non-cognitive aspects of applicants, such as integrity, which are relevant for a variety of workplace outcomes (Iddekinge et al., 2012).

Another potential non-cognitive KSAO which is likely measureable through gameplay is persistence. Persistence has long been suggested to be an important component predicting job performance as an aspect of motivation (Kipnis, 1962; Kipnis & Glickman, 1962). In particular, some studies have found evidence to suggest that persistence is related to performance for those lower in natural ability (Kipnis 1962; Ventura & Shute 2013). More recent studies have linked perseverance to both job performance ($r = .33$) and counterproductive work behaviors ($r = -.35$) indicating it may be an important character strength for employees to possess (Littman-Ovadia & Lavy, 2016). Ventura and Shute (2013) demonstrated a measure of persistence using time spent on problems (both solved and unsolved) in a physics-based video game. Their measure of persistence was found to significantly correlate ($r = .51$) with other behavioral measures of persistence (Ventura, Shute, & Zhao, 2013). Assessment games may give us a valuable tool to better measure persistence by creating a task which is both engaging and difficult requiring engaged concentration to perform (Shute et al., 2015).

7.7 Cognitive Abilities

Historically, one of the best predictors of job performance has been cognitive abilities (Ones et al., 2012; Lang et al., 2010; Schmidt & Hunter, 1998; 2004). As these cognitive abilities are strongly related to one another, they are often combined as an overall general mental ability (GMA) or g, rather than as more specific abilities (Carroll, 1993). Some research has supported the importance of specific cognitive abilities over GMA in particular for lower-complexity jobs (Lang et al., 2010). Game-based assessments offer a variety of tools for measuring GMA as well as more specific cognitive abilities (Table 7.2).

Work by Baniqued et al. (2013) found that many different cognitive abilities are tapped by casual video games. Casual games are generally fairly simple in nature and lack the depth and commitment of full-length commercial games. Using a form of cognitive task analysis (Militello & Hutton, 1998), Baniqued et al. (2013) identified a set of twenty freely available games that were believed to rely on specific cognitive abilities. While they were able to find strong relationships between some game play components and specific cognitive abilities (e.g., working memory: $r = 0.55$), they found that game performance was generally most strongly related to measures of fluid intelligence which has been conceptualized as a measure of GMA (Kvist & Gustafsson, 2008).

Similarly, the work of Quiroga et al. (2009, 2011, 2015) has consistently found videogames can reliably and validly measure general mental ability. In their early work (Quiroga et al., 2009, 2011) identified some meaningful boundary conditions of the videogame cognitive ability relationship. Notably, different games had different relationships with GMA even within a commercial game marketed as having a relationship to cognitive abilities (e.g., Nintendo's Big Brain Academy) (Quiroga et al., 2009, 2011). While some mini-games had fairly consistent relationships with GMA across practice sessions, other were found to have none or to deteriorate as practice continued (Quiroga et al., 2009). In general, the authors concluded that in order for a game to effectively tap GMA it must have moderate levels of complexity (relative to the participant being evaluated), maintain novelty over time, and have no benefits from practice by relying on working memory rather than semantic memory (Quiroga et al., 2011). Using a composite of scores from 12 of these commercial games, Quiroga et al. (2015) were able to show a strong positive correlation ($r = 0.93$) with a traditional measure of GMA.

Buford and O'Leary (2015) took a slightly different approach by modifying an existing video game (e.g., Portal 2, n.d.) to use as an assessment tool to measure fluid intelligence. Split-half reliabilities across game levels (0.92) indicated that their game-based measure was a highly reliable measure comparable to other standardized cognitive measures. While Portal 2 performance indicators (e.g., time to completion, number of levels, steps taken) were found to correlate with other measures of fluid intelligence including Raven's Standard Progressive Matrices (RPM) (Raven, Raven, & Court, 2003) ($r = 0.46$) and the Shipley 2 Block Patterns measure (Shipley et al., 2012) ($r = 0.49$), there was notably no significant relationship found with the Wonderlic Personnel Quicktest which is designed for use in personnel selection.

7.8 Assessment Games Designed for Personnel Assessment and Selection

Several organizations have begun to actively market assessment games as tools that are designed for personnel recruitment and selection. For example, Arctic Shores (n.d.) had developed games such as Cosmic Cadet, Yellow Hook Reef, and most recently Skyrise City. Each of these games is designed to assess both cognitive and non-cognitive characteristics of job applicants. At Arctic Shores, experienced psychologists work hand in hand with professional game designers to create interactive experiences that will initially seem identical to many other commercially developed casual games.

These games are designed as psychological assessment tools from the ground up. Game designers work directly with psychologists to examine ways to present and connect the assessments in an engaging thematic manner. Skyrise City, for example, is themed around working within a skyscraper. Elevators advance you through stages as you climb the skyscraper. Each level consists of a theme-based mini game such as a memory test themed as identifying which flyers to mail out, a risk assessment tool where you fill up balloons to display logos, and an emotional intelligence test where you are teaching a computer to recognize emotions in tower guests. After each game is completed, a score is immediately given to provide performance feedback to the candidate before the elevator advances them to the next level.

In contrast, Revelian's (n.d.) Cognify program involves similar mini-game principles, but removes the theme-based elements to create a very direct example of a serious game. Cognify was developed based on the Cattell-Horn-Carroll

(CHC) theory of intelligence (Carroll, 1993; McGrew, 2005) with mini-games that are targeted at measuring different stratum-two broad cognitive abilities. Simple games such as Gridlock appear to examine visuospatial skills involving mental rotation in an appealingly simple Tetris-like game. The games are designed with presentation in mind and make smart use of vibrant colors and simple interaction mechanics such as clicking and dragging with a mouse. Participants are awarded with stars during gameplay to track their scores on each game as they progresses through the battery of measures.

Landers et al. (2017) found that Cognify was both a reliable and valid measure of GMA in addition to being preferred over traditional general cognitive ability tests by college students. Furthermore, while composite scores from Cognify were strongly related to a composite score derived from more traditional measures ($r =$ .77), the Cognify measure was able to add incremental validity over the traditional measures to the prediction of GPA. Studies such as this suggest that assessment games may actually have a greater propensity for assessing cognitive abilities than traditional measures.

Although personnel selection is the main focus of many of these assessment games, they also serve as a useful tool to identify high potential candidates. Knack (n.d.)is an interactive digital platform that allows anyone to play games that have been designed to assess KSAOs of interests to employers. As people play the games, they are awarded with one of three types of "Knacks." Regular Knacks measure specific KSAOs while "Superknacks" identify specific sets of talents that are related to success in a given careers. Knacks awarded from these games can be used to show people the career paths that most align with their skill set similar to interest inventories (Campbell, 1987). "Ultraknacks," by comparison, are custom developed algorithms that identify players with high success potential at specific companies. In this way, Knack serves to connect potential job applicants directly with organizations that can make use of their demonstrated gaming skills. Exploring the potential for assessment games to serve as voluntary recruitment tools is not unique to Knack. Companies such as Pymetrics (n.d.) (Narayanan, 2017) and Symphony Talent (n.d.) (Kalinoski, 2017) offer similar services where they market the use of voluntarily taken assessment games as a form of interest inventory and initial screening process. Ideally, this process would then incorporate further assessments for only those candidates who have already demonstrated an aptitude toward a given career path (Kalinoski, 2017). Collectively, companies such as these are actively forging ahead in the field of assessment games and demonstrating the value of these methods to organizations.

7.9 Limitations of Assessment Games and Gamified Assessments

Despite the many advantages that assessment games and gamified assessment methods present, these methods may not be equally appropriate for all socio-demographic groups. In particular, not everyone may have equal access to and familiarity with the technological advances which make these assessment methods possible. The concept of the "digital divide" refers to the growing gap between those that do and do not have adequate access to computers and the internet (Turner, 2016). Research has found that technological access and familiarity varies across many socio-demographic characteristics including gender (Owens & Lilly, 2017), ethnicity (Turner, 2016), rural-living (Walker, 2017), age (Hwang & Nam, 2017), and disability status (Duplaga, 2017). These differences could lead assessment games and gamified assessment practices which are dependent on this technology to create an artificial selection bias whereby they may unintentionally cause adverse impact against certain protected groups.

Turner (2016) describes how inequality results in disproportionately low broadband placement and competition in communities of color and in rural areas in particular. This in turn results in communities of racial minorities often being considered the "internet have nots" of the digital divide. Even amongst the poorest segments of the population, there is still a pronounced digital divide between members of different racial and ethnic groups, with poor Whites being more likely to have internet access than poor Blacks, Hispanics, Native Americans, and Pacific Islanders (Turner, 2016). Similarly, while smartphone usage is increasing, estimates indicate that only about 77 percent of American adults have a smartphone (Pew Research Center, 2017) while 10 percent of Americans only have access to the internet through their smartphones (Smith, 2015). These smartphone-dependent individuals are more likely to come from ethnic minority groups, live in low-income households, and have lower educational attainment levels than those with access to broadband home internet. This may be part of the reason why mobile assessments for personnel selection are more likely to be completed by ethnic minorities (Arthur et al., 2014).

The presence of this digital divide creates a number of obstacles for organizations seeking to utilize assessment games and gamified assessment methods in their selection practices. Looking just at the professionally developed assessment games, some are being specifically designed for administration on mobile devices (e.g., Skyrise City) while others are reliant on computer access (e.g., Cognify). Due to the digital divide, neither platform alone is sufficient to provide equal access to all Americans, let alone to a global talent pool. The same problem exists with attempting to use commercially available games as an assessment method as access to these games will likely similarly vary across socio-demographic characteristics. Even simple adjustments such as including multi-media components as part of a gamification process may result in reduced access for those struggling to get adequate internet connections.

Researchers also need to more thoroughly address how perceptions of assessment games and gamified assessment practices may differently impact various socio-demographic groups. For example, age-based stereotype threats may cause negative performance in particular on cognitive based tasks (Lamont, Swift, & Abrams, 2015) due to negative stereotypes associated with older adults and cognitive decline. Despite some evidence to the contrary (Fleming, Becker, & Newton, 2017; Niemelä-Nyrhinen, 2007), older adults are typically stereotyped as being more reluctant to embrace new technologies. Similar stereotype threat has been found to affect female performance in online games (Kaye & Pennington, 2016) and may have a greater impact on those that identify as "gamers" (Vermeulen et al., 2016). Even simple gamification elements such as the presence of a leaderboard may be sufficient to trigger these stereotype threats if gender is indicated in the ranking (Albuquerque et al., 2017). Practitioners looking to implement assessments games and gamified assessment methods should be mindful of how obstacles such as the digital divide and stereotype threats may interact to keep away qualified applicants or create bias in their selection procedures.

While organizations have been quick to adopt gamification principles, research on the specifics of applying gamification in organizations has often lagged behind application (Chamorro-Premusic et al., 2016). Widespread adoption of gamification assessment practices is still in much need of additional research. One of the greatest challenges associated with developing best practices for gamifying assessments comes from the large number of game elements which can be incorporated under the umbrella term of "gamification" (Marczewski, 2017). Future research is needed to further refine these elements into a more parsimonious list of those that directly apply to assessment practices (see Bedwell et al., 2012, for an example with learning). Lack of a clear understanding surrounding the best practices for applying these different elements of gamification to a given assessment program might ultimately be the biggest limiter to their effectiveness.

Recent conferences such as SIOP have begun to see vendors share information on the validity and reliability of their gamified assessments (Popp, 2014a & b) and assessment games (Landers, 2017). It is important to note that much of the specific scoring and measurement techniques used in these assessments are still considered proprietary. Since assessment games require a heavy investment of time and resources to develop, which many academics might not possess, our field's continued exploration of the utility and limitations of these tools will rely heavily on collaboration between academics and practitioners. This has been noted as one area in which we are presently seeing practice jump ahead of the scientific research contributing to the all too familiar "scientist–practitioner gap" in the I-O community (Popp, 2014a & b).

7.10 Future Directions for Assessment Games and Gamified Assessments

Several studies have begun to address many of these limitations through successful partnering of scientists and practitioners (Landers, 2017). The few available studies that have examined the impacts of assessment games and gamified forms of assessment have generally found them to be both reliable and able to contribute predictive validity above and beyond more traditional measures (Landers et al., 2017; Sydell & Brodbeck, 2014). In general, applicant reactions to the use of these assessment tools has generally been positive (Landers et al., 2017; Popp, 2014). In particular, these new tools may be best targeted toward attracting and engaging millennials or digital natives who thrive on connections to rich media (Prensky, 2001).

Much of what we know about assessment through serious games still comes from studying educational games (Hainey, et al., 2014; Moseley 2014; Shute, 2011; Wang, Shute, & Moore, 2015). Researchers seeking to better understand the use of assessment games should seek to gain a better understanding of techniques such as stealth assessment (Shute, 2011; Wang et al., 2015), mental chronometry (Medina, et al., 2015), and other mathematical processes related to developing gaming scoring metrics (Dickinson, 2014). Additionally, further exploration on commercial games using established data mining methods (Lewis & Wardrip-Fruin, 2010) could begin to further enhance our understanding of the cross-domain generalizability of game behaviors (see Short, Weidner, & Sirabionian, 2017).

Recent research has suggested that behavioral measures, like those used in assessment games, may be better able to accurately measure decision-making styles and processes than traditional methods (Connors, Rende, & Colton, 2016). Additionally, evidence suggests that ability-based measures may suffer less from retesting or training to improve scores (Villado, Randall, & Zimmer, 2016). Much of this may depend on the fakability of the measures, or rather the ability of applicants to accurately identify evaluation criteria from the assessment games themselves. Research needs to explore the potential for fakability of gamified and game-based assessments. Although faking cognitive skills is unlikely, it may be possible to modify play style in such a way that it conveys differences in personality or decision-making style. Participants engaging in a gamified SJT, for example, may be more likely to role-play as a character that behaves differently than they normally would.

Of particular concern for the game-based assessments is the body of research examining the impact of videogame play on the development of various cognitive skills that has been growing since the 1980s (Latham, Patston, & Tippett, 2013). Video game play has been linked to numerous cognitive skills which may impact subsequent assessment and measurement using game-based assessments (Boot, Blakely, & Simons, 2011). For example, faster hand-eye reaction times (Castel, Pratt, & Drummond 2005; Moisala et al., 2017), improved mental rotation skills (Okagaki & Frensch, 1994), better visual skills (Clark, Fleck, & Mitroff, 2011), improved working memory (Moisala et al., 2017), and higher capacity to switch between tasks (Green et al., 2012). This could potentially give experienced game players an edge in game-based assessments which may rely on some of these skills (e.g., hand-eye coordination, task-switching). Future researchers examining game-based assessments should be sure to take careful steps to examine the impact of prior gaming experience on the validity and accuracy of their measures. It is important to note that any study of the impacts of prior gameplay experience should include details such as genre of play, as it is often specific genres of games that are associated with specific skill improvements (e.g., visuomotor control and action games (Li, Chen, & Chen, 2016) or Tetris and metal rotation skills (Karolyi, 2013)). Additionally, they may be order effects due to skill priming when presenting a battery of game-based assessments (Nelson & Stracham, 2009). These elements and many more should be carefully considered during the design process (see Geimer & O'Shea, 2014) and require further study to understand their potential impact on employee assessment practices specifically.

7.11 Conclusions

Ideally, assessment games and gamified assessments would improve the evaluation of applicants during the employee selection process by collecting better quality information in a more engaging way. As games are meant to be fun, these methods may hold the power to transform stressful high-stakes assessment procedures into a more engaging and enjoyable experience for the applicant. This could involve using highly engaging low-stakes assessment games designed to help organizations better target their recruitment efforts as well as transforming high-stakes assessments by gamifying them to reduce stress allowing for more accurate measurement. Assessment games often rely on alternative scoring and measurement techniques which may be less fakeable since the constructs being assessed aren't as easily identified. Additionally, using gameplay as part of an assessment could lead to more behaviorally oriented measures which should be more proximal measures of our criterion variables than self-reports. This should improve the validity and ultimately the utility of our selection systems as a whole.

While early research has begun to demonstrate the great potential of game thinking (Armstrong et al., 2015) in assessment practices, these methods still require time to be properly developed. As has been noted by others (Armstrong et al., 2016) research and practice will both benefit greatly from a taxonomy of gamification elements that are relevant for assessment practices and theoretically linked to meaningful assessment outcomes. This may help to better guide practitioners both in the process of gamifying current assessment practices as well as in the potential development of high quality assessment games. Furthermore, much research is still needed to close the expanding scientist–practitioner gap in the use of these methods. In particular, research is needed to address the concerns surrounding the potential for the digital divide to exacerbate issues of adverse impact and stereotype threat when using these methods of assessment. Provided these issues can be addressed properly, game thinking may begin to have a more recognizable place in high-stakes assessment practices.

References

Albuquerque, J., Bittencourt, I.I., Coelho, J. A. P.M., & Silva, A. P. (2017). Does gender stereotype threat in gamified educational environments cause anxiety? An experimental study. *Computers & Education*, *115*, 161–170.

Anderson, P. H. & Lawton, L. (2009). Business simulations and cognitive learning. *Simulation & Gaming*, *40*(2), 193–216.

Apperley, T. H. (2006). Genre and game studies: Toward a critical approach to video game genres. *Simulation & Gaming, 37*(1), 6–23.

Arctic Shores (n.d.). People insights from game technology. Retrieved from www .arcticshores.com/.

Armstrong, M. B., Ferrell, J. Z., Collmus, A. B., & Landers, R. N. (2016). Correcting misconceptions about gamification of assessment: More than SJTs and badges. *Industrial and Organizational Psychology, 9*(3), 671–677.

Armstrong, M. B., Landers, R. N., & Collmus, A. B. (2015). Gamifying recruitment, selection, training, and performance management. In H. Gangadharbatla & D. Davis (Eds.), *Emerging research and trends in gamification* (pp. 140–165). Hershey, PA: Information Science Reference.

Arthur, W., Doverspike, D., Muñoz, G. J., Taylor, J. E., & Carr, A. E. (2014). The use of mobile devices in high-stakes remotely delivered assessments and testing. *International Journal of Selection and Assessment, 22*(2), 113–123.

Ashton, M. C. & Lee, K. (2001). A theoretical basis for the major dimensions of personality. *European Journal of Personality, 15*(5), 327–353.

Ashton, M. C. & Lee, K. (2007). Empirical, theoretical, and practical advantages of the HEXACO model of personality structure. *Personality and Social Psychology Review, 11*(2), 150–166.

Avolio, B. J., Waldman, D. A., & Einstein, W. O. (1988). Transformational leadership in a management game simulation: Impacting the bottom line. *Group & Organization Management, 13*(1), 59–80.

Bainbridge, W. S. (2012). *The warcraft civilization: Social science in a virtual world.* Cambridge, MA: MIT Press.

Baniqued, P. L., Lee, H., Voss, M. W., Basak, C., Cosman, J. D., DeSouza, S., Severson, J., Salthouse, T.A., & Kramer, A. F. (2013). Selling points: What cognitive abilities are tapped by casual video games? *Acta Psychologica, 142*(1), 74–86.

Barrick, M. R. & Mount, M. K. (1991). The big five personality dimensions and job performance: A meta-analysis. *Personnel Psychology, 44*(1), 1–26.

Barrick, M. R. & Mount, M. K. (2012). Nature and Use of Personality in Selection. In N. Schmitt (Ed.), *The oxford handbook of personnel assessment and selection* (pp. 225–251). New York, NY: Oxford University Press.

Bartle, R. A. (1996). Hearts, clubs, diamonds, spades: Players who suit MUDs. *Journal of MUD Research, 1*(1), 19.

Bateman, C. & Nacke, L. E. (2010). The neurobiology of play. Proceedings of the International Academic Conference on the Future of Game Design and Technology – Futureplay '10.

Baumert, A., Schlösser, T., & Schmitt, M. (2014). Economic games. *European Journal of Psychological Assessment, 30*(3), 178–192.

Bean, A. M., Ferro, L. S., Vissoci, J. R., Rivero, T., & Groth-Marnat, G. (2016). The emerging adolescent World of Warcraft video gamer: A five factor exploratory profile model. *Entertainment Computing, 17*, 45–54.

Bedwell, W. L., Pavlas, D., Heyne, K., Lazzara, E. H., & Salas, E. (2012). Toward a taxonomy linking game attributes to learning: An empirical study. *Simulation and Gaming, 43*(6), 729–760.

Boot, W. R., Blakely, D. P., & Simons, D. J. (2011). Do action video games improve perception and cognition? *Frontiers in Psychology, 2*(226) 1–6.

Boyle, E. (2014). Psychological aspects of serious games. In T. Connolly, T. Hainey, E. Boyle, G. Baxter, & P. Moreno-Ger (Eds.), *Psychology, pedagogy, and assessment in serious games* (pp. 1–18). Hershey, PA: Information Science Reference.

Braun, B., Stopfer, J. M., Müller, K. W., Beutel, M. E., & Egloff, B. (2016). Personality and video gaming: Comparing regular gamers, non-gamers, and gaming addicts and differentiating between game genres. *Computers in Human Behavior*, *55*, 406–412.

Breaugh, J. A. (2009). The use of biodata for employee selection: Past research and future directions. *Human Resource Management Review*, *19*(3), 219–231.

Bruk-Lee, V., Lanz, J., Drew, E. N., Coughlin, C., Levine, P., Tuzinski, K., & Wrenn, K. (2016). Examining applicant reactions to different media types in character-based simulations for employee selection. *International Journal of Selection and Assessment*, *24*(1), 77–91.

Buford, C. C. & O'leary, B. J. (2015). Assessment of fluid intelligence utilizing a computer simulated game. *International Journal of Gaming and Computer-Mediated Simulations*, *7*(4), 1–17.

Campbell, V. L. (1987). Strong-Campbell interest inventory, fourth edition. *Journal of Counseling & Development*, *66*(1), 53–56.

Carroll, J. B. (1993). *Human cognitive abilities: A survey of factor-analytic studies*. Cambridge: Cambridge University Press.

Cardador, M. T., Northcraft, G. B. & Whicker, J. (2017). A theory of work gamification: Something old, something new, something borrowed, something cool? *Human Resource Management Review*, *27*, 353–365.

Cassady, J. C. & Johnson, R. E. (2002). Cognitive test anxiety and academic performance. *Contemporary Educational Psychology*, *27*(2), 270–295.

Castel, A. D., Pratt, J., & Drummond, E. (2005). The effects of action video game experience on the time course of inhibition of return and the efficiency of visual search. *Acta Psychologica*, *119*(2), 217–230.

Casual Games Association. (n.d.). CGA | Casual Games Association. Retrieved from www.cga.global/.

CESIM. (n.d.). Business Simulation Games. Retrieved from www.cesim.com/.

Chamorro-Premuzic, T., Winsborough, D., Sherman, R. A., & Hogan, R. (2016). New talent signals: Shiny new objects or a brave new world? *Industrial and Organizational Psychology*, *9*(3), 621–640.

Cheema, A. & Bagchi, R. (2011). The effect of goal visualization on goal pursuit: Implications for consumers and managers. *Journal of Marketing*, *75*, 109–123.

Chin, F. B., Blair, K. P., & Schwartz, D. L. (2016). Got game? A choice-based learning assessment of data literacy and visualization skills. *Technology, Knowledge, and Learning 21*, 195–210.

Clark, K., Fleck, M. S., & Mitroff, S. R. (2011). Enhanced change detection performance reveals improved strategy use in avid action video game players. *Acta Psychologica*, *136*(1), 67–72.

Collmus, A. B., Armstrong, M. B., & Landers, R. N. (2016). Game-thinking within social media to recruit and select job candidates. In R. N. Landers & G. B. Schmidt (Eds.), *Social media in employee recruitment and selection* (pp. 103–126). Cham, Switzerland: Springer.

Collmus, A. B. & Landers, R. N. (April 2015). Game narrative in personality assessment: The development of a scale. Presented at Virginia Psychological Association's Spring Convention and Education Conference, Virginia Beach, VA.

Conlin, L. D., Chin, D. B., Blair, K. P., Cutumisu, M., & Schwartz, D. L. (2015). Guardian angels of our better nature: Finding evidence of the benefits of design thinking. In Proceedings of the American Society for Engineering Education, June 2015, Seattle, WA.

Connolly, T. M., Hainey, Boyle, Baxter, & Moreno-Ger, P. (2014). *Psychology, pedagogy, and assessment in serious games*. Hershey, PA: Information Science Reference.

Connors, B. L., Rende, R., & Colton, T. J. (2016). Beyond self-report: Emerging methods for capturing individual differences in decision-making process. *Frontiers in Psychology, 7*.

Conrad, F. G., Couper, M. P., Tourangeau, R., & Peytchev, A. (2010). The impact of progress indicators on task completion. *Interacting with Computers, 22*(5), 417–427.

Costa, P. T. & McCrae, R. R. (1992). NEO personality inventory-revised (NEO PI-R). Odessa, FL: Psychological Assessment Resources.

Cucina, J. M., Su, C., Busciglio, H. H., Thomas, P. H., & Peyton, S. T. (2015). Video-based testing: A high-fidelity job simulation that demonstrates reliability, validity, and utility. *International Journal of Selection and Assessment, 23*(3), 197–209.

Cutumisu, M., Blair, K. P., Chin, D. B., & Schwartz, D. L. (2015). Posterlet: A game-based assessment of children's choices to seek feedback and to revise. *Journal of Learning Analytics, 2*(1), 49–71.

Dickey, M. D. (2007). Game design and learning: A conjectural analysis of how massively multiple online role-playing games (MMORPGs) foster intrinsic motivation. *Educational Technology Research and Development, 55*(3), 253–273.

Dickinson, J. R. (2014). A mathematical law for assessing outcome values of games. *Simulation & Gaming, 45*(3), 318–331.

Downes-Le Guin, T., Baker, R., Mechling, J., & Ruyle, E. (2012). Myths and realities of respondent engagement in online surveys. *International Journal of Market Research, 54*(5), 613–633.

Duplaga, M. (2017). Digital divide among people with disabilities: Analysis of data from a nationwide study for determinants of internet use and activities performed online. *PLoS One, 12*(6), e0179825.

ETC. (n.d.). Simulating environments for training, testing, and research and development. Retrieved from www.etcusa.com/.

Fetzer, M. (2015). Serious games for talent selection and development. *The Industrial-Organizational Psychologist, 52*, 117–125.

Finkelstein, M. A. & Penner, L. A. (2004). Predicting organizational citizenship behavior: Integrating the functional and role identity approaches. *Social Behavior and Personality: An International Journal, 32*(4), 383–398.

Fleming, J., Becker, K., & Newton, C. (2017). Factors for successful e-learning: Does age matter? *Education + Training, 59*(1), 76–89.

Gallagher, A. G., Ritter, E. M., Champion, H., Higgins, G., Fried, M. P., Moses, G., Smith, C. D., & Satava, R. M. (2005). Virtual reality simulation for the operating room. *Annals of Surgery, 241*(2), 364–372.

Geimer, J. L. & O'Shea, P. G. (May, 2014). Design Considerations to Maximize the Utility of Gamification for Selection. Presentation as part of the Challenges and Innovations of Using Game-Like Assessments in Selection. Symposium presented at the 29th Annual meeting of the Society for Industrial-Organizational Psychology. Honolulu, HI.

Gibbons, C. J. (2017). Turning the page on pen-and-paper questionnaires: Combining ecological momentary assessment and computer adaptive testing to transform psychological assessment in the 21st century. *Frontiers in Psychology, 7*(1933), 1–4.

Gnambs, T. & Appel, M. (2017). Is computer gaming associated with cognitive abilities? A population study among German adolescents. *Intelligence, 61,* 19–28.

Goldberg, L. R. (1993). The structure of phenotypic personality traits. *American Psychologist, 48*(1), 26–34.

Graham, L. T. & Gosling, S. D. (2013). Personality profiles associated with different motivations for playing World of Warcraft. *Cyberpsychology, Behavior, and Social Networking, 16*(3), 189–193.

Greco, M., Baldissin, N., & Nonino, F. (2013). An exploratory taxonomy of business games. *Simulation & Gaming, 44*(5), 645–682.

Green, C. S., Sugarman, M. A., Medford, K., Klobusicky, E., & Bavelier, D. (2012). The effect of action video game experience on task-switching. *Computers in Human Behavior, 28*(3), 984–994.

Griffith, J. L., Voloschin, P., Gibb, G. D., & Bailey, J. R. (1983). Differences in eye-hand motor coordination of video-game users and non-users. *Perceptual and Motor Skills, 57*(1), 155–158.

Grossman, R., Heyne, K., & Salas, E. (2015). Game and simulation-based approaches to training. In K. Kraiger, J. Passmore, N. R. dos Santos, S. Malvezzi, K. Kraiger, J. Passmore, . . . S. Malvezzi (Eds.), *The Wiley Blackwell handbook of the psychology of training, development, and performance improvement* (pp. 205–223). Malden, MA:Wiley-Blackwell.

Hainey, T., Connolly, T. M., Chaudy, Y., Boyle, E., Beeby, R., & Soflano, M. (2014). Assessment Integration in Serious Games. In T. Connolly, T. Hainey, E. Boyle, G. Baxter, & P. Moreno-Ger (Eds.), *Psychology, pedagogy, and assessment in serious games* (pp. 317–341). Hershey, PA: Information Science Reference.

Hainey, T., Connolly, T., Stansfield, M., & Boyle, E. (2011). The differences in motivations of online game players and offline game players: A combined analysis of three studies at higher education level. *Computers & Education, 57*(4), 2197–2211.

Hamari, J. (2017). Do badges increase user activity? A field experiment on the effects of gamification. *Computers in Human Behavior, 71,* 469–478.

Howland, A. C., Rembisz, R., Wang-Jones, T. S., Heise, S. R., & Brown, S. (2015). Developing a virtual assessment center. *Consulting Psychology Journal: Practice and Research, 67*(2), 110–126.

Hurtz, G. M. & Donovan, J. J. (2000). Personality and job performance: The big five revisited. *Journal of Applied Psychology, 85*(6), 869–879.

Hwang, H. & Nam, S. (2017). The digital divide experienced by older consumers in smart environments. *International Journal of Consumer Studies, 41*(5), 501–508.

Iddekinge, C. H., Roth, P. L., Raymark, P. H., & Odle-Dusseau, H. N. (2012). The criterion-related validity of integrity tests: An updated meta-analysis. *Journal of Applied Psychology, 97*(3), 499–530.

Illingworth, A. J., Morelli, N. A., Scott, J. C., & Boyd, S. L. (2015). Internet-based, unproctored assessments on mobile and non-mobile devices: Usage, measurement equivalence, and outcomes. *Journal of Business and Psychology, 30*(2), 325–343.

Industrial Training International. (n.d.). Virtual Reality Crane & Rigging Simulations. Retrieved from www.iti.com/vr.

Job Simulator. (2016). Owlchemy Labs. Retrieved from http://jobsimulatorgame.com/.

Judge, T. A., Higgins, C. A., Thoresen, C. J., & Barrick, M. R. (1999). The big five personality traits, general mental ability, and career success across the life span. *Personnel Psychology, 52*(3), 621–652.

Kahn, A. S., Shen, C., Lu, L., Ratan, R. A., Coary, S., Hou, J., Meng, J., Osborn, J., & Williams, D. (2015). Trojan player typology: A cross-genre, cross-cultural, behaviorally validated scale of video game play motivations. *Computers in Human Behavior, 49*, 354–361.

Kalinoski, Z. T. (April, 2017). Empowering Job Seekers by Gamifying the Recruitment and Selection Process. Presentation as part of the Serious Assessment Games and Gamified Assessment: Emerging Evidence Symposium presented at the 32nd Annual meeting of the Society for Industrial-Organizational Psychology. Orlando, FL.

Károlyi, C. V. (2013). From Tesla to Tetris: Mental rotation, vocation, and gifted education. *Roeper Review, 35*(4), 231–240.

Kaye, L. K. & Pennington, C. R. (2016). "Girls can't play": The effects of stereotype threat on females' gaming performance. *Computers in Human Behavior, 59*, 202–209.

Kipnis, D. (1962). A noncognitive correlate of performance among lower aptitude men. *Journal of Applied Psychology, 46*(1), 76–80.

Kipnis, D. & Glickman, A. S. (1962). The prediction of job performance. *Journal of Applied Psychology, 46*(1), 50–56.

Klein, R. D. & Fleck, R. A. (1990). International business simulation/gaming: An assessment and review. *Simulation & Gaming, 21*(2), 147–165.

Knack. (n.d.) Knack for unlocking the world's potential. Retrieved from www.knack.it/.

Kubisiak, C., Stewart, R. W., Thornbury, E. E., & Moye, N. (May, 2014). Development of PDRI's Learning Agility Simulation. Presentation as part of the Challenges and Innovations of Using Game-Like Assessments in Selection. Symposium presented at the 29th Annual meeting of the Society for Industrial-Organizational Psychology. Honolulu, HI

Kvist, A. V. & Gustafsson, J. (2008). The relation between fluid intelligence and the general factor as a function of cultural background: A test of Cattell's investment theory. *Intelligence, 36*(5), 422–436.

Lamont, R. A., Swift, H. J., & Abrams, D. (2015). A review and meta-analysis of age-based stereotype threat: Negative stereotypes, not facts, do the damage. *Psychology and Aging, 30*(1), 180–193.

Landers, R. N. (2014). Developing a theory of gamified learning: Linking serious games and gamification of learning. *Simulation & Gaming, 45*(6), 752–768.

Landers, R. N. (2015). Guest editorial preface: Special issue on assessing human capabilities in video games and simulations. *International Journal of Gaming and Computer-Mediated Simulations, 7*, iv-viii.

Landers, R. N. (April, 2017). Serious Assessment Games and Gamified Assessment: Emerging Evidence. Symposium presented at the 32nd Annual meeting of the Society for Industrial-Organizational Psychology. Orlando, FL.

Landers, R. N. & Armstrong, M. B. (2017). Enhancing instructional outcomes with gamification: An empirical test of the technology-enhanced training effectiveness model. *Computers in Human Behavior, 71*, 499–507.

Landers, R. N., Armstrong, M. B., Collmus, A. B., Mujcic, S. & Blaik, J. A. (April, 2017). Empirical Validation of a General Cognitive Ability Assessment Game.

Presentation as part of the Serious Assessment Games and Gamified Assessment: Emerging Evidence Symposium presented at the 32nd Annual meeting of the Society for Industrial-Organizational Psychology. Orlando, FL

Landers, R. N., Bauer, K. N., & Callan, R. C. (2017). Gamification of task performance with leaderboards: A goal setting experiment. *Computers in Human Behavior*, *71*, 508–515.

Lang, J. W., Kersting, M., Hülsheger, U. R., & Lang, J. (2010). General mental ability, narrower cognitive abilities, and job performance: The perspective of the nested-factors model of cognitive abilities. *Personnel Psychology*, *63*(3), 595–640.

Latham, A. J., Patston, L. L., & Tippett, L. J. (2013). The virtual brain: 30 years of video-game play and cognitive abilities. *Frontiers in Psychology*, *4*(629), 1–10.

Lavelle, J. J. (2010). What motivates OCB? Insights from the volunteerism literature. *Journal of Organizational Behavior*, *31*(6), 918–923.

Lawrence, A. D. & Kinney, T. B. (2017) Mobile Devices and Selection. SIOP White Paper Series. Visibility Committee Society for Industrial and Organizational Psychology, Bowling Green OH.

Lewis, C. & Wardrip-Fruin, N. (2010). Mining game statistics from web services. Proceedings of the Fifth International Conference on the Foundations of Digital Games – FDG '10.

Li, L., Chen, R., & Chen, J. (2016). Playing action video games improves visuomotor control. *Psychological Science*, *27*(8), 1092–1108.

Lievens, F. & De Soete, B. (2012). Simulations. In N. Schmitt (Ed.), *The oxford handbook of personnel assessment and selection* (pp. 383–410). New York, NY: Oxford University Press.

Lievens, F. & Patterson, F. (2011). The validity and incremental validity of knowledge tests, low-fidelity simulations, and high-fidelity simulations for predicting job performance in advanced-level high-stakes selection. *Journal of Applied Psychology*, *96* (5), 927–940.

Littman-Ovadia, H. & Lavy, S. (2016). Going the extra mile: Perseverance as a key character strength at work. *Journal of Career Assessment*, *24*(2), 240–252.

Liu, M., Huang, Y., & Zhang, D. (2018). Gamification's impact on manufacturing: Enhancing job motivation, satisfaction, and operational performance with smartphone based gamified job-design. *Human Factors and Ergonomics in Manufacturing and Service Industries*, *28*(1), 38–51.

Macan, T. (2009). The employment interview: A review of current studies and directions for future research. *Human Resource Management Review*, *19*(3), 203–218.

Marczewski, A. (April, 2017). The Periodic Table of Gamification Elements. Retrieved from: www.gamified.uk/2017/04/03/periodic-table-gamification-elements/.

Mavridis, A. & Tsiatsos, T. (2016). Game-based assessment: Investigating the impact on test anxiety and exam performance. *Journal of Computer Assisted Learning*, *33*(2), 137–150.

McGrew, K. S. (2005). The Cattell-Horn-Carroll theory of cognitive abilities. In D. P. Flanagan & P. L. Harrison (Eds.), *Contemporary intellectual assessment: Theories, tests, and issues* (pp. 151–179). New York, NY: Guilford Press.

Medina, J. M., Wong, W., Diaz, J. A., & Colonius, H. (2015). Advances in modern mental chronometry. *Frontiers in Human Neuroscience*, *9*(256), 1–3.

Mekler, E. D., Brühlmann, F., Tuch, A. N., & Opwis, K. (2017). Towards understanding the effects of individual gamification elements on intrinsic motivation and performance. *Computers in Human Behavior, 71*, 525–534. doi: 10.1016/j.chb.2015.08.048.

Merel, T. (January, 2017). The reality of VR/AR growth. Retrieved from https://techcrunch.com/2017/01/11/the-reality-of-vrar-growth/.

Michael, D., & Chen, S. (2005). *Serious games: Games that educate, train, and inform.* Mason, OH: Course Technology.

Microsoft Gamerscore. (n.d.). Xbox Live Gamerscore Leaderboards Retrieved from www.xboxgamertag.com/leaderboards/.

Militello, L. G. & Hutton, R. J. (1998). Applied cognitive task analysis (ACTA): A practitioner's toolkit for understanding cognitive task demands. *Ergonomics, 41*(11), 1618–1641.

Moisala, M., Salmela, V., Hietajärvi, L., Carlson, S., Vuontela, V., Lonka, K., Hakkarainen, K., Salmela-Aro, K., & Alho, K. (2017). Gaming is related to enhanced working memory performance and task-related cortical activity. *Brain Research, 1655*, 204–215.

Morrison, M. & Fontenla, M. (2013). Price convergence in an online virtual world. *Empirical Economics, 44*(3), 1053–1064.

Moseley, A. (2014). A Case for Integration. In T. Connolly, T. Hainey, E. Boyle, G. Baxter, & P. Moreno-Ger (Eds.), *Psychology, Pedagogy, and Assessment in Serious Games* (pp. 342–356). Hershey, PA: Information Science Reference.

Motowidlo, S. J., Dunnette, M. D., & Carter, G. W. (1990). An alternative selection procedure: The low-fidelity simulation. *Journal of Applied Psychology, 75*(6), 640–647.

Nacke, L. E., Bateman, C., & Mandryk, R. L. (2014). BrainHex: A neurobiological gamer typology survey. *Entertainment Computing, 5*(1), 55–62.

Nagygyörgy, K., Urbán, R., Farkas, J., Griffiths, M. D., Zilahy, D., Kökönyei, G.,... Demetrovics, Z. (2013). Typology and sociodemographic characteristics of massively multiplayer online game players. *International Journal of Human-Computer Interaction, 29*(3), 192–200.

Narayanan, D. Z., Samet, A. G., Blumgart, E. I., Yoo, J. J., Cohen, M. M., & Polli, F. E. (April, 2017). Gamification as a Platform to Reduce Bias. Presentation as part of the Serious Assessment Games and Gamified Assessment: Emerging Evidence Symposium presented at the 32nd Annual meeting of the Society for Industrial-Organizational Psychology. Orlando, FL.

Nelson, R. A. & Strachan, I. (2009). Action and puzzle video games prime different speed/accuracy tradeoffs. *Perception, 38*(11), 1678–1687.

Niemelä-Nyrhinen, J. (2007). Baby boom consumers and technology: Shooting down stereotypes. *Journal of Consumer Marketing, 24*(5), 305–312.

Norris, D. R. & Snyder, C. A. (1982). External validation of simulation games. *Simulation & Gaming, 13*(1), 73–85.

Oh, I., Le, H., Whitman, D. S., Kim, K., Yoo, T., Hwang, J., & Kim, C. (2014). The incremental validity of honesty–humility over cognitive ability and the big five personality traits. *Human Performance, 27*(3), 206–224.

Okagaki, L. & Frensch, P. A. (1994). Effects of video game playing on measures of spatial performance: Gender effects in late adolescence. *Journal of Applied Developmental Psychology, 15*(1), 33–58.

Ones, D. S., Dilchert, S., & Viswesvaran, C. (2012). Cognitive Abilities. In N. Schmitt (Ed.), *The oxford handbook of personnel assessment and selection* (pp. 179–224). New York, NY: Oxford University Press.

OSSO VR. (n.d.). Retrieved from http://ossovr.com/.

Owens, J. & Lilly, F. (2017). The influence of academic discipline, race, and gender on web-use skills among graduate-level students. *Journal of Computing in Higher Education, 29*(2), 286–308.

Owlchemy Labs. (October 3, 2016). OwlchemyVR Mixed Reality Tech Part 1. Retrieved from http://owlchemylabs.com/owlchemyvr-mixed-reality-tech/.

PDRI, a CEB company. (n.d.). Retrieved from www.pdri.com/.

Park, G., Lubinski, D., & Benbow, C. P. (2007). Contrasting intellectual patterns predict creativity in the arts and sciences. *Psychological Science, 18*(11), 948–952.

Pew Research Center. (January 12, 2017). Mobile Fact Sheet. Retrieved from www .pewinternet.org/fact-sheet/mobile/.

Popp, E. C. (May, 2014). Challenges and Innovations of Using Game-Like Assessments in Selection. Symposium presented at the 29th Annual meeting of the Society for Industrial-Organizational Psychology. Honolulu, HI.

Popp, E.C. (May, 2014). Addressing practical challenges in developing game-like assessments. Presentation as part of the Challenges and Innovations of Using Game-Like Assessments in Selection. Symposium presented at the 29th Annual meeting of the Society for Industrial-Organizational Psychology. Honolulu, HI.

Portal 2. (n.d.) Portal 2 Perpetual Testing Initiative. Retrieved from www.thinkwithportals .com/index.php.

Prensky, M. (2001). Digital natives, digital immigrants part 1. *On the Horizon, 9*(5), 1–6.

Pymetrics. (n.d.). Play game s to find your ideal job and optimal career path. Retrieved from www.pymetrics.com/.

Quiroga, M. Á, Escorial, S., Román, F. J., Morillo, D., Jarabo, A., Privado, J., Hernandez, M., Gallego, B., & Colom, R. (2015). Can we reliably measure the general factor of intelligence (g) through commercial video games? Yes, we can! Intelligence, *53*, 1–7.

Quiroga, M. Á, Herranz, M., Gómez-Abad, M., Kebir, M., Ruiz, J., Herranz, M., & Colom, R. (2009). Video-games: Do they require general intelligence? *Computers & Education, 53*(2), 414–418.

Quiroga, M. Á, Román, F. J., Catalán, A., Rodríguez, H., Ruiz, J., Herranz, M., Gomez-Abad, & Colom, R. (2011). Videogame performance (not always) requires intelligence. *International Journal of Online Pedagogy and Course Design, 1* (3), 18–32.

Rachman-Moore, D. & Kenett, R. S. (2006). The use of simulation to improve the effectiveness of training in performance management. *Journal of Management Education, 30*(3), 455–476.

Raven, J., Raven, J. C., & Court, J. H. (2003). *Manual for Raven's progressive matrices and vocabulary scales.* San Antonio, TX: Harcourt Assessment.

Revelian (n.d.) Cognify Next generation psychometric testing Retrieved from www.revelian .com/

Richman-Hirsch, W. L., Olson-Buchannan, J. B., & Drasgow, F. (2000). Examining the impact of administration medium on examinee perceptions and attitudes. *Journal of Applied Psychology, 85*(6), 880–887.

Rubenfire, A. (August 12, 2014). Can 'World of Warcraft' game skills help land a job? Retrieved from www.wsj.com/articles/can-warcraft-game-skills-help-land-a-job-1407885660.

Rufo-Tepper, R. (June 17, 2015). Using games for assessment. Retrieved from www.edutopia.org/blog/using-games-for-assessment-rebecca-rufo-tepper.

Sailer, M., Hense, J. U., Mayr, S. K., & Mandl, H. (2017). How gamification motivates: An experimental study of the effects of specific game design elements on psychological need satisfaction. *Computers in Human Behavior*, *69*, 371–380.

Schmidt, F. L. & Hunter, J. E. (1998). The validity and utility of selection methods in personnel psychology: Practical and theoretical implications of 85 years of research findings. *Psychological Bulletin*, *124*(2), 262–274.

Schmidt, F. L. & Hunter, J. (2004). General mental ability in the world of work: Occupational attainment and job performance. *Journal of Personality and Social Psychology*, *86*(1), 162–173.

Sears, G. J., Zhang, H., Wiesner, W. H., Hackett, R. D., & Yuan, Y. (2013). A comparative assessment of videoconference and face-to-face employment interviews. *Management Decision*, *51*(8), 1733–1752.

Shipley, W. C., Gruber, C. P., Martin, T. A., & Klein, A. M. (2012). *Shipley-2 Manual*. Los Angeles, CA: Western Psychological Services.

Short, E., Weidner, N., & Sirabionian, M. (April, 2017). Exploring Workplace Relevant Correlates of World of Warcraft Achievements. Presentation as part of the Serious Assessment Games and Gamified Assessment: Emerging Evidence Symposium presented at the 32nd Annual meeting of the Society for Industrial-Organizational Psychology. Orlando, FL.

Shute, V. J. (2011). Stealth assessment in computer-based games to support learning. In S. Tobias & J. D. Fletcher (Eds.), *Computer games and instruction* (pp. 503–524). Charlotte, NC: Information Age Publishers.

Shute, V. J., D'mello, S., Baker, R., Cho, K., Bosch, N., Ocumpaugh, J., Ventura, M., & Almeda, V. (2015). Modeling how incoming knowledge, persistence, affective states, and in-game progress influence student learning from an educational game. *Computers & Education*, *86*, 224–235.

Shute, V. J., Wang, L., Greiff, S., Zhao, W., & Moore, G. (2016). Measuring problem solving skills via stealth assessment in an engaging video game. *Computers in Human Behavior*, *63*, 106–117.

Smith, A. (April 1, 2015). U.S. Smartphone Use in 2015. Retrieved from www.pewinternet.org/2015/04/01/us-smartphone-use-in-2015/.

Spector, P. E. (2012). Self-reports for employee selection. In N. Schmitt & N. Schmitt (Eds.), *The Oxford handbook of personnel assessment and selection* (pp. 443–461). New York, NY: Oxford University Press.

Sydell, E. J. & Cox Brodbeck, C. M. (May, 2014). The predictive power of game-like assessments compared to traditional tests. Presentation as part of the Challenges and Innovations of Using Game-Like Assessments in Selection. Symposium presented at the 29th Annual meeting of the Society for Industrial-Organizational Psychology. Honolulu, HI.

Sydell, L. (October 5, 2005). 'Virtual' Virus Sheds Light on Real-World Behavior. Retrieved from www.npr.org/templates/story/story.php?storyId=4946772.

Symphony Talent (n.d.). Retrieved from www.symphonytalent.com/.

ThoroughTec (n.d.). Mining, Military and Construction Simulators. Retrieved from www
.thoroughtec.com/.

Thornton, G. C. & Gibbons, A. M. (2009). Validity of assessment centers for personnel
selection. *Human Resource Management Review, 19*(3), 169–187.

Tobias, S. & Fletcher, J. D. (2011). *Computer games and instruction.* Charlotte, NC:
Information age Pub.

Turner, S. D. (December, 2016). Digital denied: The impact of systemic racial discrimination on home internet adoption. Retrieved from www.freepress.net/sites/default/
files/resources/digital_denied_free_press_report_december_2016.pdf.

Ventura, M. & Shute, V. (2013). The validity of a game-based assessment of persistence.
Computers in Human Behavior, 29(6), 2568–2572.

Ventura, M., Shute, V., & Zhao, W. (2013). The relationship between video game use and a
performance-based measure of persistence. *Computers & Education, 60*(1),
52–58.

Vermeulen, L., Castellar, E. N., Janssen, D. Calvi, L., & Looy, J. V. (2016). Playing under
threat. Examining stereotype threat in female game players. *Computers in Human
Behavior, 57,* 377–387.

Villado, A. J., Randall, J. G., & Zimmer, C. U. (2016). The effect of method characteristics
on retest score gains and criterion-related validity. *Journal of Business and
Psychology, 31*(2), 233–248.

Virtual Aviation (n.d.). Retrieved from www.virtualaviation.co.uk/.

Walker, J. (2017). "It keeps dropping out!": The need to address the ongoing digital divide to
achieve improved health and well-being benefits for older rural Australians.
Australasian Journal on Ageing, 36(4), 262–263.

Wang, L., Shute, V., & Moore, G. R. (2015). Lessons learned and best practices of stealth
assessment. *International Journal of Gaming and Computer-Mediated
Simulations, 7*(4), 66–87.

Wiggins, B. E. (2016). An overview and study on the use of games, simulations, and
gamification in higher education. *International Journal of Game-Based
Learning, 6*(1), 18–29.

Wolfe, J. (1985). The teaching effectiveness of games in collegiate business courses:
A 1973–1983 update. *Simulation & Gaming, 16*(3), 251–288.

Wolfe, J. (2016). Assuring business school learning with games. *Simulation & Gaming, 47*
(2), 206–227.

Wolfe, J. & Roberts, C. R. (1986). The external validity of a business management game:
A five-year longitudinal study. *Simulation & Gaming, 17*(1), 45–59.

Wolfe, J. & Roberts, C. R. (1993). A further study of the external validity of business games:
five-year peer group indicators. *Simulation & Gaming, 24*(1), 21–33.

World of Warcraft (n.d.). Retrieved from https://worldofwarcraft.com/en-us/.

Worth, N. C. & Book, A. S. (2014). Personality and behavior in a massively multiplayer
online role-playing game. Computers in Human Behavior, 38, 322–330.

Worth, N. C. & Book, A. S. (2015). Dimensions of video game behavior and their relationships with personality. *Computers in Human Behavior, 50,* 132–140.

Yan, T., Conrad, F. G., Tourangeau, R. & Couper, M. P. (2011). Should I stay or should I go:
The effects of progress feedback, promised task duration, and length of question-
naire on completing web surveys. *International Journal of Public Opinion
Research, 23*(2), 131–147.

Yee, N. (2006a). The demographics, motivations, and derived experiences of users of massively multi-user online graphical environments. *Presence: Teleoperators and Virtual Environments, 15*(3), 309–329.

Yee, N. (2006b). Motivations for play in online games. *CyberPsychology & Behavior, 9*(6), 772–775.

Yee, N., Ducheneaut, N., Nelson, L., & Likarish, P. (2011). Introverted elves & conscientious gnomes. Proceedings of the 2011 Annual Conference on Human Factors in Computing Systems – CHI '11.

Zeigler-Hill, V. & Monica, S. (2015). The HEXACO model of personality and video game preferences. *Entertainment Computing, 11*, 21–26.

8 Mobile Assessment in Personnel Testing

Theoretical and Practical Implications

Winfred Arthur, Jr. and Zach Traylor

8.1 Introduction

Technology and technological advancements continue to manifest in several forms in the current hot topics in industrial/organizational (I-O) psychology (Society for Industrial-Organizational Psychology [SIOP], 2017). Within relatively nascent research streams ranging from big data to gamification to the remote administration of employment-related tests and assessments (the number one workplace trend in SIOP's list of the top ten workplace trends in 2015 [SIOP, 2015]), technology plays a central role. The ubiquitous role of technology is particularly salient in personnel testing and assessment wherein *how* and *where* job applicants (and sometimes incumbents) complete employment-related tests and assessments has drastically changed over the past several years. To that end, organizations are increasingly relying on unproctored internet-based testing (UIT; Tippins & Alder, 2011) in favor of the seemingly outdated on-site testing whereby individuals are instructed to be physically present at the organization's premises in order to complete these tests and assessments. Thus, in addition to being characterized by individuals completing employment-related tests and assessments at any location and at any time of their choosing, UIT is also characterized by test takers completing said assessments on the *device of their choosing*. Consequently, the continued growing increase in the use of mobile devices to complete these tests and assessments (Arthur et al., 2014; Illingworth et al., 2015; McClure Johnson & Boyce, 2015) is consistent not only with the relative ease with which these tests and assessments can be and are remotely administered, but also with the rapid growth in mobile device ownership in the general population as well (Pew Research Center, 2015a, 2015b, 2018).

So, with the preceding as a backdrop, based on a review of the pertinent literature, the present chapter discusses the effects of UIT device types – with an emphasis on mobile assessments – on current employment-related testing and assessment practice and its intersection with theory. The chapter first defines mobile assessments, presenting a conceptualization and operationalization of UIT device types (mobile versus nonmobile) that is psychologically grounded. Next, the chapter presents and discusses how, and the extent to which, mobile assessments have affected theory and practice in employment testing and assessment and vice versa. Within this framework, we discuss the extent to which and how current test development and validation models and paradigms are, and can potentially be influenced or changed by, mobile assessments. The chapter concludes by noting and highlighting gaps in the literature and, subsequently, providing suggestions and directions for future research, particularly those that can inform best practices.

8.2 What Is a Mobile Assessment?

Arthur, Keiser, and Doverspike (2018) defined a UIT device as "any device that a test taker can use to complete an unproctored internet test or assessment where by definition, the test taker also decides when and where to complete the assessment or test" (p. 1), and, in this context, UIT devices have also typically been described as being either mobile or nonmobile. Although on the surface it might seem pedantic, the mobile/nonmobile designation does, in terms of scientific precision (and concomitantly, from a research design and methods perspective), beg the question of, "What *is* a mobile device?" This is because structurally and technologically, a mobile device is simply a device that is untethered from the wall – that is, a wireless, nonstationary (non-fixed location) device that is used to access the internet, and, furthermore, from an I-O psychology perspective, one that can be used to complete an employment-related test or assessment. Thus, in line with this, a range of devices, from laptops, notebooks, and tablets to smartphones, would all be designated as mobile devices. So, in accordance with this delineation, mobile assessments would then refer to assessments whereby the test taker uses anything *but* a desktop computer to complete the assessment. Furthermore, as noted by Arthur, Keiser, and Doverspike (2018) in their review of the literature, it seems that although they fail to explicitly state so, most writers use the term mobile device synonymously with smartphones. For instance, out of the 23 papers that they identified that examined mobile versus nonmobile devices in personnel testing and assessment, only five noted a distinction *between* mobile device types (e.g., tablet versus smartphone).

As a counterpoint, we acknowledge that the technology industry (manufacturers and purveyors) uses the term mobile device to synonymously denote smartphones and other small-screen devices. Thus, although, for instance laptops and notebooks can be untethered and used remotely, they would not consider them to be mobile devices in their typical usage of the term. However, whether it is defined or conceptualized in terms of the technology industry's use of mobile device or a differentiation in terms of whether they are plugged into the wall (nonmobile) or not (mobile) to access the internet, these conceptualizations are certainly not psychologically very meaningful in terms of trying to understand, explain, and predict when one should and should not expect device-type effects on specified measurement and other psychological outcomes of interest. Thus, tetheredness-to-the-wall or being a mobile device, per se, cannot be the psychological mechanism that accounts for or explains the processes by which the use of different UIT devices may or may not result in different outcomes and under what conditions. So, for example, although laptops and smartphones are both mobile devices, a reasonable, conceptually grounded case can be made for them to *differentially* affect test scores and other outcomes of interest (Arthur, Keiser, & Doverspike 2018). Therefore, akin to Arthur et al., the present chapter errs on the side of using the term UIT device, and recognizes that UIT devices can be either tethered to the wall (fixed location) or unplugged (non-stationary). However, more importantly, because of the variability in the range of mobile devices (i.e., laptops, notebooks, tablets, smartphones) and the differential effects that they may engender (e.g., laptops and notebooks [perhaps even tablets?] may engender psychological properties more similar to desktops than they do smartphones), we are more precise in our use of the term mobile and nonmobile. So, when discussing others' work, we defer to the authors' designation of their UIT devices as being either mobile or nonmobile; but in our own usage, we generally indicate the *specific* UIT device type as warranted.

8.3 Effects of Mobile Assessment on Practice

With the onset of UITs in employment-related testing, there were legitimate concerns regarding test security, measurement equivalence, and malfeasant test-taking behaviors, among others (Pearlman, 2009; Tippins et al., 2006). Although this apprehension still remains, especially within the context of high-stakes testing, UIT and non-UIT assessments have not been shown to meaningfully differ in terms of measurement properties, test-score validity, and test-taker reactions (Davies & Waddlington, 2006; Do, Shepherd, & Drasgow, 2005; O'Connell, Delgado, & Kung, 2012). Hence, "UIT is here to stay" (Arthur, Doverspike, Kinney, & O'Connell, 2017, p. 968; O'Connell, Arthur, & Doverspike, 2015) primarily because it permits very high degrees of freedom for not only organizations to deliver and administer their assessments, but for job applicants to take these tests as well. In short, from an applied perspective, the "test in any location, at any time, and on any device" advantages associated with UITs are viewed by most to outweigh their disadvantages.

Although UITs have been used in practice for quite some time now, there is limited theoretically and empirically based guidance on UIT device-type effects on selection and assessment outcomes. Indeed, as observed by Arthur, et al. (2017), this is one of those domains in which practice has outpaced the science. This observation is underscored by the limited number and nature of empirical examinations of UIT effects. For instance, Arthur, Keiser, and Doverspike's (2018) review identified only 23 papers, and of these, 20 were conference presentations. Indeed, since their review, (only) one of these conference presentations has been subsequently published as a peer-reviewed journal article. Hence, to date, there have been only four peer-reviewed journal publications examining UIT device-type effects on employment-related tests and assessments. Thus, the widespread practice of allowing test takers to use *any* device of their own choosing when completing a UIT can be characterized as a practice that has outpaced theory, research in the academy, and the peer-reviewed scholarly literature. So, in accordance with the preceding, we next present summaries from Arthur et al.'s review of the personnel testing and assessment UIT device-type literature framing it in terms of the following measurement-related outcomes: (a) the measurement equivalence of device-type scores, (b) test-score differences, (c) criterion-related validity, and (d) test-taker reactions and preferences (Arthur & Villado, 2008). Finally, as previously noted, like Arthur, Keiser, and Doverspike (2018), in the review that follows, we defer to the authors' designation of their devices as being either mobile or nonmobile. That is, we use the authors' own terminology to describe the devices used when discussing their studies.

8.3.1 Measurement Equivalence of Device-Type Scores

Arthur et al. (2017) identified nine studies that had examined the measurement equivalence of UIT device-type scores, including psychometric properties such as the reliability of scores, differential item functioning, and factor structure, among others. The results generally indicated that for both cognitive and noncognitive constructs, UIT device types did not differ on these properties; that is, they displayed measurement equivalence.

8.3.2 Test Score Differences as a Function of UIT Device Type

The content of employment-related tests and assessments can broadly be classified as being either cognitive or noncognitive. Cognitive constructs are those that measure aspects of individuals' cognitive functioning, and, therefore, require cognitive effort on the part of the test taker. In contrast, noncognitive constructs refer to individual differences in domains such as personality, emotion, and volition. Arthur and Glaze (2011) further delineate between the two by noting that cognitive measures typically consist of items that have prespecified correct (or best) and incorrect responses, whereas noncognitive measures do not. Furthermore, in terms of malfeasant responding, cognitive measures are susceptible to cheating (threats) and noncognitive measures to social desirability responding.

Cognitive Constructs. Within the context of employment-related testing, UIT device-type effects on cognitively loaded tests have been documented fairly consistently. For instance, meaningful effect sizes have been found in large, operational datasets examining the difference between cognitive test scores obtained using mobile and nonmobile devices ($d = 0.90$; Arthur et al., 2014). Likewise, using a large, operational database, Wood, Stephens, and Slither (2015) found ds of 0.46 and 0.35 for two cognitive ability tests, and ds of 0.93 and 0.26 for two mechanical aptitude tests, with those using mobile devices scoring consistently lower than those using nonmobile devices.

It should be noted that not all of the empirical evidence regarding UIT device-type effects on cognitively loaded tests supports the notion that scores are lower for test takers using mobile devices. For example, both Brown, Grossenbacher, and Nguyen (2016) and Parker and Meade (2015) failed to find meaningful differences as a function of the device type used to complete cognitive tests. Arthur, Keiser, and Doverspike (2018; see also Arthur, Keiser, Hagen, & Traylor, 2018) observed that this inconsistency in findings may be attributable to the fact that studies that failed to obtain lower scores for mobile devices where all characterized by (a) being low stakes (no real-world consequences as a result of participants' scores), and (b) instead of participants selecting the device of their choice, they were randomly assigned to the device-type conditions. The self-selection of devices is important because, as noted by Arthur et al. (2014), it remains unclear whether the general pattern of lower scores on mobile devices observed in operational data is truly a device-type effect or a self-selection effect; that is, individuals on the lower end of the general mental ability (GMA) spectrum tend to use mobile devices to complete employment-related tests and assessments.

Noncognitive Constructs. Whereas there is evidence for device-type differences in scores on cognitive constructs, at least in operational contexts, the absence of *meaningful* score differences are commonplace with respect to noncognitive constructs. That is, although nonzero effect sizes are typically obtained, they are consistently small. For instance, LaPort (2016) found an effect size (d) of 0.13, which she referred to as "negligible." Similarly, McClure Johnson and Boyce (2015) found consistently small effect sizes for both noncognitive entry- and managerial-level assessments, and Arthur et al. (2014) found ds ranging from -0.13 to 0.16 for the five-factor model personality traits.

8.3.3 Criterion-Related Validity

Over the temporal span covered by Arthur, Keiser, and Doverspike's (2018) review (i.e., up to December 2016 [inclusive]), there had not been any studies, of which the authors were aware, that had comparatively examined the criterion-related validities of UIT device-types. There have since been two studies, both of which were conference symposium presentations. Kinney, Besl, Lawrence, Moretti, and Chang (2017) examined the criterion-related validity of PC and mobile assessments with 406 and 136 employees, respectively. The criterion was supervisor ratings, and the predictors were noncognitive constructs, specifically, stress tolerance, achievement motivation, and work ethic. All predictor constructs were assessed via Likert scales with the exception of stress tolerance which was assessed using both a Likert scale and a situational judgment test (SJT). Kinney et al. concluded that "the assessment predicts performance ratings regardless of the device used by the test taker."

The second study (Illingworth et al., 2017) conducted two experiments to examine the comparative criterion-related validities of cognitive (Wonderlic Personnel Test) and noncognitive (five-factor model) assessments completed on mobile and nonmobile devices. Study 1 used a between-subjects design, and Study

2 a within-subjects design. Furthermore, unlike Kinney et al. (2017), the criterion was a simulated job task, however, like Kinney et al., Illingworth et al.'s (2017) results demonstrated comparable criterion-related validities for mobile and non-mobile devices for noncognitive constructs. In addition, Study 1 obtained comparable device-type criterion-related validities for cognitive constructs as well, with said results being more tentative in Study 2. In summary, to the extent that criterion-related validity is one of the critical facets on which predictors in personnel selection are compared (Arthur & Villado, 2008), the body of research examining this issue is very limited, as reflected by only two conference presentations on the topic to date.

8.3.4 Test-Taker Reactions and Preferences

Test takers generally have less favorable reactions toward, and lower preferences for, using mobile devices compared to nonmobile devices to complete employment-related tests and assessments. For example, using a within-subjects design wherein individuals completed assessments on both mobile and nonmobile devices, Chang, Lawrence, O'Connell, and Kinney (2016) reported less favorable perceptions for screen sizes 4" or smaller. For studies using between-subjects designs, results have been mixed. Whereas some studies have found differences in reactions (e.g., Fursman & Tuzinski, 2015; Gutierrez & Sanderson, 2015) – with the use of mobile devices being viewed less favorably and less preferred – others have failed to obtain differences (e.g., Fursman, 2016; Rossini, 2016). However, it is worth noting that for the aforementioned studies that found either (a) no, or (b) a very limited difference, preferences and reactions toward using mobile devices to complete the assessments were not higher than those for nonmobile devices.

In summary, in terms of the effects of mobile assessment on practice, depending on the type of construct being assessed (i.e., cognitive or noncognitive), the type of device a test taker chooses to use may have an adverse effect on their test scores. Whereas lower test scores have been observed when test takers use mobile devices (smartphones) to complete cognitively loaded tests and assessments, there seems to be no difference in scores on noncognitive tests and assessments as a function of the device type used. Additionally, test takers tend to have less favorable reactions toward using mobile devices (smartphones) to complete employment-related tests and assessments and prefer nonmobile devices for completing said tests and assessments. The implications of these results for the continued practice of allowing test takers to use *any* UIT device of their choosing are discussed in subsequent sections of the chapter. The next section examines current developments in attempts to provide psychologically meaningful explanations as to why one would or would not expect UIT device types to affect scores on employment-related tests and assessments.

8.4 Mobile Assessment: Intersection With Theory

As previously noted, UIT is now commonplace, and testing professionals are increasingly allowing applicants to complete employment-related tests and assessments on any device of their choosing. However, again, as previously noted, this is an instance of practice being well ahead of science (and empirical research), whereby industry is capitalizing on rapid technological advancements, and the academy is trying to play catch-up in order to make sense of the potential effects of UIT device type on employment-related tests (Morelli et al., 2017). So, although the literature regarding UIT device-type effects on employment-related tests and assessments is relatively nascent, a few scholars have advanced conceptual, psychologically grounded frameworks in an attempt to explain how and when UIT device types can impact testing-related outcomes of interest to organizations in the context of employment-related decision making. Subsequently, we first briefly describe the matter of interest within the context of classical test theory (CTT), followed by a review of a conceptual framework that attempts to provide a psychologically grounded explanation of UIT device-type effects, namely, the structural characteristics/information processing (SCIP; Arthur, Keiser, & Doverspike, 2018) framework. After reviewing the SCIP framework, it is then used as a referent to compare other efforts seeking to explain the effects of technology-based assessments.

8.4.1 Classical Test Theory and UIT Device-Type Effects

The following is intended to be a brief summary of UIT device-type effects within the context of classical test theory (CTT). By no means is it meant to be exhaustive, and the reader is directed to other sources such as Nunnally and Bernstein (1994) for a more in-depth discussion of CTT. Under the framework of CTT, an observed test score is a function of one's true score and error score (i.e., $X = T + E$). The error score can be further described in terms of unsystematic and systematic (or random and nonrandom, respectively) error. In theory, after repeated administrations of some test when only random error is present, one's true score is the expected value of the distribution of observed scores; thus, the expected value of the error score after repeated administrations of the same test is zero when only random error is present. With respect to UIT device-type effects, these effects would fall into the systematic or nonrandom error component. As such, even with repeated administrations of the same test, one's true score can be downwardly or upwardly biased due to nonrandom error. Using CTT as a framework, recent conceptual models have been advanced in an effort to provide an explanation of the score differences as a function of the UIT device used to complete employment-related tests and assessments.

8.4.2 The SCIP Framework

Arthur, Keiser, and Doverspike's (2018) SCIP framework is a conceptual framework wherein UIT devices are conceived in terms of the extent to which they engender *construct-irrelevant cognitive load,* which corresponds to the aforementioned systematic error as per CTT terminology. The foundational tenet of the SCIP framework is that systematic error is introduced via construct-irrelevant cognitive load attributable to the information-processing demands engendered by the UIT device's structural characteristics. That is, to the extent that cognitive information-processing resources are finite, then one would expect the addition of cognitive demands irrelevant to the task at hand to detract from one's ability to perform optimally on the focal task. The SCIP framework posits four structural characteristics, each yoked to a specific information-processing demand: (1) screen size and working memory demands, (2) screen clutter and perceptual speed and visual acuity demands, (3) response interface and psychomotor ability demands, and (4) permissibility and selective attention demands. Figure 8.1, adapted from Arthur, Keiser, and Doverspike (2017), presents a graphical illustration of the basic information processing model which has been modified to incorporate the tenets of the SCIP framework. We next review the central tenets of the SCIP framework.

Screen Size and Working Memory.   Screen size refers to the amount of viewable surface area the device has to present information, and the corresponding information-processing variable, working memory, is defined as "a brain system that provides temporary storage and manipulation of the information necessary for . . . complex cognitive tasks" (Baddeley, 1992, p. 556). The SCIP framework posits that screen size directly affects working memory demands to the extent that information must be held in working memory (Sanchez & Goolsbee, 2010). That is, for devices with smaller screens, the requisite information (e.g., item stem and alternatives) might not fit on a single screen. Thus, the use of multiple screens requires test takers to either (a) store the requisite information in working memory, or (b) continuously scroll back and forth in order to complete the assessment, both of which directly compete for cognitive resources that would otherwise be devoted toward completing the assessment. Hence, the greater the construct-irrelevant working memory demands placed on the test taker, the greater the likelihood that observed test scores will be attenuated.

Arthur, Keiser et al. (2018) provided initial empirical support for the working memory propositions advanced by the SCIP framework. Specifically, the effect size for the relationship between working memory and GMA was larger in the smartphone condition ($r = 0.29$) than the same effect size obtained for the desktop condition ($r = 0.14$). In addition, the effect sizes for the relationship between working memory and noncognitive assessment (i.e., personality) scores for each of the two conditions were similar and negligible. Contrary to what is proposed by the SCIP framework, however, no difference was found between smartphone and desktop conditions for the cognitive test ($d = 0.05$). Nevertheless, as previously noted about laboratory studies, this might be due to the fact that the data were collected as part of an experiment wherein participants were randomly assigned to conditions and the testing was low stakes.

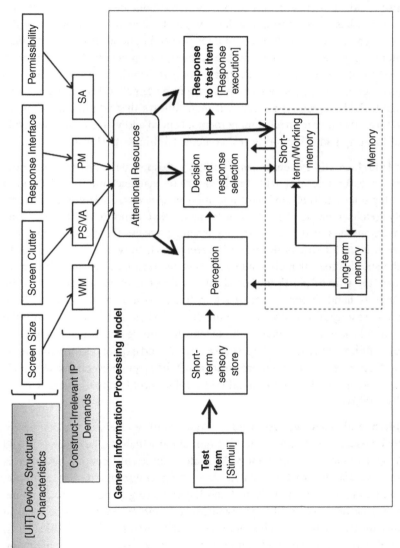

Figure 8.1 *General information processing model (Arthur, Doverspike, & Bell, 2004) modified to reflect the conceptual underpinnings of the SCIP framework. WM = working memory. PS/VA = perceptual speed and visual acuity. PM = psychomotor ability. SA = selective attention. IP Demands = information-processing demands. Adapted from Arthur, Keiser, and Doverspike (2018).*

Screen Clutter and Perceptual Speed and Visual Acuity. Screen clutter is related to screen size and, thus, also speaks to the amount of screen "real estate" that is available to present a specified amount of information. That is, it represents the density of information, or how much information is fit on the screen (Kroft & Wickens, 2002). So, for example, comparing a 32" desktop computer monitor to a 7" tablet reader, information presented on the desktop computer monitor is more readily distinguishable or spread out (less cluttered), whereas to fit the same amount of information on the tablet, the information would necessarily have to be condensed and, thus, result in a more "cluttered" display. To the extent that a device's screen has high information density, greater demands are placed on the test-taker's visual acuity (which refers to one's eyesight and ability to distinguish between items [e.g., text, pictures] on the screen), and perceptual speed (which refers to the "ability to quickly and accurately compare similarities and differences among sets of letters, numbers, objects, pictures, or patterns"; O*NET, n.d.). Thus, in reference to UIT device-type effects, it then follows that additional cognitive load in the form of construct-irrelevant perceptual speed and visual acuity demands in terms of locating and deciphering test content will hinder performance.

Response Interface and Psychomotor Ability. Response interface reflects how the user operates or interacts with the device. For instance, traditional desktop computers have an external keyboard and mouse, whereas smartphones are predominately touchscreen devices. And in terms of psychomotor ability (e.g., fine finger movement dexterity), even in the instance where the desktop also has a touchscreen interface, the desktop touchscreen interface would still be easier to use than the small screen that characterizes most smartphones. So, in reference to UIT devices, the role of psychomotor ability, which encompasses more specific abilities such as hand dexterity and reaction time, pertains to the ease with an individual can readily physically operate the device. Thus, in accordance with the SCIP framework, it is argued that to the extent that the device engenders greater psychomotor ability demands on the test taker, one would expect performance to be negatively affected (e.g., making more errors and subsequent corrections as a result of response input errors due to the so-called fat-finger problem [e.g., Siek, Rogers, & Connelly, 2005]).

Permissibility and Selective Attention. Permissibility refers to the degrees of freedom that a user has in terms of the environment in which she/he chooses to and can use the UIT device. Concomitant with greater degrees of freedom, however, is the greater potential for distractions in the testing environment. For example, desktop computers are traditionally in fixed locations (e.g., one's study at home, the office, a desk at a public library), whereas a 7" tablet reader can be used in virtually any location where wireless internet or cellular signal is available. Thus, in the case of choosing to complete employment-related tests and assessments on a tablet reader, there is a greater likelihood to complete said assessment in an environment that is not conducive to testing (e.g., the terminal of an airport). Interestingly, in an investigation of this issue in which they identified and examined the effects of three contexts (privacy [public vs. private], movement [static vs.

moving], and location [indoor vs. outdoor vs. transport]), Gray, Morelli, and McLane's (2015) results indicated that test takers (in this instance students) usually chose quieter or more private locations like a bedroom to complete the assessment; that is, the rate at which these participants completed assessments on a mobile device in a public or distracting place was not as high as they had expected. Nevertheless, to the extent that one is in a distracting environment that is not conducive to testing, greater construct-irrelevant cognitive load in the form of selective attention demands will be placed on the test taker.

It is important to reiterate that the SCIP framework is not device-specific and does not differentiate between UIT devices in terms of the rudimentary mobile/ nonmobile dichotomy. Instead, it focuses on how any particular UIT device can affect employment-related test and assessment scores in terms of the additional information-processing demands engendered by the device, when these demands are *irrelevant* to the assessment at hand. Additionally, with a myriad of different configurations of structural characteristics and their associated information-processing demands, it should be recognized that UIT device-type effects are not solely due to any structural characteristic/information-processing demand in isolation, but, rather, an amalgamation of them. As such, the effect of any current *and* future piece of technology can be modeled if it is possible to describe the device in terms of the extent to which it introduces or engenders additional construct-irrelevant cognitive load in the form of extraneous information-processing demands. This issue is further expanded on in the summary of the advantages of the SCIP framework presented in the next section.

8.4.3 Other Frameworks

Although the theoretical or conceptual work that seeks to explain UIT device-type effects on assessment and test scores is limited, there have nevertheless been other efforts to explain these effects (i.e., Lee, Kim, & Kim, 2005; Potosky, 2008; Schroeders & Wilhelm, 2010). For instance, Potosky (2008) presents a framework that speaks to the effect of technology on assessment scores. However, it is embedded in communication theory and views assessment-medium effects not in terms of individual differences in specified abilities, but instead as *communicative acts* between the test taker and the individual or anyone who wants to measure attributes of the test taker. Consequently, the focus is on how the communication channel (e.g., face-to-face versus telephone interview) or the medium's structural attributes affect the message quality and, hence, test scores. In contrast to Potosky (2008) and the SCIP framework papers, Lee et al. (2005) and Schroeders and Wilhelm (2010) are best described as presenting conceptual justifications for the posited hypotheses for their primary studies. However, a comparison of the SCIP framework to these works presents an opportunity to discuss the similarities and differences between them and, by so doing, highlight the distinctiveness and advantages of the SCIP framework.

Indeed, aspects of Lee et al.'s (2005) and Schroeders and Wilhelm's (2010) conceptual descriptions correspond with features of the SCIP framework. These prior descriptions identify specific individual differences and characteristics of device types that are purported to affect test-taker behavior and subsequently lead to test score differences. For instance, Schroeders and Wilhelm (2010) described four factors that they argue threaten the comparison of ability assessments across test media – perceptual demands, motor skill requirements, modes of item presentation, and familiarity with electronic devices. Lee et al. (2005) view the use of various devices as contextually bound and categorize the influences of test-taker behavior within various personal (i.e., emotion, time, movement) and environmental (i.e., physical, social) contextual factors. Thus, features of these descriptions coincide with some of the information-processing demands (i.e., perceptual speed and visual acuity, psychomotor ability) and structural characteristics (i.e., permissibility) inherent in the SCIP framework.

In spite of these similarities, the SCIP framework offers a comprehensive, individual-differences-based, construct-driven framework for understanding device-type score differences, explaining and accounting for observed device-type effects reported in the literature, in addition to advancing several empirically testable propositions (e.g., criterion-related validity, subgroup differences). In contrast, as previously noted, Lee et al.'s (2005) and Schroeders and Wilhelm's (2010) presentations are best described as conceptual justifications for the posited hypotheses and research for their primary studies. As such, they are not formal frameworks that present a series of interrelated testable propositions that go beyond the specific hypotheses and research questions investigated in the specified papers. Furthermore, they rely on the aforementioned mobile versus nonmobile categorization of devices. In contrast, the SCIP framework represents a broader framework that seeks to explain and predict the conditions under which UIT devices have different effects on a range of assessment-related outcomes (test performance, test completion time, test-taker reactions and perceptions, criterion-related validity, subgroup differences) as a function of the construct assessed (cognitive versus noncognitive), and the interaction between construct-irrelevant information-processing demands and the associated structural characteristics of the UIT device. Additionally, the breadth of the SCIP framework is reflected in the proposition that the tenets of the framework apply to not only a wide range of UIT device-type configurations, but to any assessment media or context in which construct-irrelevant information-processing demands associated with the testing method or medium are germane.

As previously noted, unlike Lee et al. (2005) and Schroeders and Wilhelm (2010), Potosky (2008) presents a more formal framework. Potosky's framework is embedded in communication theory; that is, Potosky views personnel tests and assessments as a *communicative act* between the test taker and organization. Various attributes of the test administration medium (i.e., transparency, social bandwidth, interactivity, and surveillance) are used in this communication process that can, in turn, affect assessment outcomes. Thus, as frameworks for conceptually explaining and accounting for UIT device-type test score differences, Potosky's (2008) framework and the SCIP framework are fundamentally dissimilar. Potosky conceptualizes attributes of test medium based on how they influence communication or message quality and test scores, whereas the SCIP framework explains test score differences as a function of a finite pool of cognitively loaded information-processing resources differentially drawn from test takers as they complete assessments (see Figure 8.1). As such, consonant with the pivotal role that individual differences play in personnel assessment and testing (Sackett et al., 2017), the SCIP framework conceptualizes assessment device-type effects in terms of how individual differences of the test taker on specified information-processing attributes interact with the structural characteristics of the assessment device to generate construct-irrelevant cognitive load on the test taker that subsequently influences the individual's performance on the assessment. Phrased another way, the SCIP framework explains device-type test score effects in terms of processes (e.g., cognitive load) that similar to or the same as those pertaining to the measured attribute (e.g., cognitive ability). Consequently, construct-irrelevant variance serves as a meaningful explanatory mechanism.

In summary, the SCIP framework offers a number of advantages and distinguishing features. Specifically: (1) It explains and accounts for UIT device-type score differences by relying on theories of individual differences, associated information-processing demands, and their interaction with device-type structural characteristics; (2) It advances several empirically testable formal propositions, and support, or lack thereof, for them should ultimately determine the viability of the framework as an explanatory framework; (3) It provides guidance to future research on how to classify and describe UIT device-types in comparative studies, that is, psychologically and conceptually instead of technologically (i.e., mobile [wireless] versus nonmobile [wired]); (4) It permits the examination of a wide range of UIT device-type configurations (e.g., an Xbox on a 53" TV; a desktop with a touchscreen interface; a tablet with an external keyboard) as well as even newer technologies as they emerge – as long as they engender and, subsequently, can be conceptualized in terms of the level of construct-irrelevant information-processing demands; and (5) it conceptually informs discussions of a wider range of assessment methods and modes, particularly in any domain in which construct-irrelevant information-processing demands associated with the testing method or medium are pertinent.

Finally, as previously noted, the conceptual structure of the SCIP framework permits it to model the effects of any current *and* future piece of (assessment) technology as long as it is possible to describe the device or technology in terms of the extent to which it introduces or engenders additional construct-irrelevant cognitive load in the form of extraneous information-processing demands. Consonant with this, Arthur, Keiser, and Doverspike (2018) comment on how the SCIP framework can inform the potential effects of other technologically mediated assessment methods such as virtual role-plays, immersive simulations, and gamified assessments. To further expand on this, to the extent that the use of voice, for instance, becomes a prevalent means of responding to and completing assessments, the tenets of the SCIP framework would suggest that the use of voice as a response interface should reduce the cognitive load and demands associated with the physical response interface and, correspondingly, reduce the role of psychomotor ability and its effect as a source of construct-irrelevant variance. An extension of this line of reasoning is the potential use of the tenets of the SCIP framework to design assessments that minimize the role of the specified construct-irrelevant information-processing variables. Thus, in accordance with the tenets of responsive design (e.g., Groves & Heeringa, 2006), a test designer could proactively use the SCIP framework as a model to design assessments and tests that mitigate or minimize differences across platforms, devices, or mobile-dedicated assessments; that is, assessments that, by virtue of their design, do not engender extra construct-irrelevant cognitive load on mobile assessments.

8.4.4 Mobile Assessment and the Prototypical Employment Process

Using the illustration presented in Figure 8.2 of the prototypical personnel psychology functions with which an applicant, and, subsequently, an incumbent, interacts with a hiring organization as an organizing framework, this section discusses the role of mobile assessments in the context of each of these functions.

The first function is the recruitment of applicants by the organization. Next, the organization makes a selection decision on the basis of the pre-employment tests and assessments administered to the applicant. If unsuccessful, the process ends here, as the organization is not interested in hiring the applicant. However, if successful, the process typically goes one of two ways: (a) the applicant, now an employee, is placed in a role that the organization deems fit, or (b) the organization places the new employee in a training program and, upon completion, makes a placement decision. After some specified period of time on the job, performance appraisal information can serve as the basis for a host personnel decisions including (a) promotion into new positions, (b) initiation of additional remedial training, or (c) termination for poor performance.

The increasing use of UIT – allowing applicants to complete employment-related tests and assessments anywhere, anytime, and on any device of their choosing – has actual and potential implications for several of the personnel psychology functions described here. Granted, mobile assessments cannot

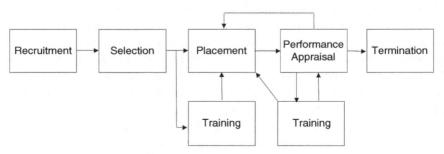

Figure 8.2 *Applicant/employee flow-through and interactions with various personnel psychology functions and systems*

necessarily be incorporated into each of these personnel functions, however, they are relevant for the majority of them. And in those instances where mobile assessment is not directly germane to the personnel psychology function, per se, we make note of how technological advancements, more broadly speaking, have, or can potentially have, an impact on said function.

Recruitment.   Although there is no testing and assessment component with respect to applicant recruitment, technological advancements have nevertheless impacted organizations' recruitment efforts. For instance, in addition to traditional recruitment (e.g., newspaper advertisements, word of mouth), organizations have been using e-recruiting (Stone et al., 2015) for quite some time now (e.g., Indeed .com, Monster.com). Additionally, although there is presently no scholarly literature of which we are aware on the topic, the use of geofencing has become a relatively newfound method of recruitment. Geofencing allows for organizations to send out job advertisements via push notifications based on the location of the user. Assuming individuals (a) possess mobile devices that allow for this feature, and (b) have it enabled, they can receive job advertisements directly to their mobile device when they are within a certain radius of the hiring organization.

Selection.   As noted in the previous section, *Effects of Mobile Assessment on Practice*, the preponderance of the mobile assessment literature has focused on selection, and of the three common outcomes on which predictors are compared – criterion-related and incremental validity, subgroup differences, and test-taker reactions (Arthur & Villado, 2008) – test-taker reactions are what have been most widely examined in the mobile device literature. As previously summarized, this literature indicates that test takers generally have less favorable reactions toward, and lower preferences for, using mobile devices to complete employment-related tests and assessments.

Although there is a very limited examination of the comparative criterion-related validity of UIT device types in the literature, Arthur, Keiser, and Doverspike (2018) commented on and discussed this. Specifically, while conceptualized as sources of construct-irrelevant cognitive load because they are not the focal constructs of interest in the assessment (see Figure 8.1), many of the SCIP information-processing variables have established demonstrable relationships with organizationally relevant outcomes and performance. For instance, working memory has been shown to be predictive of performance on a wide range of simple and complex tasks and activities that are relevant across jobs, including problem solving, multitasking, and decision making (e.g., Colom et al., 2010; Cowan et al., 2005; Edwards et al., 2017).Consequently, whereas they may not be the focal constructs of interest, to the extent that the specified SCIP information-processing variables may be relevant in the context of the job in question (e.g., perceptual speed for air traffic controllers [Ackerman & Cianciolo, 2000]; psychomotor ability for utility workers [Levine et al., 1996]), then the use of UIT devices that engender the additional cognitive load may unintendedly contribute to the criterion-related validity of the measure. That is, for instance, although the use of a smartphone to complete a GMA test may increase the role of working memory in the assessment score (more so than using a desktop), to the extent that working memory is relevant to successful performance on the criterion, then using a smartphone in this context should result in a higher criterion-related validity than the use of a desktop computer. It is worth noting that for both of the previously reviewed studies (i.e., Illingworth et al., 2017; Kinney et al., 2017) that examined and obtained comparable criterion-related validities across UIT device types, the information provided suggested that these were jobs in which one would not expect the SCIP information-processing variables to play a pivotal role. Hence, in this regard, the finding of comparable UIT device-type criterion-related validities is not at odds with the tenets of the SCIP framework (see Arthur, Keiser, & Doverspike 2018, Proposition 5).

Concerning subgroup differences, and, subsequently, adverse impact potential, the literature indicates that whereas there are no mean differences on noncognitive (e.g., personality) assessments taken on "mobile" and "nonmobile" devices (and when present, they are very small), under high-stakes conditions where test takers select their assessment device, there are pronounced differences for cognitive constructs with scores on mobile devices being substantially lower. However, whether these effects would interact with race/ethnicity to augment the well-documented subgroup differences on cognitive measures, empirically, remains unknown. Nevertheless, if taking cognitive tests on mobile devices results in lower scores, and the tendency to take assessments on mobile devices covaries with specified protected group status, then this raises the specter of observed subgroup differences and higher adverse impact potential resulting from the use of certain UIT devices (e.g., smartphone) in employment-related assessments but not others. In an effort to speak to this issue, Arthur, Keiser, and Doverspike (2017) further examined Arthur et al.'s (2014) results which reported an overall d of 0.90, reflecting lower scores on mobile devices. Disaggregating these results by race/ethnicity indicated that the White–African American d was 0.68 for mobile devices and 0.84 for nonmobile devices; that is, in Arthur et al. (2014), UIT device type did not interact with demography to result in larger subgroup differences. Arthur, Keiser, and Doverspike (2017) observed that this pattern of result, where the use of mobile devices appears to make the subgroup differences (unexpectedly) smaller, is similar to those reported by Arthur, Edwards, and Barrett (2002), and Edwards and Arthur (2007) in their comparisons of constructed-response and multiple-choice tests.

Training.   Training can be described as comprising three processes, specifically, design and development, delivery, and evaluation. With a focus on the latter two, advancements in wireless technologies and mobile devices have allowed for the use of said devices to deliver and present web-based training materials, for better or for worse. For instance, there is empirical evidence indicative of unfavorable outcomes such as lower trainee satisfaction (Richardson & Swann, 2003) when the training content is web-based, although this is likely to be less of an issue when web-based approaches are preferred by trainees (Hornik, Johnson, & Wu, 2007).

The incorporation of mobile assessments into training evaluation is not dissimilar to mobile assessments within the context of personnel selection. For example, mobile assessments can be readily incorporated into the first two levels of Kirkpatrick's (1976) training evaluation model. That is, the evaluation of reactions and learning both lend themselves to being assessed via mobile devices, as they are no different from the traditional attitude assessments and knowledge tests commonly used for other employment-related functions (e.g., selection). Hence, for the assessment of training reactions, one should not expect any UIT device-type effects. However, for evaluations of learning, one should expect effects similar to those observed for completing cognitive tests on mobile devices for employment-related testing purposes; namely, the use of mobile devices for cognitive tests seems to attenuate test scores. Kirkpatrick's third level of training evaluation criteria, behavioral criteria, represents the extent to which there are changes in on-the-job-related behaviors and performance that can be attributed to training. Harari et al.'s (2016) work on using smartphones to collect behavioral data in psychological science raises the possibility of using the functions and features of these devices to unobtrusively collect behavioral data, such as those pertaining to social interactions, daily activities, and mobility patterns. The challenge, of course, is one of ensuring that inferences can be made from these data as to the extent to which they are germane to and represent organizationally relevant work-related behaviors.

Performance Appraisal/Management. Performance appraisal/management does not lend itself to mobile assessments in the traditional sense, per se, but there nevertheless lie unique opportunities for the incorporation of mobile devices and other related technologies within this domain. For instance, electronic performance management (ePM) systems are becoming increasingly commonplace (Sierra-Cedar, 2016), although they are most often employed on desktop and laptop computers. ePM is subsumed under the broader electronic human resource management (eHRM) system that houses several human resource functions, including administrative-related functions (e.g., payroll), time management (e.g., scheduling), and talent management (e.g., performance management; Payne, Mendoza, & Horner, 2018). One of the primary benefits of eHRM is the ability for users to access and update information without assistance from the human resource department, which simplifies many common human resource functions.

The incorporation of mobile devices within ePM has many potentially beneficial outcomes. For instance, some mobile-enabled ePM applications allow for real-time anonymous feedback, which may bolster feedback acceptance (Cleveland & Murphy, 2016). Additionally, the use of mobile devices could allow for more frequent, on-the-fly performance appraisals, which, in turn, may provide a more accurate portrayal of employees' performance over time compared to the sole annual performance evaluation that is currently a commonplace practice. Finally, as described in the preceding *Training* section, this gathering and use of work performance data could also be utilized as Level 3 behavioral criteria for training evaluation purposes as well.

8.4.5 Mobile Assessments and Obsolescence in Test Development and Validation?

It is not unreasonable to inquire about the extent to which the use of mobile devices in employment-related testing and assessment have impacted, if at all, current test development and validation models and paradigms, as well as practices. Arthur et al. (2017) identified four major steps in the prototypical test development and validation process and concluded that three of these had been or could potentially be impacted by emerging technologies including mobile devices. For instance, concerning work/job analysis, the influence of mobile devices could take the form of aids in the collection of data such as online job analysis surveys, video recording of performance episodes, or critical incidents. Furthermore, the potential ease of data collection vastly increases the ease with which large numbers of raters can be sampled to complete said surveys. Likewise, because mobile devices offer alternative methods for assessing specified constructs, they have the potential to impact two additional steps of the test development and validation sequence, specifically, the selection or development of the test/assessment tool and the conduction of the validation study. Concerning the latter, this is particularly the case because mobile devices serve as the means by which the construct scores are obtained. So, in summary, although the use of mobile devices has not made current test development and validation models and paradigms obsolete, they nevertheless have the potential to vastly impact these practices (Arthur et al., 2017).

8.4.6 Legal and Ethical Implications

The legal and ethical implications and concerns for mobile assessments are similar to, if not the same as, those raised in Pearlman (2009) and Tippins et al. (2006)'s discussion of UIT. Specifically, mobile assessments, by their very nature, are almost exclusively taken in unproctored settings, and, thus, are fundamentally just a variation in the medium one chooses to take a UIT. So, in accord with what Pearlman (2009; Tippins et al., 2006) notes, UITs, and by inference, mobile assessments as well, are technically in violation of several sections of the *Ethical Principles of Psychologists and Code of Conduct* (American Psychological Association [APA], 2017), *Standards for Educational and Psychological Testing* (American Educational Research Association [AERA], American Psychological Association [APA], & National Council on Measurement in Education, 2014) and the *Principles for the Validation and Use of Personnel Selection Procedures* (SIOP, 2003). For instance, one of the many concerns with UIT is the inherent lack of standardization – an issue raised by each of the three aforementioned sources of professional principles as well as the *Uniform Guidelines* (Equal Employment Opportunity Commission, Civil Service Commission, Department of Labor, 1978). This is clearly the case with respect to "mobile" assessments to the extent that test takers are allowed to choose the device they use to complete said assessments. That is, allowing test takers to use a UIT device of their choosing is, in essence, another layer of non-standardization in addition to the standardization issues that have already been noted elsewhere with respect to UIT, namely, environmental standardization.

In addition to standardization concerns, mobile assessments also bring forth a host of other issues worth considering. From a legal and ethical standpoint, for example, to the extent that GMA and other cognitively loaded tests are the most valid predictors of job performance (Schmidt & Hunter, 1998, 2004), then differential access to UIT devices (e.g., desktops, laptops) that *do not* display UIT device-type effects on tests of this sort is potentially a serious concern. Indeed, if this is the case, then one of the promulgated benefits of UIT and mobile assessments – a larger, more diverse applicant pool (Tippins, 2015) – could potentially turn out to be prejudicial if individuals are unable to complete said tests and assessments to the best of their ability due to the inability to access proper equipment. In summary, whereas the issues noted above have failed to garner much traction in the applied and scholarly literatures since first raised by Pearlman (2009; Tippins et al., 2006), they are nevertheless worthy of serious consideration.

8.5 The Future of Mobile Assessments

It would not be unwarranted to observe that the integration of current and future forms of technology within employment-related HR functions (e.g., personnel selection, post-training assessments) and UIT is here for the long haul (Arthur et al., 2017). Consequently, the onus is on researchers and practitioners to examine both the potential adversities and benefits of replacing the old (e.g., in-house testing environments) with the new (e.g., UIT). At the present time, the literature regarding the use of new technologies for personnel psychology and other employment-related functions is relatively nascent, with the majority of the published literature devoted to using mobile devices for personnel selection purposes. Hence, this final section aims to delineate current gaps in the literature as well as future directions for both the academy and industry, including some best practices recommendations for practitioners.

8.5.1 Criterion-Related Validity

The stream of research regarding mobile assessments is still in its infancy, and one of the more acute gaps in the literature is the very limited number of studies examining the comparative criterion-related validity of test scores obtained using different UIT devices. Indeed, we could locate only two (Illingworth et al., 2017; Kinney et al., 2017; both conference symposium presentations). So, the important question of whether or not test scores have similar criterion-related validity, or, perhaps, display differential validity, has yet to receive the research attention that it warrants. And to the extent that criterion-related validity is paramount to the field of personnel psychology, these questions are of great import.

8.5.2 Subgroup Differences and Adverse Impact Potential

Another pertinent question from an ethical and legal standpoint is whether or not subgroup differences, and resultant adverse impact, arise from or are exacerbated by allowing test takers to complete employment-related tests and assessments on any device of their choosing. For example, Arthur et al. (2014), using a large, operational dataset, found that there were noticeable differences in terms of the demographics of individuals who used mobile versus nonmobile devices. Specifically, it was found that women, African Americans, and Hispanics were more likely to use mobile devices, a pattern that is consistent with the national mobile phone ownership data (Pew Research Center, 2015a, 2015b, 2018). This difference in demographic characteristics between those who use mobile versus nonmobile devices, coupled with observed subgroup differences on cognitively loaded constructs (e.g., Bobko & Roth, 2013) and observed cognitive test score differences between those using mobile versus nonmobile devices (in favor of nonmobile devices; Arthur et al., 2014; Arthur, Keiser, & Doverspike 2018), could potentially exacerbate test score differences, and, subsequently, adverse impact.

Self-selection. Differences between demographic groups in terms of the use of mobile versus nonmobile devices to complete employment-related assessments begs the question of whether the observed cognitive test score differences between UIT devices may be a self-selection instead of a device-type effects (Arthur et al., 2014). Brown and Grossenbacher (2017) sought to answer this question, but their design failed to conclusively do so. Specifically, they randomly assigned test takers into conditions, which, by definition, removed any possibility of examining a self-selection effect, contrary to their claim to do so, because participants did not choose the UIT device they used to complete the assessment. Indeed, to the contrary, as noted by Arthur et al. (2014), this issue would be best resolved by a research design in which test takers are first tested on a GMA test using the UIT device that they choose, along with the time and place of their choice, and are then retested in a controlled, proctored laboratory setting on a desktop computer (nonmobile device), irrespective of the device used for the first assessment.

So, at present, this issue remains unresolved. However, should subsequent research be more indicative that it is a self-selection phenomenon, then practitioners may want to consider incorporating a recommendation pertaining to the use of specific devices in addition to other best test-taking practices, such as those environments recognized as being most conducive to testing (e.g., quiet; Lawrence et al., 2017). That being noted, it is also acknowledged that this differential use of mobile and nonmobile devices could very well be attributed to demography. Specifically, mobile devices (smartphones in particular) could conceivably be the primary, if not the only means to access the internet (Tippins et al., 2006) for meaningful segments of some demographic groups. So, to the extent that this is indeed the case, then UITs, namely, the reliance on smartphones for employment-related assessments, have the potential to amplify observed subgroup differences. Thus, clearly, this is an area that warrants further research attention beyond the previously noted reanalysis of Arthur et al.'s (2014) data, and Brown and Grossenbacher (2017) as well.

8.5.3 Mobile Assessment Best Practices

On the basis of our review of the literature, and our research and applied experiences, coupled with input from similarly situated colleagues, we conclude this chapter by presenting some recommended best practices for the use of mobile assessments. These recommendations are enumerated only to facilitate clarity of presentation and are not indicative of importance. Finally, where there is empirical evidence that substantiates the best-practice claim, we briefly summarize said research and evidence.

1. Specify or communicate to test takers the conditions under which UIT assessments should be taken.

   In accordance with propositions made by the SCIP framework as well as empirical evidence (e.g., Arthur et al., 2014; King et al., 2015; Wood et al., 2015), this might include encouraging test takers to use devices on the lower end of the device-engendered construct-irrelevant cognitive load continuum (e.g., desktops, laptops); this is especially so for cognitively loaded assessments. Based on the conceptual tenets of the SCIP framework, Figure 8.3 from Arthur, Keiser, and Doverspike (2018) presents an illustration of device-type clusters on which one would and would not expect device-type differences. Furthermore, test takers should be advised to complete the assessment in a quiet space when they have sufficient blocks of uninterrupted time (Lawrence et al., 2017).

2. Notify test takers or provide warnings to the effect that taking assessments under less than optimal or desirable conditions (as per #;1 above) will likely negatively impact their test scores for cognitively loaded assessments.
3. Organizations should consider preventing test takers from completing cognitive assessments (more so if they are speeded) on devices that engender high levels of construct-irrelevant cognitive load (see Figure 8.3).

   Of course, this depends on the practical and business considerations under which one is operating. Adhering to this recommendation would allow for organizations to capitalize on the maximal informational value that can be obtained from the use of remotely delivered assessments for human resources decision-making.

4. Be wary of the completion of cognitive assessments on devices at the higher end of the device-engendered construct-irrelevant cognitive load continuum; or at the very least, in the context of high-stakes assessments where test takers choose their own assessment device, be very cognizant of the expected device mean differences and potential for higher levels of subgroup differences and, thus, adverse impact potential.

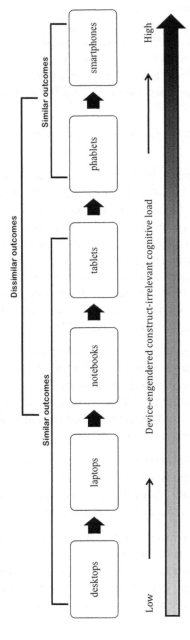

Figure 8.3 *Illustrative example of how current prototypical UIT devices might be classified on construct-irrelevant information-processing cognitive load with hypothesized similar and dissimilar device-type effect outcomes. Adapted from Arthur, Keiser, and Doverspike (2018).*

5. Ensure that the assessment is optimized for, and not simply accessible by, devices at the high end of the construct-irrelevant cognitive load continuum (e.g., smartphones; Parker & Meade, 2015).

For instance, this may entail starting with designing the assessment for smartphones and then adapting it for desktop computers. That is, design the desktop computer application to match the smartphone application; not the other way around.

6. Avoid the presentation of high-fidelity work samples and simulations on devices at the high end of the construct-irrelevant cognitive load continuum.

Due to the nature of these types of assessments, they are likely to engender even higher levels of construct-irrelevant cognitive load on devices at the high end of the construct-irrelevant cognitive load continuum.

7. Permit liberal administration times on noncognitive measures.
8. Where it is possible, allow test takers to switch devices when completing the assessment battery should they decide to do so (Arthur et al., 2014; Dages & Jones, 2015).
9. Collect and review device-type data; track or know the type of device used. This is important and required if one is to be informed about the issues noted in the preceding points.

8.6 Conclusion

Based on the limited empirical evidence to date, it would seem that the use of specific devices for employment-related tests and assessments results in adverse outcomes under some circumstances in the form of lower test scores. These deleterious effects, however, have yet to be extensively examined, and examinations of the specific mechanisms that account for or explain these effects is nascent. With that as a backdrop, the present chapter, based on a review of the pertinent literature, discussed the effects of UIT device types, with an emphasis on mobile assessment, on current employment-related testing and assessment, and its intersection with theory. Concerning the latter, the SCIP framework was reviewed and examined as a plausible conceptual framework, for positing when one should and should not expect device-types effects, and the conditions under which one should do so. Gaps in the current employment-related mobile assessment literature, such as the very limited number of comparative criterion-related validity studies, and subgroup differences and adverse impact, were also noted and explored, with suggestions for future research.

Finally, the chapter concluded with some best practices recommendations. Concerning these, they are best considered as tentative and preliminary; they are not intended to preclude the need and call for additional research within the domain of mobile assessments. As noted throughout this chapter, UIT and mobile assessments have already permeated industry; hence, the academy is, at the present time, trying to play catch-up. As was demonstrated in this chapter, gaps exist within the mobile assessment literature, but examinations of historical usage or specific research questions in applied settings would be best served by theoretical or conceptual approaches such as the SCIP framework (see also Morelli et al., 2017). More exploratory research should focus on examining best practices or innovative mobile assessment development methods. To help the field play catch-up, a forward-looking, inquisitive eye for understanding how to optimize or maximize mobile assessments is needed, rather than a backward-looking, skeptical one. In conclusion, in order to keep up with practice, concerted research devoted to addressing the issues brought about by allowing test takers to complete employment-related tests and assessments on a device of their choosing is called for.

References

Ackerman, P. L. & Cianciolo, A. T. (2000). Cognitive, perceptual-speed, and psychomotor determinants of individual differences during skill acquisition. *Journal of Experimental Psychology: Applied, 6*, 259–290.

American Educational Research Association, American Psychological Association, & National Council on Measurement in Education. (2014). *Standards for educational and psychological testing*. Washington, DC: American Educational Research Association.

American Psychological Association. (2017). Ethical principles of psychologists and code of conduct (2002, Amended June 1, 2010, and January 1, 2017). Retrieved from www.apa.org/ethics/code/index.aspx.

Arthur, W., Jr., Doverspike, D., & Bell, S. T. (2004). Information processing tests. In M. Hersen & J. C. Thomas (Eds.), *Comprehensive handbook of psychological assessment: Volume 4, Industrial and organizational assessment* (pp. 56–74). New York, NY: John Wiley & Sons, Inc.

Arthur, W., Jr., Doverspike, D., Kinney, T. B., & O'Connell, M. (2017). The impact of emerging technologies on selection models and research: Mobile devices and gamification as exemplars. In J. L. Farr, & N. T Tippins (Eds.), *Handbook of employee selection* (2nd edn., pp. 967–986). New York, NY: Taylor & Francis/Psychology Press.

Arthur, W., Jr., Doverspike, D., Muñoz, G. J., Taylor, J. E., & Carr, A. E. (2014). The use of mobile devices in high-stakes remotely delivered assessments and testing. *International Journal of Selection and Assessment, 22*, 113–123.

Arthur, W., Jr., Edwards, B. D., & Barrett, G. V. (2002). Multiple-choice and constructed-response tests of ability: Race-based subgroup performance differences on alternative paper-and-pencil test formats. *Personnel Psychology, 55*, 985–1008.

Arthur, W., Jr. & Glaze, R. M. (2011). Cheating and response distortion on remotely delivered assessments. In N. T. Tippins, & S. Adler (Eds.), *Technology-enhanced assessment of talent* (pp. 99–152). San Francisco, CA: Jossey-Bass.

Arthur, W., Jr., Keiser, N. L., & Doverspike, D. (2018). An information processing-based conceptual framework of the effects of unproctored internet-based testing devices on scores on employment-related assessments and tests. *Human Performance, 31*, 1–32.

Arthur, W., Jr., Keiser, N. L., Hagen, E., & Traylor, Z. (2018). Unproctored internet-based testing device-type score differences: The role of working memory. Intelligence, 67, 67–75.

Arthur, W. Jr. & Villado, A. J. (2008). The importance of distinguishing between constructs and methods when comparing predictors in personnel selection research and practice. *Journal of Applied Psychology*, 93, 435–442.

Baddeley, A. (1992). Working memory. *Science*, 25, 181–185.

Bobko, P. & Roth, P. L. (2013). Reviewing, categorizing, and analyzing the literature on Black-White mean differences for predictors of job performance: Verifying some perceptions and updating/correcting others. *Personnel Psychology*, 66, 91–126.

Brown, M. I. & Grossenbacher, M. A. (2017). Can you test me now? Equivalence of GMA tests on mobile and non-mobile devices. *International Journal of Selection and Assessment*, 25, 61–71.

Brown, M. I., Grossenbacher, M., & Nguyen, D. (2016). *Can you score me now? GMA testing using mobile devices*. Paper presented at the presented at the 31st Annual Conference of the Society for Industrial and Organizational Psychology, Anaheim, CA.

Chang, L., Lawrence, A. D., O'Connell, M. S., & Kinney, T. B. (2016). Mobile vs. PC delivered simulations: Screen size matters. In T. D. McGlochin (Chair), Mobile equivalence: Expanding research across assessment methods, levels, and devices. Symposium presented at the 31st Annual Conference of the Society for Industrial and Organizational Psychology, Anaheim, CA.

Cleveland, J. N. & Murphy, K. R. (2016). Organizations want to abandon performance appraisal: Can they? Should they? In D. L. Stone & J. H. Dulebohn (Eds.), *Human resource management theory and research on new employment relationships* (pp. 15–46). Charlotte, NC: Information Age.

Colom, R., Martínez-Molina, A., Shih, P. C., & Santacreu, J. (2010). Intelligence, working memory, and multitasking performance. Intelligence, 38, 543–551.

Cowan, N., Elliott, E. M., Saults, J. S., Morey, C. C., Mattox, S., Hismjatullina, A., & Conway, A. R. (2005). On the capacity of attention: Its estimation and its role in working memory and cognitive aptitudes. *Cognitive Psychology*, 51, 42–100.

Dages, K. D., & Jones, J. W. (2015). Mobile device administration: Does length or level of assessment matter? In N. Morelli (Chair), Mobile devices in talent assessment: The next chapter. Symposium presented at the 30th Annual Conference of the Society for Industrial and Organizational Psychology, Philadelphia, PA.

Davies, S. A. & Wadlington, P. L. (2006). Factor and parameter invariance of a five factor personality test across proctored/unproctored computerized administration. Paper presented at the 21st Annual Conference of the Society for Industrial and Organizational Psychology, Dallas, TX.

Do, B., Shepherd, W., & Drasgow, F. (2005). Measurement equivalence across proctored and unproctored administration modes of web-based measures. Paper presented at the 20th Annual Conference of the Society for Industrial and Organizational Psychology, Los Angeles, CA.

Edwards, B. D. & Arthur, W., Jr. (2007). An examination of factors contributing to a reduction in subgroup differences on a constructed-response paper-and-pencil test of scholastic achievement. *Journal of Applied Psychology*, 92, 794–801.

Edwards, B. D., Franco Watkins, A. M., McAbee, S. T., & Faura, L. (2017). The case for using working memory in practice. *The Industrial-Organizational Psychologist*, 55(1), 4–7.

Equal Employment Opportunity Commission, Civil Service Commission, Department of Labor, & Department of Justice. (1978). Adoption by four agencies of uniform guidelines on employee selection procedures. *Federal Register, 43*, 38290–38315.

Fursman, P. (2016). Warning message impact on assessment scores delivered on mobile devices. In T. D. McGlochin (Chair), Mobile equivalence: Expanding research across assessment methods, levels, and devices. Symposium presented at the 31st Annual Conference of the Society for Industrial and Organizational Psychology, Anaheim, CA.

Fursman, P., & Tuzinski, K. (2015). Reactions to mobile testing from the perspective of job applicants. Paper presented at the 30th Annual Conference of the Society for Industrial and Organizational Psychology, Philadelphia, PA.

Gray, C., Morelli, N. A., & McLane, W. (2015). Does use context affect selection assessments via mobile devices? In N. A. Morelli (Chair), Mobile devices in talent assessment: The next chapter. Symposium presented at the 30th Annual Conference of the Society for Industrial and Organizational Psychology, Philadelphia, PA.

Groves, R. M. & Heeringa, S. G. (2006). Responsive design for household surveys: Tools for actively controlling survey errors and costs. *Journal of the Royal Statistical Society: Series A (Statistics in Society), 169*, 439–457.

Gutierrez, S. L. & Sanderson, K. (2015). Applicant reactions: What we know about testing on the go. In H. Payne (Chair), *Future of assessment: Reactions to innovative formats and delivery methods.* Symposium presented at the 30th Annual Conference of the Society for Industrial and Organizational Psychology, Philadelphia, PA.

Harari, G. M., Lane, N. D., Wang, R., Crosier, B. S., Campbell, A. T., & Gosling, S. D. (2016). Using smartphones to collect behavioral data in psychological science: Opportunities, practical considerations, and challenges. *Perspectives on Psychological Science, 11*, 838–854.

Hornik, S., Johnson, R. D., & Wu, Y. (2007). When technology does not support learning: Conflicts between epistemological beliefs and technology support in virtual learning environments. *Journal of Organizational and End User Computing, 19*, 23–42.

Illingworth, A. J., Moon, S. M., Morelli, N., McLance, W. L., Wilgus, S. J., Green, D. K., & Thompson, I. B. (2017). Criterion validity of assessments delivered on mobile and non-mobile devices. In N. A. Morelli (Chair), Mobile testing "in the wild": Apps, reactions, images, and criterion-related validity. Symposium presented at the 32nd Annual Conference of the Society for Industrial and Organizational Psychology, Orlando, FL.

Illingworth, A. J., Morelli, N. A., Scott, J. C., & Boyd, S. L. (2015). Internet-based, unproctored assessments on mobile and non-mobile devices: Usage, measurement equivalence, and outcomes. *Journal of Business and Psychology, 30*, 325–343.

King, D. D., Ryan, A. M., Kantrowitz, T., Grelle, D., & Dainis, A. (2015). Mobile internet testing: An analysis of equivalence, individual differences, and reactions. *International Journal of Selection and Assessment, 23*, 382–394.

Kinney, T., Besl, A., Lawrence, A., Moretti, D., & Chang, L. (2017). Demonstrating criterion-related validity equivalence with PC and mobile test-takers. In N. A. Morelli (Chair), Mobile testing "in the wild": Apps, reactions, images, and criterion-related validity. Symposium presented at the 32nd Annual Conference of the Society for Industrial and Organizational Psychology, Orlando, FL.

Kirkpatrick, D. L. (1976). Evaluation of training. In R.L. Craig (Ed.), *Training and development handbook: A guide to human resource development* (2nd edn., pp. 301–319). New York, NY: McGraw-Hill.

Kroft, P. & Wickens, C. D. (2002). Displaying multi-domain graphical database information: An evaluation of scanning, clutter, display size, and user activity. *Information Design Journal, 11*, 44–52.

LaPort, K. (2016). Mobile assessment: Comparing traditional cognitive, cognitive reasoning, and non-cognitive performance. In T. D. McGlochin (Chair), Mobile equivalence: Expanding research across assessment methods, levels, and devices. Symposium presented at the 31st Annual Conference of the Society for Industrial and Organizational Psychology, Anaheim, CA.

Lawrence, A. D., Kinney, T. B., O'Connell, M. S., & Delgado, K. M. (2017). Stop interrupting me! Examining the relationship between interruptions, test performance and reactions. *Personnel Assessment and Decisions, 3*, 15–24.

Lee, I., Kim, J., & Kim, J. (2005). Use contexts for the mobile internet: A longitudinal study monitoring actual use of mobile internet services. *International Journal of Human-Computer Interaction, 18*, 269–292.

Levine, E. L., Spector, P. E., Menon, S., & Narayanan, L. (1996). Validity generalization for cognitive, psychomotor, and perceptual tests for craft jobs in the utility industry. *Human Performance, 9*, 1–22.

McClure Johnson, T. K. & Boyce, A. S. (2015). Selection testing: An updated look at trends in mobile device usage. In N. Morelli (Chair), Mobile devices in talent assessment: The next chapter. Symposium presented at the 30th Annual Conference of the Society for Industrial and Organizational Psychology, Philadelphia, PA.

Morelli, N. A., Potosky, P., Arthur, W., Jr., & Tippins, N. T. (2017). A call for conceptual models of technology in I-O psychology: An example for technology-based talent assessment. Industrial and Organizational Psychology: *Perspectives on Science and Practices, 10, 634–653.*

Nunnally, J. C. & Bernstein, I. H. (1994). *Psychometric theory.* New York, NY: McGraw-Hill.

O'Connell, M. S., Arthur, W., Jr., & Doverspike, D. (2015). Mobile device assessment: The horses have left the barn. . . now what? Invited workshop presented at the 30th Annual Conference of the Society for Industrial and Organizational Psychology, Philadelphia, PA.

O'Connell, M. S., Delgado, K., & Kung, M. C. (2012). Does proctoring impact measurement methods differently? An evaluation in a high stakes testing environment. Paper presented at the 26th Annual Conference of the Society for Industrial and Organizational Psychology, San Diego, CA.

O*NET (n.d.). www.onetonline.org/find/descriptor/result/1.A.1.e.3 (accessed June 10, 2017).

Parker, B. N. & Meade, A. W. (2015). Smartphones in selection: Exploring measurement invariance using item response theory. In N. Morelli (Chair), Mobile devices in talent Assessment: The next chapter. Symposium presented at the 30th Annual Conference of the Society for Industrial and Organizational Psychology, Philadelphia, PA.

Payne, S. C., Mendoza, A. M., & Horner, M. T. (2018). Electronic performance management: Does altering the process improve the outcome? In D. L. Stone & J. H. Dulebohn (Eds.), *Human resource management theory and research on eHRM* (pp. 189–215). Charlotte, NC: Information Age.

Pearlman, K. (2009). Unproctored internet testing: Practical, legal, and ethical concerns. *Industrial and Organizational Psychology: Perspectives on Science and Practice*, *2*, 14–19.

Pew Research Center. (2015a). Technology device ownership: 2015. www.pewinternet.org /2015/10/29/technology-device-ownership-2015/ (accessed June 10, 2017).

Pew Research Center. (2015b). Device ownership. www.pewresearch.org/data-trend /media-and-technology/device-ownership/ (accessed June 10, 2017).

Pew Research Center. (2018). Mobile fact sheet. Retrieved from www.pewinternet.org/fact-sheet/mobile/ (accessed June 10, 2017).

Potosky, D. (2008). A conceptual framework for the role of the administration medium in the personnel assessment process. *Academy of Management Review*, *33*, 629–48.

Richardson, J. C. & Swan, K. (2003). Examining social presence in online courses in relation to students perceived learning and satisfaction. *Journal of Asynchronous Learning Networks*, *7*, 68–88.

Rossini, J. (2016). Mobile device testing: A five-year look across job level. In T. D. McGlochlin (Chair), Mobile equivalence: Expanding research across assessment methods, levels, and devices. Symposium presented at the 31st Annual Conference of the Society for Industrial and Organizational Psychology, Anaheim, CA.

Sackett, P. R., Lievens, F., Van Iddekinge, C. H., & Kuncel, N. R. (2017). Individual differences and their measurement: A review of 100 years of research. *Journal of Applied Psychology*, *102*, 254–273.

Sanchez, C. A. & Goolsbee, J. Z. (2010). Character size and reading to remember from small displays. *Computers & Education*, *55*, 1056–1062.

Schmidt, F. L. & Hunter, J. E. (1998). The validity and utility of selection methods in personnel psychology: Practical and theoretical implications of 85 years of research findings. *Psychological Bulletin*, *124*, 262–274.

Schmidt, F. L. & Hunter, J. (2004). General mental ability in the world of work: Occupational attainment and job performance. *Journal of Personality and Social Psychology*, *86*, 162–173.

Schroeders, U. & Wilhelm, O. (2010). Testing reasoning ability with handheld computers, notebooks, and paper and pencil. *European Journal of Psychological Assessment*, *26*, 284–292.

Siek, K. A., Rogers, Y., & Connelly, K. H. (2005). Fat finger worries: How older and younger users physically interact with PDAs. In M. F. Costabile, & F. Paternò (Eds.), Human-Computer interaction – INTERACT 2005, Lecture notes in computer science (vol. 3585, pp. 267–280). Heidelberg, Germany: Springer Berlin Heidelberg.

Sierra-Cedar (2016). 2016–2017 HR Systems Survey White Paper (19th annual edn.). Alpharetta, GA: Sierra-Cedar.

Society for Industrial and Organizational Psychology. (2003). *Principles for the validation and use of personnel selection procedures* (4th edn.). Bowling Green, OH: Society for Industrial and Organizational Psychology.

Society for Industrial and Organizational Psychology. (2015). Top 10 workplace trends for 2015. www.siop.org/siop_newsbriefs/2015/january/january/ (accessed June 10, 2017).

Society for Industrial and Organizational Psychology. (2017). Top 10 workplace trends for 2017. www.siop.org/article_view.aspx?article=1610 (accessed June 10, 2017).

Stone, D. L., Deadrick, D. L., Lukaszewski, K. M., & Johnson, R. (2015). The influence of technology on the future of human resource management. *Human Resource Management Review, 25,* 216–231.

Tippins, N. T. (2015). Technology and assessment in selection. *Annual Review of Organizational Psychology and Organizational Behavior, 2,* 551–582.

Tippins, N. T. & Alder, S. (Eds.), (2011). *Technology-enhanced assessment of talent.* San Francisco, CA: Jossey-Bass.

Tippins, N. T., Beaty, J., Drasgow, F., Gibson, W. M., Pearlman, K., Segall, D. O., & Shepherd, W. (2006). Unproctored internet testing in employment settings. *Personnel Psychology, 59,* 189–225.

Wood, E., Stephens, K., & Slither, K. (2015). Apples to oranges? Use and comparative scores for mobile and nonmobile selection assessments. Paper presented at the 2015 Annual Conference of the International Personnel Assessment Council, Atlanta, GA.

9 The State of Technology-Enabled Simulations

Where Are We? Where Are We Going?

Seymour Adler, Anthony S. Boyce, Nicholas R. Martin, and Rachel C. Dreibelbis

Simulation-based assessments have a long and distinguished history within the field of Industrial-Organizational psychology, dating back at least to World War II (Highhouse & Nolan, 2012). Simulation methods like work samples, inbox exercises, role-plays, and assessment centers have been used to assess candidates for a broad range of organizational roles – from entry-level customer service and sales representatives or lathe machine operators to military and executive positions at the most senior levels. Simulation-based assessments are used throughout the employee life cycle, from pre-hire screening, for mastery assessment during training, for the identification of leadership potential, as input into promotional decisions, as the basis for individual developmental planning and associated coaching, or other developmental interventions (O'Leary, Forsman, & Isaacson, 2017). Simulations have been proven, when properly designed, to provide valid assessments of target capabilities, in part because they offer an opportunity to directly observe a candidate's behaviors in situations often representative of actual work challenges (Thornton, Rupp, & Hoffman, 2014).

Technological developments in recent decades – and at an accelerating pace in the last decade – have changed the design, participant experience, and delivery channels characterizing the use of simulations in assessment. Notwithstanding the strong impact of technology changes on the design and delivery of simulation-based assessment, the core science remains unchanged: well-designed simulations remain a valid and credible way to assess the job-relevant capabilities of applicants and incumbents. Indeed, as we will explore, if anything, technology can have a positive effect on both the validity and credibility of the simulation as an assessment tool.

In this chapter, we first describe the advantages of, and a key barrier to, using simulations as a vehicle to assess target capabilities, and how technology influences the magnitude of the advantages and barrier. We then describe some key dimensions of simulation design, and how technology affects those design and implementation considerations. To give a flavor of the current state of technology-delivered simulations – a state that will be relevant but certainly not *current* by the time you read this chapter – we next describe some illustrative simulations in a range of settings.

We then raise some concerns around the evolving effects of technology on simulation-based assessment and, in the process, raise questions that require more careful and rigorous research. Finally, we take a speculative peek at what assessment simulations might look like as technology evolves further over the next decade.

9.1 Benefits and Downside of Simulations

As an assessment tool, simulations have some notable advantages and at least one notable disadvantage. The advantages and disadvantages of simulations are addressed at length by Boyce, Corbet, and Adler (2013). Here we address more specifically the impact of technology on magnifying or mitigating these benefits and downside.

9.1.1 Validity

Simulations have consistently demonstrated strong criterion-related validities in assessing performance potential (e.g., Fluckinger, Dudley, & Seeds, 2014; Schmidt & Hunter, 1998; Thornton, et al., 2014), across a wide range of settings and target jobs, from entry-level to management and from stand-alone simulations to simulations delivered in the context of elaborate multi-method assessment centers (Thornton & Gibbons, 2009). What accounts for the strong validity of simulations in predicting performance?

Simulations are less subject to threats to validity arising from faking and social desirability-based response distortion than other non-cognitive tools (Boyce et al., 2013). During simulations, candidates react in real time to stimuli, situational cues, and challenges. Simulations elicit demonstrated behavior and the assessment process uses that behavior to make inferences about where the candidate falls on underlying job-relevant abilities, knowledges and traits. As such, effective or ineffective behaviors displayed during simulated work challenges are likely to be displayed again at a later point in time on the job when facing those same or similar challenges. In the classical formulation articulated by Wernimont and Campbell (1968) a half-century ago, simulations measure behavioral *samples*, not *signs*.

There are a number of ways that technology can enhance the validity advantage of simulations. For one, technology can be used to more objectively, consistently, and hence more validly combine individual assessor ratings to produce an overall assessment of target attributes. Unlike the early use of simulations, when assessors participated in qualitative consensus discussions to arrive at overall judgments of attribute scores (Moses & Byham, 2013), assessors today more commonly enter ratings into a system based on their observations of candidates during the simulation. In delivering face-to-face simulations, these ratings are typically entered by assessors on hand-held devices. The system then combines those ratings consistently, following a pre-determined algorithm, thereby generating more valid composite attribute scores. We have long known the advantages of the actuarial combination of assessment information over individual human judgment to arrive at composite evaluations (Kuncel et al., 2013). Relying on a technologically based scoring algorithm, then, can contribute to the enhanced validity of simulations.

Second, the technology itself can be used to score behaviors elicited by the simulation. For example, in the midst of a complex managerial simulation, the candidate might be asked to complete a SWOT analysis or to prioritize a series of tasks. An algorithm can be programmed to score the candidate on one or more dimensions, applying a validated set of evaluation standards to assess the degree to which the response reflects strengths or weaknesses in target attributes. Algorithms based on natural language processing and machine learning can score open-field text more consistently and hence more reliably than human assessors (Park et al., 2015), for example, "reading" emails or text messages that are part of a managerial simulation. It is likely this greater reliability extends to increased validity as well.

Third, as we will see, evolving technology can also enhance the *scope* of attributes measured through simulation performance. Using the ubiquitous camera on our smart devices or laptops, a candidate's performance on a simulation can be recorded and subjected to analysis that instantly produces scores across multiple dimensions (Tippins, 2015). Tone, speech pattern (pauses, speed, and verbal tics), response content, vocal and facial reactions at both the visible and micro-expression levels, shifts in posture, and a vast range of other behavioral information can be captured in the video and audio recording. Machine learning algorithms can process the thousands of data points that are automatically generated for a single 10-minute recorded role-play exercise and convert those data sets into an assessment of candidate suitability, greatly expanding the size and scope of the predictor set (Cascio & Montealegre, 2016). In addition, technology provides the ability to capture how candidates engage behaviorally with the assessment itself (Gonzalez-Sabate et al., 2015). For instance, capturing how many times and for how long a candidate opens and/or reviews reference materials. Or, with a virtual in-basket, whether the candidate opens and starts multiple tasks simultaneously or engages them in a linear manner, starting and completing one before moving on to the next. Technology, then, opens up access to measuring a broader set of target simulation behaviors and attributes that, if representatively sampled from those behaviors and attributes critical to effective performance on the job, can contribute to stronger simulation validity (Shon, Lobene, & Prager, 2017).

Of course, nothing guarantees that this expanded set of attributes *will* yield higher validity – the constructs measured still need to relate empirically to job performance. Nonetheless, applying recording and tracking technologies to candidate performance on a simulation does provide access to an expanded set of behavioral dimensions that *might* be related to job performance and can consequently enhance the overall validity of inferences drawn from that simulation performance.

9.1.2 The Experience

Organizations are increasingly recognizing that candidate assessment experiences can support, or detract from, the organization's brand as an attractive employer

(Cascio, 2014; Yu & Cable, 2012). This has become particularly critical in a free-agent world, with unprecedented transparency of job opportunities for both active and passive job seekers, and intense competition for top talent (Hoffman, Casnocha, & Yeh, 2014) and particularly for free-agent star talents (Adler & Segal, 2016). Candidate experiences through an assessment process – positive or negative – are widely shared today through social media ("The Candidate Experience," 2014). For many businesses, especially those serving a mass market (e.g., quick service restaurants, retail, and media), there is a growing realization that job candidates are often also customers. People's experiences as they are assessed can affect how current and prospective customers perceive the organization's brand as a provider of goods or services and whether and with what tone those experiences are shared by candidates with other potential candidates and customers within their respective social networks (Ployhart, Schmitt, & Tippins, 2017).

A key feature of simulations is their fidelity to real-world job experiences. While simulation fidelity can vary to a great extent, simulations as a whole have higher fidelity than other assessment techniques (O'Leary et al., 2017). Only during a simulation can candidates be confronted with vividly representative job challenges. They can be given the freedom to respond in ways – by speaking, writing, making decisions, standing, sitting, leaning in, smiling, frowning – that reflect how they would actually respond in a target position. Research has demonstrated that perceived job relevance, ability to perform to the best of one's abilities, and the perceived value of potential feedback, are all factors that affect the perceived credibility of assessment procedures and the perceived fairness of outcomes coming from those procedures (Hausknecht, Day, & Thomas, 2004). Not surprisingly, then, meta-analytic findings have found simulations to be consistently perceived as more favorable by candidates than all other selection techniques, with the exception of interviews (e.g., Hausknecht, et al., 2004).

Technology is likely to enhance candidate engagement with simulation-based experiences. One obvious reason is that the work most of us perform is increasingly mediated by technological tools. Hence technology-mediated simulations are more representative of target on-the-job situations, often incorporating the very same technologies (e.g., email, video conferencing, multi-dimensional visual displays) as those that would be used to perform the job. So in addition to enhancing candidate engagement, performance in these high- fidelity simulated challenges is likely to be even more predictive of performance on the job as well (O'Leary et al., 2017).

To be engaging, of course, the simulation experience needs to be credible. The experience not only has to *be* job-related, it has to *appear* job-related. As such, the technology employed in simulation design needs to keep up with the technology employed in today's work environment. Credibility becomes particularly important in situations where feedback on simulation performance is used to guide the individual development of incumbent employees, often in the context of leadership development and/or coaching programs (e.g., Stomski, Ward, & Battista, 2011). Participant acceptance of feedback on capability strengths or gaps is critical to the effectiveness of those programs. To the extent that assessment feedback is based on a simulation that reflects genuine work challenges, it is more likely that feedback will be accepted.

As a reflection of the impact of technological progress on the evolution of simulation design, consider the in-basket exercise (in some parts of the world, called the in-tray). This exercise type, a core and valid element of managerial assessment for over 60 years (Bray, Campbell, & Grant, 1974), is named after a piece of office equipment that is rarely seen on managerial desktops today. Not surprisingly, then, the exercise is rarely used today in its original format despite its strong track record of validity (Hoffman, Kennedy, & LoPilato, 2015). Just two decades ago, the use of remote, telephonic delivery of role-play simulation exercises was cutting-edge, controversial, and viewed as artificial, compared with more traditional face-to-face exercises (Gowing et al., 2008). Critics argued that remotely delivered role-plays – where, say, a "manager" and a "subordinate" conducted a role-play performance coaching discussion over the phone – lacked the realism of a face-to-face interaction. Of course, in today's world of virtual teams connected through multiple technologies (text, email, video, conference calls, tele-presence, and other collaboration tools), telephone role-plays seem unrealistic, this time because they are seen as anachronistic (what, no video?!).

The extent to which the degree of simulation fidelity directly affects simulation validity is still a bit of an open question, with surprisingly limited empirical experimental research (see Boyce et al., 2013 for a comprehensive discussion). Funke and Schuler (1998) looked at the fidelity of simulation response modality (natural free-form versus defined multiple choice) on situational judgment test validity and in that narrow context found greater fidelity is associated with stronger validity. Fidelity and engagement is also enhanced by building branching into the simulation experience, creating a dynamic interaction between the actions or decisions of the participant and the stimuli subsequently presented by the simulation. Branching promotes perceptions of fidelity because it more accurately mirrors how people operate on the job, and is seen as more interactive (Kanning et al., 2006). However, building branching into a simulation increases the complexity of content generation and scoring.

Tippins (2015) further introduces the notion of *matching* stimulus and response modalities in simulation design. Some simulation stimuli (e.g., an email from your boss) might require a highly interactive response (e.g., sending an email back) in order to have fidelity, while others (e.g., making an investment decision from a set of options) might only require a low-interaction response (e.g., selecting from a defined list of multiple choice response options). Whatever the final verdict on fidelity and validity, from the perspective of candidate engagement and credibility, simulations have a clear advantage over other forms of assessment. Beyond actually *being* valid for assessing target attributes, they *look* valid given their greater degree of fidelity to target real-life work situations.

An interesting trend that can be used to both enhance and detract from the fidelity of a simulation is the trend toward leveraging technology to gamify psychological assessments (Armstrong, Landers, & Collmus, 2016). Increasingly, simulations – including those used in high-stakes assessments –

are adopting features of video games (e.g., feedback, adaptation, humor, time pressure; Collmus, Armstrong, & Landers, 2016). These game-like features are intended to enhance applicant engagement and promote more contemporary branding (Bhatia & Ryan, 2018; Werbach & Hunter, 2015). We will describe a few illustrative examples of these game-like simulations later in this chapter. Game-like simulations can provide a more immersive and vivid experience than traditional simulation formats like face-to-face role-plays. These types of game-like experiences are also very familiar to and comfortable for at least two generations of employees who have grown up with video games as a prime mode of entertainment. Some of these simulations take the candidate completely out of the work context and into a setting that reflects fantasy or fun (Palmer, Lunceford, & Patton, 2012). The downside is that a game-like assessment experience may be seen as potentially inconsistent in tone from the reality of being in a rigorous high-stakes testing situation.

The trend toward attempting to build game-like elements into simulations raises a core issue: Games often – indeed according to some, definitionally (Werbach & Hunter, 2015) – provide the player with on-going feedback on performance. Accepted practice in high-stakes contexts, as opposed to contexts employing assessments as part of employee development, has been to withhold providing real-time feedback on performance while the candidate is still engaged in the assessment. The impact of providing within, say, the pre-employment testing context the type of ongoing performance feedback often provided by games is an unknown that future research will need to address (Bhatia & Ryan, 2018). Future research needs to experimentally investigate the effect of the full spectrum of game-like elements available to enhance the candidate experience on the psychometric soundness that simulations have historically displayed.

9.1.3 The Downside: Resources

Historically, the key negative to implementing simulations has been the relatively high cost of administering the assessment (O'Leary et al., 2017). For most applications of simulations, this included having to bring candidates to a physical facility and have trained, skilled assessors administer the simulation (e.g., role-plays, leaderless group discussions) and evaluate participants' performance, using physical materials (e.g., paper-based exercises and scoring reports). Though technology allows for the remote administration of simulations (Tippins, 2015), there are still many circumstances where candidates – individually and in groups – are assembled at a physical facility and administered technology-mediated business games and other simulations.

Another real downside of simulations today is the relatively high cost of production. It is not unusual for the custom-design of a simulation to take four to eight months from inception to deployment. In the best cases, this product requires the labor of highly skilled technologists working alongside psychometricians and organizational psychologists. Cost barriers are not limited to simulations developed in-house. The often-large investment in the commercial development of an off-the-shelf simulation, of course, can translate into substantial licensing or per-use fees as well.

Given the rapid evolution of jobs themselves, the technology we routinely use at work, and the regular updates to the technology used to design and deliver technology-mediated simulations, these tools are likely to require more frequent and costly updating than traditional simulations. Another source of cost for global organizations is the need to translate simulation content to reflect the language, culture, and visual look and feel of the environment the assessment is targeted to simulate. Content might need to be created in multiple languages, in different work environments, with actors – or avatars – wearing different clothes, reflecting different cultural nuances, representing different ethnicities. Organizations need to think long and hard before making these substantial investments and consider individual or batteries of alternate assessment solutions that may yield adequate validities at a fraction of the cost and time to develop and deliver.

9.2 Illustrative Examples

In the following section we will describe a number of specific technology-enhanced simulations currently in use. This is by no means an exhaustive list of technology-enabled simulation solutions. The range of available solutions is as broad as their applicability, covering the entire span of the human capital life cycle. From realistic job previews to executive succession, technology is being integrated into legacy simulation solutions and driving us into a new frontier of possibility, solving for the problems of today and tomorrow, by leveraging technologies that are predicated on ever-evolving, future-forward thinking. Some of these technologies are akin to building on the blocks of yesterday while others are exploring nascent areas.

9.2.1 Multimedia Web-Based Simulation

Many providers have begun to offer web-based simulations completely tailored to specific jobs and organizations. Technology advances have greatly enhanced the fidelity, flexibility, and cost effectiveness of these types of simulations. In addition to leveraging traditional situational judgment-style content and response formats enhanced with video or audio, these types of simulations tend to include simulated work samples, elements of realistic job previews, and traditional psychometric assessments woven together with an immersive and over-arching narrative story. In these types of simulations, candidates are introduced to their role and work their way through the simulation story line encountering varying situations for which they have to choose how they would respond and what an ideal response would be, engage in a novel work sample (e.g., identifying cargo that is considered a security threat), or take a personality assessment as part of an onboarding initiative which is woven into the story line.

Highly immersive simulations such as these provide not only high-fidelity situations akin to a day-in-the-life of an employee but, through the use of engaging, organizationally branded imagery and video, provide candidates with a realistic preview of not only the job or role of interest but also the organization within which they would work.

Hiring managers and participants alike benefit from the increased amount of information and data they have available to support decision-making. Candidates get to learn about the organization and job role to help inform a possible "self-selection out" decision if they perceive it to be a bad fit. Hiring managers at a minimum benefit from learning about candidates' situational specific behaviors coupled with psychometric assessment data that provides in-depth insight into candidates' standing on constructs related to performance. Reporting combines relevant data into a configured output, combining data across assessments to paint a holistic picture of the candidate vs. the more traditional presentation of individual assessment results. These types of solutions can also leverage para-data, or how the participant interacts with simulation content (Gonzalez-Sabate et al., 2015; Shon et al., 2017). Examples include analyzing the various paths which candidates take to reach the end of the simulation, assessing how much time is spent on any one assessment module, or noting how many times candidates access instructions or supplemental story-derived materials (e.g., viewing the simulation organization chart). These measures can further enhance prediction of performance, largely predicated on the application of algorithmically driven formulas that have the potential to combine a nearly limitless number of variables into a predictive formula.

9.2.2 Digital Interview Enabled Simulation

While simulations are garnering more and more attention due to their ability to provide robust data and an engaging experience, in general, they still fall a distant second to interviews in both how often they are used in high-stakes assessment and how favorably they are perceived by job applicants (e.g., Hausknecht et al., 2004). The standard situational interview where a candidate is asked about how they would behave in a given situation has been a mainstay of hiring managers for decades, and its digital version is becoming increasingly popular (Tippins, 2015). In recent years, several providers have created proprietary software systems allowing candidates to record "selfie" videos of their responses to bot-delivered situationally based interview questions (e.g., watching a video of a customer service representative interacting with an angry customer) and/or behaviorally based open-ended questions (e.g., "describe a recent time when you had to use your reasoning skills to solve a particularly challenging problem"). The former clearly falls into the category of technology-enabled simulations of focus in this chapter.

In addition to enabling the digital recording of situational interviews for later evaluation by recruiters or hiring managers, providers have also started offering automated scoring of these recordings (e.g., Chen et al., 2016). As noted above, automated scoring purports to measure key performance indicators through the use of inferential analysis of a candidate's tone, word choice, and manifestations of nonverbal communication. Similar to the simulation description above, this technology is capturing para-data of every kind through voice and facial recognition. In one case, the provider claims to capture and analyze over 25,000 data points for each candidate in arriving at an assessment outcome. The data are fed into a scoring engine that leverages machine-learning algorithms to evaluate and rank candidates on future job performance potential. More research is needed to evaluate the reliability, generalizability, and defensibility of these types of automated scoring techniques (Chamorro-Premuzic et al., 2016). Even in the absence of solid validity evidence thus far, these techniques have proven popular with organizations looking to enhance efficiency of recruiting processes through automation.

9.2.3 Instant-Messaging-Based Simulation

One provider has capitalized on the trend toward the short-burst communication preferences of younger generations by creating an instant messaging style simulation platform. The platform has the look and feel of WhatsApp, an instant messaging communication app used by over a billion people globally (Darrow, 2017). This solution's psychometric soundness is largely predicated on a tried-and-true assessment methodology, situational judgment items, albeit delivered in a digitally dynamic framework on any type of device leveraging item content that is customized for specific jobs and organizations.

Candidates engage the assessment by way of responding to incoming instant messages from fictional colleagues and must choose their response from a predefined list of choices. The system engages in a "conversation" with the candidate based on prior responses, engaging in a back-and-forth instant message exchange, leveraging underlying branching algorithms that guide the flow of the conversation. A feature that enhances the sense of reality for the participant is that there are multiple conversations the candidate engages in with different colleagues requiring the candidate to prioritize which conversations or tasks to address next. Content is not just text based; multi-media, emojis, and other material can also be embedded, which serves to diversify the content and enhance fidelity.

9.2.4 Digital Assessment Centers

Traditional assessment center simulations relied heavily on real-life actors to create the simulated environment. In-person assessment centers have largely become too resource intense and expensive to implement and maintain, requiring large numbers of actors/assessors, physical space, and an army of logisticians to manage the process, materials, and candidate schedules. Advances in online technological capabilities now allow coordination and delivery of real-time, high-touch – albeit virtual – assessment centers, still using real actors/assessors through a web-based interface (Gibbons et al., 2013). Participants have the ability to schedule their testing time and review advanced prep materials, such as a business case study, to provide them context that they will then use in the live simulation, all within their personal schedules. Several solution providers have created virtual day-in-the-life assessments that utilize real-time emails, dynamic intra-net web-sites, and the candidate's webcam for live role-playing, creating a fully immersive environment. Many providers are using automated scoring and at least one provider is also leveraging machine-learning-based scoring algorithms to evaluate simulation performance as a supplement to trained assessor ratings (Cascio & Montealegre, 2016). Most of the large providers of these types of simulations are also heavily leveraging technology to automate much of the narrative report generation. While providers generally have not yet moved beyond template if/then style report statement generation, there is likely to be significant movement toward more advanced report generation based on natural language generation (NLG) technologies over the next few years.

9.2.5 Coding-Focused Simulation

Traditional, multiple-choice, knowledge tests have been perceived as inadequate for assessing coding skills, so several providers have begun to offer simulation-based assessments of these skills. These types of simulations require candidates to generate code to demonstrate their ability to solve conceptual programming challenges in a targeted language (e.g., C, C++, Java). The candidate-generated code is then compiled and automatically evaluated against criteria (e.g., completeness, performance, efficiency). The technological savviness of this candidate population presents particular challenges in the prevention of cheating. In response to this risk, coding simulation providers not only routinely refresh content but many also deploy technology-based defensive measures aimed at identifying code that is too similar to that generated by other candidates. These algorithms function similarly to those used by universities in detecting student essay plagiarism (Gipp, 2014). At least one coding simulation also actively uses remote monitoring technology to further protect against cheating by monitoring candidates via webcam, tracking window switching, and logging IP addresses. Coding simulations will continue to evolve rapidly as the demand for employees with these skills continues to increase exponentially.

9.3 Technology-Based Assessment: Some Concerns

There are a number of practical issues that need to be considered with respect to implementing technology-mediated simulations that uniquely stem from the technology they employ. Each of these issues raises concerns about how we should interpret a participant's results on a technology-mediated simulation.

9.3.1 Bandwidth

The richer and more complex the simulation, the greater the amount of information being transmitted to and from the device being used by the participant. Even in developed countries, the available bandwidth varies by location. Within a local network, the bandwidth of available Wi-Fi connectivity varies a great deal and this issue is exacerbated in developing countries. The sophistication of the technology designed into the simulation may often outpace the capability of transmission technology to support the administration of those simulations. Similarly, designers need to address a series of bandwidth-related questions: Do all the devices on which participants might interface with the simulation support the assessment, given the media (e.g., audio, graphics, video), compression technology, and frame rates built into the simulation? Are the participant's scores on the assessment confounded with variations in the speed and quality of the internet connection? How would a candidate perceive an organization as a prospective employer if the available technology used to administer the assessment process was not sufficiently robust to support reliable interaction with the simulation? It is important to place the end-user experience first and foremost in determining whether the technology infrastructure is right for a particular simulation solution.

9.3.2 Standardization

One hallmark of rigorous assessment processes of all types is standardization, assuring that testing conditions are equal for all participants. By administering assessments to multiple participants under comparable conditions, the capabilities of these participants can reasonably be compared based on the results of those assessments. Early on, simulations were administered in tightly controlled environments, often in the context of in-person leadership assessment centers (Bray, et al., 1974) or physical ability assessments (Hogan, 1991). Today, technology-delivered simulations are taken by participants on a wide range of devices, on platforms that vary significantly in basic features like screen size, resolution, and sound quality, in settings that range from the office or factory floor to an airplane seat or coffee shop. Research shows that participants are more likely to encounter interruptions when completing assessments on mobile devices (Chang et al., 2016), an outgrowth, undoubtedly, of their very mobility. Nagata (2003) examined the impact of disruptions while completing a task on a mobile device compared to a desktop computer and, not unexpectedly, found that interruptions on the mobile device resulted in longer task completion times compared to a desktop.

The environment in which technology-mediated simulations are completed is in most cases chosen by participants themselves. Variation is almost limitless in the physical conditions (e.g., auditory and visual distractions), time, visual field, and other factors within which participants interface with simulations. This makes it difficult to claim that the testing environment is in any way standardized across participants, introducing "noise" when candidates' assessment results are compared (Arthur et al., 2017).

To be sure, there is no turning the clock back to a time when assessment conditions were tightly standardized. The benefits to organizations of increased efficiency, more positive participant convenience, always-on accessibility, and, in the pre-employment case, the ability to reach broader pools of candidates, all far outweigh any potential risks of measurement error associated with the lack of standardization. The reduced control over standardization makes it even more important than ever for simulation developers to ensure these assessments are well-designed and validated. We also need to develop a stronger set of guidelines based on experimental research on how different environmental conditions actually impact simulation performance.

9.3.3 Accommodating Participant Limitations

In many countries, including the United States, the law requires reasonable accommodation for those with disabilities taking high-stakes assessments. It goes without saying that this is also ethical and responsible organizational practice. Some traditional assessments can more easily be adapted to accommodate, for example, visual or auditory disabilities by magnifying on-screen font sizes, amplifying sound, or having text converted to speech. Accommodation becomes much more difficult, expensive, and potentially impossible when using many of the more technologically advanced simulation interfaces, given the complexity of both stimuli and response channels employed across multiple sensory modalities.

Given that simulations are intended – to a greater or lesser degree – to represent the core elements of the target role, organizations need to explore whether the accommodations made for an incumbent's disabilities in the work itself can also reasonably be applied to the simulation.

9.3.4 Additional Potential Technology-based Contaminants

Technology advances may introduce new potential contaminants into simulation-based assessments. For one, practice and comfort with the particular interface used in the simulation can contaminate simulation performance. A long-time gamer adept at navigating open worlds employed in a simulation may perform better and hence *appear* to have more skill on a target capability than a participant with less practice and comfort, even though in reality the latter is stronger in the target attribute. There may be demographically based differences that could generate biased results on an assessment simply based on prior familiarity with the simulation interface. Documented gender- and age-based differences exist in the USA, for example, in the use of game-like interfaces (e.g., Jenson & de Castell, 2010), potentially disadvantaging women and older populations. One can envision the challenge faced by an immigrant from a developing country encountering a touch-screen tablet interface for the first time when completing a simulation-based assessment and the degree to which the challenge contaminates measurement of target attributes.

Another example of potential technology-based contamination emerges from the use of avatars in simulations. Research has demonstrated that an avatar's characteristics can influence a participant's behavior on the simulation, a phenomenon that has been labelled the Proteus Effect (Ratan & Dawson, 2016; Yee & Bailenson, 2007). For instance, men or women controlling a male avatar on a math task perform better than those controlling a female avatar, perhaps reflecting stereotype threat or differences in expectations (Ratan & Sah, 2015). Even differences in the height of avatars can influence participants; the taller the avatar, the more confident the participant (Yee & Bailenson, 2007). As a final example, both male and female participants are more likely to seek and receive help when their avatars are female than when their avatars are male (Lehdonvirta et al., 2012). The strength of the Proteus Effect in simulations, and the characteristics of avatars that influence participant behavior in those simulations, represent a potential threat to valid interpretation of assessment results. Only through systematic research can we generate the knowledge to help mitigate that threat.

9.4 Open Research Questions

As the last section makes clear, there are many open questions regarding the impact of technology on key dimensions of simulation design and, ultimately, on simulation validity. Practitioners are designing and implementing simulations to be delivered through increasingly sophisticated technology based mainly on their own judgment and perhaps based on prior experience in designing traditional hard-copy simulations or other non-simulation, technology-driven assessments, instead of on the basis of solid, relevant empirical research. Key research questions need to be addressed in a number of areas.

First, how do basic structural characteristics of simulation stimuli (e.g., image size, figure and ground color, sound volume) and response interface affect participant behavior during the simulation? Recently, Arthur and his colleagues (e.g., Morelli et al., 2017) have proposed a taxonomy of these structural characteristics, a taxonomy they label the SCIP model (screen size, screen clutter, response interface, permissibility). These dimensions are hypothesized to impact the cognitive load introduced into the assessment process. Understanding the impact of these and other structural characteristics of technology-mediated simulations on simulation performance will require programs of systematic research where these characteristics can be experimentally varied. Beyond simulation performance, there is a need to better understand through systematic experimental research the impact of these same features of simulation design on candidate reactions (Tippins, 2015). A better understanding is especially needed to inform simulations applied to high-stakes settings where perceptions of fairness are so critical and, with the power of social media, the candidate experience can quickly translate into praise or complaint that impacts the organization's employment brand. In marketing applications directed at high-volume user populations, such A-B testing is common and the output valuable (e.g., Benartzi, 2015). Simulation designers need similarly to be equipped with knowledge founded on a rich base of evidence to guide simulation design.

Relatedly, even assuming the equivalence of actual participant capability across different platforms, how do the characteristics on which these platforms vary affect the *measurement* of target attributes? As Morelli et al. (2017) put the question: "What are the theoretical reasons we should expect construct-*irrelevant* variance to change due to the use of technology?" (p. 13). Potential sources of measurement error they highlight include latent or observed score differences associated with:

- How the test taker interacts with the technology (e.g., anxiety level, familiarity, visual acuity, and reaction perceptual-motor ability when that is not what is being assessed).
- How the simulation interacts with the participant's technology (e.g., web browser, operating system, screen resolution).
- How the technology interacts with the environment (e.g., strength of Wi-Fi signal, brightness of image relative to brightness of light in ambient environment).

The requirement for assessment science is for systematic research to assure measurement equivalence (Scott & Mead, 2011) across these key method characteristics and identification of measurement confounds.

Another key question is how should game-like elements be incorporated in simulation design? Note that we do not believe the question today is *whether* features typically incorporated into technology-mediated games should be incorporated in high-stakes simulations. Given the popularity of technology-mediated games throughout the world and their place in contemporary culture, and recognizing the factors that make simulations attractive as an assessment tool as described above, we believe the trend toward the incorporation of game elements in simulation design is unstoppable. Bhatia and Ryan (2018) review a number of different taxonomies that attempt to define the elements of what constitutes a game. Common to many of these taxonomies are elements like interactivity, problem solving, specific goals/rules, adaptive challenges (that is, increasing difficulty based on the user demonstrating skill at easier tasks or levels), control, ongoing feedback, and uncertainty. We know little about the effects of these elements individually on a range of simulation-relevant variables such as performance, feelings of engagement, perceived fairness, reliability, and validity. In addition, note that the transformation of simulations to be more game-like can happen in two primary ways: more of the features of games can be added to enhance traditional simulations or simulation games, in a form some have labelled serious games (Armstrong, et al., 2016), or these features can be either intentionally built or harnessed after the fact to generate assessments (Landers, 2015). Thus far, there are few examples of successfully repurposing games or building games specifically for assessment purposes and those few examples are largely in the educational rather than organizational domain. But, if a more comprehensive level of gamification has not happened yet in the assessment domain, it will soon. This inevitable move will require assessment practitioners to rethink some basic assumptions about the design of assessments. To pick just one example, ongoing feedback (levels achieved, points scored, distance travelled in a virtual landscape) is, according to some (e.g., Werbach & Hunter, 2015), a definitional element of games (Bhatia & Ryan, 2018) but is seen as inappropriate in high-stakes assessments. The enhanced employment of game-like features in simulations should at the very least prompt systematic research to test the direct and interaction effects of, to take one popular feature, ongoing feedback, and other possible game elements on the range of simulation-relevant dependent variables.

Finally, how should a candidate's simulation performance be scored? With highly interactive simulations, using multiple interfaces (video, audio, text, etc.) generating hundreds or thousands of data points, what is the best way to aggregate these data into a score profile on target attributes? The answer extends beyond the pragmatic issue of assembling a predictor set that maximizes validity against a particular criterion. What is the internal reliability and construct validity of the composite scores generated? Are these larger sets of scores still plagued by the old debate (Sackett & Wilson, 1982) about whether distinct individual difference attributes (e.g., competencies) or situational dimensions (e.g., discrete exercise situations) drive aggregate assessment scores (Lievens & Christiansen, 2012), and to what extent does scoring automation mitigate the influence of situational dimensions? We also need to better understand scoring equivalence across participants on simulations characterized by dynamic, complex branching, where the number and type of observations scored can vary greatly across participants. There are a host of questions regarding the psychometric characteristics of non-linear assessment design (e.g., as produced by branching). The use of artificial intelligence in simulation design will likely accelerate the use of branching in order to enhance fidelity (after all, real-life is frustratingly non-linear!). Note that these questions have largely been ignored in the simulation literature – traditional simulation exercises like leaderless group discussions, or a simulated performance-appraisal meeting, are also non-linear, and typically non-linearity is introduced in less systematic and less controlled ways than branching in a technology-mediated simulation. Clearly this is an area that requires more systematic research in the years to come.

9.5 Peering Toward the Future

With the rate of technology development, it is very daunting to prognosticate on the future of simulation-based assessment. This may well be the area of assessment that will be most transformed by technology over the next decade. Simulations of the future will likely be:

- **Adaptive.** The architecture of simulations will be modular, and artificial intelligence will automatically synthesize and sequence elements of simulation scenarios to target only those competencies where additional information is required. The adaptive nature of simulations will also help preserve the security of simulation content as, drawing on a large pool of elements, hundreds of unique combinations can be created.

- **Attractive.** Enhancing the game-like qualities of simulations will position organizations to successfully push the invitation to engage in simulations to passive job candidates. Like games, these simulations will have a narrative thread, challenges that increase as the user progresses, feedback throughout, and sophisticated and more natural interfaces (Palmer et al., 2012). These assessments will create a user experience that will entice candidates to participate, providing organizations with fact-based competency profiles of a wider pool of candidates, including passive candidates.

- **Cheaper.** Decreasing expense as the cost of technology goes down and third-party simulation providers build platforms that are more easily customizable to specific roles, organizations, and capabilities. Today, developers often rely on the same common software engine to create different video games. The same approach is likely to apply to create multiple simulations, especially around related themes, looks, and feels.

- **The Death of Multiple-Choice.** Simulations will simply listen to and read what a candidate says or types, and interpret it all through the use of natural language processing (NLP). Recordings will capture and analytics will score participants simply behaving in the ways they are likely to behave on the job. The 100-year era when the multiple-choice method dominated psychological measurement will surely end.

- **Interactive.** Simulations will mimic live human, face-to-face interactions, leveraging NLP and NLG algorithms predicated on machine learning principles and algorithms. Bots and avatars, and when simulations are delivered in person, robots, will be stand-ins for human assessors and role-players. These stand-ins will respond conversationally to simulate the interactions with colleagues, customers, and direct reports commonly represented today in simulation exercises.

- **Construct Range.** Much has been written about the construct of learning agility (De Meuse, 2017), especially in the context of high-potential leadership assessment. Simulations may well be an ideal way to measure learning agility or related constructs in that the simulation can provide guidance or feedback on task performance and then assess the degree the participant actually incorporates that learning into subsequent task performance. This format can be looped repeatedly, and in different contexts, throughout a simulation to create a strong, behaviorally based measure of this construct. Similarly, we hear discussion among human resources professionals of a construct they label digital mindset (Lipman, 2017). While it is far from clear exactly what is meant by that term, it does suggest that simulations, to target this attribute, could require participants to address challenges by making use of technology tools embedded in the simulation that could be arrayed on the basis of their complexity, comprehensiveness, or even currency (leading-edge versus "so two-releases ago"). As a final example, one increasingly characteristic feature of games that can be incorporated into simulation design is the creation of virtual, ad-hoc teams that attempt to work cooperatively on a common challenge. Historically, simulations have been used to assess individuals, although at times the individuals being assessed are embedded in team settings (e.g., leaderless group discussion exercise). But simulations could challenge intact teams – especially the increasingly common virtual teams – and assess the team's ability as a whole to function effectively. For example, the speed with which in the simulation context the team arrives at basic rules of conduct, the degree to which violators of these norms are held accountable, the percentage of team members participating actively at each phase of team activity, the degree to which the contributions of individual team members are complementary and add up to better collective performance, are just samples of the team-level constructs that could be assessed.

- **Real.** Even more promising than virtual reality as a vehicle for delivering simulations is the technology behind augmented reality, which superimposes computer-generated images on the user's view of the real world. These images can be transmitted via heads-up displays or eyeglasses, but soon may be projected directly onto the retina. Simulations then can take place within the actual target work environment but with imposed context that is intended to assess for particular capabilities (e.g., Grabowski & Jankowski, 2015). Augmented reality can be used, for instance, to assess participant skill in dealing with dangerous and even life-threatening situations (say a fire or active shooter situation) simulated within an actual work setting.

- **Moving from Gamified to Games**. To this point, game characteristics have been incorporated into simulation-based assessment design but in general high stakes simulation-based assessments have not truly been turned into *games*. For example, simulations in the future will contain 3D environments, interactive problem solving, goal setting, manipulation and control features, and reward and punishment features. Rather than just being layered onto the design of existing assessment content (i.e., gamified), these elements will be built into the structure of the process, such that they aid in the measurement of desired constructs instead of just changing the interface of the simulation. This process will change simulations from being game-like, to actual game-based assessments (Bhatia & Ryan, 2018).

- **The Death of Formal Assessment?** Of course, more and more of our lives is captured through technology – think of the many facets of our on-line behavior, GPS tracking, and ubiquitous video monitoring both in private and public premises. Add the information captured by wearables, from the glasses that capture everything we see, the watch-like devices that record our steps, stress levels, and more, and the implanted sensors that monitor what goes on under our skin. To that, add the findings of a DNA analysis. Powerful analytical tools will be able to extract from that mass of data valid assessments on a wide range of capabilities without ever administering a formal test of any sort (Chamorro-Premuzik et al., 2016). Questions have been, and will continue to be raised, about exactly what attributes are being assessed through these black-box methods (Adler & Boyce, 2016). Of greater societal concern, questions of privacy and ethics have already been raised and these questions will only become thornier as increasingly sophisticated technology is applied to these more passive methods of assessment. Pushing the paranoid side of this perspective even further, there are hundreds of millions of people around the world playing technology-mediated games, alone, on teams, and in competition. Their performance on these games is, for the most part, being recorded through the game platform for all eternity. As assessment methodology evolves, it will be possible to review this accumulated game performance data and validly measure identified people individually on an increasing range of work-relevant attributes (beyond the obvious ones, like reaction time). These recorded individual-level data will have great value as they will reflect prior performance across hundreds or thousands of repeated instances over long periods of time across multiple games, generating a huge amount of individual-based data that employers in the future could use – in the absence of regulatory controls – to make recruitment or hiring decisions. So the games a twelve-year-old is innocently enjoying today and will continue to enjoy over the next eight years as entertainment potentially can one day be turned into assessment-based inferences on job-related attributes that will determine high-stakes employment decisions. Fun games that over time and unbeknownst to the player become serious games (Armstrong et al., 2016). To us, a sobering thought.

In looking to the future, we end with a scenario. The well-rounded candidate recruitment and assessment process described below may well be implemented in your organization in the next few years, leveraging the power of technology.

It's the year 2021 and Amelia is graduating from university in a few months and is just starting to think about her career opportunities. She wasn't considering your organization, however your artificial recruitment agent, Rey, notices that Amelia is graduating soon and identifies her as a prospect. Rey creates a preliminary competency profile for Amelia by capturing and collecting publicly available data from Amelia's digital footprint – including her public profiles and social media posts – and judges that your organization might be a good fit for her. Rey then automatically verifies her basic qualifications (e.g., major, GPA, employment eligibility) and employment experience with external databases and determines that Amelia is indeed a good potential fit for a management trainee role.

Rey identifies from Amelia's online activity that the best time to contact her about the role is on Thursday between 6 and 8 p.m. Rey's algorithms also judge that Amelia's preference is to receive a personalized message with a virtual reality-based realistic job preview, tailored to outline exactly what her prospective job entails. Rey sends a message to Amelia introducing "himself," the organization, and the prospective role.

Amelia goes through the job preview and replies to Rey to say she is very interested in the job. This interest is automatically verified behaviorally by the fact that the time Amelia spent on the realistic job preview was at the 95th percentile compared to other job seekers. Rey automatically sends another message asking her to complete an assessment experience that is tailored to fill the gaps in Rey's passively created competency profile of Amelia.

This tailored assessment experience replaced your organization's traditional psychometric tests, but captures the same information as the previous cognitive ability, personality, and values-fit tests, though in a much shorter, visually appealing, interactive, adaptive, fair, and job-relevant manner. This is no simple multiple-choice, or one-way video-based interview. Rey, via his digital avatar, is dynamically interacting with Amelia within a simulation, using sophisticated language analysis, facial recognition and other technology to tailor the assessment experience, on-the-fly, to Amelia's natural responses as the virtual reality-based simulation unfolds. Simultaneously, Amelia gets a first-hand, vivid look at the context of the role and the everyday situations that she'll be likely to experience at your organization.

At the conclusion of the assessment, Rey provides Amelia with some high-level feedback around the parts of the role and aspects of the organization's culture that are likely to be a great fit for her, as well as information on areas that may be more challenging to her, based on her profiled personal interests and style.

Amelia's complete profile is now compared against those of successful employees, potential team members, potential managers, and currently available job opportunities within your business to determine if she is likely to be successful at your organization and, if so, in which role, team, and department she will likely have the greatest positive impact, based on detailed profiling of the composition and culture of each.

A match is found! Amelia is invited by Rey to schedule a live virtually delivered interview with the human hiring manager. The questions for the competency-based interview are automatically generated based on her competency profile and tailored to probe around any areas where more information or clarifications about Amelia's suitability are required.

After the interview, the tone, style, and content of Rey's automated messages are now even more closely tailored to reflect Amelia's personality, attitudes, and interests for maximum impact. For example, Rey detects that work-life balance is important to Amelia, so the organization's flexible work arrangements and generous leave policies are emphasized. Similarly, if Amelia had been a less successful candidate, Rey would have sent a tailored, tactful, and empathic rejection message outlining the reasons why she was unsuccessful – for example, she didn't have the right fit or specific mix of skills or behaviors required, and offered feedback and suggestions that might help her with other employers in the future. The helpful feedback leaves Amelia with a more positive view of your organization as an attractive employer, and with a perception that your organization's assessment process is fair and credible, a perception she shares with her extensive social network.

References

Adler, S. & Boyce, A. S. (2016). In defense of practical theory. *Industrial and Organizational Psychology, 9*(3), 641–645. Retrieved from www.cambridge.org/core/journals/industrial-and-organizational-psychology/article/in-defense-of-practical-theory/8DDD3B03B7E36F98422B238170599CDE.

Adler, S. & Segal, L. (2016). Reaching for the stars: Managing performance in the era of free agency. *Talent Quarterly: The Performance Issue*. Retrieved from www.talent-quarterly.com/reaching-for-the-stars-managing-performance-in-the-era-of-free-agency-seymour-adler-levi-segal.

Armstrong, M. B., Landers, R. N., & Collmus, A. B. (2016). Gamifying recruitment, selection, training, and performance management: Game-thinking in human resource management. In H. Gangadharbatla & D. Z. Davis (Eds.), *Emerging Research and Trends in Gamification* (pp. 140–165). IGI Global. Retrieved from www.researchgate.net/publication/281065589_Gamifying_Recruitment_ Selection_Training_and_Performance_Management_Game-Thinking_ in_Human_Resource_Management.

Arthur, W., Jr., Doverspike, D., Kinney, T. B., & O'Connell, M. (2017). The impact of emerging technologies on selection models and research: Mobile devices and gamification as exemplars. In J. L. Farr & N. T. Tippins (Eds.), *Handbook of employee selection* (2nd edn., pp. 967–986). New York, NY: Taylor & Francis/Psychology Press. Retrieved from www.routledge.com/Handbook-of-Employee-Selection-2nd-Edition/Farr-Tippins/p/book/9781138915497.

Bhatia, S. & Ryan, A.M. (2018). Hiring for the win: Game-based assessment in employee selection. In D. Stone & J. Dubebohn (Eds.), *The brave new world of eHRM 2.0*. Charlotte, NC: Information Age Publishing.

Benartzi, S. (2015). *The smarter screen*. New York, NY: Penguin Random House. Retrieved from www.penguinrandomhouse.com/books/318133/the-smarter-screen-by-shlomo-benartzi-with-jonah-lehrer/9780143108757/.

Boyce, A. S., Corbet, C. E., & Adler, S. (2013). Simulations in the selection context: considerations, challenges, and opportunities. In M. Fetzer & K. Tuzinski (Eds.), *Simulations for personnel selection* (pp. 17–41). New York, NY: Springer. Retrieved from link .springer.com/chapter/10.1007/978–1-4614–7681-8_2.

Bray, D. W., Campbell, R. J., & Grant, D. L. (1974). *Formative Years in Business: A Long-Term AT&T Study of Managerial Lives*. Wiley-Interscience. Retrieved from www.worldcat .org/title/formative-years-in-business-a-long-term-att-study-of-managerial-lives/oclc/ 924716692/editions?referer=di&editionsView=true.

Cascio, W. F. (2014). Leveraging employer branding, performance management and human resource development to enhance employee retention. *Human Resource Development International*, *17*(2), 121–128. Retrieved from www.tandfonline .com/doi/abs/10.1080/13678868.2014.886443.

Cascio, W. F. & Montealegre, R. (2016). How technology is changing work and organizations. *Annual Review of Organizational Psychology and Organizational Behavior*, *3*, 349–375. Retrieved from www.annualreviews.org/doi/abs/10.1146 /annurev-orgpsych-041015–062352.

Chamorro-Premuzic, T., Winsborough, D., Sherman, R. A., & Hogan, R. (2016). New talent signals: Shiny new objects or a brave new world?. *Industrial and Organizational Psychology*, *9*(3), 621–640. Retrieved from http://hoganx.io/wp-content/uploads/ sites/15/2017/01/New-Talent-Signals-Hogan-Winsborough-Tomas-Sherman.pdf.

Chang, L.C., Lawrence, A.D., Kinney, T.B. & O'Connell, M.S. (2016). What was that? Investigating distractions on test performance and reactions. Paper presented at the 31st annual conference of the Society for Industrial and Organizational Psychology, Anaheim, CA.

Chen, L., Feng, G., Leong, C. W., Lehman, B., Martin-Raugh, M., Kell, H., & Yoon, S. Y. (October, 2016). Automated scoring of interview videos using Doc2Vec multi-modal feature extraction paradigm. In Proceedings of the 18th ACM International Conference on Multimodal Interaction. ACM, pp. 161–168. Retrieved from https://dl.acm.org/citation.cfm?id=2993203.

Collmus, A. B., Armstrong, M. B., & Landers, R. N. (2016). Game-thinking within social media to recruit and select job candidates. In R. N. Landers & G. B. Schmidt (Eds.), *Social media in employee selection and recruitment* (pp. 103–124). Switzerland: Springer International Publishing. Retrieved from https://link .springer.com/chapter/10.1007/978–3-319–29989-1_6.

Darrow, B (July, 2017) Whatsapp says 1 billion people use its chat app every day. *Fortune*. Retrieved from: http://fortune.com/2017/07/28/whatsapp-one-billion-daily-users/.

De Meuse, K P. (2017). Learning agility: Its evolution as a psychological construct and its empirical relationship to leader success. *Consulting Psychology Journal: Practice and Research*, *69*(4), 267–295. Retrieved from http://psycnet.apa.org/record/ 2017–52546-002.

Duggan, M. (2015). *Gaming and gamers*. Pew Research Center, December 2015. Retrieved from www.pewinternet.org/2015/12/15/gaming-and-gamers/.

Fluckinger, C. D., Dudley, N. M., & Seeds, M. (2014). Incremental validity of interactive multimedia simulations in two organizations. *International Journal of Selection and Assessment*, *22*(1), 108–112. Retrieved from http://onlinelibrary.wiley.com /doi/10.1111/ijsa.12061/abstract.

Funke, U. & Schuler, H. (1998). Validity of stimulus and response components in a video test of social competence. *International Journal of Selection and Assessment*, *6*, 115–123. Retrieved from http://onlinelibrary.wiley.com/doi/10.1111/1468–2389 .00080/abstract.

Gibbons A., Hughes D.E., Riley P, Thornton, G.C., & Sanchez, D. (2013). Is the future here? Assessment center technology use and benefits. *Academy of Management. Proceedings*. Retrieved from http://proceedings.aom.org/content/2013/1/14819 .short.

Gipp, B. (2014). Citation-based plagiarism detection. In *Citation-based plagiarism detection* (pp. 57–88). Wiesbaden: Springer Vieweg,

Gonzalez-Sabate, L., Olive, A., Oriol, J., Cuadros, J., & Menacho, J. (2015). Tracking the behavior of players in a cost accounting simulation and identifying work patterns. *Procedia – Social and Behavioral Sciences*, *182*, 203–212. Retrieved from www .sciencedirect.com/science/article/pii/S1877042815030323.

Gowing, M. K., Morris, D. M., Adler, S., & Gold, M. (2008). The next generation of leadership assessments: Some case studies. *Public Personnel Management*, *37*(4), 435–455. Retrieved from http://journals.sagepub.com/doi/abs/10.1177 /009102600803700405.

Grabowski, A. & Jankowski, J. (2015). Virtual Reality-based pilot training for underground coal miners. *Safety Science*, *72*, 310–314. Retrieved from www.sciencedirect.com /science/article/pii/S0925753514002276.

Hausknecht, J. P., Day, D. V., & Thomas, S. C. (2004). Applicant reactions to selection procedures: An updated model and meta-analysis. *Personnel Psychology*, *57*(3), 639–683. Retrieved from http://digitalcommons.ilr.cornell.edu/cgi/viewcontent .cgi?article=1126&context=articles.

Highhouse, S. & Nolan, K. P. (2012). One history of the assessment center. In D. J. R. Jackson, C. E. Lance, & B. J. Hoffman (Eds.), *The psychology of assessment centers* (pp. 25–44). London, UK: Taylor & Francis. Retrieved from https://books.google.com/ books?id=eszFBQAAQBAJ&pg=PT50&lpg=PT50&dq=One+history+ of+the+assessment+center&source=bl&ots=8n3fmB0pLI&sig= MgpC2CF7YFxnmQ5n6D5c3tUwLKo&hl=en&sa=X&ved=0ahUKEwidspr1pvLY AhUGMqwKHeWuDjkQ6AEIJzAA#v=onepage&q=One%20history%20of%20the %20assessment%20center&f=false.

Hoffman, R., Casnocha, B., & Yeh, C. (2014). *The alliance: Managing talent in the networked age*. Boston, MA: Harvard Business Press. Retrieved from https://hbr .org/product/the-alliance-managing-talent-in-the-networked-age/14046-HBK-ENG.

Hoffman, B. J., Kennedy, C. L., LoPilato, A. C., Monahan, E. L., & Lance, C. E. (2015). A review of the content, criterion-related, and construct-related validity of assessment center exercises. *Journal of Applied Psychology, 100*, 1143. Retrieved from www.ncbi.nlm.nih.gov/pubmed/25798555.

Hogan, J. C. (1991). Physical abilities. In M. D. Dunnette & L. M. Hough (Eds.), *Handbook of industrial and organizational psychology* (pp. 753–831). Palo Alto, CA: Consulting Psychologists Press. Retrieved from http://psycnet.apa.org/record/ 1993–97200-011.

Jenson, J. & de Castell, S. (2010). Gender, simulation, and gaming: Research review and redirections. *Simulation & Gaming, 41*(1), 51–71. Retrieved from http://journals .sagepub.com/doi/abs/10.1177/1046878109353473.

Kanning, U. P., Grewe, K., Hollenberg, S., & Hadouch, M. (2006). From the subjects' point of view: Reactions to different types of situational judgment items. *European Journal of Psychological Assessment, 22*(3), 168–176. Retrieved from http:// psycnet.apa.org/buy/2006–10198-004.

Kuncel, N. R., Klieger, D. M., Connelly, B. S., & Ones, D. S. (2013). Mechanical versus clinical data combination in selection and admissions decisions: A meta-analysis. *Journal of Applied Psychology, 98*(6), 1060–1072. Retrieved from www.ncbi.nlm .nih.gov/pubmed/24041118.

Landers, R. N. (2015). An introduction to game-based assessment: Frameworks for the measurement of knowledge, skills, abilities and other human characteristics using behaviors observed within videogames. *International Journal of Gaming and Computer-Mediation Simulations, 7*(4), iv–viii. Retrieved from www.research gate.net/publication/281274750_An_Introduction_to_Game-based_Assessment_ Frameworks_for_the_Measurement_of_Knowledge_Skills_Abilities_and_Other_ Human_Characteristics_using_Behaviors_Observed_within_Videogames.

Lehdonvirta, M., Nagashima, Y., Lehdonvirta, V., & Baba, A. (2012). The stoic male: How avatar gender affects help-seeking behavior in an online game. *Games and Culture, 7*(1), 29–47. Retrieved from http://vili.lehdonvirta.com/files/fhbx4348/ Lehdonvirta-2012-Avatar-gender-and-help-seeking.pdf.

Lievens, F. & Christiansen, N. (2012). Core debates in assessment center research: Dimensions versus exercises. In D. Jackson, C. E. Lance, & B. Hoffman (Eds.), *The psychology of assessment centers* (pp. 68–94). New York, NY: Routledge. Retrieved from www .researchgate.net/publication/303347238_Core_debates_in_assessment_ center_research_Dimensions_'versus'_exercises.

Lipman, V. (July 19, 2017). Practical tips to help companies develop a digital mindset. *Forbes*. Retrieved from www.forbes.com/sites/victorlipman/2017/07/19/practi cal-tips-to-help-companies-develop-a-digital-mindset/#615ae6c97fe5.

Morelli, N., Arthur, W., Potosky, D., & Tippins, N. (2017). A call for conceptual models of technology in I-O psychology: An example from technology-based talent assessment. *Industrial Organizational Psychology 10*(4), 634–653. doi:10.1017/iop.2017.70.

Moses, J. L. & Byham, W. C. (Eds.). (2013). *Applying the Assessment Center Method: Pergamon General Psychology Series* (vol. 71). New York, NY: Pergamon Press.

Nagata, S. F. (October, 2003). Multitasking and interruptions during mobile web tasks. In *Proceedings of the human factors and ergonomics society annual meeting* (vol. 47, no. 11, pp. 1341–1345). Los Angeles, CA: SAGE Publications. Retrieved from http://citeseerx.ist.psu.edu/viewdoc/download?doi=10.1.1.139 .1216&rep=rep1&type=pdf.

O'Leary, R. S., Forsman, J. W., & Isaacson, J. A. (2017). The Role of Simulation Exercises in Selection. In H. W. Goldstein, J. P. Pulakos, & C. Semedo (Eds.), *The Wiley Blackwell handbook of the psychology of recruitment, selection and employee retention* (pp. 247–270). Chichester, UK: John Wiley & Sons. Retrieved from http://onlinelibrary.wiley.com/doi/10.1002/9781118972472.ch12/summary.

Palmer, D., Lunceford, S., & Patton, A. J. (2012). The engagement economy: How gami-fication is reshaping business. Deloitte Insights. Retrieved from https://dupress .deloitte.com/dup-us-en/deloitte-review/issue-11/the-engagement-economy-how -gamification-is-reshaping-businesses.html.

Park, G., Schwartz, H. A., Eichstaedt, J. C., Kern, M. L., Kosinski, M., Stillwell, D. J., & Seligman, M. E. (2015). Automatic personality assessment through social media language. *Journal of Personality and Social Psychology, 108*(6), 934. Retrieved from www.researchgate.net/publication/267753920_Automatic_ Personality_Assessment_Through_Social_Media_Language.

Ployhart, R. E., Schmitt, N., & Tippins, N. T. (2017). Solving the supreme problem: 100 years of selection and recruitment at the Journal of Applied Psychology. *Journal of Applied Psychology, 102*(3), 291–304. Retrieved from http://psycnet.apa.org/record/2017–03588-001.

Ratan, R. A. & Dawson, M. (2016). When mii is me: A psychophysiological examination of avatar self-relevance. *Communication Research*, *43*(8), 1065–1093. Retrieved from www.researchgate.net/publication/273501249_When_Mii_Is_Me_A_ Psychophysiological_Examination_of_Avatar_Self-Relevance.

Ratan, R. & Sah, Y. J. (2015). Leveling up on stereotype threat: The role of avatar customization and avatar embodiment. *Computers in Human Behavior*, *50*, 367–374. Retrieved from www.sciencedirect.com/science/article/pii/ S0747563215002940.

Sackett, P. R. & Wilson, M. A. (1982). Factors affecting the consensus judgment process in managerial assessment centers. *Journal of Applied Psychology*, *67*(1), 10. Retrieved from http://psycnet.apa.org/record/1982–10896-001.

Schmidt, F. L. & Hunter, J. E. (1998). The validity and utility of selection methods in personnel psychology: Practical and theoretical implications of 85 years of research findings. *Psychological Bulletin*, *124*, 262–274. Retrieved from http://citeseerx.ist .psu.edu/viewdoc/download?doi=10.1.1.172.1733&rep=rep1&type=pdf.

Scott, J. C. & Mead, A. D. (2011). Foundations of measurement. In N. T. Tippins & S. Adler (Eds.), *Technology-enhanced assessment of talent* (pp. 21–65). San Francisco, CA: Jossey-Bass. Retrieved from http://onlinelibrary.wiley.com/doi/10.1002/9781118256022.ch2/summary.

Shon, D., Lobene, E. V., & Prager, R. Y. (2017). Personality, responsiveness, and performance in technology-enabled work environments. Paper presented at the 32st annual conference of the Society for Industrial and Organizational Psychology, Orlando, FL.

Stomski, L., Ward, J., & Battista, M. (2011). Coaching programs: Moving beyond the one-on-one. In G. Hernez-Broome & L. A. Boyce (Eds.), *Advancing executive coaching: Setting the course for successful leadership coaching* (pp. 177–204). San Francisco, CA: Jossey-Bass.

The Candidate Experience Playbook. (January 27, 2014). Retrieved from www.icims.com/hiring-insights/for-employers/ebook-the-candidate-experience-playbook.

Thornton III, G. C. & Gibbons, A. M. (2009). Validity of assessment centers for personnel selection. *Human Resource Management Review, 19*(3), 169–187. Retrieved from www.researchgate.net/publication/257471770_Validity_of_assessment_centers_for_personnel_selection.

Thornton III, G. C., Rupp, D. E., & Hoffman, B. J. (2014). *Assessment center perspectives for talent management strategies*. New York, NY: Routledge. Retrieved from www.worldcat.org/title/assessment-center-perspectives-for-talent-management-strategies/oclc/882464181.

Tippins, N. T. (2015). Technology and assessment in selection. *Annual Review of Organizational Psychology and Organizational Behavior, 2*(1), 551–582. Retrieved from www.annualreviews.org/doi/abs/10.1146/annurev-orgpsych-031413-091317.

Werbach, K. & Hunter, D. (2015). *The gamification toolkit: Dynamics, mechanics, and components for the win*. Philadelphia, PA: Wharton Digital Press. Retrieved from https://books.google.com/books/about/The_Gamification_Toolkit.html?id=RDAMCAAAQBAJ.

Wernimont, P. F. & Campbell, J. P. (1968). Signs, samples, and criteria. *Journal of Applied Psychology, 52*, 372–376. Retrieved from http://psycnet.apa.org/record/1968-19528-001.

Yee, N. & Bailenson, J. (2007). The Proteus effect: The effect of transformed self-representation on behavior. *Human Communication Research, 33*(3), 271–290. Retrieved from https://vhil.stanford.edu/mm/2007/yee-proteus-effect.pdf.

Yu, K. Y. T. & Cable, D. M. (2012). Recruitment and competitive advantage: A brand equity perspective. In S. W. J. Kozlowski (Eds.), *The oxford handbook of organizational psychology* (vol. 1, pp. 197–220). New York, NY: Oxford University Press. Retrieved from www.oxfordhandbooks.com/view/10.1093/oxfordhb/9780199928309.001.0001/oxfordhb-9780199928309-e-7.

10 The Use of Social Media in Staffing

Daly Vaughn, Nicole Petersen, and Carter Gibson

Social media (SM) has become interwoven into all aspects of society, including the workplace. The rapidly advancing technological capabilities available via SM continue to offer varied and advanced benefits and applications to users. The pervasiveness of SM requires organizations and job seekers to weigh the benefits and consequences and ultimately choose the most appropriate way to use those resources during the staffing process. The staffing process includes each part of the hiring cycle from the early stages of recruitment (e.g., corporate image and reputation) to when a candidate receives a job offer. Although the staffing process continues into onboarding, this chapter will focus on pre-employment staffing.

SM content is not only readily available to organizations and decision makers, it is now the most commonly reported medium that decision makers at organizations use to interact with, identify, and source talent (SHRM, 2016a). According to survey research conducted by the Society for Human Resource Management (SHRM), an estimated 70 percent (SHRM, 2016a) to 84 percent (SHRM, 2016b) of hiring managers and HR professionals reportedly use SM as a, if not the primary, recruitment method. These estimates eclipse all other endorsed strategies including traditional methods like collaborating with educational institutions (58 percent), increasing advertising efforts (49 percent), and working with recruitment agencies (44 percent; SHRM, 2016a). In addition to use by employers in sourcing contexts, ample survey data and popular press evidence show that employers often review SM content as part of the screening process. As an example, the 2017 press release from CareerBuilder's perennial survey indicates that 70 percent of US hiring managers and human resource professionals surveyed are using SM to screen applicants, which marks a new all-time high and continues the general trend of year-over-year increases in use for screening purposes (CareerBuilder, 2017). To say that SM has "arrived" in the world of work, and staffing in general, would be an understatement.

To date, evidence-based research has not kept pace with the burgeoning use in applied settings. Promisingly, a growing number of review and theoretical articles and chapters have been written by industrial-organizational (I/O) psychologists and other HR professionals that include calls to make an impact in this domain (e.g., Roth et al., 2016). Despite some progress in recent years, Davison, Bing, Kluemper, and Roth (2016) have pointed out that there is still much of a "'Wild West' world of personnel selection that is occurring in the realm of social media"

(p. 16), and we as I/O and HR professionals cannot afford to be dismissive of the real impact it is having on recruiting and hiring in practice.

The purpose of this chapter is to provide an update on what is known and what needs to be investigated further by organizational researchers in relation to SM and staffing decisions. We review and highlight the purported benefits of SM use in recruitment and selection, the potential negative consequences of decision makers involved in the recruitment and hiring process using information gleaned from SM, and discuss practical recommendations for both job seekers and employers. We close with a discussion of emerging trends and opportunities for further research and exploration. As has been called for in prior reviews (e.g., Landers & Schmidt, 2016b; Roth et al., 2016), we pull from broad existing psychological research with the goal of combining the varied perspectives into the beginnings of a shared science and framework to accelerate research in this area.

10.1 Defining and Describing the Staffing Process

This chapter focuses on behaviors by decision makers and job seekers associated with recruitment- and selection-related activities. Recruitment encompasses any organizational practice that impacts the number and type of individuals who willingly apply or accept a job offer for an open position (Rynes, 1991). Personnel selection involves making hiring or promotion decisions through the evaluation of knowledge, skills, abilities, and other characteristics (KSAOs) related to the job activities or performance outcomes of interest to the organization (Guion, 2011). Within the study of selection, emphasis is often placed on the validity of the predictor procedures deployed (Schmitt & Sinha, 2011). Professional guidelines including the SIOP Principles for Validation and Use of Personnel Selection and Standards for Educational and Psychological Testing, commonly referred to as the *Principles* and *Standards,* provide direction to researchers and practitioners on proper procedures to ensure validity (American Educational Research Association [AERA], American Psychological Association [APA], & National Council on Measurement in Education [NCME], 1999; Society for Industrial and Organizational Psychology [SIOP], 2003).

The increased use of interactive and engaging technology has blurred the lines between an exclusively recruitment-oriented activity and an exclusively selection-oriented activity (Ferrell et al., 2015). While understanding the distinction between the two types of staffing activities is important, we discuss the impact of SM on the recruitment and selection stages generally, rather than bifurcating the review to focus exclusively on one or the other.

10.2 Defining and Describing SM

In its early years, the internet was primarily a rotary or reference resource for various organizations (primarily marketing and PR departments) to provide information to consumers (Landers & Goldberg, 2014). Since that time, technology and the ways people use it have changed dramatically. As Landers and Goldberg (2014) describe, the resultant SM boom has origins in the Web 2.0 movement, when technology and user preferences began to morph into creating a more user-centric experience.

The outcome of this movement is the continuing proliferation of content generated via SM applications. However, researchers have noted that the rapid changes in features and functionality have made SM difficult to define (Roth et al., 2016). As an example, certain aspects of the definition provided by Landers and Goldberg (2014) appeared very broad and flexible at the time, but now could be questioned based on the current SM zeitgeist. While content is still generated and shared at the will of users, activity such as the recent surge in "fake news" (e.g., US presidential election of 2016; Said-Moorhouse, 2017) may damage the perception that SM can generally be a trusted source of information coming from credible sources. Furthermore, this may serve as a prelude at a macro level to some of the concerns that have been raised about the use of SM information in staffing contexts for typical job seekers (i.e., veracity of information presented about a prospective candidate). Given the very fluid nature of SM, we use Landers and Schmidt's broad definition describing SM as "a broader set of social technologies . . . including any Internet technology that enables the sharing of content created by users with other users" (2016a, p. 5).

SM can take a variety of forms, although many people strongly associate the concept of SM with a specific category of SM known as social networking sites (Landers & Schmidt, 2016a). Social networking sites (SNS) are a highly interactive form of SM (Landers & Goldberg, 2014). According to Boyd and Ellison (2008), a SNS has three defining features: (1) users provide a description of themselves via online profiles and share those profiles with others, (2) users select others with whom they want to connect, and (3) users' social networks are explicitly articulated and made visible to others. A SNS allows people to connect in a variety of ways beyond simply including someone in your network. For example, people can communicate by posting a comment, tagging another person, sending a private or group chat message, endorsing a user's skills, or joining groups and communicating on their pages. In addition to individuals, organizations can communicate with consumers and prospective candidates via SM content affiliated with the organization's SM presence as well as targeted advertisements.

Similar to other types of SM, SNSs vary on a number of factors including, for example, purpose and communication options. An important distinction for the purposes of this chapter should be made between professional sites (e.g., LinkedIn) and personal ones (e.g., Facebook, Twitter; Aguado et al., 2017). The primary purpose of professional sites is to enable networking between people with common interests related to their vocations. People most often post business-related content on these sites. The primary purpose of personal sites is to facilitate informal connections and are most often used for sharing information related to personal interests. Although the lines are often blurred by mixed use of these sites (e.g., company Facebook pages), the primary purpose is an important distinction and has potential consequences for interpreting organizations' and individuals' behavior related to staffing. We will revisit this topic throughout the chapter.

While much of the available research and practitioner-oriented work in this space tends to focus on SNSs, many other forms of SM are available. For example, blogs (web logs) and vlogs (video web logs) provide users a private platform to share information on a topic of interest to them. Social interaction takes the form of reading or viewing entries and possibly leaving comments on them (Landers & Goldberg, 2014). Microblogs, extremely short-form blogs, gained popularity with Twitter, the world's largest microblogging service (Hampton & Shalin, 2017). Website development platforms such as WordPress and Weebly and video hosting platforms such as YouTube and Vimeo have made it relatively easy for users to create and share blogs and vlogs (Siegchrist, 2017).

Many other forms and applications of SM exist, and new forms of SM are being developed every day to varying degrees of commercial success. For example, sites such as Wikipedia, reddit, and Medium offer open platforms for users to publicly share information on topics of their choosing. Multi-user virtual environment (MUVE) is another variation on SM. It offers an immersive experience where users interact in a virtual world (e.g., through avatars; Landers & Goldberg, 2014). As newer concepts emerge, such as experiencing SM through the augmented or virtual reality of the unfolding "metaverse" and technology focused on voice interfaces and brain-machine interfaces, it is safe to assume that how users experience and engage with SM will continue to evolve. The examples presented herein are not intended to be exhaustive but do provide a brief introduction to the wide (and growing) variety of SM platforms available today.

10.3 Increasing Popularity and Use

Since its inception, SM's popularity has skyrocketed. According to Pew Research Center (2017) survey data, in 2005, just five percent of adults in the United States used at least one SM site. That number doubled in the next year and a half, and by 2011, 50 percent of adults sampled in the United States reported using at least one SM site. The most recent survey data suggests that as of November 2016, 69 percent of US adults use SM (Pew Research Center, 2017).

Although SM has increased in popularity across the board, some applications are more popular than others. In 2016, a Pew Research Center survey asked US adults to indicate which SM sites they used. All SM platforms surveyed (i.e., Facebook, Pinterest, Instagram, LinkedIn, and Twitter) experienced growth in popularity across a five-year span from 2012 to 2016; however, Facebook was consistently the most popular by a large margin (Pew Research Center, 2017). Sixty-eight percent of American adults reported using Facebook in 2016 compared to 54 percent in 2012 (Pew Research Center, 2017). Twitter's use increased from just 13 percent in 2012 to 21 percent in 2016, and LinkedIn experienced similar growth from 16 percent to 25 percent (Pew Research Center, 2017).

As SM has become increasingly popular among individuals, many companies have increased their SM presence as well. Organizations have been quick to recognize that the internet is no longer just a means for advertising their products or services. Rather, through SM, organizations can create a space to interact with their customers, clients, employees, and prospective candidates. Many companies now have a presence on multiple SM platforms, including Facebook, Twitter, Instagram, LinkedIn, WeChat, and others. Organizations use their presence for a variety of purposes including advertising, engagement, and as a component of the staffing process (SHRM, 2016a; 2016b).

10.4 Purported Benefits of SM in Staffing Context

Following a review of research, survey data, and popular press publications, several themes emerged related to potential benefits for both job seekers and employers that may be made possible through the widespread use of SM in staffing activities.

Purported Benefits for Job Seekers. A few benefits to job seekers, discussed in further detail below, include opportunity to promote skills and attributes, increased exposure to new employment opportunities, and reduced effort and investment required to engage in professional networking.

Platform to Promote Skills and Attributes. If properly curated, SM platforms provide users with the opportunity to promote and showcase their self-reported skills, talents, and interests publicly (Sinar et al., 2017). Akin to how companies market their products and services to consumers, individuals can now market their personal brand to prospective employers by creating content that promotes their skills and abilities (Chen, 2013; Labrecque et al., 2011). As described later in this chapter, empirical data has been fairly limited and what has been published in the peer-reviewed literature has not supported validity of SM content assessments in the prediction of subsequent job success (e.g., Van Iddekinge et al., 2016). However, use of SM can certainly increase content that can be made visible to prospective employers. As an example, themes emerging from qualitative interviews of five New York-based hiring managers and recruiters support the notion that employers do look for evidence of relevant skills and expertise when reviewing SM content, in addition to observing the number of connections, professionalism exhibited in photo and email address, number of recommendations received or given, and hobbies and interests (Zide et al., 2014).

The future workforce is becoming more contingent and contract-based (Horowitz & Rosati, 2014). Many workers face more uncertainty because of these short-term agreements with employers based on a particular project or amount of time. Because of these short-term commitments, individuals often need to be continually proactive about soliciting their skills, abilities, and attributes. SM provides an excellent avenue for marketing oneself. At the extreme end, SM celebrities and influencers with many followers can be sponsored by major corporations to promote, wear, or endorse their products or services through their SM presence (The Data Team, 2016). Additionally, in the gig economy, characterized by short-term contracts or freelance work, individuals can solicit their services and be noticed or generate new business by posting ads, creating informational blogs and vlogs, participating in podcasts, or posting information in forums where they share their expertise or describe and showcase prior work (for examples of all the above, see real estate investor SNS BiggerPockets).

An entire cottage industry is emerging around coaching individuals on how best to brand themselves for career purposes using SM (e.g., General Assembly, 2016). Additionally, a number of sites offer advice for removing potentially negative or damaging information that might dissuade potential employers if discovered (Fertik, 2007). For those with the right combination of marketing, SM navigation, and content creation skills, the benefits of showcasing one's strengths and talents virtually provides a great platform for job seekers to self-promote.

Exposure to More Job Opportunities. When organizations use SM to advertise job openings, both passive and active applicants are exposed to those opportunities with little effort. The opportunities may appear via a variety of methods such as a private message from a recruiter, a recommendation from a friend or colleague with a link to the posting, an appearance on one's SM dashboard or in one's SM feed, or a recommendation provided directly by the SM platform via automated matching algorithms. In these ways, workers can more quickly and easily be made aware of opportunities, improving the efficiency and ease of their search process.

Reduced Effort and Investment to Network Widely. For job seekers, meeting other professionals, including prospective employers, once might have required attending events hosted by professional or community organizations and becoming affiliated as a member representative in local, regional, national, and global organizations, which can mean costly membership dues and travel to optimize exposure. However, SM platforms empower job seekers to connect with professionals who have common interests. Additionally, users are able to easily generate content that attracts attention at a much lower cost.

Purported Benefits for Employers. Use of SM in staffing contexts is also believed to have some benefits for employers. These benefits include allowing for more targeted recruiting efforts, increased ability to contact prospective candidates directly, access to more candidate information, cost savings, perceived comfort in reducing uncertainty about a candidate, and perception that the employer is gaining candidate information in a format perceived to be less susceptible to impression management.

Enabling Targeted Recruitment. SM used in sourcing contexts may enable practitioners to execute more targeted recruitment strategies (SHRM, 2016b). Recruiters can reach out to passive job seekers they perceive as being a good fit for the company and position. At the time of this writing, the founder of the world's largest SNS, Mark Zuckerberg, announced that for the first time Facebook was changing the organization's social mission from "[making] the world more open and connected" to "[giving] people the power to build community and bring the world closer together" (Chaykowski, 2017). As Facebook and other SM outlets create more channels to build groups around communities of interest, organizational decision makers have the increased capability to search for talent in a more targeted manner. SM community groups may potentially allow employers to target prospective candidates with shared values, specific skills, or increased diversity representation. Some groups that have emerged may offer employers a pool of prospective candidates that address multiple organizational recruitment goals (e.g., see LinkedIn and Facebook groups "Women Who Code").

Increased Access to Prospective Candidates. In today's workplace, competition for top talent is increasingly high (Collmus, Armstrong, & Landers, 2016; SHRM, 2017b). SM channels can be leveraged to increase awareness and recruit some of the most sought-after prospective employees, including those not actively seeking employment. Not only can organizations reach out individually to specific people that may be a good fit, SM channels provide avenues by which organizations can demonstrate and share information about themselves and their specific roles to a wide range of prospective applicants. Hence, SM enables employers to easily expose job seekers to opportunities they may be interested in, even if they aren't actively searching.

Access to More Candidate Information. SM platforms can provide an abundance of search engine optimized information about both passive and active job seekers throughout the staffing process. The term cybervetting refers to the act of gathering information from informal, online sources that will be used by employers to make hiring decisions about the job seeker (Berkelaar, 2010). These searches often start with entering someone's name into a search engine (e.g., "googling" a candidate) and result in extracting an abundance of information about the candidate, including publically available SM content and other traditional types of information that might be available online (e.g., public records, news releases; Roth et al., 2016).

The information gleaned through SM channels offers informal sources of input that are not accessible through conventional channels. Some have argued that it is prudent to gather and use as much information as is available on candidates and that it could be viewed as negligent to not thoroughly vet candidates by ignoring SM (e.g., Berkelaar, 2014; Elzweig & Peeples, 2009). Taken to the natural extreme, an argument could be made that failing to review information made publicly available via SM may increase the risk of negligent hiring (i.e., hiring without performing proper due diligence; Berkelaar, 2014; Schmidt & O'Connor, 2016). In fact, in a qualitative study of 45 decision makers working for a diverse group of US employers from different industries and differently sized organizations, Berkelaar (2014) found that even among participants that did not generally support the practice of cybervetting, most supported the practice for jobs involving the public trust and community-oriented professions (e.g., teachers, military, police). Further, in *Howard v. Hertz* (2014), Hertz was held liable for an insensitive Facebook comment made by an employee toward a customer as the employee had records of two prior derogatory Facebook comments about other customers. Thus, there is some legal precedent suggesting that employers may be held legally responsible for performing some due diligence on prospective employees vis-à-vis publicly available SM posts. As will be discussed later, this liability should be considered carefully against all of the risks associated with use of SM in staffing contexts.

Reduced cost. SM has the potential to reduce the effort and cost of the job search process for both the job seeker and the organizational decision maker (Brown & Vaughn, 2011). Historically, to meet prospective applicants, organizations might advertise the position on the company website, the local newspaper, and a variety of job boards. In addition, the employer might have conducted job fairs, visited local colleges, and engaged in a variety of other active recruitment activities. While these modes of recruitment certainly have not disappeared, the use of SM channels as a recruitment platform (sometimes referred to as "social recruiting") has greatly increased (CareerBuilder, 2017). Organizations are able to source both passive and active prospective candidates and can also continue to generate and post content that promotes their brand and provides information to stay visible to job seekers.

Depending on the structure and rigor of the policies governing how SM content is used within an organization, very little ramp-up and deployment time may be required. For many organizations and decision makers, this process likely still begins with a broad internet search, as previously discussed. Thus, in current practice, the effort required is extremely low compared to traditional recruitment and assessment practices. Additionally, it does not take as much time to implement or administer because the information being used already exists and will be used in its obtainable form, and many applicants could be assessed in quick succession (Berkelaar, 2014; Van Iddekinge et al., 2016). Job opportunity and company information can be promoted in a manner most fitting with the way users engage with each SM channel. For example, an organization could release a photo and caption representing their employee brand and the fun aspects of their culture on Instagram, a video on YouTube, and a link to a job posting on LinkedIn. For a lot of organizations today, the flexibility SM platforms allow, coupled with the actual time, cost, and effort spent in using such methods, enables decision makers to reach a variety of applicants and prospects with relatively low effort compared to more traditional methods of recruitment and assessment (Berkelaar, 2014).

Reducing Uncertainty. Accessing SM activity during the hiring process appeals to recruiters and hiring managers because they feel they can really get to know a candidate through their profiles and online activity (Berkelaar, 2014; Van Iddekinge et al., 2016). At the most basic level, it allows a means by which a candidate's identity and qualifications can be confirmed through another public or quasi-public source (Brown & Vaughn, 2011; SHRM, 2016b). Some decision makers also believe they can better assess culture fit by learning additional details about potential new hires such as their interests and hobbies.

Carr (2016) provides a detailed review elaborating on how uncertainty reduction theory (Berger & Calabrese, 1975) may be beneficial in explaining the psychological mechanisms driving our desire to scour available SM content as decision makers in staffing contexts. Such theory may contribute to understanding why the lack of a SM presence may lead to the decreased chance of being advanced in the hiring process. In support of this proposed explanation, the majority of US decision makers and HR professionals included in CareerBuilder's 2017 survey (57 percent) suggested that they would be less likely to move forward with an interview if a candidate did not have a SM presence (a 16 percent increase from the year prior; CareerBuilder, 2017).

As of the time of this writing, the most directly job-related SM channel, LinkedIn, allows others to provide written recommendations and skill endorsements that appear on a user's profile, even highlighting endorsements from those highly skilled in the area endorsed. Endorsement of a candidate's specific skills or certain other qualities from an expert in a given area may increase a recruiter's and hiring manager's comfort level with a prospective candidate's qualifications to perform the job.

This particular benefit also represents a positive user experience. That is to say, the research supports managers' *perceptions* of evaluating fit, though, as will be discussed later, empirical data currently does not provide a clear link to their *ability* to do so accurately. Nevertheless, it is important for assessment tools to elicit positive reactions from both applicants and internal decision makers.

Reduced Impression Management. While some researchers have raised concerns about the susceptibility and vulnerability of SM to impression management and related forms of response distortion (e.g., Frantz et al., 2016; Roulin & Levashina, 2016), certain information gleaned from SM content may be *less* susceptible to impression management than traditional sources of predictor information in selection contexts (Berkelaar, 2014; Brown & Vaughn, 2011; Carr, 2016). Berkelaar (2014) argued that the type of information available via SM may be less susceptible to impression management because it provides access to candidates from outlets presumably less dedicated to career advancement. In support, researchers have found that close acquaintances of SNS users report that users present themselves accurately (Gosling et al., 2007). Carr (2016) similarly hypothesized that because applicants self-present on traditional tools such as resumes, cover letters, interviews, and references to maximize chances of getting a job, information extracted from SM might offer a more realistic representation of actual knowledge, skills, and abilities as well as personality information.

Summary of Purported Benefits. As evidenced in the review, there are several *potential* benefits of using SM in staffing contexts that continue to be discussed by researchers, practitioners, and the popular press. These potential benefits warrant continued exploration of the utility of SM channels. However, the chasm between what is perceived to be a potential benefit and what has been theoretically and empirically supported in the research literature remains wide. Several of these proposed benefits need to be more thoroughly tested before stronger statements can be made about information gleaned from SM applications and the potential to create a stronger workforce that matches good fit candidates to the right opportunities. Some of the lingering concerns will be addressed next.

10.5 Challenges of Using SM in Staffing Contexts

Many researchers have raised concerns and noted serious challenges associated with using SM in staffing contexts (e.g., Chambers & Winters, 2017; Davison et al., 2016; Frantz et al., 2016; Landers & Schmidt, 2016a, 2016b; Roth et al., 2016; Ruggs et al., 2016; Van Iddekinge et al., 2016). These concerns include limited reliability and validity evidence, lack of robust theoretical framework, questions of practical utility, legal risks, ethical considerations, lack of standardization, lack of procedural consistency in use, and the rapid rate of change of SM technology and functionality (Landers & Schmidt, 2016a; McFarland & Ployhart, 2015; Roth et al., 2016). Next, we describe and elaborate on these key themes derived from the challenges most commonly raised in the existing literature.

Limited Reliability and Validity Evidence.   Despite the popularity of perusing SM for employee recruitment and selection purposes, the evidence as to whether job-relevant information can be extracted from the available wealth of information is mixed at best (e.g., Back et al., 2010; Kluemper, Rosen, & Mossholder, 2012; Van Iddekinge et al., 2016). From an I/O psychology and HR management perspective, it would appear that a vast majority of researchers examining this area are fairly uncomfortable with what little evidence exists related to reliability and validity of information ascertained via SM channels (e.g., Davison et al., 2016; Landers & Schmidt, 2016a, 2016b; Van Iddekinge et al., 2016). In examining the reliability and construct validity of predictor constructs assessed via SM channels, it is important to emphasize that SM serves as a vehicle by which information can be gathered on psychological constructs of interest (Arthur & Villado, 2008; Brown & Vaughn, 2011; Landers & Goldberg, 2014). We present a review of the literature pertaining to what reliability and validity evidence exists.

Reliability.   Reliability estimates of constructs assessed based on a review of SM content can readily be assessed through examining internal consistency reliability, test–retest reliability, and interrater reliability (Davison et al., 2016). In examining internal consistency evidence, several studies we reviewed used multiple trained evaluators to rate participants on constructs of interest following a review of a user's SNS profiles (e.g., Big 5; Kluemper & Rosen, 2009; Kluemper et al., 2012). These two studies evidenced sufficient levels of internal consistency reliability estimates in the personality constructs being assessed (Davison et al., 2016).

More recently, Van Iddekinge et al. (2016) collected ratings of predictors of interest based on a review of Facebook content pulled from actual job seekers nearing the job market. Ratings of these predictor constructs were provided by 86 recruiters, hiring managers, or HR specialists and evidenced internal consistency estimates ranging from 0.78 for the evaluation of contextual aspects of work (interpersonal skills, adaptability, and creativity) to 0.93 for an overall composite scale assessing an applicants' general suitability for the role. These early empirical studies provide promising signs that psychological constructs can be assessed reliably using information made available via SM. However, some concerns still exist in terms of internal consistency in measurement within practical, commonly applied settings, as will be discussed in more detail later.

To date, little research has examined test–retest reliability of predictor constructs (Davison et al., 2016). In an examination of test–retest reliability with four sequential six-month time points using language-based assessment, Park and colleagues (2015) did observe average test–retest correlations of 0.70 for consecutive time sequences lending credibility that there might be consistency over time. Interestingly, some of the features specific to SM content raise the potential for unique challenges related to the examination of test–retest reliability. For example, while test–retest typically assumes examining consistency in relative standing over some pre-determined time interval, it is possible that a photo or an older "memory" is posted on one's page or the general public feed of the target candidate during the time interval (i.e., time 1 and time 2). These features may present additional noise not typical in most test–retest reliability provided they span broader durations that could indicate changes in behaviors across one's life (Davison et al., 2016).

Observed interrater reliability estimates in early empirical studies suggest that constructs assessed via SM content can evidence moderate to high degrees of interrater reliability (Davison et al., 2016). For example, Kluemper and Rosen (2009) found intra-class correlations (ICCs) between 0.93 and 0.99 on the Big 5 personality constructs when five trained raters were used. Scholastic ability was also reliably rated. Park and colleagues (2015) found only moderate levels of interrater reliability when examining correlations between human and computer assessments of personality (rs ranging from 0.20s–0.30s). Across the three methods of estimating construct reliability, there is preliminary evidence that getting modest to high levels of reliability is possible under the right conditions for a limited set of constructs to date (i.e., primarily personality). However, an expansion of constructs assessed and a better understanding of best techniques and procedures to obtain construct information in a reliable manner is needed to properly evaluate the robustness of these early findings.

Validity. In examining the validity of construct information gleaned from SM content, we considered content-related, construct-related, and criterion-related validity evidence (Binning & Barrett, 1989; Guion, 2011). Much of the content created on SM channels is irrelevant to the workplace (Roth et al., 2016; Van Iddekinge et al., 2016). With much of the information available via SM not being directly conceptually related to work-related KSAOs, building the case for content-related validity evidence could prove challenging (Binning & Barrett, 1989; Davison et al., 2016). As noted by Roth et al. (2016), of the major SNSs currently popular, LinkedIn may be the exception at present as it was designed with the purpose of facilitating professional interactions and activities.

Additionally, in assessing whether construct validity can be successfully demonstrated in constructs assessed via SM channels, several studies have now demonstrated evidence of convergent validity (e.g., Back et al., 2010; Kluemper & Rosen, 2009). One of the challenges of studying this domain is that the published research is scattered across a wide range of disciplinary perspectives including social and personality psychology, communications, sociology, and technology, among others. Evidence of construct validity can be provided in these areas despite a direct focus on applications to organizational researchers. A broad scan of the peer-reviewed, empirical research published provides examples of evidence of ability to accurately assess personality traits like agreeableness, extraversion, and narcissism (e.g., Back et al., 2010; Buffardi & Campbell, 2008; Kluemper & Rosen, 2009; Vazire & Gosling, 2004), cultural fit (Danescu-Niculescu-Mizil et al., 2013), emotions (Kramer, Guillory, & Hancock, 2014), language (Schwartz et al., 2013), and social networking (Ugander et al., 2011).

Robinson, Sinar, and Winter (2013) reported modest relationships with intention to stay, engagement, and LinkedIn coded turnover. One particularly interesting recent application examined personality via review of Facebook "likes" and found that computer modeling applications using machine-learning techniques found stronger relationships with a self-reported personality questionnaire ($r = 0.56$) than did human assessors that were close acquaintances and friends of the participants ($r = 0.49$; Youyou, Kosinski, & Stillwell, 2015). Van Iddekinge et al. (2016) also demonstrated some evidence of convergent validity. As an example, Facebook ratings of cognitive items were related to participants' self-reported ACT scores ($r = 0.23$) and self-reported GPA ($r = 0.26$). Thus, early evidence does suggest that obtaining modest evidence of construct-related validity via content gleaned from SM channels is possible, but more research is needed.

While early evidence is emerging to suggest that under the right conditions, job-relevant characteristics may be measurable via SM, the early research investigating whether the information extracted for decision-making will relate to subsequent work performance is less optimistic (Van Iddekinge et al., 2016). Where sparse research has been conducted, there have been noted study limitations. For example, Kluemper et al. (2012) found significant correlations between others' ratings of Big 5 personality traits as well as hirability based on a review of users SM profile with job performance. However, the design utilized college students, with job performance defined as cumulative GPA, and required multiple raters to ascertain standing on personality traits and hirability).

In one of the only peer-reviewed, empirical studies to date assessing criterion-related validity evidence for an actual job, Van Iddekinge et al. (2016) supported hypotheses that content gleaned from SM via ratings of a variety of predictors generally *did not* relate to a variety of key outcomes of interest. In this study, recruiters assessed the Facebook profiles of individuals entering the job search on dimensions such as overall suitability for employment, specific KSAOs thought to be obtainable from SM content based on a review of the literature, and specific predictor dimensions from scales of conscientiousness, and cognitive and contextual items. In addition, other traditional and well-established predictors were assessed for participants. Van Iddekinge et al. (2016) found that ratings of these key dimensions generally did not relate to in-role or extra-role performance, turnover intentions, actual turnover, or an overall assessment of performance provided by supervisors post-hire. This study provides one of the most striking and concerning results to date highlighting a substantial drawback and risk associated with using SM in the selection process, particularly given its popularity. Even very rigorous studies that have used a structured rating process were unable to provide strong criterion-related validity evidence, much less evidence of incremental validity over traditional selection predictors.

Lack of Theoretical Clarity. Recent work (e.g., Morelli et al., 2017) has called for increased attention to conceptual models of technology in I/O psychology. And while these calls have merit, practitioners and the market in general have moved forward without these models to guide their decisions (Gibson, Vaughn, & Hudy, 2017). Though some may see practice outpacing theory as unfortunate or mis-guided, we see this as an opportunity to use data to build new theories or refine old ones rather than believing that theory should come at the expense of empirical research (Hambrick, 2007). So while we are optimistic about the future regarding theory in the context of SM, the present leaves much room for improvement. A good theory can help guide, frame, and buttress the defensibility of decisions. In the absence of such theory regarding SM, practitioners who want to use it in the staffing process are left to rely on their own expertise and experiences. This will leave many practitioners making the same mistakes in similar situations in other organizations. The field greatly benefits from robust and evolving theory to help us understand the present, but also to better predict what may happen in the future. The lack of theory to guide decision makers is one of the many drawbacks to the use of SM in the staffing process.

With this general concern noted, some promising scholarly work has started to build more concrete frameworks around which research on SM can be performed (McFarland & Ployhart, 2015; Roth et al., 2016). While these conceptual frame-works built on existing theory are very encouraging, we still lack significant empirical work elaborating how these existing theories may or may not apply to new contexts and what new theories may emerge that help us better understand SM. McFarland and Ployhart (2015) do a good job of shifting the focus of research from a specific platform and a specific topic (e.g., Facebook on selection) to the different aspects of a platform, such as its permanence or verifiability of information. This framing shift helps increase the generalizability of research in this domain.

Several established and respected theories such as social contagion theory (Barsade & Gibson, 2002) can be reinterpreted or extended to produce predictions or enhance understanding of behavior or its effects in the context of SM. For example, Twitter provides a much wider audience than afforded to job applicants in the past. It has reduced latency and increased permanence (McFarland & Ployhart, 2015) relative to historic methods of transmission like email or face-to-face communication. A negative application experience may have once been keep relatively close to the original applicant, but today an applicant has the ability to post negative information on Glassdoor or even turn some aspect of the application into a hashtag (e.g., #taleo) to express their emotions about some aspect of the experience. Given that for many organizations their applicants may also be their customers, a positive or negative experience during the hiring process may have a more significant impact on an organization than it once did. Understanding how these attitudes and beliefs spread through a network of individuals could be an important avenue for organizations to consider when creating an application process. An engaging and memorable application experience may be a viable marketing tool if it leads to applicants sharing their positive experiences with friends (i.e., viral recruitment of job applicants).

Other existing theories could inform deeper understanding of the interplay between job seeker and organization in SM contexts to assess mutual fit such as Schneider's person-centered attraction-selection-attrition (ASA) framework (Schneider, 1987; Schneider, Smith, & Goldstein, 2000). Exploring and applying established frameworks such as person-job (PJ) and person-organization (PO) fit may also guide deeper understanding of staffing phenomenon occurring in these modern contexts (Carr, 2016; Kristof-Brown, 2000). In addition, applying attributional uncertainty theory (Carr & Walther, 2014) may help in understanding the urge to perform informal, unstructured cybervetting during the process of recruitment and selection.

Although progress has been made in the creation of more centralized conceptual frameworks for organizational researchers to draw upon (see Roth et al., 2016), little empirical research exists that has begun testing and refining these new posited frameworks or creating new theoretical models. While this is currently a challenge, we are optimistic about the creation of new or refined theory providing future value to both researchers and practitioners in ways that may live beyond the current applications and allow deeper and more sustainable understanding and prediction.

Practical Utility. In addition to lingering concerns related to the validity or conceptual clarity of using this source content under ideal study conditions, many concerns exist about whether developing methodology to extract information from SM channels (that allows for a procedurally fair and rigorous approach) will be practically useful in applied settings (Landers & Schmidt, 2016a). There are some concerns about realistic capability to get access to content that may be set to private in applied settings by job seekers. As an example, in Van Iddekinge et al. (2016), participants had to accept a Facebook "friend request" from a profile set up for the study to gain access to full and consistent Facebook information across the study participants. Much of the previously cited research from less applied disciplinary perspectives that have demonstrated relationships between SM content and outcomes of interest have also made use of laboratory-based design features that may not be repeatable or standardized in applied organizational contexts. As an example, Dorethy, Fiebert, and Warren (2014) used recently posted photos from randomly selected "friends" of research assistants to gain access to photos, comments, and likes for analyzing relationships between photo qualities and subsequent social interaction (i.e., likes) for those photos. While some employers may still request access to SM profiles, this practice has been responded to very poorly from the public, and in several states, it is now illegal to ask candidates for passwords to their SM accounts (Guerin, 2017).

In addition, as popular press draws attention to the common practice of employers scanning SM content, SM users and SM platforms are growing more sophisticated in managing the privacy of content (e.g., what is shared publicly and for how long), and this is impacting how SM platforms are being used. While one of the purported benefits of scanning SM content is the likelihood of this content to be less biased by impression management, as users become more aware of the use of this content in employment decisions, the same mechanisms of impression management and socially desirable responding plaguing other selection procedures may impact information they share (Frantz et al., 2016; Van Iddekinge et al., 2016). For example, Facebook use by college students has decreased dramatically in recent years (Boyle et al., 2017). Boyle and colleagues (2017) evidenced that users of SNSs may compartmentalize their use for different purposes, with SNS sites like the photo-oriented Instagram more likely to display images glamorizing drinking and Snapchat, with its disappearing image feature, more likely to be used to share embarrassing or incriminating photos.

In addition, some of the nuanced complexity related to SM use is that the content being examined includes situation-specific behavioral outcomes and artifacts that will differ somewhat from person to person (Landers & Schmidt, 2016a). This puts pressure on the decision maker in the hiring process to make determinations based on information from a person-situation interaction (Funder, 2001, 2006). Thus, decision makers would need to consider the influence of the situation on the person's behavior (Tett & Burnett, 2003). The archival nature of information available to review from SM further exacerbates this challenge.

Lastly, other practical risks associated with the accuracy of information reviewed by decision makers exist. For example, individuals often cannot control all of the potential (mis)information published online about them (Smock, 2010). Also, it could be easy for a hiring manager or recruiter to misattribute information from a different SM user, perhaps with the same name, as belonging to a candidate of interest (Davison et al., 2012). Assuming validity data did support use of SM content, drawing conclusions based on a review of inaccurate base content would certainly introduce noise and mitigate utility of the screening procedure, not to mention the lack of fairness to the candidate.

Lack of Standardization of Content. Because SM is a personal platform for sharing an endless variety of information (Hoseini & Mansoori; 2016), it lacks standardization (Brown & Vaughn, 2011; Van Iddekinge et al., 2016), a key characteristic of fair hiring practices. Using a SNS as an example, a host site provides users with the opportunity to include a variety of information ranging from basic demographic information (e.g., age, sex, marital status) to details about occupation, hobbies, and interests. Users can share more information about their political opinions, religious beliefs, etc. by choosing what content to share on their profiles and how they react to the content of others with emojis or likes. Additionally, through comments or posts with text, photos, and videos, users have the opportunity to share anything they wish. Each person may provide more or less information compared to others through their frequency of activity, privacy settings, etc. Furthermore, not all of the information posted on a person's SM content was posted by that individual, which adds another aspect of variability. Other users can post information to that person's profile, and there is no guarantee that information is accurate (Smock, 2010). All the choices provided to users make it difficult to standardize SM as a selection methodology.

In many ways, SM content can be considered similar to resumes. The content is personalized, and the type of content included varies from person to person. Therefore, it can be difficult, if not impossible, to extract standardized pieces of information. In the absence of standardized information, decision makers may rely on holistic judgments. However, this approach is susceptible to activating biases and heuristics and may result in poorer quality evaluations (e.g., Highhouse, 2002; Van Iddekinge et al., 2016).

Lack of Procedural Consistency. In addition to the lack of standardization in what is publicly shared by job seekers, another concern is the lack of consistency in how decision makers use the information available on SM in the staffing process (Chambers & Winter, 2017). For hiring practices to be considered fair, it is necessary to collect the same information from all applicants. This challenge is akin to the need to use structured interviews as opposed to unstructured interviews, except the organizations do not have control over the delivery mechanisms and procedures available to users (i.e., SM platforms). Structure allows for an apples-to-apples comparison between candidates and (ideally) helps ensure job-relevant information is assessed (AERA, APA, & NCME, 1999; Equal Employment Opportunity Commission [EEOC], 1978; SIOP, 2003). Furthermore, it cuts the assessment into manageable pieces and isolates key aspects of job-relevant infor-mation. Despite the best intentions, and regardless of the assessor's experience, humans lack the ability to synthesize large, varied pieces of information to arrive at a holistic judgment (e.g., Highhouse, 2002).

While there have been some attempts at algorithmic approaches to using SM data (see Youyou et al., 2015), much of the applied use in this area still appears to be conducted in a very unstructured, lightly monitored environment (Landers & Schmidt, 2016a). Such opportunities present a weak (or ambiguous) situation to the decision maker (Mischel, 1979). When presented with a weak situation, there is more opportunity for the use of personal discretion and preferences to dictate the process used to make decisions as opposed to the environmental forces that may exist when behaviors and decisions are being more closely monitored. When we are presented with more information than we can process, we often resort to using biases and heuristics to arrive at a judgment (Tversky & Kahneman, 1974).

Provided all of these considerations, the lack of clear process guidance in many organizational applied settings may suggest that the preliminary reliability and validity estimates found in published peer-reviewed literature may represent the high end of expectations for human evaluators in practice for two reasons. First, these studies assess constructs using measures and scales that are well designed and have established multi-item scales built to assess psychological constructs (e.g., Big 5 personality dimensions; Costa & McRae, 1992). However, there are hundreds of constructs that could potentially be assessed via SM channel content by practi-tioners often not using any type of formal rating scale or theoretical model

(Davison et al., 2016). Second, in practice, it is unclear what (if any) training or instruction decision makers are provided before performing evaluations. While there is some early evidence that it is possible to gather predictor measures with sufficient internal consistency reliability for assessing personality constructs, KSAOs, and general suitability when rating scales are gathered on these constructs, some skepticism may be warranted for whether similar psychometric properties would be found "in the wild" currently with human evaluators.

Further, as noted by Roth et al. (2016) in several of the empirical studies to date, multiple judges or evaluators were used (e.g., Kluemper et al., 2012). While this makes for stronger psychometric properties for peer-reviewed published research, this process very likely does not mimic how end users are using SNSs today. In current practice, most of these reviews are likely typically performed in a silo by one decision maker sifting through SM content of prospective hires, applying their own candidate narratives and mental models to how to interpret the data available.

Legal Risks. As previously discussed, studies documenting evidence of job relevance and criterion-related validity have yet to be firmly established (Van Iddekinge et al., 2016). In addition, these procedures have increased risk of inadvertent and intentional discrimination against protected class groups as covered by a variety of current and longstanding federal legislation (Brown & Vaughn, 2011; Frantz et al., 2016; Ruggs et al., 2016; Schmidt & O'Conner, 2016). Protected class information on SM platforms is readily accessible, and certain ethnic groups are more likely to post about their ethnic identity on SM (Grasmuck, Martin, & Zhao, 2009). Decision makers are seeking out and accessing information that was not necessarily volunteered by the job seeker (Van Iddekinge et al., 2016). The manner and environment in which this information is accessed often presents a weak environment to the decision maker (Mischel, 1979), making it easier to engage in discriminatory behaviors early in the screening process with low perceived risk of detection (Berkelar et al., 2014; Brown & Vaughn, 2011). Unintentional discrimination may also be a risk provided the potential for manifestations of implicit biases in evaluations (Frantz et al., 2016). Van Iddekinge et al. (2016) observed that the recruiters and organizational decision makers did rate some of the predictor constructs differently for gender and ethnicity. As the researchers suggested, while this cannot be absolutely concluded as bias, as traditional selection research has found real differences in standing on some of the relevant constructs across protected class groups, these findings are particularly problematic since the local validation study lacked supportive evidence of validity.

In addition to risk of improper use on the part of organizational decision makers, researchers have also raised concerns that the use of SM by protected class groups may differ both within various SM applications and across all SM platforms relative to the representativeness in the broader population (e.g., Davison et al., 2016). Although accessibility to computers and the internet is increasing, evidence still suggests that older, less well-educated, low-income, African-American, or disabled people are more likely to lack basic computer skills and less likely to have access to the internet, and, therefore, a SM presence (Mead, Olson-Buchanan,

& Drasgow, 2013). According to recent survey data, 80 percent or more of Americans under 50 reported using at least one SM site compared to 64 percent of those over 50 and just 30 percent of people over 65 (Pew Research Center, 2017). This pattern was similar across all SM platforms; every platform is more popular among younger Americans (Pew Research Center, 2017). SM use also varies by sex. Women (72 percent) are slightly more likely than men (66 percent) to use SM, though their preferences vary somewhat (Pew Research Center, 2017). They are equally likely to use Facebook and Twitter. However, women are more likely to use Instagram and Pinterest, whereas men are more likely to be on LinkedIn (Pew Research Center, 2017). Sixty-nine percent, 63 percent, and 74 percent of Caucasian, Black, and Hispanic Americans, respectively, report using some form of SM (Pew Research Center, 2017).

Understanding and continuing to track the macro-level differences in SM usage and engagement across protected class groups is important, as not having an active presence on SNSs may be as damaging as negative information (SHRM, 2016a; Berkelaar, 2014). Unfortunately, legal precedent for researchers and practitioners currently remains mostly void or ambiguous. With legislation unclear, employers must come to terms with resolving conflicting legal liabilities and potential for opportunities independently (Berkelaar, 2014; Schmidt & O'Connor, 2016). In a review of some of the more recent courts cases related to SM in staffing contexts, many questions still remain.

While the majority of the available research in this area currently focuses on US-based case study and legal guidelines, international legal issues with SM use in staffing makes establishing policy more complicated (Schmidt & O'Connor, 2016). Schmidt and O'Connor (2016) recommend in these cases attempting to create very general SM policies, but then localizing them to the countries in which a business may operate. For a more robust and detailed review of legal considerations in SM staffing, see Schmidt and O'Connor (2016). Before advancing, we discuss some recent, intriguing cases being addressed as of the time of this writing.

SM and Web Scraping. One of the largest unanswered questions relates to the Computer Fraud and Abuse Act (CFAA), a law passed in 1986 that made computer hacking a crime. Applying a law made in 1986 to technologies it could not have anticipated brings up a lot of potential ambiguity. A case in progress as of the time of this writing is occurring between LinkedIn, a large SNS, and hiQ, a small company specializing in web scraping. hiQ's business model is to scrape data on large quantities of LinkedIn profiles to package for sale to employers. LinkedIn issued a cease and desist letter in the summer of 2017 claiming that this data scraping was illegal and violated the CFAA. In response to this letter, hiQ sued LinkedIn. A preliminary ruling has suggested that the CFAA is not violated by scraping a website even if the owner of the website requests the scraping to stop.

The CFAA states that to "access a computer without authorization or exceed authorized access" is illegal, but it is unclear if a website owner can revoke access to individual users or companies on an otherwise publicly available website. Companies such as LinkedIn and Facebook have used technical measures such as

IP-based blocking (e.g., to block IP addresses owned by hiQ) or robots.txt (a file on a website that could tell a data scraper not to scrape data from a specific site) to rescind authorization to data scrapers. Judge Edward Chen concluded that by publishing a website you implicitly give users and the general public permission to access the website and that removing access on an individual basis could have potentially negative consequences. This case will be an interesting one to continue to monitor as the preliminary ruling favors the third-party vendor (hiQ) in contrast to an earlier case study of a similar but not identical situation that ruled in favor of the SNS (*Facebook, Inc. v. Power Ventures, Inc., 2009*). The way courts ultimately rule on allowing web scrapers to access SM content has major implications for researchers and practitioners looking to explore advanced SM scraping methodologies in practice. Thus, regarding automated scoring algorithms involving third-party entities that implement scraping methodologies, there is still some degree of risk inherent in determining long-term feasibility of these approaches.

Private Message Conversations and Selection Decisions. In a different situation involving ten prospective members of the Harvard College Class of 2021, offers of admission were revoked after the discovery of a Facebook group chat where students presented sexually explicit and often racist memes to each other (Natanson, 2017). This ostensibly private forum was used by the university as a justification to rescind offers to students involved in the group. As this decision was made in Spring of 2017, long after most college application deadlines, this decision may have had significant implications for the careers of the students, as well as establishing precedent for organizational decision makers that discover damaging "private" SM content. This type of action by Harvard is not new and has become more common over the last few years (Singer, 2013). While college admission practices are not the same as those for staffing organizations, it is an instance of high-stakes selection, and the cases and usage patterns in this domain are echoed across organizations. The Harvard decision supports a suggestion by Schmidt and O'Connor (2016) that, generally speaking, privacy in SM use is not as well protected as commonly thought based on assumptions of SM settings or features (see *Facebook, Inc. v. Power Ventures, Inc., 2009* for another interesting example).

Ethical and Privacy Concerns. Although it is not currently illegal for employers to use publicly available SM content in hiring decisions within the United States, questions still remain about whether this practice is ethical. Several scholars (Berkelaar, 2014; Landers and Schmidt, 2016a) highlight the ethical and privacy concerns by describing what parallel activities might look like if conducted in the real world (i.e., following an applicant home from work or peeking into the applicant's open window).

As users of SM have become increasingly aware of the ease of accessibility and potential work and non-work consequences of sharing aspects of their lives more publicly, SM applications have adapted to users' concerns by enhancing their privacy features (Davison et al., 2016). Further, while Facebook is still the most popular SM platform by far, many competing SM platforms (e.g., Bumble, Snapchat), which specifically cater to the desire for enhanced privacy and transient characteristics, have emerged and become more popular in recent years, particularly among 18–24-year-old users (Wagner, 2017). This is exemplified in the popularity of Snapchat, which provides an ephemeral nature to any content shared including the ability to send photos and videos to others that disappear after ten seconds and "stories" documenting the most recent day's activities before disappearing from the site after 24 hours. As discussed in the last section, while privacy settings and evanescent features offer additional layers of protection, they may not be as impervious as users believe in instances when a SM platform is requested to provide information for legal purposes (Schmidt & O'Connor, 2016) or should the data otherwise be compromised or made discoverable.

On the extreme end, some organizations have gone as far as to request usernames and passwords for all SM accounts held by applicants. This practice has generally been met with public backlash as an invasion of privacy. While not yet banned at the federal level, many states have enacted legislation to prevent this practice (Drouin et al., 2015; Schmidt & O'Connor, 2016).

With the exception of sites where the user profile is intended for professional networking and passive or active job seeking (e.g., LinkedIn), the information displayed on profiles is most often intended for sharing within personal social circles (i.e., friends and family) and not with potential employers. When candidates perceive the information is being used inconsistently with how it was intended, they may feel that they should have the right to be notified, much the same as they would be notified of a background or reference check. However, applicants are often not notified that this process is taking place (Drouin et al., 2015).

Not notifying applicants about the perusal of SM information also raises concerns as no formal opportunity is presented for them to confirm or correct information obtained (Berkelaar, 2014). Indeed, when surveyed, roughly 75 percent of candidates reported concerns that information will be misinterpreted or inaccurate (Berkelaar, 2014).

Concerns by candidates of unfair treatment, lack of face validity, and unsolicited access to EEOC protected class information all increase the risk of a legal challenge to the process (Stoughton, Thompson, & Meade, 2015). Even if applicants successfully navigate the hiring process and accept a job offer, employees who feel they were treated unfairly during the hiring process are less productive on the job and more likely to quit (Schinkel, van Vianen, & Dierendonck, 2013).

Despite these concerns, job seekers are beginning to begrudgingly accept that organizations will review SM content as a fact of life (Berkelaar, 2014). There appears to be a general understanding that information made publicly available via SM will potentially be reviewed by organizational decision makers in staffing contexts and that this exchange is most often going to occur in a one-way communication paradigm with the exchange for the prospect being an opportunity for gainful employment (Berkelaar, 2014; referred to by this scholar as the *digital social contract*). Attitudes and perspectives toward SM use in staffing contexts may be more positive among younger SM users. In a recent survey including more than 1,400 US and UK college students and recent graduates aged 20–25, the majority expressed that they did not believe SM would negatively impact their career and in fact viewed SM as something that they could use to their benefit for career purposes (Red Bull Wingfinder, 2017).

Rapid Rate of Change of SM.   Another key challenge facing I/O psychology, HR, and organizational behavior researchers studying SM and staffing is the fluidity and rapidly evolving nature of the technology, functionality, and user preferences (Landers & Schmidt, 2016a, 2016b). The growth in use of SM within staffing contexts in practice is outpacing research efforts in organizational sciences. Landers & Schmidt (2016a) noted that even if a fair, valid, and legally defensible tool were developed with local validation data, the procedure, associated guidelines, and best practices could risk functional obsolescence within a short time horizon (e.g., five years). User preferences and SM capabilities shift very quickly and new functionality is added all the time. For example, some recent trends include the shift toward video sharing including live streams that can be viewed in real time or after the fact (Rohampton, 2017). In addition, SM use in one-on-one and selected groups of interest messaging applications have increased in popularity and use. SM sites also frequently now most prominently display recent activity including posts, shares, "likes," etc. Much of the early research in this area has been more reliant upon examination of user profiles that in practice may not be as consistent with how SM consumers, including decision makers, most frequently engage with SM platforms today.

Researchers have proposed new frameworks to investigate how SM can be used in staffing, including game-thinking in SM (GSM; Collmus et al., 2016). Drawing upon research conducted in the area of applications of serious games and gamification (e.g., Armstrong, Landers, & Collmus, 2015), Collmus et al. suggests that GSM may help explain and understand the current and future manifestations of SM applications and the underlying motivations driving SM behaviors.

Many researchers in the organizational sciences have also expressed concern about the current peer-reviewed cycle lag preventing timely dissemination to practitioners and the general researcher-practitioner gap limiting the relevance and thought leadership of scholarly work in leading practice and pushing the field forward (e.g., Gibson et al., 2017; Morelli et al., 2017). Scholars have called for more overarching multidisciplinary theoretical frameworks (e.g., Landers & Schmidt, 2016b; Roth et al., 2016) or broad and robust models that address technology more generally at the underlying construct level, rather than trying to keep up with individual applications or platforms of technology (e.g., Potosky, 2008). However, it is difficult to predict how SM will continue to evolve and change and to build models that will be robust enough to explain future uses. Adding to this lofty challenge, as noted by Landers and Schmidt (2016b), sometimes the incentives are low for private organizations to share proprietary practitioner research as publishing and presenting detailed validity data opens the methods to increased external scrutiny and liability risk as well as increased risk of "giving away the farm" by sharing intellectual property that may be useful in creating a competitive advantage in the market and increasing an organization's profitability.

Summary of Challenges. While the challenges are numerous and steep, we believe organizational researchers cannot afford to ignore this established technology and the impact it is having as a methodology being used to inform or guide the recruitment and selection process in practice. In the closing section, we will share practical recommendations for organizational decision makers and job seekers, discuss a few emerging trends, and offer a few suggestions for future research.

10.6 Recommendations for Organizations and HR Professionals

Fortunately for practitioners, there are now several reviews providing guidance on some of the current best practices for organizations and HR professionals. For example, near the time of this writing, SIOP released a white paper on this topic (Chambers & Winter, 2017). SHRM also released a how-to guide detailing best practices for SM in the applicant screening process (SHRM, 2016b). In this section, we review some of the most common recommendations for practitioners across the literature we have reviewed.

Recommendation 1: Avoid Use without Criterion-Related Validity Evidence. Our first recommendation is to be cautious when using SM for screening purposes. Several researchers have strongly advised against practitioners using SM during the staffing process at all until stronger validity evidence can be found (e.g., Davison et al., 2016; Landers & Schmidt, 2016b; Roth et al., 2016; Van Iddekinge et al., 2016). For many of these experts, without traditional test validation evidence, the legal risks are simply not worth the reward potential currently provided, not to mention the many other concerns raised herein (for a nice summary of the opinions of 13 experts in this area, see Landers & Schmidt, 2016b).

Recommendation 2: Explore Internally with Extreme Caution. As mentioned, most scholars in this area would caution against current use of SM today in actual hiring decisions without better criterion-related validity evidence to support the procedure's use. However, some researchers (the authors of this chapter included) remain cautiously optimistic that value will eventually be derived pending innovative new applications that might address or mitigate present concerns (Chambers & Winter, 2017; see Landers & Schmidt, 2016b). Therefore, we recommend that organizations proceed with the utmost caution in studying, developing guidelines, and attempting to validate various forms of predictor constructs gathered via various SM outlets so that we can be part of the solution to the current challenge.

This practice may take the form of conducting a carefully designed research-only predictive validation study with the SM predictor content not used in any of the organization's current selection practices. This work could be carried out in partnership with an academic working in this domain. To be legally defensible, it is necessary to demonstrate that any assessment used for selection purposes predicts performance for the job (AERA, APA, & NCME, 1999; SIOP, 2003). Although it is common practice to conduct a local validation study for selection assessments, it is especially prudent to do this when the validity evidence in the literature is weak, as it is in the case of SM predictors (AERA, APA, & NCME, 1999; Equal Employment Opportunity Commission [EEOC], 1978; SIOP, 2003). Because measurement methods and constructs vary across different uses, and the scholarly research on this topic at present is sparse (Roth et al., 2016; Van Iddekinge et al., 2016), it is critical to demonstrate validity evidence for the specific strategies implemented within an organization. In addition, the increased model development and empirical research using field data can only enhance our shared understanding of whether this avenue may be tenable.

Recommendation 3: Stay Current and Apply Known Best Practices. Practitioners have yet to heed cautions to avoid SM use altogether (Roth et al., 2016; Davison et al., 2016). To the contrary, use continues to grow. While experts can continue to advise against use, we must also support practitioners by providing updates on best practices and training for organizations that are either (a) insistent upon allowing continued use by their decision makers or (b) concerned that it would be practically unrealistic to completely restrict practitioners from using SM reviews even if a "no use" policy is in place.

If the use of SM in sourcing and screening practices continues to increase and the technology continues to advance at the rapid clip we've observed (and we expect it will), then it is up to us to continue to stay current on best practices with use considering the latest legal, ethical, fairness, validity, and other developments so that we can provide optimal guidance using timely information (e.g., Chambers & Winter, 2017; SHRM, 2016b). For an excellent resource guide on how to stay current on the latest developments in this area, see Black, Washington, and Schmidt (2016).

Recommendation 4: Apply Strategies to Reduce Legal Risk. If SM will be used as part of the selection process, it must align as closely as possible to the same professional guidelines other assessments do (AERA, APA, & NCME, 1999; EEOC, 1978; SIOP, 2003). SM presents challenges due to lack of standardization and abundant opportunities to assess information that is not relevant to the job. To help ensure decision makers are focused on job-relevant information, the constructs assessment must be built upon a job analysis. Practitioners should develop and clearly articulate a SM policy specific to how SM is used for staffing (Chambers & Winter, 2017). Furthermore, if human raters are used, they should be trained to conduct the assessment in a systematic way (Davison et al., 2016). Specifically, they should be trained to only assess the characteristics identified as job-relevant and look for certain indicators of those characteristics based on a common definition. Consider using multiple assessors to increase reliability of construct measures (Roth et al., 2016). Using assessors who are not interviewers may help prevent bias later in the process based on information seen on SM (Roth et al., 2016).

Recommendation 5: Monitor and Evaluate Group Differences. Some sources have suggested that the disproportionate use of SM sites across various demographic groups presents another legal concern for using SM for applicant screening by increasing the possibility of discrimination (e.g., Pew Research Center, 2017). For example, older people are less likely to be on SM of any form, and women are less likely to use LinkedIn than men (Pew Research Center, 2017). To reduce the risk of adverse impact, organizations may consider using SM screening later in the process when protected class information may have already been disclosed (Davison et al., 2016). In this way, this step becomes similar to a background check, drug test, etc., rather than an early disqualifier.

Recommendation 6: Monitor Candidate Perceptions of Privacy and Ethical Concerns. We believe organizations should consider perceptions of fairness and ensure appropriate levels of candidate privacy are protected. In addition to ethical considerations associated with a lack of employer transparency, practical considerations should also be made in monitoring candidate reactions. For many employers, candidates are also consumers of their products and services, and it is important that candidates feel good about the application process. Evidence suggests that some applicants may view potential employers looking through their SM activity as an invasion of privacy (Berkelaar, 2014). As case law continues to develop (Schmidt & O'Connor, 2016), the courts may provide more definitive guidance about what constitutes private versus public information available on the internet. It is advised at this time to restrict the review to career-oriented sites, such as LinkedIn (Roth et al., 2016). Applicants will be less likely to perceive viewing their LinkedIn profiles as an invasion of privacy than their personal SM applications, like Facebook.

Some scholars have gone so far as recommending complete transparency in the process with candidates, including notifying applicants and asking their permission before their profiles are reviewed (e.g., Berkelaar, 2014), then giving applicants the opportunity to elaborate on any information gleaned from their pages, particularly any negative information. This gives them the opportunity to prevent misunderstandings and flag any misinformation. Of course, providing negative feedback to candidates may expose an organization to increased risk of litigation if the candidate believes the feedback is not valid or the procedure is not fair. In addition, candidates may be more likely to engage in impression management if they are aware their profiles will be reviewed as part of the formal screening process. Each organization must weigh the potential benefits associated with the completely transparent approach against the potential drawbacks and make decisions on policy until firmer guidance is provided via court legislation and research.

Recommendation 7: Consider SM as Part of Targeted Recruitment Strategy. Many if not most experts would agree that SM can be used as a tool for targeted and proactive recruiting efforts, even if practitioners are advised not to use it for screening purposes at present (see Landers & Schmidt, 2016b). The competition for talent is steep. Qualified applicants for technical jobs and positions requiring advanced skills are hard to find and attract. Many prospects are currently employed but would consider other opportunities if they arose. SM is one tool that can be used to identify and contact passive job seekers. In addition, diversity goals can also be pursued via sourcing strategy with communities of interest on SM platforms.

10.7 Recommendations for Job Seekers

It's clear from recent history that using SM during the hiring process is on the rise. Practically speaking, despite the many concerns discussed at length in the prior sections, those not actively engaging in SM may be inadvertently putting themselves at a disadvantage to those more willing to share information publicly via SM (Chambers & Winter, 2017). An applicant's lack of SM presence may make them less likely to advance in the hiring process (CareerBuilder, 2017). In fact, 57 percent of over 2,000 hiring managers and HR professionals endorsed being less likely to follow up with a candidate with no online presence (CareerBuilder, 2017). As noted by Roth et al. (2016), one possible theoretically based explanation can be drawn from different models out of the cognitive psychology and judgment and decision-making research domains, such as the inferred information model (Johnson, 1987; Johnson & Levine, 1985). Within this framework, missing information is viewed with suspicion. This phenomenon has also been discussed in terms of increasing job seekers "attributional certainty" about a candidate in comparison to no information, with a stronger impact from the discovery of positive information than that of negative information (Carr & Walther, 2014).

These statistics speak to perceptions of a "digital social contract" (Berkelaar, 2014). A shared understanding of job seekers' responsibility to maintain and manage online content has developed between the public and employers. For many job seekers and organizational decision makers, any information that can be found online is perceived to be fair to use for evaluation just by its public presence. But it takes more than simply being visible on SM. To maximize the potential benefits, and minimize the potential pitfalls, it is very important to put some effort into managing your content. Both active and passive candidates should curate the content posted on their profiles ongoing, avoiding information that could be perceived negatively, and highlighting aspects that could result in more positive work-related reviews of content (Carr & Walther, 2014; Chambers & Winter, 2017). In fact, two of the most commonly endorsed reasons decision makers do not move forward with a candidate included observed inappropriate behavior and typos in posts (CareerBuilder, 2017).

Not only is the removal of information that may be damaging to career opportunities very important, candidates can and should create and promote their individual brand. SM affords users the opportunity to promote themselves in a variety of ways that would communicate their purported skills and fit to potential employers. For example, job seekers might connect and communicate with other people who work in their field, join professional groups, follow organizations, share or create posts, or add a description of their background and skills to their profiles. Winners and losers in the new world of ubiquitous SM presence may in part be defined by those willing to embrace and optimize these uses of SM for their own professional advancement.

10.8 Future Research and Practice

Our field has an excellent opportunity to provide data-driven and theoretically supported evidence to inform proper use of SM information. Just as I/O psychologists and HR professionals have championed using job-relevant practices with other assessment methodologies for some of the world's biggest and most respected brands (e.g., Google's transition to structured job-relevant interviews versus less structured and creative interviews; Bock, 2015; Schmidt & Hunter, 1998), we can inform guidelines for whether and how to use SM as part of the recruitment and applicant screening process.

One risk to the impact of organizational sciences research is the lag between when research is conducted and when it is made available to practitioners. We recommend considering ways to disseminate research and guidance more quickly. Landers & Schmidt (2016b) noted that the lag is not as prominent in some disciplines of study, citing computer science as an area where research often leads breakthroughs in practice. Within computer science, conference presentations and associated proceedings that follow are often more highly cited and have more challenging standards than traditional research articles (Landers & Schmidt, 2016b). In addition, engagement in open source journals, blogs, and more informal release outlets may offer a means by which research and guidance can be disseminated more quickly among peers.

In addition to the need to get new information out quickly, we must determine how to enhance organizations' adoption of best practices based on new research that is generated. As we accumulate this knowledge and develop recommendations for improving practice, we must find ways to communicate the importance of following the guidelines to recruiters, hiring managers, etc.

Because this field is changing rapidly, it is important for researchers to collaborate with practitioners to share ideas about emerging challenges and how to test and apply solutions in a scientific manner. The old model of researching and disseminating information must come quicker to market to maximize relevance before advancements in technology make prior writing and reporting outdated.

Several recent reviews have presented propositions grounded in existing theoretical models from a diverse set of interdisciplinary perspectives (e.g., Landers & Schmidt, 2016b; Roth et al., 2016). These propositions offer guidance as to how I/O psychology can move this domain forward. First, it is unclear what information is being assessed when employers screen SM activity. Once this question is answered, it is important to distinguish the information that can be reliably and accurately extracted from that which cannot. Because the type of information shared through SM can vary across applications and people, it is important to continue to recognize that SM provides a potential *predictor method* by which employers can potentially gather information on a variety of *predictor constructs* (Arther & Villado, 2008; Brown & Vaughn, 2011; Christian, Edwards, & Bradley, 2010; Landers & Goldberg, 2014; Roth et al., 2016). We must avoid the tendency to make broad statements such as "social media does not provide job-relevant information" or "social media lacks validity evidence." Most of the research in this area has focused on the most common SNS, Facebook. It is possible that *some* job-relevant constructs might be reliably and accurately measured via SM and could potentially be valid for selection purposes. Future research in this area will shape and guide the methods and constructs appropriate for assessing with SM.

As previously discussed, the validity evidence for SM assessment methodologies is sparse and provides mixed support. Therefore, future research has a lot to contribute and clarify on this topic. To justify the continued exploration of SM in selection contexts, clear evidence suggesting successful prediction of important job performance criteria is necessary. Evidence of incremental prediction over existing methods and measures would strengthen the argument for SM assessments as well (Van Iddekinge et al., 2016). However, compelling evidence of prediction coupled with other benefits (e.g., reduced cost, time, less candidate involvement) could present a rationale for exploring these new methods compared to traditional ones. In sum, much more validity evidence is needed to draw strong conclusions of utility despite the growing popularity of searching SM content during staffing processes.

If SM use in the hiring process continues, we must also gain a better understanding of the potential for adverse impact. Currently, evidence in the scholarly literature is sparse and unclear (Davison et al., 2016; Van Iddekinge et al., 2016). As we gain a better understanding of the specific practices that are unlikely to result in discrimination, best practices can be developed to guide policies and procedures used by organizations.

Other topics in need of more research are applicant reactions and fairness perceptions. Using unfair hiring practices increases legal risk to employers and is therefore important to avoid. Currently, we know that applicants view some practices as an invasion of privacy, but early survey and qualitative study data suggests that perceptions may be changing among younger job seekers. More research should be conducted to better understand what practices might improve candidate reactions, perceptions of fairness, and mitigate privacy concerns. For example, what role does process transparency play in impacting the perceptions of fairness in the hiring process? Does incorporating flagged information in the interview quell negative reactions? Despite all of the expertise I/O psychologists can bring to this area, we also need to look outside our field to maximize our understanding. Collaborations with scholars and practitioners with varied backgrounds and perspectives can deepen our understanding (Landers & Schmidt, 2016b).

Additionally, much of the research and survey data available currently in this research area has involved research, legislation, guidelines, and case studies with a US-centric perspective (cf., Shields & Levashina, 2016). However, one of the benefits of examining big data from individuals' SM-enabled digital footprint is the ability to gather and study data outside the typically disproportionately WEIRD (Western, educated, industrialized, rich, democratic) samples seen in much of the current psychological sciences research (Kosinski et al., 2016). Despite the potential for increased reach, researchers must also consider the differences in local customs, preferences, uses, SM platforms, regulations, privacy concerns, and so forth that will impact how SM content is used in staffing contexts in practice. Some countries may vary quite widely in how they use such content (Schmidt & O'Connor, 2016). Therefore, research and practice is needed across geographic locations. Access capabilities to popular sites may also differ in some countries, and the implications on such limitations for recruiting and hiring purposes within global organizations warrants additional study.

10.9 Emerging Trends

While it is impossible to predict with precision what tools and functionality will be available to recruiters and selection scientists in the future, in evaluating the landscape, we see the possibility of market disruption coming from two potential sources with SM and staffing applications. In reviewing these applications, we hope to provide a glimpse of future possibilities that may have downstream implications for selection and validation procedures specifically and the look of organizational science research more generally.

Advancements in Machine Learning, Artificial Intelligence, and Web Scraping. To the authors' knowledge, no research has been published in peer-reviewed outlets examining SM content in a criterion-related validity study applying any of the advanced automated procedures being rampantly discussed. We believe that the convergence of technologies across web scraping, machine learning, and advancements in artificial intelligence may provide an exciting opportunity to process and synthesize the overwhelming amount of data available via SM trace content in a manner that simply isn't possible if left to subjective human decision-making and judgment, even under trained and rigorous assessment procedures.

Additionally, just as employers are attempting to use the power of data culled from SM contributions to learn more about their candidates, searching for job opportunities via powerful search engines that are driven by machine learning and artificial intelligence is becoming easier and more precise for job seekers. LinkedIn has offered a job search tool for users since 2005 and a tool for recruiters that can be used to source candidates since 2008 (LinkedIn Corp., 2015). However, in the last few years, LinkedIn has gone a step farther by providing job recommendations for open positions directly to users who are perceived to be a good fit. Relatedly, in the summer of 2017 (Burgess, 2017; Lincoln, 2017), Google launched Google for Jobs, a job search engine that culls postings for relevant searches from the largest job boards and postings made directly by organizations. The goal is to match employers with job seekers by sharing data between the two sources. Further, Laszlo Bock, Google's former SVP of People Operations, launched a new startup company, Humu, in May 2017 with the intent of making people better leaders, managers, and team members stated as being the first iteration of what they are working toward (Bock, 2017). Although the specifics of what the organization is looking to do are still not completely clear, the Humu website, as of the time of this writing, advertises the objective to "make work better … through science, machine learning, and a little bit of love" (Humu, 2017).

"Above the Funnel" Fit Tools. Several consulting firms (e.g., Pymetrics; Feloni, 2017) and global organizations with a large SM presence (e.g., Red Bull Wingfinder, 2017) have developed and deployed tools that seek to change the traditional vendor-client relationship that traditionally utilizes more of a business-to-business model and move toward something more closely aligned with a business-to-consumer model, with the consumer being the candidate or job seeker. We dub these tools "above the funnel" fit tools since they do not necessarily need to be completed by a prospective job seeker after officially submitting their candidacy for employment in an applicant tracking system where they may typically encounter a pre-hire assessment tool.

These types of tools are often positioned as opportunities to learn more about one's specific strengths, and often some job seeker motivator and value-add feedback element is provided to the assessment taker since it is usually completed outside the context of seeking a particular job or role with an organization. The benefit to these types of tools are that it appears they can expand the prospective candidate pool to active and passive job seekers for certain positions or opportunities while also giving some organizations very early stage information around assessment of fit and abilities.

Red Bull Wingfinder. The Wingfinder is positioned as a 35-minute experience that includes engaging, fast-paced exercises breaking the mold of what is typical of traditional personality type assessments and involving measures dubbed as a "cognitive challenge and intellect workout" (Red Bull Wingfinder, 2017). After completing the tool, the assessment taker will receive a professionally developed coaching video of a Red Bull-sponsored athlete purported to have some of the same strengths. In addition, Wingfinder assessment takers receive two reports. The first is a ten-page personal feedback report providing the assessment taker with strengths, advice, and coaching from professional athletes. They also will receive a one-page report that gives a high-level summary of strengths and that Red Bull instructs can be appended to a CV to a potential employer if the applicant chooses to share his or her results. As of the time of this writing, the Wingfinder has received fairly wide global exposure, with more than 250,000 individuals having completed the tool. Many learned about, accessed, and posted results from the tool via SM platforms. Despite the social aspect, everyone completed the same assessment and the reporting was generated automatically upon completion using automated scoring. These features address two of the major concerns presented earlier about SM assessments: standardization and procedural consistency. We have less line of sight to the underlying research, psychometric properties, and validity evidence associated with the Wingfinder, as this information is proprietary. However, the tool and tools like it represent an innovative hybrid approach to the application process that combines traditional with SM assessment.

Pymetrics Games. The Pymetrics tool is described as 12 distinct "games," suggested as having been built from neuroscience research assessing traits described as focus, memory, relationship to risk, and ability to read emotional versus contextual cues (Feloni, 2017). In one case study described in the popular press, the assessment was described in the context of use with client Unilever (Feloni, 2017). The process involved recruiting candidates (often seniors in college) through SM platforms Facebook, LinkedIn, The Muse, and WayUp. In the next step, candidates submitted their LinkedIn profile rather than a traditional resume. The Pymetrics assessment then took about 20 minutes to complete and was followed by a video interview with another third-party vendor, HireVue. If the candidate was not selected by Unilever, Pymetrics gave the candidate the opportunity to be considered at other partner clients using the tool, representing the business-to-consumer aspect of the Pymetrics business model.

10.10 Conclusion

Due to the rapid clip at which technology continues to advance, it is difficult to predict how SM will grow and evolve in the coming years and particularly what impact such changes will have on staffing. SM sites tend to develop or change in response to users' preferences changing and technological advancements enabling cool new uses or innovative combinations of uses that supersede what is available today. One thing that is clear in looking back at the survey trend data presented throughout this chapter is that usage and engagement in SM in general, and in aiding staffing functions at organizations specifically, will likely only continue to grow.

With the recent rapid growth in the popularity of SM, it is not surprising that so many challenges still exist. Despite these challenges and recommendations to the contrary, recruiters and hiring managers will likely continue to mine SM to source prospective candidates and learn more information about existing candidates. As our data is tracked at an ever-increasing level of detail, the result is a *digital footprint* left to be gleaned by decision makers and data analysts (Kosinski et al., 2016). Thus, it is imperative that we continue to advance our understanding of the potential uses and misuses at a more sophisticated level, so that I/O psychologists and related HR professionals can be in a strong position to serve as trusted advisers to job seekers and organizational decision makers. Requesting that practitioners simply ignore SM content may not be practically sustainable. In addition, simply discrediting the content provided on SM outright may put the field at risk of being perceived as out of touch. This could ultimately result in our staffing-process-related work efforts becoming functionally obsolete as it essentially overlooks something that the majority of practitioners are currently incorporating into their recruitment and hiring processes.

While risk certainly exists on a number of planes, including the threat to I/O psychology and related disciplines as we understand them to be today, amazing opportunities may also be on the horizon. In these exciting times, the ability to store and process mountains of data coupled with the powerful advanced analytical methods available may require we enhance or supplement our skillsets with the assistance of those trained in engineering and computer science. At the same time, we bring the unique theoretical framework and an understanding of the ethical standards related to studying human behavior to create substantial advances in this domain (Kosinski et al., 2016).

References

Aguado, D., Rico, R., Rubio, V. J., & Fernández, L. (2017). Applicant reactions to social network web use in personnel selection and assessment. *Journal of Work and Organizational Psychology, 32*, 183–190.

American Educational Research Association, American Psychological Association, & National Council on Measurement in Education (1999). *Standards for educational and psychological testing*. Washington, DC: American Psychological Association.

Armstrong, M. B., Landers, R. N., & Collmus, A. B. (2015). Gamifying recruitment, selection, training, and performance management: Game thinking in human resource management. In D. Davis & H. Gangadharbatla (Eds.), *Handbook of research trends in gamification* (pp. 140–165). Hershey, PA: IGI Global.

Arthur Jr, W., & Villado, A. J. (2008). The importance of distinguishing between constructs and methods when comparing predictors in personnel selection research and practice. *Journal of Applied Psychology, 93*(2), 435–442.

Back, M. D., Stopfer, J. M., Vazire, S., Gaddis, S., Schmukle, S. C., Egloff, B., & Gosling, S. D. (2010). Facebook profiles reflect actual personality, not self-idealization. *Psychological Science, 21*(3), 372–374.

Barsade, S. G. & Gibson, D. E. (2002). The ripple effects: Emotional contagion and its influence on group behavior. *Administrative Science Quarterly, 47*(4), 644–675.

Berger, C. R. & Calabrese, R. J. (1975). Some explorations in initial interaction and beyond: Toward a developmental theory of interpersonal communication. *Human Communication Research, 1*(2), 99–112.

Berkelaar, B. L. (2010). Cyber-vetting: Exploring the implications of online information for career capital and human capital decisions. Retrieved from ProQuest Digital Dissertations.

Berkelaar, B. L. (2014). Cybervetting, online information, and personnel selection: New transparency expectations and the emergence of a digital social contract. *Management Communication Quarterly, 28*(4), 479–506.

Binning, J. F. & Barrett, G. V. (1989). Validity of personnel decisions: A conceptual analysis of the inferential and evidential bases. *Journal of Applied Psychology, 74*(3), 478–494.

Black, S. L., Washington, M. L., & Schmidt, G. B. (2016). How to stay current in social media to be competitive in recruitment and selection. In R. N. Landers & G. B. Schmidt (Eds.), *Social media in employee selection and recruitment: Theory, practice, and current challenges* (pp. 197–222). Switzerland: Springer International Publishing.

Bock, L. (2015). Here's Google's secret to hiring the best people. Retrieved from www .wired.com/2015/04/hire-like-google/.

Bock, L. (2017). We're terrible at stealth mode. Retrieved from www.linkedin.com/pulse/ were-terrible-stealth-mode-laszlo-bock/?published=t.

Boyd, D. M. & Ellison, N. B. (2008). Social network sites: Definition, history, and scholarship. *Journal of Computer-Mediated Communication, 13*(1), 210–230.

Boyle, S. C., Earle, A. M., LaBrie, J. W., & Ballou, K. (2017). Facebook dethroned: Revealing the more likely social media destinations for college students' depictions of underage drinking. *Addictive Behaviors, 65*, 63–67.

Brown, V. R. & Vaughn, E. D. (2011). The writing on the (Facebook) wall: The use of social networking sites in hiring decisions. *Journal of Business and Psychology, 26*(2), 219–226.

Buffardi, L. E. & Campbell, W. K. (2008). Narcissism and social networking web sites. *Personality and Social Psychology Bulletin*, 34, 1303–1314.

Burgess, M. (2017). You can now hunt for jobs directly in Google search results thanks to AI. Retrieved from www.wired.co.uk/article/google-ai-job-search.

CareerBuilder. (2017). Number of employers using social media to screen candidates at all-time high, finds latest CareerBuilder study. Retrieved from http://press.career builder.com/2017–06-15-Number-of-Employers-Using-Social-Media-to-Screen-Candidates-at-All-Time-High-Finds-Latest-CareerBuilder-Study.

Carr, C. T. (2016). An uncertainty reduction approach to applicant information-seeking in social media: Effects on attributions and hiring. In R. N. Landers & G. B. Schmidt (Eds.), *Social media in employee selection and recruitment: Theory, practice, and current challenges* (pp. 59–78). Switzerland: Springer International Publishing.

Carr, C. T. & Walther, J. B. (2014). Increasing attributional certainty via social media: Learning about others one bit at a time. *Journal of Computer-Mediated Communication, 19*(4), 922–937.

Chambers, R. & Winter, J. (2017). Social media and selection: A brief history and practical recommendations. Retrieved from www.siop.org/WhitePapers/Visibility/ Social_Media_and_Selection_FINAL.pdf.

Chaykowski, K. (2017). Mark Zuckerberg gives Facebook a new mission. Retrieved from www.forbes.com/sites/kathleenchaykowski/2017/06/22/mark-zuckerberg-gives-facebook-a-new-mission/#71622ad91343.

Chen, C.-P. (2013). Exploring personal branding on YouTube. *Journal of Internet Commerce, 12*(4), 332–347.

Christian, M. S., Edwards, B. D., & Bradley, J. C. (2010). Situational judgment tests: Constructs assessed and a meta- analysis of their criterion-related validities. *Personnel Psychology, 63*(1), 83–117.

Collmus, A. B., Armstrong, M. B., & Landers, R. N. (2016). Game-thinking within social media to recruit and select job candidates. In R. N. Landers & G. B. Schmidt (Eds.), *Social Media in Employee Selection and Recruitment* (pp. 103–124). Switzerland: Springer International Publishing.

Costa, P. T. & McCrae, R. R. (1992). Normal personality assessment in clinical practice: The NEO Personality Inventory. *Psychological Assessment, 4*(1), 5–13.

Danescu-Niculescu-Mizil, C., West, R., Jurafsky, D., Leskovec, J., & Potts, C. (2013). No country for old members: User lifecycle and linguistic change in online communities. Proceedings of the 22nd International Conference on World Wide Web (pp. 307–318). New York, NY: ACM.

Davison, H. K., Bing, M. N., Kluemper, D. H., & Roth, P. L. (2016). Social media as a personnel selection and hiring resource: Reservations and recommendations. In R. N. Landers & G. B. Schmidt (Eds.), *Social media in employee selection and recruitment* (pp. 15–42). Switzerland: Springer International Publishing.

Davison, H. K., Maraist, C. C., Hamilton, R., & Bing, M. N. (2012). To screen or not to screen? Using the internet for selection decisions. *Employee Responsibilities and Rights Journal, 24*(1), 1–21.

Dorethy, M. D., Fiebert, M. S., & Warren, C. R. (2014). Examining social networking site behaviors: Photo sharing and impression management on Facebook. *International Review of Social Sciences and Humanities, 6*, 111–6.

Drouin, M., O'Connor, K. W., Schmidt, G. B., & Miller, D. A. (2015). Facebook fired: Legal perspectives and young adults' opinions on the use of social media in hiring and firing decisions. *Computer in Human Behavior, 46*, 123–128.

Elzweig, B. & Peeples, D. K. (2009). Using social networking web sites in hiring and retention decisions. *SAM Advanced Management Journal, 74*(4), 27–35.

Equal Employment Opportunity Commission, C. S. C., Department of Labor, and Department of Justice. (1978). Uniform guidelines on employee selection procedures. *Federal Register, 43*(166), 38290–38315.

Facebook, Inc. v. Power Ventures, Inc. (2009). 91 U.S.P.Q.2d 1430. (D. California May 11, 2009).

Ferrell, J. Z., Carpenter, J. E., Vaughn, E. D., Dudley, N. M., & Goodman, S. A. (2015). Gamification of human resource processes. In D. Davis & H. Gangadharbatla (Eds.), *Emerging research and trends in gamification* (pp. 108–139). Hershey, PA: IGI Global.

Fertik, M. (2007). Commentary on we googled you. *Harvard Business Review*, June, p. 47.

Feloni, R. (2017). Consumer-goods giant Unilever has been hiring employees using brain games and artificial intelligence – and it's a huge success. Retrieved from www .businessinsider.com/unilever-artificial-intelligence-hiring-process-2017–6.

Frantz, N. B., Pears, E. S. Vaughn, E. D., Farrell, J. Z., & Dudley, N. M. (2016). Is John Smith really John Smith? Misrepresentations and misattributions of candidates using social media and social networking sites. In R. N. Landers & G. B. Schmidt (Eds.), *Social Media in Employee Selection and Recruitment* (pp. 307–339). Switzerland: Springer International Publishing.

Funder, D. C. (2001). Personality. *Annual Review of Psychology, 52*, 197–221.

Funder, D. C. (2006). Towards a resolution of the personality triad: Persons, situations, and behaviors. *Journal of Research in Personality, 40*(1), 21–34.

General Assembly. (2016). Improve your LinkedIn profile to succeed in 2016. Retrieved from https://generalassemb.ly/education/improve-your-linkedin-profile-to-suc ceed-in-2016/san-francisco.

Gibson, P. C., Vaughn, D., & Hudy, M. J. (2017). Beyond empirical equivalence. *Industrial and Organizational Psychology: Perspectives on Science and Practice, 10*(4), 676–680.

Gosling, S. D., Gaddis, S., & Vazire, S. (2007). *Personality impressions based on Facebook profiles.* Paper presented at the 1st International Conference on Web and Social Media, Boulder, CO.

Grasmuck, S., Martin, J., & Zhao, S. (2009). Ethno-racial identity displays on Facebook. *Journal of Computer-Mediated Communication, 15*(1), 158–188.

Guerin, L. (2017). Can employers ask for passwords to my social media accounts? Retrieved from www.nolo.com/legal-encyclopedia/can-employers-ask-passwords-my-social-media-accounts.html.

Guion, R. M. (2011). *Assessment, measurement, and prediction for personnel decisions* (2nd edn.). New York, NY: Routledge/Taylor & Francis Group.

Hambrick, D. C. (2007). The field of management's devotion to theory: Too much of a good thing? *Academy of Management Journal, 50*(6), 1346–1352.

Hampton, A. J. & Shalin, V. L. (2017). Sentinels of breach: Lexical choice as a measure of urgency in social media. *Human Factors, 59*(4), 505–519.

Highhouse, S. (2002). Assessing the candidate as a whole: A historical and critical analysis of individual psychological assessment for personnel decision making. *Personnel Psychology, 55*(2), 363–396.

Horowitz, S. & Rosati, F. (2014). 53 million Americans are freelancing, new survey finds. Retrieved from https://blog.freelancersunion.org/2014/09/04/53million/.

Hoseini, E. & Mansoori, E. G. (2016). Selecting discriminative features in social media data: An unsupervised approach. *Neurocomputing, 205*, 463–471.

Howard v. Hertz (2014). 3–00645 (D. Hawaii Oct. 23, 2014).

Humu. (2017). Make work better. Retrieved from www.humu.com/.

Johnson, R. D. (1987). Making judgments when information is missing: Inferences, biases, and framing effects. *Acta Psychologica, 66*, 69–82.

Johnson, R. D. & Levine, I. P. (1985). More than meets the eye: The effect of missing information on purchase evaluations. *Journal of Consumer Research, 12*, 169–177.

Kluemper, D. H. & Rosen, P. A. (2009). Future employment selection methods: evaluating social networking web sites. *Journal of Managerial Psychology, 24*(6), 567–580.

Kluemper, D. H., Rosen, P. A., & Mossholder, K. (2012). Social networking websites, personality ratings, and the organizational context: More than meets the eye. *Journal of Applied Social Psychology, 42*(5), 1143–1172.

Kosinski, M., Wang, Y., Lakkaraju, H., & Leskovec, J. (2016). Mining big data to extract patterns and predict real-life outcomes. *Psychological Methods, 21*(4), 493–506.

Kramer, A. D. I., Guillory, J. E., & Hancock, J. T. (2014). Experimental evidence of massive-scale emotional contagion through social networks. *Proceedings of the National Academy of Sciences of the United States of America, 111*, 8788–8790.

Kristof-Brown, A. L. (2000). Perceived applicant fit: Distinguishing between recruiters' perceptions of person-job and person-organization fit. *Personnel Psychology, 53* (3), 643–671.

Labrecque, L. I., Markos, E., & Milne, G. R. (2011). Online personal branding: Processes, challenges, and implications. *Journal of Interactive Marketing, 25*(1), 37–50.

Landers, R. N. & Goldberg, A. S. (2014). Online social media in the workplace: A conversation with employees. In M. D. Coovert & L. F. Thompson (Eds.), *Psychology of workplace technology* (pp. 284–306). New York, NY: Routledge Academic.

Landers, R. N. & Schmidt, G. B. (2016a). Social media in employee selection and recruitment: An overview. In R. N. Landers & G. B. Schmidt (Eds.), *Social media in employee selection and recruitment: Theory, practice, and current challenges* (pp. 3–14). Switzerland: Springer International Publishing.

Landers, R. N. & Schmidt, G. B. (2016b). Social media in employee selection and recruitment: Current knowledge, unanswered questions, and future directions. In R. N. Landers & G. B. Schmidt (Eds.), *Social media in employee selection and recruitment: Theory, practice, and current challenges* (pp. 343–367). Switzerland: Springer International Publishing.

Lincoln, J. (2017). Why Google for Jobs is a total game changer for recruiters, employers, and job sites. Retrieved from www.inc.com/john-lincoln/why-google-for-jobs-is-a-game-changer-for-recruite.html.

LinkedIn Corporation. (2015). A brief history of LinkedIn. Retrieved from https://ourstory
.linkedin.com/#year-2014.

McFarland, L. A. & Ployhart, R. E. (2015). Social media in organizations: A theoretical
framework to guide research and practice. *Journal of Applied Psychology, 100*(6),
1653–1677.

Mead, A. D., Olson-Buchanan, J. B., & Drasgow, F. (2013). Technology-based selection. In
M. D. Coovert & I. F. Thompson (Eds.), *The psychology of workplace technology*
(pp. 21–42). New York, NY: Routledge Academic.

Mischel, W. (1979). On the interface of cognition and personality: Beyond the person-
situation debate. *American Psychologist, 34*(9), 740–754.

Morelli, N., Potosky, D., Arthur, Jr., W., & Tippins, N. (2017). A call for conceptual models
of technology in I-O psychology: An example from technology-based talent
assessment. *Industrial and Organizational Psychology: Perspectives on Science
and Practice, 10*(4), 634–653.

Natanson, H. (2017). Harvard rescinds acceptances for at least ten students for obscene
memes. Retrieved from www.thecrimson.com/article/2017/6/5/2021-offers-
rescinded-memes/.

Park, G., Schwartz, H. A., Eichstaedt, J. C., et al. (2015). Automatic personality assessment
through social media language. *Journal of Personality and Social Psychology, 108*
(6), 934–952.

Pew Research Center (2017). Social media fact sheet. Retrieved from www.pewinternet.org/
fact-sheet/social-media/

Potosky, D. (2008). A conceptual framework for the role of the administration medium in the
personnel assessment process. *Academy of Management Review, 33*(3), 629–648.

Red Bull Wingfinder (2017). New survey finds college graduates do not fear social media's
impact on hiring. Retrieved from www.prnewswire.com/news-releases/new-sur
vey-finds-college-graduates-do-not-fear-social-medias-impact-on-hiring-
300501887.html.

Robinson, S., Sinar, E., & Winter, J. (2013). LinkedIn as a tool for turnover research. Paper
presented at the 28th annual conference of the Society for Industrial and
Organizational Psychology, Houston.

Rohampton, J. (2017). 5 social media trends that will dominate 2017. Retrieved from www
.forbes.com/sites/jimmyrohampton/2017/01/03/5-social-media-trends-that-will-
dominate-2017/#4c5585146ffe.

Roth, P. L., Bobko, P., Van Iddekinge, C. H., & Thatcher, J. B. (2016). Social media in
employee-selection-related decisions: A research agenda for uncharted territory.
Journal of Management, 42(1), 269–298.

Roulin, N. & Levashina, J. (2016). Impression management and social media profiles. In R.
N. Landers & G. B. Schmidt (Eds.), *Social media in employee selection and
recruitment: Theory, practice, and current challenges* (pp. 307-339).
Switzerland: Springer International Publishing.

Ruggs, E. N., Walker, S. S., Blanchard, A., & Gur, S. (2016). Online exclusion: Biases that
may arise when using social media in talent acquisition. In R. N. Landers & G. B.
Schmidt (Eds.), *Social media in employee selection and recruitment: Theory,
practice, and current challenges* (pp. 289–306). Switzerland: Springer
International Publishing.

Rynes, S. L. (1991). Recruitment, job choice, and post-hire consequences: A call for new
research directions. In M. D. Dunnette & L. M. Hough (Eds.), *Handbook of*

Industrial and Organizational Psychology (vol. 2, 2nd edn, pp. 399–444). Palo Alto, CA: Consulting Psychologists Press.

Said-Moorhouse, L. (2017). Kenya election: Facebook takes out full-page ads over fake news. Retrieved from www.cnn.com/2017/08/03/africa/kenya-election-facebook-fake-news-strategy/index.html.

Schinkel, S., van Vianen, A., & Dierendonck, D. (2013). Selection fairness and outcomes: A field study of interactive effects on applicant reactions. *International Journal of Selection and Assessment, 21*(1), 22–31.

Schmidt, F. L. & Hunter, J. E. (1998). The validity and utility of selection methods in personnel psychology: Practical and theoretical implications of 85 years of research findings. *Psychological Bulletin, 124*(2), 262–274.

Schmidt, G. B. & O'Connor, K. W. (2016). Legal concerns when considering social media data in selection. In R. N. Landers & G. B. Schmidt (Eds.), *Social media in employee selection and recruitment: Theory, practice, and current challenges* (pp. 265–288). Switzerland: Springer International Publishing.

Schmitt, N. & Sinha, R. (2011). Validation support for selection procedures. In S. Zedeck (Ed.), *APA Handbook of Industrial and Organizational Psychology* (vol. 2, pp. 399–420). Washington, DC: American Psychological Association.

Schneider, B. (1987). The people make the place. *Personnel Psychology, 40*(3), 437–453.

Schneider, B., Smith, D. B., & Goldstein, H. W. (2000). Attraction–selection–attrition: Toward a person–environment psychology of organizations. In W. B. Walsh, K. H. Craik, & R. H. Price (Eds.), *Person–environment psychology: New directions and perspectives* (pp. 61–85). Mahwah, NJ: Lawrence Erlbaum Associates.

Schwartz, H. A., Eichstaedt, J. C., Kern, M. L., et al. (2013). Personality, gender, and age in the language of social media: The open-vocabulary approach. *PLOS ONE, 8*(9), 1–16.

Shields, B. & Lavashina, J. (2016). Comparing the social media in the United States and BRIC Nations, and the challenges faced in international selection. In R. N. Landers & G. B. Schmidt (Eds.), *Social media in employee selection and recruitment: Theory, practice, and current challenges* (pp. 157–174). Switzerland: Springer International Publishing.

SHRM (2016a). The new talent landscape: Recruiting difficulty and skills shortages. Retrieved from www.shrm.org/hr-today/trends-and-forecasting/research-and-sur veys/pages/talent-landscape.aspx.

SHRM (2016b). Using social media for talent acquisition– recruitment and screening. Retrieved from www.shrm.org/hr-today/trends-and-forecasting/research-and-sur veys/pages/social-media-recruiting-screening-2015.aspx.

Siegchrist, G. (2017). Choosing a website for your video blog. Retrieved from www .lifewire.com/video-blog-websites-1082183.

Sinar, E. F., Ballard, D. W., Moon, M. M., Poeppelman, T. R., & Thoresen, P. (2017). From likes to impact: The payoffs of social media involvement. Panel presented at the 32nd annual conference of the Society for Industrial and Organizational Psychology, Orlando.

Singer, N. (2013). They loved your G.P.A. Then they saw your tweets. Retrieved from www .nytimes.com/2013/11/10/business/they-loved-your-gpa-then-they-saw-your-tweets.html?mcubz=3.

Smock, A. (June, 2010). The impact of second-party content on self-presentation within a social network site environment. Paper presented at the 60th Annual Conference of the International Communication Association, Singapore.

Society for Industrial and Organizational Psychology. (2003). *Principles for the validation and use of personnel selection procedures*, 4th edn. Bowling Green, OH: Author.

Stoughton, J. W., Thompson, L. F., & Meade, A. W. (2015). Examining applicant reactions to the use of social network sites in pre-employment screening. *Journal of Business and Psychology, 30*(1), 73–88.

Tett, R. P. & Burnett, D. D. (2003). A personality trait-based interactionist model of job performance. *Journal of Applied Psychology, 88*(3), 500–517.

The Data Team. (2016). Celebrities' endorsement earnings on social media. Retrieved from www.economist.com/blogs/graphicdetail/2016/10/daily-chart-9.

Tversky, A. & Kahneman, D. (1974). Judgment under uncertainty: Heuristics and biases. *Science, 185*(4157), 1124–1131.

Ugander, J., Karrer, B., Backstrom, L., & Marlow, C. (2011). The anatomy of the Facebook social graph. *Computing Research Repository*, 1–17.

Van Iddekinge, C. H., Lanivich, S. E., Roth, P. L., & Junco, E. (2016). Social media for selection? Validity and adverse impact potential of a Facebook-based assessment. *Journal of Management, 42*(7), 1811–1835.

Vazire, S. & Gosling, S. D. (2004). e-Perceptions: Personality impressions based on personal websites. *Journal of Personality and Social Psychology, 87*(1), 123–132.

Wagner, K. (2017). Snapchat is still bigger than Instagram for younger U.S. millennials. Retrieved from www.recode.net/2017/8/24/16198632/snapchat-instagram-teens-comscore-study-growth-users.

Youyou, W., Kosinski, M., & Stillwell, D. J. (2015). Computer-based personality judgements are more accurate than those made by humans. *Proceedings of the National Academy of Sciences of the United States of America, 112*, 1036–1040.

Zhao, J., Wang, X., & Jin, P. (2015). Feature selection for event discovery in social media: a comparative study. *Computers in Human Behavior, 51*(B), 903–909.

Zide, J., Elman, B., & Shahani-Denning, C. (2014). LinkedIn and recruitment: How profiles differ across occupations. *Employee Relations, 36*, 583–604.

PART III

Technology in Training and Development

11 Gamification of Adult Learning: Gamifying Employee Training and Development

Richard N. Landers, Elena M. Auer, Adrian B. Helms, Sebastian Marin, and Michael B. Armstrong

Gamification is now commonly used in adult learning contexts, but its effects remain unclear. This has happened in part because of the initially trendy and faddish nature of gamification leading to high rates of adoption without significant critical evaluation. This was most problematic in the years leading up to peak hype in 2013 (Gartner, 2012), at which point "gamification" was used as a catchall faddish buzzword that did not refer to any particular construct or approach, instead being used primarily as a marketing strategy (Bogost, 2011). Since then, as gamification has been explored in the academic research literature, these broader problems have been largely addressed via carefully considered theoretical and empirical studies. Nevertheless, empirical work in particular is still relatively sparse; the last major published summary of such work only identified nine empirical gamification studies in the learning context as of 2014 (Hamari, Kovisto & Sarsa, 2014). Since then, the literature has grown, but there are still many unanswered questions among both gamification practitioners and academics. Among non-specialists, there is still substantial construct confusion stemming directly from gamification's initially faddish definition. Given this, the purpose of this chapter is threefold. First, we define gamification and provide a comprehensive introduction to it, contrasting it with existing approaches. Second, we explore which theories describe its known and potential effects. Third, we provide extensive practical literature-driven recommendations for those seeking to gamify training themselves.

11.1 Defining Gamification

The most critical issue to address when a new research literature forms around a seemingly new organizational construct is to develop a formal definition. As noted earlier, the lack of an agreed-upon definition of *gamification* for the early years of its popularity harmed both public perception of its value and researcher progress in studying it. In short, anything branded "gamification" was immediately suspect, first because *gamification* was itself not considered a new or unique concept, and second, because many of the gamification implementations getting press coverage were at best gimmicky and at worst actively harmful. The term *gamification* was most often used to capitalize on hype in the consulting marketplace as a means of generating profit (see Bogost, 2011). Since that hype subsided, it has been replaced with an understanding that gamification has significant potential but is easy to conduct poorly. In the academic community, a relatively strong consensus has emerged around definitions developed by a small set of researchers, and the term *gamification* now means something much more specific than it did previously. This view of gamification has even become the center of a new *gamification science* (Landers et al., 2018). We will explore definitions of gamification in the remainder of this section.

11.1.1 Distinguishing Games, Serious Games, and Gamification

Despite their apparent similarity, games, serious games, and gamification are distinct concepts focused on different objectives and principles. Games and serious games are most closely related. Though researchers do not agree upon a singular definition, games can be generally defined as "a voluntary activity, obviously separate from real life, creating an imaginary world that may or may not have any relation to real life and that absorbs the player's full attention" (Michael & Chen, 2005, p. 8). Michael and colleagues (2005) further clarified that "games are played out within a specific time and place, [and] are played according to established rules" (p. 8). Such games are typically created for entertainment purposes as a composite of many game elements working in combination. Game elements can be defined as features or mechanics of play typically found in games (e.g., fantasy, control, environment; Deterding et al., 2011). In contrast, serious games, also referred to as educational games or games for learning, are "game[s] in which education (in its various forms) is the primary goal, rather than entertainment" (Michael & Chen, 2005, p.10). Serious games can be used to directly facilitate learning in several educational and training contexts, including military, government, education, business, and healthcare (Garris, Ahlers, & Driskell, 2002). For example, the game America's Army (www. americasarmy.com) is a video game created by the US military that trains players on military tactics using single-player and multi-player missions as a way to teach them about military combat and to encourage them to enlist. In the context of employee training and development, both games and serious game can be considered an instructional method, where individual game elements can be designed to teach the player some targeted knowledge or skill. In this model, the game acts as a virtual instructor, providing information to the learner. In America's Army, for example, the user learns about military tactics by playing the game. Without playing America's Army, there would be no instruction. Both games and serious games have been shown to be effective methods in improving learning outcomes (e.g., Sitzmann, 2011) and, given their similarity in composition, can inform gamification research and practice. However, gamification is fundamentally distinct from games and serious games.

Instead, gamification in learning contexts is an instructional design process, and not an instructional method, applied to existing instructional methods to improve target outcomes. More generally, gamification is the process of adding game design elements to non-game contexts (Deterding et al., 2011), and learning can be considered a non-game context. Serious games and gamification are unified by their use of game elements to improve learning outcomes. However, gamified instructional methods, instead of being standalone game experiences with many game elements, only include one or a few game elements added to an existing instructional program. Existing instructional methods, such as online training videos, are what deliver instructional content to the learner, and the addition of game elements to those methods is intended to alter intermediary proximal learning behaviors or attitudes to improve learning outcomes more distally. In summary, a user can learn directly from a game but not from gamification. Instead, gamification is used to improve learning that is already occurring or to overcome some psychological roadblock preventing learning in a system that is otherwise functional (Landers, 2015). For example, a gamification intervention could be as simple as adding a progress bar to an employee leadership training slide presentation. In this case, a progress bar would not be the method by which a user learned, and consequently could not improve the training if the existing content was inadequate. However, if the instructional content facilitated learning, the progress bar could indirectly improve learning by increasing a user's motivation to learn by providing progress feedback.

11.1.2 Theory of Gamified Learning

The theory of gamified learning can be used to understand the potential impact of gamification and consists of two components: game element attribute categories and a process model (Landers, 2015). In summary, game element attribute categories (see Table 11.1), originated by Bedwell and colleagues (2012) in the context of serious games, provide a theoretically based yet practical framework for implementing individual game elements in the learning context. These categories organize game elements that have been previously linked to learning outcomes for application to non-game instructional methods. The process model (see Figure 11.1), the second component of the theory, explains the indirect effect of these elements on learning outcomes (Landers, 2015). In this model, gamification affects learning through learning-related behaviors and attitudes by way of either mediating or moderating processes. In the mediating process, game elements drive learning-related behaviors and attitudes, which are the underlying mechanism for improving learning outcomes. In the moderating process, game elements strengthen or weaken the existing relationship between learning-related behaviors and learning outcomes. In combination, the game element attribute categories and process model provide a parsimonious theoretical framework of gamification in a training and development context.

Game element attribute categories can be defined as broad groupings of learning-related game elements, organized by shared psychological attribute (Landers, 2015). Using Wilson and colleague's (2009) list of game elements, Bedwell and colleagues (2012) taxonomized game elements into nine categories of attributes that facilitate learning related behaviors or attitudes. The categories of elements include action language, assessment, conflict/challenge, control, environment, game fiction, human interaction, immersion, and rules/goals. This taxonomy,

Table 11.1 *Theory of gamified learning game element attribute categories and definitions*

Game Element Attribute Categories	Definition
Action Language	The method and interface by which communication occurs between a player and the game itself.
Assessment	The method by which accomplishment and game progress are tracked.
Conflict/Challenge	The problems faced by players, including both the nature and difficulty of those problems.
Control	Degree to which players are able to alter the game, and the degree to which the game alters itself in response.
Environment	The representation of the physical surroundings of the player.
Game Fiction	The fictional game world and story.
Human Interaction	The degree to which players interact with other players in both space and time.
Immersion	The affective and perceptual experience of a game.
Rules/Goals	Clearly defined rules, goals, and information on progress toward those goals, provided to the player.

Note. Table excerpted from Landers (2015).

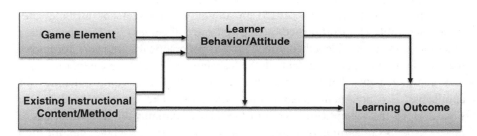

Figure 11.1 *Causal path model of the theory of gamified learning (Adapted from Landers, 2015).*

while not comprehensive or exhaustive, was empirically derived from existing research on serious games to provide guidance on which attribute categories are most likely to affect learning outcomes (Bedwell et al., 2012). For example, adding assessment to a training activity might include adding points that track correct answers in an existing training module to track a learner's progress.

The application of each of these elements to a learning context can also be described in terms of a variety of psychological theories (Landers, Armstrong, & Collmus, 2017). For example, according to self-determination theory, which posits that motivation is rooted in the fulfillment of autonomy, competence, and relatedness needs (Ryan & Deci, 2000), control game elements may satisfy a learner's need for autonomy and ultimately improve their motivation (Landers, Armstrong,

& Collmus, 2017). Similarly, according to the theory of test-enhanced learning (Roediger & Karpicke, 2006), adding assessment game elements may improve learning by triggering cognitive retrieval of previously learned content (Landers, Armstrong, & Collmus, 2017).

These learning-related elements can also be adopted individually or in meaningful combinations. In practice, adding combinations of elements may increase the change in learning behaviors or attitudes over any particular element in isolation. However, in research, it is important to isolate elements individually or in meaningful combinations so that specific guidance can be provided on which gamification elements lead to which behaviors. For example, Landers and Callan (2011) added several game elements to instructional material, including assessment, challenge, human interaction, and rules/goals. These elements were intentionally chosen to motivate students to complete optional training tests that would increase time spent on learning materials and ultimately improve learning outcomes (Landers & Callan, 2011). Although students reported favorable reactions to the gamified system when compared to the non-gamified system, the specific elements that led to favorable reactions could not be determined because the effect of each element could not be differentiated. It is impossible to determine post hoc if the effect was caused by particular elements (i.e., main effects) or their combination (i.e., an interaction).

The process model in the theory of gamified learning presents several types of causal relationships among instructional content, learning-relevant behaviors and attitudes, learning outcomes, and game characteristics. One fundamental causal relationship in the model is of the effect of instructional content on behaviors/ attitudes (Landers, 2015). Improved instructional content has repeatedly been shown to alter learner behaviors and attitudes (e.g., Arthur et al., 2003; Graham & Perin, 2007; Kulik, Kulik, & Cohen, 1980; Norris & Ortega, 2000; Seidel & Shavelson, 2007). This relationship is fundamental because gamification cannot replace instructional content and therefore will not improve learning outcomes in cases of completely ineffective existing content. For example, if a leadership training model only covers material trainees are already familiar with, adding game elements to the model will not improve learning behaviors or attitudes. Instead, training needs should be re-evaluated, and content should be altered to fit those needs. Another causal relationship is between behaviors/attitudes and learning outcomes, meaning learning attitudes affect learning outcomes (e.g., Carini, Kuh, & Klein, 2006; Paas et al., 2005; Zhao & Kuh, 2004). For example, increased student engagement can improve performance on critical thinking tests (Carini et al., 2006) and increased motivation to learn can lead to improved skill acquisition (Colquitt, LePine, & Noe, 2000). A third causal relationship exists between game characteristics and behaviors/attitudes (e.g., Bedwell et al., 2012; Hamari et al., 2014; Tay, 2010; Wilson et al., 2009). For example, the use of more specified goals can improve motivation, and ability-dependent adaptation of content may improve learner cognitive strategies (Wilson et al., 2009). Because of this causal relationship, improving learner behaviors and attitudes is the primary goal of theoretically derived gamification interventions. All three of these direct causal relationships exist in both the mediating and moderating process, which describe how game elements indirectly affect learning outcomes.

The model presents two specific paths by which game elements affect learning. The first is the mediation of the relationship between game elements and learning outcomes by learning-relevant behaviors and attitudes. *Mediation* refers to sequential causal effects between constructs (Baron & Kenny, 1986). Here, game characteristics affect learning outcomes via behaviors and attitudes, the causal mediator (Landers, 2015). For example, adding game elements that increase the amount of time a trainee spends on the training can ultimately improve learning outcomes, but only because time-on-task causes increased learning (Landers, 2015). In the case of Landers and Callan's (2011) study, gamified practice tests were meant to improve learning by increasing time spent on learning material, which has been shown to improve learning outcomes (Brown, 2001). In this example, the relationship between game characteristics (assessment, challenge, human interaction, and rules/goals) and learning outcomes is mediated by time spent on the training (behavior). In a training context, gamification is most effective via mediation when game element(s) specifically encourage a behavior/attitude that will improve learning outcomes. Targeting a behavior or attitude with gamification that does not relate to a learning outcome would likely be ineffective or result in an unexplained improvement in learning outcomes. For example, using gamification to make training more fun would likely not improve learning outcomes if increased fun did not itself improve learning outcomes. Furthermore, if learning outcomes did improve despite a lack of relationship between fun and learning outcomes, this implies the designer's understanding of why their gamification worked is incomplete; another, unmeasured mediational variable has been affected. Similarly, choosing game elements that do not influence target desired behaviors or attitudes would also likely lead to a failed intervention. For example, if fun did improve learning yet gamification did not lead to fun, gamification would likely not improve learning outcomes (Landers, 2015). Finally, it is also important to note that instructional content simultaneously affects behaviors and attitudes, leading to learning outcomes. So, it is important to consider how instructional content is beneficially contributing to behaviors and attitudes and where gamification can approve upon behaviors and attitudes.

The second process by which game elements affect learning is the moderation of the relationship between instructional content and learning outcomes by learning-relevant behaviors and attitudes altered by game characteristics. *Moderation* occurs when the effect of one construct on another varies based on the value of a third, the moderator (Baron & Kenny, 1986). In this moderating process, a game element affects an attitude/behavior, which strengthens or weakens the relationship between instructional content and learning outcomes. For example, gamifying a training module with fantasy may increase trainee engagement, strengthening the relationship between instructional content and learning outcomes (Landers, 2015). Gamification is most effective as a moderator when the game element(s) encourages a behavior/attitude that will increase learning outcomes by improving upon instruction materials. Targeting a behavior or attitude that does not moderate the relationship between instructional content and learning outcomes would likely render the gamification intervention ineffective or, in the case of an effective intervention, result in an unexplained improvement. For example, if narrative is added to an existing training module to improve learner motivation, it should already be known that learner motivation is linked to improved learning outcomes. If not, increasing motivation with a gamification intervention may not lead to improved learning outcomes. Similarly, when there is ineffective instructional content, incorporating a game element to improve behavior and attitudes would not be useful; it merely focuses learner attention on something already known to be ineffective. Without sound instructional content, gamification cannot improve learning outcomes through moderating effects.

11.1.3 Common Outcomes of Interest

The ultimate outcome of a gamification intervention is whatever change the practitioner chooses, which in a training context is most commonly learning or transfer. Learning is typically defined as the learning outcomes produced by experience and practice, which can be a change in cognitive, affective, or skill capacities (Kraiger, Ford, & Salas, 1993). Transfer is the application of learning, how well a trainee applies the knowledge, attitudes, or skills they learned in the program to their task or job (Burke & Hutchins, 2007). In the context of the process model, learning and transfer are distal learning outcomes. This means that although both learning and transfer are common targets of gamification interventions, it is difficult to target those outcomes directly. Instead, the practitioner must target a mediating or moderating process that is related to learning and transfer. For example, to indirectly target learning, an action language can be added to a training module to improve trainee engagement. In this scenario, trainee engagement, which is improved by the gamification intervention, is intended to strengthen the relationship between instructional material and learning outcomes. Similarly, to target transfer, a mediating process could be targeted. For example, to improve training transfer, a driving training module could be gamified by incorporating challenge via time pressure. This game element may serve to increase training fidelity, ultimately improving transfer of driver training.

Training reactions is another outcome frequently targeted by gamification interventions. Training reactions are post-training opinions regarding the training program, including affective reactions, perceptions of the training's utility, and difficulty in justifying the effort required to perform the training well (Kirkpatrick, 1959; Warr & Bunce, 1995). Training reactions are important for organizational decision-making, feedback, and marketing (Kraiger, 2002), and similar to learning and transfer, they are a distal outcome that can be indirectly affected by gamification interventions. For example, Armstrong and Landers (2017) examined the effects of adding narrative to a training module and found that trainees were more satisfied with gamified training than a non-gamified version and that declarative knowledge gained was similar between conditions; however, the narrative version appeared to adversely affect procedural knowledge. Thus, prioritizing target outcomes before gamifying becomes critical. Other learning outcomes may be unintentionally affected by targeting trainee satisfaction, which may or may not be acceptable depending on the priorities of the designer. Prior to using a gamification intervention, it is also important to differentiate which type of reaction is the target (i.e., affective, utility, or justification reactions) to better match game elements to it. For example, if trainees find the training content itself to be of low value, it might be more impactful to redevelop the instructional material than to intervene with gamification. In contrast, if trainees have negative affective perceptions of the training, an intervention like Armstrong and Landers' (2017) narrative intervention may be useful.

Training motivation is a commonly targeted mediator in gamification interventions to improve learning or transfer. Motivation explains the variation in intensity, persistence, quality, and direction of behavior, and in a training context reflects the direction, intensity, and persistence of learning-directed behavior (Kanfer, 1991; Mitchell, 1982). Numerous game elements have been shown to affect motivation (e.g., Malone, 1981; Sailer et al., 2013). For example, Malone (1981) examined the effect of a variety of game elements, including assessment, game fiction, and immersion, on student motivation to learn. He found that game fiction motivated students the most, followed by immersion and assessment. Sailer and colleagues (2013) also identified specific game elements that are most likely to increase motivation in gamification interventions: points, badges, leaderboards, progress bars, quests, meaningful stories, and avatars. For example, they suggested that badges cause motivation by fulfilling a player's need for success, by acting as a status symbol, by having a goalsetting function, and by fostering a player's feeling of competence (Sailer et al., 2013). Similarly, they suggested that avatars allow players to have choices, which can foster feelings of autonomy and ultimately drive motivation (Sailer et al., 2013). Increasing motivation using game elements has also been demonstrated to ultimately improve learning outcomes (e.g., Parker & Lepper, 1992). Parker and Lepper (1992) applied fantasy elements to children's instructional materials to target motivation and found improved motivation and learning and transfer. Because motivation typically makes pre-existing instruction better, rather than explicitly improve learning, in the context of the process model, motivation is typically a moderator of the existing relationship between instructional content and learning outcomes. In addition to the theory of gamified learning, Landers, Bauer, Callan, and Armstrong (2015) identified four additional motivational frameworks that explain how gamification effects training motivation including classic learning theories, expectancy theory, goal-setting theory, and self-determination theory. Each of these motivational frameworks will be discussed in more depth during later sections of the chapter.

11.1.4 Common Moderators of Interest

Moderators in gamified learning affect how gamification interventions affect outcomes differently across people because of trait or situational context variation.

Person-level moderators are psychological constructs, or proxies for those constructs, that affect how well gamification interventions work across different people. In other words, trainee characteristics can influence the effectiveness of gamification. In the gamification literature, person-level moderators typically include experience with games and game attitudes (e.g., Landers & Callan, 2012; Landers and Armstrong, 2015; Landers, Armstrong, & Collmus, 2017), as well as proxy variables such as gender (e.g., Greenberg et al., 2010; Shen et al., 2016) and age (e.g., Koivisto, & Hamari, 2014; Thiel, Reisinger, & Röderer, 2016). Experience with games and game attitudes have been shown to moderate the relationship between gamified instructional content and the anticipated value of gamified instruction, which is likely to persist to some degree post-training given the relationship between pre-training and mid-training motivation (Landers & Armstrong, 2015). For learners with high game experience and positive game attitudes, gamification led to improved anticipated learning outcomes. For learners with little game experience and more negative game attitudes, however, gamification led to diminished outcomes. Proxy variables, which include gender and age, are not causally related to the effectiveness of gamification but correlated with psychological constructs that are. For example, age moderates the effectiveness of gamification interventions in part because older adults tend to find gamified instruction more difficult to use than non-gamified instruction (Kovisto & Hamari, 2014). In this case, age is not necessarily causing gamified instruction to be more difficult to use; instead, generational differences in traits related to technology may be contributing to this effect. Gender, another proxy variable, tends to affect gaming preferences, in that males on average are more motivated by achievement game elements, and females on average are more motivated by social game elements (Greenberg et al., 2010). Ultimately, because gamification can be helpful to some but harmful to others, it is critical to consider the particular characteristics of any targeted trainee population.

Situational and contextual level moderators affect how well gamification interventions work across different situations and in different organizational contexts. When implementing gamification, it is important to consider a variety of situational moderators of training effectiveness, including climate/culture, supervisor support, and employee buy-in. Further, it is important to understand how each of these contextual influences is uniquely affected by gamification interventions. Climate and culture, which include factors like organizational commitment for training and transfer (Darden, Hampton, & Howell, 1989) and the opportunity or need for training (Ford et al., 1992), can affect non-gamified training effectiveness and should be considered when implementing any training intervention (Ostroff, Kinicki, & Muhammad, 2013). When gamifying, consideration of organizational climate for gamification is critical (Landers & Goldberg, 2014; Landers & Armstrong, 2015). Perceived supervisor support is another contextual-level moderator that affects the success of a training interventions (e.g., Ford et al., 1992; Foxon, 1997; Lim, 2001; Noe & Schmitt, 1986). If supervisors view gamification negatively, the trainee will likely be less motivated or have less favorable reactions toward the training (Landers & Callan, 2012). Lastly, employee buy-in and consent are critical to the success of gamfied training interventions (Heeter et al., 2011; Mollick & Rothbard, 2014). When implementing gamified training, consent can moderate the response to the gamification such that consent to gamification can increase positive affect while lack of consent can decrease positive affect (Mollick & Rothbard, 2014). Given the potential for situational and contextual variables to impact the effectiveness of a gamified training intervention, it is important to consider the impact of these variables prior to gamifying existing training.

11.2 Relevant Psychological Theory

Although gamification is the process of modifying existing training using game elements and design approaches derived from game science, this does not imply that the psychology underlying gamification is new or unexplored. Most motivational concepts in gamification science are themselves derived from psychology and contextualized to the context of playing games. Because of this, the games and gamification literatures have explored contextualized psychological theories sometimes to a greater extent than psychology has, and it is this literature that gamification leans on. In short, games researchers often know more about how to use psychology to influence people's behaviors in the context of a gameful experience than psychologists do. Thus, understanding how to gamify training effectively requires knowledge of relevant psychological theory as well as how such theory can be operationalized in a gameful way. The remainder of this section will explore and provide an example of each of these perspectives for each major set of gamification-relevant psychological theories.

11.2.1 Operant Conditioning

Operant conditioning is enacting a desired response by modifying behavior through two types of operants: reinforcers and punishers (Skinner, 1953). Reinforcers, which are stimuli either added (i.e., positive reinforcers) or removed (i.e., negative reinforcers) from a baseline situation, increase the probability that a behavior will be repeated. Positive reinforcement refers to the strengthening of behavior through consequences that an individual believes to be rewarding, whereas negative reinforcement strengthens behavior by removing an unpleasant stimulus. In contrast, punishers decrease the probability of repeated behavior or discourage tendencies of behaving in targeted ways (Skinner, 1953). Reinforcement schedules are specific plans for implementing positive or negative reinforcement (Staddon & Cerutti, 2003). There are four types of reinforcement schedules: fixed-interval, fixed-ratio, variable-interval, and variable-ratio. A fixed-interval schedule issues a response to a reinforcing stimulus after a specific time interval has passed, while in a fixed-ratio schedule issues a fixed number of responses per stimulus (Ferster & Skinner, 1957). In a variable-interval schedule, the intervals for reinforcement occur periodically, within randomized time-frames, whereas variable-ratio schedules issue reinforcers randomly after a specific number of responses (Ferster & Skinner, 1957; Zieler,

1968). Implementing reinforcement schedules can reinforce a desired set of behaviors, which, in the case of gamification, can lead to improved training outcomes if target behaviors, reinforcers, and punishers are chosen carefully.

Game elements like points and badges can be used as reinforcers to drive an individual to complete a specific task or engage in a target behavior (Kapp, 2012). For example, Antin and Churchill (2011) explained how badges could be utilized as reinforcers by attributing status, reputation, and group identification to their attainment. Thus, if a badge can be designed to be perceived as a reward, individuals will be more likely to engage in behaviors necessary for badge collection. Badge possession may be viewed as rewarding if it elevates others' perceptions of the badge holder; provides information about the badge holder's skills, expertise, and accomplishments; or creates a shared experience amongst badge holders. In addition to designing game elements as reinforcers, reinforcement schedules can be used to improve the effectiveness of gamification (Linehan, Kirman, & Roche, 2015). For example, points, badges, and other gamified elements appear to evoke behavior based on the kind of reinforcement schedule given (Ferster & Skinner, 1957). For example, variable ratio schedules elicit high and steady response rates and can be the most economical but have been criticized because the work produced by them may be disproportional to the rewards offered, which could be viewed as exploitative (Linehan, Kirman, & Roche, 2015).

By adding game elements intended to reward learners, a learning designer can modify learner perceptions and potentially increase engagement on a subject. Stansbury and Earnest (2017), for example, gamified an Industrial-Organizational psychology course. Students were randomly assigned to gamified or traditional courses consisting of the same course material; however, the gamified course added game elements of leveling up, feedback, exposition, and choice. These game elements reinforced students' participation by associating these external motivators, which generally take the form of public achievement recognition, with exposure to course material. The gamified course led to increased perceptions of course content understanding, reinforcement of key concepts, and increased enjoyment of course content compared to the traditional condition, suggesting some success from this gamification intervention.

11.2.2 Expectancy-Based Theories

Expectancy theories describe how people are motivated based upon their beliefs regarding behaviors. The most well-known expectancy theory, proposed by Vroom (1964), describes how the interaction between an individual's expectancy, instrumentality, and valence leads to behavior (Lawler & Suttle, 1973; Parijat & Bagga, 2014). Expectancy is the perceived probability that effort will result in an immediate behavioral outcome. Instrumentality is the perceived probability that the behavior will result in a reward. Valence is the attractiveness, value, or the liking of that reward. In most VIE models, these three beliefs are quantified and multiplied to determine motivation. The expectancy-value model, which is distinct from Vroom's expectancy theory, is comprised of three slightly different factors of motivation: expectancy, value, and an affective component (Pintrich & De Groot, 1990). In an expectancy-value framework, expectancy is the individual's belief in their ability to accomplish a task, value is the individual's thoughts of the importance of the task, and the affective component refers to the emotional reaction of the individual to a task (Pintrich et al., 1993). Although they differ in a few key ways, the expectancy-value model and Vroom's expectancy theory both utilize expected outcomes of engaging in a particular behavior as a motivator of that behavior.

By leveraging expectancy theories, game elements can be used to encourage motivation to partake in specific tasks (Richter, Raban, & Rajaeli, 2015). Badges and leaderboards can be motivating by eliciting feelings of status and reputation, achievement, and accomplishment. By these theories, game elements are effective in motivating learners if the learner has high expectancies, instrumentality, and valence for the behaviors and outcomes associated with the gamification intervention. For example, badges and leaderboards can invoke competition by putting the behaviors of an individual in reference to others (Blohm & Leimeister, 2013). An individual that succeeds in obtaining badges or climbing a leaderboard may gain a sense of status and recognition, motivating them if they have high valence for status and recognition (McNamara, Jackson, & Graesser, 2010). Points can also be understood through the lens of expectancy theory. Points can provide a more evident connection between effort, performance, and outcomes, increasing the point-associated behavior (Von Ahn & Dabbish, 2008). Therefore, game-elements can increase the motivation of an individual by creating distinct relationships between targeted behaviors such as collecting badges, earning points, or ranking on leaderboards, with the benefits of that behavior. However, this is dependent upon the individual viewing these rewards as important or valuable.

Expectancy theory suggests that the connection between the expectancy of a desired outcome is what motivates an individual; therefore, the addition of game-elements can be used to fortify this connection. Using this approach, Browne, Anand, and Gosse (2014) explored the impact of gamifying a learning application on low literacy adults' ability to differentiate various homophones. The application consisted of six different groups of homophones (e.g., it's/its, your/you're), which participants needed to accurately differentiate. They gamified this process by incorporating badges (green/gold check marks), levels, and goals. Participants in the experiment were individuals who wished to enhance their literacy; therefore, they expected that their efforts would influence their behaviors on the gamified tasks. In regard to instrumentality, gold and green check marks were immediately awarded after the completion of a level; therefore, there was a clear connection between completing tasks and the rewards associated with them.

11.2.3 Self-Regulatory Theories

Self-regulation is defined as the maintenance and modification of personal goals, where goals are internal representations of desired states (Vancouver, 2008;

Vancouver & Day, 2005). An individual regulates behavior to reduce the discrepancy a goal creates between actual performance and a desired state of performance (Latham & Locke, 1991). Thus, self-regulation can act as a mediator between set goals and performance (Kanfer & Ackerman, 1989). One self-regulatory theory that captures this relationship is goal-setting theory, which states that difficult, specific goals prompt action because they direct attention and action, inspire effort, increase persistence, and motivate the pursuit of improved performance strategies (Latham & Locke, 1990; Locke & Latham, 2002). There are four key moderators of the goal-performance relationship: commitment, feedback, task-complexity, and situational constraints (Locke & Latham, 2006). People are only committed to a difficult goal when it is of personal importance and they believe in their own ability to achieve said goal (i.e., self-efficacy). Feedback enables people to neatly track their progress toward goal attainment. As tasks advance in complexity, the effectiveness of a goal is dependent on the effectiveness of one's performance strategies given the complexity of a task. Goals can drive performance when there are appropriate amounts of time and resources to achieve those goals.

Leaderboards, progress bars, and badges are elements of games that align well with goal-setting theory (Antin & Churchill, 2011; Hsu, Chang, & Lee, 2013). More specifically, leaderboards have been shown to elicit motivation to regulate behavior similarly to goal-setting; when presented with a leaderboard containing scores corresponding to impossible, difficult, moderate, and easy goals, participants tended to perform at the level of a difficult goal (Landers, Bauer, & Callan, 2017), as would be expected in a traditional goal-setting intervention. Progress bars serve as useful feedback that regularly tracks performance outcomes (Hsu et al., 2013). As for badges, they are identifiable and quantifiable signs of accomplishment that vary in task-complexity and personal importance. Badges are specifically awarded to an individual who has performed and completed an explicit task or goal.

To utilize goal-setting theory in gamification, game elements should be accompanied with, or serve as a function of, the four key moderators of the goal-performance relationship, which should maximize goal attainment. Using this approach, Singer and Schneider (2012) gamified a computer science course to elicit best practice behavior when developing software. They implemented "milestones," which were given to students if they achieved a certain number of goals on software development projects. Earning milestones became increasingly difficult over time as project tasks became more complex, which encouraged more effort throughout the course. Weekly reports were also given to students, enabling them to gauge their progress. In quantitative analyses, the researchers revealed patterns as predicted by goal-setting theory: the increasing difficulty of earning milestones, accompanied with weekly feedback, proved to be motivating, regardless of a student's valence toward the way in which he or she was being motivated. Hamari and Koivisto (2013) conducted an exploratory field experiment to determine whether the use of badges affected user activity of an online trading service. They found that badges *themselves* did not automatically yield significant increases in activity from users. However, users who were committed to the personal goal of badge attainment, and who regularly monitored badge count as a form of feedback, showed increased activity in the trading service.

11.2.4 Self-Determination Theory

Self-determination theory (SDT; Ryan & Deci, 2000b) states that humans regulate their behavior depending on their intrinsic and extrinsic motivations to fulfill three basic psychological needs: competence, autonomy, and relatedness. On its most basic level, SDT differentiates between intrinsic motivation and extrinsic motivation to explain the personal will to act (Gagné & Deci, 2005) and contrasts these from amotivation, defined as a lack of intention and self-determination (Ryan & Deci, 2000b). Intrinsic motivation is defined as the drive to engage in an activity for its enjoyment and inherent satisfaction, and according to previous work on self-determination, situational factors that facilitate or undermine self-motivated autonomy and competence can have a lasting impact intrinsic motivation (Deci & Ryan, 1985). Extrinsic motivation is defined as the performance of an action in order "to attain some separable outcome" (Ryan & Deci, 2000a, p.55) that does not prioritize the enjoyment of performing an action itself. The degree to which someone internalizes regulatory processes, and integrates those processes into his or her sense of self, distinguishes regulatory styles of motivation that vary in level of autonomy. For example, relevant regulatory processes of extrinsic motivation include external rewards and punishments, self-control, or maintenance of identity and values.

There have been several efforts to establish Ryan and Deci's work on SDT as a theoretical foundation for gamification. There has been increasing evidence that game elements can be used to encourage enjoyment and increase intrinsic motivation by satisfying basic psychological needs of autonomy, competence, and relatedness (Ryan, Rigby, & Przybylski, 2006; Sheldon & Filak, 2008). Providing learners with positive feedback on their performance and consistent, achievable challenges satisfies a need for competence (Ryan, Rigby, & Przybylski, 2006). This could include increasing level difficulty and providing positive feedback in the form of badges. Giving learners opportunity for self-direction and acknowledging their feelings satisfies a need for autonomy, which could include choosing avatar features and different storylines. Team play and shared social attitudes toward gamified systems satisfy the need for relatedness (Hamari & Koivisto, 2013; Ryan, Rigby, & Przybylski, 2006). An important effect of enjoyment is that it promotes a higher quality of learning and creativity (Ryan & Deci, 2000b), implying that training can potentially be more enjoyable when game elements are designed effectively. The integration of gamification and SDT has been a burgeoning line of research, but few studies have determined exactly which gaming elements are most appetitive to our basic psychological needs (Seaborn & Fels, 2015).

Overall, researchers have been attempting to devise ways to appropriately operationalize SDT within a gamified system. A group of researchers have validated the conceptualization of enjoyment under SDT by presenting evidence that specific antecedents accounted for 51 percent of the variance in enjoyment during a gaming task (Tamborini et al., 2010). They found that perceived game skill predicted autonomy, intuitive mapping of the controller predicted autonomy and competence, and co-playing predicted relatedness. More recently, Mekler, Brühlmann, Tuch, and Opwis (2017) examined the nature of intrinsic and extrinsic motivations within gamified systems. Mekler et al. showed that specific game elements (i.e., points, levels, and leaderboards) increased overall efforts to perform an image annotation task. Despite this evidence, they could not conclude there were changes in intrinsic motivation. However, the gamified task itself may have not been intrinsically motivating in general, and thereby preventing researchers from accurately capturing intrinsic motivation under a gamified system. That is, the image annotation task employed might have not been inherently satisfying enough to motivate participants intrinsically, regardless of whether the task was gamified.

11.3 Practical Recommendations for Gamifying Training and Development

Because gamification is inspired by the psychology of games and the psychology of games is inspired by psychology itself, it can be difficult to identify which aspects of the literature are most useful when creating gamified training. At first glance, it may appear that basic psychological theories alone are sufficient; however, the serious game design literature and growing gamified learning literatures provide a wealth of information regarding how these theories play out in authentic learning contexts. In the remainder of this chapter, we will summarize the current lessons of these literatures for those seeking to gamify their own training programs.

11.3.1 Implementation into the Training Design Process

Critically, gamification of training should not be attempted unless there is a specific, identifiable problem with a training as it currently exists. It is assumed that the instructional designer has already conducted a training needs assessment to identify performance gaps, developed and implemented training intended to close those gaps, and conducted a training evaluation study. Gamification is most effective when used to enhance training when the results of a training evaluation suggest specific motivational or affective deficits. Although a growing research literature has demonstrated the merits of games and gamification in learning (Bedwell et al., 2012), this pales in comparison to the vast pre-existing training literature. When unsure of how to improve a training design, it is recommended to thoroughly explore the recommendations already firmly established in the training literature before attempting to use novel approaches like gamification. The empirical evidence supporting gamified learning is still sparse, and the recommendations within the literature may not be complete or well-validated. It is possible that learning may be improved by using simple techniques rather than attempting to develop a complex game-like learning context. For example, in addition to post-training learning measures, practice tests may be used throughout the training to enhance recall (Roediger & Karpicke, 2006). This addition is easily implemented and supported by the literature (Rowland, 2014). In general, if your training is not "broken," do not try to "fix" it with gamification. Gamifying an already effective training could possibly worsen outcomes, as not all gamification leads to improved learning (Armstrong & Landers, 2017).

Gamification of training is a process in which training content and methods are modified using game elements. This process is incremental in nature, whereby the instructional designer modifies pieces of the training bit by bit to improve learning outcomes. The instructional designer may choose to incrementally modify the training content with game elements or the training method. For example, the training content could be modified by adding elements of narrative, or game fiction. Armstrong and Landers (2017) modified company laptop security training content by incorporating a narrative component to relay the training material. Instead of presenting training content via slideshow or webpage, the content was woven into a storyline in which trainees learned the content in the process of reading a story. This gamified training was incremental in that the learning material was only slightly changed so that the material could be expressed as a story. The training method may also be enhanced with game elements. For example, a self-paced online training method may be gamified by the addition of progress bars or badges for completing different modules. Again, this change is incremental over the original training method. Trainees learn by reading or viewing material, but the process is gamified to provide feedback to the trainee on their progress. It is possible that with the addition of enough game elements, the training design might eventually become a game. As more game elements are added to the training, such as images, sounds, stories, challenges, feedback, and social aspects, the training certainly becomes more game-like. However, this is not necessarily the end goal of the gamification of training. It should only be a by-product of modifying existing training to improve specific outcomes.

To gamify an underperforming training program, the instructional designer must first understand what needs to be improved about the existing training process. This necessitates a training evaluation study, where outcomes like reactions, learning, behavioral transfer, organizational-level performance outcomes, or return-on-investment are measured. Once it is known which outcome is lacking, the instructional designer can work backwards to determine what changes to make to the training. For example, if reactions to the training are poor, designers should try to hone in on which type of reaction is lacking. If trainees dislike the training (i.e., poor affective reactions), it suggests a different remedy than if they find the training to be useless (i.e., poor utility reactions; Alliger et al., 1997). If trainees are not demonstrating learning, designers should try to hone in on the type of learning that the training targets. A deficit in demonstrated declarative knowledge of facts would suggest a different remedy is needed compared to a deficit in procedural knowledge or skill. If trainees' motivations or attitudes are not changed by the training as intended (i.e., affective learning; Kraiger, Ford, & Salas, 1993), this would suggest another different remedy. Once the specific outcome discrepancy has been identified, psychological theory and training theory can be used to continue to identify the root of the problem. Once the root of the problem has been identified, it is time for the instructional designer to consider whether game elements can be used to solve that problem. For example, if trainees are not demonstrating declarative knowledge learning, the designer might consider what mediators may be at play influencing learning. Colquitt, LePine, and Noe (2000) found meta-analytic evidence suggesting that motivation to learn is a key mediator in the training-learning relationship. Game elements intended to improve motivation to learn would be most appropriate in this instance (e.g., game fiction, conflict/challenge, rules/goals, control; Bedwell et al., 2012). To give another example, if behavioral transfer is not occurring post-training, the instructional designer may need to consider what moderators may be influencing the effects of the training design on the outcome. Blume, Ford, Baldwin, and Huang (2010) found meta-analytic evidence suggesting that transfer of skill-based training may depend on the type of skill being trained (i.e., open skills like leadership vs. closed skills like computer programming). In this case, game elements would not necessarily be helpful in improving transfer because the training material itself may impact the likelihood of it being transferred to the workplace.

11.3.2 Targeting Psychological Mediators with Game Elements

To target psychological mediators with game elements, the instructional designer must conduct a needs analysis (Surface, 2012) for gamification. This needs analysis starts by identifying the psychological characteristic that is problematic. To do this, the instructional designer may use surveys or focus groups to collect data about the training, which can be part of the training evaluation process mentioned previously. The data collection effort should try to investigate the typical culprits of ineffective training, while also including open-ended components to gather more contextual information and catch any unexpected findings. The typical problem constructs in a training design are the learning outcomes and mediators between training and those outcomes. Thus, in conducting a training evaluation, it would be prudent to collect data on learning retention, learning application (i.e., transfer), and reactions or satisfaction with the training. In addition, measures of motivation to learn or attitudes regarding the training content or method are good to include, as motivation and attitudes likely impact the success of most trainings. Asking open-ended questions of trainees about what they liked or did not like, what they found to be effective, what they learned, or what they believed the purpose of the training to be can help round out a full picture of the effectiveness of the training in the event the problem construct is out of the ordinary.

After the data are collected, the instructional designer should try to identify which criterion construct is most likely the problem. Each criterion measured should have an ideal point or level at which the instructional designer or organization desires trainees to be. This desired point or level could be a percent of answers correct on a training test (e.g., 80 percent correct to pass a test), familiarity with a given training topic where the maximum possible level is desirable (e.g., 5.0 out of 5.0 on familiarity with Microsoft Office products), or a motivational or attitudinal construct where the maximum possible level is desirable (e.g., 5.0 out of 5.0 on a motivation-to-learn scale). To determine problematic criterion constructs, criterion scores should be measured and subtracted from desired levels to assess training gaps. These training gaps can then be prioritized based on a variety of criteria and resolved accordingly (Watkins, Meiers, & Visser, 2012). Assuming all gaps in training criteria are equally important, the largest gap may take priority and gamification may be implemented to improve that gap. However, training outcomes are not always equally important. In these situations, the gaps that result in the largest costs to the organization or the greatest consequences if left unaddressed should take precedence, even if the gap itself is not the largest among all constructs measured. Once gaps have been prioritized, each gap can be investigated in turn, exploring the root causes of the gap. For a given training gap, the root cause may be any number of issues: the psychological measure may be unreliable or invalid, the training content may be confusing, the trainees may be lacking attention or motivation, etc. Root cause analysis may require further surveys, interviews, focus groups, or data analysis, but will lead the instructional designer to the exact cause of the gap, yielding a psychological construct to target for improvement. Once a criterion construct has been targeted for improvement, the instructional designer should select game elements that are theoretically tied to that construct. The theory of gamified learning game attribute taxonomy (Landers, 2014; see Table 11.1) provides a list of possible game element categories to consider adding to a training context to improve outcomes, and ties between these elements and target constructs vary in both quality of evidence and strength of tie. This taxonomy provides a good start for reasoning through a solution to the problematic training construct. Next, we provide several examples of game elements that are theoretically or logically tied to training-related constructs to demonstrate the process of gamifying training. First, if post-training knowledge retention is deficient, the instructional designer may conclude that trainees need to spend more time reviewing and practicing the material during the training session. According to the testing effect (Roediger & Karpicke, 2006), practicing recall is more effective than large amounts of studying at improving knowledge retention. In order to promote practicing recall, the instructional designer could integrate a practice quiz into the training by creating a review game (e.g., Jeopardy! or any other popular game show format). Adding game elements like rules/goals, feedback via points or a score, and social aspects like teamwork can incrementally improve on the practice quiz training method to provide a more memorable and enjoyable experience during the training process. To give a second example, trainees may be inattentive during a lecture-style training. To keep trainees attentive, the instructional designer could create a task to keep trainees focused on the presenter and materials. Different images and symbols or specific topics and keywords may be included within a lecture slideshow and trainees could be tasked with finding these images or keywords and marking them on a bingo card. This game-like task may not improve learning per se, but the activity will keep trainees engaged with the presentation and paying attention to the slideshow to complete the task. For a third example, perhaps training motivation is the root cause of the problem. Adding media to the training may make the training more fun and enjoyable, improving trainee motivation. Using humorous but relevant images, videos, activities, and discussions can improve the intrinsic motivation to participate in the training session. This example may not appear to be as game-like as the previous examples, but this approach would still be considered gamification, as media, humor, and other activities are still pieces of games that make them enjoyable.

Once game elements have been implemented into training, data must be collected once again to evaluate the new training design. If a problem persists, the instructional designer will need to repeat the entire process. As with any training, a needs assessment or gap analysis must be conducted, training must be designed with the intention to close prioritized gaps, the training must again be implemented, and evaluation data must be collected. As the training development cycle continues, iterations can be made based on what is working or failing to meet the goals of the training. For example, perhaps motivation to learn is initially identified as the issue and a point and leaderboard system is implemented to improve motivation via competition. If the evaluation data do not indicate improved motivation after implementing the gamified training, perhaps a different game element should be used that better aligns with the theoretical target construct. Alternatively, if motivation improves, but another learning outcome decreases, the instructional designer may need to conduct a more thorough needs assessment as another construct may be at play in affecting learning besides motivation. Once the problem has been finally resolved, the scientist-practitioner should publish his or her work so that other instructional designers do not make the same mistakes. In this manner, a scientific literature can be built, which is especially important for the nascent field of gamified learning.

11.4 Conclusions

Although gamification is sometimes presented as a "new" approach to training, this chapter describes how the techniques used in gamification often involve existing training design techniques. Instead, the "new" aspects of gamification are (1) the systematic, science-based targeting of meaningful outcomes using this game element toolkit and (2) the acceptance of both psychological and games research as valuable sources of information regarding how to make learning more engaging and compelling. Specifically, psychological theory serves as an effective and sizable foundation on which to build gamification interventions, and games research provides a record of how psychological theory has already been implemented to create fun and compelling experiences. This knowledge is what is harnessed in gamification. To enable this for the reader, we provide specific guidance on how to translate this advice into training design practice. With this chapter, we hope that training designers will be able to gamify their training content in a cost-effective and impactful way to better meet their training goals.

References

Alliger, G. M., Tannenbaum, S. I., Bennett, W., Jr., Traver, H., & Shotland, A. (1997). A meta-analysis of the relations among training criteria. *Personnel Psychology, 50*, 341–358. doi:10.1111/j.1744–6570.1997.tb00911.x.

Antin, J. & Churchill, E. F. (2011). Badges in social media: A social psychological perspective. In *CHI 2011 Gamification Workshop Proceedings* (pp. 1–4). New York, NY: ACM.

Armstrong, M. B. & Landers, R. N. (2017). An evaluation of gamified training: Using narrative to improve reactions and learning. *Simulation & Gaming, 48*, 513–538. doi:10.1177/1046878117703749.

Arthur Jr, W., Bennett Jr, W., Edens, P. S., & Bell, S. T. (2003). Effectiveness of training in organizations: a meta-analysis of design and evaluation features. *Journal of Applied Psychology, 88*, 234–245. doi:10.1037/0021–9010.88.2.234.

Baron, R. M. & Kenny, D. A. (1986). The moderator–mediator variable distinction in social psychological research: Conceptual, strategic, and statistical considerations. *Journal of Personality and Social Psychology, 51*, 1173–1182.

Bedwell, W. L., Pavlas, D., Heyne, K., Lazzara, E. H., & Salas, E. (2012). Toward a taxonomy linking game attributes to learning: An empirical study. *Simulation & Gaming, 43*, 729–760. doi:10.1177/1046878112439444.

Blohm, I. & Leimeister, J. M. (2013). Gamification. *Business & Information Systems Engineering, 5*, 275–278. doi:10.1007/s12599-013–0273-5.

Blume, B. D., Ford, J. K., Baldwin, T. T., & Huang, J. L. (2010). Transfer of training: A meta-analytic review. *Journal of Management, 36*, 1065–1105. doi:10.1177/0149206309352880.

Bogost, I. (2011). Gamification is bullshit. In S. P. Waltz & S. Deterding (Eds.), *The Gameful World* (pp. 65–79). Cambridge, MA: MIT Press.

Brown, K. G. (2001). Using computers to deliver training: Which employees learn and why? *Personnel Psychology, 54*, 271–296. doi:10.1111/j.1744–6570.2001.tb00093.x.

Browne, K., Anand, C., & Gosse, E. (2014). Gamification and serious game approaches for adult literacy tablet software. *Entertainment Computing, 5*(3), 135–146.

Burke, L. A. & Hutchins, H. M. (2007). Training transfer: An integrative literature review. *Human Resource Development Review, 6*, 263–296. doi:10.1177/1534484307303035.

Carini, R. M., Kuh, G. D., & Klein, S. P. (2006). Student engagement and student learning: Testing the linkages. *Research in Higher Education, 47*, 1–32. doi:10.1007/s11162-005–8150-9.

Colquitt, J. A., LePine, J. A., & Noe, R. A. (2000). Toward an integrative theory of training motivation: A meta-analytic path analysis of 20 years of research. *Journal of Applied Psychology, 85*(5), 678–707. doi:10.1037//0021–9010.g5.5.678.

Darden, W. R., Hampton, R., & Howell, R. D. (1989). Career versus organizational commitment: Antecedents and consequences of retail salespeople's commitment. *Journal of Retailing, 65*, 80–106.

Deci, E. L. & Ryan, R. M. (1985). *Intrinsic motivation and self-determination in human behavior*. New York, NY: Plenum. John Wiley & Sons.

Deterding, S., Sicart, M., Khaled, R., Nacke, L., O'Hara, K. E., & Dixon, D. (2011). Gamification: Toward a definition. Proceedings of the CHI 2011 Gamification Workshop, Vancouver, BC. doi:10.1145/2181037.2181040.

Ferster, C. B. & Skinner, B. F. (1957). *Schedules of reinforcement* (pp. 44–137). East Norwalk, CT: Appleton-Century-Crofts. doi:http://dx.doi.org/10.1037/10627–004.

Ford, J. K., Quiñones, M. A., Sego, D. J., & Sorra, J. S. (1992). Factors affecting the opportunity to perform trained tasks on the job. *Personnel Psychology, 45*, 511–527.

Foxon, M. (1997). The influence of motivation to transfer, action planning, and manager support on the transfer process. *Performance Improvement Quarterly, 10*, 42–63.

Gagné, M. & Deci, E. L. (2005). Self-determination theory and work motivation. *Journal of Organizational Behavior, 26*, 331–362. doi:10.1002/job.322.

Garris, R., Ahlers, R., & Driskell, J. E. (2002). Games, motivation, and learning: A research and practice model. *Simulation & Gaming, 33*(4), 441–467. doi:https://doi.org/10.1177/1046878102238607.

Gartner. (2012). Gartner says by 2014, 80 percent of current gamified applications will fail to meet business objectives primarily due to poor design [press release]. Retrieved from www.gartner.com/newsroom/id/2251015.

Graham, S. & Perin, D. (2007). A meta-analysis of writing instruction for adolescent students. *Journal of Educational Psychology, 99*, 445–476. doi:10.1037/0022–0663.99.3.445.

Greenberg, B. S., Sherry, J., Lachlan, K., Lucas, K., & Holmstrom, A. (2010). Orientations to video games among gender and age groups. *Simulation & Gaming, 41*, 238–259. doi:10.1177/1046878108319930.

Hamari, J. & Koivisto, J. (June 2013). Social motivations to use gamification: An empirical study of gamifying exercise. In *ECIS 2013 Completed Research*. http://aisel.aisnet.org/ecis2013_cr/105

Hamari, J., Koivisto, J., & Sarsa, H. (January 2014). Does gamification work? – A literature review of empirical studies on gamification. In *System Sciences (HICSS)*, 2014 47th Hawaii International Conference on System Sciences (pp. 3025–3034). IEEE.

Heeter, C., Lee, Y. H., Magerko, B., & Medler, B. (2011). Impacts of forced serious game play on vulnerable subgroups. *International Journal of Gaming and Computer-Mediated Simulations (IJGCMS), 3*, 34–53. doi:10.4018/jgcms.2011070103.

Hsu, S. H., Chang, J. W., & Lee, C. C. (2013). Designing attractive gamification features for collaborative storytelling websites. *Cyberpsychology, Behavior, and Social Networking, 16*, 428–435. https://doi.org/10.1089/cyber.2012.0492.

Kanfer, R. (1991). Motivation theory and industrial and organizational psychology. In M. D. Dunnette & L. M. Hough (Eds.), *Handbook of industrial and organizational psychology* (vol. 1, pp. 75–170.). Palo Alto, CA: Consulting Psychologists Press.

Kanfer, R. & Ackerman, P. L. (1989). Motivation and cognitive abilities: An integrative/aptitude-treatment interaction approach to skill acquisition. *Journal of Applied Psychology, 74*(4), 657–690. http://dx.doi.org/10.1037/0021–9010.74.4.657.

Kapp, K. M. (2012). *The gamification of learning and instruction: Game-based methods and strategies for training and education.* San Francisco, CA: John Wiley & Sons.

Kirkpatrick, D. L. (1959). Techniques for evaluating training programs. *Journal of the American Society of Training Directors, 13*, 3–9.

Koivisto, J. & Hamari, J. (2014). Demographic differences in perceived benefits from gamification. *Computers in Human Behavior, 35*, 179–188. doi:https://doi.org/10.1016/j.chb.2014.03.007.

Kraiger, K. (2002). *Creating, implementing, and managing effective training and development: State-of-the-art lessons for practice*. San Francisco, CA: Jossey-Bass.

Kraiger, K., Ford, J. K., & Salas, E. (1993). Application of cognitive, skill-based, and affective theories of learning outcomes to new methods of training evaluation. *Journal of Applied Psychology, 78*, 311–328. http://dx.doi.org/10.1037/0021–9010.78.2.311.

Kulik, J. A., Kulik, C. L. C., & Cohen, P. A. (1980). Effectiveness of computer-based college teaching: A meta-analysis of findings. *Review of Educational Research, 50*, 525–544.

Landers, R. N. (2015). Developing a theory of gamified learning: Linking serious games and gamification of learning. *Simulation & Gaming, 45*, 752–768. doi:10.1177/1046878114563660(6).

Landers, R. N., Auer, E. M., Collmus, A. B. & Armstrong, M. B. (2018). Gamification science, its history and future: Definitions and a research agenda. Simulation & Gaming *49*, 315–337.

Landers, R. N. & Armstrong, M. B. (2015). Enhancing instructional outcomes with gamification: An empirical test of the technology-enhanced training effectiveness model. *Computers in Human Behavior, 71*, 499–507. https://doi.org/10.1016/j.chb.2015.07.031.

Landers, R. N. & Callan, R. C. (2011). Casual social games as serious games: The psychology of gamification in undergraduate education and employee training. In M. Ma, A. Oikonomou, & L. C. Jain (Eds.), *Serious games and edutainment applications* (pp. 399–423). New York, NY: Springer. doi:10.1007/978–1-4471–2161-9_20.

Landers, R. N. & Callan, R. C. (2012). Training evaluation in virtual worlds: Development of a model. *Journal of Virtual Worlds Research, 5*, 1–20. doi:10.4101/jvwr.v5i3.6335.

Landers, R. N. & Goldberg, A. S. (2014). Online social media in the workplace: A conversation with employees. In M. D. Coovert & L. F. Thompson (Eds.), *Psychology of workplace technology* (pp. 284–306). New York, NY: Routledge Academic..

Landers, R. N., Armstrong, M. B., & Collmus, A. B. (2017). How to use game elements to enhance learning: Applications of the theory of gamified learning. In M. Ma, A. Oikonomou, & L. C. Jain (Eds.), *Serious* games *and* edutainment applications (vol. 2, pp. 457483). Surrey, UK: Springer. doi:10.1007/978–3-319–51645-5_21.

Landers, R. N., Bauer, K. N., & Callan, R. C. (2017). Gamification of task performance with leaderboards: A goal setting experiment. *Computers in Human Behavior, 71*, 508–515. https://doi.org/10.1016/j.chb.2015.08.008.

Landers, R. N., Bauer, K. N., Callan, R. C., & Armstrong, M. B. (2015). Psychological theory and the gamification of learning. In T. Reiners & L. Wood (Eds.), *Gamification in education and business* (pp. 165–186). Cham, Switzerland: Springer.

Latham, G. P. & Locke, E. A. (1990). *A theory of goal setting and task performance*. Eaglewood Cliffs, NJ: Prentice Hall.

Latham, G. P. & Locke, E. A. (1991). Self-regulation through goal setting. *Organizational Behavior and Human Decision Processes, 50*, 212–247. https://doi.org/10.1016/0749–5978(91)90021-K.

Lawler, E. E. & Suttle, J. L. (1973). Expectancy theory and job behavior. *Organizational Behavior and Human Performance, 9*, 482–503. https://doi.org/10.1016/0030–5073(73)90066–4.

Lim, D. H. (2001). The effect of work experience and job position on international learning transfer. *International Journal of Vocational Education and Training, 9*, 59–74.

Linehan, C., Kirman, B. & Roche, B. (2015) Gamification as behavioral psychology. In S. P. Walz & S. Deterding (Eds.), *The gameful world: Approaches, issues, applications* (pp. 81–105). Cambridge, MA : MIT Press.

Locke, E. A. & Latham, G. P. (2002). Building a practically useful theory of goal setting and task motivation: A 35-year odyssey. *American Psychologist, 57*, 705–717. http://dx.doi.org/10.1037/0003-066X.57.9.705.

Locke, E. A. & Latham, G. P. (2006). New directions in goal-setting theory. *Current Directions in Psychological Science, 15*, 265–268. doi:10.1111/j.1467–8721.2006.00449.x.

Malone, T. W. (1981). Towards a theory of intrinsically motivating instruction. *Cognitive Science, 4*, 333–369. doi:10.1016/S0364-0213(81)80017–1.

McNamara, D. S., Jackson, G. T., & Graesser, A. (2010). Intelligent tutoring and games (TaG). In Y. Baek (Ed.), *Gaming for classroom-based learning: Digital role playing as a motivator of study* (pp. 44–65). Hershey, PA: IGI Global.

Mekler, E. D., Brühlmann, F., Tuch, A. N., & Opwis, K. (2017). Towards understanding the effects of individual gamification elements on intrinsic motivation and performance. *Computers in Human Behavior, 71*, 525–534.

Michael, D. & Chen, S. (2005). *Serious games: Games that educate, train, and inform.* Boston, MA: Thomson Course Technology.

Mitchell, T. R. (1982). Motivation: New direction for theory, research, and practice. *Academy of Management Review, 7*(1), 80–88. doi:10.5465/AMR.1982.4285467.

Mollick, E. R. & Rothbard, N. (2014). Mandatory fun: Consent, gamification and the impact of games at work. The Wharton School Research Paper Series. Retrieved from: http://ssrn.com/abstract=2277103.

Noe, R. A. & Schmitt, N. (1986). The influence of trainee attitudes on training effectiveness: Test of a model. *Personnel Psychology, 39*, 497–523. doi:10.1111/j.1744–6570.1986.tb00950.x.

Norris, J. M. & Ortega, L. (2000). Effectiveness of L2 instruction: A research synthesis and quantitative meta-analysis. *Language Learning, 50*, 417–528. doi:10.1111/0023–8333.00136.

Ostroff, C., Kinicki, A. J., & Muhammad, R. S. (2013). Organizational culture and climate. In I. B. Weiner (Ed.), *Handbook of Psychology* (2nd edn., pp. 643–676). Hoboken, N.J.: John Wiley & Sons. doi:10.1002/0471264385.wei1222.

Paas, F., Tuovinen, J. E., Van Merrienboer, J. J., & Darabi, A. A. (2005). A motivational perspective on the relation between mental effort and performance: Optimizing learner involvement in instruction. *Educational Technology Research and Development, 53*, 25–34.

Parijat, P. & Bagga, S. (2014). Victor Vroom's expectancy theory of motivation: An evaluation. *International Research Journal of Business and Management (IRJBM), 7*, 1–8.

Parker, L. E. & Lepper, M. R. (1992). Effects of fantasy contexts on children's learning and motivation: Making learning more fun. *Journal of Personality and Social Psychology, 62*, 625–633. doi:10.1037/0022–3514.62.4.625.

Pintrich, P. R. & De Groot, E. V. (1990). Motivational and self-regulated learning components of classroom academic performance. *Journal of Educational Psychology, 82*(1), 33–40.

Pintrich, P. R., Smith, D. A., Garcia, T., & McKeachie, W. J. (1993). Reliability and predictive validity of the Motivated Strategies for Learning Questionnaire (MSLQ). *Educational and Psychological Measurement, 53*, 801–813.

Richter, G., Raban, D. R., & Rafaeli, S. (2015). Studying gamification: The effect of rewards and incentives on motivation. In T. Reiners, L. C. Wood (Eds.), *Gamification in Education and Business* (pp. 21–46). Switzerland: Springer International Publishing. doi:10.1007/978–3-319–10208-5_2.

Roediger III, H. L. & Karpicke, J. D. (2006). Test-enhanced learning: Taking memory tests improves long term retention. *Psychological Science, 17*, 249–255. doi:10.1111/j. 1467–9280.2006.01693.x.

Rowland, C. A. (2014). The effect of testing versus restudy on retention: A meta-analytic review of the testing effect. *Psychological Bulletin, 140*, 1432–1463. doi:10.1037/a0037559.

Ryan, R. M. & Deci, E. L. (2000a). Intrinsic and extrinsic motivations: Classic definitions and new directions. *Contemporary Educational Psychology, 25*, 54–67. https://doi .org/10.1006/ceps.1999.1020.

Ryan, R. M. & Deci, E. L. (2000b). Self-determination theory and the facilitation of intrinsic motivation, social development, and well-being. *American Psychologist, 55*, 68. http://dx.doi.org/10.1037/0003-066X.55.1.68.

Ryan, R. M., Rigby, C. S., & Przybylski, A. (2006). The motivational pull of video games: A self-determination theory approach. *Motivation and Emotion, 30*, 344–360. doi:10.1007/s11031-006–9051-8.

Sailer, M., Hense, J., Mandl, H., & Klevers, M. (2013). Psychological perspectives on motivation through gamification. *IxD&A, 19*, 28–37.

Seaborn, K. & Fels, D. I. (2015). Gamification in theory and action: A survey. *International Journal of Human-Computer Studies, 74*, 14–31. https://doi.org/10.1016/j.ijhcs .2014.09.006.

Seidel, T. & Shavelson, R. J. (2007). Teaching effectiveness research in the past decade: The role of theory and research design in disentangling meta-analysis results. *Review of Educational Research, 77*, 454–499. doi:10.3102/0034654307310317.

Sheldon, K. M. & Filak, V. (2008). Manipulating autonomy, competence, and relatedness support in a game-learning context: New evidence that all three needs matter. *British Journal of Social Psychology, 47*, 267–283. doi:10.1348/014466607X238797.

Shen, W. C. M., Liu, D., Santhanam, R., & Evans, D. A. (June 2016). Gamified Technology-Mediated Learning: the Role of Individual differences. In PACIS 2013 Proceedings (p. 47).

Singer, L., & Schneider, K. (June 2012). It was a bit of a race: Gamification of version control. In Games and Software Engineering (GAS), 2012 2nd International Workshop on (pp. 58). IEEE. doi:10.1109/GAS.2012.6225927.

Sitzmann, T. (2011). A meta-analytic examination of the instructional effectiveness of computer-based simulation games. *Personnel Psychology, 64*, 489–528. doi:10.1111/j.1744–6570.2011.01190.x.

Skinner, B. F. (1953). *Science and human behavior*. Simon and Schuster.

Staddon, J. E. & Cerutti, D. T. (2003). Operant conditioning. *Annual Review of Psychology, 54*, 115–144. https://doi.org/10.1146/annurev.psych.54.101601.145124.

Stansbury, J. A. & Earnest, D. R. (2017). Meaningful gamification in an industrial/organizational psychology course. *Teaching of Psychology, 44*, 38–45. https://doi.org/10 .1177/0098628316677645.

Surface, E. A. (2012). Training needs assessment: Aligning learning and capability with performance requirements and organizational objectives. In M. A. Wilson, W. Bennett, Jr., S. G. Gibson, & G. M. Alliger (Eds.), *Series in applied psychology.*

The handbook of work analysis: Methods, systems, applications and science of work measurement in organizations (pp. 437–462). New York, NY: Routledge/ Taylor & Francis Group.

Tamborini, R., Bowman, N. D., Eden, A., Grizzard, M., and Organ, A. (2010), Defining media enjoyment as the satisfaction of intrinsic needs. *Journal of Communication*, *60*: 758–777. doi:10.1111/j.1460–2466.2010.01513.x.

Tay, L. (2010). Employers: Look to gaming to motivate staff. itnews for Australian Business. Retrieved from www.itnews.com.au/News/169862,employers-look-to-gaming-to-motivate-staff.aspx.

Thiel, S. K., Reisinger, M., & Röderer, K. (December 2016). I'm too old for this!: influence of age on perception of gamified public participation. In Proceedings of the 15th International Conference on Mobile and Ubiquitous Multimedia (pp. 343–346). ACM. doi:10.1145/3012709.3016073.

Vancouver, J. B. (2008). Integrating self-regulation theories of work motivation into a dynamic process theory. *Human Resource Management Review, 18*, 1–18. https://doi.org/10.1016/j.hrmr.2008.02.001.

Vancouver, J. B. & Day, D. V. (2005). Industrial and organisation research on self-regulation: from constructs to applications. *Applied Psychology, 54*, 155–185. doi:10.1111/j.1464–0597.2005.00202.x.

Von Ahn, L. & Dabbish, L. (2008). Designing games with a purpose. *Communications of the ACM, 51.* 58–67. doi:10.1145/1378704.1378719.

Vroom, V. H. (1964). *Work and motivation.* New York, NY: John Wiley and Sons.

Warr, P. & Bunce, D. (1995). Trainee characteristics and the outcomes of open learning. *Personnel Psychology, 48*, 347–375. doi:10.1111/j.1744–6570.1995.tb01761.x.

Watkins, R., Meiers, M. W., & Visser, Y. (2012). *A guide to assessing needs: Essential tools for collecting information, making decisions, and achieving development results.* Washington, DC: The World Bank.

Wilson, K. A., Bedwell, W. L., Lazzara, E. H., Salas, E., Burke, C. S., Estock, J. L., . . . Conkey, C. (2009). Relationships between game attributes and learning outcomes. *Simulation & Gaming, 40*, 217–266. doi:10.1177/1046878108321866.

Zeiler, M. D. (1968). Fixed and variable schedules of response-independent reinforcement. *Journal of the Experimental Analysis of Behavior, 11*, 405–414. doi:10.1901/ jeab.1968.11–405.

Zhao, C. M. & Kuh, G. D. (2004). Adding value: Learning communities and student engagement. *Research in Higher Education, 45*, 115–138.

12 Real Career Development with Virtual Mentoring

Past, Present, and Future

Suzanne C. de Janasz and Wendy Murphy

The ability to get work done through virtual means is not only increasingly common but also increasingly necessary (Bailey, Leonardi, & Barley, 2012; Tannenbaum et al., 2012). As organizations expand offices and serve customers globally, it is no surprise that more and more business professionals report working often or very often with people using technology or have worked remotely during their career (96 percent and 37 percent, respectively, according to recent surveys) (Brooks, 2015; Harter, Agrawal, & Sorenson, 2014). Computer-mediated communication (CMC) will only increase, as each year 74 trillion emails are sent worldwide, and with 3.7 billion email users, that means 54 percent of the planet uses email.[1] This growth of virtual one-to-one interactions – much of which evolves organically, occurs intermittently, and is unmonitored (Makarius & Larson, 2017) – is responsible for virtual work becoming the norm for many employees (Reyt & Wiesenfeld, 2015; Thomas, 2016).

In a business climate characterized by layoffs, worker mobility, boundaryless careers, and increased work demands, today's tech-savvy employees must recognize the need for using both traditional and electronic means to expand their network of developmental relationships critical for career success (de Janasz, Sullivan, & Whiting, 2003; Dobrow et al., 2012; Higgins & Kram, 2001; Sproull & Kiesler, 1999). Such a network of developmental relationships features mentors and other developers who provide career and psychosocial support to a focal individual, enhancing his or her performance and career satisfaction (Higgins & Kram, 2001). This support is more critical than ever, as turbulent times force even the most promising individuals to rethink their careers and strategies for navigating amidst the new normal, where individuals change jobs about every 4.5 years (more frequently for millennials) (de Janasz et al., 2003; Casselman, 2015). As virtual work becomes the norm, virtual mentoring – a process in which the primary channel of communication between mentors and protégés is electronic (Hamilton & Scandura, 2003) – is likely to become more common within one's developmental network. Scholars have theorized that e-mentoring has great potential as a complement or augmentation to traditional mentoring (Ensher, Heun, & Blanchard, 2003; Hamilton & Scandura, 2003), however, there have been few empirical studies of e-mentoring in the management field (for exceptions see de

---

[1] www.lifewire.com/how-many-emails-are-sent-every-day-1171210; www.lifewire.com/how-many-email-users-are-there-1171213. Accessed 6/3/17.

Janasz, Ensher, & Heun, 2008; de Janasz & Godshalk, 2013; Murphy, 2011; and Smith-Jentsch et al., 2008).

In this chapter, we trace the growth of e-mentoring from the intersection of mentoring and computer-mediated communication (CMC) in a context of the changing nature of careers. Next, we review the current state of the literature – focusing on antecedents (e.g., dyad characteristics), mentoring received (e.g., instrumental support), and outcomes (e.g., increased network), including opportunities and challenges for this research. Finally, we offer suggestions for future research on and practical implications of e-mentoring in this rapidly changing career landscape.

12.1 Research on E-Mentoring

Today's careers reflect the ongoing trends of economic uncertainty, globalization, evolving technology, and workforce diversity. These careers have been called boundaryless (Arthur & Rousseau, 1996), emphasizing the trend toward mobility and flexibility, particularly for knowledge workers who change organizations more frequently, perform their jobs from home or anywhere in the world, and often organize in team or network structures rather than within traditional hierarchies. Along with how work gets done, such careers have evolved to be more self-directed because organizations can no longer offer job security, weakening the psychological contract (Arthur & Rousseau, 1996) and shifting the burden of career development to the individual (Hall, 2002; Sullivan, 1999). Developing a career through a series of opportunities across organizations requires individuals to identify and engage in continuous learning opportunities to develop and apply their skills in new roles. In order to thrive across these diverse and changing environments, workers must adapt quickly to evolving organizational and professional needs. Within this context, mentoring has been recognized as a key developmental tool for individuals to continue to learn and grow in their careers (Chandler, Kram, & Yip, 2001).

E-mentoring evolved from an increasing recognition that there were opportunities for building developmental relationships through CMC, connecting protégés to mentors whom they would otherwise not be able to access. Beyond this, there are several other reasons e-mentoring is beginning to realize its significant potential. First, the millennial generation (born 1980–1996) has grown up with technology; they exhibit a comfort and willingness to engage in work, as well as relationships, through CMC (Gallup, 2016). This generation is now the largest and fastest growing demographic in the global workforce, and organizations that seek ways to attract and retain them are experimenting with internal and external mentoring platforms (e.g., Triple Creek, cf. Francis, 2007) that develop millennials in ways that align with their preferences (Owens, 2006). Second, e-mentoring is significantly less expensive and more flexible than traditional mentoring as communication can occur when and where it is convenient for the parties involved. It also allows personalized, frequent, shorter interactions, which are preferred by millennials (e.g., DeLong, Gabarro, & Lees, 2008). Finally, e-mentoring may remove or reduce some of the barriers inherent in initiating and sustaining a relationship between diverse parties because surface level characteristics (e.g., age, race/ethnicity, gender) are unlikely to be identified or salient (see de Janasz et al., 2008; Murphy, 2011).

Mentoring increases protégés' performance, career satisfaction, and commitment (Chandler et al., 2001; Kram, 1985) because of the support that mentors provide. Investigating e-mentoring relationships, scholars have found that the support received by protégés parallels that found in traditional (i.e., face-to-face) mentoring relationships. This support includes career (or instrumental) development – such as sponsorship, coaching, exposure and visibility, protection – and psychosocial support – such as counseling, acceptance and confirmation, and friendship (de Janasz & Godshalk, 2013; Kram, 1985; Murphy, 2011; Ragins & Kram, 2007). However while e-mentors may provide career and psychosocial support as effectively as face-to-face mentors, Hamilton and Scandura (2003) suggest that they may not be as effective in providing role modeling. Other studies have confirmed that role modeling (a form of vicarious learning) is received by protégés, and may be transmitted through mentors' storytelling and recounting of experiences (e.g., de Janasz & Godshalk, 2013).

Beyond support functions, studies on e-mentoring have identified important antecedents including characteristics of the protégé and of the dyad (protégé-mentor relationship), and found empirical support for several outcomes such as learning, self-efficacy, and satisfaction (de Janasz & Godshalk, 2013; de Janasz, Ensher, & Heun, 2008; Murphy, 2011; Single & Single, 2005). These empirical findings and how the variables relate to one another are depicted in Figure 12.1. Below we will discuss what we know about e-mentoring antecedents and outcomes from the current literature.

12.2 Protégé Characteristics

Individual differences have long been important in the mentoring literature because they may influence the quality of support received through the relationship (Turban & Lee, 2007). In the e-mentoring literature, protégés' comfort with CMC, personality, and previous experience with a mentor were all identified as potentially important predictors of support and success (Hamilton & Scandura, 2003). Early studies on computer training found that users' attitudes toward technology significantly affected their experiences (Torkzadeh, Pflughoeft, & Hall, 1999). Thus, protégés' comfort with CMC has consistently been hypothesized as a critical consideration (Ensher & Murphy, 2007; Single & Single, 2005). However empirical work has shown that this variable is not significant (de Janasz & Godshalk, 2013), likely due to the ubiquity of CMC in our current school and workplace environments.

Similarly, in the traditional face-to-face mentoring research, personality characteristics of protégés were found to affect the extent and quality of interactions

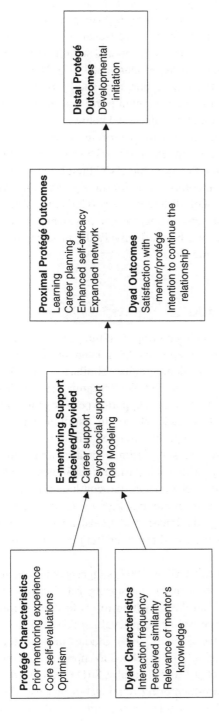

Figure 12.1 *Empirical model of E-mentoring Research*

with their mentors (Wanberg, Kammeyer-Mueller, & Marchese, 2006). Thus, two personality variables were included in Murphy's (2011) empirical study of e-mentoring – core self-evaluations and optimism. Core self-evaluations include the four affective traits of self-esteem, locus of control, emotional stability (or neuroticism), and generalized self-efficacy (Judge, Locke, & Durham, 1997). Neither core self-evaluations nor optimism were related to support received by protégés, however both characteristics were related to career planning and subsequently the more distal outcome of developmental initiation (discussed below).

Finally, protégés' previous experience with mentoring is positively related to interaction frequency in their e-mentoring relationship (DiRenzo et al., 2010). This is consistent with channel expansion theory in the CMC literature, which suggests that experience with a topic (e.g., mentoring relationships) enables individuals to communicate more effectively through different media (Carlson & Zmud, 1999). Therefore, it is useful to include protégé characteristics in e-mentoring research as they may be related to how much and how effectively the protégé–mentor dyad interact, as well as important outcomes.

12.3 Dyad Characteristics

In the traditional face-to-face mentoring literature, several characteristics of the dyad have been shown to be significantly related to support received, including frequency of interaction, demographic similarity, and knowledge exchanged (Wanberg, Welsh, & Hezlett, 2003). Research has confirmed that these characteristics are also important for the support experienced in e-mentoring relationships (e.g., de Janasz & Godshalk, 2013). In addition, having a prior existing relationship also facilitates support provided through an e-mentoring relationship. With a pre-existing relationship, intimacy is accelerated through the recognition of the complementary skills each partner contributes (Kelley et al., 1983). Since it takes time to build a relationship, the continuation of an existing relationship allows for building trust more quickly via CMC (Hinde, 1995). Confirming this line of reasoning, de Janasz and Godshalk (2013) found that a prior relationship with a mentor increased role modeling perceived by protégés via e-mentoring.

The similarity-attraction hypothesis (Allen, 2007) suggests that both actual and perceived similarity are helpful in forming mentoring relationships. Scholars distinguish actual or surface-level similarity, which refers to demographics such as gender, race, and age, from perceived or deep-level similarity, which refers to attitudes and values (Harrison, Price, & Bell, 1998). Studies in e-mentoring have consistently shown that perceived similarity is related to support received whereas actual similarity is not (de Janasz, et al., 2008; Murphy, 2011). Perceived similarity may increase in importance in an e-mentoring relationship because CMC eliminates the availability of surface-level characteristics and instead enables participants to focus on the content of their exchange. This contrasts with traditional mentoring studies that have found satisfaction increases when protégés perceive they are more similar (matched race or gender) to their mentors (Ensher, Grant-Vallone, & Marelich, 2002; Ensher & Murphy, 1997; Turban, Dougherty, & Lee, 2002).

Both social network theory (Dobrow et al., 2012; Higgins, Chandler, & Cram, 2007) and CMC theory (Carlson & Zmud, 1999; Walther, 1996) suggest that the frequency of interaction between protégés and mentors will increase positive outcomes. Studies show that frequent interaction is positively associated with both instrumental and psychosocial support received by protégés in traditional as well as e-mentoring relationships (de Janasz et al., 2008; Eby & Lockwood, 2005; Grant-Vallone & Ensher, 2000; Murphy 2011). Interaction frequency has also been shown to mediate e-mentoring program antecedents and self-efficacy outcomes (DiRenzo, et al., 2010). This is consistent with the CMC literature, which argues that more frequent interaction between electronic partners builds and enhances the relationship (Walther, 1996). In addition, online community studies demonstrate that CMC environments enable participants to obtain social support through frequent interaction with one another and through the identification of common interests (Rheingold, 1993; Wellman & Gulia, 1999), which also boosts perceived similarity.

Traditional mentoring research has shown that mentor characteristics affect mentoring functions provided (Ensher & Murphy, 1997; Koberg, Boss, & Goodman, 1998). Protégés seek mentors with enhanced abilities, knowledge, interpersonal skills, and respect (Gaskill, 1991; Olian et al., 1988). de Janasz and Godshalk (2013) developed the construct "relevant mentor knowledge" to assess protégés' perceptions of how their mentor's skill set complemented protégés' learning needs. They found protégés' perception of the relevance of their e-mentor's knowledge to be positively associated with the career development and role modeling functions. In e-mentoring, effective CMC is central to the process of protégés' assessment of mentors' knowledge, highlighting the salience of content exchanged within the dyad.

12.4 E-Mentoring Outcomes

Research on mentoring has consistently found that these relationships may provide protégés both career (vocational) support and psychosocial support (Allen et al., 2004; Chandler, et al., 2001; Kram, 1985). Career support enhances protégés' learning and provides instrumental assistance, such as coaching and help with challenging assignments, while psychosocial support enhances protégés' sense of competence, clarity of identity, and effectiveness in a professional role (Kram, 1985). Role modeling was originally included as part of the psychosocial function (Kram, 1985) but other studies have found that role modeling is a distinctive type of support in a mentoring relationship (see Pelligrini & Scandura, 2005). Studies on e-mentoring have found that all three functions have been received by protégés (de Janasz, et al., 2008). Similar to traditional mentoring, support is the most direct and proximal outcome of e-mentoring relationships and it is through support received that protégés then experience distal outcomes (de Janasz, et al., 2008; de Janasz & Godshalk, 2013; Murphy, 2011).

Protégé Outcomes. In e-mentoring programs that match students with mentors who are working professionals, researchers have found that more career planning (Murphy, 2011), increased self-efficacy (de Janasz & Godshalk, 2013), and enhanced academic performance (de Janasz, et al., 2008) are all significant outcomes for protégés. Before entering the workforce, career planning, a type of goal setting (Hall & Foster, 1977), is particularly salient for students. Career planning is helpful for student protégés because it is related to subsequent salary and career satisfaction (Gould, 1979; Wayne, et al., 1999).

Self-efficacy is defined as an individual's belief that he or she can successfully perform a specific task or activity (Bandura, 1986). de Janasz, and Godshalk (2013) found that both career support and psychosocial support from e-mentors were related to enhanced self-efficacy. Similarly, Lewis (2002) showed that protégés had improved self-confidence and were more motivated to learn after interactions with their e-mentor. It is likely that these positive effects from e-mentors' support are also reflected in students' increased academic performance (de Janasz, et al., 2008).

Protégé learning is often a key outcome for mentoring programs and several studies demonstrate that learning occurs in traditional mentoring relationships (Eby & Lockwood, 2005; Godshalk & Sosik, 2003; Ragins, Cotton, & Miller, 2000; Wanberg et al., 2003). Similarly, studies of online relationships have suggested that learning and satisfaction are based on the active involvement of both the students and the professionals they engaged (Alavi, Wheeler, & Valacich, 1995; Alavi, Yoo, & Vogel, 1997; Arbaugh, 2005; Arbaugh & Benbunan-Fich, 2006; Fuller, Vician, & Brown, 2006). Affirming these findings, deJanasz and Godshalk (2013) demonstrated that career development was positively associated with enhanced learning in university e-mentoring programs. Through e-mentoring, protégés also learn job-related and discipline-specific information (Single & Single, 2005). Past research demonstrates that when student protégés interact more frequently and receive more support from their e-mentors, they have increased career efficacy (DiRenzo et al., 2010) and receive more job opportunities (de Janasz et al., 2008). In addition, because of the support provided by e-mentors, protégés will expand their own network of professional relationships (de Janasz et al., 2008) which creates opportunities for developmental initiation (see below).

Dyadic Outcomes. Research on traditional mentoring relationships has shown that both career and psychosocial support are positively related to quality of and satisfaction with the relationship (Ensher et al., 2002; Godshalk & Sosik, 2000; Ragins et al., 2000; van Emmerik, 2004), which has been a consistent finding in e-mentoring research as well (de Janasz et al., 2008; Murphy, 2011). Qualities of the relationship itself (i.e., of the dyad) are important predictors of support exchanged and other outcomes. deJanasz and Godshalk (2013) found e-mentor relationship satisfaction was positively related to the psychosocial support and role modeling functions received. In a review of the mentoring literature, Wanberg, Welsh, and Hezlett (2003) emphasize the positive link between satisfaction with their mentor and a protégé's job satisfaction, career satisfaction, life satisfaction, and career commitment. Studies on e-mentoring confirm that protégés who received more support were more likely to continue the relationship with their e-mentors beyond the program requirements (de Janasz & Godshalk, 2013), essentially adding their mentor to their developmental network (Murphy, 2011).

12.5 Distal outcomes: Enhancing Developmental Initiation

Due to the changing nature of careers, it is critical that individuals acquire the skills to enlist new mentoring relationships to assist in their development. Developmental initiation is conceived as developmental relationship-seeking behaviors to improve one's skills, knowledge, performance, or learning (Higgins, Chandler, & Kram, 2007). Unlike mentor initiation, which focuses on seeking relationships only with higher level managers in the workplace (Turban & Dougherty, 1994), developmental initiation includes pursuing relationships within or across organizations including peers and supervisors as well as senior colleagues. This is important because research on developmental networks has shown that mentoring relationships at all levels both within and outside the workplace are related to a variety of outcomes including salary, career satisfaction, and life satisfaction (Murphy & Kram, 2010). Developmental initiation is also distinctive from networking, which is the process of building relationships that are primarily instrumental in helping with one's career, particularly by providing information on new job opportunities (Forret & Dougherty, 2001; Granovetter, 1973; Hwang, Kessler, & Francesco, 2004; Wanberg, Kanfer, & Banas, 2000). Receiving support from mentors is related to networking ability (Blass et al., 2007) and networking skills likely enhance developmental initiation (Murphy, 2011). A key difference from networking is that developmental initiation involves seeking mutually beneficial relationships through a full range of support (Higgins et al., 2007). In one study on e-mentoring, Murphy (2011) found that support received by student protégés increased career planning and intentions to continue the relationship (after the formal program ended), which then increased developmental initiation. Furthermore, levels of developmental initiation increased just from participating in the e-mentoring program.

12.6 Implications for Research and Practice of E-Mentoring

CMC may alter some of the variables that are typically important in face-to-face interactions and relationships. For example, research on traditional face-to-face mentoring has demonstrated that the duration of the relationship moderates the relationship between similarity and support (Turban et al., 2002), and that similarity is more important for shorter term relationships (Allen, 2007). In classroom studies, the duration of the e-mentoring relationships has only been one semester (de Janasz, et al., 2008; de Janasz & Godshalk, 2013; Murphy, 2011), thus one would expect that both dimensions of similarity (perceived and actual) may be important. However, these studies consistently demonstrated that perceived similarity, based on deep-level similarity regarding attitudes, values, and goals, is significantly related to important e-mentoring outcomes whereas actual similarity, based on demographics, is not significant. This means that CMC is fundamentally altering how protégés and mentors engage with one another from the start of the relationship. It also signals great opportunity in organizations that struggle to provide mentoring opportunities to women and people of color. Whereas reports of challenges in the initiation and outcomes of traditional (face-to-face) cross-gender and cross-cultural mentoring pairs are unfortunately common (e.g., Ragins et al., 2000), communicating with one's mentor via CMC helps the pair engage on the basis of deep-level similarity without the distraction of demographic differences.

CMC enables more frequent interaction, characterized by ongoing comments contingent on the previous dialogue (Smith-Jentsch et al., 2008), while simultaneously rendering demographic characteristics unimportant. In reality, e-mentoring often leads to *blended* communication, supplementing email with talking on the phone or meeting in-person (DeRouin, Fritzsche, & Salas, 2005; Ensher et al., 2003), which was found to increase the amount of support received by protégés (Murphy, 2011). Future research should explore whether such support increases the frequency and ease with which mentor and protégé communicate across platforms, and therefore, facilitates higher quality outcomes.

Technology has also enabled several firms to offer external support for large organizations implementing formal mentoring, accessing external mentors, or expanding their program offerings. Such companies provide different forms of support via technology, for example, matching mentors and protégés or a proprietary platform for interaction among participants. We share some key examples of organizations that provide technology resources as external partners. The reality of the mentoring relationships that emerge however is that participants may begin online and evolve to include a phone call, videoconference, or face-to-face meeting as well as utilize other mediums of communication (e.g., social media).

Facilitating the matching process between mentors and protégés can be complex when several variables are taken into consideration (e.g., personality, demographics, functional expertise, learning goals) such that technology can offer a more reliable method. A well-known nonprofit firm, MentorNet, has connected thousands of students to STEM (science, technology, engineering, and mathematics) professionals to create high-quality e-mentoring relationships that expose young people to potential careers in the sciences (see mentornet.org). For over two decades, Menttium based in St. Paul, Minnesota, has facilitated cross-company corporate mentoring relationships for high potential women protégés with senior executives (male or female). Outsourcing the mentor role allows companies to tap into the expertise of other senior executives for their employees and provides opportunities for protégés to develop cross-organizational networks (P-Sontag, Vappie, & Wanberg, 2007). Finally, River in Denver, Colorado (formerly known as Triple Creek), offers a platform through their proprietary software for matching participants, managing relationships, and measuring the outcomes of large-scale mentoring initiatives. These examples are a few among an array of technology-facilitated mentoring processes used in large corporations and nonprofits. It is essential that organizations considering an e-mentoring approach clarify the goals of the program to determine how additional technology might assist their initiative.

12.7 Future Research for E-mentoring's Unasked and Unanswered Questions

While the practice of e-mentoring has existed for about 20 years, empirical study of the phenomenon has barely scratched the surface. Drawing from several research streams, including traditional mentoring, computer-mediated communication, and virtual work, we have begun to discover what is inside the black box of e-mentoring. However, there is much to learn and even more to study as the practice and pace of e-mentoring soars.

12.8 Individual Factors

Several areas in which further study is needed include the individual participants, the context, and the process of interacting. We begin with the individuals. Building on the work of Makarius and Larson (2017), additional research is needed to understand who is most likely to initiate and be successful in a virtual mentoring relationship. For example, in their study of networking behaviors, Forret and Dougherty (2001) found that self-esteem and extraversion were significantly correlated with proactive networking behaviors, which provides opportunities for virtual developmental initiation. While individuals who are introverted or have low self-esteem may be unlikely to initiate a face-to-face mentoring relationship, future research might determine whether they are more or less likely than extroverts to do so in a virtual setting (de Janasz & Godshalk, 2013). It may be that despite the clear-cut benefits of traditional mentoring, introverts who might not be engaging at the rate of their extroverted counterparts would do well to consider e-mentoring to facilitate career development and satisfaction. Another individual difference – learning goal orientation – may also be instructive. Introduced by Dweck and her colleagues (e.g., Bempechat, London, & Dweck, 1991; Dweck & Leggett, 1988), this orientation describes individuals' motivation to understand something new and challenging or build their competence, even if their current skill assessment is low. Godshalk and Sosik (2003) found that protégés with high learning goal orientation (and similarity with their mentor on this characteristic) received more mentoring support, which positively influenced outcomes such as career development and satisfaction, thus, interventions to improve protégés' learning goal orientation may be helpful. Given that visible mentoring conversations (compared to online ones) may be sought as much for learning as for building one's visibility and network, future research might examine whether learning goal orientation may predispose individuals to seek and benefit from online versus traditional mentoring relationships. Finally, mentoring scholars may build on burgeoning research on factors that predict successful completion of fully-online courses. Despite the growing availability of online courses and MOOCs, some suggest that attrition rates are as high as 90 percent or more. One reason offered reflects the social isolation and personal disconnection of the online learner (Molinari, Freshman, & Tan, 2015). While this disconnectedness may happen in a 1:100+ (teacher:students) environment, it is less likely to occur in a mentoring relationship that is by design a 1:1 environment. Nonetheless, future research might discover whether and in what situations individuals who succeed in online learning environments also succeed in e-mentoring relationships – a computer-mediated learning platform between two individuals.

One of the moderating factors that may facilitate e-mentoring's process and outcomes relates to the generation/s represented by and generational similarity of the dyad. Millennials – the first generation to have been born into households with computers and to have grown up surrounded by digital media (Gorman, Nelson, & Glassman, 2004; Raines, 2002) – are used to and comfortable with communication and information technologies. They see work in flexible terms (i.e., place and time) and desire flexible work schedules to achieve their work/life balance goals (Randstad Work Solutions 2007; SHRM, 2009), giving them both aptitude and interest in virtual work (Meyers & Sadaghiani, 2010). One might predict that millennial protégés will report more satisfying and valuable e-mentoring relationships than would protégés who represent an older generational cohort. In addition, we would expect that if the protégé were a millennial but the mentor were a Gen Xer, the process and outcomes might be less favorable than if both members of the dyad were millennials. There are at least two reasons for this. First, several mentoring studies – both traditional and electronic – confirm that perceived similarity is a significant predictor of mentoring received (e.g., Ensher & Murphy, 1997; de Janasz, et al., 2008; de Janasz & Godshalk, 2013). As generational differences reflect the value alignment (or lack thereof) across generational cohorts, one would expect that generational similarity of the dyad would be positively related to mentoring received. Moreover, the nature of virtual communication through flexible technologies (vs. traditional mentoring), wherein the schedules of two parties must be in sync in order for mentoring to be received), we might expect a greater amount of mentoring received in relationships where both participants are millennials, who as a group have the highest technological proficiency (Powers & Myers, 2017).

12.9 Contextual Factors

In terms of the context, in the few settings in which e-mentoring has been empirically examined, the subjects have been primarily university students (e.g., de Janasz, et al., 2008, de Janasz & Godshalk 2013; Murphy, 2011; Smith-Jentsch, et al., 2008) who participated in a required online mentoring assignment. These constraints beg additional research on several fronts. First, given the growing prevalence and importance of mentoring in the workplace, research examining e-mentoring processes and outcomes in a variety of organizational contexts is needed to expand the generalizability of e-mentoring research. Second, whereas in traditional mentoring research, findings indicate that informal mentoring (i.e., without the aid of a formal program or person arranging the dyads) is more effective than formal mentoring, future research on e-mentoring may find that the more informal medium of exchange (virtual vs. face-to-face) neutralizes the differences between dyad self-selection (dyads choose each other without regard to level, organizational, or even geographical constraints) and formalized selection processes. It may also be that the informal, virtual medium supports greater levels of psychosocial support (i.e., friendship) and lower levels of instrumental and role modeling support. Finally, future research should be undertaken in both high-tech and low-tech environments. In a university environment, where students spend multiple hours per day on their computers and phones, the use of CMC-aided mentoring may be more readily received and effective than in organizations less dependent upon technology. Another question concerns whether individuals are assigned to the mentoring relationship. In a study by Smith-Jentsch and colleagues (2008), 51 college seniors were assigned to mentor 102 college freshmen (two protégés per mentor – one in which communication was constrained to a scheduled, virtual chat, while the other was face-to-face). In the two studies by de Janasz and her colleagues (de Janasz et al., 2008 and de Janasz & Godshalk, 2013), protégés initiated a virtual mentoring relationship with a mentor of their choosing. Research in this area suggests that trust may form more quickly when one or both members of the dyad choose their partner (Blake-Beard, O'Neill, & McGowan, 2007). However, there is also research that suggests that over time, the effect of earlier-developing trust evens out (Weinberg & Lankau, 2011). Given these findings, we might predict that the positive effects of choosing a mentor (versus having one chosen for you) may be moderated by time. Or, building on research on virtual teams and the importance of an initial face-to-face meeting (e.g., Martins, Gilson, & Maynard, 2004), trust may be developed earlier and more quickly in an e-mentoring relationship if the dyad uses videoconferencing for communicating early in the relationship.

Whether mentor and protégé both work for the same company (i.e., internal v. external) may also affect the context in which the relationship takes place. In traditional mentoring, protégés whose mentors work in the same company are rightly more concerned about disclosures coming back to haunt them. Given the perceived ease that admitted weaknesses or failures would get back to a protégé's superior, a protégé may alter his or her communication in an effort to look good to an internal mentor (de Janasz, et al., 2003); however, doing so would inhibit learning. When stakes are particularly high, as in the case of CEO protégés, an external mentor is absolutely essential, as de Janasz and Peiperl (2015) found in their research. Even with an external mentor, both parties may engage in a formal conversation if not "contract" about the importance of confidentiality. In their study, de Janasz and Peiperl (2015) learned that senior members of an organization who arranged for the mentoring of their CEO protégés would, on occasion, attempt to glean information from the mentor, who, despite being external, might be part of the inquirer's network. Despite a lack of formal training, the mentors typically demurred, no doubt informed by onboarding conversations and documents discouraging such disclosure. Future research might explore these design characteristics of formal e-mentoring programs, namely, whether mentors and protégés receive training, the formality of a confidentiality agreement, and the degree to which knowledge of a written account of the conversations may moderate the degree to which a protégé will honestly disclose weaknesses or learning gaps, and thereby report amount of mentoring received (and value therein).

12.10 Process Factors

One of the challenges in conducting e-mentoring research rests in the difficulty of isolating individuals who utilize exclusively virtual (i.e., non-face-to face) communication. The reality of today's myriad options for effective communication, means that protégés and mentors are most likely to be connected across multiple mediums, including email, texts, social media (e.g., LinkedIn, Twitter), and video conferencing (e.g., Skype, FaceTime). This means that blended mentoring, defined as the use of multiple channels to provide developmental support (Murphy, 2011), may in fact be the most realistic and effective approach. Nonetheless, prior research and practical implications lead us to offer the following.

In the study by de Janasz and Godshalk (2013), study participants were asked to self-report the percent of time they utilized various methods to communicate (e.g., phone, fax, email). Because these channels offer varying levels of richness (allowing for nonverbal as well as verbal cues), it may be that a greater proportion of time spent in richer channels (i.e., videoconferencing being the richest) is positively related to satisfaction with the e-mentoring relationship. However, it is unclear whether greater richness would predict significant differences in outcomes such as increased learning, self-efficacy, and network size/quality. As research by Ragins and her colleagues demonstrates, salient demographic differences in the conversation may adversely affect the quality of the relationship (e.g., Ragins, et al., 2000).

Another element of the process concerns the formality of the agenda that may guide the mentoring conversation. In practice, mentors are advised to not steer the conversation too much, lest the protégé lack buy-in to any actions she or he might take in pursuit of learning or career development (P-Sontag, Vappie, & Wanberg, 2007). What works for the mentor – considering their gender, ethnicity, hierarchical level, socioeconomic and marital status, education, ambition, and so on – may not be ideal for the protégé. However, in recent research on CEOs being mentored primarily face-to-face (de Janasz & Peiperl, 2015), planned meeting agendas were considered critical to a successful meeting by both protégé and mentor. In primarily virtual interactions between the dyad, given that the work is more organic and ad hoc (Makarius & Larson, 2017), it may be difficult for individuals to evaluate the formality of their conversations and its effect on mentoring functions. It may be that informality is positively associated with psychosocial support (i.e., friendship) and formality is correlated with instrumental support. Future research that explores the use of multiple media (and the proportion of time using each) and the degree to which conversations are planned in advance are essential to test these ideas. It may be that conversations that utilize media that are less rich – ranging from text to email to phone to videoconference – enable both the sender and recipient of the message to ask for or provide support in a manner that is more informal and at the discretion of the parties' needs and schedules as compared with a phone call or videoconference. It may be that the more these norms are violated, for example, an emailed request for an immediate response, the less effective or satisfying the mentoring process may seem to the participants.

12.11 Conclusion

While empirical research has a long way to go to catch up with the practice of e-mentoring, we see a promising future for developing the current and future workforce. Whereas traditional mentoring is constrained by time, place, and physical availability of mentors, e-mentoring – despite some limitations – offers protégés (and presumably mentors) similar benefits as those afforded through traditional modes of engagement (i.e., face-to-face) with fewer logistical constraints. Mentoring remains one of several critical pathways for enhancing learning, self-efficacy, networks, and career satisfaction for individuals participating in mentoring relationships, as well as socialization and knowledge transfer benefits for organizations. Owing to the rapid changes in technology, global competition, and demographics, success in careers requires continuous learning, ideally through the proactive initiation of employees. Increasingly prevalent and valuable, e-mentoring enables individuals to connect electronically with mentors of their choosing, on their terms, and without the need of a formal program. While not a perfect substitute for face-to-face communication, the few empirical studies of e-mentoring to date suggest that losses due to a lack of richness in the communication channel are made up for in terms of increased access, a critical de-emphasis of demographic differences, and surprisingly high levels of trust and disclosure necessary for effective mentoring. The receipt and outcomes of developmental support in virtual mentoring relationships are valuable to individual participants and organizations alike, and as such, implore additional practice and examination of e-mentoring.

References

Alavi, M., Wheeler, B. C., & Valacich, J. S. (1995). Using IT to reengineer business education: An exploratory investigation of collaborative tele-learning. *MIS Quarterly*, *19*, 293–312.

Alavi, M., Yoo, Y., & Vogel, D. R. (1997). Using information technology to add value to management education. *Academy of Management Journal, 40*, 1310–1333.

Allen, T. D. (2007). Mentoring relationships from the perspective of the mentor. In B. R. Ragins & K. E. Kram (Eds.), *The handbook of mentoring at work: Theory, research, and practice* (pp. 123–148). Los Angeles, CA: Sage.

Allen, T. D., Eby, L. T., Poteet, M. L., Lentz, E., & Lima, L. (2004). Career benefits associated with mentoring for protégés: A meta-analysis. *Journal of Applied Psychology, 89*(1): 127–136.

Arthur, M. B. & Rousseau, D. M. (1996). *The boundaryless career: A new employment principle for a new organizational era.* New York, NY: Oxford University Press.

Arbaugh, J. P. (2005). Is there an optimal design for on-line MBA courses? *Academy of Management Learning and Education, 4*, 135–149.

Arbaugh, J. P. & Benbunan-Fich, R. (2006). An investigation of epistemological and social dimensions of teaching in online learning environments. *Academy of Management Learning and Education, 5*, 435–447.

Bailey, D. E., Leonardi, P. M., & Barley, S. R. (2012). The lure of the virtual. *Organization Science, 23*(5), 1485–1504.

Ba, A. (1986). *Social foundations of thought and action: A social cognitive theory.* Englewood Cliffs, NJ: Prentice-Hall.

Bempechat, J., London, P., & Dweck, C. (1991). Children's conceptions of ability in major domains: An interview and experimental study. *Child Study Journal, 21*, 11–36.

Blake-Beard, S. D., O'Neill, R. M., & McGowan, E. M. (2007). Blind dates? The importance of matching in successful formal mentoring relationships. In B. R. Ragins and K. E. Kram (Eds.). *The handbook of mentoring at work: Theory, research, practice* (pp. 617–632). Los Angeles, CA: Sage.

Blass F. R., Brouer R. L., Perrewe P. L., & Ferris G. R. 2007. Politics understanding ability and networking ability as a function of mentoring: The roles of gender and race. *Journal of Leadership and Organizational Studies, 14*(2): 93–105

Brooks, C. (April 23, 2015). Are remote workers better workers? Business News Daily. Retrieved from www.businessnewsdaily.com/8311-remote-work-iscommonplace .html.

Carlson, J. R. & Zmud, R. W. (1999). Channel expansion theory and the experiential nature of media richness perceptions. *Academy of Management Journal, 42*: 153–170.

Casselman, B. (2015). Enough already about the job-hopping millennials, FiveThirtyEight – Economics (May 5). Retrieved August 25, 2017, from https://fivethirtyeight.com /datalab/enough-already-about-the-job-hopping-millennials/.

Chandler, D. E., Kram, K. E., & Yip, J. (2001). An ecological perspective on mentoring at work: A review and future prospects. *Academy of Management Annals, 5*, 519–570.

de Janasz, S. C., Ensher, E. A. & Heun, C. (2008). Using e-mentoring to connect business students with practicing managers: Virtual relationships and real benefits. *Mentoring & Tutoring: Partnership in Learning, 16*(4), 394–411.

de Janasz, S. C. & Godshalk, V. M. (2013). The role of e-mentoring in protégés' learning and satisfaction. *Group & Organization Management, 38*(6), 743–774.

de Janasz, S. C. & Peiperl, M. A. (2015). CEOs need mentors too. *Harvard Business Review, 93*(4), 100–103.

de Janasz, S. C., Sullivan, S. E., & Whiting, V. R. (2003). Mentor networks and career success: Lessons for turbulent times. *Academy of Management Executive, 17*(4),: 78–91.

Bandura, A. (1986). *Social foundations of thought and action: A social cognitive theory.* Englewood Cliffs, NJ: Prentice-Hall.

DeLong, T.J., Gabarro, R.J., & Lees, J.J. (2008). Why Mentoring matters in a hypercompetitive world. Harvard Business Review (January), 115–121.

DeRouin R. E., Fritzsche B. A., Salas E. 2005. E-learning in organizations. *Journal of Management, 31*(6), 920–940.

DiRenzo, M. S., Linnehan, F., Shao, P., & Rosenberg, W. L. (2010). A moderated mediation model of e-mentoring. *Journal of Vocational Behavior, 76,* 292–305.

Dobrow, S. R., Chandler, D. E., Murphy, W. M., & Kram, K. E. (2012) A review of developmental networks: Incorporating a mutuality perspective. *Journal of Management, 38*(1), pp. 210–242.

Dweck, C. S. & Leggett, E. L. (1988). A social-cognitive approach to motivation and personality. *Psychological Review, 95*(2), 256–273

Eby L. T. & Lockwood A. (2005). Protégés and mentors' reactions to participating in formal programs: A qualitative investigation. *Journal of Vocational Behavior, 67*(3), 441–458.

Ensher, E. A., Grant-Vallone, E. J., & Marelich, W. (2002). Effects of perceived attitudinal and demographic similarity on protégés support and satisfaction gained through their mentoring relationships. *Journal of Applied Social Psychology, 37,* 1407–1430.

Ensher, E. A., Heun, C., & Blanchard, A. (2003). Online mentoring and computer-mediated communication: New directions in research. *Journal Vocational Behavior, 63*(2), 264–288.

Ensher, E. A. & Murphy, S. E. (1997). Effects of race, gender, perceived similarity, and contact on mentor relationships. *Journal of Vocational Behavior, 50,* 460–481.

Ensher, E. A. & Murphy, S. E. (2007). E-mentoring: Next-generation research and strategies. In B. R. Ragins & K. E. Kram (Eds.), *The handbook of mentoring at work: Theory, research and practice* (pp. 299–322). Thousand Oaks, CA: Sage.

Forret, M. L. & Dougherty, T. W. (2001). Correlates of networking behavior for managerial and professional employees. *Group & Organization Management, 26,* 283–311.

Francis, L. (July, 2007). Mentoring makeover: How the web is transforming the entire mentoring process. *Training and Development, 61*(7), 52–57.

Fuller, R. M., Vician, C., & Brown, S. A. (2006). E-learning and individual characteristics: The role of computer anxiety and communication apprehension. *Journal of Computer Information Systems, 46,* 103–115.

Gallup. (2016). *How millennials want to work and live: The six big changes leaders have to make.* Washington, DC: Gallup.

Gaskill, L. R. (1991). Same-sex and cross-sex mentoring of female protégés: A comparative analysis. *Career Development Quarterly, 40,* 48–63.

Godshalk, V. M. & Sosik, J. 2003. Aiming for career success: The role of learning goal orientation in mentoring relationships.*Journal of Vocational Behavior 63,* 417–437.

Gorman, P., Nelson, T., & Glassman, A. (2004). The Millennial generation: A strategic opportunity. *Organizational Analysis, 12*(3), 255–270.

Gould S. 1979. Characteristics of career planners in upwardly mobile occupations. *Academy of Management Journal, 22*(3), 539–550.

Granovetter M. (1973). The strength of weak ties. *American Journal of Sociology, 78*(6), 1360–1380.

Grant-Vallone, E. J. & Ensher, E. A. (2000). Effects of peer mentoring on types of mentor support, program satisfaction, and graduate student stress: A dyadic perspective. *Journal of College Student Development, 41*, 637–642.

Hall, D. T. 2002. *Careers in and out of organizations*. Thousand Oaks, CA: Sage.

Hall D. T. & Foster L. W. 1977. A psychological success cycle and goal setting: Goals, performance, and attitudes. *Academy of Management Journal, 20*(2), 282–290.

Hamilton, B. A. & Scandura, T. A. (2003). E-mentoring: Implications for organizational learning and development in a wired world. *Organizational Dynamics, 31*, 388–402.

Harrison D. A., Price K. H., & Bell M. (1998). Beyond relational demography: Time and the effects of surface and deep level diversity or work group cohesion. *Academy of Management Journal, 41*, 96–107.

Harter, J., Agrawal, S., & Sorenson, S. (2014). Most U.S. workers see upside to staying connected to work. Gallup Inc. R.eved June 29, 2016, from www.gallup.com/poll/168794/workers-upside-staying-connected-work.aspx

Higgins, M. C., Chandler, D. E., & Kram, K. E. (2007). Developmental initiation and developmental networks. In B. R. Ragins & K. E. Kram (Eds.), *The handbook of mentoring at work: Theory, research and practice* (pp. 349–372). Thousand Oaks, CA: Sage.

Higgins, M.C. & Kram, K.E. (2001). Reconceptualizing mentoring at work: A developmental network perspective. *Academy of Management Review, 26*, 264–288.

Hinde, R. A. (1995). A suggested structure for a science of a relationship. *Personnel Relationships, 2*, 1–15.

Hwang, A., Kessler E. H., & Francesco, A. M. (2004). Student networking behavior, culture, and grade performance: An empirical study and pedagogical recommendation. *Academy of Management Learning and Education, 3*(2), 139–150

Judge, T. A., Locke, E. A., & Durham, C. C. (1997). The dispositional causes of job satisfaction: A core evaluations approach. *Research in Organizational Behavior, 19*, 151–188.).

Kelley, H. H., Berscheid, E., Christensen, A., Harvey, J. H., Huston, T. L., & Levinger, G. (1983). Analyzing close relationships. In H. H. Kelley, E. Berscheid, A. Christensen, J. H. Harvey, T. L. Huston, G. Levinger, E. McClintock, L. A. Peplau, & D. R. Peterson (Eds.), *Close relationships* (pp. 20–67). New York, NY: W.H. Freeman and Company.

Koberg, C. S., Boss, R. W., & Goodman, E. (1998). Factors and outcomes associated with mentoring among health-care professionals. *Journal of Vocational Behavior, 53*, 58–72.

Kram, K. E. (1985). Mentoring at work. Glenview, IL: Scott, Foresman and Company.

Lewis (2002). Telementoring: A teacher's perspective of the effectiveness of the international telementor program. *Journal of Interactive Online Learning, 1*(1).

Makarius, E. & Larson, B. (2017). Changing the perspective of virtual work: Building virtual intelligence at the individual level, *Academy of Management Perspectives, 31*, 159–178.

Martins, L. L., Gilson, L. & Maynard, M. T. (2004). Virtual teams: What do we know and where do we go from here? *Journal of Management, 30*(6), 805–835.

Meyers, K. K. & Sadaghiani, K. 2010). Millennials in the workplace: A communication perspective on millennials' organizational relationships and performance, *Journal of Business and Psychology, 25*(2), 225–238.

Molinari, C., Freshman, B., & Tan, R. Y. 2015). Mindful awareness training in online and face-to-face learning environments: A comparative analysis, *The Journal of Health Administration Education, 32*(4), 579–604.

Murphy, W. M. (2011). From e-mentoring to blended mentoring: Increasing students' developmental initiation and mentors' satisfaction. *Academy of Management Learning & Education, 10*(4), 606–622.

Murphy, W. M. & Kram, K. E. (2010). Understanding nonwork relationships in developmental networks. *Career Development International, 15*(7): 637–663.

Olian, J. D., Carroll, S. J., Giannantonio, C. M., & Feren, D. B. (1988). What do protégés look for in a mentor? Results of three experimental studies. *Journal of Vocational Behavior, 33*, 15–37.

Owens, D. M. (March, 2006). Virtual mentoring. *HR Magazine*, 51(3), 105–107.

Pellegrini, E. K. & Scandura, T. A. 2005. Construct equivalence across groups: An unexplored issue in mentoring research. *Educational and Psychological Measurement*, 65(2), 323–335.

Powers, S. R. & Myers, K. K. (2017). Millennials in the workplace: Research findings and managerial implications. In M. Sharabi (Ed.), *Generational differences in work values and work ethic: An international perspective* (pp.163–182). Commack, NY: Nova Science Publishers.

P-Sontag, L., Vappie, K., & Wanberg, C. R. (2007). The practice of mentoring: MENTTIUM Corporation. In B. R. Ragins and K. E. Kram (Eds.). *The handbook of mentoring at work: Theory, research, practice* (pp. 593–616). Los Angeles, CA: Sage.

Ragins, B. R., Cotton, J. L., & Miller, J. S. (2000). Marginal mentoring: The effects of type of mentor, quality of relationship, and program design on work and career attitudes. *Academy of Management Journal, 43*, 1177–1194.

Ragins, B. R. & Kram, K. E. (2007). The roots and meaning of mentoring. In B. R. Ragins & K. E. Kram (Eds.), *The handbook of mentoring at work: Theory, research and practice* (pp. 3–15). Thousand Oaks, CA: Sage.

Raines, C. (2002). *Connecting generations: The sourcebook for a new workplace*. Berkeley, CA: Crisp Publications.

Randstad Work Solutions (2007). *The world of work 2007*. Retrieved July 26, 2009, from: www.us.randstad.com/the%20world%20of%20work%202007.pdf.

Reyt, J. N. & Wiesenfeld, B. M. (2015). Seeing the forest for the trees: Exploratory learning, mobile technology, and knowledge workers' boundary integration behaviors. *Academy of Management Journal, 58*(3), 739–782.

Rheingold, H. (1993). *The virtual community: Homesteading on the electronic frontier.* Reading, MA: Addison-Wesley.

Single, P. B. & Single, R. M. (2005). E-mentoring for social equity: Review of research to inform program development. *Mentoring and Tutoring, 13*, 301–320.

Smith-Jentsch, K. A., Scielzo, S. A., Yarbrough, C. S., & Rosopa, P. J. (2008). A comparison of face-to-face and electronic peer-mentoring: Interactions with mentor gender. *Journal of Vocational Behavior, 72*, 193–206.

Society for Human Resource Management (SHRM). (2009). *The multigenerational workforce: Opportunity for competitive success*. Retrieved July 26, 2009, from www.shrm.org/Research/Articles/Articles/Documents/090027_RQ_March_2009_FINAL_noad.pdf.

Sproull, L. & Kiesler, S. (1999). Computers, networks and work. *Scientific American, 265*, 116–123.

Sullivan, S. E. (1999). The changing nature of careers: A review and research agenda. *Journal of Management, 25*, 457–484.

Tannenbaum, S. I., Mathieu, J. E., Salas, E., & Cohen, D. (2012). Teams are changing: Are research and practice evolving fast enough? *Industrial and Organizational Psychology, 5*, 2–24.

Thomas, M. (May 10, 2016). 4 Organizational mistakes that plague modern knowledge workers. *Harvard Business Review*, May. Retrieved from https://hbr.org/2016/05/4-organizational-mistakes-that-plague-modern-knowledge-workers.

Torkzadeh, G., Pflughoeft, K., & Hall, L. (1999). Computer user attitudes, training effectiveness, and self-efficacy: An empirical study. *Behaviour & Information Technology, 18*, 299–309.

Turban, D. B. & Dougherty, T. W. (1994). Role of protégé personality in receipt of mentoring and career success. *Academy of Management Journal, 37*, 688–702.

Turban, D. B., Dougherty, T. W., & Lee, F. K. (2002). Gender, race, and perceived similarity effects in developmental relationships: The moderating role of relationship duration. *Journal of Vocational Behavior, 61*, 240–262.

Turban, D. B. & Lee, F. K. (2007). The role of personality in mentoring relationships: Formation, dynamics, and outcomes. In B. R. Ragins & K. E. Kram (Eds.). *The handbook of mentoring at work: Theory, research, and practice* (pp. 21–50). Los Angeles, CA: Sage.

van Emmerik, I. J. H. (2004). The more you can get the better: Mentoring constellations and intrinsic career success. *Career Development International, 9*, 578–594.

Walther, J. B. (1996). Computer-mediated communication: Impersonal, interpersonal, and hyperpersonal interaction. *Communication Research, 23*, 3–43.

Wanberg, C. R., Kammeyer-Mueller, J., & Marchese, M. (2006). Mentor and protégé predictors and outcomes of mentoring in a formal mentoring program. *Journal of Vocational Behavior, 69*, 410–423.

Wanberg C. R., Kanfer R., & Banas J. T. (2000). Predictors and outcomes of networking intensity among unemployed job seekers. *Journal of Applied Psychology, 85*(4), 491–503.

Wanberg, C. R., Welsh, E. T., & Hezlett, S. A. (2003). Mentoring research: A review and dynamic process model. *Research in Personnel and Human Resources Management, 22*(1), 39–124.

Wayne S. J., Liden R. C., Kraimer M. L., & Graf I. K. (1999). The role of human capital, motivation and supervisor sponsorship in predicting career success. *Journal of Organizational Behavior, 20*(5), 577–595.

Weinberg, F. J. & Lankau, M. J. (2011). Formal mentoring programs: A mentor-centric and longitudinal analysis. *Journal of Management, 37*(6), 1527–1557.

Wellman, B. & Gulia, M. (1999). Net surfers don't ride alone: Virtual community as community. In B. Wellman (Ed.), *Networks in the global village* (pp. 331–367). Boulder, CO: Westview.

13 Professional Coaching

The Impact of Virtual Coaching on Practice and Research

Niloofar Ghods, Matt Barney, and Jonathan Kirschner

13.1 Introduction

For some coaching practitioners, the term virtual coaching is a source of apprehension. Dark visions of automation come to mind, like the opening scene from *The Terminator*, where machines take over society with the sole mission of destroying mankind. The comparison may be extreme, but the notion that virtualizing the coaching experience will eventually replace coaches with technology is one that worries many practitioners. In fact, some thought leaders in coaching have even argued this point as a plausible future for the practice (Peterson, 2017).

However realistic that outcome may be, the fact remains that the world is changing – very quickly. In the business world, globalization, increased competition, matrixed management, and the general increase of business demands put pressure on technology to accelerate business performance. Even in our personal lives, connecting virtually rather in person – using Facebook, Twitter, Snapchat, Slack, Google Hangouts, Skype, Facetime, or any of countless other applications – has become the norm. Therefore, it isn't too surprising to see recent trends indicating virtual coaching is on the rise and that fewer people are relying on traditional in-person engagements. For example, in Berry, Ashby, Gnilka, and Matheny's (2011) study, 100 percent of coaches reported using some technology as part of their coaching. Frazee (2008) found 26 percent of coaches in her study engaging with clients primarily or exclusively virtually, and with little or no in-person interaction. Furthermore, the 2016 Executive Coaching survey by Sherpa found only 37 percent of coaching conducted in person, representing a steep drop over the last seven years (Corbett & Valeri, 2016).

The speed of technological advancement is turning what seemed unthinkable a few years ago into reality. And it is becoming increasingly difficult to keep track of what technologies are being developed, tested, or used consistently in coaching, making it harder to evaluate their impact on the practice. Today, while technology becomes ever more integral to the practice, there is still much we don't know about the benefits and drawbacks of using technology for coaching. This chapter is an effort to gather what we do know – and offer a glimpse of what's ahead.

Acknowledgments: Jared Brey, Phoebe Flint, Hannah Murphy, and Robert Kovach.

13.1.1 Benefits of Technological Advancement

In the past five years, changes to the coaching practice have been especially drastic and impactful, as technological innovation has proliferated (Corbett & Valeri, 2016). And although technology has historically been used to supplement in-person coaching (Wilson, Hannum, & CCL, 2006; Young & Dixon, 1996) the trend continues to evolve as technology becomes more cost effective. We are seeing a greater adoption and variation of its use for coaching. As a grounding, Boyce and Clutterbuck (2011) provide a very useful comprehensive list of benefits of virtual coaching within three client-centered categories – convenience, service, and support – which have been highlighted in the virtual coaching literature as advantages to coaching. Below, we focus on a few of the most commonly noted benefits, based on our experience.

13.1.1.1 Accessibility

One of the benefits of leveraging technology in coaching has been to enhance the client experience with additional access to the coach outside the traditional in-person session. Technology has created easier access points between coaches and business leaders, whose interactions traditionally would require a scheduled, in-person meeting. Tools such as the telephone, video conferencing, email, and chat can now allow access to the coach at any given time.

Technology enables people to connect and have access to one another across time zones, work environments, and cultural boundaries (Boyce & Hernez-Broome, 2010). A coach who is physically located in London can coach a leader in California after her dinner time and when her kids are in bed. A sales leader who is constantly on the road can receive video coaching through his mobile phone or tablet en route to a customer meeting. And a coach in Australia can expand her experience and cultural competency of Indian culture by working remotely with more leaders based in Bangalore. These are just some real-life examples that demonstrate how technology expands access to a service historically only available to a few. Virtual coaching also enables additional connection points between coach and client to increase continuity of learning and even allow greater accountability.

13.1.1.2 Convenience

Convenience is another key benefit of technology-enabled coaching. Similar to the scenarios described above, having access to a coach in the comforts of your own home office, hotel room, or on your commute can be a meaningful and useful convenience. Some people feel more comfortable discussing difficult issues or disclosing confidential information in the environment of their own choosing. While some may prefer the visual connection with their coach via video conferencing, others feel safer or more protected without a visual connection (Day & Schneider, 2002). Still others simply don't have the time to connect with a coach in person because of their demanding schedules, leaving virtual coaching as the only viable option.

13.1.1.3 Cost and Scalability

For many, the main benefit for offering virtual coaching is its lower cost. And given that coaching has historically been affordable only for senior leaders, virtual coaching democratizes coaching, enabling organizations to offer coaching at multiple levels in an organization, often people most neglected, rather than just senior executives (Boyce & Hernez-Broome, 2010; Peterson, 2017). In practice, senior leaders in some companies, like Cisco Systems, are taking advantage of the lower cost of virtual coaching and offering coaching to their entire leadership team in an effort to accelerate the leadership capability of their organization (Ghods & Kovach, 2017).

All the benefits described above – reduction of rates, access to broader coaching networks, and the convenience of preferred working time zones or being coached in the comforts of one's preferred environment – combine to create the possibility of bringing coaching to scale. Given the many benefits described above, we believe that advancement of technology is in fact a game changer for the coaching industry, revolutionizing the practice and producing both exciting opportunities and challenging implications. As scientist-practitioners, we use this chapter to dive into what we know today about technologies used in coaching, existing research in virtual coaching, and what we anticipate the virtual coaching practice will look like in the future. Finally, we will discuss the implications of these advancements in technology for coaches, clients and researchers.

We recognize that, despite our efforts, we are unable to cover every advancement in the field in this chapter. And we are neither advocating for nor discouraging the use of virtual coaching. Instead, our hope and intention with this chapter is to provide our colleagues a grounding on what we know exists today and what we anticipate to exist in the near future. Ideally, this chapter will encourage our colleagues to start experimenting, explore how technology can benefit their practice, and share their learning to advance the field. Coaching continues to be an under-researched area and we need the help of our colleagues to continue building our collective intelligence on this evolving topic.

13.1.2 Definitions

13.1.2.1 Coaching

For this chapter we ground our definition of coaching in Kilburg's (1996) definition of executive coaching. This usage defines coaching narrowly as a practice meant to enhance leadership capability within an organizational context. It excludes coaching for the purposes of personal life, sports, and enhancing job-specific skills (e.g. sales capability or other non-leadership goals). Our definition includes coaching at different levels in an organization, from first line manager to middle management and executives. It excludes coaching conducted between a leader and his or her direct or indirect line manager or supervisor. According to Kilburg, executive coaching is:

A helping relationship formed between a client who has managerial authority and responsibility in an organization and a consultant who uses a wide variety of behavioral techniques and methods to help the client achieve a mutually identified set of goals to improve his or her professional performance and personal satisfaction and consequently, to improve the effectiveness of the client's organization within a formally defined coaching agreement. (p. 142)

13.1.2.2 Virtual Coaching

Virtual coaching, e-coaching, distance coaching, telephone coaching, video coaching, online coaching, and blended coaching have all been synonymously used to refer to coaching conducted between a coach and client who are in different physical locations and use some form of technology to collaborate, such as the telephone, video conferencing, email, chat or other online tools representing synchronous (real-time) or asynchronous (delayed-time) means of connecting (Boyce & Hernez-Broome, 2010; Clutterbuck & Hussain, 2010; Frazee, 2008; Ghods, 2009; Hernez-Broome, Boyce, & Whyman, 2007). In order to remain consistent with other prominent virtual coaching publications, we leverage Center for Creative Leadership's (CCL) definition of virtual coaching for this chapter. According to CCL, virtual coaching is defined as:

a "formal one-one" relationship between a coach and client, in which the client and coach collaborate using technology to assess and understand the client and his or her leadership development needs, to challenge current constraints while exploring new possibilities, and to ensure accountability and support for reaching goals and sustaining development. (Boyce & Hernez-Broome, 2010, p. 141; adapted from Ting & Hart, 2004, p. 116)

13.1.2.3 In-person Coaching

Face-to-face coaching, in-person coaching, or live-coaching have all been used interchangeably to describe traditional coaching conducted in the same physical location. For the purposes of this study, we will refer to this type of coaching as "in-person" coaching rather than "face-to-face" coaching given video conferencing technology enables a face-to-face experience without the physical presence of either party.

13.2 Research on Virtual Coaching

Similar to the general coaching literature, research on virtual coaching has been limited and outpaced by the practice. There are many obstacles in conducting research in virtual coaching, some of which overlap with challenges facing research on in-person coaching. These obstacles include the confidential nature of coaching (Kilburg, 1996, 1997; O'Brien, 1997; Peterson, 1996; Witherspoon & White, 1996), as many coaches, wanting to protect the comfort and confidentiality of their client relationships, are reluctant to subject their clients to being "studied." Another common reason is cost, defined in terms of the time and resources needed to coach without a guarantee of achieving meaningful outcomes. In other words, even if the coach and client decide to invest a substantial amount of time and money into finding meaningful information through coaching research, they might only walk away with that research experience (Linley, 2006).

Practitioners may find it hard to justify spending time on research unless it is part of their daily work or they have extensive free time. Unlike practitioners who work in academia or have research as one of their primary responsibilities, they will have little incentive to contribute to the scholarship around the practice. And since industry is paving the way forward, with most useful insights coming from the practice rather than academia, we are at a disadvantage in terms of the availability of research. Researchers have limited awareness of or access to coaching that is being conducted in the field, since that access would require them to be invited to partner in conducting research or be practitioners themselves. Unless practitioners partner with scholars, it is very difficult to accelerate the advancement of our research in this area.

In this section, we will briefly review existing research in virtual coaching to help expand our understanding of this new form of coaching delivery. The studies found in the literature include two industry publications (Wilson et al., 2006; Young & Dixon, 1996), three peer-reviewed studies (Berry et al., 2011; Bowles & Picano, 2006; Geissler et al., 2014), four unpublished dissertations (Charbonneau, 2002; Frazee, 2008; Ghods, 2009; Wang, 2000), and, most recently, a time-lagged field experiment in collaboration with three institutions (Passarelli et al., 2017). Ghods & Boyce (2012) provide detailed review and reconciliation of all studies in virtual coaching and related fields in their chapter, but given the paucity of research in the field we also review the virtual coaching studies briefly – including more recent studies since Ghods & Boyce's publication. Although most of this research investigated outcomes of virtual coaching, each study varies widely on experimental variables, making it difficult to draw strong generalizations about the field. In order to help build our aggregate knowledge from these studies, we have grouped their outcomes and conclusions into the following categories:

- Blended coaching, i.e. use of multiple technologies and/or complementing in-person coaching using technology
- Virtual coaching used to transfer learning as part of a training
- Virtual coaching outcomes, i.e. client satisfaction with virtual coaching
- Impact of virtual coaching on the coaching relationship
- The prevalence of and preference for modality of coaching, i.e. in-person versus virtual

Finally, although most of these studies overlap in some of these categories, we bucketed them in their most salient component to help drive clearer conclusions.

13.2.1 Blended Approach

The studies that examined the blended approach, leveraged both in-person and virtual coaching as part of the overall engagement or combining different technologies to deliver virtual coaching. The earliest study was conducted by Young and Dixon (1996) from the Center for Creative Leadership (CCL) in the form of an industry publication, reiterating our earlier point that the coaching practice, rather than academia, has paved the path for research in virtual coaching. The study examined the impact of coaching on participants of a six-month leadership-development program that included classroom learning and in-person coaching while attending class, as well as telephone communications when participants were back on the job. In this study, virtual coaching was used both as a supplement to in-person coaching as well as a transfer of learning from the training. Although it was difficult to identify which part of the program accounted for significant positive outcomes when compared to control groups, participants rated coaching as the most helpful component of their learning. It was unclear which modality, in-person or virtual coaching, was seen as most beneficial. A more recent study by Geissler et al. (2014), however, did find that telephone coaching with an internet-based program achieved positive results with 14 clients. Clients also reported more decisive advantages of combined virtual modalities in comparison to in-person coaching.

13.2.2 Transfer of Training

Two other studies examined virtual coaching within the context of knowledge transfer. For example, in Wang's (2000) study, virtual coaching was used as a post-training supplement to help transfer the knowledge gleaned from the training to the participants' home organizations. Virtual coaching in this study was defined as using multiple online tools rather than simply the telephone or video conferencing traditionally used in one-on-one coaching. The tools were email, synchronous text chat, asynchronous web-board postings, a database that captured their progress report, online and archive resources, and a help desk. The study found a positive relationship between activities supportive of virtual coaching and transfer of the knowledge from the training. Supportive activities included the relationship and interaction with the coach, coaches' encouragement, and provision of resources to participants.

CCL further examined virtual coaching in the form of quarterly conference calls intended as a follow-up supplement to classroom instruction (Wilson et al., 2006). In this study, the coaching and classroom instruction were integral to a leadership-development initiative for corporate staff and high-potential managers. Coaching calls were held with the same instructors as in the classroom training so that an established relationship existed before transitioning to a virtual working relationship. As with Young and Dixon, it was again difficult to separate what components of the program were the primary drivers of positive results. However, the overall program showed positive findings in a number of areas, including the integration of learned material into daily work, leadership performance, improved relationships, knowledge sharing and job performance.

13.2.3 Preference for Modality

Several studies surveyed the prevalence of different virtual coaching modalities, as well as the preferences of coaches and clients for specific technologies. Charbonneau (2002) conducted semi-structured interviews with ten executive coaches and ten of their clients around their experiences using different types of technologies in virtual coaching. The technologies included the telephone, video conferencing and email, in comparison to in-person coaching. Both coaches and clients perceived in-person coaching to be more effective than telephone coaching, particularly for the first session, when they were establishing trust, reviewing feedback or sharing sensitive information. However, consistent with our discussion of the key benefits of using technology in coaching, coaches in this study highlighted access to clients, convenience, and cost as benefits to telephone coaching. Additionally, coaches highlighted that virtual coaching enabled them to provide focus and accountability and promote follow-through for the client. Furthermore, Charbonneau postulated that good telephone coaches can compensate for the lack of visual cues through verbalizing the process to the client and asking powerful questions. The most important finding in Charbonneau's study, however, is a recognition of the need to have three fits as essential to virtual coaching effectiveness. They are "The fit between the coach and his/her preferred coaching medium …, the fit between the client and that medium …, and the fit between the coach and the client as people" (p.122).

Frazee (2008) explored the use of virtual coaching in organizations and in executive coaches' practice by interviewing 20 coaches and surveying 191 coaches and organizational professionals. She found that most coaching was conducted in-person as opposed to virtual coaching, and virtual coaching was primarily used as an alternative to in-person coaching. Consistent with other studies and our earlier discussion, the reasons for using virtual coaching included cost, access to the coach and real-time support across geographic distance, and the convenience of addressing scheduling issues. Technologies used for virtual coaching included telephone, email, online file sharing tools and – the least used – videoconferencing. Similarly to Charbonneau's study, Frazee found that most participants felt in-person coaching was necessary for addressing deeper issues and providing feedback on sensitive topics. Also consistent with Charbonneau's study, Frazee found compatibility and ease of technology use was most important for coaches when choosing what technology to use for coaching.

13.2.4 Coaching Outcomes and the Coaching Relationship

The following studies examine the outcomes of virtual coaching and the impact of virtual coaching on the coaching relationship. The first study is by Bowles and Picano (2006). They examined the impact of telephone coaching on 19 US Army recruiter-managers over a six-month time span. Although the study demonstrated positive outcomes with respect to work-life balance, virtual coaching had a negative impact on overall quality of work. In other words, as participants achieved their coaching goals, they perceived that their recruitment efforts were of lower quality overall.

The largest empirical study on virtual coaching to date involved 404 participants, including 152 coaching clients and 252 of their multi-raters (the client's immediate boss, peers, and direct reports). Ghods (2009) examined the coach-client relationship and observed sustained coaching outcomes (by self-ratings and multi-raters), client satisfaction with virtual coaching, and the impact of virtual coaching on the coach-client relationship. The telephone was the only technology used for virtual coaching and no pre-existing relationship existed between coaches and clients. The study found empirical support for virtual coaching leading to observable change (by self- and multi-raters). And although these findings sustained for several months, they did start to diminish over time. Finally, the study found empirical support for coaches and clients developing and maintaining a strong coaching relationship over the telephone.

Just like Ghods, Berry et al. (2011) examined the relationship between the working alliance (i.e., coach-client relationship) and client problem resolution from the perspective of coaches in in-person versus telephone coaching engagements. Results from 102 coaches surveyed revealed no significant differences between working alliance or problem resolution in either in-person or virtual coaching sessions, suggesting that telephone coaching may be a viable option, comparable to in-person coaching. Coaches also self-reported strong levels of working alliance in both virtual and in-person conditions. This is consistent with both Ghods' and Charbonneau's findings that good coaches can develop rapport with clients regardless of the medium used.

Finally, the most recent and most robust study on virtual coaching is by Passarelli et al. (2017). Researchers examined how media richness predicts the relationship quality in executive coaching. Media richness refers to the ability of a communication medium to reproduce information without loss or alteration (Daft & Lengel, 1986). For example, video conferencing is a richer communication medium than a telephone, where visual cues are lost. Using a field experiment, researchers used random assignment of coaching clients to three different coaching modalities (all coaching conducted via the telephone, video-conferencing or in-person). Participants included 10 female coaches and 88 clients (55 female and 33 male managers with minimum of three direct reports) from five organizations in the Midwest USA. Researchers made efforts to standardize the coaching engagements (i.e., coaching process, coaching framework, use of 360-degree feedback on emotional and social competence, the length of each coaching session, length of time between each coaching session, and collection of survey data throughout), while still honoring the individual needs of each client. Researchers also controlled for all coaches' proficiency for Cisco Webex videoconferencing technology. Results found client perception of in-person sessions significantly richer than telephone and videoconferencing. They also found that this relationship is moderated by the client's attitude toward and comfort level with the technology. In other words, if the client is comfortable with the videoconferencing technology then they perceive less difference in richness among the different modalities. Finally, both the coaches and clients perceived media richness as having a positive effect on the quality of their coaching relationship.

13.2.5 Research Summary

Several key themes have emerged from these studies which help us draw tentative conclusions about virtual coaching. First, industry has played a strong role in expanding our knowledge of virtual coaching in the form of applied research. And despite some experimental design shortcomings, these studies add incremental value in the practical application of coaching with professionals rather than traditional samples of students. Second, aside from Bowles and Picano's 2006 study, all studies found generally positive outcomes from the use of virtual coaching. In a few studies where coaching supplemented a training or program, it was more difficult to parse out which piece of the program yielded the greatest impact. However, in those same studies, clients did disclose preferring the coaching component of their training over other parts of the program.

About half of the studies examined only the clients' perspective on the outcomes, while the other half examined multiple raters' perspectives, i.e. coaches and their clients, clients and their stakeholders, coaches and organizational professionals, and so on. Telephone was the most used technology to conduct virtual coaching and it was in lieu of in-person coaching. In fact, aside from Geissler et al. (2014), Passarelli et al. (2017), and Wang (2000), all studies used telephone solely for conducting virtual coaching. When multiple tools were used for virtual coaching, it surpassed in-person coaching alone. Furthermore, comfort with technology impacts the experience with and preference for the modality of coaching. This reinforced the importance of investigating technological comfort before proceeding with a coaching engagement. And while some coaching activities were better suited to in-person coaching than virtual, multiple studies found that a strong coaching relationship can be developed virtually and that the coaches' skill is an important element in establishing that.

In addition to studies in virtual coaching, a few notable publications provide insight into the practice of virtual coaching. Clutterbuck and Hussain (2010) provide an overview of some reasons virtual coaching has grown in popularity, the relative strengths and weaknesses of virtual coaching technologies in comparison to in-person coaching, as well as some best practices on how to conduct virtual coaching. Boyce and Hernez-Broome (2010) provide a framework for leadership coaching in a virtual environment. Leveraging systems theory, they propose an input-process-output (I-P-O) model with the following components: the characteristics of the coach and client, the coach-client matching, the coaching process, and the coaching outcomes. They also highlight critical issues and alternative considerations for conducting virtual coaching. Boyce and Clutterbuck (2011) provide a foundation for thinking about virtual coaching, and highlight key issues to consider when building a virtual coaching practice and practical guidance to support its success. Finally, Ghods and Boyce (2012) provide a critical review of virtual coaching literature inclusive of published and unpublished research studies as well as a review of literature in related fields such as the helping professions, i.e. virtual therapy, virtual counseling, and telepsychiatry.

These publications, in combination with the studies discussed, provide us a basic grounding and understanding of the virtual coaching. However, more research is desperately needed to better understand the benefits and implications of this practice.

13.3 Technologies Used in Coaching

Today, coaches and clients use an array of tools – from telephone, email, and text messaging to videoconferencing, document sharing, and other innovative communication apps – to establish deeper, more frequent, and more immediate connections than were possible in the past. Below, we consider the most prevalent technologies in use for coaching today. This discussion begins with synchronous and asynchronous communication methods and then turns to the convergence of these methods in comprehensive coaching platforms.

13.3.1 Synchronous Tools: Telephone, Video Conferencing and Telepresence

As seen in both research and practice, telephone has been the most common modality of conducting virtual coaching (Berry et al., 2011; Bowles & Picano, 2006; Charbonneau, 2002; Frazee, 2008; Geissler et al., 2014; Ghods, 2009; Sherpa, 2016; Wilson et al., 2006; Young & Dixon, 1996). The telephone has been a familiar technology for decades and is commonly used when conducting business, giving virtually all users a high level of competency and comfort with this technology. From their survey about distance and in-person coaching practices, Berry et al. (2011) found that 72 percent of coaches reported using telephone communication with their clients. As discussed earlier in the chapter, results from this study indicated no difference between telephone and in-person modalities when considering the development of the working alliance and problem resolution. Additional research from Geissler et al. (2014), who studied a combined approach to coaching using telephone and online communication, found high levels of satisfaction among clients involved in the program.

Videoconferencing has also been on the rise. Since 2006, there has been a clear decline in the reliance of in-person and telephone modalities, and during that same period a steady increase in both forms of videoconferencing tools (Sherpa, 2016). Videoconferencing refers to two or more individuals meeting by web camera (e.g. desktop) or built-in cameras (e.g. laptops and mobile devices). Telepresence refers to a more immersive, high-definition form of videoconferencing that traditionally requires a dedicated conference room, IT support, and hardware. Due to its costs,

Table 13.1 *The evolution of synchronous tools*

Pre 1990	1990–2000	2000–2010	2010–2018	Future
Telephone	Telephone	–Telephone –Video (e.g. Skype; Oovoo; Facetime; Zoom) & telepresence (e.g. Cisco Telepresence; Polycom; Vidyo)	–Telephone –Video & telepresence –Web meeting technology (e.g. Cisco Webex; Zoom Meetings; Appear.in)	–Telephone –Video & telepresence –Web meeting technology –Internet of Things (IoT) (e.g. Fitbit; Apple Watch; Firstbeat) –Augmented Reality (AR)

Implications for Coaching

The proliferation of synchronous technologies for coaching presents greater optionality for coaching, but with that, more complexity. With the expansion of meeting modalities, coaches will need to proactively plan and discuss a meeting technology strategy with their client in order to select the appropriate tools for their engagement

telepresence tends to be limited to large enterprise boardrooms rather than accessible to consumers en masse. Although Cisco Systems (the originators of Telepresence) have more recently introduced more cost effective collaborative technologies like their DX series that provides a desktop monitor with the same high definition camera at a fraction of the price of traditional Telepresence. Videoconferencing and telepresence tools allow coaches and clients to recreate the traditional in-person coaching experience without having to travel.

By allowing coaches and clients to communicate important nonverbal behavior (e.g. affect expression, eye-gaze, nodding, smiling), videoconferencing enables opportunities for fuller communication than is possible over the telephone, which is limited to content and paraverbal communication (e.g. tone, volume, speed). Capturing these various cues and allowing for a swift exchange of feedback gives videoconferencing a high degree of richness, as suggested by Daft, Lengel, and Trevino's (1987) media richness theory. Communication methods high in richness help resolve differences in interpretation, align viewpoints on topics, and enable more complex discussion beyond basic information sharing. Rich media, typified by in-person communication, is especially useful for addressing issues of equivocality – discrepancies in understanding – by allowing parties to share ideas and come to mutual agreements. Unlike phone calls, videoconferencing engages visual cues, which, by enhancing its richness, makes collaboration more efficient and effective. There is experimental evidence for this idea, too.

When researchers compared audio- and video-mediated communication, they found that pairs of participants in the videoconferencing condition were better able to ascertain the attentional availability of their partner. In other words, they knew when their partner was ready to attune to their comments (Daly-Jones, Monk, & Watts, 1998). When the experiment was replicated with four collaborators, participants in video conditions reported greater conversational fluency cues than those in the audio-only group, measured by how people traded off speaking turns and the overlapping of speech. Video conferencing, with higher attentional fluency and conversational fluency than possible over the phone, is closer to in-person conversation.

This "naturalness" has been studied in the counseling literature as well. The practicality and effectiveness of using video conferencing for psychotherapy sessions has been documented in numerous studies that conclude that clients experience similar clinical outcomes with video technology as traditional counseling sessions provide (Backhaus et al., 2012; Richardson et al., 2009).

The benefits of video technology only go as far as the quality of the experience itself. Sometimes, technical issues impede the many benefits associated with video (Passarelli et al., 2017). Low-quality video and audio and delayed feedbacks can often interfere with coaching sessions. In earlier phases of video conferencing especially, performance was highly variable. Applications such as Skype required both parties to have strong, stable internet connections for the duration of a session.

In addition to delays, many videoconferencing tools have suffered from poor video resolution and audio quality. Low-resolution video and low-fidelity audio signals prevent coaches and clients from establishing the connections that lead to the naturalness of a conversation that the video format is intended to replicate. These challenges were documented in the clinical psychology literature which suggests that the unreliability of video conferencing technology could produce dismissive and uncertain feelings about using the technology among psychologists (Rees & Haythornthwaite, 2004).

Yuen et al. (2012) recommend that all parties receive some level of training on how to use the technology and troubleshoot issues. They also suggest that a preliminary troubleshooting meeting and instructional resources would be helpful to dispel difficulties in accessing the technology. In order to surmount technical problems during services, the American Telemedicine Association established guidelines for using video-based communications, which emphasize the importance of establishing good connections through internet speed, meeting recommended bandwidth capabilities, and ensuring that devices provide high resolution images (Turvey et al., 2013).

Over the past decade, increased internet speeds, improved video technologies, and improving hardware have made higher-quality video communication more commonplace in the delivery of coaching services. In 2009, a Harvard Business Review study asked 140 coaches how they interact with their coaching clients with the options of in-person, phone, and email (Coutu & Kaufmann, 2009). Video was not even mentioned as a meeting option. In contrast, research conducted in 2016 by the International Coaching Federation (Corbett & Valeri, 2016) evidences that 24 percent of coaches choose to utilize an audio-video platform. Though the studies cannot be directly compared, the negation of an entire modality in 2009 that now comprises up to 24 percent in research conducted in 2016 is notable and indicative of the recent adoption of video conferencing in the industry.

In addition to quality enhancements, the functionality of videoconferencing has expanded, providing coaches more flexibility in how video calls can be conducted. Today, most tools allow for multi-platform videoconferencing, enabling a coach and client to meet virtually using their laptop, mobile phone, and tablet in addition to desktop computers, where videoconferencing traditionally occurred. Multi-party video conferencing options have expanded the possibilities for coaching sessions as well. Whereas single-point meetings were once the standard, newer video technologies, such as Zoom, allow for over 200 participants to join a video call at once. Importantly, this allows for multi-person stakeholder meetings or group coaching sessions to occur by video, even when meeting participants are not in the same location.

Advances in video conferencing software have been accompanied by improvements in hardware. Computer processing is better and faster today than it was in years past and cloud computing presents a whole new promising avenue for communication methods ("After Moore's law," 2016). The shift to the cloud has benefited video conferencing quality, speed, cost, and convenience. In a survey conducted by Liu et al. (2015) on videoconferencing technology in telemedicine, the researchers found that cloud-based video conferencing services may surmount many obstacles imposed by traditional videoconferencing hardware. The cloud allows many kinds of devices, including smartphones, to tap into videoconferencing services from anywhere and allow access to the machine's microphone, speaker, and camera equipment. Avoiding the need for specialized, immobile hardware setup to facilitate traditional videoconferencing, cloud videoconferencing can be accessed anywhere from a variety of devices.

13.3.2 Asynchronous Tools

While the real-time coaching session is almost always thought of as the primary component of a coaching engagement (Charbonneau, 2002; Frazee, 2008), the interactions that occur in between sessions are crucial to the success of an engagement. Asynchronous technologies such as email and text messaging have allowed coaches and clients to establish higher-frequency communication with relative ease. Emailing and texting, for example, provide opportunities to establish goals, share fast-paced feedback, and monitor to ensure client success in meeting their objectives (Pascal et al., 2015).

Email is the oldest asynchronous technology, with its predecessor being a physical letter in the mail. In 1995, CEO of Intel Andy Grove proclaimed that email would be nothing short of revolutionary for business. In his management classic, *High Output Management*, he writes, "Everything today is going to a digital format ... And everything that's digital can be shipped around the world just as fast as it can be shipped down the hall at your workplace" (p. xi). Prior to email, a coach might make a photocopy of an article and send it in the mail with a letter explaining the context. Through email, that coach can send a digital version of that article, along with videos, photos, and web links at the click of a button. Just as email transformed management, it has become a powerful tool for coaching. Email in coaching can be used for communication on coaching activity (i.e., sharing updates and progress), dealing with scheduling and logistics (i.e., determining the best time for the next session), and sharing information and resources.

Table 13.2 *The evolution of asynchronous tools*

Pre-1990	1990–2000	2000–2010	2010–2018	Future
–Letter by traditional mail	–Email (e.g., Aol; Yahoo; Gmail) –SMS (e.g., T9 text messaging)	–Email –SMS (e.g. Palm Pilot; Blackberry; iPhone 1st Generation)	–Email –SMS –MIM (e.g.,WhatsApp; SnapChat) –MDM (e.g., LeaderAmp; Nagbot.io) –Chatbot coaches (e.g., BOLDR; PocketConfidant)	–Email –SMS –MIM –Rich Media MDM (voice, video, and text) –AI Coaching –AI Performance Support –Virtual Reality (VR)

Implications for Coaching

Email and text messaging have enabled valuable information sharing in between sessions. The mobile revolution has made asynchronous communication more frequent and more immediate than ever. On the one hand, the lines between asynchronous and synchronous communication are blurring, while on the other hand, advances in MDM technology allows for strategic, titrated messaging to occur with minimal human involvement. While asynchronous communication was once limited to email exclusively, coaches now have a full portfolio of options to leverage strategically. Yet, billing practices for coaching largely center on the actual synchronous time spent in coaching sessions. Importantly, coaches will need to factor in the time involved in using email, MIM, and MDM as part of their coaching deliverables and align their billing practices accordingly.

Without email, all of these functions would otherwise have waited until clients could review these items at their next face-to-face session.

Messaging by mobile device involves briefer messages than email and the use of this medium is on the rise today (Tang & Hew, 2017). In the early days of text messaging, users had to click through keys with letters that corresponded to numbers on a flip phone (T9 text messaging). With smartphones, the technology evolved to include a full keypad and receipts so senders could see when recipients opened a message. Today, parties can even see when another user is typing. Furthermore, Mobile Instant Messaging (MIM), compared with traditional Short Message Service (SMS) texting through carriers, transmits messages through the internet and allows for even higher frequency and more social communication. Using this means of supporting higher frequency communication, coaching can achieve more effective chatting, sharing, planning and group coordination (Church & de Oliveira, 2013).

Through SMS or MIM messaging, coaches can easily share updates with their clients and exchange logistical information. Messages can also serve as reminders or motivators associated with the coaching itself. For example, a coach might wish her client good luck before an important meeting or presentation. Other coaches may use messaging as an accountability mechanism, sending messages tied to coaching objectives such as, "Have you looked at your development plan today? Have you delegated? Have you been assertive today?"

The counseling psychology literature shows the benefits of messaging. When supplementing traditional psychological services, text messaging increases client engagement with therapy and reduces attrition (Aguilera et al., 2017). In clinical settings across a range of disorders, messaging helps with information sharing, reminds clients about appointments, provides encouragement, and helps track one's progress. It also receives overwhelmingly positive client acceptance and can create an important feeling of connectedness (Berrouiguet et al., 2016).

13.3.3 Benefits of Asynchronous

Although client needs differ in important ways between psychotherapy and executive coaching, the interventions are similar in that they rely on client success through achieving behavioral goals (Cooper & Neal, 2015). Since clients must ultimately apply learned concepts to their daily work, it follows that having more frequent communication in between sessions about coaching objectives and related information could lead to stronger application of the learning. Thanks to asynchronous messaging modalities, the client's development is more continuous, rather than a series of events that occurs every two to four weeks, which is the typical cadence of face-to-face coaching (Jarvis, 2004). Results are bolstered as well. In the cognitive behavioral therapy literature, treatment outcomes increase when clients adhere to homework assignments in between counseling sessions (Mausbach et al., 2010). Internal research conducted at AIIR Consulting (2018) also affirms this. An analysis of more than 300 client feedback surveys collected over two years indicated that the sharing of additional resources in between sessions from coach to client through AIIR's coaching communication platform, Coaching Zone®, was associated with a ten-point increase in the net promoter score (NPS) of that coaching engagement.

13.3.4 Recent Developments in Asynchronous Tech

Recent developments in asynchronous technology contain promising applications for coaching practices. Virtual assistants such as Apple's Siri, Amazon's Alexa, or Google's Home facilitate ease of communication through voice-to-speech capabilities. With the ability to send emojis, animojis, GIFs, and short voice recordings – not just through text messages but on applications such as WhatsApp, Snapchat, and Slack – coaches and clients are able to be more expressive than ever before.

In addition, developments in mobile delayed messaging (MDM), the ability to preset messages for strategically timed delivery, has found applications in coaching practices. One example of both MIM and MDM is LeaderAmp, a cloud/mobile platform for expert and AI coaching. LeaderAmp measures a baseline of a client's potential and performance with computer-adaptive assessments and helps that client set goals before enabling MIM with a client's coach that is complemented by MDM with a new form of human-authored and calibrated AI. By allowing a coaching client to schedule tailored "eCoaching" into their regular day, they can "drip" ideas for practicing behaviors that are neither too hard, nor too easy, but just right for them. Clients using LeaderAmp schedule two mobile push notifications. First, they schedule calibrated eCoaching on the mornings they wish to practice, and receive mobile push notifications that suggest specific actions they should try to take to develop. These eCoaching messages are authored by expert or famous leaders, and calibrated to match the user's current level of proficiency. On the days and times each client has scheduled, they receive digital coaching and attempt to apply the eCoaching throughout their day and work tasks. Then, at the end of their day, they receive a second scheduled mobile notification to remind them to journal about the lessons they learned from this experience. Crucially, the journal entry becomes an elegant way a human coach can see how clients are making progress in-between synchronous coaching sessions, and send MIM of encouragement, praise, or nudge them when the client may be struggling or veering off course.

13.3.5 Convergence: The Rise of Coaching Platforms

At any given time, a coach and client could be using a multitude of applications and technologies with varying landing pages and credentials. For example, for a single client, a coach may use a calendar application for scheduling, a business email for long communication, mobile messaging for short messages, phone for scheduling, video for sessions, and a cloud-based information sharing application to share files. As synchronous and asynchronous communication technologies continue to proliferate, there is a growing need to have all of these valuable tools streamlined in one virtual place.

Table 13.3 *Convergence coaching platforms*

2010–2018	Future
• Platforms with coach/client interfaces (e.g. Coaching Zone®; LeaderAmp) • Platforms with coach access (e.g. Coach.me; BetterUp) • Platforms with enterprise program management functionality (e.g. Enterprise Coaching Manager®; CoachLogix)	• Platforms with multi-stakeholder interfaces, for managers, HR leaders, as well as coaches and clients • Platforms with coach access that also provide "just in time" access to coaching services • Platforms with enterprise program management functionality that collects and leverages big data analytics and has incorporated algorithmic coach-client matching

Implications for Coaching

Coaching platforms have the potential to strengthen the coaching relationship and transfer of information by creating a dedicated environment shared exclusively between coach and client. The addition of coaching pools makes it easier and more convenient for clients to contract with a coach. Coach management systems for enterprise coach practice leaders allow for coaching activities to be more scalable than ever

As we have seen in the field of counseling psychology, there is an increasing trend to promote the use of apps for communication and information sharing to support the delivery of services (Luxton et al., 2011). Coaching platforms have emerged to bring together the capabilities of videoconferencing, direct messaging, time tracking, and document sharing all in one place, providing coaches and clients with a single access point to manage the coaching experience from end to end. In bringing together disparate functionalities into a unified platform, coaching platforms create efficiency for the end users (coach and client). These efficiencies also make coaching more scalable (Gurbaxani, 2016).

One such tool is the Coaching Zone®, a cloud-based platform created by AIIR Consulting, where a coach and client log into a virtual dashboard environment. A coach or client who logs in to the system can see all of his or her sessions, and the themes of those sessions. The asynchronous communication functions of the Coaching Zone® include the ability to schedule a coaching session with a meeting invite, share and retrieve content (e.g. assessments, development plans, and resources), and exchange notes through its coaching notes feature. For asynchronous communication, it also features integrated videoconferencing capability. Thus, over the course of several hours a client can login to review his or her notes prior to a session, review an article or homework assignment, engage in a video coaching session, and then accept a meeting invitation for the next session, all within a single virtual environment.

13.3.6 Platforms with Coach Access

Coaching platforms continue to evolve by addressing an increasing amount of the coaching lifecycle. The latest coaching platform technologies possess the streamlined capability of various synchronous and asynchronous tools, while also providing access to a pool of coaches. For example, services like Ternio and mobile apps like Coach.me allow users to log in, browse a range of coaches by category (like productivity or mindfulness), and connect with a coach of their choice on the spot. The app also has functionalities that allow users to track their habits over time. Other technologies, like BetterUp, allow users to connect with a dedicated coach from an established network. Many of these tools are relevant not only to organizations but also consumers. A person looking to increase their time management skills, for example, can download Coach.me, enter payment information, search for a coach, and then schedule a session within about 10–15 minutes.

Other advances in coaching platforms include the personalized tailoring of coaching programs. Platforms such as LeaderAmp allow the customization of the entire coaching engagement, from the dimensions to be assessed and coached, and whether or not to include artificial intelligence to complement expert coaching. Once it is set up, platforms like LeaderAmp further enable "just-in-time" coaching, MIM and MDM so that the relationship of the coach is extended through the client's mobile device, even when they are not together.

13.3.7 Coaching Operations Applications

According to the International Coach Federation, there are more than 53,300 professional coach practitioners worldwide generating nearly $2.4 billion in revenue (International Coach Federation & PricewaterhouseCoopers, 2016). With a 19 percent increase since 2011, it is clear coaching continues to be in a growth mode. With the increased use of coaching, there is much more information and more variables to track and manage. Whereas tracking data and client information was once possible through manual entry on a spreadsheet, the expanding use of coaching across enterprises is requiring more advanced tools to capture and manage project data. Technology holds the potential for companies to more effectively oversee, manage, and evaluate coaching engagements (Pascal et al., 2015). As a result, a new category of coaching technology is emerging in the form of coach management systems, such as AIIR Consulting Enterprise Coaching Manager® (ECM), Chronus, and CoachLogix. Coach management systems provide a way to see, track, and manage coaching activities in an organization. Some of these systems also provide data analytics that yield insights into the effectiveness and business impact of coaching engagements, allowing talent-development managers to make strategic decisions about their coaching programs through aggregate data.

While coach management systems are increasingly being developed by coaching and technology companies, some corporations have decided to build their own customized internal applications. For instance, GE has created their own app for promoting managerial coaching as part of ongoing performance management. Google has leveraged its own internal technology resources to deploy their scalable Guru+ program. The technology is leveraged by a client looking to identify a coach and schedule a session. The technology also captures a coach's rating from the client (Abel, Ray, & Nair, 2016).

Table 13.4 *Coaching platform technologies*

Platform	Coach-Client Platform	Administrators Dashboard	Closed Coach Pool	Artificial Intelligence	Open Coach Pool (Sharing Economy)
BetterUp	x	x	x		
Enterprise Coaching Manager®	x	x	x		
CoachLogix		x			
Coach Director	x	x			
Chronus	x	x			
LeaderAmp	x	x		x	
Everwise	x	x			x
Coach.me	x	x			x

Before turning to the implications and applications of future technological advancements for coaching, it is important to note some of the limitations and risks of using technologically mediated forms of communication. As coaching services adopt virtual methods, practitioners must ensure privacy and confidentiality by using secure online mediums, creating authentication measures to validate the correct identity of the user, and provide resources to clients explaining risks in using the technology (Richardson et al., 2009; Turvey et al., 2013; Yuen et al., 2012).

Another obstacle for the adoption of virtual coaching is the willingness and technological competency of coaches themselves. Although research suggests that virtual coaching can help clients achieve their goals and establish an effective partnership with their coaches (Berry et al., 2011), there are still practitioners who may remain skeptical (Rees & Stone, 2005). Otte et al. (2014) found that receptiveness to virtual coaching was mediated by a coach's internet self-efficacy, feelings of confidence to effectively use technology, and support for using evidence-based and goal-oriented coaching methodologies. And as discussed in earlier virtual coaching studies, Charbonneau (2002) argued that fit between the coach, client, and medium is a key ingredient to virtual coaching success, while Passarelli et al. (2017) found the client's perception of richness is tied to their comfort level with the technology. In practice, this is validated by companies like Cisco Systems' use of their own collaborative technologies to conduct virtual coaching (Desrosiers, et al., 2017; Ghods & Kovach, 2017). Since all leaders are familiar with and used to using their own technology, the virtual connection is a non-issue and rather part of their normal work day. Furthermore, given their extensive experience working with their technology, they can better troubleshoot or manage technical glitches during their coaching engagement instead of experience a derailment in their session. Sharing practical examples like what Cisco Systems is doing, and demystifying virtual coaching strategies through education, could develop technological competency and efficacy in coaches and, in turn, assist in the adoption of virtual coaching strategies into more practices (Yuen et al., 2012).

13.3.8 New Trends

The newest coaching technologies are starting to illuminate new ways to improve both synchronous and asynchronous coaching. They are blurring the line between video and message-based coaching apps as early forms of (AI). In all cases, these innovations range from incremental improvements on effective coaching practices to entirely new ways of supporting clients digitally that would not have been possible previously. The most important trends are those that allow coaching to be embedded into a client's daily life, even when they're not with their expert coach.

Further, breadth of uses of coaching throughout the life cycle of the process itself is starting to expand. More organizations and people are starting to use technology platforms to find and match coaches and clients, and to manage the coaching process. In that process, it is becoming increasingly common for the line between synchronous video coaching technologies like Skype, Appear.in, or Google Hangouts to be blurred with asynchronous technologies like email, mobile coaching apps, mobile messaging, and bulletin boards.

13.3.9 Innovations in Remote Coaching

Coaches are starting to make use of several new technologies to remotely monitor and support clients either synchronously or asynchronously. First, mobile phones and tablets now make it easy for apps to include a digital journal that clients can use to capture their thoughts after deliberately practicing. By encouraging clients to use a journal on a regular basis, a coach can track their progress via a cloud portal or document and support the client in between synchronous sessions. Some platforms allow the client to set up reminders to journal, via their smartphone using voice-to-text software (e.g. Siri). This is a special-case use of Experience Sampling technologies that periodically send mobile or email messages to clients to either survey them or remind them to jot down their current affect, or experience at that moment in a given day. These platforms automatically message participants, and then allow a coach or an administrator to monitor the quality of a person's engagement in between coaching sessions, including their sentiment. Research is showing that regular daily journaling and online peer group discussions elicit deeper cognitive and affective impacts than the simple use of experience sampling that merely tracks the behaviors of a person in naturalistic settings (Miller, 2016).

Second, some teacher coaching programs are starting to use "Bug in ear" mobile technology (Rock, Zigmond, Gregg, & Gable et al., 2011). "Bug in ear" technology allows a remote coach to watch and listen to a client while he or she is teaching. This is a much more elegant approach to supporting a client's real-time performance, in contrast with traditional approaches where the coach has to sit in the classroom, and cannot communicate privately with the coach in front of his or her students. "Bug in Ear" technology allows the expert to provide discreet, real-time feedback so that behaviors can be adjusted immediately. Coaching can include short praise, when a client is teaching and does something well, or corrective if the teacher probably lost the class, and needs to adjust his or her approach. Rock et al. (2011) provide useful guidelines about how best to use "Bug in Ear" technology. In 2018, Intel released new prototypes of hardware and software that may provide a similar "Fly in Eye" technology for coaching. Unlike Google Glass, which was ultimately viewed as awkward and interpersonally insensitive to context, Intel's normal-looking glasses provide unobtrusive suggestions for behavior that can be sent by a coach or by AI (Bohn, 2018).

13.3.10 Innovations in Assessment

Computer-adaptive measurement tools are increasingly embedded into coaching platforms as well. While some coaching platforms have historically used computers or mobile devices to administer the same questions to all clients, computer-adaptive assessments are dramatically shorter and more precise than traditional approaches. In particular, one emerging trend is to have clients manage their own 360 or multi-source surveys. Rather than have a centralized or computer-based process send unwanted automated completion reminders, the newer paradigm is to insist that clients proactively seek a circle of support for their development at the beginning of a new coaching engagement. A key advantage for this use of technology is that the individual makes sure that stakeholders are ready to be contacted for feedback and support. This can increase survey completion rates and thereby yield more substantial feedback. In the most advanced platforms, coaches can actually view the progress (or lack thereof) of clients nominating, and persuading stakeholders to rate them, providing a much more seamless view of how the client is managing his or her own environment around their on-the-job application of coaching. Some platforms are even able to adjust for rater bias (e.g. severity or leniency), even when slightly different people are rating clients before and after coaching, so that results are comparable (Barney, 2015).

13.3.11 Innovations with Gamification

Another emerging technological trend is the gamification of coaching. Emerging research suggests that leaderboards, a virtual environment where people can keep score about their progress in participating in developmental activities such as coaching, are as powerful a tool in motivating learners as setting difficult but achievable goals (Landers & Landers, 2014). The new digital coaching platforms are allowing online and mobile coaching-related behaviors to be included in leaderboards. Client behaviors that can be gamified include journaling about the lessons a client learned from practice, stakeholder management such as soliciting feedback on a 360, or peer support such as answering online questions of other clients in the same cohort (Barney, 2017).

13.4 The Future of Coaching

Google's top coach, David Peterson, is convinced that human coaches will not be required at all in the future (Peterson, 2016). This is actually not a new idea; Keynes argued that all jobs will eventually be automated nearly a century ago (Keynes, 1931). At the same time, more skeptical analysts estimate the probability of coaches being replaced by artificial intelligence to be only 1.3 percent (Frey & Osborne, 2017). Regardless, there is no question that coaching tools will continue to advance rapidly, just as information technology is transforming many other professions. In this last section, we review the cutting-edge development of science and technology, and speculate on what the future of technology-enabled coaching may look like.

Just as the telephone became a commonplace tool in coaching relationships, we believe that coaches in the distant future will make everyday use of advanced technologies. While today there are clients who shy away from the use of computer-mediated approaches, we expect that as the younger, mobile-native generations enter the workplace and become more comfortable with coaching technology, they will come to expect coaching right when they want it, all the time. The need to match coach, client and technology to the problem will become increasingly quaint as coaching technology advances.

13.4.1 The Future of Virtual and Augmented Reality Coaching

We are seeing an emergence of the use of Virtual Reality (VR) in coaching, and believe that this trend will continue to accelerate because it gives clients a safe place to practice before attempting new behaviors in their real work or life. Startups like STRIVR are starting to blend traditional coaching and VR coaching, mostly for professional athletes who can afford the high price tag, as VR coaching is extremely expensive to develop and maintain. We expect VR to only become mainstreamed in coaching once development costs and the price of hardware become drastically lower.

It could be that augmented reality, where the individual wearing goggles or glasses sees both the real world and additional computer-generated information, may be more useful earlier than VR. This is because AR may evolve to be a new form of "Bug in Ear" technology whereby a coach can watch either real-time or recorded samples of situations and clients' behavior that may improve the coaching process. This technology is relatively more affordable, and as mobile networks become more stable and able to handle more information, it is likely to add value to many types of coaching situations because it is less complex and expensive than full VR simulations.

In fact, AR is beginning to take off. Given the advent of technologies like Google Glass and GoPro cameras that can capture real-time, first-person views, the startup company ScopeAR uses heads-up displays or screen-sharing with just-in-time coaches. If a client is working, he or she can get a set of measurement information on how they're performing, and an expert coach can give them guidance just as they are performing a task. Furthermore, the fact that these situations can be recorded would be a valuable opportunity for coaches to engage in retrospectives where situations are played back with clients and alternative decisions for the same situation are explored and worked through.

13.4.2 The Future of Artificially Intelligent Coaching

In contrast with VR and AR, artificial intelligence is largely software-based and very inexpensive. The improvements in artificial intelligence are likely to continue to revolutionize the field of coaching. Today's approaches try to emulate or complement a coach, using one of two approaches. Chatbot coaches, such as BOLDR, use AI to attempt to provide real-time suggestions and feedback just in time for a given client. But today's Chatbots are typically not grounded in science, nor can they have the contextual perspective of a real coach. In contrast, human-authored and psychometrically calibrated content, like LeaderAmp's, emulates the coach with a different set of tradeoffs. While the human-authored content may be more meaningful and exciting, especially when authored by a famous or well-respected expert, and the fact that users can schedule exactly when they want to get these suggestions is beneficial, they are not interactive.

The future is likely to include the best of both of these approaches – science-anchored content, with real-time human-quality feedback and support. Until such time as AI is powerful enough to match a human coach, it is likely that blended technologies will come to dominate. In this way, clients can gain both the convenience and affordability of just-in-time coaching and journaling. And expert coaches will be able to see their clients' progress, or questions, and intervene in between synchronous sessions.

13.4.3 The Future of Big Data and Artificially Intelligent Assessment with Biometrics

The use of big data and artificial intelligence in assessment is another futuristic trend that is emerging. While IBM Watson, LeaderAmp, Receptiviti, Psychobabble, and HireVue each have text or video-based AI approaches, they are largely proprietary and usually do not report research showing that they are reliable and valid for the purposes they claim. This is a serious concern with regular assessments, but it is an even bigger issue with AI because of the infamous problems that computer scientists have had with the bias of deep learning algorithms. For example, Microsoft had to turn off its chatbot that was turned into a fictitious Nazi by internet trolls (Ingram, 2016), and Google's AI algorithms inadvertently misclassified pictures of African Americans as gorillas (Zhang, 2015). While we are enthusiastic about the potential of these natural language and video-based assessments, we also encourage the reader to scrutinize technical reports for validation, reliability, and fairness that I/O psychology requires.

Because of the rapid progress and low cost of AI, we expect that this trend will be the most powerful to complement and perhaps replace coaching in the years to come. In particular, big data allows many parts of coaching to be sampled and used to train the AI, which requires large amounts of behavioral examples before it can perform reliably. Similarly, there is also some early evidence suggesting that unobtrusive biometric data, such as the activity people perform on smartphones, can be used to measure attributes such as personality (Dubey, Mehl, & Mankodiya, 2016; Moubayed et al., 2014; Yannick et al., 2017). In this way, biometric big data may make assessment and reassessment especially painless as that research progresses.

13.5 Implications and Conclusions

Coaching is already becoming more affordable and practical thanks to the progress of the information technologies. In fact, this has been echoed in popular press and through anecdotal evidence as a practical, creative, and cost-effective alternative to face-to-face coaching (Goldsmith & Lyons, 2006; Hagevik, 1998;

Hakim, 2000; Hudson, 1999; Kilburg, 2000). While technology is not a magic pill or panacea, it holds the promise of embedding coaching more deeply into people's daily lives, at affordable levels for just about anyone at work. In fact, because coaching technology makes it cost-effective to coach all levels of employees, increasingly, firms like Coaching Right Now, and BetterUp are promoting technology-delivered coaching for even individual contributors without managerial authority. This just makes it even easier to study and improve the science of coaching. Next, we review several implications of these new technologies.

13.5.1 Practical and Theoretical Implications

We believe that the technological advances revolutionizing the practice of virtual coaching are especially beneficial for today's clients. To our earlier point at the beginning of this chapter, we see several key areas yielding the most benefit: accessibility, convenience, cost, and scalability. First, because in-person coaching is so expensive, it has historically been available only to very senior leaders. But today's technology has made coaching vastly more affordable, which is key to both developing employees lower in the management hierarchy or employees who are in price-sensitive environments, such as the developing world. Second, coaching has become much more convenient for clients. When coaching is just-in-time, as with the newer mobile apps and AI techniques, clients can receive support just when they want it, and not have to wait for their personal coach. Insofar as future research can demonstrate that technology helps clients practice more deliberately or effectively, it is likely to help them develop better than they could with just a coach and limited or no technology at all. But, ultimately, this is an empirical question, and not sufficiently tested to warrant strong conclusions about efficacy.

While technology clearly presents an opportunity to democratize coaching, increase efficiency, lower costs, and provide immediate responsiveness, there may be an unintended downside for the coaching relationship. For a client who leverages coaching technology to its fullest, an engagement with a just-in-time coach can turn into a series of disjointed, problem-solving sessions that may each be valuable unto themselves, but not present an opportunity for longitudinal growth and sustained behavior change. This contrasts with the traditional coaching experience that allows for the burgeoning of a coaching relationship that in turn facilitates change. If that relationship lasts only for a few sessions, one can argue that the longer-term sustainability could be less efficacious than the traditional paradigm.

Overall, virtual coaching still lacks a solid theoretical foundation. Ghods (2009) and Berry et al. (2011) both leveraged the working alliance theory from the therapeutic literatures, Boyce and Clutterbuck (2011) and Passarelli et al. (2017) referenced the nmedia richness theories from information systems literatures and Charbonneau (2002) leveraged trait theories of media selection (i.e., access/quality theory, information richness theory, social presence theory, task technology fit theory), as well as social interaction theories and technology acceptance model. Several related theories, such as the media synchronicity theory and embodied social presence theory, have yet to be investigated in terms of their integration with coaching. As the practice of virtual coaching accelerates, the need for a strong theoretical framework, bolstered by more research, will only become more urgent.

13.5.2 Transforming the Coaching Role

Today's coaching technology has matured to a level that it portends a major transformation for the way coaches work. Since coaching has been engaged by phone and videoconference, coaches were able to service clients with less travel. The newest cloud technologies allow coaches to access a window into each client's day-to-day journal or real-time performance, yielding an unprecedented opportunity for coaches to support clients, even when they're not meeting in real time.

Perhaps the greatest disruption to the existing paradigm is how technology will impact pricing. The latest technologies will challenge coaches to responsibly offer coaching at lower price points, with great efficacy, and still achieve profitability by billing for fewer in-person, synchronous sessions. The latest cloud-based technologies enable coaches to support substantially more clients, asynchronously, than they ever could do through traditional, in-person coaching.

Not all coaches will enjoy this tradeoff. Coaches wedded to a higher touch, in-person experience will likely remain tethered to a business model that addresses very senior level clients willing and capable of paying a premium. But, with the advent of discount coaching offered by firms such as BetterUp, we suspect organizations and clients will increasingly seek out more convenient, cost-effective coaching solutions that only new technologies will be able to facilitate.

Similarly, no client or company enjoys long, tedious assessments. Today's use of computer-adaptive assessments that are up to 90 percent shorter than traditional approaches address most organizational stakeholders' complaints about over-surveying. We expect that the computer-adaptive measurement approach will continue replacing longer, less precise assessments because they allow for better identification of client needs and improvements in a less tedious process.

13.5.3 Future Research

While these advanced technologies may hold wonderful opportunities for coaching, very little research has been conducted to make recommendations based on empirical science. In particular, it is unclear to what degree the asynchronous forms of coaching, especially the artificially intelligent forms, are sufficiently useful so as to demonstrate greater efficacy than traditional coaching alone. There is good reason to believe that it should work better, given that it allows more spaced practice between coaching sessions that the literature suggests is key to many forms of skill development. But it is not clear that this form of digital coaching can play the same role, and it needs to be studied further.

What is also potentially problematic is that while traditional coaching was purely relationship based, the more sophisticated forms of AI are not just an extension of a relationship, but a potential replacement. It may seem far fetched that a purely AI approach can supplant the wisdom and emotional connection a human coach can have with a client. Further, it's not at all clear that these forms of technology can work on a sustained basis to permanently solidify new knowledge, skill, or behavior change.

Finally, it is important to note that many of these unanswered questions may be better answered by the same coaching technology platforms through assessment data. Computer-adaptive assessments allow for efficient assessment data collection that make it easy for re-measurement over time (Barney, 2015). Frequent re-measuring allows for scientists to gain statistical power, by using repeated-measures experiments. Similarly, collecting at least three measurements is a prerequisite to the use of longitudinal research designs, like latent growth modeling (Day & Lance, 2004).

Second, technological platforms make it easy for researchers to have experimental and quasi-experimental designs. This is crucial to gain strong confidence that the presence of a technology hypothesized to make the coaching process more effective actually causes the gains claimed. The fact that some of these platforms can make it easier to test these hypotheses is a key benefit to some of the newer coaching technologies we've outlined. Further, we expect that the science of coaching will increasingly use open-source experimental methods like the Psychology Experiment Building Language (PEBL) to test hypotheses with live clients, in different experimental conditions. A major implication is that coaching scientists will need to learn new skills such as programming in PEBL, or the open-source statistical language R, to fully leverage this potential.

13.6 Conclusions

Advances in technology have been changing the coaching profession for many years. The development of coaching technology has lowered the cost of coaching and improved the personalization – even when coaches and clients are not physically together. Given that the origins of coaching are from the executive suite, the role of technology in coaching is especially important to bringing the benefits of coaching to deeper parts of an organization, including middle managers, front-line leaders, and individual contributors. Companies such as Facebook, Cisco Systems, and LinkedIn now offer coaching to people at all levels, mediated through technology that makes this once elite service affordable and accessible to the broader organization.

Some of these technologies have allowed coaches to deepen their relationships with clients in between coaching sessions. Advances in text messaging have enabled more real-time support and accountability at a minimal effort. And now coaching platforms have given coaches and clients the ability to organize these tools in even more efficient ways. Organizations have also benefited from this technology by giving talent development program managers the ability to scale coaching activities without compromising on accountability, while remaining organized and capable of capturing analytics for strategic purposes.

Nevertheless, the application of technology to coaching still requires the intervention of a coach. The technology of coaching is in a moment of transition, with a future that promises both wider adoption and greater automation. But as scientist-practitioners we need to test the degree to which these technologies actually affect the quality, cost, scalability, and timeliness of coaching in favorable ways. This is especially true for the newest innovations. Advances in AI, machine learning, and robotics will present new opportunities and challenges for coaching. Fortunately, many of these platforms actually make it easier to test efficacy hypotheses than ever before, by tracking both the antecedents and outcomes of coaching – in some cases in real time. Our advice to researchers is to continue pushing for better, higher-quality research that continues to explore new technologies used in coaching. Our advice to coaches and practitioners is to incessantly strive to remain agile and relevant through continuous learning and being open to new technologies. This is the future and it's right around the corner. If you want to remain relevant and effective, you have no choice but to be open to change.

References

Abel, A. L., Ray, R. L., & Nair, S. (2016). Global Executive Coaching Survey 2016. The Conference Board.

After Moore's law: The future of computing. (March 12, 2016). *The Economist* . Retrieved January 16, 2018, from www.economist.com/news/leaders/21694528-era-predict able-improvement-computer-hardware-ending-what-comes-next-future.

Aguilera, A., Bruehlman-Senecal, E., Demasi, O., & Avila, P. (2017). Automated text messaging as an adjunct to cognitive behavioral therapy for depression: A clinical trial. *Journal of Medical Internet Research*, *19*(5), e148. http://doi .org/10.2196/jmir.6914.

AIIR Consulting. (2018). Usage and Survey Data (Version 4). [Data file]. Philadelphia, PA: AIIR Consulting.

Backhaus, A., Agha, Z., Maglione, M. L., Repp, A., Ross, B., Zuest, D., Thorp, S. R. (2012). Videoconferencing psychotherapy: A systematic review. *Psychological Services*, *9*(2), 111–131. http://dx.doi.org/10.1037/a0027924

Barney, M. F. (2015). *Amplifying leaders: Using quantified self technologies to grow leaders like Olympians*. California: LeaderAmp Press.

Barney, M. F. & Goparaju, S. (2017). *Better coaching: Elevating potential and performance with innovative methods*. California: LeaderAmp Press.

Berrouiguet, S., Baca-García, E., Brandt, S., Walter, M., & Courtet, P. (2016). Fundamentals for future mobile-health (mHealth): A systematic review of mobile phone and web-based text messaging in mental health. *Journal of Medical Internet Research*, *18*(6), e135. http://doi.org/10.2196/jmir.5066.

Berry, R. M., Ashby, J. S., Gnilka, P. B., & Matheny, K. B. (2011). A comparison of face-to-face and distance coaching practices: Coaches' perceptions of the role of the working alliance in problem resolution. *Consulting Psychology Journal: Practice and Research, 63,* 243–253.

Bowles, S. V. & Picano, J. J. (2006). Dimensions of coaching related to productivity and quality of life. *Consulting Psychology Journal: Practice and Research, 58,* 232–239.

Bohn, D. (2018). Intel made smart glasses that look normal. Exclusive first look at Vaunt, which uses retinal projection to put a display in your eyeball. Downloaded February 5, 2018, from www.theverge.com/2018/2/5/16966530/intel-vaunt-smart-glasses-announced-ar-video.

Boyce, L. A. & Clutterbuck, D. (2011). E-coaching: Accept it, it's here, and it's evolving! In G. Hernez-Broome & L. A. Boyce (Eds.), *Advancing executive coaching: Setting the course for successful leadership coaching* (pp. 285–215). San Francisco, CA: Jossey-Bass.

Boyce, L. A. & Hernez-Broome, G. (2010). E-coaching: Consideration of leadership coaching in a virtual environment. In D. Clutterbuck & Z. Hussain (Eds.), *Virtual coach, virtual mentor* (pp. 139–174). Charlotte, NC: Information Age Publishing.

Charbonneau, M. A. (2002). Participant self-perceptions about the cause of behavior change from a program of executive coaching . Unpublished doctoral dissertation, Alliant International University, Los Angeles, CA.

Church, K. & de Oliveira, R. (2013). What's up with WhatsApp?: Comparing mobile instant messaging behaviors with traditional SMS. In *Proceedings of the 15th International Conference on Human-Computer Interaction with Mobile Devices and Services* (pp. 352–361). New York, NY: Association for Computing Machinery.

Clutterbuck, D. & Hussain, Z. (2010). *Virtual coach, virtual mentor.* Charlotte, NC: Information Age Publishing.

Cooper, S. E. & Neal, C. (2015). Consultants' use of telepractice: Practitioner survey, issues, and resources. *Consulting Psychology Journal: Practice and Research, 67*(2), 85–99. http://dx.doi.org/10.1037/cpb0000015.

Corbett, K. & Valeri, J. (2016). *The eleventh annual executive coaching survey.* Cincinnati, OH: Sherpa Consulting.

Coutu, D. & Kaufmann, C. (2009). *The realities of executive coaching .* HBR Business Report.

Daft, R., & Lengel, R. (1986). Organizational information requirements, media richness and structural design. *Management Science*, 32(5), 554–571.

Daft, R., Lengel, R., & Trevino, L. (1987). Message equivocality, media selection, and manager performance: Implications for information systems. *MIS Quarterly, 11* (3), 355–366. doi:10.2307/248682.

Daly-Jones, O., Monk, A., & Watts, L. (1998). Some advantages of video conferencing over high-quality audio conferencing: Fluency and awareness of attentional focus. *International Journal of Human-Computer Studies, 49*(1), 21–58.

Day, D. V. & Lance, C. E. (2004). Understanding the development of leadership complexity through latent growth modeling. In D. V. Day, S. J. Zacarro, & S. M. Halpin (Eds.), *Leader development for transforming organizations: Growing leaders for tomorrow* (pp. 41–69). Mahwah, NJ: Erlbaum.

Day, S. X. & Schneider, P. L. (2002). Psychotherapy using distance technology: A comparison of face-to-face, video, and audio treatment.*Journal of Counseling Psychology, 49*, 499–503.

Desrosiers, E., Ghods, N., Grubb, A., McHenry, J., & Nieberding, A. O. (2017). Coaching in Organizations: Today's reality and future decisions. Panel presentation in "Innovations in Executive Coaching: Deepening Your Expertise in a Dynamic World" The Society for Industrial and Organizational Psychology 13th Annual Leading Edge Consortium, Minneapolis, Minnesota.

Dubey, H., Mehl, M. R., & Mankodiya, K. (2016). BigEar: Inferring the ambient and emotional correlates from smartphone-based acoustic big data. ArXiv:1606.03636 [cs.SD], DOI10.1109/CHASE.2016.46.

Frazee, R. V. (2008). E-coaching in organizations: A study of features, practices, and determinants of use . Unpublished doctoral dissertation, University of San Diego, San Diego, CA.

Frey, C. B. & Osborne, M. A. (2017). The future of employment: How susceptible are jobs to computerisation? *Technological Forecasting & Social Change, 114*(c), 254–280. doi:10.1016/j.techfore.2016.08.019#.

Geissler, H., Hasenbein, M., Kanatouri, S., & Wegner, R. (2014). E-coaching: Conceptual and empirical findings of a virtual coaching programme. *International Journal of Evidence Based Coaching and Mentoring, 12*(2), 165–187.

Ghods, N. (2009). Distance coaching: The relationship between the coach-client relationship, client satisfaction, and coaching outcomes. Unpublished doctoral dissertation, Alliant International University, San Diego, CA.

Ghods, N. & Boyce, C. (2012). Virtual coaching and mentoring. In J. Passmore, D. B. Peterson, & T. Freire (Eds.), *The Wiley-Blackwell handbook of the psychology of coaching and mentoring* (pp. 501–523). Chichester, UK: Wiley.

Ghods, N. & Kovach, R. (2017). Disrupting a thriving practice in the face of new business demands: Cisco's Story. Presentation in "The Next Wave of Leadership: Accelerating Development, Increasing Impact" The Society of Consulting Psychology Conference, Seattle, WA.

Goldsmith, M. & Lyons, L. S. (2006). *Coaching for leadership: The practice of leadership coaching from the world's greatest coaches* (2nd edn.). San Francisco, CA: Pfeiffer.

Grove, A. S. (1995). *High Output Management*. New York, NY: Vintage Books.

Gurbaxani, V. (April 20, 2016). You don't have to be a software company to think like one. *Harvard Business Review*. Retrieved from https://hbr.org/2016/04/you-dont-have-to-be-a-software-company-to-think-like-one.

Hagevik, S. (1998). Choosing a career counseling service. *Journal of Environmental Health, 98*(4), 31–32.

Hakim, C. (2000). Virtual coaching: Learning, like time, stops for no one.*Journal for Quality and Participation, 23*(1), 42–44.

Hernez-Broome, G., Boyce, L. A., Whyman, W. (2007). Critical Issues of Coaching with Technology. In L. A. Boyce & G. Hernez-Broome (Chair), E-coaching: Supporting leadership coaching with technology. Symposium conducted at the 22nd Annual Conference of the Society for Industrial and Organizational Psychology, New York, NY.

Hudson, F. M. (1999).*The handbook of coaching: A comprehensive resource guide for managers, executives, consultants, and human resource professionals*. San Francisco, CA: Jossey-Bass.

Ingram, M. (March 24, 2016). Microsoft's chat-bot was fun for awhile, until it turned into a racist. *Fortune*. Downloaded January 22, 2018, from http://fortune.com/2016/03/24/chat-bot-racism/.

International Coach Federation & PricewaterhouseCoopers. (2016).*2016 ICF Global Coaching Study*.

Jarvis, J. (June 2004). *Coaching and buying coaching services: A guide* (Reference No. 2995). London, UK: Chartered Institute of Personnel and Development.

Keynes, J. M. (1931). *Essays in Persuasion*. Macmillan.

Kilburg, R. R. (1996). Toward a conceptual understanding and definition of executive coaching.*Consulting Psychology Journal: Practice and Research*, *48*, 134–144.

Kilburg, R. R. (1997). Coaching and executive character core problems and basic approaches.*Consulting Psychology Journal: Practice and Research*, *49*, 281–299.

Kilburg, R. R. (2000). *Executive coaching: Developing managerial wisdom in a world of chaos*. Washington, DC: American Psychological Association.

Landers, R. N. & Landers, A. K. (2014). An empirical test of the theory of gamified learning: The effect of leaderboards on time-on-task and academic performance.*Simulation & Gaming*, *45*(6), 769–785. doi:10.1177/1046878114563662.

Linley, P. A. (2006). Coaching research: Who? what? when? why? *International Journal of Evidence Based Coaching and Mentoring*, *4*(2), 1–7. Retrieved August 7, 2007, from www.brookes.ac.uk/schools/education/ijebcm/vol4-no2-reflections.html.

Liu, W. L., Zhang, K., Locatis, C., & Ackerman, M. (2015). Cloud and traditional video-conferencing technology for telemedicine and distance learning.*Telemedicine Journal and E-Health*, *21*(5), 422–426. http://doi.org/10.1089/tmj.2014.0121

Luxton, D. D., McCann, R. A., Bush, N. E., Mishkind, M. C., & Reger, G. M. (2011). mHealth for mental health: Integrating smartphone technology in behavioral healthcare. *Professional Psychology: Research and Practice*, *42*(6), 505–512.

Mausbach, B. T., Moore, R., Roesch, S., Cardenas, V., & Patterson, T. L. (2010). The relationship between homework compliance and therapy outcomes: An updated meta-analysis.*Cognitive Therapy and Research*, *34*(5), 429–438. http://doi.org/10.1007/s10608-010–9297-z.

Miller, A. N. (2016). Media diaries. A comparison of three approaches to electronic media diaries.*Communication Research Reports*, *34*(2), 171–179. doi:10.1080/08824096.2016.1224172.

Moubayed, N. A., Vazquez-Alvarez, Y., McKay, A., & Vinciarelli, A. (November 3–7, 2014). Face-Based Automatic Personality Perception. Proceedings of the 22nd ACM International Conference on Multimedia, Orlando, Florida, pp. 1153–1156. doi:10.1145/2647868.2655014.

O'Brien, M. (1997). Executive coaching. *Supervision*, *58*(4), 6–8.

Otte, S., Bangerter, A., Britsch, M., & Wüthrich, U. (2014). Attitudes of coaches towards the use of computer-based technology in coaching.*Consulting Psychology Journal: Practice and Research*, *66*(1), 38–52. http://dx.doi.org/10.1037/a0035592.

Pascal, A., Sass, M., Gregory, J., & Kaiser, R. B. (2015). I'm only human: The role of technology in coaching. *Consulting Psychology Journal: Practice and Research*, *67*(2), 100–109.

Passarelli, A. M., Van Oosten, E. B., Varley, A., & Trinh, M. P. (2017). Effect of coaching modality on coaching effectiveness. Paper presented in symposium "High-tech or High-touch? Developmental Relationships in the Digital Age" Academy of Management Conference, Atlanta, GA. Showcase Symposium, Best Symposium Award, MED Division.

Peterson, D. B. (1996). Executive coaching at work: The art of one-on-one change. *Consulting Psychology Journal: Practice and Research, 48*, 78–86.

Peterson, D. (2016). Reinventing executive coaching: Seven paths forward. Invited keynote, The Future of Coaching: Building Bridges and Expanding Boundaries. Columbia Coaching Learning Association (CCLA). New York, NY.

Peterson, D. (2017). Imagining the future of executive coaching. Keynote presentation in "Innovations in Executive Coaching: Deepening Your Expertise in a Dynamic World" The Society for Industrial and Organizational Psychology 13th Annual Leading Edge Consortium, Minneapolis, Minnesota.

Rees, C. & Haythornthwaite, S. (2004). Telepsychology and videoconferencing: Issues, opportunities and guidelines for psychologists. *Australian Psychologist, 39*(3), 212–219.

Rees, C. S. & Stone, S. (2005). Therapeutic alliance in face-to-face versus videoconferenced psychotherapy.*Professional Psychology: Research and Practice, 36*(6), 649–653. http://dx.doi.org/10.1037/0735–7028.36.6.649.

Richardson, L. K., Frueh, B. C., Grubaugh, A. L., Egede, L., & Elhai, J. D. (2009). Current directions in videoconferencing tele-mental health research.*Clinical Psychology : A Publication of the Division of Clinical Psychology of the American Psychological Association, 16*(3), 323–338. http://doi.org/10.1111/j.1468–2850.2009.01170.x.

Rock, M. L, Zigmond, N. P., Gregg, M., & Gable, R. A. (2011). The power of virtual coaching. *Educational Leadership, 69*(2), 42–48.

Sherpa. (2016) Eleventh Sherpa Coaching Survey. Retrieved March 9, 2017, from https://www.sherpacoaching.com/.

Sinewing, C. (2006). Must coaching be couched in secrecy? *People Management, 12*(14), 44–44.

Tang, Y. & Hew, K. F. (May 2017). Is mobile instant messaging (MIM) useful in education? Examining its technological, pedagogical, and social affordances. *Educational Research Review, 21*, 85–104. doi:10.1016/j.edurev.2017.05.001.

Ting, S. & Hart, E. W. (2004). Formal coaching. In C. D. McCauley & E. Van Velsor (Eds.), *The Center for Creative Leadership handbook of leadership development* (pp. 116–150). San Francisco, CA: Jossey-Bass.

Turvey, C., Coleman, M., Dennison, O., Drude, K., Goldenson, M., Hirsch, P., & Bernard, J. (2013). ATA practice guidelines for video-based online mental health services. *Telemedicine and e-Health, 19*(9), 722–730.

Wang, L. (2000). The relationship between distance coaching and the transfer of training. Unpublished doctoral dissertation, University of Illinois at Urbana-Champaign.

Wilson, M., Hannum, K. & Center for Creative Leadership. (2006). *Center for Creative Leadership impact study: Sonoco* . Retrieved June 21, 2007. from www.ccl.org/leadership/pdf/aboutCCL/SONOCOimpactstudy.pdf.

Witherspoon, R. & White, R. P. (1996). Executive coaching: What's in it for you. *Training and Development, 50*(3), 14–15.

Yannick, S., Sutin, A. R., Bovier-Lapierre, G., & Terracciano, A. (2017). Personality and walking speed across adulthood: Prospective evidence from five samples.*Social Psychological and Personality Science*, 1–8. doi:10.1177/1948550617725152.

Young, D. P. & Dixon, N. M. (1996).*Helping leaders take effective action: A program evaluation*. Greensboro, NC: CCL Press.

Yuen, E., Goetter, E., Herbert, J., Forman, E., Roberts, M. C., & Carter, J. A. (2012). Challenges and opportunities in internet-mediated telemental health. *Professional Psychology: Research and Practice*, *43*(1), 1–8. http://dx.doi.org/10.1037/a0024485.

Zhang, M. (July 1, 2015). Google Photos tags two African-Americans as gorillas through facial recognition software. *Forbes*. Retrieved from www.forbes.com/sites/mzhang/2015/07/01/google-photos-tags-two-african-americans-as-gorillas-through-facial-recognition-software/#2863b2f7713d.

14 Virtual Reality Training in Organizations

Matt C. Howard and Chad J. Marshall

For the past several decades, the application of virtual reality (VR) for organizational training purposes has been steadily increasing (Bedwell & Salas, 2010; Howard, 2018; Nagendran et al., 2013; Palter & Grantcharov, 2014; Sitzmann, 2011). Early efforts often applied relatively basic technologies that presented unrealistic environments to develop knowledge, skills, abilities, and other characteristics (KSAOs) that were too dangerous or costly to perform in the real world. For instance, Bliss, Tidwell, and Guest (1997) tested the efficacy of a VR training (VRT) program to develop the wayfinding abilities of firefighters in an unfamiliar building, showing that the VRT program was as effective as blueprint training and both were more effective than no training at all. While the results of these early efforts were often lackluster (Goldberg, 1994; Jense & Kuijper, 1993; Kozak et al., 1993; Psotka, 1995; Regian, Shebilske, & Monk, 1992), they nevertheless demonstrated that virtual environments could be used to develop real KSAOs.

Due to recent technological breakthroughs, VR technologies have become much more affordable and efficacious, allowing organizations to use VRT programs to develop a wider array of KSAOs. Perhaps the most notable of these technological breakthroughs was the development and subsequent funding of the Oculus Rift (Dredge, 2014; Kickstarter, 2017; Oculus, 2017). The Rift is a head-mounted VR display, which the company Oculus began as a crowd-funded project. Initially, Oculus set a crowdfunding goal of $250,000 on Kickstarter.com, which was met within 24 hours. Within a month, Oculus had raised $2.5 million. About a year-and-a-half later, Oculus was sold to Facebook for $2 billion. After the success of Oculus and the Rift, several other companies have developed their own successful head-mounted VR systems, including HTC's VIVE and Samsung's Gear (Samsung, 2017; Vive, 2017). Today, customers can purchase these head-mounted VR systems for less than $1,000 (Oculus, 2017; Samsung, 2017; Vive, 2017), which is a great reduction in cost to prior VR systems that cost thousands of dollars.

With more cost-affordable technologies, practitioners have begun to apply VR for a wider array of training purposes, moving beyond the development of KSAOs that are too dangerous or costly to perform in the real world. Instead, VR is beginning to be used as a cost-saving method. Although certain KSAOs could be easily taught in the real world, such as interpersonal skills (Krupa, Jagannathan, & Reddy, 2016; Smith et al., 2014; Smith et al., 2015; Smith et al., 2016) or procedural knowledge (Duncan, Miller, & Jiang, 2012; Ferrell et al., 2015; Merchant et al., 2014), organizations are beginning to program automated VRT programs to develop these KSAOs without the need of trainer interaction. Likewise, researchers have begun to provide support for improved VRT outcomes – compared to both early VRT programs as well more traditional training programs (Brydges et al., 2015; Merchant et al., 2014; Morina et al., 2015; Uttal et al., 2013).

Due to the recent growth in the application of VR for training purposes, it is important to take stock of the field in order to understand what is known as well as what is still unknown. Doing so could help identify important future directions for both research and practice that may pose implications beyond VRT alone. For these reasons, the current chapter reviews prior research and practice on VRT with a particular focus on three considerations: (a) What is VR? (b) What is known about VRT programs? and (c) What is unknown about VRT programs? From these discussions, the current chapter notes that important progress has been made toward a deeper understanding of VRT programs, but the study of VRT is still relatively narrow. Several relevant theories have yet to be applied, and several related research domains have yet to be clearly integrated. Therefore, while VRT is quickly growing in popularity, much is still unknown about the predictors of VRT program success. Nevertheless, several directions for future research are evident, and the field appears prime to quickly grow in the future.

Lastly, two notes should be made before continuing. First, studies and discussions of VRT programs typically do *not* cover the entire training process, such as investigating procedures that aid transfer before and after the training program. Instead, VRT program studies tend to place an almost sole focus on dynamics that occur during the training process, and most discussions concentrate on the implications of novel instructional designs. Because the current chapter is a review of VRT program research, certain aspects of the training process are not discussed in-depth. Readers should refer to prior sources for comprehensive overviews of these other dynamics (Aguinis & Kraiger, 2009; Alvarez, Salas, & Garofano, 2004; Arthur et al., 2003; Cheng & Hampson, 2008; Grossman & Salas, 2011; Littrell & Salas, 2005; Saks & Belcourt, 2006; Salas & Cannon-Bowers, 2001; Salas et al., 2012; Tannenbam & Yukl, 1992).

Second, the current chapter continuously refers to VRT program success, efficacy, effectiveness, and outcomes. The most popular conceptualization of training outcomes is likely Kirkpatrick's hierarchy (1975). This hierarchy identifies four tiers of outcomes: reactions, learning, behavior, and results. It is well established that users typically have positive reactions to VRT programs, but it has been argued that these reactions are due to enjoying the novelty of VRT programs rather than their effectiveness (Bogost, 2015; Howard, 2017a; Nicholson, 2015). For this reason, the current chapter does not include reactions when referring to VRT program success, efficacy, effectiveness, and outcomes. Unless otherwise noted, these four terms are used to refer to higher-level training outcomes (learning, behaviors, and results).

Background

What Is Virtual Reality?

VR Software

VR programs present a three-dimensional digital simulation of an environment that can imitate a physical presence in real or imagined worlds (Howard, 2017a, 2017b; Merchant et al., 2014; Morina et al., 2015; Uttal et al., 2013). Typically, the phrase "three-dimensional digital simulation" refers to faux representations of three-dimensions, such that the environment is displayed on one or more two-dimensional displays (e.g., monitors) rather than truly displayed three-dimensionally (e.g., holograms). Users can perform actions that are native to three-dimensional environments (e.g., navigate around structures, move objects), but the presentation medium itself is still two-dimensional. Examples of VR when applying this definition include many popular video games, including World of Warcraft, Call of Duty, and Halo. It should be noted, however, that not all researchers and practitioners adhere to the definition provided above. Instead, this alternative perspective restricts the label of VR to only applications that utilize immersive hardware (e.g., head-mounted displays [HMDs], surround-screen displays), suggesting that VR could be defined by elements of both software and hardware. When applying this definition, World of Warcraft, Call of Duty, and Halo would constitute as VR only if they were experienced via an immersive display. In the current chapter, we adhere to the former, more inclusive definition. We consider VR to include any three-dimensional digital simulation that can imitate a physical presence, even if it is presented via a two-dimensional display.

Furthermore, users often control a representation of themselves, called an avatar, to navigate VR environments (Burdea & Coiffet,2003; Rheingold, 1991; Steuer, 1992). Users typically take a first-person perspective and view the environment from the eyes of their avatar, or they may take a third-person perspective and view the environment from a point-of-view that is above and behind their avatar. When undergoing a VRT program, trainees most often perform the desired skills in the digital environment, such as a surgical procedure, to transfer behaviors to the workplace. In these instances, the training material is integrated into the digital environment. Sometimes, however, VR is solely used to increase trainee excitement, and the material is not integrated into the environment. For example, a VR program could teach declarative knowledge by having trainees find facts scattered about the environment, such as written on hidden notes. Regardless, it is often believed that the immersive nature of VR programs generally results in better trainee reactions and learning outcomes (Fassbender et al., 2012; Shibata, 2002).

Beyond these attributes, most other elements of VR programs are highly variable. Several taxonomies and typologies have been used to define the attributes of VR software, many of which were created to more broadly define the attributes of simulations and/or serious games (Arnab et al., 2015; Bedwell et al., 2012; Deterding et al., 2011; Duncan et al., 2012; Landers, 2014; Messinger, Stroulia, & Lyons, 2008; Rego, Moreira, & Reis, 2010; Steuer, 1992). These taxonomies and typologies attempt to define most all attributes of simulations, serious games, and/ or VR programs in order to (a) identify which programs have higher or lower levels of each attribute and (b) subsequently test whether each attribute contributes to various outcomes. For instance, Arnab et al. (2015) separated serious game attributes into the two broad categories of learning mechanics and game mechanics, with over 30 attributes within each category. Some of these attributes are commonly discussed across domains (e.g., realism, incentive, feedback cooperation), whereas others are much less discussed (e.g., tiles/grids, cut scenes, shadowing).

An integrative discussion of each taxonomy, typology, and attribute would constitute its own chapter. Nevertheless, it should be recognized that (a) VRT research is moving beyond the study of entire VRT programs and instead investigating the effects of individual attributes and (b) certain taxonomies are indeed applied more often than others in these investigations. Two such taxonomies are those of Bedwell et al. (2012) and Greco et al. (2013).

Bedwell et al. (2012) identified 19 separate game attributes grouped into nine broader categories, with the belief that these attributes may influence learning. Each of these attributes could be included within a VRT program, and some initial studies have already applied this taxonomy to detail their applied VR programs (Howard, 2017b; Petty & Barbosa, 2016; Ravyse et al., 2017). Bedwell et al.'s categories include game reality, environment, conflict/challenge, assessment, action language, rules/goals, immersion, human interaction, and control. Each of these describes attributes of the VR software. On the other hand, Greco et al. (2013) created a taxonomy of business games, which adapted prior taxonomies of simulations (Maier & Grossler, 2000) and games (Aarseth et al., 2003; Elverdam & Aarseth, 2007). This taxonomy can also be used to detail VRT programs, and it includes the five macro-categories: environment of application; design elements of user interface; target groups, goal objectives, and feedback; user relation/community; and model. By differentiating a wide array of attributes, both of these taxonomies suggest that VRT programs may produce varied outcomes, although individual aspects of VRT programs may produce specific outcomes. For example, two VRT programs may provide different learning outcomes, but including assessments in VRT programs may generally result in beneficial outcomes. For this reason, the shift from studying overall VRT programs to instead studying specific attributes seems to be merited.

Further, as opposed to Bedwell et al.'s (2012) taxonomy, Greco et al. (2013) includes attributes outside the VR software, suggesting that VR programs could be distinguished by the software, hardware, target user, and other attributes. This also suggests that more than just the VR software influences VRT program success. For this reason, we also review VR hardware.

VR Hardware

Computer hardware typically used with VRT programs can be distinguished as either output hardware or input hardware. The most common computer output device is the monitor (Diemer et al., 2015; Howard, 2017b; Milgram & Kishino,

1994). The widespread use of the monitor likely stems from its low cost and wide availability, but other practical factors also support its application. Monitors are easy to use, and the information technology (IT) departments of most organizations are already trained to troubleshoot any problems with a computer monitor. Similarly, most users are familiar with a computer monitor, and they likely do not need to be extensively trained, or trained at all, on using a computer monitor.

On the other hand, immersive displays may be the most popular method to present a VRT program, which include both surround-screen displays and HMDs (Fassbender et al., 2012; Howard, 2018; Mon-Williams, Warm, & Rushton, 1993; Shibata, 2002). Surround-screen displays involve a number of two-dimensional displays placed around users to imitate an immersive environment. Alternatively, HMDs are digital screens placed in front of users' eyes, appearing similar to night-vision goggles, that encapsulate the entire field of vision and provide point-of-view changes by tracking head movements. All types of immersive displays have several common benefits. Users tend to naturally enjoy immersive displays, which can result in better trainee reactions to VRT programs (Fassbender et al., 2012; Juan & Pérez, 2009; Rand et al., 2005). Immersive displays are commonly believed to enhance the benefits of VRT programs that are discussed further below (e.g., presence and motivation; Juan & Pérez, 2009; Mania & Chalmers, 2001; Witmer & Singer, 1998). However, immersive displays also pose certain concerns. Immersive displays are much more expensive than computer monitors, which may contribute to them being less widespread. For this reason, many IT departments may be unfamiliar with solutions to problems with immersive displays, and users may need to "learn" how to use immersive displays before learning any VRT program material. Nevertheless, immersive displays are continuing to grow in popularity, and these concerns may begin to subside in the near future.

As for input hardware, the most common is the keyboard and mouse (Brydges et al., 2015; Howard, 2017a; Merchant et al., 2014; Morina et al., 2015; Uttal et al., 2013). The keyboard and mouse is widespread, and most any IT department already manages these technologies for their employees. Likewise, most any trainee has likely used a keyboard and mouse, eliminating the need to acclimate to new technology. Further, most software is designed to be controlled by a keyboard and mouse, allowing organizations to use their existing resources.

Other specialized input hardware devices are being applied at a steadily increasing rate (Chang, Chen, & Huang, 2011; Fung et al., 2006; Henriksen et al., 2016). Some VRT programs involve specialized input hardware that provide a natural interface to perform tasks. For example, a VRT program for aviation may include hardware that presents a complete replication of a cockpit. Similarly, in some cities, bus drivers are trained with hardware that faithfully reproduces a bus, which could also be incorporated into VRT programs. Other specialized input devices are motion sensors, sensor gloves, and treadmills (Chang et al., 2011; Howard, 2017a). Specialized inputs have many of the same benefits and detriments as immersive displays. Users often find them enjoyable, and they may enhance the benefits of VRT programs (Bailenson et al., 2006; Fung et al., 2006). On the other hand, they are still relatively uncommon, and most IT departments and users may be unfamiliar with their use. Nevertheless, specialized input devices are quickly becoming more popular, and these concerns may also fade in the future.

From the various combinations of VR software and hardware, each VRT program may greatly differ from the next. The following examples of two VRT programs are provided to emphasize these possible differences:

(1) Without any prerequisite training, a child is seated in front of a typical computer setup that includes a monitor, keyboard, and mouse. The child starts the VRT program, and the monitor displays the inside of a spaceship from the point-of-view of an avatar within the spaceship. The mouse controls the avatar's point of view, and the keyboard controls the avatar's movement and other actions. The child is able to use a virtual control panel to explore the solar system, and facts about each planet are shown upon a display as they fly across each planet. Afterwards, the child is given a quiz via the display about each of the planets, and they are given performance feedback in the form of a quiz score.

(2) After undergoing an initial training to learn how to use the VR hardware, a resident surgeon is wearing a HMD and seated in front of a specialized input device. The input device is a replication of two surgical tools (one for each hand) that are attached to input sensors. The surgeon starts the VRT program, and the HMD displays a patient lying before them. The specialized input device controls two surgical tools in the virtual environment, and the surgeon is able to perform an entire surgery on their virtual patient. At each step of the process, instructions are briefly presented on the screen to aid in the learning process. Once they have completed the practice surgery, the surgeon is asked to perform the same surgery again but without instructions. The surgeon is given qualitative feedback about their performance, but a numerical score is not provided.

Thus, whenever a researcher or practitioner refers to VRT programs, they may be referencing a multitude of possibilities.

Due to the varied nature of VRT programs, it is imperative for researchers to identify the mechanisms (e.g., mediators) that cause both VRT programs and individual attributes to produce (or not produce) more desirable outcomes, such that these attributes can be applied more broadly. In doing so, the most effective attributes of both VR software and hardware can be identified. To aid in this effort, we discuss the research and theory surrounding VRT programs separated into the general sections of: What is known? and What is unknown?

What Is Known?

Researchers have long known that the effectiveness of a training program is determined by more than the program itself (Bell et al., 2017; Salas et al., 2012). Instead, many researchers have identified the predictors of training success to occur before, during, as well as after the training. For example, predictors that occur before the training include pretraining interventions (Mesmer-Magnus &

Viswesvaran, 2010), and predictors that occur after the training include supervisor support of transfer activities (Montegar et al., 1977; Nijman et al., 2006). While these predictors are indeed important and influence training success, these aspects are not commonly studied in current investigations of VRT programs. This is understandable, however, as the application of VR for training purposes occurs during the training, and most studies are focused on identifying the influence of VR itself. For this reason, the current chapter primarily discusses research and theory surrounding predictors that occur during the training.

Further, Salas et al. (2012) identified two categories of predictors that occur during the training program. These are instructional designs and trainee characteristics. When reviewing what is known, the following initially addresses whether VRT programs are effective, and then discusses the known contributors to VRT program success as separated by these two categories. Relevant theory from industrial-organizational (I-O) psychology is detailed when discussing these predictors. In many cases, some precedence is evident for discussing these theories alongside the predictors, but many investigations into VRT are conducted in an atheoretical context within the fields of human-computer interaction, engineering, and others (as noted by prior authors; Arnold & Farrell, 2002; Beckett, Amaro-Jiménez, & Beckett, 2010; Djaouti et al., 2011; Hatala et al., 2014; Kotnour, Landaeta, & Lackey, 2013; Moore, 2015). Therefore, this review may be seen as an integration of I-O psychology theory with findings derived from other fields of research.

The Efficacy of Virtual Reality Training

Learning and Instruction

Before any other question, most researchers and practitioners often ask the following in regard to VRT programs: Do they work? The short answer is, yes – in general. The longer answer is, it depends on an array of factors which include (but are not limited to) characteristics of the application, context, hardware, software, trainer, and trainee. While the current chapter elaborates on this longer answer, this section provides more context for the shorter answer.

Organizational practitioners and researchers are likely most interested in the application of VRT programs for teaching and instruction. Perhaps the most popular application of VRT for this purpose is within the healthcare industry (Brydges et al., 2015; Nagendran et al., 2013; Palter & Grantcharov, 2014; Uttal et al., 2013). Hospitals have long applied VRT programs to develop the KSAOs of surgeons. These VRT programs typically include surgical instruments connected to sensors, and the instruments control realistic actions while performing surgery in a VR environment. Originally, this application arose from the need for realistic and safe opportunities to practice surgical skills, but it grew due to the efficacy and later the cost-effectiveness of the applied technologies. Today, it is widely recognized that VRT is an effective method to train surgical residents, even more so than certain prior training methods (e.g., stitching a slice on an orange), which has been supported by several systematic reviews and meta-analyses (Hatala et al., 2014; Nagendran et al., 2013; Palter & Grantcharov, 2014).

Military applications have also shown that VRT can be an effective training method. For instance, VRT programs can effectively train soldiers' object recognition abilities, such as differentiating between various types of civilian and military vehicles (Keebler, Jentsch, & Hudson, 2011; Keebler, Jentsch, & Schuster, 2014; Plummer, Schuster, & Keebler, 2017). VRT programs have also been used to train soldiers' ability to discriminate between peaceful civilians and hostile enemies. Beyond healthcare and the military, however, much remains unknown about the effectiveness of VRT programs for organizational teaching and instruction. While VRT programs have been applied in other industries (e.g., firefighting, Bliss et al., 1997), no uses are as widespread as healthcare and the military. Nevertheless, the efficacy of VRT programs can be understood by looking beyond industry.

VRT programs are effective for teaching and development purposes in education. Many authors have supported that VRT programs can effectively deliver pre-college education (Annettta et al., 2009; Kerawalla et al., 2006; Monahan, McArdle, & Bertolotto, 2008), and a recent meta-analysis provided further support that educational VRT programs are more effective than traditional instruction, 2-D instruction, or no instruction at all (Merchant et al., 2014). Typically, these educational programs are primarily intended to add excitement to the learning processes. For instance, students can learn the names and nature of the planets within our solar system by visiting them in a digital spaceship, such as the example provided above, and they can learn math abilities by interacting with digital farm animals that help them count. Further, the recent meta-analysis also showed that the efficacy of a VRT program is contingent on several factors, such as the type of KSAO developed and feedback provided (as discussed further below; Merchant et al., 2014). Thus, the overall effectiveness of VRT programs for teaching and instruction has been supported, but several factors influence the efficacy each particular VRT application.

Other Outcomes

VRT programs also appear effective for developing outcomes outside learning. Several meta-analyses have shown that VRT is effective for physical rehabilitation purposes (Booth et al., 2014; Howard, 2017a; Lohse et al., 2014). The majority of these studied VRT programs add visual feedback to physical actions, such as exploring a VR rainforest while walking on a treadmill. Some studies have likewise shown that VRT may be an effective method to develop the physical capabilities of the general population, using very similar VRT programs (Plante et al., 2003; Plante et al., 2006). These results suggest that VRT can improve the physical abilities of employees in relevant occupations, such as police officers and firefighters. More research is needed, however, before VRT programs can be considered a reliable method to develop physical abilities of the general population.

Similarly, several studies have shown that VRT is an effective method to develop the social abilities of those with autism (Irish, 2013; Smith et al., 2014; Smith et al.,

2015; Smith et al., 2016). Many of these studies investigate a VRT program that requires trainees to choose a seat on a bus (trainees should choose a seat with an adjacent vacant seat) and/or asking other passengers whether it is okay to sit next to them (when there are no seats with an adjacent vacant seat). It has been initially supported that those with autism can better conceptualize the personal space of others after undergoing this VRT program (Irish, 2013). Much less research has tested the ability of VRT to develop the social abilities of the general population. Again, while VRT may be able to develop social abilities of employees in relevant occupations, such as salespeople, more research is needed before it can be considered a reliable training method.

Lastly, Cuijpers et al.'s (2010) meta-analysis showed that self-guided VR programs may be able to address depression and anxiety disorders. These programs typically include automated therapy-related instruction and advice, but they also include scenarios in a VR environment that trainees can practice their emotional skills. Some authors have even developed VR programs in which veterans with PTSD can experience triggering scenarios in a safe environment, ranging from observing a firework display to a realistic combat experience (Gerardi et al., 2010; McLay et al., 2011; Rothbaum et al., 2001). These findings suggest that VR programs may be able to develop emotional abilities (e.g., emotional intelligence) of the general population. Developing emotional abilities could benefit those in most all occupations, but the extent that VRT programs could benefit organizations by developing these abilities is still unclear.

While these prior efforts are promising, more research is needed before VRT programs can be reliability used for organizational purposes beyond learning and instruction. Also, in these alternative applications, authors have regularly suggested that the contributors to VRT success differ from applications for learning. For example, while training programs often benefit from scaffolding (Cuevas, Fiore, & Oser, 2002), a VRT program for physical development may only need to motivate trainees. The current chapter primarily discusses the application of VRT programs for the most common organizational purpose, learning, but it is recognized that not all inferences and suggestions are applicable to applications of VRT programs for alternative purposes.

Causes of Virtual Reality Training Success

This section reviews the known mechanisms that cause VRT programs and individual attributes to influence outcomes, as separated by instructional design and trainee characteristics. It should be noted, however, that several unknown aspects and loose ends are highlighted when discussing each of the known mechanisms.

Instructional Design

Fidelity   The experiential knowledge approach to training suggests that trainees learn best by doing (Kolb, 2014; Kolb & Kolb, 2005). If a trainee needs to learn how to weld, for example, they should be required to use a welder until some standard has been reached. Likewise, media richness theory proposes, among other things, that complex tasks require mediums that can present more information in a timely manner, which is considered the media's richness (Daft &, 1986; Lan & Sie, 2010; Trevino, Lengel & Daft, 1987). For instance, videoconferencing can present more information than a written letter, and therefore video is richer than text. Most often, organizational training programs are considered complex tasks that require rich media. Thereby, both of these theories suggest that a computer-based training program, such as a VRT program, should replicate real-world transfer tasks as much as possible. The extent that a training program resembles desired real-world activities is called fidelity, and two types of fidelity have been differentiated – physical and cognitive fidelity (Campbell, 1971; Hays & Singer, 2012; Hochmitz & Yuviler-Gavish, 2011; Keinan, 1988; McMahan et al., 2012).

Physical fidelity is the extent that training activities physically represent desired real-world activities, whereas cognitive fidelity is the extent that training activities force trainees to undergo similar cognitive processes as desired real-world activities (Bos, 2009; Keinan, 1988; Liu, Macchiarella, & Vincenzi, 2008). A flight simulator, for example, may be realistic and allow trainees to perform entirely accurate behaviors, which would indicate high physical fidelity. The flight simulator, however, may provide little incentive to perform well. This would cause the trainees to feel little stress, resulting in different psychological processes than flying a plane and thereby providing low levels of cognitive fidelity. If a reward or punishment were introduced, then trainees may begin to feel stress and the training program would have improved cognitive fidelity.

Fidelity has been a popular training topic long before the development of VRT programs, and both types of fidelity have been linked to learning and transfer outcomes across many types of training programs (Campbell, 1971; Hays & Singer, 2012; Keinan, 1988). For VRT specifically, physical fidelity is among the most often cited justifications for training success (Ma et al., 2007; Maran & Glavin, 2003). Even for early VRT programs with minimal graphical capabilities, authors often attributed the success of the program to its ability to present certain scenarios that were difficult or impossible to present in real life, such as simulating plane malfunctions or medical emergencies (McMahan et al., 2012; Zyda, 2005). For modern VRT programs, this notion is even more prevalent due to increased realism and graphical capabilities.

Few empirical studies, however, have applied experimental designs that are able to isolate physical fidelity as the cause of any observed effects. Instead, a VRT program is often compared against a traditional training program, such as a lecture, and physical fidelity is cited as the cause of any group differences – even if physical fidelity is not directly measured or manipulated in a controlled manner (McMahan et al., 2012; Steuer, 1992; Zyda, 2005). Without controlled studies, it is difficult – if not impossible – to identify physical fidelity as the source of any observed effects. For example, a realistic VRT program is often believed to produce better outcomes compared to a text-based training program due to heightened physical fidelity, but trainees may simply be excited and motivated to use a technologically advanced VRT program. Alternatively, far fewer authors have discussed whether cognitive fidelity is a contributing factor to VRT success, and almost no empirical studies have directly tested this suggestion. Therefore, while it is already known that fidelity may contribute to training success, there are still several avenues of research for the study of fidelity in VRT programs. Studies of two closely related concepts, immersion and presence, may help develop this area of VRT research.

Immersion and Presence   Immersion is typically examined from one of two perspectives. The first pertains to a psychological perspective to VR technology (Grinberg et al., 2014; Jennett et al., 2008; Shin, Biocca, & Choo, 2013; Witmer, Jerome, & Singer, 2005; Witmer & Singer, 1998), referred to as psychological immersion. As it relates to VRT, psychological immersion refers to one's perception of being continuously surrounded in a VRT environment rather than one's physical environment (Witmer & Singer, 1998). Psychological immersion is an experience in one moment in time, such as engagement (Teng, 2010). In contrast, the second perspective examines immersion as a product of technology (Poncin & Garnier, 2012; Slater & Wilbur, 1997; Wilson & Soranzo, 2015). Technological immersion refers to an aspect of the VR technology mediating the experience (Slater, 2003), and it describes the environmental detail rendered (Wilson & Soranzo, 2015). This definition incorporates hardware, software, and other characteristics of VR to identify the extent of immersion for a particular application (Slater, 1999). By articulating immersion from a technological perspective, the construct can be more objectively measured and described. In general, authors refer to technological immersion when they reference the concept of immersion, perhaps due to the similarity of the popular construct, presence, to psychological immersion.

Presence, sometimes referred to as telepresence or co-presence, is generally accepted as being positively related to improved learning and training transfer (e.g., Tichon & Wallis, 2010; Witmer & Singer, 1998). Witmer et al. (2005) define presence as "a psychological state of 'being there' mediated by an environment that engages our senses, captures our attention, and fosters our active involvement." (p. 298). More simply, Slater and Wilbur (1997) refer to presence as the psychological sense of being in a virtual environment. While a general consensus regarding the definition of presence exists, the conceptual similarities between the psychological perspective of immersion and presence has resulted in some researchers using immersion and presence interchangeably (Christou, 2014; Grinberg et al., 2014). Although related, the constructs of psychological immersion and presence are distinct (Bowman & McMahan, 2007; Jennett et al., 2008). Whereas immersion describes a property of technology, presence describes a psychological state.

Further, Lee (2004) advanced three types of presence: (a) physical presence (virtual objects experienced as actual physical objects); (b) social presence (virtual actors experienced as actual social actors); and (c) self presence (virtual self is experienced as the actual self in either sensory or non-sensory ways). Recent research by Makransky, Lilleholt, and Aaby (2017) developed and provided initial validation for a 15-item presence scale for VR environments based on Lee's (2004) presence types. This multidimensional conceptualization of presence may become more popular in future research, as it has been supported that not all types of presence are the same (e.g., some users may be physically present but not socially). Researchers have also used more advanced measurement instruments, such as an electroencephalogram (EEG), to measure presence (e.g., Kober & Neuper, 2012; Seo et al., 2017), but some doubts remain regarding the construct validity of these advanced measures.

Technological immersion, through the use of immersive VR technologies, aids in the cognitive perceptions of psychological immersion and enhances learners' presence (Slater, 1999, 2003; Wilson & Soranzo, 2015), and presence is believed to, in turn, produce positive training outcomes. Across multiple conceptualizations and measurement methods, immersion and presence relate to increased trainee engagement, self-efficacy, learning, and transfer (Grinberg et al., 2014; Tichon & Wallis, 2010; Warden, Stanworth, & Change, 2016; Witmer & Singer, 1998). Thereby, both immersion and presence are believed to be necessary components of a learner's experience to enable the development of KSAOs in a VRT program; however, both also relate to detrimental outcomes. Immersion and presence can cause complications such as loss of focus due to seductive details or virtual reality induced symptoms and effects (VRISE, both discussed further below; Brooks et al., 2010; Lo & So, 2001; Sharples et al., 2008). Akin to most other dynamics of VRT programs, immersion and presence are not a simple concept with clear outcomes.

Researchers should continue studying the implications of immersion and presence, with a particular focus on possible negative outcomes. Perhaps more importantly, more theoretical work is needed that integrates the concepts of immersion and presence with physical and cognitive fidelity. Many researchers seem to consider physical fidelity and immersion as synonyms, leaving cognitive fidelity largely absent from prior studies regarding the relation of immersion and presence. The influence of cognitive fidelity may be more evident when applying Lee's (2004) three-dimensional conceptualization of presence. While physical fidelity may relate to a feeling of physical presence, cognitive fidelity may relate to feelings of social and self presence. Of course, these proposals are only speculation, and further research is certainly needed to better understand the implications of fidelity, immersion, and presence.

Gamification   Over just the last few years, gamification has grown into an expansive research topic covering multiple domains, including education, healthcare, management, and I-O psychology. In general terms, gamification is the use of design elements of games in non-game contexts (Deterding et al., 2011). In the context of learning environments, gamification is the use of game-based mechanics and aesthetics to promote learning (Barata et al., 2017; Kapp, 2012). This can include a wide range of additions to VRT programs, as exemplified by the several taxonomies of game attributes (Bedwell et al., 2012; Dicheva et al., 2015; Greco et al., 2013; Seaborn & Fels, 2015). When designed and applied correctly, gamification has great potential to improve VRT outcomes (Dicheva et al., 2015).

An array of theories has been applied to understand the effects of game attributes, both in general and for specific attributes. Many of these theories differ from those typically applied for general VRT programs (Barata et al., 2017; Dicheva et al., 2015; Nicholson, 2015; Seaborn & Fels, 2015), suggesting that game elements may improve learning and transfer outcomes due to separate mechanisms than VR itself. Because game elements may influence outcomes via separate mechanisms, game elements are often believed to provide benefits above and beyond VR (Bedwell et al., 2012; Deterding et al., 2011; Greco et al., 2013; Kapp, 2012).

Perhaps the most popular theory applied to understand gamification is self-determination theory (Deterding et al., 2011; Dicheva et al., 2015; Hamari, Koivisto, & Sarsa, 2014; Nicholson, 2015; Seaborn & Fels, 2015). Self-determination theory identifies three basic needs that spur human motivation: autonomy, competence, and relatedness (Deci & Ryan, 2011; Ryan and Deci, 2000). Many game elements directly relate to these three basic motivational needs. For instance, customization, choice, and control promote a sense of autonomy; scoring systems, badges, and trophies promote a sense of competence; and collaboration, competition, and interaction promote a sense of relatedness. Some elements even simultaneously satisfy multiple needs, such as rankings systems promoting a sense of competence as well as relatedness.

Authors have also applied other theoretical foundations to understand the effect of game elements, including situational relevance, situated motivational affordances, universal design for learning, and user-centered design (Dicheva et al., 2015; Seaborn & Fels, 2015). The current chapter does not discuss the other theoretical foundations in depth, but it should be emphasized that the study of gamification typically requires theory that is unique to VRT programs.

Further, research has supported that game elements can improve learning and other important outcomes. For instance, the game element of points (numerical representation of progression) has been shown to improve engagement and post-test scores (Dicheva et al., 2015; Hamari et al., 2014; Pedreira et al., 2015). However, not all game design features yield the same magnitude of results – or even positive results (Hamari et al., 2014). Some design elements should be used with caution in VRT, such as visual displays of achievements (e.g., leaderboards, badges, trophies). Recent research has suggested that leaderboards may represent a proxy for difficult goals (Landers, Bauer, & Callan, 2017), which has been well established to yield higher performance (e.g., Kleingeld, van Mierlo, & Arends, 2011; Locke & Latham, 2002); however, the resulting increase in competition among employees may subsequently harm motivation, satisfaction, and empowerment (Ferrell et al., 2015; Hamari et al., 2014; Hanus & Fox, 2015).

Thus, while certain game elements are known to be effective in certain circumstances, gamification in VRT programs is also a promising area of research for future examination, and research into gamification in organizational training programs is in its infancy. More research is needed to identify the exact game elements (e.g., points, avatars, leaderboards, unlocking, levels, aesthetics) that are effective for learning and transfer – both in general and in certain circumstances. Also, as noted by others (e.g., Hamari et al., 2014), much of extant gamification research lacks methodological rigor and the application of psychometrically sound measures. Approaches to quantitatively evaluate gamification in interactive applications have begun to be developed (Lopez & Tucker, 2017), which may offer an opportunity for extension or adoption into VRT research. These methodological shortcomings and others are discussed further below. Lastly, most current research investigates whether game attributes are effective across applications in general, but it should be further explored whether certain game attributes are particularly effective when applied in a VRT program. For example, game attributes that prompt a sense of relatedness may be more effective in a VRT program, as the VR environment may cause trainees to be more aware of social interactions with others.

Heightened Motivation   As mentioned, several authors have supported that trainees tend to naturally enjoy VRT programs, perhaps due to the novelty of the technology (Bogost, 2015; Howard, 2017a; Nicholson, 2015). Often, it is assumed that this enjoyment results in better training outcomes due to heightened trainee motivation; however, this notion does not have firm empirical support. Studies have shown that trainees may exhibit greater effort during a VRT program compared to alternatives, such as a VR treadmill training and a standard treadmill training (Howard, 2017a; Mirelman et al., 2013), but this effect has not been replicated across applications relevant to organizational outcomes. Thus, while initial evidence may exist for the relationships between enjoyment, motivation, and outcomes, further research is required before VRT programs can be assumed to naturally elicit heightened trainee motivation.

Trainee Characteristics

In addition to instructional design, certain individual differences have also been shown to influence VRT outcomes. The first set of these individual differences relates to prior experience with technology, which is perhaps best understood through self-regulation theory (Sitzmann et al., 2009; Sitzmann & Ely, 2010). Self-regulation theory proposes that people must devote conscious effort to maintain certain standards of desirable behavior, and maintaining this effort can be both difficult and demotivating. In a training context specifically, self-regulation thereby refers to these "learner cognitions that help them sustain focused attention on learning through self-monitoring of performance, comparison of progress to an end goal, and adjustment of learning effort and strategy as appropriate" (Salas et al., 2012, p. 87). Because training programs can be boring and/or cognitively taxing, many authors have suggested and supported that effective self-regulatory processes can result in better training outcomes.

During a VRT program, required training activities may be even more so cognitively taxing if the trainee is not familiar with advanced technologies. Users must become acclimated to their digital environments, and this is especially true if specialized hardware devices are applied (e.g., immersive displays, specialized inputs). A person with prior experience with VR, however, may require less time to acclimate to the digital environment, allowing these people to more effortlessly interact with a VRT program – thereby resulting in greater learning and transfer outcomes. For example, some trainees may already be familiar with typical methods to navigate VR environments and therefore able to entirely focus on the required training material, whereas other trainees may need to learn how to perform these activities in addition to learning the required training material. This latter trainee may have greater difficulty at managing self-regulatory processes and obtain worse training outcomes. Likewise, the former trainee may have heightened training self-efficacy compared to the latter trainee, and may thereby work harder and persist longer (Salas et al., 2012; Tannenbam & Yukl, 1992). Thus, individual differences that relate to prior experience with technology may indeed influence VRT success.

Unsurprisingly, the most studied of these individual differences may be prior technology experience itself (Harper et al., 2007; Nicholson et al., 2006; Schuemie et al., 2001; Van Dongen et al., 2007), and similar sentiments have been expressed for other closely related variables, such as video game experience and computer self-efficacy (Pellas, 2014; Plummer, Schuster, & Keebler, 2017; Walshe et al., 2003). Research has often supported that these variables influence VRT effectiveness, which emphasizes their importance for VRT programs.

Gender and age have often been suggested to influence VRT outcomes with males and younger trainees experiencing better outcomes (Annetta et al., 2009; Grantcharov et al., 2003; Parsons & Rizzo, 2008). Most often, these suggested effects are presumed to be due to males and females, as well as younger and older people, having differing experiences with technology – particularly video games. Males are more likely to be "gamers" than females, and younger people tend to play video games more often than older people. From general trends, however, it seems that these group differences may no longer exist in the near future (Denner et al., 2014; Fox & Tang, 2014). Video games are becoming more inclusive, and gaming companies are beginning to target the female demographic more often. Also, the initial series of popular video game consoles were released in the early 1980s. The range of ages that have grown-up with video games is ever-increasing, suggesting that the relationship of video game experience and age may disappear in only a few decades. Therefore, while the relationship of gender and age with VRT outcomes may currently exist (and should be considered for research and practical purposes), it is expected that these differences may begin to subside in the future.

Beyond individual differences related to self-regulation, some personality variables have been suggested to influence VRT success. Among these are one's general tendency to try new experiences (e.g., openness, sensation seeking) and one's tendency to become immersed in experiences (e.g., hypnotizability, absorption) (Merchant et al., 2014; Morina et al., 2015; Wiederhold & Wiederhold, 2000). Those willing to try new experiences may be more motivated to complete VRT programs due to their novelty, and those with a tendency to become immersed in experience may become more cognitively engaged in VRT programs. Despite such suggestions, few studies have tested the relationship of these variables with VRT outcomes (Parsons & Rizzo, 2008). Thus, much remains unknown about *who* benefits from VRT.

What Is Unknown?

While much has been achieved regarding our understanding of VRT, much has still yet to be done. For this reason, it is important to detail some of the primary unknown aspects of VRT programs. The following is divided into the same three primary sections as above with an added fourth: the efficacy of virtual reality training, instructional design, trainee characteristics, and before the virtual reality training.

Further, many of these unknowns involve the application of theory novel to training research. Because VR has unique characteristics compared to other technologies commonly applied for training purposes, it is plausible that novel theories should be applied to best understand the technology. In doing so, we draw from fields outside I-O psychology, in the hopes that these theories and perspective will become better integrated into I-O psychology. Each of these fields has particular benefits, such as a better understanding of technological (e.g., engineering, computer science, human factors, human-computer interaction), procedural (e.g., management information systems, human resources), or psychological (e.g., cyberpsychology, education) factors associated with VRT. Currently, only modest overlap can be seen across these fields (Merchant et al., 2014; Morina et al., 2015), but researchers should take a more integrative approach and analyze VRT programs from multiple simultaneous perspectives. Thus, while the following reviews VRT research, it is intended to shift traditional theorizing in I-O psychology.

The Efficacy of Virtual Reality Training

Authors have repeatedly shown that VRT programs can be an effective training method, but these authors also acknowledge VRT may only be effective for certain applications (Brydges et al., 2015; Nagendran et al., 2013; Palter & Grantcharov, 2014; Uttal et al., 2013). As noted, VRT programs appear to be effective overall for learning and instruction when applied with a general population. While VR to develop physical, social, and emotional abilities has been successfully used with specialized populations, it is unclear whether a VRT program to develop these abilities would be effective for the general population. More research is needed before VRT for these purposes can be applied in a widespread manner.

Perhaps more importantly, finer-grained research is needed regarding the ability of VRT programs to develop certain KSAOs associated with learning and instruction. As also mentioned, experiential learning theory has regularly been applied to identify the effective applications of VRT programs, and it suggests that people learn best by doing (Kolb, 2014; Kolb & Kolb, 2005). The performance of certain KSAOs can be more readily integrated into a VR environment (e.g., wayfinding, object identification), whereas others may be largely independent from the VR environment (e.g., arithmetic). Experiential learning theory thereby suggests that these former KSAOs may be more effectively trained via a VRT program than the latter KSAOs. A study, such as a meta-analysis or systematic review, comparing the efficacy of VRT programs across an array of applications could provide fruitful inferences in this regard. Further research incorporating prior technology-oriented theories could also identify appropriate applications, and task-technology fit theory is discussed further below to exemplify such an integration.

Task-Technology Fit

Task-technology fit describes the "degree to which a technology assists an individual in performing his or her portfolio of tasks" (Goodhue & Thompson, 1995, p. 216), and it was created to understand the interface between all tasks and technologies – not just VR. Since the identification of task-technology fit, authors have repeatedly shown that technologies with greater task-technology fit result in better user performance (Dishaw & Strong, 1999; Goodhue & Thompson, 1995; Maruping & Agarwal, 2004; Zigurs & Buckland, 1998). These repeated findings have led to the idea that technologies designed for a particular purpose often perform better than those created to be applied across a range of scenarios.

This idea is often reflected in research on VRT, even when task-technology fit is not specifically mentioned. Authors often apply a VRT program that was specifically developed for a certain task – often within a particular organization. For instance, various authors have created and tested different VRT programs to develop welding skills (Chambers et al., 2012; Mavrikios et al., 2006; Porter et al., 2006; Wang et al., 2006). These programs often teach a specific set of procedures and skills that are applied at a certain organization, and this may even include where to find certain objects around the specific workplace. When testing these specifically catered VRT programs, the program is regularly shown to produce satisfactory learning outcomes (Chambers et al., 2012; Mavrikios et al., 2006; Porter et al., 2006; Wang et al., 2006).

It is still unknown, however, whether these VRT programs remain effective when task-technology fit is worse. Using the example above, it is still relatively unclear whether employees from another organization would likewise benefit from the same VRT program, although the VRT program may have a slightly different set of procedures and/or building layout. It is likewise unclear whether any detriments to learning and/or transfer due to poor task-technology fit may be offset by the natural benefits of VR, such as immersion and presence. Thus, while it is generally known that task-technology fit relates to improved outcomes, much is still unknown about the exact dynamics surrounding task-technology fit in regards to VRT programs.

Further, task-technology fit may have additional implications for VRT programs compared to other types of training programs. Many authors have discussed the differing effects of VRT programs regarding whether the training is integrated into the digital environment (Kaufmann, Schmalstieg, & Wagner, 2000; Pan et al., 2006; Zyda, 2005). For example, a VRT program may require the use of a digital environment, and trainees may need to use virtual tools to complete a task. On the other hand, a VRT program may present a digital environment as a backdrop for the presentation of information, and trainees may not need to interact with any virtual objects to learn. The former of these would be an integrated training, whereas the latter would not. Typically, integration is often treated as a dichotomous variable, as shown in this example, but task-technology fit is measured as a continuous variable (Goodhue & Thompson, 1995; Psotka, 1995). Through applying the concept of task-technology fit, researchers can identify other aspects of VRT programs that contribute to this fit, and integration could be reconceptualized as a continuous variable. In doing so, greater variation regarding the integration of tasks with VRT programs can be identified and subsequently studied.

Causes of Virtual Reality Training Success (or Failures!)

Another reoccurring theme in the above review is the dearth of research regarding the explanatory mechanisms that prompt VRT program success. Currently, most studies on VRT (and training studies in general) perform randomized confirmatory trials that compare a VRT group against an alternative treatment group (Nagendran et al., 2013; Palter & Grantcharov, 2014; Van Dongen et al., 2007). While these studies are informative, authors rarely tested for mediating mechanisms that explain the cause of VRT success or failure. While some suggestions have been provided, such as fidelity and presence, robust empirical support using appropriate experimental designs has yet to be shown – a clear direction for future research.

Relatedly, more research is needed on boundary conditions that influence VRT outcomes. While little is known about *how* and *why* VRT programs may be effective, even less is known about *when, where, for whom*, and *for what KSAOs* are VRT programs effective.

Fortunately, many aspects of instructional design, trainee characteristics, as well as events before the training program may be possible mediating mechanisms and boundary conditions of the relationship between VRT programs and outcomes. We address this gap in extant research when discussing the unknowns below. Also, it should be noted that many of the unknowns reflect possible concerns with the application of VRT programs, such as mediators that lead to negative outcomes and boundary conditions that may reduce beneficial outcomes. This is a stark contrast to current VRT research that almost wholly investigates positive aspects of the technology, and it is hoped that these detrimental topics are discussed further in future research.

Instructional Design

Seductive Details
Training research has long held the assumption that user reactions are closely related to learning and transfer outcomes (Brown, 2005; Orvis, Fisher, & Wasserman, 2009; Sitzmann et al., 2008). This assumption may be due to the belief that happy trainees learn better, but also because user reactions are the first level of Kirkpatrick's (1975) hierarchy of training outcomes. It is certainly true that most people find VR to be interesting, and thereby most trainees find VRT programs to also be interesting (Bogost, 2015; Howard, 2017a; Nicholson, 2015). It is possible,

however, that VRT programs may be *too* interesting, which may be better under-stood through research on seductive details and self-regulation theory.

Seductive details are interesting features of instructional material that are irre-levant to learning goals, and they were first studied in the field of education in order to maximize student learning (McCrudden & Corkill, 2010; Park & Lim, 2007; Park et al., 2011; Wang & Adesope, 2014). Most textbooks contain seductive details, such as entertaining pictures, to hold reader attention with hopes of improving learning outcomes. Studies have repeatedly shown, however, that seductive details reduce learning, prompting researchers to coin the seductive detail effect – the phenomenon that learning outcomes increase when extraneous information is excluded from learning material (Goetz & Sadoski, 1995; Lehman et al., 2007; Towler et al., 2008). This notion is consistent with self-regulation theory, such that seductive details force trainees to allocate more cognitive resources toward staying focused on the training material.

It should be considered whether only certain attributes of VRT programs are seductive details. For example, Greco et al.'s (2013) taxonomy identifies the attribute of appearance, which is closely related to realism and fidelity. VRT programs that are extremely realistic may captivate and distract trainees, whereas less realistic VRT programs may allow trainees to better focus on the training material. It is possible that VR itself is not a seductive detail, but rather excessive amounts of certain attributes produce seductive detail effects when included in a VRT program. Similar sentiments have been expressed for the broader gamifica-tion movement, such that authors have questioned whether game elements typically contribute to learning goals or whether they are more often seductive details (Bogost, 2015; Nicholson, 2015).

Further, it should also be considered whether VRT programs are seductive details in only certain circumstances. For instance, some VRT programs integrate the training material into the digital environment, such as flying a plane in a virtual cockpit. On the other hand, some VRT programs do not integrate the training material into the digital environment, such as learning math abilities by solving problems in a fun virtual environment. The former instance may not result in VR being a seductive detail, but this may not be the case in the latter instance. If this is the case, then investigating seductive details in VR could help determine the KSAOs that can be effectively trained via a VRT program.

Together, practitioners should question whether the possible increases to dis-traction and cognitive load outweigh the benefits of VR whenever the technology is applied for training purposes, and researchers should question which attributes of VRT programs serve as seductive details. The answer to both questions should be determined by looking toward other theories outside I-O psychology, and the uncanny valley theory is discussed below as an example of this theoretical integration.

Uncanny Valley

The uncanny valley theory was created to explain human reactions to animatronic robots (Burleign, Schoenherr, & Lacroix, 2013; Ho & MacDorman, 2010;

MacDorman et al., 2009; Mori, MacDorman, & Kageki, 2012). Specifically, the theory suggests that people prefer the appearance of humanoid robots that are dissimilar or extremely similar in appearance to humans; however, people dislike the appearance of humanoid robots that only somewhat appear similar to humans. The cause of this "valley" in preference may be due to evolutionary benefits (MacDorman et al., 2009; Mori et al., 2012). Prior to robots, objects that only approach a human-like appearance are those that likely cause disease, such as a corpse. Having natural tendencies to be disgusted and repulsed by these objects caused humans to be more likely to avoid them, thereby aiding the survival of humans.

Recently, Howard (2017b) suggested that the uncanny valley theory may hold true for simulations, including VRT programs. That is, users may be comfortable with simulations that have unrealistic attributes (e.g., limited control, basic graphics) as well as simulations that have realistic attributes (e.g., ample control, advanced graphics), but they may be uncomfortable with simulations that have mismatched attributes (e.g., limited control with advanced graphics, ample control with basic graphics). From this discomfort, users then cognitively realize this mismatch and become distracted, and thereby the specific attributes of control and realism may serve as seductive details under certain circumstances (e.g., the mismatch of attributes). Howard (2017b) supported this notion in two studies by showing that users participating in training simulations with matched control and realism had better post-test scores than those who participated in a training simulation with mismatched attributes. In both studies, realism was manipulated by having users watch a video or use a VRT program, thereby also supporting that certain attributes of VRT programs can be seductive details.

More research is needed before the uncanny valley theory can be reliability applied to understand simulations, but the application of this theory highlights the complexity of developing effective VRT programs. The noted study also demonstrates that theories typically applied outside I-O psychology, such as within the field of human-computer interaction, may be readily applied to better understand VRT programs.

Embodiment

VRT programs pose certain unique psychological effects that are currently understudied, and a sense of embodiment may be the *most* unique of these. Sense of embodiment refers to the "ensemble of sensations that arise in conjunction with being inside, having, and controlling a body" (Kilteni et al., 2012, p. 375). Typically, people experience the world through their own bodies; however, trainees are immersed in a digital experience when participating in a VRT program, and they are intended to be mentally engaged in their activities. This mental engagement is believed to be beneficial, but it may separate participants' digital experiences from their physical bodies. This separation of mind from body may result in trainees processing certain aspects of their digital bodies (e.g., avatar) in a similar manner to their physical bodies, which may produce unique effects (Fox, Arena, & Bailenson, 2009; Ries et al., 2008; Spanlang et al., 2014).

Some of these effects may be beneficial. For instance, trainees may develop a sense of agency, in which they perceive themselves as being in control of their digital body's actions and outcomes (Kilteni et al., 2012; Spanlang et al., 2014). Presumably, this would cause the trainee to be more mentally engaged and possibly motivated in their training. On the other hand, some of these effects may be detrimental. Trainees may also develop a sense of body ownership, in which they perceive their digital body as being their own (Kilteni et al., 2012; Ries et al., 2008). This may cause trainees to learn how to perform behaviors using their digital bodies rather than cognitively translating these behaviors to the real world. After the training, participants may be experts at flying a digital plane, for example, but still relatively unskilled at flying a real plane.

Also, people can develop multiple different self-concepts, such as a real-life self-concept and a virtual self-concept (Arriaga et al., 2008; Fox et al., 2009; Gillath et al., 2008). While the emergence of these self-concepts may be due to a variety of reasons, some authors have suggested that the demand to satisfy the self-guides identified by self-discrepancy theory (actual, ideal, and ought) may cause people to develop multiple self-concepts that satisfy these self-guides in certain contexts, thereby reducing general feelings of self-discrepancy (Kwon, Chung, & Lee, 2011; Li, Liau, & Khoo, 2011). Further, people may act very differently based on the saliency of these different self-perceptions (Li et al., 2011). Someone may be reserved and quiet in real life, but then become gregarious and assertive when interacting in a digital environment. Research has also shown that these effects can develop rather quickly, perhaps after only a few minutes. It should be questioned whether trainees have similar self-perceptions and behavioral patterns in a VRT environment as they do a real-world training environment. While this implication may have modest effects on a VRT program for learning purposes, it may have a large impact on VRT programs for social or emotional development. If trainees cannot be certain to perform similar social and emotional behaviors in the transfer environment, then the VRT program may only be effective at reinforcing digital KSAOs. Thus, these differences between real-life and virtuality could result in reduced training outcomes, due to an added barrier to transfer.

From these effects of embodiment, certain KSAOs trained in a digital environment may produce lackluster transfer to a real environment due to the effects of embodiment. If this is the case, then alternative technologies that blend digital environments with the real-world, such as augmented reality, may prove to be more useful technologies for training purposes. On the other hand, researchers could identify pre-training interventions that may encourage trainees to remain cognizant of their real-world bodies and self-perceptions, as discussed further below. Also, a sense of embodiment is believed to emerge from immersion and presence (Arriaga et al., 2008; Fox et al., 2009; Gillath et al., 2008). If embodiment does have negative effects on VRT program outcomes, then these negative effects could also be attributed to immersion and presence. While these two concepts are typically believed to be beneficial, research on embodiment could provide an avenue to understand their negative effects. Lastly, the study of embodiment also emphasizes the need to incorporate theory outside those typically applied in training research, such as theories regarding the development of self-concepts.

Virtual Reality Induced Symptoms and Effects

The application of VR for training purposes may also require the incorporation of theory from psychophysiology. Virtual reality induced symptoms and effects (VRISE), sometimes called VR induced sickness or cybersickness, is a general feeling of illness or motion sickness that occurs during or after experiencing VR (Brooks et al., 2010; Lo & So, 2001; Sharples et al., 2008). The extent of associated symptoms varies, but they often include nausea, fatigue, disorientation, vertigo, and eyestrain (Kim et al., 2005; Min et al., 2004; So et al., 2001a, 2001b).

Some authors have studied the outcomes of VRISE, showing that it is negatively related to reaction time (Karl et al., 2013), as well as positively related to activations of the autonomic nervous system (Emoto, Sugawara, & Nojiri, 2008; Kim et al., 2005). Specific to VRT, however, much is still unknown about the outcomes of VRISE. It is reasonable to believe that VRISE may negatively relate to beneficial training outcomes, such as learning and transfer, while positively relate to detrimental training outcomes, such as negative trainee reactions; however, few – if any – of these relations have been shown in prior research, which is a clear need for future research.

Further, due to identified and assumed effects of VRISE on outcomes, some authors have likewise studied the antecedents of VRISE. These authors have largely tested the relation of certain technology characteristics with VRISE, showing that users' experiences of VRISE may differ depending on the display hardware, amount of user control, and amount of visual movement – among other features (Emoto et al., 2008; Sharples et al., 2008; So et al., 2001a, 2001b). Some authors have also studied the relationship of certain individual differences, such as age and gender (Arns & Cerney, 2005; Knight & Arns, 2006), with VRISE; however, these investigations rarely utilize prior theory, leaving much unknown as to why VRISE may be related to these antecedents.

We suggest that an important and novel use of theory may come from prior research in psychophysiology. Particularly, the study of vision-induced motion sickness (VIMS) could greatly benefit research on VRISE, and three primary theories have been used to understand the dynamics of VIMS. These are sensory conflict theory (Reason & Brand, 1975), poison theory (Treisman, 1977), and postural instability theory (Ricco & Stoffregen, 1991). Sensory conflict theory argues that VIMS occurs when the visual system differs from the vestibular system (involved in detecting movement and orientation; Reason & Brand, 1975). Poison theory argues that the human body perceives any biological system discrepancy as indicative of ingesting poison, and VIMS is the body's attempt at riding this poison (Treisman, 1977). Postural instability theory argues that VIMS occurs when uncontrolled movements occur (Ricco & Stoffregen, 1991). When using VR, uncontrolled movements may occur when a user attempts to stabilize themselves, such as leaning forward during perceived motion, but the VR system does not provide feedback to this movement. Each of these three theories may also be used to explain the causes of VRISE, and future researchers could identify how certain individual differences, such as age and gender, contribute to discrepancies in biological systems.

Lastly, we propose that VRISE may be the most needed future direction of all VR research. As mentioned, authors have discovered a relationship between both age and gender with VRISE, and VRISE is detrimental to most all studied outcomes. This indicates that VRT may produce different outcomes depending on a trainee's age and/or gender, thereby suggesting that legal action could be taken against organizations that use VRT programs due to differential and/or unfair treatment of employees. Thus, future research and practice could greatly benefit from further investigation into VRISE – particularly methods to reduce VRISE.

Trainee Characteristics
In general, the only trainee characteristics widely studied in conjunction with VRT programs relate to prior technology experience; however, other trainee character-istics that may specifically influence VRT program outcomes can be identified via the incorporation of prior training theory. As mentioned, VRT programs may incur additional distractions and/or cognitive loads that worsen outcomes, as predicted by self-regulation theory. Trainees with a predisposition to address such difficulties may be more trainable via a VRT program. Relevant individual differences may be cognitive abilities and emotional intelligence, which have been shown to relate to better self-regulation abilities (Hofmann, Schmeichel, & Baddeley, 2012; Mayer & Geher, 1996). Few, if any, studies have investigated the effect of such individual differences on training success, which is a possible avenue for future research.

Before the Virtual Reality Training
While most prior studies of VRT programs have focused on dynamics during the program itself, it should be questioned whether the application of VR may also influence dynamics before the program.

Pretraining Interventions
As mentioned, having little prior experience with technology may result in greater difficulties with self-regulation during a VRT program. Certain methods should be considered to counteract their potential detrimental effects, such as pretraining interventions (Mesmer-Magnus & Viswesvaran, 2010). Pretraining interventions are meant to amplify or mitigate particular aspects of training programs. For instance, the pretraining intervention of attentional advice involves providing instruction on cognitive "process[es] or strategy[ies] that can be used to achieve optimal learning outcome[s] during training" (Cannon-Bowers et al., 1998, p. 294). For a VRT program, this may involve instruction on aspects of the VR environment that are most relevant for learning, so that trainees do not devote needless attention to irrelevant aspects of the VR environment. Alternatively, an appropriate pretrain-ing intervention may allow trainees to explore their VR environments before the training program begins, and the trainees can become acclimated before needing to devote their attention to learning material.

Furthermore, those with certain individual differences, such as little prior technology experience, may particularly benefit from these pretraining interventions, thereby counteracting any negative effect that the individual difference may pose. While VRT programs may be relatively ineffective for certain trainees, pretraining interventions may allow these programs to benefit everyone. Pretraining interventions have rarely been studied alongside VRT programs, but it is nevertheless believed that this area of research may be particularly fruitful.

Other Theoretical Perspectives
It should be noted that the current chapter only reviewed theoretical perspectives that have particular implications for VRT programs. Many other theoretical perspectives are believed to apply to VRT programs in a similar manner that they apply for all other training programs (Bell et al., 2017), and thereby should not be ignored when determining the effectiveness of VRT programs. For example: in regards to design characteristics, active learning programs tend to produce better outcomes than highly structured training programs (Bell & Kozlowski, 2008); in regards to trainee characteristics, those with a learning goal orientation are more likely to receive better training outcomes (Kozlowski et al., 2001); in regards to events after the training program, organizations with a better climate for transfer are more likely to produce more beneficial training outcomes (Rouiller & Goldstein, 1993). While these dynamics are not unique to VRT programs, they should not be ignored moving forward.

Methodological Recommendations

The current chapter concludes with certain methodological recommendations for the study of VRT programs, which reflect the concerns noted by prior authors regarding the study of VRT programs (Hamari et al., 2014; Lopez & Tucker, 2017). Most studies compare a VRT program against a comparable alternative training program, and some studies simply test whether a VRT program is able to meet a specified standard (Brydges et al., 2015; Nagendran et al., 2013; Palter & Grantcharov, 2014; Uttal et al., 2013). These studies can provide information regarding the overall effectiveness of a VRT program, but they struggle with identifying the effect of individual VRT program attributes. Future research should move beyond these randomized confirmatory trials, and instead apply more sophisticated methods to identify overall effects of training programs as well as individual attributes. For example, the multiphase optimization strategy is a training evaluation method that utilizes factorial designs to identify the influence of specific training attributes (Howard & Jacobs, 2016). Such an approach could allow for the easier and more accurate investigation into the influence of VRT attributes, rather than omnibus analyses of entire VRT programs.

Also, many authors have expressed concern regarding the measures applied in VRT studies (Hamari et al., 2014; Lopez & Tucker, 2017; Makransky et al., 2017). Measures are regularly applied without any prior evidence regarding their validity or psychometric properties, making it unclear whether they gauge their intended construct. Perhaps more problematically, researchers often assume that certain aspects of VRT programs necessarily produce certain effects without explicitly measuring such effects, which are then attributed to be the cause of any subsequent beneficial outcomes. For example, researchers sometimes test the outcomes of VRT programs and subsequently attribute any beneficial outcomes to the mediating effect of presence, even if presence was not measured. Future research should strive to develop relevant measures using appropriate processes identified by prior researchers (Howard, 2016; Makransky et al., 2017), and subsequently apply the measures to ensure that any observed effects of VRT programs are actually due to the attributed cause.

While it is difficult to attribute these concerns to any particular cause, it is possible that a large proportion of VRT research is performed outside fields that commonly study training. While some VRT research is conducted in I-O psychology, a large proportion of this research is performed in fields that study technology (e.g., engineering, human-computer interaction) or in which the VRT program is applied (e.g., healthcare). While collaboration across fields can be beneficial, it is unsurprising that researchers in these other fields may be relatively unfamiliar with the nuances of training research. For this reason, we urge more authors within I-O psychology to study the dynamics of VRT programs.

Conclusion

VRT is a promising method to train employees, and it is expected to become more promising in the future. Current studies on VRT have supported that it is an effective method to train employees for certain applications, but very little is known about the more nuanced dynamics of VRT programs. For this reason, the current chapter suggests that future research should explore the boundary conditions and explanatory mechanisms to better understand VRT outcomes. In doing so, authors should explore the application of theories that are atypical for computer-based training research. Because VRT programs are a unique training method, it is likely that the dynamics surrounding the method are likewise unique.

References

Aarseth, E., Smedstad, S. M., & Sunnanå, L. (November 2003). A multidimensional typology of games. In M. Copier & J. Raessens (Eds.), *Level Up: Digital Games Research Conference Proceedings*. Utrecht, the Netherlands: Universteit Utrecht.

Aguinis, H. & Kraiger, K. (2009). Benefits of training and development for individuals and teams, organizations, and society. *Annual Review of Psychology, 60*, 451–474.

Alvarez, K., Salas, E., & Garofano, C. M. (2004). An integrated model of training evaluation and effectiveness. *Human Resource Development Review, 3*(4), 385–416.

Annetta, L., Mangrum, J., Holmes, S., Collazo, K., & Cheng, M. T. (2009). Bridging realty to virtual reality: Investigating gender effect and student engagement on learning through video game play in an elementary school classroom. *International Journal of Science Education, 31*(8), 1091–1113.

Arnab, S., Lim, T., Carvalho, M. B., Bellotti, F., Freitas, S., Louchart, S., & De Gloria, A. (2015). Mapping learning and game mechanics for serious games analysis. *British Journal of Educational Technology, 46*(2), 391–411.

Arnold, P. & Farrell, M. J. (2002). Can virtual reality be used to measure and train surgical skills? *Ergonomics, 45*(5): 362–379.

Arns, L. L. & Cerney, M. M. (March, 2005). The relationship between age and incidence of cybersickness among immersive environment users. In *Virtual Reality, 2005. Proceedings. VR 2005. IEEE* (pp. 267–268). Bonn: IEEE.

Arriaga, P., Esteves, F., Carneiro, P., & Monteiro, M. B. (2008). Are the effects of unreal violent video games pronounced when playing with a virtual reality system? *Aggressive Behavior, 34*(5), 521–538.

Arthur Jr, W., Bennett Jr, W., Edens, P. S., & Bell, S. T. (2003). Effectiveness of training in organizations: A meta-analysis of design and evaluation features. *Journal of Applied Psychology, 88*(2), 234.

Bailenson, J. N., Blascovich, J., Beall, A. C., & Noveck, B. (2006). Courtroom applications of virtual environments, immersive virtual environments, and collaborative virtual environments. *Law & Policy, 28*(2), 249–270.

Barata, G., Gama, S., Jorge, J., & Gonçalves, D. (2017). Studying student differentiation in gamified education: A long-term study. *Computers in Human Behavior, 71,* 550–585.

Bedwell, W. L., Pavlas, D., Heyne, K., Lazzara, E. H., & Salas, E. (2012). Toward a taxonomy linking game attributes to learning: An empirical study. *Simulation & Gaming, 43*(6), 729–760.

Bedwell, W. L. & Salas, E. (2010). Computer-based training: Capitalizing on lessons learned. *International Journal of Training and Development, 14*(3), 239–249.

Beckett, G. H., Amaro-Jiménez, C., & Beckett, K. S. (2010). Students' use of asynchronous discussions for academic discourse socialization. *Distance Education, 31*(3), 315–335.

Bell, B. S. & Kozlowski, S. W. (2008). Active learning: Effects of core training design elements on self-regulatory processes, learning, and adaptability. *Journal of Applied Psychology, 93*(2), 296.

Bell, B. S., Tannenbaum, S. I., Ford, J. K., Noe, R. A., & Kraiger, K. (2017). 100 years of training and development research: What we know and where we should go. *Journal of Applied Psychology, 102*(3), 305–323.

Bliss, J. P., Tidwell, P. D., & Guest, M. A. (1997). The effectiveness of virtual reality for administering spatial navigation training to firefighters. *Presence: Teleoperators and Virtual Environments, 6*(1), 73–86.

Bogost, I. (2015). Gamification is bullshit. In S, Walz & S., Deterding (Eds.), *The Gameful World: Approaches, Issues, Applications*, pp. 65-80. Cambridge, MA: The MIT Press.

Booth, V., Masud, T., Connell, L., & Bath-Hextall, F. (2014). The effectiveness of virtual reality interventions in improving balance in adults with impaired balance compared with standard or no treatment: a systematic review and meta-analysis. *Clinical Rehabilitation, 28*(5), 419–431.

Bos, B. (2009). Technology with cognitive and mathematical fidelity: What it means for the math classroom. *Computers in the Schools*, *26*(2), 107–114.

Bowman, D. A. & McMahan, R. P. (2007). Virtual reality: How much immersion is enough? *Computer*, *40*(7), 36.

Brooks, J. O., Goodenough, R. R., Crisler, M. C., Klein, N. D., Alley, R. L., Koon, B. L., . . . & Wills, R. F. (2010). Simulator sickness during driving simulation studies. *Accident Analysis & Prevention*, *42*(3), 788–796.

Brown, K. G. (2005). An examination of the structure and nomological network of trainee reactions: A closer look at "smile sheets." *Journal of Applied Psychology*, *90*(5), 991.

Brydges, R., Hatala, R., Zendejas, B., Erwin, P. J., & Cook, D. A. (2015). Linking simulation-based educational assessments and patient-related outcomes: a systematic review and meta-analysis. *Academic Medicine*, *90*(2), 246–256.

Burdea, G. C., & Coiffet, P. (2003). *Virtual reality technology*. Hoboken, NJ: John Wiley & Sons.

Burleigh, T. J., Schoenherr, J. R., & Lacroix, G. L. (2013). Does the uncanny valley exist? An empirical test of the relationship between eeriness and the human likeness of digitally created faces. *Computers in Human Behavior*, *29*(3), 759–771.

Campbell, J. P. (1971). Personnel training and development. *Annual Review of Psychology*, *22*(1), 565–602.

Cannon-Bowers, J. A., Rhodenizer, L., Salas, E., & Bowers, C. A. (1998). A framework for understanding pre-practice conditions and their impact on learning. *Personnel Psychology*, *51*(2), 291–320.

Chambers, T. L., Aglawe, A., Reiners, D., White, S., Borst, C. W., Prachyabrued, M., & Bajpayee, A. (2012). Real-time simulation for a virtual reality-based MIG welding training system. *Virtual Reality*, *16*(1), 45–55.

Chang, Y. J., Chen, S. F., & Huang, J. D. (2011). A Kinect-based system for physical rehabilitation: A pilot study for young adults with motor disabilities. *Research in Developmental Disabilities*, *32*(6), 2566–2570.

Cheng, E. W. & Hampson, I. (2008). Transfer of training: A review and new insights. *International Journal of Management Reviews*, *10*(4), 327–341.

Christou, G. (2014). The interplay between immersion and appeal in video games. *Computers in Human Behavior*, *32*, 92–100.

Cuevas, H. M., Fiore, S. M., & Oser, R. L. (2002). Scaffolding cognitive and metacognitive processes in low verbal ability learners: Use of diagrams in computer-based training environments. *Instructional Science*, *30*(6), 433–464.

Cuijpers, P., Donker, T., van Straten, A., Li, J., & Andersson, G. (2010). Is guided self-help as effective as face-to-face psychotherapy for depression and anxiety disorders?: A systematic review and meta-analysis of comparative outcome studies. *Psychological Medicine*, *40*(12), 1943–1957.

Daft, R. L. & Lengel, R. H. (1986). Organizational information requirements, media richness and structural design. *Management Science*, *32*(5), 554–571.

Deci, E. L. & Ryan, R. M. (2011). Self-determination theory. *Handbook of Theories of Social Psychology*, *1*(2011), 416–433.

Denner, J., Ortiz, E., Campe, S., & Werner, L. (2014). Beyond stereotypes of gender and gaming: Video games made by middle school students. In H. Agius & M. Angelides (Eds.), *Handbook of Digital Games* (pp. 667–688). Hoboken, NJ: John Wiley & Sons.

Deterding, S., Dixon, D., Khaled, R., & Nacke, L. (September 2011). From game design elements to gamefulness: Defining gamification. In *Proceedings of the 15th international academic MindTrek conference: Envisioning future media environments* (pp. 9–15). ACM.

Dicheva, D., Dichev, C., Agre, G., & Angelova, G. (2015). Gamification in education: A systematic mapping study. *Educational Technology & Society*, *18*(3), 75–88.

Diemer, J., Alpers, G. W., Peperkorn, H. M., Shiban, Y., & Mühlberger, A. (2015). The impact of perception and presence on emotional reactions: a review of research in virtual reality. *Frontiers in Psychology*, *6*, 26.

Dishaw, M. T. & Strong, D. M. (1999). Extending the technology acceptance model with task–technology fit constructs. *Information & Management*, *36*(1), 9–21.

Djaouti, D., Alvarez, J., Jessel, J. P., & Rampnoux, O. (2011). Origins of serious games. In *Serious games and edutainment applications* (pp. 25–43). London: Springer.

Dredge, S. (2014). Facebook closes its $2bn Oculus Rift acquisition. What next? The Guardian. Retrieved from www.theguardian.com/technology/2014/jul/22/facebook-oculus-rift-acquisition-virtual-reality

Duncan, I., Miller, A., & Jiang, S. (2012). A taxonomy of virtual worlds usage in education. *British Journal of Educational Technology*, *43*(6), 949–964.

Elverdam, C. & Aarseth, E. (2007). Game classification and game design: Construction through critical analysis. *Games and Culture*, *2*(1), 3–22.

Emoto, M., Sugawara, M., & Nojiri, Y. (2008). Viewing angle dependency of visually-induced motion sickness in viewing wide-field images by subjective and autonomic nervous indices. *Displays*, *29*(2), 90–99.

Fassbender, E., Richards, D., Bilgin, A., Thompson, W. F., & Heiden, W. (2012). VirSchool: The effect of background music and immersive display systems on memory for facts learned in an educational virtual environment. *Computers & Education*, *58*(1), 490–500.

Ferrell, J. Z., Carpenter, J. E., Vaughn, E. D., Dudley, N. M., & Goodman, S. A. (2015). Gamification of human resource processes. In D. Davis & H. Gangadharbatla (Eds.), *Emerging research and trends in gamification* (pp. 108–139). Hershey, PA: IGI Global.

Fox, J., Arena, D., & Bailenson, J. N. (2009). Virtual reality: A survival guide for the social scientist. *Journal of Media Psychology*, *21*(3), 95–113.

Fox, J. & Tang, W. Y. (2014). Sexism in online video games: The role of conformity to masculine norms and social dominance orientation. *Computers in Human Behavior*, *33*, 314–320.

Fung, J., Richards, C. L., Malouin, F., McFadyen, B. J., & Lamontagne, A. (2006). A treadmill and motion coupled virtual reality system for gait training post-stroke. *CyberPsychology & Behavior*, *9*(2), 157–162.

Gerardi, M., Cukor, J., Difede, J., Rizzo, A., & Rothbaum, B. O. (2010). Virtual reality exposure therapy for post-traumatic stress disorder and other anxiety disorders. *Current Psychiatry Reports*, *12*(4), 298–305.

Gillath, O., McCall, C., Shaver, P. R., & Blascovich, J. (2008). What can virtual reality teach us about prosocial tendencies in real and virtual environments? *Media Psychology*, *11*(2), 259–282.

Goetz, E. T. & Sadoski, M. (1995). Commentary: The perils of seduction: Distracting details or incomprehensible abstractions? *Reading Research Quarterly*, *30*(3), 500–511.

Goldberg, S. (1994). Training dismounted soldiers in a distributed interactive virtual environment. *US Army Research Institute Newsletter, 14*, 9–12.

Goodhue, D. L. & Thompson, R. L. (1995). Task-technology fit and individual performance. *MIS Quarterly, 2*, 213–236.

Grantcharov, T. P., Bardram, L., Funch-Jensen, P., & Rosenberg, J. (2003). Impact of hand dominance, gender, and experience with computer games on performance in virtual reality laparoscopy. *Surgical Endoscopy and Other Interventional Techniques, 17*(7), 1082–1085.

Greco, M., Baldissin, N., & Nonino, F. (2013). An exploratory taxonomy of business games. *Simulation & Gaming, 44*(5), 645–682.

Grinberg, A. M., Careaga, J. S., Mehl, M. R., & O'Connor, M. F. (2014). Social engagement and user immersion in a socially based virtual world. *Computers in Human Behavior, 36*, 479–486.

Grossman, R. & Salas, E. (2011). The transfer of training: What really matters. *International Journal of Training and Development, 15*(2), 103–120.

Hamari, J., Koivisto, J., & Sarsa, H. (2014). Does gamification work?: A literature review of empirical studies on gamification. In *Proceedings of the annual Hawaii international conference on system sciences* (pp. 3025–3034).

Hanus, M. D. & Fox, J. (2015). Assessing the effects of gamification in the classroom: A longitudinal study on intrinsic motivation, social comparison, satisfaction, effort, and academic performance. *Computers & Education, 80*, 152–161.

Harper, J. D., Kaiser, S., Ebrahimi, K., Lamberton, G. R., Hadley, H. R., Ruckle, H. C., & Baldwin, D. D. (2007). Prior video game exposure does not enhance robotic surgical performance. *Journal of Endourology, 21*(10), 1207–1210.

Hatala, R., Cook, D. A., Zendejas, B., Hamstra, S. J., & Brydges, R. (2014). Feedback for simulation-based procedural skills training: A meta-analysis and critical narrative synthesis. *Advances in Health Sciences Education, 19*(2), 251–272.

Hays, R. T. & Singer, M. J. (2012). *Simulation fidelity in training system design: Bridging the gap between reality and training*. New York, NY: Springer Science & Business Media.

Henriksen, B., Nielsen, R., Szabo, L., Evers, N., Kraus, M., & Geng, B. (2016). A virtual reality system for treatment of phantom limb pain using game training and motion tracking. *International Journal of Virtual Reality, 16*(1).

Ho, C. C. & MacDorman, K. F. (2010). Revisiting the uncanny valley theory: Developing and validating an alternative to the Godspeed indices. *Computers in Human Behavior, 26*(6), 1508–1518.

Hochmitz, I. & Yuviler-Gavish, N. (2011). Physical fidelity versus cognitive fidelity training in procedural skills acquisition. *Human Factors, 53*(5), 489–501.

Hofmann, W., Schmeichel, B. J., & Baddeley, A. D. (2012). Executive functions and self-regulation. *Trends in Cognitive Sciences, 16*(3), 174–180.

Howard, M. C. (2016). A review of exploratory factor analysis decisions and overview of current practices: What we are doing and how can we improve? *International Journal of Human-Computer Interaction, 32*(1), 51–62.

Howard, M. C. (2017a). A Meta-Analysis and Systematic Literature Review of Virtual Reality Rehabilitation Programs. *Computers in Human Behavior, 70*, 317–327.

Howard, M. C. (2017b). Investigating the simulation elements of environment and control: Extending the Uncanny Valley Theory to simulations. *Computers & Education, 109*, 216–232.

Howard, M. C. (2018). Virtual reality interventions for personal development: A meta-analysis of hardware and software. *Human–Computer Interaction*, DOI: 10.1080/07370024.2018.1469408.

Howard, M. C. & Jacobs, R. R. (2016). The multiphase optimization strategy (MOST) and the sequential multiple assignment randomized trial (SMART): Two novel evaluation methods for developing optimal training programs. *Journal of Organizational Behavior*, *37*(8), 1246–1270.

Irish, J. E. (2013). Can I sit here? A review of the literature supporting the use of single-user virtual environments to help adolescents with autism learn appropriate social communication skills. *Computers in Human Behavior*, *29*(5), A17–A24.

Jennett, C., Cox, A. L., Cairns, P., Dhoparee, S., Epps, A., Tijs, T., & Walton, A. (2008). Measuring and defining the experience of immersion in games. *International Journal of Human-Computer Studies*, *66*(9), 641–661.

Jense, G. J. & Kuijper, F. (1993). Virtual Environments for Advanced Trainers and Simulators. In *Proceedings of the International Training Equipment Conference*, (pp. 49–57). ITEC.

Juan, M. C. & Pérez, D. (2009). Comparison of the levels of presence and anxiety in an acrophobic environment viewed via HMD or CAVE. *Presence: Teleoperators and Virtual Environments*, *18*(3), 232–248.

Kapp, K. M. (2012). *The gamification of learning and instruction: Game-based methods and strategies for training and education*. San Francisco, CA: John Wiley & Sons.

Karl, I., Berg, G., Ruger, F., & Farber, B. (2013). Driving behavior and simulator sickness while driving the vehicle in the loop: Validation of longitudinal driving behavior. *IEEE Intelligent Transportation Systems Magazine*, *5*(1), 42–57.

Kaufmann, H., Schmalstieg, D., & Wagner, M. (2000). Construct3D: A virtual reality application for mathematics and geometry education. *Education and Information Technologies*, *5*(4), 263–276.

Keebler, J. R., Jentsch, F., & Hudson, I. (September 2011). Developing an effective combat identification training. In *Proceedings of the Human Factors and Ergonomics Society Annual Meeting* (vol. 55(1), pp. 1554–1558). Los Angeles, CA: Sage Publications.

Keebler, J. R., Jentsch, F., & Schuster, D. (2014). The effects of video game experience and active stereoscopy on performance in combat identification tasks. *Human Factors: The Journal of the Human Factors and Ergonomics Society*, *56*(8), 1482–1496.

Keinan, G. (1988). Training for dangerous task performance: The effects of expectations and feedback. *Journal of Applied Social Psychology*, *18*(4), 355–373.

Kerawalla, L., Luckin, R., Seljeflot, S., & Woolard, A. (2006). "Making it real": Exploring the potential of augmented reality for teaching primary school science. *Virtual Reality*, *10*(3–4), 163–174.

Kickstarter. (2017). Oculus Rift: Step into the Game. Retrieved from www.kickstarter.com/projects/1523379957/oculus-rift-step-into-the-game/updates.

Kilteni, K., Groten, R., & Slater, M. (2012). The sense of embodiment in virtual reality. *Presence: Teleoperators and Virtual Environments*, *21*(4), 373–387.

Kim, Y. Y., Kim, H. J., Kim, E. N., Ko, H. D., & Kim, H. T. (2005). Characteristic changes in the physiological components of cybersickness. *Psychophysiology*, *42*(5), 616–625.

Kirkpatrick, D. L. (1975). Techniques for evaluating training programs In D. L. Kirkpatrick (Ed.). *Evaluating training programs*. Alexandria, VA: ASTD.

Kleingeld, A., van Mierlo, H., & Arends, L. (2011). The effect of goal setting on group performance: A meta-analysis. *Journal of Applied Psychology*, *96*(6), 1289–1304.

Knight, M. M. & Arns, L. L. (July 2006). The relationship among age and other factors on incidence of cybersickness in immersive environment users. In ACM SIGGRAPH 2006 research posters (p. 196). ACM.

Kober, S. E. & Neuper, C. (2012). Using auditory event-related EEG potentials to assess presence in virtual reality. *International Journal of Human-Computer Studies, 70* (9), 577–587.

Kolb, D. A. (2014). *Experiential learning: Experience as the source of learning and development.* Upper Saddle River, NJ: Prentice Hall.

Kolb, A. Y. & Kolb, D. A. (2005). Learning styles and learning spaces: Enhancing experiential learning in higher education. *Academy of Management Learning & Education, 4*(2), 193–212.

Kotnour, T., Landaeta, R., & Lackey, S. (2013). Defining training system impact assessment measures from a stakeholder perspective: Case study of the NEW-IT project. *International Journal of Technology Enhanced Learning, 5*(1), 1–23.

Kozak, J. J., Hancock, P. A., Arthur, E. J., & Chrysler, S. T. (1993). Transfer of training from virtual reality. *Ergonomics, 36*(7), 777–784.

Kozlowski, S. W., Gully, S. M., Brown, K. G., Salas, E., Smith, E. M., & Nason, E. R. (2001). Effects of training goals and goal orientation traits on multidimensional training outcomes and performance adaptability. *Organizational Behavior and Human Decision Processes, 85*(1), 1–31.

Krupa, A. L., Jagannathan, A., & Reddy, S. K. (2016). Importance of virtual reality job interview training in today's world. *The Journal of Nervous and Mental Disease, 204*(10), 799.

Kwon, J. H., Chung, C. S., & Lee, J. (2011). The effects of escape from self and interpersonal relationship on the pathological use of internet games. *Community Mental Health Journal, 47*(1), 113–121.

Lan, Y. F. & Sie, Y. S. (2010). Using RSS to support mobile learning based on media richness theory. *Computers & Education, 55*(2), 723–732.

Landers, R. N. (2014). Developing a theory of gamified learning: Linking serious games and gamification of learning. *Simulation & Gaming, 45*(6), 752–768.

Landers, R. N., Bauer, K. N., & Callan, R. C. (2017). Gamification of task performance with leaderboards: A goal setting experiment. *Computers in Human Behavior, 71,* 508–515.

Lee, K. M. (2004). Presence, explicated. *Communication Theory, 14*(1),27–50.

Lehman, S., Schraw, G., McCrudden, M. T., & Hartley, K. (2007). Processing and recall of seductive details in scientific text. *Contemporary Educational Psychology, 32*(4), 569–587.

Li, D., Liau, A., & Khoo, A. (2011). Examining the influence of actual-ideal self-discrepancies, depression, and escapism, on pathological gaming among massively multiplayer online adolescent gamers. *Cyberpsychology, Behavior, and Social Networking, 14*(9), 535–539.

Littrell, L. N., & Salas, E. (2005). A review of cross-cultural training: Best practices, guidelines, and research needs. *Human Resource Development Review, 4*(3), 305–334.

Liu, D., Macchiarella, N. D., & Vincenzi, D. A. (2008). Simulation fidelity. In D. A. Vincenzi, J. A. Wise, M. Mouloua, & P. A. Hancock (Eds.), *Human Factors in Simulation and Training* (pp. 61–73). New York, NY: CRC Press.

Lo, W. T. & So, R. H. (2001). Cybersickness in the presence of scene rotational movements along different axes. *Applied Ergonomics, 32*(1), 1–14.

Locke, E. A. & Latham, G. P. (2002). Building a practically useful theory of goal setting and task motivation. A 35-year odyssey. *The American Psychologist, 57*(9), 705–717.

Lohse, K. R., Hilderman, C. G., Cheung, K. L., Tatla, S., & Van der Loos, H. M. (2014). Virtual reality therapy for adults post-stroke: A systematic review and meta-analysis exploring virtual environments and commercial games in therapy. *PloS One, 9*(3), 1–13.

Lopez, C. E. & Tucker, C. S. (2017). A quantitative method for evaluating the complexity of implementing and performing game features in physically-interactive gamified applications. *Computers in Human Behavior, 71*, 42–58.

Ma, M., McNeill, M., Charles, D., McDonough, S., Crosbie, J., Oliver, L., & McGoldrick, C. (2007). Adaptive virtual reality games for rehabilitation of motor disorders. *Universal Access in Human-Computer Interaction. Ambient Interaction*, 681–690.

MacDorman, K. F., Green, R. D., Ho, C. C., & Koch, C. T. (2009). Too real for comfort? Uncanny responses to computer generated faces. *Computers in Human Behavior, 25*(3), 695–710.

Maier, F. H. & Grossler, A. (2000). What are we talking about?: A taxonomy of computer simulations to support learning. *System Dynamics Review, 16*(2), 135.

Makransky, G., Lilleholt, L., & Aaby, A. (2017). Development and validation of the Multimodal Presence Scale for virtual reality environments: A confirmatory factor analysis and item response theory approach. *Computers in Human Behavior, 72*, 276–285.

Mania, K. & Chalmers, A. (2001). The effects of levels of immersion on memory and presence in virtual environments: A reality centered approach. *CyberPsychology & Behavior, 4*(2), 247–264.

Maran, N. J. & Glavin, R. J. (2003). Low-to high-fidelity simulation: A continuum of medical education? *Medical Education, 37*(1), 22–28.

Maruping, L. M. & Agarwal, R. (2004). Managing team interpersonal processes through technology: a task-technology fit perspective. *Journal of Applied Psychology, 89*(6), 975.

Mavrikios, D., Karabatsou, V., Fragos, D., & Chryssolouris, G. (2006). A prototype virtual reality-based demonstrator for immersive and interactive simulation of welding processes. *International Journal of Computer Integrated Manufacturing, 19*(3), 294–300.

Mayer, J. D. & Geher, G. (1996). Emotional intelligence and the identification of emotion. *Intelligence, 22*(2), 89–113.

McCrudden, M. T. & Corkill, A. J. (2010). Verbal ability and the processing of scientific text with seductive detail sentences. *Reading Psychology, 31*(3), 282–300.

McLay, R., Wood, D., Webb-Murphy, J., Spira, J., Wiederhold, M., Pyne, J., & Wiederhold, B. (2011). A randomized, controlled trial of virtual reality-graded exposure therapy for post-traumatic stress disorder in active duty service members with combat-related post-traumatic stress disorder. *Cyberpsychology, Behavior, and Social Networking, 14*(4), 223–229.

McMahan, R. P., Bowman, D. A., Zielinski, D. J., & Brady, R. B. (2012). Evaluating display fidelity and interaction fidelity in a virtual reality game. *IEEE Transactions on Visualization and Computer Graphics, 18*(4), 626–633.

Merchant, Z., Goetz, E. T., Cifuentes, L., Keeney-Kennicutt, W., & Davis, T. J. (2014). Effectiveness of virtual reality-based instruction on students' learning outcomes in K-12 and higher education: A meta-analysis. *Computers & Education*, *70*, 29–40.

Mesmer-Magnus, J. & Viswesvaran, C. (2010). The role of pre-training interventions in learning: A meta-analysis and integrative review. *Human Resource Management Review*, *20*(4), 261–282.

Messinger, P. R., Stroulia, E., & Lyons, K. (2008). A typology of virtual worlds: Historical overview and future directions. *Journal for Virtual Worlds Research*, *1*(1).

Milgram, P. & Kishino, F. (1994). A taxonomy of mixed reality visual displays. *IEICE TRANSACTIONS on Information and Systems*, *77*(12), 1321–1329.

Min, B. C., Chung, S. C., Min, Y. K., & Sakamoto, K. (2004). Psychophysiological evaluation of simulator sickness evoked by a graphic simulator. *Applied Ergonomics*, *35*(6), 549–556.

Mirelman, A., Rochester, L., Reelick, M., Nieuwhof, F., Pelosin, E., Abbruzzese, G., & Hausdorff, J. M. (2013). V-TIME: A treadmill training program augmented by virtual reality to decrease fall risk in older adults: Study design of a randomized controlled trial. *BMC Neurology*, *13*(1), 15.

Mon-Williams, M., Warm, J. P., & Rushton, S. (1993). Binocular vision in a virtual world: Visual deficits following the wearing of a head-mounted display. *Ophthalmic and Physiological Optics*, *13*(4), 387–391.

Monahan, T., McArdle, G., & Bertolotto, M. (2008). Virtual reality for collaborative e-learning. *Computers & Education*, *50*(4), 1339–1353.

Montegar, C. A., Reid, D. H., Madsen, C. H., & Ewell, M. D. (1977). Increasing institutional staff to resident interactions through in-service training and supervisor approval. *Behavior Therapy*, *8*(4), 533–540.

Moore, M. (2015). Historical perspectives on e-learning. In B. H. Khan & M. Ally (Eds.), *International handbook of e-learning: Theoretical perspectives and research* (vol. 1, pp. 41–49). New York, NY: Routledge.

Mori, M., MacDorman, K.F., & Kageki, N. (2012). The uncanny valley [from the field]. *Robotics & Automation Magazine, IEEE*, *19*(2),98–100.

Morina, N., Ijntema, H., Meyerbröker, K., & Emmelkamp, P. M. (2015). Can virtual reality exposure therapy gains be generalized to real-life? A meta-analysis of studies applying behavioral assessments. *Behaviour Research and Therapy*, *74*, 18–24.

Nagendran, M., Gurusamy, K. S., Aggarwal, R., Loizidou, M., & Davidson, B. R. (2013). Virtual reality training for surgical trainees in laparoscopic surgery. *Cochrane Database of Systematic Reviews* (8).

Nicholson, S. (2015). A recipe for meaningful gamification. In T. Reiners & L. Wood (Eds.), *Gamification in education and business* (pp. 1–20), New York, NY; Springer.

Nicholson, D. T., Chalk, C., Funnell, W. R. J., & Daniel, S. J. (2006). Can virtual reality improve anatomy education? A randomised controlled study of a computer-generated three-dimensional anatomical ear model. *Medical Education*, *40*(11), 1081–1087.

Nijman, D. J. J., Nijhof, W. J., Wognum, A. A. M., & Veldkamp, B. P. (2006). Exploring differential effects of supervisor support on transfer of training. *Journal of European Industrial Training*, *30*(7), 529–549.

Oculus. (2017). Rift Homepage. Retrieved from www.oculus.com/rift/.

Orvis, K. A., Fisher, S. L., & Wasserman, M. E. (2009). Power to the people: Using learner control to improve trainee reactions and learning in web-based instructional environments. *Journal of Applied Psychology, 94*(4), 960.

Palter, V. N. & Grantcharov, T. P. (2014). Individualized deliberate practice on a virtual reality simulator improves technical performance of surgical novices in the operating room: A randomized controlled trial. *Annals of Surgery, 259*(3), 443–448.

Pan, Z., Cheok, A. D., Yang, H., Zhu, J., & Shi, J. (2006). Virtual reality and mixed reality for virtual learning environments. *Computers & Graphics, 30*(1), 20–28.

Park, S. & Lim, J. (2007). Promoting positive emotion in multimedia learning using visual illustrations. *Journal of Educational Multimedia and Hypermedia, 16*(2), 141.

Park, B., Moreno, R., Seufert, T., & Brünken, R. (2011). Does cognitive load moderate the seductive details effect? A multimedia study. *Computers in Human Behavior, 27* (1), 5–10.

Parsons, T. D. & Rizzo, A. A. (2008). Affective outcomes of virtual reality exposure therapy for anxiety and specific phobias: A meta-analysis. *Journal of Behavior Therapy and Experimental Psychiatry, 39*(3), 250–261.

Pedreira, O., Garcia, F., Brisaboa, N., & Piattini, M. (2015). Gamification in software engineering: A systematic mapping. *Information and Software Technology, 57* (1),157–168.

Pellas, N. (2014). The influence of computer self-efficacy, metacognitive self-regulation and self-esteem on student engagement in online learning programs: Evidence from the virtual world of Second Life. *Computers in Human Behavior, 35*, 157–170.

Petty, M. D. & Barbosa, S. E. (2016). Improving air combat maneuvering skills through self-study and simulation-based practice. *Simulation & Gaming, 47*(1), 103–129.

Plante, T. G., Aldridge, A., Bogden, R., & Hanelin, C. (2003). Might virtual reality promote the mood benefits of exercise? *Computers in Human Behavior, 19*(4), 495–509.

Plante, T. G., Cage, C., Clements, S., & Stover, A. (2006). Psychological benefits of exercise paired with virtual reality: Outdoor exercise energizes whereas indoor virtual exercise relaxes. *International Journal of Stress Management, 13*(1), 108.

Plummer, J. P., Schuster, D., & Keebler, J. R. (2017). The effects of gender, flow and video game experience on combat identification training. *Ergonomics, 60*(8), 1101–1111.

Poncin, I. & Garnier, M. (2012). Immersion in a new commercial virtual environment: The role of the avatar in the appropriation process. *Advances in Consumer Research, 40*, 475–482.

Porter, N. C., Cote, J. A., Gifford, T. D., & Lam, W. (2006). Virtual reality welder training. *Journal of Ship Production, 22*(3), 126–138.

Psotka, J. (1995). Immersive training systems: Virtual reality and education and training. *Instructional Science, 23*(5), 405–431.

Rand, D., Kizony, R., Feintuch, U., Katz, N., Josman, N., & Weiss, P. L. T. (2005). Comparison of two VR platforms for rehabilitation: Video capture versus HMD. *Presence: Teleoperators and Virtual Environments, 14*(2), 147–160.

Ravyse, W. S., Blignaut, A. S., Leendertz, V., & Woolner, A. (2017). Success factors for serious games to enhance learning: A systematic review. *Virtual Reality, 21*(1), 31–58.

Reason, J. T. & Brand, J. J. (1975). *Motion sickness.* London, UK: Academic Press.

Regian, J. W., Shebilske, W. L., & Monk, J. M. (1992). Virtual reality: An instructional medium for visual-spatial tasks. *Journal of Communication, 42*(4), 136–149.

Rego, P., Moreira, P. M., & Reis, L. P. (June 2010). Serious games for rehabilitation: A survey and a classification towards a taxonomy. In *Proceedings of the 5th Iberian conference on Information systems and technologies (CISTI)* (pp. 1–6). IEEE.

Rheingold, H. (1991). *Virtual reality: Exploring the brave new technologies of artificial experience and interactive worlds–From cyberspace to teledildonics.* Secker & Warburg.

Riccio, G. E. & Stoffregen, T. A. (1991). An ecological theory of motion sickness and postural instability. *Ecological Psychology, 3*(3), 195–240.

Ries, B., Interrante, V., Kaeding, M., & Anderson, L. (October, 2008). The effect of self-embodiment on distance perception in immersive virtual environments. In *Proceedings of the 2008 ACM symposium on virtual reality software and technology* (pp. 167–170). ACM.

Rothbaum, B. O., Hodges, L. F., Ready, D., Graap, K., & Alarcon, R. D. (2001). Virtual reality exposure therapy for Vietnam veterans with posttraumatic stress disorder. *The Journal of Clinical Psychiatry, 62,* 617–622.

Rouiller, J. Z. & Goldstein, I. L. (1993). The relationship between organizational transfer climate and positive transfer of training. *Human Resource Development Quarterly, 4*(4), 377–390.

Ryan, R. M. & Deci, E. L. (2000). Self-determination theory and the facilitation of intrinsic motivation, social development, and well-being. *American Psychologist, 55*(1), 68.

Saks, A. M. & Belcourt, M. (2006). An investigation of training activities and transfer of training in organizations. *Human Resource Management, 45*(4), 629–648.

Salas, E. & Cannon-Bowers, J. A. (2001). The science of training: A decade of progress. *Annual Review of Psychology, 52*(1), 471–499.

Salas, E., Tannenbaum, S. I., Kraiger, K., & Smith-Jentsch, K. A. (2012). The science of training and development in organizations: What matters in practice. *Psychological Science in the Public Interest, 13*(2), 74–101.

Samsung. (2017). Wearables homepage. Retrieved from www.samsung.com/us/mobile/wearables/

Schuemie, M. J., Van Der Straaten, P., Krijn, M., & Van Der Mast, C. A. (2001). Research on presence in virtual reality: A survey. *CyberPsychology & Behavior, 4*(2), 183–201.

Seaborn, K. & Fels, D. I. (2015). Gamification in theory and action: A survey. *International Journal of Human-Computer Studies, 74,* 14–31.

Seo, Y., Kim, M., Jung, Y., & Lee, D. (2017). Avatar face recognition and self-presence. *Computers in Human Behavior, 69,* 120–127.

Sharples, S., Cobb, S., Moody, A., & Wilson, J. R. (2008). Virtual reality induced symptoms and effects (VRISE): Comparison of head mounted display (HMD), desktop and projection display systems. *Displays, 29*(2), 58–69.

Shibata, T. (2002). Head mounted display. *Displays, 23*(1–2), 57–64.

Shin, D.-H., Biocca, F., & Choo, H. (2013). Exploring the user experience of three-dimensional virtual learning environments. *Behaviour & Information Technology, 32*(2), 203–214.

Sitzmann, T. (2011). A meta-analytic examination of the instructional effectiveness of computer-based simulation games. *Personnel Psychology, 64*(2), 489–528.

Sitzmann, T., Bell, B. S., Kraiger, K., & Kanar, A. M. (2009). A multilevel analysis of the effect of prompting self-regulation in technology-delivered instruction. *Personnel Psychology, 62*(4), 697–734.

Sitzmann, T., Brown, K. G., Casper, W. J., Ely, K., & Zimmerman, R. D. (2008). A review and meta-analysis of the nomological network of trainee reactions, *Journal of Applied Psychology, 93*(2), 280–295.

Sitzmann, T. & Ely, K. (2010). Sometimes you need a reminder: The effects of prompting self-regulation on regulatory processes, learning, and attrition. *Journal of Applied Psychology, 95*(1), 132.

Slater, M. (2003). A note on presence terminology. *Presence Connect, 3*, 3.

Slater, M. (1999). Measuring presence: A response to the Witmer and Singer presence questionnaire. *Presence: Teleoperators & Virtual Environments, 8*(5), 560.

Slater, M. & Wilbur, S. (1997). A framework for immersive virtual environments (FIVE). *Presence: Teleoperators & Virtual Environments, 6*(6), 603.

Smith, M. J., Bell, M. D., Wright, M. A., Humm, L. B., Olsen, D., & Fleming, M. F. (2016). Virtual reality job interview training and 6-month employment outcomes for individuals with substance use disorders seeking employment. *Journal of Vocational Rehabilitation, 44*(3), 323–332.

Smith, M. J., Ginger, E. J., Wright, K., Wright, M. A., Taylor, J. L., Humm, L. B., . . . & Fleming, M. F. (2014). Virtual reality job interview training in adults with autism spectrum disorder. *Journal of Autism and Developmental Disorders, 44*(10), 2450–2463.

Smith, M. J., Fleming, M. F., Wright, M. A., Losh, M., Humm, L. B., Olsen, D., & Bell, M. D. (2015). Brief report: Vocational outcomes for young adults with autism spectrum disorders at six months after virtual reality job interview training. *Journal of Autism and Developmental Disorders, 45*(10), 3364–3369.

So, R. H., Ho, A., & Lo, W. T. (2001a). A metric to quantify virtual scene movement for the study of cybersickness: Definition, implementation, and verification. *Presence: Teleoperators and Virtual Environments, 10*(2), 193–215.

So, R. H., Lo, W. T., & Ho, A. T. (2001b). Effects of navigation speed on motion sickness caused by an immersive virtual environment. *Human Factors: The Journal of the Human Factors and Ergonomics Society, 43*(3), 452–461.

Spanlang, B., Normand, J.-M., Borland, D., Kilteni, K., Giannopoulos, E., Pomés, A., . . . & Slater, M. (2014). How to build an embodiment lab: achieving body representation illusions in virtual reality. *Frontiers in Robotics and AI, 1*, 9.

Steuer, J. (1992). Defining virtual reality: Dimensions determining telepresence. *Journal of Communication, 42*(4), 73–93.

Tannenbaum, S. I. & Yukl, G. (1992). Training and development in work organizations. *Annual Review of Psychology, 43*(1), 399–441.

Teng, C.-I. (2010). Customization, immersion satisfaction, and online gamer loyalty. *Computers in Human Behavior, 26*, 1547–1554.

Tichon, J. G., & Wallis, G. M. (2010). Stress training and simulator complexity: why sometimes more is less. *Behaviour & Information Technology, 29*(5), 459–466.

Towler, A., Kraiger, K., Sitzmann, T., Van Overberghe, C., Cruz, J., Ronen, E., & Stewart, D. (2008). The seductive details effect in technology-delivered instruction. *Performance Improvement Quarterly, 21*(2), 65–86.

Treisman, M. (1977). Motion sickness: An evolutionary hypothesis. *Science, 197*, 493–495.

Trevino, L. K., Lengel, R. H., & Daft, R. L. (1987). Media symbolism, media richness, and media choice in organizations: A symbolic interactionist perspective. *Communication Research*, *14*(5), 553–574.

Uttal, D. H., Meadow, N. G., Tipton, E., Hand, L. L., Alden, A. R., Warren, C., & Newcombe, N. S. (2013). The malleability of spatial skills: A meta-analysis of training studies. *Psychological Bulletin*, *139*(2),352–402.

Van Dongen, K. W., Tournoij, E., Van der Zee, D. C., Schijven, M. P., & Broeders, I. A. M. J. (2007). Construct validity of the LapSim: Can the LapSim virtual reality simulator distinguish between novices and experts? *Surgical Endoscopy*, *21*(8), 1413–1417.

Vive (2017). Homepage. Retrieved from www.vive.com/us/.

Walshe, D. G., Lewis, E. J., Kim, S. I., O'Sullivan, K., & Wiederhold, B. K. (2003). Exploring the use of computer games and virtual reality in exposure therapy for fear of driving following a motor vehicle accident. *CyberPsychology & Behavior*, *6*(3), 329–334.

Wang, Y., Chen, Y., Nan, Z., & Hu, Y. (2006, December). Study on welder training by means of haptic guidance and virtual reality for arc welding. In *IEEE International Conference on Robotics and Biomimetics* (pp. 954–958). IEEE.

Wang, Z. & Adesope, O. (2014). Effects of seductive details on multimedia learning. *Journal of Studies in Education*, *4*(3), 32–44.

Warden, C. A., Stanworth, J. O., & Chang, C.-C. (2016). Full length article: Leveling up: Are non-gamers and women disadvantaged in a virtual world classroom? *Computers in Human Behavior*, *65*, 210–219.

Wiederhold, B. K. & Wiederhold, M. D. (2000). Lessons learned from 600 virtual reality sessions. *CyberPsychology & Behavior*, *3*(3), 393–400.

Wilson, C. J., & Soranzo, A. (2015). The use of virtual reality in psychology: A case study in visual perception. *Computational & Mathematical Methods in Medicine*, 2015, 1–7.

Witmer, B. G., Jerome, C. J., & Singer, M. J. (2005). The factor structure of the presence questionnaire. *Presence: Teleoperators & Virtual Environments*, *14*(3),298–312.

Witmer, B. G. & Singer, M. J. (1998). Measuring presence in virtual environments: A presence questionnaire. *Presence: Teleoperators & Virtual Environments*, *7* (3), 225.

Zigurs, I. & Buckland, B. K. (1998). A theory of task/technology fit and group support systems effectiveness. *MIS Quarterly*, 22(3), 313–334.

Zyda, M. (2005). From visual simulation to virtual reality to games. *Computer*, *38*(9), 25–32.

PART IV

Technology in Leadership and Teams

15 Leading from a Distance

Advancements in Virtual Leadership Research

Bradford S. Bell, Kristie L. McAlpine, and N. Sharon Hill

Fueled by advances in technology and globalization, recent years have witnessed significant growth in virtual work arrangements. Flexible work arrangements, such as telecommuting, have enabled a growing number of employees to work outside the office for some or all of their workweek (Allen, Golden, & Shockley, 2015; WorldAtWork, 2013). In addition, there has been a tremendous increase in the use of virtual teams, which enable organizations to access and connect relevant expertise regardless of where it may be located in the world (Bell & Kozlowski, 2002; Kirkman, Gibson, & Kim, 2012). These changes are reshaping not only how work gets done in organizations but also how leaders interface with their followers. As leaders increasingly find themselves physically separated from the individuals and teams they are charged with leading, direct, face-to-face interactions with followers are giving way to a greater dependence on technology-mediated communication.

Although it is clear that the context of leadership in modern organizations is changing, there is less agreement about what these changes mean for effective leadership. Some have argued that physical distance and electronic communication may make effective leadership impossible (Kerr & Jermier, 1978) or make it difficult for leaders to display certain leader behaviors, such as those associated with transformational leadership (Puranova & Bono, 2009). Others have expressed greater confidence that virtual leadership can approximate traditional, face-to-face leadership, in part because of recent and ongoing advances in electronic communication technologies (Antonakis & Atwater, 2002; Avolio & Kahai, 2003). Still others have proposed that distance may be an essential ingredient for leadership emergence (Antonakis & Jacquart, 2013) and may confer certain advantages, such as allowing leaders to hide their weaknesses and maintain detachment from the daily operational minutiae (Shamir, 2013).

It is currently difficult to reconcile these different perspectives because advances in technology and the adoption of virtual work arrangements in organizations have thus far outpaced the science of leadership (Avolio et al., 2014). Bligh and Riggio (2013, p. 2), for example, argue, "The majority of our theories of leadership implicitly suggest that it does not matter how often, across what distances, and through what media leaders and followers interact." Although these assumptions are increasingly being challenged, research on virtual leadership has been limited. In their review of virtual teams research, for instance, Kirkman et al. (2012, p. 808) contend that, "not nearly enough has been done to understand virtual team leadership." Similarly, Avolio et al. (2014) conclude that although it is possible to derive some broad conclusions about virtual leadership from the literature, more specific recommendations and guidelines remain elusive.

In the current chapter, we provide a review of research on virtual leadership, or what is sometimes alternatively referred to as e-leadership or remote leadership, with the aim of not only cataloging what we have learned but also identifying where research in this area should be heading in the future. We begin with an overview of the changing leadership context. In particular, we examine the factors that have led to the growing adoption of virtual work arrangements and consider the potential implications of this trend for the role of leaders in today's organizations. We then review the conceptual and empirical advances that have emerged from the extant research on virtual leadership. Although we acknowledge that leadership is inherently a multilevel phenomenon with interdependencies across levels (Day, 2012), we organize our review into two sections representing the loci that have been the primary focus of virtual leadership research to date: leader-follower dyads and teams. By considering each of these areas separately, we are better able to trace their evolution and consider the unique elements of virtual leadership within each of these contexts (Kirkman et al., 2012). Finally, we conclude with a discussion of future directions for advancing virtual leadership research.

15.1 The Changing Leadership Context

Virtual work arrangements have become a staple in organizations. These arrangements can take the form of flexible work arrangements (FWA), such as a telecommuting arrangements that enable employees to work offsite for some or all of the workweek (Allen et al., 2015; Gajendran & Harrison, 2007), or virtual team membership, in which employees rely on electronic tools to coordinate with one another and are often distributed across multiple geographic locations (Bell & Kozlowski, 2002; Gibson et al., 2014; Kirkman & Mathieu, 2005). Indeed, recent survey data illustrates a vast and growing virtual work landscape. A 2013 WorldAtWork survey of compensation and benefits professionals found that 88 percent of organizations offered some form of telecommuting to employees, with 34 percent offering full-time telecommuting arrangements (WorldAtWork, 2013). Moreover, data from the Society for Human Resource Management's (SHRM) 2016 benefits survey documented a threefold increase in telecommuting over the past 20 years (Society for Human Resource Management, 2016a). This striking growth in FWA use has been accompanied by an increased reliance on virtual teams. For example, data from a 2012 SHRM survey of HR professionals found that approximately half of organizations used virtual teams, with multinational organizations utilizing virtual teams the most (66 percent; Society for Human Resource Management, 2012).

15.1.1 Factors Responsible for the Trend in Virtual Work Arrangements

There are a number of factors fueling the growth in virtual work arrangements. Globalization, technological advancements, increased focus on diversity and inclusion and the work-life interface, and fundamental changes in our understanding of how organizations are structured and how work is conducted have all contributed to employees' ability, motivation, and opportunity to engage in virtual work.

With the rise of globalization, organizations are increasingly spanning national boundaries and employing workers across the globe. To respond to increased global competition, organizations must effectively mobilize employees to address complex, dynamic problems. Virtual work arrangements enable organizations to connect top talent that is distributed across multiple locations in a cost effective manner. Indeed, engaging and connecting talent located in different geographic regions is frequently cited as the chief reason for the use of virtual teams (Society for Human Resource Management, 2012). Not only is this a critical function when collaboration across global business units is becoming more prevalent, but it is also vital at a time when organizational leaders are identifying talent acquisition and talent development as their greatest ongoing challenges (Center for Creative Leadership, 2007).

The development of advanced communication technology has given rise to greater engagement in virtual work by enabling employees working across the globe – or just across the office – to coordinate via multiple forms of electronic media. Beyond the near-universal use of email and mobile devices in today's organizations, recent advances in audio/visual technology and virtual messaging platforms have allowed teams to share richer information in real time. One key development in audio/visual technology is the telepresence system, which enables employees to connect virtually with a level of richness that more closely approximates face-to-face physical presence than traditional video conferencing systems (Cascio & Montealegre, 2016). Employees working in two locations can meet virtually through a telepresence system and feel as if they are sitting on two sides of the same room together. In a different approach, the development of embodied social proxy technology enables individual employees working remotely to have a greater presence in the office by physically representing them through a life-size monitor or tablet, enabling them to participate in team activities and meetings as if they were in the office in person (Venolia et al., 2010). Alongside developments in audio/visual technology, the growth in virtual platforms has given rise to integrated virtual workspaces like Slack, an app now used by over 75 percent of Fortune 100 organizations (Hesseldahl, 2016). Slack enables employees to simultaneously share files, archive ongoing conversations about multiple topics, and send instant messages to stay in continuous contact. Other electronic tools, like the recently released app Twist, facilitate team coordination but de-emphasize synchronous communication (Deahl, 2017), which can be a challenge for teams spanning multiple time zones and with members who often feel the pressure to be perpetually online. In light of these and other technological advancements, organizations have more choices than ever before for addressing traditional barriers to virtual work. In fact, the pace at which technological tools are upgraded and replaced underscores the importance of focusing not on the particularities of any given technology, but rather on how technology can be used to foster high-quality interactions.

In addition to technological advancements, a greater focus on the work-life interface and diversity and inclusion in organizations has made virtual work an increasingly strategic tool for attracting and retaining talent in a diverse workforce (Society for Human Resource Management, 2016b). For example, the workforce now includes more dual-career couples, single-parent households, older workers, and workers with disabilities than ever before (Bureau of Labor Statistics, 2017). Virtual work arrangements help employees navigate the work-life interface by providing them with autonomy over where and when they work and enabling them to enact their preferred boundaries between work and non-work domains to reduce conflict between them (Allen et al., 2013; Kossek & Michel, 2011). Virtual work arrangements can also serve as a tool for integrating workers with disabilities, as the Equal Employment Opportunity Commission has indicated that telecommuting may be considered a reasonable accommodation under the Americans with Disabilities Act (Equal Employment Opportunity Commission, 2005). Moreover, virtual work arrangements can play an important role in engaging older workers, as organizations seek to retain experienced employees and facilitate knowledge transfer (Bale et al., 2012; Beehr & Bennett, 2014).

Finally, two themes that underlie all of these developments are changes in organizational structure and a shift in how work is conceptualized. As traditional organizational hierarchies have flattened and organizations have adopted alternative structures, such as matrices, employees and teams are becoming increasingly interdependent. Employees are often members of more than one team, reporting to leaders both face-to-face and virtually. Moreover, as work becomes more dynamic and complex, organizations are turning to systems of teams to coordinate work, necessitating virtual communication and synchronization across multiple teams that are often geographically distributed (O'Leary, Woolley, & Mortenson, 2012). In tandem with these changes, work is more often conceived of as a set of behaviors that people engage in, rather than a place where people go. As such, virtual work arrangements have enabled us to fundamentally challenge traditional assumptions of how work is done. Employees can work from their homes and across the globe, connecting virtually with coworkers and organizational leaders through technological tools. Taken together, the growth in virtual work arrangements presents a rich opportunity for researchers and practitioners to better understand the changing nature of interactions among leaders and employees and the importance of effective leadership in virtual settings.

15.1.2 The Importance of Leadership in the Context of Virtual Work Arrangements

These recent developments have created a new organizational reality for leaders. Leading individuals and teams in a virtual environment is more challenging than in traditional face-to-face settings (Bell & Kozlowski, 2002; Hoch & Kozlowski,

2014), yet the vast majority of senior leaders agree that virtual leadership is a necessary skill for leaders in their organizations (Center for Creative Leadership, 2007). When leaders and employees rely on electronic communication to connect with one another and complete their work, there is a greater possibility for misunderstandings to occur, greater barriers to fostering trust, and greater difficulty in coordinating tasks (Liao, 2017). Thus, virtual settings require leaders to employ a unique set of skills to facilitate the coordination of the group's work and build relationships with followers, whether it be a dyadic relationship with a single telecommuting employee or a set of relationships with members of a virtual team. Data from a survey of leaders conducted by the Center for Creative Leadership reflects widespread agreement that virtual leadership requires more from leaders: 87 percent of leaders – and 92 percent of senior executives – agreed or strongly agreed that virtual leadership requires a different set of skills than face-to-face leadership (Center for Creative Leadership, 2007).

Not only do virtual leaders need to draw from the same set of skills that enables them to lead effectively in traditional settings, but they must also hone an additional set of skills, including their facility with technology and the ability to set norms for technology use. Leaders must role-model the appropriate use of communication technology, exhibiting an awareness of the appropriate type of media to use for a given situation or task and show adaptability and a willingness to learn new technologies (Blackburn, Furst, and Rosen, 2003). They must also be capable of adapting communication technology to help their followers respond to emerging problems or address shifting task requirements over time (Thomas & Bostrom, 2010b). Virtual leaders must also develop and communicate norms about how and when technology should be used. For instance, because it is more difficult to observe what others are working on in virtual settings, leaders must set clear expectations around transparency, open communication, and knowledge sharing in order to facilitate the effective coordination of work tasks (Blackburn et al., 2003). Moreover, when leaders are not working face-to-face with their employees, they must communicate clear expectations about when employees are expected to be available and how quickly they are expected to respond to others. Communicating appropriate technology and work-time norms is especially important in the context of global virtual teams, when non-overlapping time zones mean that employees could be working twenty-four hours a day, seven days a week. The use of real-time messaging platforms and other forms of electronic communication tools can mean that employees are always accessible, which can have negative consequences on their ability to manage work and non-work boundaries (Butts, Becker, & Boswell, 2015).

Virtual leaders must also be able to lead employees with varying levels of skill and motivation for working virtually, as well as with different demographic characteristics and cultural backgrounds. A recent study by Hill and Bartol (2016), for example, found that empowering leadership was critical for enabling virtual team members to utilize their knowledge and judgment about how to operate in dispersed team situations to engage in effective virtual collaboration and achieve higher individual performance. Past research also suggests that personality and culture are two key factors that leaders should take into consideration (Makarius & Larson, 2017; Schulze & Krumm, 2017). For example, one study found that employees working in virtual arrangements who were more conscientious engaged in more self-management tactics, such as planning scheduled work times and following through with set goals (O'Neill, Hambley, & Chatellier, 2014). Moreover, another study found that teams engaging in decision-making using computer-mediated communication performed better when team members had higher levels of openness to experience (Colquitt et al., 2002). Past work has also found that employees from individualistic cultures exhibit greater virtual team self-efficacy than employees from collectivistic cultures (Hardin, Fuller, & Davidson, 2007). Apart from personality and culture, other factors, such as generational differences, have received more limited attention in the literature. Despite being frequently cited as an important issue for virtual leaders, there is little empirical work examining generational differences among employees and their impact on virtual team processes and outcomes (Gilson et al., 2015). As new generations of employees who have grown up communicating virtually enter organizations in higher numbers, it is possible that some of the aspects associated with virtual work arrangements that have been traditionally viewed as challenges will be reduced, removed, or even leveraged as benefits.

15.2 Virtual Dyadic Leadership

The earliest explorations of the relationship between distance and leadership focused on dyadic interactions between supervisors and their subordinates (e. g., Bogardus, 1927; Katz & Kahn, 1978; Napier & Ferris, 1993; Shamir, 1995). Later, as work increasingly shifted from individual jobs to team-based work structures (Kozlowski & Bell, 2013), research expanded to consider leader distance at not only the individual but also the group level of analysis (e.g., Antonakis & Atwater, 2002). We review virtual team leadership research in the following section, but first examine the conceptual and empirical advances that have emerged from studies on virtual leadership in the context of dyadic supervisor-subordinate relationships. We begin by discussing how leader distance has been conceptualized in the literature and its potential implications for virtual supervisor-subordinate interactions. We then review important developments in virtual dyadic leadership research, highlighting the different forms of leadership that have been examined and key conceptual advances and empirical findings in each area.

15.2.1 Leader Distance

Although the concept of distance in leadership relationships was originally proposed by Bogardus (1927) and appeared in writings over subsequent years (e.g., Katz & Kahn, 1978; Kerr & Jermier, 1978), Napier and Ferris (1993) were the first to offer an explicit definition of leader distance. In their integrative review of distance and supervisory leadership, they presented a model of Dyadic Distance consisting of three dimensions: psychological, structural, and functional. According to Napier and Ferris (1993, pp. 328–329), psychological distance refers to "the psychological effects of actual and perceived demographic, cultural, and value differences between the supervisor and subordinate." Structural distance addresses those aspects of distance that stem from physical structure (e.g., actual physical distance between work locations of a supervisor and subordinate), organizational structure (e.g., degree of centralization), and supervision structure (e.g., amount of task contact between a supervisor and subordinate). Napier and Ferris argue that all of these structural variables are associated with the amount of supervisor-subordinate interaction that is allowed or encouraged. Finally, functional distance describes the quality of the supervisor-subordinate relationship, or whether the employee is a member of the supervisor's in-group or out-group. In their model, Napier and Ferris position functional distance as mediating the relationships of psychological and structural distance with subordinate outcomes (e.g., performance, satisfaction, withdrawal).

Building on the work of Napier and Ferris, Antonakis and Atwater (2002) present an updated review and theory of leader distance in which they propose three independent dimensions of distance. The first, perceived social distance, generally equates to the psychological distance dimension proposed by Napier and Ferris (1993) in that it deals with perceived differences in status, rank, social standing, and power. The second dimension, physical distance, captures how near or far followers are located relative to their leader. The third and final dimension they propose is perceived frequency of leader-follower interaction. Unlike Napier and Ferris (1993), they argue that this dimension is independent of social and physical distance. A physically distal leader, for example, may use technology to maintain frequent contact with followers. Antonakis and Atwater (2002) use these three dimensions to develop eight typologies of distant leadership, which they then link to leader outcomes at both the individual and group levels of analysis.

Researchers interested in virtual leadership in the context of dyadic supervisor-subordinate relationships have generally focused on two dimensions of leader distance. The first, and by far the most widely used, dimension is the physical distance or separation between the supervisor and subordinate. Although physical distance would seem to be a relatively straightforward construct, observers have noted that there exists considerable variation in how it has been defined and used within the literature (Kiesler & Cummings, 2002; Lewandowski & Lisk, 2013). For example, a number of studies have examined physical distance as a dichotomous variable representing whether or not the leader and follower are located in the same city or state/province (e.g., Bonet & Salvador, 2017; Kelley & Kelloway, 2012), whereas others have asked employees to rate the extent to which they have regular contact with their supervisors (e.g., Neufeld, Wan, & Fang, 2010), or have focused on the proportion of time employees spend working outside the office (e.g., Golden, 2006; Golden & Veiga, 2008). A second dimension involves the nature of leader-follower interactions, specifically in terms of the degree to which they are mediated by technology. In their conceptualization of e-leadership, for example, Avolio and colleagues have emphasized the role of advanced information technology in mediating the effects of leadership as a social influence process (e.g., Avolio, Kahai, & Dodge, 2001; Avolio et al., 2014).

Although there are differences in how researchers have conceptualized and operationalized virtuality in supervisor-subordinate relationships, there are also some commonalities that cut across these various treatments. First, most studies have conceptualized virtuality as a characteristic of the context in which the leadership relationship exists, although some have examined it as an attribute of the leader relationship itself (Shamir, 2013). As Avolio et al. (2001, p. 616) state, "In the case of e-leadership the context not only matters, it is part of the construct being studied." Second, these different conceptualizations are functionally similar, in that greater virtuality, whether due to physical distance or technological mediation, is viewed as inhibiting opportunities for leaders and followers to engage in direct observation and contact (Kiesler & Cummings, 2002; Shamir, 2013). It is important to note that although virtuality may present a barrier to direct leader-follower interactions, other forms of interaction may not be similarly affected. Observers have noted, for example, that technology can make it easier for leaders to reach others (Avolio & Kahai, 2003), so the scope and frequency of leader-follower contact may increase (Kahai, 2013).

As discussed earlier, virtuality is generally assumed to add a layer of complexity to the supervisor-subordinate dynamic. Consistent with this view, research has provided evidence that virtual leader-follower relationships are often characterized by lower levels of trust and support than more conventional relationships (Merriman, Schmidt, & Dunlap-Hinkler, 2007) and that greater leader-follower distance is associated with negative follower outcomes, such as reduced in-role performance (Podsakoff, MacKenzie, & Bommer, 1996). However, recent research has begun to adopt a more nuanced approach to studying the effects of virtuality on the leadership dynamic; one that examines how virtuality shapes the effects of different forms of leadership and how these effects may depend on various contingencies. The evolution of these research streams are reviewed below.

15.3 Behavioral Leadership

One approach that has been used to study the effects of virtuality in the context of supervisor-subordinate dyads is the behavioral leadership perspective. In particular, research has explored how virtuality influences the relative effectiveness of different types of leadership behaviors, relying primarily on transformational-transactional leadership theory (Bass, 1985; Burns, 1978), which is one of the most widely used leadership theories in the broader leadership literature. Transformational leadership focuses on inspiring and motivating team members to rise above self-interest and act in the interests of the group. Transactional leadership is based on an exchange process of contingent rewards and punishment. Research has revealed that transformational leadership is generally associated with positive outcomes, whereas findings have been more mixed across the different dimensions of transactional leadership (i.e., contingent reward leadership, active and passive management-by-exception). A meta-analysis by Judge and Piccolo

(2004) found that contingent reward leadership exhibited a positive relationship with leader and follower criteria, whereas both active and passive management-by-exception were more inconsistently related to the criteria.

Researchers have argued that more distal leader-follower relationships may make it difficult for leaders to demonstrate transformational leadership behaviors, such as providing meaning for the followers' work and listening to followers' concerns and needs. A series of studies by Howell and colleagues (Howell & Hall-Merenda, 1999; Howell, Neufeld, & Avolio, 2005) provides some support for this argument. They found that transformational leadership led to higher follower and business-unit performance in close versus distant situations. Results for the different dimensions of transactional leadership were more mixed. Whereas contingent reward leadership led to higher follower and business-unit performance when distance was high versus low, both active and passive management-by-exception leadership produced lower follower performance when followers were more physically distant. A study by Neufeld et al. (2010) on leader-follower dyads varying in physical distance found that ratings of leader effectiveness were positively related to transformational leadership but unrelated to either contingent reward leadership or physical distance. Unfortunately, Neufeld et al. (2010) did not examine whether the degree of distance in the leader-follower dyads moderates the effects of the different types of leadership behaviors. Finally, Kelley and Kelloway (2012) found that the effects of transformational leadership on several employee outcomes (i.e., job satisfaction, organization commitment, and manager trust) were similar in virtual and proximal leader-follower samples. Overall, these studies suggest that virtuality may moderate the effectiveness of transformational and transactional leader behaviors in leader-follower dyads. However, caution should be exercised since research in this area remains limited and has at times produced mixed findings, which, as we discuss below, is also true for research that has examined the effects of transformational-transactional leadership in virtual team settings.

15.3.1 Leader-Member Exchange

A second and related perspective that has been used to study the effects of virtuality in supervisor-subordinate dyads is leader-member exchange (LMX) theory, which focuses on the relationship between an employee and his or her supervisor (Dienesch & Liden, 1986; Graen & Uhl-Bien, 1995). In high-quality LMX relationships, followers are considered members of the supervisor's in-group and receive greater levels of trust, special privileges, and other treatment that extend beyond simply economic exchange. Employees in low-quality LMX relationships do not receive these benefits and are treated in accordance with the employment contract. A recent meta-analysis by Dulebohn, Bommer, Liden, Brouer, and Ferris (2012) showed that high-quality LMX relationships are generally associated with more positive consequences (e.g., reduced turnover, higher performance, commitment, and justice).

Empirical research that has examined how virtuality influences the effects of LMX has yielded somewhat mixed findings. Several studies have found that the positive effects of high-quality LMX relationships are strengthened in situations characterized by a greater degree of virtuality (Gajendran & Joshi, 2012; Golden, 2006; Golden & Veiga, 2008; Hill, Kang, & Seo, 2014). Golden and Veiga (2008), for example, found that LMX quality exhibited a stronger, positive relationship with organizational commitment, job satisfaction, and job performance among workers who spent more time working virtually. However, others studies have found virtuality to have no effect on LMX-outcome relationships or to dampen the effects of LMX. Howell and Hall-Merenda (1999), for example, found that physical distance failed to moderate the relationship between LMX and follower performance. In a series of two studies, Kacmar, Witt, Zivnuska, and Gully (2003) found that LMX had a weaker relationship with employees' performance ratings when individuals reported infrequent communication with their supervisor.

15.3.2 Contingency Leadership Approaches

The mixed pattern of findings reviewed above suggest that the effects of virtuality on the supervisor-subordinate dynamic might be more complex than previously assumed. As Kahai (2013, p. 101) states, "the difference that IT can be expected to make for leadership is not likely to be uniform or simple." To better understand the influence of virtuality in the context of dyadic leader-follower relationships, research in this area may need to be more contingency based (Kirkman et al., 2012). That is, future research may need to focus greater attention on identifying the circumstances that determine when leader-follower virtuality is more or less challenging. A few studies have already started down this path. Bonet and Salvador (2017), for example, examined the effect of manager-worker separation on the performance of programmers and analysts working in a software maintenance center. They found that manager-worker separation led to lower levels of worker performance when tasks were high in technical and coordinative complexity, but not when they were low in complexity. In addition, they found that the costs of manager-worker separation were weaker when employees were collocated with a greater proportion of their project team members. Adopting a somewhat different approach, Kelley and Kelloway (2012) examine how several elements of the leader-follower relationship context differentially influence leadership in virtual versus proximal environments. They find that, in both virtual and proximal settings, employees' perceptions of control and unplanned communication positively predicted ratings of managers' transformational leadership style, which in turn related positively to several employee outcomes (job satisfaction, organizational commitment, manager trust). However, regularly scheduled communication and an employee's familiarity with his/her manager exhibited a positive relationship with transformational leadership style in only the virtual context. These findings suggest that certain contextual factors may have a unique or disparate impact on supervisory leadership effectiveness in virtual environments.

15.4 Virtual Team Leadership

Virtual teamwork refers to collaboration that occurs between team members who are geographically dispersed and/or interact using technology rather than face-to-face (Bell & Kozlowski, 2002; Kirkman et al., 2012). Due to the demonstrated challenges of collaborating in a dispersed and technology-mediated team environment, researchers have identified leadership as critical for virtual team success and suggested that leadership may play a stronger role when teams are more virtual (Blackburn et al., 2003; Kirkman et al., 2012; Kozlowski & Bell, 2013). However, despite this general recognition of the importance of virtual team leadership, research in this area is still relatively nascent. In their 2004 review of the virtual team literature, Martins, Gilson, and Maynard (2004) identified leadership as a critical area in need of future research. Although a decade later, researchers have noted that "research on VT leadership has grown precipitously" (Gilson et al., 2015, p. 7), they also acknowledge that significant research gaps still remain in understanding virtual team leadership (Kirkman et al., 2012).

In this section, we trace important developments in virtual team leadership research. We highlight the different forms of leadership that have been examined and review key conceptual developments and empirical research findings in each area. In addition, we discuss important moderators and mediating mechanisms that underlie leadership's effects. We start by describing how virtuality has been conceptualized in teams and its implications for virtual team leadership.

15.4.1 Team Virtuality

Virtual team leadership researchers have focused on two dominant dimensions that are most commonly included in conceptualizations of team virtuality. The first dimension, technology dependence, is the extent to which team members rely on technology-mediated communication (e.g., email, videoconference, group decision support systems) rather than face-to-face communication (Bell & Kozlowski, 2002; Gibson & Gibbs, 2006; Kirkman & Mathieu, 2005). Some researchers also differentiate between different types of communication media (Kirkman & Mathieu, 2005), suggesting that a team is more virtual the more it uses media that limits the ability to convey rich and valuable information and restricts real-time interaction (e.g., email). The second dimension is the extent to which team members are geographically dispersed (O'Leary & Cummings, 2007). Geographic dispersion encompasses different measures of physical distance (e.g., spatial dispersion, time zone differences) and configurations of team member dispersion (e.g., geographic subgroups, isolated team members).

There is a strong body of research to show that technology dependence and geographic dispersion can create challenges to effective task execution and relationship development in teams. For example, greater reliance on technology and separation across physical distance and time zones can impede information sharing, task coordination, trust building, and conflict management (for a review, see Kirkman et al., 2012). In addition, the configuration or pattern of team member dispersion has implications for virtual team functioning (O'Leary & Mortensen, 2010; Polzer et al., 2006). For example, O'Leary and Mortensen (2010) found that geographic subgroups in teams led to stronger in-group/out-group categorization effects that weakened team member identification with the team and increased conflict and coordination problems. Further, uneven subgroups created an imbalance that exacerbated these effects with larger subgroups having greater influence on team decisions. Where leaders are co-located relative to the different subgroups in the team also has implications for team functioning, since there is a risk that team members who are in the same subgroup as the leader may receive more attention from and build stronger relationships with the leader (Ocker et al., 2011).

Given the challenges team virtuality can pose to effective team functioning and performance, a key focus of virtual team leadership research is to understand how different types of leadership help to mitigate these challenges and their effects. Virtual team leadership research began with a focus on understanding the role of the formal or hierarchical team leader, but has grown to encompass informal emergent and shared leadership on the part of team members (Gibbs, Sivunen, & Boyraz, 2017). We trace this development in our review, starting with the different types of hierarchical leadership perspectives examined in a virtual team context.

15.4.2 Behavioral Leadership

Early virtual team leadership research adopted a dominant perspective used to study dyadic leadership, the behavioral leadership perspective. This perspective has also been broadly applied in more traditional team research (e.g., Burke et al., 2006; Fleishman et al., 1991; Salas et al., 1992). The behavioral approach to team leadership distinguishes between two main categories of leader behaviors: relationship-focused (those addressing team members' concerns, well-being, and development of effective interpersonal interactions) and task-focused (those that help to facilitate task accomplishment by orchestrating and monitoring the work of the team). Conceptual models of virtual team leadership based on the behavioral perspective (Dulebohn & Hoch, 2017; Liao, 2017) have suggested these behaviors are likely to have a stronger influence on team outcomes for more highly virtual teams. They argue that relationship-focused leader behaviors can help to compensate for challenges to relationship development resulting from virtuality in teams, such as difficulty in building trust and managing conflict. Similarly, task-focused leadership behaviors provide structure and coordination that help to mitigate the effects of the communication and coordination challenges caused by virtuality.

Empirical virtual team leadership research aligned with the behavioral approach has focused to a large extent on the transformational (relationship focused)/transactional (task focused) leadership framework (Bass, 1985; Burns, 1978). There is empirical evidence from research using experimental teams that transformational leadership has a stronger effect on team outcomes that are more virtual due to their greater use of leaner vs. richer communication media (e.g., Huang, Kahai, & Jestice, 2010; Kahai, Huang, & Jestice, 2012; Purvanova & Bono, 2009). Similarly, transformational leadership (Joshi, Lazarova, & Liao, 2009) and other forms of relationship-focused leadership, such as leader-member exchange (Gajendran & Joshi, 2012), have demonstrated stronger effects in organizational teams that are more highly dispersed. However, there have also been mixed results. For example, some researchers have found no difference in effects of transformational leadership in teams using electronic communication media vs. face-to-face (e.g., Hambley, O'Neill, & Kline, 2007). Also, Hoch & Kozlowski (2014) found that higher levels of virtuality (assessed as a composite of geographic dispersion, electronic communication, and cultural diversity) weakened the positive relationship between transformational leadership and team performance. Similarly, for transactional leadership, some studies have found stronger effects for transactional leadership when teams use leaner communication media (Huang et al., 2010); however, other studies have found no significant differences based on the media used (Hambley et al., 2007; Hoyt & Blascovich, 2003).

In summary, as in more traditional teams, relationship-focused and task-focused leadership appear to have a positive impact in virtual teams. There is also some evidence that their effects may be stronger for teams that are more reliant on leaner communication media. Research has also demonstrated a stronger effect of relationship-focused leadership in teams where members are more geographically dispersed. However, there have also been mixed findings in this area, suggesting that there may be important moderators of relationship-focused and task-focused leadership effects. We discuss this further in a later section related to contingency effects in virtual team leadership research.

15.4.3 Functional Leadership

Researchers have also used the functional perspective (Morgeson, DeRue, & Karam, 2010) to understand the role of leadership in teams. This perspective is based on functional leadership theory (Lord, 1977; McGrath, 1962), which conceptualizes team leadership as the process of satisfying team needs in order to make teams more effective. Defining leadership functions as any leadership actions that contribute to need satisfaction allows for a broader examination of the different ways in which leadership can contribute to effective virtual team functioning. In addition, although most virtual team leadership research has focused on formal leadership enacted by the assigned hierarchical team leader, the functional perspective suggests that leadership functions can be enacted by different sources of leadership beyond the formal team leader, including informal leadership (i.e., shared or emergent leadership) enacted by team members (Morgeson et al., 2010).

Based on a functional team leadership perspective, Morgeson et al. (2010) developed a taxonomy of team leadership functions that can be enacted by different sources of leadership in the team at different phases of the team's task life cycle. Although these functions were mostly derived from a review of traditional team research, these researchers propose that some functions might have a stronger impact on team need satisfaction in more highly virtual teams. For example, when the level of geographic dispersion in a team is higher, the leadership functions of setting clear expectations, structuring and planning the team's work, and monitoring team performance may assume greater importance because of the increased risk of virtual team members becoming disconnected from the team.

Drawing on the functional approach, researchers have developed models of leadership functions that are particularly germane to addressing the challenges encountered in global virtual teams (Bell & Kozlwoski, 2002; Carter et al., 2015; Malhotra, Majchrzak, & Rosen, 2007). For example, based on observations of thirty global virtual student teams working on a complex innovation task, Carter et al. (2015) linked the taxonomy of leadership functions proposed by Morgeson et al. (2010) to a global virtual team context by describing how these functions specifically apply to collaboration in global virtual teams. For example, in their framework, Carter et al. propose that leadership functions related to setting goals and expectations should include specific norms related to collaborating across different time zones and cultures. Further extending the functional leadership approach into the realm of virtual teams, researchers have also proposed new leadership functions that specifically support virtual teamwork, for example, functions related to managing the team's technology and technology support, ensuring that dispersed team members have sufficient information about other team members and their expertise, as well as reconciling differences in work approaches and processes resulting from different work locations and organizational membership (Bell & Kozlowski, 2002; Corderoy & Soo, 2008; Malhotra et al., 2007). However, despite these conceptual developments, empirical virtual team leadership research based on the functional perspective remains sparse.

15.4.4 Empowering Leadership

Virtual team researchers have argued that the challenges of dispersed collaboration over time and space using technology-mediated communication increases demands on team leadership, which makes it difficult for a single hierarchical team leader to effectively lead the team (Bell & Kozlowski, 2002; Hill, 2005; Lipnack & Stamps, 2000). As a result, they have examined forms of leadership where the hierarchical leader shares leadership responsibility with team members (Bell & Kozlowski, 2002; Dulebohn & Hoch, 2017). For example, Bell and Kozlowski (2002) proposed that in more highly virtual teams, the role of the formal team leader is to create an environment in which team members can regulate their own performance. This requires that they share leadership responsibility for functions related to developing and shaping team processes as well as monitoring and managing team performance. Dulebohn and Hoch (2017) also proposed a model of virtual team effectiveness that emphasized formal team leaders sharing leadership responsibility with team members. They argued that this helps to compensate for the potential attenuation of leader influence in virtual teams.

One form of leadership that fits this distributed leadership approach is empowering leadership. Empowering leaders share power with team members while at the same time raising their level of intrinsic motivation and providing support for team members to effectively use the power that has been delegated to them (Arnold et al., 2000). Although limited, empirical research that has examined empowering leadership in conjunction with virtuality in teams suggests that this form of leadership is more important when teams are more highly virtual (Hill & Bartol, 2016; Kirkman et al., 2004). Hill and Bartol (2016) found that the impact of the formal team leader's empowering leadership behaviors on the effectiveness of their team's virtual collaboration, and ultimately on team performance, was stronger for teams that were more geographically dispersed. In addition, although they did not measure leadership directly, Kirkman et al. (2004) found that team empowerment was more positively related to team effectiveness in teams that met less frequently face-to-face.

15.4.5 Shared and Emergent Leadership

Shared leadership, conceptualized at the team level, refers to team members sharing responsibility for leadership as part of a lateral influence process (Pearce & Conger, 2003; Pearce & Sims, 2002). Emergent leadership, an individual-level construct, refers to an individual team member who takes on the informal role of team leader even though that member has no formal assignment to that position (Schneider & Goktepe, 1983). As a natural extension of the distributed leadership approaches discussed above, researchers have theorized that informal leadership by team members in the form of shared and emergent leadership will positively impact virtual team functioning and performance (Hill, 2005; Hoch & Dulebohn, 2017). Further, researchers propose such leadership will play a stronger role when teams are more virtual, because greater involvement from team members is needed when the formal team leader has more limited ability to interact with and monitor the team (Bell & Kozlowski, 2002; Hill, 2005; Hoch & Dulebohn, 2013).

Empirical research examining emergent and shared leadership in virtual teams generally shows that these forms of informal leadership benefit team performance in teams with a high level of technology dependence and/or geographic dispersion (Carte, Chidambaram, & Becker, 2006; Cogliser et al., 2012; Hoch & Kozlowski, 2014; Muethel, Gehrlein, & Hoegel, 2012; Ocker et al., 2011; Pearce, Yoo, Alavi, 2004; Tyran, Tyran, & Shepherd, 2003). In one of the rare empirical investigations of leadership specific to geographic subgroups in teams, Ocker et al. (2011) also found that the geographic configuration of the team (e.g., degree of distance, relative subgroup size) and the pattern of leader emergence in the team (e.g., relative size of subgroup where emergent leader is located) impacted leadership dynamics in partially distributed teams. In their study, teams benefited from decentralized leadership with emergent leaders in each subgroup.

Although several studies have examined informal leadership in virtual teams, they differ in the types of leadership behaviors that are the focus of the study. For example, Carte et al. (2006) found that geographically dispersed student teams had higher levels of performance when team members shared responsibility for monitoring the timeliness and quality of their team's task, and when these behaviors were exhibited early in the team's life. Hoch and Kozlowski (2014) found that shared leadership behaviors focused on facilitating important cognitive, affective, and behavioral processes were positively related to team performance in geographically dispersed research and development teams. Finally, Cogliser et al. (2012) found that task-oriented emergent leadership in the aggregate predicted team performance in student teams communicating using an electronic communication tool.

Although there is general agreement that hierarchical and shared/emergent leadership can exist simultaneously in teams (Bell & Kozlowski, 2002; Hill, 2005; Hoch & Kozlowski, 2014; Morgeson et al., 2010), as noted earlier, some researchers have proposed that shared leadership might be more important than formal hierarchical leadership in virtual teams (Hill, 2005). Empirical research comparing the effects of formal and informal leadership sources provides some support for this view. For example, Ocker et al.'s (2011) study of leadership effects in partially distributed student teams showed that emergent and shared leadership had stronger effects on team performance than the assigned team leader. In addition, Pearce et al. (2004) found that shared leadership explained more unique variance than did vertical leadership in teams of geographically dispersed social workers participating in an action-learning project as part of an educational program. However, evidence that shared leadership is more strongly related to team performance in more highly virtual teams is still lacking. Hoch and Kozlowski (2014) examined the interactive effects of shared leadership and virtuality measured as a composite that included geographic dispersion and degree of electronic communication in teams on team performance, but the interaction was not significant.

15.4.6 Contingency Leadership Approaches

The research discussed thus far paints a picture of virtual team leadership that has had mixed empirical results in several areas. As a result, researchers have discussed the need for a contingency approach where the effectiveness of a particular type of leadership depends on various team and task characteristics. For example, Eisenberg, Gibbs, and Erhardt (2016) proposed that shared leadership has a stronger impact when task interdependence and task complexity is high, and Gibbs et al. (2017) suggested that hierarchical leadership is more effective in virtual teams composed of organizational members whereas shared leadership is more effective for student teams.

Empirical research supports a contingency perspective. Specifically, the effects of leadership behaviors on virtual team outcomes have been found to vary depending on certain contextual factors such as team member anonymity (transformational and transactional leadership: Kahai, Sosik, Avolio, 2003; Sosik, 1997) and task type (participative and directive leadership: Kahai, Sosik, & Avolio, 2004) for teams interacting electronically using a group decision support system, and leader-member communication frequency in geographically dispersed teams (leader-member exchange: Gajendran & Joshi, 2012). This contingency perspective is also relevant to research that has compared the effectiveness of different types of leadership. For example, empirical research comparing the relative importance of transformational vs. transactional leadership in student laboratory teams using different communication media have shown mixed results (Hambley et al., 2007; Hoyt & Blascovich, 2003; Kahai et al., 2003; Ruggieri, 2009; Sosik, 1997; Sosik, Avolio, Kahai, 1997). These comparative studies suggest that the type of leadership that is most effective is contingent on the task environment (e.g., team member anonymity, task type), the types of technology used, and the particular aspect of transformational or transactional leadership examined.

15.4.7 Mediating Factors

Although past research has focused primarily on the question of which types of leadership have the most positive impact on virtual team performance, researchers are increasingly seeking to understand the mediating mechanisms through which different types of leadership influence team effectiveness. As noted earlier, a dominant view is that virtuality challenges the development of team cognitive, motivational, and affective emergent states as well as the team processes that foster effective team outcomes. Therefore, the role of leadership is to help the team address these challenges. Mediators from traditional team research that have received particular attention in theoretical models of virtual team leadership are emergent states and team processes such as trust, cohesion, shared mental models, and team conflict (Carter et al., 2015; Dulebohn & Hoch, 2017; Liao, 2017). In addition, more recent theorizing has also included mediators that are specific to a virtual team environment such as virtual collaboration behaviors, which are behaviors that are particularly functional in dealing with the challenges of interacting with teammates in technology-mediated, geographically dispersed teamwork environments (Hill & Bartol, 2016).

Although limited, some empirical studies have examined the mediating role of team processes and emergent states in the relationship between leadership and virtual team effectiveness (e.g., performance, satisfaction, cohesion). These studies support the notion that the effects of leadership on team outcomes are transmitted through intervening variables commonly examined in the traditional team literature – e.g., trust in leader and team trust (Chen, Wu, Yang, & Tsou, 2008; Hoyt & Blascovich, 2003), cooperative climate (Huang et al., 2010), and feedback positivity (Kahai et al., 2012). With regard to processes specific to virtual teamwork, Hill and Bartol (2016) found that team members' aggregate virtual collaboration behaviors mediated the relationship between team-empowering leadership and team performance and that this indirect relationship was stronger for teams that were more geographically dispersed.

15.5 Future Research Directions

At the outset of this chapter we noted that advances in technology and the growing adoption of virtual work arrangements are rapidly reshaping not only how work gets done in organizations but also how leaders interface with their followers. To better understand the implications of these changes for effective leadership we have reviewed research on virtual leadership in the context of leader-follower dyads and teams. As summarized in Tables 15.1 and 15.2, this work has yielded

Table 15.1 *Summary of virtual dyadic leadership research*

Leadership Theory	Representative Studies	Key Findings
Behavioral Leadership Leader behaviors categorized as relationship-focused (e.g., transformational leadership) and task-focused (e.g., transactional leadership)	Howell & Hall-Merenda (1999) Howell, Neufeld, & Avolio (2005) Kelley & Kelloway (2012) Neufeld, Wan, & Fang (2010)	• Some empirical evidence that distance may weaken the effects of transformational leadership, although one study found no difference in the effects of transformational leadership across virtual and proximal leader-follower samples • Some empirical evidence that contingent reward leadership has more positive effects when distance is high • Some empirical evidence that both active and passive management-by-exception have more negative effects when distance is high
Leader-Member Exchange Focuses on the quality of the relationship between an employee and his or her supervisor	Gajendran & Joshi (2012) Golden & Veiga (2008) Hill, Kang, & Seo (2014) Howell & Hall-Merenda (1999) Kacmar, Witt, Zivnuska, & Gully (2003)	• Several studies have found that the positive effects of high-quality LMX relationships are strengthened in situations characterized by greater virtuality • Other studies have failed to find an effect of virtuality on LMX-outcome relationships or have found that virtuality weakens the effects of LMX
Contingency Leadership Effectiveness of team leadership depends on other factors (e.g., task characteristics, familiarity)	Bonet & Salvador (2017) Kelly & Kelloway (2012)	• Some evidence that leader-follower separation is more detrimental when workers' tasks are high in technical and coordinative complexity • Some evidence that regularly scheduled communication and an employee's familiarity with his/her manager is more important for leader effectiveness in virtual settings

Table 15.2 *Summary of virtual team leadership research*

Leadership Theory	Representative Studies	Key Findings
Behavioral Leadership Leader behaviors categorized as relationship-focused (e.g., transformational leadership) and task-focused (e.g., transactional leadership)	Hambley, O'Neill, & Kline (2007) Hoyt & Blascovich (2003) Huang, Kahai, & Jestice (2010) Joshi, Lazarova, & Liao (2009) Liao (2017) Purvanova & Bono (2009)	Mixed empirical results: • Some evidence that relationship-focused and task-focused leadership have stronger effects in teams that make more use of leaner vs. richer communication media • Other studies have found no difference in the effect of relationship-focused and task-focused leadership based on the type of communication media • Relationship-focused leadership shown to have a stronger effect in teams where members are more geographically dispersed
Functional Leadership Leadership conceptualized as the process of satisfying team needs in order to make teams more effective; describes leadership functions that contribute to team-need satisfaction	Bell & Kozlowski (2002) Carter et al. (2015) Corderoy & Soo (2008)	• Research in this area is mainly theoretical • Focused on understanding how leadership functions identified in traditional team research apply in virtual teams as well as identifying new leadership functions that are particularly germane to virtual teamwork
Empowering Leadership Leadership behaviors that involve a hierarchical leader sharing leadership responsibility with team members	Bell & Kozlowski (2002) Dulebohn & Hoch (2017) Hill & Bartol (2016) Kirkman, Rosen, Tesluk, & Gibson (2004)	• Theoretical research proposing that in more highly virtual teams, empowering leadership is more strongly related to team effectiveness • Some empirical evidence that empowering leadership has stronger effects in teams that are more highly dispersed or meet less frequently face-to-face

Table 15.2 (*cont.*)

Leadership Theory	Representative Studies	Key Findings
Emergent and Shared Leadership Informal leadership by an individual team member (emergent leadership) or shared among members of the team (shared leadership)	Carte, Chidambaram, & Becker (2006) Cogliser, Gardner, Gavin, & Broberg (2012) Hill (2005) Hoch & Kozlowski (2014) Muethel, Gehrlein, & Hoegel (2012) Ocker, Huang, Benbunan-Fich, & Hiltz (2011) Pearce, Yoo, & Alavi (2004)	• Theoretical research proposing that in more highly virtual teams, informal emergent/shared leadership is more strongly related to team effectiveness, but empirical evidence is lacking • Empirical studies generally show that informal emergent/shared leadership benefits team performance in highly virtual teams, but the focal leadership behaviors differ between studies • Some evidence that shared leadership is more strongly related to team effectiveness than formal hierarchical leadership in more highly virtual teams
Contingency Leadership Effectiveness of team leadership depends on other factors (e.g., team and task characteristics, team context)	Eisenberg, Gibbs, & Erhardt (2016) Gajendran & Joshi (2012) Hambley, O'Neill, & Kline (2007) Hoyt & Blascovich (2003) Kahai, Sosik, & Avolio (2003) Ruggieri (2009) Sosik, Avolio, & Kahai (1997)	• Contingency effects have been examined in relation to different types of leadership, including formal vs. informal leadership, transformational vs. transactional leadership, participative vs. directive leadership, leader-member exchange • The leadership contingencies examined include team characteristics (e.g., student vs. organizational team), task characteristics (e.g., task interdependence, task type), and team contextual factors (e.g., team member anonymity, leader-member communication frequency)

a number of valuable insights. At the same time, it is clear that research in this area is still relatively nascent and there remains much to learn about virtual leadership. Given the rapid adoption of virtual work within organizations and the recognized importance of leadership in virtual environments, we are surprised by the limited number of empirical studies that have been done in this area. Although others have expressed a similar sentiment (e.g., Kahai, 2013; Kirkman et al., 2012), it is critical that we take immediate action or risk falling farther behind ongoing developments in technology and work (Avolio et al., 2014). In this final section we highlight several new and necessary areas to be pursued by future research.

15.5.1 Considering the Advantages

Research on virtual leadership has generally assumed that physical dispersion and technology dependence represent obstacles to be overcome. Even research that has adopted more of a contingency-based approach has often sought to understand the circumstances under which virtual leadership is more or less problematic (e.g., Bonet & Salvador, 2017). Researchers have suggested, however, that virtuality may confer a number of advantages to both leaders and followers. Shamir (2013), for example, shares how distance can allow leaders to hide their errors and vulnerabilities as well as provide greater opportunity for them to reflect and recharge. He also notes that distance from the leader may provide followers with greater autonomy and empowerment. These potential advantages have received some attention in research on the implications of psychological/social distance for leadership (e.g., Antonakis & Jacquart, 2013; Cole, Bruch, & Shamir, 2009; Katz & Kahn, 1978; Shamir, 1995), but have been essentially ignored in research on physical distance.

There is some evidence, however, that it may be worthwhile to focus greater attention on the bright side of virtuality for leaders and their followers. Bonet and Salvador (2017), for example, found that when workers were collocated with most of their team members, having the manager situated at a different location not only did not harm the workers' performance, it actually improved it. They suggest that coworker collocation can serve as a substitute for leadership, which then makes manager collocation dysfunctional. They also found that when managers were inexperienced, separation resulted in higher levels of employee performance. Thus, distance may serve to insulate employees from managers who, due to inexperience, may interfere with their work activities. These findings, which emerged unexpectedly in their investigation, suggest that virtuality may, under certain circumstances, confer advantages that have thus far been largely over-looked. Kahai (2013) also discusses how advances in information technology are providing new opportunities for leaders to increase their effectiveness. For instance, by deploying social media, leaders may be able to develop a more accurate view of their network and the communication activities of others.

15.5.2 Adopting a Multifaceted Approach

The majority of studies that have been conducted in the virtual leadership domain have focused on a single dimension of virtuality, such as physical distance/dispersion or technological dependence. When researchers have measured multiple dimensions of virtuality, most often they have combined them into a single composite measure (e.g., Gajendran & Joshi, 2012; Hoch & Kozlowski, 2014). The result is that our understanding of how different facets of virtuality influence the leadership dynamic remains limited. There is some evidence, however, to suggest that the effects of different dimensions may not be uniform. Gibson and Gibbs (2006), for example, examined four characteristics of virtuality – geographic dispersion, electronic dependence, structural dynamism, and national diversity – and found that not only were they not highly intercorrelated but that they also had independent and differential effects on innovation in aerospace design teams. Similar research is needed to examine how different dimensions of virtuality influence the effects of leadership on leader and follower outcomes.

At the same time, future research is needed that considers how aspects of physical distance influence and interact with other dimensions of distance, such as social distance and perceived interaction frequency. Antonakis and Atwater (2002) stress that the different dimensions of distance are independent and, therefore, may emerge as various combinations that have different implications for leadership. For instance, the implications of a leader being physically distant but socially close to followers, may be quite different than if distance on both dimensions is high. Research to date has not focused attention on the interactive effects of different types of distance. As Avolio et al. (2014, p. 126) state, "We know of no research that has actually examined both social and physical distance together to determine how it effects the appropriation of AIT [advanced information technology] and in turn the impact it has on the appropriation of virtual leadership tools and processes."

15.5.3 Defining Virtual Leadership Functions

As noted earlier, the functional perspective has received considerable attention in both the broader team leadership literature (Morgeson et al., 2010) and theorizing about virtual team leadership (Bell & Kozlowski, 2002). However, empirical virtual team leadership research based on the functional perspective remains limited. The functional perspective holds considerable potential for understanding how leaders contribute to virtual team effectiveness and for uncovering the unique functions that team leaders need to perform in the virtual environment. For example, recent research provides evidence that effective virtual team leaders actively manage team adaptation of communication and collaboration technologies to improve interactions and team productivity (Thomas & Bostrom, 2010a), highlighting a potential important extension of functional leadership theory to the virtual team context. In addition, clearly defining virtual leadership functions will enable researchers to conceptualize and test relevant mechanisms that mediate the effects of leadership on team effectiveness. To date, virtual team leadership research that has explored mediating factors has focused primarily on variables commonly examined in the traditional team literature. Greater attention to the functions virtual team leaders need to perform may help to uncover processes specific to virtual teamwork. The study by Hill and Bartol (2016) reviewed earlier is a first step in this direction, but more work is needed. As Kirkman et al. (2012, p. 808) state, "The radically different environment in which virtual team leaders lead will likely call for novel leadership theories and models that may be specific to virtual teams."

15.5.4 Setting Expectations and Managing Boundaries

As the introduction of new, synchronous technologies make it possible for virtual leaders and their employees to connect at any time, it is critical to understand how to strike an effective balance between fostering real-time interactions, which enable fast information sharing and immediate feedback (Daft & Lengel, 1984; Dennis, Fuller, & Valacich, 2008), and preserving time for distraction-free work. The ability to engage in "deep work," or work that is conducted during an uninterrupted period of concentration (Newport, 2016), is increasingly important as the pace of work quickens and jobs become more complex. Yet, informatics researchers have documented the startling frequency of interruptions and multitasking, which they find negatively impact productivity and performance on complex cognitive tasks (Mark, 2015; Mark, Gonzalez, & Harris, 2005; Mark, Gudith, & Klocke, 2008; Mark, Iqbal, Czerwinski, & Johns, 2015). Although these dynamics are relevant for all virtual work arrangements, they may be intensified in global virtual teams whose members may work from different time zones and have non-overlapping business hours.

   In the face of this tension, it is crucial for future research to identify ways that leaders can actively establish and manage communication and work-time norms with their employees. Future studies could examine how virtual leaders can facilitate the timely coordination of work tasks while also accounting for differences in employee work/non-work boundary management preferences (Kossek & Lautsch, 2012). Furthermore, research could consider how leaders of global virtual teams can effectively establish communication norms when employees are nested within different cultural and regulatory contexts. As cultures vary in their orientation toward work time and establishing work/non-work boundaries (Allen, Cho, & Meier, 2014; Ollier-Malaterre & Foucreault, 2016), leaders must consider how the norms they establish fit with the cultural context in which employees are embedded. Moreover, the regulative institutions concerning work hours and technology vary across countries, which impact employee boundary dynamics (Piszczek & Berg, 2014) and have implications for how leaders structure communication with and among employees. A recent example of this is the French "right to disconnect" law that gives workers in companies with 50+ employees the right to negotiate over the conditions of electronic communication use (Boring, 2017).

15.5.5 Examining Virtual Leadership in Context

Observers have noted that our current understanding of virtual leadership is based largely on research that has been case-study driven or conducted in the laboratory (e.g., Kirkman et al., 2012). However, the future directions we laid out above call for more research that examines virtual leadership in organizational contexts. In addition, field settings present an opportunity to examine issues, such as time and history, which have been relatively neglected within the virtual leadership literature to date. Furst, Reeves, Rosen, and Blackburn (2004), for example, tracked six virtual project teams over an eight-month period, from inception to project delivery, and found that the teams encountered different challenges at various points in their life cycles. These findings suggest that different virtual leadership functions may be important at different phases of a team's life cycle (Bell & Kozlowski, 2002). In recent years, a number of virtual leadership studies have utilized field samples (e.g., Gajendran & Joshi, 2012; Hill & Bartol, 2016; Hill et al., 2014), suggesting the locus of research in this area may be shifting from the laboratory to real-world contexts.

15.6 Conclusion

Recent advances in technology and the growing adoption of virtual work arrangements introduce additional complexity and challenges for leaders, while also creating new opportunities for them to reach and influence others (Avolio & Kahai, 2003). Research conducted over the past two decades has made a number of important contributions to our understanding of virtual leadership in organizations, although much more work is needed to help leaders respond to the challenges and harness the opportunities that exist in virtual contexts. Our hope is that by detailing where we have been and where we need to go, the current chapter will help guide these future efforts.

References

Allen, T., Cho, E., & Meier, L. L. (2014). Work–family boundary dynamics. *Annual Review of Organizational Psychology and Organizational Behavior*, *1*(1), 99–121. https://dx.doi.org/10.1146/annurev-orgpsych-031413-091330.

Allen, T. D., Golden, T. D., & Shockley, K. M. (2015). How effective is telecommuting? Assessing the status of our scientific findings. *Psychological Science in the Public Interest*, *16*(2), 40–68. https://dx.doi.org/10.1177/1529100615593273.

Allen, T. D., Johnson, R. C., Kiburz, K. M., & Shockley, K. M. (2013). Work-family conflict and flexible work arrangements: Deconstructing flexibility. *Personnel Psychology*, *66*(2), 345–376. doi:10.1111/peps.12012.

Antonakis, J. & Atwater, L. (2002). Leader distance: A review and a proposed theory. *The Leadership Quarterly*, *13*, 673–704.

Antonakis, J. & Jacquart, P. (2013). The far side of leadership: Rather difficult to face. In M. C. Bligh & R. E. Riggio (Eds.), *Exploring* distance *in* leader-follower relationships (pp. 155–187). New York, NY: Routledge.

Arnold, J. A., Arad, S., Rhoades, J. A., & Drasgow, F. (2000). The empowering leadership questionnaire: The construction and validation of a new scale for measuring leader behaviors. *Journal of Organizational Behavior, 21*(3), 249–269.

Avolio, B. J., Kahai, S., & Dodge, G. E. (2001). E-leadership: Implications for theory, research, and practice. *The Leadership Quarterly, 11*(4), 615–668.

Avolio, B. J. & Kahai, S. S. (2003). Adding the "E" to E-leadership: How it may impact your leadership. *Organizational Dynamics, 31*(4), 325–338.

Avolio, B. J., Sosik, J. J., Kahai, S. S., & Baker, B. (2014). E-leadership: Re-examining transformations in leadership source and transmission. *The Leadership Quarterly, 25*, 105–131.

Bal, P. M., De Jong, S. B., Jansen, P. G. W., & Bakker, A. (2012). Motivating employees to work beyond retirement: A multi-level study of the role of i-deals and unit climate. *Journal of Management Studies, 49*(2), 306–331. https://dx.doi.org/10.1111/j.1467–6486.2011.01026.x.

Bass, B. M. (1985). *Leadership and performance beyond expectations*. New York, NY: Free Press.

Beehr, T. A. & Bennett, M. M. (2014). Working after retirement: Features of bridge employment and research directions. *Work, Aging, and Retirement*, 112–128. https://dx.doi.org/10.1093/workar/wau007.

Bell, B. S. & Kozlowski, S. J. (2002). A typology of virtual teams: Implications for effective leadership. *Group & Organization Management, 27*, 14–49.

Blackburn, R., Furst, S., & Rosen, B. (2003). Building a winning virtual team: KSAs, training, and evaluation. In C. B. Gibson & S. G. Cohen (Eds.), *Virtual* teams that work (pp. 95–120). San Fransisco, CA: Jossey-Bass.

Bligh, M. C. & Riggio, R. E. (2013). Introduction: When near is far and far is near. In M. C. Bligh & R. E. Riggio (Eds.), *Exploring* distance *in* leader-follower relationships (pp. 1–9). New York, NY: Routledge.

Bonet, R. & Salvador, F. (2017). When the boss is away: Manager-worker separation and worker performance in a multisite software maintenance organization. *Organization Science, 28*(2), 244–261.

Bogardus, E. S. (1927). Leadership and social distance. *Sociology and Social Research, 12*, 173–178.

Boring, N. (2017). France: Right to disconnect takes effect. United States Library of Congress: Global Legal Monitor. Retrieved from www.loc.gov/law/foreign-news/article/france-right-to-disconnect-takes-effect/.

Burke, C. S., Stagl, K.C., Klein, C., Goodwin, G.F., Salas, E., & Halpin, S.M. (2006). What type of leadership behaviors are functional in teams? A meta-analysis. *The Leadership Quarterly, 17*, 288–307.

Burns, J. M. (1978). *Leadership*. New York, NY: Free Press.

Bureau of Labor Statistics. (2017). Labor force statistics from the Current Population Survey. Retrieved from www.bls.gov/cps/demographics.htm.

Butts, M., Becker, W., & Boswell, W. (2015). Hot buttons and time sinks : The effects of electronic communication during nonwork time on emotions and work–nonwork conflict. *Academy of Management Journal, 56*(3), 763–788. https://dx.doi.org/10.5465/amj.2014.0170.

Carte, T. A., Chidambaram, L., & Becker, A. (2006). Emergent leadership in self-managed virtual teams: A longitudinal study of concentrated and shared leadership behaviors. *Group Decision and Negotiation, 15*, 323–343.

Carter, D. R., Seely, P. W., Dagosta, J., DeChurch, L. A., & Zaccaro, S. J. (2015). Leadership for global virtual teams: Facilitating teamwork processes. In J. L. Wildman, R. L. Griffith (Eds.), *Leading global teams: Translating multidisciplinary science to practice* (pp. 225–252). New York, NY: Springer.

Cascio, W. F. & Montealegre, R. (2016). How technology is changing work and organizations. *Annual Review of Organizational Psychology and Organizational Behavior, 3*(1), 349–375. https://doi.org/10.1146/annurev-orgpsych-041015–062352.

Center for Creative Leadership. (2007). What's next? The 2007 changing nature of leadership survey. Retrieved from www.ccl.org/wp-content/uploads/2015/04/WhatsNext.pdf.

Chen, C. C., Wu, J., Yang, S. C., & Tsou, H. Y. (2008). Importance of diversified leadership roles in improving team effectiveness in a virtual collaboration learning environment. *Educational Technology & Society, 11*(1), 304–321.

Cogliser, C. C., Gardner, W. L., Gavin, M. B., & Broberg, J. C. (2012). Big five personality factors and leader emergence in virtual teams relationships with team trustworthiness, member performance contributions, and team performance. *Group & Organization Management, 37*, 752–784.

Cole, M. S., Bruch, H., & Shamir, B. (2009). Social distance as a moderator of transformational leadership effects: Both a neutralizer and an enhancer. *Human Relations, 62*, 1697–1733.

Colquitt, J. A., Hollenbeck, J. R., Ilgen, D. R., LePine, J. A., & Sheppard, L. (2002). Computer-assisted communication and team decision-making performance: The moderating effect of openness to experience. *Journal of Applied Psychology, 87*(2), 402–410.

Cordery, J. L. & Soo, C. (2008). Overcoming impediments to virtual team effectiveness. *Human Factors and Ergonomics in Manufacturing, 18*(5), 487–500.

Daft, R. L. & Lengel, R. H. (1984). *Information richness: A new approach to managerial behavior and organization design*. In L. L. Cummings & B. M. Staw (Eds.), *Research in organizational behavior* (vol. 6, pp. 191–233). Homewood, IL: JAI Press.

Day, D. (2012). Leadership. In S. W. J. Kozlowski (Ed.), *The Oxford handbook of organizational psychology* (pp. 696–729). New York, NY: Oxford University Press.

Deahl, D. (2017). Todoist's Slack competitor is for people who hate constant notifications. Retrieved from www.theverge.com/2017/6/21/15848640/twist-communications-app-doist-slack-competitor

Dennis, A. R., Fuller, R. M., & Valacich, J. S. (2008). Media, tasks, and communication processes: A theory of media synchronicity. *MIS Quarterly, 32*(3), 575–600.

Dienesch, R. M. & Liden, R. C. (1986). Leader-member exchange model of leadership: A critique and further development. *Academy of Management Review, 11*, 618–634.

Dulebohn, J. H., Bommer, W. H., Liden, R. C., Brouer, R. L., & Ferris, G. R. (2012). A meta-analysis of antecedents and consequences of leader-member exchange: Integrating the past with an eye toward the future. *Journal of Management, 38*(6), 1715–1759.

Dulebohn, J. H. & Hoch, J. E. (2017). Virtual teams in organizations. *Human Resource Management Review, 27*(4), 678–693. doi:10.1016/j.hrmr.2016.12.004.

Eisenberg, J., Gibbs, J., & Erhardt, N. (2016). The role of vertical and shared leadership in virtual team collaboration. In C. Graham (Ed.), *Strategic* management *and* leadership *for* systems development *in* virtual spaces (pp. 22–42). Hershey, PA: IGI Global.

Equal Employment Opportunity Commission. (2005). Work at home/telework as a reasonable accommodation. Retrieved from www.eeoc.gov/facts/telework.html.

Fleishman, E. A., Mumford, M. D., Zaccaro, S. J., Levin, K. Y., Korotkin, A. L., & Hein, M. B. (1991). Taxonomic efforts in the description of leader behavior: A synthesis and functional interpretation. *The Leadership Quarterly, 2*, 245–287.

Furst, S. A., Reeves, M., Rosen, B., & Blackburn, R. S. (2004). Managing the life cycle of virtual teams. *Academy of Management Executive, 18*(2), 6–20.

Gajendran, R. S. & Harrison, D. A. (2007). The good, the bad, and the unknown about telecommuting: Meta-analysis of psychological mediators and individual consequences. *Journal of Applied Psychology, 92*(6), 1524–1541. https://dx.doi.org/10.1037/0021–9010.92.6.1524.

Gajendran, R. S. & Joshi, A. (2012). Innovation in globally distributed teams: The role of LMX, communication frequency, and member influence on team decisions. *Journal of Applied Psychology, 97*(6), 1252.

Gibbs, J. L., Sivunen, A., & Boyraz, M. (2017). Investigating the impacts of team type and design on virtual team processes. *Human Resource Management Review, 27*(4), 590–603. https://doi.org/10.1016/j.hrmr.2016.12.006.

Gibson, C. B. & Gibbs, J. L. (2006). Unpacking the concept of virtuality: The effects of geographic dispersion, electronic dependence, dynamic structure, and national diversity on team innovation. *Administrative Science Quarterly, 51*, 451–495.

Gibson, C. B., Huang, L., Kirkman, B. L., & Shapiro, D. L. (2014). Where global and virtual meet: The value of examining the intersection of these elements in twenty-first-century teams. *Annual Review of Organizational Psychology and Organizational Behavior, 1*(1), 217–244. https://dx.doi.org/10.1146/annurev-orgpsych-031413–091240.

Gilson, L. L., Maynard, M. T., Young, N. C. J., Vartiainen, M., & Hakonen, M. (2015). Virtual teams research: 10 years, 10 themes, and 10 opportunities. *Journal of Management, 41*(5), 1313.

Golden, T. D. (2006). The role of relationships in understanding telecommuter satisfaction. *Journal of Organizational Behavior, 27*, 319–340.

Golden, T. D. & Veiga, J. F. (2008). The impact of superior-subordinate relationships on the commitment, job satisfaction, and performance of virtual workers. *The Leadership Quarterly, 19*, 77–88.

Graen, G. B. & Uhl-Bien, M. (1995). Relationship-based approach to leadership: Development of leader-member exchange (LMX) theory of leadership over 25 years: Apply a multi-level multi-domain perspective. *The Leadership Quarterly, 6*, 219–247.

Hambley, L. A., O'Neill, T. A., & Kline, T. J. B. (2007). Virtual team leadership: The effects of leadership style and communication medium on team interaction styles and outcomes. *Organizational Behavior and Human Decision Processes, 103*, 1–20.

Hardin, A. M., Fuller, M. A., & Davison, R. M. (2007). I know I can, but can we? Culture and efficacy beliefs in global virtual teams. Small Group Research, *38*(1), 130–155. https://doi.org/10.1177/1046496406297041.

Hesseldahl, A. (2016). Three million people now use Slack every day. Retrieved from www .recode.net/2016/5/25/11772938/slack-usage-numbers-scale.

Hill, N. S. (2005). Leading together, working together: The role of team shared leadership in building collaborative capital in virtual teams. In M. Beyerlein, S. Beyerlein, & F. Kennedy (Eds.), *Collaborative capital: Advances in interdisciplinary studies of work teams* (vol. 11, pp. 183–209). New York, NY: Elsevier JAI.

Hill, N. S. & Bartol, K. M. (2016). Empowering leadership and effective collaboration in geographically dispersed teams. *Personnel Psychology, 69*(1), 159–198.

Hill, N. S., Kang, J. H., & Seo, M-G. (2014). The interactive effect of leader-member exchange and electronic communication on employee psychological empowerment and work outcomes. *The Leadership Quarterly, 25*, 772–783.

Hoch, J. E. & Dulebohn, J. H. (2013). Shared leadership in enterprise resource planning and human resource management system implementation. *Human Resource Management Review, 23*(1), 114–125.

Hoch, J. E. & Dulebohn, J. H. (2017). Team personality composition, emergent leadership and shared leadership in virtual teams: A theoretical framework. *Human Resource Management Review, 27*, 678–693.

Hoch, J. E. & Kozlowski, S. W. J. (2014). Leading virtual teams: Hierarchical leadership, structural supports, and shared team leadership. *Journal of Applied Psychology, 99*, 390–403.

Howell, J. M. & Hall-Merenda, K. E. (1999). The ties that bind: The impact of leader-member exchange, transformational and transactional leadership, and distance on predicting follower performance. *Journal of Applied Psychology, 84*(5), 680–694.

Howell, J. M., Neufeld, D. J., & Avolio, B. J. (2005). Examining the relationship of leadership and physical distance with business unit performance. *The Leadership Quarterly, 16*, 273–285.

Hoyt, C. L. & Blascovich, J. (2003). Transformational and transactional leadership in virtual and physical environments. *Small Group Research, 34*, 678–715.

Huang, R., Kahai, S., & Jestice, R. (2010). The contingent effects of leadership on team collaboration in virtual teams. *Computers in Human Behavior, 26*, 1098–1110.

Joshi, A., Lazarova, M. B., & Liao, H. (2009). Getting everyone on board: The role of inspirational leadership in geographically dispersed teams. *Organization Science, 20*, 240–252.

Judge, T. A. & Piccolo, R. F. (2004). Transformational and transactional leadership: A meta-analytic test of their relative validity. *Journal of Applied Psychology, 89*(5), 755–768.

Kacmar, K. M., Witt, L. A., Zivnuska, S., & Gully, S. M. (2003). The interactive effect of leader-member exchange and communication frequency on performance ratings. *Journal of Applied Psychology, 88*(4), 764–772.

Kahai, S. S. (2013). Leading in a digital age: What's different, issues raised, and what we know. In M. C. Bligh & R. E. Riggio (Eds.), *Exploring* distance *in* leader-follower relationships (pp. 63–108). New York, NY: Routledge.

Kahai, S. S., Huang, R., & Jestice, R. J. (2012). Interaction effect of leadership and communication media on feedback positivity in virtual teams. *Group & Organization Management, 37*, 716–751.

Kahai, S. S., Sosik, J. J., & Avolio, B. J. (2003). Effects of leadership style, anonymity, and rewards on creativity-relevant processes and outcomes in an electronic meeting system context. *The Leadership Quarterly, 14*(4–5), 499–524.

Kahai, S. S., Sosik, J. J., & Avolio, B. J. (2004). Effects of participative and directive leadership in electronic groups. *Group & Organization Management, 29,* 67–105.

Katz, D. & Kahn, R. L. (1978). *The social psychology of organizations.* New York, NY: Wiley.

Kelley, E. & Kelloway, E. K. (2012). Context matters: Testing a model of remote leadership. *Journal of Leadership & Organizational Studies, 19(4),* 437–449.

Kiesler, S. & Cummings, J. N. (2002). What do we know about proximity and distance in work groups? A legacy of research. In P. J. Hinds & S. Kiesler (Eds.), *Distributed work* (pp. 57–80). Cambridge, MA: The MIT Press.

Kerr, S. & Jermier, J. M. (1978). Substitutes for leadership: Their meaning and measurement. *Organizational Behavior and Human Performance, 22,* 375–403.

Kirkman, B. L., Gibson, C. B., & Kim, K. (2012). Across borders and technologies: Advancements in virtual team research. In S. W. J. Kozlowski (Ed.), *The Oxford handbook of organizational psychology* (pp. 789–859). New York, NY: Oxford University Press.

Kirkman, B. L. & Mathieu, J. E. (2005). The dimensions and antecedents of team virtuality. *Journal of Management, 31*(5), 700–718.

Kirkman, B. L., Rosen, B., Tesluk, P. E., & Gibson, C. B. (2004). The impact of team empowerment on virtual team performance: The moderating role of face-to-face interaction. *Academy of Management Journal, 47*(2), 175–192.

Kossek, E. & Lautsch, B. A. (2012). Work-family boundary management styles in organizations: A cross-level model. *Organizational Psychology Review, 2*(2), 152–171. https://dx.doi.org/10.1177/2041386611436264.

Kossek, E. E. & Michel, J. S. (2011). Flexible work schedules. In S. Zedeck (Ed.), *APA handbook of industrial and organizational psychology* (vol. 1, pp. 535–572). Washington, DC: American Psychological Association.

Kozlowski, S. W. J. & Bell, B. (2013). Work groups and teams in organizations. In D. N. Schmitt & S. Highhouse (Eds.), *Handbook of psychology: Industrial and organizational psychology* (vol. 2, pp. 412–469). Hoboken, NJ: Wiley.

Lewandowski, J. & Lisk, T. C. (2013). Foundations of distance. In M. C. Bligh & R. E. Riggio (Eds.), *Exploring* distance *in Leader-follower relationships* (pp. 13–38). New York, NY: Routledge.

Liao, C. (2017). Leadership in virtual teams: A multilevel perspective. *Human Resource Management Review, 27*(4), 648–659. https://doi.org/10.1016/j.hrmr.2016.12.010.

Lipnack, J. & Stamps, J. (2000). *Virtual teams: People working across boundaries with technology* (2nd edn.). New York, NY: Wiley.

Lord, R. G. (1977). Functional leadership behavior: Measurement and relation to social power and leadership perceptions. *Administrative Science Quarterly, 22,* 114–133.

Makarius, E. E. & Larson, B. Z. (2017). Changing the perspective of virtual work: Building virtual intelligence at the individual level. *Academy of Management Perspectives, 31*(2), 159–178. https://doi.org/10.5465/amp.2014.0120.

Malhotra, A., Majchrzak, A., & Rosen, B. (2007). Leading virtual teams. *Academy of Management Perspectives, 21*(1), 60–70.

Mark, G. (2015). Multitasking in the digital age. *Synthesis Lectures On Human-Centered Informatics, 8*(3), 1–113.

Mark, G., Gonzalez, V. M., & Harris, J. (2005). No task left behind? Examining the nature of fragmented work. In CHI 2005: Proceedings of the SIGCHI Conference on Human Factors in Computing Systems. https://dx.doi.org/10.1145/1054972.1055017.

Mark, G., Gudith, D., & Klocke, U. (2008). The cost of interrupted work: More speed and stress. In CHI 2008: Proceedings of the SIGCHI Conference on Human Factors in Computing Systems. https://dx.doi.org/10.1145/1357054.1357072.

Mark, G., Iqbal, S., Czerwinski, M., & Johns, P. (2015). Focused, aroused, but so distractible: A temporal perspective on multitasking and communications. In CSCW 2015: Proceedings of the 18th ACM Conference on Computer Supported Cooperative Work & Social Computing. https://dx.doi.org/10.1145/2675133.2675221.

Martins, L. L., Gilson, L. L., & Maynard, M. T. (2004). Virtual teams: What do we know and where do we go from here? *Journal of Management, 30*(6), 805–835.

McGrath, J. E. (1962). *Leadership behavior: Some requirements for leadership training.* [Mimeographed]. Washington, DC: U.S. Civil Service Commission.

Merriman, K. K., Schmidt, S. M., & Dunlap-Hinkler, D. (2007). Profiling virtual employees: The impact of managing virtually. *Journal of Leadership & Organizational Studies, 14*(1), 6–15.

Morgeson, F. P., DeRue, D. S., & Karam, E. P. (2010). Leadership in teams: A functional approach to understanding leadership structures and processes. *Journal of Management, 36*(1), 5–39.

Muethel, M., Gehrlein, S., & Hoegl, M. (2012). Socio-demographic factors and shared leadership behaviors in dispersed team: Implications for human resource management. *Human Resource Management, 51*, 525–548.

Napier, B. J. & Ferris, G. R. (1993). Distance in organizations. *Human Resource Management Review, 3(4)*, 321–357.

Neufeld, D. J., Wan, Z., & Fang, Y. (2010). Remote leadership, communication effectiveness, and leader performance. *Group Decision and Negotiation, 19*, 227–246.

Newport, C. (2016). *Deep work: Rules for focused success in a distracted world.* New York, NY: Grand Central.

Ocker, R. J., Huang, H., Benbunan-Fich, R., & Hiltz, S. R. (2011). Leadership dynamics in partially distributed teams: An exploratory study of the effects of configuration and distance. *Group Decision Negotiation, 20*, 273–292.

O'Leary, M. B. & Cummings, J. N. (2007). The spatial, temporal, and configurational characteristics of geographic dispersion in teams. *MIS Quarterly, 31*(3), 433–452.

O'Leary, M. B. & Mortensen, M. (2010). Go (con)figure: Subgroups, imbalance, and isolates in geographically dispersed teams. *Organization Science, 21*(1), 115–131.

O'Leary, M. B., Woolley, A. W., & Mortenson, M. (2012). Multiteam membership in relation to multiteam systems. In S. J. Zaccaro, M. A. Marks, & L. DeChurch (Eds.), *Multiteam systems: An organization form for dynamic and complex environments* (pp. 141–172). New York, NY: Routledge. https://doi.org/10.4324/9780203814772.

O'Neill, T. A., Hambley, L. A., & Chatellier, G. S. (2014). Cyberslacking, engagement, and personality in distributed work environments. *Computers in Human Behavior, 40*, 152–160.

Ollier-Malaterre, A. & Foucreault, A. (2016). Cross-national work-life research: Cultural and structural impacts for individuals and organizations. *Journal of Management, 20*(10), 1–26. https://dx.doi.org/10.1177/0149206316655873.

Pearce, C. L. & Conger, J. A. (2003). *Shared leadership: Reframing the hows and whys of leadership*. Thousand Oaks, CA: Sage Publications.

Pearce, C. L. & Sims, H. P., Jr. (2002). Vertical versus shared leadership as predictors of the effectiveness of change management teams: An examination of aversive, directive, transactional, transformational, and empowering leader behaviors. *Group Dynamics: Theory, Research, and Practice*, 6, 172–197.

Pearce, C. L., Yoo, Y., & Alavi, M. (2004). Leadership, social work, and virtual teams: The relative influence of vertical versus shared leadership in the nonprofit sector. In R. E. Riggio & S. S. Orr (Eds.), *Improving leadership in nonprofit organizations.* (pp. 180–203). San Francisco, CA: Jossey-Bass.

Piszczek, M. M. & Berg, P. (2014). Expanding the boundaries of boundary theory. *Human Relations*, 67(12), 1491–1512.

Podsakoff, P. M., MacKenzie, S. B., & Bommer, W. H. (1996). Meta-analysis of the relationships between Kerr and Jermier's substitutes for leadership and employee job attitudes, role perceptions, and performance. *Journal of Applied Psychology*, *81(4)*, 380–399.

Polzer, J. T., Crisp, C. B., Jarvenpaa, S. L., & Kim, J. W. (2006). Extending the faultline model to geographically dispersed teams: How colocated subgroups can impair group functioning. *Academy of Management Journal*, 49(4), 679–692. doi:10.5465/AMJ.2006.22083024.

Purvanova, R. K. & Bono, J. E. (2009). Transformational leadership in context: Face-to-face and virtual teams. *The Leadership Quarterly*, 20, 343–357.

Ruggieri, S. (2009). Leadership in virtual teams: A comparison of transformational and transactional leaders. *Social Behavior & Personality: An International Journal*, 37, 1017–1021.

Salas, E. Dickinson, T. L., Converse, S. A., & Tannenbaum, S. I. (1992). *Toward an understanding of team performance and training.* In R. W. Swezey & E. Salas (Eds.), *Teams: Their training and performance* (pp. 3–29). Norwood, NJ: Ablex.

Schneider, C. E. & Goktepe, J. R. (1983). Issues in emergent leadership: The contingency model of leadership, leader sex, leader behavior. In H. H. Blumberg, A. P. Hare, V. Kent, & M. F. Davies (Eds.), *Small groups and social interaction* (pp. 413–421). Chicester, England: John Wiley.

Schulze, J. & Krumm, S. (2017). The "virtual team player": A review and initial model of knowledge, skills, and abilities and other characteristics for virtual collaboration. *Organizational Psychology Review*, 7(1), 66–95. https://doi.org/10.1177/2041386616675522.

Shamir, B. (1995). Social distance and charisma: Theoretical notes and an exploratory study. *The Leadership Quarterly*, 6(1), 19–47.

Shamir, B. (2013). Notes on distance and leadership. In M. C. Bligh & R. E. Riggio (Eds.), *Exploring distance in Leader-follower relationships* (pp. 39–60). New York, NY: Routledge.

Society for Human Resource Management. (2012). Virtual teams. Retrieved from www .shrm.org/research/surveyfindings/ articles/pages/virtualteams.aspx.

Society for Human Resource Management. (2016a). 2016 employee benefits: Looking back at 20 years of employee benefits offerings in the U.S. Retrieved from www.shrm .org/hr-today/trends-and-forecasting/research-and-surveys/pages/2016-employee-benefits.aspx.

Society for Human Resource Management. (2016b). SHRM survey findings: 2016 strategic benefits – Flexible work arrangements. Retrieved from www.shrm.org/hr-today/trends-and-forecasting/research-and-surveys/Documents/SHRM-Survey-Findings-Strategic-Benefits-Flexible-Work-Arrangements.pdf.

Sosik, J. J. (1997). Effects of transformational leadership and anonymity on idea generation in computer-mediated groups. *Group & Organization Management*, *22*(4), 460–487.

Sosik, J. J., Avolio, B. J., & Kahai, S. S. (1997). Effects of leadership style and anonymity on group potency and effectiveness in a group decision support system environment. *Journal of Applied Psychology*, *82*(1), 89–103.

Thomas, D. M. & Bostrom, R. P. (2010a). Team leader strategies for enabling collaboration technology adaptation: Team technology knowledge to improve globally distributed systems development work. *European Journal of Information Systems*, *19*, 223–237.

Thomas, D. M. & Bostrom, R. P. (2010b). Vital signs for virtual teams: An empirically developed trigger model for technology adaptation interventions. *MIS Quarterly*, *34*(1), 115–142.

Tyran, K. L., Tyran, C. K., & Shepherd, M. (2003). Exploring leadership in virtual teams. In C. B. Gibson & S. G. Cohen (Eds.), *Virtual teams that work* (pp. 183–195). SanFrancisco, CA: Jossey-Bass.

Venolia, G., Tang, J., Cervantes, R., Bly, S., Robertson, G., Lee, B., & Inkpen, K. (2010). Embodied social proxy: Mediating interpersonal connection in hub-and-satellite teams. In CHI 2010: Proceedings of the 28th International Conference on Human factors in Computing Systems. New York: ACM Press. https://doi.org/10.1145/1753326.1753482.

WorldatWork. (2013). Survey on workplace flexibility 2013. Retrieved from www.worldatwork.org/adimLink?id=73898.

16 Managing Distributed Work

Theorizing an IPO Framework

Julia E. Hoch

Distributed work refers to employment arrangements that enable workers to access company resources they need to do their jobs outside the traditional dedicated on-site physical office space at their company. Distributed work arrangements may be grouped in terms of on-site and off-site work places (Gilleard & Rees, 1998). On-site and off-site work places may be further delineated by sites within those categories. For example, on-site work places include shared office space. Off-site work places include telecommuting, satellite offices, and home offices. To qualify as a distributed workforce, a company's workers conduct their work in different locations and the medium for their interaction with the organization and organizational resources, needed to do their jobs, is typically web-based, asynchronous electronic communication media (Roper & Ha Kim, 2007).

Thus, distributed work reaches beyond the restrictions of a traditional physical office environment. Distributed workforces may be dispersed geographically over a relatively small area (e.g., such as a metropolitan area where a company's workers telecommute) to much wider areas – domestically or internationally (i.e., where workers work at satellite offices or virtually). By installing key technologies, organizations enable remote employees to access required company resources they need to perform their work through software applications without working within the confines of a physical company-operated facility. Despite growing attention and interest in distributed work, surprisingly little is still known about successful management of a distributed workforce (e.g., Gibbs et al., 2015; Harrison, Wheeler & Whitehead, 2003; Hoch & Kozlowski, 2014).

Reasons for employing a distributed workforce are manifold and, according to recent surveys (Knoll, 2011; O'Neill & Wymer, 2010), corporations who employ a distributed workforce enjoy several substantial benefits: First, there are substantive cost savings of an average 33 percent first-year cost avoidance over conventional workspace, with consistent savings thereafter. That is, remote organizations attain greater space utilization than conventional ones. Second, they also attain higher levels of employee satisfaction in that about two-thirds of employees are satisfied with the impact of distributed work programs on their individual performance and 80 percent feel this way about their performance.

Precisely, a recent study by O'Neill and Wymer (2010) reveals two key strategic drivers for what motivates organizations to implement distributed workforce programs. First are cost savings and second are strategic benefits, such as supporting more effective collaboration, satisfaction, and retention. With regard to cost savings, the square foot space requirements for a company's workers have dropped dramatically over time (Knoll, 2011; O'Neill & Wymer, 2010). Specifically, large meeting rooms are especially underused (they only have a 44 percent utilization rate, whereas small meeting rooms have a 73 percent utilization rate, Knoll, 2011). This has important implications for the lease of a shared workspace, especially in the large, metropolitan areas where office space is often limited and costlier than in suburban or rural areas.

With regard to strategic issues, such as supporting effective work processes, collaboration, or retention, it is important to find what attracts, motivates, and retains top talent in these organizations, as well as how to best structure distributed work for optimal distributed work processes to emerge (Harrison et al., 2003). While there is increasing interest in creating and successfully leveraging a distributed workforce, especially since the 1990's, little empirical research has been devoted toward identifying the "hows" and "whys" of successfully leveraging and making efficient use of such distributed workforces (e.g., Dulebohn & Hoch, 2017; Eisenberg & Mattarelli, 2016; Hoch & Dulebohn, 2017; Hoch & Kozlowski, 2014; Valkenburg, Peter, & Walther, 2016).

Commonly, distributed work is considered to be more difficult to manage than work in non-distributed work settings (e.g., Harrison, et al., 2003). In response to these challenges, it has been argued that the management of distributed work should be augmented by structural supports (e.g., Dulebohn & Hoch, 2017; Hoch & Kozlowski, 2014), such as reward systems, resources, or communication infrastructure; the delegation of management and leadership responsibilities toward distributed employees; and the staffing of distributed work with employees whose traits make them well-suited for distributed work (e.g., Bell & Kozlowski, 2002; Dulebohn & Hoch, 2017; Eisenberg, Gibbs, & Erhardt, 2016; Hoch & Kozlowski, 2014). All of these have implications for HR activities, such as developing and reinforcing proper HR processes and strategies, developing and strengthening managerial leadership, and toward training and personnel selection.

The present review presents a framework that applied the input-process-output (IPO) model toward the management of a distributed workforce. The IPO model has originated in the systems analysis and software engineering areas to describe the structure and processes, or nature, of information processing processes (Curry, Flett, & Hollingsworth, 2006). Most introductory programming and systems analysis texts present the IPO as the most basic framework for describing a process of information management and work flow. It can also be applied to inputs such as materials, human resources, financial parameters, or information. It can also be transformed into outputs, such as consumables, services, new information, or financial incentives (Goel, 2010; Grady, 1995; Zelle, 2010). The IPO has been used to review and integrate the literature on groups and teams (e.g., Hackman, 1987; McGrath, 1991) or virtual teams (Hoch & Kozlowski, 2014). In the context of this literature review, the goal is to identify the important inputs, processes, and outcome factors that are relevant to the context of managing a distributed workforce.

A second theoretical approach that is essential with regard to managing a distributed workforce is the media richness theory (Daft & Lengel, 1984; 1986). Media richness theory holds that the electronic media used by organizations to manage face-to-face and distributed work vary in the extent of richness. That is, the media and sources differ in respect to the extent of the richness of the media used. Media and sources that are richer, typically contain content such as nonverbal gestures, such as in the case of face-to-face conversation, whereas the absence of rich media is indicated through media such as email or text-messages, that do not contain face-to-face components, or gestures. The degree of the media richness of these sources matters, as it influences the effects that the various input factors, such as structural support mechanisms, managerial leadership, or employee characteristics, have on the processes and on the outcomes of distributed work.

In Figure 16.1, I present the IPO framework. First, input factors include structural support mechanisms, such as reward systems and communication management, managerial leadership, and individual differences, such as KSAOs of the distributed employees. These input factors are antecedents of three types of processes: cognitive processes, such as knowledge of employees work task; emotional processes, such as affective preference toward working in distributed settings; and motivational processes, such as work engagement. Outputs may include job satisfaction and performance, commitment, and reduced turnover. Lastly, Figure 16.1 presents media richness as a moderating variable in the input-process-output model. I expect that media richness will strengthen the association between the antecedents and processes and between the processes and outcomes.

16.1 Theoretical Background

16.1.1 Managing a Distributed Workforce

New technologies are changing important aspects of how we live and work, and the ways we manage distance within the work environment. The management of distance requires more than just technical artifacts. In fact, techniques, social conventions and norms, and organizational structures and institutions are also required. In this section, I will take a look at the ways "distributed work" has evolved over the past several centuries, specifically covering the last fifty decades. Distributed work is different from a *virtual business*, in that a virtual business employs electronic means to transact business as opposed to a traditional brick and mortar business that relies on face-to-face transactions with physical documents and physical currency or credit. Distributed work is also different from *distributed teams*, whereupon work has to be performed in a group or team settings. In comparison to that, distributed work does not, per se, contain a work structure that is organized around teams. Instead, distributed work, per se, is a broader term and it may or may not contain a team or group work component.

In the mid 1900s, the most prominent business strategy was based on a mechanistic view of office workers as units of production to be housed in a unified and controlling space. Since then, in the 1960s, a perspective emerged in which the office was seen as a communication system, toward the human relations movement, with the floor plan opening up to facilitate the free flow of information. This office space was designed with the intention of fostering communication and coordination within the physical location. Then, in the 1980s, there was a major workplace revolution as the computer moved from the computer room to the desktop. In the 1990s, a second workplace revolution saw the introduction of "new ways of working," a response to the realization that information technology was transforming cultural, social, technological, and developmental processes.

This digital revolution has led to a convergence between communications and computing technologies, which now allow individuals and organizations to connect in ways and on scales that were previously inconceivable. Today, the new economy is characterized by an increasing virtualization of products, processes, organizations, and relationships. In the new economy, production no longer necessitates workers to occupy the same physical space in order to access the tools and resources they need to share in producing their work product. In today's work environment, distributed work provides for equally, or even more efficient, work production processes (Harrison, et al., 2003).

A review of the literature on distributed work reveals that most scholars agree that managing a distributed workforce is more difficult than managing workers at a dedicated physical workplace site (e.g., Davis & Bryant, 2003; Dulebohn & Hoch, 2017; Harrison et al., 2003; Hoch & Dulebohn, 2017; Hoch & Kozlowski, 2014; Martins et al., 2004). As a result of lower levels of co-presence, managers often have less influence and less information about their employees' work situation, and the management of their workforce is more difficult due to reduced levels of direct, face-to-face interaction. The challenges of managing a distributed workforce are manifold, ranging from developing practices to uncover and resolve conflicts, to motivating employees and monitoring their performance to managing principles of communication and information exchange (e.g., Hinds & Kiesler, 2002). While these challenges have been widely discussed, different solutions have been proposed toward the management of a distributed workforce.

One approach to managing a distributed workforce involves broadening the perspective of what is considered to be effective management of distributed work (Dulebohn & Hoch, 2017; Hoch & Kozlowski, 2014), such as positing that management functions should be augmented by structural substitutes and HR practices; delegating leadership and management tasks toward the distributed workforce; and selecting employees based on their willingness, capability, and motivation to work remotely. For example, HR practices may place added weight on reward systems and communication or information management as well as augmenting and increasing the amount of the work tasks and responsibilities delegated and distributed amongst individual employees.

16.1.2 An IPO Framework for Managing a Distributed Workforce

The following presents an integrative model of management in applying the IPO approach to enhancing distributed work processes and effectiveness. The model portrayed in Figure 16.1 proposes three different antecedents: structural support mechanisms, managerial leadership, and employee characteristics. Following an input-process-output model approach (Hackman, 1987; McGrath, 1991), three groups of inputs are structural supports, managerial leadership, and characteristics of the distributed workforce, which are considered as three groups of input-variables, which lead to development of three groups of cognitive, affective, and motivational work processes, which then predict different outcomes, such as job satisfaction, organization performance, increased organizational commitment, and reduced turnover, as core organizational outcomes.

Input factors include: structural supports, which could be performance management, reward and resources systems, or communication and information management; managerial leadership facilitating goal and process clarity; and KSAOs of the distributed workforce in terms of employee or member characteristics (Hackman, 1987; McGrath, 1991). Mediating processes explain how and why certain inputs, such as structural supports, leadership, and employee characteristics, affect the effectiveness of the distributed workforce and their work outcomes, such as job satisfaction, performance, commitment, and turnover indicators.

All of these factors are integrated in our model in Figure 16.1. Three groups of processes are conceptualized as mediating the relationship between input and output factors (Hackman, 1987): cognitive processes, motivational processes, and affective processes of the distributed workforce toward their organization. Outcomes in our model are presented last in our framework, since these represent the core result of work activity, and the reason for the organization's existence (Hackman, 1987). Among these are performance indicators, such as sales or production units, as well as job satisfaction, commitment, and retention.

Finally, drawing upon the media richness theory (Daft & Lengel, 1984; 1986), the media richness is posited to moderate the junctions between inputs, process

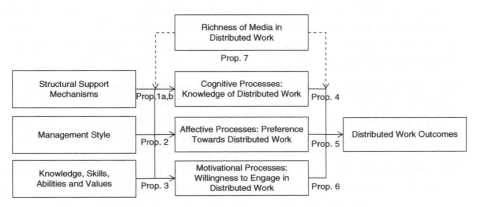

Figure 16.1 *Conceptual model: managing distributed work*

factors, and outcomes, and between process factors and outcomes. We posit these moderations, in such that structural support mechanisms, managerial leadership, and characteristics of the workforce will be more instrumental in relation to performance and other outcomes with richer information media (e.g., video conferencing) than when media are less dense (e.g., email, text). Thereby, previous research has shown that, next to density or the richness of the media being applied, the synchronicity of media can be equally important (Carlson & George, 2004; Valkenburg et al., 2016). As outlined in the paragraphs on the moderating effects, the effects will ultimately depend on the manager and employees' capability to select the "right" communication and information technology for the specific content and under specific conditions.

16.1.3 Input Factor: Structural Supports

Distributed work has been made possible by advances in information and communication technologies (Hoch & Kozlowski, 2014). With regard to structural support systems for distributed work, a significant amount of the "support infrastructure" is provided through an organization's reward systems, and by its communication and information management systems (Bell & Kozlowski, 2002; Hoch & Kozlowski, 2014). In fact, structural supports, as displayed in Figure 16.1, describe a form of indirect influence, via support mechanisms and contingencies, on employee attitudes and work-related behaviors (Hoch, 2007). The conceptualization of structural supports is based on the "leadership substitutes" theory (Howell & Dorfman, 1986; Kerr, 1977; Kerr & Jermier, 1978). The idea of reward systems and communication management, as two separate dimensions of structural support mechanisms, has been introduced by Hoch and Dulebohn (2013) and by Hoch and Kozlowski (2014).

With respect to distributed work, structural support mechanisms provide stability by compensating for challenges inherent in the lack of structure and formal elements (e.g., shared office building, physical meeting rooms). As noted by Hoch and Kozlowski (2014), an important function of structural support mechanisms is that of creating structures and routines to substitute for structure and organize the workflow. For example, when it comes to managing distributed work, the impact of reward systems becomes particularly important, since the stability emerging from rewards and resources management will mitigate the turbulences, flexibility/instability, and unpredictability, in distributed work arrangements (Dulebohn & Martocchio, 1998; Rynes, Gerhart, & Parks, 2005; Zaccaro & Bader, 2003; Zigurs, 2003).

Structural Supports of Performance and Reward Systems. The model in Figure 16.1 includes the two structural support components of performance management, reward systems and communication systems, which is based on Hoch and Dulebohn (2013; Hoch & Kozlowski, 2014). Structural supports with respect to reward and communication systems and mechanisms are more important in distributed work because, as employees meet less frequently, support mechanisms might compensate for the lack of physical structure surrounding the employees, such as shared office buildings and physical meeting rooms (Dulebohn & Hoch, 2017; Hoch & Kozlowski, 2014).

Reward systems should be fair (& Martocchio, 1998), and they also should be transparent and under the control of the affected employees (Rynes & Gerhart, 2000; Rynes et al., 2005). Fairness, in terms of both procedural and distributive fairness of reward systems (Dulebohn & Martocchio, 1998), is positively associated with higher levels of performance in conventional work settings and in role performance, innovation, commitment, work satisfaction, reducing withdrawal behavior, and others (Colquitt et al., 2011; Dulebohn & Martocchio, 1998). Similar relationships to these could also be expected as a result of compensation fairness in distributed work, and resources management (Fleishman, et al., 1991).

So far, limited research has examined the role of reward systems, or has compared the effects of reward systems in distributed work and conventional, non-distributed work. Thus, based on the central role of compensation and pay fairness to employees, and their influence on their motivation and other attitudes and work behaviors, the use of compensation as part of structural leadership in distributed work also needs to be designed in such a way that employees are rewarded for their distributed work performance. We posit:

Proposition 1a: *Structural support mechanisms of fairness of reward systems are positively related to distributed work outcomes.*

Structural Supports of Communication and Information Management.

Structural support mechanisms, as displayed in our model in Figure 16.1, also include communication and information management. Information and communication management is important in distributed work for a number of reasons (Dulebohn & Hoch, 2017). First, remote or teleworkers perform mostly "white-collar" cognitive, complex, and interdependent tasks and, therefore, the management of communication and information is necessary to deliver comparable or higher quality work relative to traditional, physically centralized work settings. Here, information has to be transparent and organized, timely and reliable, encoded and stored, transferred and managed, all of which is enabled and facilitated by communication and information management networks (e.g., Clampitt & Downs, 2004). Accordingly, empirical results show that communication processes produce greater efficiency for distributed work, when structured in a more uniform way, that is, more formalized, structured, and in a more centralized organizational setting (DeSanctis & Monge, 1998).

While researchers studied organizational information management in non-distributed, traditional, office workplace settings (Downs & Adrian, 2004; Griffith, Sawyer, & Neale, 2003; Warkentin & Beranek, 1999), less research has explored the role of these same factors in the distributed work setting. However, based on the previous results, we expect that role of the structural support mechanisms will be just as important in the distributed work setting than in the face-to-face work. Thus, we posit that structural supports of communication and information management are positively related to the core processes and outcomes in distributed work. Further, these associations will be stronger when the work is more distributed than under lower degrees of distribution. We posit:

Proposition 1b: *Structural supports in terms of information and communication management are positively related to distributed work outcomes.*

16.1.4 Input Factor: Managerial Leadership

The second predictor is the managerial leadership, as presented in Figure 16.1. Managerial leadership describes a formal, hierarchically structured form of influence, whereby an external manager exerts influence on one or more employees toward the achievement of one or more organizational goals (Yukl, 2009). It describes a direct form of influence as compared with the indirect means of influence derived from structural support mechanisms (Dulebohn & Hoch, 2017; Hoch & Dulebohn, 2013; Hoch & Kozlowksi, 2014).

Managerial leadership may include alternating and mutual-exchange processes between leaders and employees, and reciprocal and multidirectional forms of relationships, in addition to the solely top-down processes (Yukl, 2009). In this review we suggest that the leaders should implement management by objective and goal-setting procedures, with the ultimate purpose of facilitating the efficient distribution and clear assignment of responsibilities among employees in their remote workforce. As displayed in our model in Figure 16.1, managerial leadership is primarily reflected through management by objectives (MBO) that comprises systematic goal setting as well as feedback.

Management by Objectives (MBO).   As displayed in the model in Figure 16.1, the management by objectives approach (MBO), which suggests a combination of goal setting and according feedback, is proposed as a managerial leadership technique in distributed work settings. According to goal setting theory, the impact of specific, challenging goals on performance and effectiveness has shown to exert strong effects on different measures of organizational effectiveness. This is essentially what is reflected in the MBO approach.

MBO describes a more structured leadership technique because, once goals are installed, only limited further direct interaction is necessary, as structural goals are performance motivating and compensate for interaction. MBO has the potential to encourage process development by stimulating a shared vision and shared goals (Kouzes & Posner, 2009), creating goal interdependencies, increasing morale, preventing negative behaviors, and encouraging self-management skill development (Manz, 1986). Individuals generally tend to respond favorably to leaders who inspire and motivate them (Judge & Piccolo, 2004). This positive response may extend into the context of distributed work settings.

In a lab study of remote work, researchers observed that managers who adapted their leadership to changing situational contexts and conducted their role accordingly were perceived as more effective (Purvanova & Bono, 2009). Thus, despite the fact that management and leadership may be more difficult to perform in distributed work settings, leadership is not necessarily less effective in more distributed work environments (Avolio & Kahai, 2003; Avolio, Kahai & Dodge, 2000). In fact, in distributed work, managerial leadership may play a much more vital role and requires enhanced levels of creativity and interpersonal skill to effectively engage employees and deliver a positive work atmosphere that is both practical and personal. Effectiveness of managerial leadership may have an important role in reducing the challenges presented by the elements of distributed work settings.

Empirical research indicates that, while the impact of managers might be weaker in more distributed work environments when compared with traditional work settings, the impact of managerial leadership is still significant in distributed work (Howell & Hall-Merenda, 1999; Howell, Neufeld, & Avolio, 2005). Similarly, Hoch and Kozlowski (2014) found that associations between supervisor management and employee work outcomes were weaker in distributed work than in traditional work settings. Howell and Hall-Merenda (1999) examined the effects of managerial leadership on performance in varying degrees of distribution and found no differences in leadership effectiveness.

Since the MBO approach is a more structural approach that requires less personal, direct human engagement and interaction, we expect that it may be more easily applied in a virtual, distributed work environment. The MBO approach provides clarity of structure and responsibility, as well as specific feedback to successfully guide the distributed employee. This will lead distributed employees to perform more successfully. It is proposed:

Proposition 2:   *Managerial leadership with regard to management by objectives (MBO) is positively related to distributed work outcomes.*

16.1.5 Input Factor: KSAOs and Individual Differences

As displayed in the model in Figure 16.1, several characteristics of the remote employee are associated with distributed work outcomes. Specifically, several types of Knowledge, Skills, Abilities and Others, such as personality traits (KSAOs) are positively associated with the processes and outcomes in distributed work. These factors are summarized and referred to as KSAOs in the model in Figure 16.1.

Knowledge.   First, employees in distributed work need to possess superior knowledge in their fields of training and education to perform their tasks success-fully. Further, they need specific knowledge about the nature of distributed work and how the concept is effectively put into practice. Furthermore, in distributed work, knowledge about differences between the respective legal systems of various governing bodies dictating rule of law over the territory in which the distributed or remote employees physically reside, are considered highly relevant.

Generally, knowledge can be acquired through formal education and training, as well as informally, through on-the-job training and real-world experience. As with all practical implementation of classroom-based knowledge, educational back-ground does not provide all the task- and job-related knowledge conditional to effective work performance. In distributed work, both of these approaches are relevant. In total, as displayed in Figure 16.1, we posit that these and several other types of knowledge are important predictors of distributed work effectiveness.

Skill.   In general, skills that are important in distributed work include role-specific technical skills and expertise. This is the foremost integral component for distributed work effectiveness. Role-specific experience is critical to this component, as skill and proficiency reflective of one's grasp of a specific area of expertise typically grow exponentially with experience. Skills relevant with respect to working remotely are technical skills ("tech savviness") and fluency in multiple languages, English language verbal fluency and writing skills, time management skills, and self-management skills. The skills required in distributed work are not expected to remain stable and, instead, will change over time. In this regard, self-management is a core, conservative, and more persistent requirement.

Self-management represents a broad spectrum of cognitive and behavioral self-management concepts that incorporate strategies of self-regulation and self-control (Houghton & Neck, 2002). There are three strategies associated with self-leadership: behavior-focused, natural reward, and constructive thought strategies (Manz & Neck, 2004; Neck & Houghton, 2006). While employee self-leadership competencies have not been examined with respect to the impact they may have on distributed work (Neck & Houghton, 2006), it has been argued that employees who engage in positive self-management strategies are more likely to develop and engage in behaviors that are related to effectiveness in distributed work (Dulebohn & Hoch, 2017; Hoch & Kozlowski, 2014). Therefore, we expect self-leadership in distributed work will facilitate the development of more effective distributed work processes and outcomes.

Ability.   An ability refers to an individual's capacity to perform the various tasks requisite in any work assignment. Intellectual abilities are those that are required to perform activities involving analysis, cognition, comprehension, and communication. Physical abilities are required to perform activities demanding stamina, dexterity, strength, and coordination. Distributed work employee performance is enhanced when employee's personal strengths are efficiently deployed toward natural and consistent successful execution of tasks associated with a given role. In the modern economy, with its ever-increasing move toward computer automation, most human tasks require intellectual, rather than physical, ability. Intellectual abilities can be multi-faceted, comprising specific focusses such as numeric or verbal abilities, and others.

In fact, in this developing era of far flung, globally distributed work, which is in large part the product of the internet revolution, traditional measures of mental aptitude and acumen appear increasingly ill-suited to quantifying employee value. Albeit from a slightly altered perspective, physical traits may remain an important factor for consideration with respect to workforce valuation. In a global economy, the ability to rapidly adjust to travel across different time zones or to adjust a sleep schedule to allow for the conducting of business at unusual hours, may prove integral. For example, employees might need to be willing to travel across regional and national boundaries and tolerate or adjust to cultural and time zone differences.

Personality.   Finally, we expect several personality traits to be an antecedent of distributed work effectiveness. A recent review summarized the literature on the associations between the Big Five personality dimensions and core outcomes in distributed work (Hoch & Dulebohn, 2017). One such trait might be proactive personality, which refers to an individual's propensity to take actions, or pursue initiatives, to influence their environment (Bateman & Crant, 1993). Proactive personality represents a personality disposition, or relatively stable tendency, to effect change and take personal initiative in a range of situations and activities (Brown et al., 2006). Bateman and Crant (1993) described a person who is high in proactive personality as one who identifies opportunities, shows personal initiative, identifies and solves problems, and perseveres in bringing about change that positively impacts their surroundings. Individuals differ in their propensity to seek, identify, and solve problems, thereby taking it upon themselves to effect change.

Thompson (2005), in his study of proactive personality and job performance, concluded that such initiative taking appears to have a positive association with job performance. Kirkman and Rosen (1999) found proactive personality to positively relate to outcomes such as productivity and satisfaction. Because of this, we expect that high levels of proactive personality will facilitate the development and exercise of distributed work. In total, as displayed in the model in Figure 16.1, we expect that KSAOs of employees in distributed work settings positively relate to outcomes in distributed work. We posit:

Proposition 3:   *Knowledge, Skills, Ability, and Personality of distributed workforce employees are positively associated with distributed work outcomes.*

16.1.6 Mediating Processes

As displayed in the model in Figure 16.1, three types of mediating processes are presented. The first are cognitive processes, the second are affective processes, and third are motivational processes. As outlined in the following, we expect that all three groups of processes explain the associations between the three types of input factors and the distributed work outcomes.

Cognitive Processes   are "higher mental processes, such as perception, memory, language, problem solving, and abstract thinking" (Gerrig & Zimbardo, 2002). Cognitive processes refer to a composite of cognitive activities or operations that demands analysis, comprehension, and decision-making. Other cognitive processes may comprise comprehension, retention, and problem solving. Cognitive processes are necessary to acquire task related, declarative inputs and transform them into outcomes, such as job performance.

A variety of different jobs can be performed under distributed work arrangements. Different jobs will require different types of job-related knowledge and job content. Consequently, different jobs require declarative knowledge and different types of cognitive processes. However, the nature of distributed work as and of itself will pose a set of shared, additional demands toward the distributed workforce, in addition to the specific job requirements.

Cognitive processes relevant for distributed work across different types of jobs are those of information sharing, information processing, information storage, and information retrieval, among others (Faraj & Sproull, 2000). Furthermore, a set of shared task characteristics that is required across distributed work settings is that of information media usage. Employees in remote work settings need to be able to navigate the technical support system infrastructure (c.f. Faraj & Sproull, 2000).

The development of cognitive processes will benefit from employees bringing the "right" set of KSAOs to the work place. In this regard, self-management and self-leadership skills, proactivity, and error monitoring, reflect but a few of the necessary KSAOs to enhance development of the according cognitive processes. These KSAOs will enable employees to perform distributed work well. In consequence, they will lead to higher levels of distributed work outcomes. Consequently, we posit that the association between KSAOs and distributed work outcomes is indirectly explained, through cognitive processes. This is displayed in the model in Figure 16.1.

Next, we posit that the development of appropriate cognitive processes will benefit from the presence of structural support mechanisms, such as information and communication technology management systems. Managerial styles such as management by objectives, leading through goal setting and feedback-oriented adjustments, will also support the development of important cognitive processes. We posit that structural supports, managerial leadership, and employee KSAOs will benefit the development of the appropriate cognitive processes which, in turn, will explain the associations with distributed work outcomes.

Cognitive processes are defined as "the processes necessary to [facilitate] the [...] acquisition of knowledge" to successfully perform distributed work (Kozlowski & Bell, 2003, p.346). They may include activities such as learning, feedback, error monitoring, or process improvement (Edmondson, 1999), or shared memory systems (Lewis, 2003), which describe "an organized understanding of relevant knowledge" (Mohammed & Dumville, 2001, p.89).

Previous research documented that cognitive processes are related positively to organizational performance, effectiveness, satisfaction, and commitment (e.g., Kozlowski & Bell, 2003; Mohammed & Dumville, 2001). For example, feedback seeking and process improvement have been shown to be associated with enhanced performance (Edmondson, 1999, 2002; Edmondson, Bohmer, & Pisano, 2001). Numerous studies have documented positive relations between cognitive processes and performance (Austin, 2003; Ellis, 2006; Mohammed & Dumville, 2001). Consequently, we posit cognitive processes to be positively associated with distributed work outcomes. Furthermore, as displayed in the model in Figure 16.1, cognitive processes will explain the association between structural supports, managerial leadership, and employee characteristics, with the distributed work outcomes. Thus, we posit:

Proposition 4: *Structural support mechanisms, managerial leadership, and employee KSAOs are positively associated with cognitive processes, which are positively associated with distributed work outcomes.*

Affective Processes. Affect is the experience of feeling or emotion (Hogg, Abrams, & Martin, 2010). Employees in distributed work settings are likely to report lower levels of affective or emotional attachment to their work and co-workers due to the lack of physical connection. However, if employees in distributed work settings possess a preference toward working across distance or using of new, modern electronic communication media, they may benefit from this circumstance. In these instances, the affective processes, or preference toward distributed work, may compensate for the challenges of lacking face-to-face contact.

Research has documented that affective processes, which include well-being or positive affect, have been found to relate to a number of positive organizational outcomes, which has been found to result from positive relations with others, environmental mastery, social integration, and social contribution (Lyubomirsky, King, & Diener, 2005). For example, research has demonstrated that positive affect, or positive mood, leads to higher levels of performance in organizations (George, 1990). Consequently, as displayed in the model in Figure 16.1, we posit that beneficial affective processes will be positively associated with work outcomes.

Compared to traditional work settings, distributed work generally represents a more ambiguous situation in which it is more difficult to assess work accountability, such as determining the degree to which an employee contributes to the work product. When communication structures are clear and employees are rewarded appropriately and according to their work performance, distributed work might become more enjoyable for the employees. Consequently, as portrayed in Figure 16.1, we posit that structural supports are positively associated with affective processes and affective processes are expected to explain the association between structural supports and work outcomes.

The existence of managerial leadership is necessary to develop agreement on the employee's objectives and how to achieve them. Thus, when managerial leadership is lacking, remote employees will have difficulty coming to agreements and reaching their goals. Consequently, they will find their work less enjoyable and more frustrating. Thus, we expect a beneficial managerial style to positively relate to employee's preference toward distributed work, and the role of affect to mediate the association between managerial leadership and distributed work outcomes.

Individual differences with respect to KSAOs, such as values and personality, represent a third input factor that, as displayed in our model in Figure 16.1, will influence work processes and consequently, distributed work outcomes. If employees are more proactive, and bring higher levels of self-management skills to work, they will also be more successful in distributed work arrangements, and therefore be more likely to enjoy their work. Also, if employees are more tech savvy, they will likely prefer distributed work. Employees who enjoy their distributed work will more likely perform highly. Consequently, we propose that the positive affect and preference toward distributed work explains the associations between the three groups of input factors, as displayed in the model in Figure 16.1, and distributed work outcomes. We posit:

Proposition 5: *Structural support mechanisms, managerial leadership, and employee KSAOs are positively associated with affective processes, which are positively associated with distributed work outcomes.*

Motivational Processes. Motivation is defined as: "the process of starting, directing, and maintaining physical and psychological activities; it includes mechanisms involved in preferences for one activity over another and the vigor and persistence of responses" (Gerrig & Zimbardo, 2002). Motivational processes are further described as "a positive, fulfilling, work-related state of mind that is characterized by vigor, dedication, and absorption" (Schaufeli et al., 2001: p. 22). Motivational processes comprise work engagement and effort. They are important because they enable employees in remote work settings to connect with each other and their shared work.

Specifically, motivational processes are relevant because the forgone physical presence inherent in distributed work groups presents additional disadvantages and challenges to employee motivation that must be overcome. Motivational processes are important for the performance of distributed work, as scholars repeatedly stated that a challenge of distributed work settings is to overcome the motivational difficulties that result from the challenges of the distributed work settings (e.g., Avolio et al., 2000; Howell et al., 1999; Purvanova & Bono, 2009).

As displayed in the model in Figure 16.1, the development of motivational processes will benefit from the presence of structural support mechanism, managerial leadership and employee characteristics. First, structural support mechanisms, such as reward systems, are important for performing distributed work. Reward systems are an important predictor of motivational work processes in traditional work settings (e.g., Dulebohn & Martocchio, 1998; Rynes & Gerhart, 2000; Rynes et al., 2005). Employees are more likely to overcome the disadvantages inherent to distributed work groups when they are appropriately rewarded for their work. Motivation, effort, and engagement will likely help overcome the challenges of the impersonal nature of distributed work groups, and attendant feeling of anonymity and sense of isolation caused by the greater physical distances separating one another.

Second, prior research has shown that managerial leadership leads to an increase in confidence and a sense of mastery among the employees, as an important motivational process (Sivasubramaniam et al., 2002). A managerial style that provides clarity and direction will encourage employees in distributed work settings to accomplish their goals. In comparison, poor managerial leadership will lead employees to become frustrated and unmotivated. We expect that these same motivational processes that emerge during non-distributed work will manifest in distributed work in that a positive managerial style will subsequently enhance distributed work outcomes and the association with work outcomes will be explained through work engagement (Dulebohn & Hoch, 2017).

Employees in distributed work groups who bring proactivity, determination, and focused self-management skills (Hoch & Dulebohn, 2017), will be more likely to perform distributed work tasks efficiently and will experience a higher level of success in completing their tasks. This experience of success will encourage employees to stay motivated and remain successful in their distributed work.

Therefore, as portrayed in Figure 16.1, we expect that the association between KASOs and distributed work outcomes will be explained through motivational processes. In sum, as displayed in the model in Figure 16.1, we posit that all three groups of input factors will encourage motivational processes and these will explain the positive effects on the outcomes. We posit:

Proposition 6: *Structural support mechanisms, managerial leadership, and employee KSAOs are positively associated with motivational processes, which are positively associated with distributed work outcomes.*

16.1.7 Moderator: Media Richness

Media richness theory (e.g., Daft & Lengel, 1984; 1986) classifies communication media in terms of their relative information-carrying properties. A medium is rich to the extent that it provides immediate feedback, multiple cues through body language, voice modulation, and natural spoken language. In general, richer communication media are more personal as they include nonverbal and verbal cues, body language, inflection, and gestures that signal a person's reaction to a message. The richer the medium, the better it facilitates collaboration and enhances clarity and understanding among employees.

The general proposition is that the associations between the distributed work input factors with the processes and the outcomes will be stronger under higher degrees of media richness compared to when media richness is lower (Hoch & Dulebohn, 2017). In work settings with high levels of distribution, high levels of structural support mechanisms, managerial leadership, and employee characteristics will contribute enhanced processes and outcomes. The degree of media richness and increased levels of synchronicity of media use, will strengthen the association between input factors, processes, and outcomes, in such that these associations might be augmented, when more information-rich media are applied.

Recent empirical research supports this assumption. For example, a recent study that examined the role of media richness theory (Simon & Peppas, 2004) suggests that, at least under certain conditions, there are more positive attitudes and higher levels of satisfaction with regard to information-rich content than under less information-rich conditions. However, moderating factors, such as self-presentation goals, relational goals, complexity of the message itself, and others, may moderate the strength of these associations (e.g., Sheer & Chen, 2004; Valkenburg et al., 2016). For example, employees can be overwhelmed by large amounts of poorly structured information (e.g., Carlson & Zmud, 1999).

Since its inception, media richness theory has repeatedly been expanded, refined, and explicated (e.g., Dennis & Valacich 1999). For example, some state that synchronicity, rather than media richness, is more relevant to communicating core content (e.g., Dennis, Fuller, & Valacich, 2008). Indeed, there is empirical evidence to suggest that, beyond "media richness," other aspects such as synchronicity or density of the message are also important (Carlson & George, 2004). These are notable extensions and the importance of "fit" between the media in use, the participants and the information content have been highlighted when further developing the media richness theory (Carlson & George, 2004; Goodhue & Thompson, 1995). In this respect, the assumption is that distributed employees, manager, and leaders are capable of evaluating and choosing the appropriate media to convey the appropriate message. Thus, while positing media richness and synchronicity as a moderating variable, the expectation is not that more is always better. Instead, it is important to highlight that the media effects can and will go both ways. While being relevant, the appropriateness of the media usage depends on the managers' and employees' capability to select the right media for the appropriate type of communication.

Media richness theory classifies face-to-face interaction as being the highest in terms of media richness (Daft & Lengel, 1984; 1986). It is our expectation that all input and mediating factors will play a more important role in generating efficient processes and augmenting positive outcomes in distributed work when information-rich media are used than when work and media are less interdependent. A primary cause is related to the communication challenges in distributed work. Precisely, the use of more information-rich media will further augment the effects of strong input and mediating factors, whereas low media richness may further complicate matters as it may lead to misinterpretations when communicating among employees.

Based on Daft and Lengel (1984; 1986), there are several key terms associated with co-located work and distributed work. The most important concepts are common ground, coupling in work, collaboration readiness, and technology readiness. Common ground refers to the knowledge that participants have in common, when they are aware that they have this information in common. Coupling refers to the extent and kind of communication required by work wherein highly interdependent structures require more frequent, complex communication among employees. Collaboration readiness refers to a remote employee's willingness to work together and share ideas. Technology readiness is a company's or remote employee's willingness and ability to use technology.

Overall, the more common ground people can establish, the easier the communication and the greater the productivity. It has been noted that those who are remote often complain about the difficulty of establishing common ground. For example, when employees participating in distributed work are connected via audio conference call, it is difficult to tell who is speaking when employees do not know each other well. Employees who are able to connect with video can engage the subtle visual nuances that help establish local common ground, regardless of whether what was said was understood as intended or whether the conversation needs repair.

In sum, as displayed in the model in Figure 16.1, we posit that the degree of media richness and synchronicity will moderate the associations between input and outcomes, between input and processes, and between processes and outcomes, in that higher levels of structural supports, managerial leadership, and more well-suited employee characteristics will have a more positive effect under the presence of more information-rich media than when media are less rich. However, if the levels of structural supports, managerial leadership, and KSAOs of the employees are low, presence of information-rich media will unveil these weaknesses and might further complicate things. In sum, we posit:

Proposition 7: *The associations between the distributed work input factors with the processes and the outcomes will be stronger under higher degrees of media richness than when media richness is lower.*

16.2 Discussion

Distributed work represents alternative work arrangements where workers conduct their jobs outside a traditional dedicated office. The use of distributed workplaces has greatly increased due to the growth in computer technologies, company intranets and IT infrastructure, and the internet. These technologies enable workers to access resources, interact with co-workers, and complete work remotely. It makes sense that, in our knowledge economy where much work is conducted using computer technologies, the actual physical location becomes less relevant for many types of work. Although the use of distributed workforces by companies has grown exponentially in the last decade or so, there has been little systematic research and limited theoretical models to assist companies in implementing distributed work and improving the effectiveness of these work arrangements.

The primary goal of the present article was to summarize the literature on the management of distributed work and provide practical implications. In this respect, following initial assessment, the IPO model may provide guidance or direction for distributed work training, development, and other interventions. For example, examining the structural elements, such as reward systems and information systems, may reveal that certain employees lack motivation due to a failure of the organization to tie their rewards to their actual performance, or that employees are under-utilizing certain types of communication media. As noted earlier, management of distributed work is facilitated through web enabled components of the workflow management. Organizations need to make an effort to leverage these capabilities to monitor, motivate, and connect distributed employees. This could require an active approach such as using time and attendance functions, or performance and project management tools, where distributed work members record their accomplishments.

The secondary goal of the present article was to summarize the literature on the management of distributed work and derive direction for future research. Specifically, the model presents an example of a useful classification typology, with regard to management tools that can be used to encourage distributed work effectiveness. So far not all of the components of the model presented have been tested empirically. Consequently, our model might also provide direction for future research efforts on the effective management of distributed work.

In sum, our model emphasizes the importance of future research on the importance of distributed work. The IPO approach, with its emphasis on structural supports, managerial leadership and employees' characteristics, and cognitive, affective and motivational processes, might provide insight into identifying factors that can be enhanced in a particular situation. That is, by assessing distributed work using the model and evaluating factors in relation to organization effectiveness, it serves as a conceptual framework for evaluating the quality of distributed work.

References

Austin, J. R. (2003). Transactive memory in organizational groups: The effects of content, consensus, specialization, and accuracy on group performance. *Journal of Applied Psychology*, *88*, 866–878.

Avolio, B. J. & Kahai, S. S. (2003). Adding the "E" to e-leadership: How it may impact your leadership. *Organizational Dynamics*, *31*, 325–338.

Avolio, B. J., Kahai, S. S., & Dodge, G. E. (2000). E-leadership: Implications for theory, research, and practice. *The Leadership Quarterly*, *11*, 615–670.

Bateman, T. S. & Crant, J. M. (1993). The proactive component of organizational behavior: A measure and correlates. *Journal of Organizational Behavior*, *14*, 103–118.

Bell, B. S. & Kozlowski, S. W. J. (2002). A typology of virtual teams: Implications for effective leadership. *Group & Organization Management*, *27*, 14.

Brown, D. J., Cober, R. T., Kane, K., Levy, P. E., & Shalhoop, J. (2006). Proactive personality and the successful job search: A field investigation with college graduates. *Journal of Applied Psychology*, *91*, 717–726

Carlson J. R. & George, J. F. (2004). Media appropriateness in the conduct and discovery of deceptive communication: The relative influence of richness and synchronicity. *Group Decision and Negotiation*, *13*, 191–210.

Carlson, J. R. & Zmud, R. W. (1999). Channel expansion theory and the experimental nature of media richness perceptions. *Academy of Management Journal*, *42*, 153–170.

Clampitt, P. G. & Downs, C. W. (2004). Downs-Hazen communication satisfaction questionnaire. In C. W. Downs & A. D. Adrian (Eds.), *Assessing organizational communication*. New York, NY: Guilford Press.

Colquitt, J. A., Wesson, M. J., Porter, C. O. L. H., Conlon, D. E., & Ng, K. Y. (2001). Justice at the millennium: A meta-analytic review of 25 years of organizational justice research. *Journal of Applied Psychology*, *86*, 425–445.

Curry, A., Flett, P., & Hollingsworth, I. (2006). Managing information and systems: The business perspective. Routledge.

Daft, R. L. & Lengel, R. H. (1984). Information richness: A new approach to managerial behavior and organizational design. Research in Organizational Behavior. *6:*, 191–233.

Daft, R. L. & Lengel, R. H. (1986). Organizational information requirements, media richness and structural design. *Management Science*, *32*, 554–571.

Davis, D. D. & Bryant, J. L. (2003). Influence at a distance: Leadership in global virtual teams. *Advances in Global Leadership*, *3*, 303–339.

Dennis A. R. & Valacich J. S. (1999). Rethinking media richness: Towards a theory of media synchronicity. Proc. 32nd Hawaii International Conference System Science, 1–10.

Dennis, A. R., Fuller, R. M., & Valacich, J. S. (2008). Media, tasks, and communication processes: A theory of media synchronicity. *MIS Quarterly, 32*, 575–600.

DeSanctis, G., & Monge, P. R. (1998). Communication processes for virtual organizations. *Journal of Computer-Mediated Communication, 3*(4). https://academic.oup.com/jcmc/article/3/4/JCMC347/4584413.

Downs, C. W. & Adrian, A. D. (2004). *Assessing organizational communication*. New York, NY: Guilford Press.

Dulebohn, J. H. & Martocchio, J. J. (1998). Employee perceptions of the fairness of work group incentive plans. *Journal of Management, 24*, 469–488.

Dulebohn, J. H. & Hoch, J. E. (2017). Virtual teams in organizations. *Human Resource Management Review, 27*, 569–574.

Edmondson, A. (1999). Psychological safety and learning behavior in work teams. *Administrative Science Quarterly, 44*, 350–383.

Edmondson, A. (2002). The local and variegated nature of learning in organizations: A group-level perspective. *Organization Science, 13*, 128–146.

Edmondson, A., Bohmer, R. M., & Pisano, G. P. (2001). Disrupted routines: Team learning and new technology implementation in hospitals. *Administrative Science Quarterly, 46*, 685–716.

Eisenberg, J. & Mattarelli, E. (2016). Building bridges in global virtual teams: The role of multicultural brokers in overcoming the negative effects of identity threats on knowledge sharing across subgroups. *Journal of International Management Studies, 23*, 399–411.

Eisenberg, J., Gibbs, J. L., & Erhardt, N. (2016). The role of vertical and shared leadership in virtual team collaboration. In C. M. Graham (Ed.), *Strategic management and leadership for systems development in virtual spaces*. Hershey, PA: IGI Global.

Ellis, A. P. J. (2006). System breakdown: the role of mental models and transactive memory in the relationship between acute stress and team performance. *Academy of Management Journal, 49*, 576–589.

Faraj, S. & Sproull, L. (2000). Coordinating expertise in software development teams. *Management Science, 46*, 1554–1568.

Fleishman, E. A., Mumford, M. D., Zaccaro, S. J., Kevin, K. Y., Korotkin, A. L., & Hein, M. B. (1991). Taxonomic efforts in the description of leader behavior: A synthesis and functional interpretation. *The Leadership Quarterly, 2*, 245–287.

George, J. M. (1990). Personality, affect, and behavior in groups. *Journal of Applied Psychology, 75*, 107–116.

Gerrig, R. J. & Zimbardo, P. G. (2002). Psychology and life, 16/e. Boston, MA: Allyn and Bacon; Pearson Education.

Gibbs, J., Eisenberg, J., Rozaidi, N., & Gryaznova A. (2015). The "Megapozitiv" role of enterprise social media in enabling cross-boundary communication in a distributed Russian organization. *American Behavior Scientist, 59*, 103–123.

Gilleard, J. D. & Rees, D. R. (1998). Alternative workplace strategies in Hong Kong. *Facilities, 16* (5/6), 133–137.

Goel, A. (2010). *Computer fundamentals*. Dehli: Pearson Education India.

Goodhue D. & Thompson R. (1995). Task-technology fit and individual-performance. *MIS Quart, 19*, 213–236.

Grady, J. O. (1995). *System engineering planning and enterprise identity*. Boca Raton, FL: Taylor & Francis.

Griffith, T. L., Sawyer, J. E., & Neale, M. A. (2003). Virtualness and knowledge in teams: Managing the love triangle of organizations, individuals, and information technology. *MIS Quarterly, 27*, 265–287.

Hackman, J. R. (1987). The design of work teams. In J. Lorsch (Ed.), *Handbook of organizational behavior* (pp. 315–342). Englewood Cliffs, NJ: Prentice-Hall.

Harrison, A., Wheeler, P., & Whitehead, C. (2003). *Distributed workplace: Sustainable work environments*. London: Spon Press.

Hinds, S. & Kiesler, S. (2002). *Distributed work*. Cambridge, MA: MIT Press.

Hoch, J. E. (2007). Verteilte Führung in virtuellen Teams: Zum Einfluss struktureller, interaktionaler und teambasierter Führungstechniken auf den Teamerfolg [Distributed leadership in virtual teams]. Unpublished doctoral dissertation.

Hoch, J. E. & Dulebohn, J. H. (2013). Shared leadership in enterprise resource planning and human resource management systems implementation. *Human Resource Management Review, 23*, 114–125.

Hoch, J. E. & Dulebohn, J. H. (2017). Team personality composition, emergent leadership and shared leadership in virtual teams: A theoretical framework. *Human Resource Management Review, 27*, 678–693.

Hoch, J. E. & Kozlowski, S. W. J. (2014). Leading virtual teams: Hierarchical leadership, structural supports, and shared team leadership. *Journal of Applied Psychology, 99*, 390–403.

Hogg, M.A., Abrams, D., & Martin, G.N. (2010). Social cognition and attitudes. In Martin, G.N., Carlson, N.R., & Buskist, W. (Eds.), *Psychology* (pp. 646–677). Harlow: Pearson Education Limited.

Houghton, J. D. & Neck, C. P. (2002). The revised self-leadership questionnaire: Testing a hierarchical factor structure for self-leadership. *Journal of Managerial Psychology, 17*, 672–91.

Howell, J. M. & Hall-Merenda, K. (1999). The ties that bind: The impact of leader-member exchange, transformational and transactional leadership, and distance on predicting follower performance. *Journal of Applied Psychology, 84*, 680–694.

Howell, J. M., Neufeld, D. J., & Avolio, B. J. (2005). Examining the relationship of leadership and physical distance with business unit performance. *The Leadership Quarterly, 16*, 273–285.

Howell, J. P. & Dorfman, P. W. (1986). Leadership and substitutes for leadership among professional and non-professional workers. *Journal of Applied Behavioral Science, 22*, 39–46.

Judge, T. A. & Piccolo, R. F. (2004). Transformational and transactional leadership: A meta-analytic test of their relative validity. *Journal of Applied Psychology, 89*, 755–768.

Kerr, S. (1977). Substitutes for leadership: Some implications for organizational design. *Organization and Administrative Sciences, 8*, 135–146.

Kerr, S. & Jermier, J. M. (1978). Substitutes for leadership: Their meaning and measurement. *Organizational Behavior and Human Performance, 22*, 375–403.

Kirkman, B. L. & Rosen, B. 1999. Beyond self-management: Antecedents and consequences of team empowerment. *Academy of Management Journal, 42*, 58–74.

Kirkman, B. L., Rosen, B., Gibson, C. B., Tesluk, P. E., & McPherson, S. O. (2002). Five challenges to virtual team distributed work success: Lessons from Sabre. *Academy of Management Executive, 16*, 67–79.

Kirkman, B. L., Rosen, B., Tesluk, P. E., & Gibson, C. B. (2004). The impact of team empowerment on virtual team performance: The moderating role of face-to-face-interaction. *Academy of Management Journal, 47,* 175–192.

Kouzes, J. M. & Posner, B. Z. (2009). To lead, create a shared vision. *Harvard Business Review, 87,* 20–21.

Kozlowski, S. W. J. & Bell, B. S. (2003). Work groups and teams in organizations. In W. C. Borman, D. R. Ilgen & R. J. Klimoski (Eds.), *Comprehensive handbook of psychology: Industrial and organizational psychology* (pp. 333–375). New York, NY: John Wiley.

Lewis, K. (2003). Measuring transactive memory systems in the field: Scale development and validation. *Journal of Applied Psychology, 88,* 587–604.

Lyubomirsky, S., King, L., & Diener, E. (2005). The benefits of frequent positive affect: Does happiness lead to success? *Psychological Bulletin, 131,* 803–855.

Manz, C. (1986). Self-leadership: Toward an expanded theory of self-influence processes in organizations. *Academy of Management Review, 11,* 585–600.

Manz, C. C. & Neck, C. P. (2004). *Mastering self-leadership: Empowering yourself for personal excellence* (3rd edn). Upper Saddle River, NJ: Prentice-Hall.

Martins, L. L., Gilson, L. L., & Maynard, M. T. (2004). Virtual teams: What do we know and where do we go from here? *Journal of Management, 30,* 805–835.

McGrath, J. E. (1991). Time, interaction, and performance (TIP). *Small Group Research, 22,* 128–147.

Mohammed, S. & Dumville, B. C. (2001). Team mental models in a team knowledge framework: Expanding theory and measurement across disciplinary boundaries. *Journal of Organizational Behavior, 22,* 89–106.

Neck, C. P. & Houghton, J. D. (2006). Two decades of self-leadership theory and research: Past developments, present trends, and future possibilities. *Journal of Managerial Psychology, 21,* 270–95.

O'Neill, M. & Wymer, T. D. (2010). The metrics of distributed work: Financial and performance benefits of an emerging work model. Retrieved from www.knoll.com/document/1352940439564/WP_DistributedWork.pdf.

Purvanova, R. K. & Bono, J. E. (2009). Transformational leadership in context: Face-to-face and virtual teams. *The Leadership Quarterly, 20,* 343–357.

Roper, K. O. & Ha Kim, J. (2007). Successful distributed work arrangements: A developmental approach. *Journal of Facilities Management, 5*(2), 103–114.

Rynes, S. L. & Gerhart, B. (2000). *Compensation in organizations: Current research and practice.* San Francisco, CA: Jossey-Bass.

Rynes, S. L., Gerhart, B., & Parks, L. (2005). Personnel psychology: Performance evaluation and pay for performance. *Annual Review of Psychology, 56,* 571–600.

Schaufeli, W. B., Salanova, M., Gonzalez-Roma, V., & Bakker, A. B. (2002). The measurement of engagement and burnout and: A confirmative analytic approach. *Journal of Happiness Studies, 3,* 71–92.

Sheer, C. V. & Chen, L. (2004). Improving media richness theory: A study of interaction goals, message valence, and task complexity in manager-subordinate communication. *Management Communication Quarterly, 18,* 76–83.

Simon, S. J. & Peppas, S. C. (2004). An examination of media richness theory in product Web site design: An empirical study. *Digital Policy, Regulation and Governance, 6* (4), 270–281.

Sivasubramaniam, N., Murry, W. D., Avolio, B. J., & Jung, D. I. (2002). A longitudinal model of the effects of team leadership and group potency on group performance. *Group & Organization Management*, *27*, 66–96.

Valkenburg, P. M., Peter, J. & Walther, J. B. (2016). Media effects: Theory and research. *Annual Review of Psychology*, *67*, 315–338.

Warkentin, M. & Beranek, P. M. (1999). Training to improve virtual team communication. *Information Systems Journal*, *9*, 271–289.

Yukl, G. (2009). Leading organizational learning: Reflections on theory and research. *The Leadership Quarterly*, *20*, 49–53.

Zaccaro, S. J. & Bader, P. (2003). E-leadership and the challenges of leading e-teams: Minimizing the bad and maximizing the good. *Organizational Dynamics*, *31*, 377–387.

Zelle, J. (2010). *Python programming: An introduction to computer science* (2nd edn.) Portland, OR: Franklin, Beedle, & Associates.

Zigurs, I. (2003). Leadership in virtual team distributed works: Oxymoron or opportunity? *Organizational Dynamics*, *31*, 339–351.

17 Virtual Teams

Conceptualization, Integrative Review, and Research Recommendations

Stanton Mak and Steve W. J. Kozlowski

With the advent of the decentralization and globalization of work processes, organizations are finding it necessary to coordinate activities that span temporal, spatial, and geographic boundaries. As a result, many organizations have moved toward using virtual teams, in which members are geographically dispersed and collaborate using communication technologies (e.g., email, videoconferencing). This trend has accelerated in the last two decades, fueled by the rapid development of new communication technologies and their adoption by organizations worldwide. Indeed, a survey conducted by the Society for Human Resource Management revealed that nearly half of all organizations now use virtual teams (Minton-Eversole, 2012).

As the communication technologies evolved over the past two decades, so too did our conceptualization of "virtuality," which refers to the extent to which a team is more or less virtual. In early research, scholars tended to make a categorical distinction between "purely" virtual and face-to-face (FTF) teams; virtual team members were posited to be geographically dispersed and collaborated predominantly through the rudimentary communication technologies available at the time (i.e., email and audioconferencing), whereas co-located teams were said to interact almost exclusively FTF. However, the ensuing decades have witnessed a rapid proliferation of new communication technologies in the workplace – from text messages to video phone calls, online meetings, and document-sharing systems – that have gotten progressively less expensive, easier to use, and more robust. Recent conceptualizations have therefore stressed the omnipresence of virtual interactions, noting that a purely FTF team that does not use any electronic communication media is now exceptionally rare. From this perspective, most modern teams lie on a continuum somewhere between completely virtual and completely FTF, and where a team exists on this continuum is believed to be a function of several factors (Bell & Kozlowski, 2002). Although there has yet to be agreement on what the key dimensions are, core elements of virtuality that have been proposed include the degree of reliance on computer-mediated communication (CMC) and indicators of geographic dispersion such as the average distance between members or the number of working sites represented in the team together with the number of members at each site.

In parallel with the growing prevalence of teams with some degree of virtuality, the past few decades have seen an extensive amount of empirical research on virtual teams across multiple disciplines, and there have been several reviews in that time. For example, Hertel, Geister, and Konradt (2005) summarized empirical research on virtual teams, organized around a life cycle model of team development. Other reviews evaluated the virtual team literature with respect to the input-process-output (IPO) model of team effectiveness (McGrath, 1964), which conceptualizes team performance in systems terms such that inputs influence team processes, which in turn impact critical team outcomes. Using the IPO model as an organizing framework, Martins, Gilson, and Maynard (2004) reviewed the research findings related to team inputs, processes, and outputs. Ten years later, they updated their review by highlighting some of the research advancements that have been made since their original review (Gilson et al., 2015). Kirkman, Gibson, and Kim (2012) also used the IPO framework to synthesize the empirical literature published up to 2008; however, while the other reviews focused on findings at the team level, Kirkman et al. (2012) included attention toward inputs, processes, and outputs at multiple levels of analysis (i.e., individual, team, organizational).

The purpose of this review is to take a focused look at the recent empirical literature on virtual teams, drawing upon the concept of a multilevel IPO model that Kirkman et al. (2012) proposed and using it to evaluate the extensive amount of new research that has been conducted during the last nine years since the ending date of their review (i.e., 2008). In doing so, we extend previous reviews of the virtual team literature in three ways. First, in contrast to previous reviews that primarily used the IPO model as an organizing framework to summarize research findings, we conceptually map the literature to the IPO model and consider how well the studies encompass all key components. This allows us to determine the extent to which the literature makes full use of a theoretically comprehensive IPO model. For this review, we evaluate the literature with respect to a contemporary version of the IPO model that includes multiple levels of analysis, feedback loops, and moderators (Ilgen et al., 2005; Kozlowski & Bell, 2003; Kozlowski & Ilgen, 2006). Second, we focus greater attention on the ways in which virtuality has been defined and studied. Although scholars have acknowledged that virtuality is comprised of various dimensions, the empirical research has often take the concept of virtuality for granted and has not always been explicit on what dimensions of virtuality are examined in given studies. Therefore, the goal is to identify the extent to which different features of virtuality have been examined in the literature, and what features have been relatively neglected. Third, we add a greater focus to the methodological rigor of the literature and highlight needed advances in research design and methods.

We first explore the theoretical conceptualization of virtuality, tracing its evolution over time and posing a taxonomy of virtuality features that will be used for our review. Then, we review the recent empirical literature, which can be categorized based on whether the phenomena investigated in the study is primarily at the team level, the individual level, or at multiple levels. For each category of studies, we consider (a) how well the research makes use of the full IPO model, (b) the types of moderators that are studied, and (c) the features of virtuality that are typically examined. Next, we evaluate the research settings and design of virtual team research. In the final section, we conclude with recommendations designed to advance future research.

Using search engines and electronic databases such as PsychINFO and ProQuest, we identified and collected empirical articles published in academic journal articles between 2008 and 2017 within the fields of management, psychology, information technology, and communication. We used search terms such as "virtual team," "distributed team," "virtuality," and computer-mediated communication." For our review, we focused on work that is explicitly situated in a team or group context. Additionally, we excluded qualitative, non-empirical, or case studies as their informational value for this review is limited. The entire search process produced a total of 165 empirical studies for our review.

17.1 The Conceptualization of Team Virtuality

In the 1980s and early 1990s, rapid advancements in computer hardware and networking infrastructure began to dramatically reshape the workplace. In contrast to the computers in the 1960s that were expensive and bulky, the early 1980s saw the introduction of compact and economical personal computers that have since become ubiquitous in our daily lives. Initially, personal computer usage was limited to solitary users interacting with isolated computer systems. However, the emergence of corporate networks and then the World Wide Web in the early 1990s soon enabled computers across the world to connect with each other, creating new possibilities for collaborative work that transcends the limitations of time and space.

Motivated by these technological developments, researchers within the field of computer-supported cooperative work began devoting efforts to understanding how technology might best support teamwork. Studies were conducted to examine the impact of various communication tools on team functioning, usually comparing computer-supported teams to traditional FTF teams that did not use the technology. Although early efforts primarily focused on the use of simple email systems available at the time, successive waves of technology and falling prices enabled new communication tools, broadening the scope of research over time. Text messaging, voicemail, and voice conferencing provided employees new ways to collaborate both synchronously (at the same time) or asynchronously (at different times). Videoconferencing systems, which once involved dedicated meeting rooms that were costly to set up and maintain, were soon available at a fraction of the cost and made possible richer levels of communication among team members. As the use of these technologies expanded, so did research on issues related to their use.

By the mid 1990s, these technological advancements began to provide organizations the ability to build effective teams in which members are spread over wide geographic distances, may never meet FTF, but are instead primarily linked together via electronic communication tools. Scholars introduced the term "virtual teams" to refer to this new form of work unit, and they began to devote research attention to the benefits and costs associated with their use. Most of the earlier research on virtual teams contrasted them with purely FTF teams (e.g., Lea & Spears, 1992; Straus & McGrath, 1994). However, as the communication technologies became more affordable over time, virtual interactions soon became ubiquitous in the workplace, prompting scholars to recognize that most teams can be described on a continuum of virtuality. This shifted the research focus onto the dimensions that underlie the degree of virtuality in teams.

The nature of team virtuality has been explored in several conceptual papers. Bell and Kozlowski (2002) were perhaps the first to propose that virtual teams should be conceptualized using characteristics that treat virtuality as a continuum, rather than as a discrete "ideal type" to be contrasted with FTF teams, with task complexity determining the extent to which such teams were more or less virtual. They proposed two characteristics that distinguish virtual teams from conventional FTF teams – (a) spatial distance and (b) information, data, and communication requirements. First, virtual team members are distributed across space (and time), whereas conventional teams are co-located. Members of conventional teams work in close proximity to each other; in contrast, members of virtual teams are separated by different cities, countries, or even continents. Second, because virtual team members are physically separated, often by thousands of miles, they are not able to meet FTF and are therefore dependent on the use of communication technologies to collaborate.

With respect to virtuality, Bell and Kozlowski (2002) postulated that task complexity would influence the nature of team virtuality; that is, that task complexity would serve "as a moderator of virtual team structure and process" (p. 19). As shown in Figure 17.1, they characterized team task complexity as ranging from low to high with associated workflow interdependence (i.e., pooled, sequential, reciprocal, to intensive; Van de Ven, Delbecq, & Koenig, 1976), internal coupling (i.e., asynchronous, weak linkages to synchronous, strong linkages), external coupling (i.e., loosely coupled to tightly coupled), and task environment (i.e., static to dynamic) dimensions. Essentially, as task complexity increases, virtual team collaboration and coordination requirements necessitate more advanced, information-rich, and real-time communication media that mitigate the experience of spatial and temporal separation. In other words, richer and more synchronous communication technology would make the psychological experience less "virtual" and distant and more like that of conventional FTF teams.

This is illustrated in Figure 17.2 (Bell & Kozlowski, 2002), which postulates four facets that characterize a continuum of team virtuality that ranges from more virtual (i.e., member roles-multiple, boundaries-multiple, temporal distribution-distributed, and lifecycle-discrete) to less virtual and more like conventional FTF

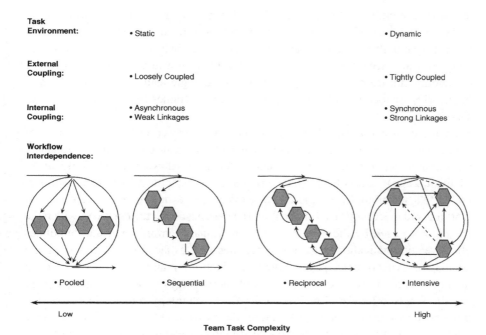

Figure 17.1 *Characteristics of simple vs. complex team workflows*
From:
Bell, B. S., & Kozlowski, S. W. J. (2002). A typology of virtual teams:
Implications for effective leadership. *Group and Organization Management,*
27, 14–49.
Reprinted with permission.

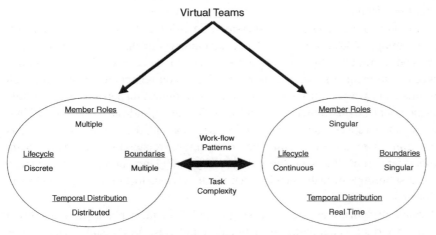

Figure 17.2 *Facets that characterize a virtuality continuum*
From:
Bell, B. S., & Kozlowski, S. W. J. (2002). A typology of virtual teams:
Implications for effective leadership. *Group and Organization Management,*
27, 14–49.
Reprinted with permission.

teams (i.e., member roles, singular; boundaries, singular; temporal distribution, real time; and life cycle, continuous). In other words, team members in more virtual teams juggle multiple roles and team boundaries, are distributed in time (as well as geographical space), and often have a concise lifespan whereas, at the other end of the continuum, teams are virtual but linked to a single team with fixed roles and boundaries, operate in real time, and over long time frames (e.g., air traffic control systems).

Building on that perspective, researchers have focused on different aspects of communication technologies used by virtual teams, including technology reliance, information richness, and synchronicity (Bell & Kozlowski, 2002; Kirkman & Mathieu, 2005). Technology reliance refers to the extent to which team members use virtual technologies to coordinate work activities and communicate (versus working and meeting FTF). Information richness describes the degree to which the technologies used by the team convey rich, valuable information that facilitates effective communication (e.g., nonverbal cues such as facial expression and body language). Synchronicity is the extent to which communications between team members occur in real time (e.g., instant messaging) or incur a time lag (e.g., email). Teams are more virtual as the level of technology reliance increases, the information value in communication tools decreases, and the level of synchronous interactions decreases. Recently, Mesmer-Magnus, DeChurch, Jiminez-Rodriguez, Wildman, and Shuffler (2011) conducted a meta-analysis to examine how the level of virtuality (as defined by where a team lies on these three communication dimensions) may impact team information sharing. They found that high virtuality teams tended to share more unique pieces of information than low virtuality teams, possibly because virtual communication helped to equalize status differences. However, high virtuality teams shared less information overall, likely because they relied on communication technologies with less informational value and greater time delays.

Expanding on the geographic dispersion dimension of team virtuality, O'Leary and Cummings (2007) proposed three characteristics of dispersion: spatial, temporal, and configural. Spatial dispersion refers to the actual physical distance between team members, whereas temporal dispersion reflects the extent to which team members work in different time zones. Configural dispersion refers to how team members are distributed across different locations, and can be subdivided into three separate aspects: site configuration describes to the number of locations where team members work; isolation configuration relates to how isolated team members are from others on the team; finally, imbalance describes the balance between subgroups of team members across the various locations where members are located.

Because organizations are increasingly global in their reach, they are often relying on virtual teams that span national boundaries. As a result, virtual teams are often composed of members with different cultural backgrounds, meaning that the members may have different value systems, behavioral norms, or even native languages. This adds difficulty to virtual team interactions. Some scholars have therefore included national or cultural diversity as a defining characteristic of

Table 17.1 *Features of team virtuality and complicating characteristics*

Features of Team Virtuality

Communication Technology
- Technology Reliance
- Information/Media Richness
- Synchronicity

Geographic Dispersion
- Spatial Dispersion
- Site (Configural)
- Isolation (Configural)
- Imbalance (Configural)

Complicating Characteristics

Task Complexity
National/Cultural Diversity

---

virtual teams (e.g., Chudoba et al., 2005; Gibson & Gibbs, 2006; Hoch & Kozlowski, 2014). Even when cultural diversity is not formally included in the definition of virtuality, it is frequently recognized as an important feature that often coincides with virtual collaborations. We think there is value in capturing diversity facets, but keeping it distinct from the conceptualization of virtuality.

Summarizing across these theoretical efforts, in Table 17.1 we propose a taxonomy that integrates the core features of communication technology and geographic dispersion that combine to create a continuum of team virtuality. There is continuing debate about whether geographic dispersion should be considered an antecedent of virtuality, rather than as one if its core features (Kirkman & Mathieu, 2005). Nonetheless, we believe that these facets are interconnected, and research on virtual teams should therefore incorporate both of these features in some fashion. For example, in the review of studies on virtual teams by Gibson and Gibbs (2006), both of these features were dominant for characterizing virtual teams (138 and 122 studies, respectively). Additionally, we highlight two factors – task complexity and national/cultural diversity – that are not necessarily core features of virtuality, but often complicate virtual team functioning. The review findings will demonstrate that researchers are often not specific regarding team virtuality features incorporated in their studies or selectively pick specific features with little conceptual justification for what was included/excluded. Moreover, task complexity and cultural diversity, which can complicate and moderate the effects of team virtuality are often not specified.

Finally, although we have not included the facet of fluid membership (i.e., multiple member roles, permeable boundaries, member churn; Bell & Kozlowski, 2002; Gibson & Gibbs, 2006) in the typology because it is rarely noted, it may be useful to consider as a complication. We advise that researchers should use the full taxonomy or, if they do not, should at a minimum provide a conceptual justification for their inclusion and exclusion choices. With this in mind, we begin our review of the recent empirical literature on virtual teams.

17.2 Integrative Review

A relatively recent review by Kirkman et al. (2012) synthesized the extensive literature on virtual teams published up to 2008. Their review used the IPO model as an organizing framework to summarize research findings at multiple levels of analyses. The authors concluded that, although progress has been made in our understanding of virtual team functioning, greater attention should be paid to topics such as time and stages of team development, virtual team leadership, and phenomena at multiple levels of analysis. In the following parts, we review the empirical research that has been conducted since 2008. We also use the IPO model as an organizational framework for our review, but in a different way. Specifically, we conceptually map the literature to a multilevel IPO model with moderators and feedback loops, and evaluate the extent to which studies encompass all key components. As shown in Figure 17.3, we expect research to examine inputs, processes, and outcomes at both the individual and team level, with potential interplay between persons, the team, and contextual factors. Studies are categorized as primarily at the team level, the individual level, or at multiple levels. For each category, we examine how well the research makes use of the full IPO model, the types of moderators studied, and the features of virtuality that are examined. Following this conceptual assessment, we review the methods employed in the research and critique its methodological rigor.

17.2.1 Team-Level Virtual Team Research

The majority of the virtual team studies we reviewed are at the team level (78 studies, or 47 percent of all studies). Researchers primarily use the team as the focal unit of theory, assess data at the individual level, and then aggregate to the team level in order to examine between-team differences. Such research increases our understanding of factors that affect virtual teams as a whole.

We also found 32 studies (19 percent of all studies) in which the theory and hypotheses are specified at the team level, but data are assessed and analyzed at the individual level. This is a misspecification that makes the drawing of meaningful inferences problematic. Therefore, we do not review these studies in this part, and we will elaborate on this issue in the Discussion and Recommendations part.

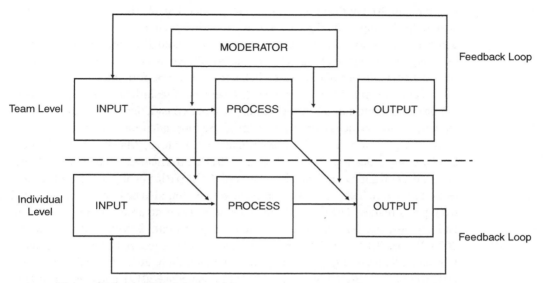

Figure 17.3 *Multilevel IPO model*

17.2.1.1 Mapping to the IPO Framework

Input – Process – Output. Looking across the team-level studies, we found 17 studies (22 percent of team-level studies) that examined process and emergent states as mediators between team inputs and team outcomes, thus fitting the structure of the IPO heuristic.[1] These studies most frequently examine team virtuality as an input. For example, CMC teams have been found to be less successful than FTF teams in exchanging and processing information (Kerr & Murthy, 2009) and developing an accurate shared mental model (Andres, 2011), resulting in lower levels of team performance and satisfaction.[2] Several researchers have also investigated the role of team composition (e.g., personality, functional diversity, deep-level diversity) on team processes and outcomes. For example, Pinjani and Palvia (2013) found that deep-level diversity had a positive relationship with trust and knowledge sharing in virtual teams, which leads to higher levels of team effectiveness.

Additionally, a handful of these studies have examined team leadership, both as an input and as a process. With respect to leadership as an input, research has examined transformational/transactional leaders (Huang, Kahai, & Jestice, 2010; Kahai, Huang, & Jestice, 2012) and theory X/theory Y leaders (Thomas &

---

[1] Marks et al. (2001) distinguished between behavioral processes than enable team work from perceptual measures of processes that they referred to as emergent process states. This distinction is conceptually meaningful, but it is not an important distinction for the purpose of this review. We use the terms process or processes to refer to the intervening mechanisms in the IPO heuristic.

[2] We use the term CMC teams instead of virtual teams when referring to studies that solely focus on the effects of different communication medium/technologies within a laboratory context.

Bostrom, 2008). On the other hand, Muethel, Gehrlein, & Hoegl (2012) examined shared leadership behaviors as a team process; their study demonstrated that demographic factors that are common in virtual teams (i.e., high female-to-male ratio, high mean age, and high levels of national diversity) are positively related to shared leadership behaviors, which helps foster team performance.

Process – Output. Nineteen studies (24 percent of team-level studies) examined the process-output link in virtual teams, without considering any inputs. In these studies, teamwork behaviors have received the most attention; for example, cooperation (e.g., Lin et al., 2016), coordination (Montoya, Massey, & Lockwood, 2011), communication (Montoya et al., 2011), information exchange (McLeod, 2013), organizational citizenship behaviors (OCB) (Rico et al., 2011), and conflict (e.g., de Jong, Schalk, & Curseu, 2008) have been found to be key drivers of virtual team performance. The positive influence of goal-setting processes on satisfaction and performance has also been examined (e.g., Brahm & Kunze, 2012; Haines, 2014; Pazos, 2012). Finally, some of these studies have focused on emergent states. For example, trust (e.g., Altschuller & Benbunan-Fich, 2013; Crisp & Jarvenpaa, 2013), cohesion (Brahm & Kunze, 2012; Carlson et al., 2013), and team identification (Lin et al., 2016) have been found to be positively related to virtual team performance.

Input – Process/Output. Researchers have sometimes examined the direct effect of inputs on both processes and outputs (12 studies, or 15 percent of team-level studies); that is, team processes were not examined as a mediator between the inputs and outputs, but are treated as criterion variables alongside outputs. A large majority of these studies compare FTF teams with teams using a variety of computer technologies on teamwork processes such as communication (van der Kleij, Schraagen, Werkhoven, & de Dreu, 2009), information exchange (van der Kleij, Lijkwan, Rasker, & De Dreu, 2009), and synergy (Pazos & Beruvides, 2011); and team effectiveness outcomes such as creativity (Han et al., 2011), satisfaction (Zornoza, Orengo, & Penarroja, 2009), and team performance (e.g., Pazos & Beruvides, 2011). Additionally, some studies have examined team familiarity as an input; in particular, virtual teams in which members were more familiar with each other relayed less task-irrelevant information during high workload (Espevik, Johnson, & Eid, 2011), were more likely to detect group deception (Giordano & George, 2013), and displayed higher levels of team performance (Espevik et al., 2011; Giordono & George, 2013).

Input – Output. Eleven studies (14 percent of team-level studies) examined the input-output link but did not examine any team processes. These studies have frequently examined how various team composition dimensions influence virtual team performance, including role composition (Eubanks et al., 2016; Zheng, Zeng, & Zhang, 2016), extraversion (Turel & Zhang, 2010), conscientiousness (Turel & Zhang, 2010), and ability (Zheng et al., 2016). Additionally, several researchers have examined the impact of a variety of contextual characteristics (e.g., structural supports, leadership type [vertical vs shared], problem-solving requirement) on virtual team performance (e.g., Hoch & Kozlowski, 2014; Turel & Zhang, 2010).

Finally, some studies have examined the influence of team virtuality on team effectiveness (e.g., Schweitzer & Duxbury, 2010; Tzabbar & Vestal, 2015).

Input – Process. Ten studies (13 percent of team-level studies) investigated the input-process link but did not examine any outputs. Some of these studies examined the effect of team virtuality on team processes, including group style (Branson, Clausen, & Sung, 2008), organizational citizenship behaviors (Ganesh & Gupta, 2010), team trust, collaborative behaviors, and information exchange (Peñarroja et al., 2013). Other studies examined the influence of task characteristics on team processes in virtual teams (Ganesh & Gupta, 2010; Xie, Zhu, & Wang, 2009). For example, Xie et al. (2009) found that the amount of task-relevant information positively influenced the sharedness of mental models in CMC teams, but had a negative impact on the sharedness of mental models in FTF teams. These results suggest that CMC teams can focus more on the task and less on interpersonal issues than FTF teams. Finally, a few studies have evaluated interventions designed to improve virtual team processes. For example, Peñarroja et al. (2015) found that providing teams with a feedback intervention that conveyed process and outcome information resulted in higher levels of team learning and group information elaboration.

Miscellaneous. Six studies examined how processes relate to other processes, without examining any inputs or outputs. These studies often focus on intragroup conflict, with virtuality as a moderator. For example, Lira, Ripoll, Peiro, and Orengo (2008) found that relationship conflict had a stronger negative influence on group potency in CMC teams than in FTF teams, whereas task conflict had a stronger positive influence on group potency in FTF teams compared to CMC teams. Likewise, Martinez-Moreno, Zornoza, Gonzalez-Navarro, and Thompson (2012) found that early task conflict predicted relationship conflict during later collaborations for FTF or videoconferencing teams, but not for teams that use text messaging. This suggests that communication technologies with less media richness can mitigate conflict escalation. Finally, two studies examined the direct effects of input and process on output (MacDonnell et al., 2009; Magni et al., 2013), and one examined the effect of output on process (Lira et al., 2008). In particular, Lira et al. (2008) found that group effectiveness had a positive influence on group potency in both CMC and FTF teams.

17.2.1.2 Moderators

We found that thirty-five of the seventy-eight team-level studies examined moderating variables. They can generally be organized into four categories: team virtuality dimensions, task characteristics, team processes, and team composition characteristics. Team virtuality has received the most attention as a moderator in team-level studies. Most often, studies compared the effects of a wide array of communication media (e.g., FTF, videoconferencing, virtual world) on group processes and outcomes (e.g., Huang et al., 2010; Swaab, Phillips, & Schaerer, 2016). Different virtuality dimensions have also been examined, such as the degree of geographic dispersion (e.g., McLeod, 2013; Suh & Shin, 2010), the degree of electronic communication (e.g., Bradley et al., 2013), or both (de Jong et al., 2008; Hoch & Kozlowski, 2014). In general, studies that use virtuality as a moderator propose that the input-process-output relationships found for "traditional" teams are generally supported in virtual teams, but the strength of many relationships in the model are moderated by the degree of virtuality of the team.

Task characteristics have been examined in a number of studies, including task interdependence (e.g., Ganesh & Gupta, 2010; Maynard et al., 2012; Pinjani & Balvia, 2013), task routineness (Malhotra & Majchrzak, 2014), time pressure (van der Kleij, Lijkwan et al., 2009), task complexity (Colazo & Fang, 2010), and task type (Stone & Posey, 2008). For example, Malhotra and Majchrzak (2014) examined whether using communication technologies that allow distributed team members to be aware of the work that their colleagues are performing (task knowledge awareness) would have positive effects on team functioning, particularly when virtual teams work on non-routine tasks as opposed to routine tasks. Indeed, the results demonstrated that the use of communication technologies that promote task knowledge awareness in virtual teams is positively associated with team performance, but only when the task is non-routine in nature.

Several researchers have examined the moderating effect of team processes, such as trust (e.g., Brahm & Kunze, 2012; Zornoza et al., 2009), process conflict (Martinez-Moreno et al., 2012), social attraction (Chiu & Staples, 2013), and task elaboration (Chiu & Staples, 2013). For example, Brahm and Kunze (2012) proposed that the association between goal setting and team cohesion is stronger under conditions of high trust climate. Using a field study of fifty geographically distributed teams, the researchers confirmed their proposed model; team goal setting was related to higher levels of team cohesion, and this relationship was stronger when teams had higher levels of team trust climate. Additionally, team cohesion was positively associated with team performance.

Characteristics related to team composition have been examined as a moderator in some studies, including ability disparity (Zheng et al., 2016) and experience with CMC (Carlson et al., 2013). For example, in a laboratory study with 152 student teams, Carlson et al. (2013) found that team cohesion and team openness was positively related to virtual team effectiveness. Additionally, the effects of openness on team effectiveness are stronger for teams that have higher levels of CMC experience.

17.2.1.3 Dimensions of Virtuality Examined

Looking across the team-level studies, we found that the majority did not measure or manipulate any dimensions of virtuality (39 studies, or 50 percent of team-level studies). Studies that used ongoing employee teams tended to simply include teams in their sample if they met the researchers' broadly defined virtuality criteria, without directly assessing any specific virtuality dimensions. Likewise, many studies employed simulated virtual teams, but the dimensions of virtuality were held constant across all teams and were not variables of interest in the study.

Of the studies that measured or manipulated virtuality dimensions, the majority evaluated the effects of different communication media, primarily within a laboratory context (27 studies, or 35 percent of team-level studies). These studies typically compared FTF teams with CMC teams that used one type of computer technology (e.g., videoconferencing, virtual world, texting). Some studies included multiple types of computer technology options, which allows for the examination of how different technologies with varying levels of media richness and/or synchronicity may influence team functioning (e.g., Han et al., 2011; Martinez-Moreno et al., 2012; Nowak, Watt, & Walther, 2009; Zornoza et al., 2009).

Other aspects of virtuality have been examined less frequently; less than 10 percent of team-level studies assessed or manipulated geographic dispersion, reliance on communication technologies, or national/cultural diversity. Additionally, rather than operationalizing virtuality as a multidimensional construct, studies tend to only examine a single dimension of virtuality. Therefore, the team-level studies are not as informative as they could be about all dimensions of virtuality. As an illustrative example, we looked across the eighteen team-level studies that fit with the IPO framework and found only two studies that measured the degree of technology reliance (Bradley et al., 2013; Maynard et al., 2012) and we did not find any studies that measured the degree of geographic dispersion or national diversity. Although we applaud these efforts for making full use of the IPO framework, we encourage researchers to add a focus toward measuring or manipulating these other dimensions of virtuality.

17.2.1.4 Summary

The vast majority of virtual team studies are at the team level of analysis. This provides researchers the opportunity to elaborate the effects of different virtuality dimensions on core processes that contribute to team effectiveness. A moderate number of the studies map to the IPO framework at the team level. However, many studies do not, as they often examine the process-output link without considering any inputs, or they only examine the direct effect of inputs on both processes and outputs. Furthermore, only half the team-level studies we reviewed assessed or manipulated any dimension of virtuality, and those that do, primarily focus on the effects of the different types of technology used. Dimensions such as geographic dispersion, degree of technology reliance, or national/cultural diversity have been relatively neglected.

17.2.2 Individual-Level Virtual Team Research

We found 31 studies (19 percent of all studies) that were strictly at the individual level, focusing on processes and outcomes of individual team members. Such research contributes to our knowledge of virtual teams by providing an understanding of how individuals perceive functioning within a virtual team context.

17.2.2.1 Mapping to the IPO Framework

Input – Process – Output. Looking across the research that focuses solely at the individual level, we found only three studies (10 percent of individual-level studies) that examined processes and psychological states as mediators between inputs and outputs (Arling & Subramani, 2011; Sarker, Kirkeby, Sarker, & Chakraborty, 2011; Sohrabi, Gholipour, & Amiri, 2011). Two of these studies examined how individual perceptions or subjective experiences of virtuality are related to various individual processes and outcomes (Arling, 2011; Sohbrabi et al., 2011). For example, Sohbrabi et al. (2011) found that an individual's perception of virtuality negatively influences organizational identification, resulting in lower levels of job satisfaction, organizational commitment, job involvement, and OCB. Additionally, one study found that individuals with higher levels of knowledge and expertise are more likely to transfer more knowledge to other team members; as a result, that individual will be viewed as being a high performer by other team members (Sarker, Kirkeby et al., 2011).

Input – Process. A majority of individual-level studies investigated the input-process link, without considering any outputs (16 studies, or 52 percent of individual-level studies). These studies commonly focus on input factors that relate to trust in virtual teams (e.g., Altschuller & Benbunan-Fich, 2013; Kuo & Thompson, 2014). For example, Kuo and Thompson (2014) found that social ties and propensity to trust influenced perceptions of a new teammate's trustworthiness as well as the willingness to trust the new teammate. Some studies have examined input factors that influence an individual's motivation to engage in teamwork behaviors (e.g., Tran, Oh, & Choi, 2016; Yilmaz & Pena, 2014). As an example, Tran et al. (2016) found that virtual team members with a global mindset had higher self-efficacy, which translated to greater willingness to cooperate with others in the team. Finally, although perceptions of virtuality tends to be conceptualized as an input factor, we found one study in which it is examined as a process variable. Specifically, Stark, Bierly, and Harper (2014) found that when individuals perceive that relationship conflict is high among team members, but they are still willing to cooperate with one another to complete the task, they reduced FTF interactions and worked more virtually. Likewise, they found that high perceptions of task interdependence was positively related to perceptions of virtuality when perceived cooperation was high.

Input – Process/Output. Five studies (16 percent of individual-level studies) examined the direct effect of inputs on both processes and outputs. Some studies examined how working in teams with various reward structures may influence individual processes and outcomes (McLeod, 2011; Rack et al., 2011). For example, Rack et al. (2011) found that individuals who worked in teams in which rewards were distributed equally (each team member receives an equal share), as opposed to equitably (each team member's share depends on their contribution) had higher levels of communication behavior and pay satisfaction. However, individuals who worked in teams in which rewards were distributed equitably showed higher levels of individual performance when they had an assertive personality. Other studies have examined individual differences in the attitudes or skills regarding the use of CMC (Fuller, Vician, & Brown, 2016; Walther & Bazarova, 2008). For example, Fuller et al. (2016) found that individuals who had high CMC anxiety participated less, sent fewer task-oriented messages, introduced fewer novel communication topics, and had lower levels of perceived performance compared to individuals with low CMC anxiety.

Miscellaneous. We found four studies that examined the process-output link but did not consider any inputs. Most of these studies examined how individual processes affect trust in virtual teams, and how trust affects various individual outcomes (e.g., Romeike, Nienaber, & Schewe, 2016; Sarker, Ahuja, Sarker, & Kirkeby, 2011). For example, adopting a social network perspective, Sarker, Ahuja et al. (2011) demonstrated that individuals with high communication centrality were more likely to be trusted by team members, resulting in higher levels of individual performance. Romeike et al. (2016) found that individuals who perceived his or her own performance to be better than the team's performance had lower levels of trust toward team members, and this resulted in lower levels of job satisfaction. Additionally, two studies examined how processes relate to other processes, without examining any inputs or outputs (Turel & Connelly, 2012; Xieu et al., 2012). These studies focus on process factors that influence future intentions. For example, Turel and Connelly (2012) found that psychological collectivism influences confidence in the team's capability and perceived usefulness of e-collaboration tools, and these factors both affect future usage intentions. Finally, one study examined the input-output link but did not examine any processes (Medina & Srivastava, 2016). Specifically, Medina and Srivastava (2016) found that individuals who reported greater FTF communication with the team had higher levels of satisfaction with the team; however, online communication was not related to satisfaction with the team.

17.2.2.2 Moderators

We found that nine of the thirty-one individual-level studies examined moderating variables. A number of studies have examined the moderating role of individual process variables, such as perceived risk (Robert, Dennis, & Hung, 2009), positive impression formation (Altschuller & Benbunan-Fich, 2013), perceived cohesion (Sarker, Sarker, & Schneider, 2009), perceived cooperation (Stark et al., 2014), and perceived behavioral differences of members within a team (Bazarova & Walther, 2009). Individual behavioral variables have also been studied as moderators, including self-disclosure (Altschuller & Benbunan-Fich, 2013), and individual performance (Belogolovsky et al., 2016). Some personality-related variables have been examined, including assertiveness (Rack et al., 2011) and extraversion (Medina & Srivastava, 2016).

Finally, we found one study that examined a moderator situated at the individual-within-teams level, resulting from comparison processes with other team members in the group (i.e., a frog-pond effect). Perry, Lorinkova, Hunter, Hubbard, and McMahon (2013) examined whether a team member's level of family responsibility and dissimilarity from team members in terms of family responsibility (calculated as the average difference of each team member from his or her participating teammates) would jointly moderate the relationship between team virtuality and perceived social loafing in teams. Using 275 students across 80 teams in a field study, they found that individuals with high family responsibility who worked with others who also had similarly high levels of family responsibility reported more team social loafing if the teams were more virtual. In contrast, individuals who reported low family responsibility and worked with others who also had similarly low levels of family responsibility reported less social loafing in teams as virtuality increased.

17.2.2.3 Dimensions of Virtuality Examined

Like the team-level studies we reviewed, the majority of individual-level studies did not include the level of virtuality as a focal variable (19 studies, or 61 percent of individual-level studies). Rather, studies tend to keep all dimension of virtuality constant across conditions for simulated virtual teams, or simply list the virtuality criteria for team inclusion without measuring any dimension of virtuality for ongoing employee teams.

However, we were pleased to see that the other twelve studies measured or manipulated a wide variety of virtuality dimensions, and many of them examined multiple dimensions. Some studies used subjective or perceptual measures of spatial and temporal dispersion (Sohrabi et al., 2011; Weber & Kim, 2015), cultural diversity (Sohrabi et al., 2011), and degree of technology reliance (e.g., Medina & Srivastava, 2016; Perry et al., 2013; Stark et al., 2014). Other studies assessed or manipulated objective measures of virtuality, typically related to geographic dispersion and communication medium (6 studies, or 19 percent of individual-level studies). For example, Arling and Subramani (2011) assessed individuals' average level of spatial, configural, and temporal dispersion from other team members. Conceptually, this is at the individual-within-teams level, resulting from comparison processes with other team members in the group (i.e., a frog-pond effect). Cheshin, Kim, Nathan, Ning and Olsen (2013) employed teams in which some members were co-located with each other and could interact FTF, whereas other members were put in separate rooms and could only communicate with fellow team members through text. Mean differences between the co-located team members and "remote" team members were examined. Finally, some studies manipulated both the configural dispersion and communication medium of teams in order to examine mean differences of individual outcomes (e.g., Bazarova & Walther, 2009; Marett & George, 2013; Walther & Bazarova, 2008).

17.2.2.4 Summary

Individual-level research helps shed light on how individual team members function within a virtual context. As such, it is an important part of our understanding of virtual teams. Researchers now recognize that individuals may vary within a team in the extent to which they perceive or experience virtuality. Indeed, current work suggests that certain dimensions of virtuality (e.g., geographic dispersion) may operate at the individual level or individual-within-teams level to impact critical individual processes and outcomes. We commend these efforts in understanding individuals' experiences of virtuality and hope it continues. However, our review shows that the vast majority of the individual-level studies make limited use of the IPO framework; indeed, only 10 percent of the studies we reviewed encompassed the full IPO framework. Part of the reason is because individual-level virtual team studies tend to focus on individual inputs and processes, but have often neglected outcomes. Thus, there is a need to devote more research attention not just to individual processes, but how those processes may influence outcomes such as individual performance or satisfaction.

17.2.3 Multilevel-Level Virtual Team Research

Previously, we reviewed research that is strictly at the team level or strictly at the individual level. However, virtual teams are inherently hierarchical entities involving individual team members within teams. A key implication is that team functioning and processes must be regarded as multilevel phenomena (Kozlowski & Klein, 2000). Consistent with this conceptualization, we found 24 studies (15 percent of all studies) that examined phenomena at multiple levels. This provides researchers an opportunity to model the impact of factors that may be variable across team members, and well as factors that may impact the whole team. Additionally, research can consider top-down effects of contextual factors on individual processes, as well as bottom-up influences of individuals on teams. Thus, multilevel research provides an opportunity to capture collective and individual processes, as well as the interplay between person and team.

17.2.3.1 Mapping to the IPO Framework

Input – Process – Output. Looking across the multilevel research, we found six studies (25 percent of multilevel studies) that fit the IPO framework. These studies predominantly focus on virtual team leadership, and the level of team virtuality tends to be treated as a moderator. For example, Hill and Bartol (2016) found a cross-level effect of empowering leadership, such that under conditions of high empowering leadership, the relationship between an individual's situational judgment and their virtual collaborative behaviors increased, which resulted in better individual performance. At the team level, empowering leadership had an indirect positive impact on team performance through higher levels of aggregate collaborative behaviors, especially under high levels of team dispersion. A study by Andressen, Konradt, and Neck (2012) found that individual perceptions of transformational leadership fostered higher levels of self-leadership. Additionally, self-leadership had a significant positive impact on individual motivation, commitment, and performance, especially under high levels of team virtuality.

Input – Process. Eight studies (33 percent of multilevel studies) examined the input-process link, but did not examine any outputs. Most of these studies examine the input-process relationship at the individual level, with a team-level moderator. For example, Charlier, Stewart, Greco, and Reeves (2016) found that text-based communication ability was positively related to leadership emergence, and communication apprehension was negatively related to leadership emergence, especially when team virtuality was high. Similarly, Balthazard, Waldman, and Warren (2009) found that personality factors lead to the emergence of transformational leadership, but only when team virtuality was low.

Other studies have examined the input-process relationship at the team level, while also assessing processes variables at a lower level of analysis. As an example, O'Leary and Mortensen (2010) found that teams with geographically defined subgroups experienced lower identification with the team, less effective transactive memory, more conflict, and more coordination problems than teams without subgroups. Additionally, differences were found at the subgroup level: among teams with geographically defined subgroups, members of minority subgroups experienced these problems more seriously than members of majority subgroups.

Process – Output. We found five studies (21 percent of multilevel studies) that examined the process-output link, but did not examine any inputs (e.g., Fuller, Marett, & Twitchell, 2012; Paul, Drake, & Liang, 2016; Turel & Zhang, 2011). Typically, these studies examine the process-output relationship at the team level, while also assessing process variables at the individual level. For example, Turel and Zhang (2011) found that individual perceptions of social loafing negatively affected the perceived usefulness of an e-collaboration system, which reduced usage intentions. At the team level, the collective social loafing in a team negatively affected team potency, which was detrimental to team performance. A cross-level effect was also found, such that low levels of team potency at the team level reduced individual usage intentions.

Miscellaneous. Three studies examined the process-process link, without examining any inputs or outputs (Cheshin, Rafaeli, & Bos, 2011; Erez et al., 2013; Robert, 2016). Additionally, two studies examined the input-output link at the team level, but did not examine any mediating processes; however, various outcomes at the individual level were examined as well. For example, Purvanova and Bono (2009) found that team-level transformational leadership had a stronger positive effect on team performance in virtual than FTF teams. At the individual level, team members who perceived high levels of transformational leadership had equally high levels of satisfaction in virtual and FTF teams.

17.2.3.2 Moderators

Moderating variables were investigated in fifteen of the twenty-four multilevel studies, and almost all of them were team-level. The vast majority of the moderators relate to team virtuality, and they tend to examine the degree of geographic dispersion (e.g., Charlier et al., 2016; Cummings & Haas, 2012) or the degree of technology reliance (Andressen et al., 2012), although a handful of studies compared FTF with virtual teams (Balthazard et al., 2009; Williams & Castro, 2010). Beyond virtuality, the moderators are few but diverse in nature, and they include racial and gender diversity (Robert, 2016), team trust (Erez et al., 2013), and team leadership (Hill & Bartol, 2016). As an example, Robert (2016) found that individuals' perceptions of subgroup formation negatively impact their perceptions of teamwork quality, but only when team gender and racial diversity is high. This finding suggests that subgroup formation based on race or gender are more likely to invoke in-group/out-group comparisons and hinder team functioning, whereas subgroup formation based on other characteristics does not.

Finally, we found one study that included an individual-level moderator (Gajendran & Joshi, 2012). Gajendran and Joshi (2012) used data from forty globally distributed teams and found that, at the individual level, LMX is positively related to member influence on team decisions when the frequency of leader-member communication is high. Additionally, at the team level, member influence on team decisions has a positive effect on team innovation.

17.2.3.3 Dimensions of Virtuality Examined

Looking across the multilevel studies, we found eight studies (33 percent of multilevel studies) that did not include the degree of virtuality as a focal variable. These studies use simulated student teams, and the elements of virtuality are kept consistent across teams. On the other hand, we were pleased to see that the majority of multilevel studies examined at least one dimension of virtuality. Studies most frequently assessed or manipulated the degree of geographic dispersion (13 studies, or 50 percent of multilevel studies); spatial and configural dispersion are primarily examined (e.g., Charlier et al., 2016; Cummings & Haas, 2012), whereas temporal dispersion has received less attention (e.g., Hill & Bartol, 2016; Joshi, Lazarova, & Liao, 2009). We also found ten studies (38 percent of multilevel studies) that compared FTF teams with CMC teams, usually within a laboratory context. Unfortunately, dimensions such as teams' reliance on communication technologies and national/cultural diversity have been rarely examined. As an example, we looked across the six studies that map to the IPO framework and found that all six studies examined aspects of geographic dispersion. Only one study measured the degree of technology reliance (Andressen et al., 2012) and we did not find any studies that measured national/cultural diversity. This represents an obvious need for future research attention.

17.2.3.4 Summary

Multilevel studies are an important part of our understanding of virtual team effectiveness, as they allow the examination of the interplay of individuals within a team as well as the team as a whole. We were therefore encouraged to see that research has begun to take a multilevel view of virtual teams. However, our review shows that most of the multilevel studies do not fit with the IPO framework; studies tend to examine the input-process link without examining any outputs, or they examine the process-output link without examining any inputs. Moreover, the multilevel studies have primarily focused on the effects of geographic dispersion; while we were pleased to see that studies often include multiple dimensions of dispersion, future research should add a focus toward dimensions such as the degree of technology reliance and national/cultural diversity.

17.2.4 Methods and Research Design

17.2.4.1 Research Settings

When reviewing the type of setting in which VT research is conducted, we found that 67 studies (41 percent of all studies) occurred in a laboratory setting, and they predominantly employ ad-hoc student teams. A small number of the laboratory studies (five studies) used a correlational design and did not manipulate any variables, making causal inference murky (e.g., Altschuller & Benhbunan-Fich, 2010; Wang, Fan, Hsieh, & Meenefee, 2009). We suspect that these studies were conducted in a laboratory setting to reduce the variation in situational conditions that were not the focus of the study design by providing common technologies, task, and incentives to each team. Nevertheless, they do not maximize the strengths of the laboratory, which are measurement and causal precision. In contrast, a majority of the laboratory studies (62 studies) used an experimental design that allows for the testing of the causal effect of key variables in controlled settings. Most often, they assign teams into different communication media conditions in order to ascertain differences in team outcomes such as communication quality, conflict, performance outcomes, and satisfaction. Some studies used confederates embedded in the teams to examine how positive or negative team member behaviors influence individual outcomes (e.g., Fuller et al., 2012; Yilmaz & Pena, 2014). Another set of studies evaluated the effectiveness of a specific tool or intervention designed to enhance virtual team functioning (e.g., Rentsch et al., 2014; Martinez-Moreno et al., 2015). Finally, some laboratory experiments examined the influence of structural attributes, such as the type of reward (McLeod, 2011; Rack et al., 2011) and the degree of task complexity (Giordano & George, 2013).

In the past decade, scholars have stressed that laboratory research is often limited because they employ ad hoc student teams that are relatively homogenous and have no prior history. Responding to calls for more work that focuses on real-world virtual teams, we found 98 studies (59 percent of all studies) that occurred within a field-based setting. A majority of these studies investigated organizational employees in ongoing work groups, although a moderate number of studies used student teams within a university setting (43 studies). Compared to laboratory studies, which tend to examine the implications of different communication media usage in virtual teams, the field studies are more likely to assess the degree of team virtuality along a continuum (e.g., degree of geographic dispersion, degree of computer technology use), and incorporate a broader variety of contextual variables, leader characteristics/behaviors, and team characteristics. The field studies are predominantly correlational in nature (88 studies) or employ quasi-experimental designs (three studies; Crisp & Jarvenpaa, 2013; O'Leary & Mortensen, 2010; Purvanova, 2013), which limits causal conclusions. In contrast, a small number of field studies (seven studies) used an experimental design. These experimental studies tend to recruit students from multiple universities, and randomly assign them to teams with different degrees of configural dispersion (i.e., the proportion of members spread out among n locations and the resulting number of subgroups in each site) in order to examine its effect on factors such as situational/dispositional attributions (Bazarova & Walther, 2009), group decision-making processes (Bazarova, Walther, & McLeod, 2012; McLeod, 2013), and trust and satisfaction (Schiller et al., 2014). Other team inputs that have been experimentally manipulated in a field setting include team structure (e.g., hierarchical vs. nonhierarchical teams) (Liu, Magjuka, & Lee, 2008) and leadership style (transformational vs transactional leadership) (Ruggieri, 2009).

17.2.4.2 Research Design

Correlational Studies. Looking across the ninety-six correlational laboratory and field studies, we found that a majority are cross-sectional (eighty studies). For example, using 141 hybrid-virtual teams in a field study, Lin et al. (2016) examined whether team affective tone was related to team performance indirectly through team identification and team cooperation. The study data was collected through a questionnaire at a single point in time, whereby team members were surveyed to measure the antecedents (team affective tone) and mediating variables (team identification and team cooperation), while team leaders were surveyed to measure team performance. Mediation analyses generally supported their model. However, the cross-sectional nature of the data limits the ability to draw causal inferences, creates potential issues of common method variance (in instances of single-source data), and precludes the examination of change over time.

Some of the correlational studies temporally separated the predictors, mediators, and criterion variables across two to four measurement occasions (twelve studies), which suggests some attempt to mitigate causal ambiguity and the potential biasing effects of common method variance. As an example, using eighty-one student teams that collaborated on a class project over a period of three weeks, Connelly and Turel (2016) examined the mediating influence of team trust and teamwork behaviors on the relationship between team emotional authenticity and team performance in virtual teams. Students completed survey measures of team-level authenticity and interpersonal trust while they worked on the project (time 1). After the teams had submitted their team assignment, they completed another survey to reflect on the quality of teamwork behaviors that their teammates displayed (time 2). One week later, teams were provided grades on their team assignment, which served as the measure of team performance (time 3).

In contrast to the studies that employ cross-sectional or simple time-lagged designs, we found one correlational study that performed two waves of repeated measurement on focal variables (Fuller et al., 2016), and three studies that performed three or more waves of repeated measurement on focal variables (Erez et al., 2013; Haines, 2014; Kuo & Yu, 2009). As an example, Erez et al. (2013) conducted a longitudinal field study using 1221 students assigned to 312 four-person virtual multicultural teams in order explore whether working on a project in a multicultural context helps develop team members' cultural intelligence, global identity, and local identity over time. These variables were assessed at three time points: before the project was assigned, in the middle of the project, and six months after the project had ended. Hierarchical linear modeling analyses at the individual level revealed that participants' cultural intelligence and global identity significantly increased from the beginning to the end of the project, and these results remained stable six months after the end of the project.

Experimental Studies. When reviewing the lab and field experiments, we found that a majority examined the processes and outcomes of teams at a single point in time (fifty-two studies). A typical example is a study by Kerr and Murthy (2009), which compared the effectiveness of FTF and synchronous CMC when using a chat tool in solving a hidden profile case. Results showed that, in comparison to the CMC groups, the FTF groups exchanged a greater number of information items, were more successful in solving the hidden profile problem, and were able to recall more information after completing the case. As in most of the experimental studies we reviewed, the groups only engaged in a single performance episode.

In contrast, we found eleven studies that examined change in focal variables across two time points. One study examined change over time by computing simple difference scores (Lira et al., 2008). Likewise, some studies have used repeated-measures analysis to examine change over time (e.g., Cheshin et al., 2011; Gonzalez-Navarro et al., 2010). Other studies have examined the level of a variable during the final performance episode, while controlling for the initial level of the variable. This allows the investigators to examine the effects of a predictor on that part of final level of the variable that is not predicted by the baseline level of the variable (i.e., degree of improvement) (e.g., Fan et al., 2014; Konradt et al., 2015; Lira et al., 2008; Martinez-Moreno et al., 2012; Monanzi et al., 2014).

Finally, we found six experimental studies that examined change in focal variables across three or more time points (e.g., Ellwart et al., 2015; Pazos & Beruvides, 2011; van der Kleij, Schraagen et al., 2009). For example, van der Kleij, Schraagen et al. (2009) conducted a longitudinal laboratory experiment to examine how FTF and videoconferencing teams differ in their communication patterns, task performance, and satisfaction, and how these variables change over time. Twenty-two three-person teams took part in four experimental sessions separated by two-week intervals. During each session, the teams completed a task in which team members were required to debate about and select the correct answer out of a set of three alternatives. Repeated measures analysis of variance demonstrated that, although there were no performance differences between FTF and teleconferencing groups, the FTF groups were more satisfied than videoconferencing groups across all sessions. Additionally, the videoconferencing groups had more difficulty regulating their conversations compared to FTF groups. They took fewer turns in discussing how to complete the task, required more time for turns, and interrupted each other less often – indicating that the interaction process of teleconferencing groups were more formal and lecture-like. However, their longitudinal analyses showed that these initial differences in communication patterns disappeared over time, which suggests that the videoconferencing teams were able to adapt to their communication environment.

17.2.4.3 Self-Report vs. Multisource Method

Correlational Studies. Looking across the ninety-six correlational studies, we found forty-six studies that make use of multisource data. Typically, these studies combine self-report survey data with data from one or more additional sources, such as objective measures, observer ratings, or supervisor surveys. For example, rather than relying on team members' perceptions of their own performance, some studies used a measure of team performance that is based on objective indicators (e.g., Haines, 2014; Montoya et al., 2011; Zheng et al., 2016), judgment of external raters (e.g., Bradley et al., 2013; Cogliser et al., 2013; Eubanks et al., 2016; Ortega et al., 2010), or perceptions of the team leader or manager (e.g., Hoch & Kozlowski 2014; Joshi et al., 2009). Additionally, rather than using perceptions of virtuality (e.g., asking participants how virtual their team is), many studies use more objective indicators, such as the number of sites, the level of isolation of members, the spread across zones, and/or the degree of electronic media usage. As an example, Andressen et al. (2012) assessed the use of different electronic media (i.e., email, telephone, videoconference, and chat) in relation to the overall frequency of communication between team members. They also measured the team's geographic dispersion through indices such as the total number of sites used by the team, the degree of spatial dispersion of team members, the percentage of team members with no other team members at their site, and the number of hours the team members can communicate synchronously. The indices for CMC and geographic dispersion were then combined into a single overall index of virtuality. Finally, we found a handful of studies that used a social network approach to observe phenomena underlying virtual work (e.g., Sarker, Ahuja, Sarker, & Kirkeby 2011; Suh et al., 2011). The social network approach consists of mapping the location of entities and the presence and strength of relationships between entities with statistical properties (e.g., average tie strength, network centrality), thus providing a rich understanding of the underlying team structure.

Regrettably, a majority of the correlational studies measure all study variables using self-report surveys from the same rater or source (fifty studies). This is problematic because most of the studies that solely rely on self-report surveys are cross-sectional as well, with all focal variables collected from the same rater at the same point in time (forty-five studies). As a typical example of this type of research design, Pazos (2012) conducted a study with thirty-nine student teams that worked on a class project in order to explore the potential mediating role of conflict management on the relationship between goal commitment and team outcomes such as performance and satisfaction. After the student teams had submitted their project, they completed a self-report questionnaire that assessed their perceptions of the predictor, mediator, and criterion variables. Such correlational research is particularly vulnerable to method biases and is not very informative.

Experimental Studies. It is often assumed that common method variance is less of a concern in experimental studies because one or more of the focal variables have predetermined levels that are manipulated. Therefore, not all study variables are self-reported from the same person at the same point in time. However, even experimental designs may be susceptible to the effects of CMV in some circumstances. For example, we found three experimental studies in which researchers manipulated an independent variable and/or a moderator variable, and obtained measures of other independent variables, potential mediators, and dependent variables using cross-sectional surveys at a single point in time (Chiu & Staples, 2013; Penarroja et al., 2015; Schiller et al., 2014). In such cases, CMV may potentially bias observed relationships between the self-reported variables.

With these aforementioned exceptions aside, however, the majority of the experimental studies make use of multisource data. For example, they frequently assess team performance or decision quality using objective measures (e.g., Andres, 2011; Bartelt et al., 2013) or judgment of external raters (e.g., Rentsch et al., 2014; Schreiber & Engelmann, 2010). Although personality and attitudinal variables (e.g., extraversion, trust, cohesion, and satisfaction) are strictly measured through self-assessments (as expected), other process variables have frequently been measured through other sources. For example, the quality of teams' mental models has been measured through cognitive mapping techniques (Xie et al., 2009) or independent raters (Andres, 2011). To assess the degree to which an individual emerged as a leader, studies have asked participants to rate each of their team members on distinct leadership dimensions, which helps avoid self-report bias (e.g., Balthazard et al., 2009; Charlier et al., 2016). Likewise, the quality of team communication or information exchange tend to be measured through content analysis of communication transcripts (Kerr & Murthy, 2009; O'Neill et al., 2016).

17.3 Discussion and Recommendations

The growing globalization of markets, along with technological advancements to support collaboration, have led to a steady increase in scholarly attention toward virtual team collaboration. We conducted a focused review of the empirical research on virtual teams published since 2008 by situating it within a multilevel IPO framework, examining how virtuality tends to be conceptualized, and evaluating the rigor of its research design (i.e., research settings, source of data, and treatment of time). In our discussion below, we summarize key findings and make recommendations for future research, focusing on three areas: (a) conceptualization of virtuality; (b) alignment with a multilevel IPO framework; and (c) rigor in research methods and design. All recommendations for future research are presented in Table 17.2.

17.3.1 Conceptualization of Virtuality

Almost two decades ago, Bell and Kozlowski (2002) critiqued the research on virtual teams for treating the concept categorically, typically contrasting FTF teams with virtual teams, and argued treating virtuality as continuum. Since then, the core dimensions of team virtuality have been further elaborated (i.e., Chudoba et al., 2005; Gibson & Gibbs, 2006; Kirkman & Mathieu, 2005; O'Leary & Cummings, 2007) to the point that we think that there is reasonable conceptual consensus on the core dimensions of team virtuality as a continuum. Yet, our review of the literature indicates that the concept of virtuality has tended to be neglected in empirical research. In fact, a large number of studies did not measure or manipulate any virtuality dimensions. Teams are simply selected for inclusion into the study if they meet the predefined selection criteria, but team virtuality facets are not measured or included in hypothesis testing. Thus, although these studies are situated in a virtual

Table 17.2 *Recommendations for future research on virtual teams*

Conceptualization of Virtuality

Recommendation 1: Future virtual teams research should measure or manipulate dimensions of virtuality and complicating factors, and treat them substantively.
Recommendation 2: Researchers should investigate multiple dimensions of virtuality, and should examine whether the various dimensions have different effects on team functioning.
Recommendation 3: To help generalize findings appropriately, researchers are advised to characterize all dimensions of virtuality and complicating factors of their study sample, even when they are not the primary research focus.
Recommendation 4: Future research should focus greater attention on the complicating factor of national/cultural diversity in virtual teams.

Alignment with Multilevel IPO Framework
Recommendation 5: Research on virtual teams should map more completely to a multilevel IPO framework.
Recommendation 6: Researchers should ensure that the level of theory, measurement, and analyses are aligned.

Research Methods and Design
Recommendation 7: Researchers should take advantage of recent developments in data collection methods that allow for objective data to be collected longitudinally and unobtrusively.
Recommendation 8: Future research can employ computational modeling to model virtual team phenomenon, and then use traditional lab or field research to validate simulation findings.

team context, they are not particularly informative about virtuality itself. We can only understand the effects of team virtuality facets by comparing teams that have varying levels of core virtuality dimensions. We strongly encourage future research to measure the communication/spatial distance clusters and complicating factors that we identified in the taxonomy, and include them as part of their theoretical rationale, hypotheses, and analyses.

Recommendation 1: *Future virtual teams research should measure or manipulate dimensions of virtuality and complicating factors, and treat them substantively.*

Additionally, although most scholars agree that virtuality is a multidimensional construct, it is seldom operationalized using multiple dimensions in the empirical research. Oftentimes, studies loosely define the term "virtual teams" that implies multiple dimensions, but only measure or manipulate a single dimension. For example, a large number of laboratory studies we examined focus primarily on the effects of using different communication media, whereas many field studies only examine geographic dispersion or only measure the degree of communication technology use. Some recent studies have begun to move away from these single indicators of virtuality and utilized multi-item measures that tap into multiple virtuality dimensions. For example, by conceptualizing virtuality as multidimensional and treating it as a continuum rather than at two extremes (FTF versus virtual), Mesmer-Magnus et al. (2011) clarified contradictory findings of past research regarding the impact of virtuality on team informational processes. We applaud these efforts and encourage future research to recognize and study multiple dimensions of virtuality, as this will enable more systematic investigations of the effects of various dimensions on team effectiveness. Additionally, more research should examine these virtuality dimensions separately, as they may have differential impacts on team functioning depending on contextual moderators.

Recommendation 2: *Researchers should investigate multiple dimensions of virtuality, and should examine whether the various dimensions have different effects on team functioning.*

At the same time, we recognize that focusing solely on the effects of one dimension of virtuality has its place in research, as it allows researchers to isolate specific features of virtuality to tease out their effects. Nevertheless, in such studies, it is important that researchers be explicit about which virtuality dimensions are examined and which are not. Our taxonomy of virtuality that we developed for this review can serve as a useful framework to help researchers identify what features of virtuality are the focus in their studies. Even when certain dimensions are not the primary research focus, they should still be assessed because it would provide an understanding of how the virtual teams in the sample are similar to or different from virtual teams in other studies. This will help researchers adequately compare empirical findings across studies, as well as help bound their own study findings and generalize appropriately.

Recommendation 3: *To help generalize findings appropriately, researchers are advised to characterize all dimensions of virtuality and complicating factors of their study sample, even when they are not the primary research focus.*

Previous reviews noted a trend of comparing FTF teams with CMC teams in order to examine how technologies with varying levels of media richness and/or synchronicity may influence team functioning. Our review of the recent literature shows that these aspects of virtuality are still predominantly studied, whereas other aspects of virtuality have been examined less frequently. Specifically, there has been limited empirical attention devoted to the effects of national or cultural diversity within virtual teams thus far. This is surprising, since scholars often conceptualize national or cultural diversity as a defining characteristic of virtuality (or at least coincides with it), particularly with the increasing proliferation of global virtual teams. While many of the studies we reviewed included teams that consist of members from different countries, it is very rare that researchers measure the degree of national or cultural diversity and include it as a key variable in the relationships investigated. Therefore, future research should add a focus toward measuring and testing the effects of the cultural aspect of virtuality.

Recommendation 4: *Future research should focus greater attention on the complicating factor of national/cultural diversity in virtual teams.*

17.3.2 Alignment with Multilevel IPO Framework

Thus far, there has been limited use of a theoretically comprehensive multilevel IPO framework. Researchers have predominantly focused their efforts at the team level of analysis without examining important individual-level processes in team contexts. We also found a small number of studies that are strictly at the individual level; although it is conceptually meaningful to consider individual processes and outcomes within a team context, such research does not contribute to our knowledge about team effectiveness. Therefore, we expect to see more studies take a multilevel perspective on virtual team phenomena in the future.

Examples are provided to illustrate how the multilevel nature of virtual team phenomena can be explored. We may be able to characterize teams or subunits based on the degree to which the team as a whole exhibits the different dimensions of virtuality. At the same time, it is possible to also assess each individual participant's perception, experience, or extent of each dimension, given individuals may vary within teams or subunits in the extent to which they perceive the element as a defining characteristic of the team. Individuals within the same team can experience virtuality differently based upon their perceptions of a specific dimension or interactions with other members. For instance, depending on the configural dispersion of a virtual team, some team members may be more isolated from the rest of the team than others. Thus, one can envision a multilevel model in which team-level virtuality dimensions are linked to between-team mediating processes and outcomes, while individuals' variable experiences of virtuality are linked to individual mediating processes and outcomes. This would provide a fuller examination of the effects of virtuality on team functioning across multiple levels.

As another example, Liao (2017) proposed a multilevel model of virtual team leadership that theoretically describes how some leadership functions may be applied consistently to the team as a whole, whereas other functions may be individually tailored to specific team members. Leader behaviors directed at the entire team may help shape team processes that are particularly important to virtual team effectiveness (e.g., shared mental models, trust, and virtual conflict). On the other hand, leader behaviors directed at individual team members may be critical for individual processes (e.g., cognitive, affective, and motivational states) that contribute to individual effectiveness in a virtual context. Liao (2007) also explicated the potential cross-level impact of team processes on individual processes. By drawing on this conceptualization, future research can examine leader collective processes and leader individuation processes within the team, as well as the interplay between person and team.

Recommendation 5: *Research on virtual teams should map more completely to a multilevel IPO framework.*

Additionally, we noted early in our review that a number of the studies suffer from a misalignment in the level of theory, measurement, and analysis. For example, some of these studies conceptualized the phenomena examined at the team level, but then collected data for all study variables through individual perceptions of team constructs from only one respondent per team. Likewise, some studies collected data from multiple team members, but they did not aggregate the measures to the team level or examine the interplay across levels; instead, they simply analyzed the data at the individual level, and then went on to generalize the results to the team level. Such generalizations to the team level are invalid. It is important that constructs, data, and analyses are aligned with the level to which conclusions are to be drawn. We offer three general recommendations to address this issue. These recommendations are more general in nature and not specific to the virtual teams literature per se, but we believe they are important in enhancing the quality of virtual teams research and, indeed, all team research. First, all future research should clearly specify the level(s) of analysis of all study constructs and their expected relationships. Second, researchers should ensure that the constructs are measured at, or aggregated appropriately to, the same level of analysis represented in the theory and hypotheses. Lastly, researchers should employ the appropriate analytical methods that allow the relationships specified by the theory and hypotheses to be tested.

Recommendation 6: *Researchers should ensure that the level of theory, measurement, and analyses are aligned.*

17.3.3 Research Methods and Design

Our review found that almost all of the field studies were cross-sectional, and most of them rely exclusively on self-reported data. Such research is methodologically weak. Clearly, more field studies should employ data collection methods that provide more objective data to supplement perceptual measures, and do so for longer periods of time. This is a recommendation that applies to team research in general. One promising new method is the use of sociometric badges or team interaction sensors, which are small sensor devices that can measure team interaction networks (Pentland, 2010) and also capture physiological reactions of participants wearing them (Kozlowski & Chao, 2018). The badges can automatically record who has FTF interactions with whom, which can be used to construct and track FTF social networks and reactions over extensive periods of time. This data can then be combined with social network data from email communications (or other collaborative tools); thus, researchers would have continuous data that provides a dynamic view of not only FTF social network ties, but also links between team members that are primarily through virtual tools. As another example, researchers can analyze the content of a team's communication records. Sources such as email texts and conversation transcripts can be coded to identify knowledge-sharing behaviors, psychological states, as well as team member relationships. These measures will take time to develop and validate, but they have the potential to provide rich longitudinal data of individual and group processes that are collected in an unobtrusive manner.

Recommendation 7: *Researchers should take advantage of recent developments in data collection methods that allow for objective data to be collected longitudinally and unobtrusively.*

Finally, virtual team phenomena may be researched using computational models (CM) and agent-based simulation (ABS). A CM is a precise, theoretically based model that mathematically or logically describes the core process mechanisms that drive group dynamics. These mechanisms can then be instantiated in an ABS, which allows computer-based agents to emulate how micro-level interactions yield macro-level outcomes over time (Kozlowski et al., 2013). Researchers can simulate different degrees of virtuality, different types of teams, and different environmental contexts in order to observe how they influence the interaction processes of team members and the emergence of higher-level, collective phenomena (e.g., cohesion, performance). Virtual experiments can be conducted using simulated teams in order to fully explore a theoretical space and identify process dynamics of interest. Traditional lab or field research using human teams can then be conducted to verify interesting findings derived from the ABS (Grand et al., 2016; Kozlowski et al., 2013).

Recommendation 8: *Future research can employ computational modeling to model virtual team phenomenon, and then use traditional lab or field research to validate simulation findings.*

17.4 Conclusion

We have reviewed the recent empirical literature on virtual teams by evaluating how well it maps to all the key components of a multilevel IPO model, the extent to which it encompasses all the key dimensions of virtuality, and how rigorous the research designs and methodologies are. Although considerable progress has been made in our understanding of virtual team functioning, we highlighted a number of substantive and methodological issues in the current literature. In particular, we believe that more can be learned by (a) being more comprehensive and systematic in the conceptualization and operationalization of virtuality dimensions; (b) mapping more completely to a multilevel IPO model; and (c) employing innovative research methodologies. Virtual teams are here to stay. They are growing in number and importance. Even teams that are primarily FTF are increasingly interacting virtually to some extent. It is important that we extend foundational knowledge from the science of team effectiveness to virtual teams. To do so well, virtual team research needs to advance conceptually, methodologically, and rigorously.

17.5 Acknowledgments

We gratefully acknowledge the US Army Research Institute for the Behavioral and Social Sciences (ARI; W911NF-14–1-0026, S.W.J. Kozlowski & G.T. Chao, Principal Investigators), the National Aeronautics and Space Administration (NASA; NNX13AM77G and NNX16AR52G, S.W.J. Kozlowski, Principal Investigator), and the National Science Foundation (NSF, 1533499, S.W.J. Kozlowski & G.T. Chao, Principal Investigators) for support that in part contributed to the composition of this article. Any opinions, findings, conclusions, and recommendations expressed are those of the authors and do not necessarily reflect the views of ARI, NASA, or NSF.

References

Altschuller, S. & Benbunan-Fich, R. (2013). The pursuit of trust in ad-hoc virtual teams: How much electronic portrayal is too much? *European Journal of Information Systems*, *22*(3),619–636.

Andres, H. P. (2011). Shared mental model development during technology-mediated collaboration. *International Journal of e-Collaboration*, *7*(3), 14–30.

Andressen, P., Konradt, U., & Neck, C. P. (2012). The relation between self-leadership and transformational leadership: Competing models and the moderating role of virtuality. *Journal of Leadership and Organizational Studies, 19*(1), 68–82.

Arling, P. A. and Subramani, M. (2011). The effect of virtuality on individual network centrality and performance in on-going, distributed teams. *International Journal of Internet and Enterprise Management, 7*(4), 325–348.

Balthazard, P. A., Waldman, D. A., & Warren, J. E. (2009). Predictors of the emergence of transformational leadership in virtual decision teams. *Leadership Quarterly, 20* (5), 651–663.

Bartelt, V., Dennis, A.R., Yuan, L., and Barlow, J.B. (2013). Individual priming in virtual team decision-making. *Group Decision and Negotiation, 22*(5), 873-896

Bazarova, N. N. & Walther, J. B. (2009). Attributions in virtual groups: Distances and behavioral variations in computer-mediated discussions. *Small Group Research, 40*(2), 138–162.

Bazarova, N. N., Walther, J. B., & McLeod, P. L. (2012). Minority influence in computer-mediated groups: A comparison of four theories of minority influence. *Communication Research, 39*(3), 295–316.

Bell, B. S. & Kozlowski, S. W. J. (2002). A typology of virtual teams. *Group & Organization Management, 27*(1), 14–49.

Belogolovsky, E., Bamberger, P., Alterman, V., & Wagner, D. T. (2016). Looking for assistance in the dark: Pay secrecy, expertise attribution and efficacious help seeking among members of newly formed virtual work groups. *Journal of Business and Psychology, 31*, 459–477.

Bradley B. H., Bauer J. E., Banford C. G., & Postlethwaite B. E. (2013). Team players and collective performance: How agreeableness affects team performance over time. *Small Group Research, 44*(6), 680–711.

Brahm, T. & Kunze, F. (2012). The role of trust climate in virtual teams. *Journal of Managerial Psychology, 27*(6), 595–614.

Branson, L., Claussen, T., & Sung, C. H. (2008). Group style differences between virtual and FTF teams. *American Journal of Business, 23*(1), 65–70.

Carlson J. R., Carlson D. S., Hunter E. M., Vaughn R. L., & George J. F. (2013). Virtual team effectiveness: Investigating the moderating role experience with computer-mediated communication on the impact of team cohesion and openness. *Journal of Organizational and End User Computing, 25*(2), 1–18.

Charlier, S. D., Stewart, G. L., Greco, L. M., & Reeves, C. J. (2016). Emergent leadership in virtual teams: A multilevel investigation of individual communication and team dispersion antecedents. *Leadership Quarterly, 27*(5), 745–764.

Cheshin, A., Bos, D. N., Kim, Y., Ning, N., & Olson, S. J. (2013). Emergence of differing electronic communication norms within partially distributed teams. *Journal of Personnel Psychology, 12*(1), 7–21.

Cheshin, A., Rafaeli, A., & Bos, D. N. (2011). Anger and happiness in virtual teams: Emotional influences of text and behavior on others' affect in the absence of non-verbal cues. *Organizational Behavior and Human Decision Processes, 116* (1), 2–16.

Chiu, Y. & Staples, D.S. (2013). Reducing faultlines in geographically-dispersed teams: Self-disclosure and task elaboration, *Small Group Research: An International Journal of Theory, Investigation, and Application, 44*(5), 498–531.

Chudoba, K. M., Wynn, E., Lu, M., & Watson-Manheim, M. B. (2005). How virtual are we? Measuring virtuality and understanding its impact in a global organization. *Information Systems Journal, 15*(4), 279–306.

Cogliser, C. C., Gardner, W., Trank, C. Q., Gavin, M., Halbesleben, J., & Seers, A. (2013). Not all group exchange structures are created equal: Effects of forms and levels of exchange on work outcomes in virtual teams. *Journal of Leadership & Organizational Studies, 20*(2), 242–251.

Colazo, J. A. & Fang, Y. (2010). Following the sun: temporal dispersion and performance in open source software project teams. Journal of the Association for Information Systems, *11*(11), 684–707.

Connelly, C. & Turel, O. (2016). Effects of team emotional authenticity on virtual team performance. *Frontiers in Psychology, 7*(7), 1–13.

Crisp, C. B. & Jarvenpaa, S. L. (2013). Swift trust in global virtual teams: Trusting beliefs and normative actions. *Journal of Personnel Psychology, 12*(1), 45–56.

Cummings, J. N. & Haas, M. R. (2012). So many teams, so little time: Time allocation matters in geographically dispersed teams. *Journal of Organizational Behavior, 33*(3), 316–341.

de Jong, R., Schalk, R., & Curseu, P. L. (2008). Virtual communicating, conflicts and performance in teams. *Team Performance Management. An International Journal, 14*, 364–380.

Ellwart T., Happ C., Gurtner A., & Rack O. (2015). Managing information overload in virtual teams: Effects of a structured online team adaptation on cognition and performance. *European Journal of Work and Organizational Psychology, 24*(5), 812–826.

Erez M., Lisak A., Harush R., Glikson E., Nouri R., & Shokef E. (2013). Going global: Developing management students' cultural intelligence and global identity in culturally diverse virtual teams. *Academy of Management Learning & Education, 12*(3), 330–355.

Espevik, R., Johnsen, B. H., & Eid, J. (2011). Outcomes of shared mental models of team members in cross training and high-intensity simulations. *Journal of Cognitive Engineering and Decision Making, 5*(4), 352–377.

Eubanks D., Palanski M., Olabisi J., Joinson A., & Dove J. (2016). Team dynamics in virtual, partially distributed teams: Optimal role fulfillment. *Computers in Human Behavior, 61*, 556–568

Fan, K.T., Chen, Y.H., Wang, C.W., & Chen, M. (2014). E-leadership effectiveness in virtual teams: Motivating language perspective, *Industrial Management & Data Systems, 114*(3), 421–437.

Fuller, C., Marett, K., & Twitchell, D. (2012). An examination of deception in virtual teams: Effects of deception on task performance, mutuality, and trust. *IEEE Transactions on Professional Communication, 55*(1), 20–35.

Fuller, R. M., Vician, C. M., & Brown, S. A. (2016). Longitudinal Effects of Computer-Mediated Communication Anxiety on Interaction in Virtual Teams. *IEEE Transactions on Professional Communication, 59*(3), 166–185.

Gajendran, R. & Joshi, A. (2012). Innovation in Globally Distributed Teams: The Role of LMX, Communication Frequency, and Member Influence on Team Decisions. *Journal of Applied Psychology, 97*(6), 1252–1261

Ganesh, M. P. & Gupta, M. (2010). Impact of virtualness and task interdependence on extra-role performance in software development teams. *Team Performance Management, 16*(3/4), 169–186.

Gibson, C. B. & Gibbs, J. L. (2006). Unpacking the concept of virtuality: The effects of geographic dispersion, electronic dependence, dynamic structure, and national diversity on team innovation. *Administrative Science Quarterly*, *51*(3), 451–495.

Gilson, L. L., Maynard, M. T., Young, N. C. J., Vartiainen, M., & Hakonen, M. (2015). Virtual teams research: 10 years, 10 themes, and 10 opportunities. *Journal of Management*, *41*(5), 1313–1337.

Giordano, G. & George, J. (2013). The effects of task complexity and group member experience on computer-mediated groups facing deception. *IEEE Transactions on Professional Communication*, *56*(3), 210–225.

González-Navarro, P., Orengo, V., Zornoza, A., Ripoll, P., & Peiró, J. M. (2010). Group interaction styles in a virtual context: The effects on group outcomes. *Computers in Human Behavior*, *26*(6), 1472–1480.

Grand, J. A., Braun, M. T., Kuljanin, G., Kozlowski, S. W. J., & Chao, G. T. (2016). The dynamics of team cognition: A process-oriented theory of knowledge emergence in teams [Monograph]. *Journal of Applied Psychology*, *101*, 1353–1385.

Haines, R. (2014). Group development in virtual teams: An experimental reexamination, *Computers in Human Behavior*, *39*, 213–222.

Han, H. J., Hiltz, S. R., Fjermestad, J. & Wang, Y. (2011). Does medium matter? A comparison of initial meeting modes for virtual teams. *IEEE Transactions on Professional Communication*, *54*(4),376–391.

Hertel, G. S., Geister, S., & Konradt, U. (2005). Managing virtual teams: A review of current empirical research. *Human Resource Management Review*, *15*(1), 69–95.

Hill, N. S. & Bartol, K. M. (2016). Empowering leadership and effective collaboration in geographically dispersed teams. *Personnel Psychology*, *69*(1), 159–198.

Hoch, J. E. & Kozlowski, S. W. J. (2014). Leading virtual teams: Hierarchical leadership, structural supports, and shared team leadership. *Journal of Applied Psychology*, *99* (3), 390–403.

Huang R., Kahai S., & Jestice R. (2010). The contingent effects of leadership on team collaboration in virtual teams. *Computers in Human Behavior*, *26*(5), 1098–1110

Ilgen, D. R., Hollenbeck, J. R., Johnson, M., & Jundt, D. (2005). Teams in organizations: From input-process-output models to IMOI models. *Annual Review of Psychology*, *56*, 517–543.

Joshi, A., Lazarova, M. B., & Liao, H. (2009). Getting everyone on board: The role of inspirational leadership in geographically dispersed teams. Organization Science, *20*(1), 240–252.

Kahai, S., Huang, R., & Jestice, R. (2012). Interaction effect of leadership and communication media on feedback positivity in virtual teams. *Group & Organization Management*, *37*(6), 716–751.

Kerr, D.S. & Murthy, U.S. (2009). Beyond brainstorming: The effectiveness of group support systems for convergence and negotiation tasks, *International Journal of Accounting Information Systems*, *10*(4), 245–262.

Kirkman, B. L. & Mathieu, J. E. (2005). The dimensions and antecedents of team virtuality. *Journal of Management*, *31*(5), 700–718.

Kirkman, B. L., Gibson, C. B., & Kim, K. (2012). Across borders and technologies: Advancements in virtual teams research. In S. W. J. Kozlowski (Ed.), *Oxford handbook of organizational psychology* (vol. 2, pp. 789–858). New York, NY: Oxford University Press.

Konradt, U., Schippers, M., Garbers, Y., & Steenfatt, C. (2015). Effects of guided reflexivity and team feedback on team performance improvement: The role of team regulatory processes and cognitive emergent states. *European Journal of Work and Organizational Psychology, 24*(5), 777–795.

Kozlowski, S. W. J. & Bell, B. S. (2003). Work groups and teams in organizations. In W. C. Borman, D. R. Ilgen, & R. J. Klimoski (Eds.), *Handbook of psychology: Industrial and organizational psychology* (vol. *12*, pp. 333–375). London: Wiley.

Kozlowski, S. W. J., & Chao, G. T. (2018). Unpacking team process dynamics and emergent phenomena: Challenges, conceptual advances, and innovative methods. American Psychologist, *73*(4), 576–592.

Kozlowski S.W.J, Chao, G.T, Grand J.A, Braun, M.T, & Kuljanin, G. (2013). Advancing multilevel research design: Capturing the dynamics of emergence. *Organizational Research Methods, 16*(4), 581–615.

Kozlowski, S. W. J. & Ilgen, D. R. (2006). Enhancing the effectiveness of work groups and teams [Monograph]. *Psychological Science in the Public Interest, 7*(3), 77–124.

Kozlowski, S. W. J. & Klein, K. J. (2000). A multilevel approach to theory and research in organizations: Contextual, temporal, and emergent processes. In K. J. Klein & S. J. Kozlowski (Eds.), *Multilevel theory, research, and methods in organizations: Foundations, extensions, and new directions* (pp. 3–90). San Francisco, CA: Jossey-Bass.

Kuo, E. W. & Thompson, L. F. (2014). The influence of disposition and social ties on trust in new virtual teammates. *Computers in Human Behavior, 37*, 41–48.

Kuo, F. & Yu, C. (2009). An exploratory study of trust dynamics in work-oriented virtual teams. *Journal of Computer-Mediated Communication, 14*(4), 823–854.

Lea, M. & Spears, R. (1992). Paralanguage and social perception in computer-mediated communication. *Journal of Organizational Computing, 2*, 321–342.

Liao, C. (2017). Leadership in virtual teams: A multilevel perspective. *Human Resource Management Review, 27*(4), 648–659.

Lin, C.P., He, H., Baruch, Y., & Ashforth, B. E. (2017). The effect of team affective tone on team performance: The roles of team identification and team cooperation. Human Resource Management.

Lira, E., Ripoll, P., Peiró, J.M. & Zornoza, A. (2008). The role of information and communication technologies on the relationship between group effectiveness and group potency. A longitudinal study. *Small Group Research, 39*(6), 728–745.

Lira, E. M., Ripoll, P., Peiró, J. M., & Orengo, V. (2008). How do different types of intragroup conflict affect group potency in virtual compared with face-to-face teams? A longitudinal study. *Behaviour & Information Technology, 27*(2), 107–114.

Liu, X., Magjuka R., & Lee, S. (2008). An examination of the relationship among structure, trust, and conflict management styles in virtual teams. *Performance Improvement Quarter, 21*(1),77–93.

MacDonnell R. M., O'Neill T., Kline T., & Hambley L. (2009). Bringing group-level personality to the electronic realm: A comparison of face-to-face and virtual contexts. *The Psychologist-Manager Journal, 12*(1), 1–24

Magni, M., Maruping, L. M., Hoegl, M., & Proserpio, L. (2013). Managing the unexpected across space: Improvisation, dispersion and performance in NPD teams. *Journal of Product Innovation Management, 30*(5), 1009–1026.

Malhotra, A. & Majchrzak, A. (2014). Enhancing performance of geographically distributed teams through targeted use of information and communication technologies. *Human Relations*, *67*(4), 389–411.

Marett, K. & George, J.F. (2013). Barriers to deceiving other group members in virtual settings. *Group Decision and Negotiation*, *22*(1), 89–115.

Marks, M. A., Mathieu, J. E., & Zaccaro, S. J. (2001). A temporally based framework and taxonomy of team processes. Academy of Management Review, *26*(3), 356–376.

Martínez-Moreno, E., Zornoza, A., González-Navarro, P., & Thompson, L. F. (2012). Investigating face-to-face and virtual teamwork over time: When does early task conflict trigger relationship conflict? *Group Dynamics: Theory Research and Practice*, *16*(3), 159–171.

Martínez-Moreno, E., Zornoza, A., Orengo, V., & Thompson, L. F. (2015). The effects of team self-guided training on conflict management in virtual teams. *Group Decision and Negotiation*, *2*(5)*4*, 905–923.

Martins, L. L., Gilson, L. L., & Maynard, M. T. (2004). Virtual teams: What do we know and where do we go from here? *Journal of Management*, *30*(6), 805–835.

Maynard, M. T., Mathieu, J. E., Rapp, T. L., & Gilson, L. L. (2012). Something(s) old and something(s) new: Modeling drivers of global virtual team effectiveness. *Journal of Organizational Behavior*, *33*(3): 342–365.

McGrath, J. E. (1964). *Social psychology: A brief introduction*. New York, NY: Holt, Rinehart & Winston

McLeod, P. L. (2011). Effects of anonymity and social comparison of rewards on computer-mediated group brainstorming. *Small Group Research*, *42*(4), 475–503.

McLeod, P. L. (2013). Distributed people and distributed information: Vigilant decision-making in virtual teams. *Small Group Research*, *44*(6), 627–657.

Medina, M.N. & Srivastava, S. (2016). The role of extraversion and communication methods on an individual's satisfaction with the team. *Journal of Organizational Psychology*, *16*(1).

Mesmer-Magnus, J. R., DeChurch, L. A., Jimenez-Rodriguez, M., Wildman, J., & Shuffler, M. (2011). A meta-analytic investigation of virtuality and information sharing in teams. *Organizational Behavior and Human Decision Processes*, *115* (2), 214–225.

Minton-Eversole, T. (2012). *Virtual teams used most by global organizations, survey says*. Alexandria, VA: Society for Human Resource Management.

Monzani, L., Ripoll, P., Peiro, J.M., & Van Dick, R. (2014). Loafing in the digital age: The role of computer mediated communication in the relation between perceived loafing and group affective outcomes. *Computers in Human Behavior*, *33*, *279–285*.

Montoya, M.M., Massey, A.P., & Lockwood, N.S. (2011). 3D collaborative virtual environments: Exploring the link between collaborative behaviors and team performance. *Decision Sciences*, *42*(2), 451–476.

Muethel, M., Gehrlein, S., & Hoegl, M. (2012). Socio-demographic factors and shared leadership behaviors in dispersed teams: Implications for human resource management. *Human Resource Management*, *51*(4), 525–548.

Nowak, K., Watt, J. H., & Walther, J. B. (2009). Computer mediated teamwork and the efficiency framework: Exploring the influence of synchrony and cues on media satisfaction and outcome success. *Computers in Human Behavior*, *25*(5), 1108–1119.

O'Leary, M. B. & Cummings, J. N. (2007). The spatial, temporal, and configurational characteristics of geographic dispersion. *MIS Quarterly, 31*(3), 433–452.

O'Leary, M. B. & Mortensen, M. (2010). Go con(figure): Subgroups, imbalance, and isolates in geographically dispersed teams. *Organization Science, 21*(1), 115–131.

O'Neill, T. A., Hancock, S. E., Zivkov, K., Larson, N. L., and Law, S. J. (2016). Team decision making in virtual and face-to-face environments. *Group Decision and Negotiation, 25*(5), 995–1020.

Ortega, A., Sánchez-Manzanares, M., Gil, F., & Rico, R. (2010) Team learning and effectiveness in virtual project teams: The role of beliefs about interpersonal context. *The Spanish Journal of Psychology, 13*(1), 266–275.

Paul, R., Drake, J. R., & Liang, H. (2016). Global virtual team performance: The effect of coordination effectiveness, trust, and team cohesion. *IEEE Transaction on Professional Communication, 59*(3), 186–202.

Pazos, P. & Beruvides, M. G. (2011). Performance patterns in face-to-face and computer-supported teams. *Team Performance Management, 17*(1/2), 83–101.

Pazos, P. (2012). Conflict management and effectiveness in virtual teams. *Team Performance Management, 18*(7/8), 401–417.

Peñarroja, V., Orengo V., Zornoza A., & Hernandez A. (2013). The effects of virtuality level on task-related collaborative behaviors: The mediating role of team trust. *Computers in Human Behavior, 29*, 967–974.

Peñarroja, V., Orengo, V., Zornoza, A., Sánchez, J., & Ripoll, P. (2015). How team feedback and team trust influence information processing and learning in virtual teams: A moderated mediation model. Computers In Human Behavior, *48*, 489–516.

Pentland, A. S. (2010). To signal is human. Real-time data mining unmasks the power of imitation, kith and charisma in our face-to-face social networks. *American Scientist, 98*(3), 204–211.

Perry, J. S., Lorinkova, N. M., Hunter, E. M., Hubbard, A., & McMahon, J. T. (2013). When does virtuality really "work"? Examining the role of work-family and virtuality in social loafing. *Journal of Management, 2*, 345–357.

Pinjani, P. & Palvia, P. (2013). Trust and knowledge sharing in diverse global virtual teams. *Information & Management, 50*, 144–153.

Purvanova, K.R. & Bono, E.J. (2009). Transformational leadership in context: Face-to-face and virtual teams. *The Leadership Quarterly, 20*, 343–57.

Purvanova, R. (2013). The role of feeling known for team member outcomes in project teams. *Small Group Research, 44*(3), 298–331.

Rack, O., Ellwart, T., Hertel, G. & Konradt, U. (2011) Team based rewards in computer-mediated groups. *Journal of Managerial Psychology, 26*, 419–438.

Rentsch, J. R., Delise, L. A., Mello, A. L., & Staniewicz, M. J. (2014). The integrative team knowledge building training strategy in distributed problem-solving teams. *Small Group Research, 45*(5), 568–591.

Rico, R., Bachrach, D. G., Sánchez-Manzanares, M., Collins, & B. J. (2011). The interactive effects of person-focused citizenship behaviour, task interdependence, and virtuality on team performance. *European Journal of Work and Organizational Psychology, 20*(5), 700–726.

Robert, L. P. (2016). Healthy divide or detrimental division? Subgroups in virtual teams. *The Journal of Computer Information Systems, 56*(3), 253–260.

Robert, L. P., Denis, A. R., & Hung, Y. T. C. (2009). Individual swift trust and knowledge-based trust in face-to-face and virtual team members. *Journal of Management Information Systems, 26*(2), 241–279.

Romeike, P., Nienaber, A.-M, & Schewe, G. (2016). How differences in perceptions of own and team performance impact trust and job satisfaction in virtual teams. *Human Performance, 29*(4), 291–309.

Ruggieri, S. (2009). Leadership in virtual teams: A comparison of transformational and transactional leaders. *Social Behavior and Personality, 37*, 1017–1022

Sarker, S., Ahuja, M., Sarker, S., & Kirkeby, S. (2011). The role of communication and trust in global virtual teams: A social network perspective. *Journal of Management Information Systems, 28*(1), 273–309.

Sarker S., Sarker S., & Schneider C. (2009). Seeing remote team members as leaders: A study of US–Scandinavian teams. *IEEE Transactions on Professional Communication, 52*(0), 75–94.

Sarker, S., Kirkeby, S., Sarker, S., & Chakraborty, S. (2011) Road to "stardom" in globally distributed teams: An examination of a knowledge-centered perspective using social network analysis, *Decision Sciences Journal, 42*(2), 339–370

Schiller, S., Mennecke, B., Nah, F., & Luse, A. (2014). Institutional boundaries and trust of virtual teams in collaborative design in a virtual environment, *Computers in Human Behavior, 35*, 565–577.

Schreiber, M. & Engelmann, T. (2010). Knowledge and information awareness for initiating transactive memory system processes of computer-supported collaborating ad hoc groups. *Computers in Human Behavior, 26*(6), 1701–1709.

Schweitzer, L. & Duxbury, L. (2010). Conceptualizing and measuring the virtuality of teams. *Information Systems Journal, 20*(3), 267–295.

Sohrabi, B., Gholipour, A., & Amiri, B. (2011). The influence of information technology on organizational behavior: Study of identity challenges in virtual teams. *International Journal of e-Collaboration, 7*(2), 19–34.

Stark, E., Bierly, P., & Harper, S.R. (2014). The interactive influences of conflict, task interdependence and cooperation on perceptions of virtualness in co-located teams. *Team Performance Management: An International Journal, 20*(5/6), 221–241.

Stone, N. J. & Posey, M. (2008). Understanding Coordination in Computer-Mediated versus Face-to-Face Groups. *Computers in Human Behavior, 24*(3), 827–851.

Straus, S. G. & McGrath, J. E. (1994). Does the medium matter: The interaction of task and technology on group performance and member reactions. *Journal of Applied Psychology, 79*(1), 87–97

Suh, A. & Shin, K. (2010). Exploring the effects of online social ties on knowledge sharing: A comparative analysis of collocated vs dispersed teams. *Journal of Information Science, 36* (4), 443–463

Suh, A., Shin, K.-S., Ahuja, M., & Kim, M. S. (2011). The influence of virtuality on social networks within and across work groups: A multilevel approach. *Journal of Management Information Systems, 28*(1), 351–386.

Swaab, R. I., Phillips, K. W., & Schaerer, M. (2016). Secret conversation opportunities facilitate minority influence in virtual groups: The influence on majority power, information processing, and decision quality. *Organizational Behavior and Human Decision Processes, 133*, 17–32.

Thomas, D. & Bostrom, R. (2008). Building trust and cooperation through technology adaptation in virtual teams: Empirical field evidence, *Information Systems Management*, *25*(1), 45–56.

Tran, T. B., Oh, C. H., & Choi, S. B. (2016). Effects of learning orientation and global mindset on virtual team members' willingness to cooperate in: The mediating role of self-efficacy. *Journal of Management & Organization*, *22*(3), 311-327.

Turel, O. & Connelly, C. (2012). Team spirit: The influence of psychological collectivism on the usage of e-collaboration tools. *Group Decision and Negotiation*, *21*(5), 703–725

Turel O. & Zhang Y. (2010). Does virtual team composition matter? Trait and problem-solving configuration effects on team performance. *Behaviour & Information Technology*, *29*(4), 363–375.

Turel, O. & Zhang, Y. J. (2011). Should I e-collaborate with this group? A multilevel model of usage intentions. *Information & Management*, *48*, 62–68.

Tzabbar, D. & Vestal, A., 2015. Bridging the social chasm in geographically distributed R&D teams: The moderating effects of relational strength and status asymmetry on the novelty of team innovation. *Organization Science*, *26*(3), 811–829.

Van der Kleij, R., de Jong, A., te Brake, G., & de Greef, T. (2009). Network-aware support for mobile distributed teams. *Computers in Human Behavior*, *25*(4), 940–948.

Van der Kleij, R., Lijkwan, J. T. E., Rasker, P. C., & De Dreu, C. K. W. (2009). Effects of time pressure and communication environment on team processes and outcomes in dyadic planning. *International Journal of Human-Computer Studies*, *67*(5), 411–423.

van der Kleij, R., Schraagen, J. M., Werkhoven, P., & De Dreu, C. K. W. (2009). How conversations change over time in face-to-face and video-mediated communication. *Small Group Research*, *40*(4), 355–381.

Van de Ven, A. H., Delbecq, A. L., & Koenig, R. (1976). Determinants of coordination modes within organizations. *American Sociological Review*, *41*, 322–328.

Walther, J. B. & Bazarova, N. N. (2008). Validation and application of electronic propinquity theory to computer-mediated communication in groups. *Communication Research*, *35*(5), 622–645.

Wang, C., Hsieh, C., Fan, K., Menefee, M. L. (2009). Impact of motivating language on team creative performance. Journal of Computer Information Systems, *50*(1), 133–140.

Weber, M. & Kim, H. (2015). Virtuality, technology use, and engagement within organizations. *Journal of Applied Communication Research*, *43*(4), 385–407.

Williams, E. A. & Castro, S. L. (2010) The effects of teamwork on individual learning and perceptions of team performance: A comparison of face-to-face and online project settings. *Team Performance Management: An International Journal*, *16*(3/4), 124–147.

Xie, X., Zhu, Y. & Wang, Z. (2009). Effect of the amount of task-relevant information on shared mental models in compute-mediated and face-to-face teams: Is more always better? *Social Behavior & Personality: An International Journal*, *37*(9), 1153–1160.

Xue, Y., Liang, H., Hauser, R., & O'Hara, M. (2012). An empirical study of knowledge sharing intention within virtual teams. *International Journal of Knowledge Management*, *8*(3), 47–61.

Yilmaz, G. & Peña, J. (2014). The influence of social categories and interpersonal behaviors on future intentions and attitudes to form subgroups in virtual teams. *Communication Research*, *41*(3), 333–352.

Zheng, S., Zeng, X., & Zhang, C. (2016). The effects of role variety and ability disparity on virtual group performance. *Journal of Business Research*, *69*(9), 3468–3477.

Zornoza, A., Orengo, V., & Penarroja, V. (2009). Relational capital in virtual teams: The role played by trust. *Social Science Information*, *48*(2), 257–81.

18 Social Media and Teamwork

Formation, Process, and Outcomes

Ioana C. Cristea, Paul M. Leonardi, and Emmanuelle Vaast

Teams play an ever-increasing role in today's organizations. Traditionally, teams have been viewed as complex, dynamic, adaptive entities (Ilgen, 1999) that are "composed of two or more individuals who (a) exist to perform organizationally relevant tasks, (b) share one or more common goals, (c) interact socially, (d) exhibit task interdependencies (i.e., work flow, goals, outcomes), (e) maintain and manage boundaries, and (f) are embedded in an organizational context that sets boundaries, constrains the team, and influences exchanges with other units in the broader entity" (Kozlowski & Bell, 2003, p. 334). In fact, scholars have begun to argue that teams are not simply entities that exist inside organizations, but rather that organizations themselves are best viewed as collections of teams (Zaccaro, Marks, & DeChurch, 2012). As a senior vice president at a large healthcare manufacturing company told us recently, "Everywhere you look you see teams. It's so easy to form teams these days that we do it all the time. I bet the average employee is on four or five teams. It seems like my job is really about organizing all the teams." The increased prevalence of teaming within organizations (Edmondson, 2012) has emerged on the back of an increasingly capable but easy-to-use technological infrastructure within organizations. In the past three decades, email, FTP sites, and teleconferencing technologies enabled the proliferation of virtual teams – i.e. teams distributed in time and space – within organizations (Griffith, Sawyer, & Neale, 2003; Kozlowski & Bell, 2003; Lipnack & Stamps, 1999; Mankin, Cohen, & Bikson, 1996; Miles & Hollenbeck, 2013).

Today, a host of enterprise social media technologies like Jive, Yammer, and Chatter enable organizational members to connect with each other in a digital platform and work together in real time with all of their activities and interactions recorded. Lightweight social media technologies like Slack or Microsoft Teams use the Cloud to enable employees to assemble, share documents, track conversations, and manage all of their interactions in real time on a consistent platform. Even technologies like Jira or Asana that are routinely utilized for project management have incorporated social media capabilities that allow teams to conduct their work and communication in a single, easy-to-access platform. Teams today really are socio-technical systems in every sense of the term (Fiore & Wiltshire, 2016).

Although research examining the interplay of technology and teams flourished in the 1990s and early 2000s, such research has stagnated in recent years at the same time that these new social media capabilities have begun to enter organizations at a quickening pace forcing teams to adapt and change more frequently than ever before (Tannenbaum et al., 2012). As Treem and Leonardi (2012) argue, social media technologies, such as blogs, wikis, social networking sites, social tagging, and microblogging, warrant examination by organizational scholars interested in the role of technology in social dynamics, because these new technologies provide a number of affordances that were difficult to achieve with prior technologies: visibility, persistence, editability, and association. Their argument is that by integrating the features of several existing technologies into one social media platform that is accessible to all members of an organization, social media technologies have the potential provide capabilities for action that shape organizational action in profound ways. Leonardi, Huysman, and Steinfield (2013, p. 2) define social media used in organizations as technologies that enable workers to: (1) communicate messages with specific coworkers or broadcast messages to everyone in the organization; (2) explicitly indicate or implicitly reveal particular coworkers as communication partners; (3) post, edit, and sort text and files linked to themselves or others; and (4) view the messages, connections, text, and files communicated, posted, edited, and sorted by anyone else in the organization at any time of their choosing. Given the capabilities of these new technologies, it is not surprising that a small amount of research has begun to suggest that they may be useful for improving team effectiveness (Ellison, Gibbs, & Weber, 2015; Weber & Shi, 2016).

The argument linking social media to team effectiveness rests on the assumption that after nearly three quarters of a century of scientific inquiry into the conduct of teams, teamwork, and teaming, we know quite a lot about what leads people to form teams, how team processes play out, and what kinds of actions lead to effective team outputs (Cohen & Bailey, 1997). But despite this knowledge, many teams simply do not work well. One potential explanation as to this disconnect between scholarly insights and team performance is that many of the recommendations developed from rigorous studies of teams are simply hard to execute. As one small example, take diversity. Ample evidence exists to suggest that for teams looking to innovate, develop new ideas, or improve product development, more functional and cognitive diversity is better (Cummings, 2004). But with many employees in an organization unaware of what but a small number of their coworkers know (Ren & Argote, 2011) along with strong tendencies toward homophily in team selection, many organizations fail to follow the scientific advice regarding diverse team membership.

However, because social media provide capabilities for action that other technologies before them have not, there is some optimism that social media may help teams to overcome some of those obstacles and follow scholarly advice. For example, as Leonardi (2015) has suggested, the fact that social media technologies enable broader visibility into what and whom others know across the organizations means that individuals looking to form teams may have a more accurate cognitive map of the organization and, consequently, be more able to choose from a diverse set of potential teammates than they would otherwise. Of course, these speculations are just that: speculation. Scholars and pundits alike have long forecasted that whatever the newest technology on the block is, it would have dramatic impacts on the way that teams form, work together, and execute on their plans.

With a healthy dose of skepticism about the role of social media in teams, but also with strong intrigue about the potential ways these new technologies might aid in the production and accomplishment of teams, we surveyed the literature on social media and teams. We quickly discovered that while there are many papers on the role of social media in people's personal lives and a sizeable number of papers on the role of social media in the process of organizing, there is very little research that has explored social media and teams.

Given the increasing empirical importance of the topic and the absence of theory about the role of social media and teams we decided to examine the existing literature that discusses the use of social media at work and cull from it insights that may apply to three main areas of interest to team scholars: team formation, team processes, and team outputs. After conducting this review, we turn our attention to discussing three other areas. First, we point scholars to areas in which increased testing and experimentation is necessary to determine and validate relationships between social media and teams that are inferred from the existing literature. Second, we use our review to raise several new areas of research for scholars of social media, scholars of teams, or scholars who are interested in both. We believe that the use of social media to create teams and to work through their processes provide exciting avenues for future research. Third, and finally, we explore new avenues for exploring the changing nature of teams, work, and teamwork in the era of social technologies in the workplace.

18.1 Team Formation

Organizational researchers have long been interested in how to design and develop high-performing teams (Hackman & Oldham, 1980; Ilgen et al., 2005), and with the rapid diffusion of social media in organizations, team researchers have recently called for a closer look at how technologies impact team design and composition (Mathieu et al., 2014; Tannenbaum et al., 2012). Depending on the need, teams can be designed to stay together for longer periods of time (most teams), or for shorter ones, i.e., flash teams (generally, task force or crews) (Arrow, McGrath, & Berdahl, 2000). Formation is not always permanent, and with the recent rise of social media capabilities, teams have experienced this new way of coming together for a short time in ways not possible before, e.g., by connecting and managing paid experts from a crowd to work together on new projects (Retelny et al., 2014). In what follows, we review the literature on the effects that social media in organizations have on team formation, specifically, on team structure, membership, and maintenance.

18.1.1 Structure

The structure of a team has been traditionally defined as a web of interconnected relationships reflecting the task distribution, responsibilities, interaction patterns, and authority within the team (Ilgen et al., 2005; Stewart & Barrick, 2000). The introduction of social media in organizations, with its unprecedented power to connect employees across different parts of the organization (Treem & Leonardi, 2012), allows for a more dynamic approach to the classic view on team structure (Leonardi & Vaast, 2017).

Through its unique capabilities (see definition, Treem & Leonardi, 2012; Leonardi et al., 2013) social media could increase visibility within teams, allowing them to be structured in a way that focuses on the unique and distinctive cognitive elements of each team member. Such a structure was not possible in the classical team designs, where, according to research on transactive memory systems (Wegner, 1986), team members were unaware of who knew what within the team (Ilgen et al., 2005). The distinctive characteristics of social media help alleviate this problem. In their conceptual paper, Fulk and Yuan (2013) speak to the possibilities of increasing transactive memory systems in teams. According to their research, it is possible to have people with very different backgrounds on a team, as social media technologies allow team members to bridge across those differences and learn who knows what and who knows whom (Leonardi, 2015). Whereas, before the rise of social media within organizations, team designers built high-performing teams by recruiting individuals with similar cognitive backgrounds (Mohammed & Dumville, 2001). Through its visibility and persistability features, social media technologies afford employees the opportunity to access their colleagues' personal pages, network of contacts, previously shared posts, or discussion boards they were part of. These features are important as they allow employees to learn what their colleagues know (Treem & Leonardi, 2012). By making it possible for team members with different cognitive elements to work together toward a shared goal in an effective way, social media allow them to discover their similarities and boost their collective knowledge.

Social media adoption could also disrupt traditional managerial roles, restructuring them to account for more flexibility and greater access to knowledge. For example, Ford and Mason (2013) explored the perceived tensions that arise for managers who try to keep their traditional role attributions tied to the organizational level and found that, due to social media's unique affordances, managers have access to a much wider pool of employees than ever before, surpassing traditional organizational boundaries. Ford and Mason (2013) also found that such an openness to employees and knowledge can be daunting for traditional managerial styles, but could work well for promoting a more flexible managerial role, and thus a team structure characterized by a greater level of sense-making and knowledge accessibility.

Increased access to knowledge contributes to more flexible managerial roles (Ford & Mason, 2013) and to employees' rapid expansion of their organizational network of contacts (Weber & Shi, 2016), potentially affecting traditional team relationships, as reported by Mark, Guy, Kremer-Davidson, and Jacovi (2014). The authors found that team members who possess smaller individual networks look down on their colleagues with larger individual networks. Such perspective shifting could potentially damage team relationships between contenders of large personal networks and team members with small networks, disrupting team structure.

18.1.2 Membership

If traditional team formation involved a rather stable team membership, with clear team boundaries (Tannenbaum et al., 2012), social media allow for a more dynamic approach to team composition models (Mark et al., 2014; Mathieu et al., 2014), leading researchers to conclude that "movement is the new normal" (Tannenbaum et al., 2012, p. 5).

Social media are a relatively unique case for an organizational technology because of employees' interaction with similar social media technologies through personal use prior to being introduced to them in the workplace (Treem & Leonardi, 2012). As a result, employees who are highly experienced in using social media technologies through their out-of-work usage, might be reluctant to use such platforms in the workplace (Treem et al., 2015). Employees' choice of using social media technologies in the workplace also depends on their perceived coworker and supervisor support (Charoensukmongkol, 2014). Reluctance to adopt the technology or a lack of interest in using it, could have negative consequences for the knowledge sharing process within the team as employees might opt out of key social media groups. On the other side, should employees be avid users of social media, they could potentially persuade other employees to join (network effects), leading to an expansion of the team from within the system. Koch, Leidner, and Gonzalez (2013) found that when employees choose to socialize using internal social media technologies they start to develop an affective commitment toward the organization, stimulating them to stay longer with the company. When team members resist using the internal social media they risk being excluded from team talks and feeling disconnected from their team colleagues.

Lastly, team membership fluctuations might happen when team members successfully persuade their coworkers to expand their networks. Majchrzak, Faraj, Kane, and Azad (2013) propose that when employees start to learn more about their network members, they are more eager to share knowledge. However, if they show preferential treatment to some members of their networks, and not to others, team conflicts might develop, as well as a loss of productivity or a change in the number of team members. Team membership could go down, due to misunderstandings, or up, if knowledge conversations determine other colleagues to join the team. The latter could be a result of social media's visibility and association affordances allowing employees to learn about each other's similarities and build on them, even when they are not part of the same team (Fulk & Yuan, 2013).

18.1.3 Relationship Building and Maintenance

A key element in building and maintaining relationships within high performing teams where the level of work interdependence is high (Beal et al., 2003) is bonding: "Bonding reflects affective feelings that team members hold toward each other and the team. [...] Bonding goes beyond trust and reflects a strong sense of rapport and a desire to stay together, perhaps extending beyond the current task context" (Ilgen et al., 2005, p. 526). Team bonding is achieved when team composition is either homogenous or highly heterogeneous and a single culture exists within the team (Earley & Mosakowski, 2000). Team members can also build relationships through extensive communication or by showing their support for each other's problems. Bonding this way helps them develop common frames of reference (Klimoski & Mohammed, 1994) and an "organized understanding of relevant knowledge that is shared by team members," or shared mental models (Mohammed & Dumville, 2001, p. 89). As such, social media technologies can promote bonding and thus tighten work relationships as they facilitate deep interactions between team members at any level.

Research by Steinfield, DiMicco, Ellison, and Lampe (2009) uncovered that employees' perceptions of connectedness across cultures and large time zone differences increased when they used social media for internal collaboration. Ellison, Steinfield, and Lampe (2011) have proposed that one of the main ways that employees built and maintained social capital on social media was by personally connecting and building relationships with the others. Jackson, Yates, and Orlikowski (2007) tried to understand employees' motivation behind using internal corporate blogs at a global IT company to connect with others. They found that blogging positively affected employees' social well-being. The employees they talked to recounted how they felt like belonging to a well-knit community, spanning from their immediate colleagues to employees from other parts of the company. Besides the social capital increase, bloggers were also motivated by the easy access to knowledge and information that aided them in solving work issues. Heavy bloggers and moderate users reported similar benefits.

Social media have also shown to facilitate relationship building on purpose (DiMicco et al., 2009). One famous example is IBM's Beehive social networking platform. Beehive was launched in mid 2007 and had a similar design to Facebook. It was only accessible to IBM employees and soon after launching it reached 30,000 users. Team members reported building relationships with both close and distant colleagues via Beehive and found that it improved content sharing with distant colleagues. Their result resonates with Bharati, Zhang, and Chaudhury's (2015) findings indicating that an increased level of knowledge sharing is proof of healthy relationship building and maintenance. Yet this relationship can turn unhealthy for teams when team members use social media platforms to actively seek and bond with peers who are cognitively similar to them, leading to team homophily (McPherson, Smith-Lovin, & Cook, 2001).

18.2 Team Processes

The rise of social media in organizations (Leonardi & Vaast, 2017) is also likely to have an effect on team processes (O'Leary & Cummings, 2007), i.e., the interactions between team members (Hackman, 1987). Here we summarize the potential effects social media use can have on communication, knowledge sharing, and collective cognition in teams.

18.2.1 Communication

Communication within geographically dispersed, diverse, and culturally rich teams (Tannenbaum et al., 2012) has benefited tremendously from the leap forward made by social media in organizations. Access to instant communication, as well as to individual and content visibility that persists over time (DiMicco et al., 2009; Treem & Leonardi, 2012), allows team members to talk to one another across time zones and physical distance, synchronously and asynchronously, to easily identify who knows what and whom within the team, to broadcast their messages to larger audiences when needed, as well as to be part of discussion groups that offer insights into what other groups within their team are working on, diminishing the feelings of missing out.

Social media technologies are powerful tools for improving the communication process as they allow messages to be largely visible and available for a long period of time through their visibility and persistence affordances. On social media, messages can persist online for an indefinite time, remaining linked to the person who wrote them (unless purposefully untagged) making communication between individuals, and individuals and teams, transparent and easy to exchange (Leonardi et al., 2013). Before social media technologies became commonplace in organizations, employees were typically unaware of the conversations between two colleagues as they happened through private communication channels (Cross, Borgatti, & Parker, 2002). In a team context supported by social media, a significant amount of information can nowadays be observed by third-parties. Thus team members may be reluctant to share too much information and to communicate on social media due to fear of losing power or importance through the leakage of information (Leonardi et al., 2013).

Social media can also influence the type of information exchanged, the privacy of the information shared, as well as the way communication flows within teams, favoring some groups to the detriment of others. Gibbs, Eisenberg, Rozaidi, and Gryaznova (2014) studied the introduction of a social media platform in a large Russian telecommunications company and the degree to which it promoted communication across geographical and hierarchical boundaries within the company. After analyzing data from server logs and conducting fourteen in-depth interviews, they found that local managers used social media for communication with local colleagues more than with remote colleagues. They also found that non-work discussions happened during work time, while work discussions usually happened after work, with non-work discussions also contributing to building and maintaining better quality relationships. Their findings also revealed that remote employees felt closer to their in-house colleagues who were exchanging information with them on social media. On the other hand, in the case study of another telecommunications company, Denyer, Parry, and Flowers (2011) found that in spite of a strong managerial push for using social media to accomplish everyday tasks, communication suffered and was not as open as employees were led to believe. Surprisingly, employees perceived the platform as a means for their managers to promote themselves and impose their views upon others. And, even if the capabilities for fruitful and open communication and information exchange were available, employees were still reluctant to communicate via social media out of fear of top management surveillance. Employees might also show reluctance to using social media when they perceive their environment as psychologically unsafe (Monge, Cozzens, & Contractor, 1992). The key for social media to positively impact team communication might lie in creating an environment that encourages spontaneous, frequent, and informal communication, as well as trust between team members (Gibbs et al., 2014).

18.2.2 Knowledge Sharing

Social media are favored by organizations due to the rich opportunities they afford for creating and distributing knowledge both within and across organizational team boundaries, leading to a considerable amount of user-generated content (Beck, Pahlke, & Seebach, 2014; Weber & Shi, 2016). For example, social media features like persistability and social tagging allow users to quickly localize knowledge, which means that regardless of employees' physical location in the organization, it is easy for them to search and access relevant knowledge (Ellison et al., 2015), at any point they need it (Treem & Leonardi, 2012). Affordances such as these, unique to social media, make it easy for team members to connect to anyone sharing an interest in the same type of knowledge (von Krogh, 2012). But it is also not unlikely that such quick and easy access to knowledge could result in team members using social media strategically (e.g., impressing managers with blogging activities) (Jarrahi & Sawyer, 2015).

There are two main reasons behind a team member's decision to strategically increase the knowledge shared: One reason is the desire to expand one's network (Fulk & Yuan, 2013) and the other reason is the desire to gain visibility and good performance reviews from upper management (Jarrahi & Sawyer, 2015). First, team members can tactically decide the frequency and the type of knowledge they share through social media. For example, Fulk and Yuan (2013) theorized that knowledge sharing is likely to increase when employees are in need of expanding their networks and stagnate when they are happy with them. They argued that employees who use social media are capable of managing and articulating their network at their own pace and to their best interest. Yet Majchrzak et al. (2013) found that when looking to expand their networks, team members tend to connect with other colleagues who have either common or complimentary backgrounds. Gibbs Rozaidi, & Eisenberg (2013) also suggested that team members approach the knowledge sharing process strategically, but with other underlying reasons. Exploring the engineering division of a distributed technology start-up, they discovered that team members were careful about the image they projected when engaging in knowledge sharing over social media as they were concerned about the potential effects it had on their career. Second, in their field-based study of management consultants, Jarrahi and Sawyer (2015) showed how consultants spent generous amounts of time contributing to online discussion forums and sharing knowledge with their peers when they knew they were being rewarded for it, and not because they genuinely wanted to contribute to the creation of a common pool of knowledge. Brzozowski (2009) also found that employees' motivation to participate and contribute to the knowledge sharing process was ensured when they saw that their contributions received feedback or when they saw that their managers and coworkers were active as well. On the opposite end, Vuori and Okkonen (2012) found that employees were likely to help other colleagues when needed and were eager to share knowledge not necessarily because of the possibility of a career promotion as much as for the desire to help.

Social media's distinct features provide openness to the networking process and allow a wealth of knowledge and information to stay available, accessible, and associated to the employees who shared it. And, regardless of the intent behind the process, if the quality of the knowledge shared is good, it could encourage companies to continue promoting social media as the preferred technology for sharing knowledge internally (Bharati et al., 2015).

18.2.3 Collective Cognition

Social media affords team members the opportunity to gain visibility into the communications of their peers, learning about each other's shared experiences (Cohen & Bailey, 1997; Treem & Leonardi, 2012). This awareness of each other's communication is known as ambient awareness (Leonardi & Meyer, 2015). According to Leonardi and Meyer's (2015) findings from a large telecommunications company in Peru, ambient awareness is extremely helpful in allowing knowledge seekers to access the knowledge pool of knowledge givers and use that knowledge for creating new knowledge. Due to social media's visibility affordance, employees can capture knowledge through casual observations and are able to gather information about the knowledge shared and the knowledge provider, even if they have never interacted with the provider directly. Similarly, Leonardi (2015) demonstrated how social media can increase team members' meta-knowledge, i.e., knowledge of "who knows what" and "who knows whom" at work. As he explains, employees become aware of the interactions and communications between their colleagues through messages they have access to, which helps them learn about each other's interests and expertise and develop a better and general understanding of what everyone is working on (Leonardi, 2015; Treem & Leonardi, 2012).

Being able to identify commonalities between team members' knowledge exchanges is important for teams wanting to create a shared cognition (Gibson & Vermeulen, 2003). Shared cognition develops when communication is open and easily available (Gibson, 2001). Unique information collected from different team members needs to be integrated through team members' interactions, where team members have the opportunity to learn from one another and develop a collective knowledge (Dahlin, Weingart, & Hinds, 2005; Sole & Edmondson, 2002).

Achieving such a level of knowledge integration is hard in teams, because team members do not always share the common cognitive ground necessary to connect all parts and develop a shared understanding (Krauss & Fussell, 1990).

Social media can help bridge this gap by making it feasible to identify experts (Brzozowski, 2009). According to Brzozowski's (2009) virtual watercooler study, employees reported positive experiences using HP's social media technology (similar to a company's RSS feed), stating that it helped them stay up to date with what their colleagues knew, as well as who they knew. Identifying experts could also be helpful when trying to fill in a position on a team. For example, knowledge-based companies could search through their social media database to find the perfect profile that fits an open position (Alavi, Kayworth, & Leidner, 2005), when not long ago, managers had to perform that task manually (Peters, Waterman, & Jones, 1982). Social media also afford mangers easy access to employee analytics and graphics showing their team members' interactions with one another (Ransbotham, Kane, & Lurie, 2012). The downside of easy managerial access to employee data is that it could trigger the big brother effect, with employees feeling like they are being watched constantly. Under such circumstances, employees could protest by showing their disagreement and by having their right to privacy cited (McCreary, 2008), or they could embrace the behavior and support research on their actions collected through social media (Kane et al., 2014).

18.3 Team Outcomes

As social media have become pervasively used in organizations and, in particular, in organizational teams, a growing body of scholarship has tackled the crucial question of the outcomes associated with their use (Dong & Wu, 2015; Koch et al., 2013; Luo, Zhang, & Duan, 2013). Findings have revealed nuanced implications, whereby actual outcomes are highly, but not deterministically, related to, such things as management involvement, team characteristics, and the features and affordances of actual social media applications (Leidner, Koch, & Gonzales, 2010; Schmidt, Lelchook, & Martin, 2016). Scholarship has specifically highlighted outcomes associated with teams' use of social media that were positive, ambivalent, and unanticipated.

18.3.1 Positive Outcomes

With regard to positive outcomes, the use of social media can be associated with team and job performance (Ali-Hassan, Nevo, & Wade, 2015; Shami, Nichols, & Chen, 2014). Social media also participate in transforming the very nature of the work performed in teams (Leftheriotis & Giannakos, 2014; Lin et al., 2016). Moreover, of particular importance for contemporary teams, social media use makes it possible to engage in more open innovation (Bayus, 2013; Kane, Johnson, & Majchrzak, 2014). We detail next how existing scholarship has depicted these three important dimensions of the positive outcomes related to team social media use.

Considering how social media use can participate in team and job performance, research has highlighted the importance of the social context and of the social capital of its members. Ali-Hassan et al. (2015), in particular, showed how the use of social media had an indirect but positive effect on employees' routines. They noticed that the introduction of enterprise social media occasioned three types of use: social, hedonic, and cognitive. Specifically, while hedonic use of social media had a direct negative impact on routine performance, this negative effect was offset somewhat by its positively influencing the development of social ties, and, consequently, improving the company's innovative ability. Moreover, researchers have started to question how the use of social media participates in patterns of change in the ways in which work is performed in organizations (Bertot, Jaeger, & Grimes, 2010; Charoensukmongkol, 2014; Gibbs, Rozaidi, & Eisenberg, 2013). Lin et al. (2016) in particular, focused upon how software development teams used Slack, a recent social media platform dedicated to the needs of various teams. They found that the use of Slack had wide-ranging implications for teams, which included replacing other, older technologies such as email, but also supporting the integration of the team's work with external services and bots. Doing so, the use of this particular social media application contributed to drastic transformations of the processes and nature of the work accomplished by software development teams. For these teams, and the software engineers that worked in them, the effects of the use of this social media application were strongly positive.

The transformation of patterns of work in teams with social media use has also been associated with the integration of leisure and work enabled by certain features of social media (Thom, Millen, & DiMicco, 2012). In other words, the ways in which team members use social media for non-work related purposes also affects what they do. Leftheriotis and Giannakos (2014) directly asked whether employees using social media for non-work-related purposes during work hours were merely wasting their time. They found that even non-work-related social media use was related to higher performance. Thom et al. (2012) also dealt with this issue as they investigated how the availability of gamification features could affect participation and contribution in an enterprise social networking site. In a related manner, Huang, Singh, and Ghose (2015) discovered that prohibiting leisure activities on social media in organizations was counterproductive because it also led to a decrease in work-related contributions. Leisure activities on social media had positive spillover effects for organization's performance and employees' expertise.

Another key positive outcome of teams' use of social media has to do with innovation. In particular, scholarship has highlighted how organizational innovation can be enhanced by outsiders' participation and, more generally, user-generated content (Kallinikos & Tempini, 2014; Miller & Tucker, 2013). Social media are therefore associated with critical developments related to open innovation (Scuotto et al., 2017; Uratnik, 2016). Bayus (2013), for instance, examined the effect of outsiders' input on organizations' innovation capabilities. They found that the outsiders who provided the organization with ideas, the "ideators," differed widely in terms of frequency and the implementability of their suggestions into actual innovation processes.

18.3.2 Ambivalent Outcomes

Other outcomes associated with teams' social media use have been shown to be more mixed: some consequences have been positive for teams and organizations, while others, often at the same time, have been negative, leading to ambivalent implications. The diversity of findings in scholarship reflects this heterogeneity of outcomes (Cardon & Marshall, 2015; Schlagwein & Hu, 2016).

Van Osch and Steinfield (2016), for instance, focused on how social media applications may be used for team boundary spanning activities. They found that the use of social media helped represent the team to outsiders and, thus, improved the recognizability of the team to outsiders. Yet, the use of social media provided limited support for information search and coordination. Nissen and Bergin (2013) also reported ambivalent team outcomes from social media use. They examined the implications for team performance of knowledge work through social media use. They argued that these implications depend upon team members' experience and skills with the use of social media for workplace integration. Whether social media use may result in better knowledge management or organizational performance, therefore, relies upon team members' acquired competences and training.

Iyer and Katona (2016) noted as well some differentiated patterns of participation and outcomes associated with social media use. They developed a model of online social communication that underlined increased connectivity, the low cost of scaling messages, and the role of social differentiation. They concluded that senders start competing among each other for receivers' attention, which leads to high participation inequality in online social networks.

In a related manner, social media may lead to ambivalence for team members as they need to manage their self-presentation. Ensuring that one appears and remains professional on social media can be costly in terms of time and effort. Drawing upon Goffman's (1959) seminal ideas, Hogan (2010) conceptualized the content that people put on social media in terms of a "curation" of one's appearance. Rather than merely performing on social media, people produce "exhibitions" for others to see and engage with. In a similar way, Ollier-Malaterre, Rothbard, and Berg (2013) emphasized the effort it takes for employees to maintain their professional image on social media. In other words, social media can enable team members to self-present as professional and effective, which can enhance team's processes, but this takes effort and time (Vaast, Davidson, & Mattson, 2013).

Research has, more generally, started to unearth the mixed outcomes that may emerge from the openness of social media (Gibbs et al., 2013). It has showed the inherent ambivalence associated with opening up communication processes in and among teams with social media (Leonardi et al., 2013; Oostervink, Agterberg, & Huysman, 2016; Vaast & Kaganer, 2013). Social media may fortify teams and their identification (Ferguson et al., 2013; Lin et al., 2016), but this can also lead to leaks of information and to inconsistencies in the messages that a company and its employees send (Miles & Mangold, 2014). With social media, employees have a "voice" that is distinct from, yet related to, that of management and organizations (Miles & Mangold, 2014). The impact of employees' voices depends upon what employees actually say and may differ widely depending upon whether they express satisfaction or dissatisfaction toward the organization. In other words, social media may lead managers to have less control over what employees, teams, and other stakeholders of the organization say about the organization (Pfeffer, Zorbach, & Carley, 2014), which opens the way to unanticipated consequences (Vaast & Kaganer, 2013).

18.3.3 Unanticipated Outcomes

Seminal scholarship has also started to delve into some of the more unanticipated, and often detrimental, outcomes associated with social media use. In particular, the use of social media can lead to new forms of communications with paradoxical effects (Leonardi et al., 2013; Pfeffer et al., 2014). Social media use can be associated to new ethics and privacy-related issues (Mitrou et al., 2014; Sánchez Abril, Levin, & Del Riego, 2012) and can participate in increases in employees' stress (Bucher, Fieseler, & Suphan, 2013).

With regard to paradoxical effects associated with new forms of communications afforded by social media use, research has highlighted the risks associated with "online firestorms" (Pfeffer et al., 2014) as well as "negative word-of-mouth" (Munnukka & Järvi, 2014) that organizations may experience as multiple stakeholders use social media to communicate actively and negatively about them (Vaast et al., 2017. Even within organizations and their teams, communications via social media do not always fare well. Leonardi and Treem (2012), in particular, noted that the information posted on social media is often difficult to access and assess. As employees benefit from high volume and low cost storage, the maintenance of the content posted on social media can be laborious. Therefore, in many companies, wikis and blogs may become abandoned or end up having limited effect on intra-organization communication ability. Moreover, there can at times be even counter-productive consequences associated with communication via social media. In this regard, Leonardi et al. (2013) argued that enterprise social networks could have opposing implications for within and among team communications by generating "echo chambers." These effects arise from the ability of team members to use social media to select with whom they communicate. Echo chambers appear as employees actively ignore other teams' or management messages and, thus, remain immune to conflicting perspectives. All in all, enterprise social media may enhance within-team communications but, critically, decrease communications among them.

Other unanticipated outcomes associated with social media use have to do with the rise of unprecedented ethical and privacy issues for organizations and their employees. In this regard, in particular, some have noted the inequities associated with new forms of value production via social media (Duffy, 2015). Other scholarship has questioned the implications of new forms of social and, at times, romantic relationships that may emerge from the use of enterprise social media (Mainiero & Jones, 2013). This scholarship has, in this regard, noted the need for organizations to develop a communications ethics policy to deal with potential harassment concerns (Mainiero & Jones, 2013). More generally, the use of social media in organizations has generated privacy issues (Berkelaar, 2014; Mitrou et al., 2014). Sánchez Abril et al. (2012), articulating the tension between, on the one hand, employees' desire to disclose much information about themselves online while remaining protected from their companies' gaze, and their employers' own constraints. They concluded that social media will continue to shape the demands of workplace and individual autonomy. In a related vein, Berkelaar (2014) noted that "cybervetting," i.e., companies' use of social media information for personnel selection, carried with it new ethics and privacy-related dilemmas for organizations and employees. They thus called for the elaboration of a "digital social contract" articulating normative expectations regarding employees' visibility on social media.

These new ethical issues also participate in another unexpected outcome of social media use in organizations and their teams, the rise in employees' stress (Bucher et al., 2013). Some of this stress also originates from the need for employees to manage multiple identities to respond variously to different audiences (boyd, 2010) in electronically mediated contexts (Zappavigna, 2014). Bucher et al. (2013) examined the stress potential associated with employees' access to information and interaction possibilities, which can become overwhelming. Employees thus need to learn to cope to avoid becoming "technostressed" by social media. They found that employees' ability to thrive with social media depends on their ability to extract and interpret information from electronic social settings as well as to develop ways to cope with information overload and uncertainty.

18.4 Discussion

As this review demonstrates, the use of social media within organizational settings can have many important impacts on the work of teams. From team formation, to process, to output, the affordances of social tools stand to provide individuals capabilities that were heretofore difficult to achieve; consequently, actions of and on teams may look very different in the future than they have in the past.

We began this chapter by noting that despite the abundance of research on what makes teams work, there is increasing evidence that teams in the real world do not function as effectively as they should – in other words, they do not always or even regularly follow the recommendations that are typically derived from scholarly research about teams. We suggested that perhaps one reason is that many of the recommendations emerging out of scholarship are difficult to implement and that social media may provide individuals and teams with capabilities that enable them to begin to do those kinds of things that research suggests really do work.

Our review of the literature on the use of social media in the workplace provides insights into why this might be the case. But because most of the studies conducted about social media use to date have not focused specifically on teams, our insights are necessarily speculative. In what follows, we provide suggestions for how to verify these speculations. First, we point out a number of assumptions derived from our review that would merit testing in the specific context of social media use in and around teams. Next, based on this review, we identify several emerging areas of research and point scholars to new research questions that will help advance our understanding of how social media and teams fit together. Finally, we provide suggestions on how scholars might continue to study the changing nature of teams, work, and teamwork as social tools become a central part of organizational life. Table 18.1 collects and summarizes questions for future research from each of these sections.

Table 18.1 *Research foci for studies of social media and teams*

	Team Formation	Team Processes	Team Outcomes
Assumptions	1. Social media usage frequency is likely to influence team size. 2. Social media allows a set of diverse team members to learn about one another on the platform, but also allows them to band together based on similarities, likely turning diversity into a weakness for team formation. 3. Social media is likely to increase the team boding levels for globally distributed team members.	1. Social media is likely to build a directory development of a transactive memory system to increase team metaknowlegde. 2. Social media, through its design and algorithms, is likely to encourage the formation of echo chambers within a team.	1. Social media usage is likely to impact the psychological safety climate for team members. 2. Information shared on social media can leak, likely influencing the way team members choose to share what they know on the platform. 3. Social media usage and usage expectations are likely to negatively impact team members' mental health.
Areas of Future Research	1. How are teams formed in the era of social media and what is the process of enrolling new members on a team?	1. How can collective cognition help to ease coordination and knowledge transfer processes across teams considering the increased	1. What type of information will team members choose to focus their attention on from the large amount of information made

Table 18.1 (*cont.*)

	Team Formation	Team Processes	Team Outcomes
	2. What is the proper size of a team so that team members can keep up with the knowledge shared without being overwhelmed? 3. How much diversity is too much for a well-functioning team? 4. How can social media help encourage informal relationship building within and across teams to enhance team dynamics?	metaknowledge provided by social media? 2. How can teams build momentum and purpose when working together on social media? 3. How likely are team members to leave current teams and join new ones, as a result of employees across the organization gaining more awareness into everyone else's expertise?	available through social media? 2. How can team members cope with the high levels of information available and managerial expectation to be constantly up to date without reaching mental exhaustion?
Exploring the Changing Nature of Teams	1. What is the level of overlap or differentiation in terms of participation and content between formal and informal types of teams formed on social media? 2. How will multi-team members benefit from, and cope with, the potential exponential increase in the number of teams they can belong to on social media?	1. How will team processes be affected by the interactions between formal and informal teams enabled by social media?	1. What will teamwork look like on social media and what are the implications for team functioning? 2. How can managers foster pleasant work contexts on social media that also enhance team effectiveness?

18.4.1 Assumptions to be Tested

Based on the literature reviewed in this chapter, one key assumption is that social media make it easy for everyone in the organization to see what their peers are working on, as posts are visible and persist over time (Treem & Leonardi, 2012). This could mean that social media enable the creation of the directory development of a transactive memory system by allowing team members to learn what their colleagues already know in a transparent manner (Jackson, 2012;

Wegner, 1986). Such transactive memory systems can be thought of as a network of cognitive elements about "who knows what" in the network (Hollingshead & Contractor, 2002; Monge & Contractor, 2003; Wegner, 1986). For example, IBM's social networking site Beehive, later called SocialBlue, was designed to help employees make new connections, keep track of old ones, and reactivate old connections, such as colleagues they used to work with. Employees had personal pages on the SocialBlue platform where they entered information about the projects they were working on or had previously worked on (DiMicco et al., 2008). That particular feature afforded employees across the platform the opportunity to identify what their colleagues were working on, i.e. learn about "who knows what" within the company (Treem & Leonardi, 2012). Directory development is the first of three transactive memory system components, together with information allocation and information retrieval (Wegner, 1995), and is fundamental for the functioning of the system. The main challenge with directory development has always been the difficulty in actually knowing what knowledge exists, and where it can be found (Lave & Wenger, 1991). Social media, through its visibility and persistency features, removes this barriers making the knowledge shared visible and persistent for easy retrieval (Treem & Leonardi, 2012), allowing it to be used effectively at a later point (Alavi & Leidner, 2001).

Collective cognition has the potential to improve the directory development component of a transactive memory system (Yuan et al., 2010). This could have implications for team formation by challenging the current modes of bringing people together on a team, as well as for team processes, by making it hard to know how the team dynamics will play out when team members have access to everyone else's knowledge base. It might also be that team members are overloaded with information and resist it by pulling out of the system, in which case, even if the technological capabilities allowed for an improved directory development, the results produced at a collective level would not be satisfactory. As Yuan et al. (2010) also pointed out, when teams are too large, team members experience difficulty in learning about each other's expertise by directly engaging with each other. Team members have a limited amount of time and energy to engage in grooming relationships, also due to the exhaustion they experience from a large amount of interruptions (Turel & Serenko, 2012). This raises questions about the proper size of a team, as well as the level of cognitive diversity on the team.

Even if social media, through its affordances, could make it possible to have team members with distinctive cognitive elements on the same team (Leonardi, 2015), it could also have the opposite effect, by promoting homophily on teams (McPherson et al., 2001), as team members would likely find it easier to begin conversations with colleagues who are like them or who share similar cognitive orientations (Ibarra, 1992). Researchers should test whether teams formed with diverse employees could develop a collective cognition and remain together, given that current research shows that teams consisting of individuals with ties between non-similar individuals tend to disband at a high rate (McPherson et al., 2001). How similar, or how diverse should teams be to work well together? Why does social media allow for individuals with similar interests and ideas to associate with one another and band into echo chambers (Pariser, 2011)?

When social media in organizations are configured in ways similar to the technologies designed for personal use, e.g., Facebook, users might only be shown content that is similar to their viewpoint (Yavaş & Yücel, 2014). As a result, the chances of similar employees bonding together could increase, as well as the amount of information overlooked due to the social media's news feed algorithm, purposefully avoiding showing information not in line with the user's ideology. In such contexts, echo chambers could thrive to the detriment of collective cognition (Leonardi et al., 2013). The positive side of echo chambers could be the strengthening of relationships between employees with similar interests and needs, which could be especially beneficial when teams are not co-located (Yuan & Gay, 2006), as research found that members of global teams reported feelings of connectedness across cultures when using social media in teams (Steinfield et al., 2009). These paradoxical findings make further research on the development of echo chambers in organizations exciting.

The reviewed literature surfaces other assumptions about the impact of social media on team bonding and the extent to which social media use can create high levels of connectedness between employees who are part of globally distributed teams. It also raises questions about the creation of chat rooms and if they are beneficial or, on the contrary, detrimental to a healthy team functioning. For example, earlier research (Brzozowski, 2009) at HP on a system called WaterCooler, which was created to bring together information scattered across the organization to make it easier for employees to access it, revealed that it helped employees (active and passive users) increase access to both new knowledge and people. This type of interaction can also raise questions about what happens when employees create their own "watercoolers" to share delicate information. Can information leak? Privacy concerns have already been gaining interest (Bélanger & Crossler, 2011) and are likely to garner even more due to the drastic implications they might have on employees' organizational lives (Stuart et al., 2012). Are employees more careful about the image they are projecting when typing sensitive information that can leak? As we know, employees tend to engage in defensive self-presentation behaviors in daily social media interactions out of caution for the potential career consequences (Gibbs et al., 2013). Employees also risk being excluded from certain groups, such as "watercoolers," which could endanger their psychological safety, even if, social media are recognized for creating environments with high levels of psychological safety by enabling people who would otherwise be more introverted to connect with others (boyd & Ellison, 2007).

18.4.2 New Areas of Research

Our review has revealed several areas that are either grossly understudied in the existing literature or have yet to receive attention given the relatively recent availability of social media technologies within organizations. In this section, we examine these new potential areas of research.

On the whole, the amount of research into team formation is quite small. Throughout the twentieth century, team formation within organizations consisted of teams formed from the top down, by managers and other leaders who assembled people into teams based on needs or preferences. Findings from scholarly research has show a shift in the way managers thought about the formation of teams (Williams & O'Reilly, 1998). Recent literature frequently provides examples of teams that are formed from the bottom-up by future team members. In fact, the idea of teaming rests on the assumption that teams can form and disband with increasing agility such that their memberships are fluid and dynamic (O'leary, Mortensen, & Woolley, 2011).

Social media technologies are likely to play an important role in teaming. As individuals have increasingly broader and shared metaknowledge about who knows what and whom across the organization, their ability to skillfully decide who should become a member of a team increases. On the flip side, as people across the organization gain more awareness about the kinds of teams forming or the kinds of problems experienced by their coworkers daily, they may decide to join existing teams or form new ones. Membership may mean joining a group on a social media platform and contributing to a discussion. As such, a promising new direction for research on social media and teams could be to dive deeper into how team members come to recognize that new teams should be formed, how they make decisions about who should be involved with the team, how they enroll others in those teams, and how those teams build momentum and purpose. These dynamics will be increasingly important as organizations continue to become collections of teams.

As the literature suggests, individuals are frequently teaming with a wider array of people across the organization (Edmondson, 2012). In the case of such purposive multi-teaming, scholars often conceptualize organizations in which individuals are embedded in multiple teams as multi-team systems (Zaccaro et al., 2012). Sometimes, this expansive teaming leads to disagreements about who is actually on a team (Mortensen, 2004). Yet there are also many cases in which membership in multi-team systems can help increase important organizational outcomes such as innovation and performance returns (Asencio et al., 2012).

Our review suggests that social media may particularly affect organizational processes in the area of multi-team systems and multi-teaming. Knowledge sharing and information exchange may benefit from membership in multiple embedded teams as individuals are able to move knowledge from one team context to another where it is needed. Further, enhanced metaknowledge via social media may help team members to have collective cognition about who does what work on what team. Such collective cognition may help to ease coordination and knowledge transfer processes across teams in a way that produces positive organizational benefits. Our review also makes clear that social media can aid in the sharing personal or non-work information that seeds work-related interactions. Interpersonal connection and cohesion are important for strong teams, thus social media use may help to encourage the kinds of informal relationship building within and across teams that will enhance team dynamics.

Our review surfaced positive, ambivalent, and negative team outcomes associated with social media use in organizations. Across all of these, issues of boundary spanning and attention loomed large. One important new area for future research concerns the allocation of attention to content on social media. Clearly, if social media enable boundary spanning such that individuals are exposed to a diversity of information that they can usefully combine into new ideas or products, managers and organizations will be happy. But as the content of information available on social media increases, it seems unlikely that individuals will be able to have the kinds of serendipitous encounters that generate novelty. Instead, it is possible that individuals will use some heuristics to guide their attention allocation. Perhaps, for example, they will focus their attention on team members or people in adjacent teams who are doing work they perceive as relevant. Focusing attention based on relevancy would potentially reduce exposure to unique information from other domains that could be usefully recombined to generate novelty. Or, individuals might focus their attention on information coming from powerful actors – whether team leads, managers, or executives. Too much collective attention from across the team on powerful actors would again stymie the novelty of information brought into the team for processing. Understanding attention allocation patterns in the era of social media is an extremely important area of research for explaining team functioning and effectiveness.

Another area for future research related to team outputs concerns the disbanding of teams. Across the various papers included in our review was evidence of individuals learning about teammates by observing them interacting with others online, even though the observers did not interact with the others themselves. Given that teams in organizations are rapidly contracting and disbanding (Miles & Hollenbeck, 2013), it seems important to understand how team members stay connected to others when they are not teaming such that they can reactivate their ties if they need to team again in the future. Social media afford the ability for individuals to have latent ties in the sense that a tie still exists (e.g., a person can signal someone as a "friend" and still observe their behavior and actions) even if the actors are not actively engaging with each other. These latent ties are new resources that scholars know very little about. Research into how actives ties are transitioned into latent ties, how latent ties are retained, and how they are reactivated into active ties deserves much scholarly research if we are to understand the dynamics of today's teaming environment.

18.4.3 Exploring the Changing Nature of Teams

Colbert, Yee, and George (2016) pointed out how the "workplace of the future" would be shaped by the use of digital technologies such as social media. We believe that the nature of teams and of their work may also become substantially transformed as social media themselves become more prevalent and sophisticated. Future research could fruitfully explore these deep transformations of teams and teamwork with social media, in at least three areas: that of the effects on teams of the erosion of the boundaries between organizations and their environment; that of the interactions between formal and informal teams enabled by social media; and that of the transformation of the nature of teamwork made possible in part by social technologies. For one, the rise of open innovation (Fleming & Waguespack, 2007), and, more generally, open collaboration (Baldwin & Hippel, 2011; Levine & Prietula, 2014) has contributed to making the boundaries between organizations and their environment more porous. Team membership may thus be based not only on organizational affiliations. Increasingly, customers and freelance workers, for instance, may participate more or less fully in organizational teamwork. More research is needed to understand how the fluidity of participation in teams, afforded by social media, affects the processes and outcomes associated with teams. Moreover, the trend toward open teams raises new questions associated with the origins, development, and protection of organizational capabilities when teams are increasingly open and heterogeneous in their composition. It would also be fascinating to investigate transformations in the relationships developing within teams with the increased diversity of forms and statuses of participation.

Regarding the interactions between formal and informal teams, a notable recent trend in enterprise social media is to offer social platforms not only for preexisting, formal teams, but also for emergent, informal teams. Social technologies may be used by teams that mirror some formal structures of organizations (e.g., new product development teams, marketing teams, accounting teams) as well as by teams that arose thanks to the technology. A platform such as Slack, for instance, enables formal and informal teams to self-organize and develop their own content (Lin et al., 2016). Informal teams may use such applications to form and interact on the basis of common interests and social relationships rather than formal affiliation. Much remains to be investigated regarding how these different types of teams may work alongside and interact with one another. One may ask, for instance, whether there is a lot of overlap or differentiation in terms of participation and content between these two types of teams. Also, scholars may study how multi-team members may both benefit from and need to cope with the potential exponential increase in the number of teams they can belong to. At the organizational level of analysis, furthermore, scholarship is needed to understand how these emerging and informal teams may affect important processes of coordination and control.

Finally, the growing use of social media participates in substantial transformations in the very nature of teamwork. So far, existing scholarship has highlighted how social media implementation and use can be complemented with the addition of gamification features in order to stimulate desired benefits such as increased adoption or idea contributions (Dale, 2014; Thom et al., 2012). It has also theorized how people need to adjust their self-presentation as the boundary between the personal and the professional becomes blurred (Ollier-Malaterre et al., 2013). There are avenues for exciting new research that would deal more directly with what becomes of "work" for teams with social media. Future scholarship tackling this important issue could lead to insights for managers associated with how to foster pleasant work contexts that also enhance team effectiveness. It would also have theoretical and practical implications for the teams' training and socialization.

18.5 Conclusion

With the rapid spread of social media across organizations – and with social features finding their way into routinely used productivity apps – the time is ripe for scholars interested in technology and teams to focus their collective gaze on the way that these new technologies can aid, transform, or complicate teams and the work they do. The findings from this review suggest that social media have the potential for shifts in the way teams form, how team members conduct their processes, and the kinds of outputs that teams work toward. We have highlighted a number of areas for future research that will help teams and the organizations in which they operate make smart decisions about how to carry out important activities in the age of social technologies.

References

Alavi, M., Kayworth, T. R., & Leidner, D. E. (2005). An empirical examination of the influence of organizational culture on knowledge management practices. *Journal of Management Information Systems*, *22*(3), 191–224.

Alavi, M. & Leidner, D. E. (2001). Knowledge management and knowledge management systems: Conceptual foundations and research issues. *MIS Quarterly*, *25*(1), 107–136.

Ali-Hassan, H., Nevo, D., & Wade, M. (2015). Linking dimensions of social media use to job performance: The role of social capital. *The Journal of Strategic Information Systems*, *24*(2), 65–89. doi:10.1016/j.jsis.2015.03.001.

Arrow, H., McGrath, J. E., & Berdahl, J. L. (2000). *Small groups as complex systems: Formation, coordination, development, and adaptation*. Thousand Oaks, CA: Sage Publications.

Asencio, R., Carter, D. R., DeChurch, L. A., Zaccaro, S. J., & Fiore, S. M. (2012). Charting a course for collaboration: A multiteam perspective. *Translational Behavioral Medicine*, *24*(2), 487–494.

Baldwin, C. & Hippel, E. v. (2011). Modeling a paradigm shift: From producer innovation to user and open collaborative innovation. *Organization Science*, *22*(6), 1399–1417. doi:10.1287/orsc.1100.0618.

Bayus, B. L. (2013). Crowdsourcing new product ideas over time: An analysis of the Dell IdeaStorm community. *Management Science*, *59*(1), 226–244.

Beal, D. J., Cohen, R. P., Burke, M. J., & McLendon, C. L. (2003). Cohesion and performance in groups: A meta-analytic clarification of construct relations. *Journal of Applied Psychology*, *88*, 989–1004.

Beck, R., Pahlke, I., & Seebach, C. (2014). Knowledge exchange and symbolic action in social media-enabled electronic networks of practice: A multilevel perspective on knowledge seekers and contributors. *MIS Quarterly*, *38*(4), 1245–1270.

Bélanger, F. & Crossler, R. E. (2011). Privacy in the digital age: a review of information privacy research in information systems. *MIS Quarterly*, *35*(4), 1017–1042.

Berkelaar, B. L. (2014). Cybervetting, Online Information, and Personnel Selection New Transparency Expectations and the Emergence of a Digital Social Contract. *Management Communication Quarterly*, *28*(4), 479–506.

Bertot, J. C., Jaeger, P. T., & Grimes, J. M. (2010). Using ICTs to create a culture of transparency: E-government and social media as openness and anti-corruption tools for societies. *Government Information Quarterly, 27*(3), 264–271.

Bharati, P., Zhang, W., & Chaudhury, A. (2015). Better knowledge with social media? Exploring the roles of social capital and organizational knowledge management. *Journal of Knowledge Management, 19*(3), 456–475.

boyd, d. m. (2010). Social network sites as networked publics: Affordances, dynamics, and implications. In P. Papacharissi (Ed.), *The networked self: Identity, community, and culture on social network sites* (pp. 39–58). New York, N.Y.: Routledge.

boyd, d. & Ellison, N. B. (2007). Social network sites: Definition, history, and scholarship. *Journal of Computer-Mediated Communication, 13*(1), 210–230.

Brzozowski, M. J. (2009). WaterCooler: exploring an organization through enterprise social media. Paper presented at the Proceedings of the ACM 2009 international conference on Supporting group work.

Bucher, E., Fieseler, C., & Suphan, A. (2013). The stress potential of social media in the workplace. *Information, Communication & Society, 16*(10), 1639–1667.

Cardon, P. W. & Marshall, B. (2015). The hype and reality of social media use for work collaboration and team communication. *International Journal of Business Communication, 52*(3), 273–293.

Charoensukmongkol, P. (2014). Effects of support and job demands on social media use and work outcomes. *Computers in Human Behavior, 36*, 340–349. doi:10.1016/j.chb.2014.03.061

Cohen, S. G. & Bailey, D. E. (1997). What makes teams work: Group effectiveness research from the shop floor to the executive suite. *Journal of Management, 23*(3), 239–290. doi:10.1177/014920639702300303.

Colbert, A., Yee, N., & George, G. (2016). The digital workforce and the workplace of the future. *Academy of Management Journal, 59*(3), 731–739.

Cross, R., Borgatti, S. P., & Parker, A. (2002). Making invisible work visible: Using social network analysis to support strategic collaboration. *California Management Review, 44*(2), 25–46.

Cummings, J. N. (2004). Work groups, structural diversity, and knowledge sharing in a global organization. *Management Science, 50*(3), 352–364.

Dahlin, K. B., Weingart, L. R., & Hinds, P. J. (2005). Team diversity and information use. *Academy of Management Journal, 48*(6), 1107–1123.

Dale, S. (2014). Gamification making work fun, or making fun of work? *Business Information Review, 31*(2), 82–90.

Denyer, D., Parry, E., & Flowers, P. (2011). "Social", "open" and "participative"? Exploring personal experiences and organizational effects of Enterprise2.0 use. *Long Range Planning, 44*(5–6), 375–396.

DiMicco, J., Millen, D. R., Geyer, W., Dugan, C., Brownholtz, B., & Muller, M. (2008). Motivations for social networking at work. Paper presented at the Proceedings of the 2008 ACM conference on Computer supported cooperative work.

DiMicco, J. M., Geyer, W., Millen, D., Dugan, C., & Brownholtz, B. (2009). People sensemaking and relationship building on an enterprise social networking site. Paper presented at the HICSS'09. 42nd Hawaii International Conference, Hawaii.

Dong, J. Q. & Wu, W. (2015). Business value of social media technologies: Evidence from online user innovation communities. *The Journal of Strategic Information Systems, 24*(2), 113–127.

Duffy, B. E. (2015). Gendering the labor of social media production. *Feminist Media Studies*, *15*(4), 710–714.

Earley, C. P. & Mosakowski, E. (2000). Creating hybrid team cultures: An empirical test of transnational team functioning. *Academy of Management Journal*, *43*(1), 26–49.

Edmondson, A. C. (2012). *Teaming: How organizations learn, innovate, and compete in the knowledge economy*. New York, NY: John Wiley & Sons.

Ellison, N. B., Gibbs, J. L., & Weber, M. S. (2015). The use of enterprise social network sites for knowledge sharing in distributed organizations. *American Behavioral Scientist*, *59*(1), 103–123. doi:10.1177/0002764214540510.

Ellison, N. B., Steinfield, C., & Lampe, C. (2011). Connection strategies: Social capital implications of Facebook-enabled communication practices. *New Media & Society*, *13*(6), 873–892. doi:10.1177/1461444810385389.

Ferguson, J., Soekijad, M., Huysman, M., & Vaast, E. (2013). A vision for development? Blogging in ICT4D. *Information systems journal*, *23*(4), 307–328.

Fidelman, M. (2012). IBM study: If you don't have a social CEO, you're going to be less competitive. *Forbes*. Retrieved from www.forbes.com/sites/markfidelman/2012/05/22/ibm-study-if-you-dont-have-a-social-ceo-youre-going-to-be-less-competitive/.

Fiore, S. M. & Wiltshire, T. J. (2016). Technology as teammate: Examining the role of external cognition in support of team cognitive processes. *Frontiers in Psychology: Cognitive Science*, *7*, 1–17.

Fleming, L. & Waguespack, D. M. (2007). Brokerage, boundary spanning, and leadership in open innovation communities. *Organization Science*, *18*(2), 165–180.

Ford, D. P. & Mason, R. M. (2013). A multilevel perspective of tensions between knowledge management and social Media. *Journal of Organizational Computing and Electronic Commerce*, *23*(1–2), 7–33. doi:10.1080/10919392.2013.748604.

Fulk, J. & Yuan, Y. C. (2013). Location, motivation, and social capitalization via enterprise social networking. *Journal of Computer-Mediated Communication*, *19*(1), 20–37. doi:10.1111/jcc4.12033.

Gibbs, J. L., Eisenberg, J., Rozaidi, N. A., & Gryaznova, A. (2014). The "Megapozitiv" role of enterprise social media in enabling cross-boundary communication in a distributed Russian organization. *American Behavioral Scientist*, *59*(1), 75–102. doi:10.1177/0002764214540511.

Gibbs, J. L., Rozaidi, N. A., & Eisenberg, J. (2013). Overcoming the "ideology of openness": Probing the affordances of social media for organizational knowledge sharing. *Journal of Computer-Mediated Communication*, *19*(1), 102–120.

Gibson, C. & Vermeulen, F. (2003). A healthy divide: Subgroups as a stimulus for team learning behavior. *Administrative Science Quarterly*, *48*(2), 202–239.

Gibson, C. B. (2001). From knowledge accumulation to accommodation: Cycles of collective cognition in work groups. *Journal of organizational Behavior*, *22*(2), 121–134.

Goffman, E. (1959). *The presentation of self in everyday life*. Garden City, NY: Doubleday.

Griffith, T. L., Sawyer, J. E., & Neale, M. A. (2003). Virtualness and knowledge in teams: Managing the love triangle of organizations, individuals, and information technology. *MIS Quarterly*, *27*(2), 265–287.

Hackman, J. R. (1987). The design of work teams. In J. W. Lorsch (Ed.), *Handbook of organizational behavior* (pp. 315–342). Englewood Cliffs, NJ: Prentice-Hall.

Hackman, J. R., & Oldham, G. R. (1980). *Work redesign*. Reading, MA: Addison-Wesley.

Hogan, B. (2010). The presentation of self in the age of social media: Distinguishing performances and exhibitions online. *Bulletin of Science, Technology & Society, 30*(6), 377–386.

Hollingshead, A. B. & Contractor, N. S. (2002). New media and organizing at the group level. *The Handbook of New Media,* 221–235.

Huang, Y., Singh, P. V., & Ghose, A. (2015). A structural model of employee behavioral dynamics in enterprise social media. *Management Science, 61*(12), 2825–2844.

Ibarra, H. (1992). Homophily and differential returns: Sex differences in network structure and access in an advertising firm. *Administrative Science Quarterly, 37*(3), 422–447.

Ilgen, D. R. (1999). Teams embedded in organizations: Some implications. *American Psychologist, 54*(2), 129–139.

Ilgen, D. R., Hollenbeck, J. R., Johnson, M., & Jundt, D. (2005). Teams in organizations: From input-process-output models to IMOI models. *Annual Review of Psychology, 56,* 517–543. doi:10.1146/annurev.psych.56.091103.070250.

Iyer, G. & Katona, Z. (2016). Competing for attention in social communication markets. *Management Science, 62*(8), 2304–2320.

Jackson, A., Yates, J., & Orlikowski, W. (2007). Corporate Blogging: Building community through persistent digital talk. Paper presented at the System Sciences, 2007. HICSS 2007. 40th Annual Hawaii International Conference on.

Jackson, P. (2012). Transactive directories of organizational memory: Towards a working data model. *Information & Management, 49*(2), 118–125.

Jarrahi, M. H. & Sawyer, S. (2015). Theorizing on the take-up of social technologies, organizational policies and norms, and consultants' knowledge-sharing practices. *Journal of the Association for Information Science and Technology, 66*(1), 162–179. doi:10.1002/asi.23161.

Kallinikos, J. & Tempini, N. (2014). Patient data as medical facts: Social media practices as a foundation for medical knowledge creation. *Information Systems Research, 25* (4), 817–833.

Kane, G., Alavi, M., Labianca, G., & Borgatti, S. P. (2014). What's different about social media networks? A framework and research agenda. *MIS Quarterly, 38*(1), 275–304.

Kane, G. C., Johnson, J., & Majchrzak, A. (2014). Emergent life cycle: The tension between knowledge change and knowledge retention in open online coproduction communities. *Management Science, 60*(2), 3026–3048.

Klimoski, R. & Mohammed, S. (1994). Team mental model: Construct or metaphor? *Journal of Management, 20*(2), 403–437.

Koch, H., Leidner, D. E., & Gonzalez, E. S. (2013). Digitally enabling social networks: resolving IT–culture conflict. *Information Systems Journal, 23*(6), 501–523.

Kozlowski, S. W. & Bell, B. S. (2003). Work groups and teams in organizations. In W.C. Borman, D.R. Ilgen, & R.J. Klimoski (Eds.), *Handbook of Psychology: Industrial and organizational psychology,* Vol. 12 (pp. 333–375). London, UK: Wiley.

Krauss, R. M. & Fussell, S. R. (1990). Mutual knowledge and communicative effectiveness. In J. Galegher, R. E. Kraut, & C. Egido (Eds.), Intellectual teamwork: Social and technological foundations of cooperative work (pp. 111–146). New York, NY: Lawrence Erlbaum Associates.

Lave, J., & Wenger, E. (1991). *Situated learning: Legitimate peripheral participation*: New York, NY: Routledge.

Leftheriotis, I. & Giannakos, M. N. (2014). Using social media for work: Losing your time or improving your work? *Computers in Human Behavior, 31,* 134–142.

Leidner, D. E., Koch, H., & Gonzales, E. (2010). Assimilating generation Y IT new hires into USAA's workforce: The role of an Enterprise 2.0 system. *MIS Quarterly Executive, 9*(4), 163–176.

Leonardi, P. M. (2014). Social media, knowledge sharing, and innovation: Toward a theory of communication visibility. *Information Systems Research, 25*(4), 796–816.

Leonardi, P. M. (2015). Ambient awareness and knowledge acquisition: Using social media to learn "who knows what" and "who knows whom". *MIS Quarterly, 39*(4), 747–762.

Leonardi, P. M., Huysman, M., & Steinfield, C. (2013). Enterprise social media: Definition, history, and prospects for the study of social technologies in organizations. *Journal of Computer-Mediated Communication, 19*(1), 1–19.

Leonardi, P. M. & Meyer, S. R. (2015). Social media as social lubricant: How ambient awareness eases knowledge transfer. *American Behavioral Scientist, 59*(1), 10–34.

Leonardi, P. M. & Treem, J. W. (2012). Knowledge management technology as a stage for strategic self-presentation: Implications for knowledge sharing in organizations. *Information and Organization, 22*(1), 37–59.

Leonardi, P. M. & Vaast, E. (2017). Social media and their affordances for organizing: A review and agenda for research. *Academy of Management Annals, 11*(1), 150–188.

Levine, S. S. & Prietula, M. J. (2014). Open collaboration for innovation: Principles and performance. *Organization Science, 25*(5), 1414–1433. doi:10.1287/orsc.2013.0872.

Lin, B., Zagalsky, A., Storey, M.-A., & Serebrenik, A. (2016). Why developers are slacking off: Understanding how software teams use Slack. Paper presented at the Proceedings of the 19th ACM Conference on Computer Supported Cooperative Work and Social Computing Companion.

Lipnack, J. & Stamps, J. (1999). Virtual teams: The new way to work. *Strategy & Leadership, 27*(1), 14–19.

Luo, X., Zhang, J., & Duan, W. (2013). Social media and firm equity value. *Information Systems Research, 24*(1), 146–163.

Mainiero, L. A. & Jones, K. J. (2013). Workplace romance 2.0: Developing a communication ethics model to address potential sexual harassment from inappropriate social media contacts between coworkers. *Journal of Business Ethics, 114*(2), 367–379.

Majchrzak, A., Faraj, S., Kane, G. C., & Azad, B. (2013). The contradictory influence of social media affordances on online communal knowledge sharing. *Journal of Computer-Mediated Communication, 19*(1), 38–55. doi:10.1111/jcc4.12030.

Mankin, D. A., Cohen, S. G., & Bikson, T. K. (1996). *Teams and technology: Fulfilling the promise of the new organization.* Boston, MA: Harvard Business Press.

Mark, G., Guy, I., Kremer-Davidson, S., & Jacovi, M. (2014). Most liked, fewest friends. In Proceedings of the 17th ACM conference on computer supported cooperative work & social computing (pp. 393–404). New York, NY: ACM. doi:10.1145/2531602.2531662.

Mathieu, J. E., Tannenbaum, S. I., Donsbach, J. S., & Alliger, G. M. (2014). A review and integration of team composition models: Moving toward a dynamic and temporal framework. *Journal of Management, 40*(1), 130–160.

McCreary, L. (2008). What was privacy? *Harvard Business Review, 86*(10), 123–130, 142.

McPherson, M., Smith-Lovin, L., & Cook, J. M. (2001). Birds of a feather: Homophily in social networks. *Annual Review ofsSociology*, *27*(1), 415–444.

Miles, J. & Hollenbeck, J. R. (2013). Teams and technology. In M. D. Coovert & L. F. Thompson (Eds.), *The psychology of workplace technology* (pp. 99–117). New York, NY: Routledge.

Miles, S. J. & Mangold, W. G. (2014). Employee voice: Untapped resource or social media time bomb? *Business Horizons*, *57*(3), 401–411.

Miller, A. R. & Tucker, C. (2013). Active social media management: The case of health care. *Information Systems Research*, *24*(1), 52–70.

Mitrou, L., Kandias, M., Stavrou, V., & Gritzalis, D. (2014). Social media profiling: A Panopticon or Omniopticon tool? Paper presented at the Proc. of the 6th Conference of the Surveillance Studies Network.

Mohammed, S. & Dumville, B. C. (2001). Team mental models in a team knowledge framework: Expanding theory and measurement across disciplinary boundaries. *Journal of organizational Behavior*, *22*(2), 89–106.

Monge, P. R. & Contractor, N. S. (2003). *Theories of communication networks*: Oxford, UK: Oxford University Press.

Monge, P. R., Cozzens, M. D., & Contractor, N. S. (1992). Communication and motivational predictors of the dynamics of organizational innovation. *Organization Science*, *3*(2), 250–274.

Mortensen, M. (2004). Fuzzy Teams: Why do teams disagree on their membership and what does it mean? Working Paper McGill University.

Munnukka, J. & Järvi, P. (2014). Perceived risks and risk management of social media in an organizational context. *Electronic Markets*, *24*(3), 219–229.

Nissen, M. E. & Bergin, R. D. (2013). Knowledge work through social media applications: Team performance implications of immersive virtual worlds. *Journal of Organizational Computing and Electronic Commerce*, *23*(1–2), 84–109.

O'Leary, M. B. & Cummings, J. N. (2007). The spatial, temporal, and configurational characteristics of geographic dispersion in teams. *MIS Quarterly*, 433–452.

O'leary, M. B., Mortensen, M., & Woolley, A. W. (2011). Multiple team membership: A theoretical model of its effects on productivity and learning for individuals and teams. *Academy of Management Review*, *36*(3), 461–478.

Ollier-Malaterre, A., Rothbard, N., & Berg, J. (2013). When worlds collide in cyberspace: How boundary work in online social networks impacts professional relationships. *Academy of Management Review*, *38*(4), 645–669.

Oostervink, N., Agterberg, M., & Huysman, M. (2016). Knowledge sharing on enterprise social media: Practices to cope with institutional complexity. *Journal of Computer-Mediated Communication*, *21*(2), 156–176.

Pariser, E. (2011). The filter bubble: How the new personalized web is changing what we read and how we think. New York, NY: Penguin.

Peters, T. J., Waterman, R. H., & Jones, I. (1982). *In search of excellence: Lessons from America's best-run companies*. New York, NY: Harper and Row.

Pfeffer, J., Zorbach, T., & Carley, K. M. (2014). Understanding online firestorms: Negative word-of-mouth dynamics in social media networks. *Journal of Marketing Communications*, *20*(1–2), 117–128.

Ransbotham, S., Kane, G. C., & Lurie, N. H. (2012). Network characteristics and the value of collaborative user-generated content. *Marketing Science*, *31*(3), 387–405.

Ren, Y. & Argote, L. (2011). Transactive memory systems 1985–2010: An integrative framework of key dimensions, antecedents, and consequences. *Academy of Management Annals*, *5*(1), 189–229.

Retelny, D., Robaszkiewicz, S., To, A., Lasecki, W. S., Patel, J., Rahmati, N.,. . . Bernstein, M. S. (2014). Expert crowdsourcing with flash teams. Paper presented at the Proceedings of the 27th annual ACM symposium on User interface software and technology.

Sánchez Abril, P., Levin, A., & Del Riego, A. (2012). Blurred boundaries: Social media privacy and the twenty-first-century employee. *American Business Law Journal*, *49*(1), 63–124.

Schlagwein, D. & Hu, M. (2016). How and why organisations use social media: Five use types and their relation to absorptive capacity. *Journal of Information Technology*, *32*(2), 194–209.

Schmidt, G. B., Lelchook, A. M., & Martin, J. E. (2016). The relationship between social media co-worker connections and work-related attitudes. *Computers in Human Behavior*, *55*, 439–445.

Scuotto, V., Del Giudice, M., della Peruta, M. R., & Tarba, S. (2017). The performance implications of leveraging internal innovation through social media networks: An empirical verification of the smart fashion industry. *Technological Forecasting and Social Change*, *120*, 184–194.

Shami, N. S., Nichols, J., & Chen, J. (2014). Social media participation and performance at work: a longitudinal study. Paper presented at the Proceedings of the SIGCHI Conference on Human Factors in Computing Systems.

Sole, D. & Edmondson, A. (2002). Situated knowledge and learning in dispersed teams. *British Journal of Management*, *13*(S2).

Steinfield, C., DiMicco, J. M., Ellison, N. B., & Lampe, C. (2009). Bowling Online: Social Networking and Social Capital within the Organization. Paper presented at the Proceedings of the fourth international conference on communities and technologies.

Stewart, G. L. & Barrick, M., R. (2000). Team structure and performance: Assessing the mediating role of intrateam process and the moderating role of task type. *Academy of Management Journal*, *43*(2), 135–148.

Stuart, H. C., Dabbish, L., Kiesler, S., Kinnaird, P., & Kang, R. (2012). Social transparency in networked information exchange: a theoretical framework. Paper presented at the Proceedings of the ACM 2012 conference on Computer Supported Cooperative Work.

Tannenbaum, S. I., Mathieu, J. E., Salas, E., & Cohen, D. (2012). Teams are changing: Are research and practice evolving fast enough? *Industrial and Organizational Psychology*, *5*, 2–24.

Thom, J., Millen, D., & DiMicco, J. (2012). Removing gamification from an enterprise SNS. Paper presented at the Proceedings of the ACM 2012 conference on Computer Supported Cooperative Work.

Treem, J. W., Dailey, S. L., Pierce, C. S., & Leonardi, P. M. (2015). Bringing technological frames to work: How previous experience with social media shapes the technology's meaning in an organization. *Journal of Communication*, *65*(2), 396–422. doi:10.1111/jcom.12149.

Treem, J. W. & Leonardi, P. M. (2012). Social media use in organizations: Exploring the affordances of visibility, editability, persistence, and association. *Communication Yearbook*, *36*, 143–189.

Turel, O. & Serenko, A. (2012). The benefits and dangers of enjoyment with social networking websites. *European Journal of Information Systems*, *21*(5), 512–528.

Uratnik, M. (2016). Interactional service innovation with social media users. *Service Science*, *8*(3), 300–319.

Vaast, E., Davidson, E. J., & Mattson, T. (2013). Talking about technology: The emergence of new actors with new media. *MIS Quarterly*, *37*(4), 1069–1092.

Vaast, E. & Kaganer, E. (2013). Social media affordances and governance in the workplace: An examination of organizational policies. *Journal of Computer-Mediated Communication*, *19*(1), 78–101.

Vaast, E., Safadi, H., Lapointe, L., & Negoita, B. (2017). Social media affordances for connective action-an examination of microblogging use during the Gulf of Mexico oil spill. *MIS Quarterly*, *41*(4), 1179–1205.

Van Osch, W. & Steinfield, C. W. (2016). Team boundary spanning: strategic implications for the implementation and use of enterprise social media. *Journal of Information Technology*, *31*(2), 207–225.

von Krogh, G. (2012). How does social software change knowledge management? Toward a strategic research agenda. *The Journal of Strategic Information Systems*, *21*(2), 154–164. doi:10.1016/j.jsis.2012.04.003.

Vuori, V. & Okkonen, J. (2012). Knowledge sharing motivational factors of using an intra-organizational social media platform. *Journal of Knowledge Management*, *16*(4), 592–603.

Weber, M. S. & Shi, W. (2016). Enterprise social media. In C. Scott and L. Lewis (Eds.), *The International Encyclopedia of Organizational Communication*, Vol. 4 (pp. 1–9). Hoboken, NJ: Wiley Blackwell. doi:10.1002/9781118955567.wbieoc072.

Wegner, D. M. (1986). Transactive memory: A contemporary analysis of the group mind. In B. M. G. R. Goethals (Ed.), *Theories of group behavior* (pp. 185–205). New York, NY: Springer-Verlag.

Wegner, D. M. (1995). A computer network model of human transactive memory. *Social Cognition*, *13*(3), 319–339.

Williams, K. Y. & O'Reilly, C. A. (1998). Demography and diversity in organizations: A review of 40 years of research. In B. M. Staw & L. L. Cummings (Eds.), *Research in organizational behavior* (vol. *20*, pp. 77–140). Greenwich, CT: JAI Press.

Yavaş, M. & Yücel, G. (2014). Impact of homophily on diffusion dynamics over social networks. *Social Science Computer Review*, *32*(3), 354–372.

Yuan, Y. C., Fulk, J., Monge, P. R., & Contractor, N. (2010). Expertise directory development, shared task interdependence, and strength of communication network ties as multilevel predictors of expertise exchange in transactive memory work groups. *Communication Research*, *37*(1), 20–47.

Yuan, Y. C. & Gay, G. (2006). Homophily of network ties and bonding and bridging social capital in computer-mediated distributed teams. *Journal of Computer-Mediated Communication*, *11*(4), 1062–1084.

Zaccaro, S. J., Marks, M. A., & DeChurch, L. A. (Eds.). (2012). *Multiteam systems: An organization form for dynamic and complex environments*. New York, NY: Routledge.

Zappavigna, M. (2014). Enacting identity in microblogging through ambient affiliation. *Discourse & Communication*, *8*(2), 209–228.

PART V

Technology in Motivation and Performance

19 Telework

Outcomes and Facilitators for Employees

T. Alexandra Beauregard, Kelly A. Basile, and Esther Canonico

Flexible work practices refer to mutual arrangements made between employers and employees that vary the hours and location of work, often with the dual aim of improving employees' work-life balance and meeting the organization's needs (Thompson, Payne & Taylor, 2015). Telework is one such arrangement, which involves working away from the office for a portion of the work week while keeping in contact via information and communications technology (ICT) (Allen, Golden & Shockley, 2015). It can be used simultaneously with other flexible work arrangements, such as flexible hours and part-time work. Telework is usually conducted from a location of the employee's choosing (e.g., home) and can thus be differentiated from remote work, which more often takes place at different business units or while travelling for business purposes.

One acknowledged difficulty in drawing any firm conclusions about the impact of telework is that studies of this work arrangement appear in numerous disciplinary literatures: management, human resource management, industrial relations, psychology, family studies, sociology, information systems, logistics, and operations, for example. For the purposes of this chapter, which is attempting to identify individual-level factors that facilitate or hinder the telework experience, we will be drawing upon each of these literatures but focusing primarily upon those relevant to interpersonal processes rather than organization-level systems.

19.1 Outcomes of Telework

Outcomes of telework manifest themselves in a number of different ways. We will first examine work-related outcomes in the form of job performance, job attitudes, and professional isolation. Following this, we will review the effects of telework on well-being, in the form of stress and work-life balance.

19.1.1 Individual Performance

Numerous studies support the positive association between telework and increased productivity (Allen et al., 2015; Bélanger, 1999; Bloom et al., 2014; Crandall & Gao, 2005). For example, results from an experiment conducted with 252 call-center employees over nine months showed a 13 percent increase in job performance of the teleworkers compared to the office-based control group (Bloom et al., 2014). Some researchers have questioned the relationship between telework and productivity, as performance is often based on self-report measures rather than on more objective evidence (Bailey & Kurland, 2002). However, there is considerable empirical evidence that telework leads to not only greater self-reported productivity but also greater supervisor-rated performance (Kossek, Lautsch, & Eaton, 2006; Telework Exchange, 2008). For instance, a recent study using field data from 323 employees and 143 matched supervisors across a variety of organizations found that telework was positively associated with task performance (Gajendran, Harrison, & Delaney-Klinger, 2015).

The positive relationship between telework and productivity can be explained by multiple factors. First, employees working from home may simply put more hours into work: they have more time than office-based workers (as they do not travel to the office) and choose to use this extra time to work, or they may feel the need to reciprocate the flexibility provided by the organization by longer hours and/or harder work (Baruch, 2000; Gajendran & Harrison, 2007; Kelliher & Anderson, 2010). Empirical studies have frequently found that teleworkers put in longer hours when working at home (Kelliher & Anderson, 2010; Mariani, 2000; Peters & van der Lippe, 2007). For instance, in a qualitative study of 62 teleworkers in the UK, including some from a local government agency, 48 percent of participants reported having increased their working hours since having changed to telework from an office-based working arrangement (Baruch, 2000).

Second, as teleworkers lack the distractions of the office and have less involvement in organizational politics (Fonner & Roloff, 2010), they may be able to focus on their job tasks more effectively than at the office. For instance, in a qualitative study of UK professionals, employees teleworking for part of the week noted putting more effort due to the absence of distractions from the office; writing documents and analyzing large volumes of data were identified as tasks that benefited the most from being performed at home rather than at the office (Kelliher & Anderson, 2010). Third, having a relatively high level of discretion over the conditions under which the work is conducted (for example, choosing to work in the hours when one is more efficient) could lead to a gain in productivity when working from home rather than in a traditional office setting (Harpaz, 2002). Lastly, the perceived increase in autonomy when working from home (Baruch & Nicholson, 1997) could help employees to meet job-related goals and respond to job demands (Gajendran et al., 2015). The practice of telework may provide employees the flexibility to better manage the demands of their jobs and private lives and become more productive (Baruch, 2000).

However, telework may negatively affect individual performance. As explained later in this chapter, there is extensive empirical evidence that telework may lead to social and professional isolation (Baruch & Nicholson, 1997). Unsurprisingly, extensive use of telework may imply less face-to-face interaction with colleagues, increasing the sense of feeling out of touch with others in the workplace. Professional isolation among teleworkers may negatively affect job performance (Golden, Veiga, & Dino, 2008). The main argument underlying this statement is that professionally isolated teleworkers are less confident in their abilities and knowledge to perform their work; they have less opportunity to interact with coworkers and acquire and accurately interpret and use information that may be essential to performing the job well. Supporting this argument, Golden et al.'s (2008) quantitative study of a matched sample of 261 professional-level teleworkers and their managers revealed that the intensity of telework accentuates the negative impact of professional isolation on job performance. Results also revealed that more face-to-face interactions and access to communication-enhancing technologies (such as audio/videoconferencing, email/web meeting software) are likely to decrease professional isolation's negative impact on job performance. Echoing these results, a study of eighty-nine employees teleworking an average of 27.4 hours a week found a positive relationship between the richness of the communication media used and teleworkers' performance and job satisfaction (Turetken et al., 2011). Teleworkers communicating more via Skype video calls, for example, reported higher levels of job satisfaction and performance than those using messaging or email. These text-based forms of communication are considered the least "rich" media as they are further removed from in-person, face-to-face communication.

In addition, telework may also influence *perceptions* of individual performance. Telework presents managers with the difficulty associated with monitoring workers who are not working from the office. Felstead, Jewson and Walters (2002) attribute this difficulty to "visibility" and "presence." Visibility allows managers to observe workers' behavior and performance first-hand, while presence facilitates worker interactions and relationships with their coworkers. When supervising remote workers, managers must rely on output-related metrics and alternative monitoring techniques, often utilizing technology as well as trust, to both evaluate and manage performance quality and quantity (Felstead et al., 2002).

Working from home has also been negatively associated with absenteeism and turnover (Gibson et al., 2002). Given the greater flexibility that employees working from home usually have compared to office-based employees, teleworkers may be able to accommodate demands from private life (for example, taking an elderly parent to a hospital appointment) without needing to request a day off. At the same time, teleworkers may believe that it would be difficult finding similar flexible conditions in other organizations (Kelliher & Anderson, 2010) and choose to stay working for their employer.

19.1.2 Team-Related Performance

One of the main reasons managers and coworkers have been opposed to the implementation of telework is the perception that if one or more members regularly work away from the office it would negatively impact team performance (Lupton & Haynes, 2000). There is evidence which suggests this may be the case, that telework may negatively affect teleworkers' relationship with coworkers, coworkers' job satisfaction, knowledge transfer, and, ultimately, team performance. However, factors such as intensity of telework (i.e., the amount of time teleworkers work away from the office), communications with colleagues, and task interdependence may help to reduce or eliminate the potential negative effects of telework on team functioning.

Concerns that telework may harm the quality of relationship of teleworkers with their colleagues have been reported in a number of studies (Igbaria & Guimares, 1999; Nardi & Whittaker, 2002; Reinsch, 1997). The diminished frequency of face-to-face interactions associated with telework may reduce the richness of employees' connection with his or her peers. Coworkers may perceive spatial distance as psychological distance (out of sight, out of mind). As the contributions of teleworkers may not be as visible as those of employees working at the office, coworkers may perceive that teleworkers contribute less to the shared team objectives (Golden, 2006a). For individuals who work mostly from home, research results indicate that telework may be linked to decreased coworker relationship quality. In a large-scale study of professional employees in a telecommunications company, where the extent of telework ranged from two hours per week to over thirty-five hours per week, greater participation in telework was significantly associated with lower quality relationships with both supervisors and coworkers (Golden, 2006a). Similarly, a meta-analysis of telework research found that "high-intensity" telework, defined as working at home more than 2.5 days per week, had a negative relationship with coworker relationship quality; however, this effect was not found with "low-intensity" telework (Gajendran & Harrison, 2007). In line with these findings, several empirical studies suggest that telework is unlikely to have any negative effect on teleworkers' relationships with colleagues when they work at home for only part of their working week. For instance, a study of over 1,000 workers in the Netherlands demonstrated that employee participation in non-exclusive telework arrangements had no effect on social and communicative behavior toward coworkers and efforts to contribute to the social atmosphere in the team, e.g., keeping in close touch with team members, helping to organize social activities, and discussing non-work issues with colleagues (ten Brummelhuis, Haar, & van der Lippe, 2010).

Results from past empirical research also suggest that the number of teleworkers in an organization is negatively associated with coworker satisfaction (Golden, 2007). This relationship is moderated by the telework intensity, the extent of face-to-face interactions, and job autonomy. For example, Golden's (2007) study of 240 professionals at a high technology firm revealed that the more time employees work from home, the more negative the impact of teleworker prevalence on coworker satisfaction. Similarly, the more face-to-face interactions and job autonomy, the less that teleworker prevalence reduces coworker satisfaction. This dissatisfaction in turn predicted higher turnover intentions for office-based coworkers.

The number of teleworkers in an organization can also have a differential impact on relationship quality among teleworkers and office workers. For instance, a qualitative case study of a local government council in Britain found that while full-time teleworkers experienced diminishing levels of support from office-based colleagues after they began working from home, support from other teleworkers grew (Collins, Hislop, & Cartwright, 2016). The same study found that office workers identified other office workers as their main sources of workplace social support (Collins et al., 2016).

Coworker relationships are important as they have significant consequences for both teleworkers and office-based staff. A study of high-intensity teleworkers (working away from the office at least three business days per week) found that teleworkers liking their peers was positively related to teleworkers' satisfaction with their informal communication with coworkers, and with their organizational commitment and job satisfaction (Fay & Kline, 2011). This study found that social support provided by coworkers predicts high-intensity teleworkers' levels of organizational commitment and identification with the employing organization. Another study, investigating 226 employees who worked at home for an average of half the working week, found that a trusting relationship with colleagues and supervisors and an interpersonal bond with coworkers predicted increased knowledge sharing with coworkers, and these links were strengthened by a greater number of face-to-face interactions (Golden & Raghuram, 2010).

Regarding knowledge sharing, it has been argued that telework can jeopardize an organization's knowledge base due to its likely detrimental effects on knowledge transfer between teleworkers and office-based workers. There is some evidence that telework may negatively affect knowledge transfer in organizations (Taskin & Bridoux, 2010). This negative effect is the result of telework having a negative impact on components of organizational socialization (i.e., shared mental schemes, quality of relationships) that are key enablers of knowledge transfer. Past research has found that employees working remotely while relying on technology to communicate may experience lower levels of communication, information sharing, discussion quality, and communications richness than those employees who mainly interact face to face (Lowry et al., 2006). In contrast, there is evidence indicating that even though working from home for at least 50 percent of the time leads to less frequency of information exchange, it does not necessarily mean that it will affect the quality of information exchange, and fewer interactions with others may even prove to be beneficial (as interactions with others may disrupt work; Fonner & Roloff, 2010). A recent study examining the performance of teams in new product development projects in telecommunications has indicated that telework has a positive effect on team performance via facilitating knowledge sharing, cross-functional cooperation, and inter-organizational involvement (Coenen & Kok, 2014). This study found that the ease and speed of communications via telework supports knowledge transfer and collaboration in groups whose members are geographically dispersed, as long as there are some basic face-to-face interactions to create and maintain trust and good interpersonal relationships. It can therefore be tentatively concluded that telework does not necessarily have a detrimental effect on knowledge transfer. This finding notwithstanding, other studies do occasionally report on teleworker perceptions that reduced communication with colleagues results in reduced information acquisition. For example, a teleworker in Beauregard, Basile and Canonico's (2013, p. 58) qualitative study of public sector employees is quoted as saying: "Again it goes back to the fact that you are, potentially, away from hearing and subconscious learning. Lifting your head up and asking a question."

Related to communications and knowledge sharing, task interdependence is an important consideration when analyzing the impact of telework on teamwork. Past research suggests that higher levels of task interdependence are associated with lower productivity of teams with teleworkers (Turetken et al., 2011). As task interdependence requires a higher degree of information exchange and interaction between teleworkers and their colleagues, greater interdependence may hinder collaboration and performance due to limited range of interactions associated with telework (Bell & Kozlowski, 2002; Bordia, 1997). For less interdependent tasks (e.g., sequential or pooled tasks), where performance is the sum of individual members' performance, telework is unlikely to produce any negative outcomes for teamwork as team members do not need much direct interaction with each other (Maynard & Gilson, 2014). Empirical evidence also indicates that when workers with lower numbers of face-to-face interactions make themselves proactively available to their colleagues, team performance can be enhanced (Corwin, Lawrence, & Frost, 2001).

Whether telework is seen as the norm or as an exception in an organization may help to explain its effects on team performance. Some scholars speculate that in organizations that view telework as an exception, teleworkers may feel responsible for minimizing any negative impact of not being physically present at the office, for instance, by working longer hours to indicate their commitment to their office-based coworkers (Gajendran et al., 2015). In contrast, in organizations where telework is the norm, office-based workers may have adapted their processes to accommodate teleworkers (for example, by not starting team meetings earlier than 10:00 to allow employees working from home to travel to the office) in order to maximize the benefits for telework, which, ultimately, would lead to an increase in team performance and teleworkers are more likely to feel like legitimate, valued members of the team.

19.1.3 Job Attitudes

Job satisfaction is one of the most commonly reported consequences of telework arrangements (Manochehri & Pinkerton, 2003; Stephens & Szajna, 1998; Tremblay, 2002). The main explanatory factor for the link between telework and job satisfaction is that having the flexibility to work away from the office (and being able to exercise discretion over where, when, and how to work), may lead to an increased sense of job control and autonomy (Kelliher & Anderson, 2008; Tietze & Musson, 2005). This autonomy, in turn, is positively associated with job satisfaction (Gajendran & Harrison, 2007). However, empirical evidence regarding the impact of telework on job satisfaction remains mixed.

Past research has suggested that there is an inverted U-shaped relationship between the extent of telework and job satisfaction, with increases in job satisfaction dropping off as telework becomes more extensive (Golden, 2006a; Golden & Veiga, 2005). When the extent of telework is small (teleworking up to twelve hours per week), teleworkers can minimize negative effects from telework (such as isolation and frustration) and benefit from the perception of increased autonomy and report higher job satisfaction (Feldman & Gainey, 1998). However, extensive use of telework intensifies reliance on technology to communicate with others at the workplace, and also increases the likelihood of isolation and frustration, which may counteract the benefits of telework and reduce job satisfaction (Golden, 2006a). In contrast, a study with a sample of 192 participants (89 teleworkers and 103 office-based workers) found that employees extensively using telework (those who worked at home three days or more per week) remained more satisfied than office-based employees, questioning assumptions regarding the value of frequent face-to-face interactions in the workplace (Fonner & Roloff, 2010). This study helps to explain that satisfaction can be associated with working away from the stress of a traditional office setting; stress caused by meetings, interruptions and awareness of organizational politics.

Work-life conflict has also been studied as a mediator in the relationship between telework and job satisfaction. Results from this research have not been entirely consistent. Some researchers have found that telework was associated with a reduction of work-life conflict, leading to an increase in job satisfaction (Fonner & Roloff, 2010: Gajendran & Harrison, 2007). They also found the highest reduction in work-life conflict among employees who used telework more extensively. In contrast, other scholars argue that telework may increase work-life conflict as it may blur the lines between the work and non-work domains, making boundary violations more likely and, as a result, create conflict (Anderson & Kelliher, 2009).

The perception of greater autonomy among teleworkers is also positively related to greater commitment to the employer. Increased organizational commitment may reflect teleworkers' desire not to lose their working arrangement and its associated benefits; employees working flexibly and experiencing higher levels of autonomy have reported beliefs that it would be difficult to find comparable working arrangements in another organization (Anderson & Kelliher, 2009; Kelliher & Anderson, 2010). This link between telework and organizational commitment has been echoed in other studies, which have found that teleworkers are less likely to express a desire to leave their employer or, in some cases, to change jobs within the same organization (Glass & Riley, 1998; Golden, 2006b; Igbaria & Guimares, 1999; Kossek et al., 2006). In at least one case, however, this relationship has been found to be contingent upon the degree of telework performed. There is evidence of a positive relationship between telework and organizational commitment for moderate use of telework, but no significant effect for intensive use of telework (Hunton & Norman, 2010). In contrast, there is some research that suggests that telework is associated with lower organizational commitment, as teleworkers may become more committed to work from home than to their organization and have a more transactional view of the relationship with their employer (Tietze & Nadin, 2011).

Past research on the impact of telework on employee engagement, another important job-related attitude, is contradictory. On the one hand, empirical research has suggested that telework may have a positive relationship with employee engagement. For instance, Anderson and Kelliher (2009) found that flexible workers (who include teleworkers) were likely to be more engaged than non-flexible workers, as they reported higher levels of organizational commitment, job satisfaction, and organizational citizenship behavior than non-flexible workers. Having a choice over their working pattern and feeling the support and trust of their employer, who allowed their individual needs to be accommodated, are some of the factors that explained the referred positive outcomes of flexible working.

On the other hand, there is contrasting evidence that shows a negative relationship between telework and employee engagement, mediated by increased isolation (Arora, 2012; Davis & Cates, 2013; Sardeshmukh, Sharma, & Golden, 2012). An explanation for this finding is that social relationships drive human motivation and if the social need is thwarted, perceptions of isolation will emerge, which can have a negative influence on engagement among teleworkers (Davis & Cates, 2013). This relationship can be contingent upon the frequency of telework. Frequent use of telework has been associated with high level of isolation, which in turn, negatively impacts work engagement (Arora, 2012). Furthermore, a US survey of 417 teleworkers has found that telework is associated with lower employee engagement mediated by job demands and resources (Sardeshmukh et al., 2012). This study revealed that teleworkers may experience greater role ambiguity (job demand) and reduced social support and feedback (job resources) and, as a result, report lower levels of engagement.

A final note on telework's effect on job attitudes relates to the importance of a good fit between managers and subordinates. A quantitative study of over 11,000 workers and managers found that compared to colleagues whose managers were office-based, subordinates with telework managers reported lower levels of job satisfaction and increased intentions to leave the organization (Golden, 2011). However, telework subordinates whose managers were also teleworkers experienced more positive outcomes than teleworkers with office-based managers: more feedback, greater opportunities for professional development, higher job satisfaction, and lower turnover intentions. Based on these results, it seems that individuals with similar working arrangements may have an advantage when it comes to forging a successful working relationship.

19.1.4 Isolation

Closely linked to the impact of telework on coworker relationships are telework outcomes that are associated with isolation. The conduct of work activities in a space that is distant from the office and one's coworkers can lead to physical, social, and/or professional isolation among coworkers. Physical isolation refers to an employee conducting work activities in an environment that is separate from the work environment of their colleagues (Bartel, Wrzesniewski, & Wiesenfeld, 2012). Social isolation refers to an individual's feelings of lack of inclusion or connectedness within their work environment (Bentley et al., 2016). Last, professional isolation is linked to reduced development opportunities offered to employees; employees may be concerned that telework limits their opportunities for networking, learning, and/or informal mentoring (Cooper & Kurland, 2002). However, it is important to note that isolation is not a phenomenon specific to telework; employees can experience isolation even when working in the same physical location as their colleagues (Rokach, 1997; Smith, 1998). Conversely, some employees experience sustained connections with colleagues despite regular absences from the workplace (Duxbury & Neufeld, 1999; Vega & Brennan, 2000; Venkatesh & Speier, 2000). In addition, concerns about isolation and telework may actually exceed the degree of isolation experienced. In a study of 394 teleworkers, more than half indicated that prior to teleworking they were concerned about the loss of professional (53.5 percent) or social (54 percent) interactions; however, far fewer indicated that they actually experienced the loss of professional (24.2 percent) or social (32.7 percent) interactions after initiating telework (Maruyama & Tietze, 2012). However, despite the discrepancy between perceptions and experiences of isolation, research has identified some important outcomes associated with isolation resulting from telework.

In many organizations, teleworkers have concerns about the impact of isolation on their career prospects, fearing that they are not only out of sight, but also out of mind when it comes time for managers to allocate key assignments or nominate candidates for promotion (Baruch, 2001; Gibson et al., 2002; Khalifa & Davidson, 2000). A qualitative study of seventy-six remote workers at a Canadian subsidiary of a multi-national organization found that workers feared that, despite strong performance and higher productivity levels, due to their ability to work from home, they would be forgotten in terms of career advancement due to their lack of visibility in the office (Richardson & Kelliher, 2015). Research has also found that these fears may not be unfounded (McCloskey & Igbaria, 2003). In Golden et al.'s (2008) study of 261 teleworkers and their managers, self-reported professional isolation among teleworkers was negatively related to their job performance, as rated by their managers. This effect was particularly pronounced for teleworkers who worked extensively from home and engaged in limited amounts of face-to-face interaction with colleagues and managers. Further research examines the contributing factors to concerns about telework and career advancement. A study of 394 British Telecom teleworkers observed that lack of professional interaction was an important outcome associated with telework that led to concerns about the ability to advance in one's career (Maruyama & Tietze, 2012). In particular, lack of professional interaction reduced employees' opportunities to share knowledge, learn from their colleagues, and build their professional networks.

Research has sought to explain the linkage between telework, isolation, and employee attachment to or identification with their organization. For example, work by Bartel et al. (2012) has linked experiences of isolation with employees' perceived respect from their colleagues and organizational identification. Conducting surveys with participants in alternative work programs across two companies, Bartel and colleagues found that at higher levels of physical isolation, workers perceived that they were regarded with lower levels of respect by their colleagues. This, in turn, reduced their own identification with the organization. Belle, Burley and Long's (2015) qualitative study of high-intensity teleworkers further explored factors contributing to employees' sense of belonging in the workplace. The research found three contributing factors to teleworker perceptions of belonging: the sense that they had a choice in their telework arrangement; the sense that they were able to negotiate the specifics of their telework arrangement; and having strong knowledge of how the organization operates prior to engaging in telework. These are important considerations for managers of teleworkers, because organizational identification and attachment have been associated with positive organizational outcomes such as increased individual performance (He & Brown, 2013).

19.1.5 Well-Being: Work-Life Balance

One of the most frequently reported outcomes of telework is that it affords individuals more opportunities to manage the demands of their work and non-work roles, reducing experiences of work-to-life conflict (Gajendran & Harrison, 2007). For instance, a survey of 454 professional-level employees who divided their work time between an office and home found that the more time per week individuals worked at home, the lower their work-to-life conflict (Golden, Veiga, & Simsek, 2006). This effect was even more pronounced for employees reporting higher levels of job autonomy and scheduling flexibility, which presumably allowed them to arrange their work tasks in such a way as to accommodate their family or other non-work commitments. The lower levels of work-to-life conflict experienced by teleworkers have been found to predict, in turn, higher job satisfaction, perceptions of performance, reduced intentions to leave the organization, and decreased levels of job-related stress for teleworkers (Fonner & Roloff, 2010; Gajendran & Harrison, 2007; Vega, Anderson, & Kaplan, 2015; Wheatley, 2012).

Qualitative research helps to explain why telework has such beneficial effects on work-to-life conflict. Telework saves employees time, because it reduces or eliminates commuting time that cannot be used for work, family, or leisure activities (Hill, Ferris, & Martinson, 2003). It also allows employees to determine the timing of their task completion; for instance, interviews with forty-seven dual-earner couples with children found that many of the participants chose to work at times when their children would be busy with other activities or already asleep for the evening (Haddock et al., 2006). By doing so, participants could complete greater amounts of work without having job-related obligations interfere with their family time. This has knock-on effects on family relationships. In a qualitative study of sixty-two UK teleworkers, including some employed by a local government, participants reported that since they began working at home, they had noticed improvements in their relationships with family members (Baruch, 2000). In addition, telework also allows employees to be more flexible in meeting the needs of their employers. A qualitative study of eleven teleworkers in the UK found that the ability to telework was helpful in balancing their non-work obligations as well as giving them greater flexibility to manage work demands, such as evening conference calls (Grant, Wallace, & Spurgeon, 2013).

These beneficial effects on work-to-life conflict notwithstanding, telework does not appear to be a quick ticket to better work-life balance for all employees. Because work is taking place in the same physical space allocated to an individual's personal or family life, it can sometimes be difficult to erect and maintain clear boundaries between work and non-work domains. The time and place separations between home and work that exist for office-based workers do not arise as naturally for teleworkers; telework increases the permeability of boundaries between life domains, making it easier for one domain to intrude upon the other (Standen, Daniels, & Lamond, 1999). A study drawing on data from the 2001, 2006, and 2012 Skills and Employment Survey (SES) series found that telework was associated with higher levels of organizational commitment, enthusiasm, and job satisfaction; however, it was also associated with working beyond formal working hours, expending voluntary effort, and work-life spillover (Felstead & Henseke, 2017).

Suppressing work-related thoughts, emotions, and behaviors can be challenging, because the simultaneous presence of work and non-work cues can blur the boundary between the two domains (Raghuram & Wieselfeld, 2004). For example, research conducted with UK telework professionals found that some experienced difficulty in putting an end to the working day (Kelliher & Anderson, 2010). The presence of work-related materials in visible areas of the home seems to exacerbate this boundary permeability. A study of public sector teleworkers in the UK showed the differential effects of having designated versus common spaces for work and non-work activities (Basile & Beauregard, 2016). Those with designated spaces for work activities seemed better able to disengage from work versus those that utilized shared spaces for work and home activities. Quotes from a teleworker with a designated space (p. 107) versus one who conducted his work activity out of his dining room (p. 108), respectively, illustrate this phenomenon:

> I am one of the lucky ones, I actually have a dedicated office. I've got a door and a lock. So I didn't have to do the mental changing of shoes, it's a case of switching my computer off and closing the door.

> So I worked in the dining room for two years . . . So for two years whilst we had dinner, tea, lunch, the computers and my files sat next to us. It was far from ideal especially if the children had time off.

Research suggests that teleworkers engage in boundary work to manage the integration of work and home roles exacerbated by telework. For example, Fonner and Stache's (2012) qualitative study of 142 teleworkers who engaged in telework at least one day per month found that teleworkers used space, time, communications, and technology strategies to manage the boundaries between their home and work activities. Participants identified closing their door of their home office at the end of the day as a space-related strategy for managing the work/non-work boundary and clearly communicating their work hours to both managers and family members as a time related strategy. Similarly, teleworkers used communications and technology to manage work/non-work boundaries, for example by sending emails to notify colleagues that they were making the transition from home to work or shutting down work-related computers and turning off phones to mark the end of the workday.

Interestingly, technology seems to have become a doubled-edged sword in terms of managing work and home boundaries. The "always-on" culture promulgated by advances in ICT encourages workers to remain contactable and responsive beyond regular working hours (McDowall & Kinman, 2017). This pressure is exacerbated for teleworkers, who rely on technology to display their virtual presence and thus prove that they are working. Fonner and Roloff's (2012) study comparing the experiences of 89 high-intensity teleworkers and 104 office-based employees found that teleworkers struggled with the need to utilize technology to maintain a social presence and social interactions with colleagues, while at the same time managing technology so that they were able to disconnect from work during personal time. Therefore, the same resource teleworkers might use to manage their work-home boundary might reduce their ability to foster connections with others in the workplace. Similarly, Sewell and Taskin (2015) found that teleworkers' use of technology to engage in display behaviors that enhance their visibility and availability lead to feelings of being "shackled to their workstations at home" (p. 1519). Another study of work-related social media use found that the use of social media for work-related activities, such as finding experts in specific occupations or making others aware of one's own professional activities, results in both greater work-to-life and life-to-work conflict (van Zoonen, Verhoeven, & Vliegenthart, 2016).

Research has also sought to examine whether the impact of telework differs in terms of the direction of work-to-life and life-to-work conflict. Allen, Johnson, Kiburz and Shockley's (2013) meta-analysis found that there are, indeed, differences in the conflict experienced when flexible working is an alternative. Their study demonstrated that flexible working arrangements were negatively associated with work-to-life conflict and that the degree of this association was stronger than that for life-to-work conflict. The meta-analysis also found some interesting differences in terms of whether time-based or place-based (telework) flexibility was used, with flexibility in terms of time leading to greater work-to-life conflict than flexibility in terms of place.

There is, however, research showing evidence that increased participation in telework is linked to higher levels of life-to-work conflict – particularly for those individuals with heavier caregiving responsibilities for children or adult dependents, which can intrude upon work activities more easily when the workplace is also the family home (Golden et al., 2006). Kossek et al.'s (2006) research on how people manage the boundaries between their work and personal lives has found that teleworkers who prefer to integrate their work and non-work activities – for instance, by switching back and forth between work and personal tasks throughout the day – are more likely to experience life-to-work conflict as a result of blurred boundaries.

19.1.6 Well-Being: Stress

The general consensus in the research literature is that telework is associated with significantly lower levels of work-related stress than those experienced by office-based staff (Gajendran & Harrison, 2007; Golden, 2006b; Raghuram & Wieselfeld, 2004). Teleworkers who work at least three days a week at home report less stress generated by frequent meetings and interruptions by colleagues, and perceive less exposure to office-based politics (Fonner & Roloff, 2010). Other research has found that teleworkers encounter fewer job stressors, such as role conflict and ambiguity, than office-based staff, and that their resultant lower levels of work-related stress are in turn predictive of increased job satisfaction and commitment to the organization (Igbaria & Guimares, 1999).

These positive results may be explained by the Job Demands-Resources Model (Demerouti et al., 2001) of occupational stress and motivation. The model defines demands as physical or social aspects of a job that require effort and thus have physical and mental costs, and resources as workplace or organizational aspects that help with the achievement of work goals, reduce demands, or stimulate growth and development. Job demands lead to strain, whereas job resources lead to motivation. Telework would therefore appear to function more as a resource than as a demand.

However, this classification of telework may depend on individual differences among workers. For some, telework may function as a demand. For example, Anderson, Kaplan and Vega's (2015) diary study of 102 US government employees found that generally, employees had higher levels of positive affect and lower levels of negative affect on days when they worked from home. Individual differences impacted these affective experiences, however; employees with high levels of social connectedness and those rated highly on openness to experience were more likely to have positive affective gains on telework days, while those with a tendency toward rumination were less likely to experience positive affective gains. In addition, some scholars have found greater evidence of mental health problems among teleworkers, compared to their office-based colleagues (Mann & Holdsworth, 2003). For instance, Kossek et al. (2006) found that formal participation in a telework arrangement was significantly associated with higher rates of depression – although for one specific group, female teleworkers with dependent children, rates of depression were actually lower than those of office-based staff.

Research also suggests that there may be a threshold at which the amount of time spent engaged in telework no longer yields positive outcomes. Golden and Veiga's (2005) study of 321 teleworkers at a high tech firm found a curvilinear relationship between levels of telework and job satisfaction, whereby satisfaction was highest at moderate levels of telework, but declined among extensive teleworkers. Another study of 261 teleworkers and their managers found that professional isolation increased at more extensive levels of telework, reducing performance outcomes (Golden et al., 2008).

There is mixed evidence regarding the nature of teleworkers' work-related stress. We know that teleworkers tend to put in longer hours of work and may exert greater intensive effort on the job, as discussed earlier in this chapter, and these factors may lend themselves to work-related stress in a way not experienced by office-based staff (Tietze & Musson, 2005). However, research seems to indicate that although teleworkers may work more overtime, they also report reduced feelings of time pressure compared to office-based workers, and this is particularly the case for those who spend more than one day per week working at home (Hill et al., 2001; Peters & van der Lippe, 2007). A qualitative study of work intensification among UK telework professionals found that workers did not experience negative outcomes from this intensification; instead, teleworkers appeared to be voluntarily increasing their levels of effort in exchange for the privilege of being able to work at home (Kelliher & Anderson, 2010). The element of choice, or autonomy, involved in this extension of the working day and intensification of effort may serve to counteract any potentially stressful effects of longer work hours.

Other research examines teleworker engagement and exhaustion from a job-demands and resources model. Sardeshmukh et al.'s (2012) study of 471 teleworkers at a US-based supply chain organization found that while telework had a negative relationship with time pressure and role conflict, it was positively related to both autonomy and role ambiguity. However, findings also indicated that job demands and resources mediated the relationship between amount of time spent teleworking, exhaustion, and engagement, again suggesting that contextual factors such as level of time pressure and degree of autonomy will impact telework outcomes. Further research suggests that gender may be an important indicator of stress-related outcomes associated with telework. A study of 101 Swedish government employees who recently began engaging in telework found that while all workers indicated that working from home relieved some of the stress associated with commuting and balancing work and family, women reported reduced levels of "restoration" from being in the home environment, while men reported enhanced levels (Hartig, Kylin, & Johansson, 2007). This suggests that, for women, the benefits they accrue in terms of balancing work and family may be diminished due to increased levels of stress associated with the home environment.

19.1.7 Concluding Thoughts on Outcomes of Telework

The majority of the studies reviewed here are based on research conducted among workers who work from home part of the time but not all of the time. Working at home for the entirety of one's working week appears to be a relatively rare arrangement, and there are conflicting views among scholars about whether telework works best as a moderate (one or two days a week) or a high-intensity (half the working week or more) activity. The practitioner-oriented literature is less equivocal, and tends to be of the opinion that to avoid the potential risks of telework, a non-exclusive telework arrangement is advisable for most organizations (Pyöriä, 2011).

A prospective counter-argument to this perspective derives from research findings that employee experience with telework intensifies the ability of working at home to decrease levels of work-to-life conflict and work-related stress. This suggests that there is a learning curve associated with telework, and that as workers adjust to the arrangement, they adapt over time to its advantages and disadvantages and develop ways to maximize the former while reducing the latter (Gajendran & Harrison, 2007). This can involve modifying one's use of technology to communicate with others, and amending one's work processes to better suit an environment free of office-based distractions but also lacking face-to-face contact and cues for taking breaks or finishing work for the day.

In addition to individual employees developing strategies to overcome some of the potential drawbacks of telework, managers can take steps to smooth the way. Scholars have suggested that managers reduce social isolation among teleworkers by scheduling regular staff meetings, providing intranet systems with which teleworkers and office-based staff can communicate with one another, releasing information bulletins to keep all employees informed of work-related news, and organizing social events at which teleworkers and office-based staff can interact (Mann, Varey, & Button, 2000). Some have argued for the creative use of communication technologies to substitute for face-to-face interaction, such as telephone conference calls, videoconferencing, and Web-enabled meetings (Potter, 2003). For instance, some organizations have created virtual "watercoolers" online where employees can post jokes and photos, and comment on workplace social events, football matches, or television programs (McAdams, 2006).

19.2 Contributing Factors to Effective Telework

Having examined the outcomes of telework, we now turn our attention to factors that contribute to a successful telework experience. These can be grouped into three main categories: characteristics of the job, characteristics of the individual teleworker, and characteristics of the teleworker's manager(s). Compared to the number of studies conducted on the outcomes of telework, there is relatively little published research on any of these contributing factors.

19.2.1 Characteristics of the Job

Jobs characterized by individual control of work pace and little need for face-to-face interaction with colleagues or clients are generally thought to be most suitable for telework arrangements (Bailey & Kurland, 2002), but little empirical research has been conducted in this area. A notable exception is work by Turetken et al. (2011), who found that low task interdependence is associated with greater teleworker productivity, and that work output measurability is most important determinant of teleworker success as reported by HR managers. A common theme in the literature is the extent to which idiosyncratic details of individual jobs, rather than general job traits, are more likely to determine whether a particular employee can successfully engage in telework. Based on direct knowledge of what their work requires them to do, employees will often choose not to request or engage in a telework arrangement due to the belief that their jobs are not capable of being successfully performed away from the office. What this means is that perceptions of job suitability, generated by personal knowledge of specific jobs, may be a better predictor of who is suitable for telework than an assessment of general job categories.

19.2.2 Characteristics of the Teleworker

It is a generally acknowledged truth that in the majority of organizations, little is known about how to select the most suitable individuals to participate in telework arrangements, and this is supported by research conducted among employers (Verbeke et al., 2008). Surprisingly little research has investigated or found evidence for specific traits, skills, or motivations common to successful teleworkers. There is a great deal of guidance based upon common sense assumptions or anecdotal evidence generated from observations of small numbers of teleworkers. For instance, managers have been advised that successful teleworkers must have the ability to work independently with little supervision, the ability to work without much social contact, and the personality traits of dependability and honesty (Baruch, 2001; Harpaz, 2002). Employers have also been warned to ensure that teleworkers are self-disciplined, organized and motivated, in order to segment work and home activities and manage effectively the distractions associated with the home environment (Mello, 2007; Raghuram & Wieselfeld, 2004).

Some research has asked teleworkers themselves about necessary qualities an individual should possess in order to be suitable for working at home. The teleworkers' responses largely echo the advice given to managers, by listing self-discipline, self-motivation, ability to work alone, and organizational skills as required attributes of a successful teleworker. Other features they identified were tenacity, self-confidence, time-management skills, and integrity (Baruch, 2000; Greer & Payne, 2014).

Moving beyond the realm of opinions and personal experience, more rigorously designed research finds that diligence and organizational skills are no more important for teleworkers than they are for office-based staff (O'Neill et al., 2009). O'Neill et al.'s (2009) large-scale study of teleworkers and their office-based colleagues showed that need for autonomy, however, was much more strongly associated with self-rated job performance and job satisfaction for teleworkers than for office-based workers. People with a higher need for autonomy are those who prefer to set their own hours of work, plan their own work processes and schedules, and generally "be their own boss": all activities congruent with telework. This trait has been advocated by scholars as an important one for telework, as teleworkers are usually expected to work without direct supervision and set their own schedule and methods for accomplishing their job tasks (Harris, 2003; Konradt, Hertel, & Schmook, 2003).

Several personality traits have also been linked to success in telework. While individuals high in openness to experience find the prospect of telework more attractive (Gainey & Clenney, 2006), those who are highly extroverted may have a more difficult time participating in this arrangement. In O'Neill et al.'s (2009) study, higher levels of sociability in teleworkers were related to lower job performance. People who are highly sociable are probably more likely to feel the absence of a workplace setting populated by others, and to feel socially isolated when working at home by themselves (Weisenfeld, Raghuram, & Garud, 2001).

19.2.3 Characteristics of Management

Scholars have argued that a successful telework program is more a function of leadership than of technology, with a creative and progressive leadership mentality being required to design and implement telework schemes effectively (Offstein, Morwick, & Koskinen, 2010). The consensus in the telework literature is that managers must be willing and able to relinquish traditional notions of how best to manage performance – usually based on direct supervision – and adopt new ways of motivating and monitoring their staff. Four themes that dominate the literature on management of teleworkers are those of trust, performance management, communication, and training.

19.2.3.1 Trust

In order for an organization to adopt a telework program, management must exhibit at least some trust in employees (Pyöriä, 2011). That having been said, managing teleworkers does represent a special challenge for managers, especially those who prefer to engage in direct supervision of their staff, with their employees in sight as often as possible. Managers may be concerned about their loss of direct control over teleworkers (Potter, 2003; Robertson, Maynard, & McDevitt, 2003), and may not be able to detect if or when an employee is experiencing difficulties, is working too much, or is not working enough (Manochehri & Pinkerton, 2003). Those managers who subscribe to "Theory X" (McGregor, 1960) believe that workers are inherently lazy and motivated primarily by money and the threat of punishment. Theory X managers may therefore assume that teleworkers are likely to take advantage of the opportunity to slack off undetected at home. Managers who subscribe to "Theory Y," in contrast, believe that intrinsic motivation plays a more important role than extrinsic motivation and that workers enjoy taking responsibility for their work and do not require direct supervision to complete their tasks. These managers are therefore more likely to exhibit trust in their teleworking subordinates.

One of the greatest barriers to telework success is the presence of traditional managerial attitudes about employees needing to be seen in order to be considered productive (Lupton & Haynes, 2000). These attitudes can often be quite resistant to change. Despite the advent of communications technology that enables individuals to work anywhere, at any time, many organizations continue to value and reward face-time and operate under the assumption that visibility equates to productivity and commitment (Beauregard, 2011). There is little evidence that many organizations take the time to develop new management approaches geared toward alternative working arrangements such as telework. Research shows that in the telework context, trust is positively related to employee perceptions of good performance and job satisfaction, and negatively related to job stress (Grant et al., 2013; Staples, 2001). A culture of trust requires a re-evaluation of what it means to be "working," and how managers recognize and evaluate work. A critical component of such a culture is a results-based management system.

19.2.3.2 Performance Management

To adapt effectively to a telework program, managers often need to change their monitoring strategies from behavior-based to output-based controls (Cooper & Kurland, 2002; Konradt et al., 2003). Behavior-based controls refers to the relatively common practice of assessing performance based on employees' observable actions, whereas output-based controls involve assessing performance based on output, products, or other deliverables of the work rather than on the process or behaviors used to generate the output. Madlock's (2012) study of full-time teleworkers found that managers of teleworkers were more likely to use a task-oriented rather than a relational-oriented leadership style, and that this task-oriented leadership was a significant predictor of teleworkers' job satisfaction, organizational commitment, and satisfaction with communication. Managers who cannot – or will not – modify their supervisory styles are likely to experience a deterioration of their relationships with telework subordinates (Shin et al., 2000).

Teleworkers' attitudes and behaviors will also be affected by the performance management system used. For example, research by Virick, DaSilva and Arrington (2010) has found that when objective criteria such as goals and measurable targets are used to evaluate performance outcomes, there is no link between the extent of participation in telework and teleworkers' job satisfaction. However, when use of objective criteria in performance evaluation is low, and the organizational culture rewards visibility in the workplace, teleworkers exhibit higher job satisfaction when they work at home only one or two days per week rather than exclusively.

19.2.3.3 Communication

Scholars and practitioners alike have occasionally expressed concern than an organization's culture may lose strength as a telework program gathers speed, because inculcating that culture in telework employees will be more difficult than doing so with office-based staff whose frequent face-to-face interactions sustain and reinforce organizational norms (Manochehri & Pinkerton, 2003; Mills et al., 2001). This potential for weakened culture will obviously depend on the organization; research evidence suggests that some cultures can easily be kept alive and well if constant communication among employees is not necessary (Gainey, Kelley, & Hill, 1999).

In almost all organizations, of course, some degree of communication among staff is required. Research investigating effective managerial communication approaches has determined that managers should stay in close contact with teleworkers, but this contact should emphasize information-sharing rather than close monitoring of work processes. Teleworkers with managers using an information-sharing approach have been found more likely to report lower work-to-life conflict, better performance, and higher rates of helping their coworkers (Lautsch, Kossek, & Eaton, 2009). Other communication strategies linked to greater job satisfaction, output, and loyalty among teleworkers include communicating job expectations in a clear and concise manner; communicating job responsibilities, goals and objectives clearly; and clearly communicating deadlines (Ilozor, Ilozor, & Carr, 2001).

Communication strategies can be linked to leadership style. Brunelle's (2013) research with mobile workers describes their work context as one in which managers must be able to influence subordinates by means of asynchronous, remote communications rather than rely upon face-to-face interactions. Transformational leadership, which involves communicating a vision, creating meaning, empowering employees, and delegating, improves teleworkers' mental representations of effective behaviors to be adopted and facilitates teleworkers' identification with the organization and/or with their manager (Larsson et al., 2007). Using a transformational leadership style may, therefore, enable managers to compensate for the potentially negative effects of distance on teleworkers' job-related attitudes (Brunelle, 2013).

The relative ease of face-to-face communication compared to making a phone call or composing an email plays a role in determining managerial attitudes toward telework. Research conducted in an Italian call center demonstrated that although line managers were technically capable of relying upon electronic monitoring to supervise their staff, the managers preferred that employees remained directly visible to them (Valsecchi, 2006). Having all staff physically present in the workplace and being able to wander around in sight of the call center operatives assisted the line managers in their exercise of control over the pace and quality of work, and in communicating with employees during crisis situations that arose and disappeared in rapid succession.

This idea that communication is enhanced when it is done face-to-face is reinforced by a remark from a teleworker in Beauregard et al.'s (2013, p. 53) study of a large, public sector organization: "I find when you ring in sometimes, if your other colleagues are there when you are on the phone, you can hear what's going on but I suppose you don't feel part of it because you can't read people's expressions or anything to see a problem."

19.2.3.4 Training

The need for training has been discussed in much of the telework literature, with the general consensus being that teleworkers should be trained on the use of equipment, time management, and establishing boundaries between home and work (Greer & Payne; 2014; Haines III, St. Onge, & Archambault, 2002). The results of a telework study involving IBM employees demonstrated that good training is of vital importance to both teleworkers and their managers, and should focus not only on technology but also on social and psychological adjustments to be made by teleworkers (Hill et al., 1998). There is empirical evidence that organizational support and training can promote teleworkers' resilience and well-being. A quantitative research with a sample of 804 teleworkers from 28 organizations suggests that social organizational support (including supervisor, coworker, and organizational support) can help reduce psychological strain and social isolation (Bentley et al., 2016). Another study shows that teleworking employees participating in guided health discussions report less stress regarding time manage-ment, communication, and ergonomic issues (e.g., body position while working) compared with a control group of teleworkers (Konradt et al., 2000).

Training companies providing client organizations with training for teleworkers cover topics such as setting up a home office, maintaining work relationships and professional credibility, and managing one's time, workload, and performance; specific training for managers of teleworkers addresses the creation and mainte-nance of a work environment that supports telework (Johnson et al., 2007). Despite the discussion surrounding telework training and the innovations exhibited by select organizations, many employers lauded for their successful telework pro-grams (such as Allianz Insurance UK, Ernst & Young UK, Intel, and LaSalle Investment Management) fail to offer any training specific to engaging in telework or managing teleworkers (Beauregard et al., 2013; Johnson et al., 2007).

19.2.4 Concluding Thoughts on Contributing Factors to Successful Telework

In general, the literature advocates a number of conditions to be met in order for a successful telework experience to take place. Some of these are technical in nature: job responsibilities must be able to be performed away from the office, and work spaces at employees' homes should be safe, secure, and reasonably distrac-tion-free. Some conditions are concerned with the teleworkers themselves: suc-cessful teleworkers need to be able to work without close supervision, should be able to separate their work from their personal lives, and must be capable of overcoming the threats posed by working in isolation (O'Neill et al., 2009). Finally, scholars and practitioners emphasize that successful telework programs are characterized both by broad institutional support, and by the presence of managers who understand the value of telework and have confidence in the benefits it can bring (Mello, 2007).

19.3 New Directions

While this chapter has reviewed a great deal of what we do know about telework's outcomes for the individual and how these might best be facilitated, there are undoubtedly gaps in our knowledge regarding the repercussions of tele-work for employees and organizations. Two such areas of note are the impact of telework on employees' extra-role performance, and on organizations' succession planning.

Although there are few studies of the relationship between telework and extra-role behaviors, recent empirical evidence suggests that those working from home are likely to exhibit enhanced citizenship behavior. Gajendran et al. (2015) found a positive link between telework and contextual performance, defined as "a set of interpersonal and volitional behaviors that contribute to the organization by creat-ing a positive social and psychological climate" (p. 3). Employees with access to the flexibility of working from home are likely to feel obligated toward those who granted them that access (their employer). To relieve that obligation, employees may not only work longer or harder but also reciprocate through discretionary citizenship behaviors.

This sense of reciprocity should be examined over time, however. Gajendran et al. (2015) found that telework normativeness moderated the relationship between telework and contextual behavior. In other words, when telework was a relatively customary or normative aspect of a workplace, it weakened the intensity of the need to reciprocate the provision of telework. The moderating effect of normativeness can be explained by social exchange theory with the norm of reciprocity (Blau, 1964; Gouldner, 1960). When telework is perceived as a "special" arrangement (i.e., individuals who telework are a small fraction of the work group), employees are more likely to feel indebted to the managers and organization that provided them with special treatment and, thus, reciprocate by engaging in discretionary citizenship behaviors. Conversely, if telework is widely established in a workplace, teleworkers are likely to perceive such an arrangement as customary or normative. This normativeness may diminish teleworkers' level of indebtedness toward their managers and organization, as the practice of telework is no longer perceived as a special arrangement (Canonico, 2016). Might employees who avail themselves of telework arrangements develop a similar reduction in feelings of indebtedness over time, as telework becomes an established routine and perceptions of it being an extra benefit decline? This question calls for further longitudinal research on the long-term impact of telework on teleworker perceptions of reciprocity and discretionary behavior.

With regard to succession planning, extended telework may influence this process in two ways. First, research has demonstrated that teleworkers' less visible presence in the workplace may reduce their opportunities for learning and development, potentially limiting their career advancement opportunities (Cooper & Kurland, 2002). In addition, teleworkers may find that the advantages they incur by giving up these opportunities in exchange for greater work-life balance outweigh the monetary or professional advantages associated with a higher-level position. For instance, Beauregard et al.'s (2013) study of teleworkers in a UK public sector organization found that full-time teleworkers were less likely than occasional teleworkers to seek promotion if that required returning to office-based work. When asked about any potential drawbacks of telework for this organization, one senior manager confirmed that the lack of teleworker interest in taking on roles that would require an increased presence in the office was likely to generate difficulties for organizational succession (Canonico, 2016). Further investigation of these links between telework and succession planning, over time and using quantitative as well as qualitative methods, might help to clarify the processes in play and assist researchers and practitioners to design telework policy and job-design practices to overcome any problems that may exist.

In addition to further research investigating the gaps of which we are aware, research also needs to consider what telework practices may look like in the future.

Research has found that the growth of telework statistically surpasses many of the common economic and demographic factors we often ascribe as its drivers. For example, an analysis of trend data from the 1981–2015 Labour Force Series (LFS) surveys found that the increasing trend of work being completed away from a physical workplace far outpaces the growth of the "knowledge economy," the increase in flexible working arrangements, and demographic shifts in the workforce (Felstead & Henseke, 2017). Therefore this calls for research on telework across a broader spectrum of contextual factors.

One possible avenue for research might be to look at the growing impact of multiple layers of cultural contexts, across organizations, industries, and nations, in order to better explain the conditions under which telework will result in positive or negative effects. Beauregard, Basile and Thompson (2018) have proposed a model that examines the impact of national culture on organizational policy, organizational culture, and individual work-life role preferences. For example, an individual's national culture may influence their preferences as to how they manage their work and non-work roles; women from countries with low levels of gender egalitarianism may be more likely to take on a telework role to meet their family obligations than men (Powell, Francesco & Ling, 2009). In addition, national culture will also influence the more formal (institutional) industrial/organizational work-life policies, as well as attitudes toward the usage of these policies (Ollier-Malaterre & Foucreault, 2017; Piszczek & Berg, 2014). For example, Sweden's recent adoption of a six-hour workday will influence both formal organizational work-life policies as well as more informal practices amongst workers with reduced scheduled (Matharu, 2015). The model suggests that when there is alignment between national culture, organizational culture and individual preferences, individuals are able to develop a "coherent work-family role orientation" resulting in organizational citizenship behaviors (OCBs), well-being, and satisfaction with work-life balance; misalignment results in a "dissonant work-family role orientation" resulting in work-life conflict, stress, reduced OCBs and productivity, and higher turnover (Beauregard, Basile & Thompson, 2018).

19.4 Implications for Theory and Practice

Based on the evidence presented in this chapter, we can conclude that the effects of telework on performance and well-being are becoming more and more nuanced. This can be attributed to an increasing number of contextual factors that influence the telework experience, such as telework intensity, task interdependence, communications richness and frequency, as well as organizational and national culture. Therefore, extant theory must be re-examined and new theory developed to account for the more complex landscape in which telework takes place. For example, Piszczek and Berg's (2014) article on the impact of regulatory institutions on HR practices and individual integration segmentation preferences helped to expand on boundary theory, thus addressing one area of contextual importance.

Research on telework and work-life boundary management has clearly identified that individuals react differently to differing levels of home and work integration (Beauregard et al., 2013; Shockley & Allen, 2010). In addition, research has also established the importance of autonomy and control in telework experiences (Kelliher & Anderson, 2008; Kurland & Egan, 1999; Kossek et al., 2006). Eligibility for participation in telework arrangements should therefore take into account individual preferences and abilities for independent, self-directed scheduling and work performance in order to gain the intended benefits of these programs. Assessing employees for these preferences and telework-related abilities before they engage in working away from the office on a regular basis may help to predict telework success, and could be used to screen candidates for their suitability. Such an assessment could also form part of telework induction training, and help both employees and managers to plan for the new arrangement and to anticipate problems that might arise.

Organizations may also seek to do further assessment and engage in the development of more tailored approaches to telework for employees with differing preferences and boundary management tactics. For example, one group of researchers has created a tool named the Work-Life Indicator, which could be of use to both individuals and organizations in terms of assessing an individual's boundary management profile (Kossek et al., 2012). This instrument assesses role transition behaviors, the centrality of work and non-work roles, and perceptions of control over the management of their work and non-work boundaries. Another researcher has developed an assessment tool to measure the impact of telework on employees by assessing eight dimensions, including work effectiveness, management style, trust, role conflict, boundary management, and well-being, both before and after engaging in a telework arrangement (Grant, 2017). This too could be used by organizations to help managers identify and address any difficulties employees encounter in adjusting to their new work arrangement, via coaching or training.

Based on this review of the telework research literature, we recommend that evidence-based guidelines be developed and made available to organizations for the successful implementation and management of telework. These recommended guidelines are summarized in Table 19.1 and should address (1) implementation requirements, (2) employee eligibility, (3) employee suitability, (4) trial period and training, (5) intensity of telework, and (6) termination. Basic conditions for the successful implementation of telework in an organization include having senior leaders who are strong advocates of the practice, work that is easily measured and quantified, a robust business case to overcome potential internal resistance to telework, IT systems that can support telework, and written formal policies that clarify expectations and conditions of work (Meadows, 2007). These policies should be visible and easily accessible to all members of the organization (Beauregard et al., 2013). Employee eligibility criteria should require having a space to work at home that complies with health and safety regulations, assigned tasks that can be performed remotely without adverse effect on the business (e.g., that continue to fulfill clients' needs), and a good track record in terms of performance (Beauregard et al., 2013; Busch, Nash, & Bell; 2011). For instance, research

Table 19.1 *Summary of Best Practices*

Implementation	• Top leaders who are strong advocates of telework • Work that is easily measured and quantified • A robust business case to overcome potential internal resistance to telework • IT systems that can support telework • Written formal policies that clarify expectations and conditions of work and that are visible and easily accessible to organizational members
Employee eligibility	• Space to work at home that complies with health and safety regulations • Assigned tasks that can be performed remotely without negatively impacting the business • Good track record of performance
Employee suitability	• Communication skills, self-motivation, ability to work independently • Preference for telework
Trial period and training	• Test or trial for employees to telework for a determined period of time • Formal process with paperwork (e.g., contractual change, consent form) and physical set-up (e.g., internet connection, IT equipment, furniture) • Guidance for managers of teleworkers including agreeing to formal communications, fostering informal frequent communications with teleworkers, and conducting regular assessments of teleworking conditions • Guidance for teleworkers including actively engaging in regular formal communications and frequent informal communications with their manager and coworkers, and making use of good time management practices
Intensity of telework	• A maximum of two to three days per week spent working from home
Termination	• Organizations reserve the right to cancel the telework arrangement at any time and base the teleworker at an office • Teleworker is commonly consulted and given notice in advance of termination of telework agreement
General organizational best practices	• A "trust and openness" culture • Adequate systems in place (communications, IT equipment and support) • Objectives-based performance management system • An adapted physical workplace to allow teleworkers to work and interact with their colleagues when they come to the office

clearly identifies that the ability to work in a separate location within the home leads to more beneficial telework outcomes (Mustafa & Gold, 2013; Sullivan, 2000).

In terms of employee suitability, employees should have appropriate skills (e.g., communication skills, self-motivation) and express a preference for teleworking. While more research is needed to fully understand the impact of voluntary vs. involuntary telework, inconsistent findings from prior research may be explained by differences in employee attitudes toward telework (Allen et al., 2013). For example, a study of 251 sales professionals found that involuntary telework led to higher levels of strain-based work-to-family conflict and, among those who indicated low self-efficacy for managing the multiple demands of the home and work environment, there was an increase in both time and strain-based work-to-family conflict (Lapierre et al., 2016). This suggests that attitudes toward telework are unlikely to be positive if telework has been imposed on rather than chosen by employees, and negative attitudes are more likely to produce negative outcomes. Managers should therefore avoid obliging employees to engage in telework, especially without adequate training in place for those who do not already possess preferences and abilities for working independently and alone.

It is common amongst organizations that offer telework to their employees to require a test or trial for a determined period of time. Actual implementation of telework usually involves a formal process with paperwork (e.g., contractual change to terms and conditions of employment, consent form), physical set-up (e.g., internet connection, IT equipment, furniture), and procedures and guidance that are made available to both employees and managers (Beauregard et al., 2013). This guidance includes recommendations to managers of teleworkers to agree to a regular schedule of formal communications, to foster frequent, informal communications with teleworkers, and to conduct regular assessments of telework conditions. Teleworkers are advised to actively engage in regular, formal communications and frequent, informal communications with their manager and coworkers and to make use of good time management practices.

Extent or intensity of telework may also be an important contributing factor to telework success. Research suggests that moderate versus extensive telework leads to better outcomes in terms of exhaustion, job satisfaction, isolation, and recovery (Golden, 2012; Golden & Veiga, 2005; Hartig et al., 2007). Regarding termination, organizations usually reserve the right to cancel the telework arrangement at any time and base the teleworker at an office. Good practice involves consulting the teleworker and giving notice in advance that the provision of telework is being retracted (Beauregard et al., 2013).

Lastly, there are some crucial organizational elements that need to be in place for telework to succeed. These include an organizational culture characterized by trust and openness, an objectives-based performance management system, and an adapted physical workspace that can accommodate teleworkers when they come to the office. Telework programs should be designed with these specifications in mind in order to facilitate the best outcomes for both employees and the organization.

References

Allen, T. D., Golden, T. D., & Shockley, K. M. (2015). How effective is telecommuting? Assessing the status of our scientific findings. *Psychological Science in the Public Interest, 16*(2), 40–68.

Allen, T. D., Johnson, R. C., Kiburz, K. M., & Shockley, K. M. (2013). Work–family conflict and flexible work arrangements: Deconstructing flexibility. *Personnel Psychology, 66*(2), 345–376.

Anderson, A. J., Kaplan, S. A., & Vega, R. P. (2015). The impact of telework on emotional experience: When, and for whom, does telework improve daily affective well-being? *European Journal of Work and Organizational Psychology, 24*(6), 882–897.

Anderson, D. & Kelliher, C. (2009). Flexible working and engagement: The importance of choice. *Strategic HR Review, 8*(2), 13–18.

Arora, S. A. (2012). *Does workplace isolation matter? Examining the impact of workplace isolation on telecommuter work engagement.* Melbourne, FL: Florida Institute of Technology.

Bailey, D. E. & Kurland, N. B. (2002). A review of telework research: Findings, new directions, and lessons for the study of modern work. *Journal of Organizational Behavior, 23*, 383–400.

Bartel, C. A., Wrzesniewski, A., & Wiesenfeld, B. M. (2012). Knowing where you stand: Physical isolation, perceived respect, and organizational identification among virtual employees. *Organization Science, 23*(3), 743–757.

Baruch, Y. (2000). Teleworking: Benefits and pitfalls as perceived by professionals and managers. *New Technology, Work and Employment, 15*, 34–49.

Baruch, Y. (2001). The status of research on teleworking and an agenda for future research. *International Journal of Management Reviews, 3*(2), 113–129.

Baruch, Y. & Nicholson, N. (1997). Home, sweet work: Requirements for effective home working. *Journal of General Management, 23*(2), 15–30.

Basile, K. A. & Beauregard, T. A. (2016). Strategies for successful telework: How effective employees manage work/home boundaries. *Strategic HR Review, 15*(3), 106–111.

Beauregard, T. A. (2011). Corporate work-life balance initiatives: Use and effectiveness. In S. Kaiser, M. Ringlstetter, M. Pina e Cunha, & D. R. Eikhof (Eds.), *Creating balance? International perspectives on the work-life integration of professionals* (pp. 193–208). Berlin: Springer.

Beauregard, T. A., Basile, K. A., & Canonico, E. (2013). *Home is where the work is: A new study of homeworking in Acas – and beyond. Acas research paper* (Ref. 10/13). London: Acas.

Beauregard, T.A., Basile, K.A., & Thompson, C. A. (2018). Organizational culture in the context of national culture. In K. Shockley, W. Shen & R. Johnson (Eds.), *The cambridge handbook of the global work-family interface* (pp. 555–569). Cambridge: Cambridge University Press.

Bélanger, F. (1999). Workers' propensity to telecommute: An empirical study. *Information and Management, 35*, 139–153.

Bell, B. S. & Kozlowski, S. W. J. (2002). A typology of virtual teams: Implications for effective leadership. *Group & Organization Management, 27*, 14–49.

Belle, S. M., Burley, D. L., & Long, S. D. (2015). Where do I belong? High-intensity teleworkers' experience of organizational belonging. *Human Resource Development International, 18*(1), 76–96.

Bentley, T. A., Teo, S. T. T., McLeod, L., Tan, F., Bosua, R., & Gloet, M. (2016). The role of organisational support in teleworker wellbeing: A socio-technical systems approach. *Applied Ergonomics, 52*, 207–215.

Blau, P. M. (1964). *Exchange and power in social life.* New York, NY: Wiley.

Bloom, N., Liang, J., Roberts, J., & Ying, Z. J. (2014). Does working from home work? Evidence from a Chinese experiment. *The Quarterly Journal of Economics*, *130* (1), 165–218.

Bordia, P. (1997). Face-to-face versus computer-mediated communication: A synthesis of the experimental literature. *Journal of Business Communication*, *34*, 99–120.

Brunelle, E. (2013). Leadership and mobile working: The impact of distance on the superior-subordinate relationship and the moderating effects of leadership style. *International Journal of Business and Social Science*, *4*(11), 1–14.

Busch, E., Nash, J., & Bell, B. S. (2011). *Remote work: An examination of current trends and emerging issues*. Ithaca, NY: Center for Advanced Human Resource Studies, Cornell University. Retrieved December 11, 2017, from https://distantjob.com/ Spring2011_CAHRSRemoteWorkReport.pdf.

Canonico, E. (2016). Putting the Work-Life Interface into a Temporal Context: An Empirical Study of Work-Life Balance by Life Stage and the Consequences of Homeworking (Doctoral dissertation, London School of Economics and Political Science (LSE)).

Coenen, M. & Kok, R. A. (2014). Workplace flexibility and new product development performance: The role of telework and flexible work schedules. *European Management Journal*, *32*(4), 564–576.

Collins, A. M., Hislop, D., & Cartwright, S. (2016). Social support in the workplace between teleworkers, office-based colleagues and supervisors. *New Technology, Work and Employment*, *31*(2), 161–175.

Cooper, C. D. & Kurland, N. B. (2002). Telecommuting, professional isolation and employee development in public and private sector organizations. *Journal of Organizational Behavior*, *23*, 511–532.

Corwin, V., Lawrence, T., & Frost, P. (2001). Five strategies of successful part-time work. *Harvard Business Review*, *79*, 121–7.

Crandall, W. & Gao, L. (2005). An update on telecommuting: Review and prospects for emerging issues. *SAM Advanced Management Journal*, *70*(3), 30–37.

Davis, R. & Cates, S. (2013). The dark side of working in a virtual world: An investigation of the relationship between workplace isolation and engagement among teleworkers. *Journal of Human Resource and Sustainability Studies*, *1*(2), 9–13.

Demerouti, E., Bakker, A. B., Nachreiner, F., & Schaufeli, W. B. (2001). The job demands-resources model of burnout. Journal of Applied Psychology, *86*(3), 499–512.

Duxbury, L. E. & Neufeld, D. (1999). An empirical evaluation of the impacts of telecommuting on intra-organizational communication. *Journal of Engineering and Technology Management*, *16*, 1–28.

Fay, M. J. & Kline, S. L. (2011). Coworker relationships and informal communication in high-intensity telecommuting. *Journal of Applied Communication Research*, *39* (2), 144–163.

Feldman & Gainey. (1998). Patterns of telecommuting and their consequences: Framing the research agenda. *Human Resource Management Review*, *7*(4), 369–388.

Felstead, A. & Henseke, G. 2017. Assessing the growth of remote working and its consequences for effort, well-being and work-life balance. *New Technology Work and Employment*, *32*(3), 195–212.

Felstead, A., Jewson, N., & Walters, S. 2003. Managerial control of employees working at home. *British Journal of Industrial Relations*, *41*(2), 241–264.

Fonner, K. L. & Roloff, M. E. (2010). Why teleworkers are more satisfied with their jobs than are office-based workers: When less contact is beneficial. *Journal of Applied Communication Research*, *38*(4), 336–361.

Fonner, K. L. & Roloff, M. E. (2012). Testing the connectivity paradox: Linking teleworkers' communication media use to social presence, stress from interruptions, and organizational identification. *Communication Monographs*, *79*(2), 205–231.

Fonner, K. L. & Stache, L. C. (2012). All in a day's work, at home: Teleworkers' management of micro role transitions and the work–home boundary. *New Technology, Work and Employment*, *27*(3), 242–257.

Gainey, T. W. & Clenney, B. F. (2006). Flextime and telecommuting: Examining individual perceptions. *Southern Business Review*, *32*(1), 13–21.

Gainey, T., Kelley, D., & Hill, J. (1999). Telecommuting's impact on corporate culture and individual workers: Examining the effect of employee isolation. *SAM Advanced Management Journal*, *64*(4), 4–11.

Gajendran, R. S. & Harrison, D. A. (2007). The good, the bad, and the unknown about telecommuting: Meta-analysis of psychological mediators and individual consequences. *Journal of Applied Psychology*, *92*(6), 1524–1541.

Gajendran, R. S., Harrison, D. A., & Delaney-Klinger, K. (2015). Are telecommuters remotely good citizens? Unpacking telecommuting's effects on performance via i-deals and job resources. *Personnel Psychology*, *68*(2), 353–393.

Gibson, J., Blackwell, C., Dominicis, P., & Demerath, N. (2002). Telecommuting in the 21st century: Benefits, issues, and a leadership model which will work. *Journal of Leadership and Organizational Studies*, *8*(4), 75–86.

Glass, J. & Riley, L. (1998). Family responsive policies and employee retention following childbirth. *Social Forces*, *76*(4), 1401–1435.

Golden, T. D. (2006a). The role of relationships in understanding telecommuter satisfaction. *Journal of Organizational Behavior*, *27*, 319–340.

Golden, T. D. (2006b). Avoiding depletion in virtual work: Telework and the intervening impact of work exhaustion on commitment and turnover intentions. *Journal of Vocational Behavior*, *69*(1), 176–187.

Golden, T. D. (2007). Co-workers who telework and the impact on those in the office: Understanding the implications of virtual work for co-worker satisfaction and turnover intentions. *Human Relations*, *60*, 1641–1667.

Golden, T. D. (2011). Does it matter where your manager works? Comparing managerial work mode (traditional, telework, virtual) across subordinate work experiences and outcomes. *Human Relations*, *64*(11), 1451–1475.

Golden, T. D. (2012). Altering the effects of work and family conflict on exhaustion: Telework during traditional and nontraditional work hours. *Journal of Business and Psychology*, *27*(3), 255–269.

Golden, T. D. & Raghuram, S. (2010). Teleworker knowledge sharing and the role of altered relational and technological interactions. *Journal of Organizational Behavior*, *31*(8), 1061–1085.

Golden, T. D. & Veiga, J. F. (2005). The impact of extent of telecommuting on job satisfaction: Resolving inconsistent findings. *Journal of Management*, *31*(2), 301–318.

Golden, T. D., Veiga, J. F., & Dino, R. N. (2008). The impact of professional isolation on teleworker job performance and turnover intentions: Does time spent teleworking, interacting face-to-face, or having access to communication-enhancing technology matter? *Journal of Applied Psychology, 93*(6), 1412–1421.

Golden, T. D., Veiga, J. F., & Simsek, Z. (2006). Telecommuting's differential impact on work-family conflict: Is there no place like home? *Journal of Applied Psychology, 91*(6), 1340–1350.

Gouldner, A. W. (1960). The norm of reciprocity: A preliminary statement. *American Sociological Review, 25*(2), 161–178.

Grant, C. A. (2017). Ework-Life Balance Assessment Solutions. Retrieved June 22, 2017, from https://ework.coventry.ac.uk.

Grant, C. A., Wallace, L. M., & Spurgeon, P. C. (2013). An exploration of the psychological factors affecting remote e-worker's job effectiveness, well-being and work-life balance. *Employee Relations, 35*(5), 527–546.

Greer, T. W. & Payne, S. C. (2014). Overcoming telework challenges: Outcomes of successful telework strategies. *The Psychologist-Manager Journal, 17*(2), 87–111.

Haddock, S. A., Zimmerman, T. S., Ziemba, S. J., & Lyness, K. (2006). Practices of dual earner couples successfully balancing work and family. *Journal of Family and Economic Issues, 27*(2), 207–234.

Haines, V.Y. III, St. Onge, S., & Archambault, M. (2002). Environmental and person antecedents of telecommuting outcomes. *Journal of End User Computing, 14* (3), 32–50.

Harpaz, I. (2002). Advantages and disadvantages of telecommuting for the individual, organization, and society. *Work Study, 51*(2/3), 74–80.

Harris, L. (2003). Home-based teleworking and the employment relationship: Managerial challenges and dilemmas. *Personnel Review, 32*(4), 422–437.

Hartig, T., Kylin, C., & Johansson, G. (2007). The telework tradeoff: Stress mitigation vs. constrained restoration. *Applied Psychology, 56*(2), 231–253.

He, H. & Brown, A. D. (2013). Organizational identity and organizational identification: A review of the literature and suggestions for future research. *Group & Organization Management, 38*(1), 3–35.

Hill, E. J., Ferris, M., & Martinson, V. (2003). Does it matter where you work? A comparison of how three work venues (traditional office, virtual office, and home office) influence aspects of work and personal/family life. *Journal of Vocational Behavior, 62*, 220–241.

Hill, E. J., Hawkins, A. J., Ferris, M., & Weitzman, M. (2001). Finding an extra day a week: The positive influence of perceived job flexibility on work and family life balance. *Family Relations, 50*, 49–58.

Hill, E. J., Miller, B. C., Weiner, S. P., & Colihan, J. (1998). Influences of the virtual office on aspects of work and work/life balance. *Personnel Psychology, 51*, 667–683.

Hunton, J. E. & Norman, C. S. (2010). The impact of alternative telework arrangements on organizational commitment: Insights from a longitudinal field experiment. *Journal of Information Systems, 24*(1), 67–90.

Igbaria, M. & Guimares, T. (1999). Exploring differences in employee turnover intentions and its determinants among telecommuters and non telecommuters. *Journal of Management Information Systems, 16*(1), 147–164.

Ilozor, D.B., Ilozor, B.D., & Carr, J. (2001). Management communication strategies determine job satisfaction in telecommuting. *Journal of Management Development, 20* (5/6), 495–507.

Johnson, B., Hartstrom, G., Griffith, A., & Neff, J. (2007). *Trends in Telework Outreach and Training.* Eugene: University of Oregon: Community Planning Workshop.

Kelliher, C. & Anderson, D. (2008). For better or for worse? An analysis of how flexible working practices influence employees' perceptions of job quality. *International Journal of Human Resource Management, 19,* 419–431.

Kelliher, C. & Anderson, D. (2010). Doing more with less? Flexible work practices and the intensification of work. *Human Relations, 63*(1), 83–106.

Khalifa, M. & Davidson, R. (2000). Exploring the telecommuting paradox. *Communications of the ACM, 43*(3), 29–30.

Konradt, U., Hertel, G., & Schmook, R. (2003). Quality of management by objectives, task-related stressors, and non-task related stressors as predictors of stress and job satisfaction among teleworkers. *European Journal of Work and Organizational Psychology, 12,* 61–79.

Konradt, U., Schmook, R., Wilm, A., & Hertel, G. (2000). Health circles for teleworkers: Selective results on stress, strain and coping styles. *Health Education Research, 15*(3), 327–338.

Kossek, E. E., Lautsch, B. A., & Eaton, S. C. (2006). Telecommuting, control, and boundary management: Correlates of policy use and practice, job control, and work-family effectiveness. *Journal of Vocational Behavior, 68*(2), 347–367.

Kossek, E. E., Ruderman, M. N., Braddy, P. W., & Hannum, K. M. (2012). Work–nonwork boundary management profiles: A person-centered approach. *Journal of Vocational Behavior, 81*(1), 112–128.

Kurland, N. B., & Egan, T. D. (1999). Telecommuting: Justice and control in the virtual organization. *Organization Science, 10*(4), 500–513.

Lapierre, L. M., Steenbergen, E. F., Peeters, M. C., & Kluwer, E. S. (2016). Juggling work and family responsibilities when involuntarily working more from home: A multiwave study of financial sales professionals. *Journal of Organizational Behavior, 37*(6), 804–822.

Larsson, G., Sjöberg, M., Nilsson, S., Alvinius, A., & Bakken, B. (2007). Indirect leadership: A quantitative test of a qualitatively developed model. *Leadership and Organization Development Journal, 28*(8), 771–783.

Lautsch, B. A., Kossek, E. E., & Eaton, S. C. (2009). Supervisory approaches and paradoxes in managing telecommuting implementation. *Human Relations, 62*(6), 795–827.

Lowry, P. B., Roberts, T. L., Romano Jr., N. C., Cheney, P. D., & Hightower, R. T. (2006). The impact of group size and social presence on small-group communication: Does computer-mediated communication make a difference? *Small Group Research, 37*(6), 631–661.

Lupton, P. & Haynes, B. (2000). Teleworking: The perception-reality gap. *Facilities, 18*(7/8), 323–337.

Madlock, P. E. (2012). The influence of supervisors' leadership style on telecommuters. *Journal of Business Strategies, 29*(1), 1–24.

Mann, S. & Holdsworth, L. (2003). The psychological impact of teleworking: Stress, emotions and health. *New Technology, Work and Employment, 18,* 196–211.

Mann, S., Varey, R., & Button, W. (2000). An exploration of the emotional impact of teleworking via computer-mediated communication. *Journal of Managerial Psychology, 15*(7), 668–682.

Manochehri, G. & Pinkerton, T. (2003). Managing telecommuters: Opportunities and challenges. *American Business Review, 21*(1), 9–16.

Mariani, M. (2000). Exploring the telecommuting paradox. *Communications of the ACM*, *42*, 29–50.

Maruyama, T. & Tietze, S. (2012). From anxiety to assurance: Concerns and outcomes of telework. *Personnel Review*, *41*(4), 450–469.

Matharu, H. (October 1, 2015). Sweden introduces six-hour work day. The Independent. Retrieved from www.independent.co.uk/news/world/europe/sweden-introduces-six-hour-work-day-a6674646.html.

Maynard, M. T. & Gilson, L. L. (2014). The role of shared mental model development in understanding virtual team effectiveness. *Group & Organization Management*, *39* (1), 3–32.

McAdams, J. (2006). Telecommuters. *Computer World*, *40*(20), 36–37.

McCloskey, D. W. & Igbaria, M. (2003). Does "out of sight" mean "out of mind"? An empirical investigation of the career advancement prospects of telecommuters. *Information Resources Management Journal*, *16*(2), 19–34.

McDowall, A. & Kinman, G. (2017). The new nowhere land? A research and practice agenda for the "always on" culture. *Journal of Organizational Effectiveness: People and Performance*, *4*(3), 256–266.

McGregor, D. M. (1960). *The human side of Enterprise*. New York, NY: McGraw-Hill.

Meadows, V. (2007). Versatile bureaucracy: A telework case study. *Public Manager*, *36*(4), 33–37.

Mello, J. A. (2007). Managing telework programs effectively. *Employee Responsibilities and Rights Journal*, *19*(4), 247–261.

Mills, J., Wong-Ellison, C., Werner, W., & Clay, J. (2001). Employer liability for telecommuting employees. *Cornell Hotel and Restaurant Quarterly*, *42*(5), 48–59.

Mustafa, M. & Gold, M. (2013). "Chained to my work"? Strategies to manage temporal and physical boundaries among self-employed teleworkers. *Human Resource Management Journal*, *23*(4), 413–429.

Nardi, B. & Whittaker, S. (2002). The role of face-to-face communication in distributed work. In P. Hinds & S. Kiesler (Eds.), *Distributed work: New ways of working across distance using technology* (pp. 83–110). Cambridge, MA: MIT Press.

O'Neill, T. A., Hambley, L. A., Greidanus, N. S., MacDonnell, R., & Kline, T. J. (2009). Predicting teleworker success: An exploration of personality, motivational, situational, and job characteristics. *New Technology, Work and Employment*, *24*, 144–162.

Offstein, E. H., Morwick, J. M., & Koskinen, L. (2010). Making telework work: Leading people and leveraging technology for competitive advantage. *Strategic HR Review*, *9*(2), 32–37.

Ollier-Malaterre, A. & Foucreault, A. (2017). Cross-national work-life research: Cultural and structural impacts for individuals and organizations. *Journal of Management*, *43*(1), 111–136.

Peters, P. & van der Lippe, T. (2007). The time-pressure reducing potential of telehome-working: The Dutch case. *International Journal of Human Resources Management*, *18*(3), 430–447.

Piszczek, M. M. & Berg, P. (2014). Expanding the boundaries of boundary theory: Regulative institutions and work–family role management. *Human Relations*, *67* (12), 1491–1512.

Potter, E. (2003). Telecommuting: The future of work, corporate culture, and American society. *Journal of Labor Research*, *24*(1), 73–84.

Powell, G. N., Francesco, A. M., & Ling, Y. (2009). Toward culture-sensitive theories of the work–family interface. *Journal of Organizational Behavior*, 30(5), 597–616.

Pyöriä, P. (2011). Managing telework: Risks, fears and rules. *Management Research Review*, 34(4), 386–399.

Raghuram, S. & Wieselfeld, B. (2004). Work–nonwork conflict and job stress among virtual workers. *Human Resource Management*, 43(2), 259–277.

Reinsch, N. L. Jr. (1997). Relationships between telecommuting workers and their managers: An exploratory study. *Journal of Business Communication*, 34(4), 343–369.

Richardson, J. & Kelliher, C. (2015). Managing visibility for career sustainability: A study of remote workers. In A. De Vos & B. Van der Heijden (Eds.), *Handbook of research on sustainable careers* (pp. 116–130). Cheltenham, UK: Edward Elgar.

Robertson, M., Maynard, W., & McDevitt, J. (2003). Telecommuting: Managing the safety of workers in home office environments. *Professional Safety*, 48(4), 30–36.

Rokach, A. (1997). Relations of perceived causes and the experience of loneliness. *Psychological Reports*, 80, 1067–1074.

Sardeshmukh, S. R., Sharma, D., & Golden, T. D. (2012). Impact of telework on exhaustion and job engagement: A job demands and job resources model. *New Technology, Work and Employment*, 27(3), 193–207.

Sewell, G. & Taskin, L. (2015). Out of sight, out of mind in a new world of work? Autonomy, control, and spatiotemporal scaling in telework. *Organization Studies*, 36(11), 1507–1529.

Shin, B., El Sawy, O. A., Sheng, O. R. L., & Higa, K. (2000). Telework: Existing research and future directions. Journal of Organizational Computing and Electronic Commerce, 10(2), 85–101.

Shockley, K. M. & Allen, T. D. (2010). Investigating the missing link in flexible work arrangement utilization: An individual difference perspective. *Journal of Vocational Behavior*, 76(1), 131–142.

Smith, J. W. (1998). Preliminary development of an alternative measure of isolation: The construct of institutional isolation. *Psychological Reports*, 82, 1323–1330.

Standen, P., Daniels, K. & Lamond, D. (1999). The home as a workplace: Work-family interaction and psychological well-being in telework. *Journal of Occupational Health Psychology*, 4, 368–381.

Staples, D. S. (2001). A study of remote workers and their differences from non-remote workers. *Journal of End User Computing*, 13(2), 3–14.

Stephens, G. K. & Szajna, B. (1998). Perceptions and expectations: Why people choose a telecommuting work style. *International Journal of Electronic Commerce*, 3(1), 70–85.

Sullivan, C. (2000). Space and the intersection of work and family in homeworking households. *Community, Work & Family*, 3(2), 185–204.

Taskin, L. & Bridoux, F. (2010). Telework: A challenge to knowledge transfer in organizations. *The International Journal of Human Resource Management*, 21 (13), 2503–2520.

Telework Exchange (March 11, 2008,). National Science Foundation and Telework Exchange Study Validates Telework Productivity Hypothesis. Press release. Retrieved May 11, 2017, from www.businesswire.com/news/home/20080311005147/en/National-Science-Foundation-Telework-Exchange-Study-Validates.

ten Brummelhuis, L., Haar, J., & van der Lippe, T. (2010). Collegiality under pressure? The effects of family demands and flexible work arrangements in the Netherlands. *International Journal of Human Resource Management*, *21*(15), 2831–2847.

Thompson, R. J., Payne, S. C., & Taylor, A. B. (2015). Applicant attraction to flexible work arrangements: Separating the influence of flextime and flexplace. *Journal of Occupational and Organizational Psychology*, 88(4), 726–749.

Tietze, S. & Musson, G. (2005). Recasting the home-work relationship: A case of mutual adjustment? *Organization Studies*, *26*(9), 1331–1352.

Tietze, S. & Nadin, S. (2011). The psychological contract and the transition from office-based to home-based work. *Human Resource Management Journal*, *21*(3), 318–334.

Tremblay, D.-G. (2002). Balancing work and family with telework? Organizational issues and challenges for women and managers. *Women in Management Review*, *17*(3/4), 157–170.

Turetken, O., Jain, A., Quesenberry, B., & Ngwenyama, O. (2011). An empirical investigation of the impact of individual and work characteristics on telecommuting success. *IEEE Transactions on Professional Communication*, *54*(1), 56–67.

Valsecchi, R. (2006). Visible moves and invisible bodies: The case of teleworking in an Italian call centre. *New Technology, Work and Employment*, *21*, 123–138.

van Zoonen, W., Verhoeven, J. W., & Vliegenthart, R. (2016). Social media's dark side: Inducing boundary conflicts. *Journal of Managerial Psychology*, *31*(8), 1297–1311.

Vega, G. & Brennan, L. (2000). Isolation and technology: The human disconnect. *Journal of Organizational Change Management*, *13*, 468–481.

Vega, R. P., Anderson, A. J., & Kaplan, S. A. (2015). A within-person examination of the effects of telework. *Journal of Business and Psychology*, *30*(2), 313–323.

Venkatesh, V. & Speier, C. (2000). Creating an effective training environment for enhancing telework. *International Journal of Human-Computer Studies*, *52*, 991–1005.

Verbeke, A., Schulz, R., Greidanus, N., & Hambley, L. A. (2008). *Growing the virtual workplace: The integrative value proposition for telework*. Northampton: Edward Elgar.

Virick, M., DaSilva, N., & Arrington, K. (2010). Moderators of the curvilinear relation between extent of telecommuting and job and life satisfaction: The role of performance outcome orientation and worker type. *Human Relations*, *63*(1), 137–154.

Weisenfeld, B.M., Raghuram, S., & Garud, R. (2001). Organizational identification among virtual workers: The role of need for affiliation and perceived work-based social support. *Journal of Management*, *27*, 213–229.

Wheatley, D. (2012). Good to be home? Time-use and satisfaction levels among home-based teleworkers. *New Technology, Work and Employment*, *27*(3), 224–241.

20 A Review and Extension of Cyber-Deviance Literature

Why It Likely Persists

Dianne P. Ford, Mahyar Garmsiri, Amanda J. Hancock, and Robert D. Hickman

Since the 1970s, industrial-organizational scientists have been examining the dark side of human behavior within the workplace, such as withdrawal (Rosse & Hulin, 1985), fraud (Darby & Karni, 1973), sexual harassment (MacKinnon, 1979), and unethical decision-making (Hegarty & Sims, 1978). Behaviors like these come with significant legal, production, reputation, and recovery costs to organizations. They also present significant consequences to individuals who are targeted and to those who witness these negative behaviors. Thus, managers and organizations are usually motivated to prevent these costly behaviors.

In 1995, Robinson and Bennett proposed a typology to organize the different forms of these workplace deviance behaviors. Workplace deviance is defined as "voluntary behavior that violates significant organizational norms and in so doing threatens the well-being of an organization, its members, or both. Employee deviance is voluntary in that employees either lack the motivation to conform to normative expectations of the social context or become motivated to violate those expectations" (Kaplan, 1975; c.f., Robinson & Bennett, 1995, p. 557). While the majority of deviance is considered negative with harmful effects, it is important to note that some forms of workplace deviance may actually be societally beneficial, like whistleblowing or union organization. Some workplace deviance behaviors may be illegal, like theft/shrinkage or violating human rights legislation, conversely other unethical or illegal behaviors could be deemed not deviant as they follow organizational norms and aid the organization (e.g., collusion). We will not make a distinction between legality, ethics, and deviance; rather, we take the perspective of workplace deviance solely within the context of the organization.

Robinson and Bennett (1995) identified four types of workplace deviance: production deviance (leaving early, taking excessive breaks, intentionally working slow, and wasting resources), property deviance (sabotaging equipment, accepting kickbacks, lying about hours worked, stealing from the company), political deviance (showing favoritism, gossiping about coworkers, blaming coworkers, competing non-beneficially), and personal aggression (sexual harassment, verbal abuse, stealing from coworkers, endangering coworkers). Two dimensions defined these four types: level of seriousness or harmfulness (minor to serious), and nature of the impact (interpersonal to organizational; Robinson & Bennett, 1995).

Since the late 1990s, the modus operandi of organizations shifted significantly to an online format via various modes of computer-mediated communications, and researchers began to consider how these newer technologies would impact work-life (Kiesler, 1986). Now, technology has evolved to be ubiquitous and all-encompassing from personal, professional, and social use, prompting many organizations to develop policies in response (e.g., Fontein, 2017). Along with this technological evolution, organizational behaviors have also evolved to a virtual presence. Accordingly, Weatherbee (2010) adapted Robinson and Bennett's deviance typology for computer-mediated communications to: production cyber-deviance, property cyber-deviance, political cyber-deviance, and personal aggression (which we shall call personal cyber-aggression).

Political cyber-deviance is characterized by minor counterproductive work behaviors committed online at an interpersonal level. Example behaviors include: e-politics, playing zero-sum games, selective informing, blame shifting, and gossip (Weatherbee, 2010). Whistleblowing and cyber-smearing are other examples of political cyber-deviance, both of which may occur on social media, and have wider social implications for the organization than more traditional forms of whistle-blowing or smear campaigns (Workman, 2012). Whistleblowing occurs through stealing and exposing private information (Väyrynen, Hekkala, & Liias, 2013). Another behavior potentially perceived as political cyber-deviance from an organizational perspective (not societal perspective) is sending union-organizing emails using a company-supplied home-computer (Cole, 2002).

Production cyber-deviance is the misuse of technology (Weatherbee, 2010), and violates the organizational norms regarding minimal quantity of production; it occurs when employees waste time using company resources. Cyberloafing, personal email, chain email, online banking, and online shopping are examples of production cyber-deviance (Weatherbee, 2010). Similar behaviors include cyber-slacking (Greengard, 2000), personal web usage (Mahatanankoon, Anandarajan, & Igbaria, 2004), and non-work-related computing (Pee, Woon, & Kankanhalli, 2008). Cyberloafing (the most studied) is defined as the "voluntary act of employees using their companies' internet access during office hours ... for personal purposes" (Lim, 2002, p. 675), which consists of two dimensions: personal email and browsing the web. Additional dimensions have since been proposed to reflect the expanded use of the internet and Web 2.0 activities (online videos, blogging: e.g., Anandarajan, Devine, & Simmers, 2004). (See Vitak, Crouse, and LaRose [2011] for a summary.)

Property cyber-deviance is the damaging of company property or the theft and leaking of important company information using information technologies (Johnson, 2011). Examples are online gambling, web pornography, software piracy, data diddling (the removal or alteration of data at time of entry), and hacking (Weatherbee, 2010). In addition, property cyber-deviance includes employee behaviors that harm the reputation of employers, such as blogs or social media posts from personal accounts, and intentionally using technology to provide poor customer service (excessive waiting or wrong phone transfers: Skarlicki, van Jaarsveld, & Walker, 2008). Tampering with employers' information technologies is another form of property cyber-deviance, like hacking into company databases to access user activity records in the company database to hide prohibited internet activity, or even add inappropriate activity to the log of other employees (Barlow, Bean, & Hott, 2003).

Personal cyber-aggression consists of a range of behaviors, and is defined as computer-mediated communications that are "either used intentionally for the expression of aggression, or where it is used in such a way that it results in the perception of aggression by a focal target" (Weatherbee, 2010, p. 37). These behaviors are interpersonal; they target an individual or group of individuals. Personal cyber-aggression includes a range of behaviors from low-intensity cyber-incivility, virtual harassment, to severe-intensity cyber-bullying and cyberstalking (e.g., Barnes & Biros, 2007; D'Cruz & Noronha, 2013; Ford, 2013; Giumetti et al., 2012). The terms vary across national borders; cyber-mobbing (Germany), virtual or cyber-bullying (Italy), and harassment via internet or mobile phone (Spain) are used to describe the same behavior of "cyber-bullying" (Nocentini, et al., 2010). Other example behaviors that constitute personal cyber-aggression are cyber-aggression, e-harassment, and identity theft (Weatherbee, 2010).

Workplace cyber-deviance does not follow the traditional workplace deviance typography as cleanly as traditional. Cyber-whistleblowing, for example, is not only political deviance, but if company technologies are used for the act, it is also property deviance. The impacts of workplace cyber-deviance also included external others (i.e., other organizations or individuals who are not members of the organization: Weatherbee, 2010). In other words, the impacts (effect) of the cyber-behavior is no longer contained solely within the organization as it is easier to publicly broadcast through cyber means (Weatherbee & Kelloway, 2006). Finally, there are effect shifts among the four types of deviance through cyber whistleblowing and workplace blogging, and the effects of one form of behavior can now trigger or shift to related and secondary outcomes (Weatherbee, 2010).

In this chapter, we examine the existing literature regarding these four forms of workplace cyber-deviance and synthesize what is known about them. We theoretically examine each from multiple levels of analysis, from a process model of antecedents–behavior–outcomes, starting with the minor forms of cyber-deviance followed by the serious forms. Any gaps in the literature will be highlighted in the discussion section. Then, we discuss potential feedback loops which may lead to the perpetuation or reinforcement of these negative workplace behaviors. We conclude with a discussion of implications.

20.1 Political Cyber-Deviance

Classic indicators of political deviance at the workplace are struggles for power, knowledge hiding, or gossiping/smearing campaigns (Weatherbee, 2010). An example of political cyber-deviance was the "Diversity Manifesto," authored by a senior engineer at Google. The unofficial manifesto, which had harmful, biasing comments targeting females, was a statement decrying Google's diversity efforts (e.g., Oreskovic, 2017). The response by witnesses within Google resulted in a very public airing of disapproval via Twitter and other media outlets, and the author was ultimately fired. The reasons and effects for such behaviors are still not fully understood, but the research on political cyber-deviance suggests that many of the antecedents of political cyber-deviance mirror the antecedents of in-person political deviance. The two major differences can be seen where (1) technology augments the capabilities of individuals so individuals and communities outside the organization may also be impacted by political cyber-deviance outcomes, and (2) technology media characteristics increases the equivocality of conversations and makes individuals more inclined to commit their deviant behaviors online rather than offline.

20.1.1 Antecedents of Political Cyber-Deviance

Individual.   The primary focus of the research to date has been on what personal factors appear to be related to someone engaging in political cyber-deviance. Two related factors seem to influence the extent and likelihood of political cyber-deviance enacted by individuals: (1) exploitive personality traits, and (2) a desire for power (e.g., Rogers, Smoak, & Liu, 2006; Workman, 2010). Narcissism is also linked to both exploitiveness and need for power (Raskin, Novacek & Hogan, 1991) but the current political cyber-deviance literature is scarce (e.g., Workman, 2010) and warrants further research before any conclusions can be made regarding narcissism. The two factors, exploitiveness and need for power, underlie the typical example of an employee playing political games using influence tactics to win struggles for power for self-gain within the organization (Pfeffer, 1992; Vigoda-Gadot & Drory 2006).

For example, exploitive manipulative behaviors mediate the relationship between the Big-5 personality traits and politically cyber-deviant behaviors (guessing others' passwords, browsing others' personal files, or changing others' files: Rogers, et al., 2006). Workman (2010) suggested exploitation is just one driving factor of deviant behaviors like cyber-smearing. According to theories of assertion, individuals with a need for power, control, and dominance over others are driven to assert success and power to confer status and self-esteem, satisfying the need of power (Alonzo & Aiken, 2004; McGuire, 1974).

Aside from an exploitive personality and desire for power, some studies report observed gender and age differences in committing political cyber-deviance. Males were found to be more likely than females to commit specific types of political cyber-deviance, such as flaming (Alonzo & Aiken, 2004), meanwhile females were found more likely than males to commit other types of political cyber-deviance, such as cyber-gossiping (Oluwole, 2009). Late adolescents were also more likely than young adolescents to cyber-gossip (Oluwole, 2009). However, a word of caution is provided as there is not a substantive number of studies replicating these results and they may not be generalizable to a larger population.

Dyadic.   Dyadic interactions may exacerbate inclinations to be politically cyber-deviant when the interactions impact perpetrators' power status. Perpetrators, who feel their coworker caused them a loss of power or autonomy or caused a sense of procedural unfairness, may resist through less severe acts of deviance like political cyber-deviance (Lawrence & Robinson, 2007). The coworker's action, or even inaction, may create feelings of rage, need for power and control, and anger issues that lead to cyber-stalking behaviors during which the perpetrator collects information for identify theft, intimidation, or emailing harassing messages or viruses to their coworker and seizing power (Pittaro, 2007).

Perpetrators are also more able to be politically cyber-deviant when they have personal information of the victim. Perpetrators may (il)legally access an organization's private databases to steal personal data about employees' assets, lives, employment history, information about violent behaviors, and even information about affairs between coworkers to gain insight into their target's personality and vulnerabilities for political advantage (Civiello, 1999). Individuals can publish this type of information to blackmail, humiliate, shame, or intimidate and gain power over their coworker (Douglas, 2016). However, this is not possible unless the victims first disclose this information somewhere and it is stored unsafely. Unfortunately, sometimes it is unavoidable to disclose this information in which case it becomes a matter of how well the organization can protect the information.

Organizational. The major organizational antecedent is how vulnerable a company's database is to unauthorized use. Sometimes organizational systems enable political cyber-deviance, like leaving known system vulnerabilities open (Larson, 2017). Other times, perpetrators attempt to force access to organizational systems; for example, the most common computer deviant behaviors for undergraduates were guessing others' passwords and browsing others' files without permission (Rogers et al., 2006). Perpetrators require access to relevant information to successfully commit politically cyber-deviant behaviors such as cyber-stalking, cyber-smearing, and leaking of information. These vulnerabilities can be addressed by password protecting private folders and having two-factor authentication for passwords (Jin, Ling, & Goh, 2004).

When organizations permit access to organizational computer resources via home computers, they create a vulnerability where anyone in the employee's home may have access to sensitive information (Cole, 2002). It is even possible that others near but outside the home may compromise the employee's home Wi-Fi network to interrupt, modify, or destroy the transmission of personal information between the home computer and the workplace (Aime, Calandriello, & Lioy, 2007; Sturgeon, 1996). Organizations not implementing policies against inappropriate access and use of private information or providing software to protect home computers make themselves vulnerable to political cyber-deviance (Väyrynen et al., 2013).

Beyond the IT structures, high workloads and competitive workplaces may also lead to political cyber-deviance. There is little research identifying connections between these two. However, when workplaces with power imbalances and competitive environments cause employees to impede or eliminate competitors (Salin, 2003b), some of those behaviors are politically motivated (Salin, 2003a) and it is believable that those behaviors may be expressed as political cyber-deviance. For example, employees refuse to share knowledge with coworkers or only share part of the knowledge requested (Connelly et al., 2012) to protect the competitive advantage they have over their coworkers (Michailova & Husted, 2003). This example can manifest as political cyber-deviance when employees do not include specific coworkers in emails intentionally or do not give coworkers access to data.

20.1.2 Outcomes of Political Cyber-Deviance

Perpetrator. What little research there is on perpetrator outcomes identifies satisfaction as the main perpetrator outcome. Very assertive individuals require control, dominance and power over others to strengthen their status of power, driving some individuals to be politically deviant until those needs are satisfied (e.g., Alonzo & Aiken, 2004; Bissett & Shipton, 2000). Unsuccessful political cyber-deviance may instead just fuel the need for power and compel an individual to engage in more cyber-deviance until this need is met (Pittaro, 2007).

Target.   Targets of cyber-attacks struggle with losing a feeling of safety in the workplace and social media. Targets of political cyber-deviance may view their computer as a new source of harassment, misinformation, and personal information to be potentially leaked (Bissett & Shipton, 2000). If the perpetrator is anonymous, the target also loses trust in their coworkers since it is unknown which coworker is a threat. Workman (2010, 2012) claims in-person harassment in organizations has considerable negative impacts on individuals' social relations and business performance, suggesting that these same outcomes are seen from cyber-harassment and political cyber-deviance.

Social media publicizes political cyber-deviant behaviors, like doxing and cyber-smearing, by increasing an audience's access to misinformation (Douglas, 2016; Workman, 2012). Especially problematic is perpetrators' anonymity and indiscriminate spread of misinformation across international borders. The degree of publicity of the political cyber-deviance, and viewers' inclination to tune into the misinformation, increase the audience impacted by doxing and cyber-smearing (Douglas, 2016; Hemsley & Mason, 2013; Workman, 2012). Perpetrators may also add inappropriate activity to a coworker's internet usage (Davis & Braun, 2004); if this is publicized, the target risks receiving an unjust termination. The outcomes of personal cyber-aggression for targets are also relevant for targets of political cyber-deviance as many of these behaviors may fit both categories (e.g., flaming, cyber-stalking).

Organization.   While political deviance is an interpersonal type of deviance, political cyber-deviance has outcomes that reach beyond the interpersonal relationship. Organizations failing to protect and manage their knowledge will experience compromised and damaged reputation, management of social media, and database of private information (Civiello, 1999; O'Sullivan, 2017; Väyrynen et al., 2013). Leaks and whistleblowing blurs the line between political cyber-deviance and property cyber-deviance as damaged reputation and failed protection of private knowledge manifests as financial losses (Väyrynen et al., 2013). After such leaks, companies may incur expenses from paying ransom for their data, hiring lawyers and cyber-security experts to consult for security and response options, and large losses of share value within hours. The integration of technology into political cyber-deviance allows for the deviant behavior to have larger and more considerable outcomes. This further illustrates the concept of effect shift highlighted earlier (Weatherbee, 2010).

20.1.3 The Context: Media Characteristics

Some of the research above has considered the context of the media characteristics. For example, the media richness of online interactions may be what prompts individuals to take their political deviance online. According to the media richness theory, online textual media are considered lean because they lack the social cues and conversational content associated with face-to-face communications; this creates uncertainty and equivocality in the messages received (Daft, Lengel, & Trevino, 1987). Perpetrators may use this equivocality (multiple interpretations possible) to hide their intentions and declare they were misinterpreted (Coyne, et al., 2017).

Adding to the issue of low media richness, the increased geographical and temporal space between online conversation partners may depersonalize online social interactions (Workman, 2012). Depersonalization subsequently weakens the social influences facilitating mutual understanding between conversation partners (Tajfel, 1982; Workman, 2012). This is also partially attributed to the characteristic of anonymity in virtual environments since individuals are more inclined to engage in cyber-deviant behaviors under the protection of anonymity (Barlett et al., 2017). Taken together, the research suggests that technology makes it easier to be politically cyber-deviant whether the deviance is intentional or not.

20.2 Production Cyber-Deviance

Similar to traditional production deviance, variables that predict production cyber-deviance include individual and organizational-level factors. Explanations of production cyber-deviance rely on psychological theories of motivation, which posit that an individual's intentions are the strongest predictor of their behavior (Ajzen, 1991). Intentions are determined by how an individual's unique knowledge, skills, attitudes, and beliefs interact with more stable characteristics of personality and demography (e.g., Lim, 2002). Intentions are formed within a context of organizational considerations, including subjective norms and ability to hide the production cyber-deviance behavior (Sheikh, Atashgah, & Adibzadegan, 2015).

20.2.1 Antecedents for Production Cyber-Deviance

Individual. Similar to general deviance stereotypes, young males are most likely to engage in production cyber-deviance; younger workers may be more likely because they rely on computer-mediated communications and prefer to socialize online more than older workers (Caplan, 2007). While this is consistent across a number of contexts, age and gender do not fully explain why production cyber-deviance occurs; other personal characteristics (like extroverted personalities, higher status in the organization, and higher technological-savviness) can counteract demographic effects (e.g., Andreassen, Torsheim, & Pallesen, 2014; Baturay & Toker, 2015; Garrett & Danziger, 2008). Individuals of higher status and more technologically savvy individuals are less likely to be caught, and may have more opportunity; whereas extroverts use social media (cyberloafing) to express their social tendencies (Andreassen et al., 2014).

Finally, based on theories of stress and cognitive resources, it is suggested that burnout and low sleep quality may lead to production cyber-deviance (Aghaz & Sheikh, 2016; Hobfoll, 1998; Wagner, et al., 2012). Both conditions suggest an employee may lack the cognitive resources required for difficult job tasks, so they choose the less demanding task of production cyber-deviance instead (Askew et al., 2014). Similarly, low engagement (Blau, Yang, & Ward-Cook, 2006), role overload, role ambiguity, and role conflict (Henle & Blanchard, 2008) contribute to an employee's desire to cyberloaf (Andreassen et al., 2014), due to the stress or reduced cognitive (or physical) resources associated with these experiences.

Organizational.   Much like political cyber-deviance, justice theory helps explain production cyber-deviance (e.g., de Lara, 2007; Restubog, et al., 2011). When employees feel their organization has treated them unfairly, they are more likely to cyberloaf as a form of reprisal (Lim, 2002).

Shifting to broader considerations, subjective and social norms and the extent to which an employee can hide the behavior also contribute to production cyber-deviance. An employee's perceptions of supervisor and coworkers' lack of support for cyberloafing (Liberman, et al., 2011) can deter employee's computer misuse (Malhotra & Galletta, 2005). If employees perceive an organizational culture in which their supervisor and coworkers frown upon cyberloafing, they may seek to avoid negative social consequences of production cyber-deviance by not doing it (e.g., Blanchard & Henle, 2008). Similarly, characteristics of organizational environments that make it difficult to conceal one's cyber-deviant behaviors act as a deterrent of this behavior (Liberman, et al., 2011). A high degree of contextual consideration is required for social and subjective norms assessments, as this fluctuates between and within organizations, departments and jobs (e.g., Garrett & Danziger, 2008); for example, a workstation setup that offers a clear view of an employee's computer screen to passersby may deter the employee from engaging in production cyber-deviance.

Organizational best practices for mitigating production cyber-deviance have been discussed. These include a clearly communicated internet usage policy that is specific to the organizational context (Stewart, 2000), rigorous employee screening and training (Case & Young, 2001), as well as monitoring and enforcement of the policy (Churchman, 2003). Human resource practices also play a role in deterrence when employees become aware that production cyber-deviance could implicate their performance appraisal, compensation, or opportunity for advancement (Alshuaibi, Subrananiam, & Shamsudin, 2014).

20.2.2 Outcomes for Production Cyber-Deviance

Due to its easily disguised nature (Akbulut, Donmez, & Durson, 2017), the outcomes of production cyber-deviance are difficult to quantify. The internet is a double-edged sword for organizations: it is harmful for diminishing productivity, wasting resources, and creating liability, yet beneficial for fostering creativity, allowing time for relaxation, recovery, and learning (Lim & Chen, 2012).

Perpetrator.   In accordance with general deterrence theory, if repercussions for violating company policy are linked with human resource policies, the perpetrator may receive poor performance evaluations, reduced compensation, miss opportunities for advancement (e.g., Alshuaibi et al., 2014), and face formal or informal reprimands, such as warnings, suspensions, loss of privileges, or termination (Case & Young, 2001). Beyond these potential sanctions, cyberloafing distracts employees from their main job duties and reduces productivity, thus employees may miss deadlines, important meetings, and other important work engagements (Caplan, 2007). There are also relational costs for the perpetrator, ranging from increased conflicts, loss of trust with supervisor or peers, to increased job stress (Aghaz & Sheikh, 2016; Koay, Soh, & Chew, 2017). For example, Roberts and David (2017) introduce the construct of "boss phubbing" (p. 206) to describe the extent to which a supervisor is distracted by their smartphone while in the presence of subordinates. Boss phubbing is associated with lower trust in their supervisor and lower organizational engagement (Roberts & David, 2017; Roberts & Wasieleski, 2012).

Conversely, employees who engage in production cyber-deviance may derive some benefits. Consistent with Hobfoll's (1998) conservation of resources theory, cyberloafing may offer employees an opportunity to recover (Lim & Chen, 2012). The results of an experimental study suggest that web-surfing can be restorative and pleasurable (Chen & Lim, 2011), and may decrease exhaustion, stress, and boredom (Andreassen et al., 2014). Web browsing may also have a positive effect on mood (Lim & Chen, 2012), knowledge, and skills (Belanger & Van Slyke, 2002).

Witnesses.   Unregulated internet use at work is a socially learned behavior (Moody & Siponen, 2013). As per social cognitive theory (Bandura, 1989), observers formulate impressions about the frequency with which their coworkers engage in cyberloafing and form perceptions about the degree of support for cyberloafing behavior within that context (Blanchard & Henle, 2008). When observers perceive that coworkers and supervisors support production cyber-deviance, then this may reproduce the behavior due to socialization and modeling.

Organization.   Cyberloafing can hurt an organization's bottom-line in the form of lost wages, reduced output, and reduced profitability (Henle & Kedharnath, 2012). It can also lead to exhaustive use of company resources through network degradation and use of bandwidth (Mills et al., 2001), which can negatively impact system performance (Sipior & Ward, 2002) and lower productivity for other users (Pee, et al., 2008). This may lead to direct and indirect financial losses, such as IT expenditures (Sharma & Gupta, 2003). Additionally, production cyber-deviance can pose a security risk and increase legal liability through the potential for defamation, libel, negligence, and wrongful termination (Johnson & Indvik, 2003).

While theory leads us to believe that burnout is a predictor of cyberloafing behavior, it could also be an outcome. In this case, other well-established correlates of burnout, specifically increased turnover intentions and decreased organizational commitment, may also be associated with cyberloafing (Aghaz & Sheikh, 2016). Additionally, if organizational policies prohibiting production cyber-deviance are applied, organizations may experience higher turnover as the organization termi- nates employees who cyberloaf (Glassman, Prosch, & Shao, 2015). Since this requires organizational resources to be directed toward disciplinary actions, profit and performance may be negatively affected (Shamsudin, Subramaniam, & Alshuaibi, 2012).

20.2.3 The Context: Media Characteristics

Technological advancements continue to obscure the boundaries between work and home and change perceptions of how easy or difficult it is to conceal one's online behaviors (Barlett et al., 2017); media characteristics shape research in this area.

Initially, the ability to access a computer at work that had faster internet than at home was integral to one's ability to engage in production cyber- deviance (e.g., Garrett & Danziger, 2008; Mastrangelo, Everton, & Jolton, 2003). As computers with high-quality internet access became the norm, research shifted to more nuanced considerations such as which social media sites should be accessible on work computers and who is more likely to use them (Andreassen et al., 2014; Caplan, 2007; Mahatanankoon et al., 2004). Time spent on the computer and sophistication of computer skills are posi- tively related to engaging in production cyber-deviance as these employees have more opportunity and skill to enact production cyber-deviance (e.g., Anandarajan et al., 2004; Baturay & Toker, 2015).

Investigations soon expanded to include other devices that provide internet access at work to determine which were more problematic (e.g., handheld phones or computers; Askew, et al., 2014), and the degree of sophistication required for work technologies (Roberts & Wasieleski, 2012). While a shift toward more distributed and mobile work facilitates more production cyber- deviance in some contexts (e.g., O'Neill, Hambley, & Bercovich, 2014), enhanced security and monitoring systems deter it in other contexts. These developments represent technologically changing subjective norms that may increase or decrease production cyber-deviance (Askew et al., 2014; Barlett et al., 2017).

20.3 Property Cyber-Deviance

With social media, employers are at risk for employees posting content defaming their employer. In 2008, a school teacher posted disparaging comments toward her school on her Facebook account, stating she was "teaching in the most ghetto school in Charlotte" (New York Times, 2008). In another example, an employee posted comments about her coworkers on her online blog, calling them "imbeciles" and "idiot savants" (Harris, 2008). Both cases exemplify property cyber-deviance as the employee endangers the company's reputation.

Property cyber-deviance behaviors are becoming increasingly common and diverse, as employees are becoming more technologically savvy (Davis & Braun, 2004). Increases in employees' technological skills and capabilities put employers at risk for property cyber-deviant behaviors, such as accessing unauthorized files; the altering, deleting, or copying of data; and installation of harmful software. The most common type of unauthorized computer behavior is copying and modifying data, which could include copying credit card numbers or other sensitive financial information (Davis & Braun, 2004). Targets of property cyber-deviance can be the organization, other employees, or customers (e.g., Barlow, et al., 2003; Davis & Braun, 2004; Mastrangelo, Everton, & Jolton, 2006), with the most common being the employer.

20.3.1 Antecedents of Property Cyber-Deviance

Individual. Reasons employees engage in property cyber-deviance that targets coworkers (e.g., accessing coworker's sensitive/secure files) have not yet been empirically studied; therefore, antecedents of these behaviors cannot be confidently identified. However, these behaviors usually require greater technological expertise (Davis & Braun, 2004). Employees' level of self-control is associated with digital piracy; those with lower self-control more frequently engaged in risky and impulsive computer behavior at work (Higgins & Wolfe, 2008).

Property cyber-deviant acts that harm company property, such as online gambling or pornography, are more common in cyber-deviance literature, thus their antecedents are well understood. Generally, young male workers more commonly engage in this type of cyber-deviant behavior (Mastrangelo, et al., 2006). Employees were also more likely to engage in online gambling or pornography at work if they work multiple jobs, as these employees reported more stressful work-life situations (Mastrangelo, et al., 2006). All of these factors – self-control, youth, and stressful work-life situations – may be related to the functioning of the frontal cortex, where impulse control and higher-order decision-making functioning resides. Research on sleep deprivation and adolescence neuropsychological development highlight the impacts on reduced frontal cortex functioning (e.g., Chambers & Potenza, 2003; Christian & Ellis, 2011), thus future research may want to examine the neurophysiological factors as potential explanatory factors instead of relying on correlations of age, impulse control and stress.

An individual's morals and moral identity (i.e., the symbolization and internalization levels of employees) impact their tendency to engage in property cyber-deviance toward customers. Internalization is based on moral identity theory, in which an individual's traits and morals are central to one's identity, while symbolization is rooted in social identity theory, and refers to the degree in which individuals engage in acts of self-presentation and avoid "threats to one's moral identity" (Skarlicki, et al., 2008, p. 1338). Employees with low internalization more frequently engage in deviant acts toward customers, as they have a higher tendency to engage in immoral behavior. Employees high in symbolization more frequently engage in deviant acts toward customers since they are more likely to view demeaning behavior from customers as threats to their status and identity.

Dyadic.   Acts like purposefully leaving customers on hold, transferring their phone call to the wrong department, or disconnecting their call can be triggered by experiencing rude treatment from the targeted customer (Skarlicki, et al., 2008). As the interactional justice theory explains, when an employee perceives that they are treated unjustly by a particular customer and the employee has low internalization and high symbolization, the employee will engage in deviant behaviors to restore the level of interactional justice between the employee and customer (Skarlicki, et al., 2008).

Organizational.   Similar to production cyber-deviance, organizational justice and the fair treatment of employees is important; employees' perceptions of being unfairly treated by their organization were an antecedent to online gambling and pornography (Blau et al., 2006). Similarly, if an employee feels they are unfairly treated through either unmet financial or relationship needs, then they may steal intellectual property or trade secrets from the employer to sabotage the organization (Civiello, 1999).

In a few serious cases of property cyber-deviance, employees have infected company computer systems with a virus that either deleted significant amounts of company data or made the company's computer system inoperable. Bissett and Shipton (2000) identify several conscious aims of individuals who design and release computer viruses, including non-specific malice, revenge (due to employee disgruntlement), ideological motives (political, freedom of information), commercial sabotage (like bankruptcy), and warfare (espionage). Out of the motives listed by different authors, employee disgruntlement seems to be a common factor. In a few cases, the disgruntled perpetrator cited their motives as retribution for being told that they were being fired (e.g., Barlow et al., 2003). Therefore, employers must be careful when terminating employees with considerable technological capabilities. Also, it is important for organizations to be aware of who has access to sensitive company information. Carelessly sharing information with employees and other third-party organizations increases the risk of sensitive information being leaked or exposed by disgruntled employees seeking retribution (e.g., Aldhizer III, 2008; Scheier, 2001).

Another organizational factor is a company's technological system security level. Although this has not yet been examined empirically, it has been suggested that some forms of property cyber-deviance, such as hacking, installation of harmful software, and data deletion, are all more likely when an employee has a significant level of technological capabilities (Davis & Braun, 2004). Therefore, it is possible that increased technology system security could reduce the ability of tech-savvy employees from being able to engage in such forms of property cyber-deviance.

20.3.2 Outcomes of Property Cyber-Deviance

Perpetrator. Acts of property cyber-deviance have the potential to benefit or disadvantage the perpetrator. One behavior benefitting perpetrators is the altering or deleting of one's own internet activity, as an employee can hide inappropriate computer usage from their employer (Barlow, et al., 2003). Another benefit for perpetrators is the perceived readdressing of interpersonal injustice between the perpetrator and customers or their employer. For example, by disconnecting a customer's telephone call, the perpetrator may feel as though they have reduced the imbalance of interpersonal justice that was caused by previous poor treatment of the employee by that customer (Skarlicki, et al., 2008). If an employee feels as though they have been treated unjustly by their employer, the employee might engage in cyber-deviant acts such as the altering/deleting of data or downloading of a virus to address the imbalance of justice between the employee and employer; however, the subsequent outcomes (e.g., satisfaction, remorse, sanctions) have not been examined (Davis & Braun, 2004).

Lastly, employees have claimed to engage in unproductive computer usage, such as online gambling or pornography, as it provides stress relief (Klotz & Buckley, 2013). However, the few potential benefits of engaging in property cyber-deviance are heavily outweighed by the potential negative impacts for perpetrators. For starters, employees engaged in computer misuse may see a reduction in performance as it would also constitute production cyber-deviance, not just property cyber-deviance (e.g., Mastrangelo, et al., 2006). Also, engaging in property cyber-deviance, such as hacking sensitive company information, or accessing coworkers' usernames or passwords can result in serious consequences for perpetrators such as termination (e.g., Harris, 2008). In more serious instances, such as the deletion of important company information or the deactivation of a company's computer system, perpetrators risk being sentenced to jail or subject to large fines, if caught (Davis & Braun, 2004).

Organization. The most common organizational consequence of property cyber-deviance is decreased organizational performance. In the instance of non-productive computer activity, company resources are being wasted while important work is often left undone, reducing organizational efficiency (Mastrangelo, et al., 2006). Deletion of important company data negatively impacts organizations since losing critical company information reduces organizational performance (Davis & Braun, 2004). Another negative outcome of property cyber-deviance for organizations is the potential breach of confidentiality or leak of sensitive information. For example, tech-savvy employees hacking confidential company information may release the sensitive information internally or externally (Davis & Braun, 2004). Leaked information or trade secrets reflect poorly on the organization's security capabilities and reputation (Civiello, 1999). The last consequence of property cyber-deviance for employers is the potential harm to the company's reputation. If an employee makes a defamatory post about their company on their social media account, this content is publically viewable. Thus, it has the potential to damage the reputation of the company (Harris, 2008).

20.3.3 The Context: Media Characteristics

When examining the prevalence and likelihood of property cyber-deviance in the workplace, it is important to consider the media characteristics associated with the technology available to employees. However, the only characteristic examined to date is anonymity, which has been shown to lead to digital piracy, as one feels as if they are less likely to get caught (Higgins & Wolfe, 2008).

20.4 Personal Cyber-Aggression

As noted in the introduction, there are many different forms of personal cyber-aggression; for our purposes, we will focus on three related behaviors: cyber-incivility, virtual (sexual) harassment, and cyberbullying, as these behaviors have been most researched and organizations are highly motivated to reduce or eradicate these behaviors. Each of these behaviors has been researched extensively in their traditional forms, and cyber-aggression research has sought to replicate findings and understand the frequency of cyber-aggression (e.g., Lee, 2017; Privitera & Campbell, 2009). Virtual sexual harassment and cyberbullying is rarely studied in workplace contexts, with the vast majority of cyberbullying research done on adolescents. However, this research may be highly relevant as this population (teenagers) is the largest age group in precarious jobs (involuntary part-time and temporary; Fleury, 2016), and cyberbullying does occur within the workplace.

20.4.1 Antecedents of Personal Cyber-Aggression

Individual.   Most of the research examines individual factors given the interpersonal nature of personal cyber-aggression. Males are more likely to actively engage in cyber-incivility (Lim & Teo, 2009) and post nonverbal aggressive posts on Facebook (Shelton & Skalski, 2014); whereas, females are more likely to enact passive forms of cyber-incivility (Lim & Teo, 2009). These gender effects are not deemed to be deterministic biological factors, but due to socialization and psychological aspects, as per cultivation theory (Shelton & Skalski, 2014) or gender identity (e.g., Maas, et al., 2003).

Personality is another perpetrator trait commonly examined within the aggression literature. Individuals high in emotional stability and extroversion exhibit lower rates of cyber-incivility than those who are lower in these personality traits when they are also high in conscientiousness (Krishnan, 2016). Personality traits may also interact with other psychological factors, like frustration (e.g., Reio, 2011). Frustration may be viewed as a situational context; however, according to frustration theory (Amsel, 1992), people have propensities (called dispositional learning) toward certain responses to frustration; one of these, invigoration, can be expressed as aggression. Similarly, perpetrator trait anger (e.g., Ak, Ozdemir, & Kuzueu, 2015; Lee, 2017) is positively associated with cyberbullying. Individuals high in trait anger have a predisposition to respond to triggers more aggressively than individuals low in trait anger due to several cognitive processes (e.g., Wilkowsky & Robinson, 2008).

Perpetrators' belief that physical stature is irrelevant for online bullying is a factor for cyber-bullying. The strength differential hypothesis partially explains traditional bullying (physically stronger individuals are more likely to bully others who are not as physically strong), but it appears to not apply to cyberbullying (Barlett, et al., 2017). Rather, perpetrators' cyberbullying attitude, and witnesses' normative beliefs about verbal and cyber-aggression, are positively related to incidents of cyberbullying by the perpetrator (Barlett, et al., 2017) or the reinforcement of cyberbullying by witnesses (Machockova & Pfetch, 2016). In other words, similar to theory of reasoned action (Fishbein & Ajzen, 1975), positive beliefs regarding the behavior increase the likelihood of the individual intending or actually enacting that behavior, they do not require physical stature like they do for in-person bullying.

According to the victim precipitation model (Wolfgang, 1957), certain target characteristics make an individual more susceptible to personal cyber-aggression, like sexual orientation, religion, and appearance (Lee, 2017). For example, in one experiment, if the target was known to be a feminist, the perpetrator was more likely to sexually harass her (send soft pornographic material: Maas et al., 2003), presumably because the feminist status was a threat to his gender identity and served as a trigger.

The target's behaviors may also trigger personal cyber-aggression. For example, the theory of self-presentation explains that certain social media posting behaviors (i.e., posting risky or inappropriate posts) increase the likelihood of becoming a target (Peluchette, et al., 2015). Also, the larger an individual's social media network size is, the more likely he or she is to become a target (Peluchette, et al., 2015). According to social information processing theory, people use the information available to them to form opinions then act in accordance to those opinions. Individuals who have large online social networks and spend more time on social media become more likely to be targeted, as they may appear to be more "promiscuous" in their friending behaviors or increase the chance of posting something that is less filtered/more likely to be negatively construed (Peluchette, et al., 2015). Relatedly, individuals high in extroversion and openness are more likely to become targets of cyberbullying (Peluchette, et al., 2015).

Organizational. Like the previously discussed forms of cyber-deviance, workloads, justice, and policies explain some of the occurrences. Increasing workloads is associated with higher rates of cyber-incivility (e.g., Francis, Holmvall, & O'Brien, 2015). Interestingly, as per social exchange theory, this also interacted with a dyadic/situational aspect of the level of civility of the original email; uncivil emails would get more incivility in return (Francis, et al., 2015). Other similar "situational constraints," like work-life spillover, time pressure, and having an inadequate supply of equipment and job resources may be associated with more incidents of cyber-incivility because of their link with frustration (Reio, 2011), as per the frustration-aggression model (Dollard, et al., 1939). Without adequate organizational support, perpetrators more frequently engage in cyberbullying (Gardner, et al., 2016). Again, this may be due to social exchange theory, the frustration-aggression model, or a combination thereof. Finally, without clear cues from the organization on the unacceptability of personal cyber-aggression behaviors, cyberbullying is more likely to occur (Gardner, et al., 2016).

20.4.2 Outcomes of Personal Cyber-Aggression

Perpetrator. There is limited literature examining outcomes for perpetrators of personal cyber-aggression. We found discussion of the enjoyment or anticipation of the target's response for cyberbullying (Dooley, Pyzalski, & Cross, 2009), and the over-estimation of effect on target (Giménez Gualdo, et al., 2015). Together, these reinforce the cyberbullying behaviors. However, these studies were not within the organizational context, and both used youth as the target population. Adult perpetrators may face internal organizational sanctions if an in-house complaint is laid, other remedy requirements if a complaint is filed with a human rights legislative body, or criminal charges if offenses are deemed criminal. These should reduce the probability of the occurrence of the behaviors; however, they may only work if they are known and salient, enacted, and sufficiently severe to counter any reinforcers of the behavior for the perpetrator.

Target. The personal cyber-aggression research mainly examines the impact of cyber-aggression on targets, predominantly using the stressor-strain model (e.g., Barling, 1996) to explain how perceived severity, stress, and strain relate to personal cyber-aggression and each other. Perceived severity has been examined with respect to cyberbullying (e.g., D'Cruz & Noronha, 2013; Nocentini, et al., 2010; Sticca & Perren, 2013) and virtual harassment (Biber, et al., 2002), but not cyber-incivility. Given incivility refers to acts which are low in severity, this makes sense. Gender may impact how severity of cyber-aggression is perceived. In a scenario-based experiment, gender moderated perceptions of severity of virtual sexual harassment. Women rated jokes and pictures as more harassing than men; there were no gender differences in ratings of severity between traditional means and online (cyber) (Biber, et al., 2002).

Stress, in its various forms, has been a more popular research topic for personal cyber-aggression. Same-day distress (Park, Fritz, & Jex, 2015), anxiety (Byron, 2008), fear (which may be long-lasting: e.g., Ford, 2013), and feelings of intimidation (Ophoff, et al., 2015) all result from exposure to workplace personal cyber-aggression. Another form of stress is anger and negative affect, which has been found in all forms of personal cyber-aggression (Farley, et al., 2015; Ford & Clarke, 2017; Giumetti, et al., 2012). What has not been addressed is how these different forms of stress may (dis)empower targets. Do they motivate more withdrawal or retribution, more individually/organizationally harmful behaviors? Distress, anxiety, and fear increase strain, as does anger and negative affect; however, what has not been discussed is the use of anger to motivate and support restitutive actions. D'Cruz and Noronha (2013) found that evidence from cyberbullying could be used to instigate restitution; however, they did not examine the role of anger or the impact of the anger-restitution relationship on target strain.

Finally, according to stressor-strain model, strain (i.e., lowered psychological and physical well-being) is a distal outcome (e.g., Coyne, et al., 2017; Ford, 2015). Somewhat contrary to the stressor-strain model, Ford (2013, 2015) found strain was only partially mediated by fear; while traditional harassment was fully mediated by fear of future workplace aggression. Strain may also show as diminished self-esteem (Ophoff, et al., 2015), and some researchers examined strain as it is expressed within the workplace: decreased energy and engagement (Giumetti, et al., 2012), diminished motivation (Ophoff et al., 2015), burnout (e.g., Giumetti, et al., 2012), and decreased job satisfaction (e.g., Coyne, et al., 2017; Reio, 2011). Thus, there are a lot of different ways of operationalizing strain within the personal cyber-aggression literature; however, one thing is clear, it is not a positive effect for the target or the organization.

Dyadic.   While Byron (2008) did not explicitly discuss cyber-incivility, her explanation on how emotional cues are misinterpreted in emails explains why cyber-incivility occurs. Byron (2008) notes the outcomes of these misinterpretations of emotions, which are dyadic in nature: increased relational distance, decreased connectedness, and decreased group focus. If these outcomes were to occur due to a misinterpretation or personal cyber-aggression, a more toxic workplace environment may result. For example, several theories (e.g., kin selection, social network theory) highlight how individuals within our social networks benefit because we tend to aid them. With decreased group focus (e.g., diminished collectivism), increased relational distance, individuals may become more self-focused and less polite (i.e., increase incivility) and may even start to exclude others (social isolation is a part of workplace bullying). Finally, social support is a critical support system for targets of workplace aggression; without the buffer of social ties, the workplace becomes an isolating, lonely place to work.

Organization.   In terms of outcomes for the organization, all outcomes examined thus far have actually been individual-level behaviors or attitudes that ultimately affect the organization. For example, personal cyber-aggression is associated with the following target behaviors and attitudes: greater absenteeism (Giumetti, et al.,

2012), lower organizational commitment (Reio, 2011), higher turnover intentions (e.g., Lim & Teo, 2009), lower engagement and performance (e.g., Ophoff, et al., 2015), and higher workplace deviance (Lim & Teo, 2009). All of these individual outcomes may impact the organization's performance and bottom line as per Porter's (1985) value chain model; however, research has not followed these outcomes to the organizational level. Interestingly, increased absenteeism and lower engagement leads into the potential start of weakened social ties and the start of a toxic work environment as discussed above.

There were two factors found within the literature focusing on organizational-level factors: the level of job control that organizations provide their employees, and interactional justice. Park, et al. (2015) found that job control moderated the relationship between cyber-incivility and same-day distress. This is important as it may reduce the amount of stress and strain targets experience (e.g., stressor-strain model), but also assists in allocating energy and resources best suited for dealing with the cyber-incivility (as per the conservation of resources theory). According to organizational justice theories, interactional justice mediates cyberbullying and strain and job satisfaction (Farley, et al., 2015). This may assist in mitigating some of the negative outcomes for targets, and organizational costs (as strain and job satisfaction relate to other individual behaviors and attitudes, like commitment, turnover, absenteeism, and performance).

20.4.3 The Context: Media Characteristics

One important aspect often excluded from the research is consideration for media characteristics and their influence on perpetrator's motivations, experiences of the target or perpetrator, or organizational costs. For perpetrators, there has been no examination of media characteristics and their impact on cyber-incivility or virtual harassment. However, for cyberbullying, the ability of perpetrators to conceal their identity (i.e., anonymity) has been linked to increased probability of cyberbullying due to either the reduced relevance of strength differential (Barlett, et al., 2017) or due to lack of being held accountable (e.g., Lee, 2017).

Research is starting to examine media characteristics for target experiences. The actual choice of media has been examined in terms of impact on perceptions of severity, which was not significant (Sticca & Perren, 2013). Anonymity has been associated with severity, fear, evidence to evoke change, and strain for cyberbully-ing and virtual harassment (e.g., D'Cruz & Noronha, 2013; Ford, 2013). Media richness has been examined for virtual harassment (associated with fear: Ford, 2013, 2015) and misinterpretations of emotions (Byron, 2008). Reach (i.e., pub-licity) of cyberbullying is associated with the perception of severity (e.g., Nocentini, et al., 2010). The permanence (or persistence) of the media has also been examined with respect to impact on fear and strain on the targets of cyber-bullying and virtual harassment, along with its ability to be used as evidence to evoke restitution (D'Cruz & Noronha, 2013; Ford, 2013). Finally, the location of receipt of the harassing messages impacts fear and strain (Ford, 2013, 2015), but it has not been examined with respect to cyber-incivility or cyberbullying. It is possible that location of receipt of uncivil emails would also be relevant for stress if receiving them at home, in the evening, prevents the target's "psychological evening detachment," which (Park, et al., 2015), suggested to be an important moderator for preventing distress from cyber-incivility continuing to the next day.

20.5 The Feedback Loop: When Outcomes Lead to Antecedents

One challenge that organizations face regarding cyber-deviance is how to mitigate it, particularly when it is malevolent to other organizational members, the organization, and society. Within the literature review, we found three main possible feedback loops where outcomes may reinforce cyber-deviancy: (1) escalation due to spillover effects; (2) learning theories; and (3) general deterrence theory. We clarify how they apply to cyber-deviance.

20.5.1 The Escalation Effects

A major challenge is the chicken-versus-the-egg issue, and identifying which came first. Within the context of personal cyber-aggression, it can become difficult to ascertain who is the original bully as targets may use bullying tactics (like social isolation of the bully, or badmouthing the bully to sympathetic listeners) to protect themselves from further harm from the bully (e.g., Lee & Brotheridge, 2006). Furthermore, targets of workplace cyber-aggression may experience anger, leading to retaliation (Weatherbee, 2007).

Escalation could occur due to different reasons, including conflict escalation (e.g., Zapf & Gross, 2001), an escalation effect of ineffectual coping strategies which in turn bully the original perpetrator (e.g., Lee & Brotheridge, 2006), or instances where an incident leads to perceptions of organizational injustice which then leads to "balancing of the ledger" (e.g., Blau, et al., 2006; Lim, 2002). Similarly, a spillover effect and rumination could lead to triggered aggression if there is insufficient distraction (e.g., Bushman, et al., 2005) or psychological detachment from work in the evening (e.g., Park, et al., 2015).

A final form of escalation could come in the form of virtual "mob justice" when witnesses or the original target air their disapproval through social media, as illustrated in the "Diversity Manifesto" incident. A problem of this type of mob justice is several-fold. The original incident goes from a small audience to a very public audience as its reach (publicity) increases. As noted earlier, reach increases perceptions of severity, so the original target may experience worse effects. Second, mob justice rarely follows the principles associated with Procedural Justice (e.g., Leventhal, 1980), and, in turn, the newly shamed party experiences injustice, which increases the probability of more cyber-deviance. Finally, virtual mob justice is a severe form of positive punishment that comes with a host of other negative effects (see Operant Conditioning below).

20.5.2 Learning Theories

Social Learning Theory.   According to social cognitive theory and social learning theory, there are three main components: observation, self-efficacy, and self-regulation (Bandura, 1989). Cyber-deviance research has focused primarily on observation. For example, Moody and Siponen (2013) conclude that unregulated internet use at work is a social behavior learned through observing other employees. Witnessing a coworker's cyberloafing, especially during the socialization of a new employee, may reproduce the behavior in the witness (e.g., Blanchard & Henle, 2008). Similarly, individuals who witness acts of property, production, or political cyber-deviance may be socialized to accept these deviant behaviors as acceptable. When individuals witness episodes of cyberbullying, if they also held positive normative beliefs about cyber-aggression, they too would reinforce cyberbullying (Machackova & Pfetsch, 2016).

Self-efficacy was hypothesized to increase the probability of cyberbullies engaging in cyberbullying; however, self-efficacy regarding computer skills was not related to cyberbullying behaviors (Barlett, et al., 2017). Perhaps it is one's cyber-deviance self-efficacy that is more relevant than computer self-efficacy. Finally, self-regulation has not been examined within the context of cyber-deviance.

Operant Conditioning.   According to operant conditioning theory (e.g., Skinner, 1953), the probability of a behavior occurring again in the future increases when it is followed either by negative reinforcement (the removal of an aversive stimulus), or positive reinforcement (the addition of an enjoyable stimulus); the probability of a behavior will decrease if it is followed by either positive punishment (the addition of an aversive stimulus) or negative punishment (the removal of an enjoyable stimulus); and a behavior will ultimately extinguish if there is absolutely no feedback to the behavior. It is important to note that punishment only suppresses a behavior; it does not permanently stop (extinguish) a behavior. A suppressed behavior may recur at a later date, especially if the expectation of punishment is removed. Thus, given these premises, it is evident that if cyber-deviance continues within the organization, there is some form of reinforcement occurring, be it extrinsic reinforcement (coming from someone else) or intrinsic (emanating from the behavior itself).

Glassman et al. (2015) compared agency theory, operant conditioning, procedural justice, social norms, employee empowerment, and resource replenishment to cyberloafing to demonstrate the type of organizational policy most effective for limiting cyberloafing. It should be noted that the authors confused positive punishment and negative reinforcement when they stated, "negative reinforcers reprimand or cause displeasure for the test subject for engaging in inappropriate behaviors" (p. 172). That aside, they assessed how to minimize inappropriate internet usage.

In their study, they examined how employer-created lists of approved (full access) work-related sites, blocked sites, and the remaining "unknown" sites could be best utilized. A blocking approach created firewalls that prohibited the access to the known unapproved sites. All attempts to access these sites resulted in a prompt on the screen, reminding the employees that these were not work-related sites. A quota approach allowed end users a certain amount of time (ten-minute intervals) on known leisure sites before disallowing them after ninety minutes of use in a day. Finally, a confirmation approach used the list of approved and blocked sites, and for any unknown site, a prompt would appear on the screen to confirm the site was for work-related use. This prompt would appear at five-minute intervals. They found the confirmation model of monitoring was more effective than the blocking or quota model, which they argued was due to its empowerment of employees and alignment with procedural justice (Glassman et al., 2015). An alternative explanation is that the five minute interval "reminders" (interruptions) were a form of response cost which is a mild form of punishment (the occurrence of an aversive stimulus: the interruption to their enjoyment), as per operant conditioning theory.

There has been limited research examining the operant conditioning process with cyber-deviance; however, some researchers have highlighted perpetrators of personal cyber-aggression do derive (intrinsic or extrinsic) positive reinforcement from their behaviors (e.g., Barlett, et al., 2017; Dooley, et al., 2009). This implies that these cyber-deviant behaviors will continue due to their intrinsic reinforcement.

There are four issues present within this literature and business practices from the perspective of operational conditioning. First, there is an over-emphasis on punishment. As noted above, punishment (either the removal of an enjoyable stimulus [negative punishment] or the introduction of an aversive stimulus [positive punishment]) only suppresses a behavior, it cannot extinguish it. When monitoring ceases, these undesired behaviors will often recur. Second, one characteristic of cyber-deviance is the asynchronous nature of the communications and, if the perpetrator is knowledgeable enough, anonymous. This means that any punishment given to perpetrators is somewhat distal from the time of the behavior. This time lag diminishes the effectiveness in learning and altering behavior. Third, from a behavioral adjustment and training perspective, punishment leads to unpredictable outcomes (such as fear, anger, aggression, frustration, suppression), and it may create feelings of injustice, which only increase the likelihood of further retaliatory deviance. Therefore, it is not a very effective way of stopping a cycle of cyber-deviance within the organization. Fourth, it is hard to train the absence of behavior (e.g., "Do not do [behavior]"). Rather, it is far more effective to train an alternative "Do" behavior that is incompatible to the undesired behavior. While focusing on reinforcing the alternative behavior, the negative outcomes of punishment are avoided, and the undesired behavior has a chance to extinguish because it is not being rehearsed. These issues have been overlooked by researchers and practitioners. Yet, some of this has been started to be implemented within the prison and school systems to address violence issues (e.g., Compassion Games, http://compassiongames.org/). Future research should examine the effectiveness of reinforcing incompatible, positive behaviors to address cyber-deviance.

20.5.3 General Deterrence Theory

According to general deterrence theory, prevention, detection, and correction are required to prevent (and recover from) occurrences of deviance (e.g., Thornton, Gunningham, & Kagan, 2005). The first step is to have clear and well-known policies. Even before empirical work began on understanding individuals' cyber-loafing behavior, organizations worked to prevent and/or decrease this activity. Computer-aided monitoring of automated offices began in the late 80s (e.g., Chalykoff & Kochan, 1989). Within a decade, organizations were being advised to control cyberloafing through measures such as acceptable usage policies (e.g., de Lara, Tacoronte, & Ding, 2006; Stewart, 2000), proactive management, and communication (Case & Young, 2001) because these things were shown to reduce internet abuse at work (Churchman, 2003).

General deterrence theory has been tested empirically and confirmed; explicit prevention and detection techniques (monitoring usage and controlling web access), and employee beliefs about organizational sanctions, significantly reduced workplace internet abuse (Henle & Blanchard, 2008; Mirchandani & Motwani, 2003). More recent findings from the deterrence perspective call for a multi-dimensional measure of cyberloafing by demonstrating that although termination threats and detection mechanisms are effective against some cyberloafing activities, such as viewing pornography, managing personal finances, and personal shopping, they are less effective in preventing personal emailing and social networking (Urgin & Pearson, 2013). In order for policies to be effective, they must include all organizational members and forms of cyber-deviance. For example, Canadian universities often had incomplete cyberbullying policies as it was assumed to be an issue among students and not involve faculty or staff (Faucher, Jackson, & Cassidy, 2015).

The second step is to monitor and capture incidents of failure. To that end, researchers have been creating ways to monitor and identify likely cases of cyber-bullying through data mining (Burn-Thornton & Burman, 2012). However, monitoring for property cyber-deviance comes with a cost. Monitoring employee's online activity has shown to have significant implications for job satisfaction and intention to quit (Chalykoff & Kochan, 1989). Using Theory X (employees must be monitored and it is an employer's right) and Theory Y (some diligent employees will welcome monitoring and organizational deadweight may be eliminated), Urbaczewski and Jessup (2002) observed a productivity-satisfaction tradeoff depending on whether employees knew their internet usage was being monitored or not and the purposes of the monitoring. It is not known if this cost would apply to monitoring for cases of personal cyber-aggression, political cyber-deviance, or property cyber-deviance.

What was missing from the literature was discussion on the organizational recovery side of general deterrence theory (i.e., the correction and return to original state of organizational resources and processes), with the exception of Ophoff, et al. (2015) who noted that those targets of cyber-aggression who were able to use the messages as evidence and enacted change had more positive outcomes. However, they did not examine the impact on the perpetrator and the likelihood of it reoccurring; ergo they missed the final feedback loop.

20.6 Discussion

In this chapter, we set out to synthesize the research on the four types of cyber-deviance (Weatherbee, 2010) in terms of a process model (antecedents–behavior–outcomes–feedback loop). From the above summary of the research, several issues become evident.

Clearly, technology blurs the boundaries between the four types, even more so than first highlighted by Weatherbee (2010). We found production cyber-deviance and property cyber-deviance often involved the same behavior. For example, Weatherbee (2010) highlighted viewing pornography as property deviance; however, Greengard (2000) included visiting pornographic websites in his definition of cyberslacking. If an employee misuses their company-provided technology during workhours to engage work-unrelated behaviors, then both typologies are clearly enacted. Mastrangelo, et al. (2003) identified two types of deviant computer use: nonproductive computer use (playing games, shopping, conversing with friends) and counterproductive computer use (forwarding pornography, attempting to access confidential information, and trafficking drugs at the worksite). When aligned with Weatherbee's (2010) typology, nonproductive computer use is covered by production cyber-deviance, while counterproductive computer use is more aligned with property cyber-deviance and/or personal cyber-aggression. We also found cyber-stalking could be construed as political cyber-deviance or personal cyber-aggression, and misuse of a coworker's computer could be construed as political cyber-deviance or property cyber-deviance; the distinction between these is the effects of the perpetrator's behaviors. To that end, more research should examine spillover effects given the inter-relatedness of these typologies of cyber-deviance.

Similarly, it may be interesting to examine a temporal framework of cyber-deviance. For example, Spector and Fox (2010) argued that organizational citizenship behaviors (OCB) and counterproductive work behaviors (CWB) could be related due to processes such as compensation (OCBs follow CWB due to feelings of guilt), and entitlement (CWBs follow OCBs because the individual has "earned" the right). Is it possible that there are similar spillovers or compensatory effects with cyber-deviance? For example, could an employee who uses company computers for personal business during work hours feel guilt and conduct work business on a personal computer during personal hours? While that may address production cyber-deviance, could this action put the organization at higher risk to property cyber-deviance (e.g., accidental leaking/hacking)? Could production or property cyber-deviance (use of company resources for personal matters and social networking) lead to lower political cyber-deviance or personal cyber-aggression because of reduced stress? These potential relations have not been examined but would be an interesting and worthwhile endeavor to identify the possible long-term repercussions of cyber-deviance.

Another issue is the lack of empirical papers on political and property cyber-deviance. It may be due to these being the more "minor" form of deviance; however, given these minor forms of cyber-deviance converge with more serious forms of deviance as noted above, it behooves researchers to give these topics empirical consideration. Conversely, there is a significant amount of research on personal cyber-aggression, but not a lot within the context of the workplace (i.e., there are vast amounts on cyberbullying with youths and school systems). As individuals may bring their own IT into the organization (e.g., smartphones), young workers may be experiencing cyberbullying from their school lives within their place of employment, just like adults who have work computers or smartphones may experience workplace aggression while at home (Ford, 2013, 2015). Thus, the cyberbullying literature within the education field is relevant and should be integrated within the cyber-deviance research.

Despite the blurring of the lines of the four types of cyber-deviance, we do not see a similar convergence in the literature. Rather, we notice a lack of synergies and integration across types, and even within each of the types of cyber-deviance; there lacks a cohesive discourse within the various types of cyber-deviance, illustrated by the range of labels for the behaviors. This lack of cohesion puts this field at very high risk of silo-ism, which Kruglanski (2001) warned against. Workplace aggression research has had a call for more synergy and integrative discussion (Hershcovis, 2011); we, too, make this call for cyber-deviance. There are many possible reasons why this silo-ism is apparent within this literature, the main one being that it is multi-disciplinary. There are researchers from psychology, education, business, and information systems adding to the discussion, and there are different conversations and norms within each discipline.

Alternatively, this silo-ism may be due to a narrow focus on the IT-artifact (e.g., Benbasat & Zmud, 2003) instead of the theoretical context of the behavior and the theoretical nuances (Ford, 2003) or "spirit" (DeSanctis & Poole, 1994) of the information technology. For example, there is a trend of more recent production cyber-deviance and personal cyber-aggression articles focusing on how the behavior is done on devices (like smartphones/tablets) versus a desktop computer (e.g., Askew et al., 2014; Lee, 2017). Yet, technology has characteristics that can be examined on a theoretical level, like reach (publicity/virality), anonymity, richness (although, we do not recommend richness be considered as a deterministic perspective intrinsic to the technology, but rather the experienced richness as expressed by channel expansion theory: Carlson & Zmud, 1999), permanence, location, security, and surveillance. By including these characteristics, researchers may bridge the gap between workplace cyber-deviance and traditional workplace deviance as these characteristics may be examined within the traditional contexts as well. This has been done to a certain extent in the personal cyber-aggression literature (e.g., Barlett, et al., 2017; Ford, 2013). By focusing too much on the IT-artifact, the literature risks being outpaced by technological developments. If researchers focus on the theoretical aspects of the technological context of these behaviors, then research may remain more timely and relevant through various technological advancements.

On the positive side, we did notice, particularly within the personal cyber-aggression literature, acknowledgment or integration of existing theories and frameworks into the cyber context, and the direct examination of the technological characteristics instead of simply the IT-artifact (e.g., Coyne, et al., 2017; Dooley, et al., 2009).

Beyond these observations, we sought to synthesize a process model to understand the antecedents, outcomes, and feedback loop for the four types of cyber-deviance. The above synthesis highlights that for the antecedents, there is a fair amount of discussion and research on perpetrators' individual and organizational factors for the four types of cyber-deviance and some known target factors for personal cyber-aggression, but very little is known about dyadic or interpersonal antecedents for all four types of behavior. Personality, gender, age, attitudes, and skills are the most commonly examined perpetrator factors. Organizational justice, surveillance, and organizational norms are the most common organizational factors.

Surveillance goes hand-in-hand with policies and policies aid in creating organizational norms, but surveillance may run counter to perceptions of organizational justice. The fact some of the cyber-deviant behaviors are difficult to monitor limits the effectiveness of policies further. This leaves organizational justice, which may be the most impactful factor for organizations to interrupt the feedback loop and prevent spillover effects from one form of cyber-deviance to others. If policies focus too much on punishment, they will fail from an operant conditioning perspective and may fail from an organizational justice perspective. We suggest it is the level of fairness and quality of interpersonal skills that may have the largest potential for positive change. Future research needs to examine this possibility further given its relation to all four types of cyber-deviance.

It was surprising for us to not find any mention of organizational culture, per se, within the cyber-deviance literature. Workplace deviance needs to be understood within the context of the organizational norms and culture for it to be labelled "deviant." Yet, for the most part, the cyber-deviant behaviors were deterministically labelled as deviant as most were deviant from a societal or legal perspective (e.g., cyber-bullying, theft of data). The lack of understanding of how organizational culture (and counter-cultures) inhibit (or promote) these types of cyber-deviant behaviors is important to examine. As noted earlier, the diminishing of social ties (Byron, 2008) may imply that organizations high in individualism (e.g., Hofstede, 1991) may be more prone to various types of cyber-deviance (e.g., political, production) than collectivist organization cultures. Organizations high on sociability and solidarity (Goffee & Jones, 1996) may be more immune to some of these deviant behaviors as they enhance social connections. Organizational cultures are critical in the socialization process, thus contribute directly to the feedback loop via social learning theory. This is an important avenue for future research.

In terms of outcomes, the focus has been primarily on organizational outcomes, and for personal cyber-aggression, the target. This makes sense as these are critical to understand in terms of highlighting the importance of these behaviors and identifying their impact on the injured parties. However, there is very little research on the effects of these behaviors for the perpetrator. There is some discussion in property and production cyber-deviance; however, for the most part it is assumed or ignored. Yet, as shown in the discussion of possible feedback loops, it is evident there is some form of reinforcement occurring if these behaviors persist. This is a significant gap in the literature and future research must examine this further to provide practitioners effective points of leverage to extinguish these harmful behaviors. There is also very little research on the effect of cyber-deviance on witnesses. Again, this is critical to understand due to feedback loops: social cognitive theory highlights the effects of observing others; and escalation effects (where witnesses experience stress and strain, which may lead to them enacting cyber-deviance).

We also wish to highlight that the above summary identifies some benefits for individuals and organizations from some forms of cyber-deviance. In particular, when employees use company technology for non-productive activities, such as web-surfing, there may be benefits for the individual (reduced stress, learning), the organization (more knowledge, increased opportunities, happier workers), and other coworkers if our proposed spillover effects occur (reduced political cyber-deviance, personal cyber-aggression). Future research needs to examine this further so organizations do not reject the essential (beneficial cyber-deviance) along with the inessential (counter-productive cyber-deviance).

Finally, some of the papers cited in this paper suggest that deviant behaviors are inevitable. For example, people have a natural social inclination to cyber-gossip (Oluwole, 2009), people feel inclined to flame to assert their power (Alonzo & Aiken, 2004), and organizational data will inevitably get leaked whether it is by an outsider or insider (Scheier, 2001). Most recommendations are to put policies in place to deal with the aftermath, since prevention is almost impossible. Prevention is especially difficult when people take work computers home and they have sensitive data or access to work emails to commit cyber-deviant behaviors (Cole, 2002), or when people bring into work their personal electronic devices that provide an avenue to commit cyber-deviant behaviors. Civiello (1999) provides the following recommendations to practitioners to mitigate the risk of insider threats: (1) due diligence in hiring, applicants can be asked to provide examples of their behavior in cyberspace to see if they act appropriately; (2) a threat-reporting mechanism, a system for reporting others' threat behaviors; (3) threat assessment, prevention, and intervention mechanisms, need to balance threats of possible leaks with how useful it is to share the information with the potential recipient; (4) threat consideration when firing, treating employees with respect and kindness during termination will reduce the cyber threat they pose as former insiders who may still have some sort of access to company information, or may be able to grab company information as they exit the workplace. These recommendations are aligned with the general deterrence theory and organizational justice (escalation effects) feedback loops. However, these policies may fall short without also satisfying operant conditioning principles of positive reinforcement of desired behaviors and due consideration of the interpersonal (dyadic) nuances for organizational justice principles.

20.7 Conclusion

In conclusion, cyber-deviance has been discussed and researched since the late 1990s, evolving from general discussion or anecdotal highlights in media to more empirical and theoretical research. There are some empirical and theoretical ties to traditional forms of workplace deviance; however, there needs to be more connection of the two forms (traditional and cyber), and more theoretical examination of the technological factors. We also call for more synergies and discourse among the different types as it appears the cyber context blends these boundaries, potentially making the traditionally "minor" deviant behaviors more serious. Given the continuing trend toward distributed and mobile work, and the evidence that traditional workplace deviance may co-occur with cyber-deviance, organizations and researchers need to take on this topic to stay relevant to organizational needs and individuals' experiences. We also note there are some individual and organizational benefits to some forms of cyber-deviance, which should be considered in any actions to reduce cyber-deviance in general. Finally, we have highlighted some significant gaps in the research that need addressing if the field is to understand and help practitioners mitigate these behaviors effectively.

References

Aghaz, A. & Sheikh, A. (2016). Cyberloafing and job burnout: An investigation in the knowledge intensive sector. *Computers in Human Behavior*, *62*, 51–60.

Aime, M. D., Calandriello, G., & Lioy, A. (2007). Dependability in wireless networks: Can we rely on WiFi?. *IEEE Security & Privacy*, *5*(1).

Ajzen, I. (1991). The theory of planned behavior. *Organizational behavior and human decision processes*, *50*(2), 179–211.

Ak, S., Ozdemir, Y., & Kuzucu, Y. (2015). Cybervictimization and cyberbullying: The mediating role of anger, Don't anger me! *Computers in Human Behavior*, *49*, 437–443.

Akbulut, Y., Donmez, O., & Durson, O. (2017). Cyberloafing and social desirability bias among students and employees. *Computers in Human Behavior*, *72*, 87–95.

Aldhizer III, G. R. (2008). The insider threat: automated identity and access controls can help organizations mitigate risks to important data. *Internal Auditor*, *65*(2), 71–73.

Alonzo, M. & Aiken, M. (2004). Flaming in electronic communication. *Decision Support Systems*, *36*(3), 205–213.

Alshuaibi, A. S., Subrananiam, C., & Shamsudin, F. M. (2014). The mediating role of job satisfaction on the relationship between HR practices and cyberdeviance. *Journal of Marketing and Management*, *5*(1), 105–119.

Amsel, A. (1992). Frustration theory – many years later. *Psychological Bulletin*, *112*(3), 396–399.

Anandarajan, M., Devine, P., & Simmers, C.A. (2004). Chapter IV: A multidimensional scaling approach to personal Web usage in the workplace, in *Personal Web Usage in the Workplace: A Guide to Effective Human Resources Management* (pp. 61–79). Hershey, PA: Idea Group Publishing.

Andreassen, C. S., Torsheim, T., & Pallesen, S. (2014). Predictors of use of social network sites at work – a specific type of cyberloafing. *Journal of Computer-Mediated Communication, 19*, 906–921.

Askew, K., Buckner, J. E., Taing, M. U., Ilie, A., Bauer, J. A., & Coovert, M. D. (2014). Explaining cyberloafing: The role of the theory of planned behavior. *Computers in Human Behavior, 36*, 510–519.

Bandura, A. (1989). Human agency in social cognitive theory. *American Psychologist, 44* (9), 1175–1184.

Barlett, C.P., Prot, S., Anderson, C.A., & Gentile, D.A. (2017). An empirical examination of the strength differential hypothesis in cyberbullying behavior. *Psychology of Violence, 7*(1), 22–32.

Barling, J. (1996). Prediction, experience, and consequences of violence. In G. R. Vandenbos, & E. Q. Bulatao (Eds.), *Violence on the job: Identifying risks and developing solutions.* Washington, DC: American Psychological Association.

Barlow, J., Bean, L., & Hott, D.D. (2003). Employee "spy" software: Should you use it? *Journal of Corporate Accounting & Finance, 14*(4), 7–12.

Barnes, S. & Biros, D. (2007). An exploratory analysis of computer mediated communications on cyberstalking severity. *The Journal of Digital Forensics, Security and Law, 2*(3), 7–27.

Baturay, M. H. & Toker, C. (2015). An investigation of the impact of demographics on cyberloafing from an educational setting angle. *Computers in Human Behavior, 50*, 358–366.

Belanger, F. & Van Slyke, C. (2002). Abuse or learning? *Communications of the ACM, 45* (1), 64–65.

Benbasat, I. & Zmud, R.W. (2003). The identity crisis within the IS discipline: Defining and communicating the discipline's core properties. *MIS Quarterly, 27*(2), 183–194.

Biber, J.K., Doverspike, D., Baznik, D., Cober, A., & Ritter, B.A. (2002). Sexual harassment in online communications: effects of gender and discourse medium. *Cyberpsychology & Behavior: The Impact of the Internet, Multimedia and Virtual Reality on Behavior and Society, 5*(1), 33–42.

Bissett, A. & Shipton, G. (2000). Some human dimensions of computer virus creation and infection. *International Journal of Human-Computer Studies, 52*(5), 899–913.

Blanchard, A. L. & Henle, C. A. (2008). Correlates of different forms of cyberloafing: The role of norms and external locus of control. *Computers in Human Behavior, 24*(3), 1067–1084.

Blau, G., Yang, Y., & Ward-Cook, K. (2006). Testing a measure of cyberloafing. *Journal of Allied Health, 35*(1), 9−17.

Burn-Thornton, K. & Burman, T. (2012). The use of data mining to indicate virtual (email) bullying. 2012 Third Global Congress on Intelligent Systems, November 2012, 253–256.

Bushman, B. J., Bonacci, A. M., Pedersen, W. C., Vasquez, E. A., & Miller, N. (2005). Chewing on it can chew you up: Effects of rumination on triggered displaced aggression. *Journal of Personality and Social Psychology, 88*, 969–983.

Byron, K. (2008). Carrying too heavy a load? The communication and miscommunication of emotion by email. *Academy of Management Review, 33*(2), 309–327.

Caplan, S. E. (2007). Relations among loneliness, social anxiety, and problematic internet use. *CyberPsychology & Behavior, 10*(2), 234–242.

Carlson, J. R. & Zmud, R. W. (1999), Channel expansion theory and the experiential nature of media richness perceptions, *Academy of Management Journal*, *42*, 153–170.

Case, C. & Young, K. (2001). A preliminary investigation of employee internet misuse, *Issues in Information Systems*, *1*, 43–49.

Chalykoff, J. & Kochan, T. A. (1989). Computer-aided monitoring: Its influence on employee job satisfaction and turnover. Personnel Psychology, *42*, 807–834.

Chambers, R. A. & Potenza, M. N. (2003). Neurodevelopment, impulsivity, and adolescent gambling. *Journal of Gambling Studies*, *19*(1), 53–84.

Chen, D. J. Q. & Lim, V. K. G. (August, 2011). Impact of cyberloafing on psychological engagement. Paper presented at the Annual Meeting of Academy of Management, San Antoni, TX.

Christian, M. S. & Ellis, A. P. (2011). Examining the effects of sleep deprivation on workplace deviance: A self-regulatory perspective. *Academy of Management Journal*, *54*(5), 913–934.

Churchman, P. (2003). Technology abusing the Net – How to curb work surfers with surfing there's always the risk of getting dumped – a lesson worth heeding as the incidence of workplace internet abuse increases and both companies and employees pay the cost. New Zealand Management, 46–7. Retrieved June 3, 2017 from https://management.co.nz/article/technology-abusing-net-how-curb-work-surfers.

Civiello, C. L. (1999). Cyberspace, trusted insiders, and organizational threat. *The Psychologist-Manager Journal*, *3*(2), 149–166.

Cole, T. J. (2002). PC use at home and for union organizing: New challenges in the wired workplace. *Employment Relations Today*, *29*(1), 73–78.

Connelly, C. E., Zweig, D., Webster, J., & Trougakos, J. P. (2012). Knowledge hiding in organizations. *Journal of Organizational Behavior*, *33*(1), 64–88.

Coyne, I., Farley, S., Axtell, C., Sprigg, C., Best, L., & Kwok, O. (2017). Understanding the relationship between experiencing workplace cyberbullying, employee mental strain and job satisfaction: A disempowerment approach. *The International Journal of Human Resource Management*, *28*(7), 945–972.

Daft, R. L., Lengel, R. H., & Trevino, L. K. (1987). Message equivocality, media selection, and manager performance: Implications for information systems. *MIS Quarterly*, *11*(3), 355–366.

Darby, M. R. & Karni, E. (1973). Free competition and the optimal amount of fraud. *The Journal of Law and Economics*, *16*(1), 67–88.

Davis, H. E. & Braun, R. L. (2004). Computer fraud: Analyzing perpetrators and methods. *The CPA Journal*, *74*(7), 56–59.

D'Cruz, P. & Noronha, E. (2013). Navigating the extended reach: Target experiences of cyberbullying at work. *Information and Organization*, *23*(4), 324–343.

de Lara, P. Z. M. (2007). Relationship between organizational justice and cyber-loafing in the workplace: Has "anomia" a say in the matter? *CyberPsychology & Behavior*, *10*(3), 464–470.

de Lara, P. Z. M., Tacoronte, D. V., & Ding, J-M. T. (2006). Do current anti-cyberloafing disciplinary practices have a replica in research findings?: A study of the effects of coercive strategies on workplace Internet misuse. *Internet Research*, *16*(4), 450–467.

DeSanctis, G. & Poole, M.S. (1994). Capturing the complexity in advanced technology use: Adaptive structuration theory. *Organization Science*, *5*(2), 121–147.

Dollard, J., Miller, N. E., Doob, L. W., Mowrer, O. H., & Sear, R. R. (1939). *Frustration and aggression*. New Haven, CT: Yale University Press.

Dooley, J., Pyzalski, J., & Cross, D. (2009). Cyberbullying versus face-to-face bullying: A theoretical and conceptual review. *Zeitschrift fur Psychologie – Journal of Psychology, 217*(4), 182–188.

Douglas, D. M. (2016). Doxing: a conceptual analysis. *Ethics and Information Technology, 18*(3), 199–210.

Farley, S., Coyne, I.J., Sprigg, C.A., Axtell, C., & Subramanian, G. (2015). Exploring the Impact of Workplace Cyberbullying on Trainee Doctors. https://dspace.lboro.ac.uk/2134/20812.

Faucher, C., Jackson, M., & Cassidy, W. (2015). Governing cyberbullying at the university level. *The Canadian Journal of Higher Education, 45*(1), 102–121.

Fleury, D. (2016). Precarious employment in Canada: An overview of the situation. HillNotes Research and Analysis from Canada's Library of Parliament, January 26, 2017. Retrieved December 18, 2017, from https://hillnotes.ca/2016/01/27/precarious-employment-in-canada-an-overview-of-the-situation/.

Fishbein, M. & Ajzen, I. (1975). *Belief, attitude, intention, and behavior: An introduction to theory and research*. Reading, MA: Addison-Wesley.

Fontein, D. (2017). How to write a social media policy for your company. Hootsuite, February 23, 2017. Retrieved May 23, 2017 from https://blog.hootsuite.com/social-media-policy-for-employees/.

Ford, D. P. (2003). TAM Research: A Theoretical Critique & Call for Debate. Presentation at Administrative Sciences Association of Canada 2003 Conference, Halifax, NS, June 2003.

Ford, D. P. (2013). Virtual harassment: Media characteristics' role in psychological health. *Journal of Managerial Psychology, 28*(4), 408–428.

Ford, D. P. (2015). The relevance of media characteristics for targets' experience of workplace aggression. Platform paper presented at Work, Stress and Health Conference, May 6–9,2015, Atlanta, GA.

Ford, D. P. & Clarke, H. M. (2017). Testing the impact of media characteristics for virtual workplace aggression: Four experiments. Poster presentation at Canadian Psychological Association Conference, Toronto, ON, June 8–10, 2017.

Francis, L., Holmvall, C. M., & O'Brien, L. E. (2015). The influence of workload and civility of treatment on the perpetration of email incivility. *Computers in Human Behavior, 46*, 191–201.

Gardner, D., O'Driscoll, M., Cooper-Thomas, H. D., Roche, M., Bentley, T., Catley, B., Teo, S. T. T., & Trenberth, L. (2016). Predictors of workplace bullying and cyber-bullying in New Zealand. *International Journal of Environmental Research & Public Health, 13*(5), 1–14.

Garrett, R. K. & Danziger, J. N. (2008). On cyberslacking: Workplace status and personal internet use at work. *CyberPsychology & Behavior, 11*(3), 287–292.

Giménez Gualdo, A. M., Hunter, S. C., Durkin, K., Arnaiz, P., & Maquilón, J. J. (2015). The emotional impact of cyberbullying: Differences in perceptions and experiences as a function of role. *Computers & Education, 82*, 228–235.

Giumetti, G. W., McKibben, E. S., Hatfield, A. L., Schroeder, A. N., & Kowalski, R. M. (2012). Cyber incivility @ work: The new age of interpersonal deviance. *Cyberpsychology Behavior and Social Networking, 15*(3), 148–154.

Glassman, J., Prosch, M., & Shao, B. B. M. (2015). To monitor or not to monitor: Effectiveness of a cyberloafing countermeasure. *Information & Management*, *52*(2), 170–182.

Goffee, R. & Jones, G. (1996). What holds the modern company together? *Harvard Business Review*, *74*(6), 133–148.

Greengard, S. (2000). The high cost of cyberslacking. *Workforce*, *79*(12), 22–24.

Harris, L. (2008). Staffer fired after bad-mouthing colleagues, management in blog. *Canadian HR Reporter* (September 8, 2008), *18*. Retrieved September 29, 2018, from www.hrreporter.com/article/6313-staffer-fired-after-bad-mouthing-collea gues-manage/.

Hegarty, W. H. & Sims, H. P. (1978). Some determinants of unethical decision behavior: An experiment. *Journal of Applied Psychology*, *63*(4), 451–457.

Hemsley, J. & Mason, R. M. (2013). Knowledge and knowledge management in the social media age. *Journal of Organizational Computing and Electronic Commerce*, *23*(1–2), 138–167.

Henle, C. A. & Blanchard, A. L. (2008). The interaction of work stressors and organizational sanctions on cyberloafing. *Journal of Managerial Issues*, *20*, 383–400.

Henle, C. A. & Kedharnath, U. (2012). Cyberloafing in the Workplace 560. In Z. Yan (Eds.), *Encyclopedia of Cyber Behavior*. USA: IGI Global.

Hershcovis, M. S. (2011). Incivility, social undermining, bullying . . . Oh My! A call to reconcile constructs within workplace aggression research. *Journal of Organizational Behavior*, *32*, 499–519.

Higgins, G. E. & Wolfe, S. E. (2008). Digital piracy: An examination of three measurements of self-control. *Deviant Behavior*, *29*, 440–460.

Hobfoll, S. E. (1998). *Stress, culture, and community*. New York, NY, Plenum Press.

Hofstede, G. (1991). *Cultures and organizations: Software of the mind*. New York, NY: McGraw-Hill.

Jin, A. T. B., Ling, D. N. C., & Goh, A. (2004). Biohashing: Two factor authentication featuring fingerprint data and tokenised random number. *Pattern Recognition*, *37*(11), 2245–2255.

Johnson, M. (2011). Workforce deviance and the business case for employee engagement. *The Journal for Quality and Participation*, *34*(2), 11.

Johnson, P. R. & Indvik, J. (2003). The organizational benefits of reducing cyberslacking in the workplace. *Allied Academies International Conference Proceedings; Arden, 8*(2), 53–59.

Kaplan, H. B. (1975). *Self-attitudes and deviant behavior*. Pacific Palisades, CA: Coodyear.

Kiesler, S. (1986). The hidden messages in computer networks. *Harvard Business Review*, *64*(1), 46–48.

Klotz, A. C. & Buckley, M. R. (2013). A historical perspective of counterproductive work behavior targeting the organization. *Journal of Management History*, *19*(1), 114–132.

Koay, K. Y., Soh, P. C. H., & Chew, K. W. (2017). Antecedents and consequences of cyberloafing: Evidence from the Malaysian ICT Industry. First Monday, *22*(3). Retrieved June 16, 2017, from http://firstmonday.org/ojs/index.php/fm/article/view/7302/5968.

Krishnan, S. (2016). Electronic warfare: A personality model of cyber incivility. *Computers in Human Behavior*, *64*, 537–546.

Kruglanski, A. W. (2001). "That vision thing": The state of theory in social and personality psychology at the end of the new millennium. *Journal of Personality and Social Psychology, 80*(6), 871–875.

Larson, S. (June 19, 2017). Data of almost 200 million voters leaked online by GOP analytics firm. Retrieved from http://money.cnn.com/2017/06/19/technology/voter-data-leaked-online-gop/index.html.

Lawrence, T. B. & Robinson, S. L. (2007). Ain't misbehavin: Workplace deviance as organizational resistance. *Journal of Management, 33*(3), 378–394.

Lee, E. B. (2017). Cyberbullying. *Journal of Black Studies, 48*(1), 57–73.

Lee., R. T. & Brotheridge, C. M. (2006). When prey turns predatory: Workplace bullying as a predictor of counteraggression/bullying, coping, and well-being. *European Journal of Work and Organizational Psychology, 15*(3), 352–377.

Leventhal, G. S. (1980). What should be done with equity theory? In K. J. Gergen, M. S. Greenberg, & R. H. Willis (Eds.) *Social Exchange* (pp. 27–55). Boston. MA: Springer.

Liberman, B., Seidman, G., McKenna, K. Y. A., & Buffardi, L. E. (2011). Employee job attitudes and organizational characteristics as predictors of cyberloafing. *Computers in Human Behavior, 27*, 2192–2199.

Lim, V. K. G. (2002). The IT way of loafing on the job: Cyberloafing, neutralizing and organizational justice. *Journal of Organizational Behavior, 23*(4), 675–694.

Lim, V. K. G. & Chen, D. J. (2012). Cyberloafing at the workplace: Gain or drain on work? *Behavior and Information Technology, 31*, 343–353.

Lim, V. K.G. & Teo, T.S.H. (2009). Mind your E-manners: Impact of cyber incivility on employees' work attitude and behavior. *Information & Management, 46*(8), 419–425.

Maas, A., Cadinu, M., Guarnieri, G., &, Grasselli, A. (2003). Sexual harassment under social identity threat: The computer harassment paradigm. *Journal of Personality and Social Psychology, 85*(5), 853–870.

Machackova, H. & Pfetsch, J. (2016). Bystanders' responses to offline bullying and cyber-bullying: The role of empathy and normative beliefs about aggression. *Scandinavian Journal of Psychology, 57*(2), 169–176.

MacKinnon, C. A. (1979). Sexual *harassment* of *working women:* A *case* of *sex discrimination* (No. 19). New Haven, CT: Yale University Press.

Mahatanankoon, P., Anandarajan, M., & Igbaria, M. (2004). Development of a measure of personal Web usage in the workplace. *CyberPsychology & Behavior, 7*(1), 93–104.

Malhotra, Y. & Galletta, D. (2005) A multidimensional commitment model of volitional systems adoption and usage behavior. *Journal of Management Information. Systems, 22*(1), 117–151.

Mastrangelo, P. M., Everton, W. J., & Jolton, J. A. (2003). Deviant computer use at work: from bad to worse. Systems, Man and Cybernetics, IEEE International Conference, Washington, DC, USA.

Mastrangelo, P. M., Everton, W., & Jolton, J.A. (2006). Personal use of work computers: Distraction versus destruction. *CyberPsychology & Behavior, 9*(6), 730–741.

McGuire, W. J. (1974). Psychological motives and communication gratification. In J. G. Blumler & E. Katz (Eds.), The uses of mass communications: Current perspectives on gratifications research (pp. 167–196). Beverly Hills, CA: Sage.

Michailova, S. & Husted, K. (2003). Knowledge-sharing hostility in Russian firms. *California Management Review, 45*(3), 59–77.

Mills, J. E., Hu, B., Beldona, S., & Clay, J. (2001). Cyberslacking! A liability issue for wired workplaces. *Cornell Hotel and Restaurant Administration Quarterly, 2*(5), 34–47.

Mirchandani, D. & Motwani, J. (2003). Reducing internet abuse in the workplace. *SAM Advanced Management Journal, 68*(1), 22–28.

Moody, G. D. & Siponen, M. (2013). Using the theory of interpersonal behavior to explain non-work related personal use of the Internet at work. *Information & Management, 50*, 322–335.

New York Times. (2008). NC school employee fired over Facebook posting. New York Times Company. Retrieved April 27, 2017, from https://search.proquest.com/doc view/370252926?accountid=12378.

Nocentini, A., Calmaestra, J., Schultze-Krumbholz, A., Scheithauer, H., Ortega, R., & Menesini, E. (2010). Cyberbullying: Labels, behaviours and definition in three European countries, *Australian Journal of Guidance and Counselling, 20*(2), 129–142.

Oluwole, D. A. (2009). Spirituality, gender and age factors in cybergossip among Nigerian adolescents. *Cyberpsychology & Behavior, 12*(3), 323–326.

O'Neill, T. A., Hambley, L. A., & Bercovich, A. (2014). Prediction of cyberslacking when employees are working away from the office. *Computers in Human Behavior, 34*, 291–298.

Ophoff, J., Machaka, T., & Stander, A. (2015). Exploring the impact of cyber incivility in the workplace. In Proceedings of Information Science & IT Education Conference (InSITE) (pp. 443–504).

Oreskovik, A. (2017). A senior engineer at Google wrote a controversial diversity manifesto and employees are furious. Business Insider, August 5. Retrieved December 4, 2017, from www.businessinsider.com/google-engineer-anti-diversity-manifesto-causes-uproar-2017-8.

O'Sullivan, D. (2017). The RNC files: Inside the largest US voter data leak. UpGuard, July 19. Retrieved June 20, 2017, from www.upguard.com/breaches/the-rnc-files.

Park, Y., Fritz, C., & Jex, S. M. (2015). Daily cyber incivility and distress the moderating roles of resources at work and home. *Journal of Management, 44*(7), 2535–2557, 0149206315576796.

Pee, L. G., Woon, I. M. Y., & Kankanhalli, A. (2008). Explaining non-work-related computing in the workplace: A comparison of alternative models. *Information & Management, 45*(2), 120–130.

Peluchette, J. V., Karl., K., Wood, C., & Williams, J. (2015). Cyberbullying victimization: Do victims' personality and risky social network behaviors contribute to the problem? *Computers in Human Behavior, 52*, 424–435.

Pfeffer, J. (1992). *Managing with Power: Politics and Influence in Organizations.* Boston, MA: Harvard Business Press.

Pittaro, M. L. (2007). Cyber stalking: An analysis of online harassment and intimidation. *International Journal of Cyber Criminology, 1*(2), 180–197.

Porter, M. E. (1985). *Competitive Advantage.* New York, NY: Free Press.

Privitera, C. & Campbell, M. A. (2009). Cyberbullying: The new face of workplace bullying? *Cyberpsychology & Behavior: The Impact of the Internet, Multimedia and Virtual Reality on Behavior and Society, 12*(4), 395–400.

Raskin, R., Novacek, J., & Hogan, R. (1991). Narcissistic self-esteem management. *Journal of Personality and Social Psychology*, *60*(6), 911.

Reio Jr., T. G. (2011). Supervisor and coworker incivility: Testing the work frustration-aggression model. *Advances in Developing Human Resources*, *13*(1), 54–68.

Restubog, S. L. D., Garcia, P. R. J. M., Toledano, L. S., Amarnani, R. K., Tolentino, L. R., & Tang, R. L. (2011). Yielding to (cyber)-temptation: Exploring the buffering role of self-control in the relationship between organizational justice and cyber-loafing behavior in the workplace. *Journal of Research in Personality*, *45*, 247–251.

Roberts, J. A. & David, M. E. (2017). Put down your phone and listen to me: How boss phubbing undermines the psychological conditions necessary for employee engagement. *Computers in Human Behavior*, *75*, 206–217.

Roberts, J. A. & Wasieleski, D. M. (2012). Moral reasoning in computer-based task environments: Exploring the interplay between cognitive and technological factors on individuals' propensity to break rules. *Journal of Business Ethics*, *110*, 355–376.

Robinson, S. L. & Bennett, R. J. (1995). A typology of deviant workplace behaviors: A multidimensional scaling study. *Academy of Management Journal*, *38*(2), 555–572.

Rogers, M., Smoak, N. D., & Liu, J. (2006). Self-reported deviant computer behavior: A Big-5, moral choice, and manipulative exploitive behavior analysis. *Deviant Behavior*, *27*(3), 245–268.

Rosse, J. G. & Hulin, C. L. (1985). Adaptation to work: An analysis of employee health, withdrawal, and change. *Organizational Behavior and Human Decision Processes*, *36*(3), 324–347.

Salin, D. (2003a). Bullying and organisational politics in competitive and rapidly changing work environments. *International Journal of Management and Decision Making*, *4*(1), 35–46.

Salin, D. (2003b). Ways of explaining workplace bullying: A review of enabling, motivating and precipitating structures and processes in the work environment. *Human Relations*, *56*(10), 1213–1232.

Scheier, R. (2001). Watching the watcher. *Computer World*, *35*(34), 36–37.

Shamsudin, F. M., Subramaniam, C., & Alshuaibi, A. S. (2012). The effect of HR practices, leadership style on cyberdeviance: The mediating role of organizational commitment. *Journal of Marketing and Management*, *3*(1), 22–48.

Sharma, S. K. & Gupta, J. N. D. (2003). Improving workers' productivity and reducing Internet abuse. *Journal of Computer Information Systems*, *44*(2), 74–78.

Sheikh, A., Atashgah, M. S., & Adibzadegan, M. (2015). The antecedents of cyber-loafing: A case study in an Iranian copper industry. *Computers in Human Behavior*, *51*, 172–179.

Shelton, A. K. & Skalski, P. (2014). Blinded by the light: Illuminating the dark side of social network use through content analysis. *Computers in Human Behavior*, *33*, 339–348.

Sipior, J. C. & Ward, B. T. (2002). A strategic response to the broad spectrum of Internet abuse. *Information Systems Management*, *19*(4), 71–79.

Skarlicki, D. P., van Jaarsveld, D. D., & Walker, D. D. (2008). Getting even for customer mistreatment: The role of moral identity in the relationship between customer interpersonal injustice and employee sabotage. *Journal of Applied Psychology*, *93* (6), 1335–1347.

Skinner, B. F. (1953). *Science and Human Behavior*. New York, NY: MacMillan

Spector, P. E. & Fox, S. (2010). Counterproductive work behavior and organizational citizenship behavior: Are they opposite forms of active behavior? *Applied Psychology: An International Review*, *59*(1), 21–39.

Stewart, F. (2000). Internet acceptable use policies: navigating the management, legal, and technical issues. *Information Systems Security*, *9*, 46–53.

Sticca, F. & Perren, S. (2013). Is cyberbullying worse than traditional bullying? Examining the differential roles of medium, publicity, and anonymity for the perceived severity of bullying. *Journal of Youth and Adolescence*, *42*(5), 739–750.

Sturgeon, A. (1996). Telework: Threats, risks and solutions. *Information Management & Computer Security*, *4*(2), 27–38.

Tajfel, H. (1982). Social psychology of intergroup relations. *Annual Review of Psychology*, *33*(1), 1–39.

Thornton, D., Gunningham, N. A., & Kagan, R. A. (2005). General deterrence and corporate environmental behavior. *Law & Policy*, *27*(2), 262–288.

Urbaczewski, A. & Jessup, L.M. (2002). Does electronic monitoring of employee Internet usage work? *Communications of the ACM*, *45*(1), 80–83.

Urgin, J. C. & Pearson, J. M. (2013). The effects of sanctions and stigmas on cyberloafing. *Computers in Human Behavior*, *29*, 812–820.

Väyrynen, K., Hekkala, R., & Liias, T. (2013). Knowledge protection challenges of social media encountered by organizations. *Journal of Organizational Computing and Electronic Commerce*, *23*(1–2), 34–55.

Vigoda-Gadot, E. & Drory, A. (Eds.). (2006). *Handbook of Organizational Politics*. Cheltenham, UK: Edward Elgar Publishing.

Vitak, J., Crouse, J., & LaRose, R. (2011). Personal Internet use at work: Understanding cyberslacking. *2009 Fifth International Conference on Intelligent Computing*, *27* (5), 1751–1759.

Wagner, D. T., Barnes, C. M., Lim, V. K. G., & Ferris, D. L. (2012). Lost sleep and cyberloafing: Evidence from the laboratory and a daylight saving time quasi-experiment. *Journal of Applied Psychology*, *97*(5), 1068–1076.

Weatherbee, T. G. (2007). Cyberaggression in the workplace: Construct development, operationalization, and measurement, Sobey's School of Business, Saint Mary's University, Halifax, NS.

Weatherbee, T. G. (2010). Counterproductive use of technology at work: Information & communication technologies and cyberdeviancy. *Human Resource Management Review*, *20*(1), 35–44.

Weatherbee, T. G. & Kelloway, E. K. (2006). A case of cyberdeviancy: Cyberaggression in the workplace. In E. K. Kelloway, J. Barling, & J. J. Hurrell (Eds.), *Handbook of workplace violence* (pp. 445–487). Thousand Oaks, CA: Sage Publications.

Wilkowski, B. M. & Robinson, M. D. (2008). The cognitive basis of trait anger and reactive aggression: An integrative analysis. *Personality and Social Psychology Review*, *12*(1), 3–21.

Wolfgang, M. F. (1957). Victim precipitated criminal homicide, *Journal of Criminal Law and Criminology*, *48*(1), 1–11.

Workman, M. (2010). A behaviorist perspective on corporate harassment online: Validation of a theoretical model of psychological motives. *Computers & Security*, *29*(8), 831–839.

Workman, M. (2012). Rash impulsivity, vengefulness, virtual-self and amplification of ethical relativism on cyber-smearing against corporations. *Computers in Human Behavior*, *28*(1), 217–225.

Zapf, D. & Gross, C. (2001). Conflict escalation and coping with workplace bullying: A replication and extension. *European Journal of Work and Organizational Psychology*, *10*(4), 497–522.

21 Information Communication Technology and Employee Well-Being

Understanding the "iParadox Triad" at Work

Arla Day, Larissa K. Barber, and Jillian Tonet

Information and communication technologies (ICTs) have become a ubiquitous and integral aspect in our social lives and our work world. Smartphones, laptops, and other devices keep us easily connected to people and tasks across both work and home domains. Although heralded as time- and cost-saving initiatives that boost employee flexibility, unintended negative consequences of ICTs have led to a backlash felt in some quarters of the working world. However, these criticisms have not been explored in detail, and critical questions remain as to the seemingly paradoxical impact of ICT on worker health and functioning. In this chapter, we explore what we know about ICT paradoxes – what we refer to as the iParadox Triad related to autonomy, social connectivity, and productivity issues. We then explore whether the stress and well-being effects of the iParadox Triad can be understood through traditional occupational health psychology models. Finally, we develop a theoretical model that incorporates social psychology theory on the self and motivation to help guide future research in this area that can help address autonomy, connectivity, and productivity issues.

21.1 The iParadox Triad: Autonomy, Social Connectivity, and Productivity

ICT is defined as any technology or electronic device (such as computers and phones) that is able to gather, store, and/or send information (Steinmueller, 2000). Perhaps one of the most widely adopted ICTs in modern times is the smartphone. In just a decade after Apple's release of the first iPhone in 2007, the vast majority of adults in Western countries own some type of smartphone (e.g., 66 percent in Germany, 72 percent in Canada and the UK, 77 percent in the U.S., 79 percent in Spain and the Netherlands, and 80 percent in Sweden; Pew Research Centre, 2017).

The "i" in iPhone referred primarily to internet connection, but its meaning was also associated with the technology's capability to instruct, inform, and inspire individuals (Griffin, 2016), which is a defining feature of all smartphones. Indeed, ICTs are used to access and share information via web searches, emails, texts, and social media outlets. Such benefits serve as a key inspirational worker resource, with resource perceptions increasing work engagement and job performance (Day, Scott, & Kelloway, 2010). Yet, "i" also can stand for intrusive. ICT contributes to a unique set of demands in the workplace that require our attention and/or response, taking the form of social demands (e.g., availability, response expectations, miscommunications), cognitive demands (e.g., access to information, amount of control, learning expectations), and hassles (e.g., technological malfunctions, software incompatibility, security; Day et al., 2012). Demands arising from ICT also tend to be distinct from other work demands and stressors. For example, Day et al. (2012) found that ICT stressors tend to be related to worker stress and strain, even after controlling for the impact of other work demands, such as lack of job control, role overload, job boredom, and role ambiguity. Similarly, Barber and Santuzzi (2014) found that telepressure – a preoccupation with messages and an urge to quickly respond to them – predicted burnout, absenteeism, and poor sleep quality after controlling for work-related demands.

Throughout the literature, the potential paradox of ICT and worker well-being and functioning has been repeatedly noted. That is, ICT can have both positive and negative effects on workers (Day et al., 2010, Day et al., 2012; O'Driscoll et al., 2010; Ter Hoeven, van Zoonen, & Fonner, 2016) and organizations (Day et al., 2010; Mamaghani, 2006; O'Driscoll et al., 2010; Rennecker & Godwin, 2005). There are three interrelated ICT paradoxes, which we also refer to as the iParadox Triad (using "i" as a stand-in for internet). Each paradox can be described in terms of their unique features: autonomy and work task access; social interaction with work colleagues; and work task completion and productivity.

First, the *autonomy paradox* describes simultaneous increases and decreases in perceptions of control over how work tasks are accessed (Mazmanian, Orlikowski, & Yates, 2013). On the positive side, ICTs can provide flexibility for employees to do work from home or from other convenient locations and times. Workers greatly benefit from increased access to information without the traditional physical or temporal constraints of a one-size-fits-all workplace, which helps task completion and problem solving (Morgan, Morgan, & Hall, 2000). Similarly, ICT allows workers the flexibility to deal with home tasks while at work and to remain reachable for personal communications or emergencies during work hours, which can be helpful for individuals balancing multiple roles. These control-oriented benefits to accessibility may increase work engagement (Ter Hoeven et al., 2016) and job satisfaction (Diaz et al., 2011). However, they also may contribute to a perceived lack of control in the form of continuous interruptions inhibiting workflow or create the ironic effect of people feeling continuously tethered to their work in a way that makes it difficult to "switch off" for down time. The same autonomy-boosting accessibility characteristics also can break down desired boundaries between work and non-work, making workers feel captive to real-time notifications of new work tasks instead of enjoying leisure time or engaging in other non-work activities (i.e., taking care of household duties and family members, civic or spiritual involvement in our communities, and other personal pursuits). For example, work emails and information are easily accessible when workers desire to connect, but sometimes workers also receive instantaneous notifications of new work arriving in their inboxes or through file-sharing applications when they do not want to be working.

The *social connectivity paradox* refers to the socially oriented issues related to ICTs ranging from an isolation-to-intrusion continuum (Leonardi, Treem, & Jackson, 2010). On the positive side, ICTs can be used to reduce social isolation from coworkers when working remotely (i.e., email, text messages) and improve communication (Dewett & Jones, 2001). ICT also can be beneficial in helping to maintain positive relationships in workgroups, especially to foster the trust and cooperation necessary for virtual team work (Moser & Axtell, 2013) and to provide social interaction to stay connected to the workplace (to be aware of organizational events, staying competitive for promotion opportunities, etc.; Cooper & Kurland, 2002).

However, the same ICT tools used to reduce social isolation for people across different geographical locations also may cause social problems through issues such as technological interruptions (e.g., Rennecker & Godwin, 2005) and mis-interpretation of email tone (Day et al., 2012). Moreover, ICT can create feelings of intrusion, such that workers may feel overwhelmed by work interruptions from colleagues (e.g., chat notifications, email requests), which can easily negate benefits of working remotely to focus on work tasks uninterrupted (Leonardi et al., 2010). These negative outcomes can lead to increased burnout through increased interruptions and unpredictability (Ter Hoeven et al., 2016).

Finally, the *productivity paradox* refers to how ICTs simultaneously enhance and hinder work task completion. We borrow this term from observations in the economic literature on how macro-level investments in information technology in organizations often do not map on well with productivity gains, at least in the short-term (e.g., David, 1990; Dewan & Kraemer, 1998). In this context, we use this term to refer to individual-level concerns pertaining to task efficiencies and task hindrances. On the positive side, ICTs can boost efficiencies in how we do our work, by providing flexibility in communications (through asynchronous technologies, such as email; Barber & Santuzzi, 2015), which helps workers when collaborating with others across time zones and provides opportunities to gain information efficiently regardless of geographical locations. However, ICTs also can interfere with work completion by increasing the amount of task disruptions during the workday (O'Driscoll et al., 2010), such that workers switch tasks more frequently, which delays task completion. ICTs inflate the amount of accessible information (through emails, texts, the internet), which necessitates more time spent processing and sifting through information (Tarafdar, Tu, & Ragu-Nathan, 2010) and increases time spent on responding to communications.

Given these paradoxes, there are a few lingering questions. What are the contextual factors that influence how ICT is perceived? What factors influence whether ICT positively or negatively impacts worker functioning and well-being? We first examine this issue from the context of traditional occupational health theories related to stress and well-being. We then further expand these ideas into social psychology theory related to the self and motivation. Finally, we integrate theoretical approaches to discuss potential avenues of research for addressing the iParadox Triad to improve worker well-being and performance.

21.2 Understanding iParadoxes: Occupational Stress and Well-Being Models

An underlying theme of the iParadox Triad is the trade-offs when using ICTs. On the one hand, they can serve as a useful tool to help achieve work-related (and non-work-related) goals. On the other hand, they appear to introduce new stressors that can negatively affect well-being. In this regard, research on ICTs fits into a variety of occupational stress frameworks that dominate the organizational behavior and management literature. We discuss key aspects of popular occupational health and stress models in the context of ICT use by classifying aspects of the work environment as demands versus resources, examining the role of individual appraisals in stress responses, and understanding boundary management patterns and preferences.

Work Demands and Resources. The Job Demands-Resources (JD-R) model uses multiple theories to identify work factors that can be viewed either as demands or resources, and how these categorizations lead to differential well-being outcomes (Bakker & Demerouti, 2007; Demerouti et al., 2001). Demands are factors such as high workload and poor interpersonal relationships that are considered to require physical or psychological effort (Bakker & Demerouti, 2007; Demerouti et al., 2001). Guided by **Effort-Recovery Theory**, in which work demands, effort, and decision latitude interact to impact on physiological and psychological outcomes (Meijman & Mulder, 1998), demands are expected to deplete psychological and physical health through a *health impairment process* that ultimately results in exhaustion and work burnout if there is not a sufficient chance for recovery. In the ICT context, demands include feeling that you are on call 24/7, ineffective communications or miscommunication, and increased workload from needing to learn new technologies or processes (Day et al., 2010). It is possible that when these ICT demands are continuous, recovery does not occur; in line with Effort-Recovery Theory, "load reactions accumulate and result in longer term negative effects, such as impaired well-being and health problems" (Sonnentag, 2001, p. 196).

Alternatively, resources are factors such as support and control that are expected to foster psychological and physical health and work engagement through a *motivational process* (Bakker & Demerouti, 2007; Demerouti et al., 2001). This process is in line with **Conservation of Resources Theory (COR)**, which states that we "strive to retain, protect, and build resources" such that "the potential or actual loss of these valued resources" is threatening to us (Hobfoll, 1989, p. 516). Resources also are expected to buffer the negative impact of job demands on feelings of exhaustion. In the context of ICT use, resources can be factors such as improved access to information with technology, improved communication with colleagues in different locations, and decreased workload because of increased efficiencies (Day et al., 2010).

One limitation of JD-R theory in explaining the iParadoxes may be an assumption that the majority of individuals will evaluate certain factors as being demands or resources in a similar way. Employees are likely to have a variety of different reactions to the same ICT experiences based on individual appraisals and boundary preferences. We discuss each of these perspectives below using an example of an email request for more information on a project after usual work hours. Would this particular email request be considered an ICT demand that leads to more stress or a resource that improves well-being? It might be tempting to automatically classify this situation as a stress-inducing demand, yet there are contextual factors that alter how the email request affects a particular worker's evaluation of stress and well-being.

Individual Stress Appraisals. Lazarus and Folkman's (1984) Transactional Model of Stress is one of the seminal stress models that helps us to understand how individuals interpret the environment. Lazarus and Folkman defined demands as external events in the environment that have the potential to create negative outcomes based on (a) how individuals initially interpret events in relation to their well-being and (b) their resources to cope with demanding situations. In this vein, ICT characteristics (e.g., types of ICT use, context of ICT use) can be defined as events and features that have the *potential* to lead to negative health and well-being outcomes via individual cognitive appraisals. However, these same demands may not necessarily trigger adverse health and well-being effects – and may even produce positive outcomes.

Using the Transactional Model of Stress, ICTs would not be not seen as innately positive or negative; instead, people may view the same ICT experience as a threat to their well-being ("this is stressful to me"), a positive challenge ("this is good for me"), or irrelevant ("this is not important to me"). Each of these views represents differing *primary appraisals* that affect the person's initial evaluation of the event. Although some workers may see the email as an unwanted social intrusion on their personal time (i.e., a threat that leads to a stress response), some workers may see it as coworkers valuing their input on an important project (i.e., a positive event or challenge), and other workers may not care either way because the project is not important to them – or perhaps the timing of receiving work messages does not matter to them. Thus, the same type of evening work emails can be interpreted as stressful, challenging, or irrelevant based on individual primary appraisals.

Another key aspect of the Transactional Model of Stress is that *secondary appraisals* can alter how primary appraisals of threat affect well-being, which is based on one's personal characteristics and resources to manage the threatening situation or stressor. Stress is the result of an individualistic appraisal of an environmental event that a person sees as "taxing or exceeding his or her resources and endangering his or her well-being" (Lazarus & Folkman, 1984, p. 19). Thus, even threatening ICT events may not result in a stress response if they do not tax or exceed the worker's resources. For example, receiving that undesirable work email in the evening while taking care of family tasks may be less likely to create strain if the worker has a supportive partner to help with task or if the worker has the necessary resources (skills, knowledge) to answer the email quickly. Employees are less likely to experience anger and work-home conflict from after-hours email communications when requests take little time to read and respond to (Butts, Becker, & Boswell, 2015). However, receiving the same unwanted email when the worker is short on time or energy for dealing with the email – or if they feel that they haven't had a sufficient chance to recover from other work and email demands – would tend to exacerbate feelings of psychological strain.

The individual appraisal view also is echoed and extended in COR Theory (Hobfoll, 1989), such that stress depends on threats or potential threats to resources that people value. Resources include energies (e.g., time and energy), conditions (e. g., social status and autonomy), objects (e.g., shelter and food), and personal characteristics (e.g., self-esteem and skills/abilities). In this model, losing valued resources causes the experience of stress, which even applies to the *anticipation* of potentially losing valued resources. For example, according to COR Theory, receiving an unwanted work email during the evening could be stressful just because it merely threatens the possibility of leisure time loss, even when the worker decides not to actually invest time into responding. Some workers may take umbrage with a supervisor or coworker merely seeking to "threaten" their leisure time by requesting information during off-work hours.

Additionally, responding to the work email can be considered stressful because it represents actual leisure time loss, such as missing out on family time or a relaxing evening alone. However, receiving an off-hours email at another time may not be perceived as stressful because the specific leisure time activity is not a highly valued resource. Some people may welcome an excuse to escape an awkward holiday gathering or a quiet evening home alone. In these cases, the off-work email is not a stressful intrusion because it does not threaten a valued resource. In fact, it may be seen as a welcome activity of interest or an excuse for escaping personal life demands.

COR theory also would suggest that the perceived benefits of sacrificing a valued resource (e.g., leisure time) may be taken into consideration. For example, if the worker perceives that the small leisure time resource investment ultimately saves them more work the next day (i.e., preventing coworkers from making mistakes on the project without their input) or ultimately provides them with more resources (e. g., a promotion), then sacrificing a small amount of leisure time may not be seen as stressful, and may even be seen as a positive opportunity. However, if the worker does not perceive a net gain in resources after the leisure time investment (i.e., there is still more work to do the next day), then the evening email response may indeed be perceived as stressful. Therefore, ICT events could create stress if it reduces – or has a potential to reduce – current perceived resources or net gains in resources following resource investments such as time or effort.

Boundary Preferences. Understanding individual differences in managing work-home boundaries also may help us better understand these iParadoxes.

Boundary theory states that we have multiple roles in our life (e.g., worker, parent, friend, community member) and we use these boundaries to help organize and simplify our environment (Ashforth, Kreiner, & Fugate, 2000; Clark, 2000; Nippert-Eng, 1996). Our reactions to cross-boundary ICT issues, such as receiving an email after work, depend on the extent that we prefer to have overlapping or separate work and non-work roles. The related notions of permeability (i.e., extent of behavioral or emotional spillover between domains; Clark, 2000) and flexibility (i.e., degree to which one can engage in a role across time and place; Ashforth et al., 2000) also impact our reactions and stress. A highly permeable work-home boundary means more interruptions across those two domains (e.g., taking personal calls at work or work calls at home), whereas a highly flexible work-home boundary means easier transitions between domains (e.g., ability to leave work to manage personal issues; ability to complete work at home). Segmentation of roles occurs when the boundaries between two roles have low permeability and flexibility, whereas integration occurs when there is high permeability and flexibility between the two roles (Ashforth et al., 2000; Bulger, Matthews, & Hoffman, 2007).

Workers may manage boundaries by either increasing integration or segmentation between work-home (Hall & Richter, 1988), but there are both costs and benefits to integration and segmentation strategies (Ashforth et al., 2000). Integration can increase role permeability and flexibility, which may reduce work-home role conflict (e.g., allow workers to deal with a personal issue during work time) or exacerbate it (e.g., require workers to answer emails on weekends; Ashforth et al., 2000), which may impede recovery (Sonnentag & Fritz, 2015). Segmentation reduces blurring between roles "because each role is associated with specific settings and times" (Ashforth et al., 2000, p. 477), which may result in fewer interruptions across roles (e.g., receiving personal phone calls at work or work emails at home), but may not be desirable or realistic because most people have difficulty compartmentalizing their lives completely (Kanter, 1977). In fact, research suggests that few people tend to have a high level of segmentation behaviors in practice, and most people tend to be on the integration end of the spectrum (Bulger et al., 2007).

ICTs can be used to foster both permeability and flexibility for desired integration when needed, but may be used to undermine segmentation when workers want to keep roles separate at a given place or time. For example, technology may "provide new forms of freedom by working (partially) remotely ... [but] there might also be substantial negative impacts ... from the constant switching and loss of clear boundaries between work and private life with their distinct sets of norms, demands, and separate times and spaces" (Moser & Axtell, 2013, p. 5). Therefore, the degree to which norms align with individual preferences for integration/segmentation may impact worker well-being in response to ICT demands. Having a good fit between individual and employer preferences for segmentation/integration can reduce work-home interference (Chen, Powell, & Greenhaus, 2009). Thus, resolving iParadoxes may require taking members' preference for integration or segmentation for work communications into account.

21.3 Understanding iParadoxes: Incorporating Self-Determination Theory

Because there are attention and effort demands in both work and non-work domains that can be facilitated via ICT use, we examine the roles of attention and motivation to understand the ICT iParadoxes more fully. The extent to which demands placed on our attention by ICT use are viewed as "desirable" may be influenced by whether we *want* to use ICT, and whether we find that a particular ICT use is currently fulfilling a *need* that is personally satisfying. Self-Determination Theory (SDT; Ryan & Deci, 2000) helps us to understand individual motivations and needs in the ICT context by distinguishing between intrinsic and extrinsic motivation and by addressing three universal needs (autonomy, competency, and relatedness).

The distinction between autonomous versus controlled motivation on tasks maps onto intrinsic versus extrinsic motives, which highlights the extent to which the goal or demand is in line with our core values and interests (Sheldon & Elliot, 1999). ICTs can keep us more connected to work that we find inherently interesting and coworkers we like, but can interfere with respite from work or people that we find taxing. In both intrinsic and extrinsic motivation situations, ICT poses a work demand that requires attention and effort, but only the former is likely to produce a distress response.

A key component of SDT postulates three universal needs: autonomy (being in control of one's choices and behaviors), competency (feeling connected to others and being effective in the social environment), and relatedness (feeling connected to others and being effective in the social environment; Deci & Ryan, 1985; Deci & Ryan, 2002; Gagné & Deci, 2005). Individuals experience higher well-being and lower stress when these needs are met, and experience distress and lower well-being when these needs are undermined. Organizations that foster the satisfaction of these needs will promote intrinsic motivation, resulting in positive work outcomes, including more effective performance, more positive work attitudes, and higher psychological adjustment and well-being (Gagné & Deci, 2005). Therefore, the extent that patterns of ICT use fulfill or threaten workers' needs for autonomy, relatedness, and competence in any given situation may influence whether it is defined as a demand/stressor or resource.

Each of the three SDT needs map on to the iParadox Triad: ICTs can satisfy needs for control through flexible access or thwart control needs through constant accessibility expectations. ICTs can satisfy needs for relatedness through closer interpersonal connections to geographically dispersed team members or undermine related needs via over-inclusion (e.g., interpersonal intrusions while trying to work). ICTs can satisfy competence needs through work efficiencies and mastery over technology or threaten feelings of competence when experiencing technological overload or malfunctions that halt work progress.

Need for Autonomy. ICT may be used to meet workers' needs for autonomy by providing opportunities for increased flexibility and control over work schedules and the work environment (i.e., where and when work is completed), such that workers have greater autonomy over their work and may be able to better balance work and life responsibilities (Day et al., 2010; Standen et al., 1999). For example, asynchronous technologies (e.g., email) allow people to send and receive work-related information any time and place based on personal convenience (Barber & Santuzzi, 2015; Barley, Meyerson, & Grodal, 2011), as opposed to synchronous interactions that require time coordination issues. This fluidity of work can result in more effective functioning by allowing greater access to information and expertise across geographic areas and time zones.

In addition to increasing control over work schedules and demands, ICT also may be used to meet autonomy needs if the worker has control over their own ICT use. There is a consistent and strong relationship between a lack of job control over one's work with stress and strain (e.g., Day & Jreige, 2002; Lui, Spector, & Jex, 2005; Wall et al., 1996). Based on these studies that demonstrate that having control over one's job is important for reducing worker stress and improving health, Day et al. (2010) argued that this same relationship may apply when one has control over ICT use. Day et al. (2012) tested this hypothesis and found that control over one's use of ICT was associated with lower levels of stress, strain, and burnout. Similarly, Ohly and Latour (2014) found that workers who reported autonomous reasons (compared to controlled reasons) for smartphone use in the evenings reported feeling more recovered in the evening and had more positive emotions.

Alternatively, ICT may be used in such a way as to interfere with workers' autonomy need satisfaction. Lack of control tends to be related to concerns over work emails, often considered to be a key source of workplace stress and overload (Barley et al., 2011). Workers who feel a lack of control over their emails and report immediate email response expectations tend to view email as stressful (Hair, Renaud, & Ramsay, 2007). However, even if they have control over ICT, workers may feel compelled to comply instantaneously to work requests (e.g., respond to texts, emails) after work hours. Employees who feel the urge to respond quickly to email and other work-related messages (i.e., workplace telepressure) report more perceived stress and less recovery during non-work hours (Barber & Santuzzi, 2015).

Therefore, how ICT is implemented in day-to-day workplace practice ultimately determines the degree to which it can meet one's need for autonomy. Workers who decide what ICT they can use, when and how they use ICT to assist with completion of their work, and who are supported in their use of ICT, have increased well-being and more opportunities for work-life balance (Day et al., 2010). Conversely, workers who do not have control over their access to, availability of, and use of ICT may experience increased strain.

Need for Relatedness. Given that relatedness involves feeling connected to others (Gagné & Deci, 2005), ICT should, in theory, be able to help workers meet this need because ICTs help connect, coordinate, and increase communication among colleagues and clients from a variety of locations (Dewett & Jones, 2001). In fact, a key advantage of ICT is that it can increase flow and amount of communication to reduce work delays that arise from waiting on information from others (Renneker & Godwin, 2005). Employees who work remotely often report increased feelings of isolation from both social interactions at work and missed professional development opportunities compared to their in-office counterparts (e.g., Cooper & Kurland, 2002; Morganson et al., 2010).

Smart phones may help to strengthen social bonds, such that they expand "psychological neighborhoods" and can help maintain these bonds from a distance (Wei & Hwei-Lo, 2006, p. 53). Email communications after hours can boost feelings of happiness when they include messages of support and recognition (Butts et al., 2015). These benefits may go farther than being a simple conduit to increased social interaction: ICT can contribute to workers' sense of self (Clayton, Leshner, & Almond, 2015), which may define how, and how much, they want to interact with specific others. For example, some remote workers find that ICTs allow them to strengthen relationships with other remote workers whom they enjoy interacting with, while minimizing contact with negative relationships that are difficult to avoid in a shared office setting (Collins, Hislop, & Cartwright, 2016).

However, ICTs can make workers feel they are constantly connected to social relationships in the workplace (Leonardi et al., 2010; Ragu-Nathan, Tarafdar, & Ragu-Nathan, 2008), which may negatively impact the need for relatedness in by impeding social relationships outside work. For example, Porter and Kakabadse (2006) found that ICT enabled working longer hours, causing workers to be preoccupied thinking about emails after work, and ultimately sacrificing non-work responsibilities. To the extent that non-work activities include social interactions with friends and family, these sacrifices may impede fulfillment of one's need for relatedness.

Ironically, ICT also may have negative implications for workers' need for relatedness by *increasing social isolation* (Levy & Spiller, 1994). The ease of access of information from the internet can decrease the necessity for social interaction. Likewise, because ICT can increase one's ability to work remotely with colleagues at different geographic locations, it may increase feelings of isolation. Isolation has been identified as one of the key potential problems with telecommuting (e.g., Cooper & Kurland, 2002; Salomon & Salomon, 1984; Tomaskovic-Devey & Risman, 1993).

Another way that ICT may negatively impact well-being is the possibility that workers feel that ICT allows *too much interaction* with others in the form of social intrusions. Intrusions are a specific type of workplace interruption that is an unexpected social encounter, which can include both in-person and technological sources (Jett & George, 2003). Intrusions are considered to be taxing interpersonal demands that are linked to perceived worker stress (Lin, Kain, & Frtiz, 2013; Wilkes, Barber, & Rogers, 2017). Being constantly accessible can create an overload of social interaction via ICT that increases worker stress, especially for individuals who want less interpersonal contact. For example, introverts are more sensitive to work-home conflict in terms of a variety of well-being indicators compared to extraverts (i.e., job burnout, work engagement, and satisfaction with work-life balance; Baer, Jenkins, & Barber, 2016). Having others intrude into one's personal space via ICT may create anxiety and stress for individuals who have a lower need for relatedness.

Finally, ICT may present other difficulties for meeting the need for relatedness by introducing new conflict and miscommunication. Day et al. (2010) argued that "although the intent of using ICT within the workplace is often to create effective mechanisms to communicate to others, it often becomes a conduit for miscommunication" (p. 328), which can negatively impact one's need for relatedness. Both unintentional miscommunication (Ramirez et al., 2002) and aggressive communications (Weatherbee & Kelloway, 2006) through ICTs can negatively influence worker well-being outcomes.

Need for Competence. ICT may satisfy workers' need for competence by improving their ability to access, collect, and analyze information and data (Dewett & Jones, 2001), and by increasing lines of communication (Day et al., 2010), which may increase one's effectiveness and productivity. With the increased globalization of organizations, investing in ICTs represents a key business strategy for linking both workers and clients across the world in order to share information, knowledge, and resources (Nielsen & Koseoglu, 2007). This increased sharing of information can decrease the ambiguity of one's work tasks and work delays (Renneker & Godwin, 2005), which may be important in increasing one's sense of competence.

However, this increased information also has the potential to undermine feelings of competence in a few ways. First, wider access to information can increase feelings of information fatigue and perceptions of workload, which may lead to stress (Day et al., 2010; Day et al., 2012) or technostress (Rosen & Weil, 1997; Wood, 2001). Second, needing to learn technologies, or keeping up-to-date with new technological skills can create stress (Day et al., 2010) as it may undermine feelings of competence. Third, ICT may exacerbate stress in other ways, which can impede performance, and thus, perceptions of competence. For example, technology glitches and breakdowns may reduce feelings of competence (i.e., self-efficacy) due to unexpected loss or halting of one's work (Shu, Tu, & Wang, 2011), leading to increased levels of stress (Day et al., 2012). Fourth, the use of ICTs and wearable devices for monitoring also poses some perils for frustrating workers' competence needs. The use of wearable technology and ICT implants, is a growing interest in organizations (see Ernst, 2017). Although the underlying rationale for this type of technology may be for ensuring security and efficiency (accessing printers and opening doors), providing feedback and rewards (Miller & Weckert, 2000), or ensuring well-being (monitoring health data; Mack, 2017), if they are used to punish wrong behavior (e.g., Stanton & Weiss, 2000), then workers will perceive them as competence threats in relation to their abilities or work integrity, which may have a negative impact on worker well-being and health (Day et al., 2010; Smith et al., 1992).

Our review of the literature suggests that ICT can have both positive and negative effects on worker stress and strain because of issues surrounding worker autonomy, social connectivity, and productivity. To help guide future work in the area, we outline a research agenda to further our understanding of the degree to which ICT can help workers resolve autonomy, connectivity, and productivity issues, as well as to identify the factors that may exacerbate these issues.

21.4 Future Research

To help address the ICT paradoxes, we have created a model that identifies how ICT can act as both a demand and a stressor and how individual differences and organizational support are integral contextual issues in these autonomy, connectivity, and productivity paradoxes (see Figure 21.1). We based this model on a holistic research agenda in terms of incorporating the new conceptual ICT perspective, ensuring valid measurement of the ICT constructs, and ensuring solid research designs, not only in terms of understanding the moderators and mediators of the ICT-stress relationship, but also in terms of utilizing longitudinal designs and validating organizational initiatives that address the ICT paradoxes. Several individual factors (e.g., segmentation vs. integration preference) may play a role in how ICT is perceived and, ultimately, how ICT impacts individual health and well-being. Moreover, organizational culture and leader support around ICT issues also may influence worker health.

21.4.1 Conceptual, Measurement, and Design Issues

We can approach ICT and worker health and stress with a view that ICT can be seen as having both positive and negative effects on workers, depending on the situation. By representing research in terms of the three paradoxes (autonomy, social connectivity, and productivity), we will be better able to identify the mechanisms to promote worker health. Traditional occupational health psychology and stress and well-being models can help guide research in this area, and integrating other theoretical perspectives (e.g., self-determination theory) may help further elucidate situations in which ICTs are perceived as wanted and/or unwanted activities in relation to satisfying basic psychological needs.

More work is needed on the basics of measurement of ICT use, attitudes, and reactions to specific ICT activities. We need to more carefully define ICT use itself, in terms of what needs to be measured and how to accurately quantify its usage. Moreover, reconciling previous measures and studies with the current research framework, incorporating autonomy, connectivity, and productivity, would be beneficial. For example, it is important to examine the definitions and measurement of recovery experiences and how they may be modified to better account for the growing use of ICT during off-work time.

To comprehensively understand the iParadoxes, we call upon future research to explore the relationships that exist between the ICT use and strain, particularly addressing the mechanisms that may mediate the ICT–strain relationship and the mechanisms that may buffer and/or exacerbate perceived stress (e.g., participative leadership and employee involvement). The area also would benefit from

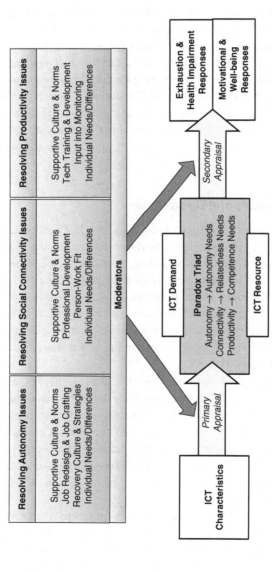

Figure 21.1 *Theoretical model of the moderators and outcomes of the iParadox Triad of autonomy, social connectivity, and productivity*

longitudinal and experimental studies to examine the impact of ICT on worker well-being and health over time and reactions to interventions, respectively. An extension of this suggestion is to acknowledge the importance of explicitly testing the capacity of organizational initiatives to resolve the autonomy, social connectivity, and productivity paradoxes. For example, can job crafting initiatives increase autonomy, and ultimately improve well-being? Can leaders create optimal levels of autonomy, connectivity, and productivity via participative leadership and employee involvement initiatives? Finally, based on the strong theoretical framework, future research should examine the validity of evidence-based interventions that address the autonomy, connectivity, and productivity paradoxes in predicting worker stress and health outcomes.

21.4.2 Resolving Autonomy Issues

In attempting to resolve the issue of ICT and autonomy, we need to look both at (a) the extent to which workers can use ICT to increase their autonomy over their work, and (b) the extent to which they have autonomy in how, when, and where they use ICTs. In doing so, we need to consider both organizational and individual factors: That is, can organizational strategies (e.g., job crafting) improve workers' autonomous motivation on work tasks and reduce the perception of work demands as threatening? Do leaders who support individual differences (such as preference for integration/separation) help to improve fit and increase control per boundary theory? How does ICT impact recovery, and does a recovery-supportive culture positively influence worker health?

Job Redesign and Job Crafting.   Job redesign that specifically targets ICT issues may be beneficial in improving autonomy issues because the core aspects of job design involve increased autonomy (Hackman & Oldham, 1980; Karasek, 1979; Oldham & Hackman, 2010). Moreover, job crafting may be an important tool in resolving the autonomy paradox. Job crafting evolved from the job design research, such that it is the "jobholders [who] are actively involved in determining what changes will be made in their jobs to improve the match with their own needs and skills" and they may "redesign their jobs on their own initiative – either with or without management assent and cooperation" (Kulik, Oldham, & Hackman, 1987, p. 292). That is, the jobholder has the ability to change the conditions and parameters of job tasks and relationships, increasing self-concordance with work goals and autonomous motivation for work tasks, and reducing the perceptions of work demands as threatening (Wrzeniewski & Dutton, 2001). Through such modification, workers can increase or incorporate crucial resources, which is positively related to increased engagement and job satisfaction, and decreased burnout (Tims, Bakker, & Derks, 2013).

This transition from externally imposed work boundaries to internally assimilated boundaries works to increase autonomous motivation for work tasks by increasing self-concordance (Deci & Ryan, 2000). Therefore, supporting job crafting strategies may increase worker control and autonomy. Job crafting may reduce

ICT demand perceptions indirectly by increasing autonomous motivation on work tasks. That is, work requests via ICTs may be seen as less of an intrusion, and workers may have more discretion in when and where they respond. Job crafting also may affect well-being directly by allowing workers to modify and prioritize ICT tasks, ICT social interactions, and cognitive appraisals of ICTs. For example, some workers may want to integrate ICTs more into their daily routine more than others, or limit ICT use to only certain types of tasks. Finally, some workers may prefer to reframe some aspects of ICT use as a way to add broader impact or meaning to their work tasks, like advertising key work accomplishments on social media or seeing ICTs as a critical tool for creatively approaching difficult or tedious tasks. Although we know that encouraging engagement in the ICT implementation process (i.e., increased involvement for how to use ICTs) tends to be associated with lower levels of strain (Coovert & Thompson, 2003), no research has examined the extent to which job crafting influences ICT use and perception and levels of stress. Future research should examine these relationships and clarify the specific mechanisms by which job crafting may reduce stress (directly or indirectly).

Supporting Individual Differences.   In providing a supportive culture, leaders can consider individual preferences for integration of roles, also known as boundary management profiles or "flexstyles." Boundary theory suggests that individuals build and maintain psychological, physical, and/or behavioral boundaries between work and personal life, through the process of segmenting and/or integrating the domains (Ashforth et al., 2000), and that individuals tend to differ in terms of the degree to which they want integration or segmentation of their work and non-work lives (Nippert-Eng, 1996). Workers tend to differ not only in terms of their preference for integration or segmentation, but also in terms of the nature in which they prefer interruptions in work versus home domains (i.e., work-to-home interruptions versus home-to-work interruptions), their perceived control over blurring work-home boundaries, and how they prioritize work versus personal life roles (i.e., work as a priority, family life as a priority, or prioritizing both equally; Kossek et al., 2011). Understanding these different flexstyles among workers is critical for improving alignment between employers' goals and workers' needs (Kossek & Lautsch, 2007).

If workers perceive ICT as being able to help facilitate the integration (or reduce segmentation), those with a strong preference for integration will tend to view ICT positively, whereas workers with a strong preference for segmentation will tend to view it negatively. These perceptions may be influenced by our role identities in terms of how we see and define ourselves: Based on Ashforth et al.'s (2000) overview of segmented and integrated roles, it is feasible to expect that the greater one's core role identities differ in each role, the greater the desire to have segmented roles. Conversely, the greater the overlap between one's role identities, the greater one's desire to have integrated roles.

Kossek, Ruderman, Braddy, and Hannum (2012) found that profiles for work–non-work boundary management styles were differentially related to positive and negative work-family outcomes depending on the amount of perceived boundary control that workers reported. Specifically, the extent to which one feels in control of boundaries and the amount of fit relevant to one's identities and values is more significant in determining well-being than the levels of integration or separation overall (Kossek et al., 2012).

Individual flexstyles and boundary management styles also encompass primary appraisals of demands or stressors. Continuing the example of the after-work email, a worker who identifies highly with work may view the off-work interruption as a welcomed opportunity to escape family/non-work roles momentarily, whereas workers who report having high separation behaviors may perceive the email as disruptive of their recovery time and in violation of their control. More research needs to be conducted that further explores flexstyles in the ICT context. Specifically, research on how organizations can accommodate and support individual flexstyles with a focus on ICT boundaries would help to further understand how to resolve autonomy iParadox issues.

Developing a Supportive Recovery Culture.   An organizational culture that is supportive of work recovery and family roles also may help resolve the autonomy paradox. According to the JD-R, COR, Effort-Recovery Theories, and the health impairment process, increased and/or sustained job demands that command sustained worker effort may exhaust vital resources and lead to energy depletion and health problems (e.g., Bakker, Demerouti, & Schaufeli, 2003). This depletion results in a need for recovery, so that resources and energy can be replenished and exhaustion abated.

In line with the Effort-Recovery Theory, recovery can be conceptualized as the process opposite to the strain process: functional systems, or internal resources, which have been taxed during a stressful experience (e.g., work demand) are restored to pre-stressor levels, often resulting in a decrease of strain indicators (Sonnentag & Fritz, 2007). This process may consist of physically and mentally distancing oneself from one's work situation (i.e., psychological detachment) in order to recover from job stress (Sonnentag & Bayer, 2005). Although detachment from work may be seen as being important for worker health and well-being (Park, Fritz, & Jex, 2011; Sonnentag & Bayer, 2005; Sonnentag & Fritz, 2015), some workers may have difficulty engaging in this type of detachment because of blurred boundaries between work and home, which is further heightened by the flexibility-enhancing accessibility characteristics of ICTs. For example, Mellner (2015) found that high levels of expectations to be available after work hours tend to be associated with a decreased ability to psychologically detach from work.

Recognizing and supporting the importance of recovery time as a symbiotic element of work life, and encouraging explicit recovery norms (e.g., planned time off, such as vacations, weekends, and evenings during which workers are not obligated to check in with work) may be valuable to workers' health, because this type of recovery-supporting culture encourages workers to have the autonomy to decide when and how they engage with work during down-time. Future recovery research should more explicitly examine the effects of ICT use on detachment, including the extent to which workers use ICT for work purposes even when they are away from the work setting and how organizational culture can help or hinder the recovery process.

Moreover, behaviors that are seen as being supportive to workers (in balancing their non-work lives) may have unintended negative effects. For example, some organizations have banned email use in an effort to promote work-life balance, reduce work-related stress, and prevent burnout (e.g., Volkswagen as reported by Tsukayama, 2011; see www.bbc.com/news/technology-16314901). Germany's legislation prohibits ministry managers from contacting workers outside work hours, except in emergency situations (Vasagar, 2013). Although these initiatives and legislation have been approached from a very supportive context of promoting work-life balance and reducing burnout, "banning" may have the ironic effect of reducing well-being given that limiting worker control can also backfire and create stress.

France introduced legislation stating that organizations must establish and communicate rules about sending and responding to work emails (Morris, 2017), which allows for workers' input on the final guidelines. This strategy further supports workers' choice of where and when to use ICT (i.e., increasing autonomy) rather than resorting to a ban, which decreases individual worker autonomy. This difference is highlighted in the example of some organizations banning the use of email of workers who are on leave, even going as far as "freezing" or deleting emails for workers away on holiday, maternity, or sick leave (e.g., Daimler; see Kremer, 2014). Employees must then rebuild their email and try to catch up when they are back in the office. Other workers who are using ICT to increase their work flexibility to accommodate family or health needs may feel censured for wanting to send emails during times that are more convenient for them (such as in the evening or on weekends), and feel obligated to do these types of communications during "regular" working hours.

In a slightly different approach to Volkswagen's move to block workers' access to emails on their work smartphones after regular working hours, BMW requested that each employee work with his/her supervisor to decide upon the amount of work to be completed outside regular work hours, based on the honor system (see Morris, 2017). From a SDT perspective, the latter approach may be seen as being more effective to meet workers' needs for autonomy (i.e., deciding what schedule works for them).

Future research should explore how different organizational strategies (e.g., the right to disconnect versus outright banning of ICT use after hours) affect worker perceptions of autonomy, and ultimately workers' attitudes, well-being, and productivity. It is important to understand whether enacted ICT-based supportive behaviors actually enhance or detract from worker control, as well as the subsequent effects on worker health. However, it is important that research clearly assesses real autonomy over how and when to use technology. If workers are still rewarded or punished by managers based on accessibility (e.g., promotional opportunities, work assignments, pay), then regularly checking in during off-hours still qualifies as controlled motivation.

21.4.3 Resolving Social Connectivity Issues

The literature suggests that ICT can both reduce (Dewett & Jones, 2001) and increase social isolation (Cooper & Kurland, 2002), help maintain positive relationships (Moser & Axtell, 2013) yet create communication problems (Ramirez et al., 2002), and empower workers (Dewett & Jones, 2001) yet create feelings of intrusion (Day et al., 2012). Moreover, because concerns about social connectivity may range from poor connectivity (not enough, or poor quality) to too much connectivity (intruding into personal time, feeling overwhelmed by too much interaction), it is important to look at this issue as a matter of balance and fit with the individual and organizational preferences. We look at how we can use group, leader, and organizational initiatives to support balanced connectivity in terms of establishing norms around ICT use, providing professional development opportunities, and understanding workers' preferences for social interactions in the workplace.

Developing and Supporting ICT Norms.   Having clear organizational and group norms pertaining to respectful social etiquette (including after-work rules) around ICT use can help to ensure that workers' boundary and interruption preferences are respected, and foster control over social connectivity. A varying degree of segmentation or integration can be promoted or discouraged through formal or informal norms, such as policies, practices, and demands (Ashforth et al., 2000; Clark, 2000; Nippert-Eng, 1996). Furthermore, the creation of these norms goes beyond the organization itself. Regulative institutions, such as laws and public policies, directly affect organizational rules and procedures by establishing codes or minimum standards to which all organizations must adhere (Piszczek & Berg, 2014), such as France's guidelines to limit work-related technology usage outside office hours (Wang, 2017). Although the larger social and political environments establish parameters within which organizations operate, leaders play a critical role in strengthening the organization's norms by promoting practices, role modeling, providing supportive leadership, and addressing individual needs.

Future research should explore how developing and supporting explicit ICT norms may affect workers' well-being when it comes to too much or too little social connectivity, and importantly, how those norms are practiced and perceived in actual work settings. Furthermore, research should investigate whether there are optimal levels of connectivity for both organizations and workers that could be put into practice.

Offering Professional Development Opportunities.   Although ICT is uniquely effective in connecting workers and teams that do not share the same physical space (Day et al., 2010), having an opportunity to commune in the same space may be beneficial for mitigating the experience of professional and social isolation reported by some remote workers. For example, Cooper and Kurland (2002) found that professional isolation of telecommuters was directly linked to worker development activities, such as interpersonal networking, informal learning, and mentoring. Specifically, they found that when organizations placed value in PD activities and telecommuters were able to participate, experiences of professional isolation decreased. By providing professional development, team-building, and connection opportunities for remote workers, organizations may be able to address concerns about a lack of social support and connectivity. Furthermore, when considering professional isolation, professional development and connection opportunities may contribute importantly to perceived social support, which is a critical resource in both JD-R and COR theories, and maps onto SDT's need for relatedness. Research needs to address the potential impact of training and development on optimizing connectivity, preventing isolation, and reducing worker stress.

Accommodating Individual Preferences.   Just as individual needs and preferences for integration or segmentation may impact the autonomy paradox, they also can affect the social connectivity paradox, in combination with understanding these preferences, as well as preferences for social interaction and work style. For example, people differ on their preferences for social interaction (i.e., extraversion levels), with introverts showing more sensitivity to work intrusions into the home domain (Baer et al., 2016). Some workers also may want to expand social interactions using ICTs, whereas others want more personal restrictions on the timing and number of social interactions via ICTs. Thus, some workers might see ICTs as more unwelcome social interactions than others outside the workplace. Future research needs to explore the effectiveness of organizations supporting more segmented work-home boundaries for people wishing to limit social interactions with colleagues during non-work hours.

Individual differences might also dictate preferences for a more focused work style to achieve high work engagement activities related to "flow" experiences; that is, the state of complete mental immersion in an activity. In particular, the absorption aspect of work engagement is likely difficult to achieve with constant workplace interruptions. For people who prefer high levels of predictability and structure (i.e., need for closure; Webster & Kruglankski, 1994), frequent social intrusions on work may be a particularly stressful experience. However, research into how individual differences affect reactions to social intrusions in the workplace while working on tasks is lacking. Therefore, future research should integrate personality theories to examine individual differences in preferences for social connectivity, the extent to which these preferences fit with job and organizational requirements (person-work fit), and the impact of these differences in these "optimal" levels of connectivity.

21.4.4 Resolving Productivity Issues

At the core of the productivity paradox is that although ICT is intended to increase productivity, its unintended consequences may be to increase overload and/or decrease effectiveness and overall productivity. A supportive culture is imperative here to ensure that there are resources to provide ICT upgrades (see for example, Day et al., 2010; 2012), training, and reasonable workloads. Managers also need to take into consideration individual differences in worker needs and skills related to ICT use.

Supporting Training and Technology Adoption. Providing sufficient training and a reasonable technology adoption pace (avoiding new tech fads) boosts competence using COR Theory (skills/abilities as a resource) and the resources aspect of JD-R. For example, Korunka and Vitouch (1999) found that workers who were adequately trained to use ICT and were involved in the implementation of new ICT experienced less stress and dissatisfaction. Chen et al. (2009) found that training to support new ICT buffered the negative impact of the new technologies on workers' levels of exhaustion and job dissatisfaction. Having supportive ICT staff assistance and organizational support for ICT resources and upgrades tends to be related to lower levels of strain and burnout (Day et al., 2012). Effective technical support may increase workers' engagement with ICT (O'Driscoll et al., 2010) and minimize work disruptions, because problems are typically solved more quickly (Ragu-Nathan et al., 2008). Moreover, having organizational support and supportive staff tend to buffer the relationships between ICT stressors (learning demands and ICT hassles) and strain/burnout outcomes (Day et al., 2012). Research should address the interplay of organizational supports (in terms of the resources given to training and new technology) and the specific needs of individual workers.

Encouraging Employee Input on Monitoring. Just as having respectful and agreed upon ground rules can increase well-being, encouraging workers' involvement and input on monitoring may increase trust and empower workers as to how ICT is used. How ICT monitoring is used and promoted in organizations may be more important for well-being than just the frequency or pervasiveness of monitoring. As highlighted in a recent Forbes article on ICT implants, although an RFID (radio frequency identification) chip "doesn't provide a record of all your movements, like say, your smartphone can, it could easily provide enough data to a nosey or unethical supervisor to give any employee pause" (Mack, 2017). That is, although ICT is not good or bad, per se, it may increase the opportunities for exploitation of workers if it is misused. Indeed, using ICT to monitor performance tends to be related to negative worker outcomes (Smith et al., 1992), especially if workers perceive that it will result in negative outcomes (Stanton & Weiss, 2000).

Researchers can consider whether organizational strategies that promote autonomous motivation when adopting technologies would be useful. For example, using participatory management strategies to come up with guidelines for acceptable monitoring practices and policies for managers would give workers more control over how new monitoring technologies are used. Involvement is especially critical for improving workers' well-being, and it can range from relatively low-level forms (i.e., suggestion forums and reaction surveys) to self-managed work teams (Grawitch, 2009). Researchers also should consider exploring the effects of workers' involvement levels in the adoption of monitoring technologies.

Accommodating Individual Differences in ICT Needs and Skills.   Part of the challenge to resolve the productivity paradox is to understand differences in workers' perception of technology (as per Lazarus & Folkman's (1984) stress model), as well as their individual needs and skills related to ICTs. In order to accurately assess these individual differences, appropriate needs analyses of the technology (i.e., "does the new ICT really fit our needs and current worker abilities?") are necessary to avoid exceeding individuals' personal resources. Differences in education, age, gender, and computer self-efficacy have been shown to affect the ease of use, adoption of, and attitudes toward ICT. Individuals with higher levels of education have been shown to learn faster and have less anxiety about new ICT training compared to individuals with lower levels of education (Agarwal and Prasad, 1999). Age may negatively influence perceived ease of ICT use (Burton-Jones & Hubona, 2005), ICT stress (Day et al., 2012), and technostress (Syvänen et al., 2016), but it does not appear to significantly affect computer-related stress. Women tend to use less ICT in the workplace (Day et al., 2012; Venkatesh & Morris, 2000). Whereas some studies have found that women experience more ICT-related anxiety (Whitley, 1997) and technostress (e.g., Syvänen et al., 2016), other studies have found no gender difference in ICT stress (e.g., Day et al., 2012), and other studies have found differential relationships between ICT variables and outcomes for men and women, depending on the specific predictor and outcome (e.g., ICT exposure was associated with depression for women, and SMS messaging was associated with depression for men; Thomée et al., 2007).

As we have argued throughout this chapter, we need to disentangle the reason underlying the (sometimes conflicting) relationships with ICT and stress, and demographics may play a role in this work. However, although future research should continue to look at demographic variables, it is likely more efficient and precise to measure ICT use, behaviors, and attitudes toward ICT directly because demographics may be only tangentially related to actual attitudes and behaviors. For example, having ICT competence and frequency of ICT may be associated with decreased technostress (Syvänen et al., 2016), yet higher overall ICT exposure may be associated with prolonged stress and depression symptoms over time (Thomée et al., 2007).

From a practical perspective, conducting appropriate needs analyses will help to avoid exceeding individuals' personal resources. Needs analysis is a systematic strategy for examining whether the new ICT fits the organizational needs and current worker abilities, which helps reduce issues of adopting ineffective technologies or ICTs that will not improve productivity (and may even hinder it). Acknowledging and assessing individual differences regarding ICT use and attitudes, as well as providing adequate training and adoption periods, is necessary for the smooth introduction of new ICT.

21.4.5 Concluding Comments

In this review, we created a model based on job stress and well-being models to help us understand what is known about the three potential paradoxes (autonomy, social connectivity, and productivity) of ICT's influence on worker well-being and to guide future work. The paradoxical nature of ICT means that the same ICT characteristics that may increase well-being also can increase stress and strain. That is, the same ICT features that allow us to connect more easily and frequently with our colleagues and clients regardless of geographic location also can create more overload and interpersonal conflict. The same ICT features that provide us with more autonomy in how and where we do our jobs also can reduce boundaries making us too accessible and even vulnerable. Therefore, ICT cannot (and should not) be defined as innately good or bad: the key factors are how it is promoted within the organization and how it is used to meet workers needs for autonomy, competence, and relatedness.

As highlighted in the model, ICT's influence on our well-being is moderated by our individual characteristics, such as boundary and work style preferences, needs, and skills, as well as social and workplace factors, such as the organizational culture and supportive leadership (i.e., the manner in which ICT is used to foster worker health or to negatively influence well-being). Given that ICT is here to stay in the workplace, the quest of trying to label ICT as being either good or bad may be secondary to the questions of how can we help workers use it effectively, and how can we advise organizations and leaders to use it responsibly and effectively, while creating a joint goal of creating healthy workplaces and creating healthy and effective workers. Based on SDT, well-being should arise from ensuring that technology is used in such a way as to allow individuals to meet their needs for autonomy, relatedness, and competence. Therefore, future research needs to address how to create organizational change and culture change to embrace this perspective on technology in the workplace. Future research also needs to take individual needs into consideration, as well as their perceptions of technology and the amount of control that they have over it.

References

Agarwal, R. & Prasad, J. (1999). Are individual differences germane to the acceptance of new information technologies? *Decision Sciences, 30*(2), 361–391. doi:10.1111/j.1540–5915.1999.tb01614.x.

Ashforth, B. E., Kreiner, G. E., & Fugate, M. (2000). All in a day's work: Boundaries and micro role transitions. *Academy of Management Review, 25*(3), 472–491. doi:10.5465/AMR2000.3363315.

Baer, S. M., Jenkins, J. S., & Barber, L. K. (2016). Home is private . . . Do not enter! Introversion and sensitivity to work–home conflict. *Stress and Health, 32*(4), 441–445. doi:10.1002/smi.2628.

Bakker, A. B. & Demerouti, E. (2007). The job demands–resources model: State of the art. *Journal of Managerial Psychology, 22*(3), 309–328. doi:10.1108/02683940710.

Bakker, A., Demerouti, E., & Schaufeli, W. (2003). Dual processes at work in a call centre: An application of the job demands–resources model. *European Journal of Work and Organizational Psychology, 12*(4), 393–417. doi:10.1016/S0001-8791(02)00030–1.

Barber, L. K. & Santuzzi, A. M. (2015). Please respond ASAP: Workplace telepressure and employee recovery. *Journal of Occupational Health Psychology, 20*(2), 172–189. doi:10.1037/a0038278.

Barley, S. R., Meyerson, D. E., & Grodal, S. (2011). E-mail as a source and symbol of stress. *Organization Science, 22*(4), 887–906. doi:10.1287/orsc.1100.0573.

Bulger, C. A., Matthews, R. A., & Hoffman, M. E. (2007). Work and personal life boundary management: Boundary strength, work/personal life balance, and the segmentation integration continuum. *Journal of Occupational Health Psychology, 12*(4), 365. doi:10.1037/1076–8998.12.4.365.

Burton-Jones, A. & Hubona, G. S. (2005). Individual differences and usage behavior: Revisiting a technology acceptance model assumption. *ACM Sigmis Database, 36*(2), 58–77. doi:10.1145/1066149.1066155.

Butts, M. M., Becker, W. J., & Boswell, W. R. (2015). Hot buttons and time sinks: The effects of electronic communication during nonwork time on emotions and work-nonwork conflict. *Academy of Management Journal, 58*(3), 763–788. doi:10.5465/amj.2014.0170.

Chen, Z., Powell, G. N., & Greenhaus, J. H. (2009). Work-to-family conflict, positive spillover, and boundary management: A person-environment fit approach. *Journal of Vocational Behavior, 74*(1), 82–93. doi:10.1016/j.jvb.2008.10.009.

Clark, S. C. (2000). Work/family border theory: A new theory of work/family balance. *Human Relations, 53*(6), 747–770. doi:10.1177/0018726700536001.

Clayton, R. B., Leshner, G., & Almond, A. (2015). The extended iSelf: The impact of iPhone separation on cognition, emotion, and physiology. *Journal of Computer-Mediated Communication, 20*, 119–135. doi:10.1111/jcc4.12109.

Collins, A. M., Hislop, D., & Cartwright, S. (2016). Social support in the workplace between teleworkers, office-based colleagues and supervisors. *New Technology, Work and Employment, 31*(2), 161–175. doi:10.1111/ntwe.12065.

Cooper, C. D. & Kurland, N. B. (2002). Telecommuting, professional isolation, and employee development in public and private organizations. *Journal of Organizational Behavior, 23*(4), 511–532. doi:10.1002/job.145.

Coovert, M. D. & Thompson, L. F. (2003). Technology and workplace health. In J. C. Quick & L. E. Tetrick (Eds.), *Handbook of occupational health psychology* (pp. 221–241). Washington, DC: American Psychological Association.

David, P. A. (1990). The dynamo and the computer: an historical perspective on the modern productivity paradox. *The American Economic Review, 80*(2), 355–361.

Day, A. L. & Jreige, S. (2002). Examining Type A behavior battern to explain the relationship between job demands and psychosocial outcomes. *Journal of Occupational Health Psychology, 7*, 109–120. doi:10.1037/1076–8998.7.2.109.

Day, A., Paquet, S., Scott, N., & Hambley, L. (2012). Perceived information and communication technology (ICT) demands on employee outcomes: The moderating effect of organizational ICT support. *Journal of Occupational Health Psychology, 17*, 473–491. doi:10.1037/a0029837.

Day, A., Scott, N., & Kelloway, E. K. (2010). Information and communication technology: Implications for job stress and employee well-being. In P. L. Perrewé & D. C. Ganster (Eds.), New developments in theoretical and conceptual approaches to job stress (vol. 8, pp. 317–350). Emerald Group Publishing. doi: 10.1108/S1479-3555 (2010)0000008011.

Deci, E. L. & Ryan, R. M. (1985). The general causality orientations scale: Self-determination in personality. *Journal of Research in Personality, 19*(2), 109–134. doi:10.1016/0092–6566(85)90023–6.

Deci, E. L. & Ryan, R. M. (2000). The "what" and "why" of goal pursuits: Human needs and the self-determination of behavior. *Psychological Inquiry, 11*(4), 227–268. doi:10.1207/S15327965PLI1104_01.

Deci, E. L. & Ryan, R. M. (2002). Overview of self-determination theory: An organismic dialectical perspective. In E. L. Deci & R. M. Ryan (Eds.), *Handbook of self-determination research* (pp. 3–33). Rochester, NY: University Rochester Press.

Demerouti, E., Bakker, A. B., Nachreiner, F., & Schaufeli, W. B. (2001). The job demands–resources model of burnout. *Journal of Applied Psychology, 86*, 499–512. doi:10.1037/0021–9010.86.3.499.

Dewan, S. & Kraemer, K. L. (1998). International dimensions of the productivity paradox. *Communications of the ACM, 41*(8), 56–62. doi:10.1145/280324.280333

Dewett, T. & Jones, G. R. (2001). The role of information technology in the organization: A review, model, and assessment. *Journal of Management, 27*, 313–346. doi:10.1177/014920630102700306.

Diaz, I., Chiaburu, D. S., Zimmerman, R. D., & Boswell, W. R. (2012). Communication technology: Pros and cons of constant connection to work. *Journal of Vocational Behavior, 80*(2), 500–508. doi:10.1016/j.jvb.2011.08.007.

Ernst, D. (July 24, 2017) Wisconsin company to offer staff microchip implants: "The next evolution in payment systems." The Washington Times. Retrieved from www.washingtontimes.com/news/2017/jul/24/three-square-market-to-offer-staff-microchip-impla/.

Gagné, M. & Deci, E. L. (2005). Self-determination theory and work motivation. *Journal of Organizational Behavior, 26*(4), 331–362. doi:10.1002/job.322.

Grawitch, M. J., Ledford Jr., G. E., Ballard, D. W., & Barber, L. K. (2009). Leading the healthy workforce: The integral role of employee involvement. Consulting Psychology Journal: Practice and Research, *61*(2), 122–135. doi:10.1037/a0015288.

Griffin, A. (February 19, 2016). This is what the 'i' in 'iPhone' stands for. Business Insider. Retrieved from www.businessinsider.com/this-is-what-the-i-in-iphone-stands-for-2016-2.

Hackman, J. R. & Oldham, G. R. (1980). *Work redesign.* Reading, MA: Addison-Wesley.

Hair, M., Renaud, K. V., & Ramsay, J. (2007). The influence of self-esteem and locus of control on perceived email-related stress. *Computers in Human Behavior, 23*, 2791–2803. doi:10.1016/j.chb.2006.05.005.

Hall, D. T. & Richter, J. (1988). Balancing work life and home life: What can organizations do to help? *The Academy of Management Executive, 2*(3), 213–223. doi:10.5465/AME.1988.4277258.

Hobfoll, S. E. (1989). Conservation of resources: A new attempt at conceptualizing stress. American Psychologist, 44, 513–524. doi:10.1037/0003-066X.44.3.513.

Jett, Q. R. & George, J. M. (2003). Work interrupted: A closer look at the role of interruptions in organizational life. *Academy of Management Review, 28*(3), 494–507. doi:10.5465/AMR.2003.10196791.

Kanter, R. M. (1977). *Work and family in the United States: A critical review and agenda for research and policy.* New York, NY: Russell Sage Foundation.

Karasek, R. A. (1979). Job demands, job decision latitude, and mental strain: Implications for job redesign. Administrative Science Quarterly, 24, 285–308.

Korunka, C. & Vitouch, O. (1999). Effects of the implementation of information technology on employees' strain and job satisfaction: A context-dependent approach. *Work & Stress*, *13*(4), 341–363. doi:10.1080/02678379950019798.

Kossek, E. E. & Lautsch, B. A. (2007). *CEO of me: Creating a life that works in the flexible job age*. Upper Saddle River, NJ: Prentice Hall, Pearson Education.

Kossek, E. E., Pichler, S., Bodner, T., & Hammer, L. B. (2011). Workplace social support and work–family conflict: A meta-analysis clarifying the influence of general and work–family-specific supervisor and organizational support. *Personnel Psychology*, *64*(2), 289–313. doi:10.1111/j.1744–6570.2011.01211.x.

Kossek, E. E., Ruderman, M. N., Braddy, P. W., & Hannum, K. M. (2012). Work–nonwork boundary management profiles: A person-centered approach. *Journal of Vocational Behavior*, *81*(1), 112–128. doi:10.1016/j.jvb.2012.04.003.

Kremer, W. (August 14, 2014). Should holiday email be deleted? BBC News. Retrieved from www.bbc.com/news/magazine-28786117.

Kulik, C. T., Oldham, G. R., & Hackman, J. R. (1987). Work design as an approach to person-environment fit. *Journal of Vocational Behavior*, *31*(3), 278–296. doi:10.1016/0001–8791(87)90044–3.

Lazarus, R. S. & Folkman, S. (1984). Coping and adaptation. In W. D. Gentry (Ed.), *The handbook of behavioral medicine* (pp. 282–325). New York, NY: Guilford.

Leonardi, P. M., Treem, J. W., & Jackson, M. H. (2010). The connectivity paradox: Using technology to both decrease and increase perceptions of distance in distributed work arrangements. *Journal of Applied Communication Research*, *38*(1), 85–105. doi:10.1080/00909880903483599.

Levy, B. & Spiller, P. T. (1994). The institutional foundations of regulatory commitment: a comparative analysis of telecommunications regulation. *The Journal of Law, Economics, and Organization*, *10*(2), 201–246. doi:10.1093/oxfordjournals.jleo.a036849.

Lin, B. C., Kain, J. M., & Fritz, C. (2013). Don't interrupt me! An examination of the relationship between intrusions at work and employee strain. *International Journal of Stress Management*, *20*(2), 77–94. doi:10.1037/a0031637.

Liu, C., Spector, P., & Jex, S. (2005). The relation of job control with job strains: A comparison of multiple data sources. *Journal of Occupational and Organizational Psychology*, *78*(3), 325–336. doi:10.1348/096317905X26002.

Mack, E. (2017). Why the company putting 'chip' Implants in employees isn't starting a trend. Forbes. Retrieved from www.forbes.com/sites/ericmack/2017/07/25/micro chips-implant-three-square-market-wisconsin-chip/#28c86179463a.

Mamaghani, F. (2006). Impact of information technology on the workforce of the future: An analysis. *International Journal of Management*, *23*(4), 845–850.

Mazmanian, M., Orlikowski, W. J., & Yates, J. (2013). The autonomy paradox: The implications of mobile email devices for knowledge professionals. *Organization science*, *24*, 1337–1357. doi:10.1287/orsc.1120.0806.

Meijman, T. F, & Mulder, G. (1998). Psychological aspects of workload. In P. J. D. Drenth & H. Thierry (Eds.), *Handbook of work and organizational psychology* (vol. 2, pp. 5–33). Hove, UK: Psychology Press.

Mellner, C. (2016). After-hours availability expectations, work-related smartphone use during leisure, and psychological detachment: The moderating role of boundary control. *International Journal of Workplace Health Management*, *9*, 146–164. doi:10.1108/IJWHM-07–2015-0050.

Miller, S. & Weckert, J. (2000). Privacy, the workplace and the internet. *Journal of Business Ethics, 28,* 255–265. doi:10.1023/A: 1006232417265.

Morgan, K., Morgan, M., & Hall, J. (2000). Psychological developments in high technology teaching and learning environments. *British Journal of Educational Psychology, 31,* 71–79. doi:10.1111/1467–8535.00136.

Morganson, V. J., Major, D. A., Oborn, K. L., Verive, J. M., & Heelan, M. P. (2010). Comparing telework locations and traditional work arrangements: Differences in work-life balance support, job satisfaction, and inclusion. *Journal of Managerial Psychology, 25*(6), 578–595. doi:10.1108/026839410110.

Morris, D. Z. (2017). New French law bars work email after hours. Fortune. Retrieved from http://fortune.com/2017/01/01/french-right-to-disconnect-law/.

Moser, K. S. & Axtell, C. M. (2013). The role of norms in virtual work. *Journal of Personnel Psychology, 12,* 1–6. doi:10.1027/1866–5888/a000079.

Nielsen, Y. & Koseoglu, O. (2007). Wireless networking in tunnelling projects. *Tunnelling and Underground Space Technology, 22*(3), 252–261. doi:10.1016/j. tust.2006.08.004.

Nippert-Eng, C. E. (1996). *Home and work.* Chicago, IL: University of Chicago Press.

O'Driscoll, M. P., Brough, P., Timms, C., & Sawang, S. (2010). Engagement with information and communication technology and psychological well-being. In P. L. Perrewé & D. C. Ganster (Eds.), *New developments in theoretical and conceptual approaches to job stress* (vol. 8, pp. 269–316). Bingley, UK: Emerald Group Publishing Limited.

Ohly, S. & Latour, A. (2014). Work-related smartphone use and well-being in the evening. *Journal of Personnel Psychology, 13,* 174–183. doi:10.1027/1866–5888/a000114.

Oldham, G. R. & Hackman, J. R. (2010). Not what it was and not what it will be: The future of job design research. *Journal of Organizational Behavior, 31*(2-3), 463–479. doi:10.1002/job.678.

Park, Y., Fritz, C., & Jex, S. M. (2011). Relationships between work-home segmentation and psychological detachment from work: The role of communication technology use at home. *Journal of Occupational Health Psychology, 16,* 457–467. doi:10.1037/a0023594.

Pew Research Center (2017). 10 facts about smartphones as the iPhone turns 10. Retrieved from www.pewresearch.org/fact-tank/2017/06/28/10-facts-about-smartphones/.

Piszczek, M. M. & Berg, P. (2014). Expanding the boundaries of boundary theory: Regulative institutions and work-family role management. *Human Relations, 67* (12), 1491–1512. doi:10.1177/0018726714524241.

Porter, G. & Kakabadse, N. K. (2006). HRM perspectives on addiction to technology and work. *Journal of Management Development, 25*(6), 535–560. doi:10.1108/0262171061067011.

Ragu-Nathan, T. S., Tarafdar, M., & Ragu-Nathan, B. S. (2008). The consequences of technostress for end users in organizations: Conceptual development and empirical validation. *Information Systems Research, 19,* 417–433. doi:10.1287/isre.1070.0165.

Ramirez, A., Walther, J. B., Burgoon, J. K., & Sunnafrank, M. (2002). Information-seeking strategies, uncertainty, and computer-mediated communication. *Human Communication Research, 28,* 213–228. doi:10.1111/j.1468–2958.2002.tb00804.x.

Rennecker, J. & Godwin, L. (2005). Delays and interruptions: A self-perpetuating paradox of communication technology use. *Information and Organization, 15*(3), 247–266. doi:10.1016/j.infoandorg.2005.02.004.

Rosen, L. & Weil, M. (1997). *TechnoStress: Coping with technology @work @home @play.* Etobicoke, ON: John Wiley & Sons Canada.

Ryan, R. M. & Deci, E. L. (2000). Self-determination theory and the facilitation of intrinsic motivation, social development, and well-being. *American Psychologist, 55*(1), 68–78. doi:10.1037110003-066X.55.1.68.

Salomon, I. & Salomon, M. (1984). Telecommuting: The employee's perspective. *Technological Forecasting and Social Change, 25*(1), 15–28. doi:10.1016/0040–1625(84)90077–5.

Sheldon, K. M. & Elliot, A. J. (1999). Goal striving, need satisfaction, and longitudinal well-being: The self-concordance model. *Journal of Personality and Social Psychology, 76*(3), 482–497. doi:10.1037/0022–3514.76.3.482.

Shu, Q., Tu, Q., & Wang, K. (2011). The impact of computer self-efficacy and technology dependence on computer-related technostress: A social cognitive theory perspective. *International Journal of Human-Computer Interaction, 27*(10), 923–939. doi:10.1080/10447318.2011.555313.

Smith, M. J., Carayon, P., Sanders, K. J., Lim, S. Y., & LeGrande, D. (1992). Employee stress and health complaints in jobs with and without electronic performance monitoring, *Applied Ergonomics, 23*, 17–27. doi:10.1016/0003–6870(92)90006-H.

Sonnentag, S. (2001). Work, recovery activities, and individual well-being: A diary study. *Journal of Occupational Health Psychology, 6*(3), 196–210.

Sonnentag, S. & Bayer, U. V. (2005). Switching off mentally: Predictors and consequences of psychological detachment from work during off-job time. *Journal of Occupational Health Psychology, 10*(4), 393–414. doi:10.1037/1076–8998.10.4.393.

Sonnentag, S. & Fritz, C. (2007). The Recovery Experience Questionnaire: Development and validation of a measure for assessing recuperation and unwinding from work. *Journal of Occupational Health Psychology, 12*(3), 204–221. doi:10.1037/1076–8998.12.3.204.

Sonnentag, S. & Fritz, C. (2015). Recovery from job stress: The stressor-detachment model as an integrative framework. *Journal of Organizational Behavior, 36*, 72–103. doi:10.1002/job.1924.

Standen, P., Daniels, K., & Lamond, D. (1999). The home as a workplace: Work-family interaction and psychological well-being in telework. *Journal of Occupational Health Psychology, 4*, 368–381.

Stanton, J. M. & Weiss, E. M. (2000). Electronic monitoring in their own words: An exploratory study of employees' experiences with new types of surveillance. *Computers in Human Behavior, 16*, 423–440. doi:10.1016/S0747-5632(00)00018–2.

Steinmueller, W. E. (2000). Will new information and communication technologies improve the "codification" of knowledge? *Industrial and Corporate Change, 9*, 361–376. doi:10.1093/icc/9.2.361.

Syvänen, A., Mäkiniemi, J. P., Syrjä, S., Heikkilä-Tammi, K., & Viteli, J. (July, 2016). When does the educational use of ICT become a source of technostress for Finnish teachers? In *Seminar. Net: Media, Technology & Life-Long Learning* (Vol. 12, No. 2).

Tarafdar, M., Tu, Q., & Ragu-Nathan, T. S. (2010). Impact of technostress on end-user satisfaction and performance. *Journal of Management Information Systems, 27*, 303–334. doi:10.2753/MIS0742-1222270311.

Ter Hoeven, C. L., van Zoonen, W., & Fonner, K. L. (2016). The practical paradox of technology: The influence of communication technology use on employee burnout and engagement. *Communication Monographs*, *83*(2), 239–263. doi:10.1080/03637751.2015.1133920.

Thomée, S., Eklöf, M., Gustafsson, E., Nilsson, R., & Hagberg, M. (2007). Prevalence of perceived stress, symptoms of depression and sleep disturbances in relation to information and communication technology (ICT) use among young adults–an explorative prospective study. *Computers in Human Behavior*, *23*(3), 1300–1321.

Tims, M., Bakker, A. B., & Derks, D. (2013). The impact of job crafting on job demands, job resources, and well-being. *Journal of Occupational Health Psychology*, *18*(2), 230. doi:10.1037/a0032141.

Tomaskovic-Devey, D. & Risman, B. J. (1993). Telecommuting innovation and organization: a contingency theory of labor process change. *Social Science Quarterly*, *74* (2), 367–385.

Vasagar, J. (August 31, 2013). Out of hours working banned by German labour ministry. The Telegraph. Retrieved from www.telegraph.co.uk/news/worldnews/europe/germany/10276815/Out-of-hours-working-banned-by-German-labour-ministry.html.

Venkatesh, V. & Morris, M. G. (2000). Why don't men ever stop to ask for directions? Gender, social influence, and their role in technology acceptance and usage behavior. *MIS Quarterly*, *24*, 115–139. doi:10.2307/3250981.

Wall, T. D., Jackson, P. R., Mullarkey, S., & Parker, S. K. (1996). The demands – control model of job strain: A more specific test. *Journal of Occupational and Organizational Psychology*, *69*(2), 153–166. doi:10.1111/j.2044–8325.1996.tb00607.x.

Wang, A. (2017). France gives employees 'right to disconnect' from work emails. The Star. Retrieved from www.thestar.com/news/world/2017/01/02/france-gives-employees-right-to-disconnect-from-work-emails.html.

Weatherbee, T. & Kelloway, E. K. (2006). A case of cyberdeviancy: Cyberaggression in the workplace. In E. K. Kelloway, J. Barling, & J. J. Hurrell (Eds.), *Handbook of workplace violence* (pp. 445–487). Thousand Oaks, CA: Sage Publications.

Webster, D. M. & Kruglanski, A. W. (1994). Individual differences in need for cognitive closure. *Journal of Personality and Social Psychology*, *67*(6), 1049–1062. doi:10.1037/0022–3514.67.6.1049.

Wei, R. & Hwei Lo, V. (2006). Staying connected while on the move: Cell phone use and social connectedness. *New Media & Society*, *8*, 53–72. doi:10.1177/1461444806059870.

Whitley, B. E. (1997). Gender differences in computer-related attitudes and behavior: A meta-analysis. *Computers in Human Behavior*, *13*(1), 1–22. doi:10.1016/S0747-5632(96)00026-X.

Wilkes, S. M., Barber, L. K., & Rogers, A. P. (2017). Development and validation of the Workplace Interruptions Measure. *Stress and Health*, *34*, 1–13. doi:10.1002/smi.2765.

Wood, C. (2001). Dealing with tech rage. *MacLean's*, *114*(12), 41–42.

Wrzesniewski, A. & Dutton, J. E. (2001). Crafting a job: Revisioning employees as active crafters of their work. *Academy of Management Review*, *26*(2), 179–201. doi:10.5465/AMR.2001.4378011.

22 Technology and the Aging Worker

A Review and Agenda for Future Research

W. Jackeline Torres, Brittany C. Bradford, and Margaret E. Beier

The US population is growing older, and this trend is likely to continue (Colby & Ortman, 2015). Adults age 55 and older are expected to see an increase in workforce participation, from 11.8 percent in 1992 to 25.6 percent in 2022. At the same time, the share of younger workers age 16 to 22 is expected to decrease, dropping from 16.9 percent in 1992 to 11.3 percent in 2022 (Bureau of Labor Statistics, 2014). The world's population is also aging. The number of adults age 60 and older is projected to increase by 56 percent worldwide between 2015 and 2030 (United Nations, 2015). A concurrent workplace trend is the ubiquitous nature of technology. It is difficult to imagine a modern industry or organization that does not rely heavily on technology to remain profitable and competitive in today's global marketplace. Deployed properly, technology can improve workflow, increase worker efficiency and productivity, and improve organizational processes such as selection and training. The advent of smartphones and other devices that provide the power of personal computers in the palm of one's hand has made technology use a constant for all people – and blurred the lines between work and leisure time. Though adults of all ages use technology (for example, 64 percent of adults age 65 and older used the internet regularly in 2016; Pew Research Center, 2017), there are special considerations at the interface of technology and the aging workforce. The focus of the current chapter is on the experiences of aging workers interacting with technology in the workplace, focusing on digital technologies (computer software, hardware, and information networks).

Technology offers workers many advantages, including increased autonomy and efficiency, multiple ways of accomplishing company goals, and improved safety standards and procedures (Cascio & Montealegre, 2016). However, technology can also be a barrier to work productivity and performance depending on the interaction between the person and the tool, and the environment in which that interaction occurs. For example, a worker may have little prior knowledge or experience with a particular software program, the program may be designed without the user experience in mind, and use of the program may be less efficient and/or may introduce unforeseen errors into work processes, particularly when the program is new to the user (Ackerman, 1988). Workers may also be reluctant to adopt new technologies, instead preferring established processes that have proven effective in the past. Managers and co-workers can also consciously or unconsciously reinforce norms, whether they are to adopt new technologies or to use well-known procedures and routines instead (Ford et al., 1992; Rouiller & Goldstein, 1997).

This chapter presents a review of the issues and opportunities posed by the increasing use of technology in the workplace and the increasing age of the average worker. The review discusses the ideas presented in Figure 22.1. We consider two major technology-related activities for workers: (1) adopting technology and (2) using technology. For the purposes of this chapter, adopting technology is defined as the choice to engage in new technology, regardless of who initiates that choice (a user, an organization, or a colleague). Using this definition, adopting new technology can be considered analogous to the goal choice process that considers the value of desired outcomes and the probability that engaging in an activity – such as adopting a new tool – will be instrumental in obtaining desired outcomes (Vroom, 1964). We define using technology as the process of engaging with a tool after the choice has been made to adopt it. It is considered analogous to the goal striving process that engages metacognitive processes such as self-efficacy and self-regulation in the successful use of technology (Campbell & Pritchard, 1976). In practice, technology adoption and use are not as cleanly delineated; that is, a person might make a choice to engage with a new tool only to abandon it, then reengage with it, and so forth. Consequently, some of what we discuss will be relevant to both technology use and adoption.

Antecedents of technology adoption and use considered in this review are (1) person-related factors such as a person's level of ability and his or her motivation to attain outcomes related to technology use and (2) the characteristics (affordances and design) of the technology. We also describe the broader context in which decisions to adopt and use technology take place, recognizing the influence of organizational policies and ageism on worker behavior.

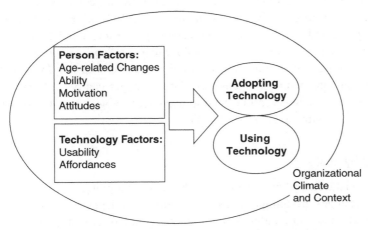

Figure 22.1 *Illustration of the person, technology, and environmental factors that influence the adoption and use of technology*

The chapter is organized in five sections. In 22.1, we describe the person-factors that influence adopting and using technology, focusing on age-related changes expected to affect these outcomes. Section 22.2 focuses on the characteristics of technology – and technological advancements – that are likely to affect the adoption and use of technology for all workers, with special consideration for older workers. Section 22.3 focuses on the organizational climate and contextual factors that support or provide barriers to successful technology use for older workers. In 22.4 we discuss the current state of technology in the workplace in the context of person (i.e., age-related changes) and contextual factors. Section 22.5 concludes with a review of interventions designed to address some of the specific challenges associated with age and technology adoption and use, and provides recommended directions for future research.

22.1 Age-Related Changes that Influence Technology Adoption and Use

Theories of workplace aging (Kanfer & Ackerman, 2004) suggest that age-related changes in cognitive abilities, motivation, and one's perception of one's own abilities (self-efficacy) affect the extent to which workers will adopt and use technologies. However, there is much confusion about the definition of older workers. In the current chapter, we examine sources of age differences, including physical, social, and psychological changes, and how these changes may facilitate or hinder successful technology use in the workplace. We discuss normative age-related changes, while acknowledging the idiosyncratic nature in which people age; that is, aging does not occur at an identical rate or pattern across the population. One 50-year-old, for instance, might resemble a 70-year-old in terms of his or her physical and cognitive abilities, while another more resembles a 30-year-old (Hertzog et al., 2008). As a result of these idiosyncrasies, there is no definitive age at which a worker becomes an "older" worker. While considering general age trajectories is instructive for understanding how older workers use technology in the workplace and how best to design technology for this population, the interaction of technology and worker age is not dependent on a specific age or even a more general age range. Even though this complicates our discussion, fortunately most interventions intended to mitigate age-related changes can benefit workers of all ages because these interventions tend to make technology easier to use for everyone (Truxillo, Cadiz, & Hammer, 2015).

22.1.1 Physical

Aging is characterized by a decline of physical functioning. Trajectories of these physical changes are unique to each individual and depend on lifestyle choices, genetics, and the social-cultural environment (e.g., Koster et al., 2006). Although cosmetic physical changes associated with aging (e.g., hair loss, graying hair, wrinkles) may affect older worker self-esteem and identity (Kwon, 2017), and these effects should not be underestimated, some physical changes more directly affect daily functioning (e.g., physical strength or movement limitations, visual changes, hearing impairment). Physical limitations make it challenging for older adults to use certain tools, such as manipulating a stylus, pressing small buttons, or using audio equipment (Chen & Chan, 2014). Charness and Boot (2009) postulate that poor design can contribute to older adults' higher levels of computer anxiety, as adults recognize that the technology with which they are interacting has not been designed to meet their needs, leading to decreased self-efficacy and reduced motivation to adopt and use new tools. A detailed discussion of the physical changes associated with aging are beyond the scope of the chapter; we direct readers to resources that discuss physical changes associated with aging in-depth (see Timiras, 2007; Whitbourne, 2002).

22.1.2 Cognitive Abilities

Cognitive aging research suggests that abilities related to memory and learning new information tend to increase up until early adulthood and then start to decline with increased age (Carroll, 1993; McGrew, 2005; Salthouse, 2010). These abilities are related to processing new knowledge and go by many names (e.g., "fluid abilities" or "reasoning abilities"); here we use the term reasoning abilities to simplify the presentation. Conversely, the knowledge that one acquires through education, job, and leisure experiences remains stable or continues to grow throughout the life-span. These abilities also have many different names, including "knowledge" and "crystallized abilities"; here we refer to them as knowledge abilities (Carroll, 1993; Cattell, 1987; Salthouse, 2010).

Ability-age trajectories affect a person's ability to use technology. For example, declines in reasoning abilities will affect learning new software or hardware (Beier, Teachout, & Cox, 2012; Carter & Beier, 2010; Kelley & Charness, 1995). Reasoning abilities support navigation and finding one's way through unknown internet websites by facilitating problem solving and memory for recent activity that permit finding one's way back after mistakes are made (Chadwick-Dias, McNulty, & Tullis, 2003). These reasoning skills are most relevant when users are completely unfamiliar with the technological environment, because in these cases users cannot rely on their prior experience (i.e., knowledge abilities) to support their new learning (Beier & Ackerman, 2005).

Conversely, situations in which users can rely on their prior learning or existing knowledge and expertise are somewhat less cognitively demanding (Beier & Ackerman, 2005). For instance, workers who have used the same word-processing program for years may be able to easily use it to solve a new problem (e.g., conduct a mail merge for the first time) because their prior experiences provide some understanding of how the program and process may be organized. However, if the word processing software is significantly re-organized or if a new word processing interface is chosen, the task will tax memory and other reasoning abilities more than it taxes existing knowledge abilities. As such, older workers would be expected to experience more difficulty than younger workers. In support of these ideas, an age and technology study by Charness, Kelley, Bosman, and Mottram (2001) found that the cost of learning new technology was minimized when older adults had previous experience with the technology, as they outperformed novice older adults.

One unique challenge at the intersection of workplace technology and the aging workforce is that technology is constantly changing, making it difficult for older workers to rely on their existing knowledge as much as they might have been able to in decades past. Extensive experience with technology would theoretically support new learning for older workers, but due to declining reasoning abilities with age, older workers can expect any new learning, and by extension the use of new technology, to be increasingly difficult as they age (e.g., the negative relationship between age and training outcomes; Kubeck et al., 1996). Moreover, increased difficulty in learning should negatively affect a worker's motivation for adopting and learning new technology. As will be described next, the relationship between effort and performance is likely to change through the lifespan in important ways that affect perceptions of the probability that adopting new technology will ultimately pay off (Kanfer & Ackerman, 2004).

22.1.3 Motivation

Motivation concerns the direction, intensity, and persistence of behavior (Kanfer, 1990). Valence-Instrumentality-Expectancy (VIE; Vroom, 1964) theory of motivation describes three components that work together to affect the motivating potential of a given activity: (1) valence of a desired outcome (e.g., a raise), (2) instrumentality, or a person's belief that a performance of a certain behavior will be instrumental in obtaining an outcome (e.g., believing that if one learns a new skill, he or she will receive a raise), and (3) expectancy, or a person's belief that increased effort will lead to desired performance on the goal-related task (e.g., believing that one can expend the effort to learn this new skill). VIE theory recognizes that motivation is idiosyncratic in that the extent to which people value outcomes and hold beliefs about instrumentality and expectations will depend on their own values, abilities, and self-efficacy.

There are some normative ways in which age affects VIE judgments, however (Kanfer & Ackerman, 2004). First, age should affect the valence that people assign certain goals. The theory of socio-emotional selectivity (SST), for instance, suggests that as people age, their goals shift from achievement-focused to socio-emotional (Carstensen, Isaacowitz, & Charles, 1999). This shift is thought to be a function of perceived time left in one's life. When a person's time horizon is perceived as unlimited, he or she is likely to pursue goals related to advancement (the future is full of possibilities!). However, when people begin to perceive their occupational time horizon as limited, such as a pending retirement, they are likely to shift their goals from self-development to developing emotional ties with others, a proposition that has been generally supported by meta-analytic research (Kooij et al., 2011). In the context of adopting technology, it is possible that older workers might not see a strong internal incentive to learn new technology because they expect to have less time to use their newly learned skills on the job given that they will retire relatively soon. To the extent that adopting new technology is associated with achievement goals (e.g., one must learn a new software program to advance in an organization), SST suggests a relatively weak relationship between adoption and age.

Selection, Optimization, and Compensation theory (SOC) is another motivation theory relevant in the context of age and technology adoption. Selection refers to the selection of a goal (i.e., what a person chooses to do); optimization refers to optimizing the talents that one has toward goal achievement (e.g., choosing strategies that align with one's expertise); compensation refers to the process of compensating for shortcomings in goal pursuit. Examples of compensation include using an organization system that relies on sticky notes to compensate for age-related changes in memory abilities or wearing glasses to compensate for age-related vision loss. SOC theory posits that as people age, they are likely to select environments or activities with which they already have some experience, enabling them to capitalize on their strengths and existing expertise (Baltes & Baltes, 1990).

Predictions about technology adoption in the context of the SOC model are not straightforward (Baltes & Baltes, 1990). On the one hand, SOC theory suggests that older workers will be less likely to adopt new technologies because of their tendency to self-select into environments in which they can take advantage of their existing technical knowledge. In this context, SOC theory would reinforce the idea that age will be negatively related to adopting new technology. On the other hand, SOC theory would suggest that older workers' motivation to adopt new technology will increase if workers believe that new technology will help them compensate for age-related losses. For example, age-related changes in vision can be mitigated through easily adjustable interface fonts and better lighting; memory can be augmented through calendaring and reminder systems (Beier et al., 2012). Moreover, case studies suggest that older workers generally embrace technology designed to accommodate age-related changes in physical and cognitive abilities (Beier, 2015). A case study at a BMW plant in Germany, for example, found that employees welcomed small changes to a manufacturing line that increased worker comfort and accommodated age-related physical changes related to joint pain, as worker productivity increased, and average retirement age rose (Economist Intelligence Unit, 2011). A study by Melenhorst, Rogers, and Bouwhuis (2006) provides further evidence that older workers embrace technology when they perceive benefits in doing so. Using focus groups consisting of American and Dutch older adults, Melenhorst et al. (2006) found that older adults demonstrated positive motivation to use communication technology (i.e., email) when its benefits were apparent. When older adults did not understand the benefits the technology would provide, they were not motivated to use the technology. The researchers suggested that older adults might avoid using new technology not because of the perceived costs in doing so (e.g., time, energy), but rather because the value of its adoption is not apparent.

Age-related changes in abilities, as described previously, affect motivation in part because older workers are aware of the changes within themselves. Through their own experiences, older workers understand that learning becomes increasingly effortful because it entails adjusting well-learned routines and/or establishing completely new ones (Beier et al., 2012). In the parlance of VIE theory (Vroom, 1964) aging affects perceptions of the effort involved in any activity (Kanfer & Ackerman, 2004), which will, in turn, affect motivation for adopting and using technology. Even if older workers value an outcome and understand the instrumentality of certain behaviors for achieving that outcome, if they perceive the effort involved in performing those behaviors to be too great, motivation for the activity will be reduced (Kanfer & Ackerman, 2004).

Self-efficacy is another component of motivation related to people's expectancy judgments. Self-efficacy, defined as a person's belief that he or she can engage the resources necessary to accomplish a specific goal (Bandura, 1982), is a function of successful experiences engaging in an activity. It can be negatively affected when one experiences failure or difficulty performing a task. For instance, as workers notice age-related changes within themselves (e.g., related to memory and difficulty in learning new things), their self-efficacy for learning and continuous development activity such as on-the-job training may suffer (Maurer, 2001). Self-efficacy has been studied in the context of aging and technology and has been shown to be an important predictor of the successful use of technology in the workplace among older adults. Computer self-efficacy, or a person's belief in his or her ability to learn new computer technology, has been a particularly influential area of research (Compeau & Higgins, 1995). For example, Reed, Doty, and May (2005) found that older employees' self-efficacy beliefs, and not the fact that they were older, *per se*, influenced their ability to learn new computer skills. Nonetheless, on average, older adults have lower computer self-efficacy than younger adults do, which in turn is related to a wide variety of work-related outcomes (Poynton, 2005; Wagner, Hassanein, & Head, 2010).

Self-efficacy can affect attitudes about technology use, and these attitudes subsequently affect actual technology use (Chen & Chan, 2014; Elias et al., 1987). Because of limited experience or due to salient negative experiences, older workers are also likely to have more negative attitudes about technology (Dyck & Smither, 1994; Poynton, 2005). Despite the expectation that older workers will have less efficacy for using technology, research suggests that older workers generally understand the benefits of technology. Focus groups conducted with 113 adults between the ages of 65 and 85 found that older adults expressed more positive attitudes toward technologies than they did negative attitudes (Mitzner et al., 2010). Reasons for positive attitudes included support for work activities (e.g., sharing documents with coworkers), the features of the technology (e.g., speed, storage), and the convenience of the technology (e.g., typing instead of handwritten notes). In summary, older workers are likely to feel somewhat ambivalent about technology – they realize its benefits but their reduced efficacy for its use makes engagement with technology less appealing – and this ambivalence is likely to affect technology adoption and use. A summary of the major challenges at the interface of age-related individual differences and technology, as well as suggested solutions to these issues, is shown in Table 22.1.

Table 22.1 *Individual differences: Barriers and solutions to workplace technology for older adults*

	Challenges	Solutions
Physical	Decline in visual perception and hearing, and reduction in physical strength or motor control	Emphasize technology designs that take into consideration physical (e.g., button distance on interfaces) and perceptual limitations (e.g., font size, availability of subtitles)
Ability (reasoning and knowledge/experience)	Declining reasoning ability, low levels of familiarity with evolving technology	Minimize working memory demands on computer tasks, update technology only when necessary
Motivation and goals	Shift away from achievement motivation, low belief that the effort will be worth it in context of upcoming retirement	Emphasize the benefits of technology beyond career advancement, including ability to compensate for age-related losses
Attitudes	Technology anxiety, low computer self-efficacy	Encourage increased computer experience, including social support, and recognition of successes

Researchers have proposed and tested models of technology acceptance and use (e.g., Davis, 1989; Venkatesh et al., 2003), such as the Technology Acceptance Model (TAM; see Davis, 1989), which proposes that perceived usefulness and perceived ease of use predict information technology acceptance, and the Unified Theory of Acceptance and Use of Technology (UTAUT), which suggests that technology acceptance (defined as actual use) is influenced by both individual factors (i.e., performance expectancy, effort expectancy) and the environment (i.e., social influence, facilitation conditions). One model is directly relevant to aging: Chen and Chan (2014) proposed a senior technology acceptance model (STAM) that uses age-related health and ability characteristics to predict technology attitudes and use. Testing of this model found that age-related health and ability characteristics were related to the use of technology while self-efficacy, along with a supportive environment, facilitated technology use. These models emphasize that the motivation to use and adopt technology is influenced by myriad factors, including those predicted by the VIE framework, such as confidence in achieving success (or self-efficacy), and the value of the predicted outcome (e.g., using technology to connect with family).

22.2 Characteristics of Technology

Research suggests that, similar to younger people, older people are likely to use a variety of technology in their daily lives (Bock, 2015). Anderson and Perrin

(2017) analyzed survey data from a 2016 Pew Research Center (2017) survey and found that many older adults aged 65 and older own smartphones (approximately 40 percent), use the internet (67 percent), own tablets (32 percent), and use social media (34 percent). Researchers also asked adult internet users how technology fits into their everyday work lives (Purcell & Rainie, 2014) and, perhaps not surprisingly, office workers identified using email, internet, and phone regularly to accomplish job tasks. These tools did not vary by age (e.g., workers of all ages are likely to use keyboards, mice, basic software; Olson et al., 2011). Younger workers reported using technology more frequently than older workers, however, and they also reported using a broader range of technologies (e.g., touchscreen devices, advanced software such as presentation software and programming software) than older workers.

Regardless of the specific tools workers use, the evolution of technology in the workplace has indisputably benefitted all workers. First and foremost, technology fundamentally changes job requirements through its ability to take over physically demanding or repetitive tasks, which can extend the work lifespan for many workers across an array of industries (from knowledge work to physical labor). Moreover, technological advancements that replace human labor can make jobs safer by reducing the likelihood that workers will suffer acute or chronic work-related injury. For jobs that continue to require workers to perform physical or repetitive tasks, technology can assist task execution through the automation of task components that are particularly demanding. For instance, robot-assisted labor to support physical job tasks, originally developed in the manufacturing industry, has now expanded to fields as diverse as aircraft production, healthcare, and construction, and many devices have been designed to extend the working lifespan of aging employees (Bock, 2015). Robotics can also supplement fine motor control, such as in the field of surgery, where there is evidence that robot-assisted surgery produces better outcomes than manual techniques in endoscopic surgery (Broeders, 2014). Automatic system monitoring and system checks can also improve safety because some work-related processes are nonoperational unless all safety precautions have been considered. These automatic system and process checks can reduce human error by reducing the memory burden of system reviews for workers.

There is a concern that automation may eventually replace workers of all ages and across industries (Fozard, 2017). Although we may eventually see technology dramatically change the way people engage in work, workers may continue to work alongside technology tools, providing needed creativity and problem-solving skills to work processes. Therefore, it is crucial to examine the factors that predict attitudes toward technology as well as its use in the workplace (e.g., trust in automation, self-efficacy) and to obtain the input of users. In sum, technology's ability to take over physical and repetitive task demands in some jobs, and its ability to monitor work-related processes can make jobs safer for employees and make many jobs accessible to older workers (Charness & Boot, 2009). For a discussion on automation in the workplace and projected trends in automation, we refer readers to additional resources (Autor, 2015; Frey & Osborne, 2017; Nokelainen, Nevalainen, & Niemi, 2018).

In addition to its impact on job demands, technology renders many work-related processes customizable to the unique needs of the worker. A simple example is the customizability of font size and computer screen brightness for jobs that rely heavily on computer work. Customization is likely to benefit all workers, but because of changes in vision, hearing, and physical abilities that accompany aging, it may be particularly important for older workers (Czaja et al., 2001). Charness and Boot (2009) summarize three ways in which technology can impact older adults in work, in leisure, and in safeguarding their health:

1. Prevention: Technology can prevent impairments associated with age. For instance, using physical input devices can prevent injury due to fine motor control degradation.
2. Augmentation: Technology can facilitate customization for individual declines from aging. For instance, interface options with bigger font sizes can counteract declines in visual acuity.
3. Substitution: Technology can be designed to execute physically demanding tasks previously performed by workers, extending the work lifespan.

These three factors can be broadly considered in the context of non-work activities that affect working adults. For instance, in terms of substitution, the ability to telecommute will minimize the need for many workers to drive to work, which could potentially extend the working lifespan for aging workers who might be experiencing declines in some driving-related abilities (De Raedt & Ponjaert-Kristoffersen, 2000). Older workers who desire greater flexibility in work schedules might be able to engage in socio-emotional goals such as mentoring, family engagement, or pursuing hobbies or opportunities that may be salient to them in retirement (Carstensen et al., 2000; Sharit et al., 2009).

An important consideration of the interface of aging and technology is the dynamic nature and interaction between the two domains. Similar to the effect of constant technological change, the effect of age on a person's abilities, traits, and goals is a moving target (Kanfer & Ackerman, 2004). Despite its benefits, technology can be perceived as a barrier for some work processes, particularly for older workers, when it is designed without regard for the end user (Charness & Boot, 2009). The diversity in how people age makes it impossible to design technology for a specific age group; rather, the goal should be to design for the dynamic diversity in how abilities change with age (Gregor, Newell, & Zajicek, 2002). The field of technology development in the workforce is increasingly focusing on user-centered design (UCD), which is a systematic process for designing products and technologies that best serve the needs of the users and the environments and circumstances under which they will use the product.

22.2.1 Design Considerations for Older Workers: Cognitive and Physical Demands

Recommendations from usability research will render systems easier to use for all workers, but they might especially benefit older workers due to the cognitive and motivational changes described earlier. Here we discuss design considerations based on UCD and gerontechnology research. *Gerontechnology* is the field of study into how aging affects technology usage, the needs of older adults as they age, and how best to design technological products that meet these needs (Czaja & Lee, 2007). Tasks with high cognitive load can be detrimental to performance for workers of all ages, particularly when the cognitive demands of the task exceed cognitive resources available (Mayhorn, Rogers, & Fisk, 2004; Sweller, 2011). However, to the extent that tasks rely on novel problem solving or reasoning abilities for performance, the negative effect of cognitive load on performance should be exacerbated for older adults because reasoning abilities decline with age. Unfortunately, many computing tasks incur a heavy cognitive load. Technology designed to provide complex information at a rapid pace will tax attentional abilities, and thus may be more difficult for older versus younger workers to use (Singh, 2000). Technology that taps multiple abilities will likewise result in high cognitive load for older workers. For example, data entry performance is dependent on psychomotor speed and attentional abilities; word processing performance depends on spatial memory and motor control; and research and writing depend on multiple cognitive skills such as learning, problem-solving, attention, and reasoning (Czaja & Lee, 2007). One caveat, however, is that performance for well-learned tasks should not be affected by age.

Due to the physical processes of aging, older employees may have reduced visual acuity, reduced hearing as well as a reduced ability to distinguish relevant auditory information from background noise, and reduced motor control (Sjölinder, 2006). For example, older adults who have experienced declines in visual acuity may struggle to interpret visual icons in an interface if the icon's design is complex (Hawthorn, 2000). Older adults may also find it more difficult to navigate computer screens with high degrees of visual clutter (Craik & Anderson, 1999). Further, a study of reading performance on many mobile computing devices found that older adults' performance was lower than younger adults' performance due to the screens having low contrast and small text sizes (Omori et al., 2002). Programs that involve responding to recorded spoken instructions by high-pitched voices or audio alerts may be difficult for older trainees to hear, as older adults frequently lose hearing sensitivity to sounds or words that are too high in pitch (presbycusis; Schieber, 2013). There is also evidence that many older adults experience loss of sensitivity to light physical pressure and high frequency vibrations on their hands (Hawthorn, 2000), meaning that tactile interactions with touchscreen devices may require different device settings for older adults to be able to interact effectively with the device. Design guidelines for older adults have been provided by researchers that address declines in vision (e.g., use appropriate lighting, reduce glare, provide adjustable light sources), hearing (e.g., use adjustable sound levels, provide an additional sensory channel such as vibration, minimize environmental noise), and speech perception (e.g., use appropriate pauses in speech, avoid speech rates that are too fast; see Fisk et al., 2009).

Precision and motor control-based mouse performance, including dragging and dropping tasks and pointing to and clicking in precise locations on the screen, are also significantly worse in older populations (Namazi & McClintic, 2003). Double-clicking, which requires rapidly clicking a mouse button twice while keeping the mouse itself still, is one of the most difficult types of mouse control for older adults to perform (Sjölinder, 2006). Technology that requires wrist rotation to use may also be especially difficult for older adults (Chaparro et al., 2000). Technological design strategies that address age-related changes in visual perception (e.g., assess color decisions), auditory perception (e.g., use semantic context to enhance speech perception), and touch and movement (e.g., consider button or control distance relative to user) are discussed in Scialfa, Ho, and Laberge (2004).

Usability is central to the UCD process: it is a multidimensional construct that includes how intuitive users find the structure and navigation of tools; how quickly users understand interfaces; how memorable the steps are to complete tasks (the users' ability to memorize and re-create the steps); identifying where users are most likely to make errors, the seriousness of errors, and the users' ability to recover from them; and how much users enjoy interacting with the tools (US Department of Health & Human Services, 2013). Best practices in usability include using interface elements that are consistent and predictable (for example, allowing multiple selections if square checkboxes are used, but only one selection if circular radio buttons are used), planning screen layouts to prioritize placing the most important elements or information in the most visible locations, carefully using typography (larger font sizes or different font faces) to create hierarchy and improve scanning speed, and using clear notifications to communicate errors, changes in states (such as a screen showing the technology is performing the requested action), and logical next steps (Martin, 1996). Pak and McLaughlin (2010) developed a list of ten suggestions to maximize technology usability for older adults, including minimizing the short-term memory demands users incur navigating between different screens of the interface, creating error messages that provide information on potential solutions to the problem, and using natural, clear language free of jargon and unnecessary dialogue. As another example of different usability needs for older workers, meta-analytic studies show that older workers benefit most from technology training that occurs at a slower rate or is self-paced (Callahan et al., 2003).

In summary, well-designed technology for older workers should minimize the effects of physical deficits and reduce cognitive load to the greatest extent possible, which would benefit workers of all ages as well. Table 22.2 provides a summary of the technology challenges employees face in the workplace, as well as suggested solutions to mitigate these concerns. Notably, the interaction between the worker and technology does not happen in a vacuum. Indeed, just as individual and technological factors influence the adoption and use of technology, so will the context in which work gets done.

Table 22.2 *Technology characteristics: Barriers and solutions to workplace technology for older adults*

	Challenges	Solutions
Physical usability	Many types of technology fail to provide optimal design for older workers, including their reduced vision, hearing, physical strength, and fine motor control	Increase user control over visual and auditory settings, reduce need for hand and wrist input devices, simplify visual interfaces
Cognitive load demands	Reduced reasoning abilities lead to difficulties processing complex information, difficulties in navigation schema due to reduced spatial ability	Decrease new information shown simultaneously, make previous information easy to re-access if working memory fails, simplify navigation options, conform to UCD best practices in interface design

22.3 Contextual Factors

22.3.1 Socioeconomic Barriers

One of the most pervasive determinants of the adoption and use of technology is income level. The digital divide, which refers to differential access and use of technology based on socioeconomic status (OECD, 2002), may be further exacerbated for older people, who may be less experienced, more anxious, and more negative about technology (Czaja et al., 2006). The effect of aging in the context of reduced technology usage has been termed the "grey digital divide" (Millward, 2003). Evidence for the grey digital divide can be seen in data on technology use; over 6,000 phone interviews with Americans found that smartphone ownership was 42 percent for older adults with annual household incomes of at least $75,000, compared to 8 percent for older adults with annual household incomes of less than $30,000 (Smith, 2014).

In addition to the grey digital divide, older workers are more likely to fall into other demographic groups that have experienced disadvantages in the availability and use of technology (Witte & Mannon, 2010). Older adults are more likely to have a lower household income and to have less formal education than other groups, both factors that are correlated with negative job outcomes, including lower computer skills, an asset that is considered critical in an internet-dependent workforce (van Deursen & van Dijk, 2011). Therefore many older workers have a fundamentally different background in technology independent of their interest or ability to use technology, a difference that must be considered when attempting to increase successful technology use among aging workers. Beyond organizational experiences, these differences in technology use and adoption based on socioeconomic status and education could limit exposure to information and opportunities for those in society who might most benefit from them (e.g., engaging in a massive open online course [MOOC] to obtain job skills; applying for jobs online).

Because research in technology access often addresses factors outside an organization, it may be tempting to disregard the importance of socioeconomic status, age, and technology use and adoption as unrelated to the worker and organizational experience and thus tangential to the concerns of organizational scientists. However, technology provides access to information that affects success in all realms of life, including work. For example, as organizations continue to use technology to advertise job openings and recruit and select employees for jobs, access to technology will have a greater impact on occupational success (Badger, Kaminsky, & Behrend, 2014). Organizations will need to consider access to technology as an important barrier to opportunities as automation in human resources (HR) practices continues to expand.

22.3.2 Ageism

Ageism is the stereotyping of, and discrimination against, older people (Butler, 1975). There is evidence that ageist attitudes permeate organizations, including older workers receiving fewer promotions and training opportunities, and more negative performance feedback than younger workers (Posthuma & Campion, 2009). Ageism is different from other discrimination aimed at specific groups, because it is more pervasive as many people – even older people themselves – subscribe to ageist beliefs (Posthuma & Campion, 2009). Some of the most pervasive age-related stereotypes are about older workers being less productive, more difficult to train, and less flexible to try new things like technology (Chiu et al., 2001; Posthuma & Campion, 2009). Not all age-related stereotypes are negative; older adults may be perceived as being reliable or trustworthy (Posthuma & Campion, 2009). Still, negative age stereotypes in the workplace can limit the opportunities (e.g., training) available to older adults. Perhaps because they are so prevalent and likely to be held by older workers themselves, age-related stereotypes are rarely recognized as a problem in organizations, and organizations have few efforts to counteract ageism against older employees (Lagacé et al., 2016).

Age-based stereotypes that hiring managers, supervisors, and co-workers hold toward aging workers may negatively influence the opportunities that older workers receive to learn new technologies (Nelson, 2004). Ilgen and Youtz (1986) discuss "lost opportunities" for minority employees in organizations, and a similar concept can be applied to older workers. For example, training opportunities might not be offered to older workers because aging workers are assumed to be uninterested in learning new technology, to be untrainable, or to be a poor business investment due to being close to retirement age (Maurer, 2001).

Social cognitive theory, which examines the processes through which people seek to understand others (Fiske & Taylor, 2013), can serve as a useful framework through which to examine how stereotypes can affect technology use among older workers. Specifically, the theory states that people use characteristics of others (such as age) to categorize them (Hummert et al., 1994). Though this process is a time-saving heuristic and not intentionally discriminatory, in practice it can invoke stereotypes, many of which are negative, in the context of aging and technology use (Davis & Songer, 2009; Hess & Blanchard-Fields, 1999). As a result of older adults' awareness of negative stereotypes of aging, they may experience stereotype threat, or the fear of fulfilling a perceived stereotype of a group they belong to (Nelson, 2004). Experiencing stereotype threat can take up cognitive resources, resulting in decrements in older adults' task performance (Chasteen et al., 2005; Hess et al., 2003).

Stereotypes that impact managers' and organizations' beliefs may also affect older workers' psychological disengagement and reduce their willingness to adopt new technologies. Psychological disengagement happens when an employee detaches his or her perceptions of success or failure in a certain domain from his or her identity in order to protect self-esteem (Major & Schmader, 1998). Older adults may use digital disengagement from learning and technology as a defense mechanism and protect their self-esteem for any past or predicted failures. This practice can create a self-fulfilling prophecy as older adults begin to avoid computer usage and thus do not gain experience in using new technology (Lagacé et al., 2016; Wandke, Sengpiel, & Sönksen, 2012).

In summary, ageism and patterns of overt or even subtle discrimination against older workers create troublesome long-term consequences. Workers might be offered fewer opportunities for significant growth in exposure and use of workplace technology. Repercussions could reverberate to the organizational level as well, as managers find themselves unable to fill positions vacated by early retirements of older workers mistakenly considered less valuable to the organization and unable to learn new technology.

22.3.3 Job Characteristics

The Demand-Control Model (DCM; Cascio, 2014; Karasek Jr., 1979) refers to the balance (or lack thereof) between job demands (such as deadlines and work overload) and job control, or the degree to which the employee has autonomy over how he or she fulfills role responsibilities. A job that is high in both demands and control is thought to be challenging yet engaging. Conversely, a job that is high in demands and low in individual control is predicted to cause job strain, which can include job anxiety, physical and mental health concerns, exhaustion, and stress (Bakker & Demerouti, 2007). Technology can be expected to influence both job-related demands and control in ways that will affect the experience of all workers, but may be particularly meaningful for older workers.

We have previously described the affordances of technology in terms of reducing job demands through customization of work processes to the unique needs of the worker and the facilitation or elimination of physically demanding or repetitive tasks. But because older workers are likely to lag behind younger workers in terms of their adoption of technology, jobs that place heavy demands on workers by requiring them to constantly update their technological skills may be more difficult for older workers to perform compared to younger workers (Ilmarinen, Tuomi, & Klockars, 1997). More generally, as the pervasiveness of technology in the workplace increases, so do expectations about the volume of work that an individual worker can and should be able to do in the course of a workday. Consider expectations about managing the volume of email a typical office worker now receives – and corresponding expected response times – versus responding to office correspondence two decades ago. Moreover, reading and responding to emails interrupts concentration on tasks from which employees are not able to immediately recover (Barley, Meyerson, & Grodal, 2011). As technology becomes more pervasive in the workplace, it will be important to weigh whether its benefits (e.g., for reducing the demands of some tasks and providing increased control) outweigh its costs (e.g., increasing expectations for the volume and rate of work) in terms of increasing job demands (Thompson & Mayhorn, 2012).

In addition to its effect on job demands, some technologies should increase worker control over job tasks by providing the means to choose how and where work gets done. One way in which technology adoption can increase worker perceptions of autonomy and control that may be particularly relevant for older workers is by facilitating flexible work schedules, providing workers the means to accomplish work virtually and the autonomy to decide when and where work gets done (Cascio, 2014). For older workers, opportunities for flexible work arrangements may play a role in delaying retirement decisions, allowing organizations to retain talented and experienced older workers. For instance, when knowledgeable older workers want to continue to contribute to the organization, but no longer desire full time work, flexible work arrangements can keep them working longer in ways that benefit the organization. As such, flexible work arrangements have been suggested as an organizational strategy that can be used to retain older workers, as they may perceive greater autonomy in their jobs and be less likely to retire (Beier, 2015).

22.3.4 Norms

Organizational norms influence how much people adopt new technology, and age may influence or interact with norms in important ways. Norms are tied to peer and supervisor influences, and may affect technology adoption (Morris & Vankatesh, 2000). In a five-month study of 118 workers within an organization who were introduced to a new software system, Morris and Vankatesh (2000) found that younger workers' intentions to adopt new technology were influenced by their judgments about how useful the technology was; older workers were more likely to be influenced by subjective norms. Organizations might be able to influence social norms through managing the messages sent to workers. For instance, Maurer (2001) proposed that one factor why older employees may participate less in career development activities is because of declines in self-efficacy for career-relevant learning. He provided examples of different strategies to increase self-efficacy, such as older employees' success stories in training and development be made known within the organization and training materials that include depictions of workers of all ages successfully learning the training material. To the extent that organizations can manage company norms, training and performance outcomes may improve, particularly for older workers. See Table 22.3 for a summary of these contextual challenges that older workers face, as well as suggestions to implement these solutions in practice.

22.4 Technology in Workplace Processes

For many workers, technology impacts most every aspect of their work experience: from the first time they apply for a job, through onboarding, training, and eventual exit from the workforce.

22.4.1 Technological Use in HR Processes

Technology use in employee selection systems has been on the rise since 2008, for both small and large organizations. Technology developments can also be seen in the digital formatting of traditional personality, interest, and ability assessments, including the use of internet testing, mobile assessments, virtual role-plays, and simulation games (Ryan & Ployhart, 2014). The use of technology in selection systems benefits organizations by generally reducing the number of resources needed (e.g., staff, physical space) to administer the assessments.

Table 22.3 *Contextual factors: Barriers and solutions to workplace technology for older adults*

	Challenges	Solutions
Socioeconomic barriers	"Grey digital divide," lower access to computers, computers were not part of early education	Increase computer access and training, increase perceptions of the value of technology
Ageism and stereotyping	More likely to be laid off, less training, fewer promotions, leads to psychological disengagement	Assign fewer routine job tasks, explicitly discourage ageist treatment and communication, provide training opportunities
Job characteristics	Difficulties in using technology may increase job demands, increased job expectations that may be higher than older workers performed in prior decades	Increase worker proficiency in technology that will increase job control, reduce job demands through customized workflow changes, offer flexible work schedules
Social changes and norms	Workplace norms may not explicitly support the value of technology use	Increase manager and organizational communication of technology norms, increase visibility of older workers' successes in using technology

The job search process increasingly requires participation in technology. Job seekers can find job openings online (e.g., company's webpage, online job board), submit applications online, and participate in job interviews remotely over the internet. Technology use for job search varies among job seekers by age. Smith (2015) found that among adults age 18 to 29, 83 percent looked up job information online and 79 percent applied for a job position online. By contrast, among adults 50 to 64, 43 percent looked up job information online and 32 percent applied for a job position online. Job seekers also use social media during the job search process. However, not all social media users engage with available social media features and services in the same way, and these use differences may be associated with age (El Ouirdi et al., 2015; Nakai et al., 2011). Smith (2015) found that among social media users, 24 percent of adults 50 years of age and older use social media during the job search process, as compared to 43 percent of adults between the ages of 18 to 29 who say they use social media during the job search process. Given the prevalence of electronic job advertisements and applications, job applicants may find themselves at a disadvantage (e.g., less likely to find job openings) without using certain technology tools during the job search process (Smith, 2015).

In the context of workplace aging, it would benefit organizations to have a clear understanding of the motivations and needs of older job seekers applying for specific positions. Nakai, Chang, Snell, and Fluckinger (2011) used a cluster analysis to identify three profiles of older job seekers: (a) those primarily interested in earning a full-time, secure wage, (b) those who had more flexibility in choosing to work or not to work and were interested in personal growth, and (c) those who had a diverse set of reasons for being interested in employment but generally wanted full-time employment that met their internal criteria for both job and organizational characteristics. As Nakai et al. (2011) discuss, different organizational policies will attract different subgroups of older workers. As such, organizations may consider intentionally targeting certain subgroups. For instance, previous research has found that the organizational attraction of retirees who were interested in bridge employment increased when job opening advertisements included statements about work arrangement flexibility and commitment to being an equal employment organization (Rau & Adams, 2005). Not all job seekers find themselves in the same career stage (e.g., interest in job advancement) and older workers have a variety of needs and motivations in seeking employment opportunities. Organizations that want to benefit from a broad applicant pool consisting of a range of ages from which they can select the best candidates should evaluate whether they are reaching their target population.

Although some selection professionals are concerned about the increasing use of technology in workplace selection (e.g., as it affects the validity of selection assessments; see Tippins, 2009 for a discussion of assessments completed over the internet), there is also concern that certain groups will be less likely to participate in such technologies in the first place (Posthuma & Campion, 2009). Arthur, Doverspike, Muñoz, Taylor, and Carr (2014) examined technology use in the application process by adults who were given the choice to complete employment assessments using mobile or non-mobile devices. They found that younger adults (i.e., under 40 years of age) participated in more assessments using a mobile device than a non-mobile device, while the opposite was true for older adults (i.e., 40 years of age and older). Though digital assessments should benefit workers by affording flexibility to complete assessments where and when they want, many older job seekers do not appear to perceive or value this arrangement. The extent to which employers form perceptions of employees based on job seeking behaviors (e.g., opting to complete a paper job application instead of on online application) is an area for future research.

22.4.2 Workplace Training and Technology

Training is one way in which organizations maintain a workforce that has the knowledge, skills, and abilities to meet work functions (Goldstein & Ford, 2002). As discussed above, older workers may be perceived as not being interested in training, in particular when technology is part of the training (Posthuma & Campion, 2009). However, research has shown that older workers are willing to complete training in technology, particularly when it will help them meet their goals (Mitzner et al., 2010). Importantly, training can occur in an autonomous learning environment which is self-directed and initiated by learners (e.g., register in an online course from home), or training can be mandated by others (e.g., instructor-led course in an organization).

Although most research on training has focused on training mandated by employers, some researchers have studied self-directed learning, sometimes called autonomous learning (Beier, Torres, & Gilberto, 2017). Autonomous learning is so pervasive in organizations that many people who engage in it do not consider it to be outside their normal job duties (e.g., on-the-job learning, cross-training; Tannenbaum, 1997). Technology can provide an array of autonomous learning and development activities, and these activities can be less formal (e.g., searching the internet for resources to assist in managing a project) or more formal (e.g., participating as a student in a MOOC about project management), but as long as they are self-directed, they would be considered autonomous (Beier et al., 2017). Although some studies have examined the use of online courses by the elderly (people past retirement age; Liyanagunawardena & Williams, 2016), additional research is needed on the factors that lead working adults to use self-directed online training.

Beyond the autonomous learning environment, research has shown that the best approach to computer training generally differs between younger and older employees due to the wide range of differences in physical, sensory, speed, and learning abilities previously described (Glass, 1996). Individual studies have identified specific design considerations such as the structure and instructions given during technology training. In a laboratory study, Carter and Beier (2010) trained 161 community adults aged 20–66 years on a database management program and found that older adults had better performance in conditions of increased structure and instructions. Wolfson and Kraiger (2014) also found evidence for positive outcomes for older workers when attention is paid to the type of instructions given during computer-based instruction. They found that older adults who were provided with an advance organizer (i.e., outline of training content provided before training begins) performed better in training than older adults who were not provided with such a tool, while no such difference was found for younger adults. Similarly, Mitzner and colleagues (2008) conducted focus groups with 119 older adults ranging in age from 65 to 85 regarding their technology learning preferences. Participants reported preferring text-based instruction to be available during training and having access to printed manuals to refer to during and after training.

Research has also highlighted the affordances of using technology to deliver training content to older learners. For instance, technology that is easy to customize for the unique needs of older learners (e.g., allowing ease of adjusting font size and increasing contrast; permitting self-pacing through training material) will benefit older learners (Beier & Ackerman, 2005; Beier et al., 2012; Callahan, Kiker, & Cross, 2003). Moreover, there is evidence that older workers will prefer training that is customized to the individual needs of the learner. For instance, Laganà (2008) conducted a study to explore the effectiveness of one-on-one versus group computer training with older adults. She found that one-on-one training was effective at improving adults' computer self-efficacy and attitudes toward computers, and that study participants reported preferring one-on-one training to group training.

Multiple studies of training interventions for older adults have also shown that effective training can affect older trainees' attitudes about technology as well as their computer self-efficacy (Laganà, 2008). For example, Morrell, Park, Mayhorn, and Echt (1996) found that brief training sessions improved attitudes toward technology. Wagner et al. (2010) further note that technology training interventions may be most effective if they target increasing computer self-efficacy, which will in turn increase trainees' computer use and proficiency. Using a systems approach to computer training with a focus on older adults, Mayhorn, Stronge, McLaughlin, and Rogers (2004) proposed guidelines, informed by structured interviews conducted with older adults, that trainers can use to evaluate their own training programs. Recommendations include the need to allow for a comfortable pace of training, to build positive attitudes toward computers while reducing computer anxiety, and to make available step-by-step references that are accessible later.

The Center for Research and Education on Aging and Technology Enhancement (CREATE) discussed similar factors that predict technology use among adults and highlighted the role of computer anxiety (Czaja et al., 2006). The researchers used a community sample of adults ranging from 18 to 91 years old to examine predictors of computer and technology use (e.g., fax machine, videocassette recorder). In addition to sociodemographic (i.e., age, ethnicity, and education) and ability (reasoning and knowledge abilities) factors, they found that computer anxiety was related to technology use. Older adults reported more computer anxiety and less self-efficacy than younger adults, and those with lower self-efficacy were less likely to use technology. Czaja et al. (2006) suggested that technology training should provide trainees with opportunities to experience success because those with higher technology self-efficacy are more likely to engage in technology behaviors in the future than those with lower self-efficacy. In summary, effective technology training for older workers should take into account psychological outcomes such as computer anxiety and self-efficacy, in addition to more concrete quantitative outcomes such as task performance.

22.5 Interventions and Recommendations for Future Research

Organizations can implement interventions aimed at improving technology-related job and psychological outcomes for older workers. There is extensive evidence that older employees can effectively learn and use technology in the workplace as effectively as their younger coworkers if they are given adequate time, opportunities to practice, and organizational support (Charness & Czaja, 2005; Dyck & Smither, 1994).

22.5.1 Workplace Interventions Associated with Age and Technology

Person-level interventions.   Researchers have considered the role of emotions of older employees in successful training outcomes using technology. Engaging with unfamiliar technology may lead older adults to experience negative reactions, such as stress, which may negatively impact training outcomes, particularly since older adults demonstrate generally more passive and potentially less effective coping strategies than younger adults do (Blanchard-Fields, Jahnke, & Camp, 1995), and because stress takes up already limited cognitive resources. Dijkstra et al. (2015) examined the extent to which coping and relaxation interventions would help older adults (60 to 92 years of age) and younger adults (17 to 37 years of age) manage stress during technology training (i.e., task training involving the use of personal digital assistant and webcam tools). They found that coping interventions helped lower physical signs of stress in both younger and older adults and that relaxation interventions helped improve task performance. This study suggests that interventions aimed at improving the experience and performance of older workers might positively affect all workers. However, trainers should consider how training will be administered (e.g., consider the benefits of self-paced training; Beier & Ackerman, 2005), as negative experiences during training may lead to negative reactions (e.g., lower self-efficacy). Overall, training characteristics may be used to promote improved learning and training experiences with technology.

The reverse side of computer anxiety is self-efficacy, and research suggests that self-efficacy is influenced by positive experiences as described above, as well as social support, encouragement, and positive feedback (Bandura, 1977). Bolstering self-efficacy in older workers' technology use in particular might include promoting a work climate that recognizes employees' successes in technology training and on-the-job results and incorporates more extensive positive feedback when employees successfully complete training or implement what they have learned in training when they are back on the job.

Technology-level interventions.   Listening to the end users is the first step – i.e., if asked, workers will often offer their own solutions or recommendations for simple accommodations (Beier, 2015; Economist Intelligence Unit, 2011). Solutions may involve selecting software and hardware that are easily customized to workers' needs (e.g., to allow larger text sizes and greater screen contrast wherever those options are available), re-working the organization's existing technology to enable interactions with a keyboard or touchscreen instead of a mouse, and/or altering individual employee computer settings to allow for slower double-clicking and mouse movement speed.

Organizational-level Interventions.   Organizations should consider the unique challenges facing older workers when implementing or purchasing new workplace technology and when exploring where existing technology can be altered to accommodate limitations. For example, internal websites and other computer-based resources that an organization manages should be reviewed to ensure best practices in terms of usability (see above). Furthermore, to reduce employees' cognitive load, computer-based job tasks should be simplified if possible to require sequential rather than concurrent cognitive demands. In addition, to ensure technology safety and data security (Mitzner et al., 2010), organizations should make sure that appropriate safety training is provided (e.g., Internet and email safety) and that established safety processes fit with the capabilities of older workers (e.g., using digitized procedural safety lists).

22.5.2 Future Research

Throughout our review of the literature, it became clear that much of the research on technology and aging is dated, conducted in the 1990s when the introduction of the personal computer began fundamentally changing our relationship with technology. Moreover, this research makes assumptions about older adults' emotional responses to technology (i.e., anxiety) and assumes a relatively limited and circumscribed role of technology in home and work life. Fast-forward almost three decades and most workers have at least some experience with technology; moreover, mobile computing is ubiquitous at home and at work. Research on age and technology has not kept up. We know very little about how older workers use technology, and whether their behaviors are different from younger workers. As such, our first research recommendation is to more closely assess older adults' experiences with technology at work. A thorough understanding of how older workers engage with technology, including the affordances, barriers, and the conditions for optimal performance, could lead to a set of best practices for the design of interventions. For example, strategies for encouraging the adoption of new technology within a day-to-day work routine given that motivation might be low (driven by increased perceptions of effort and anticipated errors) would benefit employees of all ages and the organization as a whole. After all, organizations spend millions of dollars on training every year and billions on technology; if these tools are not optimally used because they are perceived to be too much effort and/or not aligned with a worker's goals, this money will not be well spent. Further, we need to know more about the experiences that people have with technology and how this prior experience impacts future technology use as technology continues to evolve.

One question is whether young workers who have experience with technology today will have difficulty in engaging with technology in the workplace as they age. In other words, is there a cohort effect in technology attitudes, adoption, and use? Czaja et al. (2006) suggested that while older workers today were introduced to computers in later life (which may explain lower technology use rates), today's young workers will most likely have more exposure to computers. We speculate that while prior experiences with technology may facilitate technology use in later life, there will likely continue to be concerns about how to design technology that addresses age-related changes (e.g., changes in cognition, vision) and how to effectively train for changes in workplace technology.

A second, but no less important area of future research is understanding how to best design technology for older users. Although many human factors professionals have begun to understand the impact of the aging workforce on the design of workplace tools, this research is not moving quickly enough to accommodate the needs of older workers, and further research is needed. Research on age and technology has shown the need to design technology that allows for age-related changes. For example, technology that is designed with consideration for age-related cognitive changes (e.g., working memory) would allow older workers to engage with important technologies across the lifespan (see technology design using cognitive principles; Mayhorn et al., 2004). Further, technology design might leverage the positive experiences associated with aging (e.g., prior experiences and knowledge) to support the successful implementation of workplace technology. Involving older adults in the research design process would take into consideration older adults' strengths, needs, values, motivations, and preferences (see Dienel, Peine, & Cameron, 2004, for an example of designing technology tools that are appealing to older individuals).

A third area of future research is examining the contextual factors that influence the adoption and use of technology by workers of all ages. The research reviewed above suggests that older workers, in particular, are susceptible to social pressure to use technology (Morris & Venkatesh, 2000). It would be interesting to explore the contextual cues that influence technology use and adoption more broadly than peer pressure. For instance, organizational policies about purchasing and updating the newest technologies, a willingness to send workers of all ages to training to update their technology skills and a culture that rewards risk taking and innovation might be factors in encouraging technology use and adoption that might be beneficial for workers of all ages. But to date, very little research has been done on the contextual factors that encourage workers – particularly older workers – to use and adopt new technologies.

Last, there is limited research on how some of the new developments in technology we have discussed in this chapter, such as using technology for selection and recruiting, impact older workers in particular. This research recommendation focuses on understanding whether age impacts reactions to the ways in which organizations use technology (e.g., in recruiting and selection). Because workers of different ages are likely to experience varying levels of engagement, self-efficacy, and attitudes about technology in the workplace, it is reasonable to expect significant differences in perceptions of novel technology, such as use of technology for selection and recruiting. However, generational values and priorities may also interact with perceptions of these technologies in unanticipated ways. Older prospective employees, who are likely more focused on social and emotional goals, may be more likely to perceive recruitment efforts that engage smart technology as cold and detached, whereas younger prospective employees might perceive such an impersonal approach as innovative. In sum, very little research has been conducted on reactions to new technologies employed by organizations, and we recommend this as a major area of research in the future. Further, we suggest the research on recruitment and applicant reactions more broadly attend to age as a potential moderator. A summary of our suggested research directions for each area within the context of research on older workers and technology use is shown in Table 22.4.

Table 22.4 *Future research directions for older workers and technology*

Current research area	Future research directions
Technology training for older workers	Explore different training methods (group, one-on-one), pacing (self-pacing, ability to return to earlier material), and customization of program for physical/ability needs of older workers
Computer self-efficacy in older adults	Evaluate methods to increase self-efficacy (mandatory training, social support, changes in interface design, organizational policies that do not punish early mistakes)
Design for usability	Evaluate the effectiveness of different methods to optimize tools to older adults' needs (e.g., how effective interface changes are at decreasing cognitive load)
Ageism in the workplace	Evaluate interventions to change organizational culture, management training on age-related stereotypes
Technology job demands on older workers	Examine how technology can reduce job demands and increase job control for older workers, reducing job strain
Older workers as a population	Increase research on older employees in the workplace overall; much of the existing research on older adults and technology is on elderly and retired populations
Older job applicants	Explore the effect of online recruitment and selection on older applicants
Daily technology usage by older workers	Examine intra-individual differences such as self-efficacy and approach or avoidance motivation on integrating new technology into workflow and the impact of social support and norms on usage
Perceptions of technology advancements	Examine generational differences in attitudes toward new developments such as workplace monitoring, 24/7 availability expectations

22.6 Conclusion

The introduction and advancement of workplace technology has had profound implications for all employees and organizations, but perhaps none more so than older workers. It is important for organizations to recognize that young adults' interactions with and perceptions toward technology are fundamentally different from those of older adults. Older workers are often shielded from the most advanced workplace technology, due to both systematic decisions by the organization and managers and by the employee's own reluctance to learn new technology. However, older employees can benefit greatly from workplace technology if they are given the appropriate incentives to engage with new technology and are afforded sufficient time and opportunities to adopt and use technology.

References

Ackerman, P. L. (1988). Determinants of individual differences during skill acquisition: Cognitive abilities and information processing. *Journal of Experimental Psychology: General, 117*, 288–318. doi.org/10.1037//0096–3445.117.3.288.

Anderson, M. & Perrin, A. (2017). *Tech adoption climbs among older adults*. Washington, DC: Pew Research Center.

Arthur, W., Doverspike, D., Muñoz, G. J., Taylor, J. E., & Carr, A. E. (2014). The use of mobile devices in high-stakes remotely delivered assessments and testing. *International Journal of Selection and Assessment, 22*(2), 113–123. doi.org/10.1111/ijsa.12062.

Autor, D. H. (2015). Why are there still so many jobs? The history and future of workplace automation. *Journal of Economic Perspectives, 29*(3), 3–30. doi.org/10.1257/jep.29.3.3.

Badger, J. M., Kaminsky, S. E., & Behrend, T. S. (2014). Media richness and information acquisition in internet recruitment. *Journal of Managerial Psychology, 29*(7), 866–883. doi.org/10.1108/JMP-05–2012-0155.

Bakker, A. B. & Demerouti, E. (2007). The job demands resources model: State of the art. *Journal of Managerial Psychology, 22*(3), 309–328. doi.org/10.1108/02683940710733115.

Baltes, P. B. & Baltes, M. M. (1990). Psychological perspectives on successful aging: The model of selective optimization with compensation. In P. B. Baltes & M. M. Baltes (Eds.), *Successful aging: Perspectives from the behavioral sciences* (pp. 1–34). New York, NY: Cambridge University Press.

Bandura, A. (1977). Self-efficacy: Toward a unifying theory of behavioral change. *Psychological Review, 84*(2), 191–215. doi.org/10.1037//0033-295x.84.2.191.

Bandura, A. (1982). Self-efficacy mechanism in human agency. *American Psychologist, 37*(2), 122–47. doi.org/10.1037//0003-066x.37.2.122.

Barley, S. R., Meyerson, D. E., & Grodal, S. (2011). E-mail as a source and symbol of stress. *Organization Science, 22*(4), 887–906. doi.org/10.1287/orsc.1100.0573.

Beier, M. E. (2015). Strategies for engaging and retaining mature workers. SHRM-SIOP Science of HR Series. Retrieved from www.shrm.org/hr-today/trends-and-fore

casting/special-reports-and-expert-views/Documents/SHRM-SIOP%20Engaging %20and%20Retaining%20Mature%20Workers.pdf.

Beier, M. E. & Ackerman, P. L. (2005). Age, ability, and the role of prior knowledge on the acquisition of new domain knowledge: Promising results in a real-world learning environment. *Psychology and Aging, 20(2)*, 341–355. doi.org/10.1037/ 0882–7974. 20. 2.341.

Beier, M. E., Teachout, M. S., & Cox, C. B. (2012). The training and development of an aging workforce. In J. W. Hedge & W. C. Borman (Eds.), *The Oxford handbook of work and aging* (pp. 436–453). New York, NY: Oxford University Press.

Beier, M. E., Torres, W. J., & Gilberto, J. M. (2017). Continuous development throughout a career: A lifespan perspective on autonomous learning. In J. E. Ellingson & R. A. Noe (Eds.), *Autonomous learning in the workplace* (pp. 179–200). New York, NY: Routledge.

Blanchard-Fields, F., Jahnke, H. C., & Camp, C. (1995). Age differences in problem-solving style: The role of emotional salience. *Psychology and Aging, 10*(2), 173–180. doi. org/10.1037/0882–7974.10.2.173.

Bock, T. (2015). The future of construction automation: Technological disruption and the upcoming ubiquity of robotics. *Automation in Construction, 59*, 113–121. doi.org/ 10.1016/j.autcon.2015.07.022.

Broeders, I. A. (2014). Robotics: The next step? *Best Practice & Research Clinical Gastroenterology, 28*(1), 225–232. doi.org/10.1016/j.bpg.2013.12.001.

Bureau of Labor Statistics, US Department of Labor. (2014). Share of labor force projected to rise for people age 55 and over and fall for younger age groups. Retrieved from www.bls.gov/opub/ted/2014/ted_20140124.htm.

Butler, R. N. (1975). Psychiatry and the elderly: An overview. *The American Journal of Psychiatry, 132*(9), 893–900. doi.org/10.1176/ajp.132.9.893.

Callahan, J. S., Kiker, D. S., & Cross, T. (2003). Does method matter? A meta-analysis of the effects of training method on older learner training performance. *Journal of Management, 29*(5), 663–680. doi.org/10.1016/s0149-2063(03)00029–1.

Campbell, J. P. & Pritchard, R. (1976). Motivation theory in industrial and organizational psychology. In *Handbook of industrial and organizational psychology* (pp. 63–130). Chicago: Rand McNally.

Carroll, J. B. (1993). *Human cognitive abilities: A survey of factor-analytic studies.* New York, NY: Cambridge University Press.

Carstensen, L. L., Isaacowitz, D. M., & Charles, S. T. (1999). Taking time seriously: A theory of socioemotional selectivity. *American Psychologist, 54*(3), 165–181. doi.org/ 10.1037/0003-066X.54.3.165.

Carstensen, L. L., Pasupathi, M., Mayr, U., & Nesselroade, J. R. (2000). Emotional experience in everyday life across the adult life span. *Journal of Personality and Social Psychology, 79*(4), 644–655. doi.org/10.1037/0022–3514.79.4.644.

Carter, M. & Beier, M. E. (2010). The effectiveness of error management training with working-aged adults. *Personnel Psychology, 63*(3), 641–675. doi.org/10.1111/ j.1744–6570.2010.01183.x.

Cascio, W. F. (2014). Looking back, looking forward: Technology in the workplace. In M. D. Coovert, L. F. Thompson, M. D. Coovert, & L. F. Thompson (Eds.), *The psychology of workplace technology* (pp. 307–313). New York, NY: Routledge/ Taylor & Francis Group.

Cascio, W. F. & Montealegre, R. (2016). How technology is changing work and organizations. *Annual Review of Organizational Psychology and Organizational Behavior*, *3*(1), 349–375. doi.org/10.1146/annurev-orgpsych-041015–062352.

Cattell, R. B. (1987). *Intelligence: Its structure, growth and action* (vol. 35). New York, NY: Elsevier.

Chadwick-Dias, A., McNulty, M., & Tullis, T. (2003). Web usability and age: How design changes can improve performance. In CUU '03 proceedings of the 2003 conference on universal usability (pp. 30–37). doi.org/10.1145/960201.957212.

Chaparro, A., Rogers, M., Fernandez, J., Bohan, M., Sang Dae, C., & Stumpfhauser, L. (2000). Range of motion of the wrist: Implications for designing computer input devices for the elderly. *Disability and Rehabilitation*, *22*(13–14), 633–637. doi.org/10.1080/09638280050138313.

Charness, N. & Boot, W. R. (2009). Aging and information technology use: Potential and barriers. *Current Directions in Psychological Science*, *18*(5), 253–258. doi.org/10.1111/j.1467–8721.2009.01647.x.

Charness, N. & Czaja, S. J. (2005). Older worker training: What we know and don't know (No. AARP Public Policy Institute #2006–22.). Washington, DC: AARP. Retrieved from https://assets.aarp.org/rgcenter/econ/2006_22_worker.pdf.

Charness, N., Kelley, C. L., Bosman, E. A., & Mottram, M. (2001). Word-processing training and retraining: Effects of adult age, experience, and interface. *Psychology and Aging*, *16*(1), 110–127. doi.org/10.1037//0882–7974.16.1.110.

Chasteen, A. L., Bhattacharyya, S., Horhota, M., Tam, R., & Hasher, L. (2005). How feelings of stereotype threat influence older adults' memory performance. *Experimental Aging Research*, *31*(3), 235–260. doi.org/10.1080/03610730590948177.

Chen, K. & Chan, A. H. S. (2014). Gerontechnology acceptance by elderly Hong Kong Chinese: A senior technology acceptance model (STAM). *Ergonomics*, *57*(5), 635–652. doi.org/10.1080/00140139.2014.895855.

Chiu, W. C. K., Chan, A. W., Snape, E., & Redman, T. (2001). Age stereotypes and discriminatory attitudes towards older workers: an east-west comparison. *Human Relations*, *54*(5), 629–661. doi.org/10.1177/0018726701545004.

Colby, S. L. & Ortman, J. M. (2015). Projections of the size and composition of the US population: 2014 to 2060 (Current Population Reports No. P25-1143). Washington, DC: US Census Bureau, pp. 1–13.

Compeau, D. R. & Higgins, C. A. (1995). Computer self-efficacy: Development of a measure and initial test. *MIS Quarterly*, *19*(2), 189–211. doi.org/10.2307/249688.

Craik, F. I. & Anderson, N. D. (1999). Applying cognitive research to problems of aging. In D. Gopher & A. Koriat (Eds.), *Attention and performance XVII – Cognitive regulation of performance: Interaction of theory and application* (pp. 583–615). Cambridge, MA: The MIT Press.

Czaja, S. J., Charness, N., Fisk, A. D., Hertzog, C., Nair, S. N., Rogers, W. A., & Sharit, J. (2006). Factors predicting the use of technology: Findings from the Center for Research and Education on Aging and Technology Enhancement (CREATE). *Psychology and Aging*, *21*(2), 333–352. doi.org/10.1037/0882–7974.21.2.333.

Czaja, S. & Lee, C. C. (2007). Information technology and older adults. In A. Sears & J. A. Jacko (Eds.), *Human-computer interaction: Designing for diverse users and domains* (2nd edn., pp. 777–792). New York, NY: Erlbaum.

Czaja, S. J., Sharit, J., Charness, N., Fisk, A. D., & Rogers, W. (2001). The Center for Research and Education on Aging and Technology Enhancement (CREATE): A program to enhance technology for older adults. *Gerontechnology*, *1*(1), 50–59. doi.org/10.4017/gt.2001.01.01.005.00.

Davis, F. D. (1989). Perceived usefulness, perceived ease of use, and user acceptance of information technology. *MIS Quarterly*, *13*(3), 319–340. doi.org/10.2307/249008.

Davis, K. A. & Songer, A. D. (2009). Resistance to IT change in the AEC industry: Are the stereotypes true? *Journal of Construction Engineering and Management*, *135*(12), 1324–1333. doi.org/10.1061/(asce)co.1943–7862.0000108.

De Raedt, R. & Ponjaert-Kristoffersen, I. (2000). The relationship between cognitive/neuropsychological factors and car driving performance in older adults. *Journal of the American Geriatrics Society*, *48*(12), 1664–1668. doi.org/10.1111/j.1532–5415.2000.tb03880.x.

Dienel, H. L., Peine, A., & Cameron, H. (2004). New participative tools in product development for seniors. In D. C. Burdick & S. Kwon (Eds.), *Gerotechnology: Research and practice in technology and aging* (pp. 18–41). New York, NY: Springer.

Dijkstra, K., Charness, N., Yordon, R., & Price, J. (2015). The role of coping, relaxation, and age on stress and task performance with new technology. *Gerontechnology*, *13*(4), 388–395. doi.org/10.4017/gt.2015.13.4.003.00.

Dyck, J. L. & Smither, J. A. A. (1994). Age differences in computer anxiety: The role of computer experience, gender and education. *Journal of Educational Computing Research*, *10*(3), 239–248. doi.org/10.2190/E79U-VCRC-EL4E-HRYV.

Economist Intelligence Unit. (2011). A silver opportunity? Rising longevity and its implications for business. Retrieved from http://graphics.eiu.com/upload/eb/Axa_Longevity-EIU_Web.pdf.

El Ouirdi, M., Segers, J., El Ouirdi, A., & Pais, I. (2015). Predictors of job seekers' self-disclosure on social media. *Computers in Human Behavior*, *53*, 1–12. doi.org/10.1016/j.chb.2015.06.039.

Elias, P. K., Elias, M. F., Robbins, M. A., & Gage, P. (1987). Acquisition of word-processing skills by younger, middle-age, and older adults. *Psychology and Aging*, (*4*), 340–348. doi.org/10.1037//0882–7974.2.4.340.

Fisk, A. D., Czaja, S. J., Rogers, W. A., Charness, N., & Sharit, J. (2009). *Designing for older adults: Principles and creative human factors approaches* (2nd edn.). Boca Raton, FL: CRC Press.

Fiske, S. T. & Taylor, S. E. (2013). Social cognition: From brains to culture. Los Angeles, CA Sage.

Frey, C. B. & Osborne, M. A. (2017). The future of employment: How susceptible are jobs to computerisation? *Technological Forecasting and Social Change*, *114*, 254–280. doi.org/10.1016/j.techfore.2016.08.019.

Ford, J. K., Quiñones, M. A., Sego, D. J., & Sorra, J. S. (1992). Factors affecting the opportunity to perform trained tasks on the job. *Personnel Psychology*, *45*(3), 511–527. doi.org/10.1111/j.1744–6570.1992.tb00858.x.

Fozard, J. L. (2017). Epilogue: A 10-year growth spurt in applications to aging in human factors and ergonomics. In S. Kwon & S. Kwon (Eds.), *Gerontechnology: Research, practice, and principles in the field of technology and aging* (pp. 485–502). New York, NY: Springer Publishing.

Glass, J. C. J. (1996). Factors affecting learning in older adults. *Educational Gerontology, 22* (4), 359–372. doi.org/10.1080/0360127960220405.

Goldstein, I. L. & Ford, K. (2002). *Training in organizations: Needs assessment, development, and evaluation* (4th edn.). Belmont, CA: Wadsworth.

Gregor, P., Newell, A. F., & Zajicek, M. (2002). Designing for dynamic diversity: Interfaces for older people. In *Proceedings of the fifth international ACM conference on assistive technologies* (pp. 151–156). New York, NY: Association for Computer Machinery. doi.org/10.1145/638249.638277.

Hawthorn, D. (2000). Possible implications of aging for interface designers. *Interacting with Computers, 12*(5), 507–528. doi.org/10.1016/s0953-5438(99)00021-1.

Hertzog, C., Kramer, A. F., Wilson, R. S., & Lindenberger, U. (2008). Enrichment effects on adult cognitive development: Can the functional capacity of older adults be preserved and enhanced? *Psychological Science in the Public Interest, 9*(1), 1–65. doi.org/10.1111/j.1539–6053.2009.01034.x.

Hess, T. M., Auman, C., Colcombe, S. J., & Rahhal, T. A. (2003). The impact of stereotype threat on age differences in memory performance. *The Journals of Gerontology: Series B, 58*(1), 3–11. doi.org/10.1093/geronb/58.1.p3.

Hess, T. M. & Blanchard-Fields, F. (1999). *Social cognition and aging.* San Diego, CA: Academic Press.

Hummert, M. L., Garstka, T. A., Shaner, J. L., & Strahm, S. (1994). Stereotypes of the elderly held by young, middle-aged, and elderly adults. *Journal of Gerontology, 49*(5), 240–249. doi.org/10.1093/geronj/49.5.p240.

Ilgen, D. R. & Youtz, M. A. (1986). Factors affecting the evaluation and development of minorities in organizations. In K. Bowland & G. Ferris (Eds.), *Research in personnel and human resource management: A research annual* (pp. 307–337). Greenwich, CT: JAI Press.

Ilmarinen, J., Tuomi, K., & Klockars, M. (1997). Changes in the work ability of active employees over an 11-year period. *Scandinavian Journal of Work, Environment & Health, 23*, 49–57.

Kanfer, R. (1990). Motivation theory and industrial and organizational psychology. In M. D. Dunnette & L. M. Hough (Eds.), *Handbook of industrial and organizational psychology* (vol. 1, 2nd edn., pp. 75–170). Palo Alto, CA: Consulting Psychologists Press, Inc.

Kanfer, R. & Ackerman, P. L. (2004). Aging, adult development, and work motivation. *The Academy of Management Review, 29*(3), 440–458. doi.org/10.2307/20159053.

Karasek Jr, R. A. (1979). Job demands, job decision latitude, and mental strain: Implications for job redesign. *Administrative Science Quarterly, 24*(2), 285–308. doi.org/10.2307/2392498.

Kelley, C. L. & Charness, N. (1995). Issues in training older adults to use computers. *Behaviour & Information Technology, 14*(2), 107–120. doi.org/10.1080/01449299508914630.

Kooij, D. T. A. M., de Lange, A. H., Jansen, P. G. W., Kanfer, R., & Dikkers, J. S. E. (2011). Age and work-related motives: Results of a meta-analysis. *Journal of Organizational Behavior, 32*(2), 197–225. doi.org/10.1002/job.665.

Koster, A., Bosma, H., Broese van Groenou, M. I., Kempen, G. I., Penninx, B. W., van Eijk, J. T., & Deeg, D. J. (2006). Explanations of socioeconomic differences in changes in physical function in older adults: results from the Longitudinal Aging Study Amsterdam. *BMC Public Health*, *6*(1). doi.org/10.1186/1471–2458-6–244.

Kubeck, J. E., Delp, N. D., Haslett, T. K., & McDaniel, M. A. (1996). Does job-related training performance decline with age? *Psychology and Aging*, *11*(1), 92–107. doi. org/10.1037/0882–7974.11.1.92.

Kwon, S. (2017). Synopsis: Lessons learned, long-term guidelines, and how to live a livable life in old age with likable technologies. In S. Kwon & S. Kwon (Eds.), *Gerontechnology: Research, practice, and principles in the field of technology and aging* (pp. 463–483). New York, NY: Springer Publishing.

Lagacé, M., Houssein, C., Zaky, R., & Firzly, N. (2016). From psychological to digital disengagement: Exploring the link between ageism and the "grey digital divide." *Revista Română de Comunicare Şi Relaţii Publice*, *18*(1), 65–75. doi.org/ 10.21018/rjcpr.2016.1.202.

Laganà, L. (2008). Enhancing the attitudes and self-efficacy of older adults toward computers and the Internet: Results of a pilot study. *Educational Gerontology*, *34*(9), 831–43. doi.org/10.1080/03601270802243713.

Liyanagunawardena, T. R. & Williams, S. A. (2016). Elderly learners and massive open online courses: A review. *Interactive Journal of Medical Research*, *5*(1), e1. doi. org/10.2196/ijmr.4937.

Major, B. & Schmader, T. (1998). Coping with stigma through psychological disengagement. In J. K. Swim & C. Stangor (Eds.), *Prejudice: The target's perspective* (pp. 219–241). San Diego, CA: Academic Press.

Martin, S. (1996). Effective visual communication for graphical user interfaces. Retrieved from http://web.cs.wpi.edu/~matt/courses/cs563/talks/smartin/int_design.html.

Mayhorn, C. B., Rogers, W. A., & Fisk, A. D. (2004). Designing technology based on cognitive aging principles. In D. C. Burdock & S. Kwon (Eds.), *Gerotechnology: Research and practice in technology and aging; A textbook and reference for multiple disciplines* (pp. 43–53). New York, NY: Springer.

Mayhorn, C. B., Stronge, A. J., McLaughlin, A. C., & Rogers, W. A. (2004). Older adults, computer training, and the systems approach: A formula for success. *Educational Gerontology*, *30*(3), 185–203. doi.org/10.1080/03601270490272124.

Maurer, T. J. (2001). Career-relevant learning and development, worker age, and beliefs about self-efficacy for development. *Journal of Management*, *27*(2), 123–140. doi.org/10.1016/S0149-2063(00)00092–1.

McGrew, K. S. (2005). The Cattell-Horn-Carroll theory of cognitive abilities: Past, present, and future. In D. P. Flanagan & P. L. Harrison (Eds.), *Contemporary intellectual assessment: Theories, tests, and issues* (pp. 136–181). New York, NY: Guilford Press.

Melenhorst, A.-S., Rogers, W. A., & Bouwhuis, D. G. (2006). Older adults' motivated choice for technological innovation: Evidence for benefit-driven selectivity. *Psychology and Aging*, *21*(1), 190–195. doi.org/10.1037/0882–7974.21.1.190.

Millward, P. (2003). The "grey digital divide": Perception, exclusion and barriers of access to the Internet for older people. First Monday, 8 (7). Retrieved from http://first monday.org/ojs/index.php/fm/article/view/1066/986.

Mitzner, T. L., Fausset, C. B., Boron, J. B., Adams, A. E., Dijkstra, K., Lee, C. C., . . . Fisk, A. D. (2008). Older adults' training preferences for learning to use technology. *Proceedings of the Human Factors and Ergonomics Society Annual Meeting*, *52*(26), 2047–2051. doi.org/10.1177/154193120805202603.

Mitzner, T. L., Boron, J. B., Fausset, C. B., Adams, A. E., Charness, N., Czaja, S. J., ... Sharit, J. (2010). Older adults talk technology: Technology usage and attitudes. *Computers in Human Behavior, 26*(6), 1710–1721. doi.org/10.1016/j.chb. 2010.06.020.

Morrell, R., Park, D., Mayhorn, C., & Echt, K. (1996). Electronic technology and older adults. Presented at the International Conference on Memory, Albano Terme, Italy.

Morris, M. G. & Venkatesh, V. (2000). Age differences in technology adoption decisions: Implications for a changing work force. *Personnel Psychology, 53*(2), 375–403. doi.org/10.1111/j.1744–6570.2000.tb00206.x.

Nakai, Y., Chang, B., Snell, A. F., & Fluckinger, C. D. (2011). Profiles of mature job seekers: Connecting needs and desires to work characteristics. *Journal of Organizational Behavior, 32*(2), 155–172. doi.org/10.1002/job.697.

Namazi, K. H. & McClintic, M. (2003). Computer use among elderly persons in long-term care facilities. *Educational Gerontology, 29*(6), 535–550. doi.org/10.1080/713844391.

Nelson, T. D. (2004). *Ageism: Stereotyping and prejudice against older persons*. Cambridge, MA: MIT Press.

Nokelainen, P., Nevalainen, T., & Niemi, K. (2018). Mind or machine? Opportunities and limits of automation. In C. Harteis (Ed.), *The impact of digitalization in the workplace* (pp. 13–24). Cham: Springer. doi.org/10.1007/978–3-319–63257-5_2.

Olson, K. E., O'Brien, M. A., Rogers, W. A., & Charness, N. (2011). Diffusion of technology: frequency of use for younger and older adults. *Ageing International, 36*(1), 123–145. doi.org/10.1007/s12126-010–9077-9.

Omori, M., Watanabe, T., Takai, J., Takada, H., & Miyao, M. (2002). Visibility and characteristics of the mobile phones for elderly people. *Behaviour & Information Technology, 21*(5), 313–316. doi.org/10.1080/0144929021000048466.

Organisation for Economic Co-operation and Development (OECD) (2002). OECD information technology outlook. Retrieved from www.oecd.org/sti/ieconomy/1933354.pdf.

Pak, R. & McLaughlin, A. (2010). *Designing displays for older adults*. Baton Rouge, LA: CRC Press.

Pew Research Center (2017). Internet/broadband fact sheet. Washington, DC. Retrieved from www.pewinternet.org/fact-sheet/internet-broadband/.

Posthuma, R. A. & Campion, M. A. (2009). Age stereotypes in the workplace: Common stereotypes, moderators, and future research directions. *Journal of Management, 35*(1), 158–188. doi.org/10.1177/0149206308318617.

Poynton, T. A. (2005). Computer literacy across the lifespan: A review with implications for educators. *Computers in Human Behavior, 21*(6), 861–872. doi.org/10.1016/j.chb.2004.03.004.

Purcell, K. & Rainie, L. (December 30, 2014). Technology's Impact on Workers. Retrieved April 1, 2017, from www.pewinternet.org/2014/12/30/technologys-impact-on-workers/

Rau, B. L. & Adams, G. A. (2005). Attracting retirees to apply: Desired organizational characteristics of bridge employment. *Journal of Organizational Behavior, 26*(6), 649–660. doi.org/10.1002/job.330.

Reed, K., Doty, D. H., & May, D. R. (2005). The impact of aging on self-efficacy and computer skill acquisition. *Journal of Managerial Issues, 17*(2), 212–228. www.jstor.org/stable/40604496.

Rouiller, J. Z. & Goldstein, I. L. (1997). The relationship between organizational transfer climate and positive transfer of training. In D. F. Russ-Eft, H. S. Preskill, & C. Sleezer (Eds.), *Human resource development review: Research and implications* (pp. 330–347). Thousand Oaks, CA: Sage Publications.

Ryan, A. M. & Ployhart, R. E. (2014). A century of selection. *Annual Review of Psychology*, *65*(1), 693–717. doi.org/10.1146/annurev-psych-010213-115134.

Salthouse, T. A. (2010). *Major issues in cognitive aging*. New York, NY: Oxford University Press.

Schieber, F. (2013). Aging and the senses. In J. E. Birren, G. D. Cohen, R. B. Sloane, B. D. Lebowitz, D. E. Deutchman, M. Wykle, & N. R. Hooyman (Eds.), *Handbook of mental health and aging* (pp. 251–305). San Diego, CA: Academic Press.

Scialfa, C. T., Ho, G., & Laberge, J. (2004). Perceptual aspects of gerontechnology. In D. C. Burdick & S. Kwon (Eds.), *Gerotechnology: Research and practice in technology and aging* (pp. 18–41). New York, NY: Springer.

Sharit, J., Czaja, S. J., Hernandez, M. A., & Nair, S. N. (2009). The employability of older workers as teleworkers: An appraisal of issues and an empirical study. *Human Factors and Ergonomics in Manufacturing*, *19*(5), 457–477. doi.org/10.1002/hfm.20138.

Singh, S. (2000). Designing intelligent interfaces for users with memory and language limitations. *Aphasiology*, *14*(2), 157–177. doi.org/10.1080/026870300401531.

Sjölinder, M. (2006). Age-related cognitive decline and navigation in electronic environments. (Unpublished doctoral dissertation). Stockholm University, Stockholm, Sweden.

Smith, A. (2014). Older adults and technology use. Retrieved from www.pewinternet.org/2014/04/03/older-adults-and-technology-use/

Smith, A. (2015). Searching for work in the digital era. Retrieved from www.pewinternet.org/2015/11/19/searching-for-work-in-the-digital-era/

Sweller, J. (2011). Cognitive load theory. In J. P. Mestre, & B. H. Ross (Eds.), *The psychology of learning and motivation: Cognition in education* (vol. 55, pp. 37–76). San Diego, CA: Elsevier Academic Press.

Tannenbaum, S. I. (1997). Enhancing continuous learning: Diagnostic findings from multiple companies. *Human Resource Management*, *36*(4), 437–452. doi.org/10.1002/(sici)1099-050x(199724)36:4<437::aid-hrm7>3.3.co;2-4

Thompson, L. F. & Mayhorn, C. B. (2012). Aging workers and technology. In J. W. Hedge & W. C. Borman (Eds.), *The Oxford handbook of work and aging* (pp. 341–361). New York, NY: Oxford University Press.

Timiras, P. S. (2007). *Physiological basis of aging and geriatrics*. Boca Raton: CRC Press.

Tippins, N. T. (2009). Internet alternatives to traditional proctored testing: Where are we now? *Industrial and Organizational Psychology*, *2*(1), 2–10. doi.org/10.1111/j.1754-9434.2008.01097.x.

Truxillo, D. M., Cadiz, D. M., & Hammer, L. B. (2015). Supporting the aging workforce: A review and recommendations for workplace intervention research. *Annual Review of Organizational Psychology and Organizational Behavior*, *2*(1), 351–381. doi.org/10.1146/annurev-orgpsych-032414-111435.

United Nations Department of Economic and Social Affairs, Population Division. (2015). World population ageing 2015 (No. ST/ESA/SER.A/390). Retrieved from www.un.org/en/development/desa/population/publications/pdf/ageing/WPA2015_Report.pdf.

U. S. Department of Health & Human Services (October 8, 2013). *Usability evaluation basics*. Retrieved from www.usability.gov/what-and-why/usability-evaluation .html

van Deursen, A. & van Dijk, J. (2011). Internet skills and the digital divide. *New Media & Society, 13*(6), 893–911. doi.org/10.1177/1461444810386774.

Venkatesh, V., Morris, M. G., Davis, G. B., & Davis, F. D. (2003). User acceptance of information technology: Toward a unified view. *MIS Quarterly, 27*(3), 425–478. doi.org/10.2307/30036540.

Vroom, V. H. (1964). *Work and motivation*. New York, NY: John Wiley & Sons.

Wagner, N., Hassanein, K., & Head, M. (2010). Computer use by older adults: A multi-disciplinary review. *Computers in Human Behavior, 26*(5), 870–882. doi.org/10.1016/j.chb.2010.03.029.

Wandke, H., Sengpiel, M., & Sönksen, M. (2012). Myths about older people's use of information and communication technology. *Gerontology, 58*(6), 564–570. doi.org/10.1159/000339104.

Whitbourne, S. K. (2002). *The aging individual: Physical and psychological perspectives* (2nd edn.). New York, NY: Springer Publishing.

Witte, J. C. & Mannon, S. E. (2010). *The Internet and social inequalities*. New York, NY: Routledge.

Wolfson, N. E. & Kraiger, K. (2014). Cognitive aging and training: The role of instructional coherence and advance organizers. *Experimental Aging Research, 40*(2), 164–186. doi.org/10.1080/0361073X.2014.882206.

23 The Role of Technology in the Work-Family Interface

Jeremiah T. McMillan and Kristen M. Shockley

23.1 Introduction

Recently, researchers have heralded the need to consider the role of technology in the work-family (WF) interface (e.g., Kossek, Baltes, & Matthews, 2011). Spanning many interrelated topics, the intersection of technology and WF issues has been considered from a broad range of disciplines, including psychology (e.g., Ferguson et al., 2016; Shockley, 2018), management (e.g., Hislop & Axtell, 2007), sociology (e.g., Edley, 2001; Glavin & Schieman, 2010), communication studies (e.g., Berkowsky, 2013; Wright et al., 2014), information technology (e.g., Turel, Serenko, & Bontis, 2011), and bioethics (e.g., Goold & Savulescu, 2009). The goal of the present chapter is to review past empirical evidence regarding the role of technology in the WF interface, as well as explore the implications of such technology for future theory and practice in this area.

The term WF interface is rather broad in scope, but we use it to refer to any intersection between work and family roles. Regarding terminology, researchers in this area have sometimes focused on slightly different conceptualizations of the "family" side of the interface, using other labels such as work-home, work-life, and work–non-work (Kossek et al., 2011). Due to conceptual similarity, we use the overarching label work-family when summarizing findings as this is the most commonly researched construct, but use the authors' nomenclature in discussing study-specific findings.

Within the past two decades, technology has fundamentally altered the way individuals communicate, manage their social identities, and plan their future careers and families (Steiner-Adair & Barker, 2013). Because the interface between work and family is inherently socially constructed (Kreiner, Hollensbe, & Sheep, 2009), the degree to which technology has shifted societal values generally and the symbolic meanings of work and family specifically have clear implications for individual experiences within and across these domains. Although research focused on the implications of these changes for the WF interface has only recently begun in earnest, a recurring theme is that technological advances act as a double-edged sword, facilitating greater freedom in where and when work is conducted but simultaneously threatening employee well-being (e.g., Day, Scott, & Kelloway,

2010). It is therefore imperative to examine and synthesize the current state of the literature to understand what we currently know – and do not know – to inform future theory development and guide empirical research that is practically useful.

This chapter reviews four broad technological trends pertinent to the WF interface. Although these areas are somewhat disparate in terms of content and amount of available evidence, we focus on these areas based on theoretical relevance to the interface between work and family. We begin by examining the rise of the "always on, always connected" culture and the crucial role of technology in facilitating this phenomenon. Given that this area has received by far the most research attention, we devote the bulk of our chapter to reviewing issues related to it. We then explore the impact of social media on managing work and non-work identities. Next, we examine the emerging literature on egg cryopreservation and the implications for family formation, career decision-making, and employee well-being. Finally, we discuss how technologically driven economic changes impact work-family dynamics. We conclude by providing suggestions for future research within each of these categories.

23.2 Always on, Always Connected: The Role of Information and Communication Technology

Information and communication technology (ICT) refers to a broad class of technologies that allow for the storage and transmission of data, including email, texting, mobile phone calls, Skype, or any other internet or telephone-enabled connection (Day et al., 2012). Up to 63 percent of individuals check work-related email while at home more than once per day (Berkowsky, 2013), and 44 percent do so even while on vacation (American Psychological Association, 2013). These statistics represent the rise of an "always on, always connected" culture, a sweeping societal trend in which ICT has become ubiquitous in everyday life and results in the experience of always being electronically accessible to others (Mazmanian, Orlikowski, & Yates, 2005; Richardson & Benbunan-Fich, 2011). One critical implication of this phenomenon is the facilitation of conducting work outside the temporal and spatial confines of the workplace (Dettmers, 2017a; Middleton, 2007). Work facilitated by the use of ICT outside the physical workspace has been termed work extension (Towers et al., 2006), boundary-spanning work (Voydanoff, 2005), organizational pervasive technology use (Turel et al., 2011), technology-assisted supplemental work (TASW; Fenner & Renn, 2010), work connectivity after-hours (Richardson & Benbunan-Fich, 2011), and mobile work (Middleton, 2008).[1] We use the broader term "ICT use" to encompass both utilizing ICT in the home for work-related purposes and in the workplace for family-related purposes, although extant research has focused much more on the former.

---

[1] Scholars have occasionally opted for more colorful, pejorative terms including "corporate colonization of the lifeworld" (Edley, 2001) and "techno-invasion" (Tu, Wang, & Shu, 2005).

Importantly, telecommuting is a related trend that has also been made possible largely due to the emergence of new ICTs but is outside the scope of the current review. Whereas telecommuting is relatively formally embedded within the psychological contract pertaining to one's role and is marked by relatively consistent expectations regarding when and how work is to be performed at home (cf. Chapter 19), use of ICT to perform work after hours is much more ambiguous (Derks & Bakker, 2014). Thus, the two phenomena may have distinct correlates and are worthy of separate examination (Fenner & Renn, 2010).

In the following sections, we begin by examining predictors of ICT use, including organizational availability expectations and individual differences. We then explore the association of both organizational availability expectations and actual ICT use with employee well-being, outcomes in the family domain, and outcomes in the work domain. We conclude by presenting a model summarizing the current literature and highlighting potential future directions.

23.2.1 Predictors of ICT Use for Work-Related Purposes at Home

Organizational Factors.   A small body of research has examined organizational factors that predict employees' use of ICT during non-work hours. Much of this research has focused on organizational availability expectations, which refer to an organization's culture surrounding the desirability and necessity of performing supplemental work using ICT outside the workplace. These expectations may be communicated explicitly (e.g., directly telling an employee that being ready to answer phone calls after work is expected) or implicitly (e.g., an employee witnesses rapid responses from coworkers when a group email is sent after-hours; Dettmers, 2017a).

Not surprisingly, availability expectations are generally associated with higher employee availability behaviors, such as responding quickly to requests sent via ICT (Dettmers, 2017b; Fenner & Renn, 2010). Intricately related to availability expectations, a norm of responsiveness refers to the value that organizations place on employees being ready and willing to respond quickly to after-hour communications (Barley, Meyerson, & Grodal, 2011). When norms of responsiveness are high, those who respond quickly are perceived by managers or co-workers as more attentive and committed. On the other hand, those who do not conform are often perceived negatively by coworkers. Norms of responsiveness are often strictly enforced; employees may take actions to alter the behavior of non-compliant team members by marking emails as urgent or by CCing other stakeholders when requesting action (Barley et al., 2011). Some researchers have opted for examining more proximal predictors of ICT use than organizational climate. For instance, the actual frequency of requests from coworkers has been found to predict employee ICT use for after-hours work (Arlinghaus & Nachreiner, 2013; Grotto & Lyness, 2010; Voydanoff, 2005). The number of different sources of requests (e.g., both organizational insiders and outsiders) also predicts ICT use (Matusik & Mickel, 2011).

Telepressure refers to the extent that individuals think about ICT and feel an internal urge to quickly respond to ICT communications (e.g., email) while not at work. Previous research emphasizes that telepressure is associated not only with organizational factors discussed above (e.g., response expectations, work demands) but also with individual antecedents (e.g., self-consciousness/impression management, affective commitment), which are discussed in the following section in greater detail (Barber & Santuzzi, 2015). Importantly, telepressure may serve to mediate the relationship between demands and use, although this evidence is cross-sectional in nature (Barber & Santuzzi, 2015).

Organizational availability expectations, norms of responsiveness, specific behaviors of co-workers, telepressure, availability behaviors (i.e., being ready to respond via ICT), actual employee use of ICT, and even addiction to ICT use are all linked in a complex pattern of relationships. Table 23.1 provides an overview of each of these constructs to provide additional conceptual clarity.

Individual Differences.   Individuals may differ in their frequency and patterns of ICT use based on a variety of individual factors. Previous research suggests that individuals differ significantly in the amount of ICT use both within and outside the workplace based upon occupation (Chesley, 2006). Specifically, professionals (e.g., lawyers, doctors) report the highest rates of use of ICT at home among all occupational categories, followed by clerical/office/sales staff, in turn followed by semi-skilled tradespeople (e.g., truck driver; Chesley, Siibak, & Wajcman, 2013; Wajcman et al., 2010). Certain job characteristics may help elucidate these occupational differences. For instance, the degree to which one has control of scheduling time and place of work is associated with higher ICT use (Chesley, 2006). Additionally, perceived total workload and weekly work hours are positively associated with frequency of ICT use, although without experimental evidence, it is not possible to tease apart whether ICT use is adopted to cope with a heavy workload or if ICT use in fact leads to a greater amount of work to be completed (Towers et al., 2006). Finally, both job involvement – the centrality of one's work to one's identity – and ambition – the drive to attain career success – are positively associated with ICT use (Boswell & Olson-Buchanan, 2007).

Men appear more likely than women to use ICT for work purposes at home. This finding may be due to a number of factors, including gendered occupational segregation (i.e., men work in more time-intensive positions; Wajcman, Bittman, & Brown, 2008) and gender role expectations (i.e., men are expected to devote more resources to the work role than are women; Gutek, Searle, & Klepa, 1991). Indeed, very little current evidence exists regarding the role of demographic variables on ICT use for work-related purposes at home, controlling for occupational factors. However, it has been found that use of ICT is negatively associated with age and positively associated with education level (Chesley et al., 2013). Thus, those with less familiarity with ICT may be more resistant to its adoption.

Individual attitudes toward (1) technology, (2) the way work and family boundaries are managed, and (3) the combination of both play an important role in ICT use. *Technology means efficacy* is defined as the belief that technology will help an

Table 23.1 *Disentangling ICT constructs*

Construct	Operational definition	Key Source(s)
Demands		
Availability expectations	Organizational climate pertaining to the expectation that employees are available across time and space to perform work	Bergman & Gardiner, 2007; Dettmers, 2017a
Norms of responsiveness	Organizational climate pertaining to an expectation that employees are willing to respond quickly to after-hours ICT requests	Barley, Meyerson, & Grodal, 2011
Frequency of ICT requests	Number of ICT requests received by an employee from organizational insiders or outsiders after hours	Arlinghaus & Nachreiner, 2013; Grotto & Lyness, 2010; Voydanoff, 2005
Psychological State		
Telepressure	Frequency and intensity of employee urges to check and respond to after-hours ICT requests; conceptualized as emerging from person by environment interaction	Barber & Santuzzi, 2015
Behaviors		
ICT use – General	Irrespective of purpose, the frequency and intensity of ICT use; often used as proxy for after-hours work via ICT	Chesley, 2005; Derks & Bakker, 2014
ICT use – After-hours work	Frequency and intensity of ICT use for conducting after-hours work	Fenner & Renn, 2010; Park & Jex, 2011
Extended work availability	Psychological and instrumental preparedness to perform ICT after-hours work, irrespective of whether requests are received	Dettmers, 2017a
ICT addiction	Compulsive use of ICT, including frequent checking for new requests, which interferes with other responsibilities and provokes anxiety when ICT use is blocked	Porter & Kakabadse, 2006; Turel, Serenko, & Bontis, 2011

individual meet work demands (Fenner & Renn, 2010). *Preference for polychronicity* is defined as the desire and motivation to engage in multiple activities simultaneously (Richardson & Benbunan-Fich, 2011). Both attitudes are positively associated with ICT use. But individuals are likely to evaluate the impact of ICT use not only on performance of work responsibilities but also on the family role. According to boundary theory, individuals establish physical and psychological boundaries around the separate roles they inhabit (e.g., work and family) in order to structure and make sense of their identity and external environment (Ashforth, Kreiner, & Fugate, 2000). Importantly, individuals differ in the degree to which they prefer to integrate or segment roles, resulting in differential "boundary work" behaviors to maintain integration or segmentation (Nippert-Eng, 1996). Previous research demonstrates that individuals with high segmentation preferences use ICT for work-related purposes at home less frequently than those with low segmentation preferences (Olson-Buchanan & Boswell, 2006; Richardson & Benbunan-Fich, 2011). This may occur in part because integrators perceive higher control over when and how they transition between work and family roles while using ICT. On the other hand, segmentors perceive lower control (Piszczek, 2017). In conclusion, appraisals regarding both ICT utility and desirability may coalesce prior to ICT use decisions.

23.3 Consequences of ICT Expectations and Use for Work-Related Purposes at Home

Compared with antecedents of ICT adoption, the outcomes of availability expectations and ICT use have received considerably more research attention. Presently we discuss the association of ICT use behaviors and availability expectations with employee well-being (i.e., subjective user reactions, recovery, and physical and psychological health), family outcomes (i.e., crossover to other family members), work outcomes (i.e., job attitudes), and outcomes that span both domains of work and family (i.e., work-family conflict). Where appropriate, we also explore the role of moderators on these relationships.

Subjective User Reactions. A basic issue related to work-related ICT use during non-work hours pertains to an individual's perceptions about how use impacts his or her ability to manage work and family. Regarding global perceptions, some individuals report overall that ICT is helpful, some that it is harmful, and some that the impact on their lives is neutral (Towers et al., 2006). When probed to qualitatively describe their feelings about their devices, most users of ICT – specifically, BlackBerries – chose descriptors such as freeing or useful and rarely reported negative attributes (Middleton, 2007). In fact, across job levels, 78 percent of workers indicated that having email/internet at home has improved their ability to do their job to at least some extent (Chesley et al., 2013). Middleton (2008) found that executives report that they gain more work-life balance with the use of ICT as they are able to attend family events or take vacations while knowing they can address pressing work issues should they arise. Employees may also feel that ICT enables better time management and efficiency by making otherwise nonproductive time productive, such as checking emails during one's morning train commute (Towers et al., 2006; Townsend & Batchelor, 2008).

Although having the *option* to use ICT is associated with positive reactions, the pressure and expectations surrounding ICT use tend to elicit primarily negative reactions. In one study, 78 percent of ICT users identified that availability expectations were a concern (Matusik & Mickel, 2011). More specifically, another study found that 41 percent of employees felt that ICT use had increased overall demands, and 43 percent indicated that the presence of ICT made it harder to forget about work on nights and weekends (Chesley et al., 2013). In addition to perceptions of an overall higher quantity of demands, perceptions of greater work pressure may also occur (Chesley, 2006). Lastly, despite evidence cited above that individuals are more likely to take vacations because ICT ensures they can keep up on work responsibilities, employees simultaneously report the inability to truly enjoy vacations because of the pressure to continually check messages and emails (Heijstra & Rafnsdottir, 2010).

Reactions to ICT expectations may be negative, positive, or a combination of the two. Qualitative research on American employees from a variety of occupations revealed that mobile phone use led to a mix of both positive and negative reactions (Lowry & Moskos, 2008). A qualitative study of Icelandic professors – a profession marked by very high levels of work autonomy – noted that participants felt simultaneously empowered by ICT to help them continually be engaged in their research but also exhausted by the perpetual stream of requests from students (Heijstra & Rafnsdottir, 2010). Matusik and Mickel (2011) identified three distinct profiles of individual reactions to ICT: *enthusiastic* users reported primarily positive psychological and instrumental outcomes from ICT use; *balanced* users reported benefits and drawbacks for both the work and family domains, resulting in efforts to moderate ICT use; and *trade-off* users focused on the work-related benefits of ICT use and the subsequent detriment to the family domain. The motivation for ICT use was closely tied to profile membership such that enthusiastic users were more likely to report voluntary adoption of ICT for its utility, whereas balanced and trade-off users were more likely to cite organizational requirements.

ICT use spans a broad range of devices and types of use. Regarding differences among specific devices, BlackBerries elicited the strongest user opinions, both negative and positive, compared with mobile phones (pre-smartphones), PDAs, laptops, and home PCs (Towers et al., 2006). BlackBerries and other smartphones are unique among ICT in the variety of tasks that they allow and the ease of mobile use, which may explain the simultaneous perceptions of utility and frustrations associated with their intrusion into family life (Matusik & Mickel, 2011). Drilling down to specific communication medium, research suggests that email, compared to telephone use, may be particularly stressful, and hence associated with greater overload and perceived inability to cope. One explanation is the sheer volume of emails received in comparison to other media. Employees often fear that they may fall behind and lose control of their inbox or will miss important information because of the constant onslaught (Barley et al., 2011).

Overall, it seems that the primary benefit of ICT use is that it increases flexibility by allowing work to be done at different times and in different places, resulting in greater ability to meet both family and work demands (Towers et al., 2006). This can relieve stress and create higher self-perceptions of productivity. But it also may increase expectations of being available at all times, increasing overall demands (Middleton, 2007) and can lead to role overload or perceived inability to stop thinking about work (Chesley et al., 2013).

Recovery. Adequate recovery from work-related stressors is associated with a plethora of positive outcomes (Sonnentag & Bayer, 2005; Sonnentag & Fritz, 2015; Sonnentag, Kuttler, & Fritz, 2010). Psychological detachment represents a highly researched recovery state marked by being both physically and psychologically disengaged from work, not merely absent from the workplace but also free from work-related thoughts (Etzion, Eden, & Lapidot, 1998). In the short-term, psychological detachment is associated with positive mood, lower emotional exhaustion, and lower fatigue after work (Sonnentag & Bayer, 2005; Sonnentag et al., 2010). Over longer periods of time, detachment from work is associated with higher life satisfaction and lower levels of burnout (Sonnentag & Fritz, 2015).

Inability to psychologically detach is predicted by organizational expectations and coworker ICT requests (Dettmers, Vahle-Hinz, et al., 2016); each account for incremental variance in detachment, suggesting that the two are not always in perfect alignment (Dettmers, Bamberg, & Seffzek, 2016). Similar to availability expectations, actual ICT use displays a significant relationship with psychological detachment. For instance, Derks, van Mierlo, and Schmitz (2014) found that excessive use of an employer-provided smartphone for work purposes while at home was negatively associated with detachment. In an attempt to tie together all of the above, Dettmers (2017a) tested a mediation model, finding that the relationship between availability expectations and detachment is partially mediated through actual ICT use. In a similar manner, preference for integration is associated with a lack of detachment, and the relationship between the two is mediated by ICT use (Park, Fritz, & Jex, 2011). Although the literature is slightly disjointed in terms of the relationships under focus, the best evidence currently suggests that both availability expectations and preference for integration are associated with increased ICT use, which is in turn associated with an inability to psychologically detach.

Numerous boundary conditions may impact the relationships above. Among employees who are expected to be available after hours, those who perceive greater ability to control when and how they receive ICT requests experience greater psychological detachment than those who perceive less control (Dettmers, Bamberg, et al., 2016). Also, counterintuitive outcomes may occur when organizational expectations shift unexpectedly. Due to their expectation that work be segmented from family life, employees in an organization with high segmentation norms may experience relatively less ability to detach on days wherein they must utilize ICT after hours compared with employees in organizations with high integration norms (Derks et al., 2014). This may be because such work is unexpected, and employees thus lack the necessary coping mechanisms.

Physical and Psychological Health. Recent evidence suggests that ICT expectations and use may be associated with general somatic complaints, sleep disturbances, mood impairments, exhaustion, and physiological markers of stress. In a large European sample, controlling for a wide range of demographic and work-related variables, being contacted via ICT outside work hours for work-related purposes was significantly associated with an increased likelihood of endorsing any of sixteen different health impairments, such as mental health problems and musculoskeletal complaints (Arlinghaus & Nachreiner, 2013). Research on American workers has found a similar link between being contacted outside work and psychological and physical strain reactions, including perceived inability to cope and complaints of headaches and stomach upset (Voydanoff, 2005).

A burgeoning area of interest is the relationship between ICT use and sleep. Availability expectations are associated with increased risk of insomnia (Voydanoff, 2005). More specifically, use of ICT at home has been linked to poorer sleep outcomes, including quantity, quality, and consistency – defined as how frequently one maintains the same sleep schedule across nights. Furthermore, lack of detachment was found to significantly mediate the effect of ICT use at home on poor sleep outcomes (Barber & Jenkins, 2014). Thus, poor sleep may result via two related pathways: individuals are spending more time working instead of sleeping, and even while not actively using their device, they experience the emotional and cognitive aftereffects of telepressure (Barber & Santuzzi, 2015). Fortunately, the degree to which individuals create boundaries around the specific times and ways in which ICT is utilized in the home may mitigate the negative association between ICT use and sleep outcomes (Barber & Jenkins, 2014). In particular, utilizing ICT only on certain days or times, only for outbound rather than inbound work, and only for emergencies were all associated with better sleep quality, quantity, and consistency.

Research has found that, within individuals, greater daily required extended work availability is positively associated with the next day's cortisol awakening response (an important indicator of the body's stress level and precursor to numerous health conditions). It is also associated with emotional exhaustion (Derks et al., 2014; Dettmers, Bamberg, et al., 2016) and next-day morning mood (i.e., lower energetic arousal, lower calmness, and more negative valence). Furthermore, the relationship between extended work availability and next-day mood is mediated by perceived lack of control over off-hours activities, an important psychological recovery experience (Dettmers, Vahle-Hinz, et al., 2016). Overall, this research demonstrates the potential links between the psychological experience of recovery, affect, and health consequences.

Work-Family Conflict. Work-family conflict occurs when pressures from the work role and family role are incompatible in some respect (Greenhaus & Beutell, 1985). Work-family conflict may be time-based, strain-based, or behavior-based. Time-based conflict occurs when the time spent in one domain directly reduces time that can be devoted to the other, such as staying late at work instead of attending a child's soccer game. Strain-based conflict occurs when stressors in one domain carry over into strain reactions in the other, such as fighting with one's coworkers because of negative emotions experienced at home. Finally, behavior-based conflict occurs when the behaviors of one domain are inappropriately applied to the other, such as an employee enacting stern management tactics with his or her children (Greenhaus & Beutell, 1985). Conflict can occur in two distinct directions: work-to-family and family-to-work (Frone, Russell, & Cooper, 1992; Greenhaus & Beutell, 1985).

Typically variables in the work domain are studied as predictors of work-to-family conflict; thus, research on work-related ICT use at home has largely focused on this direction of conflict. The following related constructs have all been found to have significant associations with work-to-family conflict: frequency of general ICT use (Derks et al., 2015; Fenner & Renn, 2010), frequency of mobile device use for work (Ferguson et al., 2016; Schieman & Young, 2013), intensity of smartphone use (Derks & Bakker, 2014), perceived availability expectations from coworkers (Harris, Marett, & Harris, 2011), frequency of ICT requests from coworkers (Grotto & Lyness, 2010), perceived supervisor expectations (Derks et al., 2015), and organizational availability expectations transmitted through actual availability behaviors (Dettmers, 2017a).

Evidence suggests that ICT expectations and use are associated with all three types of work-to-family conflict (i.e., time-based, strain-based, and behavior-based; Ferguson et al., 2016). Although ICT use naturally implies time-based conflict (i.e., time is devoted to work-related tasks instead of family-related tasks), conflict may occur via strain as well, particularly emotional exhaustion (Ferguson et al., 2016). Taking an episodic, within-person approach to ICT use, Butts, Becker, and Boswell (2015) found that negative affective tone of after-hour email communications and the time required to address email requests were both associated with greater work-to-family conflict, and both relationships were mediated by the experience of anger.

A point worth considering is that work-related ICT use at home and personal-related ICT use in the workplace are behaviors that may actually represent a form of work-family conflict, rather than just acting as a correlate. That is, these behaviors represent cross-domain intrusions, which may impede performance in the domain where one is physically located. Such behaviors are not captured in typical measures of work-life/family conflict (e.g., Carlson, Kacmar, & Williams, 2000; Netemeyer, Boles, & McMurrian, 1996), which were developed before the proliferation of ICT. We urge future researchers to consider measurement of work-family conflict in light of technological changes, as current measures may not be capturing the full content domain.

Researchers have also examined how individual traits and behaviors mitigate or exacerbate the relationship between ICT use and work-to-family conflict. At the trait level, negative affectivity intensifies the strength of the relationship between technology use pressures and work-to-family conflict (Harris et al., 2011). Time management skills moderate the relationship between ICT use and work-to-family conflict, such that greater time management skills weaken the relationship between the two (Fenner & Renn, 2010). The authors explain this relationship by arguing that those with greater time management skills are more adept at setting goals and priorities for work-related ICT use and thus presumably had fewer time demands as a result.

At the daily, within-person level, researchers have found that the relationship between daily smartphone use and work-home interference is moderated by daily work engagement, such that the relationship is weaker when work engagement is higher (Derks et al., 2015). The authors speculate that work engagement is associated with completing work activities while at work, thus reducing the need to bring them home, and that high activation at work may spill over into high activation in fulfilling responsibilities at home. Additionally, stable boundary management preferences moderate the relationship between the amount of time required to complete emailed tasks and daily work-to-family conflict, such that when preference for segmentation is high, the amount of time required is more strongly associated with perceptions of conflict (Butts et al., 2015).

Crossover to Other Family Members. Crossover refers to the process by which the experiences of an employee in the workplace impact the experiences of his or her family members (Kossek et al., 2011; Westman & Etzion, 2005). "Absent presence" is a term that has emerged to reflect the way in which those using ICT for work purposes at home are not able to devote attention to family members, effectively taunting them with their physical but not psychological presence (Middleton, 2008; Middleton & Cukier, 2006). Evidence suggests that quality time, more so than quantity of time, between parents and children is crucial for relationship quality. This connotes maintaining a psychological focus with full attention on the present situation (Galinsky, 1999). When employees are not focused at home due to work-related ICT use, spouses and children may express strong feelings of resentment, frustration, exasperation, and loneliness (Lowry & Moskos, 2008; Middleton, 2008; Steiner-Adair & Barker, 2013). Such attitudes may also extend to the employee's organization. For instance, ICT-related work-to-family conflict has been associated with spousal resentment toward the family member's employer (Ferguson et al., 2016).

Beyond immediate reactions, use of technology by one family member may be associated with future technology use by other family members. For instance, in a longitudinal study, a husband's use of communications technology significantly predicted his wife's use of communications technology two years later – although, interestingly, the reverse was not true (Chesley, 2006). These study findings may be specific to the historical context in which they were collected (i.e., during widespread adoption of cell phones but before complete ubiquity), but they could potentially generalize to current ICT adoption patterns. Thus, preliminary evidence suggests that couples may not only experience stress as a result of their spouse's technology use but also become more alike over time in their technology use.

Additionally, parental use of ICT sends powerful messages to children about the role of technology in life, modeling behavior that may be adopted as children grow older (Steiner-Adair & Barker, 2013). Additional research is needed to identify the relationship between parents' use of ICT for work and children's own technology use, both in childhood and in later years. Such research is warranted considering the negative impact that personal excessive technology use can have on children's healthy psychological development (Steiner-Adair & Barker, 2013).

Job Attitudes. The relationship between use of ICT during off-work hours for work-related purposes and job attitudes is not entirely straightforward. For instance, different studies suggest organizational commitment demonstrates a negative (Lim & Teo, 2000), positive (Golden & Geisler, 2007), or null (Boswell & Olson-Buchanan, 2007) relationship with ICT use. These conflicting findings may be due in part to the multiple potential mechanisms through which organizational commitment and use of ICT are related. Namely, use of ICT may lead to lower organizational commitment via work overload-related frustration and exhaustion, or high organizational commitment may lead to more willingness to use ICT (Turel et al., 2011). With regard to job satisfaction, the perception that one's ICT use interferes with family responsibilities is negatively associated with job satisfaction, but the objective time spent using ICT is not related to job satisfaction (Wright et al., 2014).

The fit between employee preferences for segmentation and organizational policies that promote segmentation (i.e., not having strong after-hours ICT use norms) may predict job attitudes better than either variable in isolation. For instance, Rothbard, Phillips, and Dumas (2005) found that job satisfaction and organizational commitment are lower for individuals who value segmentation when policies promote integration, whereas job satisfaction and organizational commitment are higher for individuals who value integration when these policies are instituted. Although this particular study assessed the organizational policies and practices of onsite childcare and flextime, it is conceivable that policies around technology use have similar interactions with employee segmentation preferences.

Job attitudes, such as organizational commitment and job satisfaction, may have important downstream consequences. Mobile telephone use for work purposes at home is related to turnover intentions with the effect serially mediated via strain-based work-to-family conflict to higher burnout to lower organizational commitment to higher turnover intentions (Ferguson et al., 2016). As another causal explanation, the impact of employee work-to-family conflict on spousal resentment toward an employee's organization was also associated with higher employee turnover intentions. Hence, ICT use outside work may predict turnover intentions not only through the employee's attitudes but also the attitudes of the employee's family.

23.3.1 Summary

Drawing on the study findings reviewed in this section, the relationships among predictors of ICT use, perceived pressure (i.e., telepressure), actual ICT use behaviors, and outcomes are summarized in Figure 23.1. Several important take-aways emerge from this model. Whether ICT is "good" or "bad" for employee outcomes is ultimately an oversimplification of the issue (Day et al., 2010) because ICT may serve as either a demand or resource (Bakker & Demerouti, 2007; Demerouti et al., 2001) depending on the attributes of the organization and the individual. Additionally, organizational and individual characteristics may be

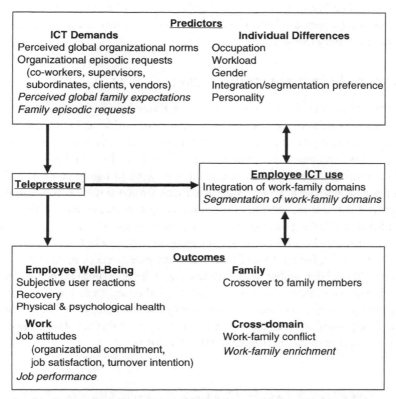

Figure 23.1 *The role of cross-domain information and communication technology use on employee outcomes. Italicized terms represent suggested areas for future research*

associated with important outcomes via their impact on employee behaviors or directly through the telepressure experienced as a result of demands.

This model is intended to illustrate time-based, dynamic relationships. Specifically, general expectations from family and work may be best suited to predicting between-person differences in outcomes, whereas specific episodes of demands from either domain may help uncover within-person differences in outcomes across time. Additionally, ICT use exhibits bidirectional relationships with both predictors and outcomes. Previous longitudinal research suggests that organizational expectations and availability behaviors demonstrate a bidirectional relationship, such that (1) higher expectations are associated with more availability behaviors in the future, and (2) making oneself more available is associated with increased organizational expectations. This may result in a positive feedback loop of continually increasing demands (Dettmers, 2017a). An employee's ICT use may also have an influence on family expectations (Steiner-Adair & Barker, 2013). Regarding the link between ICT use and outcomes, boundary management via ICT represents an ongoing process that may shift depending on the results of previous behavior. For instance, neglect of family responsibilities due to ICT use may be followed by a period of less ICT use in order to achieve greater balance between work and family (Shockley & Allen, 2015).

23.3.2 Family-Related ICT Use at Work

The previous sections on ICT use have been devoted entirely to the correlates of ICT use *for work-related purposes at home*. We were unable to locate any studies that directly examine predictors of ICT use *for family-related purposes at work*, but several studies have examined the consequences of this behavior. Similar to the manner in which use of ICT at home is associated with work-to-family conflict, ICT use for family-related issues at work is associated with family-to-work conflict. In particular, there is a stronger association between checking personal email and family-to-work conflict than checking Facebook or texting (Berkowsky, 2013). However, just as ICT use at home may be seen as a tool for meeting work demands, ICT use at work may be vital for meeting family demands, such as when parents check in on children at home (Edley, 2001). Highlighting gender differences, Chesley (2005) found that technology use is not associated with family-to-work conflict for men, but it is for women, suggesting that men and women differentially use technology for fulfillment of work and family roles. In turn, there is research to suggest that non-task-related ICT use hinders short-term task performance (Brooks, 2015).

23.4 Social Media and Work and Non-Work Selves

Another prominent technological change that has blossomed in the 2000s is the ubiquity of social media, such as Facebook, Instagram, Twitter, and Snapchat. Over 1.5 billion people around the globe are active Facebook users, including 68 percent of adults in the United States (Pew Research Center, 2017). This brings up an interesting question regarding the blurring of work and non-work identities, as before the social media era it was much easier to keep work and non-work identities completely separated (Fieseler, Meckel, & Ranzini, 2015). To date, there is limited empirical research linking social media use to specific work-family outcomes. However, there is a body of work focused on understanding strategies people use to manage multiple identities via social media.

van Zoonen, Verhoeven, and Vliegenthart (2016) conducted the only known study empirically investigating social media use and work-life conflict. They focused specifically on work-related social media use and theorized that processing and publishing information on social media creates cognitive demands for employees beyond normal work demands, resulting in a depletion of resources, which results in less ability to manage multiple life roles and in turn perceptions of work-life conflict. The data gathered from Dutch employees supported these hypothesized relationships, but the association between work-related social media use and life-to-work conflict was stronger than that of work-to-life conflict, which is counterintuitive given theory regarding domain specific predictors (Frone et al., 1992).

A small stream of research has developed that focuses on how people manage multiple role identities via social media. Understanding this process is critical given the potential repercussions of mismanagement, which may include losing respect of professional colleagues for personal-life social media actions. Real-life examples of these repercussions have made headlines. In 2011, an American teacher was forced to resign for simply posting a picture on Facebook where she was holding a beer (Fastenberg, 2011). Several people have been fired for making racist remarks in the context of non-work situations on social media (Blake, 2016; Boroff, 2016; Ronson, 2015). On the other hand, personal self-disclosure to one's professional network can also have positive benefits, increasing liking and respect (Ollier-Malaterre, Rothbard, & Berg, 2013).

In a theoretical paper, Ollier-Malaterre et al. (2013) propose a taxonomy of four different social media boundary management styles: *open* (no restrictions on who can view content and no differentiation between professional and personal contacts), *audience* (designate certain social media sites as personal and others as professional; deny friend requests from professional networks on those deemed personal and make the profile private), *content* (post only flattering and noncontroversial content; highly monitor appearance in other people's postings and comments), and *hybrid* (create "groups" within social media content and cater content to each group). The authors assert that there are two main drivers behind people's management style: (1) preference for segmentation versus integration of work and non-work roles and (2) self-verification motives, which can include self-enhancement (i.e., presenting the self in a positive, socially desirable manner) and self-verification (i.e., behaving in a way that confirms one's own view of the self, whether positive or negative). Additionally, they argue that each management style is likely to result in different levels of liking and respect from professional colleagues. Content and hybrid approaches are likely to generate the most respect and liking but are also the most time-consuming and cognitively demanding.

There is no known data reporting on the percentage of people that fall into these various categories. However, one study found that 91 percent of people who have received coworker friend requests on Facebook accepted them and 75 percent did so without adjusting their privacy settings (Frampton & Child, 2013). This suggests that the *open* method is quite common. On the other hand, a qualitative study based on a small sample of Indian IT workers found that the common approaches most closely align with the *audience* and *hybrid* methods (Gonibeed & Ravishankar, 2016). Larger studies of diverse workers are needed for clarification regarding prevalence. Moreover, Batenburg and Bartels (2017) tested the effects of various strategies on liking and respect using an experimental methodology. Participants reviewed a Facebook profile of a possible colleague that displayed one of the four strategies and rated the individual on likeability and respect. The *content* strategy resulted in the highest liking ratings. These results should be interpreted with the caveat that this design is likely not able to capture social media dynamics as they unfold in the real world, given that exposure to a colleague's social media content and subsequent reactions takes place over time and people are likely not aware of the specific management strategy that a colleague is using.

An important avenue for future research is to examine how these various strategies relate to work-family outcomes. For example, it is conceivable that the *open* strategy increases stress and feelings of work-family conflict, if one ruminates over coworkers' responses to a given posting. Conversely, the *open* approach could facilitate coworkers having a better understanding of one's personal life and in response being more supportive when instrumental assistance is needed to manage work-family conflict (e.g., offering to cover a shift because she has seen through social media how difficult a child's recent illness is). This parallels Ollier-Malaterre et al.'s (2013) idea that the *open* approach may lead to increased coworker liking. It would be useful to also determine if this liking translates into actual supportive behaviors, which have been shown to be critical in mitigating work-family conflict (Hammer et al., 2009).

23.5 Technology and Economic Changes

Technology has brought about several economic changes that impact the way work is conducted. The ability to work remotely, easily communicate with people across the globe, and use online marketplaces that connect workers and clients have allowed for the emergence of a freelance economy. In fact, estimates suggest that the number of freelance workers has increased by around 27 percent more than the number of payroll employees over the past twenty years (Hathaway & Muro, 2016). This changing nature of work grants employees more autonomy and discretion over their work, which can help in managing work and family roles (e.g., Michel et al., 2011) but can also introduce new levels of job insecurity and instability, which can negatively impact the work-family interface (e.g., Lawrence et al., 2013).

There is limited research specifically focused on freelancers or independent contractors in relation to work-family outcomes. Prottas and Thompson (2006) analyzed data from a nationally representative sample of American workers, comparing independent contractors, owners (self-employed people who had others on their payroll), and traditional employees. Independent contractors reported significantly lower work-family conflict than both owners and traditional employees, but these differences were no longer significant when controlling for work and demographic characteristics. Other research has focused on how being self-employed impacts the division of labor between parents of young children. Using an Australian sample, Craig, Powell, and Cortis (2012) found that mothers use self-employment as a way to combine paid labor with childcare, often working from home, whereas fathers' involvement in childcare does not vary as a function of their employment type. This suggests that freelancing may serve as a method for women, more so than men, to cope with competing work and family demands.

A related idea is the concept of perceived flexibility requirements, which are "new" managerial strategies that organizations have adopted to face the changing economy that aim to enhance organizations' flexibility, adaptability, and efficiency (Höge, 2011). This includes practices that generally give employees more discretion in how and when tasks are completed as well as taking responsibility for one's own career development and growth and learning. Höge and Hornung (2013) tested a model linking four types of perceived flexibility requirements (task responsibility, career development, learning, and time) to work-family conflict. They found that only perceived flexibility in working time related to work-family conflict, and the association was positive such that greater flexibility lead to higher conflict. This finding highlights some of the potential negative consequences of increased flexibility. Other researchers have also noted how the changing nature of work has potential to negatively impact workers, including the intensification of job demands (Kubicek, Paškvan, & Korunka, 2015), and autonomy itself as a job demand in that it requires job redesign (Bredehöft et al., 2015). A second technology-enabled economic change is the increasing automation of work. A recent PwC estimates that close to 38 percent of jobs in the USA will be replaced by robots in the next fifteen years (Berriman & Hawksworth, 2017). Researchers have not yet studied this issue in relation to the WF interface to our knowledge, but we speculate that it has potential to impact family dynamics in many ways. With a reduction of available low-skill jobs, a large sector of the workforce will be forced to find different types of employment. Some of these opportunities will require higher levels of education, adding time and financial demands to family, whereas difficulty finding employment for those who opt to not gain new skills clearly adds financial strain. Some have argued that the appropriate societal response to automation is a universal basic income, in which every citizen is guaranteed a certain level of income (e.g., Murray, 2016). If this economic change were to be instituted, it has the potential to shift individuals' attention to caring for family due to work no longer being an economic necessity. Or, drawing on the argument that work may be defined loosely as agentic creation (Weiss, 2014), work will simply alter its form from the current paradigm of employment to one in which individuals maximize their strengths and their identity as a worker.

Lastly, technology has enabled globalization and an increase in multi-national corporations. There is considerable variation across countries in terms of cultural norms, economic conditions, and legislation (House et al., 2004; Olliere-Malaterre & Foucreault, 2017). These macro factors can interact with organizational policies to impact people's successful management of WF issues (Powell, Francesco, & Ling, 2009; Shockley, French, & Yu, 2018). With this in mind, it is important for multi-national organizations to consider the local context when implementing policies, as a "one size fits all countries" approach is not likely to be successful (Biga et al., 2016). For example, Lu et al. (2010) found that employees residing in a country high in the cultural value of power distance (i.e., Taiwan), defined as the degree that cultures expect power to be unequally distributed (House et al., 2004), benefit more from family-supportive supervisors in terms of reduced work-family conflict than people in a lower power distance culture (i.e., Great Britain). The authors argued this was because people in such cultures are not used to receiving support, making it more impactful. Similarly, organizations may not need to offer as extensive parental leave policies in countries where this is a part of state-sponsored welfare, or, conversely, may find that offering generous policies in places where state-mandated policies are weak is an effective recruiting and retention tool.

23.6 Biomedical Advances

As a relatively new technological advancement, *oocyte cryopreservation* (OC; i.e., the process of cryogenically preserving women's eggs, or ova) has received very little research attention as it pertains to the WF interface. With the advent of OC, families may be both rewarded with new options for family planning but also faced with challenging new considerations. Generally speaking, women face the issue of whether or not to prioritize having children or advancing their careers during peak child-bearing years. The option to preserve their eggs indefinitely could provide a crucial opportunity for women to "have it all," investing the necessary energy into their early career to eventually reach top positions and having children later in life (success with this method has even been achieved for post-menopausal women; Goold & Savulescu, 2009). The cost of OC can be prohibitive (i.e., approximately US $15,000 depending on the number of rounds of egg retrieval), including fees for multiple hormone treatments and egg retrieval procedures, annual storage, and the eventual fertilization procedure (USC Fertility, 2017). However, large organizations, including Intel, Apple, and Facebook, are beginning to subsidize this process, removing the financial burden and potentially making it a feasible option for female employees (Zoll, Mertes, & Gupta, 2015).

Bioethicists disagree on the merits and dangers of OC utilization generally, aside from the issue of employer involvement. Despite the lifting of the "experimental" label for OC by the American Society for Reproductive Technology in 2012, some suggest that insufficient scientific evidence has amassed to support its widespread use in healthy women (Zoll et al., 2015). In fact, production of viable offspring utilizing OC is less likely than natural reproduction, inviting the possibility that women will inadvertently harm their ultimate chances at motherhood (Zoll et al., 2015). On the other hand, others reason that if a female employee unequivocally plans to postpone pregnancy until her late 30s, it is superior for her to have the option of reclaiming a healthier egg from her youth than conceiving naturally (Goold & Savulescu, 2009). Ultimately, the ethical crux of the issue may be the degree to which healthy women are provided sufficient resources to make a fully informed decision after weighing the health risks against the potential gains to their career.

23.7 Future Research Directions

Through our review of the intersection of technology and the work-family interface, we identified several areas that are ripe for future research. Below, we present eight areas for future research; the first five are related specifically to ICT use and are also embedded in Figure 23.1 in italics. The last three are related to social media, economic changes, and biomedical advances.

Switching Off: Individual and Organizational Tactics. Research regarding the implications of ICT use on employee boundary management has focused almost exclusively on the role of technology in blurring boundaries (cf. Towers et al., 2006). However, what is lacking in this research paradigm is empirical assessment of the efficacy of individual and organizational tactics that aim to reduce the impact of ICT use at home. From an individual standpoint, employees have reported managing the pressure from ICT use by turning technology off, limiting individuals who have their contact information, physically leaving technology at work, and establishing a set routine for after-hours activities (Towers et al., 2006). On a smaller scale, employees may contend with "micro-decisions" related to subscribing/unsubscribing from mailing lists, using the "do not disturb" feature on one's smartphone for certain hours, allowing "push" notifications for emails, and using filters for incoming email (Barley et al., 2011). Both the processes impacting these decisions as well as the health and performance implications of these decisions warrant future investigation because it is presently unknown if such behaviors serve to help or harm employees. As an example, individuals may exhibit complex patterns of reducing availability as a function of both work and family demands; these decisions may be associated both with reduced workload but also anxiety around failing to meet organizational expectations.

Additionally, several technological tools have recently become available specifically for employees to manage the demands of work and family. For instance, BlackberryBalance® offers its smartphone users the capability of maintaining completely separate work and personal accounts on their device with differing security clearances, applications, and stored data (Reimer, 2013). In a seeming contradiction, this tool may serve to increase role integration by maintaining all data in the same physical device but also increase segmentation by allowing users to switch over to the personal account when one is done working. As another example, Cozi®, a free smartphone application, boasts a shared calendar and to-do list for all family members to coordinate appointments and activities (Cozi Inc., 2017). Future research efforts should systematically investigate the ability of these and other similar tools to decrease conflicts and increase perceptions of balance, as well as identify the mechanisms through which this occurs.

On a larger scale, organizations are beginning to experiment with counteracting the always on, always connected mentality. In 2011, Volkswagen experimented with shutting down email servers after work hours, in effect making connectivity impossible for its German employees (Ferguson et al., 2016). Similarly, Google implemented a policy in its Dublin, Ireland, office to shut down all work after 6:00 PM, requiring workers to physically turn in their laptops before heading home. Anecdotal evidence suggests that employees were initially disgruntled but then came to appreciate the change (Bock, 2015). Certainly organizational culture, as well as broader industry standards and national culture, are likely to have important implications for the efficacy of these burgeoning initiatives (Perlow & Porter, 2009). As a case in point, France has recently passed legislation requiring that large employers negotiate after-hours email policies with employees to minimize work-family conflict (Rubin, 2017).

Drawing on theory and past evidence, it stands to reason that reducing after-hours connectivity may lead to greater psychological health and recovery (Perlow & Porter, 2009; Sonnentag & Fritz, 2015). However, the results of turning off, particularly when mandated by the organization, are likely to impact individuals in different ways. Indeed, anecdotal evidence suggests that highly engaged workers, or those favoring integration, may choose to disregard organizational policies regarding disengaging from work after hours (Middleton, 2007).

ICT Use and Work-Family Enrichment. Another potential area for future research is to examine if ICT use in the workplace for family-related issues may actually enrich performance on the job, and vice versa. Work-family enrichment represents the process by which resources or positive experiences in one domain transfer over into positive experiences in another domain, flowing either from work-to-family or from family-to-work (Greenhaus & Powell, 2006). For instance, the self-esteem boost that arises from using ICT to solve a work-related issue may transfer into more goal-directed behavior in fulfilling one's role at home and the experience of more positive emotions (Greenhaus & Powell, 2006).

In one study, ICT use was not associated with work-to-family or family-to-work enrichment, even though it was associated with interference in both directions (Chesley, 2005). However, this study did not capture the specific purposes of ICT use, which limits conclusions regarding how performing work tasks in the home and family tasks at work are associated with enrichment. We discovered only one study that purports to find a positive association between ICT use and family-to-work enrichment; however, in reality the study operationalized enrichment as participants' ability to fulfill family requirements while at work, which does not meet typical definitions (Lowry & Moskos, 2008). Thus, there exists a gap in the literature regarding the potentially positive implications of ICT use across domains.

Family Predictors of ICT Use Across Domains. As shown throughout this review, a variety of work-related variables (e.g., workload and organizational availability expectations) have been examined as predictors of ICT use at home. However, very little research has been devoted to examining the other side of the issue: family-related variables that predict ICT use in the home or in the workplace. This is an omission in that it is unlikely that individuals consider only the demands of work when determining whether to make themselves available via ICT at home. Rather, individuals probably weigh the costs and benefits of doing so. Understanding this mental calculus is challenging without examining the number and characteristics of other family members and family-level norms surrounding the appropriate use of ICT. Research suggests that, cutting across job levels and occupation, ICT use for family-related purposes at work is actually more common than for work-related purposes at home (Wajcman et al., 2010). Thus, it would be valuable to understand family variables related to both types of ICT use.

ICT Use and Job Performance. Despite (highly valuable) research efforts examining the association between ICT use and employee well-being, there is a dearth of research on outcomes directly pertaining to organizational effectiveness. Rather, it is reasonably assumed that using ICT at home will allow for the production of a greater quantity of work. But this approach may fail to take into account less immediate outcomes of importance to organizations. For instance, there exists scant evidence on the relationship between ICT use and the quality of work performed while at home and subsequently in the workplace. ICT requests from work may act as an interruption from family, potentially resulting in process loss and less focus than if the same tasks were reserved for the following workday (Chesley et al., 2013).

Furthermore, both the objective frequency of contacts via ICT for work-related purposes outside work and the subjective experience of telepressure are associated with increased likelihood of absenteeism, although the mechanism of this relationship is not well understood (Arlinghaus & Nachreiner, 2013; Barber & Santuzzi, 2015). Theoretically, even if employees do not exhibit absenteeism, the emotional exhaustion (Dettmers, Bamberg, et al., 2016) and heightened stress response (Dettmers, Vahle-Hinz, et al., 2016) that result from a failure to psychologically detach from work may accumulate over time. Psychological detachment has been found previously to be associated with increased work engagement (Kühnel, Sonnentag, & Westman, 2009) and feeling refreshed upon returning to work (Perlow & Porter, 2009). However, we are not aware of a study that has directly assessed if detachment experiences mediate the relationship between ICT use and work engagement, nor if this translates to more effective performance. Research that examines these potential processes, as well as the extent to which ICT policies and practices impact outcomes at higher levels of analysis (e.g., overall organizational effectiveness) would be highly beneficial.

Temporal Approaches to ICT Use. A small body of literature has emerged examining the role of ICT use on outcomes at the within-person level, particularly work-to-family conflict, as discussed earlier in this review (Derks & Bakker, 2014; Derks et al., 2014; Dettmers, Vahle-Hinz, et al., 2016). Until recently, research had almost exclusively examined the association between ICT use and outcomes from a between-person perspective, signifying that employees are asked to identify, on the aggregate, how often they engage in these behaviors and how often certain outcomes occur (Maertz & Boyar, 2011). However, within-person relationships may show different patterns and can help better elucidate temporal order. They are also well-suited to research questions that involve discrete episodes of behaviors, which is the case with ICT use. Therefore, we advocate that longitudinal and experience-sampling methodology should continue to be leveraged to address numerous technology and WF-related questions.

Social Media. Regarding social media, an area of research that remains virtually untapped is the role that social media plays in helping people cope with work-family struggles. The work-family coping literature is quite disjointed and no universally accepted taxonomy of coping strategies exist, but there is some consensus around the idea that people seek emotional support as one way to cope (e.g., Aryee et al., 1999; Neal & Hammer, 2009). Social media may serve as a means for people to cope with work-family concerns by posting about their struggles.

Reactions from others who can empathize might be a useful way to deal with the emotional effects of work-family conflict, such as "working mommy guilt" (Borelli et al., 2017). Indeed, research has found that social media users report receiving more social support than non-users (Hampton et al., 2011). On the other hand, social media use could exacerbate feelings of inadequacy that stem from work-family struggles, given the common social comparison processes induced by social media (Vogel et al., 2014).

Economic Considerations. Empirical research focused on freelancing as it relates to work-family concerns is relatively scant and research related to automation is non-existent. There is however a substantial literature focused on globalization and understanding work-family concerns across the world (cf. Shockley, Shen, & Johnson, 2018). Thus, we recommend that future researchers concentrate efforts on the first two issues. Although a few studies have examined freelancers and self-employed individuals in relation to those in salaried jobs, this research is descriptive in nature, examining main effects. To enhance the practical application of this research we suggest that scholars investigate the specific conditions under which freelancing is beneficial for work-family management. Speculatively, motivation for freelancing may be one important boundary condition. When freelancers are motivated by wanting greater work-life balance, this may facilitate such balance, but when they are motivated by wanting to earn a larger income by being self-employed, this could result in working longer hours and creating additional work demands. Other factors such as the type of occupation and family situation are also likely relevant. In terms of research on automation, this shift is a gradual one and the downstream impact on the labor force is relatively nascent. Changes of this nature are ripe grounds for longitudinal research, and we urge researchers to pre-emptively consider these changes and plan studies that follow employees in different occupational groups over time, assessing changes in their work and family dynamics. Whereas the theoretical bases of the work-family literature, such as boundary theory (Ashforth et al., 2000) and role theory (Katz & Kahn, 1978) are positioned to provide a general framework for understanding how individuals manage the roles in their life, development of theoretical extensions may be critical for driving investigation of how individuals manage roles when these roles are no longer distinct due to economic advances.

Biomedical Advances. Many questions specifically regarding the impact of organizationally sponsored oocyte cryopreservation (OC) on employee behaviors and attitudes remain. It is currently unclear, for instance, whether these subsidies are perceived by employees as a caring gesture made by organizations or rather as a more self-serving attempt to keep women engaged in the workforce instead of prioritizing raising a family. Women may experience some degree of pressure to take advantage of the service, as the act of merely offering it may signal that the organization values or expects prioritization of career over family (Zoll et al., 2015). Examining the primary personal motivations for taking advantage of these programs would be a valuable endeavor. Utilizing longitudinal designs, the long-term impact of OC on work-family conflict should be examined, considering that it may reduce conflict or it may simply shift the modal peak of work-family conflict from middle adulthood to late adulthood. Finally, it remains to be seen if alternative work-family programs, such as extended paid maternal leave and job security, are better for women and society than OC. One set of recommendations is that if an employer chooses to subsidize OC, this should be in combination with other family-friendly policies, not endorsed as a sole solution; the voluntariness of the program should be made clear; and the risks of participation should be thoroughly explained (Mertes, 2015).

Additional advances in medicine may have far-reaching implications for the WF interface that have not yet received research attention. For instance, surrogacy represents another relatively new reproductive option. Although motivations to use a surrogate may be largely related to one's physical health, it may be valuable to identify psychosocial factors that factor into this decision. Specifically, the desire to advance (or maintain) one's career or the desire to avoid pregnancy-related discrimination (cf. Morgan et al., 2013) could be important drivers for women considering this option.

23.8 Conclusion

Advances in technology have changed many aspects of people's lives, and the work-family interface is no exception. The majority of extant research in the area focuses on the impact of work-related ICT use during non-work time, highlighting both the beneficial and detrimental aspects of such technology. Other issues of importance include social media, the freelance on-demand economy, and technology related to fertility. We hope that our chapter spurs future research on these important dynamic topics.

References

American Psychological Association. (2013). Americans stay connected to work on weekends, vacation and even when out sick. Retrieved from www.apa.org/news/press/releases/2013/09/connected-work.aspx.

Arlinghaus, A. & Nachreiner, F. (2013). When work calls: Associations between being contacted outside of regular working hours for work-related matters and health. *Chronobiology International, 30*(9), 1197–1202. doi:10.3109/07420528.2013.800089.

Aryee, S., Luk, V., Leung, A., & Lo, S. (1999). Role stressors, interrole conflict, and well-being: The moderating influence of spousal support and coping behaviors among employed parents in Hong Kong. *Journal of Vocational Behavior, 54*(2), 259–278. doi:10.1006/jvbe.1998.1667.

Ashforth, B. E., Kreiner, G. E., & Fugate, M. (2000). All in a day's work: Boundaries and micro role transitions. *Academy of Management Review, 25*(3), 472–491. doi:10.5465/amr.2000.3363315.

Bakker, A. B. & Demerouti, E. (2007). The Job Demands-Resources model: State of the art. *Journal of Managerial Psychology, 22*(3), 309–328. doi:10.1108/02683940710733115.

Barber, L. K. & Jenkins, J. S. (2014). Creating technological boundaries to protect bedtime: Examining work-home boundary management, psychological detachment and sleep. *Stress Health, 30*(3), 259–264. doi:10.1002/smi.2536.

Barber, L. K. & Santuzzi, A. M. (2015). Please respond ASAP: Workplace telepressure and employee recovery. *Journal of Occupational Health Psychology, 20*(2), 172–189. doi:10.1037/a0038278.

Barley, S. R., Meyerson, D. E., & Grodal, S. (2011). E-mail as a source and symbol of stress. *Organization Science, 22*(4), 887–906. doi:10.1287/orsc.1100.0573.

Batenburg, A. & Bartels, J. (2017). Keeping up online appearances: How self-disclosure on Facebook affects perceived respect and likability in the professional context. *Computers in Human Behavior, 74*, 265–276.

Berkowsky, R. W. (2013). When you just cannot get away. *Information, Communication & Society, 16*(4), 519–541. doi:10.1080/1369118x.2013.772650.

Bergman, A. & Gardiner, J. (2007). Employee availability for work and family: Three Swedish case studies. *Employee Relations, 29*(4), 400–414. doi:10.1108/01425450710759226.

Berriman, R. & Hawksworth, J. (2017). Will robots steal our jobs? The potential impact of automation on the UK and other major economies. *PwC*. Retrieved from www.pwc.co.uk/economic-services/ukeo/pwcukeo-section-4-automation-march-2017-v2.pdf.

Biga, A. M., Church, A. H., Wade, C., Pratt, A. K. Kiburz, K. M., & Brown-Davis, M. (2016). Inside organizations: Work–life issues from a practice perspective. In T. Allen & L. Eby (Eds.), *Oxford handbook of work and family* (pp. 455–65). New York, NY: Oxford University Press.

Blake, A. (December 3, 2016). Denver institutions cut ties with doctor who called Michelle Obama a 'monkey face' on Facebook. *The Washington Times*. Retrieved from www.washingtontimes.com/news/2016/dec/3/denver-institutions-cut-ties-doctor-who-called-mic/.

Bock, L. (2015). *Work rules!: Insights from inside Google that will transform how you live and lead*. New York, NY: Twelve.

Borelli, J. L., Nelson, S. K., River, L. M., Birken, S. A., & Moss-Racusin, C. (2017). Gender differences in work-family guilt in parents of young children. *Sex Roles, 76*, 356–368. doi:10.1007/s11199-016-0579-0.

Boroff, D. (November 25, 2016). Trump supporter in Alabama fired from prestigious bank job after referring to President as "Barrack, socialist Muslim O'Bama." *New York Daily News*. Retrieved from www.nydailynews.com/news/national/trump-supporter-fired-bank-job-racist-obama-comments-article-1.2887173.

Boswell, W. R. & Olson-Buchanan, J. B. (2007). The use of communication technologies after hours: The role of work attitudes and work-life conflict. *Journal of Management, 33*(4), 592–610. doi:10.1177/0149206307302552.

Bredehöft, F., Dettmers, J., Hoppe, A., & Janneck, M. (2015). Individual work design as a job demand: The double-edged sword of autonomy. *Psychology of Everyday Activity, 8*(2), 12–24.

Brooks, S. (2015). Does personal social media usage affect efficiency and well-being? *Computers in Human Behavior, 46*, 26–37.

Butts, M. M., Becker, W. J., & Boswell, W. R. (2015). Hot buttons and time sinks: The effects of electronic communication during nonwork time on emotions and work-nonwork conflict. *Academy of Management Journal*, *58*(3), 763–788. doi:10.5465/amj.2014.0170.

Carlson, Dawn S., Kacmar, K. M., & Williams, L. J. (2000). Construction and initial validation of a multidimensional measure of work–family conflict. *Journal of Vocational Behavior*, *56*(2), 249–276. doi:10.1006/jvbe.1999.1713.

Chesley, N. (2005). Blurring boundaries? Linking technology use, spillover, individual distress, and family satisfaction. *Journal of Marriage & Family*, *67*(5), 1237–1248. doi:10.1111/j.1741–3737.2005.00213.x.

Chesley, N. (2006). Families in a high-tech age. *Journal of Family Issues*, *27*(5), 587–608. doi:10.1177/0192513X05285187.

Chesley, N., Siibak, A., & Wajcman, J. (2013). Information and communication technology use and work-life integration. In D. A. Major & R. Burke (Eds.), *Handbook of work-life integration among professionals: Challenges and opportunities* (pp. 245–268). Cheltenham, UK: Edward Elgar Publishing.

Cozi Inc. (2017). Feature overview. Retrieved from www.cozi.com/feature-overview/.

Craig, L, Powell, A., & Cortis, N. (2012). Self-employment, work-family time and the gender division of labour. *Work, Employment and Society*, *26*, 716–734.

Day, A., Paquet, S., Scott, N., & Hambley, L. (2012). Perceived information and communication technology (ICT) demands on employee outcomes: The moderating effect of organizational ICT support. *Journal of Occupational Health Psychology*, *17*(4), 473–491. doi:10.1037/a0029837.

Day, A., Scott, N., & Kelloway, E. K. (2010). Information and communication technology: Implications for job stress and employee well-being. In P. L. Perrewe & D. C. Ganster (Eds.), *New developments in theoretical and conceptual approaches to job stress* (vol. 8, pp. 317–350). Bingley, UK: Emerald Group Publishing.

Demerouti, E., Bakker, A. B., Nachreiner, F., & Schaufeli, W. B. (2001). The job demands-resources model of burnout. *Journal of Applied Psychology*, *86*(3), 499–512. doi:10.1037/0021–9010.86.3.499.

Derks, D. & Bakker, A. B. (2014). Smartphone use, work-home interference, and burnout: A diary study on the role of recovery. *Applied Psychology: An International Review*, *63*(3), 411–440. doi:10.1111/j.1464–0597.2012.00530.x.

Derks, D., van Duin, D., Tims, M., & Bakker, A. B. (2015). Smartphone use and work-home interference: The moderating role of social norms and employee work engagement. *Journal of Occupational and Organizational Psychology*, *88*(1), 155–177. doi:10.1111/joop.12083.

Derks, D., van Mierlo, H., & Schmitz, E. B. (2014). A diary study on work-related smartphone use, psychological detachment and exhaustion: Examining the role of the perceived segmentation norm. *Journal of Occupational Health Psychology*, *19*(1), 74–84. doi:10.1037/a0035076.

Dettmers, J. (2017a). The differentiated voluntary or expected availability effects on work-family-conflict. Paper presented at the 18th European Association of Work and Organizational Psychology Congress, Dublin, Ireland.

Dettmers, J. (2017b). How extended work availability affects well-being: The mediating roles of psychological detachment and work-family-conflict. *Work and Stress*, *31* (1), 24–41. doi:10.1080/02678373.2017.1298164.

Dettmers, J., Bamberg, E., & Seffzek, K. (2016). Characteristics of extended availability for work: The role of demands and resources. *International Journal of Stress Management*, *23*(3), 276–297. doi:10.1037/str0000014.

Dettmers, J., Vahle-Hinz, T., Bamberg, E., Friedrich, N., & Keller, M. (2016). Extended work availability and its relation with start-of-day mood and cortisol. *Journal of Occupational Health Psychology, 21*(1), 105–118. doi:10.1037/a0039602.

Edley, P. P. (2001). Technology, employed mothers, and corporate colonization of the lifeworld: A gendered paradox of work and family balance. *Women & Language, 24*(2), 28–35.

Etzion, D., Eden, D., & Lapidot, Y. (1998). Relief from job stressors and burnout: Reserve service as a respite. *Journal of Applied Psychology, 83*(4), 577–585. doi:10.1037/0021–9010.83.4.577.

Fastenberg, D. (October 14, 2011). Facebook post fallout puts Georgia teacher out of a job. aol.com. Retrieved from www.aol.com/2011/10/14/georgia-teacher-fired-for-posting-drinking-photos-on-facebook/.

Fenner, G. H. & Renn, R. W. (2010). Technology-assisted supplemental work and work-to-family conflict: The role of instrumentality beliefs, organizational expectations and time management. *Human Relations, 63*(1), 63–82. doi:10.1177/0018726709351064.

Ferguson, M., Carlson, D., Boswell, W., Whitten, D., Butts, M. M., & Kacmar, K. M. (2016). Tethered to work: A family systems approach linking mobile device use to turnover intentions. *Journal of Applied Psychology, 101*(4), 520–534. doi:10.1037/apl0000075.

Fieseler, C., Meckel, M., & Ranzini, G. (2015). Professional personae: How organizational identification shapes online identity in the workplace. *Journal of Computer-Mediated Communication, 20*(2), 153–170. doi:10.1111/jcc4.12103.

Frampton, B. D. & Childs, J. T. (2013). Friend or not to friend: Coworker Facebook friend requests as an application of communication privacy management theory. *Computers in Human Behavior, 29*, 2257–2264.

Frone, M. R., Russell, M., & Cooper, M. L. (1992). Antecedents and outcomes of work-family conflict: Testing a model of the work-family interface. *Journal of Applied Psychology, 77*(1), 65–78. doi:10.1037/0021–9010.77.1.65.

Galinsky, E. (1999). *Ask the children: What America's children really think about working parents*. New York, NY: William Morrow.

Glavin, P. & Schieman, S. (2010). Interpersonal context at work and the frequency, appraisal, and consequences of boundary-spanning demands. *The Sociological Quarterly, 51*(2), 205–225. doi:10.1111/j.1533–8525.2010.01169.x.

Golden, A. G. & Geisler, C. (2007). Work-life boundary management and the personal digital assistant. *Human Relations, 60*(3), 519–551. doi:10.1177/0018726707076698.

Gonibeed, A. & Ravishankar, M. N. (2016). Exploring how individuals manage their image when interacting with professional contacts online. Conference on e-Business, e-Services and e-Society, 401–410.

Goold, I. & Savulescu, J. (2009). In favour of freezing eggs for non-medical reasons. *Bioethics, 23*(1), 47–58. doi:10.1111/j.1467–8519.2008.00679.x.

Greenhaus, J. H. & Beutell, N. J. (1985). Sources of conflict between work and family roles. *Academy of Management Review, 10*(1), 76–88. doi:10.5465/AMR.1985.4277352.

Greenhaus, J. H. & Powell, G. N. (2006). When work and family are allies: A theory of work-family enrichment. *Academy of Management Review, 31*(1), 72–92. doi:10.5465/AMR.2006.19379625.

Grotto, A. R. & Lyness, K. S. (2010). The costs of today's jobs: Job characteristics and organizational supports as antecedents of negative spillover. *Journal of Vocational Behavior*, *76*(3), 395–405. doi:10.1016/j.jvb.2009.09.004.

Gutek, B. A., Searle, S., & Klepa, L. (1991). Rational versus gender role explanations for work-family conflict. *Journal of Applied Psychology*, *76*, 560–568.

Hammer, L. B., Kossek, E. E., Yragui, N. L., Bodner, T. E., & Hanson, G. C. (2009). Development and validation of a multidimensional measure of Family Supportive Supervisor Behaviors (FSSB). *Journal of Management*, *35*(4), 837–856. doi:10.1177/0149206308328510.

Hampton, K.N., Goulet, L.S., Rainie, L., & Purcell, K. (2011). Social networking sites and our lives: How people's trust, personal relationships, and civic and political involvement are connected to their use of social networking sites and other technologies. Pew Internet and American Life Project. Retrieved from http://pewinternet.org/Reports/2011/Technology-and-social-networks.aspx

Harris, K. J., Marett, K., & Harris, R. B. (2011). Technology-related pressure and work-family conflict: Main effects and an examination of moderating variables. *Journal of Applied Social Psychology*, *41*(9), 2077–2103. doi:10.1111/j.1559-1816.2011.00805.x.

Hathaway, I. & Muro, M. (2016). Tracking the gig economy: New numbers. Brookings Institute. Retrieved from www.brookings.edu/research/tracking-the-gig-economy-new-numbers/.

Heijstra, T. M. & Rafnsdottir, G. L. (2010). The Internet and academics' workload and work–family balance. *The Internet and Higher Education*, *13*(3), 158–163. doi:10.1016/j.iheduc.2010.03.004.

Hislop, D. & Axtell, C. (2007). The neglect of spatial mobility in contemporary studies of work: The case of telework. *New Technology, Work & Employment*, *22*(1), 34–51. doi:10.1111/j.1468-005X.2007.00182.x.

Höge, T. (2011). Perceived flexibility requirements at work and the entreployee-work-orientation: Concept and measurement. *Psychology of Everyday Activity*, *4*(1), 3–21.

Höge, T. & Hornung, S. (2013). Perceived flexibility requirements: Exploring mediating mechanisms in positive and negative effects on worker well-being. *Economic and Industrial Democracy*, *36*(3), 407–430. doi:10.1177/0143831X13511274.

House, R. J., Hanges, P. J., Javidan, M., Dorfman, P. W., & Gupta, V. (2004). *Culture, leadership, and organizations: The GLOBE study of 62 societies*. Thousand Oaks, CA: Sage Publications.

Katz, D. & Kahn, R. L. (1978). *The social psychology of organizations*. New York, NY: Wiley.

Kossek, E. E., Baltes, B. B., & Matthews, R. A. (2011). How work–family research can finally have an impact in organizations. *Industrial and Organizational Psychology*, *4*(3), 352–369. doi:10.1111/j.1754-9434.2011.01353.x.

Kreiner, G. E., Hollensbe, E. C., & Sheep, M. L. (2009). Balancing borders and bridges: Negotiating the work-home interface via boundary work tactics. *Academy of Management Journal*, *52*(4), 704–730. doi:10.5465/amj.2009.43669916.

Kubicek, B., Paškvan, M., & Korunka, C. (2015). Development and validation of an instrument for assessing job demands arising from accelerated change: The intensification of job demands scale (IDS). *European Journal of Work and Organizational Psychology*, *24*(6), 898–913. doi:10.1080/1359432X.2014.979160.

Kühnel, J., Sonnentag, S., & Westman, M. (2009). Does work engagement increase after a short respite? The role of job involvement as a double-edged sword. *Journal of Occupational and Organizational Psychology, 82*(3), 575–594. doi:10.1348/096317908X349362.

Lawrence, E. R., Halbesleben, J. R. B., & Paustian-Underdahl, S. C. (2013). The influence of workplace injuries on work–family conflict: Job and financial insecurity as mechanisms. *Journal of Occupational Health Psychology, 18*(4), 371–383. doi:10.1037/a0033991.

Lim, V. G. & Teo, T. H. (2000). To work or not to work at home: An empirical investigation of factors affecting attitudes towards teleworking. *Journal of Managerial Psychology, 15*, 560–582. doi:10.1108/02683940010373392.

Lowry, D. & Moskos, M. (2008). Mobile phones, spillover and the work–life balance. In D. Hislop (Eds.), *Mobility and technology in the workplace* (pp. 167–179). London: Routledge.

Lu, L., Cooper, C. L., Kao, S.-F., Chang, T.-T., Allen, T. D., Lapierre, L. M., . . . Spector, P. E. (2010). Cross-cultural differences on work-to-family conflict and role satisfaction: A Taiwanese-British comparison. *Human Resource Management, 49*, 67–85.

Maertz, C. P. & Boyar, S. L. (2011). Work-family conflict, enrichment, and balance under "levels" and "episodes" approaches. *Journal of Management, 37*(1), 68–98.

Matusik, S. F. & Mickel, A. E. (2011). Embracing or embattled by converged mobile devices? Users' experiences with a contemporary connectivity technology. *Human Relations, 64*(8), 1001–1030. doi:10.1177/0018726711405552.

Mazmanian, M. A., Orlikowski, W. J., & Yates, J. (2005). Crackberries: The social implications of ubiquitous wireless e-mail devices. In C. Sorensen, Y. Yoo, K. Lyytinen, & J. DeGross (Eds.), *Designing ubiquitous information environments: Socio-technical issues and challenges* (pp. 337–344). New York, NY: Springer.

Mertes, H. (2015). Does company-sponsored egg freezing promote or confine women's reproductive autonomy? *Journal of Assisted Reproduction and Genetics, 32*(8), 1205–1209. doi:10.1007/s10815-015–0500-8.

Michel, J. S., Kotrba, L. M., Mitchelson, J. K., Clark, M. A., & Baltes, B. B. (2011). Antecedents of work–family conflict: A meta-analytic review. *Journal of Organizational Behavior, 32*(5), 689–725.

Middleton, C. A. (2007). Illusions of balance and control in an always-on environment: A case study of BlackBerry users. *Continuum, 21*(2), 165–178. doi:10.1080/10304310701268695.

Middleton, C. A. (2008). Do mobile technologies enable work-life balance? In D. Hislop (Eds.), *Mobility and technology in the workplace* (pp. 209–224). London: Routledge.

Middleton, C. A. & Cukier, W. (2006). Is mobile email functional or dysfunctional? Two perspectives on mobile email usage. *European Journal of Information Systems, 15* (3), 252–260. doi:10.1057/palgrave.ejis.3000614.

Morgan, W. B., Walker, S. S., Hebl, M. M., & King, E. B. (2013). A field experiment: Reducing interpersonal discrimination toward pregnant job applicants. *Journal of Applied Psychology, 98*(5), 799–809. doi:10.1037/a0034040.

Murray, C. (June 3, 2016). A guaranteed income for every American. *The Wall Street Journal.* Retrieved from www.wsj.com/articles/a-guaranteed-income-for-every-american-1464969586.

Neal, M.N. & Hammer, L.B. (2009). Dual-earner couples in the sandwiched generation: Effects of coping strategies over time. *The Psychologist-Manager Journal, 12*(4), 205–234.

Netemeyer, R. G., Boles, J. S., & McMurrian, R. (1996). Development and validation of work–family conflict and family–work conflict scales. *Journal of Applied Psychology, 81*(4), 400–410. https://doi.org/10.1037/0021–9010.81.4.400.

Nippert-Eng, C. E. (1996). *Home and work: Negotiating boundaries through everyday life.* Chicago, IL: University of Chicago Press.

Ollier-Malaterre, A., Rothbard, N. P., & Berg, J. M. (2013). When worlds collide in cyberspace: How boundary work in online social networks impacts professional relationships. *Academy of Management Review, 38*(4), 645–669.

Ollier-Malaterre, A. & Foucreault, A. (2017). Cross-national work-life research: Cultural and structural impacts for individuals and organizations. *Journal of Management, 43*(1), 111–136.

Olson-Buchanan, J. B. & Boswell, W. R. (2006). Blurring boundaries: Correlates of integration and segmentation between work and nonwork. *Journal of Vocational Behavior, 68*(3), 432–445. doi:10.1016/j.jvb.2005.10.006.

Park, Y., Fritz, C., & Jex, S. M. (2011). Relationships between work-home segmentation and psychological detachment from work: The role of communication technology use at home. *Journal of Occupational Health Psychology, 16*(4), 457–467. doi:10.1037/a0023594.

Park, Y. & Jex, S. M. (2011). Work-home boundary management using communication and information technology. *International Journal of Stress Management, 18*(2), 133–152. doi:10.1037/a0022759.

Perlow, L. A. & Porter, J. L. (2009). Making time off predictable – and required. *Harvard Business Review, 87*(10), 102–109. Retrieved from http://europepmc.org/abstract/MED/19839447.

Pew Research Center (January 12, 2017). Social media fact sheet. Retrieved from www.pewinternet.org/fact-sheet/social-media/.

Piszczek, M. M. (2017). Boundary control and controlled boundaries: Organizational expectations for technology use at the work-family interface. *Journal of Organizational Behavior, 38*(4), 592–611. doi:10.1002/job.2153.

Porter, G. & Kakabadse, N. K. (2006). HRM perspectives on addiction to technology and work. *Journal of Management Development, 25*(6), 535–560. doi:10.1108/02621710610670119.

Powell, G. N., Francesco, A. M., & Ling, Y. (2009). Toward culture-sensitive theories of the work-family interface. *Journal of Organizational Behavior, 30*, 597–616.

Prottas, D. J. & Thompson, C. A. (2006). Stress, satisfaction, and the work-family interface: A comparison of self-employed business owners, independents, and organizational employees. *Journal of Occupational Health Psychology, 11*, 366–378.

Reimer, L. (2013). BlackBerry Balance enables a true work and personal experience on BlackBerry 10. Retrieved from http://bizblog.blackberry.com/2013/01/blackberry-10-balance/.

Richardson, K. & Benbunan-Fich, R. (2011). Examining the antecedents of work connectivity behavior during non-work time. *Information and Organization, 21*(3), 142–160. doi:10.1016/j.infoandorg.2011.06.002.

Ronson, J. (February 12, 2015). How one stupid tweet blew up Justine Sacco's life. *The New York Times*. Retrieved from www.nytimes.com/2015/02/15/magazine/how-one-stupid-tweet-ruined-justine-saccos-life.html?_r=0.

Rothbard, N. P., Phillips, K. W., & Dumas, T. L. (2005). Managing multiple roles: Work-family policies and individuals' desires for segmentation. *Organization Science*, *16*(3), 243–258. doi:10.1287/orsc.1050.0124.

Rubin, A. J. (2017). France lets workers turn off, tune out and live life. *The New York Times*. Retrieved from www.nytimes.com/2017/01/02/world/europe/france-work-email.html.

Schieman, S. & Young, M. C. (2013). Are communications about work outside regular working hours associated with work-to-family conflict, psychological distress and sleep problems? *Work and Stress*, *27*(3), 244–261. doi:10.1080/02678373.2013.817090.

Shockley, K. M. (2018). Managing the work-family interface. In N. Anderson, D. S. Ones, H. K. Sinangil, & C. Viswesvaran (Eds.), *The SAGE handbook of industrial, work, & organizational psychology* (2nd edn.). London: SAGE Publications.

Shockley, K. M. & Allen, T. D. (2015). Deciding between work and family: An episodic approach. *Personnel Psychology*, *68*(2), 283–318. doi:10.1111/peps.12077.

Shockley, K.M., French, K., & Yu, P.P. (2018). An overview of cross-cultural work-family research. In K.M. Shockley, W. Shen, & R.C Johnson (Eds.), *Handbook of the global work-family interface*. Cambridge, UK: Cambridge University Press.

Shockley, K.M., Shen, W., & Johnson, R.C (2018). *Handbook of the global work-family interface*. Cambridge Industrial and Organizational Psychology Series. Cambridge, UK: Cambridge University Press.

Sonnentag, S. & Bayer, U. V. (2005). Switching off mentally: Predictors and consequences of psychological detachment from work during off-job time. *Journal of Occupational Health Psychology*, *10*(4), 393–414. doi:10.1037/1076–8998.10.4.393.

Sonnentag, S. & Fritz, C. (2015). Recovery from job stress: The stressor-detachment model as an integrative framework. *Journal of Organizational Behavior*, *36*(S1), S72-S103. doi:10.1002/job.1924.

Sonnentag, S., Kuttler, I., & Fritz, C. (2010). Job stressors, emotional exhaustion, and need for recovery: A multi-source study on the benefits of psychological detachment. *Journal of Vocational Behavior*, *76*(3), 355–365. doi:10.1016/j.jvb.2009.06.005.

Steiner-Adair, C. & Barker, T. H. (2013). *The big disconnect: Protecting childhood and family relationships in the digital age*. New York, NY: HarperCollins Publishers.

Towers, I., Carr, A. N., Duxbury, L., Higgins, C., & Thomas, J. (2006). Time thieves and space invaders: Technology, work and the organization. *Journal of Organizational Change Management*, *19*(5), 593–618. doi:10.1108/09534810610686076.

Townsend, K. & Batchelor, L. (2008). Freedom and flexibility with a ball and chain: Managers and their use of mobile phones. In D. Hislop (Eds.), *Mobility and technology in the workplace* (pp. 180–191). London: Routledge.

Tu, Q., Wang, K., & Shu, Q. (2005). Computer-related technostress in China. *Communications of the ACM*, *48*, 77–81.

Turel, O., Serenko, A., & Bontis, N. (2011). Family and work-related consequences of addiction to organizational pervasive technologies. *Information & Management*, *48*(2–3), 88–95. doi:10.1016/j.im.2011.01.004.

USC Fertility. (2017). *Frequently asked questions about egg freezing.* Retrieved from http://uscfertility.org/egg-freezing-faqs/.

van Zoonen, W., Verhoeven, J.W.M., & Vliegenthart, R. (2016). Social media's dark side: Inducing boundary conflicts. *Journal of Managerial Psychology, 31*(8), 1297–1311.

Vogel, E. A., Rose, J. P., Roberts, L. R., & Eckles, K. (2014). Social comparison, social media, and self-esteem. *Psychology of Popular Media Culture, 3*(4), 206–222. doi:10.1037/ppm0000047.

Voydanoff, P. (2005). Consequences of boundary-spanning demands and resources for work-to-family conflict and perceived stress. *Journal of Occupational Health Psychology, 10*(4), 491–503. doi:10.1037/1076–8998.10.4.491.

Wajcman, J., Bittman, M., & Brown, J. E. (2008). Families without borders: Mobile phones, connectedness and work-home divisions. *Sociology, 42*(4), 635–652. doi:10.1177/0038038508091620.

Wajcman, J., Rose, E., Brown, J. E., & Bittman, M. (2010). Enacting virtual connections between work and home. *Journal of Sociology, 46*(3), 257–275. doi:10.1177/1440783310365583.

Weiss, H. M. (2014). Working as human nature. In J. K. Ford, J. R. Hollenbeck, & A. M. Ryan (Eds.), *The nature of work: Advances in psychological theory, methods, and practice* (pp. 35–47). Washington, DC: American Psychological Association.

Westman, M. & Etzion, D. L. (2005). The crossover of work-family conflict from one spouse to the other. *Journal of Applied Social Psychology, 35*(9), 1936–1957. doi:10.1111/j.1559–1816.2005.tb02203.x.

Wright, K. B., Abendschein, B., Wombacher, K., O'Connor, M., Hoffman, M., Dempsey, M., ... Shelton, A. (2014). Work-related communication technology use outside of regular work hours and work life conflict: The influence of communication technologies on perceived work life conflict, burnout, job satisfaction, and turnover intentions. *Management Communication Quarterly, 28*(4), 507–530. doi:10.1177/0893318914533332.

Zoll, M., Mertes, H., & Gupta, J. (2015). Corporate giants provide fertility benefits: Have they got it wrong? *European Journal of Obstetrics, Gynecology, and Reproductive Biology, 195*, A1-2. doi:10.1016/j.ejogrb.2015.10.018.

24 Work in the Developing World

Technology as a Barrier, Technology as an Enabler

Lori Foster and Benjamin Kumpf

During a recent meeting at the United Nations General Assembly, UN Deputy Secretary-General Amina Mohammed underscored technology's profound potential to accelerate progress toward sustainable development worldwide. She warned, however, that technological progress also risks exacerbating existing inequalities if it is not managed carefully. Mohammed then asked an attendee by the name of Sophia what the UN can do to help people in the many parts of the world who lack access to the internet. Quoting science fiction writer William Gibson, Sofia noted in reply, "The future is already here. It's just not very evenly distributed" (United Nations News Centre, 2017). Sophia is a humanoid robot recently granted citizenship in Saudi Arabia and is now advocating for women's rights in a country where work-related opportunities, for example opening a business, require male oversight (Williams, 2017).

Technology has a demonstrated track record of both contributing to socioeconomic marginalization, and freeing people from such constraints. Technology's effect on sustainable development can be considered, in part, through the lens of decent work. Decent work serves as an important antecedent to well-being and sustainable development – one that can be enabled or hindered through technology. A key question is: How can emerging innovations be shaped and deployed to facilitate universal access to decent work? Considered in this manner, technological innovation is not an end in and of itself, but rather a means to a somewhat more proximal end known as decent work, as well as a more distal end known as sustainable development.

It is difficult to fully appreciate technology's perils and potential to foster empowerment through employment without a clear understanding of development, including the role of decent work. Decent work and the concept of development are briefly discussed next, to set the stage for a subsequent consideration of technology's role in the developing world of work.

24.1 Decent Work as a Basic Human Right

Access to decent work is not only important to well-being and development, it is a basic human right. Article 23 of the United Nations Universal Declaration of Human Rights states that "Everyone has the right to work, to free choice of employment, to just and favourable conditions of work and to protection against unemployment." Similarly, in her development of Amartya Sen's Capability Approach, Martha Nussbaum (2007) provides a list of ten Central Human Capabilities, which include the right to seek employment on an equal basis with others and "being able to work as a human being, exercising practical reason and entering into meaningful relationships of mutual recognition with other workers" (Nussbaum, 2007, p. 24).

Employment allows for financial security, which is critical. Under the right circumstances, it also provides an opportunity for psychological empowerment. It is an avenue through which we can form relationships with others and develop a sense of autonomy (freedom to make choices) and competence (mastering skills; Deci, Olafsen, & Ryan, 2017). Indeed, the recently established Psychology of Working Theory spells this out, showing how the opportunity to engage in decent work leads to fulfillment and well-being by meeting people's needs for survival, social connection, and self-determination (Duffy et al., 2016).

Of course, not everyone lives and works under the aforementioned right circumstances. Some people cannot find employment. Some work in sweatshops or other hazardous settings that endanger their health. Many children and adults around the world endure forced labor conditions. Clearly, work and workplaces can be a source of oppression, especially when conditions fail to meet what might be considered decent work, a term commonly used by a specialized agency of the United Nations (UN) known as the International Labour Organization (e.g., ILO, 2017).

The Psychology of Working Theory (Duffy et al., 2016) outlines the conditions that facilitate and hinder the attainment of decent work, pointing first and foremost to two impediments: economic constraints and marginalization. It is in this context that the work-related risks and opportunities posed by technology in less-developed regions of the world may be considered. To the extent that technology such as automation, mobile phones, online training, and other innovations contributes to economic constraints and marginalization, access to decent work and its positive psychological outcomes will be limited. However, technology that bridges divisions and helps people overcome current economic and social constraints can be economically and psychologically liberating, fostering individual, community, national, and international development.

24.2 Developed vs. Developing Countries: Operationalizing Development

In order to understand technology's role in accessing decent work in lower-income regions of the world, it is important to understand the concept of development – how it is viewed, how it is measured, and how it is meant to be achieved. We begin by noting that the boundaries of the so-called developing world are not unanimously set. The World Bank defines low-income economies in the 2018 fiscal year as those with a Gross National Income (GNI) per capita, calculated using the World Bank Atlas method, of $1,005 or less (World Bank, 2018). The United Nations Secretariat's Department of Economic and Social Affairs (UN/DESA) proposes three broad categories: developed economies, economies in transition, and developing economies. Economic productivity and growth are the main criteria for this categorization (United Nations, 2018).

However, the definition of human development has transcended concepts that solely focus on economic productivity. The United Nations Development Programme (UNDP) established the Human Development Index (HDI) in 1990 to emphasize that people and their capabilities should be the ultimate criteria for assessing the development of a country, not solely economic growth and productivity. The HDI is a summary measure of average achievement in three key dimensions of human development: a long and healthy life (health), being knowledgeable (education), and having a decent standard of living (income). The HDI is the geometric mean of normalized indices for each of the three dimensions.

Any given country can be quantified with respect to this index of development. The health dimension is assessed by life expectancy at birth. The education dimension is measured by mean of years of schooling for adults aged 25 years and older as well as expected years of schooling for children of school-entering age. The standard of living dimension is measured by Gross National Income (GNI) per capita. The HDI uses the logarithm of income, to reflect the diminishing importance of income with increasing levels of GNI (UNDP, 2016). Since 2010, UNDP expanded its country typology from three to four categories: very high, high, medium, and low human development based on the HDI.

24.3 Development and the World of Work

Volatility, uncertainty, complexity, and ambiguity (VUCA) has been coined the new normal for global development and nation-states in the developed world alike. But for much of the workforce in developing countries, volatility and uncertainty are by no means new. Many people living in developing countries depend on subsistence farming for their livelihoods and work in the informal sector. Broadly, the informal sector comprises labor market activities that are not regulated by the government and accordingly on which taxes are not paid. In developing countries, job opportunities in the formal sector are scarce compared to the labor supply, and the informal sector provides individuals with income through activities that range from subsistence farming to street vending. A recent statistical analysis by Jacques Charmes (2016) on the size of the informal economy in terms of its contribution to employment and to gross domestic product (GDP) suggests that:

• more than half of all non-agricultural employment in most middle- and low-income economies is informal, reaching over 80 percent in Central Africa;
• the proportion of informal employment has risen in many regions over recent decades; and

- the informal economy accounts for nearly a third of GDP in Latin America, more than half in India and well over 60 percent of the total GDP of sub-Saharan Africa.

While employment in the formal sector guarantees neither fair wages nor decent working conditions, the informal sector is often coined the unprotected sector due to the absence of any regulatory oversight and protective policies for workers. To enter either the formal sector or leverage opportunities in the informal sector, women and men, particularly youth, depend on accessing relevant opportunities for education and training.

There are many connections between the world of work and development as operationalized by the HDI's three components: income, health, and education. Access to employment has obvious implications for income. A living wage can go a long way toward attaining a decent standard of living (Carr et al., 2016). Technology also opens up opportunities for jobs, such as driving gigs (e.g., Uber, Lyft) and other chances for self-employment. But will wages be sufficient to lead a healthy life that fosters one's capabilities? Technology also takes jobs away, as advances in automation shift tasks and duties from people to machines. This poses major threats to people's financial livelihoods.

In addition, work and health intersect. Dangerous jobs and stressful working conditions can pose physical and social hazards that impair health (Krieger et al., 2006). Occupational hazards, shift work, overtime work, and adverse psychosocial work environments contribute to work-related diseases; accordingly, work and employment contribute to social inequalities in adult health (Siegrist, 2014). Machines are poised to take over some dangerous jobs, such as search and rescue operations, for example. In addition to the direct effects of work on health, an adequate income from employment can buy access to healthcare for oneself and one's family. In some cases, employers provide health insurance. Meanwhile, an inflexible work schedule can impede access to healthcare. For example, employees who are unable to take time off from work have trouble getting to the doctor to attend to their own or their family members' medical needs. Telework offers autonomy and flexibility to attend to such needs, though it may simultaneously contribute to stressful forms of work-family conflict (Lapierre et al., 2016).

The world of work also contributes to human development by providing opportunities for basic and continuing education. Consider, for example, the case of the Khayelitscha Cookie Company in South Africa (Holt & Littlewood, 2013). This organization focuses on hiring women from the local community, many of whom have never been in formal employment before. In addition to teaching job skills relevant to cookie production, the employer offers training in other areas, such as financial management and banking, including how to open a bank account, which is new to many employees. Training is also provided to improve long-term employment prospects, including basic computer skills courses (Holt & Littlewood, 2013). This is just one example of how education, technology skills, and lifelong learning can be promoted through work.

24.4 Achieving Development

Given the differences in geography and climate conditions, population density, the occurrence of violent conflicts, as well as the uneven wealth distribution among citizens as measured by the Gini coefficient, the developing world cannot be understood as a homogenous category. The HDI has registered substantial progress on average in every region since 1990 – across educational attainment, health status, and income levels. Yet when one looks beneath the averages, it is clear that a significant number of lives have been scarcely touched by that progress. One third of the world's population continues to live in low human development, and hundreds of millions of those people live in countries classified as having medium, high, or very high human development overall. Discussions around technology's availability and impact parallel these concerns. It is important to consider not only technology's average reach and influence in the world of work, but also to disaggregate these effects to examine which subsets of the world's working population may be benefiting from technological innovations, and which segments may be getting left behind.

The tendency to focus on potentially misleading averages was one of the major criticisms of the United Nations Millennium Development Goals (MDGs). Adopted in 2000 for a duration of fifteen years, the MDGs were a set of eight development goals primarily aimed at lower-income countries. For example, MDG #1 was labeled "Eradicate Extreme Hunger and Poverty," and its main target was to halve, between 2000 and 2015, the proportion of people in the world whose income is less than $1.25 a day. This global goal was largely achieved due to China's considerable economic growth which had sufficient trickle-down effects on its vast population. However, such progress did not characterize all regions of the world: more than 40 percent of the population in sub-Saharan Africa still lived in extreme poverty when the MDGs expired in 2015 (United Nations, 2015).

In 2015, the United Nations member states adopted the next global development agenda: The Sustainable Development Goals, or SDGs – seventeen goals with a fifteen-year timespan from 2015–2030. Each SDG is further broken down into more specific targets (United Nations General Assembly, 2015). The SDGs emphasize the disaggregation of development data, reflecting a growing global consensus among UN Member States that averages disguise inequalities.

A number of the 17 SDGS are directly or indirectly related to technology's risks and opportunities to promote empowerment through employment. Table 24.1 provides examples of selected SDGs and targets. As shown in Table 24.1, the SDGs intersect with technology and the world of work in a variety of ways. For example, technology can be developed and used to provide skills to women and girls previously denied training and education opportunities (Table 24.1, Target 4.5). It can be used to recruit and engage youth who are not in education, employment, or training (Target 8.6). Innovations can help integrate people with disabilities into the world of work (Target 8.5). Partnerships between the public sector, governments, civil society, and private sector companies can facilitate such initiatives (Target 17.17). And, advances in big data analytics can support efforts to

Table 24.1 *Selected Sustainable Development Goals and targets*

Goal 4: Ensure inclusive and equitable quality education and promote lifelong learning opportunities for all.

- **Target 4.4:** By 2030, substantially increase the number of youth and adults who have relevant skills, including technical and vocational skills, for employment, decent jobs and entrepreneurship.
- **Target 4.5:** By 2030, eliminate gender disparities in education and ensure equal access to all levels of education and vocational training for the vulnerable, including persons with disabilities, indigenous peoples and children in vulnerable situations.
- **Target 4.b:** By 2020, substantially expand globally the number of scholarships available to developing countries, in particular least developed countries, small island developing States and African countries, for enrolment in higher education, including vocational training and information and communications technology, technical, engineering and scientific programmes, in developed countries and other developing countries.

Goal 5: Achieve gender equality and empower all women and girls.

- **Target 5.1:** End all forms of discrimination against all women and girls everywhere.
- **Target 5.b:** Enhance the use of enabling technology, in particular information and communications technology, to promote the empowerment of women.
- **Target 5.c:** Adopt and strengthen sound policies and enforceable legislation for the promotion of gender equality and the empowerment of all women and girls at all levels.

Goal 8: Promote sustained, inclusive and sustainable economic growth, full and productive employment and decent work for all.

- **Target 8.2:** Achieve higher levels of economic productivity through diversification, technological upgrading and innovation, including through a focus on
- high-value added and labour-intensive sectors.
- **Target 8.3:** Promote development-oriented policies that support productive activities, decent job creation, entrepreneurship, creativity and innovation, and encourage the formalization and growth of micro-, small- and medium-sized enterprises, including through access to financial services.
- **Target 8.5:** By 2030, achieve full and productive employment and decent work for all women and men, including for young people and persons with disabilities, and equal pay for work of equal value.
- **Target 8.6:** By 2020, substantially reduce the proportion of youth not in employment, education or training.
- **Target 8.8:** Protect labour rights and promote safe and secure working environments for all workers, including migrant workers, in particular women migrants, and those in precarious employment.
- **Target 8.10:** Strengthen the capacity of domestic financial institutions to encourage and expand access to banking, insurance and financial services for all.

Goal 9: Build resilient infrastructure, promote inclusive and sustainable industrialization and foster innovation.

- **Target 9.3:** Increase the access of small-scale industrial and other enterprises, in particular in developing countries, to financial services, including affordable credit, and their integration into value chains and markets.

Table 24.1 (*cont.*)

- **Target 9.c:** Significantly increase access to information and communications technology and strive to provide universal and affordable access to the internet in least developed countries by 2020.

Goal 17: Strengthen the means of implementation and revitalize the Global Partnership for Sustainable Development.
- **Target 17.6:** Enhance North-South, South-South and triangular regional and international cooperation on and access to science, technology and innovation and enhance knowledge sharing on mutually agreed terms, including through improved coordination among existing mechanisms, in particular at the United Nations level, and through a global technology facilitation mechanism.
- **Target 17.7:** Promote the development, transfer, dissemination and diffusion of environmentally sound technologies to developing countries on favourable terms, including on concessional and preferential terms, as mutually agreed.
- **Target 17.8:** Fully operationalize the technology bank and science, technology and innovation capacity-building mechanism for least developed countries by 2017 and enhance the use of enabling technology, in particular information and communications technology.
- **Target 17.16:** Enhance the Global Partnership for Sustainable Development, complemented by multi-stakeholder partnerships that mobilize and share knowledge, expertise, technology and financial resources, to support the achievement of the Sustainable Development Goals in all countries, in particular developing countries.
- **Target 17.17:** Encourage and promote effective public, public-private and civil society partnerships, building on the experience and resourcing strategies of partnerships
- **Target 17.18:** By 2020, enhance capacity-building support to developing countries, including for least developed countries and small island developing States, to increase significantly the availability of high-quality, timely and reliable data disaggregated by income, gender, age, race, ethnicity, migratory status, disability, geographic location and other characteristics relevant in national contexts.
- **Target 17.19:** By 2030, build on existing initiatives to develop measurements of progress on sustainable development that complement gross domestic product, and support statistical capacity-building in developing countries.

Excerpts from United Nations General Assembly (2015, September 25). *Transforming our world: The 2030 agenda for sustainable development*, A/RES/70/1.

measure developmental progress at all levels, in a manner that is disaggregated while still protecting anonymity (Targets 17.18 and 17.19).

In short, positive synergies among work, technology, and development are entirely possible. However, such synergies are not guaranteed. Noting the economically destabilizing effects that rising levels of inequality can have, Sharafat and Lehr (2017) acknowledge that "Managing the growth of ICTs so the net social benefits are maximized presents a complex challenge" (p. 5). Fundamental questions concern the degree to which the working age population in less developed countries has access to technology, and the skills to capitalize on it, and will reap the benefits that technology can bring.

24.5 The Persistent Digital Divide: Availability and Accessibility of Technology and Related Skills

Technological progress follows an unprecedented growth curve in human history. For example, computer chips have become increasingly powerful while their prices have dropped consistently. Over the last five decades, the number of transistors on a single chip has been doubling regularly. This growth curve – an exponential one known as Moore's Law (Mack, 2011) – is a reason why modern smartphones can combine so many capabilities in a relatively small package. Whether one coins the current technological growth curve exponential or simply unprecedented, its implications for virtually all humans, the way we think, interact, work, make sense of the world, and learn remain to be fully understood. Following the unevenness of human development across and within countries, the positive effects of technological progress are unevenly distributed. The role of technology in the present and future of work is embedded in and constituted by dynamics between geographical, socio-economic, political, and legal subsystems of national systems.

An important barrier is the persistent digital divide between geographic locations and demographic groups as outlined by the World Bank's Development Report 2016, which estimates that nearly 60 percent of the world's people are still offline (World Bank, 2016). Usage remains much higher in some parts of the world than others. For example, according to the International Telecommunications Union (ITU) only about 20 percent of Europeans are offline whereas more than 75 percent of people in Africa are not using the internet (ITU, 2017). In 2017, the proportion of women using the internet was estimated to be 12 percent lower than the proportion of men using the internet worldwide. In lower-income regions, this gap is even wider: in the least developed countries, only one out of every seven women is using the internet, compared to one out of five men (ITU, 2017). Moreover, people who are less educated, residing in rural communities, and living with disabilities are also reportedly less likely than their counterparts to be using information and communication technologies (Sharafat & Lehr, 2017). Nevertheless, the number of internet users has more than tripled in a decade – from 1 billion in 2005 to an estimated 3.2 billion at the end of 2015 according to the 2016 World Development Report (World Bank, 2016). There is without a doubt an increasing pace of progress in accessibility – partially based on infrastructure investments by governments, and partially based on private sector investments in telecommunication networks, particularly in cell phone coverage.

The current understanding of the digital divide is largely based on understanding availability of digital infrastructure, skills, and opportunities. While much focus has been dedicated to understanding infrastructural barriers, there is not yet a globally accepted framework to assess barriers related to accessibility and digital literacy. In April 2017, the G20 Ministers responsible for the digital economy published a declaration titled "Shaping Digitalisation for an Interconnected World," which called for global cooperation and coordination to maximize the benefits and mitigate the risks associated with digitalization (G20 Digital Economy

Ministerial Declaration, 2017). The declaration recognizes technology's potential to advance progress toward the SDGs, especially if the global community together focuses on improving the availability and affordability of broadband connectivity, enhancing digital skills and literacy, and promoting greater digital entrepreneurship. The declaration specifically points out that, "Connectivity and digital access alone are not enough to create an inclusive, sustainable digital future for all" and underscores the importance of efforts "examining how employment and social policies could be adapted in order to shape the future of work in the areas of skills development and adjustment, social policies and job quality" (p. 4). The declaration includes a recognition that "all forms of education and life-long learning may need to be adjusted to take advantage of new digital technologies and to develop the skills required by the labour market" (p. 4) and welcomes initiatives to build digital skills into and through apprenticeships, vocational training, and on-the job training. The notion that digital literacy is key to sustainable development is clear in the G20 Ministers' declaration.

A widely accepted framework from the United Nations Educational, Scientific and Cultural Organization (UNESCO, 2011) describes digital literacy as a set of basic skills required for working with digital media, information processing and retrieval. However, focusing uniquely on technical aspects of digital literacy falls short as workers also need to be able to critically assess the content, process and evaluate it. Knowing how to assess and ultimately judge what is appropriate and how to derive meaning while using digital technologies is as important as being able to use the technology itself. Yet, internet content in local languages is lacking. Typically, the content most important to people is that which is in their own language and relevant to the communities in which they live and work. At present, a disproportionate amount of the content on the internet is in English, and of Western origin, causing the Organisation for Economic Co-operation and Development (OECD) and its collaborators to point out a *content* divide. This situation is improving, as content is becoming more diverse with time. Nevertheless, contributing local content requires specific skills and tools which are unequally distributed across the world (OECD/ISOC/UNESCO, 2013).

24.6 Gender Divide

Access to the digital revolution remains uneven – not only across regions, but also across sexes and other demographic groups (UNDP, 2015). At the same time, access to decent work is also unevenly distributed (Duffy et al., 2016). Gender, ethnicity, nationality, religion, disability, sexual orientation, extreme poverty, age, and other factors all present barriers. While space constraints preclude a consideration of each of these important factors in turn, we consider here the special case of gender in order to illustrate the dynamic and complex interactions among work, technology, and marginalization.

Achieving gender equality (Table 24.1, SDG 5) is one of the most daunting struggles of humanity. Viewed as a moral imperative by some, it also makes economic sense. Equality between men and women in all aspects of life, from access to health and education to political power and earning potential, is fundamental to whether and how societies thrive. The World Economic Forum concluded in 2015 that at current rates, it would take the world another 118 years – or until 2133 – to close the economic gap between women and men. In the ten years the Forum has been reporting on the gap between men and women in health, education, economic opportunity, and political representation, the gap has only narrowed by 4 percent overall (World Economic Forum, 2015).

Technology serves as both a source of concern and optimism in efforts to promote gender equality in the developing world of work. To date, men and women have not equally accessed the digital revolution. A 2015 study from the Women's Rights Online (WRO) initiative found that women in poor, urban communities are 50 percent less likely to be online than men (World Wide Web Foundation, 2015). While more and more people across the globe can connect to the internet, the gender digital divide seems to be growing. The International Telecommunication Union's most recent estimate indicates that the global internet user gender gap has grown from 11 percent in 2013 to 12 percent in 2016. Internet penetration rates remain higher for men than women in all regions in the world, especially in the Least Developed Countries, where the gap is estimated to be 31 percent (United Nations Broadband Commission for Sustainable Development, 2017). Women face additional barriers in accessing digital opportunities because many household devices are owned and controlled by men. Women also use digital technologies differently: the WRO study found that women are 30–50 percent less likely than men to speak out online, or to use the web to access information related to their rights. Controlling for the effects of age, education, employment status and income, women are also 25 percent less likely to use the internet for job-seeking than men (World Wide Web Foundation, 2015).

Research is needed to better understand the degree to which the type of content offerings as well as the design and linguistics of available online content constitute barriers. It should be noted that the tech industry globally employs predominantly men. In the United States, for example, women comprise far less than half of information technology professionals and are also underrepresented among those earning bachelor's degrees in computer science (Hill, Corbett, & St. Rose, 2010). Accordingly, online content, including content related to educational and job opportunities, is coded, designed, and branded mainly by men. This is even true when women and men are given theoretically equal opportunities to contribute. For example, research suggests that while nearly half the people who use Wikipedia are female, only a small fraction (approximately 16 percent) of the editors contributing content to Wikipedia are female (Lam et al., 2011). This gap, which does not appear to be shrinking (Lam et al., 2011) has been explained in terms of masculine norms for behavior in Wikipedia that lead to psychological experiences for women that discourage contributions (Bear & Collier, 2016). According to Frenkel (2008) the "global hi-tech industry constitutes a deeply masculine environment in which women are welcome as long as they perform as surrogate men" (p. 352).

Years of research in the social, behavioral, and organizational sciences provide insight into this issue. A recent meta-analysis reveals that men are preferred for male-dominated jobs, a phenomenon known as gender-role congruity bias (Koch, D'Mello, & Sackett, 2015). Male decision-makers are especially likely to exhibit this bias. Meanwhile, this phenomenon does not appear to work the other way around: meta-analysis shows no evidence for a strong preference for either gender for female-dominated jobs (Koch et al., 2015). Experimental studies reveal some of the dynamics at play. For example, Heilman, Wallen, Fuchs, and Tamkins (2004) investigated 242 subjects in three experimental studies investigating reactions to a woman's success in a male gender-typed job. Results indicated a trade-off between success and likeability: When women were shown to succeed in male arenas, they were less liked and more personally derogated than equally successful men.

Findings such as these suggest that access to technology and related skills are necessary but not sufficient for achieving equal access to decent work. Solutions are also needed to ensure both women and men can use their skills and tools in an environment that values, supports, respects, and encourages contributions from everyone, regardless of sex, ethnicity, nationality, religion, disability, sexual orientation, extreme poverty, age, and other factors that currently serve to marginalize members of the workforce.

24.7 Technology as an Enabler, Technology as a Barrier

There is no doubt that challenges and opportunities abound as key technologies develop and are leveraged in the evolving digital economy. Technologies at the forefront of development policy discussions include mobile phones, Information and Communication Technologies for Development (ICT4Ds), advanced robotics, artificial intelligence, cloud computing, the Internet of Things, big data analytics, and three-dimensional (3D) printing (UNDP, 2015). Technological implants are also being considered given recent and ongoing advances in this domain (Pelegrín-Borondo, Reinares-Lara, & Olarte-Pascual, 2017). Technology can serve as a barrier to inclusive development, reinforcing and exacerbating the marginalization of disadvantaged groups. It can also serve as an enabler, creating unprecedented opportunities for vulnerable populations to access meaningful work. Therein lies great concern and hope, as well as a vast number of unanswered questions.

The following pages discuss technology-related opportunities and risks. We begin with more micro, individual-level considerations – namely, technology's role in people's access to decent work and related opportunities: banking, education and training, information, global markets, and new forms of work. This is followed by a discussion of more macro issues pertaining to automation, workforce development, and bioengineering policy.

24.7.1 Access to Banking

About two billion adults are currently unbanked (World Bank, 2017). Most of the women and men without access to banking services live in developing countries and face barriers to services and tasks such as receiving wages and setting a certain percentage of their salaries aside for saving or sending money to family members. Without access to banking services, their finances are more likely to be unstable due to the barriers to saving for the future or borrowing in times of need.

SDG Target 8.3 in Table 24.1 reveals important connections among sustainable development, decent work, entrepreneurship, innovation, and access to financial services. The successful development of Micro, Small, and Medium-sized Enterprises (MSMEs) requires human capital and financial capital alike. Money and loans are commonly needed to start businesses of all sizes. Without a bank account, it is difficult to secure the credit and materials needed to begin even a small business – which is at times the only viable option for a sustainable livelihood when other job opportunities are scarce. This helps explain why SDG Target 8.10 in Table 24.1 emphasizes the importance of "access to banking, insurance and financial services for all." Mobile banking, in particular, has an important role to play. Far more than a mere convenience, mobile banking is commonly required for micro-entrepreneurship in rural parts of the developing world where financial institutions lack economic incentives to provide physical banking services (Sharafat & Lehr, 2017).

The growing uptake of mobile phones has resulted in many countries historically lacking broadband leapfrogging to online connectivity. This has affected access to banking, which has improved with the advent of mobile phones generally and mobile banking in particular. Between 2011 and 2014, the percentage of adults with a bank account increased from 51 percent to 62 percent, a trend driven by a 13 percentage point rise in account ownership in developing countries and the role of technology. Mobile money accounts in sub-Saharan Africa are a major factor in this trend (Demirguc-Kunt et al., 2014). Systems such as M-Pesa in Kenya are helping to rapidly expand and scale up access to financial services. Data from the World Bank's 2014 Findex Report also shows growing opportunities for boosting financial inclusion of women: In 2011, 47 percent of women and 54 percent of men had a bank account while in 2014, 58 percent of women had an account, compared to 65 percent of men (Demirguc-Kunt et al., 2014).

The number of unbanked adults is likely to continue to decrease at an accelerated pace, opening up opportunities particularly for women who face greater barriers to financial inclusion. This, in turn, may stimulate entrepreneurship (Table 24.1, Target 4.4) and support women's empowerment (Target 4.4).

24.7.2 Access to Education and Training

It is no secret that the quality of education and training varies greatly between and within countries. As implied by SDGs #4 and #8 in Table 24.1, factors such as sex and social class continue to dictate access to knowledge and skills in many parts of the world by determining, for example, who is allowed to and who can afford to go to school. Open educational resources such as Massive Open Online Courses (MOOCs) represent a noteworthy innovation that can provide educational opportunities for members of marginalized groups. MOOCs are offered by world-class educational institutions, are free of cost, and have the potential to democratize education (e.g., Osuna-Acedo et al., 2017). They allow people to complete courses on a range of topics and gain a wide variety of technical and non-technical skills. To date, however, MOOCs have failed to realize their full potential to level the metaphorical playing field when it comes to education and training. Indeed, a 2013 study from the University of Pennsylvania points to existing inequalities being perpetuated in the uptake of MOOCs (Emanuel, 2013). The study analyzed 34,779 responses to a survey of people from more than 200 countries in 32 MOOC course sessions. Results suggested that most MOOC students are well-educated young men seeking to advance their careers. Approximately 83 percent of MOOC students studied already had a two- or four-year diploma or degree, and 56 percent were male. The percentage of men was even higher in lower-income regions of the world. In addition, nearly 80 percent of the MOOC students from the BRICS countries (i.e., Brazil, Russia, India, China and South Africa) came from the wealthiest and most well-educated 6 percent of the population. The study concluded that despite their promise, MOOCs are not typically reaching the disadvantaged.

Thus, opportunities exist, but access and uptake continue to be concerns. One important question is whether work-related education, training, and skills development can follow the banking trend described above, capitalizing on movements toward mobile connectivity in lower-income regions of the world. Mobile learning has the added benefit of being portable, which is a necessity in some cases. Consider, for example, the plight of migrants, refugees, and asylum seekers. Such individuals' education, training, and work opportunities are often severely disrupted once they leave their home country. Mobile technologies could enable them to continue their education and gain marketable job skills through programs of study that can be picked up and continued during relocations. Both hope and uncertainty about this prospect are reflected in the agenda of a 2017 meeting co-hosted by UNESCO and the UN Refugee Agency (UNHCR), which focused on mobile learning for displaced individuals. Table 24.2 outlines the areas of inquiry at the forefront of policy discussions about how technology can be utilized to support the education, training (and thus employment) of migrants, refugees, and asylum seekers (UNESCO, 2017). These include questions such as how to teach e-skills to displaced individuals, and how mobile learning can support work opportunities.

One concern with mobile learning pertains to the fact that not every web site and service was built for a small device. This may limit users' engagement with the internet and consequently their learning as a whole, potentially reducing learners' self-efficacy for online learning in the process. Napoli and Obar (2013) describe a number of usage studies reinforcing this concern by demonstrating, for example, very limited information gathering among mobile users in six sub-Saharan countries. Another usage study found that PC-based users habitually access far more (8.64, on average) categories of websites compared to mobile-based users, who

Table 24.2 *Technology, learning, work, and refugees: Open questions*

E-skills for mobile learning and sustainable development:
1. How do countries identify and teach essential e-skills?
2. How can countries take advantage of newly affordable mobile technologies to improve e-skills education and lay foundations for mobile learning and sustainable development?
3. What policy solutions exist to continuously update e-skills education and keep pace with rapidly changing technology?

E-skills and mobile learning for socio-economic inclusion:
1. What policies can ensure universal access to e-skills and mobile learning?
2. How can e-skills be acquired by vulnerable and displaced populations?
3. How can mobile learning create stronger bridges to work, aid social inclusion in national systems and promote protection for refugees and other displaced people arriving in new communities?

Partnerships for e-skills and mobile learning:
1. How can public–private dialogue about e-skills and mobile learning be organized at national level?
2. What are examples of successful partnerships to improve and expand e-skills education?
3. What roles should national authorities, mobile network operators and technology companies play in the development and provision of e-skills programs, especially those conducted with and through mobile devices?

The big picture and the way forward:
1. How can e-skills and mobile learning support progress toward the SDGs, in particular SDG4?
2. How can countries ensure the new and powerful technologies support inclusion and equity in education and beyond?

Excerpts from UNESCO (2017, March 24). *Mobile learning week: Education in emergencies and crises.* www.unesco.org/new/fileadmin/MULTIMEDIA/HQ/ED/pdf/ mlw2017_ProvisionalProgramme.pdf.

tended to access an average of 3.58 categories of websites (Napoli & Obar, 2013). These usage statistics raise concerns about mobile learning opportunities that require engagement with content that is not mobile-friendly. Such usability concerns also extend beyond mobile learning, applying as well to other online opportunities such as filling out a job application or completing a job screening test on a platform that is not optimized for mobile phones.

24.7.3 Access to Information

In recent years, a number of digital tools, platforms, systems, and job aids have been designed and deployed to connect lower income workers in developing regions of the world with information. This reflects a trend toward Information and Communication Technologies for Development (ICT4D or ICTD), a field that has emerged and grown rapidly (Heffernan, Lin, & Thomson, 2016). ICT4D aims to leverage ICTs for socioeconomic growth and development, with a particular focus on poverty alleviation.

While ICT4D as a field addresses various aspects of development, some ICT4D initiatives focus specifically on supporting workers. Mobile phone-based tools for community health workers and smallholder farmers provide examples of ICT4D tools applied to work settings. In many regions, healthcare tasks such as HIV testing and educating pregnant women on nutrition and prenatal care have shifted from physicians to non-skilled or semi-skilled community health workers or frontline healthcare workers, who deliver services in rural villages. Sometimes, these workers are remunerated; other times, they are unpaid volunteers. Work-related responsibilities include providing advice, information, and education to patients, offering limited medical services, and recording data during household visits to send back to a central office or clinic. Challenges include difficult terrain, high workload, inadequate training, isolation, and attrition (Meyer, Kanfer, & Burrus, 2016; Vallières et al., 2017). Mobile phone tools have been developed to put relevant information at these workers' fingertips. Mobile-health tools can help community health workers do their jobs more efficiently by sending them reminders about household visits, allowing them to look up information as needed, enabling them to track their own progress, and supporting their efforts to collect data from clients and households (e.g., Vallières et al., 2013). The ultimate aim is for such efficiency gains to translate into lower rates of infant mortality and better health outcomes for patients, families, and communities. Questions remain, however, about how to ensure such workers are best trained and motivated to use the technology at hand. Mobile phone-based tools that transmit patient data to a central office can improve healthcare data accuracy and potentially eliminate or reduce requirements to check in with a supervisor or team at a central office. Yet, even in the best of circumstances in which the technology is intuitive and reliable, such autonomy could lead to isolation, reducing fulfillment of social connection needs, which is important to feelings of work fulfillment and well-being (Duffy et al., 2016).

Another classic example of ICT4D occurs in the context of farming. To produce at a profitable level, farmers need information about what, where, when, and how to plant, as well as market information, including who prospective buyers are, where they reside, what they need, and the going market rate or price to sell at. Historically, access to such information has been difficult and costly. Mobile phones have the potential to change that. Botswana start-up Modisar, for example, uses text messaging to track cattle and give farmers advice on feed, vaccinations, and financing. Another system called Esoko not only gives farmers advice, but also links them with traders in a virtual marketplace (Brock, 2015). However, the literature suggests that mobile phones have not reached their full potential to support smallholder farmers' marketing and pricing decisions (Tadesse & Bahiigwa, 2015). There is a need for more research to better understand the barriers to uptake, adoption, and effective use of such systems. Models from the social, organizational, behavioral, and management sciences may help identify such barriers. As discussed in greater depth later in this chapter, the Technology Acceptance Model (TAM) and related theories would suggest looking at the degree to which farmers perceive this tool as easy to use and useful (Davis, 1989; Verma & Sinha, 2016). Perceived usefulness could be threatened by a lack of relevant, localized market information to which to connect. The Theory of Planned Behavior and TAM2 suggests also looking at social norms around ICT usage for farming practices (Ajzen, 1991; Maji & Pal, 2017; Venkatesh & Davis, 2000).

A number of ICT4D initiatives fail (Dodson, Sterling, & Bennett, 2012). Various reasons for this have been suggested, including prioritizing the technology over the community in which it is to be deployed, approaches that are too top-down in nature without sufficient input from end users, and inadequate consideration of human elements such as work motivation (Behrend, Gloss, & Foster Thompson, 2013; Dodson et al., 2012). Sometimes, issues as fundamental as a lack of reliable access to electricity to power the technology at hand are responsible for ICT4D failures (Fife & Pereira, 2016). Interestingly, the adoption of mobile phones in the Global South has stimulated a demand for small-scale solar panels to recharge phones. This has led to overall improvements in household access to electricity (Heffernan et al., 2016), which enables other positive developments. In this sense, technology can breed innovation. Indeed, UNDP (2015) points to energy storage as one of the technologies with the greatest potential to change work by bringing affordable electricity to more than a billion people who currently lack access, and by creating jobs. In 2014 alone, the renewable energy sector employed an estimated 7.7 million people directly and indirectly (UNDP, 2015).

24.7.4 Access to Global Markets

The United Nations Conference on Trade and Development's (UNCTAD) flagship *Information Economy Report 2017* clearly asserts up front that "digital technologies are changing the economy, with implications for development" (UNCTAD, 2017, p. xiii). Internet connectivity not only allows access to local markets, as implied by the farming example above. It also allows access to global markets (Table 24.1, Target 9.3). Consider, for example, a woman in rural India with the skills to make handbags out of material from recycled plastic bags and recycled saris (e.g., Norris, 2010). The internet gives her access to information about the market value of this product, as well as a connection to potential consumers from around the world who are willing to pay a fair price for her handcraft. Technology has enabled the establishment of organizations designed to connect artisans in less developed countries to global markets (e.g., www.serrv.org/category/about-us). Handmade jewelry, clothing, toys, and other items can be ordered online, purchased, sold, and shipped at fair prices around the world. This can help artisans become entrepreneurs. It can enable them to remain in their local villages if they so desire, including villages where job and livelihood opportunities are otherwise scarce. The common alternative is poverty and/or migration away from family to seek work in larger cities, sending money back to parents and children as it is earned.

Participation in global trade can help Micro, Small, and Medium Enterprises (MSMEs) cut costs, giving them access to global supply chains and talent supplies. Unfortunately, however, these benefits and possibilities often go unrealized. Connectivity limitations and skills gaps are two notable barriers. In many less-developed countries, reliable and affordable connectivity is still too inefficient for MSMEs to compete online (UNCTAD, 2017). In addition, capitalizing on the digital economy requires technological knowledge and skills, as well as an understanding of global trade, which need to be acquired. People and countries lacking relevant skills are at a disadvantage.

24.7.5 Access to New Forms of Work

Online labor platforms have also created opportunities for *digital labor*. An example familiar to many readers comes from Amazon's Mechanical Turk service. Employers of sorts can post tasks requiring human intelligence, such as completing a survey. Workers can opt to complete the task for pay. The employer posting the task has the freedom to pay whatever rate he or she sees fit. The worker has the freedom to accept whatever work he or she chooses to do. This is but one small example of a much larger trend toward cloud work. In discussing digital labor, UNCTAD (2017) makes a distinction between cloud work and gig work. Cloud work is that which can be performed from anywhere via the internet, including microtasks such as Mechanical Turk and contest-based platforms such as 99designs. The term *gig work* refers to location-based work facilitated by digital platforms. Examples include services such as transportation (e.g., Uber), accommodation (e.g., Airbnb), and household repairs (e.g., Taskrabbit). While such work offers employment opportunities by reducing barriers to entry, there has been some concern that such commodification of work, accompanied by a large oversupply of job-seekers in these platforms, suppresses wages below what is needed to sustain a livelihood, resulting in a so-called "race to the bottom" with respect to wages and working conditions (UNCTAD, 2017).

The preceding concern relates to a broader point about the potential for innovations to backfire. Enthusiasm about technology's capacity to connect people to global markets, new forms of work, and other opportunities should be accompanied by efforts to consider technology's second- and third-order effects, not only on collective wages and the economy, but also on individuals' lives. History is replete with examples of innovations with unforeseen consequences that exacerbate inequalities and change lives for the worse. For example, Eli Whitney's late eighteenth century invention of the cotton gin in the Southern United States was intended to make growing cotton more profitable by automating the removal of seeds from cotton bolls, which was an otherwise time- and labor-intensive process. This invention decreased the need for slave labor to remove cotton seeds and increased the profitability of growing cotton. The consequence, however, was an increased demand for land and slaves to grow and pick the cotton amid worsening labor conditions as the work became more regimented, with longer hours needed to cover the output of ever-larger plantations (Schur, 2016).

How might initial successes starting a recycled sari business or participating in the gig economy, for example, affect household and community power dynamics, resources, and relationships? What happens if a more powerful corporation takes note of a MSME's early successes and decides to replicate the business model with more labor, better technology, and more sophisticated marketing strategies? It is not difficult to imagine a situation in which a MSME entrepreneur is unable to compete against a more powerful and better-resourced company, resulting in an inability to support local employees, tensions in the household, and a loss of esteem in the community. While it is impossible to foresee every consequence of innovation, there is value in thinking about how advances could backfire and setting up systems that help head off such risks to individuals and societies at large.

24.7.6 Automation and Jobs

Automation driven by advanced robotics and artificial intelligence is an area that has generated a great deal of discussion about the individual and societal dangers of innovation. In some circles, automation trends have come to be known as the Fourth Industrial Revolution – a term popularized by Klaus Schwab (2016), founder and executive chairman of the World Economic Forum. In this context, the industrial revolution is considered the first machine age, electricity the second, and electronics the third (Peters, 2017). The fourth industrial revolution, advances in automation, will cause some jobs to disappear as they are overtaken by technology. The demand for other jobs will increase or decrease, depending on their connection to trends in automation. Still other, new jobs will emerge. However, the skills profile needed for new jobs and those growing in demand will not match the skills possessed by those whose jobs are becoming obsolete, resulting in a gap between labor market supply and demand, with the potential for those lacking relevant skills to slip into poverty. This concern is by no means limited to developing countries. A prominent 2017 report titled *Information Technology and the U.S. Workforce: Where Are We and Where Do We Go from Here?* addresses this topic in depth, pointing to a number of areas that are likely to advance in coming years at a level that will affect the workforce, including: mobile robots; assembly line automation; computer perception of speech, video, and other sensory data; automatic language translation by computers; text reading by computers (which will automate even knowledge work jobs); and work flow automation (National Academies of Sciences, Engineering, and Medicine, 2017).

Whether these trends are dubbed the fourth industrial revolution (Schwab, 2016), technological unemployment (Peters, 2017), or jobless growth (OECD, 2015), there is believed to be "consensus that robots and big data systems will disrupt labor markets, kill jobs and cause social inequalities" (Peters, 2017, p. 25). The effects of automation on polarization and income inequalities remain concerns for developing and developed countries alike (National Academies of Sciences, Engineering, and Medicine, 2017; UNDP, 2015). Of course, higher-income countries have the technological capacity to make this happen more quickly. Lower-income countries are starting at a lower level of technological capacity and adoption, which may in some ways lower and slow the impact of automation. At the same time, a number of jobs in developing economies – such as textile and clothing jobs in Cambodia and Vietnam – are those that have been outsourced by higher-income countries due to relatively cheap labor costs. Countries whose economies depend on such outsourcing may be hit hard, and quickly, as jobs are lost to automation and re-shoring (ILO, 2016).

24.7.7 Workforce and Human Resource Development

As machines are assigned responsibility for rote tasks, there will be an increasing need for labor supplies with strong cognitive, creative, innovative, and adaptive capacities – that is, capabilities that cannot be easily replaced by computers. Workers will need skills that allow them to use artificial intelligence (AI) and complement the work being carried out by AI (UNCTAD, 2017). This has implications for education and training systems at local, regional, and national levels. Training and retraining will be needed to compete in the digital economy. Systems, policies, and cultures supportive of lifelong learning will also be required, as skill demands will continue to change, requiring adaptability, flexibility, and an openness to evolve in order to succeed.

The need for such skills has implications for human resource development on individual, regional, national, and international levels. High-quality labor market data are needed to drive human resource development policy. Here, technology has the potential to provide useful insights in new and innovative ways. For instance, Verhulst and Young (2017) describe a competition designed to use big data generated by users of LinkedIn to provide labor market insights – namely, to glean information about what kinds of skills employers are looking for (labor market demand) and what kinds of jobs workers possess (labor market supply). This is consistent with other analyses of LinkedIn data which revealed, for example, the most in-demand soft skills employers are seeking, including communication, organization, teamwork, punctuality, critical thinking, social skills, creativity, and adaptability (Davidson, 2016; Verhulst & Young, 2017). Using data analytics to unearth such powerful insights has the potential to support lower-income regions of the world lacking systems and resources to produce high-quality labor market information to drive workforce development strategy – but only to the extent that the country's inhabitants are online and producing big data to analyze. Otherwise, lower income regions of the world could be left farther behind as higher-income counterparts respond to, utilize, and capitalize on the results of labor market information gleaned from data analytics, which is not available in less connected regions of the world.

Analyses of workforce development needs have not been limited to so-called soft skills. They have also included an assessment of the more technical skills projected to be increasingly important in the days to come. As noted earlier, technology opens access to training, information, jobs, global markets, and more. However, relevant skills are needed in order for individuals and countries to benefit from this access. Drawing on earlier work from the European Commission (2004), UNCTAD (2017) describes, in the form of a pyramid, three distinct types or tiers of skills that countries will need to thrive in the digital economy. The first tier at the base of the pyramid consists of foundational digital skills, which include digital literacy skills, such as how to go online and use the internet; digital information literacy skills, such as how to distinguish reliable from unreliable sources of information; and digital/ICT user skills, such as how to send email and use software packages. The second tier consists of more advanced, digital specialist skills, which encompass skills needed for hardware and systems design, data analytics, app development, and so forth. The third tier at the top of the pyramid encompasses the relatively sophisticated digital entrepreneurship, e-business, and e-leadership skills needed to thrive and move the digital economy forward. Developed and developing countries alike will need an adequate supply of these distinct types of skills to take advantage of digital technologies.

24.7.8 Bioengineering

Lastly, there is a need to think about innovations on the horizon that could quickly transform an individual and a country's capacity to compete in the workforce and beyond. Specifically, technological implants may become increasingly available, allowing workers and job candidates to transform for advantage. Already, implants intended to enhance attractiveness (e.g., breast augmentation) are relatively common in higher-income settings. So are technologies designed to address physical disabilities. For example, cochlear implants for people with hearing impairments and pacemakers for people with heart problems have seen widespread adoption (Pelegrín-Borondo et al., 2017). Researchers are now working on neuroprosthetics that function as memory implants, which improve humans' innate capacity (Cohen, 2013). This moves us from an era of wearable technology to one of insideables (Pelegrín-Borondo et al., 2017). Most likely, people and countries with greater access to financial resources will have better access to such technologies, allowing those with greater means to transform for advantage – and become more capable – more rapidly than their less privileged counterparts. In effect, economic inequality will translate into biological inequality (NPR, 2017). This has the potential to substantially widen individual and national inequalities within and outside the employment sphere, prompting people such as author Yuval Noah Harari to call for global guidelines and governance of bioengineering (NPR, 2017).

24.8 Behavioral Insights

Many questions remain about how to best ensure technology fulfills its promising potential to promote socio-economic development and access to decent work, rather than contributing to problematic inequalities. Insights from the social and behavioral sciences provide a people-centered, theoretical, evidence base upon which to answer such questions. "There is nothing so practical as a good theory," Kurt Lewin famously stated (Lewin, 1951). A more intentional integration of psychological and organizational theory into the design and deployment of technologies can help scientists, practitioners, and policy makers understand and guide the digital revolution in desired directions.

Realizing such a vision requires behavioral insights from a range of different disciplines, including but not limited to industrial-organizational psychology, vocational psychology, human factors, management information systems, and behavioral economics. The following pages illustrate ways in which each of these disciplines can contribute to a better understanding of work, technology, and sustainable development.

24.8.1 Industrial-Organizational Psychology (IOP)

Research and theory from industrial-organizational psychology (IOP) provide particularly useful insights about the broader work context in which innovations are introduced. For example, there has been a great deal of scholarship on telework, virtual teams, and multi-cultural interactions in the workplace (e.g., Breuer, Hüffmeier, & Hertel, 2016; Golden, Veiga, & Dino, 2008; Kopelman et al., 2016; Vignovic & Foster Thompson, 2010). This research base can provide useful insights as cloud work, gig work, and other forms of labor bring together people from a variety of cultures and socioeconomic backgrounds, while also offering opportunities to work outside traditional brick and mortar organizational structures. In addition, this chapter has noted the need to train people on digital literacy skills, digital specialist skills, and digital entrepreneurship skills including e-leadership – a topic that has certainly received attention in the IOP literature (e.g., Hoch & Kozlowski, 2014). More broadly, the IOP training literature has seen a great deal of theory development in recent decades, providing insights into how people learn and how to evaluate training effectiveness (Bell et al., 2017). Such theory can be useful in considering human resource development at individual, community, and national levels.

Some of the needed efforts to train digital skills will continue to occur online, for example through a mobile device. In certain cases, such training programs include an intelligent tutor. Research in IOP has looked at similarity between training avatars and learners, suggesting that deep-level features such as similarity in feedback delivery style may be more important that surface-level features such as similarity in appearance (Behrend & Foster Thompson, 2011). Such insights can be useful to the development and delivery of ICT4D training programs.

Of course, training for digital skills will also continue to occur via live trainers, who are connected to learners virtually and in-person. Research and theory on the Pygmalion effect is relevant in this context and beyond. Stereotypes abound, including in education, training, and employment settings. The fulfillment of others' beliefs as well as the potential power of self-expectations are worth considering as ICT4D applications for work evolve in the developing world. Experimental and meta-analytic evidence from IOP has indicated that trainers' and managers' expectations influence how well people learn and perform in work settings (McNatt, 2000). This Pygmalion effect is especially powerful for persons for whom low expectations were initially held (McNatt, 2000). The Pygmalion effect does not just influence individuals; it extends to entire groups (Eden, 1990). In other words, individuals and groups learn more and perform better when trainers and managers have high expectations for them at the outset. This is due in part to the positive self-efficacy that workers develop when dealing with instructors and managers who exhibit leadership conveying a belief in trainees' and subordinates' ability to master the responsibility at hand (Eden, 1992). These are important points to bear in mind, for those concerned with the Sustainable Development Goals related to education and training. Whether designing digital tutors or training online instructors, efforts to build efficacy among trainers and workers are needed.

"The internet is never our friend", a collaborator from a less developed country recently told one of this chapter's authors during a Skype-based team kickoff meeting in which all team members were quickly asked to turn their videos off to save precious bandwidth, in hopes of minimizing technological glitches during the call. The unfortunate consequence of this decision was that the team members were not able to see each other during the initial phases of their team formation, which may have been important to establishing trust and rapport. Israeli psychologist Dov Eden distinguishes between internal and external sources of efficacy (Eden, 2001). Internal sources of efficacy entail one's subjective assessments of one's skill, talent, knowledge, willpower, endurance, intelligence, resourcefulness, and any other traits deemed important for successful performance. External efficacy entails subjective assessments of task-relevant external resources used to facilitate performance (Eden et al., 2010). Means efficacy is an external type of efficacy defined as belief in the utility of the tools available for task performance (Eden et al., 2010). Eden et al. (2010) conducted two field experiments in work and educational settings showing how the mere belief in the quality of one's technology (workplace computer system, online course web site, etc.) affects learning and performance in organizational and educational settings. This IOP research is significant because it suggests the potential for a double hurdle for those learning and working in less developed parts of the world. First, there is the very real possibility of inferior technology, such as connectivity that is slow or unreliable. In addition, the mere belief that one's technology is inferior can have detrimental effects.

Another illustrative line of IOP research and theory worth considering pertains to job design. Hackman and Oldham's (1976) classic Job Characteristics Model suggests that three psychological states are important antecedents to favorable work outcomes such as job satisfaction, work motivation, and strong performance. Those three states are: experienced meaningfulness of work; experienced responsibility for outcomes of work; and knowledge of work results. According to the Job Characteristics Model, jobs vary in the degree to which they possess the core characteristics (skill variety, task identity, task significance, autonomy, and feedback) known to trigger the three important psychological states. This is relevant as tasks, duties, and functions shift from people to machines. Will automation affect the level of autonomy workers are afforded? The Job Characteristics Model and other such theories can help us understand the motivating potential of remaining jobs as they are reconfigured, and how to proactively design work that is satisfying and motivating. Research and theory in work analysis (e.g., Wilson et al., 2012) can also prove useful as job and labor requirements shift on account of automation.

The examples above are just a small sampling of ways in which IOP theory and research can inform the developing world of work as technology continues to evolve. In addition to considering how IOP can inform ICT4D, there is value in asking the opposite question: How can and should what we know about work and technology in the developing world influence IOP theory, research, and practice moving forward? Box 24.1 considers this question.

Box 24.1   Considerations and Implications for the Field of Industrial-Organizational Psychology (IOP)

The majority of the working-age population lives in developing regions of the world, where the role of technology in work and well-being continues to evolve. Whether IOP will play a meaningful role in this evolution remains an open question with implications for IOP's growth, reach, and future. The answer depends in part on the degree to which IOP adapts to take into account the realities faced by people living, working, and using technology in resource-constrained settings.

It is worth noting that IOP has expanded in recent years to include an explicit focus on humanitarian work psychology (HWP), which entails applying IOP research and practice to poverty reduction and development (Gloss et al., 2017; McWha-Hermann, Maynard, & Berry, 2016). Given the close and well-documented linkages between technology and development, HWP researchers and practitioners need to take technology access (e.g., equipment, skills) into account when going about their work. For example, a goal-setting app or intervention designed to improve self-efficacy in an online training program in a developing part of the world may fail if the technology is (or is believed to be) substandard. This example illustrates how technology can affect IOP *practice* – such as delivering a training program to upskill people for decent work opportunities. Technology also has the unrealized potential to shape IOP and HWP *theory*. Guszcza (2015) notes that "much of what we call 'big data' is in fact behavioral data" (p. 73). By enabling the collection of detailed behavioral data (for example, through mobile devices gathering big data), technology can expand our theoretical understanding of work in the developing world by providing volumes of moment-to-moment information about how people engage with each other and with work. Such insights can help inform theory in parts of the world that have been largely neglected by IOP, thus addressing a major criticism of an overly WEIRD (Western, Educated, Industrialized, Rich, Democratic) understanding of the psychology of work (Gloss et al., 2017).

Given current trends in sustainable development and decent work, could IOP theories be made obsolete if technology is ignored? The answer to this question probably depends on the theory. Many useful theories (e.g., goal setting theory) are likely relevant to human behavior at work, whether or not it is mediated through technology. However, the relevance of some IOP theories may be called into question to the extent that technology fundamentally changes engagement with work. For example, the rise of gig and cloud work may require IO psychologists to re-think some conceptualizations of organizational commitment. In addition, there will be an increasing need for IOP theories that accommodate informal and unpaid work forms of work. Both of these two forms of work are inextricably linked to technology. Innovations enable new forms of entrepreneurship, some of which will lead to informal employment. Finally, automation may render paid work opportunities scarce in the days to come. This could encourage people to seek work fulfillment from volunteerism and other unpaid forms of labor. Such projections suggest a need to broaden IOP's scope, as many of its theories at present assume formal, paid employment. What may be needed is a broader conceptualization of work, beyond the paid labor focus that has typically dominated the scientific study of work in IOP (Jiranek, Brauchli, & Wehner, 2014). Work, some would argue, is a much broader concept that not only encompasses jobs and employment, but also includes unpaid care work, voluntary work, and creative expression (Jiranek et al., 2014; UNDP, 2015). Theory development taking into account the experience of work outside the job and employment sphere may become increasingly important as automation results in job losses in the shorter or longer term.

IOP theory is not currently an integral part of labor policy and practice in lower-income settings. This raises obvious concerns. But it also provides an opportunity. As the movement toward humanitarian work psychology grows, IOP theory can and likely will be applied and adapted to less-developed countries with increasing frequency. As this occurs, there is an opportunity – perhaps even an imperative – to continually consider, as a matter of course, the role that technology can or should play in such application and

Box 24.1

adaptation. Technology is already highly connected to issues of training and work in the developing world. Compared with technology, IOP has had a far weaker influence on how training and work in the developing world unfolds. An important question, going forward, is not how IOP *remains* engaged, but rather how IOP *becomes* engaged with technology in lower-income settings. Part of the answer involves regularly interfacing and collaborating with those designing and implementing technology for the purpose of enabling access to decent work, such that IOP theories of human behavior at work are "baked into" the way technology is built, rolled out, and implemented.

24.8.2 Vocational Psychology

As noted earlier, the Psychology of Working Theory (PWT; Duffy et al., 2016) provides a useful basis on which to consider how technology may facilitate or disrupt access to decent work. Heavily influenced by the field of vocational psychology, the PWT is not a technology theory. However, it clearly articulates the economic, social, and psychological factors that influence the attainment of decent work – from economic constraints and marginalization, to work volition and career adaptability – while outlining the variables (proactive personality, critical consciousness, social support, and economic conditions) that moderate the effects of the proposed antecedents. There is value in considering the degree to which emerging innovations affect and interact with these variables. For example, work volition is the perceived capacity to make career decisions. How might innovations intentionally or unintentionally affect this perception? The same question could be asked of critical consciousness, which is defined as "a careful and systematic analysis of one's social conditions, the perceived capacity to change them, and individual or collective action to reduce societal inequality" (Duffy et al., 2016, p. 129). Research is needed to understand the conditions under which digital innovations and movements influence critical consciousness in ways that help people from marginalized groups overcome barriers to decent work.

PWT also describes the positive outcomes of decent work. They are not limited to economically driven survival needs, but also include psychosocial variables: social connection, self-determination, work fulfillment, and well-being. This right-hand side of the PWT model detailing the outcomes of decent work is just as important to consider as the factors leading up to it, given the possibility of job losses driven by the fourth industrial revolution. PWT implies that psychological as well as economic concerns should be attended to as we prepare for the changes brought on by automation. There may be a temptation for policy makers to focus solely on solutions (e.g., a universal basic income) that soften the economic blows incurred when jobs are lost to automation. However, such solutions may be dangerously incomplete if they fail to consider the concomitant psychosocial consequences of not being afforded the opportunity to work.

24.8.3 Human Factors

Another discipline with obvious potential to contribute is human factors, ergonomics, and related areas that rely on principles of human-centered design. Human-centered design focuses on the people who will use an innovation during the design phase of technology. This methodology includes deep observation of people in their natural environment followed by an iterative cycle of ideation, prototyping, and testing (Hewer, 2015). Psychologist Donald Norman, author of *The Design of Everyday Things* (2013), underscores the importance of having psychologists involved in design, suggesting that psychologists' absence often results in an unproductive incorporation of amateur, folk-psychology into design processes and outcomes (Hewer, 2015).

Collaboration with cross-cultural psychologists and behavioral scientists who are indigenous to the country or culture where the technology is to be deployed could also bear fruit with respect to technology design, acceptance, uptake, and usefulness in the context of decent work and sustainable development. Consider, for example, a 2016 *Human Factors* study published by Kisaalita, Katimbo, Sempiira, and Mugisa, an authorship team spanning the United States and Uganda. Kisaalita et al. (2016) discuss the asset gap between women and men in sub-Saharan Africa, noting its linkages to the disproportionate amount of unpaid housework women are responsible for. Labor-saving devices for the home, the authors argue, can free women up to produce for the market, which can lead to greater financial stability, family well-being, and sustainable livelihoods. Kisaalita et al. (2016) suggest that labor-saving innovations for women in such contexts can fail due to insufficient attention to women's cultural practices and physical characteristics (i.e., insufficient anthropometry). The authors describe the redesign and usability testing of a milk churner using a human-centered participatory design approach with groups of women from two dominant ethnolinguistic groups of Bantu and Nilotic of Uganda. The experience inspired six pieces of advice to complement human-centered design principles in low-resource settings, as follows (Kisaalita et al., 2016, pp. 38–40):

1. Start with the local cultural, civic, and/or spiritual leadership for "blessing" the design project.
2. Make sure you have the relevant anthropometry data.
3. Make sure you have the relevant strength data.
4. Be mindful of the solution being consistent with prevailing gender roles.
5. Be mindful of the relationship between solution adoption and the prevailing household decision-making process.
6. If asset ownership is important to success of the solution, devise strategies to overcome lack thereof.

Kisaalita et al.'s (2016) approach illustrates human-centered design and the important role of human (physical, cultural, interpersonal) factors in developing innovations. While their research focused on a physical rather than a digital innovation, many of the same principles likely apply when developing information and communication technologies for development in lower income regions of the world.

24.8.4 Management Information Systems and Human-Computer Interaction

Of course, theories addressing human-technology interaction at work will also be useful going forward. As noted earlier, the Technology Acceptance Model and related theories provide insight into who is more and less inclined to adopt technological innovations, including those central to ICT4D.

For example, a recent study looked at how personality may influence Taiwanese university students' attitudes toward mobile learning (m-learning) tools. Such tools are a gateway to education, allowing students to download teaching materials, access information and announcements, upload assignments, and engage in discussions with teachers and peers (Hsia, 2016). Consistent with research findings from a corporate e-learning context (Hsia, Chang, & Tseng, 2014), locus of control played a key role in acceptance of m-learning technology. Locus of control is a personality characteristic reflecting the degree to which people believe that life's rewards and outcomes stem from their own actions (internal locus of control) vs. outside influences (external locus of control) such as fate or other people (Rotter, 1966; Wang, Bowling, & Eschleman, 2010). According to Hsia (2016), learners with a more internal locus of control were more inclined to accept m-learning technology. Specifically, locus of control was associated with perceptions that the m-learning technology was useful and easy to use, as well as perceptions of behavioral control, which the authors defined as students' confidence in mastering the new learning approach. All three of these beliefs were significantly related to the behavioral intention to use m-learning. Thus, personality likely plays a role in the adoption of ICT4D.

Gender may also matter, with implications for the digital divide described earlier. The relationship between gender and technology acceptance has been explored quite a bit in the research literature and is modeled in Venkatesh, Morris, Davis, and Davis's (2003) Unified Theory of Acceptance and Use of Technology (UTAUT). UTAUT resulted from a consideration and integration of various theoretical frameworks relevant to technology acceptance and usage including the theory of reasoned action, technology acceptance model, motivational model, theory of planned behavior, model of PC utilization, innovation diffusion theory, and social cognitive theory. UTAUT looks at behavioral intentions to use a new technology and examines factors that shape those intentions, including: (a) performance expectancy – that is, perceived usefulness, or the belief that using the technology will lead to gains in job performance; (b) effort expectancy, or the perceived ease of using the technology; and (c) social influences, or the belief that important others think the new technology should be used. UTAUT indicates that performance expectancy is more important for men than it is for women, while effort expectancy and social influences are more important for women than they are for men considering whether to use a new technology (Venkatesh et al., 2003).

Acknowledging the need for practitioners and policy makers to better understand the factors that shape people's acceptance of new technologies such as e-learning systems, Tarhini, Hone, and Liu (2014) surveyed university students in England about the use of a web-based learning system offered by their university.

Respondents were asked to report their intentions to use the system to do various things, such as downloading lecture notes. They also rated whether and how frequently they planned to use the system in the future, as well as their perceptions of the system and the social factors surrounding its usage. Perceived ease of use (effort expectancy), usefulness (performance expectancy), and social norms played a role in usage intentions, as did self-efficacy, or students' confidence in their ability to use the web-based learning system. Consistent with UTAUT predictions, gender moderated the effect of perceived ease of use and social norms on behavioral intentions; women put more emphasis on both of these factors when deciding on whether to fully adopt the e-learning system.

He and Freeman (2012) explored the concept of self-efficacy in more depth in a sample of American college students. They concluded that, relative to their male counterparts, women tend to feel more anxious about using computers and less confident with computers because they have learned and practiced less. This indicates that women and men may not always approach ICT4D opportunities with the same level of comfort and confidence, and also suggests a relatively straightforward solution – namely exposure, high-quality training, and practice opportunities.

Brown, Dennis, and Venkatesh (2010) expressed the need to better understand the adoption of collaboration technologies in particular, noting that innovations facilitating electronic collaboration have become an important aspect of day-to-day life both within and outside the workplace. They conducted two studies examining Finnish adults' intentions to use short message services (SMS; study 1) and a workplace-based collaboration technology (study 2). Results supported their hypotheses that the intention to use SMS and the workplace collaboration technology are shaped by (a) performance expectancy, especially for younger men; (b) effort expectancy, especially for older women with little experience; and (c) social influences, especially for older women with little experience.

Maity (2014) surveyed people from low socio-economic groups in five Southeast Asian countries, inquiring about their intentions to use mobile phones in the future for SMS as well as voice calls. Contrary to Brown et al.'s (2010) findings, perceived ease of use was positively associated with intentions to use the technology for men but not for women. Consistent with previous research, subjective norms were more important to women considering their future mobile phone usage. Subjective norms involved perceived social influences, namely the desire to use the same service as others and the sense that mobile phone usage is common in the community.

As technology evolves, so too do the theories explaining its adoption. For example, Pelegrín-Borondo et al. (2017) recently published a cognitive-affective-normative model to explain and predict reactions to potentially controversial new technologies, such as high-tech implants. Newer research models as well as more established ones like UTAUT can help predict the degree to which a new technology, if introduced, will be used (Venkatesh et al., 2003). Such models can also help decision makers – including those designing and deploying ICT4D technologies – understand the determinants of technology acceptance for different user groups in order to proactively design interventions for populations less inclined to adopt new tools such as e-learning platforms, collaboration tools, and other technologies meant to support development. Connecting the relatively mature stream of management information systems research on technology adoption to ICT4D initiatives – including those aimed at encouraging women's participation in skills development and work opportunities – is an important direction for future research and practice.

24.8.5 Behavioral Economics

Malcolm MacLachlan (2014) recently called for the development of a macro perspective in psychology, like that found in macroeconomics. Macropsychology is defined as psychology's application to factors that influence the settings and conditions of our lives (MacLachlan, 2014). Meanwhile, economics has become more behavioral in nature, setting the stage for greater convergence, collaboration, and cooperation between the psychological sciences and economics. In 2002, psychologist Daniel Kahneman was awarded the Nobel Prize in Economics for his work in applying psychological insights on judgment and decision-making to economic theory (Kahneman, 2011; Smith, 2002). Fifteen years later, Richard Thaler won the 2017 Nobel Prize in Economics for his related work in behavioral economics, recognizing that human behavior is not always strictly rational, but rather influenced by biases and heuristics (Appelbaum, 2017). Thaler co-wrote the book *Nudge* (Thaler & Sunstein, 2008), which advocates policy that is built on a fundamental understanding of how people actually behave and make decisions in their everyday lives. Historically, the more common alternative has been policy built on a vision of humans as perfectly rational emotion-less beings who consistently make optimal decisions in their own best interests. Such policy does not always play out as intended due to its unrealistic assumptions about people. The work of Kahneman, Thaler, Sunstein, and colleagues has entered policy circles in a variety of ways, including in the form of behavioral insights teams comprised of social and behavioral scientists, which are embedded in governments and institutions around the world and devoted to applying social and behavioral science methods, theories, and findings to policy (OECD, 2017).

Behavioral economics approaches often involve efforts to narrow the gap between what people intend to do and the way they actually behave. This is relevant in a variety of circumstances, such as saving money for the future, applying for a scholarship, enrolling in a training program, completing a MOOC, learning a new app, or refraining from email and texts during a meeting or family dinner. Recognizing natural human limitations in attention and self-control as well as tendencies such as unrealistic optimism and loss aversion, behavioral economics interventions use a range of tools to encourage or nudge people toward particular courses of action. These include carefully crafting forms and policies such that the desired course of action is the default course of action (default rules); simplifying the information and choices given to people; leveraging the power of social norms; increasing the ease or convenience of a desired choice; disclosures; warnings and graphics; pre-commitment strategies; reminders; eliciting implementation intentions; and informing people of the nature and consequences of their own past choice (Sunstein, 2014).

Methods borrowed from the behavioral economics community could be useful at the intersection of work, technology, and socioeconomic development. For example, efforts to educate young adults or train employable skills may be more successful if organized and framed in a behaviorally informed manner that starts with an analysis of the behavioral barriers or bottlenecks that prevent people from taking advantage of relevant education, training, and employment opportunities. A study by Castleman and Page (2015) illustrates this approach. These authors sought to address a problem whereby US high school graduates intending to go to college fail to matriculate the year following high school. Using a multi-site randomized controlled trial design, Castleman and Page (2015) tested the effects on postsecondary enrollment of a behaviorally informed, personalized, automated text messaging campaign to remind college-intending students of required pre-matriculation tasks and to connect them to counselor-based support. The intervention had a positive effect on enrollment among college-intending high school graduates from urban school districts, with effects concentrated among students with little access to college planning supports and students with less-developed college plans (Castleman & Page, 2015). This text message reminder technique was later replicated and applied by the US Social and Behavioral Sciences Team, leading to a 5.7-percentage-point increase in college enrollment among low-income students (Congdon & Shankar, 2015). Pilot studies from the United Kingdom's Department for Business, Innovation and Skills have also used behaviorally informed text messages and other communications to (a) encourage adults with low English and Math skills to persevere with adult education programs, and (b) increase Small and Medium Enterprises' demand for entrepreneurial mentorship (OECD, 2017).

Nudges themselves could be more effective when tailored and adapted to individual learners and employees. Enabled through technology, big data, and advanced analytics, the practice of smart nudges has already seen some early successes, including in workplace settings (Guszcza, 2015; OECD, 2017; Risdon, 2017).

24.8.6 Conclusion

Overall, the research, theory, and insights suggested above are but a small sampling of perspectives from the social and behavioral sciences that could help leverage the opportunities offered by emerging technologies and address the challenges presented when considering how best to use innovation to foster empowerment through employment. However, two caveats are in order. First, relevant theoretical perspectives such as those illustrated above should not be considered in isolation. Greater cross-fertilization of ideas and integration of theories from economics, psychology, computer science, development, and related disciplines is needed in bolster technology's potential to contribute to decent work and sustainable development (Behrend et al., 2013). Second, much of the existing research and theory remains rooted in WEIRD traditions. This is a major criticism of our current understanding of human behavior within and outside the workplace (Henrich, Heine, & Norenzayan, 2010). There is no doubt that these theories will need to be refined or at times even replaced to ensure relevance in other parts of the world. Nevertheless, they may provide a good starting place, moving forward.

References

Ajzen, I. (1991). The theory of planned behavior. *Organizational Behavior and Human Decision Processes*, *50*, 179–211.

Appelbaum, B. (October 9, 2017). Nobel in economics is awarded to Richard Thaler. *New York Times*. Retrieved from www.nytimes.com/2017/10/09/business/nobel-economics-richard-thaler.html.

Bear, J. B. & Collier, B. (2016). Where are the women in Wikipedia? Understanding the different psychological experiences of men and women in Wikipedia. *Sex Roles*, *74*, 254–265.

Behrend, T. S. & Foster Thompson, L. (2011). Similarity effects in online training: Effects with computerized trainer agents. *Computers in Human Behavior*, *27*, 1201–1206.

Behrend, T. S., Gloss, A. E., & Foster Thompson, L. (2013). Global development through the psychology of workplace technology. In M. D. Coovert & L. Foster Thompson (Eds.), *The psychology of workplace technology* (pp. 261–283). New York, NY: Routledge Academic.

Bell, B. S., Tannenbaum, S. I., Ford, J. K., Noe, R. A., & Kraiger, K. (2017). 100 years of training and development research: What we know and where we should go. *Journal of Applied Psychology*, *102*, 305–323.

Breuer, C., Hüffmeier, J., & Hertel, G. (2016). Does trust matter more in virtual teams? A meta-analysis of trust and team effectiveness considering virtuality and documentation as moderators. *Journal of Applied Psychology*, *101*, 1151–1177.

Brock, J. (March 16, 2015). Africa business: With iCow and M-Farm, smartphones reboot African agriculture. *Reuters Market News*. Retrieved from www.reuters.com/article/africa-farming/africa-business-with-icow-and-m-farm-smartphones-reboot-african-agriculture-idUSL5N0WB34920150316.

Brown, S. A., Dennis, A. R., & Venkatesh, V. (2010). Predicting collaboration technology use: Integrating technology adoption and collaboration research. *Journal of Management Information Systems*, *27*, 9–53.

Carr, S. C., Parker, J., Arrowsmith, J., & Watters, P. A. (2016). The living wage: Theoretical integration and an applied research agenda. *International Labour Review*, *155*, 1–24.

Castleman, B. L. & Page, L. C. (2015). Summer nudging: Can personalized text messages and peer mentor outreach increase college going among low-income high school graduates? *Journal of Economic Behavior & Organization*, *115*, 144–160.

Charmes, J. (2016). The informal economy: Definition, size, contribution, and main characteristics. In E. Kraemer-Mbula & S. Wunsch-Vincent (Eds.), *The informal economy in developing nations: Hidden engine of innovation?* (pp. 13–52). New York, NY: Cambridge University Press.

Cohen, J. (2013). Memory implants: A maverick neuroscientist deciphered the code by which the brain forms long-term memories. *MIT Technology Review.* Retrieved from www.technologyreview.com/s/513681/memory-implants/.

Congdon, W. J. & Shankar, M. (2015). The White House Social & Behavioral Sciences Team: Lessons learned from year one. *Behavioral Science & Policy, 1,* 77–86.

Davidson, K. (August 30, 2016). The "soft skills" employers are looking for. *Wall Street Journal.* Retrieved from https://blogs.wsj.com/economics/2016/08/30/the-soft-skills-employers-are-looking-for/.

Davis, F. D. (1989). Perceived usefulness, perceived ease of use, and user acceptance of information technology. *MIS Quarterly, 13,* 319–340.

Deci, E. L., Olafsen, A. H., & Ryan, R. M. (2017). Self-determination theory in work organizations: The state of science. *Annual Review of Organizational Psychology and Organizational Behavior, 4,* 19–43.

Demirguc-Kunt, A., Klapper, L., Singer, D., & Van Oudheusden, P. (2014). The global findex database 2014: Measuring financial inclusion around the world. World Bank Policy Research Working Paper 7255. Retrieved from http://documents.worldbank.org/curated/en/187761468179367706/pdf/WPS7255.pdf#page=3.

Dodson, L. L., Sterling, S. R., & Bennett, J. K. (2012). Considering failure: Eight years of ICTD research. Paper presented at the meeting of the International Conference on Information and Communications Technologies and Development (ICTD), Atlanta, GA.

Duffy, R. D., Blustein, D. L., Diemer, M. A., & Autin, K. L. (2016). The psychology of working theory. *Journal of Counseling Psychology, 63,* 127–148.

Eden, D. (1990). Pygmalion without interpersonal contrast effects: Whole groups gain from raising manager expectations. *Journal of Applied Psychology, 75,* 394–398.

Eden, D. (1992). Leadership and expectations: Pygmalion effects and other self-fulfilling prophecies in organizations. *Leadership Quarterly, 3,* 271–305.

Eden, D. (2001). Means efficacy: External sources of general and specific subjective efficacy. In M. Erez, U. Kleinbeck, & H. Thierry (Eds.), *Work motivation in the context of a globalizing economy* (pp. 73–86). Hillsdale, NJ: Lawrence Erlbaum.

Eden, D., Ganzach, Y., Flumin-Granat, R., & Zigman, T. (2010). Augmenting means efficacy to boost performance: Two field experiments. *Journal of Management, 36,* 687–713.

Emanuel, E. J. (2013). MOOCs taken by educated few. *Nature, 503* (7476), 342.

European Commission (2004). E-skills for Europe: Towards 2010 and beyond. European E-Skills Forum Synthesis Report. Brussels. Retrieved from www.cedefop.europa.eu/files/etv/Upload/Projects_Networks/Skillsnet/Publications/EskillForum.pdf

Fife, E. & Pereira, F. (2016). The promise and reality: Assessing the gap between theory and practice in ICT4D. *Telecommunications Policy, 40,* 595–601.

Frenkel, M. (2008). Reprogramming femininity? The construction of gender identities in the Israeli hi-tech industry between global and local gender orders. *Gender, Work and Organization, 15,* 352–374.

G20 Digital Economy Ministerial Declaration (April, 2017). Shaping digitalisation for an interconnected world. Retrieved from http://unctad.org/meetings/es/Contribution/dtl_eWeek2017c02-G20_en.pdf.

Gloss, A., Carr, S. C., Reichman, W., Abdul-Nasiru, I., & Oestereich, W. T. (2017). From handmaidens to POSH humanitarians: The case for making human capabilities the business of I-O psychology. *Industrial-Organizational Psychology, 10,* 329–369.

Golden, T. D., Veiga, J. F., & Dino, R. N. (2008). The impact of professional isolation on teleworker job performance and turnover intentions: Does time spent teleworking, interacting face-to-face, or having access to communication-enhancing technology matter? *Journal of Applied Psychology, 93*, 1412–1421.

Guszcza, J. (2015). The last-mile problem: How data science and behavioral science can work together. *Deloitte Review, 16*, 65–79.

Hackman, J. R. & Oldham, G. R. (1976). Motivation through the design of work: Test of a theory. *Organizational Behavior and Human Performance, 16*, 250–279.

He, J. & Freeman, L. A. (2012). Are men more technology-oriented than women? The role of gender on the development of general computer self-efficacy of college students. *Journal of Information Systems Education, 21*, 203–212.

Heffernan, C., Lin, Y., & Thomson, K. (2016). Drawing from development: Towards unifying theory and practice of ICT4D. *Journal of International Development, 28*, 902–918.

Heilman, M. E., Wallen, A. S., Fuchs, D., & Tamkins, M. M. (2004). Penalties for success: Reactions to women who succeed at male gender-typed tasks. *Journal of Applied Psychology, 89*, 416–427.

Henrich, J., Heine, S. J., & Norenzayan, A. (2010). The weirdest people in the world? *Behavioral and Brain Sciences, 33*, 61–83.

Hewer, M. (2015). Design with humans in mind. *APS Observer*. Retrieved from www .psychologicalscience.org/observer/design-with-humans-in-mind.

Hill, C., Corbett, C., & St. Rose, A. (2010). *Why so few? Women in science, technology, engineering, and mathematics*. Washington, DC: American Association of University Women. Retrieved from www.aauw.org/files/2013/02/Why-So-Few-Women-in-Science-Technology-Engineering-and-Mathematics.pdf.

Hoch, J. E. & Kozlowski, S. W. J. (2014). Leading virtual teams: Hierarchical leadership, structural supports, and shared team leadership. *Journal of Applied Psychology, 99*, 390–403.

Holt, D. & Littlewood, L. (2013). Case study 4 – The Khayelitsha Cookie Company: Creating opportunity one bite at a time. Trickle Out Africa Project Case Study Series, Queen's University Management School, Queen's University Belfast, ISSN 2052–0026 (Online).

Hsia, J.-W. (2016). The effects of locus of control on university students' mobile learning adoption. *Journal of Computing in Higher Education, 28*, 1–17.

Hsia, J.-W., Chang, C.-C., & Tseng, A.-H. (2014). Effects of individuals' locus of control and computer self-efficacy on their e-learning acceptance in high-tech companies. *Behaviour & Information Technology, 33*, 51–64.

International Labour Organization (2016). ASEAN in transformation: How technology is changing jobs and enterprises. Geneva.

International Labour Organization (2017). Sustainable enterprises and jobs: Formal enterprises and decent work. *World Employment Social Outlook*. Retrieved from www .ilo.org/wcmsp5/groups/public/–dgreports/–dcomm/–publ/documents/publica tion/wcms_579893.pdf.

International Telecommunications Union (2017). ICT facts and figures 2017. Retrieved from www.itu.int/en/ITU-D/Statistics/Documents/facts/ICTFactsFigures2017 .pdf.

Jiranek, P., Brauchli, R., & Wehner, T. (2014). Beyond paid work: Voluntary work and its salutogenic implications for society. In G. F. Bauer & O. Hämmig (Eds.), *Bridging occupational, organizational and public health: A transdisciplinary approach* (pp. 209–229). Dordrecht: Springer.

Kahneman, D. (2011). *Thinking, fast and slow.* New York, NY: Farrar, Strous and Giroux.

Kisaalita, W. S., Katimbo, A., Sempiira, E. J., & Mugisa, D. J. (2016). Cultural influences in women-friendly labor-saving hand tool designs: The milk churner case. *Human Factors, 58,* 27–42.

Koch, A. J., D'Mello, S. D., & Sackett, P. R. (2015). A meta-analysis of gender stereotypes and bias in experimental simulations of employment decision making. *Journal of Applied Psychology, 100,* 128–161.

Kopelman, S., Hardin, A. E., Myers, C .G., & Tost, L. P. (2016). Cooperation in multi-cultural negotiations: How the cultures of people with low and high power interact. *Journal of Applied Psychology, 101,* 721–730.

Krieger, N., Waterman, P. D., Hartman, C., Bates, L. M., Stoddard, A. M., Quinn, M. M., Sorensen, G., & Barbeau, E. M. (2006). Social hazards on the job: Workplace abuse, sexual harassment, and racial discrimination – a study of black, Latino, and white low-income women and men workers in the United States. *International Journal of Health Studies, 36,* 51–85.

Lam, S. K., Uduwage, A., Dong, Z., Sen, S., Musicant, D. R., Terveen, L., & Riedl, J. (October, 2011). WP: Clubhouse? An exploration of Wikipedia's gender imbalance. Paper presented WikiSym '11, the ACM's International Symposium on Wikis and Open Collaboration, Mountain View, CA. Retrieved from www.ideas geek.net/wp-content/wp-gender-wikisym2011.pdf.

Lapierre, L. M., Van Steenbergen, E. F., Peeters, M. C. W., & Kluwer, E. S. (2016). Juggling work and family responsibilities when involuntarily working from home: A multiwave study of financial sales professionals. *Journal of Organizational Behavior, 37,* 804–822.

Lewin, K. (1951). *Field theory in social science: Selected theoretical papers* D. Cartwright (Eds.), New York, NY: Harper & Row.

Mack, C. A. (2011). Fifty years of Moore's Law. *IEEE Transactions on Semiconductor Manufacturing, 24,* 202–207.

MacLachlan, M. (November, 2014). Macropsychology, policy, and global health. *American Psychologist,69,* 851–863.

Maity, M. (2014). Mobile phone users from low socio-economic strata in Asia: The moderating roles of age and gender. *International Journal of Technology Management & Sustainable Development, 13,* 177–200.

Maji, S. K. & Pal, K. (2017). Factors affecting the adoption of e-filing of income tax returns in India: A survey. *The IUP Journal of Accounting Research & Audit Practices, 16,* 46–66.

McNatt, D. B. (2000). Ancient Pygmalion joins contemporary management: A meta-analysis of the result. *Journal of Applied Psychology, 85,* 314–322.

McWha-Hermann, I., Maynard, D. C., & Berry, M. O. (Eds.). (2016). *Humanitarian work psychology and the global development agenda: Case studies and interventions.* London: Routledge

Meyer, R. D., Kanfer, R., & Burrus, C. (2016). Improving motivation and performance among frontline healthcare workers in rural India: The role of team-based goals and incentives. In I. McWha-Hermann, D. C. Maynard, & M. O'Neill Berry (Eds.), *Humanitarian work psychology and the global development agenda: Case studies and interventions* (pp. 100–112). London: Routledge.

Napoli, P. M. & Obar, J. A. (2013). Mobile leapfrogging and digital divide policy: Assessing the limitations of mobile internet access. Retrieved from http://web.archive.org/web/20140814122050/http://oti.newamerica.net/sites/newamerica.net/files/policydocs/MobileLeapfrogging_Final.pdf.

National Academies of Sciences, Engineering, and Medicine (2017). *Information technology and the U.S. workforce: Where are we and where do we go from here?* Washington, DC: The National Academies Press.

NPR (2017). Are cyborgs in our future? 'Homo Deus' author thinks so. All Things Considered: Author Interviews. Retrieved from www.npr.org/2017/02/21/516484639/are-cyborgs-in-our-future-homo-deus-author-thinks-so

Norman, D. (2013). *The design of everyday things*. New York, NY: Basic Books.

Norris, L. (2010). *Recycling Indian clothing: Global contexts of reuse and value*. Indianapolis, IN: Indiana University Press.

Nussbaum, M. (2007). Human rights and human capabilities. *Harvard Human Rights Journal*, *20*, 21–24.

OECD. (2017). *Behavioural insights and public policy: Lessons from around the world*. Paris: OECD Publishing.

OECD. (2015). *Securing livelihoods for all: Foresight for action*. Paris: OECD Publishing.

OECD, ISOC, & UNESCO. (2013). The relationship between local content, internet development and access prices. OECD Digital Economy Papers, No. 217, OECD Publishing. Retrieved from http://dx.doi.org/10.1787/5k4c1rq2bqvk-en.

Osuna-Acedo, S., Frau-Meigs, D., Camarero-Cano, L., Bossu, A., Pedrosa, R., & Jansen, D. (2017). Intercreativity and interculturality in the virtual learning environments of the ECO MOOC project. In M. Jemni, Kinshuk, & M. K. Khribi (Eds.), *Open education: From OERs to MOOCs* (pp. 161–187). Berlin: Springer.

Pelegrín-Borondo, J., Reinares-Lara, & Olarte-Pascual (2017). Assessing the acceptance of technological implants (the cyborg): Evidences and challenges. *Computers in Human Behavior*, *70*, 104–112.

Peters, M. A. (2017). Technological unemployment: Educating for the fourth industrial revolution. *Journal of Self-Governance and Management Economics*, *5*, 25–33.

Risdon, C. (2017). Scaling nudges with machine learning. *Behavioral Scientist*. Retrieved from http://behavioralscientist.org/scaling-nudges-machine-learning/

Rotter, J. B. (1966). Generalized expectancies for internal versus external control of reinforcement. *Psychological Monographs: General and Applied*, *80*, 1–28.

Schur, J. B. (2016). Eli Whitney's patent for the Cotton Gin. National Archives. Retrieved from www.archives.gov/education/lessons/cotton-gin-patent.

Schwab, K. (2016). *The fourth industrial revolution*. New York, NY: Crown Publishing Group.

Sharafat, A. R. & Lehr, W. H. (2017). ICT4SDGs: ICT-centric economic growth, innovation and job creation. International Telecommunication Union. Retrieved from www.itu.int/dms_pub/itu-d/opb/gen/D-GEN-ICT_SDGS.01–2017-PDF-E.pdf.

Siegrist, J. (2014). Social inequalities in work and health in a globalized economy. In G. F. Bauer & O. Hämmig (Eds.), *Bridging occupational, organizational and public health: A transdisciplinary approach* (pp. 15–28). Dordrecht: Springer.

Smith, D. (2002). Psychologist wins Nobel Prize. *APA Monitor*, *33*(11), 22.

Sunstein, C. R. (2014). Nudging: A very short guide. *Journal of Consumer Policy*, *37*, 583–588.

Tadesse, G. & Bahiigwa, G. (2015). Mobile phones and farmers' marketing decisions in Ethiopia. *World Development, 68*, 296–307.

Tarhini, A., Hone, K., & Liu, X. (2014). Measuring the moderating effect of gender and age on e-learning acceptance in England: A structural equational modeling approach for an extended technology acceptance model. *Journal of Educational Computing Research, 51*, 163–184.

Thaler, R. H. & Sunstein, C. R. (2008). *Nudge: Improving decisions about health, wealth, and happiness*. New York, NY: Penguin.

United Nations. (2015). The Millennium Development Goals report 2015. New York: Inter-Agency and Expert Group on MDG Indicators, Department of Economic and Social Affairs. Retrieved from www.un.org/millenniumgoals/2015_MDG_Report/pdf/MDG%202015%20rev%20(July%201).pdf.

United Nations. (2018). World economic situation and prospects 2018. Report jointly produced by the United Nations Department of Economic and Social Affairs (UN/DESA), the United Nations Conference on Trade and Development (UNCTAD), Economic Commission for Africa (ECA), Economic Commission for Europe (ECE), Economic Commission for Latin America and the Caribbean (ECLAC), Economic and Social Commission for Asia and the Pacific (ESCAP), and Economic and Social Commission for Western Asia (ESCWA). New York. Retrieved from www.un.org/development/desa/dpad/wp-content/uploads/sites/45/publication/WESP2018_Full_Web-1.pdf.

United Nations Broadband Commission for Sustainable Development. (March, 2017). Recommendations for action: Bridging the gender gap in internet and broadband access and use. Working group on the digital gender divide. Retrieved from http://broadbandcommission.org/Documents/publications/WorkingGroupDigitalGenderDivide-report2017.pdf.

United Nations Conference on Trade and Development. (2017). Information economy report 2017: Digitalization, trade, and development. Retrieved from http://unctad.org/en/PublicationsLibrary/ier2017_en.pdf.

United Nations Development Programme. (2015). Human development report 2015: Work for human development. Retrieved from http://hdr.undp.org/sites/default/files/2015_human_development_report.pdf.

United Nations Development Programme. (2016). Human development index (HDI). Retrieved from http://hdr.undp.org/en/content/human-development-index-hdi.

United Nations Educational, Scientific and Cultural Organization. (May, 2011). Digital literacy in education. UNESCO Institute for Information Technologies in Education. Retrieved from http://unesdoc.unesco.org/images/0021/002144/214485e.pdf.

United Nations Educational, Scientific and Cultural Organization. (March 24, 2017). *Mobile learning week: Education in emergencies and crises*. Programme delivered by UNESCO in partnership with UNHCR, the United Nations refugee agency, and in collaboration with ITU, the United Nations specialized agency for ICT. Retrieved from www.unesco.org/new/fileadmin/MULTIMEDIA/HQ/ED/pdf/mlw2017_ProvisionalProgramme.pdf.

United Nations General Assembly. (September 25, 2015). Transforming our world: The 2030 agenda for sustainable development, A/RES/70/1. Retrieved from www.un.org/ga/search/view_doc.asp?symbol=A/RES/70/1&Lang=E.

United Nations News Centre. (October 11, 2017). At UN, robot Sophia joins meeting on artificial intelligence and sustainable development. Retrieved from www.un.org/apps/news/story.asp?NewsID=57860#.Wl-qXKinE2w.

Vallières, F., McAuliffe, E., Hyland, P., Galligan, M., & Ghee, A. (2017). Measuring work engagement among community health workers in Sierra Leone: Validating the Utrecht Work Engagement Scale. *Journal of Work and Organizational Psychology*, *33*, 41–46.

Vallières, F., McAuliffe, E., Palmer, I., Magbity, E., & Bangura, A. S. (2013). Supporting & strengthening maternal, neonatal, and child health services using mobile phones in Sierra Leone: A research protocol. *Africa Policy Journal*, *8*, 46–51.

Venkatesh, V. & Davis, F. D. (2000). A theoretical extension of the technology acceptance model: Four longitudinal field studies. *Management Science*, *46*, 186–204.

Venkatesh, V., Morris, M. G., Davis, G. B., & Davis, F. D. (2003). User acceptance of information technology: Toward a unified view. *MIS Quarterly*, *27*, 425–478.

Verhulst, S. G. & Young, A. (September, 2017). The potential of social media intelligence to improve people's lives: Social media data for good. GovLab. Retrieved from www.thegovlab.org/static/files/publications/social-media-data.pdf.

Verma, P. & Sinha, N. (2016). Technology acceptance model revisited for mobile based agriculture extension services in India. *Management Research and Practice*, *8* (4), 29–38.

Vignovic, J. A. & Foster Thompson, L. (2010). Computer-mediated cross-cultural collaboration: Attributing communication errors to the person versus the situation. *Journal of Applied Psychology*, *95*, 265–276.

Wang, Q., Bowling, N. A., & Eschleman, K. J. (2010). A meta-analytic examination of work and general locus of control. *Journal of Applied Psychology*, *95*, 761–768.

Williams, J. (December 5, 2017). Sophia the robot wants women's rights for Saudi Arabia. *Newsweek*. Retrieved from www.newsweek.com/sophia-robot-saudi-arabia-women-735503.

Wilson, M. A., Bennett, W., Jr., Gibson, S. G., & Alliger, G. M. (Eds.). (2012). *The handbook of work analysis: Methods, systems, applications and science of work measurement in organizations*. New York, NY: Routledge.

World Bank. (2017). Financial inclusion. Retrieved from www.worldbank.org/en/topic/financialinclusion/overview#1.

World Bank. (2018). World Bank country and lending groups. Retrieved from https://datahelpdesk.worldbank.org/knowledgebase/articles/906519-world-bank-country-and-lending-groups

World Bank. (2016). *World development report 2016: Digital dividends*. Washington, DC: World Bank. Retrieved from http://documents.worldbank.org/curated/en/896971468194972881/pdf/102725-PUB-Replacement-PUBLIC.pdf.

World Economic Forum. (2015). The global gender gap report 2015. Retrieved from www3.weforum.org/docs/GGGR2015/cover.pdf.

World Wide Web Foundation. (October, 2015). Women's rights online: Translating access into empowerment. Retrieved from http://webfoundation.org/docs/2015/10/womens-rights-online21102015.pdf.

25 Electronic Surveillance and Privacy

David L. Tomczak and Tara S. Behrend

25.1 Introduction

Employees at a London banking company arrived at work one day to find that management had installed black boxes underneath their desks. The boxes, created by a company called OccupEye, used heatmapping technology to track the employee's locations. The company claimed that the boxes are used for tracking real estate costs and building usage, not performance or employee whereabouts (Morris, Griffin, & Gower, 2017). Nonetheless, given the computing power of the boxes, employees were suspicious of how the data collected from the box would be used. At the same time in the US, a Wisconsin technology company installed rice-sized microchips in the hands of volunteer employees. The microchips have Radio Frequency Identification (RFID) capabilities, allowing employees to gain access to the building and pay for cafeteria lunches with the wave of a hand. That company also claims that the technology will not be used to monitor personal location within or outside working hours, but cybersecurity experts are skeptical; they note that such technology is often easy to hack and could reveal more personal information about these employees than was originally intended (Astor, 2017).

These are a couple examples of the new ways that organizations are gathering employee data in the ever-changing world of work. In fact, after this chapter is published, monitoring capabilities will no doubt continue to evolve and render these examples obsolete. These two examples demonstrate, however, the importance of discussions concerning the present and future implications of electronic monitoring. The first example demonstrates how computing power and data-capturing capabilities are evolving at great speeds, allowing organizations to analyze large amounts of employee behavior data for organizational decision-making. The second is an example of human-computer embeddedness that we previously had seen only in science-fiction. These may sound like extreme cases, but approximately 80 percent of organizations monitor employee behavior in some way, and this number will only rise with technological trends (Ribitzky, 2007). As companies continue to adopt increasingly complex computing capabilities, it is important to understand their effects on organizational surveillance practices, including methods, uses, and consequences, as well as what implications these practices have for privacy.

This chapter accomplishes the following: we define and organize past and present electronic performance monitoring (EPM) methods and their uses; we review the empirical research on the attitudinal and behavioral responses to monitoring at all levels of the organization (employee, manager, and organization); we discuss the practical, legal, and ethical limitations of monitoring; and we identify research gaps as well as future research directions.

25.2 The Evolution of EPM

Electronic performance monitoring (EPM) was originally conceived as an umbrella term for any electronic system with the capability to collect and analyze employee behavior in the workplace or on the job (Alge, 2001). Early studies of EPM focused on monitoring single employee tasks, such as data entry or customer service calls. These early studies suggested that EPM generally elicits the same feelings as being physically observed by a supervisor (Aiello & Svec, 1993; Griffith, 1993). Employers were using monitoring to gauge how much time an employee allocated to a task, how frequently they completed tasks, and how accurately the task was completed. Electronic systems can capture this data more quickly, more objectively, and with less human capital than direct supervisor observation. Less complex jobs, such as call center positions, were more likely to be monitored because the positions did not require immense cognitive effort to perform satisfactorily, so performance could be summarized with a few measurable outputs (Vorvoreanu & Botan, 2000).

As technology becomes more integrated and advanced, the types of jobs that can be monitored have expanded. EPM is now applicable to high-complexity jobs because computers, laptops, phones, and other data-gathering products can communicate with each other, making digital traces of behavior accurate and representative measures of how employees operate in an organization (Cascio & Montealegre, 2016). Company-provided computers and tools are all capable of collecting and storing digital traces of employees, such as emails, messages, location, internet site visits, and phone calls (Lohr, 2013), all of which can be used to construct an accurate depiction of how an employee behaves in workplace. For example, data collected from an employee's RFID badge can be linked with the employee's laptop usage, allowing the organization to not only confirm an employee's absence from the company building but also to track what the employee was doing on the computer during working hours.

The concept of ubiquitous computing is possible because, per Moore's law, the price of computers has decreased over time and the computing power has become increasingly more complex, creating systems that seamlessly link the physical world and digital world (Cascio & Montealegre, 2015). Not only are personal computers abundant, but they have stronger capabilities, such as thumbprint reading, eye-tracking, and GPS location tracking. Modern computer programs, such as videoconferencing programs, have user-friendly interfaces adjusted to fit human interaction, allowing individuals to complete relatively complex computing tasks with minimal effort (Cascio & Montealegre, 2015).

25.3 EPM Types, Capabilities, and Uses

At this point, we believe it is important to distinguish between surveillance and EPM, although these terms are often used interchangeably. The word surveillance is derived from the Latin "super" (meaning "over") and "vigilantia" (meaning "watchfulness") (Surveillance, n.d.). Based on the word's origin, surveillance inherently assumes a power differential – that is, the ability of a superior to watch over another object or person is an exercise of power over that object. Historically, the word has been synonymous with watching over suspicious individuals (BBC, 2015). EPM does not inherently assume a power differential; the observational capabilities of EPM go beyond deterring suspicious behavior, by gathering large amounts of employee behavior data that can be used to drive organizational decision-making. As we will discuss throughout this chapter, however, EPM can function much like surveillance, either intentionally or unintentionally, simply because data-capturing and analysis capabilities are becoming more sophisticated, allowing us to analyze more behavioral data points than before. In the midst of these advancements, there is greater organizational responsibility in handling employee data, and thus we emphasize the ethical and legal ramifications of these functions.

25.3.1 Early Uses of EPM

In contrast to the integrative EPM that we have today, early forms of surveillance were predictable and authoritarian because they were mainly used for quality control and deterring bad employee behavior. As described in Sewell and Wilkinson (1992), Just-In-Time and Total Quality Management systems in manufacturing and industrial workplaces were designed to limit deviations from desired employee behaviors to increase efficiency and performance, all while using as few supervisors as possible on the factory floor. Electronic tests of final products were used to set manufacturing standards for other factories nationwide. The same tests could also pinpoint inadequacies and identify which employee or department did not perform up to standards. Researchers describe this surveillance as putting employees "under the gun" because the intimidating watchful eye of monitoring aims to direct employees toward better behaviors, and at the time, there was little consideration for the stress that employees may experience under such scrutiny. Only within the past few decades have the potential negative ramifications of computer monitoring capabilities been studied as a threat to employee welfare (Ajunwa, Crawford, & Schultz, 2017).

25.3.2 Complex Monitoring for Complex Jobs

Industrial monitoring methods do not translate well to more complex jobs because work can involve several different types of tasks, and each task may vary in autonomy and complexity. Rather than following specified procedures to create end products, a worker may have several simultaneous projects in which there is no specified procedure for reaching each goal and thus, there are several criteria for job performance. For example, if we were to measure the performance of an outside sales representative, we could assess performance from the number of sales closed and the dollar value of the sales. Our choice of criteria, however, excludes a representative's ability to research a target market and to maintain correspondence with major accounts, both of which may also contribute to overall performance. Modern EPM allows an organization to collect data on each of these aspects to assess performance. Monitoring for such jobs consequently can take several different forms, such as, but not limited to, those listed in Table 25.1.

The list presented in Table 25.1 is not exhaustive, but it provides an overview of the various ways that organizations can collect digital traces. Taken together, a compilation of data from these methods can paint a vivid picture of exactly how an employee "spends company time." Returning to our previous example, the sales representative's organization can gather performance data on her market research skills by monitoring website history and tracking computer usage. Email and messaging archives provide data on communication skills, and the GPS location data extracted from the company phone and vehicle can verify the time and location of her on-site client meetings. Although each of these data points are subject to criterion deficiency and cannot paint the full picture of her performance, the organization now has more data to inform her performance appraisal.

The methods in Table 25.1 contain important distinctions, such as monitoring vs. blocking internet usage, and tracking location via RFID vs. GPS. Research suggests that employees react differently based on EPM characteristics, and that types of EPM serve different purposes for managers. For example, EPM can vary in monitoring intensity – low intensity or "passive" EPM is summary performance data that is either delayed or asynchronous, whereas high intensity or "active" EPM is continuous and highly detailed. When monitoring computer use, an organization may use low intensity EPM to routinely take screenshots of an employee's desktop and view the screenshots later to summarize an employee's computer usage. Conversely, the organization may use high intensity EPM to monitor an employee's computer, employing remote access on the user's desktop to see all computer actions in real time (Alge, Ballinger, & Green, 2004; McNall & Roch, 2009). Moreover, managers are more likely to use more intense EPM methods when they highly depend on the employee or wish to closely monitor a struggling employee (Alge et al., 2004).

These examples illustrate how research has previously discussed EPM characteristics, and as monitoring tactics continue to evolve, we add to this literature by proposing a typology of monitoring characteristics that is robust to technological evolution (see Table 25.2). Previous frameworks for EPM have listed the many

Table 25.1 *EPM types, capabilities, and uses (based on AMA Monitoring Survey, 2007)*

Type of EPM	Capability	Examples of Use
Surveillance Cameras	Collecting and storing physical movement data	Ensuring employee safety, deterring theft and counterproductive work behaviors, recording employee location
Telephone Audio Recordings	Collecting and storing the timing, duration, and content of work-related phone conversations	Assessing quality of customer service, establishing call length standards, deterring personal calls at work
Computer Monitoring	Collecting and storing computer-use data including number of keystrokes, time spent at computer, and real-time monitoring	Assessing how employees spend their time at work, assessing building usage, deterring counterproductive work behaviors such as excessive socializing
Internet Monitoring	Collecting and storing internet site visits and/or real-time monitoring	Deterring cyberloafing (i.e., social media usage, gaming, online shopping, personal email accounts)
Website Blocking	Prohibiting employee access to certain types of websites (i.e., social media sites, adult content, job applications)	Deterring cyberloafing (i.e., social media usage, gaming, online shopping), preventing offensive content
Email and Messaging Archives	Collecting and storing internal email and instant messages	Tracking internal and external communications, ensuring confidential information is handled appropriately, tracking personal use, observing inappropriate language
GPS	Collecting and storing location data from company-issued cell phones and vehicles and/or real-time location monitoring	Recording employee whereabouts during working hours, verifying deliveries, recording and analyzing routes to ensure time efficiency
RFID Badges	Providing access to company buildings, collecting and storing employee access data	Tracking and recording building access, inventory and logistics
Wearable Technology	Collecting and storing location and physiological data via heart rate monitors and pedometers (i.e., Fitbits)	Providing employees with health-related information to encourage healthy habits, promoting health and wellness programs/challenges
Work-Related Mobile Applications	Collecting employee data specific to the position or organization (i.e., Castlight employee health app, Xora workforce management app)	Providing employees with tailored resources to do their jobs and/or improve decision-making, collecting information in a manner specific to the organization's interests

Table 25.2 *EPM Typology*

EPM Element 1: Purpose
The main function and/or reason for EPM implementation.

Sub-Elements	Categories
	Administrative & Safety Legal, compliance, recordkeeping, etc. *Performance, Loss Prevention & Profit* Employee behavior and financial productivity. *Motivation, Development & Feedback* EPM is linked with organizational feedback/appraisal process. *Surveillance & Authoritarian Power* Employee data collection without clear instrumentality.

EPM Element 2: Invasiveness
The who, what, and how of employee monitoring.

Sub-Elements	Categories
Target Level	*Individual* *Group*
Monitoring Target	*Task Quality* How well a product was produced. *Task Quantity* Number of products produced in a period of time. *Thoughts & Feelings* Employee work-related attitudes (e.g., monitoring employee email content and/or social media feeds). *Location & Safety Behaviors* Location/movement of employee body and/or organizational property (e.g., vehicles).
Constraints	*High* Clear bounds regarding how EPM data is used (e.g. strictly for performance), and who can access it (e.g., manager only). *Low* Data can be used in any way, and many organizational members can access it.
Control	*High* Employee can delay and/or stop monitoring for a period of time. *Low* Employee has no control over monitoring timing.

EPM Element 3: Synchronicity

The frequency, pervasiveness, and regularity of monitoring and monitoring feedback.

Sub-Elements	Categories
Collection	*High* Continuous monitoring; real-time location tracking. *Low* Intermittent monitoring; Summarized information about employee behavior over period of time.
Feedback *Delivery*	*High* Customized feedback in close proximity to the employee behavior. *Low* Summarized reports of employee behaviors over a period of time.

EPM Element 4: Transparency

The who, what, and how of communicating EPM to the employee and the extent to which an employee is aware of monitoring.

Sub-Elements	Categories
	High Employee is informed of how data is collected (timing, level, monitoring targets), how the data aligns with performance standards and disciplinary consequences, and who has access to the data. *Low* Organization does not communicate full extent of employee monitoring; employee is unaware of timing, content, and consequences of monitoring.

possible monitoring characteristics (Stanton, 2000a), and we attempt to synthesize these past efforts. Our typology draws from literature on employee reactions to monitoring and incorporates the various purposes of monitoring, including EPM that does not clearly benefit the employee or organization (surveillance and authoritarian power). We identify sub-elements and categories within four overarching elements (purpose, invasiveness, transparency, and synchronicity) in which EPM can differ, and it is the variance in these categories that may explain why and how employees respond to EPM differently, as we discuss later. The *purpose* of EPM varies depending on organizational need, which has implications for how EPM is integrated in the employee's job. For example, EPM for compliance, legal, and safety issues may satisfy higher-order organizational needs, whereas feedback and employee development purposes suggest that there will be greater interaction between EPM and the employee. This interaction can vary greatly in *invasiveness* as well – for example, the perception that an individual's contributions may go unnoticed (group monitoring) can elicit a different response than when the individual is aware that only their actions are scrutinized (individual monitoring). Likewise, EPM directed at a task, rather than the employee's body or thoughts, will elicit different perceptions of privacy invasion. The *synchronicity* element accounts for differences in EPM capabilities: fine-grained, customized feedback can provide recommendations for employee behavioral change in real time, whereas summarized reports generate aggregates of employee behavior that can be used for general guidance. Thus, the amount and type of feedback can vary considerably. Lastly, *transparency* considers the extent to which the organization has communicated and clarified the role and capabilities of EPM; well-informed employees may react more positively than individuals that are unaware of the role of monitoring in their job.

Even in the midst of changing surveillance and monitoring capabilities, this typology of EPM characteristics should be relatively enduring and provide guidance on understanding employee reactions to monitoring. We provide further review and description of employee reactions to monitoring in the sections to follow.

25.4 Why Organizations Use EPM

In addition to some of the brief examples we have provided thus far, there are several additional reasons why organizations use EPM: measuring employee performance, loss prevention, and profit; employee safety and wellness; disciplinary consequences; and organizational decision-making (Stanton & Stam, 2006).

25.4.1 Employee Performance, Loss Prevention, and Profit

25.4.1.1 Combatting Rater Issues

One of the key advantages of EPM is that it provides organizations with objective evidence and data of employee behavior to provide an unbiased assessment of employee task performance (Grant & Higgins, 1991). Objective performance data is advantageous because without proper rater training, biases (i.e., leniency, halo) can influence supervisor ratings of performance (Landy & Farr, 1980). Supervisor ratings of performance are multidimensional, such that supervisors often consider both task and contextual performance when rating employees (Motowidlo & Van Scotter, 1994). It is important, however, that supervisors can distinguish between task and extra-role behaviors because experience is closely related to task performance, whereas personality closely relates to contextual performance (Motowidlo & Van Scotter, 1994). In situations where an organization is interested in how an employee performed on a single task, without risk of rating bias, EPM data can be very helpful.

25.4.1.2 Addressing Criterion-Related Issues

EPM can be particularly useful in situations where performance is difficult to observe, and in these cases, monitoring can provide a wider range of performance criteria for managers to conduct performance appraisals. As such, EPM can be used to combat criterion-deficiency or contamination in performance assessments because it can provide more employee information than a supervisor may be able to gather from physical presence alone. Further, EPM can assist with identifying the employee behaviors that are responsible for job performance, and identify the factors that may have contributed to low output. Returning to our sales representative example, EPM data can identify that the sales representative has engaged in the right behaviors, but that conditions out of their control, such as economic downturn, are responsible for low sales numbers.

It is important to emphasize, though, that performance is still a multi-determined, complex phenomenon, and EPM will not fix all criterion woes. EPM data itself is subject to criterion deficiency or contamination if monitoring is directed at the wrong behavior or if the monitored behavior is not an accurate depiction of the entire job.

25.4.1.3 Job Analysis

Although it has been discussed less frequently, EPM data can be used for job analysis. An organization may use this data in several ways including updating the job description, adjusting the job qualifications, job reclassification, and creating performance standards. For example, employee behavior data regarding off-site client visits can give an organization a better view of the requirements of the sales representative position, alerting job applicants that a certain amount of travelling is required to satisfy the job requirements adequately. By collecting this information electronically, organizations gather accurate behavioral data without relying on observations, focus groups, or interviews. Few researchers have explored EPM's usefulness for job analysis, and such studies would be advantageous for informing organizational practice.

25.4.1.4 Establishing Performance Standards

EPM can assist in constructing performance standards or personalized employee metrics that motivate employees to achieve greater performance (Ambrose & Kulik, 1994). Providing employees with feedback from monitoring can increase an employee's desire to improve (Alder, 2007). For example, platforms like WorkIQ combine real-time computer, internet, and location monitoring to give employers a measure of employee productivity. Companies can condense this information into weekly or quarterly reports that are emailed directly to the employee, outlining how the employee has used their computer time throughout the week, and even how productive they are in the office compared to remote working situations. The process aims to help employees become cognizant of their habitual work behaviors and provide recommendations for improvement, but it may also be used to make employment, promotion, or disciplinary decisions.

25.4.1.5 Managing Virtual Employees

Trends in remote or virtual working environments also generate interest in EPM. The percentage of companies using virtual teams has grown to 46 percent (Minton-Eversole, 2012), and 63 percent of companies allow employees to telework at least occasionally (Shockley, 2014). Because virtual teams have less opportunity to be observed and directed, many virtual teams rely on self-management (Bell & Kozlowski, 2002). Nonetheless, electronic monitoring can offer several advantages for team members and their supervisors. EPM provides an opportunity for managers to maintain and control project progress even when employees are away from the office (Alge et al., 2004). Virtual team members and remote employees often must communicate through computer-mediated communication (CMC), such as email, instant messaging, and videoconferencing. Using EPM, managers can remotely track employee communications and internet use in real time or summarized reports, and see how long employees are at their computers. Virtual team members benefit from the awareness monitoring capabilities of CMC programs. Signals that a coworker is "Away" or "Online" are helpful for optimizing virtual communication (Zweig & Webster, 2002).

Whether organizations *should* closely examine employee communication logs is another question that we address in our section on the ethical and legal implications of EPM.

25.4.1.6 Disciplinary Consequences

Reasons for implementing EPM are usually directed at deterring negative behaviors at the employee level, such as surveilling for theft and monitoring use of company time for personal use. Organizations are often interested in curtailing cyberloafing, instances where employees are surfing the internet (i.e., online shopping, gaming, social networking) and engaging in non-work behaviors on company time. Companies want to optimize human labor because it is typically their greatest expense, and reports indicate that cyberloafing costs organizations $85 billion a year (Zakrzewski, 2016).

Although a monitoring system may be directed at surveilling for theft, it can still produce data that supports organizational development. A Dallas restaurant used a complex tracking software to analyze every aspect of server behavior (i.e., all tickets and orders) to detect patterns of theft (Lohr, 2014). This rich source of employee data could also identify exceptional workers, which the restaurant owners selected as next-in-line for management positions in new restaurant openings (Lohr, 2014).

25.4.1.7 Satisfying Legal Requirements

Lastly, in addition to controlling costs and using evidence to target training initiatives, EPM fulfills some basic organizational needs such as satisfying legal compliance, avoiding liability, and protecting company assets (Stanton & Stam, 2006; Vorvoreanu & Botan, 2000). EPM creates digital traces of nearly all organizational actions, including file storage and email communications with third parties. These digital traces can be retrieved in cases of serious organization harm or employee disputes, such as data breaches or confidentiality cases.

25.4.2 Safety and Employee Wellness

EPM can be directed at improving employee health and safety by using employee behavior data and providing recommendations. Ryder, the transportation and logistics company, installed a tracking system in all semi-trucks to record driver speeds, abrupt braking, unexpected stops, and turning radii. This system allows Ryder to track driving and delivery performance, as well as provide personalized feedback and recommendations to drivers for making safer turns and stops (Bowman, 2014; Tomczak, Lanzo, & Aguinis, 2018).

EPM can also assist employees with making the right decisions. Organizations like Walmart and Time-Warner reportedly encouraged their employees to download a mobile application called Castlight (Tomczak, Lanzo, & Aguinis, 2018; Zarya, 2016). The Castlight interface allowed employees to enter information regarding their general health (i.e., blood pressure, etc.) and health behaviors (i.e., exercising, sleeping and eating habits), and the application provided them with recommendations for engaging in better behaviors based on their likelihood of disease (i.e., risk for diabetes and heart disease; Zarya, 2016). The application also allowed employees to enter symptoms or health-related questions to gain simple, generic medical advice. By encouraging employees to use this application, these companies expressed genuine interest in employee health, but as we will discuss later, wellness applications such as these gather an alarming amount of personal data from employees – data that can harm employees over time.

25.4.3 Organizational Performance and Decision-Making

25.4.3.1 Allocating Resources and Improving Operations

Employee behavior data is a useful resource that allows organizations to make data-driven adjustments to increase productivity, decrease undesirable behaviors, and more. Using this data, organizations better understand where to allocate training or developmental resources, depending on which departments or employees have low performance. Moreover, EPM can help identify which aspects of employee performance (e.g., knowledge, skills) are suffering, which in turn provides guidance for selecting the training and development interventions that will be most useful (Noe et al., 1994). Organizations that gather more data have an advantage in making better decisions and allocating organizational resources.

Returning to the example of Ryder semi-trucks, monitoring all aspects of a driver's route can put Ryder at a distinct advantage over its competitors. GPS tracking analysis can indicate areas where routes are less time-efficient, and the organization can then use this data to adjust the route, eliminate it, or assign additional drivers. Locational data can be analyzed continuously to find areas of improvement. OccupEye's data on employee location might also suggest that the organization decrease their building size since many employees telework, saving money on real estate.

25.4.3.2 Building Competency Models and Clarifying Selection Criteria

Insights gained from big data analyses can be used to identify employee characteristics that are related to performance (Chamorro-Premuzic et al., 2016), and thus

EPM data can be a tool for building competency models and clarifying selection criteria. Specifically, organizations can analyze the EPM data from high-performing employees to understand individual differences associated with high performance. Chamorro-Premuzic et al. (2016) report that in addition to being used as performance criteria, phone call data (e.g., duration, frequency, location) can reliably predict personality traits (de Montjoye et al., 2013), and similar results have been found using location data, such that the amount and type of locations that people visit predict their level of conscientiousness and neuroticism (Chorley, Whitaker, & Allen, 2015). Verbal speech patterns extracted from video/audio recordings can be compared to ideal standards, providing feedback on intonation and emotion in speech patterns (Chamorro-Premuzic et al., 2016). These speech analyses can be used for performance management, and also assessing audio-video interview candidates. Monitoring data often contains these types of behavioral data (e.g., phone activity, location, speech), and thus EPM can be a tool for selection processes. While we do not anticipate EPM to change selection theory, we do expect EPM to contribute to big data in selection practices.

25.5 The Effects of EPM at Each Organizational Level

Understanding how EPM affects various organizational actors is essential to ensuring that EPM accomplishes what it was designed to accomplish. If the invasiveness of EPM results in negative employee behaviors, then the design of EPM contradicts its goals – that is, a system aimed at measuring productivity may instead be harming productivity (Vorvoreanu & Botan, 2000). The following sections review the research on EPM effects at all levels of an organization.

25.5.1 Employee-Level Effects

Much of the EPM literature has been directed at understanding how employees respond to monitoring practices. Here we provide an overview of EPM's known effects on attitudes, behaviors, and performance at the individual level.

25.5.1.1 Privacy Invasion and Fairness

Monitoring infiltrates psychological barriers; it invades interpersonal and spatial boundaries, such that individuals are less certain about the times that they have privacy in the workplace (Zweig & Webster, 2002). Indeed, it is well established that monitored individuals experience feelings of privacy invasion (McNall & Roch, 2009; Moorman & Wells, 2003; Stanton, 2000a), and individuals respond differently to various monitoring methods. Using latent class analysis, Willford et al. (2015a) found that email, computer, and phone monitoring, as well as video surveillance, were viewed as most invasive, while blocking internet sites was less invasive. Thus, monitoring that allows employers to observe employee behavior rather than simply direct it is considered more invasive. Perceived invasion of privacy is even higher when employees believe non-performance data is being gathered from EPM tools or if the data is released without permission, is used for things outside the organization, and concludes in unfavorable results (i.e., disciplinary actions; Tolchinsky et al., 1981). It is important to note that employees do not respond negatively to monitoring because they are concealing some sort of negative behavior. Rather, individuals prefer to have control over their information in general; they wish to control how their information is being used and control which pieces of information are available to others (Drexel University, 2016).

In addition to privacy invasion, monitoring affects how people feel about their jobs and the organization. Monitored individuals find EPM to be an unfair practice (McNall & Roch, 2007; Moorman & Wells, 2003; Stanton, 2000b), and EPM negatively correlates with job satisfaction and organizational commitment (Wells, Moorman, & Werner, 2007). Given the established negative relationships among satisfaction, commitment, and turnover intentions (Tett & Myer, 1993), organizations may face turnover costs if monitoring negatively affects employees.

25.5.1.2 Deviance and Counterproductive Work Behaviors (CWBs)

Another major issue with EPM is that negative attitudes often lead to counterproductive or destructive employee behaviors. Yost et al. (2018) suggest that these feelings of privacy invasion may cause an individual to "lash out" against the organization, as being monitored was found to be associated with increased counterproductive work behaviors directed at the organization (CWB-O), such as arriving to work late without permission (Willford et al., 2017). In other cases, reactions are more extreme: perceptions of injustice provoked by monitoring are associated with computer abuse, such as purposely damaging or sabotaging internal computer systems and files, purposely making errors, or abusing company computer policies by accessing unauthorized files and stealing computer-system resources (Posey et al., 2011). Thus, tech-savvy employees could seriously harm the organization and put key assets in jeopardy.

25.5.1.3 Personal Control and Feedback Reactions

Despite the potential for negative effects of EPM, organizational conditions can mitigate negative attitudes and promote desirable work behaviors. Stanton and Barnes-Farrell (1996) found that if the monitored employee can control the onset of EPM in some way (e.g., delay or prevent monitoring), they experience greater personal control and task performance than those with no control. The researchers suggest that this control is the electronic equivalent to being able to "close the office door" (p. 744) for a moment of privacy in the workplace. Privacy control is also important for virtual teams and electronic communication. Awareness monitoring systems that indicate whether an individual is online and able to talk cause individuals to feel like they have less control over the timing and way they complete work tasks (Zweig & Webster, 2002). The abilities to disconnect from these systems or indicate that one is "busy" are helpful for restoring employee control and autonomy.

When the communicated purpose of monitoring is commensurate with the expectations of the position, employees respond favorably. Bartels and Nordstrom (2012) observed participant reactions to a monitored or unmonitored data entry task, and manipulated the communicated purpose of the monitoring (no purpose, research-based, developmental, and administrative). Surprisingly, when individuals were instructed that EPM would be administrative (to distribute rewards or punishments), participants performed well and were highly motivated with relatively low reported stress; thus, EPM was conducive to their performance. Earley (1988) also found similar positive effects of EPM feedback. When individuals used a computer system to generate feedback on their task performance, they trusted and used the feedback more than supervisor ratings because they felt that the feedback was specifically tailored to their work actions. These studies provide information about the positive effects of EPM: simple, repetitive tasks can be monitored according to reward/punishment with little negative impact on the individual, and employees may even prefer the customized feedback from EPM over traditional supervisor feedback.

25.5.1.4 Social Facilitation and Observer Effects

Although much of EPM occurs outside the employee's awareness (Stanton, 2000a), monitoring elicits reactions that are like being physically supervised. Social facilitation theory asserts that the presence of another person can affect the performance of an individual positively or negatively (Zajonc, 1965). This effect has been found in monitoring situations, such that monitoring causes low-skilled workers to perform worse on monitored tasks compared to high-skilled individuals, and low-skilled workers may experience more stress (Aiello & Kolb, 1995). A study using a three-day monitored task demonstrates that these performance and stress issues can worsen over time (Schleifer, Galinsky, & Pan, 1996). Workload dissatisfaction increased for the monitored low performance group, and irritation increased for medium performance groups. These findings show how EPM affects employees differently, and that effects may be most negative for low-skilled or low-performing employees. Even though EPM can provide employees with useful performance feedback, it may not help underperforming individuals achieve greater productivity.

There is also growing evidence that the mere presence of monitoring can affect performance, even without communicated task demands. Becker and Marique (2014) found that monitored individuals performed with lower quantity output on a simple work task than non-monitored participants, even after controlling for cognitive ability and emotion. Work demands were not communicated to either group of participants, so it appears that individuals engage in more precautionary thinking when they are being monitored. Rather than finishing the task quickly and potentially making a mistake, monitored employees think through the process more slowly. It is important to note that the study was exploratory, and thus the authors induced conclusions about the participants' thought processes based on the data.

More research on the cognitive processes occurring while being monitored is needed to further understand how monitoring affects decision-making.

The social facilitation effect can also be responsible for lower satisfaction in learning tasks. Being monitored during learning tasks elicits evaluation apprehension, and depending on the type of monitoring (asynchronous vs. real time), both individuals with an avoid-performance orientation and a prove-performance orientation, respectively, can experience lower skill attainment (Watson et al., 2013). Furthermore, when individuals perceive monitored learning tasks as performance evaluation, they have negative perceptions of feedback and have subsequently worse learning outcomes than individuals that view such tasks as developmental (Karim, 2015). These negative reactions to monitored learning elicit physiological responses as well. Thompson, Sebastianelli, and Murray (2009) demonstrated through measured heart rates that participants in monitored learning tasks experience a greater mental overload than their unmonitored counterparts. When monitoring was made salient to the learners, they reported lower satisfaction with the training exercises. The results of these studies have serious implications for organizations that wish to train employees using online modules and the message is clear: monitoring learning tasks will have a negative impact on the employee experience.

25.5.1.5 Direction of Effort

EPM can signal to employees about to which tasks/behaviors they should direct their attention. For example, when EPM appears to favor quantity, participants focus on quantity (Stanton & Julian, 2002). When EPM focuses on quality, however, participants are more satisfied with the task and are more motivated to complete it. Interestingly, if quality is not emphasized, participants default to stressing quantity, demonstrating that organizations must carefully choose which tasks are monitored.

EPM can unfortunately direct effort in counterproductive ways. Brewer (1995) found that employees tend to allocate more effort toward monitored tasks than unmonitored tasks when they perceived that their individual performance is being evaluated. There was no difference in effort when supervisors evaluated the performance of the group, rather than the individual. These findings suggest that social loafing will still occur in monitored groups if employees do not feel that they are being monitored directly.

Contrary to findings of negative behavioral reactions to EPM, other researchers have found employee performance to increase with supervisory use of EPM, especially when EPM is used more frequently (Bhave, 2014). There are two explanations for these findings. Frequent EPM can cause evaluation apprehension, encouraging employees to work their hardest because they feel they are constantly being watched. EPM may also increase performance because job tasks that are monitored closely are perceived by the employee to be more important to the organization, and thus they are likely to allocate more time and effort toward these tasks (Larson & Callahan, 1990).

Recent studies have observed EPM's effect on extra-role behaviors. Bhave (2014) found that EPM use was associated organizational citizenship behaviors (OCBs) but not counterproductive work behaviors (CWBs). The positive effects of EPM may occur because the direction of EPM may signal what tasks are of importance to the organization, and thus employees direct more effort toward them (Stanton & Julian, 2002). The rationale for this behavior stems from self-presentation theory, such that employees adjust their behaviors because they know they are being watched (Baumeister, 1982; Bhave, 2014). If employees wish to present themselves favorably to the organization, monitoring allows the employee's altruistic actions to be noticed.

25.5.1.6 Physical and Affective Reactions

EPM elicits not only psychological reactions, but physical reactions as well. Through interviews with insurance company workers, Aiello (1993) found that monitored individuals experience more stress and reported more physical issues such as headaches. Employees also felt that their social interactions were suffering. Once the organization integrated more technology into their work processes, employee workspaces housed all the tools and access that they needed to perform their job, and they were suddenly lacking purposeful and impromptu social interactions with coworkers. These findings suggest that monitoring pressures employees to stay at their desks, which can result in unanticipated social and physical distress.

EPM affects employee mood. EPM is associated with state reactance and anger, and feelings of anger are associated with increased CWB-O and decreased OCB-O (Yost et al., 2018). Davidson and Henderson (2000) also found evidence of EPM's effect on mood – participant mood was higher in monitored easy tasks rather than difficult ones, and subjects experienced greater stress during complex tasks. Considering that monitoring can induce stressful reactions, including employee participation in any new technological implementation can help employees adjust to new organizational methods and garner support (Smith, Conway, & Karsh, 1999). In fact, when employees expect to be monitored and anticipate helpful performance feedback from monitoring practices, much of the negative effects of monitoring are diminished, and EPM can be conducive to goal-setting and expectancy (Nebeker & Tatum, 1993).

The seemingly never-ending list of negative monitoring effects on employees is at odds with the managerial benefits of monitoring – managers would like to know what their employees are up to, but such actions appear to negatively affect the employee. Although EPM can be implemented in such a way as to minimize these effects, such as providing employee control and developmental feedback, organizations must always be aware of the negative repercussions.

25.5.2 Managerial-Level Effects

Early studies of monitoring perceptions concluded that most managers consider electronic surveillance to be a vital aspect of organizational functioning. Managers claim that surveillance "keeps employees on their toes" to deter undesirable behaviors and keep employees on task. On a more positive note, managers also report that they are better able to see if an employee is using proper technique and procedures on the job, which offers opportunities for feedback and behavior adjustment when necessary (Chalykoff & Kochan, 1989). Managers are more likely to decide to electronically monitor subordinates if the supervisors depend heavily on them or if they anticipate future performance as being low (Alge et al., 2004). When these conditions are met, supervisors are also more likely to secretly monitor, or monitor employees without their awareness.

Empirical research has generated some recommendations for managers who use EPM. First, EPM should not be the only source of performance appraisal data; supervisors need to use other criteria in addition to monitoring for evaluation, especially since EPM data can be inconsistent or manipulated by the employee (Ball, 2010). Second, although there are no legal requirements to detail monitoring methods, supervisors should clearly communicate monitoring criteria (i.e., timing, capabilities, uses) because those who are less informed of monitoring practices elicit some of the strongest negative reactions to EPM (Ball, 2010; Jeske & Santuzzi, 2015; Willford et al., 2015b).

Third, supervisors must be aware that the format of the EPM data can influence how supervisors judge employee performance. Ambrose and Kulik (1994) found that summarized results of EPM data influenced supervisor ratings of performance and anticipated future performance. Participants underestimated the success of rising performers and overestimated declining performers. Managers may avoid summarized performance data if they wish to reward rising performers and provide training or motivational interventions for declining performers.

Lastly, monitoring may influence the ways that managers evaluate employees. Drawing from theory on decision-making and judgment in performance appraisal, managers tend to automatically categorize employees without being conscious of their reasoning (Feldman, 1981), and monitoring research has begun to explore how EPM influences this process. Kulik and Ambrose (1993) found that when EPM data suggests an unfavorable appraisal of an employee, the manager will likely maintain that judgment and not revise the appraisal. This finding reiterates the importance of ensuring that EPM is directed at the appropriate employee behaviors and that the data results in an accurate depiction of performance. It also stresses the importance of having other appraisal criteria in addition to EPM results.

25.5.3 Organizational-Level Effects

Few studies have addressed the effects of EPM at the organizational level, but this research area is ripe for interesting new directions. Findings from existing research provide some guidance for considering organizational characteristics when deciding to monitor.

25.5.3.1 Employee Trust and Fairness

When organizations fail to elicit the participation of employees in decisions that affect the working conditions of the employee, organizational trust is undermined (Westin, 1992); thus, organizations should provide notice of monitoring methods before implementation to enhance employee trust. Hovorka-Mead, Ross, Whipple, and Renchin (2002) studied a sample of seasonal student workers, reporting that notice of monitoring resulted in more favorable fairness perceptions of the monitoring, and that perceptions of fairness were positively related to returning to the position the following year. Furthermore, in a laboratory setting, the researchers found that even weak justifications for monitoring can elicit greater procedural justice beliefs rather than no justification. Alder, Noel, and Ambrose (2006) support the importance of communicating organizational EPM; they found that greater employee trust in EPM was positively associated with job satisfaction, organizational commitment, and turnover intentions. Thus, organizations should always be transparent about monitoring employees as it may mitigate some of EPM's negative outcomes.

25.5.3.2 Alignment with Organizational Goals

Organizations should ensure that the performance metrics and standards originating from EPM align with organizational or departmental goals. Grant, Higgins, and Irving (1988) note that EPM may create confusion regarding performance metrics. In some situations, employees will report that quantity is more important for performance on monitored tasks, although supervisors intend to communicate that both quantity and quality are considered in performance ratings. Reactions to EPM are also influenced by perceived characteristics of the EPM, such as its accuracy, the timing, and the bias of the system (Kidwell & Bennett, 1994).

Organizational efforts to improve employee self-management and encourage discretionary behavior may be undermined by close surveillance (Jensen & Raver, 2012). This is because close supervision is a conflicting signal to the employee; the organization wants the employee to self-manage, but the supervisor still closely monitors the employee, which leads to perceptions of distrust and subsequently counterproductive work behaviors. To mitigate confusion regarding performance expectations and monitoring capabilities, monitoring discussions should include a description of the advantages and limitations of EPM, and the ways that EPM will be used to supplement performance appraisals. Furthermore, monitoring should not conflict with other efforts to encourage employee autonomy.

25.5.3.3 Organizational Characteristics and Monitoring Acceptance

Organizational characteristics can be instrumental in employee reactions to monitoring. As organizational size increases, employee perceptions of procedural fairness diminish because decision-making takes place further away from the employee level (Schminke, Ambrose, & Cropanzano, 2000). Large organizations that wish to monitor employees may struggle more with having employees agree with EPM methods. Furthermore, if the organization is experiencing volatile restructuring or personnel concerns in which job security is threatened, employees will be less likely to accept new monitoring practices (Ball, 2010). In general, if employees have low perceptions of procedural justice, it will be more difficult to garner support for monitoring because the organization is already considered to have unfair practices (Westin, 2003).

EPM can also be a major concern for employers because employees tend to view managers as an extension of the organization; thus, any poor monitoring practices exhibited by managers will be projected onto the organization. When employees perceive procedural justice violations from monitoring, they can attribute them to poor supervisory practices, rather than organizational policy (Zweig & Scott, 2007).

25.6 Legal Implications and Ethics of Monitoring

Although research recommends that organizations and managers be transparent about their monitoring practices, privacy laws have not kept pace with monitoring best practices and technological advancements. In the previous sections, we demonstrated the potential benefits and drawbacks of employee monitoring for performance and employee well-being. In the following sections, we address the legal and societal implications of monitoring. We also use legal cases to discuss the current protections of employee data, and the ethics of monitoring employees.

25.6.1 Privacy Protections

Technology changes rapidly and the ways that organizations gather employee data become continually more invisible, but privacy laws in the United States have not kept pace, offering insufficient legal protection over employee personal information. The Privacy Act of 1974 sets forth requirements for organizations to communicate, in some way, that they are gathering employee data, but does not require them to inform employees of when or how it is happening, or how the data might be used. The lack of legal protections for employees is especially troubling considering the sensitivity of data collected; for example, wellness applications collect employee health data but because these companies are not health care providers, HIPAA laws do not apply (Ajunwa, Crawford, & Schultz, 2017).

When we think of the privacy implications of EPM, it is also important to stress that monitoring is taking place in an environment where not all pieces of personal information are equal. Knowing an employee's web-surfing habits is not equivalent to knowing if an employee will be pregnant soon – one piece of information is intimate and has legal protection. Because EPM data contains deeply personal employee information, the onus is on the organization to provide sufficient cyber-security to ensure that external hacking does not put employee data at risk for theft.

25.6.2 New Technology as Accidental Monitoring

Whereas previous EPM methods were imposed upon employees in a hierarchical manner, Ajunwa, Crawford, and Schultz (2017) argue that surveillance has now become participatory, such that employees are expected to engage with EPM voluntarily to improve productivity, improve their work behaviors, and receive employee benefits. Even more concerning is the abundance of "shiny new toys" that IT companies offer to organizations to improve productivity that have not been properly tested to see if employee performance does indeed improve.

Even if new technologies do not clearly state monitoring capabilities, accidental monitoring can occur. In their case study of new technology implementation in a hospital, Lankshear and Mason (2001) discuss "surveillance capable technologies" (p. 231), electronic systems that are intended to assist with non-monitoring orga-nizational functions (i.e., instructional resources, data collection), but nonetheless contain information that employees would prefer to keep private. In this example, a hospital introduced a voluntary computerized instructional program to reinforce cardiotocography (CTG) interpretation skills. Data from the computerized program could identify the employee, the number of times that they accessed the program, and the score that they achieved during the session. Without clear explanation of how the results would be used, employees soon became concerned about who would have access to their scores and what disciplinary action, if any, would occur if scores were unsatisfactory, leading to uneasiness toward the program. Perhaps it is not the organization's intention to violate privacy, but most modern technology has basic capabilities that can identify employees and their behaviors, and compa-nies can put personal information at risk without being aware of it. Thus, it is the organization's responsibility to ensure that employee behavior data is handled appropriately when integrating new technologies.

25.6.2.1 The Boundaries of Acceptable Monitoring

The following example from Tomczak, Lanzo & Aguinis (2018) provides a closer look at unethical monitoring that resulted in substantial legal ramifications:

> Employees at Intermex, a money-wiring company, were required to download a mobile application to assist with job-related duties. The app, Xora, used GPS capabilities to track and optimize driver routes, verifying the time and location of trips and deliveries. The GPS capabilities could track the exact location of an employee at any time – it could even tell managers how fast the person was driving. One employee, Myrna Arias, likened the app to a "tracking bracelet" (Gardella, 2015), and was concerned about her employer tracking her location outside working hours. She requested to delete the app or turn off the phone outside work, but Intermex asserted that the application and her phone must be active so that she could accept client calls. Concerned about her privacy, she deleted the app when she was not using it. Despite being a good employee, she was

soon fired for not complying with organizational policies. She sued the company for privacy invasion and wrongful termination in the total of $500,000 in fees and lost wages (Gardella, 2015).

The case demonstrates the boundaries of acceptable monitoring and the legal ramifications for invasive monitoring systems that extend into an employee's personal life. Cases such as these, however, will continue to occur because privacy laws are still lacking the proper clarity and scope to regulate organizational monitoring practices. As of this writing, organizations supply employees with tools to complete their work, and employees are provided with minimal privacy rights when using company property (West & Bowman, 2016). Indeed, laws in the United States require organizations to protect employee personal information "only where an actual and reasonable expectation of privacy exists" (Determann & Sprague, 2011, p. 1034). Because of these ambiguous terms, when employees are given company tools, organizations can navigate these vague requirements and assert that they are entitled to see all data on any company device.

25.6.2.2 The Black Box of Employee Data

Monitoring also requires ethical scrutiny because it is difficult to ascertain if organizations are using personal information gathered from monitoring to make employment decisions (i.e., promotion, termination, etc.; Lohr, 2013). For instance, consider the Castlight employee wellness app discussed earlier. The app provided seemingly well-meaning recommendations to employees, but after digging through the data capabilities, product managers reported that the app could reliably indicate which employees were considering pregnancy (Zarya, 2016).

If an employee wellness application has the capability to suggest that an employee is pregnant and management uses this information to deny a promotion, it would be difficult to prove legally that the organization used such information in their decision. Furthermore, Ajunwa (2017) asserts that wellness programs may put employee data in danger because the data-collection companies can sell employee information to other companies. Wellness companies are not health-care providers and are not required to abide by HIPAA protections, so they are free to use employee health data as they wish. Because some wellness applications collect private health information such as medical exams, employees are at risk of losing great amounts of personal information from a single data breach.

25.6.2.3 The Ethics of Monitoring

As our examples illustrate, even well-intentioned monitoring practices can have unintended negative results – organizations can abuse the knowledge that they wield over individuals, or the technology can reveal more personal information than was anticipated. Thus, it is important to note: there is no difference between well-intentioned EPM with accidental negative employee impact and EPM with intentionally negative employee impact. When we consider the ethics of using EPM, there must be a goal in mind that clearly identifies the boundaries of acceptable and unacceptable use. For example, if phone call length is a meaningful performance outcome for a call center representative position, auditory EPM should be used to track phone call length only, not the content of the phone conversation. When these boundaries are established, organizations clearly articulate the function of EPM and mitigate the risk of invading the privacy of their employees.

There is also evidence to suggest that monitoring for the sake of monitoring results in poor organizational outcomes. Church and Oliver (2006) find that when organizations survey employees but do not take action on the survey results, employees respond with less satisfaction, and may be less likely to participate in future surveys. Although this has not been explored empirically, we expect that monitoring without appropriate feedback or organizational action may be met with similar levels of dissatisfaction and resistance. Revisiting our distinction between "surveillance" and "monitoring," monitoring without purpose may be seen as an authoritarian action in which the employer wields a disproportionate amount of personal information over an employee without sufficient instruction of how or if this information will affect their employment. Considering that monitoring devices like smartphones can collect a vast amount of personal employee information, and that this information can predict intimate aspects of a person's life, organizations are encountering a complex ethical dilemma as technology rapidly advances and big data capabilities become commonplace.

There is an expectation, especially in the workplace, that if an employer is deliberately measuring a behavior/attitude, that behavior/attitude is of importance to the employer, and employees are cognizant of that. We see this in how people allocate their effort and attention to tasks based on whether or not they are monitored. This ethical concern is relevant to big data in general, and it is important to keep in mind – all data collection should be purposeful and beneficial to the employee. We run the risk of exacerbating perceptions of privacy invasion if we conduct ourselves otherwise.

West and Bowman (2016) analyzed the ethics of monitoring through several different lenses including results-, rule-, and virtue-based ethics. From a results-oriented perspective, a major concern is whether the ends justify the means: do the benefits of monitoring (i.e., improved organizational decision-making, productivity) outweigh the drawbacks (i.e., increased employee stress, fatigue, privacy invasion perceptions)? Monitoring allows the organization to better understand how their resources are used, but is that enough to justify an employee's loss of privacy? From a rule-based perspective, monitoring keeps employees accountable for their actions and provides evidence for performance disputes. Organizational monitoring and surveillance rarely solicits employee consent, and employees are not aware of the actions that are being scrutinized. From the virtue-based perspective, monitoring encourages integrity, but through implementation, does monitoring assume the worst of employees – that they cannot be trusted?

Ultimately, the state of privacy in monitoring boils down to one essential question: just because organizations can see everything an employee does, should they? A recent court case in Europe has brought this question to light.

An employee in good standing at an organization was fired, weeks after the company discovered that he had been using his instant messaging account to have personal conversations with his wife and friends. The courts originally sided with the organization, asserting that personal matters were not to be handled during working hours. A court revision, however, sided with the employee, stating that the employee was never informed of the company's monitoring capabilities. There was also no legitimate reason (i.e., poor performance, illegal behavior) for the company to dissect his messages. Legal experts argue that the court ruling is a step in the right direction for establishing boundaries to company monitoring and protecting employee personal information. The case illustrates that work and social interaction are inseparable, and that privacy protections can vary considerably by country (Chan, 2017). Furthermore, it presents an interesting question about monitoring global teams: what legal privacy protections can virtual team members exercise and how might cross-cultural differences complicate privacy concerns? Are American companies able to closely monitor virtual team members in Europe, or are these companies restricted by European law?

Ambiguous legal scenarios such as these have yet to be addressed, but we anticipate this issue to receive greater public attention in the near future. The big data capabilities of EPM can be immensely helpful, but curiosity can lead organizations to engage in more invasive monitoring of employee behavior, arriving to legal issues that can be easily avoided otherwise. Organizations must clarify and adhere to the original purpose of the monitoring system to prevent organizational members from arriving at erroneous conclusions or exploiting deeply personal employee information.

25.7 Opportunities for Future Research

Technological advancements and the future of automated work offer a wealth of research opportunities. As we look to the future of EPM, we can already observe how the collection of employee behavior data has the potential to change not only the workplace, but also the ways that we relate to each other. Popular press has recently covered automation and monitoring trends among truck drivers (Roberts, 2016). Trucking companies have installed monitoring devices to maximize the productivity of their drivers, providing them with helpful metrics on driving schedules to reduce the amount of driving that is done on low amounts of sleep. Data from these same devices, however, can be used to train AI for driverless vehicles that will eventually replace these truckers. Interviews with drivers reveal that they are aware of automation's threat to their job security, and consequently, they report a range of negative reactions to these monitoring systems. With the inevitability of automation, truckers resent the monitoring devices and view them as a threat to not only their job security, but also their way of life. As they accumulate long hours in their vehicles, these workers become attached to their trucks and view them as a second home. Moreover, with the loss of autonomy, they feel extraneous. Without these job characteristics to sustain, truckers lose the sense of competence and self-sufficiency that they value. Thus, the combination of EPM and the threat of automation can influence the ways that we think of ourselves as human beings and how we fit into our societal roles.

The effect of monitoring on how we relate and interact with each other can even be seen everyday behaviors – take the example of email. The differences in informational content between verbal and electronic communication can differ simply based on the knowledge that our emails can be recorded, stored, and accessed at another time. The rehearsability that email affords us causes us to think carefully about what we send, and the recordkeeping and accessibility of online communication can make us reconsider the types of information that we divulge online in general.

We believe that these discussions about how EPM fits into the future of automation and the role of the human in the workplace have yet to be adequately explored. Specific to the theoretical and practical applications to the field of I-O psychology, we have identified several opportunities for future research.

Effects on Motivation. Ideally, EPM can be used to construct performance standards that motivate employees to achieve a desired performance level. Organizations that wish to deter poor internet habits such as cyberloafing may consider electronic monitoring to be a guidance tool for staying on task, but considering the number of negative reactions to EPM, it is unclear if EPM can improve employee motivation (Thompson, Meriac, & Cope, 2002). Although EPM can be a signal of where to direct employee effort (Brewer, 1995), it can also hinder task performance (Aiello & Kolb, 1995). Conflicting results such as these have urged researchers to establish deliberate theory on technology's effect on motivation (Kanfer & Chen, 2016), and understand work in virtual environments (Aiello & Douthitt, 2001). We see how monitoring could affect motivation both positively and negatively. Monitoring feedback could positively affect goal-setting by providing evidence of goal progress, yet monitoring may also restrict employee autonomy and perhaps impede task progress. More research is needed to explore these propositions.

Research Design. There is a need for more longitudinal, quasi-experimental studies. Many empirical studies are survey based or experimental with one simple work task. Longitudinal and quasi-experimental studies in organizations can contribute to understanding of EPM's role on complex full-time jobs over time, and can address the question: do employees assimilate to monitoring procedures over time and learn to accept them, or is there is a constant struggle against EPM? There is evidence to suggest that the effects of EPM can worsen over time (Schleifer et al., 1996), but further research is needed to understand the contextual variables that influence this longitudinal effect.

Managerial Focus. At this point, few research studies have fully delved into managerial motivations for using EPM. Bhave (2014) suggests that differences in individual managerial characteristics may affect the EPM – performance relationship, and research has not yet explored how leadership behaviors interact with monitoring. For example, would close electronic surveillance undermine the positive impacts of transformational leadership behaviors or high leader-member exchange, much like the counterintuitive effects of close surveillance found by Jensen and Raver (2012)? Given the various methods of monitoring and the contexts in which it may take place, we must better understand the contexts in which EPM is useful for managerial decisions, and why managers choose to closely monitor employees (i.e., reading message content) rather than use summarized EPM data.

Organization-Level Effects. Individuals' information privacy values, attitudes, and beliefs differ based on the type of organization in which they are employed; for example, private employers and governmental agencies (IRS, law enforcement agencies) report significantly higher information privacy beliefs than insurance companies and credit grantors (Stone et al. 1983). Stone et al. (1983) reports differences in privacy attitudes for employees based on their organization, but in this study, all private employers were categorized together, irrespective of industry. Decades later, research is still needed to update these findings and categorize companies by industry to observe industry-level differences in beliefs and behaviors. The number and size of organizations that monitor employees, as well as the amount of work behaviors that can now be monitored, have grown greatly since the 1980s, and it would be useful to understand how feelings toward monitoring and privacy have changed.

Furthermore, studies on the negative reactions to EPM suffer from a chicken-vs.-egg debate because much of the research is cross-sectional. Do negative reactions to monitoring occur because an individual already has a negative perception of the organization? Can a good organization lose trust/justice simply from monitoring employees? How much of these negative reactions can we attribute to only EPM and not feelings about the organization?

Individual Differences. So far, little research has attended to individual differences and reactions to monitoring, yet the existing research looks promising. From individual differences approach, researchers found that those with an internal locus of control experience greater stress levels during monitored simple tasks than those with external locus of control (Kolb & Aiello, 1996). Brown, Badger, Behrend, and Jensen (2012) also found an effect of personality characteristics with reactions to monitoring, demonstrating that regardless of the different kinds of EPM characteristics available, reactions to EPM will still be affected by stable characteristics of the individual. Further research on stable characteristics would help organizations understand why some employees may be more receptive to EPM or experience less adverse effects than others.

We also propose that the field of I-O psychology be open to exploring new individual differences, ones that are in direct relation to the growing trend in behavior tracking. We anticipate that amid the popularity of behavior tracking, whether it is from EPM or personal tracking (e.g., health data from Fitbits, productivity data and computer usage from Rescue Time), there may be a bifurcation in how people react to the possibility of a fully quantified self in which we have metrics for all aspects of our lives (Swan, 2013). On the one hand, individuals may embrace such tracking capabilities and find goal-setting and behavior change to be much easier with these continual feedback loops; on the other hand, individuals may react negatively to the collection and storage of all intimate details of their lives, and they may respond by avoiding all tracking at all costs. With the popularity of fitness trackers, as well as the public discourse regarding online privacy, either one of these situations may come to fruition.

EPM Characteristics.   As illustrated in Tables 25.1 and 25.2, monitoring capabilities can differ widely. It is important to note distinctions between monitoring practices because such distinctions can cause employees to react in different ways (Willford et al., 2017). There is still much research to be conducted on the relationships between monitoring characteristics and employee reactions, and the typology proposed in this chapter serves as guide for future research. For example, some of the core characteristics that require more research are feedback frequency, control, and medium or device effects. Researchers must understand the ideal feedback characteristics for encouraging employee productivity, and the appropriate amount of control that individuals can have over their monitoring experiences. Furthermore, research is needed to understand how employee reactions differ based on differences in EPM sub-elements and categories, such as productivity differences at varying levels of control and feedback, or reactions to various EPM purposes.

Cross-Cultural Studies.   Given the differences in cultural expectations and privacy laws, there is a need for more cross-cultural research. Do research participants respond negatively to EPM because there is a WEIRD (Western, Educated, Industrialized, Rich, Democratic) expectancy to have privacy in the workplace? Furthermore, expectations of privacy may differ based on the governmental ruling of an area (Westin, 2003). Areas with authoritarian government tend to have less expectation for personal information privacy whereas democratic environments may have stronger expectations. As we discussed with the European court case, however, the differences in privacy expectation among nations with similar characteristics may be greater than anticipated.

Schoeman (1984) discusses that the maintenance of a private life is essential for a person to express their individuality and to distinguish themselves from others. From this perspective, the importance of maintaining privacy in collectivistic cultures may not be as strong as it is in the United States, and EPM could be more accepted. Panina and Aiello (2005) have incorporated the Hofstede (1997) cultural taxonomy with EPM research to present a theoretical model for studying EPM in a cultural context, but this research area has not yet been fully explored. As organizational teams become more virtual and global, it will be essential to understand the role of cultural differences in EPM acceptance and EPM reactions to drive organizational decision-making for monitoring virtual team projects.

Technological Advancement.   In general, the field must remain vigilant regarding upcoming technology improvements and new introductions to the field – for example, the peripheral issues with GPS tracking systems in mobile applications were not considered until we started observing the employee response to implementation. The world of EPM will be quickly evolving as companies use virtual reality systems and adopt more powerful wearable technologies such as Google Glass and sociometric badges. While such technologies may be pioneering the ways that we gather big data and employee experience, the field is constantly on guard against practical and legal issues that continue to hinder technological use and introduce new legal concerns that were previously inconceivable.

Privacy Concerns.   People often report invasion of privacy when they encounter monitoring in the workplace, yet several studies demonstrate the growing lack of interest in protecting personal information (Barnes, 2006; Norberg, Horne, & Horne, 2007). These studies highlight the "privacy paradox," a phenomenon in which individuals claim to be concerned over the privacy of their personal information, yet they freely share personal information on social networking sites or exchange personal information for convenient online services. In some cases, people are even willing to exchange personal information for free pizza (Athey, Catalini, & Tucker, 2017). As Gross and Acquisti (2005) discuss, very personal information can be extracted from social networking sites, and thus there is a misconception about how much privacy we have on the internet. We have found that even modern vehicles can compile and analyze large amounts of intimate data, such as a person's weight, dining preferences, and entertainment interests (Holley, 2018), and thus privacy concerns are no longer limited to only internet activity. As company-issued devices and vehicles feature more sophisticated data-capturing capabilities, should employees learn to not expect privacy when working for organizations as well? Is this all that different from the privacy that we encounter in other parts of our lives – that is, is no privacy now the social norm (Acquisti, John, & Lowenstein, 2013)? Given the growing popularity of personal tracking devices and applications (e.g., Fitbits, RescueTime), we may accept that all aspects of our lives are recorded forever and thus privacy becomes a non-issue. Nonetheless, our lives will inevitably become embedded with technology, and it is this discussion of privacy that must be on the minds of organizations as EPM continues to change.

Theoretical Updates.   Perhaps the most critical question of all for I-O psychology is how our theoretical principles will hold up in the face of technological advancements. Monitoring technologies can amass large amounts of data about just a single employee, and with these massive capabilities, digital traces of human behavior can paint a vivid picture of every aspect of employee performance. As with all big data sets, it is important that the sheer quantity of the data does not drive the analysis and conclusions; even the greatest amounts of data cannot undermine strong theoretical reasoning (Boyd & Crawford, 2012). Our models of job performance are now decades old and based on data from annual performance appraisals (Campbell, 1990), which are currently being replaced with more frequent feedback interactions. Large organizations like Bridgewater Associates have even incorporated spontaneous feedback and rating systems where employees can submit public feedback on their coworkers during meetings, or even make back-channel comments on the CEOs' presentations, fostering an environment of accountability, transparency, and performance (Fessler, 2017). As we anticipate a world where EPM is able to generate personalized performance feedback loops for employees with more data and in less time, the annual performance review is unlikely to see resurgence, and performance models based on antiquated practices become even more obsolete. Thus, the question remains: once we have data on all aspects of an employee, how well do our existing models of job performance and employee behavior apply amid new technology? And where do we go from here?

25.8 Looking to the Future

We have reviewed the EPM literature, proposed a typology to guide studies, highlighted the legal implications of workplace monitoring, and identified new opportunities for EPM research. Concomitant in this research area is the idea of privacy and how our perceptions of privacy may change as our everyday behaviors become data points for personal or organizational decision-making. In these cases where we look to the future societal impact of technological advancements, science-fiction provides hints of what may come.

In an episode "The Entire History of You" from the sci-fi series *Black Mirror*, characters have implants in their eyes that allow them to record everything that they see, and they are able to review these recordings in their own mind or project them on a public screen at any time (Armstrong & Welsh, 2011). The premise seems unimaginable in present day, but as the plot develops, we see how access to such intimate recordings can become a sort of social currency. Characters have evidence of other's actions to record the truth, refute lies, and settle arguments. They can revisit moments in their lives to scrutinize every detail, especially nonverbal communication. They use these recordings to navigate their worlds, remember key details about people, and share their experiences with others. Although our devices are not yet implanted in our eyes or brains, many of the tools we use today mimic these capabilities. Audio recordings and email monitoring can settle workplace issues and arguments by providing evidence of an agreed upon deadline or project role. Productivity applications and health monitors allow us to review our daily behavior, and identify areas where performance faltered or goals were not met. We use social networking sites to remember birthdays, prioritize our social lives, and share details about ourselves with those around us. If we were to combine and analyze the data from all of these aspects of our lives, the result would be an accurate depiction of who we are, because we find that our online selves are often representations of our true selves – after all, online behavioral data is *real* behavioral data. Perhaps the technology in *Black Mirror* is futuristic, but the social behavior associated with the technology use is very much realized in present day.

25.9 Acknowledgments

We would like to acknowledge Jerod White for assisting us with the literature review for this chapter, and our WAVE Lab members – Lili Greenstein, Gayatri Menon, Daniel Ravid, Ian Siderits, Jerod White, and Sarah Zarsky – for their collaboration in creating the EPM typology.

References

Acquisti, A., John, L. K., & Loewenstein, G. (2013). What is privacy worth? *The Journal of Legal Studies, 42*(2), 249–274.

Aiello, J. R. (1993). Computer based work monitoring: Electronic surveillance and its effects. *Journal of Applied Social Psychology, 23*(7), 499–507. doi.org/10.1111/j.1559–1816.1993.tb01100.x.

Aiello, J. R. & Douthitt, E. A. (2001). Social facilitation from Triplett to electronic performance monitoring. *Group Dynamics: Theory, Research, and Practice, 5* (3), 163–180.

Aiello, J. R. & Kolb, K. J. (1995). Electronic performance monitoring and social context: Impact on productivity and stress. *Journal of Applied Psychology, 80*(3), 339–353. doi.org/10.1037/0021–9010.80.3.339.

Aiello, J. R. & Svec, C. M. (1993). Computer monitoring of work performance: Extending the social facilitation framework to electronic presence. *Journal of Applied Social Psychology, 23*(7), 537–548. doi.org/10.1111/j.1559–1816.1993.tb01102.x.

Ajunwa, I. (Jan 19, 2017). Workplace wellness programs could be putting your health data at risk. *Harvard Business Review*. Retrieved from https://hbr.org/2017/01/work place-wellness-programs-could-be-putting-your-health-data-at-risk.

Ajunwa, I., Crawford, K., & Schultz, J. (2017). Limitless worker surveillance. *California Law Review, 105*, 735–776.

Alder, G. S. (2007). Examining the relationship between feedback and performance in a monitored environment: A clarification and extension of feedback intervention theory. *Journal of High Technology Management Research, 17*(2), 157–174. doi.org/10.1016/j.hitech.2006.11.004.

Alder, G. S., Noel, T. W., & Ambrose, M. L. (2006). Clarifying the effects of Internet monitoring on job attitudes: The mediating role of employee trust. *Information & Management, 43*(7), 894–903.

Alge, B. J. (2001). Effects of computer surveillance on perceptions of privacy and procedural justice. *Journal of Applied Psychology, 86*(4), 797–804.

Alge, B. J., Ballinger, G. A., & Green, S. G. (2004). Remote control: Predictors of electronic monitoring intensity and secrecy. *Personnel Psychology, 57*(2), 377–410.

Ambrose, M. L. & Kulik, C. T. (1994). The effect of information format and performance pattern on performance appraisal judgments in a computerized performance monitoring context. *Journal of Applied Social Psychology, 24*(9), 801–823. doi. org/10.1111/j.1559–1816.1994.tb00613.x.

American Management Association. (2007). Electronic monitoring and surveillance survey. AMA/ePolicy Institute Research. Retrieved from www.amanet.org/training/arti cles/the-latest-on-workplace-monitoring-and-surveillance.aspx.

Armstrong, J. (Writer) & Welsh, B. (Director). (Dec 18, 2011). The entire history of you [Television series episode]. In C. Brooker & A. Jones (Producer), *Black mirror.* London: Endemol UK.

Astor, M. (July 25, 2017). Microchip implants for employees? One company says yes. *The New York Times*. Retrieved from www.nytimes.com/2017/07/25/technology/ microchips-wisconsin-company-employees.html?mcubz=3.

Athey, S., Catalini, C., & Tucker, C. (2017). The digital privacy paradox: Small money, small costs, small talk (No. w23488). National Bureau of Economic Research.

Ball, K. (2010). Workplace surveillance: An overview. *Labor History, 51*(1), 87–106. doi. org/10.1080/00236561003654776.

Barnes, S. (2006). A privacy paradox: Social networking in the United States. *First Monday, 11*(9). doi:dx.doi.org/10.5210/fm.v11i9.1394.

Bartels, L. K. & Nordstrom, C. R. (2012). Examining big brother's purpose for using electronic performance monitoring. *Performance Improvement Quarterly, 25*(2), 65–77.

Baumeister, R. F. (1982). A self-presentational view of social phenomena. *Psychological Bulletin, 91*, 3–26.

BBC (July 14, 2015). The very French history of the word "surveillance". *BBC News.* Retrieved from www.bbc.com/news/blogs-magazine-monitor-33464368.

Becker, T. E. & Marique, G. (2014). Observer effects without demand characteristics: An inductive investigation of video monitoring and performance. *Journal of Business and Psychology, 29*(4), 541–553.

Bell, B. S., & Kozlowski, S. W. (2002). A typology of virtual teams: Implications for effective leadership. *Group & Organization Management*, 27(1), 14–49.

Behrend, T. S., Yost, A. B., Howardson, G. N., Badger Darrow, J., & Jenson, J. (2018). Reactance to organizational surveillance: A test of antecedents and outcomes. *Journal of Business and Psychology.*

Bhave, D. P. (2014). The invisible eye? Electronic performance monitoring and employee job performance. *Personnel Psychology, 67*(3), 605–635.

Bowman, R. (Feb 11, 2014). Is new truck-monitoring technology for safety – or spying on drivers? *Forbes*. Retrieved from www.forbes.com/sites/robertbowman/2014/02/ 11/is-new-truck-monitoring-technology-for-safety-or-spying-on-drivers.

Boyd, K. & Crawford, K. (2012). Critical questions for big data: Provocations for a cultural, technological, and scholarly phenomenon. *Information, Communication & Society, 15*(5), 662–679.

Brewer, N. (1995). The effects of monitoring individual and group performance on the distribution of effort across tasks. *Journal of Applied Social Psychology, 25*(9), 760–777.

Brown, A. R., Badger, J. M., Behrend, T. S., & Jensen, J. M. (April, 2012). Personality predicts acceptance of performance monitoring at work. Paper presented to the 27th Annual Meeting of the Society for Industrial and Organizational Psychology, San Diego, CA.

Campbell, J. P. (1990). Modeling the performance prediction problem in industrial and organizational psychology. In M. D. Dunnette & L. M. Hough (Eds.), *Handbook of industrial and organizational psychology* (pp. 687–732). Palo Alto, CA: Consulting Psychologists Press, Inc.

Cascio, W. F. & Montealegre, R. (2016). How technology is changing work and organizations. *Annual Review of Organizational Psychology and Organizational Behavior*, *3*(1), 349–375. doi.org/10.1146/annurev-orgpsych-041015–062352.

Chalykoff, J. & Kochan, T. A. (1989). Computer-aided monitoring: Its influence on employee job satisfaction and turnover. *Personnel Psychology*, *42*(4), 807–834. http://doi.org/10.1111/j.1744–6570.1989.tb00676.x.

Chamorro-Premuzic, T., Winsborough, D., Sherman, R. A., & Hogan, R. (2016). New talent signals: Shiny new objects or a brave new world? *Industrial and Organizational Psychology*, *9*(3), 621–640.

Chan, S. (Sept 5, 2017). European court limits employers' right to monitor workers' email. *The New York Times*. Retrieved from www.nytimes.com/2017/09/05/business/european-court-employers-workers-email.html.

Chorley, M. J., Whitaker, R. M., & Allen, S. M. (2015). Personality and location-based social networks. *Computers in Human Behavior*, *46*, 45–56.

Church, A. H. & Oliver, D. H. (2006). The importance of taking action, not just sharing survey feedback. In A. I. Kraut (Eds.), *Getting action from organizational surveys: New concepts, technologies, and applications* (pp. 102–130). San Francisco, CA: Jossey-Bass.

Davidson, R. & Henderson, R. (2000). Electronic performance monitoring: A laboratory investigation of the influence of monitoring and difficulty on task performance, mood state, and self-reported stress levels. *Journal of Applied Social Psychology*, *30*(5), 906–920. doi.org/10.1111/j.1559–1816.2000.tb02502.x.

de Montjoye, Y. A., Quoidbach, J., Robic, F., & Pentland, A. S. (April, 2013). Predicting personality using novel mobile phone-based metrics. In A.M. Greenberg, W.G. Kennedy, & N.D. Bos (Eds.), *International conference on social computing, behavioral-cultural modeling, and prediction* (pp. 48–55). Berlin, Heidelberg: Springer.

Determann, L., & Sprague, R. (2011). Intrusive monitoring: Employee privacy expectations are reasonable in Europe, destroyed in the United States. *Berkeley Technology Law Journal*, *26*(2), 979–1036.

Drexel University (2016). Just give me some privacy – Anonymous Wikipedia editors and Tor users explain why they don't want you to know who they are. *DrexelNow*. Retrieved from http://drexel.edu/now/archive/2016/October/Tor-Wikipedia-privacy/.

Earley, P. C. (1988). Computer-generated performance feedback in the magazine-subscription industry. *Organizational Behavior and Human Decision Processes*, *41*(1), 50–64.

Feldman, J. M. (1981). Beyond attribution theory: Cognitive processes in performance appraisal. *Journal of Applied psychology*, *66*(2), 127–148.

Fessler, L. (Sept 7, 2017). At the world's largest hedge fund, 24-year-olds use "dots" to critique their CEO. *Quartz*. Retrieved from https://qz.com/1071749/bridgewater-associates-ceo-ray-dalio-explains-the-dot-collector-feedback-tool-his-company-uses-to-rate-employees/.

Gardella, A. (June 5, 2015). Employer sued for GPS-tracking salesperson 24/7. *Forbes*. Retrieved from www.forbes.com/sites/adrianagardella/2015/06/05/employer-sued-for-gps-tracking-salesperson-247/#55fe267823e3.

Grant, R. A. & Higgins, C. A. (1991). The impact of computerized performance monitoring on service work: Testing a causal model. *Information Systems Research*, *2*(2), 116–142.

Grant, R. A., Higgins, C. A., & Irving, R. H. (1988). Computerized performance monitors: Are they costing you customers? *Sloan Management Review*, *29*(3), 39–45.

Griffith, T. L. (1993). Monitoring and performance: A comparison of computer and supervisor monitoring. *Journal of Applied Social Psychology*, *23*(7), 549–572. doi.org/10.1111/j.1559–1816.1993.tb01103.x.

Gross, R. & Acquisti, A. (2005, November). Information revelation and privacy in online social networks. In Proceedings of the 2005 ACM workshop on Privacy in the electronic society, 71–80. ACM.

Hofstede, G., 1997. *Culture and organizations: Software of the mind*. New York, NY: McGraw-Hill.

Holley, P. (Jan 15, 2018). Big Brother on wheels: Why your car company may know more about you than your spouse. *The Washington Post*. Retrieved from www.washingtonpost .com/news/innovations/wp/2018/01/15/big-brother-on-wheels-why-your-car-com pany-may-know-more-about-you-than-your-spouse/?utm_term=.b584b0e4638f.

Hovorka-Mead, Ross, A. D., Whipple, W. H., Brenchin, T., & Michella B. (2002). Watching the detectives: Seasonal student employee reactions to electronic monitoring with and without advance notification. *Personnel Psychology*, *55*(2), 329–362.

Jensen, J. M. & Raver, J. L. (2012). When self-management and surveillance collide: Consequences for employees' organizational citizenship and counterproductive work behaviors. *Group & Organization Management*, *37*(3), 308–346.

Jeske, D. & Santuzzi, A. M. (2015). Monitoring what and how: Psychological implications of electronic performance monitoring. *New Technology, Work and Employment*, *30*(1), 62–78.

Kanfer, R. & Chen, G. (2016). Motivation in organizational behavior: History, advances and prospects. *Organizational Behavior and Human Decision Processes*, *136*, 6–19.

Karim, M. N. (2015). Electronic monitoring and self-regulation: Effects of monitoring purpose on goal state, feedback perceptions, and learning (Doctoral dissertation). Retrieved from ProQuest Dissertations Publishing. (3687652)

Kidwell, R. E. & Bennett, N. (1994). Employee reactions to electronic control systems: The role of procedural fairness. *Group & Organization Management*, *19*(2), 203–218.

Kolb, K. J., & Aiello, J. R. (1996). The effects of electronic performance monitoring on stress: Locus of control as a moderator variable. *Computers in Human Behavior*, 12(3), 407–423.

Kulik, C. T. & Ambrose, M. L. (1993). Category-based and feature-based processes in performance appraisal: Integrating visual and computerized sources of performance data. *Journal of Applied Psychology*, *78*(5), 821–830.

Landy, F. J. & Farr, J. L. (1980). Performance rating. *Psychological Bulletin*, *87*(1), 72–107.

Lankshear, G. & Mason, D. (2001). Technology and ethical dilemmas in a medical setting: Privacy, professional autonomy, life and death. *Ethics and Information Technology*, *3*(3), 223–233.

Larson, J. R. & Callahan, C. (1990). Performance monitoring: How it affects work productivity. *Journal of Applied Psychology*, *75*(5), 530–538.

Lohr, S. (April 20, 2013). Big data, trying to build better workers. *The New York Times*. Retrieved from www.nytimes.com/2013/04/21/technology/big-data-tryingto-build-better-workers.html.

Lohr, S. (June 21, 2014). Unblinking eyes track employees. *The New York Times*. Retrieved from www.nytimes.com/2014/06/22/technology/workplace-surveillance-sees-good-and-bad.html?mcubz=3.

McNall, L. A. & Roch, S. G. (2007). Effects of electronic monitoring types on perceptions of procedural justice, interpersonal justice, and privacy. *Journal of Applied Social Psychology*, *37*(3), 658–682.

McNall, L. A. & Roch, S. G. (2009). A social exchange model of employee reactions to electronic performance monitoring. *Human Performance*, *22*(3), 204–224.

Minton-Eversole, T. (July 19, 2012). Virtual teams used most by global organizations, survey says. *Society for Human Resource Management*. Retrieved from www.shrm.org/resourcesandtools/hr-topics/organizational-and-employee-development/pages/virtualteamsusedmostbyglobalorganizations,surveysays.aspx.

Moorman, R. H. & Wells, D. L. (2003). Can electronic performance monitoring be fair? Exploring relationships among monitoring characteristics, perceived fairness, and job performance. *Journal of Leadership & Organizational Studies*, *10*(2), 2–16.

Morris, S., Griffin, D., & Gower, P. (Aug 18, 2017). Barclays puts in sensors to see which bankers are at their desks. *Bloomberg*. Retrieved from www.bloomberg.com/news/articles/2017-08-18/barclays-puts-in-sensors-to-see-which-bankers-are-at-their-desks.

Motowidlo, S. J. & Van Scotter, J. R. (1994). Evidence that task performance should be distinguished from contextual performance. *Journal of Applied psychology*, *79*(4), 475–480.

Nebeker, D. M. & Tatum, B. C. (1993). The effects of computer monitoring, standards, and rewards on work performance, job satisfaction, and stress. *Journal of Applied Social Psychology*, *23*(7), 508–536. doi.org/10.1111/j.1559–1816.1993.tb01101.x.

Noe, R. A., Hollenbeck, J. R., Gerhart, B., & Wright, P. M. (1994). *Human resource management: Gaining a competitive advantage*. Irwin: McGraw-Hill.

Norberg, P. A., Horne, D. R., & Horne, D. A. (2007). The privacy paradox: Personal information disclosure intentions versus behaviors. *Journal of Consumer Affairs*, *41*(1), 100–126.

Panina, D. & Aiello, J. R. (2005). Acceptance of electronic monitoring and its consequences in different cultural contexts: A conceptual model. *Journal of International Management*, *11*, 269–292. doi.org/10.1016/j.intman.2005.03.009.

Posey, C., Bennett, B., Roberts, T., & Lowry, P. B. (2011). When computer monitoring backfires: Invasion of privacy and organizational injustice as precursors to computer abuse. *Journal of Information System Security*, *7*(1), 24–47.

Ribitzky, R. (2007). Active monitoring of employees rises to 78%. *ABC News*. Retrieved from http://abcnews.go.com/Business/story?id=88319&page=1.

Roberts, D. (Aug 3, 2016). 1.8 million American truck drivers could lose their jobs to robots. What then? *Vox*. Retrieved from www.vox.com/2016/8/3/12342764/autonomous-trucks-employment.

Schleifer, L. M., Galinsky, T. L., & Pan, C. S. (1996). Mood disturbances and musculoskeletal discomfort: Effects of electronic performance monitoring under different levels of VDT data entry performance. *International Journal of Human Computer Interaction*, *8*(4), 369–384.

Schminke, M., Ambrose, M. L., & Cropanzano, R. S. (2000). The effect of organizational structure on perceptions of procedural fairness. *Journal of Applied Psychology*, *85*(2), 294–304.

Schoeman, F. (1984). Privacy: Philosophical dimensions. *American Philosophical Quarterly*, *21*(3), 199–213.

Sewell, G. & Wilkinson, B. (1992). "Someone to watch over me": Surveillance, discipline and the just-in-time labour process. *Sociology*, *26*(2), 271–289.

Shockley, K. (2014). Telecommuting. Society for Industrial Organizational Psychology White Paper Series. Bowling Green, OH: Scientific Affairs Committee of the Society for Industrial Organizational Psychology.

Smith, M. J., Conway, F. T., & Karsh, B. T. (1999). Occupational stress in human computer interaction. *Industrial Health*, *37*(2), 157–173.

Stanton, J. M. (2000a). Reactions to employee performance monitoring: Framework, review, and research directions. *Human Performance*, *13*(1), 85–113.

Stanton, J. M. (2000b). Traditional and electronic monitoring from an organizational justice perspective. *Journal of Business and Psychology*, *15*(1), 129–147.

Stanton, J. M. & Barnes-Farrell, J. L. (1996). Effects of electronic performance monitoring on personal control, task satisfaction, and task performance. *Journal of Applied Psychology*, *81*(6), 738–745.

Stanton, J. M. & Julian, A. L. (2002). The impact of electronic monitoring on quality and quantity of performance. *Computers in Human Behavior*, *18*(1), 85–101.

Stanton, J. M. & Stam, K. R. (2006). *The visible employee: Using workplace monitoring and surveillance to protect information assets–without compromising employee privacy or trust*. Medford, NJ: Information Today.

Stone, E. F., Gueutal, H. G., Gardner, D. G., & McClure, S. (1983). A field experiment comparing information-privacy values, beliefs, and attitudes across several types of organizations. *Journal of Applied Psychology*, *68*, 459–468.

Surveillance. (n.d.). In *Online Etymology Dictionary*. Retrieved from www.etymonline .com/word/surveillance.

Swan, M. (2013). The quantified self: Fundamental disruption in big data science and biological discovery. *Big Data*, *1*(2), 85–99.

Tett, R. P., & Meyer, J. P. (1993). Job satisfaction, organizational commitment, turnover intention, and turnover: Path analyses based on meta-analytic findings. *Personnel Psychology*, *46*(2), 259–293.

Thompson, L. F., Meriac, J. P., & Cope, J. G. (2002). Motivating online performance: The influences of goal setting and Internet self-efficacy. *Social Science Computer Review*, 20(2), 149–160. doi.org/10.1177/089443930202000205.

Thompson, L. F., Sebastianelli, J. D., & Murray, N. P. (2009). Monitoring online training behaviors: Awareness of electronic surveillance hinders e-learners. *Journal of Applied Social Psychology*, *39*(9), 2191–2212. doi.org/10.1111/ j.1559–1816.2009.00521.x.

Tolchinsky, P. D., McCuddy, M. K., Adams, J., Ganster, D. C., Woodman, R. W., & Fromkin, H. L. (1981). Employee perceptions of invasion of privacy: A field simulation experiment. *Journal of Applied Psychology*, *66*(3), 308–313. doi.org/ 10.1037/0021–9010.66.3.308.

Tomczak, D. L., Lanzo, L. A., & Aguinis, H. (2018). Evidence-based recommendations for employee performance monitoring. *Business Horizons*, 61(2), 251–259. doi.org/ 10.1016/j.bushor.2017.11.006.

Vorvoreanu, M. & Botan, C. H. (June, 2000). Examining electronic surveillance in the workplace: A review of theoretical perspectives and research findings. In the Conference of the International Communication Association.

Watson, A. M., Thompson, L. F., Rudolph, J. V., Whelan, T. J., Behrend, T. S., & Gissel, A. L. (2013). When big brother is watching: Goal orientation shapes reactions to electronic monitoring during online training. *Journal of Applied Psychology, 98* (4), 642–657.

Wells, D. L., Moorman, R. H., & Werner, J. M. (2007). The impact of the perceived purpose of electronic performance monitoring on an array of attitudinal variables. *Human Resource Development Quarterly, 18*(1), 121–138.

West, J. P. & Bowman, J. S. (2016). Electronic surveillance at work: An ethical analysis. *Administration & Society, 48*(5), 628–651. doi.org/10.1177/0095399714556502.

Westin, A. F. (1992). Two key factors that belong in a macroergonomic analysis of electronic monitoring: Employee perceptions of fairness and the climate of organizational trust or distrust. *Applied Ergonomics, 23*(1), 35–42.

Westin, A. F. (2003). Social and political dimensions of privacy. *Journal of Social Issues, 59* (2), 431–453. doi.org/10.1111/1540–4560.00072.

Willford, J. C., Cox, M. J., Howard, R., & Behrend, T. S. (May, 2015a). Workplace monitoring and surveillance: A mixed-methods examination of invasiveness perceptions. Poster presented at the 27th Annual Convention for the Association for Psychological Science, New York, NY.

Willford, J. C., Cox, M. J., Howard, R., Badger, J. M., & Behrend, T. S. (April, 2015b). A latent class analysis of electronic monitoring practices. Poster presented at the 30th Annual Conference of the Society for Industrial and Organizational Psychology, Philadelphia, PA.

Willford, J. C., Tomczak, D. L., Jimenez, W. P., Ravid, D., & Behrend, T. S. (April, 2017). Electronic performance monitoring type predicts monitoring perceptions and contextual performance. Poster presented at the 32nd Annual Conference of the Society for Industrial and Organizational Psychology, Orlando, FL.

Yost, A. B., Behrend, T. S., Howardson, G. N., Badger Darrow, J., & Jenson, J. (2018). Reactance to organizational surveillance: A test of antecedents and outcomes. *Journal of Business and Psychology.* doi.org/10.1007/s10869-018-9532-2.

Zajonc, R. B. (1965). Social facilitation. *Science, 149*, 269–274.

Zakrzewski, C. (March 13, 2016). The key to getting workers to stop wasting time online. *The Wall Street Journal.* Retrieved from www.wsj.com/articles/the-key-to-get ting-workers-to-stop-wasting-time-online-1457921545.

Zarya, V. (Feb 17, 2016). Employers are quietly using big data to track employee pregnancies. *Fortune.* Retrieved from http://fortune.com/2016/02/17/castlight-preg nancy-data/.

Zweig, D. & Scott, K. (2007). When unfairness matters most: Supervisory violations of electronic monitoring practices. *Human Resource Management Journal, 17*(3), 227–247. doi.org/10.1111/j.1748–8583.2007.00040.x.

Zweig, D. & Webster, J. (2002). Where is the line between benign and invasive? An examination of psychological barriers to the acceptance of awareness monitoring systems. *Journal of Organizational Behavior, 23*(5), 605–633.

PART VI

Technology in Statistics and Research Methods

26 Raising the Ante

Technological Advances in I-O Psychology

Krista L. Uggerslev and Frank Bosco

26.1 Introduction

We are surrounded by data. It is streaming continually around us in daily life – from our credit cards, wearable devices, computers, and phones, to sensor-equipped buildings, bridges, factories . . . it's everywhere. We now measure data in zettabytes, a volume surpassing the cumulative sum of total data generated since the start of human civilization only a few years ago (Xu, 2014); 90 percent of the world's data was generated within the past two years (SINTEF, 2013). What's remarkable is not that the world is producing this immensity of data, but rather that we are now able to do something with this data. Thanks to statistical and computational advances, we are able to harvest and store massive quantities of data, and analyze immense data corpuses. And now we are able to build research tools that capitalize on these technological enablements.

In this chapter we explore three of the underpinning data science advances that have paved the way for new technologies that are changing the way we conduct research in the field of I-O psychology. We then describe five technologies that are impacting our discipline from how our data is curated for future research use through the metaBUS project, to how constructs and theories may be developed in an interdisciplinary fashion through the Inter-Nomological Network (INN), to how data is shared and stored for open and reproducible use through the Open Science Framework, to how data can be analyzed and visualized using Python and R, to how we access research articles in our personal libraries through ReadCube. We touch upon some additional applications or tools that can also be handy for researchers in our field. We discuss how these technologies may influence the sorts of research questions we ask in I-O psychology, the way we ask them, and the way we answer them. We philosophize about how technological advances in analysis and data collection may evolve the way we conduct I-O psychology science.

26.2 Data Science Advances

The social science research environment is in a never-seen-before state of rapid advance and flux. Opportunities around how to manage and make sense of so-called big data led to the creation of the new research field of data science. Dominated by computer scientists, data scientists have been seeking new ways to create and collect data, novel statistical and analytic techniques, and fresh visualizations and presentations of information. Often characterized by the five Vs of *high volume* – often terabytes to exabytes per file, *high velocity* – fast generation of data, often in real time, *high variety* – from structured to semi- and unstructured data, and *lower veracity* – uncertainty or low quality data, the challenge is interpreting big data to produce *high value* (Olmedilla, Martínez-Torres, & Toral, 2016; Schroeck et al., 2012). As big data was not common prior to 2010, tools, websites, and sensors were not readily available to capture, store, analyze, and process large datasets. This meant that datasets were not inter-mixed for research purposes: structured data (i.e., data with nominal, ordinal, interval, and ratio scales) was typically analyzed separately from semi-structured (e.g., transcripts, free-form text), or unstructured data (e.g., images, audio, video, or multimedia formats; Creswell & Plano Clark, 2011).

The solutions developed by data scientists to generate, collect, and analyze big data are now transforming applied social science (Foster et al., 2016). In this section, we describe three underlying data science advances that have enabled specific technologies to impact the ways in which we conduct and share scientific research: (a) cloud-based tools, (b) database tools, and (c) OCR/data harvesting tools. We have chosen these three particular advance categories because each plays a central role in making possible existing functionality, and will likely be relied upon for future developments. As an example, consider the traditional versus modern approach to a literature search. During the early 1990s, one who wished to locate several papers on a given topic would likely have relied on (1) asking an expert to suggest a key paper; (2) traveling to the library to locate and photocopy the article; and then (3) manually locating papers whose references appeared in the key article. That was *the* process of searching the literature, and it hadn't changed very much in several hundred years. The process was incredibly time-consuming and relied on human memory. By the late 1990s and early 2000s, however, the process had become revolutionized. What had happened? What underlying data science events took place that now allow us to locate surprisingly more related articles from the comfort of our own homes, in mere minutes, without the need to consult a guru? Certainly, many changes happened during those years, especially the increased prevalence of internet access and the personal computer. However, we argue that three interrelated advances came together to bring this about this incredible level of information accessibility.

First, journal publishers began containing article information in electronic cloud-hosted databases with a standardized structure. Next, cloud-based user interfaces were built to allow virtually any individual to specify queries and view search results. Finally, and more recently, the development of OCR/data harvesting tools has allowed journal publishers to extract information from the enormous backlog of articles that were published before the internet era (i.e., late 1990s). We argue that these three powerful data science advances are at present revolutionizing the social sciences, and will continue to do so in the decades to come.

26.2.1 Cloud-Based Tools

One of the challenges previously associated with big data was the server power required to store, manage, and process the data. Relying on a network of remote servers hosted on the Internet, cloud computing solutions affably address this issue by providing shared computer processing resources on demand. Mell and Grance (2011) define cloud computing as "a model for enabling convenient, on-demand network access to a shared pool of configurable computing resources (e.g., networks, servers, storage, applications, and services) that can be rapidly provisioned and released with minimal management effort or service provider interaction." Likened to an electricity grid, cloud computing is typically available on a "pay as you go" basis, which enables users to avoid costly server infrastructure costs, with improved manageability, scalability, data security, and hardware stability.

Users are able to access cloud computing resources including infrastructure (e.g., virtual machines, servers, storage, networks), platforms (e.g., execution runtime, databases, web servers, development tools), and software applications (e.g., email, virtual desktop, CRM) via networked client devices, such as desktops, laptops, tablets, and smartphones. Some devices, like Chromebooks essentially rely on a web browser to interact with the cloud without native applications (i.e., those residing on the device itself). Thus, massive storage, analytic, and visualization resources are available without relying on local infrastructure. More and better services are becoming available to assist with big data analytics through companies like Oracle, Hadoop, Microsoft, and Amazon Web Services.

26.2.2 Database Tools

A second major data science advance is in the area of new database structures, known as NoSQL databases (Prajapati, 2013; Varian, 2014; VoltDB, 2017). Traditional databases, also called relational databases (or Relational Database Management Systems, RDBMs), have relied upon a Structure Query Language (SQL). SQL databases tend to have table-like structures (i.e., rows of data) with references, relationships, and consistency between data in those tables. They continue to provide the foundation for the world's transactions, such as credit card transactions, with mainframes and large UNIX servers in the data centers of financial services companies. When changes are required to the structure of the database, however, SQL databases require adjustments to their underlying tables, which requires work, care, and cost. NoSQL (commonly referred to as "not only SQL") databases incorporate SQL functionality, but also go beyond standard SQL functionality by allowing violations to many of the data consistency rules of SQL databases, and their table structures are relatively easier to change. They work well with large quantities of data, in particular where most activity involves reading the data from the database rather than writing to it. NoSQL offerings attracted the attention of large web-native companies like Google, Facebook, and Twitter (Mohan, 2013; WIRED, 2012), because of their ability to deal with vast inflows of unstructured data from multiple sources such as mobile devices, user status updates, and streams of comments. Some of the most popular NoSQL databases currently include MongoDB, Redis, Cassandra, CouchDB, OrientDB, and MarkLogic.

26.2.3 OCR/ Data Harvesting Tools

Another data science advance that has enabled new researcher technologies rests in Optical Character Recognition (also optical character reader, OCR), the mechanical or electronic conversion of images of typed, handwritten, or printed text into machine-encoded text (e.g., Singh, 2013). OCR technology has created new capacity for extracting or harvesting information from scanned documents, photos of documents, scene photos (e.g., pictures of text from signs or billboards), and from subtitle text superimposed on an image (e.g., subtitles from televised broadcasts; analogous technologies in voice recognition automate the generation of subtitles from an audio signal). Once digitized, information from these formerly printed records can be electronically searched, edited, indexed, stored more compactly, displayed online, and used in computational processes such as natural language processing and supervised machine learning (Bhatia, 2014; Manning, Raghavan, & Schutze, 2009). Data harvesting tools are then built to read and retrieve vast volumes of data that were previously unavailable for electronic search, thereby availing new datasets and research processes.

26.3 Research Tools Relying on Data Science Advances

The statistical and computational advances in data science described above have created opportunities for scientific advancements within our field through the creation of technology-based research tools. A number of cloud-based research tools have emerged, each using these data science advances in different ways, to improve various aspects of the research process. Everything from access to scientific findings and other research, to methods for coding and analyzing data, to sharing data and collaborating with other scientists within the field is touched by these advances.

This section provides an overview of five publicly available research tools that rely greatly on the data science advancements: metaBUS, Inter-Nomological Network, Open Science Framework, R and RStudio, and ReadCube. Numerous other technologies are referred to within these descriptions. By no means is this list meant to be exhaustive of all of the technologies that have the potential to drive our field forward. Rather, we have aimed to describe a broader variety ranging from tools to facilitate meta-analysis in I-O psychology specifically (i.e., metaBUS) to development of theory within the social sciences and beyond (i.e., the INN) to tools to enable advanced analytics and visualization (i.e., R and RStudio) and facilitate the research process (i.e., OSF, ReadCube). At the end of this section, we also briefly highlight some other technologies that you might find useful to add to your research toolkit (e.g., Google Keep) or leverage within your teaching or learning arsenal (e.g., MOOCs, analysis wikis).

26.3.1 metaBUS

metaBUS is a cloud-based open access tool for locating and meta-analyzing findings in I-O psychology (see metaBUS.org; Bosco, Uggerslev, 2018; Bosco, Uggerslev, Steel, 2017). Initiated to turn meta-analyses from a non-cumulative process taking months or years into an instant cumulative and collaborative system, the metaBUS team has extracted the correlations from about 12,000 papers from 1990 (some as far back as 1980) to current across twenty-eight I-O journals. Picture taking the "Table 1" from every published quantitative study in our field; these tables typically contain information about every variable examined in the study. For each entry, the metaBUS database contains information to identify the article from which it was extracted (e.g., author names, journal title, publication year, DOI), its sample characteristics (e.g., sample size, respondent type, geographic location), and other variable-level information (e.g., reliability, response rate). The reader is directed to Bosco et al. (2017) for a detailed description of the extraction process, coding process, and database fields. As of January 2018, there are just over 1 million rows of data (where each data row refers to a single, reported correlation coefficient) included in the metaBUS data corpus, each complemented with about twenty metadata tags (Baker et al., 2016).

Accessible at www.metaBUS.org, I-O psychologists can register for a user account and begin to explore the two main functionalities of the software. Using the *meta-analysis* function, users can specify any two concepts for which they'd like to explore the meta-analytic or overall relationship. This can be done using either a text string match (like a Google search bar) or via a hierarchical taxonomy of about 4,000 concepts designed to facilitate a search for synonymous terms (e.g., turnover, quit) and concepts that nest in specificity (e.g., procedural and distributive justice are more specific concepts that would nest within a broader justice concept). With a click of the run button, the software will scan the million-plus coefficients returning all of the matching correlations and associated metadata as individual records, and generate a series of meta-analytic data and plots. Users are provided with a link to the original publications for each correlation thereby enabling them to improve the precision of the meta-analysis using functionality to remove any unwanted records, and reverse the valence as required (e.g., dissatisfaction to satisfaction). Any noted anomalies should be flagged by users using the functionality provided so that they can be updated within the platform.

Also within the meta-analysis functionality, users are able to explore several pre-curated moderators (e.g., country of origin of the data, grant funding source), as well as input their own custom moderators for each record (e.g., a user may want to explore different job types within their returned query) to be analyzed within the system. Using the provided filters, users can specify limits to the years of data included in an analysis, as well as reliabilities for inclusion. All meta-analyses are stored within the user's MyMetaBUS page for later use and refinement. Users can also upload additional data (e.g., unpublished, translated) for inclusion in their analyses.

Although it was not the original intention for the software (which was meta-analytic in orientation), curation of all of the correlations in our field has resulted in a substantial improvement in the accuracy and comprehensiveness with which we can find studies that have examined one's topic of interest. Within the *locate* function, users can enter a single concept and examine all of the other concepts with which it has been studied, both by frequency of co-occurrence and by strength of relationship. Exploratory meta-analyses can be conducted indicating the strengths of relationships between a focal variable and all of its correlates, and reference lists are generated for all of the papers from the curated data corpus containing correlational data. Unlike traditional keyword searches in library search tools like PsycInfo and ABInform, which are limited to only the four or five keywords associated with the study, the metaBUS locate tool will reveal all of the studies that have correlational data with a particular variable from the curated data corpus. This is also a vast improvement over current full-text searches, which reveal all studies that mention a concept anywhere within the article, and which require a significant by-hand culling of studies that do not focus on the concept.

Users who are interested in building new functionality leveraging R and RShiny (described in more detail below), can add onto the metaBUS software. New plots and data visualizations, analytic algorithms, and corrections can all be added to the Shiny-based platform as they become available.

As the authors of this handbook chapter are also the co-founders of metaBUS, we are indeed pleased to be able to highlight the tool we have built in the hopes that it will foster collaboration and reduce redundant efforts required to create meta-analyses now and into the future in our field. We also believe the tool highlights the need for significantly improved methods for data curation in our field. Our hope is that others find the tool useful, and are encouraged to build and add tools that promote shared scientific advancement. Notably, however, metaBUS is certainly not the only tool with the potential to advance our field and we highlight several other tools next.

26.3.2 Inter-nomological Network

The INN (http://inn.theorizeit.org/), developed as a tool by the Human Behavior Project, enables users to build nomological networks of constructs from variables and items that have been examined in the published behavioral literature across a series of fields from psychology, education, sociology, business, nursing, information systems, and healthcare (Larsen et al., 2010; Li & Larsen, 2011). Acknowledging that construct proliferation is increasing how difficult it is to identify the nomological networks of constructs pertaining to a given research question and underpinning theories, the INN uses semantic analysis to systematically identify, categorize, and predict relationships among the constructs that define the combined cognitive interest of behavioral scientific fields.

As users, we can enter a variable (e.g., self efficacy) into the INN web-interface, and the search reveals a series of studies that have examined that variable along with the items that measured the construct, the authors' definition of the construct, and other studies that have cited that scale. Through the *similar constructs* functionality, we can examine other constructs that may be synonyms, more or less specific constructs, and related constructs. For building a nomological network of concepts, users can readily sort concepts into nested bins, and store their ongoing work in a registered account. As a ready way of finding scales to measure a construct, the INN is a quick and easy tool (Larsen, 2017). We find that the tool is also useful to examine other fields exploring similar constructs and compare operationalizations.

26.3.3 Open Science Framework

The Open Science Framework (https://osf.io/), developed as part of the Center for Open Science (COS), is a series of open-source tools designed to facilitate scholarly collaboration in research. Cloud-based tools are available to (a) structure projects and associated files, data, and protocols in a permanent storage repository, (b) control access to the projects from only collaborators to broad public access, and (c) connect easily with other research-facilitating tools including DropBox (for cloud-based storage), GitHub (for open sharing of software code), Amazon Web Services (for on-demand cloud computing platforms and interface hosting), box (a cloud content management and file sharing service), Google Drive (for cloud storage and collaborative file use), figshare (a repository for all forms of research output including figures and presentations), The Dataverse Project (to store data and link data to publications), and Mendeley (a free reference manager and academic social network).

COS has successfully secured more than $26 million in grant funds to date coupled with a series of in-kind donations of goods and services, and has amassed a team of sixty-eight, over half of whom are software developers. In addition to the Open Science Framework tools for research software and storage, COS is also aiming to connect and build open science communities including researchers and their institutions, funders, and the publishers of scientific research, and to conduct research on scientific practices and support metascience. In short, we can anticipate more and more software-based tools to facilitate the main objectives of COS, namely, openness, integrity, and reproducibility of scholarly research.

26.3.4 R and RStudio

The technological advance that is having the most radical impact on how users conduct and visualize data is R. R is a free software environment and language for statistical computing and graphics. It provides a wide variety of statistical and graphical techniques, and is extensible for data manipulation, calculation, and graphical display by any user. Users can add additional functionality by defining new functions, which may then be shared through websites such as GitHub.com, or submitted for review to become indexed and hosted by CRAN (the Comprehensive R Archive Network). Initiated back in 1997, the current R platform is the result of collaborative contributions from all around the world. There are currently more than 10,500 packages available in CRAN. More packages can be found at GitHub, including the RHadoop packages to integrate R and Hadoop, representing two of the three pieces of the framework described earlier. Exploring the "Task Views" subject list on the CRAN website (https://cran.r-project.org/web/views/) reveals the wide range of tasks – in fields as diverse as machine learning, genetics, high performance computing, medical imaging and clinical trials, the social sciences, psychometrics, and spatial statistics – for which R packages are available.

Now one of the most widely used languages for statistics and data science in the world, R has been put together a bit like a patchwork quilt and functions of all shapes and sizes have been added over the past twenty years. Most R scripts rely on one or more CRAN packages. However, packages on CRAN change daily. One previous difficulty in writing script in R stemmed from package versions changing resulting in code generating errors or incorrect results without warning. Because R is dependency-driven (i.e., some packages act as "wrappers" or "add-ons" to existing packages), as changes or upgrades are made to some packages, errors are induced in packages relying on related code. This has led to challenges for both authors of packages when their functionality "breaks" following an update to one of the source CRANs and to users who may find packages that work one day but do not the next. Microsoft R Open, launched following an acquisition in 2015, is aiming to offer reproducibility support and reliable 64-bit R code (Sirosh, 2015) that, unlike CRAN's version of R, is able to address multiple CPU cores, thus speeding up complex processes severalfold. Seemingly, reliable (and faster) R code will continue to improve in the coming years.

The R statistical platform has facilitated efforts by hundreds of researchers in our field and related fields to develop packages for a host of statistical analysis varieties. For instance, metaSEM (Cheung, 2014; 2017) provides functionality to conduct univariate, multivariate, and three-level meta-analyses using a two-stage structural equation modeling (SEM) approach to conducting fixed- and random-effects meta-analytic SEM. Viechtbauer (2010) authored a meta-analytic package called metafor, which is an open-source add-on for conducting meta-analyses including fixed-, random-, and mixed-effects models as well as moderator and meta-regression analyses (see www.metafor-project.org/doku.php). With packages available for thousands of statistical analyses with a free software license, there are advantages to learning and using R.

To write packages for R, the most commonly used graphical integrated development environment is RStudio. RStudio includes a code editor, debugging, and visualization tools to make R easier for novice users to create new packages. RShiny assists users in making interactive web applications for visualizing data. Using RShiny, users can create applications without knowledge of HTML, CSS, or JavaScript. Also a part of RStudio, RMarkdown has been extended to support fully interactive documents. Unlike the more traditional workflow of creating static reports, users can create documents that allow readers to change the parameters underlying an analysis and to see the results immediately. RMarkdown leverages Shiny at its core to make this possible.

26.3.5 ReadCube

ReadCube (www.readcube.com/) is a software tool designed to help researchers manage their libraries of scholarly publications, now typically stored in PDF form. Once ReadCube is downloaded onto your computer, you can drag your stores of PDF files into the ReadCube software and begin organizing them according to your preferences (e.g., by author, journal, topic, year); ReadCube will assist by relabeling your inconsistently named files to facilitate the process. With unlimited cloud storage, you can access your library from multiple devices (such as desktops, laptops, tablets, and smart phones) freeing up storage room. As you read articles, you can highlight sections, add annotations, and use hashtags which become searchable references within your library (e.g., add the annotation "#replicability paper" and you can later search for "replicability paper," and all of the PDFs you tagged with this annotation will be listed). Your library can be searched for particular papers or topics and becomes interconnected through clickable inline references (clicking on an inline reference in one paper will take you to the reference paper also in your library).

Additional features of ReadCube include a figure browser, one-click author searches, a related articles feature, full screen viewer, and customizable interface. It works easily with other reference managing tools you might already be familiar with using (e.g., EndNote, Refworks). ReadCube can then examine the library you have created and will ping you (even daily) with new articles that it identifies as potentially useful to you with one-click access through your institution's library proxy. ReadCube will also search the web for free full versions of the paper. When you open a PDF at any time, ReadCube will ask you if you'd like to add it to your library (though this can also become a point of frustration when prompted to save every PDF meeting agenda or form you open). Especially to organize and search amongst your existing downloaded PDFs, ReadCube is worth checking out. ReadCube boasts adoption in 220 countries and over 2500 institutions. With funding now from Elsevier, Mendeley offers a free alternative to many of the features offered within ReadCube, provided your library is under 2GB.

26.3.6 Other Useful Technology Tools

By no means are the tools described above the best or the only tools advancing research in I-O psychology. There are lots of other tools and applications whose primary design intention was not research per se, that are useful to try out and perhaps catch onto using. A couple of our favorites include Google Keep, Grammarly, and LastPass, which we briefly outline below. There are also recent advances that may facilitate how we learn and/or teach new research skills through various wikis and MOOCs. We will also provide a brief outline of a couple of these below.

Google Keep.   As we work, we often come across webpages, images, quotes, stats, articles, blogs etc. that are of interest. If you have not checked out Google Keep before, it is worth a look. With the Google Keep Chrome extension, you can easily save anything you come across online. As you come across a whitepaper, media release, quote, social media clip, etc., a simple click of the extension will capture the link and your note for later retrieval. You can take notes for additional detail, and add labels to quickly categorize your note, or even speak a voice memo on the go and have it automatically transcribed. As with other Google products, Google Keep syncs across your devices making it easier to capture that interesting piece. We've used this tool in writing this chapter. Each time we came across an article, a report, a stat, and so forth during our literature review stage, we simply clicked on Keep in the Chrome browser, added a short note about what was useful in the piece to ease finding it later. Then, at authorship time, we opened Keep and saw a list of all of the links we'd identified as potentially useful. This is also handy for when, at the proofs stage, one has omitted a piece of a reference or needs to verify a component – the source material is all readily linked through Keep.

Grammarly.   Especially useful for communications via social media outlets, Grammarly will check your spelling and grammar before posts onto Facebook, Twitter, LinkedIn, Tumblr, or any web comment. As we pursue more avenues to mobilize the knowledge that we create within our field, tools like Grammarly can take on a bit of an editorial role at least insofar as grammar and spelling are concerned.

LastPass.   All of the technologies described above for facilitating research in our field require user names and passwords to establish user accounts. With varying requirements for capital and/or lowercase letters, special symbols or no special symbols, character length, uniqueness, and password strength, creating and remembering usernames and passwords can be challenging. LastPass stores all of your usernames and passwords. Accessible by one master password, LastPass will enable you to access your information for every instance. It also provides an alternative to generating that 'Important Numbers' document stored on our desktops that we're cautioned are easy to hack through proximity.

MOOCs.   Many of us are now familiar with the concept of MOOCs, or massive, online, open courses. These are courses available over the internet, typically offered without charge to a very large number of people. Stanford instructors Sebastian Thrun and Peter Norvig first offered their "Introduction to Artificial Intelligence" course for free online and had over 160,000 students enroll from more than 190 countries (www.udacity.com/us). MOOCs on a myriad of topics are now offered open for attendees from around the globe. From learning about nanotechnology to the latest in augmented reality and virtual reality to obtaining certification in self-driving cars, there are MOOCs on the topic. Companies like Lynda.com (purchased by LinkedIn for $1.5 billion in 2015; Kosoff, 2015) and Udacity (founded by the same founder as Google X of famed projects including the Self-Driving Car and Google Glass) are revolutionizing education for aspiring learners around the globe albeit not all of these courses follow the free model. The face of education may change if the monopoly on many credentials such as undergraduate, Masters, and doctoral degrees is lifted from traditional educational institutions, or if new credentials from MOOC-type sources gain credibility. For instance, nanodegrees offered from Udacity are gaining credibility as an alternate form of credential on topics created at the speed of technology rather than the speed of university new course generation. Regardless of where MOOCs and other online educational opportunities go, there are substantial opportunities for I/O to influence broad audiences and for those in research and practice of our discipline to learn and leverage new skills.

There are also wikis and various other online statistical tools to facilitate many of the data analytics we regularly utilize as researchers in our field. Whereas previously, a subscription to SPSS or SAS was required for many of the statistical analyses regularly conducted in our field, one only needs to search for online tools to support basically any statistical inference and a free tool can be located. The underlying assumptions used and veracity of the online tool, however, are caveat emptor (buyer beware).

In short, there are a number of technologies that are being developed to facilitate research within our field. The increased emphasis on the importance of open science has made these and future tools openly available for broad scientific use. There are substantial opportunities for scientists to contribute to the further development of these tools, and to explore creation of further technologies that will continue to evolve science in our discipline.

26.4 How Technology Is Changing I-O Psychology Research

Advances in data science and technologies built upon the advances are impacting the core nature of the science that we produce within our field. In this section, we discuss how technologies may be changing the designs of our studies, the questions we ask, and ways in which we analyze and report data.

Study Designs.   Data science advances may broaden the data scope as well as data granularity of phenomena examined in our field (George et al., 2016). Data scope may include the comprehensiveness or range of variables examined, the number of observations collected, or proportion of the population sampled. One scope-broadening tool is the launch of web-scraping tools to extract text, audio, and video data. Application programming interfaces (APIs) facilitate access to data from the public domain and are provided by most social media services such as Twitter and Facebook, and the largest media online retailers such as YouTube, Flickr, and Amazon (Olmedilla, Martinez-Torres, & Toral, 2016). Often the APIs may not provide all of the information required by researchers, but can be supplemented with web crawlers, programs that extract information from recursive hyperlinks contained from seed webpages (Najor, 2009).

In terms of data granularity, we may be able to directly measure constituent characteristics of a construct (e.g., using wearable biometrics) rather than rely upon surveys or interviews. For instance, Bono, Glomb, Shen, Kim, and Koch (2013) and Ilies, Dimotakis, and DePater (2010) recorded employees' blood pressure at specific intervals. Greater data granularity may afford high precision in effect sizes, and also discovery of clearer causal mechanisms (George et al., 2016).

Although both data scope and data granularity may avail more data and different forms of data than has been previously available, Boyd and Crawford (2012) caution that there is a tendency by computational scientists to engage in acts of social science; both perspectives are needed (Olmedilla et al., 2016). As social scientists, we have a role in guiding the types of questions and conclusions that are drawn from data within our field.

Study Purpose. As reviewed in the special issue of the *Journal of Applied Psychology* celebrating its first century (e.g., Kozlowski, Chen, & Salas, 2017), research questions in our discipline have become more complex over time. We have moved from assessing the relationship between two variables to assessing the fit of a model to many variables (e.g., mediation and moderation), and examining multiple shapes of relationships from only linear relationships (Cortina et al., 2017).

Research questions have also become more geared toward addressing theories with introduction sections gaining pagination perhaps at the expense of method sections (Cortina et al., 2017). Indeed, trends over time show more information on psychological variables (e.g., traits; states) than intentions, behaviors, or job attitudes (Bosco et al., 2015), perhaps owing to the relative simplicity of collecting questionnaire data. With technology-facilitated big data sources now coming online, however, there are many more sources of data available to social scientists such as social media and biometrics as reviewed in other chapters in this handbook. The ease with which big data analytics may be able to assist in detecting patterns for social phenomena, as compared to establishing causal relations, has been suggested to potentially swing the pendulum toward machine-identified patterns and away from prior theories and hypotheses (Anderson, 2008). Related to availability of big data, Cowls and Schroeder (2015) argue that "the claims regarding the shift toward correlation and the 'end of theory' are exaggerated" (p. 449), but rather require embedding within theoretical frames to understand their significance.

We predict that the evolution of technology and its further adoption into research practices in the coming decade will lead to a new balance between emphasis on theory and induction in our field. Further, concerns about page length in publications will diminish in importance as online supplements increase in use and as adherence to standards aimed at transparency and reproducibility of research such as PRISMA (i.e., Preferred Reporting Items for Systematic Reviews and Meta-Analyses) and MARS (Meta-Analysis Reporting Standards) go up. For instance, producing an RMarkdown file of one's analyses, or storing raw data on the OSF, may become requirements for publishing research. Additionally, the timeline from data collection to publication has not been a critical factor to date for I-O-psychologists; however, data velocity is a fundamental element of new data science (George et al., 2016).

26.4.1 Analytic Techniques

As evidenced in publications trends over the past several decades, research studies within I-O psychology have become more varied and more complicated (e.g., multivariate designs, multilevel designs, experience sampling designs, panel/long-itudinal designs; Cortina, Aguinis, & DeShon, 2017). Whereas early forays into the accompanying more complex analyses was initially limited to fewer well-versed scientists, readily available software and macros have broadened the number of researchers able to conduct complex analyses. Unfortunately, the number of incorrectly conducted analyses has risen as well (e.g., Cortina, Green, Keeler, & Vandenberg, 2017; Holland, Shore, & Cortina, 2016). For reviewers of manuscripts, the methodological and statistical sophistication required to conduct thorough assessments has increased the challenge in providing feedback and publishing manuscripts. In the coming years, perhaps new review processes will emerge to meet conceptual and methodological requirements.

It seems logical that as data scope and data granularity evolve, as more technologies are developed to enhance the research process, and as the technological sophistication required for optimal use of technology-based tools grows, scientists' skill sets will have to evolve as well. As discussed in a dedicated chapter within this handbook, graduate school programs in I-O psychology may need to offer greater breadth in statistical training along with skill-building in a broader array of analysis tools. Eventually, doctoral students may need programming skills. Or the expectation may be that students garner these skills by leveraging online resources like MOOCs currently offered to teach how to use R and build functionality using RStudio. As one prime example of the types of offerings now available, Richard Landers (editor of this Handbook) has released about 150 hours of content including lecture videos and course materials (including a sample syllabus, final exam, final project, weekly projects, and course schedule) on R, which are designed to teach data science to social scientists online (see http://datascience.tntlab.org/). These materials are available to instructors and their students for free, or for a reasonable cost to deploy some of the related software if you engage in self-paced learning.

26.4.2 Conclusion

Klaus Schwab, founder of the World Economic Forum, stated that, "Technology is going to revolutionize almost every sector, leading to the demise of many traditional professions." Within I-O psychology, technology is permeating data analysis and data collection, as well as how we organize and communicate our findings. In this chapter we explored the potential and impacts of data science advances and tools created to leverage them for the field of I-O psychology. We provided just a sampling of some of the technologies that are changing the ways in which we conduct and share scientific research. It is an exciting time to be an I-O psychologist, and indeed, a scientist more generally. But we need to embrace the use of these tools while providing wisdom about the types of questions and conclusions that can be drawn on their basis.

References

Anderson, C. (2008). The end of theory: The data deluge makes the scientific method obsolete. *Wired Magazine 16* (7). http://archive.wired.com/science/discoveries/magazine/16-07/pb_theory/.

Baker, C. A., Bosco, F. A., Uggerslev, K. L., & Steel, P. (2016). metaBUS: An open search engine of I-O research findings. *The Industrial-Organizational Psychologist. 54* (1). http://www.siop.org/tip/july16.aspx.

Bhatia, E. N. (2014). Optical character recognition techniques: A review. *International Journal of Advanced Research in Computer Science and Software Engineering, 4* (5), 1219–1223.

Bono, J. E., Glomb, T. M., Shen, W., Kim, E., & Koch, A. J. (2013). Building positive resources: Effects of positive events and positive reflection on work-stress and health. *Academy of Management Journal, 56*: 1601–1627.

Bosco, F. A., Aguinis, H., Field, J. G., Pierce, C. A., & Dalton, D. R. (2016). HARKing's threat to organizational research: Evidence from primary and meta-analytic sources. *Personnel Psychology, 69*, 709–750.

Bosco, F. A., Aguinis, H., Singh, K., Field, J. G., & Pierce, C. A. (2015). Correlational effect size benchmarks. *Journal of Applied Psychology, 100*, 431–449.

Bosco, F. A., Steel, P., Oswald, F. L., Uggerslev, K. L., & Field, J. G. (2015). Cloud-based meta-analysis to bridge science and practice: Welcome to metaBUS. *Personnel Assessment and Decisions, 1*, 3–17.

Bosco, F. A., Uggerslev, K. L., & Steel, P. (2017). metaBUS as a vehicle for facilitating meta-analysis. *Human Resource Management Review, 27*, 237–254.

Bosco, F. A., & Uggerslev, K. L. (2018). metaBUS, http://metaBUS.org, September 25.

Boyd, D. & Crawford, K. 2012. Critical questions for big data: provocations for a cultural, technological and scholarly phenomenon, *Information, Community, & Society, 15* (5), 662–679.

Cheung, M. W.-L. (2015). metaSEM: an R package for meta-analysis using structural equation modeling. *Frontiers in Psychology, 5*, 1521. doi.org/10.3389/fpsyg.2014.01521.

Cheung, M. W.-L. (2017). metaSEM: An R package for meta-analysis using structural equation modeling. Modified from the Frontiers in Psychology 2014 manuscript. https://cran.r-project.org/web/packages/metaSEM/vignettes/metaSEM.pdf.

Cortina, J. M., Green, J. P., Keeler, K. R., & Vandenberg, R. J. (2017). Degrees of freedom in SEM: Are we testing the models that we claim to test? *Organizational Research Methods, 20*(3), 350-378. doi.org/10.1177/1094428116676345.

Cowls, J. & Schroeder, R. (2015). Causation, correlation, and Big Data in social science research. *Policy & Internet, 7, (4)*, 447–472.

Creswell, J., & Plano Clark, V. (2011). Choosing a mixed method design. In: J. Creswell & V. Plano Clark (Eds.), *Designing and Conducting Mixed Methods Research* (2nd edn., pp. 53–105). Thousand Oaks, CA: Sage.

Foster, I., Ghani, R., Jarmin, R. S., Kreuter, F., & Lane, J. (Eds.). (2016). *Big data and social science: A practical guide to methods and tools*. Boca Raton, FL: CRC Press/ Taylor & Francis Group.

George, G., Osinga, E. C., Lavie, D., & Scott, B. A. (2016). Big data and data science methods for management research, *Academy of Management Journal*, *59*(5), 1493–1507. doi: 10.5465/amj.2016.4005.

Holland, S. J., Shore, D. B., & Cortina, J. M. (2016). Review and recommendations for integrated mediation and moderation. *Organizational Research Methods*, *20*(4), 1–35. http://dx.doi.org/10 .1177/1094428116658958.

Ilies, R., Dimotakis, N., & De Pater, I. (2010). Psychological and physiological reactions to high workloads: Implications for well-being. *Personnel Psychology*, *63*, 407–436. doi:10.1111/j.1744–6570.2010.01175.x.

Kosoff, M. (2015). LinkedIn just bought online learning company Lynda for $1.5 billion, April 9, 2015. www.businessinsider.com/linkedin-buys-lyndacom-for-15-billion-2015-4.

Kozlowski, S. W., Chen, G., & Salas, E. (2017). One hundred years of the Journal of Applied Psychology: Background, evolution, and scientific trends. *Journal of Applied Psychology*, *102*(3), 237.

Larsen, K. R., Lee, J., Li, J., & Bong, C. H. (2010). A transdisciplinary approach to construct search and integration, 16th Americas Conference on Information Systems, Lima, Peru, August 12 –15.

Larsen, K. R. (2017). Inter-Nomological Network. http://inn.colorado.edu, June 14.

Li, J. & K. R. Larsen. (2011). "Establishing Nomological Networks for Behavioral Science: a Natural Language Processing Based Approach," International Conference on Information Systems (ICIS), Shanghai, China, December 4th–7th, 2011.

Manning, C. D., Raghavan, P., & Schutze, H. (2009). *Introduction to information retrieval*. Cambridge, UK: Cambridge University Press.

Mell, P. & Grance, T. (2011). The NIST Definition of Cloud Computing (Technical report). National Institute of Standards and Technology: U.S. Department of Commerce. doi:10.6028/NIST.SP.800–145. Special publication 800–145.

Mohan, C. (2013). "History Repeats Itself: Sensible and NonsenSQL Aspects of the NoSQL Hoopla". Proceedings of the 16th International Conference on Extending Database Technology. Retrieved 2017–06–26 from http://openproceedings.org/ 2013/conf/edbt/Mohan13.pdf.

Najor, M. (2009). Web crawler architecture. In: LIU L., ÖZSU M.T. (Eds) *Encyclopedia of Database Systems*. Boston, MA: Springer,

Olmedilla, M., Martínez-Torres, M.R., & Toral, S.L. (2016). Harvesting Big Data in social science: A methodological approach for collecting online user-generated content, *Computer Standards & Interfaces*, *46*, 79–87. doi.org/10.1016/j.csi.2016.02.003.

Prajapati, V. (2013). *Big data analytics with R and Hadoop*. Birmingham, UK: Packt Publishing.

Schroeck, M., Shockley, R., Smart, J., Romero-Morales, D., & Tufano, P. (2012). Analytics: The real-world use of Big Data – How innovative enterprises extract value from uncertain data, Executive Report, IBM Institute for Business Value.

Singh, S. (2013). Optical character recognition techniques: a survey. *Journal of emerging Trends in Computing and information Sciences*, *4*(6), 545–550.

SINTEF. Big Data, for better or worse: 90 percent of world's data generated over last two years. *ScienceDaily*. Retrieved June 20, 2017, from www.sciencedaily.com/releases/2013/05/130522085217.htm.

Sirosh, J. (2015). Microsoft Closes Acquisition of Revolution Analytics. Microsoft. Retrieved November 22, 2015 from blogs.technet.com.

Varian, H. R. (2014). Big data: New tricks for econometrics. *The Journal of Economic Perspectives*, *28*: 3–27.

Viechtbauer, W. (2010). Conducting meta-analyses in R with the metafor package. *Journal of Statistical Software*, *36*(3):1–48.

VoltDB. SQL vs. NoSQL vs. NewSQL. White paper retrieved on 2017–6-26 from www.voltdb.com/wp-content/uploads/2017/05/VoltDB_SQL-vs-NoSQL-vs-NewSQL.pdf.

WIRED. (Jan 19, 2012). Amazon Goes Back to the Future With "NoSQL" Database. Retrieved June 26, 2017, from www.wired.com/2012/01/amazon-dynamodb/.

Xu, Z.W. (2014). Cloud-sea computing systems: Towards thousand-fold improvement in performance per watt for the coming zettabyte era. Journal of Computer science and technology, *29*(2),177–181. doi: 10.1007/s11390-014–1420-2.

27 Data Science as a New Foundation for Insightful, Reproducible, and Trustworthy Social Science

Richard N. Landers, Elena M. Auer, Andrew B. Collmus, and Sebastian Marin

In this chapter, data science will be defined as, "an emerging area of work concerned with the collection, preparation, visualization, management, and preservation of large collections of information" (Stanton, 2013, p. ii). Data science is not a scientific discipline, per se, but instead an interdisciplinary approach to understanding data and analyzing it in a way useful to some target stakeholders. In business settings, the term *data scientist* typically suggests a person whose role is to organize, explore, and understand organizational data so that those data can be used to improve business outcomes. In social science, these stakeholders are the scientists themselves and the entities scientists serve, such as their institutions and society at large. Data science centralizes and formalizes rules and guidelines surrounding analyses of large datasets in a way that is often implicit within fields and even within labs. For example, data cleaning practices are often not explicitly taught in graduate training programs; instead, many social scientists learn how to clean data by repeating the techniques of their advisors and mentors. Data science makes practices like these explicit but also expands them to incorporate modern computer science into a broader, shared understanding of how to most meaningfully collect, store, analyze, and present data (Landers, Fink, & Collmus, 2017), both big and small.

Using this definition, we explored the current landscape of data science research and practice to identify what lessons it could teach modern social science. Overall, we identified three major potential contributions. First, insights from data science practices could be used to develop a better understanding of human behavior by revealing new sources of complex, high-complexity data (i.e., big data) as well as new techniques to organize and analyze those sources, such as machine learning, cloud computing, and interactive visualization. Second, data science practices could be used to improve the reproducibility of social science via open-source technologies, version control technologies, and the concept of data analytic pipelines, which together enable the complete reproduction of the data cleaning, analysis, and production of results of one scientist by another. Third, data science techniques could be used to improve the trustworthiness of social science, which builds on the previous two gains by enabling exploration of authentic behavior

761

instead of laboratory behaviors, triangulation of theoretical claims, and improved influence on the public and public policy. We will discuss each of these potential gains in turn.

27.1 Data Science for Creating Insightful Social Science

Data science's focus on extremely large datasets has led to the development of many tools and analytic approaches optimized for those datasets, and many of these tools and approaches bring great value to improve the conclusions developed by social science. We identified four of these. First, we describe big data, which refers to these datasets themselves. Second, we describe analytic techniques optimized for such data, generally referred to as machine learning. Third, we describe the techniques used to manage storage and processing power with such datasets in our discussion of cloud computing. Finally, we describe how data science leads the way in visualization techniques, which become especially important to understanding and explaining insights obtained from vast amounts of data. While some of these concepts are new to the field of social science, most are not as foreign as they may initially appear. Many of the statistics and practices are similar to or evolutions of traditional social science methods but offer more advanced techniques for predicting behavior and developing data-driven insights.

27.1.1 Big Data

Big data is most often characterized by the large volume, velocity, and variety, of the data of interest, attributes which are commonly referred to as the Vs of big data (Laney, 2001). The volume of the data refers to the quantity of data points, the velocity refers to the pace of data creation and analysis, and the variety refers to the various forms and sources of the data (e.g., text, numbers, audio, video). More recently, additional Vs, including the value (i.e., explanatory power), veracity (i.e., uncertainty about the information collected), and variability (i.e., inconsistency) of the data have been included as characteristics of big data (Hitzler and Janowicz, 2013). In addition to defining big data by its characteristics, the distinction between what is and is not big data is also sometimes made based upon whether the data can be processed or analyzed using traditional statistical approaches (Dumbill, 2013). Within this view, rather than differentiating between big and small data based on the Vs, the focus is on the technologies needed to handle big data (e.g., machine learning, cloud computing, visualization). More broadly, big data can be characterized as an overall shift in problem-solving approach (Tonidandel, King, and Cortina, 2016), generally described as a shift from a data modeling approach to an algorithmic approach (Brieman, 2001). A data modeling approach focuses on identifying goodness of fit of the data to a prescribed theoretical model, very much in line with common practice in social science research, most saliently in the context of structural equation modeling. In contrast, an algorithmic approach emphasizes maximizing the out-of-sample predictive accuracy of a model. In sum, big data is not just defined by the size of the dataset but also represents a potential shift in research goals. This potentially provides social scientists new ways to investigate existing social scientific research questions, which may be especially valuable at a time when current theory validation and replication have been met with criticism (Earp and Trafimow, 2015; Hambrick, 2007; Tonidandel et al., 2016). It also enables the analysis of new questions that social scientific methods were not previously able to ask.

Big data are often created by combining data from multiple existing messy sources, such as online archival data and primary trace data. In contrast to traditional data collection using live participation by research participants, which can be time consuming and costly, improvements in technology have made large and diverse data sources available to social scientists almost instantly (Lazer et al., 2009). For example, in organizational settings, big data are commonly created using an organization's Human Resource Information System (HRIS), which often includes information about employee tenure, turnover, performance scores, supervisors, incident reports, satisfaction survey scores, and any other information collected as part of the organization's human resources management function, potentially hundreds or thousands of pieces of information about each employee. When such data are further combined with video camera feeds, card swipes, or other such data collected by the organization, the datasets can truly become "big." Public archival datasets are also becoming increasingly available to researchers; for example, data.gov (www.data.gov) contains over 200,000 large datasets that cover a wide range of topics including agriculture, climate, consumer, and education data. Less obvious sources of data, such as trace datasets (e.g., time stamps, badge access logs, wearables output), can also be sources of big data. These datasets include a vast number of data points detailing microbehaviors that can be used to identify broader patterns of behavior or understand more dynamic processes. For example, data from wearables can be used to answer questions about team dynamics and performance (Kozlowski et al., 2015), and access logs of students playing serious games can provide insight about gaming behaviors that improve learning outcomes (Westera, Nadolski, & Hummel, 2014). Big data can also be created by extracting information found online. Web scraping and APIs are becoming more common sources of data for research (e.g., Landers et al., 2016). Twitter posts, for example, have been used to examine job satisfaction as well as predict crime and election results (Chen, Cho, Jang, 2015; Hernandez, Newman, & Jeon, 2016; Tumasjan et al., 2010).

Social scientists can leverage big data like these to answer existing and novel research questions, improve the utility of their research, and fundamentally improve science (Tonidandel et al., 2016; Wenzel & Van Quaquebeke, 2017). Historically, many social scientists, especially psychologists, have been concerned with explaining behavior and processes rather than predicting it (Yarkoni & Westfall, 2017). Big data, because of the considerable number of cases and features, often enables increased model complexity that can aid social scientists in improving prediction of behavior and outcomes (Wenzel & Van Quaquebeke, 2017). Additionally, while historically limited to sampling, big data can in some cases enable social scientists to examine population data. For example, an organizational scientist could examine the complete employee population of an organization, or a marketing researcher could examine the entire population of a company's consumers through their social media behavior. Big data can also improve upon research on dynamic phenomena such as team processes (Carter, Carter, & DeChurch, 2015), entrepreneurship (Huang & Knight, 2015), and stress event theories (Luciano et al., 2017; Park, 2010). Big data with multiple data points per behavior over time can make understanding and modeling these dynamic processes more practical and accessible. Finally, the use of big data can complement existing theoretical approaches with inductive approaches (McAbee, Landis, and Burke, 2017). Although big data can be used for a priori hypothesis testing, it also offers a compelling context in which to conduct empirically driven inductive research as a way to build new theory.

Although big data offer substantial new opportunities in social science, there are also numerous risks and concerns with their use, including issues of privacy, data quality, and overinterpretation of statistical tests conducted with large sample sizes. More data, both in complexity of the data and storage requirements, introduce greater risk for privacy breaches (Guzzo et al., 2015). It is therefore necessary when working with big data to take extra precautions to protect the information being collected and analyzed considering the significant consequences of accidentally releasing that information. The more data that is stored about an individual, the more serious a data breach would be. Anonymizing data has typically been considered the safest option in prior cases, but reidentification of an anonymized dataset, especially through demographic information, is becoming more of a concern (Ohm, 2010). As such, data storage security is especially important. Although small data can be stored locally in a physically protected location, big data may require cloud-based storage space, and this brings a higher risk of breach (Chen & Zhao, 2012). Another concern with the use of big data is the quality of the data. Big data sources are typically messy, unstructured, and poorly organized. They are also often incidental; they are collected as a side effect of some other process, not as the primary goal of data collection. They are rarely as carefully curated as a traditional social scientific dataset. Thus, issues of poor measurement, sampling bias, and the veracity of the data still apply and can lead to incorrect assumptions about the true predictive value or generalizability of models or conclusions built using big data. Lastly, with the use of big data, there is a risk of making inappropriate claims based on the analyses or overinterpreting the importance of results from statistical tests with such a large sample size. Cherry-picking relationships in datasets with large sample sizes creates a substantial risk of discovering spurious relationships. When using big data analytic techniques that reduce the interpretability of model coefficients, additional issues are introduced regarding how to reasonably make decisions based on those results. This is especially relevant in an employee selection setting, where the black box nature of many machine learning algorithms can lead to unwanted but unexplained problems, like adverse impact. For example, if resume text is being processed and used to predict future job performance with a black box algorithm, subgroup differences in certain words or phrases that predict job performance could lead to differential prediction of job performance based on protected class status, yet analysis of the model itself might provide little insight as to why. In sum, although it is pertinent for social scientists to explore the wealth of opportunity big data has to offer, it is equally important for researchers to consider the risks and ethical consequences of such research.

27.1.2 Machine Learning

The term "machine learning (ML) algorithm" refers to a computer program that learns from data to make new predictions without relying upon a closed-form solution. Closed-form solutions are statistical formulas; for example, in univariate ordinary least squares (OLS) regression, the slope of a predictor can be expressed as the correlation between x and y multiplied by the ratio of the standard deviation of y to the standard deviation of x, and it is known that this formula will produce the slope of the line of best fit. In machine learning, slopes (and other coefficients to be estimated) are derived without such formulas, through iterative estimation techniques, because such formulas are typically not available given the complexities of the models proposed. Thus, ML algorithms are close cousins to statistical modeling in that both procedures use data to make out-of-sample predictions from a given dataset but take different approaches to obtaining those predictions. In the case of OLS regression, coefficients can be derived either through statistical analysis (i.e., by solving known mathematical formulas for each coefficient) or by machine learning (i.e., by iterative estimation of those same coefficients). Despite the substantial conceptual difference in these approaches, the coefficients obtained given the same dataset will be identical.

Despite the similarities, the terms used in data science to refer to ML algorithms are often unfamiliar to social scientists. For example, algorithms are generally classified as supervised, unsupervised, or semi-supervised, depending upon the nature of the variables being modeled. Each of these terms refers to familiar statistical concepts. Supervised learning algorithms receive the most research attention currently and are characterized by having at least one predictor and at least one criterion variable. Typically, supervised machine learning is split between classification problems, in which the output variable has a nominal scale of measurement, and regression problems, in which the output variable has ordinal, interval, or ratio scale of measurement (Hastie, Tibshirani & Friedman, 2009; James et al., 2013; Kuhn & Johnson, 2013). Thus, logistic regression could be approached as a *supervised machine learning classification problem*, whereas OLS regression could be approached as a *supervised machine learning regression problem*, although both could alternatively be solved using closed-form solutions. In contrast, unsupervised learning is used when there is only input data, much like factor analysis or cluster analysis, both more common in the social sciences. The goal of unsupervised learning algorithms is to understand the structural aspects of input data before generating clusters or associations within the data. Semi-supervised algorithms combine aspects of both supervised and unsupervised algorithms and are used when there is a large amount of input data and only some of the outputs are specified. For example, if the goal of an algorithm is to detect shapes in a series of pictures in which not all pictures are labeled with the shape they contain, a semi-supervised algorithm might combine unsupervised estimation techniques that can be used to identify structure to the input variables (in this case, pixels) with supervised estimation techniques to predict the shape of the unlabeled pictures both within the given sample and beyond it.

One type of supervised machine learning algorithm that has recently become popular in a wide variety of applications is neural network modeling, the more complex versions of which are colloquially referred to as "deep learning." Neural network algorithms are designed to mimic neuronal functioning in the brain. In short, they involve the creation of numerous layers of interrelated predictive models. For example, consider a dataset in which pictures of digits are used as input with the goal of answering what seems like a relatively simple question to a human: "what digit is depicted in this picture?" In the language of data science, this is a *supervised classification problem*. The goal is to create a model that can be used to predict the number displayed given new out-of-sample pictures of numbers. When using a neural network, the image is first quantified as individual points of color or light. Thus, a dataset containing 1920x1080 pixel images (i.e., 1080p resolution) may be converted into 2,073,600 predictors. In a neural network model, these predictors might then be used to predict a set of intermediate latent characteristics, which are then used to predict a still smaller set of latent characteristics, and so on through as many prediction layers as the modeler decides is appropriate, until the final possible values (e.g., $0 - 9$) are predicted. Although this approach does not replicate the actual functionality of the human brain, such algorithms generally lead to better prediction than any others currently available with datasets of such complexity; the greatest gains in prediction over other methods have been found in the contexts of image and voice recognition.

Research-wise, ML differs from traditional statistical modeling in that it generally focuses on maximizing out-of-sample prediction at the expense of coefficient interpretability. In the digit prediction example above, the goal is not to determine the value of any one pixel (i.e., predictor) but rather to create generalizable overall prediction from the model as a whole. Thus, ML techniques take an approach to the model bias-variance tradeoff (Hastie et al., 2009; Kuhn & Johnson, 2013) dissimilar to that of traditional social scientific estimation. In traditional OLS regression as used in social science, to address assumptions regarding predictor multicollinearity, a relatively small number predictors are typically utilized in comparison to what could be used, a problem referred to in the machine learning literature as underfitting. Additionally, because OLS regression coefficients are unbiased estimates of population parameters only under strict assumptions, model accuracy (i.e., R^2) is often attenuated out-of-sample even with a relatively small number of predictors, a problem called overfitting. In a traditional social scientific approach, researchers use methods like OLS regression despite these weaknesses because they maximize coefficient interpretability: an OLS regression coefficient is defined clearly and precisely as the number of points change associated with a one-point increase in a predictor value multiplied by that coefficient, holding all other predictor values at zero. This allows coefficients to be interpreted directly, given certain known assumptions, particularly related to predict multicollinearity. As multicollinearity becomes more severe, which is inevitable in observed data with many predictors, overfitting will become more severe. Thus, in practice, social scientists seeking high predictive accuracy often drop predictors (i.e., underfitting by design) to reduce statistical overfitting. A major goal of machine learning is therefore to improve out-of-sample generalization, avoiding both overfitting and underfitting, by sacrificing coefficient interpretability; in short, the sample R^2 obtained via machine learning models will generally better represent the population R^2 than will those obtained via unbiased estimators, and greater out-of-sample model accuracy can generally be obtained with machine learning models. Putka, Beatty, and Reeder (2017) provide a nonmathematical discussion of common regression machine learning algorithms for regression problems (e.g. Lasso and Least Angle Regression, elastic nets, regression trees, random forests, stochastic gradient boosted trees, support vector matrices, lasso, and bagged trees), and Kotsiantis, Zaharakis, and Pintelas (2007) provide a more technical but comprehensive overview of machine learning algorithms for classification problems (decision trees, neural networks, Naïve Bayes, k nearest neighbors, and support vector matrices) for further reading on the specifics of such techniques and their potential applications to psychology and social science more broadly.

Social scientists have already begun using machine learning to predict outcomes of interest, including personality, subjective facial recognition, and job performance, among others. Kosinski and colleagues (2014) predicted a variety of traits from Facebook profile data using machine learning with accuracies ranging from $r = .05$ (agreeableness) to $r = .50$ (age). Rissman, Greely, and Wagner (2010) used machine learning to predict subjective recognition of faces using fMRI data, which has numerous implications for criminal investigations. In a study comparing the performance of different machine learning algorithms with employee selection data, Putka and colleagues (2017) found that machine learning algorithms outperform traditional methods when the number of predictors is large in comparison to the number of cases.

27.1.3 Cloud Computing

In data science, substantial computational power (i.e., CPU and GPU) and memory (i.e., RAM), beyond what a personal computer typically provides, are often necessary for data storage and analysis. Considering that big data grow by about 40 percent per year, there is a pressing need to keep up with these increases (Manyika et al., 2011) if researchers wish to take advantage of these new data to draw new scientific conclusions. Cloud computing offers a solution for meeting these requirements and has been instrumental in making big data analyses accessible to social scientists. Cloud computing is defined as "a model for enabling ubiquitous, convenient, on-demand network access to a shared pool of configurable computing resources (e.g., networks, servers, storage, applications, and services) that can be rapidly provisioned and released with minimal management effort or service provider interaction" (Mell & Grance, 2011 p.3). In other words, it refers to the use of remote computers, typically running in a data warehouse dedicated to this purpose, for storing, managing, scaling, and processing data. Cloud computing is offered by numerous vendors including Amazon (Amazon Web Services: https:// aws.amazon.com/), IBM (IBM Cloud: www.ibm.com/cloud/), and Google (Google Cloud Platform: https://cloud.google.com/). Additionally, academic researchers typically have access to university or National Science Foundation (NSF) funded cloud computing resources at little to no cost through XSEDE (https://www.xsede .org/) and Jetstream (https://jetstream-cloud.org/). With such services, social scientists can access much greater processing power and scalable data storage than possible on a personal computer. Furthermore, commercial or university cloud offerings further reduce the need for individual labs to create and maintain their own data management and storage infrastructure (see Hashem et al., 2015, for a more detailed overview). For example, when working with a large dataset with missing data, running a missing imputation algorithm or building a neural network may take days or weeks to execute on a standard computer and hard drive and devote a significant portion of the computer's resources while executing. With cloud computing, scientists can process their data with greater memory storage, take advantage of parallel processing to dramatically improve computational power, and avoid overburdening their own limited local computational resources.

In contrast to other computing paradigms, cloud computing has several unique features including scalability and on-demand services, user-centric interface, guaranteed quality of service (QoS), an autonomous system, and among commercial offerings, pay-as-needed pricing (Furht & Escalante, 2010). In terms of scalability, because cloud computing services are offered to users on demand, and because users often do not need to utilize those services simultaneously, a single cloud system can support far more users more inexpensively and more efficiently than individual systems with the same computational power would enable. Additionally, overall processing and storage in the cloud can be increased more easily than in local systems. User-centric interfaces enable accessibility of services to users regardless of location, because access to cloud services is typically through internet browsers or common internet protocols. Cloud computing guarantees QoS for users because of the almost unlimited amount of CPU performance and memory capacity; even in situations where power is lost or hard drives crash, a well-designed cloud-based system will be able to recover from these problems with no direct impact on users. Lastly, commercial cloud computing systems are autonomous and do not require a priori investment from the user, instead adopting a pay-as-needed model. There are furthermore three main types of cloud computing service models: Software as a Service (SaaS), Platform as a Service (PaaS), and Infrastructure as a Service (IaaS; Mell & Grance, 2011). SaaS service models, such as Google Docs, online payroll systems, and web-based email, are the most user-friendly cloud-based services in which providers create applications that users interact with. PaaS service models, such as the Google App Engine and Windows Azure, provide a platform for users to create applications that are then deployed to other people without having to handle any of the cloud infrastructure. Lastly, IaaS service models, which include examples like Amazon EC2 and Google Compute Engine, provide consumers with processing, storage, and networks for the consumer to run software without managing or controlling cloud infrastructure. Additionally, cloud computing can be provisioned for specified users, meaning that the cloud is available to a private organization, to a specific community such as a university, to the public, or some hybrid of these.

The complexity of social science research has grown exponentially since the advent of modern day computers, and cloud computing may help continue that trajectory of growth. There are several areas of social science research in which cloud computing can be particularly useful, including simulation research and computational modeling, storing and analysis of big data sources, and data sharing and transparency. For example, Kozlowski, Chao, Grand, Braun, and Kuljanin (2016) conducted a simulation study modeling the dynamics of multilevel phenomena in employee teams. Using a high-performance computing center, a common name for IaaS cloud-computing systems within an organization focusing upon processing power, storage, and analytic speed, the simulation analyses took three hours of computing time in contrast to the ten days it would have taken on the computers housed within the researchers' laboratory. Cloud computing can thus dramatically improve social scientist's computational power and expand upon the methodologies accessible to social scientists. Cloud computing can also be helpful for large-scale data sharing, improving efficiency and transparency. For example, in the public health field, cloud computing helps foster the transmission of information between public healthcare organizations for real-time analyses to improve health outcomes (Jalali, Olabode, and Bell, 2012).

Similarly, cloud infrastructures can also be used to synthesize and curate existing data in social science. One cloud-based system that enables real-time meta-analysis called metaBUS (http://metabus.org/) summarizes empirical evidence from over a million findings across the social science field (Bosco et al., 2015). Another cloud-based system, the Open Science Framework (OSF.io), provides a hub for project management to foster collaboration, file and data sharing, and a full history of file changes and versions. The OSF cloud-based system also integrates with a variety of commonly used services like Dropbox, GitHub, and Amazon Web Services, free of charge. Access to free and science-oriented cloud-based systems like these make it feasible and convenient for social science researchers to take advantage of the benefits of cloud computing.

27.1.4 Visualization

Patterns within data and the results of complex analyses are difficult for humans to process without the aid of visualization. Although this is not a new problem, visualization is especially important in the era of big data as a means for understanding the data, making the data and findings accessible to larger audiences, and providing transparency of the data. Specifically, data visualization is a set of techniques used for displaying information graphically for better exploration, explanation, and engagement with data (Sinar, 2015). Data visualization used for exploration involves identifying patterns and relationships in an inductive manner, to make the raw data more interpretable. In addition, this approach can point out features of the data that may not be obvious using traditional summary statistics. Checking for outliers using box plots is a common example of data exploration through visualization already familiar to social scientists. In data science, visualization to identify patterns of missing data or high frequency word usage is much more common than in most social sciences. Data visualization for explanation involves looking beyond the raw data and instead at variables of interest to explain trends or relationships that answer questions or address hypotheses. A typical example of this use of visualization is a line graph depicting the slope and intercept of a regression line. In the big data realm, visualizations such as tree maps, sunbursts, and parallel coordinate plots can be particularly useful for explaining high volume, velocity, and variety big data (Wang, Wang, Alexander, 2015). Using visualization for data explanation can democratize data by reducing the need for explaining statistical models or techniques, ultimately widening the accessibility of the data to a variety of audiences (Sinar, 2015). For example, presenting information using graphs leads to more likely attitudinal changes in audience members than presenting the same information through tables (Pandey et al., 2014). Lastly, visualization of big data can be a tool to improve general engagement with the data by increasing its utility and transparency. Interactive visualizations of big data that require user input can, in a literal sense, increase engagement with the user. For example, the open-source R package Shiny (https://shiny.rstudio.com/) provides a platform for creating web apps that connect interested people directly to datasets and are designed for interactivity. Using this type of tool makes it easier for researchers or organizations to share data in a controlled, easy to interpret, and engaging manner.

There are a theoretically infinite number of ways of visualizing data and a wide variety of tools for creating such visualizations. Choosing a visualization method is dependent on both the intended message and the audience of the visualization (Zhu, 2007). Keeping in mind the objectives and the source of the information, and leveraging a design process for the targeted audience can help scientists avoid potential pitfalls including inaccuracies in the visualization, falsely visualizing optical significance, and oversaturating the audience with too much information (Sinar, 2018). Kirk (2012) presented a popular taxonomy of data visualization methods, which include comparing categories, assessing hierarchies and part-to-whole relationships, showing changes over time, plotting connections and relationships, and mapping geo-spatial data. Example visualizations of each of these methods can be found in Table 27.1. To create these visualizations, there a variety of open-source tools already available to social scientists, such as RAWgraphs (https://rawgraphs.io/) for creative visualizations, R and Shiny (https://shiny.rstudio.com/) for creating visualizations in existing data pipelines, and Voyant (https://voyant-tools.org/) for text analysis and visualization. There are also numerous commercial tools available, including Tableau (www.tableau.com/), which focuses on making visualization accessible even to people without expertise in data analysis (Landers, 2016).

Table 27.1

Visualization Method	Examples
Category Comparisons	Dot plot
	Bar Chart
	Histogram
	Slope Graph
	Word Cloud
	Alluvial Diagram
	Radial Chart
Assessing Hierarchical and Part-to-Whole Relationships	Pie Chart
	Stacked Bar Chart
	Tree Map
	Circle Packing Diagram
	Sunburst Diagram
	Cluster Dendrogram
Changes Over Time	Line Chart
	Sparklines
	Area Chart
	Steam Graph
Plotting Connections and Relationships	Scatter Plot
	Heatmap
	Radial Network
	Network Diagram
	Bubble Plot
Mapping Geo-Spatial Data	Choropleth Map
	Dot Plot Map
	Bubble Plot Map
	Topological Map

27.2 Data Science for Creating Reproducible Social Science

Best practices from data science can help improve both the *reproducibility* and *replicability* of scientific research, on which there has been a renewed focus in recent years, due to several high-profile instances of fraud and failure to replicate (Baker, 2016; Johnson et al., 2017). Reproducibility, in this sense, refers to the ability to re-create published findings using the same raw data and procedures, whereas replicability refers to the ability to recreate published findings with new data, collected using the same materials and procedures (Bollen et al., 2015). This section focuses on techniques commonly used in data science that, when incorporated into social science research, should increase the reproducibility of any particular study. Specifically, the use of open-source software, publicly shared data analytic pipelines, and public data repositories increase the transparency and accessibility of published findings: when these tools are used, any social scientist should be able to reproduce published analyses on their own computers.

27.2.1 Open-Source Technologies

Popular open-source technologies are generally free to acquire and use, have clear and comprehensive documentation, have community support, are highly customizable, and can be used to create reproducible analytic projects. Importantly, not all open-source technologies have these characteristics, so one data science skill that social scientists must develop is the ability to recognize high quality open-source technologies. We will describe how open-source technologies commonly used in data science improve reproducibility from data import to analysis stages. The two most common open-source technologies in data science that accomplish these tasks are the R and Python programming languages, and using either brings two major strengths in regards to reproducibility.

First, use of analytic systems like R and Python enable complete reproduction of a researcher's entire interaction with data, from start to finish. To illustrate, consider how the Pandas package in Python (McKinney, 2010) and import functions in base R (R Core Team, 2017) are commonly used for importing data. In Pandas, there are import options for many different data structures and file types. For example, *read_csv* can be used to automatically infer data types and variable labels, skip blank rows or headers, and handle user-specified separators to interpret tsv or other common data storage formats. Similarly, base R has read.csv and read.table functions. Both languages can also read XML, SQL, and many other common formats for data storage, although this may require loading specific packages. Further, Python and R can directly interface with other languages. For example, a user could enter SQL queries directly in R or Python if the environment is correctly specified. The primary advantage to importing files using such approaches is that, in comparison to the techniques used within commercial analytics packages like SPSS, every decision made is recorded in a script file. In SPSS, once a user has clicked, the record of that click is gone forever. This often results in a data import strategy that is unknown after it is executed; for example, although there might be an "original dataset" and an SPSS file, it is often unknown what specific steps were taken to get between these two. By using R or Python in the way described here, any user can recreate the original data import strategy perfectly, without question. Once data are imported, Pandas and the R package *tidyverse* (Wickham, 2017) have myriad further options for cleaning and inspecting data, restructuring data as necessary, and analyzing and visualizing the imported dataset. Figures 27.1 and 27.2 demonstrate identical projects in Python, using the open-source Spyder integrated development environment, and R, using the R Studio integrated development environment, starting with data import and cleaning, then analyzing, then creating visualizations. In each, it is clear precisely

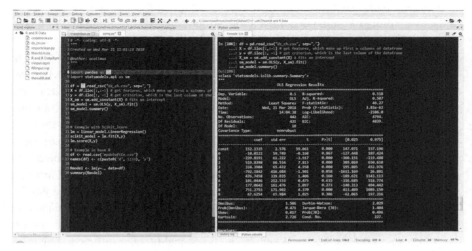

Figure 27.1 *Sample Python code, using the open-source Spyder integrated development environment.*

Figure 27.2 *Sample R code, using the open-source R-Studio development environment.*

what analytic steps were taken by the researchers from data import to results. Thus, complete analytic records are created within each environment, ensuring reproducibility of results. Analytic reproducibility can be further maximized by creating a software container using tools such as Docker or Singularity to capture the computational environment necessary to run the script. Binder (https://mybinder.org), for example, makes it easy for users to quickly create a Dockerfile by simply linking their code from their Github repository. In this way, if the original data source and the script used to conduct analyses are shared, other researchers can fully reproduce the original analyses.

A second major strength of open-source languages in regards to reproducibility is the availability of online documentation, which can not only aid in learning how to use various libraries, learning new functionality, learning the theoretical basis for functions via included references to academic statistics papers, and directly viewing source code already created by other researchers, but enables an absolutely clear understanding of precisely what mathematics and data manipulation processes were employed in any particular analytic code. Thousands of pages of official documentation are available for both Python and R, searchable for any purpose or use case. We encourage interested readers to view full Pandas documentation (http://pandas .pydata.org/pandas-docs/stable/) and base R documentation (https://cran.r-project.org/ doc/manuals/) to recognize how comprehensive they are as references. These manuals comprehensively explain functions, function arguments, and use cases. The Pandas documentation also contains links to sample code, whereas R has its own manual of source code. Such information is useful when one needs to understand exactly what is going on under-the-hood. When basic functionality is insufficient (e.g., for machine learning), Python and R allow users to import libraries, each of which contain their own documentation. Possibly the best example is from the Scikit-Learn (SKL) library in Python (Buitinck et al., 2013; Pedregosa et al., 2011). This library enables myriad complex statistical procedures used in machine learning, and many of these functions have dozens of arguments where a user can tune or optimize algorithms. Fortunately, the documentation for this library explains all of this, including parameter options, underlying statistical theory, and links citations to statistical papers on which the procedure is based. As an organized central source, such documentation offers some of the best and most comprehensive information on machine learning available anywhere, from theory to application, and it is freely available. With such documentation, it becomes possible for a researcher curious about a published analysis to not only conclude, "this is the analysis that the researcher conducted," but to be able to track down the precise mathematical approach used within the functions that accomplished that analysis. This supports reproducibility at a very fine level of detail.

Third, a major advantage of open-source technologies for reproducibility is that when existing functionality is insufficient, users can create and share their own tools created with that software with the scientific community. Specifically, because Python and R are programming languages, users can define their own functions and analytic approaches. Although many social scientists do not have the expertise or time to create widely used libraries such as previously mentioned, it is simple to write a single function to accomplish a specific task. For example, in a recent applied project, one of the present authors wanted to screen for multivariate outliers using Mahalanobis distances (MD). When a brief search did not find this existing functionality in a Python package, he wrote a function to accomplish the task by converting the statistical formula from a multivariate analysis textbook into a new algorithm. Although this may sound daunting, it is well within the capabilities of any social scientist who has learned even intermediate R or Python skills and can interpret a statistics textbook. Once the function is written, it can be applied to a dataset following the same rules and conventions as are standard in the environment. Importantly for reproducibility, this new analytic approach is then recorded in script files that can be viewed and reproduced in their entirety by later researchers.

Beyond reproducibility, open-source technologies bring other advantages to social science. For example, when documentation or specific applications are unclear, there are many forums where, after demonstrating sufficient effort, one can obtain high-quality free advice and support, sometimes from the author of the library in question. One of the most popular examples of this is the StackOverflow website, which currently provides access to discussions and answers to over 15 million programming-related questions. On this site, users gain reputation by asking and answering properly formatted questions, defined as those containing a clear and reproducible example of a problem not solvable with documentation alone and not already asked. Thus, StackOverflow, and websites like it, provide a depth of freely available assistance typically reserved to commercial technical support, in many cases from the original developers of the analytic tools being used. For example, the creators of Python's Pandas (McKinney, 2010) and machine learning library *caret* in R (Kuhn, 2017) are both active in these communities.

27.2.2 Data Analytic Pipelines and Version Control

Version control and data analytic pipelines help data scientists share and document progress and changes as they build solutions (i.e., import, inspection, cleaning, analysis, output, and visualization) to problems, creating an externally verifiable and reproducible pipeline in the process. Data science is an iterative process. One might first import a portion of a data file to understand the structure and type of variables present. Based on this information, the import command might be modified to skip rows, identify certain columns as indices (e.g., specify that participant number should not be interpreted as a continuous integer variable), and so on. As the analytic process proceeds, the code slowly changes such that a pipeline leading from raw data import to the most recent step is always maintained, enabling reproduction of the entire import and analytic process to that point whenever needed. This maximizes reproducibility; at any time, all data manipulation and analyses conducted since the raw-data stage can be recreated at will.

Because maintaining a data pipeline this way requires multiple iterations and potentially large scale "test" changes to analytic code, version control technologies have been developed that allow for comprehensively tracking updates and changes to code as it is written. For example, throughout the process of iteratively updating code to create a pipeline, it may be discovered that a previous change needs to be undone or viewed for reference. In traditional statistical environments, like SPSS syntax, such changes would be lost forever unless different versions of the syntax file were saved over time with new filenames. Such file structures quickly become overwhelming and unmanageable (e.g., code-v1, code-v2, code-v2-revised, code-v1-experiment, code-v1-experiment-revised, code-v1v2-combined). Version control systems alleviate this problem by tracking all changes within a single file at time points specified by the user and allowing for navigation between all prior versions of the file, so that any major change can be retrieved and examined whenever it is needed.

Git is a popular version control tool that enables this. Git is a simple and lightweight language that enables a user to specify when to "commit" new versions of their analytic code. Each commit version shows differences in text between itself and the previous version, similar to the track changes feature of popular word-editing software, but with much greater control. In some fields, scientists use Git to write manuscripts, as it integrates well with LaTeX (which is commonly used for typesetting manuscripts), keeps track of changes between saves, and is not very resource-intensive. Because Git only stores text, complete revision records do not require much space or computing power. When a change is committed, the commit is coupled with a user-specified message describing the changes (e.g., "reduce columns in import command; add labels"). These commit messages help track the evolution of a project and make a handy browsing tool for users wishing to review old code or revert to a previous commit. This improves reproducibility not only with other scientists but even within labs; it is easy to return to code written a few years ago and recreate the specific thinking that led to the analyses conducted.

Git also integrates with collaboration tools to make sharing even easier. GitHub is an online repository that extends the usefulness of Git in this way. First, because it is online, GitHub enables work on a project from multiple computers. Thus, it is easy for a user to "push" code from a work computer, then "pull" it from a laptop or any other computer to continue working on the latest version of the project. Second, it enables teams of data scientists to simultaneously work on a project, from disparate locations if necessary. In this way, a team can divide and allocate tasks, using comments, frequent push/pull requests, and other best practices from computer science (Chacon & Straub, 2014). In short, data scientists working in teams often "check out" a piece of code, develop it, and then push it back into the master where other team members can either approve and integrate the change or try to reconcile issues that the change introduces. Third, this approach affords data scientists the option to publicize their work. GitHub repositories can be made public so that other users can view the project history. The owner of a repository has the option to allow public editing as well, which has greatly furthered the open-source movement. In fact, popular libraries such as Pandas or Scikit-Learn can be fully viewed on GitHub, which means that users have access to the source code itself (e.g., if one wanted to check whether a standard deviation calculation used n or n–1 for degrees of freedom) and the opportunity to contribute (e.g., if a user wanted to add functionality to calculate Mahalanobis distances).

To summarize, the final pipeline of a data science project includes code that can take an external user from raw data to all analyses and output; this process reduces errors by never modifying the raw data and enables complete reproduction of the analytic approach. Additionally, data pipelines make it easy for users to make small changes in the script (e.g., after forgetting to reverse code a single survey item), or to add new data as they become available. At the beginning of the pipeline, raw data is imported and cleaned. Unlike in an SPSS file, all changes to the data occur in the R or Python development environment, so the original raw data file is never lost or replaced in a properly designed data pipeline. When the user runs an R or Python script designed this way from its beginning, the script imports raw data, cleans the data, runs all desired analyses and creates all output that will eventually be shared with others. Furthermore, in R, packages like apaTables can be used to automatically format output from standard statistical analyses into APA formatted tables that can be exported directly into Microsoft Word. With a complete data pipeline, a user can upload a new dataset or make a small change and then re-run all analyses and generate formatted tables in a matter of seconds. A complete data pipeline, in combination with version control, provides complete start-to-finish documentation of the entire progression of analyses, maximizing reproducibility.

27.2.3 Online Data Repositories

Some academics and academic journals are now promoting the idea of pre-registered research studies. During pre-registration, authors specify their data collection methods, hypotheses, analyses, and data cleaning methods prior to collecting data. The Center for Open Science, for example, provides a popular platform (https:// cos.io/prereg/) for scientists to pre-register their work in effort to increase the credibility of their results. In social sciences, in contrast to the medical field, for example, the practice of pre-registering studies is relatively new (van 't Veer & Giner-Sorolla, 2016). In medical research, the call for pre-registration in the early to mid 2000s was a reaction to publication bias and low replication rates of clinical trials. Similar calls are being made in social sciences in reaction to a "replication crisis" (Earp & Trafimow, 2015). Some journals, such as *Perspectives on Psychological Science* and *Social Psychology*, have reacted with the adoption of registered reports as a submission category, special issues of pre-registered research, and even by awarding badges for pre-registration (Kidwell et al., 2016). By pre-registering research, theoretical soundness and methodology are prioritized over the results of the study. By shifting the emphasis away from study results, publication bias and reporting bias are believed to become less prevalent. Although pre-registration does require more work up front and reduces post-data collection analytic flexibility, it encourages good scientific practice and increases the credibility of the findings, ultimately improving the quality of the social science body of literature.

Similarly, online data repositories enable researchers to store and share raw data, which, when accompanied by code and version control info, communicates the entirety of the data-analytic process. Although public data sharing in social scientific research is not typically required, there are some cases in which data sharing is required to fulfill grant or journal publication requirements. In cases where data sharing is not required, however, it still demonstrates transparency and creates better opportunities for more accurate replication. In social science, common data repositories include openICPSR (www.openicpsr.org/openicpsr/), GitHub (https:// github.com/), Academic Torrents (http://academictorrents.com/), and figshare (https://figshare.com/). To publish data on OpenICPSR, for example, users simply need to provide a name for the project, describe and upload their files, and publish, making data sharing "so easy, even your cat could do it" (openICPSR.org). Such democratization of process and data further the goals of transparent and reproducible science.

27.3 Data Science for Creating Trustworthy Social Science

Although integrating the data science techniques described up to this point as standard practices in social scientific inquiry would not itself make social science more trustworthy, it has the potential to make questionable research practices (QRPs) more difficult to hide and easier for future researchers to identify, both likely deterrents to their practice, increasing scientific trustworthiness in the long run. In short, the data science techniques described so far support and enhance science's self-corrective nature. This is critical, because one of the primary goals of science is the "production of cumulative knowledge" (Schmidt & Hunter, 2003, p. 533), and untrustworthy science slows or halts progress toward that goal. In a high profile case of QRPs, Diederik Stapel (2014), a leading social scientist at Tilburg University, was able to easily fabricate data for over a decade, affecting at least 55 publications within social psychology (Univers, 2012), in a way that would have been much more obvious if the record-keeping and transparency of data science had been standards of the field at that time. Concerns over QRPs, such as those used by Stapel, and the broader causes of scientific misconduct, have been accumulating (Baker, 2016; Crocker, 2011; Marshall, 2000; Maxwell, Lau, & Howard, 2015; Wicherts, 2011), and in a survey of 2,000 psychologists regarding QRPs, a troubling one in ten psychologists admitted to having falsified data (John, Loewenstein, & Prelec, 2012). Researchers have also found that most psychologists have engaged in other QRPs, including selective reporting, collecting more data after desired results were not found (i.e., p-hacking), and portraying unexpected findings as predicted (see discussion on HARKing in Kerr, 1998). If QRPs produce a science that is untrustworthy, and if techniques and philosophies from data science can be adopted to reduce QRPs, such integration is clearly a goal worth pursuing.

27.3.1 Reproducibility as a Necessary First Step toward Trustworthiness

Credibility in several scientific disciplines has been critically examined within the past few years due to QPRs and scientific misconduct (Stroebe, Postmes, & Spears, 2012), an effort in large part spurred by psychology's replication crisis (Baker, 2016; Open Science Collaboration, 2015), which has called into question the field's overall scientific legitimacy. One basic principle of the scientific method is that results are trustworthy, and trustworthiness is defined in part by the extent to which scientific results are both reproducible and replicable. Similar to the relationship between reliability and validity, reproducibility is necessary but insufficient to support replicability. As noted earlier, reproducibility involves the ability of external researchers to both methodologically and analytically recreate the results of primary research, whereas replicability refers to the generalizability of theories derived from those results to other appropriate contexts. Reproducibility may even include the use of different statistical techniques that are equally or more justifiable given an identical dataset (LeBel et al., 2017, p. 3). Reproducibility and replicability should not be thought as equivalent to scientific quality, as there are other core features of high-quality science researchers must prioritize to optimize the study quality (Finkel, Eastwick, & Reis, 2017), such as internal or external validity, construct validity, cumulativeness, and discovery (Finkel et al., 2017, p. 246).

Science is only self-correcting if its research is both reproducible and replicable. In such a state, findings contrary to true scores should occur only relatively infrequently; within the null hypothesis significance testing paradigm common to many social scientific fields, Type I error rates should be tightly controlled at 5 percent or less, and Type II error rates should be 20 percent or less, assuming 80 percent power. However, when QRPs are integrated, both error rates may be inflated, and lack of transparency regarding data cleaning and analysis contributes to this problem. Wicherts, Borsboom, D., Kats, and Molenaar (2006) argued that most researchers do not document their data in such a way as to let others readily verify data and results; yet this problem could be easily mitigated by integrating data science best practices, which are inherently transparent and open. As discussed earlier, it is common in data science to track and record every data manipulation and statistical test executed from raw data import to display of final results. Scripts of data pipelines can be freely published online on platforms like GitHub or the Open Science Framework (OSF). In turn, this enables verification by any interested researcher that is immediate and easy. Online platforms such as OSF let the complete life cycle of a study remain in full view, which gives social scientists the ability to publicly verify each step of the research process, including data manipulation and cleaning. Also, platforms such as these breaks down the arcane restraints journals place on researchers, such as page limits (McAbee, Grubbs, & Zickar, 2018). Moreover, not only can social scientists verify results from the same statistical techniques previous researchers employed, but they can also run simulations to rule out the likelihood of false-positive results due to random chance or statistical artifacts (Simmons, Nelson, & Simonsohn, 2011). Thus, reproducibility, as enabled by tools like these, would be a promising first step toward a replicable, trustworthy science.

27.3.2 Changes in Measurement of Behavior

Beyond improving the trustworthiness of our existing scientific methods, data science also enables new ways to measure constructs, which can be used to build a more comprehensive, and thus trustworthy, social science. Because theoretical constructs are latent and not directly observable, measurement theory has traditionally been an area of emphasis in the training of many social scientists, particularly psychologists. This is in part because measurement error can reduce statistical power (Phillips & Jiang, 2016), which is in turn related to replication (Maxwell et al., 2015). Classical problems of validity and reliability, such as lack of power (Shadish, Cook, & Campbell, 2002), still apply in the age of big data and data science, but data science can unlock innovative ways of validating novel instruments. For example, researchers could use data science methods to integrate previous psychometric findings from validation studies and continuously update validity and reliability estimates of instruments on an open-source platform, like the continuously updated validity estimates currently found within the metaBUS database. Researchers could in this way prioritize other core features of high-quality science without focusing as many resources on local measure validation.

Two relatively unexplored approaches to behavioral measurement in the social sciences, yet common in data science, are the analyses of text and microbehaviors. Text is analyzed in data science using natural language processing (NLP), a branch of artificial intelligence that helps computers create meaning from raw textual data (Bird, Klein, & Loper, 2009). When employed by social scientists, NLP systems provide the ability to capture qualitative and quantitative data simultaneously from text in a way that is traditionally difficult and time-consuming, as social scientists most commonly code or interpret such text manually and intuitively, usually labeled some variation of "content analysis." Microbehaviors, a term which refers to fleeting technology-focused behaviors like mouse clicks, key presses, the timings of such events, and other such metadata (Giles, 2012), could theoretically be used to assess a wide range of constructs (Lazer et al., 2009; McKelvey & Menczer, 2013; Shute, 2011). For example, Bogomolov, Lepri, Ferron, Pianesi, and Pentland (2014) created a machine learning model that predicted out-of-sample graduate student stress levels with 72.28 percent accuracy by combining mobile phone microbehaviors, weather patterns, and personality surveys as predictors, improving upon existing stress prediction models by combining psychological, physiological, and data sciences approaches.

Another new source of behavioral data comes from websites and the databases supporting them, and data science technologies like web scraping (i.e., mining data found on webpages) and application programming interfaces (APIs) can be used to access these data. Using such techniques can help to corroborate previous research findings and further enhance the trustworthiness of results. For example, Landers, Brusso, Cavanaugh, and Collmus (2016) presented a study using such web scraping collecting 165,527 posts from a public self-help discussion board to test existing psychological theory regarding gender and coping behaviors. The development of APIs, which permit direct communication between researchers and website data-bases, expands the availability of behavioral data. Companies including Facebook, Google, and Twitter store massive amounts of user data and online trace data, and these companies also create APIs so that different web and mobile applications can communicate with each other using this information. Social scientists can access many of these data that are publicly available, enabling new ways of testing established research questions.

Additionally, data science informs and enables new theoretical perspectives toward measurement more broadly. The hypothetico-deductive approach has domi-nated the social sciences over the last several decades (Locke, 2007), wherein researchers test the extent to which a priori theory-derived hypotheses are sup-ported by collected data. However, this exclusionary focus on deductive (i.e., top-down, theory-driven) methods may limit the progress of social scientific theory development (Locke, 2007; Spector et al., 2014). Given the rise of big data, data science enables comprehensive, inductive approaches to theory development (Tonidandel et al., 2016). Although approaches like these have been derogatively labeled "dustbowl empiricism" and criticized as "atheoretical," such methods can be used to build theory alongside deductive approaches (McAbee et al., 2017; Tonidandel et al., 2016). Furthermore, data science is not inherently either; its methods could be categorized as either deductive or inductive, depending upon application (McAbee et al., 2017).

27.3.3 Triangulating Upon Theory

Triangulation is a metaphor used in research drawn from sea navigation wherein an unknown point can be determined using the position of other fixed points (Thurmond, 2001). Pragmatically, triangulation is defined as combining multiple theoretical perspectives and methodological approaches to study a phenomenon looking for evidence that points to a consensus understanding (Jick, 1979; Thurmond, 2001). Thus, the purpose of triangulation is in part to accurately capture the richness of multidimensional phenomena (Thurmond, 2001). Triangulation has typically been used in social science to describe the integration of qualitative and quantitative perspectives in more completely understanding complex phenomena (Wenzel & Van Quaquebeke, 2017). A major goal when determining the trust-worthiness of theory should be successful triangulation, the collection of evidence supporting the accuracy of that theory regardless of the paradigm used to examine it (Denzin, 1970). Data science offers social scientists additional tools and techniques for triangulating upon theory by helping to overcome validity limitations of traditional single-method research designs (e.g., misunderstanding questionnaires, demand characteristics in experimentation, social desirability in case studies). As described earlier, the variety of data available for this purpose is ever-growing. Therefore, no single metric or method can capture multidimensional phenomena. This suggests that a phenomenon or construct should be examined through multi-method designs for more complete understanding.

In general, social science is shifting toward examination of emergent phenomena that are multilevel and unfold over time (Highhouse & Schmitt, 2013). Luchiano, Mathieu, Park and Tannenbaum (2017) show how data science can play a role in the theoretical advancement of dynamic phenomena, which have traditionally been challenging to capture. Luchiano et al. (2017) claim that dynamic phenomena can be captured using streams of data that index, store, and track behaviors (e.g., movement, posture, body position, gestures, facial expressions), patterns of speech and writing (e.g., words used, tone, pitch, interruption) and individual physiological responses (e.g., heart rate, blood pressure). For example, behavioral-related data streams can be fed (via wearable sensors) individuals' audio-visual nonverbal behavior that indicate dynamic multilevel constructs such as team cohesion (Hung & Gatica-Perez, 2010) and the degree to which the meetings people attend are collaborative in nature (Gatica-Perez, 2009). In sum, data science methods give social scientists more perspectives on dynamic multidimensional phenomenon than have been impossible to capture previously, and the availability of multiple perspectives that converge upon the same theory improves the trustworthiness of that theory.

27.3.4 Influencing the Public and Public Policy

Public mistrust of social science is not a new concept; as a result of disagreement within the social and behavioral sciences in the 1970s, government officials and the public at that time became disillusioned with social science, which threatened public funding. However, the advent of the meta-analysis demonstrated that social scientific research did have sufficient consistency to influence public policy (Schmidt and Hunter, 2003). In the same way meta-analytic techniques helped bolster the credibility of psychology and related social sciences at that time, data science can now help improve the trustworthiness of science with the public. Some such advances have even been legislated; since 2007, clinical researchers in the United States are required by law to register their studies in a public database and post a summary of results (Miguel et al., 2014). Registering studies in public databases reduces publication bias and improves decision-making when creating policy. Also, publicly available data and analyses can empower citizens to make their own informed decisions.

The overall purpose of evidence-based policy is to use research findings to drive policy decision-making. However, scientific dissemination and implementation can take years. Moreover, policy can also be ill-informed by untrustworthy findings. Thus, both the rate of scientific dissemination and lack of replication pose a threat to decision-making when legislating evidence-based policy. Key concerns for social scientists and policy makers are the quality and relevance of evidence (McKnight & McKnight, 2005). These concerns are usually addressed by the peer-review process. However, publication bias has arisen from the current peer review process (Dickersin, 1990). A more transparent social science (i.e., disclosure, registration, proposed analysis, and open data sharing) could improve this and rapidly expedite the decision-making process in evidence-based policy (Miguel et al., 2014).

Such possibilities from data science do not come without cost. Facebook and Twitter have now reached 2.2 billion and 330 million global users (We Are Social, 2018), respectively, increasing the risk of propaganda and misinformation spreading internationally. The hyperconnectivity people experience through various virtual social networks (e.g., Facebook, Twitter, email, texting) enables exchange of information that is immediate and global, which catalyzes false information to spread like "digital wildfire" through digital news outlets and social media (Howell, 2013). On the one hand, digital wildfires can be dangerous when online trace data is used to individually tailor misinformation toward targeted users to ultimately influence behavior offline, such as voting behavior (Lewis, Grierson, & Weaver, 2018). On the other hand, user activity can influence the public and combat misinformation in monumental ways. For instance, Facebook played a crucial role in the Arab Spring, a time of civil unrest and regime change in North African countries starting in 2010 with the Tunisian revolution, which allowed protesters to organize and strategically coordinate demonstrations (Mourtada & Salem, 2011). Trustworthy scientific evidence can also play a role in combating propaganda and misinformation when data are freely shared and disclosed.   Data sharing and publicly available, large datasets afford rapid scientific dissemination. Our current capabilities, offering immediate scientific results that are publicly verifiable and checked via crowdsourcing, can be integrated in browser extensions, such as Truthy (McKelvey & Menczer, 2013), that automatically fact-check and flag media for false information or misinformation.

27.4 Conclusion

In summary, the techniques already developed and being developed within the interdisciplinary approach of data science have immense potential to create new insights for social science, improve the reproducibility of social science, and improve the trustworthiness of social science both in terms of its replicability and its accuracy, within the scientific community and with the public at large. Importantly, this potential should not be interpreted to mean that emergent data science should be incorporated wholesale into modern social science, replacing all its well-established practices. Integration of data science into mainstream social science should not fundamentally transform it, nor will integration of data science automatically repair the reputational damage already done by QRPs. Instead, care is needed when considering what to borrow and integrate, to take the good and leave the bad as much as possible. With the promise of new data sources and analytic techniques always comes the threat of their misinterpretation, and as a result, we expect there will be many an uncritical, glassy-eyed stare at the extremely large sample sizes that a move toward data science is likely to bring. Despite this and other risks, we contend that the long-term benefits to our disciplines that would be brought by integration dramatically outweigh the potential drawbacks and encourage researchers to actively and critically explore such possibilities.

References

Baker, M. (2016). Is there a reproducibility crisis? *Nature*, *533*(7604), 3–5.

Bird, S., Klein, E., & Loper, E. (2009). *Natural language processing with Python: analyzing text with the natural language toolkit*. Sebastopol, CA: O'Reilly Media.

Bogomolov, A., Lepri, B., Ferron, M., Pianesi, F., & Pentland, A. S. (November, 2014). Daily stress recognition from mobile phone data, weather conditions and individual traits. In Proceedings of the 22nd ACM international conference on Multimedia (pp. 477–486). ACM.

Bollen, K., Cacioppo, J. T., Kaplan, R. M., Krosnick, J. A., & Olds, J. L. (2015). Social, behavioral, and economic sciences perspectives on robust and reliable science. Retrieved from www.nsf.gov/sbe/AC_Materials/SBE_Robust_and_Reliable_Research_Report.pdf.

Bosco, F. A., Steel, P., Oswald, F. L., Uggerslev, K., & Field, J. G. (2015). Cloud-based meta-analysis to bridge science and practice: Welcome to metaBUS. *Personnel Assessment and Decisions*, *1*, 3–17.

Brieman, L. (2001). Statistical modeling: The two cultures. *Statistical Science*, *16*, 199–231.

Buitinck, L., Louppe, G., Blondel, M., Pedregosa, F., Mueller, A., Grisel, O.,… Varoquaux, G. (2013). API design for machine learning software: experiences from the scikit-learn project. Paper presented at the European Conference on Machine Learning and Principles and Practices of Knowledge Discovery in Databases, Prague, Czech Republic.

Carter, N. T., Carter, D. R., & DeChurch, L. A. (2015). *Implications of observability for the theory and measurement of emergent team phenomena. Journal of Management,* 0149206315609402.

Chacon, S. & Straub, B. (2014). *Pro git* [pdf version]. Retrieved from https://github.com/progit/progit2/releases/download/2.1.48/progit.pdf.

Chen, D. & Zhao, H. (March, 2012). Data security and privacy protection issues in cloud computing. In International Conference Computer Science and Electronics Engineering Proceedings (ICCSEE), 2012 (vol. 1, pp. 647–651). IEEE.

Chen, X., Cho, Y., & Jang, S. Y. (April, 2015). Crime prediction using Twitter sentiment and weather. In Systems and Information Engineering Design Symposium Conference Proceedings (SIEDS), 2015 (pp. 63–68). IEEE.

Crocker, J. (2011). The road to fraud starts with a single step. *Nature, 479,* 151.

Denzin, N. K. (1970). *The research act: A theoretical introduction to sociological methods.* Chicago, IL: Aldine.

Dickersin, K. (1990). The existence of publication bias and risk factors for its occurrence. *Jama, 263*(10), 1385–1389.

Dumbill, E. (2013). Making sense of big data. Big Data, 1(1), 1–2.

Earp, B. D. & Trafimow, D. (2015). Replication, falsification, and the crisis of confidence in social psychology. *Frontiers in Psychology, 6,* 621.

Finkel, E. J., Eastwick, P. W., & Reis, H. T. (2017). Replicability and other features of a high-quality science: Toward a balanced and empirical approach. *Journal of Personality and Social Psychology, 113*(2), 244.

Furht, B. & Escalante, A. (2010). *Handbook of cloud computing* (vol. 3). New York, NY: Springer.

Gatica-Perez, D. (2009). Automatic nonverbal analysis of social interaction in small groups: A review. *Image and Vision Computing, 27*(12), 1775–1787.

Giles, J. (2012). Making the links. From e-mails to social networks, the digital traces left by the life in the modern world are transforming social science. *Nature, 488*(7412), 448–450. doi:10.1038/488448a.

Guzzo, R. A., Fink, A. A., King, E., Tonidandel, S., & Landis, R. S. (2015). Big data recommendations for industrial–organizational psychology. *Industrial and Organizational Psychology, 8,* 491–508.

Hambrick, D. C. (2007). Upper echelons theory: An update. *Academy of Management Review, 32,* 334–343.

Hashem, I. A. T., Yaqoob, I., Anuar, N. B., Mokhtar, S., Gani, A., & Khan, S. U. (2015). The rise of "big data" on cloud computing: Review and open research issues. *Information Systems, 47,* 98–115.

Hastie, T., Tibshirani, R., & Friedman, J. (2009). *The elements of statistical learning: Data mining, inference, and prediction* (2nd edn.). New York, NY: Springer.

Hernandez, I., Newman, D., & Jeon, G. (2016). Twitter analysis: Methods for data management and validation of a word count dictionary to measure city-level job satisfaction. In S. Tonidandel, E. King, & J. Cortina (Eds.), *Big data at work: The data science revolution and organizational psychology* (pp. 64–114). New York, NY: Routledge.

Highhouse, S. & Schmitt, N.W. (2013). A snapshot in time: Industrial-organizational psychology today. In I. B. Weiner (Ed.), *Handbook of psychology* (2nd edn., pp. 3–13). Hoboken, NJ: John Wiley & Sons.

Hitzler, P. & Janowicz, K. (2013). Linked data, big data, and the 4th paradigm. *Semantic Web*, *4*, 233–235.

Howell, L. (2013). Digital wildfires in a hyperconnected world. WEF Report 2013. Retrieved from reports.weforum.org/global-risks-2013/risk-case-1/digital-wild fires-in-a-hyperconnected-world.

Huang, L. & Knight, A. P. (2017). Resources and relationships in entrepreneurship: an exchange theory of the development and effects of the entrepreneur-investor relationship. *Academy of Management Review*, *42*, 80–102.

Hung, H. & Gatica-Perez, D. (2010). Estimating cohesion in small groups using audio-visual nonverbal behavior. *IEEE Transactions on Multimedia*, *12*(6), 563–575.

Jalali, A., Olabode, O. A., & Bell, C. M. (2012). Leveraging cloud computing to address public health disparities: An analysis of the SPHPS. *Online Journal of Public Health Informatics*, *4*.

James, G., Witten, D., Hastie, T., & Tibshirani, R. (2013). *An introduction to statistical learning with applications in R*. New York, NY: Springer.

Jick, T. D. (1979). Mixing qualitative and quantitative methods: Triangulation in action. *Administrative Science Quarterly*, *24*(4), 602–611.

John, L. K., Loewenstein, G., & Prelec, D. (2012). Measuring the prevalence of questionable research practices with incentives for truth telling. Psychological Science, *23*(5), 524–532. doi:10.1177/0956797611430953.

Johnson, V. E., Payne, R. D., Wang, T., Asher, A., & Mandal, S. (2017). On the reproducibility of psychological science. *Journal of the American Statistical Association*, *112*, 1–10. doi:10.1080/01621459.2016.1240079.

Kerr, N. L. (1998). HARKing: Hypothesizing after the results are known. *Personality and Social Psychology Review*, *2*(3), 196–217.

Kidwell, M. C., Lazarević, L. B., Baranski, E., Hardwicke, T. E., Piechowski, S., Falkenberg, L. S., . . . & Errington, T. M. (2016). Badges to acknowledge open practices: a simple, low-cost, effective method for increasing transparency. *PLoS Biology*, *14*(5), e1002456.

Kirk, A. (2012). *Data visualization: A successful design process*. Birmingham, UK: Packt

Kosinski, M., Bachrach, Y., Kohli, P., Stillwell, D., & Graepel, T. (2014). Manifestations of user personality in website choice and behaviour on online social networks. *Machine Learning*, *95*, 357–380.

Kotsiantis, S. B., Zaharakis, I., & Pintelas, P. (2007). Supervised machine learning: A review of classification techniques. Emerging *A*rtificial *I*ntelligence *A*pplications in Computer *E*ngineering, *160*, 3–24.

Kozlowski, S. W., Chao, G. T., Chang, C. H., & Fernandez, R. (2015). Team dynamics: Using "big data" to advance the science of team effectiveness. In S. Tonidandel, E. B. King, & J. M. Cortina (Eds.), Big data at work: The data science revolution and organizational psychology (pp. 273–309). New York, NY: Routledge.

Kozlowski, S. W., Chao, G. T., Grand, J. A., Braun, M. T., & Kuljanin, G. (2016). Capturing the multilevel dynamics of emergence: Computational modeling, simulation, and virtual experimentation. *Organizational Psychology Review*, *6*, 3–33.

Kuhn, M. & Johnson, K. (2013). *Applied predictive modeling*. New York, NY: Springer.

Kuhn, M., Wing, J., Weston, S., Williams, A., Keefer, C., ... & Hunt, T. (2017). Caret: Classification and Regression Training. R package version 6.0–78. https://CRAN .R-project.org/package=caret.

Landers, R. N. (October, 2016). A Crash Course in Data Visualization Platform Tableau. *The Industrial Organizational Psychologist*, *55*(2).

Landers, R. N., Brusso, R. C., Cavanaugh, K. J., & Collmus, A. B. (2016). A primer on theory-driven web scraping: Automatic extraction of big data from the Internet for use in psychological research. *Psychological Methods*, *21*, 475–492.

Landers, R. N., Fink, A., & Collmus, A. B. (2017). Using big data to enhance staffing: Vast untapped resources or tempting honeypot? In J. L. Farr & N. T. Tippins (Eds.), *Handbook of employee selection* (2nd edn., pp. 949–966). New York, NY: Routledge.

Laney, D. (2001). 3D data management: Controlling data volume, velocity and variety. *META Group Research Note*, 6.

Lazer, D., Pentland, A. S., Adamic, L., Aral, S., Barabasi, A. L., Brewer, D., ... & Jebara, T. (2009). Life in the network: The coming age of computational social science. *Science*, *323*(5915), 721–723.

LeBel, E. P., Vanpaemel, W., McCarthy, R., & Earp, B., & Elson, M. (2017). A Unified Framework to Quantify the Trustworthiness of Empirical Research. Manuscript under review @ Advances in Methods and Practices in Psychological Science. Retrieved from https://osf.io/preprints/psyarxiv/uwmr8.

Lewis, P., Grierson, J., Weaver, M. (March 24, 2018). Cambridge Analytica academic's work upset university colleagues. The Guardian. Retrieved from www.theguar dian.com/education/2018/mar/24/cambridge-analytica-academics-work-upset-university-colleagues.

Locke, E. A. (2007). The case for inductive theory building. *Journal of Management*, *33*(6), 867–890.

Luciano, M. M., Mathieu, J. E., Park, S., & Tannenbaum, S. I. (2017). A Fitting Approach to Construct and Measurement Alignment: The Role of Big Data in Advancing Dynamic Theories. Organizational Research Methods, 1094428117728372.

Manyika, J., Chui, M., Brown, B., Bughin, J., Dobbs, R., Roxburgh, C., & Byers, A. H. (2011). *Big data: The next frontier for innovation, competition, and productivity*. McKinsey Global Institute.

Marshall, E. (2000). Scientific misconduct. How prevalent is fraud? That's a million-dollar question. *Science*, *290*(5497), 1662.

Maxwell, S. E., Lau, M. Y., & Howard, G. S. (2015). Is psychology suffering from a replication crisis? What does "failure to replicate" really mean? *American Psychologist*, *70*(6), 487–498.

McAbee, S., Grubbs, J., & Zickar, M. (2018). Open science is robust science. *Industrial and Organizational Psychology*, *11*(1), 54–61. doi:10.1017/iop.2017.85.

McAbee, S. T., Landis, R. S., & Burke, M. I. (2017). Inductive reasoning: The promise of big data. *Human Resource Management Review*, *27*, 277–290.

McKelvey, K. R. & Menczer, F. (February, 2013). Truthy: Enabling the study of online social networks. In Proceedings of the 2013 conference on Computer supported cooperative work companion (pp. 23–26). ACM.

McKinney, W. (2010). Data Structures for Statistical Computing in Python. In S. van der Walt & J. Millman (Eds.), Proceedings of the 9th Python in Science Conference (pp. 51–56).

McKnight, K. M., Sechrest, L., & McKnight, P. E. (2005). Psychology, psychologists, and public policy. *Annual Review of Clinical Psychology*, *1*, 557–576.

Mell, P. & Grance, T. (2011). The NIST definition of cloud computing. National Institute of Standards and Technology, U.S. Department of Commerce.

Miguel, E., Camerer, C., Casey, K., Cohen, J., Esterling, K. M., Gerber, A., . . . & Laitin, D. (2014). Promoting transparency in social science research. *Science*, *343*(6166), 30–31.

Mourtada, R. & Salem, F. (2011). Civil movements: The impact of Facebook and Twitter. *Arab Social Media Report*, *1*(2), 1–30.

Ohm, P. (2010). Broken promises of privacy: Responding to the surprising failure of anonymization. *UCLA Law Review*, *57*, 1701–1776.

Open Science Collaboration. (2015). Estimating the reproducibility of psychological science. Science, *349*(6251), aac4716. doi:10.1126/science.aac4716.

Pandey, A. V., Manivannan, A., Nov, O., Satterthwaite, M., & Bertini, E. (2014). The persuasive power of data visualization. *IEEE Transactions on Visualization and Computer Graphics*, *20*, 2211–2220.

Park, C. L. (2010). Making sense of the meaning literature: an integrative review of meaning making and its effects on adjustment to stressful life events. *Psychological Bulletin*, *136*, 257.

Pedregosa, F., Varoquaux, G., Gramfort, A., Michel, V., Thirion, B., Grisel, O., . . . & Vanderplas, J. (2011). Scikit-learn: Machine learning in Python. *Journal of Machine Learning Research*, *12*, 2825–2830.

Phillips, G. W. & Jiang, T. (2016). *Measurement error and equating error in power analysis. Practical Assessment, Research & Evaluation*, 21*(9)*, 1–12.

Putka, D. J., Beatty, A. S., & Reeder, M. C. (2017). Modern prediction methods: New perspectives on a common problem. Organizational Research Methods, 1094428117697041.

R Core Team (2017). R: A language and environment for statistical computing. R Foundation for Statistical Computing, Vienna, Austria. www.R-project.org/.

Rissman, J., Greely, H. T., & Wagner, A. D. (2010). Detecting individual memories through the neural decoding of memory states and past experience. *Proceedings of the National Academy of Sciences, USA*, *107*, 9849–9854. doi:10.1073/ pnas.1001028107.

Shadish, W. R., Cook, T. D., & Campbell, D. T. (2002). *Experimental and quasi-experimental designs for generalized causal inference*. Boston, MA: Houghton Mifflin.

Schmidt, F. L. & Hunter, J. E. (2003). History, development, evolution, and impact of validity generalization and meta-analysis methods, 1975–2001. In Validity generalization: A critical review (pp. 31–65).

Shute, V. J. (2011). Stealth assessment in computer-based games to support learning. *Computer Games and Instruction*, *55*(2), 503–524.

Simmons, J. P., Nelson, L. D., & Simonsohn, U. (2011). False-positive psychology: Undisclosed flexibility in data collection and analysis allows presenting anything as significant. *Psychological Science*, *22*(11), 1359–1366.

Sinar, E. F. (2015). Data visualization. In S. Tonidandel, E. B. King, & J. M. Cortina (Eds.), *Big data at work: The data science revolution and organizational psychology* (pp. 115–157). New York, NY: Routledge.

Sinar, E. F. (2018). Data Visualization: Get Visual to Drive HR's Impact and Influence. Society for Human Resource Management (SHRM)-Society for Industrial Organizational Psychology (SIOP) Science of HR White Paper Series.

Spector, P. E., Rogelberg, S. G., Ryan, A. M., Schmitt, N., & Zedeck, S. (2014). Moving the pendulum back to the middle: Reflections on and introduction to the inductive research special issue of Journal of Business and Psychology. *Journal of Business and Psychology*, *29*(4), 499–502.

Stanton, J. M. (2013). Introduction to data science. Retrieved from https://archive.org/details/DataScienceBookV3.

Stapel, D. (2014). Faking science: A true story of academic fraud. Trans. NJL Brown.). Retrieved from https://errorstatistics.files.wordpress.com/2014/12/fakingscience-20141214.pdf.

Stroebe, W., Postmes, T., & Spears, R. (2012). Scientific misconduct and the myth of self-correction in science. *Perspectives on Psychological Science*, *7*(6), 670–688.

Thurmond, V. A. (2001). The point of triangulation. *Journal of Nursing Scholarship*, *33*(3), 253–258.

Tonidandel, S., King, E. B., & Cortina, J. M. (2016). Big Data methods: Leveraging modern data analytic techniques to build organizational science. Organizational Research Methods, 1094428116677299.

Tumasjan, A., Sprenger, T. O., Sandner, P. G., & Welpe, I. M. (2010). Predicting elections with twitter: What 140 characters reveal about political sentiment. *ICWSM*, *10*, 178–185.

Univers. (2012). Levelt: Fraud detected in 55 publications [Blog post]. Retrieved from https://universonline.nl/2012/11/28/levelt-report-fraud-detected-in-55-publications.

van 't Veer, A. E. & Giner-Sorolla, R. (2016). Pre-registration in social psychology: A discussion and suggested template. *Journal of Experimental Social Psychology*, *67*, 2–12.

Wang, L., Wang, G., & Alexander, C. A. (2015). Big data and visualization: Methods, challenges and technology progress. *Digital Technologies*, *1*, 33–38.

We Are Social. (January, 2018). Most famous social network sites worldwide as of January 2018, ranked by number of active users (in millions). Retrieved from www.statista.com/statistics/272014/global-social-networks-ranked-by-number-of-users/.

Wenzel, R. & Van Quaquebeke, N. (2017). The Double-Edged Sword of Big Data in Organizational and Management Research: A Review of Opportunities and Risks. Organizational Research Methods, 1094428117718627.

Westera, W., Nadolski, R., & Hummel, H. (2014). Serious gaming analytics: What students' log files tell us about gaming and learning. *International Journal of Serious Games*, 1(2), 35–50.

Wicherts, J. (2011). Psychology must learn a lesson from fraud case. *Nature, 480*.

Wicherts, J. M., Borsboom, D., Kats, J., & Molenaar, D. (2006). The poor availability of psychological research data for reanalysis. *American Psychologist*, *61*(7), 726–728. http://dx.doi.org.proxy.lib.odu.edu/10.1037/0003-066X.61.7.726.

Wickham, H (2017). Tidyverse: Easily Install and Load the "Tidyverse." R package version 1.2.1. https://CRAN.R-project.org/package=tidyverse.

Yarkoni, T. & Westfall, J. (2017). Choosing prediction over explanation in psychology: Lessons from machine learning. *Perspectives on Psychological Science, 12,* 1100–1122.

Zhu, Y. (2007). Measuring effective data visualization. *Advances in Visual Computing,* 4842, 652–661.

28 Lost In The Crowd

Crowdsourcing as a Research Method

Tara S. Behrend and Daniel M. Ravid

Technology has profoundly changed the way we work. Part of this shift is a change in the way we as behavioral researchers conduct our research. Just as we no longer have to rotate our factor analyses by hand, we no longer have to stand with pen and paper in hand and recruit participants for our surveys when they wander into the lunch room. Technology has given us the power to reach participants we otherwise couldn't. In addition to surveying participants more efficiently by using computers, we can reach new populations using online panel services – a method referred to as crowdsourcing. New questions have arisen about how to properly understand the samples we can now obtain via crowdsourcing. In some cases these questions have been the subject of intense debate and disagreement. In this chapter, we outline some key findings and outstanding questions related to the use of crowdsourcing to conduct behavioral research.

28.1 What is Crowdsourcing?

First coined in 2006 by columnist Jeff Howe in Wired magazine, the term *crowdsourcing* is used to refer to the partitioning of large tasks into small chunks that can be completed by multiple individuals. Although Howe (2006) did not clearly define crowdsourcing when he coined the term, he indicated that it was limited to for-profit businesses making use of the internet workforce. Indeed, crowdsourcing was originally used most commonly for two kinds of tasks – those that were difficult to automate, and those that benefited from many independent judgments (e.g., wisdom of the crowd). However, as the use of crowdsourcing expanded beyond that of for-profit business, the term crowdsourcing evolved to include "the intentional mobilization for commercial exploitation of creative ideas and other forms of work performed by consumers" (Kleemann, Voß, & Rieder, 2008).

Today, crowdsourcing refers to the "distribution of tasks to large groups of individuals via a flexible, open call" (Chandler & Shapiro, 2016). For example, SETI@home can be considered an early form of crowdsourcing. SETI@home was created in 1999 by the Berkeley Space Science Laboratory and operated as a distributed computing network with the purpose of identifying radio signs of extraterrestrial life. SETI@home operated by breaking apart massive amounts of unanalyzed audio telescope data into millions of small "work unit" data chunks, which were then distributed and analyzed by offsite personal computers, with results automatically sent back to a Berkeley mainframe. To help analyze these data chunks, anyone could download the Berkeley Open Infrastructure for Network Computing (BOINC) software program and allow the program to run as a background process which used idle computer power to run the signal analysis. At its peak, SETI@home had almost 200,000 active participants contributing personal computing power to the project. Although SETI@home largely failed to identify signs of extraterrestrial life, it did provide support for the viability of computer-based crowdsourcing projects.

Wikipedia is another not-for-profit crowdsourcing platform. Wikipedia exists as an almost totally open interweb encyclopedia, with web users responsible for creating, editing, and publishing entries. Likewise, each entry has an associated "talk" page where editors can discuss, coordinate, and debate the content of entries. Although restrictions on who is able to edit and create entries on Wikipedia have increased slightly in recent years, the platform continues to rely almost entirely on crowdsourcing to expand, maintain, and update all entries.

Platforms that support gig work, such as on-demand piecework tasks (e.g., TaskRabbit) are also supported by a variety of crowdsourcing services (Kittur et al., 2013) and can be considered crowdsourcing platforms. At the moment, perhaps the most profitable platforms that rely on crowdsourcing are carsharing and driving services (e.g., Uber, Lyft). These carsharing platforms see themselves as digital agents that connect customers and independent contractors (Prassl & Risak 2015), and rely on crowdsourcing for labor.

Although Jeff Howe did not have behavioral research in mind when he coined crowdsourcing as a term, the use of crowdsourcing for research purposes has exploded in popularity among scientists. Crowdsourcing platforms such as Amazon Mechanical Turk allow researchers to cheaply recruit participants and obtain data through the internet with relative ease. Thus, similar to carsharing or gig working platforms, research oriented crowdsourcing platforms exist as a way to connect those in need of human labor (researchers) with those willing to work (participants). As mentioned, understanding participants and samples obtained via crowdsourcing is a topic of much interest within the scientific community. Thus, the scope of this chapter covers the use of crowdsourcing as a tool for behavioral research, as well as the consideration of crowdsourcing workers as a population of interest.

28.1.1 Mechanical Turk

Far and away the most popular among social sciences researchers is a platform developed by Amazon: Mechanical Turk (MTurk). MTurk and similar crowdsourcing platforms have provided social scientists with access to large and diverse participant pools that they would likely not have access to otherwise. However, the widespread use of MTurk to conduct scientific research has also sparked debate about the proper use of MTurk and crowdsourcing as a research tool. Thus, we will focus on discussing MTurk as a primary crowdsourcing tool.

Recent estimates suggest that over 1000 published papers each year use samples derived from MTurk (Litman, Robinson, & Abberbock, 2017). Originally used internally by Amazon to improve its search and organization capabilities (e.g., by labeling images of Amazon products with tags), MTurk is now available to anyone who wishes to use it. Users are either Workers (those completing tasks) or Requestors (those providing tasks). The MTurk platform is structured like a marketplace. Requestors post jobs known as Human Intelligence Tasks (HITs), and Workers can browse among posted HITs and complete them for pay. Workers receive quality ratings based on the proportion of their work that is of high quality. Workers with low ratings may get blocked by Requestors for future studies or have their account suspended by Amazon. Likewise, Workers can also share information about Requestors, via independent web sites and forums as a means of avoiding unfair or low-quality Requesters. Thus, the maintenance of one's reputation should theoretically serve as a motivator for fair tasks from Requesters and good performance by Workers.

Because MTurk was not intended for behavioral research, various awkwardnesses and complications have arisen as researchers have expanded their research methodologies to include this tool. For example, without a knowledge of programming and a substantial time commitment, researchers using MTurk cannot easily communicate with multiple participants at once or set up longitudinal studies. In response, secondary markets have emerged that mean to assist researchers in navigating some of these complications; see for example, TurkPrime (Litman et al., 2017), an internet-based platform that offers participant management and communication services, including "excluding participants on the basis of previous participation, longitudinal studies, making changes to a study while it is running, automating the approval process, increasing the speed of data collection, sending bulk emails and bonuses, enhancing communication with participants, monitoring dropout and engagement rates" (Litman et al., 2017).

Alternative Crowdsourcing Platforms. Although MTurk is by far the most popular crowdsourcing platform for research, in recent years, several alternative crowdsourcing platforms have emerged. Unlike MTurk, many alternative platforms were developed specifically for research purposes, and thus, several of these platforms are able to address potential shortcomings in MTurk. For example, in MTurk, Requesters must design their own custom qualification tests if they desire to screen Workers for certain skills or competencies. On the other hand, Requesters in alternate platforms such as ClickWorker and CrowdFlower can apply skill restrictions to HITs which can be cleared by taking the platform's standardized skill tests. Other alternative platforms such as oDesk and CloudFactory allow Requesters to screen potential Workers via video interview. This ability to more stringently screen potential participants may be particularly useful for researchers interested in recruiting for rare populations, as a recent study showed that when solely relying on participant self-report, a substantial number of MTurk participants misrepresented theoretically relevant characteristics to meet eligibility criteria explicit in studies (Chandler & Paolacci, 2017). Of course, more lenient screening and restrictions for Workers may be one reason why MTurk continues to have the largest and most active participant workforce.

Many alternate platforms also benefit from an increased level of participant naiveté as compared to MTurk participants (Peer et al., 2017; Peer et al., 2016). Although the large participant pool and high activity of Workers on MTurk means studies can be completed very quickly, some worry that participants on MTurk have become over familiar with research manipulations, and this familiarity may affect findings. Indeed, a recent study showed that MTurk user non-naiveté significantly reduced effect sizes of research findings (see Chandler et al., 2015). In comparison, alternative platforms such as MicroWorkers, CrowdFlower, and Prolific Academic possess more naïve Workers (Peer et al., 2017; Peer et al., 2016).

A benefit of MTurk is that because it is so widely used, researchers have spent a great deal of energy examining whether data acquired through MTurk is of high quality (e.g., valid, reliable, generalizable; Behrend et al., 2011; Buhrmester, Kwang, & Gosling, 2011), and have generally found the data is of similar quality to that found in other participant pools such as university students (Casler, Bickel, & Hackett, 2013), particularly when following specific participant screening and selection guidelines (see Chandler & Paolacci, 2017; Keith, Tay, & Harms, 2017). On the other hand, there has been much less research about the quality of data obtained on many other crowdsourcing platforms. There is reason to think, however, that alternate platforms to MTurk may produce comparable quality of data to that found in MTurk. For example, crowdsourcing platforms such as CrowdFlower, MicroWorkers, and Prolific Academic have been shown to produce adequate to high data quality, with Prolific Academic as perhaps the most viable alternative to MTurk (Peer Brandimarte, Samat, & Acquisti, 2017; Peer, Samat, Brandimarte, & Acquisti, 2016). In their study of alternative crowdsourcing platforms, Peer and colleagues found that while users of Prolific Academic did show slightly lower levels of attention as compared to MTurk, this did not significantly affect measures of reliability (Peer et al., 2017). On the other hand, data collected from Prolific Academic showed comparable reproducibility to MTurk data, and users showed a lower propensity to answer questions dishonestly.

Alternate platforms also offer researchers an opportunity to access varying population pools. While the geographic origin of MTurk and Prolific Academic users are mostly US based, Crowd Flower is mainly composed of European users, with relatively little user overlap with other crowdsourcing platforms, and higher ethnic diversity as compared to MTurk and Prolific Academic (Peer et al., 2017).

Thus, although MTurk is the most frequently used crowdsourcing platform, numerous platforms exist today to aid researchers in conducting studies and collecting data through crowdsourcing. Most important for researchers is to review and understand the expectations, procedures, and types of Workers associated with their chosen platform, as this will likely impact data collection methods and impact the data they collect.

28.2 How Does Crowdsourcing Differ from Other Online Panels?

In some ways, MTurk functions similarly to an online panel. Online panels are organized with the explicit intention of generating a pool of participants with known characteristics. Qualtrics, for example, offers access to panels for a price as part of their business model. Researchers can specify the qualifications they require for a given study (e.g., age, gender, language) and the service will share the research opportunity with participants who have been pre-screened on those characteristics. Qualtrics charges a fee, and participants are compensated on a per-survey basis. Google Opinion Rewards is another survey research tool, in which users volunteer to receive survey questions and are free to accept or decline on a per-survey basis. Crowdsourcing services are different in that they are not meant to serve as research tools. Unlike online panels, the particulars of the crowdsourcing population are not totally known to those using crowdsourcing, and users may not always be able to select for a particular characteristic. Thus, despite the similarity between online panels and crowdsourcing, users of each tool may have different expectations about their role and their entitlements in using the service.

28.3 Who are Crowdsourcing Participants?

A great deal of energy has been devoted to understanding the character-istics of people who participate in crowdsourcing, particularly for Workers on MTurk. Early research, which was primarily concerned with whether these samples looked similar to other convenience samples, suggested that there were not mean-ingful demographic differences between MTurk samples and college student samples with respect to political orientation (Berinsky, Huber, & Lenz, 2012), basic biases in decision-making (Paolacci, Chandler, & Ipeirotis, 2010), or Big Five personality characteristics (Behrend et al., 2011), particularly when MTurk samples are restricted to participants in native English-speaking countries (Feitosa, Joseph, & Newman, 2015). On the other hand, MTurk samples were older, more racially diverse, and came from a wide range of industries and socioeconomic backgrounds (Berinsky et al., 2012; Paolacci et al., 2010). Over the last several years, hundreds of investigations have explored this question in more detail, concluding that MTurk samples as a whole are more representative of the popula-tion than are traditional samples in terms of age, gender, income, education levels, and ethnic background (Berinsky et al., 2012; Levay, Freese, & Druckman, 2016).

That being said, MTurk samples do consistently differ from the general popula-tion in some clear and distinct ways. For example, MTurk Workers tend to be younger on average than the general population, and tend to have lower average incomes, higher average education levels, and are less religious (Berinsky et al., 2012; Shapiro, Chandler, & Mueller, 2013). MTurk samples also tend to be less racially diverse than the general population, with black and Latino Workers particularly underrepresented (Roulin, 2015). On the other hand, a growing number of MTurk users are based in India, with a 2010 study finding that Indian MTurk Workers may make up as much as 34 percent of Workers (Ipeirotis, 2010). A large majority of MTurk Workers are drawn from urban areas, with one study finding that only 10 percent of Workers live in rural loacations (Huff & Tingley, 2015). When it comes to political ideology, MTurk samples typically consist of more Democrats and lean more liberal than the general population (Levay et al., 2016). While early studies of MTurk found that sample pools were often predominated by female Workers (Paolacci et al., 2010), more recent studies have found approximately equal representation of men and women (Chambers, Nimon, & Anthony-McMann, 2016; Huff & Tingley, 2015). It is important to note however, that demographic makeup of MTurk workers is confounded by country, with US-based Workers tending to be more heavily female, and non-US workers tending to be male (Harms & DeSimone, 2015).

As far as what industries are represented, a study of over 1,000 US-based MTurk Workers found that the top three industries for MTurk Workers were informational technology (16.1 percent), arts/entertainment (12.2 percent), and finance (12.2 percent; Harms & DeSimone, 2015). This makeup varies quite drastically from that of the general population, with the US Census reporting that informational technology, arts/entertainment, and finance makeup 2.6 percent, 2.0 percent, and 5.1 percent of the workforce, respectively. MTurk workers are also much more likely to be unemployed than the general population (Keith & Harms, 2016). While, the nonrepresentational industry makeup MTurk participant pool may pose a challenge for some researchers, it does present an opportunity for researchers who wish to study certain specific industries such as the arts, or participants who are unemployed.

It is hard to estimate exactly how large the MTurk Worker population is at any moment, as Workers are constantly entering and exiting the pool (Huff & Tingley, 2015), and Workers may be active and then inactive for intermittent stretches. A 2015 World Bank report estimated that MTurk had about half a million registered Workers worldwide, but not all of them were active (Kuek et al., 2015). On the other hand, a separate 2015 study that used capture-recapture analysis, a method often used in ecology and epidemiology, estimated that the average lab is sampling from about 7,300 active Workers, only a few times larger than typical university pools (Stewart et al., 2015).

Although MTurk Workers are paid to complete tasks, pay is not necessarily always the sole or even primary motivator. A 2011 survey asked MTurk Workers to rate the importance of five motivations for using MTurk: (1) to kill time, (2) to make money, (3) to have fun, (4) to enjoy doing interesting tasks, and (5) to gain self-knowledge (Buhrmester et al., 2011). On average, MTurk Workers responded that enjoyment was the most important motivator, followed by killing time and having fun. Making money was rated as the fourth most important motivator of the five choices. Other studies have found that financial incentives may be the primary motivator for a majority of MTurk users, but with a sizable minority reporting alternative primary motives such as curiosity or fun (Behrend et al., 2011, Hitlin, 2016).

Likewise, among active MTurk Workers, there is a high degree of variance in hours spent working. In a 2010 survey approximately 20 percent of Workers reported spending two or less hours per week on MTurk (Ipeirotis, 2010). On the other hand in the same survey, close to 15 percent of Workers reported spending 20 or more hours on MTurk each week. In a separate study, a little under 25 percent of Workers said they spent ten or less hours per month on MTurk, while about 5 percent reported spending over eighty hours per month on MTurk (Behrend et al., 2011). Thus, certain groups of Workers may account for a disproportionate amount of HITs. This is an important point for researchers using MTurk or other crowdsourcing platforms to understand. Although MTurk has been shown to have a reasonably diverse Worker pool, if a small group of Workers are indeed accounting for a disproportionate amount of hits, it may mean that researchers are over-sampling a particular group of individuals who have free time (20+hours/week) to dedicate to MTurk. Future efforts should be taken to understand who these high workload Workers are, and how they may be affecting the data or conclusions for a given study.

28.4 What Challenges Exist When Using Crowdsourcing for Research?

Because crowdsourced participants are distant and anonymous, questions about their trustworthiness are natural. Concerns about participant motivation, honesty, and identity are raised frequently by critics of this kind of sample. Landers and Behrend (2015) outlined four primary challenges that face researchers who wish to use crowdsourcing for research purposes: repeated participation, motivation and pay, selection bias, and relevance. A fairly large literature base exists that has explored some of these questions, detailed in the following sections.

Sampling/Repeat Participation. Some debate exists about the total size of the MTurk population, as well as the effective size of active users who complete most HITs. This information is important for a few reasons – first, if the population is very small, it is more likely to be unusual in some way that affects research conclusions. Speculation that MTurk users are more antisocial, or computer-savvy, or more money-conscious, for example, would be of more concern if the population were small and range-restricted on these variables. A second reason to be concerned about the population size is that a small population suggests that the same individuals are being sampled many times. Because most statistics assume independence of observations, a single individual making their way into the same study multiple times would be a significant problem. The same individuals showing up in separate but related studies would also be of concern if those studies were later included in meta-analytic research synthesis efforts. One thorough investigation of this problem found that the top 1 percent of the most active users were responsible for 11 percent of the HITs and that the top 10 percent were responsible for 41 percent of the HITs completed on the service (Chandler, Mueller, & Paolacci,

2014). The website Deneme (2009) reports that the top 22 percent of Turkers were responsible for 80 percent of HITs.

Honesty. Some researchers (e.g., Chandler & Paolacci, 2017), have presented evidence that MTurk Workers are not always honest in their responses to questions. This is not a concern that is unique to MTurk; clinical researchers have expressed this concern when recruiting participants who volunteer for multiple studies and lie about the screening criteria in order to be eligible for a greater number of studies (Devine at al., 2013). Nonetheless, concerns about the honesty of MTurk participants remain. Feitosa et al. (2015) estimated that somewhere between 5 and 10 percent of participants claiming to be from the US were actually from India or another country. Other studies of participant honesty have also identified this issue (e.g., Berinsky et al., 2012; Rand, 2012). There is indeed a subset of MTurk users who will say and do whatever they think is needed for a task, rather than respond honestly. These users might share information about pre-screening questionnaires in order to "pass" and become eligible for the study. For instance, users may test out the pre-screening questions many times to figure out the "correct" configuration (e.g., females under age 40) and then share that information with others, who can present themselves as females under 40. Researcher diligence is needed in order to encourage honest responses. Monitoring online discussions about the HIT can identify potential issues. Pre-screening questions can be concealed within bigger questionnaires. The wisest option, however, might be to permit all users to complete the questionnaire and pay them accordingly, and then conduct data screening afterwards. While this method is more expensive, it makes it more likely that the people in the sample are responding honestly about their characteristics.

Participant Motivation, Effort, and Attention. Critiques about the internal validity of MTurk samples are common. Specifically, some have expressed worry that inattentiveness or insufficient effort may act to compromise the internal validity of data (Cheung et al., 2017). A related concern has to do with whether participants are devoting sufficient effort to reading, understanding, and responding. For example, Rand (2012) reported that 4 percent of participants reported different genders across two studies.

Feitosa and colleagues (2015) used two quality control items and ended up screening out approximately 9 percent of their sample. A more recent study used extreme scores on self-reported psychopathology scales to remove 10 percent of participants (Shapiro et al., 2013). These concerns are in line with a larger worry that the absence of controls regarding the settings in which Workers complete studies may introduce extraneous factors that may too affect internal validity (Cheung et al., 2017).

Generalizability. Critiques about the external validity or generalizability of MTurk are also common. Generally, the question concerns whether MTurk Workers are similar enough to serve as proxies for Workers within traditional organizations, which are the typical domain of I-O psychology researchers. Others have wondered if there might be some characteristic of MTurk Workers that that differentiate them from non MTurk Workers (Cheung et al., 2017) Landers and Behrend (2015) encourage researchers to use reason and logic when selecting a sample. Of special concern is whether some characteristic of the sample is expected to correlate with study outcomes and predictors; if so, the model may be biased due to omitted variable effects (Meade, Behrend, & Lance, 2009). In order to determine whether some characteristic of an MTurk sample is problematic, explore prior theory and identify related constructs in the broader nomological net of all constructs being studied. Specifically, Landers and Behrend (2015) recommend:

1. Identify any variables in the target convenience sample that are likely to be range restricted or have an atypical mean at both the level of the study (e.g., individual, team) and above it (e.g., team, organization, industry, nation). In organizational samples, researchers should consider existing selection systems, organizational culture (including leadership), and the industry/work domain, in particular.
2. Decide if prior theory suggests any interactions between any variable within the nomological net of the study's constructs and the characteristics of the sample.
3. Consider all potential trade-offs as a result of these interactions and choose the sample that best addresses stated research questions. Unless probability sampling, there will always be tradeoffs.
4. Describe all of this reasoning in any submitted paper.

From this discussion, it is clear that sampling issues cannot be solved with simple rules of thumb or yes/no dichotomies. Rather, the appropriateness of an MTurk sample depends on the research question and research goals. For many research questions, the fact that MTurk Workers are not employed in traditional organizations makes them poor proxies for organization members. For other research questions, this is not a concern.

28.5 Using MTurk

What is clear to this point is that there are many concerns and considerations for those who wish to use crowdsourcing platforms such as MTurk as a research tool. Despite this, crowdsourcing has proven to be an invaluable research tool with many emerging solutions to help manage and mitigate these concerns. Next, we discuss some important considerations when using crowdsourcing for research that can promote better data gathering processes and better data quality.

Pay. For many researchers, the question of how much to pay MTurk Workers is the most vexing. In MTurk's infancy, one primary attraction was the very low cost compared with other convenience sampling alternatives. In 2008, a ten-minute task paying less than five cents was not unusual – an effective hourly wage of 30 cents, nowhere near an acceptable way to earn a living. It can be inferred that Workers during this period were willing to work for such low pay because they (a) had no other options, (b) did the tasks for fun and not to earn money, or (c) were able to complete the tasks much more quickly than the time estimates generated by Requestors. As the market evolved, however, more Workers began to see MTurk as primarily a money-making endeavor and one for which they should be paid like employees, e.g., following the standards for minimum wage. A number of initiatives have emerged to lobby for Worker rights to fair pay and to avoid what have been termed sweatshop-like conditions. Dynamo (wearedynamo.org) is among the most commonly referenced organizations for this purpose, recommending a standard "wage" of $6/hr. It is worth noting however that pay decisions can lead to a number of unintended consequences. For example, higher-paying HITs tend to attract more experienced Workers, according to one recent investigation (Casey et al., 2017). It could also be argued that treating MTurk Workers like employees is not wise for scientific reasons. Our recommendation is to weigh pay decisions carefully, acknowledging that there does indeed exist a power differential between Requestors and Workers, and that the power should not be used to exploit participants. At the same time, paying very high wages might not be advisable either.

Logistics. As mentioned earlier in the chapter, although MTurk is widely used by social science researchers, the platform was not originally designed with social scientists in mind, and as consequence, many common research tasks can be unintuitive, time-consuming, or difficult to implement. As result, a number of external resources exist to assist social science researchers who wish to use MTurk as research tool. For example, Turkgate is a program that can be downloaded and installed on a web server with a database management system, and is designed to group HITs together such that participants may only access one HIT per group. In this way, researchers are able to exclude participants who have already participated in related studies. Turkgate completion codes also allow experimenters concerned about anonymity to verify participation without using response IDs as completion codes. Because Turkgate can require some administration such as updating versions or setting up database backups, it is most commonly used by laboratories or departments where an IT professional or computer savvy member can maintain it.

Likewise, as already noted, TurkPrime is an internet-based platform that integrates with MTurk and is designed to give researchers greater control over HITs. TurkPrime is able to assist MTurk users in speeding up data collection, conducting longitudinal studies, verifying participant country and state locations, sending bulk emails and bonuses to participants, excluding participants on the basis of previous participation, making changes to a study while it is running, and monitoring dropout and engagement rates.

In addition to external platforms designed to optimize the functionality of MTurk, subreddits (internet discussion boards) and blog forums such as MTurkCrowd.com and ExperimentalTurk.Wordpress.com exist as resources where researchers using MTurk can connect, pose questions, and be kept up to date on the latest research on MTurk. Researchers can also look to books (e.g., Sheehan & Pittman, 2016), articles (e.g., Alonso & Lease, 2011; Mason, Suri,

2011), e-manuals (e.g., Amazon.com, 2017), and YouTube tutorials (e.g., Baobao Zhang, 2014), as resources to help guide them in the use of MTurk.

28.6 Considering Crowdsourcing Participants as Workers

Since the inception of crowdsourcing, questions have been raised about the motivation of people who participate in crowdsourced tasks. The amount of money earned is often small. The work is not generally very interesting. Some early writing equated MTurk with "clipping coupons" – i.e., not a way to make a living, but a way to earn a few extra dollars here and there. As the marketplace evolves, questions about motivation remain. Further, we have begun to ask questions about whether Workers in this system behave like traditional workers, and whether our models of work motivation, commitment, and engagement can apply to this context. One useful analogy might be the classic literature on piecework (Alkhatib, Bernstein, & Levi, 2017). Another may be the literature on nonstandard and temporary workers (e.g., Ashford, George, & Blatt, 2007).

Workers Rights. Crowdsourcing workers are classified by law as independent contractors as opposed to employees. In many ways this makes sense, as workers are afforded many of the flexibilities that often characterizes independent contractors. Workers are able to decide when to work, where to work, how often to work, and for how long they want to work. Workers are also able decide which tasks to accept and which to reject. At the same time, the level of worker control by crowdsourcing platforms can be quite significant and is unusual in the traditional contractor-contractee relationship (Prassl & Risak 2015). Crowdsourcing platforms often set wages, as well as specify, and sometimes supervise, how work is to be done. Worker conditions are generally poor, with a lack of union representation or organizing power and relatively few platforms for certain kinds of tasks resulting in very little bargaining power for workers. This lack of bargaining power has resulted in heavily slanted terms and conditions in platform agreements, and generally very low wages (Williamson, 2016). It is not surprising then that a district judge tasked with deciding worker status in a case dealing with crowdsource workers commented that the decision was like:

> "being handed a square peg and asked to choose between two round holes. The test the ... courts have developed over the 20th Century for classifying workers isn't very helpful in addressing this 21st century problem. Some factors point in one direction, some point in the other, and some are ambiguous." (*Cotter v. Lyft*, 2015)

Supports for Workers. In response to Worker vulnerability to exploitation and lack of means to negotiate their rights, several networks and supports have been developed that allow Workers to organize and share information as a means of avoiding overly exploitative work. Turkopticon is a website where Workers can rate Requesters on their communicativity, generosity, fairness, and promptness, write reviews about Requesters, and flag requesters whom they believe have violated the terms of service. Likewise, a number of online forums such as TurkerNation.com and MTurkgrind.com exist where Workers can gather, start discussion threads, ask questions, and post about good and bad HITs and Requestors.

A number of browser extensions/add-ons and scripts that can be downloaded and integrate with the MTurk platform have also been developed for Workers. The Turkopticon extension allows Workers to see Requestor ratings and reviews from the Turkopticon website as they scroll through potential HITs in MTurk. Likewise the Block Requestors script lets Workers block undesired Requestors from search results in MTurk by putting an "x" next to their name, and the Requestor ID script displays requestor ID's in case requesters have changed their name. Other scripts such as the Pending Earnings script, which adds up any pending earnings and displays them on the MTurk dashboard, and the Change Notifier, which shows requester changes to submitted HITs, can make the MTurk platform more functional for frequent Workers.

28.7 Future Directions

Crowdsourcing shows every sign of continuing to grow in popularity, as a means of obtaining research participants and as a means of making a living. Psychological researchers have both the opportunity and the duty to explore the implications of crowdsourcing on individuals, organizations, and society. A number of research directions are outlined in the following section.

Effects of Nonnaivete. A number of investigations have explored the potential consequences that can arise when crowdsourced participants have previous exposure to an experiment. The precise effects of exposure, or nonnaivete, will vary depending on the characteristics of a study. For example, Chandler, Paolacci, Peer, Mueller, & Ratliff (2015) demonstrated that when participants were exposed for a second time to a manipulation in a two-condition experimental study, effect sizes were markedly lower than when they were experiencing the manipulations for the first time. This problem was exacerbated in cases when the participant was assigned to a different manipulation in their second instance of participation. From this study, it becomes clear that controls should be put into place to make sure that participants do not complete the same study twice. But, this advice is obvious. A more tricky problem is when participants are exposed to many independent but similar studies.

Pay and Fairness. To date, researchers have not drawn from the vast literature in distributive and procedural justice to understand Worker reactions to pay. It is likely that Worker reactions depend on their prior expectations, their interest in the task, the way the task was communicated to them, the beliefs they have about what others receive, and many other factors. This information would be useful in guiding researchers who wish to use MTurk samples, but it may also be informative in expanding our theories of pay and justice. This is a unique context and one that may demonstrate boundary conditions which limit the explanatory power of classic theory.

MTurk as a Primary Source of Income. Another under investigated area in the crowdsourcing literature has to do with Workers who depend on the pay provided by MTurk as a primary means of income. One survey found that approximately 14 percent of US-based MTurk Workers reported MTurk as their primary source of income (Paolacci et al., 2010), with a more recent study finding that about 22 percent of MTurk Workers depend on MTurk as a main source of income (Peer et al., 2016). The fact that some MTurk Workers depend on HITs for their livelihood would presumably raise the stakes of completing each research study. Further research is needed to examine this group of Workers, the stress associated with relying on MTurk for income, and any effects on the validity of data produced by these Workers.

Worker/Requestor Relationships. Workers and requestors are not exactly like employees and supervisors. Nor are they exactly like clients and contractors. As such, it is unclear whether existing research on workplace interpersonal dynamics is relevant to this context. It is certainly the case that a Worker might return to complete many HITs for the same requestor. It is also the case that a requestor's reputation can serve as a positive or negative recruiting influence. Still, the peculiarities of these relationships are worth considering carefully.

Flash Organizations. A currently underexplored question has to do with how MTurk and other crowdsourcing Workers, such as those from Upwork, might collaborate with each other to accomplish professional or long-term tasks. Researchers have explored the concept of "flash organizations" in which skilled Workers are assigned to projects based on their skills and reputations (Retelny et al., 2014). Projects include a variety of roles, including management, and might last weeks or months. The concept of a temporary "organization" can be roughly inspired by film crews, military task forces, and other teams that come together for a short time and then disband. The difference here is that when applied to a crowdsourcing platform, the process of searching for skilled Workers, setting pay levels, and rating performance is simplified. Technology also allows for the flattening of hierarchies; every Worker can rate every other Worker's performance, and anyone can be replaced at any time, including Workers assigned to management roles.

28.8 Conclusion

Ultimately, future research will need to answer the question of what exactly crowdsourcing "is." Is it like an organization? Is it like a market? Is it a unique phenomenon? Our organizational theories may or may not apply to this context. If they do or if they don't, the theories will be strengthened by virtue of this exploration. We will identify the boundaries of existing theory, and build new models that help to understand and structure effective crowdsourcing tools.

References

Alonso, O. & Lease, M. (February, 2011). Crowdsourcing 101: Putting the WSDM of crowds to work for you. In *WSDM* (pp. 1–2). New York, NY: ACM.

Alkhatib, A., Bernstein, M. S., & Levi, M. (2017). Examining Crowd Work and Gig Work Through The Historical Lens of Piecework. Paper presented at the Proceedings of the 2017 CHI Conference on Human Factors in Computing Systems, Denver, Colorado, USA.

Amazon.com. (2017). Amazon Mechanical Turk Getting Started Guide, 2017 Retrieved from http://docs.aws.amazon.com/es_es/AWSMechTurk/latest/AWSMechanicalTurkGettingStartedGuide/amt-gsg.pdf.

Ashford, S. J., George, E., & Blatt, R. (2007). 2 old assumptions, new work: The opportunities and challenges of research on nonstandard employment. The Academy of Management Annals, 1(1), 65–117.

Behrend, T. S., Sharek, D. J., Meade, A. W., & Wiebe, E. N. (2011). The viability of crowdsourcing for survey research. *Behavior Research Methods*, *43*(3), 800.

Baobao Zhang. (August 19, 2014). How to launch a survey on Amazon Mechanical Turk (MTurk) [Video file]. Retrieved from www.youtube.com/watch?v=qPcVe4SOmz8.

Berinsky, A., Huber, G., & Lenz, G. (2012). Using Mechanical Turk as a subject recruitment tool for experimental research. *Political Analysis*, *20*, 351–368.

Buhrmester, M. D., Kwang, T., & Gosling, S. D. (2011). Amazon's Mechanical Turk: A new source of inexpensive, yet high-quality, data? *Perspectives on Psychological Science*, *6*, 3–5.

Casey, L. S., Chandler, J., Levine, A. S., Proctor, A., & Strolovitch, D. Z. (2017). Intertemporal differences among MTurk Workers: Time-based sample variations and implications for online data collection. *SAGE Open*, *7*(2), 2158244017712774.

Casler, K., Bickel, L., & Hackett, E. (2013). Separate but equal? A comparison of participants and data gathered via Amazon's MTurk, social media, and face-to-face behavioral testing. *Computers in Human Behavior*, *29*(6), 2156–2160.

Chambers, S., Nimon, K., & Anthony-McMann, P. (2016). A primer for conducting survey research using MTurk: Tips for the field. *International Journal of Adult Vocational Education and Technology (IJAVET)*, *7*(2), 54–73.

Chandler, J., Mueller, P., &Paolacci, G. (2014).Nonnaiveté among Amazon Mechanical Turk Workers: Consequences and solutions for behavioral researchers. *Behavioral Research*, *46*, 112–130.

Chandler, J. J. & Paolacci, G. (2017). Lie for a dime: When most prescreening responses are honest but most study participants are impostors. Social Psychological and Personality Science, 8, 500–508. doi: 10.1177/1948550617698203.

Chandler, J., Paolacci, G., Peer, E., Mueller, P., & Ratliff, K. A. (2015). Using nonnaive participants can reduce effect sizes. *Psychological Science*, *26*, 1131–1139. doi:10.1177/0956797615585115

Chandler, J. & Shapiro, D. (2016). Conducting clinical research using crowdsourced convenience samples. Annual Review of Clinical Psychology, *12*. 53–81. doi: 10.1146/annurev-clinpsy-021815-093623.

Cheung, J. H., Burns, D. K., Sinclair, R. R., & Sliter, M. (2017). Amazon Mechanical Turk in organizational psychology: An evaluation and practical recommendations. *Journal of Business and Psychology*, *32*(4), 347–361.

Cotter v. Lyft, Inc., 60 F. Supp. 3d 1067, 1081–82 (ND Cal. 2015).

Devine, E. G., Waters, M. E., Putnam, M., Surprise, C., O'Malley, K., Richambault, C., ... & Streeter, C. (2013). Concealment and fabrication by experienced research subjects. Clinical Trials, 10(6), 935–948.

Deneme. (December 21, 2009). Deneme: A blog of experiments on Amazon Mechanical Turk. http://groups.csail.mit.edu/uid/deneme/?p=523.

Feitosa, J., Joseph, D., & Newman, D. (2015). Crowdsourcing and personality measurement equivalence: A warning about countries whose primary language is not English. *Personality and Individual Differences*, *75*, 47–52.

George, E., & Ng, C. K. (2010). *APA Handbook of Industrial and Organizational Psychology*. APA.

Harms, P. D., & DeSimone, J. A. (2015). Caution! MTurk workers ahead—Fines doubled. Industrial and Organizational Psychology, 8(2), 183–190.

Hitlin, P. (2016). Research in the crowdsourcing age, a case study. Retrieved from http://assets.pewresearch.org/wpcontent/uploads/sites/14/2016/07/PI_2016.07.11_Mechanical-Turk_ FINAL.pdf.

Howe, J. (2006). Crowdsourcing: a definition. Wired Blog Network: Crowdsourcing. Retrieved September 2018, from http://crowdsourcing.typepad.com/cs/2006/06/crowdsourcing_a.html

Huff, C., & Tingley, D. (2015). "Who are these people?" Evaluating the demographic characteristics and political preferences of MTurk survey respondents. Research & Politics, 2(3), 2053168015604648.

Ipeirotis, P. (2010). Demographics of Mechanical Turk [Working Article]. New York University. Retrieved from www.archive.nyu.edu/bitstream/2451/29585/2/CeDER-10-01.pdf.

Keith, M. G. & Harms, P. D. (2016). Is Mechanical Turk the answer to our sampling woes?. *Industrial and Organizational Psychology*, *9*(1), 162–167.

Keith, M. G., Tay, L., & Harms, P. D. (2017). Systems perspective of Amazon Mechanical Turk for organizational research: Review and recommendations. *Frontiers in Psychology*, *8*, 1359.

Kittur, A., Nickerson, J. V., Bernstein, M., Gerber, E., Shaw, A., Zimmerman, J.,... Horton, J. (2013). The future of crowd work. Paper presented at the Proceedings of the 2013 conference on Computer supported cooperative work.

Kleemann, F., Voß, G. G., & Rieder, K. (2008). Un(der)paid innovators: The commercial utilization of consumer work through crowdsourcing. *Science, Technology & Innovation Studies*, *4*(1), 5–26.

Kuek, S. C., Paradi-Guilford, C., Fayomi, T., Imaizumi, S., Ipeirotis, P., Pina, P., & Singh, M. (2015). *The global opportunity in online outsourcing*. Washington, DC: The World Bank. Retrieved from http://documents.worldbank.org/curated/en/138371468000900555/The-global-opportunity-in-online-outsourcing.

Landers, R. & Behrend, T. (2015). An inconvenient truth: Arbitrary distinctions between organizational, Mechanical Turk, and other convenience samples. Industrial and Organizational Psychology: Perspectives on Science and Practice, 8(2), 142–164.

Levay, K. E., Freese, J., & Druckman, J. N. (2016). The demographic and political composition of Mechanical Turk samples. *Sage Open*, *6*(1),1–17.

Litman, L., Robinson, J., & Abberbock, T. (2017). Behavior Research Methods, 49(2), 433–442.

Mason, W. & Suri, S. (2011). Conducting behavioral research on Amazon's Mechanical Turk. Behavioral Research, 44, 1–23.

How, I., Meade, A. W., Behrend, T. S., & Lance, C. E. (2009). Dr. StrangeLOVE, or: How I learned to stop worrying and love omitted variables. In C. E. Lance & R. J. Vandenberg (Eds.), *Statistical and methodological myths and urban legends: Doctrine, verity and fable in the organizational and social sciences* (pp. 89-106). New York, NY: Routledge/Taylor & Francis Group.

Paolacci, G., Chandler, J., & Ipeirotis, P. G. (2010). Running experiments on Amazon Mechanical Turk. *Judgment and Decision Making, 5,* 411–419.

Peer, E., Samat, S., Brandimarte, L.,& Acquisti, A. (2016). Beyond the Turk: An Empirical Comparison of Alternative Platforms for Crowdsourcing Online Behavioral Research (May 1, 2016). Retrieved from SSRN. https://ssrn.com/abstract=2594183 or http://dx.doi.org/10.2139/ssrn.2594183.

Peer, E., Brandimarte, L., Samat, S., & Acquisti, A. (2017). Beyond the Turk: Alternative platforms for crowdsourcing behavioral research. *Journal of Experimental Social Psychology, 70,* 153–163.

Prassl, J. & Risak, M. (2015). Uber, Taskrabbit, and Co.: Platforms as ezmployers – Rethinking the legal analysis of crowdwork. *Comparative Labor Law & Policy, 37,* 619.

Rand, D. (2012). The promise of Mechanical Turk: How online labor markets can help theorists run behavioral experiments. *Journal of Theoretical Biology, 299,* 172–179.

Retelny, D., Robaszkiewicz, S., To, A., Lasecki, W. S., Patel, J., Rahmati, N.,. . . Bernstein, M. S. (2014). Expert crowdsourcing with flash teams. Paper presented at the Proceedings of the 27th annual ACM symposium on User interface software and technology.

Roulin, N. (2015). Don't throw the baby out with the bathwater: Comparing data quality of crowdsourcing, online panels, and student samples. *Industrial and Organizational Psychology, 8*(2), 190–196.

Shapiro, D., Chandler, J., &Mueller, P. (2013). Using Mechanical Turk to study clinical populations. *Clinical Psychological Science, 1,* 213–220.

Sheehan, K. & Pittman, M. (2016). *Amazon's Mechanical Turk for academics: The HIT handbook for social science research.* Irvine, CA: Melvin & Leigh.

Stewart, N., Ungemach, C., Harris, A. J., Bartels, D. M., Newell, B. R., Paolacci, G., & Chandler, J. (2015). The average laboratory samples a population of 7,300 Amazon Mechanical Turk Workers. *Judgment and Decision making, 10*(5), 479.

Williamson, V. (2016). On the ethics of crowdsourced research. *PS: Political Science & Politics, 49*(1), 77–81

29 Research in the Era of Sensing Technologies and Wearables

Markus Langer, Marianne Schmid Mast, Bertolt Meyer, Wolfgang Maass, and Cornelius J. König

29.1 Introduction

F. is a participant in a psychological experiment in which F.'s behavior is monitored the entire day. F. is wearing a smartwatch, a sociometric badge, and is carrying a smartphone. At the end of the day, these devices relay the data back to the experimenters. The experimenters know with whom F. interacted, who F. called, where F. has been, how F. had felt during the night, etc. Remember the days when participants kept track of their own behavior via diary studies?

In another experiment, V. and L. are negotiating and two cameras are recording their interaction. During the experiment, the experimenters know in real time when one of the two people smiled and when the negotiation got heated. After the interaction, the experimenters obtain an automatic evaluation of the participants' nonverbal behavior showing that L. smiled back at V. most of the time. Remember the days when student assistants had to watch recordings of interactions and manually code smiling and other behavior?

These two examples illustrate that in the near future, novel sensing devices and analysis possibilities offer great opportunities for social scientists to examine individuals, dyads, or groups. As sensing technologies can collect data more efficiently, soon, there might be no need for participants to self-report their own behavior, thoughts, or emotions or for a small army of student assistants to manually code videos. Additionally, machine learning algorithms and other approaches will facilitate automatic sense making and coding of data (Schmid Mast Gatica-Perez, Frauendorfer, Nguyen, & Choudhury, 2015), thus supporting or replacing manual coding and offering novel insights for research.

The aim of this chapter is to illustrate a variety of sensor devices and point out their potential for researchers, especially for social scientists. We propose that these devices add value for hypotheses testing as they provide additional sources of information over and above common data collection possibilities (e.g., self-report questionnaires). Therefore, in the first section, we present selected sensor devices and preconditions for their usage. In the second, third, and fourth sections we discuss what these sensor devices offer for laboratory and field research on individuals, dyads, and groups. To illustrate possible research, readers will find

Research Example Boxes where we present research and first-hand experience with sensor devices used for scientific and practical purposes. In the fifth section, we illustrate possible challenges related to the use of sensor devices like data quality, privacy concerns, and the fact that sensor devices likely deliver big data. The last section provides a conclusion and an outlook for the future of sensor-based research.

29.2 Sensors and Data Collection

All sensors are similar in that they can measure physical, biological, or chemical properties of the environment. This way, one can sense and measure behavior of individuals in the environment. For example, a microphone senses sound waves and translates them into an electric signal; this signal can then be processed and stored on a computer. In addition, researchers can use this data to recognize words or vocal features (e.g., voice pitch), and – based on this data – infer constructs like personality (Batrinca Mana, Lepri, Pianesi, & Sebe, 2011), romantic intentions (Ranganath, Jurafsky, & McFarland, 2013), or job performance (Schmid Mast Frauendorfer, Nguyen, Gatica-Perez, Choudhury, & Odobez, 2017).

Nowadays, sensors are ubiquitously available in everyday technology devices; Table 29.1 presents a (non-exhaustive) list of current sensor devices and exemplifies data gathering options available through these devices. Although there are additional sensor devices that could be covered by this chapter (e.g., eye tracker; for an excellent introduction to the eye tracking methodology see Duchovski, 2007), we selected these six sensor devices because of their largely unexplored potential for social science research purposes (and because of our own familiarity with these devices). The reader should keep in mind that sensor devices consist of one or more sensors: for instance, microphones are sensors themselves, but they can also be part of other sensor devices (e.g, smartphones). Nevertheless, we will discuss microphones and smartphones separately, focusing on different aspects and use cases. Readers should thus be aware that all the aspects discussed of microphones also apply to other sensor devices that include microphones.

Sensor devices are interesting tools that may advance research. First and foremost, sensor devices can offer novel perspectives regarding hypotheses testing. They provide data that could be used as predictors and as dependent variables, and this way they can offer additional and possibly more objective sources of data above and beyond self-report and observer data, potentially strengthening robustness and implications of research results. Second, they collect data automatically, drastically reducing the cost of observational studies. Third, they can be non-obtrusive such that participants might not even notice that data collection through sensor devices is happening. Fourth, sensor devices are able to capture everyday behavior more easily over long periods of time so researchers do not have to rely entirely on participants observing and reporting their own behavior. Fifth, sensor devices can provide a great variety of different kinds of data. For instance, they can collect audio, video, health, movement, or location data. Sixth, in the area of scientific research, it is important to note that these devices are not necessarily

Table 29.1 *List of sensor devices presented in this chapter, generated data, and possible research directions*

Device (including sources of information regarding their use)	Data	Possible research directions
External sensors		
Depth cameras (e.g., Kinect®, RealSense®; Baur et al., 2013; Wagner et al., 2013)	3-D videos and pictures of participants	Laboratory studies; nonverbal behavior detection (e.g., smiling), observing dyadic interactions, navigation, spatial cognition studies, field studies
Microphones (Boersma & Van Heuven, 2001; Eyben et al., 2016)	Voice recordings	Laboratory studies; paraverbal behavior detection (e.g., participants' voice features like speech rate), language and word analysis, field studies
Body-worn sensors		
Electronically Activated Recorder (EAR; Mehl, 2017; Mehl et al., 2001)	Ambient sound recordings during participants' day	Field studies; health research, stress research, diary studies
Vital sensors (e.g., smart watches [e.g., Apple Watch] and fitness tracker [e.g., Fitbit Charge HR]; Wallen et al., 2016)	Biometric data (e.g., heartrate, pulse, body temperature, electrodermal activity)	Laboratory and field studies; health research, stress research, sports research
Sociometric badges (Olguín & Pentland, 2007)	Movement, conversational time, proximity measure to other people, vocal features, body motion	Field research on group processes
Smartphones (Damian, Baur, & André, 2016; Damian, Dietz et al., 2016; Miller, 2012)	e.g., GPS, movement, voice, air pressure, temperature (list extendable as smartphones are flexible in adding more sensors)	Field studies; diary studies, health research, stress research

expensive. For example, the Microsoft Kinect Xbox One® camera (Microsoft Corporation, 2015) is available for around 100 USD.

These points highlight the viability of employing sensor devices in social science research and the possibilities for gaining new insights that might not be possible otherwise. In the following, we discuss two external sensor devices (i.e., depth cameras, and microphones) and four body-worn sensor devices (i.e., the electronically activated recorder, smartphones, vital sensors, and sociometric badges), and describe preconditions and advantages of their use for research.

29.2.1 Using Sensor Devices for Research

29.2.1.1 External Sensors

The first external sensor device we would like to discuss are depth cameras like Microsoft's Kinect® (Microsoft Corporation, 2015) or Intel's® RealSense™ (Intel, 2018) camera. These cameras were developed for gaming purposes and are cheap and user-friendly. They are stationary which makes them less appropriate for any setting requiring mobility of the data collection device. Therefore, depth cameras might rather be useful to support laboratory research on individuals and dyads. It is important to note that the IPhone X includes a depth camera (Apple, 2018), so in future the aforementioned restriction might not apply any more. In general, depth cameras can provide videos of participants, enriched with depth information that makes these videos interpretable in three dimensions. This data can be especially valuable for researchers interested in nonverbal behavior, emotions, and affective reactions, as well as dyadic interactions.

Stand-alone depth cameras without any additional software do not provide any more information than a video. However, such cameras sometimes come with their own data analysis software (e.g., the Kinect® Software Development Kit; Microsoft, 2017) that can detect some nonverbal behavior (e.g., smiling) in captured videos, but users still have to possess some computer skills to access this data, and to extract data that fits their research questions. Due to the fact that many researchers have asked themselves how they can adapt such cameras for their own research, there are research frameworks available for gathering data with depth cameras. Indeed, several research frameworks facilitate data collection not only with depth cameras but with multiple sensor devices. For instance, the Social Signal Interpretation Framework (SSI; Wagner Lingenfelser, Baur, Damian, Kistler, & André, 2013) incorporates a variety of frameworks to detect nonverbal and paraverbal behavior (e.g., PRAAT [the dutch word for speak] to detect voice features, OpenFace to detect facial behavior; Baltrušaitis, Robinson, & Morency, 2016). A great advantage of frameworks like the SSI is that they can synchronize data gathering through different sensors. For instance, they could synchronize depth camera data and vital sensor data (e.g., heart rate) so researchers can match video data with noticeable changes in heart rate. Furthermore, synchronization makes it possible to coordinate two depth cameras and the data they produce (e.g., in a setting in which two people interact face-to-face). This way, emotional expressions in one video can be matched with emotional expressions in the other video (e.g., capturing mimicry behavior). However, researchers need to have computer skills to adapt these frameworks to their own research (for an introduction to and the documentation of the framework SSI see www.hcm-lab.de/projects/ssi/ and Wagner et al., 2013).

Second, collecting audio with microphones can add valuable insights. Microphones might be most interesting for researchers who want to integrate information about participants' verbal and paraverbal behavior into their research. For instance, this might be viable in research regarding stress, dyadic interactions, or human-computer interaction.

The output of microphones themselves is just audio files that might not be especially useful for insight about participants, but with the development of PRAAT, Boersma and Van Heuven (2001) offered an open-source program for processing of phonetics (i.e., everything related to spoken language) that has stimulated a lot of research and practical applications (for an overview of its capabilities see www.fon.hum.uva.nl/praat/). A newer framework for acoustic data which was specifically developed for affective computing research is the Geneva Minimalistic Acoustic Parameter Set (GeMAPS; for an introduction see Eyben et al., 2016). Using PRAAT or GeMAPS, researchers can analyze participants' audio recordings for a vast number of vocal features (e.g., voice pitch, volume, harmonicity, pauses, voicebreaks, jitter, shimmer; for an example see Figure 29.1), and this data can then be used to predict outcomes of interest (e.g., job interview performance, Naim Tanveer, Gildea, & Hoque, 2015; job performance, Schmid Mast et al., 2017; mood, Ellgring & Scherer, 1996; sleepiness, Krajewski & Kröger, 2007; stress, Giddens Barron, Byrd-Craven, Clark, & Winter, 2013).

It is important to note that in studies using microphones, researchers have to be aware of the kind of data they would like to collect as there is a trade-off between data precision and intrusiveness of microphones. For instance, researchers can decide to use a room microphone, which is a non-intrusive tool to capture participants' voice data. However, these microphones will capture noise and echo, therefore potentially undermining reliability and precision of the data. This might sound like a minor issue, since most audio software (e.g., Audacity; Audacity, 2017) is able to reduce noise, but noise reduction can impact recorded vocal features of participants. To illustrate this, imagine a longitudinal study where one of the days during data collection, a window is open. It is likely that the difference in noise would be much different if the window was closed the following day. If recordings are now post-processed using noise reduction, this can lead to different alterations of participants' voice which reduces data reliability. This means that voice recordings of one participant at different days might only differ because of noise reduction instead of events during the day. It is worth mentioning, that environmental sound does not necessarily decrease data quality. In fact, it can also provide insights about contextual information. For instance, this sound can tell a story about where participants were (e.g., in a bar, in the woods) and what they did (e.g., watching a football match, doing sports), which is exactly the rationale behind the Electronically Activated Recorders (EAR; Mehl Pennebaker, Crow, Dabbs, & Price, 2001) sensor device that we describe later.

Figure 29.1 *Output example of a voice analysis with PRAAT within the graphical user interface NovA (The [Non]Verbal Annotator, Baur et al., 2013). In the middle there is the voice activity detection. For instance, it indicates that the person speaks with a voice intensity of 73.140 dB (median) during this specific voice activity (i.e., the person talked for a duration of 2990 milliseconds during this voice activity).*

Another challenge with room microphones occurs when there is more than one person speaking, as people in vocal interactions tend to overlap in their speech. When using room microphones, it is challenging to split up these overlapping parts. Therefore, instead of using external room microphones, it might be a good idea to use body-worn, close-talk microphones for every participant (i.e., microphones that are normally attached to a headset and placed near participants' mouth). These microphones counterbalance the two aforementioned problems, as they usually only record voice of one participant, resulting in an audio trace for every participant, whilst additionally cancelling out noise and all other participants' voices. However, these microphones suffer from another disadvantage: they can make interactions appear to be artificial because most people in face-to-face interactions do not usually wear headsets.

To conclude, if researchers want to use microphones for their purposes, they have to be aware of the data they want to capture. If researchers are especially interested in participants' vocal features and changes in these features, controlled laboratory settings are recommendable to ensure data quality.

29.2.1.2 Body-Worn Sensors

First, Electronically Activated Recorders (EAR; Mehl et al., 2001) are very similar to microphones, however they intentionally capture ambient sound to automatically record participants' daily activities. EARs can be carried in participants' pockets and they record snippets of ambient sound without participants recognizing these recordings (Mehl et al., 2001). These recordings can then be used to evaluate participants' behavior throughout the day. For instance, if TV sound is present on 10 percent of the recordings, this can be interpreted as participants watching TV for 10 percent of the waking day. These measurements could be used as a measurement of participants' behavior during the day in addition to self-report measures where they have to estimate the duration they have engaged in activities like watching TV. Recently, the EAR has also become available as an app (iEAR) for smartphones, so researchers do not need to buy an EAR device but can install the app on participants' smartphones. EARs might be particularly interesting for researchers conducting longitudinal field studies on participants' daily behavior, as they can add valuable information in diary studies (for an introduction to the EAR see Mehl, 2017; Mehl et al., 2001).

Obviously, some concerns pop up when EARs are used for research because there might be situations where participants do not want the device to capture ambient sound, potentially leading to lower compliance and increased perceived obtrusiveness of these sensor devices. Research by the developers of the EAR has shown, though, that the EAR is rated as relatively low in obtrusiveness, and that there is generally a high compliance in studies using it (Mehl & Holleran, 2007). However, another study by Manson and Robbins (2017) had participants wear badges saying "This conversation might be recorded" in order to ensure that interaction partners are also informed about this fact, and found that this increased reported obtrusiveness and decreased compliance. These two studies point to privacy concerns as a potential issue regarding sensor-enhanced research (for a more in-depth discussion on privacy concerns see Section 6 of this chapter and Chapter 25 of this book, Electronic Surveillance and Privacy).

Second, vital sensors are available in different variations and combinations with other sensor devices (e.g., chestbands). These sensors can be medical-grade or consumer-oriented sensors. While medical-grade sensors have been used in laboratory research for years, consumer-oriented sensors that only approximate medical sensors open up new opportunities for research. Due to their low cost, these sensors can be used in laboratory as well as field studies. Medical-grade sensors provide high quality data, whereas consumer-oriented sensors require statistical analysis for extracting data with defined qualities. Vital sensors can be further distinguished into skin sensors and invasive sensors. First, skin sensors have direct skin contact and provide data on electrocardiograms (ECG), electromyogram (EMG), electroencephalogram (EEG), heart rate, heart sounds, blood pressure, body/skin temperature, and skin conductance. Second, invasive sensors are implanted under the skin and on organs, such as heart. They are used for accessing data that are measured by skin sensors with a higher accuracy. Additionally, invasive sensors provide access to blood glucose, oxygen saturation, hormones, and other biological signals (e.g., Pantelopoulos & Bourbakis, 2010). These sensors are equally interesting for laboratory and field research as they are able to provide incremental insights into participants' vital functions during experiments or throughout the day.

It is important to note that although non-medical-grade vital signal sensors can support laboratory research, data quality has to be assessed. For instance, some fitness trackers' step-counting function have been found to accurately count steps but underestimate energy expenditure (e.g., calorie consumption; Noah Spierer, Gu, & Bronner, 2013). Accordingly, when gathering participants' amount of steps during a day, fitness trackers might be viable sensor devices, but not for energy expenditure. As another example, previous research has shown that non-medical-grade heart rate trackers can strongly correlate with medical-grade trackers (Stahl An, Dinkel, Noble, & Lee, 2016), and can therefore be a good alternative to medical-grade trackers (which are usually more expensive). However, this depends on the sensor device. For instance, there is research showing some devices differ significantly from medical grade sensors with increasing heart rate values (Wallen Gomersall, Keating, Wisløff, & Coombes, 2016; Wang, Blackburn, Desai, Phelan, Gillinov, Houghtaling & Gillinov, 2017). It is worth mentioning that developing different kinds of medical and non-medical sensors is a highly active research and business field. This means that the availability and probably also the reliability of vital sensors will continue to grow. For instance, rather novel external sensors try to recognize physical exercises by using sensor mats (Sundholm Cheng, Zhou, Sethi, & Lukowicz, 2014) or attempt to monitor respiratory rates using smart textile clothing (Ciocchetti et al., 2015).

Third, sociometric badges (sometimes called sociometers) are sensor devices designed specifically for social science purposes (for an introduction to sociometric badges see Olguín & Pentland, 2007; and www.hd.media.mit.edu/badges/). Study participants wear these white plastic boxes that are the size of a deck of cards around their neck. These badges were developed at the MIT (Olguín & Pentland, 2007) to measure interactions and behavior.

Regarding the functionality of sociometric badges, they only measure interactions between people who are all wearing them. Specifically, the devices feature two microphones (one pointing upwards, the other to the front), an infrared transmitter and receiver, a Bluetooth transmitter and receiver, and an accelerometer. The devices store the metadata generated by these sensors on a Secure Digital (SD) memory card. In other words, in the default mode, the devices do not record raw audio, but log that the front microphone picked up an audio signal at a certain volume for a certain duration. The infrared beam from the transmitter on the front of the device has a range of about 1.2 meters and a deflection of about 30°; if another device picks it up, this means that the devices were (roughly) face-to-face at a distance of 1.2 meters or less. Similarly, the devices log all Bluetooth contacts to other devices along with signal strength, which is interpreted as proximity. The accelerometer data indicates how much the wearer moved while wearing it, but the devices cannot track exact position or location.

A proprietary software triangulates all log files from all devices that are used in a given study. For each badge, it calculates speaking time of the wearer, verbal interactions with others, face-to-face contacts, and spatial proximities. For speaking, face-to-face contact, and proximity, the software calculates network matrices that can be visualized and analyzed as social networks. While the resulting data is somewhat sparse, researchers can export it to other applications such as R where they can triangulate it with other data (e.g., questionnaires).

These sensors are especially useful for research about interactions between two or more people. For instance, researchers interested in social relations in organizations might find value in the use of sociometric badges.

Fourth, smartphones are the most commonly available sensor devices (Miller, 2012) and they typically contain a large number of sensors. These include cameras, microphones, touch sensors, gyroscopes, a barometer, accelerometers, proximity sensors, and ambient light sensors (Apple, 2018; Samsung, 2017). Furthermore, it is also possible to connect external sensors (e.g., an electrocardiogram, Miller, 2012). It is highly likely that the integration of sensors into smartphones will continue, creating even more possibilities in the future (Miller, 2012). All of this makes smartphones the most flexible sensor device. In future, it is possible that all of the aforementioned functionalities of other sensor devices are integrated into smartphones. For instance, take Apple's Iphone X (Apple, 2018) to support this assumption. It is equipped with a depth camera that is able to recognize faces and emotions, a microphone, it is possible to install the iEAR app on it, vital sensors are integrated and additional external ones can be added, and with some effort it is even conceivable to imitate functionalities of sociometric badges. Up to now, the other sensor devices discussed in this chapter are still useful and may provide more reliable data than similar smartphone sensors, but it is advisable to stay up to date regarding smartphones and their sensor capabilities as they might soon be the sensor device of choice for most research goals.

Since participants are likely to possess a smartphone, they are especially interesting tools for researchers who would like to conduct field studies in longitudinal designs. These devices allow data collection for a long period of time, they are able to report live data to the researchers to supervise potential issues during data collection (e.g., early detection of participants who will drop-out), and they can collect data from multiple sources. The latter fact makes smartphones especially valuable as they can simultaneously integrate data from multiple sensors, and users' self-report data can possibly enrich this data.

Furthermore, most people see their smartphone as a very private and intimate device (Miller, 2012). In smartphone-based research, one assumption is that the latter fact can lead to data that is externally valid as participants carry their smartphone the entire day. Additionally, participants might share sensitive data with their smartphone that they would not share in a questionnaire (Miller, 2012). This might be true as participants may not be consciously aware that their smartphone is capturing data about them the entire day. However, the aforementioned circumstances make it a necessary precondition that participants are willing to share smartphone data for research purposes. For instance, participants need to be willing to install an app that records their data during the day, which, similar to the application of EARs, raises potential privacy concerns necessitating informed consent and potentially leading to issues regarding sensor-enhanced studies.

One crucial precondition of smartphone-based studies is that researchers need to have some kind of data collection tool at hand that they can install on participants' smartphones. There are some commercially available apps for this purpose (e.g., Apple's Research Kit; Apple, 2017), but using commercial products might further increase privacy concerns and they offer limited flexibility in data collection (e.g., non-customizable which sensors to use or which data to gather). An alternative would be to use custom apps developed by researchers to support other researchers with their smartphone-enhanced studies (Oksüz Biswas, Shcherbatyi, & Maass, 2017). An excellent example for such a custom app is the SSJ (see Figure 29.2; Damian, Baur et al., 2016; Damian, Dietz et al., 2016), a graphical user interface for Android smartphones to design social signal processing pipelines (for an introduction to the SSJ app see Damian, Baur, et al., 2016; Damian, Dietz et al., 2016). Such apps provide flexible ways of controlling different smartphone-included sensors, collect data through smartphones, and synchronize this data (i.e., GPS data and accelerometer), but they might require researchers to acquire deeper knowledge on

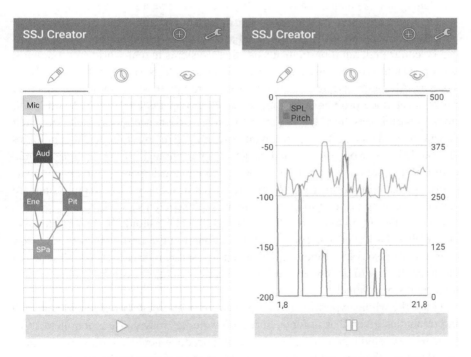

Figure 29.2 *On the left side there is an example pipeline developed with the app SSJ to gather voice data. The top rectangle (Mic) instructs the app to use the microphone sensor. The next rectangle (Aud) indicates to use the audio output of the sensor. The rectangles Ene and Pit tell the app to process the energy level (more precisely sound pressure level [SPL], a measure of the vocal energy) and voice pitch. The last rectangle (SPa) instructs the app to display the vocal features in the graphical output presented on the right side.*

how to use these apps and how to gather data with these apps – support by computer scientists specialized on sensing devices might therefore be helpful. Another option offering most flexibility would be to program a data collection app specifically for the given study, but this requires advanced programing skills. Evidently, researchers who conduct sensor-based studies might consider working together with technical experts, programmers, and computer scientists (this advice is not restricted to smartphone-based studies).

29.2.2 Considerations Regarding the Use of Sensors in Field Settings

The application of sensors in field studies is growing, as we will present in the remainder of this chapter. Nonetheless, leaving the laboratory brings uncertainties and noise into the data. Several constraints need special care in field studies with sensor technologies, such as (a) technical system implementation, (b) reducing intrusiveness, (c) set up and robustness testing of sensor environment as well as training users, (d) managing participants' study related problems (e.g., technical problems), and (e) managing data quality (i.e., real time and periodically).

The first constraint is that most sensor-based systems require permanent or periodic connections with central database systems. In laboratory settings, this can be controlled, but if participants use these systems in real-world environments, sensor systems require mediating technologies such as smartphones and Wi-Fi systems. Although researchers are tempted to provide these technologies, this may cause acceptance problems. For instance, if participants are provided with additional smartphones they are required to carry two smartphones, including their private one. In cases where participants use their own smartphones, technologies are needed that work on a broad range of smartphones otherwise biases could evolve if users of certain smartphone brands cannot participate. Although commercially available platforms (e.g., Apple HealthKit or Google Fit) integrate standard sensors, it can be difficult to integrate more sophisticated sensors.

Second, the set-up of the whole sensor-based service should be as non-intrusive as possible. However, battery power limitations require participants to regularly charge sensors and smartphones, which could possibly induce feelings of burden as participants have to be concerned about the battery status of even more devices than their own smartphone.

Third, the whole experimental setup needs to be thoroughly tested and analyzed in pre-studies given that failures during field studies may cause a complete abortion. As field studies require participants to introduce new technologies into their private lives, they might be concerned about data storage and privacy, but also about handling of the sensor devices. Therefore, detailed planning of instructions for participants and participants' training should be mandatory (e.g., training on how to wear the sensor device and how and when to recharge it).

Fourth, participants during field studies often encounter unanticipated problems that might result in them abandoning the system. Close monitoring of incoming data and contacting participants via established communication channels (e.g., telephone, chat systems, meetings) should help to quickly overcome issues.

Finally and most importantly, study designers should closely assess the quality of incoming data. Data stream break-downs, external effects on data (e.g., environmental noise in microphone-based studies), and interference with other apps are only a few examples of issues that might impact data quality.

In the following sections, we review sensor-enhanced research on individuals, dyadic interactions, and group processes. We discuss findings from laboratory and field research and show how different kind of sensors can be used to generate novel data for innovative research questions.

29.3 Research on Individuals

Researchers typically gather data using questionnaires where they rely on participants' self-reports. However, there are some issues with this kind of data. First, self-reports are subject to biases: participants (a) might answer in a socially desirable way (Podsakoff & Organ, 1986), (b) might fake answers (Ziegler, MacCann, & Roberts, 2011), (c) might employ answer tendencies (e.g., extreme answers; Van Vaerenbergh & Thomas, 2013), (d) sometimes fall for the hindsight bias (Hawkins & Hastie, 1990), (e) can get bored by the questionnaire and just answer randomly (Huang et al., 2012), and (f) might not be aware that they report biased data (Podsakoff & Organ, 1986). These issues are often addressed using multiple observers and raters. However, coding can be hard work and it is likely to be very costly and time consuming to instruct and train raters.

A variety of the aforementioned challenges could be addressed by using sensor devices as an (additional) data source. For instance, sensor devices (e.g., a depth camera) combined with automatic extraction of nonverbal behavior can assist human coders. Once an automatic extraction algorithm is developed, detection of nonverbal behavior occurs much faster and more accurately because there is less observer fatigue influencing coding. An interesting project that aims for the development of exactly such a system to algorithmically support coding of video and audio data is the (Non)Verbal Annotator (NovA; for an introduction, see Baur et al., 2013, and www.informatik.uni-augsburg.de/lehrstuehle/hcm/projects/tools/NovA/). However, it is important to note that automatic extraction algorithms are not necessarily less biased because the data on which the algorithms were trained and validated is based on human coding and thus can still be subject to bias.

Another argument for using sensor devices in research is that for data like health data and vocal features, classical methods (e.g., self-report, observers) offer limited insights into the variety of features that could possibly be evaluated. Certainly, it is possible to ask participants to provide information about their health data (e.g., heart rate) or to instruct observers to assess participants' vocal features (e.g., voice volume), but sensor devices are able to provide a deeper insight into this kind of data.

These are only some reasons why sensor devices can make research on individuals more efficient, objective, and observable. Evidently, all of the aforementioned challenges and advantages that come with sensor-based data also apply to research on dyads and groups. It is important to note that we are not implying that sensor data can or should replace self-report and observational data. Rather, we want to shed light on how using novel perspectives may enhance research, as well as outline the main advantages of sensor devices – data collection and analysis can become more cost and time-efficient.

29.3.1 Laboratory Research on Individuals

To begin with, sensor devices could strengthen conclusions drawn from self-report questionnaires. For instance, in studies investigating stress, participants respond to questionnaires, and they provide information about stressors at work or home. The latter information is then used to provide a source of validity about the stress questionnaire (i.e., if participants report that they had a conflict with customers, the stress questionnaire should show high levels of stress). A possible way to advance this research is to use vocal data as another source of information about participants' stress level, as previous research has shown that vocal features (e.g., voice pitch) can indicate stress (Giddens et al., 2013; Lu et al., 2012).[1] Therefore, data collection by microphones might provide further support for the relationships between self-report stress questionnaires and self-report stressors. Participants reporting higher levels of stress in the stress questionnaire or participants reporting a recent conflict, might also talk with a higher voice pitch (cf., Giddens et al., 2013) in a laboratory interview on their current situation, leading to validity information that does not entirely rely on self-report.

Furthermore, research on nonverbal behavior is another example where sensors will be beneficial. During such research, a depth camera together with adequate software (e.g., NovA; Baur et al., 2013) can support coding. For instance, participants are recorded with the camera whilst watching an advertisement (e.g., to measure the emotional impact of the advertisement). The software can then automatically detect nonverbal behavior of interest (e.g., smiling). Afterwards, raters might only need to look at timestamps where the software recognized nonverbal behavior and indicate that the automatic analysis was correct, making the entire process of coding nonverbal behavior more efficient (c.f., Baur et al., 2013).

Additionally, depth camera video recordings can automatically analyze participants' emotional state. For instance, the framework OpenFace by Baltrušaitis and colleagues (2011) can be applied to automatically evaluate participants' upper body and face for emotional states like sadness and anger with the help of a depth camera. For research purposes, this implies that emotional states could be analyzed from three perspectives (participants self-report, observer ratings, automatic evaluation), potentially increasing the validity of findings. More precisely, researchers can use this data as additional predictors or dependent variables and as a way to come up with new hypotheses. It is important to note that training data that build the data base to develop frameworks comparable to the one from Baltrusaitis

---

[1] These results come predominantly from Western samples; it might be that the relation between vocal features and stress is different in other cultures.

and colleagues (2011) might originate predominantly from Western samples, it is therefore possible that these frameworks will not work equally well in Eastern cultures because of differences in emotional display rules (Matsumoto et al., 2008). It is therefore necessary to clarify in advance on which kind of data these frameworks were trained and validated.

Third, both medical-grade and consumer-grade vital sensors devices can be added to laboratory studies to gather health data. In the case of laboratory studies, vital sensors present a feasible source of additional data since participants can wear them (e.g., on their wrist) during the experiment and an experimental manipulation might also lead to differences in data collected with the vital sensor device. However, vital signal sensors provide data that needs to be mapped to constructs. For instance, it can be argued that heart rate variability data correlates with cognitive stress (McDuff, Gontarek, & Picard, 2014), but clear concept definitions are yet to be defined. This is an important challenge that researchers who use sensor data will likely face – sensor data have to prove that they meet the same psychometrical standards as classical self-report scales (we will discuss this issue in Section 6 of this chapter in more depth).

Fourth, sociometric badges also deliver data on the individual level, namely speaking time and movement (energy). However, used in isolation, sociometric badges are of little use for studies that collect data purely on the individual level.

29.3.2 Field Research on Individuals

Diary studies as classical field research designs are highly complex and rely on participants' commitment (Ohly Sonnentag, Niessen, & Zapf, 2010). Participants need to monitor themselves and they need to remember to make their diary entries (e.g., every day, once a week). Tools simplifying diary studies might be smartphones, microphones, or vital sensors, as they provide constant data flow throughout participants' days.

Smartphones could be used to collect data about every single phone call participants make during the day without the need for participants' involvement. In addition, smartphone GPS data offer detailed information about where participants have been and potentially also what they have done (e.g., if they were shopping or if they were doing sports). A very interesting feature of smartphones is that this sensor data can then be paired with calendar data or with smartphone usage data (e.g., web searches). This way, sensor data can be enriched with contextual data about participants' daily behavior. For instance, during health research, it is important to know why participants' heart rate increased. Calendar information and vital sensors data could allow researchers to know if the increase was because of a stressful meeting at work or because the participant went for a hike (Luxton McCann, Bush, Mishkind, & Reger, 2011).

Other sensors that might be interesting tools to enhance field research are microphones because vocal features can reveal insights into participants' state at the time they recorded their voice (Giddens et al., 2013; Naim et al., 2015). For example, in field research where participants have to monitor their stress over time, participants could report their level of stress every evening after work using a self-report stress questionnaire. In addition, participants record themselves answering to some questions (e.g., "How was your day at work?"). Vocal features (e.g., pitch) could then provide useful insights into participants sleepiness (Krajewski & Kröger, 2007), mood (Ellgring & Scherer, 1996), and stress level (Giddens et al., 2013).

29.4 Research on Dyadic Interactions

Research on dyadic interactions suffers from similar issues that research on individuals does, as data might also be biased through self-report, and gathering observer ratings and coding is very time-consuming. Therefore, sensors can be help to overcome some of these difficulties. In addition, the entire dyadic process is demanding to observe and measure. For instance, it is hard to tell which aspects during dyadic interactions might have caused which effects (e.g., did smiling of one participant cause smiling of the other participant?), when exactly during the interaction do critical events happen that impact the rest of the interaction, or

---

Research Example Box 29.1   Vital Sensor for Health Research

Öksüz and colleagues (2017) used vital signal sensors in a study on obese children. The participants (seven female and thirteen male, aged between 11 and 17 years, BMI between 25 and 37) took part in a fitness test (Eurofit Fitness Testing Battery) plus a run test evaluated by the Dordel-Koch Test before and after a standardized obesity therapy. For every child, number of laps, number of steps during the six-minute run test, the exercise heart rate, as well as the post-exercise heart rate (cool-down period of three minutes) were measured. To measure the heart rate, the participants were equipped with a Scosche Rhythm+ heart rate monitor connected to the Pathmate2 app installed on Android smartphones via a Bluetooth Low Energy (BLE) channel and synchronized with a central server system via a RESTFul API. Heart rate data collection during the EuroFit Fitness Test and the six-minute run test is initiated by pressing a start button on the app. At the end, participants press a second button for starting the cool-down phase. All data is stored and visualized locally. If the internet is available, data is synchronized with the central server system for further analysis. During the study, it became obvious that the cool-down button was activated with a delay. By applying data analytics, turning points of heart rate data were extracted that indicate the beginning of cool-down phases.

Several data analytical processes were applied. For the purpose of predictive analysis, the authors calculated the average heart rate during steady state as the *average heart rate* during the running test (see Figure 29.3). Furthermore, the heart rate difference between the start of the cool down and the average of the last ten values of the cool down was taken as the *heart rate recovery*.

Based on these data features, the number of laps during the six-minute run test have been predicted using the linear regression model Least Absolute Shrinking and Selection Operator (LASSO). The features used to train the model were *BMI, gender, average heart rate* during the running and *heart rate recovery*. The results show that the average difference between the actual number of laps and the number of laps predicted by the model was 2.185 with an overall average error of 7.1 percent. By a second data analytical study, it was found that heart rate data of the six-minute run test plus the cool down data together with abovementioned profile are sufficient to predict positive or negative BMI changes for each participant even before the obesity therapy was applied.

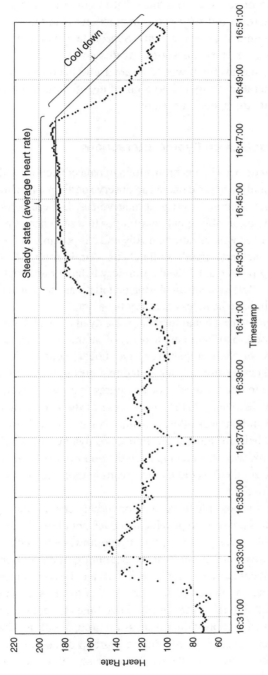

Figure 29.3 *Heart rate during the Fit test*

how does synchronization of nonverbal behavior affect interaction outcomes. For example, participants might be asked to negotiate about the price of a car and some participants agree on the price, whereas others fail to come to an agreement. In hindsight, it might be hard to tell why some interactions resulted in a negative outcome (i.e., failed to come to an agreement). Sensor devices might potentially provide useful data to answer these questions. At this point, we want to mention that it is still necessary to stay aware of what data are useful to collect. For instance, it is unlikely to help generating insights into a failed negotiation if sensor devices only collected data about atmospheric pressure.

29.4.1 Laboratory Research on Dyadic Interactions

A big advantage of sensor devices is synchronization of data collection. In the case of a laboratory negotiation study, a depth camera can observe participants while they are also wearing close-talk microphones to record their voices. If these recordings are synchronized, resulting data can offer great possibilities to researchers. For instance, nonverbal behavior can be recognized automatically and it is possible to see if, during successful negotiations, one participant's smile elicits a smile from the other participant, possibly reflecting participants' dyadic mimicry behavior and rapport building (Chartrand & Bargh, 1999). In contrast, during negotiations that failed to come to an agreement, there might have been less mimicry behavior.

In addition to dyadic nonverbal behavior, analyzing dyadic vocal features can be useful as they are supposed to affect many aspects of interactions without participants being fully aware of their impact (cf., De Looze Scherer, Vaughan, & Campbell, 2014). For instance, research suggested that during interactions, people build rapport by adapting to one another's vocal features (e.g., speech rate, accents; Louwerse Dale, Bard, & Jeuniaux, 2012). In the case of the negotiation scenario where two synchronized audio traces of participants' voices are available, machine learning algorithms can help to unravel the impact of dyadic vocal behavior on negotiation outcomes. This way, researchers have the opportunity to monitor more closely if adapting to one another's vocal features leads to more rapport, which then leads to successful negotiations.

Furthermore, because it is possible to extract nonverbal behavior during a social interaction in real time, it is possible to provide feedback about that behavior while the interaction unfolds. We have yet to explore if and how such feedback affects social interactions. Moreover, we are only at the beginning of discovering how to best provide behavioral feedback (e.g., audio or visual) and how disruptive it is for the social interaction. The following example rather fits to the section on group research, but it shows the potential of sensor-based real time interactional feedback. Several studies have shown that providing discussion groups with feedback about individual group members' speaking time during a group discussion (e.g., using sociometric badges; Kim Chang, Holland, & Pentland, 2008) led to a more egalitarian distribution of speaking time among group members (Kim et al., 2008).

Sociometric badges are also suitable for dyadic research: For a given pair of study participants, the data reveals how much two individuals speak with each other, how much time they spend in proximity of each other, and how much face-to-face contact they have. For example, in a recent study, Cook and Meyer (2017) investigated how leadership perceptions change in teams when the team task changes, and how face-to-face contact moderates this relationship. In other words, they investigated whether participants who perceived another participant as the team leader in a previous task were also inclined to perceive this person as the leader in a new and different task. Using sociometric badges, Cook, Meyer, Gockel, and Zill (in press) found that the relationship between dyadic leadership perceptions across tasks was moderated by face-to-face contact of dyad members. Specifically, team members tended to ascribe leadership in the new task to a fellow team member only if they had had face-to-face contact with that team member.

Sensor data can also be used to make research on human-computer interaction more realistic. For instance, human-computer interaction within simulations, games, or with virtual characters and robots still rely heavily on manual input by the user (e.g., users choose between some textual multiple choice answers). Cameras, microphones, and also vital sensors can provide a less artificial human-computer interaction. For instance, a depth camera could help the computer system to recognize users' nonverbal and paraverbal behavior (cf. Research Example Box 29.2). This information could then be used in real time to let the system respond or even adapt to participants' behavior. The computer system may ask participants questions and they answer through voice input; if the user is silent for a specific amount of time, the computer system asks the next question. This way, virtual reality training as described in Section 3 of this book could also be advanced. Another example might be a computer system that recognizes nodding and smiling as a method of participants' rapport building. In this case, if participants smile at a virtual character, the character can smile back, which could lead to improved user experience and evaluations of the computer system. Many novel research questions arise through these possibilities. For instance, how do participants react to virtual characters' mimicking their behavior (e.g., virtual agent scratching its head if participants are scratching their head), or which sensors are especially useful to generate realistic human-computer interactions? Regarding the latter question, an exciting direction for future research would be to use data from vital sensors to influence human-computer interaction. For instance, participants' heart rate or electrodermal activity during interactions with robots could be measured to assess participants stress levels during the interaction, which then again might provide information about how to improve features of the robots that have caused increased stress levels (e.g., strange behavior of the robot, cf., Mori, 1970; Mori, MacDorman, & Kageki, 2012).

29.4.2 Field Research on Dyadic Interactions

Dyadic field research could also be enhanced with sensor data. In the case of phone, videoconference, or digital interviews for personnel selection purposes, vocal and nonverbal features captured with cameras and microphones can provide information about the candidate and about the interviewer. For instance, nonverbal and

Research Example Box 29.2   Virtual Job Interview Training with Automatic Feedback for Nonverbal Behavior

Langer, König, Gebhard, and André (2016) used a Kinect® camera, a microphone, a virtual character and the SSI framework (Wagner et al., 2013) to train candidates for job interviews. During their training, participants were sitting in front of a monitor equipped with a close-talk microphone, whilst a Kinect® camera was placed on top of the computer. Participants went through an entire job interview, where the virtual character acted as an interviewer. This allowed participants to experience how job interviews might feel. Additionally, nonverbal and paraverbal behavior (e.g., voice volume) data were recognized using the Kinect® and the close-talk microphone. This data was used to generate feedback on participants' nonverbal and paraverbal behavior during the job interview training (see Figure 29.4). For instance, participants were asked to smile during their self-presentation, if they succeeded a feedback signal light for smiling on the right side of the screen turned green. Another example was eye contact with the virtual character; participants who did not manage to keep eye contact for a specific ratio of time were presented with a red signal light (for detailed information see Langer et al., 2016). Results showed that participants in the virtual training group, compared to a classical job interview training group (i.e., participants read information and watched videos about how to behave during job interviews), reported less interview anxiety, better nonverbal behavior, and they received higher interview performance ratings.

Figure 29.4 *The virtual job interview training environment. On the right side there are feedback signal lights providing feedback for nonverbal and paraverbal behavior (smiling, eye contact, body posture, arm position, nodding, voice loudness, vocal energy). On the left side there is the recognized skeleton of the participant and below there is a continuous smile analysis.*

vocal data seem to predict job interview performance and in some cases even job performance (see Research Example Box 29.3), and thus could be used as an additional source of information for validity research (Naim et al., 2015; Schmid Mast et al., 2017). This means, that nonverbal and vocal features could provide incremental validity over and above interviewer evaluations of applicants' performance. Another possibility would be to capture the interviewers' nonverbal and paraverbal behavior and measure how applicants react to this behavior. This way, it is possible to examine the interviewers' influence on applicant reactions (e.g., through smiling more frequently) more systematically, instead of just relying on interviewees self-report ratings of their behavior.

In addition, knowing which kind of automatically extracted nonverbal cues are related to performance in a given domain can be used for training purposes or, as mentioned above, for enhancing performance evaluations. As an example, one of the authors of this chapter investigated which verbal cues of receptionists relate to client satisfaction. In a first step, we achieved better prediction of performance impressions when adding automatically extracted audio-video nonverbal behavior to the personality traits (Muralidhar, Schmid Mast, & Gatica-Perez, 2017). In a next step, we want to use this information to either train receptionists or we can use it for selection purposes in the realm of an assessment center for selecting receptionists.

29.5 Research on Group Processes

Research on group processes faces similar issues as research on individuals and on dyads, but it also comes with its own set of challenges (see also Section 4 of this book). For instance, research on group processes is inherently more complex than the aforementioned research on individuals and dyads. Several relationships and behaviors need to be elicited simultaneously and the number of dyadic interactions within the team increases exponentially with team size. Teams give rise to dynamics that only occur in groups, such as struggles for power and hierarchy (Bunderson van der Vegt, Cantimur, & Rink, 2016) and conflicts (Jehn, 1995). Especially constructs

---

Research Example Box 29.3   Automatic Analysis of Vocal and Nonverbal Behavior to Predict Job Performance

A study by Schmid Mast and colleagues (2017, under review) investigated whether and how job applicant nonverbal behavior during a job interview predicts actual job performance and whether it predicts job performance above and beyond traditionally used selection tools such as personality questionnaires and recruiter evaluation. Job applicants ($N = 54$) were audio- and videotaped during the job interview. The applicants' vocal and nonverbal behaviors were assessed objectively via an automated sensing platform. This platform contained a high definition camera and a microphone array, able to accurately segment and register different speakers. With the exception of applicants' smiling and gazing, which were coded manually, all nonverbal cues were extracted automatically using computational methods.

Unbeknownst to them, all applicants were hired for a sales-like job. They had to convince people on the street to sign up for a study at the local university. As an objective job performance measure, the authors used the average number of people who provided their name and contact information on the sign-up sheet per hour of recruitment. Applicant vocal nonverbal behavior, but not their kinesic nonverbal behavior, significantly predicted later job performance above and beyond applicant personality and recruiter evaluation. Knowing the link between applicant nonverbal behavior and later job performance can be used for future personnel selection or for applicant job interview training.

Research Example Box 29.4   Negotiation Training

A German start-up (Affective Signals, 2017) used a videoconference tool for negotiation training. During the training, participants negotiate through webcam and microphone with each other. Dyadic video and audio data are analyzed and interpreted into a descriptive timeline of the negotiation process. This means that this training tool analyzes nonverbal and paraverbal behavior of a dyadic nature (i.e., behavior in one participant that evoked a reaction in the other participant in a short timeframe). Through analysis of this data, negotiations can be examined regarding the points in time when participants agreed on a topic, when they disagreed, and when the negotiation stalled. Furthermore, the chance of a positive outcome of the negotiation could be analyzed based on the dyadic data. This data can potentially also tell a story about participants' negotiation style, for instance, if participants are more competitive or if they are more cooperative. Insights through the sensor data are then used to provide feedback to participants about their nonverbal and verbal behavior, and they can be advised on how to strategically use their nonverbal behavior to improve negotiation success.

that capture complex team processes and interactions such as conflict or emotion elaboration can be difficult and costly to observe. In research on groups and teams, constructs can lie on different levels of analysis (individual, dyad, or group) that can exhibit cross-level interactions and reciprocal relationships. Non-independence of measurements within the group is an additional challenge, as it requires more sophisticated statistical procedures such as mixed models that can accommodate these specificities.

29.5.1 Laboratory Research on Group Processes

The first sensor that might come to mind when thinking about group processes might be cameras. Indeed, they might be useful for research on group processes as interactions can be analyzed in detail and novel research frameworks might be able to detect every participants' emotional state (e.g., during a group discussion). Regarding analysis of nonverbal behavior however, frameworks like the SSI (Wagner et al., 2013) might face challenges in cases where there is more than one person observed by a camera. For instance, current depth cameras have issues when there is more than one person visible and reliable recognition of nonverbal behavior is not yet possible.

Sensors with (currently) more potential regarding group processes are sociometric badges as they can provide useful data for laboratory research on group processes, because they facilitate collecting data on emergent team processes such as the structure or pattern of verbal interactions and leadership. For example, many studies on the effects of gender and gender composition of team behavior measure whether female team members contribute to the group and are treated differently than their male counterparts. Specifically, one study looked at how frequently team members encouraged other team members to contribute something to the group task (Chatman Boisnier, Spataro, Anderson, & Berdahl, 2008). To measure this behavior, the researchers videotaped the discussions and coded the behavior. Such video coding of behaviors is very costly and time-consuming and requires several coders for the same instance to establish inter-rater reliability. Sociometric badges offer the opportunity to automate or at least facilitate the collection of interactional data in the team context. For the given example, employing sociometric badges would measure how many seconds each member spent talking to other team members. In other words, for each team member, the researchers would obtain how many seconds this particular team member was addressed by others. While this data gives no indication about the content of the exchange, the time-stamped log files containing the speaking instances would drastically facilitate video coding: The corresponding snippets could be extracted from the video and passed through a secondary stage of manual coding. At least this way, sequencing the stream of the discussion into certain (speaking) events can be automated with sociometric badges.

29.5.2 Field Research on Group Processes

In the lab, researchers have the option to collect observational data through video. In the field, this option is typically not available due to mobility issues and due to privacy concerns. Here, small wearable sensor devices such as the sociometric badges offer interesting possibilities for collecting behavioral data that did not previously exist. Sociometric badges do not require any further technical infrastructure. Depending on the type of data that the researcher collects, the internal SD cards can store up to three days of data, therefore facilitating longer collection periods. Given that the devices only store the sensors' metadata and not actual audio, they can be used in contexts where privacy concerns prevent audio or video recordings. However, one of the authors of this chapter found that in practice, resistance to the use of these devices in organizational field contexts is extremely strong, especially among workers' councils who typically oppose the deployment of sociometric badges used in their organization (an explanation for this problem, considering the influence of surveillance and stress, is provided in another chapter of this book in Part V, technology and stress). Nevertheless, Research Example Box 29.5 presents an example for a field study using sociometric badges.

29.6 Potential Challenges

Despite many opportunities for enhancing research, there are several potential challenges with using sensor devices that need to be addressed. First, research regarding sensor technologies should follow similar standards as research using other measurement approaches (e.g., self-report), like reliability and validity. Regarding reliability, researchers using sensor devices may be required to provide support for the claim that the sensor captured reliable data. For instance, when using microphones it might be a good idea to gather data in a pre-study showing that vocal parameters of a person can be reliably measured within a specific timeframe. If the researchers find that vocal data can only be measured reliably if there is at least five minutes of voice recording, this should be accounted for in the real study. Regarding validity it might be even harder to come up with hypotheses

Research Example Box 29.5   Description of a Field Study Employing Sociometric Badges

In order to assess the capability of sociometric badges to capture leadership emergence and leadership positions, Cook and Meyer (2017) used sociometric badges to gather data from twenty-nine staff members at a German university over two days. Participants were introduced to the badges prior to data collection in order to make them aware of the sensors, the measurement variables, and the handling of the badges (e.g., recharging instructions). In the evening of each day of the study, participants completed an online questionnaire asking for the five coworkers which whom they had the most face-to-face contact at work. In addition, participants ranked these coworkers according to the estimated amount of face-to-face communication.

Afterwards, the authors used questionnaire data to compute social networks for each day. In these social networks, Cook and Meyer calculated in-degree centrality (i.e., how often this person was named as one of the five persons with whom another employee had the most communication), closeness centrality (i.e., coworkers' centrality on basis of the entire network) and betweenness centrality (i.e., how often an individual lies on the shortest path between two other individuals).

All of the aforementioned centrality indices were compared to the centrality indices derived from the sociometric badge data (i.e., derived from distance and proximity data from the infra-red and Bluetooth sensors; see Olguín, 2007, for a detailed description). The results show large and significant positive correlations, indicating a good validity of the badge-assessed interactions as a measure for face-to-face interactions in an organizational field setting.

and explanations of why sensor data should relate to a construct of interest (e.g., stress). Solutions to these challenges might be to develop and test theoretical assumptions on why sensor-based measures should relate to constructs of interest.

Second, sensors can potentially be intrusive, thus they might interfere with participants' acceptance of the experiment. However, the less intrusive some sensors are, the less precise their measures become. For instance, vital sensors can provide data very non-intrusively using only a wristband. However, data measured with wristband trackers (e.g., heartrate) can suffer from low reliability (Stahl et al., 2016) or they might only be measured every thirty seconds. For higher reliability and more frequent measurement, using an additional chestband might be an option. However, asking participants to wear a chestband throughout the day, or even only during a one-hour experiment might result in less acceptance of the experiment and to participants refusing to take part in the experiment.

For research on dyadic interactions, it is important that the interaction happens as realistically as possible. However, as we already have discussed, sensors can potentially be intrusive, thus interfering with the realism of the dyadic interaction. For instance, in the case of a negotiation scenario, participants who are constantly reminded that their data is recorded might not be able to show their usual negotiation behavior, leading to lower external validity. Therefore, it is essential to realistically pre-test the conditions under which the experiment takes place to ensure that participants are willing to take part in the experiment, and to clarify if data quality is high enough to answer the research question.

As a third challenge, participants' privacy concerns need to be addressed (for a more detailed discussion on privacy concerns, surveillance and ethical constraints see Section 5 of this book, surveillance systems/electronic performance monitoring/privacy). We have tried to make clear that sensor devices are able to capture a great variety of participants' personal data and that this can be useful for research. However, the more data researchers collect about participants, the more concerned participants might be about what happens to this data. Moreover, in cases in which sensors collect participant data, participants usually have little influence about the data that the sensors collect. In such cases, privacy concerns can be expected to be especially high as participants have the impression that they cannot control which information are gathered (Dinev & Hart, 2004).

For instance, in organizational field research on group processes, participants might be especially concerned if collected data results in heavy surveillance of their activities throughout day. Ultimately, they might be afraid that the data would indicate lower productivity and that the organization would use the information to take punitive action like decreased payment (e.g., if data showed that people who engaged in fewer conversations than other people caused productivity of the organization to drop). In fact, as we have already mentioned in the section on field research for group processes, resistance to use of sensor devices can be a severe obstacle for sensor-based research in organizational settings. Hence, prior to any sensor-based study, researchers should think about ways to improve participants' and organizations' acceptance and commitment to take part in the study (e.g., by pronouncing the scientific purpose, being transparent about gathered data, offering explanations about the study, providing clear benefits for participants/organizations).

Furthermore, handling sensor data leads to several challenges. First, sensors potentially yield large amounts of data (for a deeper understanding of this issue see Section 6 of this book, Big Data). For example, recording a dyadic interaction with a depth camera in high definition quality results in a gigabyte of data after only a few minutes. Second, recorded data can result in an overwhelming number of features that can be used for further analysis (vocal features, nonverbal features, health data, GPS data, etc.); researchers have to decide which of these captured features are valuable to answer their research questions. This is further complicated in dyadic interactions where there are even more features that can possibly analyzed. This leads to a third issue on how to interpret sensor data. Take the example of speech pauses during dyadic interactions. There are speech pauses that can indicate turn-taking (i.e., when the turn changes from one interaction partner to the other), however pauses also happen naturally within a single utterance of one interaction partner; more pauses occur if one interaction partner interrupts the other, and these pauses have different implications than pauses during turn-taking. Classical statistical methods might not be useful to support the interpretation of this data because it is very likely that researchers drown in the massive number of features that are available for analysis. An especially fruitful approach that might help to overcome these issues is data visualization, which is described in detail in Section 6 of this book, data visualization.

In the case where more advanced statistical methods like machine learning algorithms are used to support analysis and interpretation (see Section 6 of this book, methods, statistics and software), different challenges occur. For instance, it might be possible to tell that some features distinguish between a successful and an unsuccessful negotiation; however it might be much harder to tell why exactly these features should be the cause for different negotiation outcomes, which relates to the issue of data validity mentioned earlier in this section.

Accordingly, it might be advantageous to combine advanced statistical methods (e.g., investigating statistical relations when many features are included, testing for non-linear relationships) and data-driven research with hypothesis-driven research. For instance, instead of exploring relationships between all possible features and dependent variables, it might be helpful to invest in theoretical frameworks for the relationship between certain features and dependent variables. In addition, researchers could take an exploratory look at other relationships within the data to come up with new hypotheses about relationships between features and dependent variables. This could then stimulate additional hypothesis-driven research to support the former exploratory result. This way, data-driven and hypothesis-driven research can benefit from each other.

29.7 Conclusion and Outlook

This chapter presented insight into how sensor devices can be used as tools for enhancing research on individuals, dyads, and groups. One of the most crucial advantages of sensor devises is that they offer novel perspectives for most classical research paradigms. Hopefully, this chapter has inspired readers to think creatively about sensor devices as potentially useful tools to enhance their own research.

In the near future, sensor devices will become cheaper, more reliable, and hopefully also less intrusive and easier to apply without help from technical experts and computer scientists. Potentially, this will lead to an era of sensor-enhanced research where sensor data can provide novel answers for classical research questions.

29.8 Acknowledgments

Thanks to Tobias Baur for allowing us to use the screenshot from the software NovA in Figure 29.1, to Ionut Damian for allowing us to use the screenshots of the app SSJ in Figure 29.2, and to the company Charamel for the permission to use the screenshot of the virtual character displayed in Figure 29.4.

References

Affective Signals (June 14, 2017). Affective Signals. Retrieved from www.affective-sig
    nals.com/.

Apple (2017). ResearchKit and CareKit. Retrieved from www.apple.com/de/researchkit/.

Apple (2018). IPhone X Specs. Retrieved from www.apple.com/iphone-Xs/specs/.

Audacity (2017). Audacity. Retrieved from www.audacity.de/.

Baltrušaitis, T., McDuff, D., Banda, N., Mahmoud, M., El Kaliouby, R., Robinson, P., & Picard,
    R. (2011). Real-time inference of mental states from facial expressions and upper body
    gestures. Presented at the *IEEE International Conference on Automatic Face &
    Gesture Recognition*, Santa Barbara, CA. doi:10.1109/FG.2011.5771372.

Baltrušaitis, T., Robinson, P., & Morency, L.-P. (2016). Openface: An open source facial behavior
    analysis toolkit. In *2016 IEEE winter conference on applications of computer vision
    (WACV)* (pp. 1–10). Lake Placid, NY: IEEE. doi:10.1109/wacv.2016.7477553.

Batrinca, L. M., Mana, N., Lepri, B., Pianesi, F., & Sebe, N. (2011). Please, tell me about
    yourself: Automatic personality assessment using short self-presentations. In
    Proceedings of the 13th international conference on multimodal interfaces (pp.
    255–262). New York, NY: ACM Press. doi:10.1145/2070481.2070528.

Baur, T., Damian, I., Lingenfelser, F., Wagner, J., & André, E. (2013). NovA: Automated
    analysis of nonverbal signals in social interactions. *Lecture Notes in Computer
    Science*, 8212, 160–171. doi:10.1007/978–3–319–02714-2_14.

Boersma, P. & Van Heuven, V. (2001). Speak and unSpeak with PRAAT. *Glot International*,
    5, 341–347.

Bunderson, J. S., van der Vegt, G. S., Cantimur, Y., & Rink, F. (2016). Different views on
    hierarchy and why they matter: Hierarchy as inequality or as cascading influence.
    Academy of Management Journal, 42, 1265–1289. doi:10.5465/amj.2014.0601.

Chatman, J. A., Boisnier, A. D., Spataro, S. E., Anderson, C., & Berdahl, J. L. (2008). Being
    distinctive versus being conspicuous: The effects of numeric status and sex-stereo-
    typed tasks on individual performance in groups. *Organizational Behavior and
    Human Decision Processes*, 107, 141–160. doi:10.1016/j.obhdp.2008.02.006.

Chartrand, T. L. & Bargh, J. A. (1999). The chameleon effect: The perception–behavior link
    and social interaction. *Journal of Personality and Social Psychology*, 76, 893–910.
    doi:10.1037//0022–3514.76.6.893.

Ciocchetti, M., Massaroni, C., Saccomandi, P., Caponero, M., Polimadei, A., Formica, D., &
    Schena, E. (2015). Smart textile based on fiber Bragg grating sensors for respira-
    tory monitoring: Design and preliminary trials. *Biosensors*, 5, 602–615.
    doi:10.3390/bios5030602.

Cook, A. & Mayer, B. (2017). Assessing leadership behavior with observational and sensor-
    based methods: A brief overview. In B. Schyns, R. J. Hall, & P. Neves (Eds.),
    Handbook of methods in leadership research (pp. 73–102). Cheltenham, UK:
    Edward Elgar.

Cook, A. (S.) & Mayer, B., Gockel, C., & Zill, A. (in press). Adapting leadership perceptions
    across tasks: The micro origins of informal leadership transitions. *Small Group
    Research*.

Damian, I., Baur, T., & André, E. (2016). Measuring the impact of multimodal behavioural
    feedback loops on social interactions. In *Proceedings of the 18th ACM
    International Conference on Multimodal Interaction* (pp. 201–208). New York,
    NY: ACM Press. doi:10.1145/2993148.2993174.

Damian, I., Dietz, M., Gaibler, F., & André, E. (2016). Social signal processing for dummies. In *Proceedings of the 18th ACM international conference on multimodal interaction* (pp. 394–395). New York, NY: ACM Press. doi:10.1145/2993148.2998527.

De Looze, C., Scherer, S., Vaughan, B., & Campbell, N. (2014). Investigating automatic measurements of prosodic accommodation and its dynamics in social interaction. *Speech Communication, 58*, 11–34. doi:10.1016/j.specom.2013.10.002.

Dinev, T. & Hart, P. (2004). Internet privacy concerns and their antecedents: Measurement validity and a regression model. *Behaviour & Information Technology, 23*, 413–422. doi:10.1080/01449290410001715723.

Duchovski, A. (2007). *Eye tracking methodology: Theory and practice*. London, UK: Springer.

Ellgring, H. & Scherer, K. R. (1996). Vocal indicators of mood change in depression. *Journal of Nonverbal Behavior, 20*, 83–110. doi:10.1007/bf02253071.

Eyben, F., Scherer, K. R., Schuller, B. W., Sundberg, J., Andre, E., Busso, C., ... Truong, K. P. (2016). The Geneva Minimalistic Acoustic Parameter Set (GeMAPS) for voice research and affective computing. *IEEE Transactions on Affective Computing, 7*, 190–202. doi:10.1109/TAFFC.2015.2457417.

Giddens, C. L., Barron, K. W., Byrd-Craven, J., Clark, K. F., & Winter, A. S. (2013). Vocal indices of stress: A review. *Journal of Voice, 27*, 21–29. doi:10.1016/j.jvoice.2012.12.010.

Hawkins, S. A. & Hastie, R. (1990). Hindsight: Biased judgement of past events after the outcomes are known. *Psychological Bulletin, 107*, 311–327. doi:10.1037//0033–2909.107.3.311.

Huang, J. L., Curran, P. G., Keeney, J., Poposki, E. M., & DeShon, R. P. (2012). Detecting and deterring insufficient effort responding to surveys. *Journal of Business and Psychology, 27*, 99–114. doi:10.1007/s10869-011–9231-8.

Intel (2018). Intel RealSense technology. Retrieved from https://software.intel.com/en-us/realsense/d400.

Jehn, K. A. (1995). A multimethod examination of the benefits and detriments of intragroup conflict. *Administrative Science Quarterly, 40*, 256–282. doi:10.2307/2393638.

Kim, T., Chang, A., Holland, L., & Pentland, A. S. (2008). Meeting mediator: Enhancing group collaboration using sociometric feedback. In *Proceedings of the 2008 ACM conference on computer supported cooperative work* (pp. 457–466). New York, NY: ACM Press. Retrieved from http://dl.acm.org/citation.cfm?id=1460636.

Krajewski, J. & Kröger, B. J. (2007). Using prosodic and spectral characteristics for sleepiness detection. Paper presented at the *INTERSPEECH 2007*, Antwerp, Belgium. Retrieved from www.ao.i2.psychologie.uni-wuerzburg.de/fileadmin/06020230/user_upload/1-_Krajewski_Kroeger_2007_Using_prosodic_and_spectral_07_erschienen_in_interspeech.pdf.

Langer, M., König, C. J., Gebhard, P., & André, E. (2016). Dear computer, teach me manners: Testing virtual employment interview training. *International Journal of Selection and Assessment, 24*, 312–323. doi:10.1111/ijsa.12150.

Louwerse, M. M., Dale, R., Bard, E. G., & Jeuniaux, P. (2012). Behavior matching in multimodal communication is synchronized. *Cognitive Science, 36*, 1404–1426. doi:10.1111/j.1551–6709.2012.01269.x.

Lu, H., Frauendorfer, D., Rabbi, M., Mast, M. S., Chittaranjan, G. T., Campbell, A. T., ... Choudhury, T. (2012). StressSense: Detecting stress in unconstrained acoustic environments using smartphones. In *Proceedings of the 2012 ACM conference on ubiquitous computing* (pp. 351–360). New York, NY: ACM Press. Retrieved from http://dl.acm.org/citation.cfm?id=2370270.

Luxton, D. D., McCann, R. A., Bush, N. E., Mishkind, M. C., & Reger, G. M. (2011). mHealth for mental health: Integrating smartphone technology in behavioral healthcare. *Professional Psychology: Research and Practice, 42*, 505–512. doi:10.1037/a0024485.

Manson, J. H. & Robbins, M. L. (2017). New evaluation of the Electronically Activated Recorder (EAR): Obtrusiveness, compliance, and participant self-selection effects. *Frontiers in Psychology, 8*, 658. doi:10.3389/fpsyg.2017.00658.

Matsumoto, D., Yoo, S. H., & Fontaine, J. (2008). Mapping expressive differences around the world: The relationship between emotional display rules and individualism versus collectivism. *Journal of Cross-Cultural Psychology, 39*, 55–74. doi:10.1177/0022022107311854.

McDuff, D., Gontarek, S., & Picard, R. (2014). Remote measurement of cognitive stress via heart rate variability. Presented at the *36th annual international conference of the IEEE Engineering in Medicine and Biology Society*, Chicago, IL. doi:10.1109/EMBC.2014.6944243.

Mehl, M. R. (2017). The Electronically Activated Recorder (EAR): A method for the naturalistic observation of daily social behavior. *Current Directions in Psychological Science, 26*, 184–190. doi:10.1177/0963721416680611.

Mehl, M. R. & Holleran, S. E. (2007). An empirical analysis of the obtrusiveness of and participants' compliance with the Electronically Activated Recorder (EAR). *European Journal of Psychological Assessment, 23*, 248–257. doi:10.1027/1015-5759.23.4.248.

Mehl, M. R., Pennebaker, J. W., Crow, D. M., Dabbs, J., & Price, J. H. (2001). The Electronically Activated Recorder (EAR): A device for sampling naturalistic daily activities and conversations. *Behavior Research Methods, 33*, 517–523. doi:10.3758/bf03195410.

Microsoft. (February 25, 2015). Kinect for Windows. Retrieved from www.microsoft.com/en-us/kinectforwindows/.

Microsoft. (2017). Developing with Kinect for Windows. Retrieved from https://developer.microsoft.com/en-us/windows/kinect/develop.

Miller, G. (2012). The smartphone psychology manifesto. *Perspectives on Psychological Science, 7*, 221–237. doi:10.1177/1745691612441215.

Mori, M. (1970). Bukimi no tani [The uncanny valley]. *Energy, 7*, 33–5.

Mori, M., MacDorman, K., & Kageki, N. (2012). The uncanny valley. *IEEE Robotics & Automation Magazine, 19*, 98–100. doi:10.1109/MRA.2012.2192811.

Muralidhar, S., Schmid Mast, M., & Gatica-Perez, D. (2017). How May I Help You? Behavior and Impressions in Hospitality Service Encounters. In *Proceedings of 19th ACM international conference on multimodal interaction* (pp. 312–320). New York, NY: ACM Press. doi:10.1145/3136755.3136771.

Naim, I., Tanveer, M. I., Gildea, D., & Hoque, M. E. (2015). Automated analysis and prediction of job interview performance: The role of what you say and how you say it. Presented at the *11th IEEE international conference and workshops on automatic face and gesture recognition*, Ljubljana, Slovenia. doi:10.1109/fg.2015.7163127.

Noah, J. A., Spierer, D. K., Gu, J., & Bronner, S. (2013). Comparison of steps and energy expenditure assessment in adults of Fitbit Tracker and Ultra to the Actical and indirect calorimetry. *Journal of Medical Engineering & Technology, 37*, 456–462. doi:10.3109/03091902.2013.831135.

Ohly, S., Sonnentag, S., Niessen, C., & Zapf, D. (2010). Diary studies in organizational research: An introduction and some practical recommendations. *Journal of Personnel Psychology, 9*, 79–93. doi:10.1027/1866–5888/a000009.

Oksüz, N., Biswas, R. S. I., Shcherbatyi, I., & Maass, W. (2018). Measuring biosignals of overweight and obese children for real-time feedback and predicting performance. In J. vom Brocke, P.-M. Léger, & A. Randolph (Eds.), *Information systems and neuroscience– Gmunden retreat on NeuroIS 2017* (pp. 185–193). Cham, Switzerland: Springer.

Olguín, D. O. (2007). *Sociometric badges: Wearable technology for measuring human behavior* (Master thesis). Massachusetts Institute of Technology, Boston. Retrieved from http://hdl.handle.net/1721.1/42169.

Olguín, D. O. & Pentland, A. S. (2007). Sociometric badges: State of the art and future applications. In *Doctoral colloquium presented at IEEE 11th International Symposium on Wearable Computers*, Boston, MA. Retrieved from https://pdfs .semanticscholar.org/48f1/f30259586e2229682510a3ba90fa053004c8.pdf.

Pantelopoulos, A. & Bourbakis, N. G. (2010). A survey on wearable sensor-based systems for health monitoring and prognosis. *IEEE Transactions on Systems, Man, and Cybernetics, 40*, 1–12. Available at: doi:10.1109/tsmcc.2009.2032660.

Podsakoff, P. M. & Organ, D. W. (1986). Self-reports in organizational research: Problems and prospects. *Journal of Management, 12*, 531–44. doi:10.1177/014920638601200408.

Ranganath, R., Jurafsky, D., & McFarland, D. A. (2013). Detecting friendly, flirtatious, awkward, and assertive speech in speed-dates. *Computer Speech & Language, 27*, 89–115. doi:10.1016/j.csl.2012.01.005.

Samsung. (2017). Samsung Galaxy S7 Specs. Retrieved from www.samsung.com/de/smart phones/galaxy-s7/more/.

Schmid Mast, M., Frauendorfer, D., Nguyen, L. S., Gatica-Perez, D., Choudhury, T., & Odobez, J.-M. (2017). A step towards automatic applicant selection: Predicting job performance based on applicant nonverbal interview behavior. [*Under Review.*]

Schmid Mast, M., Gatica-Perez, D., Frauendorfer, D., Nguyen, L., & Choudhury, T. (2015). Social sensing for psychology automated interpersonal behavior assessment. *Current Directions in Psychological Science, 24*, 154–160. doi:10.1177/ 0963721414560811.

Stahl, S. E., An, H.-S., Dinkel, D. M., Noble, J. M., & Lee, J.-M. (2016). How accurate are the wrist-based heart rate monitors during walking and running activities? Are they accurate enough? *BMJ Open Sport & Exercise Medicine, 2*, 1–7. doi:10.1136/ bmjsem-2015–000106.

Sundholm, M., Cheng, J., Zhou, B., Sethi, A., & Lukowicz, P. (2014). Smart-mat: Recognizing and counting gym exercises with low-cost resistive pressure sensing matrix. In *Proceedings of the 16th ACM international joint conference on pervasive and ubiquitous computing* (pp. 373–382). New York, NY: ACM Press. doi:10.1145/2632048.2636088.

Van Vaerenbergh, Y. & Thomas, T. D. (2013). Response styles in survey research: A literature review of antecedents, consequences, and remedies. *International Journal of Public Opinion Research, 25,* 195–217. doi:10.1093/ijpor/eds021.

Wagner, J., Lingenfelser, F., Baur, T., Damian, I., Kistler, F., & André, E. (2013). The social signal interpretation (SSI) framework: Multimodal signal processing and recognition in real-time. In *Proceedings of the 21st ACM international conference on Multimedia* (pp. 831–834). New York, NY: ACM Press. Retrieved from http://dl .acm.org/citation.cfm?id=2502223.

Wallen, M. P., Gomersall, S. R., Keating, S. E., Wisløff, U., & Coombes, J. S. (2016). Accuracy of heart rate watches: Implications for weight management. *PLoS One, 11,* e0154420. doi:10.1371/journal.pone.0154420.

Wang, R., Blackburn, G., Desai, M., Phelan, D., Gillinov, L., Houghtaling, P., & Gillinov, M. (2017). Accuracy of wrist-worn heart rate monitors. *JAMA Cardiology, 2,* 104–106. doi:10.1001/jamacardio.2016.3340.

Ziegler, M., MacCann, C., & Roberts, R. (Eds.) (2011). *New perspectives on faking in personality assessment.* Oxford, UK: Oxford University Press.

30 Storytelling and Sensemaking through Data Visualization

Karl Giuseffi, Benjamin Sievert, Brett M. Wells, and Fran Westfall

A picture is worth a thousand words.

30.1 What is Data Visualization?

Data visualization is a technique of distilling and communicating the value of data using a visual medium: it makes answers to complicated questions available in a digestible and engaging manner, while furnishing insights to better facilitate and guide leaders' decision-making about their workforce. A simple question guides our scientist-practitioner advice and approach to data visualization: Are we providing decision-makers with valuable insights for business action? By this, we expect several touchstones are achieved: (1) we are harnessing available data and consulting around potential new data sources; (2) we are finding ways to blend seemingly disparate data sources, thereby opening new vistas for exploration and discovery; and (3) we are leveraging data to facilitate more profound and insightful conclusions using descriptive, diagnostic, and prescriptive analytics to develop compelling stories that guide decision-making. By and large, data visualization has the potential to amplify human cognition – the mental structures and processes of attention, perception, analysis, communication, and memory – for large quantities of information.

From Neanderthal cave drawings of successful hunts to the pilgrimage of the Chicago Cubs ending their 108-year World Series drought, data visualization is not a new concept, though trends and discussions in the marketplace might leave you thinking otherwise. What has evolved, is increased attention paid to the "Vs" of data: volume, variety, velocity, veracity, value, and visualization (see De Mauro, Greco, & Grimaldi, 2016). Technological advances have made visualization available to the masses (e.g., Tableau, Domo, Microsoft Power BI, Qlik, Plotly, Sisense BI), though by no means easing the burden of knowing the right questions, structures, and kinds of approaches to data in order to fully visualize it and empower leaders. In fact, the bar is set higher to use the best methods and approaches to meet organizational needs, because the potential impact of decisions from data displays and analytics are far-reaching.

Data visualization sits on the forefront of many areas that pose challenges for those consulting and conducting analyses for organizations and leaders. In the technological age, our patience for information has waned and the reality is that we all want information available at our fingertips. Because of technology, it is more possible than ever to provide data on a more immediate basis. Even so, all of the issues that confront data, such as methods, collection, structure, and analytics, are not eased by cutting-edge data displays and means for blending data together quickly. As the adage goes, "garbage in, garbage out," and this perhaps makes data science and approaches even more challenging as data become easier to quickly grasp from a compelling image, but underlying issues due to structure or analytics become less visible, especially to untrained eyes. As an expert, it is incumbent to address underlying data issues, ensure data structures are correct, and ensure the analyses underpinning data displays remain appropriate, valid, and meaningful – both statistically and practically.

We make the following suggestions regarding research and data visualizations. Ensure all of the basic data essentials are met, which makes completing data visualization contingent on the following: having all of the right data that are necessary, that the data are accurate, and that the data are structured to effectively analyze questions. In short, having everything you need to accurately and effectively answer key questions from stakeholders, even anticipating other questions or information that will arise from the data analysis and presentation. The core of research and proper analytic techniques are always core to data visualization. A major component of good data visualization is value. While "value added" seems to be understood, it is perhaps one of the most overlooked features because it is too easy to focus on the research questions, data, insights, and whether or not the questions were sufficiently answered. As such, the research and insights from the data need to do more than simply answer the questions. They need to be compelling and meaningful, so that it continuously serves as a resource for the decision-makers leverages what was uncovered from the research.

When building data visualizations, we encourage the use and consideration of the visual analytic framework (Keim et al., 2008). The visual analytic framework goal is "to turn information overload into an opportunity" through the combined use of technology and human intelligence while addressing several components of data, analytics, and the presentation of both (p. 155). The visual analytic framework is quite useful, though we propose additional dimensions to enhance the presentation of information and the retention of it, which are design thinking, aperture, and control. The objective of design thinking applied to data visualizations is to create more effective visualizations that stimulate a step-wise, deeply considered approach to thinking outside the box to address complicated stakeholder concerns. Indeed, with high-level stakeholders there is an incredibly limited margin for error – you have one shot to convince – and a windfall opportunity if done right, to change the way something is perceived and approached within an organization. In essence, the presentation uncovers several insights as easily and directly as possible, focuses leaders, and allows them the ability to make maximally informed decisions. Just as an aperture changes the depth of field to create an intended image, so too should an aperture be applied to the abstraction of data. While there are many paths to guiding discovery with data visualization, many subscribe to

Shneiderman's (1996) visual information-seeking mantra: "overview first, zoom and filter, then details on demand" (p. 336). Furthermore, like any good presentation or piece of art, once it is created it is out in the open and subject to a myriad of users, interpretations, and uses, some of which exceed or misrepresent the original intent. The reality is that, at some point, the data visualization will no longer be in the control of the creator or presenter. Rather than being approached as a problem, the lack of control is an opportunity. As such, we leverage interactive control to ensure that once the visualization is created, the end users can make the discoveries that we wanted them to uncover, but we turn it over to them to make additional discoveries, engage with it, as well as minimize the opportunity for automation bias (Skitka, Mosier, & Burdick, 2000). We treat end users like consumers, hopefully creating a sense of the IKEA effect within the end user. Indeed, there is a substantial "increase in valuation of self-made products" that can even contend with those created by experts (Norton, Mochon, & Ariely, 2012, p. 453).

Think of what we are suggesting with interactive control as a balance of control and freedom. Most people can think of a backseat driver. Why do people insist on others driving more like themselves or want others to drive the way they drive? Data visualization will inevitably meet the same issue, where the audience wants to control the information and use it in their own way. Interactive control plans for this eventuality and sets up confines so that leaders can take and use the information, slice and evaluate it as they deem fit and want, but all of the underlying data analytics and work are done so the data are still accurate, representative, and useful. The design is to enhance engagement by expanding the realm of control available to the end user, in our case, the client.

Rather than be beleaguered by the complexities of presentational features, and focusing on the challenges, let's turn the issue on its head and think of the opportunities presented and freedom granted inside data displays to meet others' needs. A goal of data visualization is to make it a great experience, so the audience is more likely to understand and recall it. How can we create compelling and engaging presentations that answer questions leaders pose about their workforce and that raise awareness regarding issues about which they were previously unaware? Rather than trying to train yourself in everything, with whom can you partner and blend your skills, knowledge, and talents? What software can you use to leverage you toward your collective success? How can you make your presentations engaging and, even better, interactive so that you can meet the unique needs of those to whom you are presenting, while answering questions in a more fluid manner? Beyond other mentioned factors we strongly rely on and use, we use humble inquiry, active listening, parsimony, teamwork, and drawing on others' insights, especially those who have backgrounds different from our own, to make a presentation stronger. We also use technologies that facilitate our ability to address many organizational questions and issues, and to do so in an intuitive, proactive way. We demand that our data science approaches have the same high rigor when we distill and display those data insights. We want people to appreciate as many features of our presentations as possible, meanwhile making the presentation more interactive and engaging, captivating their focus and allowing them to better attend to and retain the information. The goal is to move people through displays of information to action.

30.2 People's Perceptions Drive Perceptions of Results

Effective data presentations hinge on not only data components but also people. Coupled with the technological advances, data visualizations face challenges from biased information processing, selective attention, and several other factors that drive people's thoughts, attention, and behaviors. Like the visual analytic framework suggests, due to differences in human cognition and perception, it is important to pay attention to some key factors in variations in attention. People are selectively attentive, through their own volition or not, in learning new information or generally processing information (Deng & Sloutsky, 2016; Hoffman & Rehder, 2010). Studies in human cognition and learning show that, while people employ many strategies to process and encode new information, people generally optimize their processing of information through categorizing information and making inferences from it (Deng & Sloutsky, 2016). Generally, people tend to categorize and recall what they are exposed to via color, shapes, textures, and a variety of other dimensions. As such, color and shapes are an important part of data visualization, because they allow people to attach meaning and categorize the information that you are conveying and want them to remember. Colors and shapes are crucial to simplifying and clarifying the presentation of your story, but the information has to be salient and presented in a meaningful way, directly addressing concerns or interests. As a result, use images or colors to facilitate and ease mental processing. For example, presenting performance as "gold, silver, or bronze" may use heuristics and shapes to more readily attribute meaning to visuals.

There are incredibly complex mechanisms underlying the way people process information, and keep in mind that the human brain is wired for seamlessly processing information (Gazzaniga & Mangun, 2014). Human perception and attention is drawn to and influenced by movement, color, patterns, and many other features that are crucial to the way people process information. This means that these features of a presentation have the power to embolden a message or to mute it. A single color, for instance, has the potential to undercut a presentation if not carefully considered. The color red has different meanings in different contexts, and changes people's processing considerably. Red in social contexts is linked to people's perception of social dominance or aggression, such as a face flushing red (Elliot, 2015). In other contexts, like prior to performing a taxing cognitive task, red may undermine performance on the task, but red also can be beneficial in rallying team members together such as before sporting competitions (Elliot, 2015). This conversation about the color red is to make us all seriously consider the importance of color and design. The choices of colors and hues are typically considered after the fact, though they clearly will determine success in displaying information in a compelling manner. One needs to be mindful of the context in which one's displays are presented. The example of the various implications of using red also offers an important reality check. Each one of the authors of this chapter is guilty of not fully measuring the importance of color contained in a presentation and has missed the mark as a consequence. Color, shapes, and other important features present challenges. In particular, they present us with an interdisciplinary challenge, especially because data gurus are unlikely to also be trained in human differences in attention and learning patterns, though they are expected to be able to meet people's diverse needs when presenting data. From our lessons learned, we recommend immediately starting with pure black and white designs. Make certain that your intended message is clear from these alone; if it is not, then color will not clarify an already muddied message.

30.3 People Data to Solve Business Problems: An Example

Fundamentally, human resources' (HR) goal is to maximize performance. As a result, HR continuously tracks and measures a variety of work quality, quantity, and efficiency metrics: turnover rate, absenteeism rate, time to fill, performance reviews, engagement, salary, promotion, training hours, sales, revenue per full-time equivalent, among countless others. Often, these metrics are blended, augmented, and analyzed to support decision-making – for example, succession planning, a process that evaluates an employee's current performance against the employee's potential for success in higher roles to be used for employment decisions. To demonstrate the potential power of data visualization, we created a fictitious succession planning data visualization given the following scenario:

> Kokopelli Bank is a family-owned, local bank that takes a personal approach to providing a breadth of services across its twenty-six branches in Albuquerque and its surrounding area. After the District Manager's retirement announcement, Kokopelli Bank is faced with the dilemma of finding his successor. With change comes opportunity, and Kokopelli Bank is committed to developing and promoting talent from within. The Executive Committee knows that the industry is facing a difficult and uncertain period with increased regulations, and wants to leverage relevant data to guide their decisions when considering each of the twenty-six Branch Managers for promotion. Relevant data included the following:
>
> 1. Branch Manager Demographics: Name, tenure, and branch location.
> 2. Branch Manager Performance: Branch customer satisfaction score (identified as the most important indictor of a Branch Manager's performance by the Executive Committee), average annual turnover rate, and average quarterly loan volume.
> 3. Branch Manager Leadership Assessment: Validated, personal characteristics that measure leadership potential and predict future success. The assessment was administered during the pre-employment application phase to be considered for Branch or District Manager positions.

Our team acted as the external Talent Analytics Consultant, hired by the Executive Committee to harness, aggregate, and augment these data into a meaningful data visualization. Figure 30.1 presents our conceptualization of a dashboard solution that informs promotion decisions and succession planning strategies. We strongly recommend you interact with this dashboard for yourself, as if you were an Executive Committee member, by visiting: https://public.tableau.com/profile/benjamin.sievert#!/vizhome/CambridgeHandbookofTechnologyandEmployeeBehaviorStorytellingandSensemakingwithDataVisualization/SuccessionDashboard?publish=yes.

Ideally, we hope that we met our overarching goal in the eyes of the end user and target audience: the Executive Committee should be able to use these data as easily and directly as possible to make decisions. We designed our dashboard to be intuitive, yet insightful with functionality and interaction between four quadrants. Moving from the upper-left quadrant, clockwise:

1. Quadrant I plots the branch locations for each Branch Manager via a map. Each Branch Manager is represented by a unique shape marker that is consistently presented in other quadrants. When hovering over a marker, additional data are presented such as name and financial metrics. Please observe that each individual is represented by a unique indicator, recognizing their individuality and focusing the Executive Committee on the fact they are making decisions about people – they are not merely a combination of metrics.
2. Quadrant II presents a succession planning grid that plots a Branch Manager's current performance (customer satisfaction score) on the y-axis and overall leadership potential on the x-axis. Minimal thresholds for each axis are set, which creates a four-box grid. For this exercise, greater attention should be paid to those who are both high performing and high potential (i.e., upper-right quadrant), but this matrix could be subsequently used to reassign those who are low performing and low potential or coach and mentor those who are low performing but high potential. Two other sources of information are also plotted: (1) the unique shape marker's (same as in Quadrant I) color represents the Branch Manager's employee turnover rate with a gradient from green (relatively lower turnover) to red (relatively higher turnover); and (2) the linear relationship between leadership potential and current performance. To ease interpretation, no regression statistics are presented, but the statistics are referenced when hovering over the regression line. The predictive model results can be used for future pre-employment selection decisions to project what a candidate's customer satisfaction ratings will be based on his or her leadership potential.
3. Quadrant III compares leadership assessment results across ten indicators of leadership potential (e.g., confidence, forethought, partnership building, business application) for selected Branch Managers. Leadership potential scores are represented by bars, highly successful (Top Performer) and less successful (Contrast Performer) benchmarks are represented by the overshadowing lines, and the color of the leadership potential bars represent strong (green), moderate (yellow), and weak (red) potential to ease interpretation.

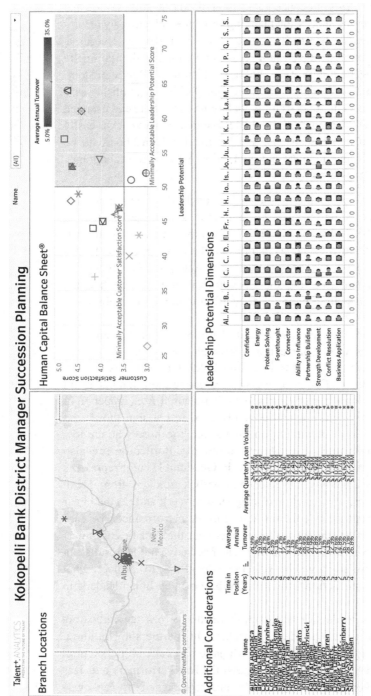

Figure 30.1 *Succession planning dashboard.*

4. Quadrant IV presents peripheral metrics that may add value when making decisions, such as tenure and average quarterly loans, after narrowing the scope to a handful of finalists.

We hope that users intuitively click and drag across a group of high performing and high potential Branch Managers, as depicted in Figure 30.2. In our example, we lassoed three of the more promising candidates: Arnulfo Alequin, Domonique Dismuke, and Mikel Marts in Quadrant II. For these individuals, their data are brought to the forefront, while others' data are suppressed, to focus attention. Notice, other quadrants are updated with their specific information. These two changes leverage movement and color (i.e., shading) to enhance attention, control, and engagement.

Among the three individuals, Domonique has the longest tenure, lowest turnover and highest loan volume, despite being located far outside the main hub of Albuquerque. Although Domonique and Mikel have identical (and strong) customer satisfaction and overall leadership potential, Domonique's profile is more stable, with no leadership indicators below the Contrast Performer benchmark. Mikel's Strength Development, on the contrary, is far below the Contrast Performer benchmark, and may be a contributing factor to his seemingly higher staff turnover – *Does Mikel continually focus on developing the strengths of his staff, or does he routinely point out and try to correct their weaknesses?* It is less important to us that all users arrive at selecting Domonique to be the next District Manager. Instead, we hope to convey that, when executed efficiently, effectively, and interactively, data visualization can foster communication and empower decision-makers to make wiser decisions – notice the ease with which complicated information is displayed and can be digested by decision-makers.

30.4 Visualizing the Bigger Picture

> *"My inventory goes home every night."*
> Michael Eisner, Former CEO of the Disney Corporation

An internal or external consultant can design the perfect study, find significant and meaningful results, but ultimately fail if data and analytics are not presented clearly and effectively. Our practical example takes over 500 data points and presents them in an approachable manner that doesn't overwhelm decision-makers with noise, but instead focuses on the few crucial signals. The example makes use of the visual analytic framework and design thinking, progressively narrows the scope of focus, and fosters a sense of ownership, moving decision-makers away from being the traditional, passive audience members and more toward being active participants in the curated discovery process.

Historically, we relied heavily on more traditional presentation tools, such as executive summaries, PowerPoint, and static charts, tables, and graphs. Although carefully analyzed and crafted, static presentations often created more stakeholder

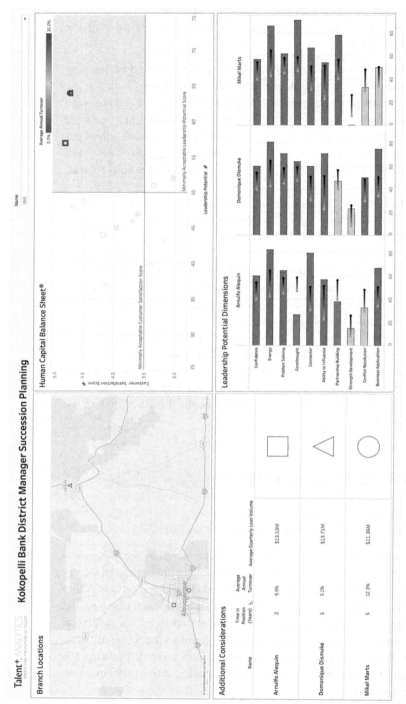

Figure 30.2 *Self-directed discovery.*

questions than we had answers to in the moment. Leaving a meeting without closure, we would return to our analytics packages to answer these questions, often with a delayed response. As a result, communication suffered and reports and presentations are soon out of sight and mind for busy executives, finding their way to the nearest recycle bin. Interactive, data visualization supports consulting in the moment and, while everyone enjoys a good story, it's even a better story when you get to choose your own adventure. With all data and significant insights in the background, questions can be answered live in the moment with as little as a click or drag. Instead of being labeled "one-hit wonders," data visualization can continue to gain popularity with integrated data feeds and new vistas for exploration and discovery.

While there is substantial literature regarding human perception of graphics and data visualizations (e.g., Cleveland & McGill, 1984; Ware, 2004), there has been a dearth of empirical evidence for its application – the "so what?" Research has weighed heavily on the scientist side of the scientist-practitioner model – understanding visual encoding features such as color, shape, size, gradation, and their combination – but less attention has been paid to the craft or art of visualization. For example, are stories told with visualizations more impactful (e.g., encoding, storage, retrieval, application, deductive and inductive reasoning) than those without visualizations? How do users act on visual information compared to information provided in other mediums? We see so much left to be researched in the realm of data visualization, especially the more recent practitioner innovations such as dynamic, interactive data visualizations. We hope that sharing our experiential knowledge can spur new research directions for academics and may shed light onto the areas that the extant literature does not cover.

Done properly, data visualization has the power to guide human cognition, ultimately leading to better decision-making. Nevertheless, we caution practitioners and consumers to not remove the human element when working with people data or creating visualizations, as subsequent decisions can often impact many lives. Lastly, remember to not simply put "lipstick on a pig." Data visualization is a complement to, but not a replacement for, sound data collection, blending, and analysis. Nevertheless, we look forward to the continuous improvement of data visualization for the mutual benefit of organizations and its many stakeholders.

References

Cleveland, W. S. & McGill, R. (1984). Graphical perception: Theory, experimentation, and application to the development of graphical methods. *Journal of the American Statistical Association*, *79*, 531–554.

Deng, W. S. & Sloutsky, V. M. (2016). Selective attention, diffused attention, and the development of categorization. *Cognitive Psychology*, *91*, 24–62. doi:10.1016/j. cogpsych.2016.09.002

De Mauro, A., Greco, M., & Grimaldi, M. (2016). A formal definition of big data based on its essential features. *Library Review*, *65*, 122–135. doi:10.1108/LR-06–2015-0061.

Elliot, A. (2015). Color and psychological functioning: A review of theoretical and empirical work. *Frontiers in Psychology*, *6*, 368. doi:10.3389/fpsyg.2015.00368.

Gazzaniga, M. S., & Mangun, G. R. (Eds.). (2014). Cognitive neurosciences (5th ed.). Cambridge, MA: MIT Press.

Hoffman, A. B. & Rehder, B. (2010). The costs of supervised classification: The effect of learning task on conceptual flexibility. *Journal of Experimental Psychology: General*, *139*, 319–340. doi:1037/a0019042.

Keim, D., Andrienko, G., Fekete, J. D., Görg, C., Kohlhammer, J., & Melançon, G. (2008). Visual analytics: Definition, process, and challenges. In A. Kerren, J. T. Stasko, J. D. Fekete, & C. North (Eds.), *Information visualization: Human-centered issues and perspectives* (pp. 154–175). New York, NY: Springer.

Norton, M. I., Mochon, D., & Ariely, D. (2012). The IKEA effect: When labor leads to love. *Journal of Consumer Psychology*, *22*, 453–60. doi:10.1016/j.jcps.2011.08.002.

Shneiderman, B. (September, 1996). The eyes have it: A task by data type taxonomy for information visualizations. Paper presented at the Proceedings of the IEEE Symposium on Visual Languages, Washington, DC.

Skitka, L. J., Mosier, K. L., & Burdick, M. (2000). Accountability and automation bias. *International Journal of Human-Computer Studies*, *52*, 701–17. doi:10.1006/ijhc.1999.0349.

Ware, C. (2004). *Information visualization: Perception for design* (2nd edn.). San Francisco, CA: Elsevier.

PART VII

Interdisciplinary Perspectives on Employees and Technology

31 Microblogging Behavior and Technology Adoption at the Workplace

Charalampos Chelmis

31.1 Introduction

Social networks have revolutionized the way people communicate and interact, while serving as a platform for information dissemination, content organization and search, expertize identification, and influence discovery. The popularity of online social networks like Facebook and Twitter has given researchers access to massive quantities of data for analysis. Such datasets provide an opportunity to study the characteristics of social networks in order to understand the dynamics of individual and group behavior, underlying structures, and local and global patterns that govern information flows.

Most of the analysis performed thus far has mainly focused on publicly available online social networks (Mislove et al., 2007). However, microblogging capabilities have been adopted by enterprise as well (Zhang et al., 2010). Contrary to online social networks, microblogging services for enterprises are primarily designed to support employees in connecting and learning about each other through personal and professional sharing (Wu, DiMicco, & Millen, 2010). Connecting employees within an organization can result in multiple benefits both for employees and corporations. Employees can "get help or advice, reach opportunities beyond those available through existing ties, discover new routes for potential career development, learn about new projects and assets they can reuse and leverage, connect with subject matter experts and other influential people within the organization, cultivate their organizational social capital, and ultimately grow their reputation and influence within the organization" (Guy et al., 2011). Enterprises on the other hand can directly benefit from increased productivity due to reduced time spent in team building and knowledge sharing. Additionally, organizations hosting internal social networking sites can benefit from mining employees' informal interaction logs so as to understand the processes of knowledge generation and sharing, as well as from identifying reliable indicators of expertise.

In this chapter, we begin by providing insights from a large-scale enterprise microblogging dataset that was collected from a multinational corporation and comprises threaded discussions in a corporate microblogging service that resembles Twitter, augmented by a snapshot of the organizational hierarchy of the company (Section 31.3). In addition to validating structural and semantic properties of the interaction network, and comparing our findings to online social networks that are available to the public (e.g., Facebook and Twitter) and thus have a much broader audience, we further provide insights into the corporate microblogging service. We observe that the world is "smaller" in the corporate environment, even though the inferred network appears to have similar structure to online networks, with a large, strongly connected core with highly connected employees exhibiting characteristics of expertise, conceptualized by frequent message exchanges with other employees. Such employees are therefore critical for the connectivity and flow of information in the corporate environment.

In Section 31.4, we examine the interplay between formal structure and information propagation at the workplace. Unlike online social networks where users create links to others who are similar to them (a phenomenon known as homophily; McPherson, Smith-Lovin, & Cook, 2011), or whose contributions they find interesting (Li et al., 2013; Weng et al., 2010), in a corporate environment, employees form bonds not because of similar tastes but due to tasks at hand or because of reporting-to relationships, i.e. organizational hierarchy. In this sense, there is no explicit social network, however, formal structures such as the organizational hierarchy may provide hints of influence at the workplace. Formal organization structures may constrain influence patterns, but informal communication outside the boundaries and restrictions of this formal backbone may also affect how users behave and ultimately how the diffusion network changes and grows. We explore the dynamics of information diffusion on an online environment at the workplace. Since our dataset does not contain explicit information regarding who influences whom, we empirically quantify the role of reporting-to relationships and local behavior (teammates), as well as the effect of global influence (overall popularity) to the spread of technology adoption at the workplace. We incorporate our findings into two simple and intuitive agent-based computational models with the least possible number of parameters. We emphasize on accurately reproducing the cumulative number of adoptions over time, rather than trying to predict which employee in the network will "infect" which other employees. In this sense, we not only model the influence each employee has on the diffusion (microscopic modeling), permitting user behavior to vary according to the behavior of the general crowd, but we also provide a simple mechanism by which adoption rate rises and decays over time (macroscopic dynamics).

31.2 Dataset Description

The company we studied is a Fortune 500, multinational company, which operates outside the IT sector. Our dataset consists of a snapshot of the organizational hierarchy, containing over 12,000 employees, and employees' join logs and threaded discussions during the first two years of adoption of a microblogging service from the enterprise (July 2, 2010, to March 22, 2012). The main purpose of the corporate microblogging service is to promote and enable collaboration and sharing (e.g., of information, knowledge, and expertise) within the enterprise. The ultimate goal of the corporate microblogging service is to become the primary platform for asynchronous collaboration and colleagues' communication. The functionality of the microblogging service resembles that of Twitter, imposing no restrictions on the way people interact or who they chose to follow. As in Twitter, users author messages in the enterprise microblogging service, and form threaded discussions. A message may (i) become available to the corporate-wide news stream, (ii) be sent to a specific group of employees (public or private), or (iii) have a single recipient. Each message may be annotated with hashtags and may receive multiple replies by other employees. A group of employees (public or private) defines a workspace dedicated to a certain topic (e.g., a project team within the organization), or a group of employees with a shared interest (e.g., data science methods). Anyone in the organization network can view messages exchanged in a public group. Conversely, a message that is being sent to a private group is accessible only to the members of the group.

As much as the corporate microblogging service is similar to online microblogging services (e.g., Twitter), it also differs in several ways. First, only employees with a valid company email address can join the company's network. This reduces spam (e.g., advertisements) and noisy text (e.g., personal status updates). Secondly, there is no character limit on messages, while at the same time, multiple number of files can be attached to a message. Usually large enterprises rely on multiple collaboration platforms such as blog, project wiki, and discussion boards to share information between employees. In fact, email is shown to be the primary communication mechanism in enterprises (Burkhart, Werth, & Loos, 2012). Messages can be posted to the service by email and received by email. Finally, the microblogging service offers both web-based access, as well as integration with all major platforms, desktop and mobile.

The company did not officially initiate usage of the microblogging service. Rather, it was independently initiated by an employee, in the beginning of July, 2010. It was not promoted or even mentioned in any formal corporate communications. Our dataset does not contain information with respect to growth and invitations. We can only speculate that growth was achieved through email and word of mouth invitations.

We obtained our dataset in two rounds; on August 2011, and March 2012. Our first snapshot (i.e., from July 2, 2010, to August 2011), which for the sake of clarity, we denote as D_1, represents 15 per cent of the entire employee population, and reflects users' activity during the first year of adoption of the microblogging service by the company. Table 31.1 summarizes the properties of this dataset. During the time period from July 2, 2010, to March 22, 2012, the number of employees who join the service increases dramatically. By August 2011, 4,213 users had joined the microblogging service. These users represent a broad spectrum of employees across 33 different business units and 228 departments worldwide. By the time we obtained our second snapshot, D_2, a broad spectrum of employees (9,421 users) had joined the microblogging service (77.35 per cent of hierarchy dataset), sharing 19,371 status updates and exchanging 20,370 replies (Chelmis, Ajitesh, &

Table 1. *Dataset D₁ high-level statistics.*

Metric	Value
Number of employees	4,213
Number of messages	16,438
Number of threads	8,139
Number of replies	8,264
Number of hashtags	637
Number of groups	88

Prasanna, 2014; Chelmis & Prasanna, 2013b). Even though, not all employees have joined the microblogging service, nor was the microblogging service equally adopted by all employees, our dataset contains a rough representative sample of all employees, as it includes users with various job functions.

31.3 Characteristics of Microblogging at the Workplace

Contrary to traditional collaboration platforms, such as blogs, project wikis, and discussion boards, microblogging offers an informal setting for communication, search for information, data and experts, and sharing of ideas and news. Instead of being project or team specific, conversations are often broader and replies are often instantaneous. The microblogging service includes a secure environment in which users can share tasks, learn about new topics of interest, ask questions, and look for information. Merging social network capabilities with discussion board features and knowledge base paradigm leads to an integrated environment with major advantages. Clutter can be minimized by subscribing to selected feeds, or by joining groups dedicated to certain topics. As a knowledge base, content is searchable and discoverable by colleagues, whereas in other mediums, such as email, content is accessible only by individuals. The interested reader may refer to, for example, Zhang, Qu, Cody, & Wu (2010) and Lin et al. (2012) for a thorough discussion on the value of social media in the workplace. In this chapter, we do not seek to discover or test the perceived benefits and barriers to adoption of microblogging services in enterprise environments.

Online communities often have a discussion thread structure, based on which users share a status update or post a question, which other users comment on, effectively contributing to the discussion, answering the question posed in the original post, or post their own (subsequent) questions (Zhang, Ackerman, & Adamic, 2007). Posting and commenting data illuminate the communication information flow among commentators and post creators (Hua & Haughton, 2012). We can use such posting and replying activity to create a post-reply network, representing each participating user as a node and linking the user starting a thread to a replier (Zhang et al., 2007). In this sense, links indicate information sharing between nodes. The direction of the link indicates how discussion flows among users through the network. A node with many inbound links indicates a user who has received many comments. A node with many outbound links, but no inbound links, indicates a user who has contributed to discussions on several occasions but received no replies in return.

Figure 31.1 shows how we map posting and replying activity into a directed post-reply graph. A bipartite graph of users and discussion threads they participate in can be created by linking post creators and repliers to threads, as shown on the left. For example, the message created by A received three comments, two comments from user C and one from B. The bipartite graph is then transformed to a directed graph where an edge is drawn from the replier to the user who made the initial post. Formally, we represent the post-reply network as a directed graph $G=(V, E)$, where V is the set of vertices, E denotes the set of edges between nodes in V, and an edge e_{ij} exists and points from node i to node j if user i has sent at least one reply message to user j. We have chosen this intuitive definition for edges to capture the information flow from user i to user j when user i sends user j a message. An undirected edge between users i and j if either user sent a message to the other would not capture the semantics of directed communication, which may or may not be reciprocal. We exclude multiple links between nodes, which would represent interaction across multiple discussion threads; instead, we used single links between nodes. We considered weighting the edges by the frequency of replies sent from user i to user j, and also weighting each message-reply occurrence differently, based on how many replies there are in a discussion thread. The addition of weights would have no effect on the structure and properties of the inferred graph; it is straightforward, however, to incorporate edge weights for other applications or studies.

This microblogging network has some interesting characteristics. First, it is not a network focused on social relationships as it is not intentionally built by its users. Instead, it reflects information flow, members' shared interests, and in case of questions being answered, knowledge transfer. Zhang et al. (2007) argued that "whether it is a community centered on questions and answers, social support, or discussion, the reason that a user replies to a topic is usually because of an interest in the content of the topic rather than who started the thread," reflecting shared

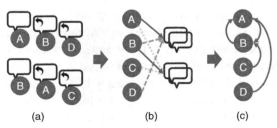

(a)   (b)   (c)

Figure 31.1 *Mapping of threaded discussions into a directed communication network. Threaded discussion (a), represented as bipartite graph (b), is projected into a directed graph (c).*

interests between the original poster and the repliers. "Furthermore in a question and answer community, the direction of the links carries more information than just shared interest. A user replying to another user's question usually indicates that the replier has superior expertise on the subject than the asker."

Whenever a user joins the service, a "join" message is automatically sent by the service to the company feed, announcing the event to the rest of the users. Users' activity is not homogeneous across users. After the join message, not all users continue sending messages. Some just stop using the service altogether, others assume a receiving role, simply reading others' messages, and some contribute to the microblogging service with status updates, which in our modeling do not contribute any edges between users. From the remaining users, 1,210 (28.7 per cent) have sent at least one message (excluding the join message). The distribution of the number of messages per user is broad and highly skewed. This highly skewed posting pattern is similar to what was found in Twitter (Krishnamurthy, Gill, & Arlitt, 2008) and is commonly observed among many online communities (Mislove et al., 2007; Schifanella et al., 2010). This suggests that participation patterns are similar to online microblogging services, where a relatively small number of users produce the bulk of content and most users either contribute sparsely or just lurk.

31.3.1 Structural Properties of Microblogging Interaction at the Workplace

In this section, we provide a brief summary of the topological properties of the microblogging interactions in our dataset. For more details on the dynamics and characteristics, and the interplay between its social and topical components, users' homophily and activity, as well as latent topical similarity and link probability, we direct the interested reader to Chelmis & Prasanna (2013a).

Figure 31.2 shows the probability distributions of the number of messages n_m and the number of replies n_r per user, the distribution of the number of groups n_g to which a user belongs, and the probability of finding a user with a number n_t of distinct hashtags in his or her vocabulary. Figure 31.2 further shows the total number t of hashtag assignments per user (e.g., a hashtag used twice is counted twice) and the total number g of group-related messages per user (i.e., the number of messages sent to a group instead of binary group membership). All activities show behavior consistent with power law networks; the majority of users show small activity patterns with a few nodes being significantly more active. All distributions are broad, indicating that the activity patterns of users are highly heterogeneous. The average number of messages per thread is 2.02, while the ratio of the messages to the number of replies is approximately 1.011: Even though these statistics indicate shallow conversations on average, we found that is not the case overall. Instead, the mean is so small due to the heavy-tailed distribution of number of messages per user. Further, even though the average number of messages per user is approximately 4, the average number of replies per user (7.3) is quite a bit higher, indicating users' tendency to directional communication instead of personal

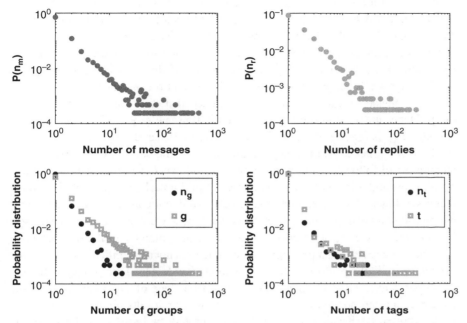

Figure 31.2 *From left to right and top to bottom, distribution of the number of (i) messages, n_m, posted by a user; (ii) replies, n_r, received by each user; (iii) distinct groups, n_g, to which a post belongs, and the total number of group-related messages, g, per user; and (iv) distinct hashtags, n_t, and the total number of hashtags used by a user.*

status updates or sharing of news. The study by Zhang et al.,(2010) reports a 25 per cent average of "conversation seeking" type of messages in an enterprise social network. We visually inspected randomly sampled messages and found that approximately 35 per cent are "share news" type of messages, which probe some sort of response. The combined average of approximately 60 per cent in the study by (Zhang et al., 2010) aligns quite well with our findings.

In many online social networks, users with shared interests may create and join groups. In the corporate microblogging service users are able to create and join groups to collaborate with smaller teams. Messages sent within group boundaries are broadcast to group members only, while private message exchanges among group members are also feasible. We found that the average number of messages per group is 24.6, indicating considerably high activity patterns across all groups. Instead, the number of hashtags per message is relatively low (approximately 0.4 hashtags per message). Tagging allows users to organize web resources (e.g., photos in Flickr, bookmarks in Delicious or tweets in Twitter). Twitter users adopted hashtags as an attempt to alleviate the significant information overload that the streaming nature of social media impose to users interested in specific topics. Huang, Thornton, & Efthimiadis (2010) examined tagging strategies followed by

Twitter users for content management and filtering. The low number of hashtags per message in our dataset is approximately similar to values reported for other Twitter datasets (e.g., Zangerle, Gassler, & Specht, 2011). Given the relatively low average number of hashtags per message, and the distribution of messages per group, we conjecture that rather than using hashtags, users of the corporate microblogging service mostly rely on group membership for content organization.

The existence of edge e_{ij} does not guarantee that the reciprocal edge e_{ji} also exists. Hence the relationship is not symmetric. If user A sends a message to user B, the edge e_{AB} is created, but not vice versa. We call user B the "follower" of user A. If B also replies to A, then they are each other's "mutual followers." By plotting the number of followees versus the number of followers, we found that the number of followers and followees is approximately equal for each user, possibly indicating reciprocal links (Chelmis & Prasanna, 2013a). High correlation of symmetric links due to users' tendency to reply back when they receive a message from other users is expected. However, our analysis of the level of symmetry in the directed post-reply network reveals that the degree of symmetry is not as significant as one would expect. Overall, the post-reply network exhibits low levels of reciprocity with only 21.49 per cent symmetric links, whereas the percentage of symmetric links in the largest connected component is 23.18 per cent. Our results align very well with those reported in (Kwak et al., 2010) for reciprocity in Twitter. Twitter users can join conversations either by replying to others (i.e., directly responding to another person's Tweet) or by mentioning them in their own Tweets (i.e., using their @username). When replying, only relevant people (e.g., the followers of the person who replied and the author of the original Tweet) will become aware of the reply in their timeline. Mentions are instead only visible to the users being mentioned unless someone explicitly searches Twitter for Tweets mentioning a given @username. Thus, the broadcasting nature of replying makes it easy for employees to both reach a lot of their colleagues relative to some other communication media (e.g., email), and from a reader's perspective, employees can choose to follow certain employees' tweets based on similar interests. In this context, our observations align very well with existing IOP studies (Zhao & Rosson, 2009; Kraut et al., 1990), aimed at gaining an in-depth understanding of how and why people use Twitter and exploring microblog's potential impacts on informal communication at work.

To quantify the extent of how densely the neighborhood of a node is connected, we examined the tendency of users in the post-reply network to cluster together. Not all nodes are connected in one cluster. There are 3,570 connected components, with the largest component encompassing 582 nodes (~13.8 per cent of the network). In addition, the clustering coefficient of nodes vary as a function of node degree. Specifically, the average clustering coefficient follows a decreasing trend with increasing node degree as shown in Figure 31.3. The clustering coefficient of a node u, with set Γ of N neighbors, is defined as the number of directed edges that exist between nodes in Γ, divided by the number of all possible directed edges between the nodes in Γ. Figure 31.3 shows that clustering coefficient is higher for nodes of low degree, suggesting significant clustering among low-degree nodes. This evidence of strong local clustering supports the intuition that people tend to be

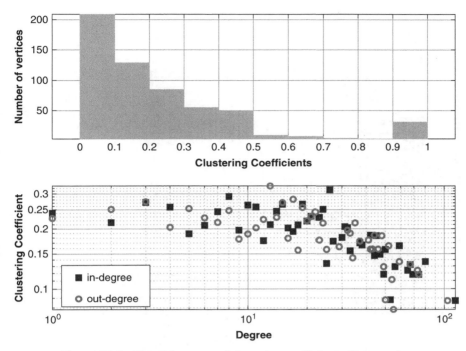

Figure 31.3 *Top: Histogram of clustering coefficients; Bottom: Average clustering coefficient as a function of degree. Both quantities refer to the largest connected component.*

introduced to others via mutual contacts, thus increasing the probability of two neighbors, u and v, of user z, to be connected themselves (Mislove et al., 2007).

31.3.2 Content Popularity and User Contribution to Discussions

In this section, we provide a brief introduction on how content and network features can influence the amount of response that messages receive, and how this can impact the growth of discussion threads. Understanding such dynamics can help employees to issue better posts, thus increasing their influence in the corporate network. Analysts may use this information to predict influential employees, identify experts and evolving or withering communities of practice, keep track of innovation and knowledge networks, and promote collaboration.

Much like Twitter, the microblogging service we study acts like an information network, where users post messages, which are then propagated to their followers, broadcasted to specific groups, or become available to the company-wide stories stream. Intuitively, one would expect a personal message that is being sent from user u to user v to trigger a reply message being sent from user v back to user u. In Section 31.3.1 we discussed that not all edges are reciprocal. Instead, we

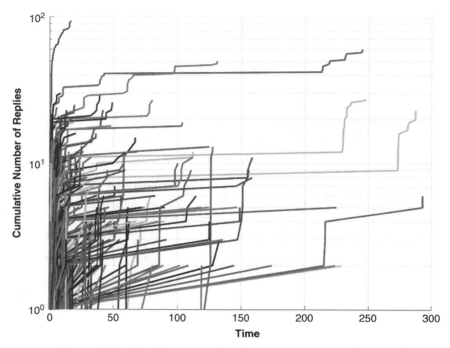

Figure 31.4 *Cumulative number of replies a message triggers over time.*

argued that, overall, the post-reply network exhibits low level of reciprocity with only 21.49 per cent symmetric links.

Figure 31.4 shows the evolution of the number of replies a message receives over a period of about one year in our D_1 dataset. Each curve corresponds to a threaded discussion, showing how much the number of replies increases daily for a single message, over a year. To make the figure readable, we randomly sample few discussion threads. The final number of replies varies widely among messages. A few messages become popular very fast, attracting numerous replies almost instantaneously, whereas others remain extremely unpopular. Overall, as messages age, accumulation of new replies slows down, and after a few days, messages typically no longer receive new replies. For some messages, the slope abruptly increases, often periodically. Messages in the post-reply network can be classified into four broad categories:

- Extremely popular posts that receive a lot of attention fast. The cumulative number of replies explodes over a small period of time.
- Extremely unpopular posts that receive small attention, in many cases just a single reply from the intended recipient of the message. Status updates of a personal nature might fall into this category, with a few comments coming mainly from "friends."
- Posts that accumulate few replies fast, often immediately, and few replies after a considerable amount of time has elapsed from the submission time of the post.
- Posts that trigger responses periodically, thus exhibiting periodic popularity.

Corporate microblogging capabilities provide users the opportunity to share day-to-day operational knowledge and domain knowledge, or discuss problem solving, relevant emerging techniques applications and technologies, trends, etc. Enterprise microblogging services mostly emphasize on the business perspective and therefore their content revolves around their main business and work culture, work practices, and everyday problems (technical or otherwise related to business). This factor may partially explain messages that fold into the third category. Messages of the form "I do not know how to run Apache Server in my machine. Can anyone help me?" could trigger messages of the form "I will look into the matter and get back to you asap," with the actual reply coming later on, often after a long time has passed, partially due to other, high priority responsibilities of repliers. Periodic attention could be the result of periodic messages being sent to groups, stimulating conversation between group members. Finally, extremely popular messages can be attributed to polls, which stimulate employees in positioning themselves with respect to a matter of interest (e.g., technology adoption).

For enterprises, the investment in money and time in maintaining microblogging services requires some sort of profit in return. Such profit may come from the sharing of ideas, leading to innovation, as well as reduction of searching time spend for data, information, and experts. A reduction in activity could be detrimental to the deployment of such services in the workplace, whereas abnormally high activity patterns may collide with employees' attention to work-related issues. Further, understanding what catches the attention of users (e.g., total number of replies a message yields) may lead to insights with respect to whom individuals choose to collaborate and for what reasons. Chelmis & Prasanna (2013a) provides a detailed analysis on the factors that can indicate the number of replies a message may receive over time.

31.4 Microblogging Technology Adoption at the Workplace

The importance of social networks on information spread has been well studied (Bakshy et al., 2012; Gomez Rodriguez, Leskovec, & Krause, 2010; Yang & Leskovec, 2010), emphasizing particularly on information dissemination. Traditionally, diffusion and cascading behavior have been formalized as transmission of infectious agents in a population, where each individual is either infected or susceptible, and infected nodes spread the contagion along the edges of the network. There are, however, differences between the way information flows, and the spread of viruses. While virus transmission is an indiscriminate process, information transmission is a selective process. Information is passed by its host only to individuals the host thinks would be interested in it. Diffusion models heavily rely on the premise that contagion propagates over an implicit network, the structure of which is assumed to be sufficient to explain the observed behavior. However, the structure of the underlying network has to be learned (Gomez Rodriguez et al., 2010) from a plethora of historical evidence, i.e. cascades. Although diffusion theory brings up the importance of friendship relations, adoption behavior is instead examined on the premises of the behavior of the entire population.

In online social networks, where individuals tend to organize into groups based on their common activities and interests, it has been hypothesized that the network structure (friendship or interaction) affects the way information spreads, and that adoption quickens as the number of adopting friends increases (Bakshy, Karrer, & Adamic, 2009). However, a node activation may not only be a function of the social network but can also depend on other factors such as imitation (Yang & Leskovec, 2010). This has lead to the development of epidemiology models (Hethcote, 2000) and computational approaches that are based on threshold models (Granovetter, 1978), deterministic or stochastic (Strang & Macy, 2001). Each agent has a threshold that, when exceeded, leads the agent to adopt an activity. When the threshold is applied within a local neighborhood (Solomon et al., 2000; Valente, 1996), local models emerge (Kempe, Kleinberg, & Tardos, 2003). Instead, global diffusion models perform thresholding to the whole population (Budak, Agrawal, & Abbadi, 2012).

Unlike online social networks where users create links to others who are similar to them (a phenomenon known as homophily; McPherson et al., 2011), or whose contributions they find interesting (Li et al., 2013), in a corporate environment, employees form bonds not because of similar tastes but due to tasks at hand (i.e., a function to be completed or an organizational need) or because of reporting-to relationships (i.e., team-members reporting to their supervisor). In this sense, there is no explicit social network, however, formal structures such us the organizational hierarchy may provide hints of influence at the workplace. As illustrated in Figure 31.5, the formal organization structure may constrain influence patterns, but informal communication outside the boundaries and restrictions of this formal "backbone" may also affect how users behave and ultimately how the diffusion network changes and grows.

31.4.1 Effect of Organization Hierarchy on Microblogging

Contrary to online social networks, microblogging services for enterprises are primarily designed to improve intra-firm transparency and knowledge sharing. However, the adoption of such collaborative environments presents certain challenges to enterprises (Günther et al., 2009). Zhang et al. (2010), provided a case study on the perceived benefits of corporate microblogging and barriers to adoption. Key factors influencing microblogging systems adoption in the workplace include privacy concerns, communication benefits, perceptions regarding signal-to -noise ratio, codification effort, reputation, expected relationships, and collaborative norms (Günther et al., 2009). Since the underlying process of influencing employees toward adopting the microblogging service is unknown and non trivial, we hypothesize that when employees choose to join the corporate microblogging service, they then have some influence on the employees who directly report to them, according to the formal organizational chart. Some of these employees will choose to join, which will in turn influence some of their team members into joining themselves and so on. Therefore, we assume that employee decisions to join depend on: (1) direct influence by managers, (2) peer influence by teammates,

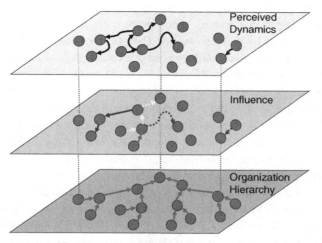

Figure 31.5 *Technology adoption dynamics at the workplace. Dynamics on and of the formal network structure are strongly coupled. The bottom layer illustrates the formal organization hierarchy, where black arrows represent "reporting-to" relationships between employees. The directionality of edges is from lower level employees to the company CEO. The middle layer depicts the flow of influence between people in the same group (red arrows), top-down influence from supervisors to team members (dashed, dark red arrows) and vice versa, bottom up team members' influence on their supervisors (dashed purple arrows). The upper layer, depicts observed adoption dynamics, i.e., a potential propagation tree.*

and (3) social influence resulting from the overall popularity of the microblogging service in the enterprise.

To quantify the influence inflicted by managers to employees reporting directly to them, we proceed as follows. Assume that manager u urges team members to join the microblogging service. A directed link e_{ju} exists if employee j directly reports to u according to the formal organizational hierarchy. If j joins the microblogging service after u, we call this join an "influenced join". We counted the number of employees who joined the microblogging service after their manager and classified employees into three classes:

- Employees who did not adopt the microblogging service even if their manager did (10.94%),
- Employees who adopted the microblogging service before their manager (36.04%), and
- Employees who adopted the microblogging service after their manager (53.01%).

Let N be the total number of employees directly reporting to manager u. Let K be the number of employees in N who joined the microblogging service after their manager u, and k be the total number of employees in N who joined the microblogging service after their manager u within the first n draws. The stochastic process according to which employees directly reporting to u choose to join the microblogging service is described by the "urn model" (Ghosh & Lerman, 2010), in which n balls are drawn without replacement from an urn containing N balls in total, of which K are white. The probability $P(X = k \mid K, N, n)$ that k of the first n employees reporting to manager u, joined the microblogging service after their manager purely by chance is equivalent to the probability that k of the n balls drawn from the urn are white. We set $n = 8$, calculating the number of employees who joined the microblogging service after their manager within the first 8 draws. This probability is given by the hypergeometric distribution (Chvátal, 1979).

The average number of employees who joined the microblogging service after their manager during the first n samples as a function of the number of employees who joined the microblogging service after their manager is shown in Figure 31.6. The plot is approximated by the Weibull cumulative distribution (Pinder, Wiener, & Smith, 1978). Using the learned parameters of this distribution, we can compute the expected number of employees to join the microblogging service after their manager within the first n joins for a manager with K employees reporting to her who joined the microblogging service after her. Additionally, we calculate the probability that k employees joined after their manager purely by chance using the hypergeometric distribution (Chvátal, 1979). We found that for $K > 3$, this probability is exceedingly small. Since it is exceedingly unlikely for employees to adopt the microblogging service after their manager purely by chance, we conclude that the number of employees who joined after their manager u is a prominent indicator of u's influence.

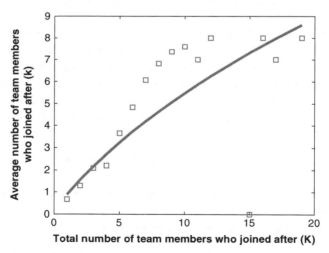

Figure 31.6 *Average number, k, of employees who joined the microblogging service after their manager, within the first n samples, versus the total number K of employees who joined after their manager, and approximation (shown as red line).*

Let N_j denote the number of employees who directly report to u and have joined the microblogging service. Also, let $\alpha \leq N_j$ be the number of employees who report to u and have joined the microblogging service after u, and let $q \leq N_j$ be the number of employees who report to u and have joined the microblogging service before u. While a high number of employees reporting to u having joined the microblogging service after u implies that u has high influence, a high q value is an indicator that one lacks influence. We use an adaptation of the z-score (Zhang et al., 2007), as a measure that combines the number of employees who have joined before and after their supervisor. Specifically, we use influence score (i.e., ι-score) to measure how different this behavior is from a user with random influence, i.e. managers the employees reporting to whom join after them with probability $p = 0.5$ and before him with probability $(1 - p) = 0.5$. We would expect such a random influencer to have N_j $p = N_j/2$ team members who joined after their supervisor with a standard deviation of $\sqrt{(N_j p(1-p))} = \sqrt{N_j}/2$. The ι-score measures how many standard deviations above or below the expected "random" value manager u lies, i.e., $\iota(u) = (\alpha-q)/\sqrt{(\alpha+q)}$.

If the employees reporting to manager u have joined the microblogging service after u about half of the time, u's ι-score will be close to 0. If they join after u more often than not, u's ι-score will be positive, otherwise, negative. We also calculate the time-independent ι-score of employees, with the difference that $\alpha \leq N$ is the number of employees who have joined the microblogging service (time invariably) and $q \leq N$ is the number of employees who have not joined the microblogging service.

Above, we measured influence at the level of individual employees, assuming that influence scores are fixed in time, but that they differ from employee to employee. A more sophisticated model of influence might include some small increase (similarly for decrease) in influence score as a function of time. We stick to the simpler model for simplicity, and because our fundamental result is not sensitive to such details.

Next, we examine the correlation between ι-score of managers and the number of employees reporting to them (team size), hoping to get a clearer picture of the relationship between the two quantities. We characterize the average ι-score of managers with λ employees reporting to them as $\iota(\lambda)$. Figure 31.7(a) shows the average ι-score of managers with λ employees reporting to them, that have joined the microblogging service. Here, we focus on managers that have themselves joined the microblogging service, so that a time comparison of joining times is meaningful. A clear increasing trend is evident, providing a supporting evidence on top-down influential flow through the formal organizational hierarchy. Figure 37.1 (b) shows the average time independent ι-score of managers with λ employees reporting to them. Figure 31.7(b) further shows different plots of the average time-independent ι-score of managers based on the premise that they have joined the microblogging service themselves or not. The average time-independent ι-score of managers that have not joined the microblogging service exhibits more fluctuations due to greater data sparsity. In every case, the average time-independent ι-score of managers who have joined the microblogging service is slightly higher than for managers who have not joined the service. Even though we cannot explain the

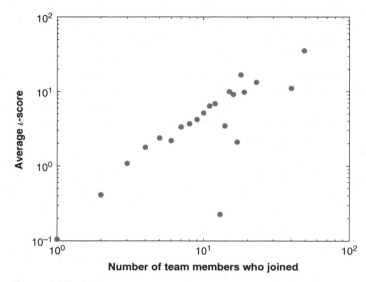

Figure 31.7 *(a) Average ι-score of managers with λ team-members who joined the microblogging service, and (b) average time-invariant ι-score of managers who have themselves adopted the new technology (similarly for those who have not joined the service) with λ team-members.*

reasons why this effect appears, the average time-independent ι-score increases for both classes as the team size λ increases, clearly indicating a strong correlation between the two quantities. We consider this a prominent indicator of influence imposed by managers to employees reporting directly to them.

Next, we assume that influence scores are characteristic of a particular level of the organization hierarchy tree, are fixed in time, and are the same for all employees at that particular level. To compute the average influence score for hierarchy level l, we first find employees m who belong to level l. We then compute the total number of employees N who directly report to managers in level l. Quantities α and q are defined as before, with the difference that they now operate on the total number of employees N who directly report to managers in level l. We then calculate the influence score for each level l as ι(l). Levels are ascending from the CEO (level 1) to lower levels. Level 13, which represents bottom level employees in our dataset, contains employees with no team members reporting to them.

Figure 31.8 shows the results. Level 13 has no influence score, thus, it does not appear in Figure 31.8. Most levels exhibit positive influence scores, with the exception of higher levels, which are closest to the CEO. Particularly, level 3, exhibits negative influence on average. As before, we measured influence at the granularity of hierarchical levels, assuming that influence scores are fixed in time, but that they differ from level to level. A more sophisticated model of influence might include some small increase (similarly for decrease) in influence score as a function of time, and also introduce a balancing factor based on the number of total employees at a level and the number of total employees reporting to them.

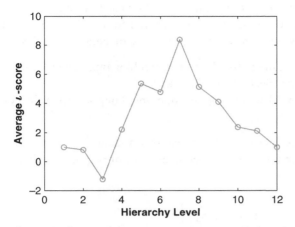

Figure 31.8 *Average ι-score as a function of hierarchy level.*

While it is intuitive to assume that higher levels in the organization would have higher impact due to the report-to relationships involved, our study suggests that middle levels are more successful in influencing employees lying lower in the hierarchy. Even though we do not have supporting evidence from other use-cases, we conjecture that middle-level managers are the most influential with respect to convincing others to adopt new technologies (in this case the new microblogging service). For reference, the influence of self-efficacy and work environment perceptions on employees' participation in development activities and its mediation by learning attitudes, perceptions of development needs, and perceived benefits were investigated in the field study by Noe & Wilk (1993). De Jong & Den Hartog (2007) explored leadership behaviors that stimulate employees' idea generation and application behavior based on a combination of literature research and in-depth interviews, whereas Bass (1990) studied the impact of manager's self-interest and values on directing employees under the influence of such managers away from their own best interests and to those of the organization as a whole. Finally, the structural model proposed by Hartline III & McKee (2000) to explain the dissemination by service firms of customer-oriented strategy to customer contact service employees indicated three "corridors of influence" between customer-oriented strategy and shared employee values.

31.4.2 Peer Pressure and Microblogging Technology Adoption

So far, we have assumed that an employee can be infected either by a direct supervisor or randomly, as a result of the overall popularity of the microblogging service in the enterprise. Widely used models of social and biological contagion (e.g., Granovetter, 1978; Newman, 2002) and observational studies of online contagion (Anagnostopoulos, Kumar, & Mahdian, 2008; Bakshy et al., 2009; Cha, Mislove, & Gummadi, 2009; Leskovec, Adamic, & Huberman, 2007) predict that the likelihood of infection increases with the number of infected contacts.

However, recent studies suggest that this correlation can have multiple causes that might be unrelated to social influence processes (Bakshy et al., 2012). Based on our empirical observations, we consider two alternative modeling scenarios:

• An employee is more likely to adopt the microblogging service if more team-mates join the service (Section 31.4.2.1), and
• An employee is more likely to adopt the microblogging service as its popularity increases (Section 31.4.2.2).

Our goal then becomes to estimate the probability of adoption for each user given the actions of their teammates (local neighborhood) or overall popularity (global influence).

31.4.2.1 Independent Peer Pressure Model

Influence of friends is generally modeled to be additive. For instance, according to the widely used Independent Cascade Model (ICM; Kempe et al., 2003), a node has n independent chances to become infected, where n is the number of infected "friends." In our case, every node can be infected only once, and once infected, it stays infected. Because of the structure of the organizational hierarchy, employee u's friends may include either (i) teammates alone, or (ii) teammates and the direct supervisor. Starting with a single employee who has joined the microblogging service, employees susceptible to infection, decide to join the microblogging service with some probability that depends on the number of their infected friends. We model the influence employees receive by their friends as multiple exposures to an infection according to ICM (Kempe et al., 2003) as $p_{ICM} = 1 - (1 - \lambda)^n$.

We measured this quantity on our dataset, by isolating the employees in two classes: those who had exactly n friends joining the microblogging service and did not join, and those who had exactly n friends joining the microblogging service before they themselves joined. We found that the likelihood of adoption when no friends have joined is remarkably high (0.7581 when considering teammates only and 0.6807 when the supervisor is also considered). In both cases, the likelihood of adoption becomes 1 when at least one friend has joined the service. We conclude that the relationship between the number of friends that have joined and likelihood of joining most probably reflects heterogeneous popularity of the microblogging service across teams (Bakshy et al., 2012). Therefore, the naive conditional probability does not directly give the probability increase due to influence via multiple joining friends (Bakshy et al., 2012).

31.4.2.2 Exponential Peer Pressure Model

Next, we consider the scenario where employees observe others adopting the micro-blogging service. In this context, they may not only be more likely to adopt the service, but the rate at which they do so may quicken as the popularity of the service increases (i.e., the more popular the microblogging service becomes, the more likely it is for employees to adopt it). We begin by splitting the employee population into two

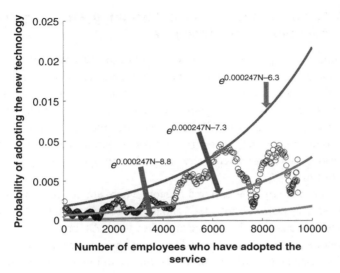

Figure 31.9 *Empirical probability of an employee adopting the new technology given that n employees have already done so. Solid lines denote probability estimates as calculated from an exponential growth model.*

compartments: those who have already joined the microblogging service and those who have not. Assuming an exponential growth model (Bass, 1969), the rate at which employees join the service should follow an increasing trend. Intuitively, as more people adopt the microblogging service, a certain buzz" around the service begins to unfold, increasing the probability of others joining the service as well. Figure 31.9 shows the probability that an employee will join the microblogging service as a function of the service popularity. Figure 31.9 reveals that the probability of employees joining the microblogging service is in fact neither constant nor monotonically increasing (similarly decreasing). Instead it exhibits increasing and decreasing regimes over time. This observation suggests that more complex dynamics take place over the organizational hierarchy. One possible explanation of this phenomenon is that whenever influential managers join the microblogging service, a period of "influenced joins" follows. In essence, this provides a hint that the adoption mechanism follows a snowball effect propagating the "epidemic" in a top-to-bottom fashion, followed by a random infection that exposes new portions of the population.

Since, the probability of joining given the number of total infections incorporates the probability of an influenced join, we fit three exponential growth models. The first model (blue line at the top) provides an "optimistic" expected probability of adoption. Contrary, the "pessimistic" model (red line at the bottom) yields a probability of adoption that increases marginally as the total number of people who join the service increases over time. Finally, the average fit (green line in the middle) shows how the probability of adoption follows on average an increasing trend as a function of previous adoptions.

31.5 Computational Models of Microblogging Technology Adoption at the Workplace

The underlying process that drives adoption of new technologies at the workplace is unknown and non trivial. In this section, we present a set of computational models that approximate the dynamics of the observed adoption of a new microblogging service given the organizational hierarchy in our dataset. Even though other social datasets with different types of enterprise hierarchies may naturally fit into our modelling, we restrict our discussion to the setting of microblogging adoption at the workplace, were we track employees joining the service over a period of time.

We study the problem of progressive diffusion, where employees who adopt the microblogging service become "infected" and do not become "healthy" again (i.e., employees do not unsubscribe the service once they join). As time progresses, more employees become infected as they adopt (join) the microblogging service. Additionally, we assume that when employees choose to join the corporate microblogging service, they then have some influence on the employees who directly report to them, according to the formal organizational chart. Some of these employees will choose to join, which will in turn influence some of their team members into joining themselves and so on.

We only observe the time t_u when a particular employee joins the microblogging service. We assert that manager u urges team members to join the microblogging service. A directed link e_{ju} exists if employee j directly reports to u according to the formal organizational hierarchy. If j joins the microblogging service after u, we call that join an "influenced join". One can think of influenced joins as an implicit indicator of the underlying influence network. In addition to being directly influenced by a manager, we assume that an employee may experience social influence from the overall popularity of the microblogging service in the enterprise.

We define n_t as the number of employees who have joined the microblogging service by time t, i.e., the number of infections at time t. We aim to accurately model the number of infections, n_t, over time as a function of individual influence functions due to reporting relationships, and general influence as a function of the service popularity.

31.5.1 Computational Model of Top-Down and Global Influence (TGI)

From the empirical analysis presented in Section 31.4, we incorporate the following dynamics into our computational model of top-down and global influence:

- Employees are influenced by their managers to join the microblogging service.
- Employees have multiple chances to get infected (join). Once employees are infected, they cannot recover, i.e., employees do not unsubscribe from the service.
- As employees observe others adopting the microblogging service, the rate at which they are more likely to adopt the service increases with its popularity.

We begin by selecting a single node from the organization hierarchy to start the infection. We chose this "seed" node to be the exact employee who first registered to the microblogging service according to our dataset. At each time step, the technology spreads as follows:

(i) Each node that was infected at time $t - 1$ has n chances to infect the n employees who directly report to it, each with probability p, at time t. Once a node is infected, it cannot be infected again. Infected employees are not allowed to infect their direct supervisor, so following this strategy, the technology can only propagate toward the leaves of the hierarchy tree.

(ii) Once all infected nodes are examined, healthy nodes have the chance to be "randomly" infected by observing the general popularity of the microblogging service up to time $t - 1$. For n_i^{t-1} employed who have adopted the technology up to time $t - 1$, the probability of "random" adoption is computed using the pessimistic exponential growth pattern from Section 31.4.2.2. The choice of the pessimistic exponential growth pattern is conservative in that it does not unfairly help our model in predicting the cumulative number of adoptions over time.

31.5.2 Computational Model of Local Influence and Global Influence (LGI)

In model we presented in Section 31.5.1 assumes that the process of adopting the microblogging service closely follows the boundaries imposed by the formal organization hierarchy. Specifically, the model in Section 31.5.1 treats the spread of the adoption as a virus and incorporates influence either by a direct supervisor or by the overall popularity of the microblogging service. However, widely used models of social and biological contagion (e.g., Granovetter, 1978; Newman, 2002) and observational studies of online contagion (e.g., Anagnostopoulos et al., 2008; Bakshy et al., 2009; Cha et al., 2009; Leskovec et al., 2007) predict that the likelihood of infection increases with the number of infected contacts. However, recent studies suggest that this correlation can have multiple causes that might be unrelated to social influence processes (Bakshy et al., 2012). As a result, we consider in this section an alternate approach based on which, nodes choose to adopt the technology after examining their immediate neighborhood (which includes both managers and employees directly reporting to them) or after examining the overall growing popularity of the microblogging service over time.

The process starts with the organization hierarchy, and two colors. Let red represent employees who have joined the microblogging service, and blue those who have not. We choose a single node to be the seed user, i.e. have color red. All other users are painted blue. Once a node is painted red, it cannot change color again. Finally, nodes have the chance to be randomly influenced by observing the general popularity of the microblogging service up to time $t - 1$. The probability of random influence at time t is based on the same function as that used in Section 31.5.1. As before, we chose the seed node to be the exact employee who first registered to the microblogging service according to our dataset. At each time step, nodes painted blue, calculate if the payoff of picking the color red (i.e., $\alpha(n_{red}/n)$) is greater than the payoff of picking the color blue (i.e., $\beta(n_{blue}/n)$). In the former case, they decide to flip colors, otherwise to remain painted blue. Parameter n_{blue} denotes the number of blue neighbors, n_{red} denotes the number of red neighbors and $n = n_{blue} + n_{red}$ is the total number of neighbors of a node. Parameters α and $\beta = 1 - \alpha$ denote the rewards for choosing red and blue accordingly.

31.5.2.1 Empirical Evaluation

In order to evaluate the ability of the computational models presented in Sections 31.5.1 and 31.5.2 to match the observed dynamics of technology adoption in our dataset, we perform extensive numerical simulations. Specifically, we begin with the organization hierarchy of 12,170 employees in our dataset, and the employee who first joined the microblogging service. In our simulations, each time step represents a day. We let our models run for 600 steps, or until all employees are predicted to have adopted the technology. We simulated our models ten times. Even though we experimented with various values of parameters p, α and β, in the end, we decided to use $p = 0.023$ for TGI and $\alpha = 0.82$, $\beta = 0.18$ for LGI.

For evaluation purposes, we performed the following comparisons:

- The *overall* number of employees who are predicted to have adopted the technology by the end of the simulation is compared to the real cumulative number of adoptions extracted from our dataset,
- The *cumulative number* of employees who are predicted to have adopted the technology by the time t is compared to the real cumulative number of adoptions at that time extracted from our dataset.
- The total time required to infect N employees as predicted by the models is compared to the actual time observed in our dataset.

We compare the models presented in Section 31.5.1 and 31.5.2 with three baselines that have shown superior performance in predicting information and innovation diffusion in social networks:

- Epidemic Models: According to the Susceptible-Infected (SI) model (Jacquez & Simon, 1993), each node can infect its neighbors, each with probability p_{SI}. We additionally considered the Susceptible-Infected-Susceptible (SIS) and Susceptible-Infected-Resistant (SIR) models (Hethcote, 2000), as well as the Susceptible-Infected-Dead (SID) model (Kamp, 2010) as alternatives to model social contagion, as these models are widely used in prior work. We found these models, however, to not appropriately capture the semantics of adoption, according to which an employee who joins the microblogging service does not unsubscribe, thus returning to the susceptible state, or becoming resistant. Further, our analysis did not provide any supporting evidence for the hypothesis that infected employees do not infect others, thus modeling them as "dead" is not appropriate in this case.

- Cascade Model: According to the Independent Cascade Model (ICM) (Kempe et al., 2003), a node has n independent chances to become infected, where n is the number of infected friends. In our context, employee u's friends may include either (i) teammates alone, or (ii) teammates and a direct supervisor due to the structure imposed by the organizational hierarchy. Every node can be infected only once, and once infected, it stays infected. Starting with a single employee who has joined the microblogging service, employees adopt the microblogging service with some probability that depends on the number of their infected friends (see Section 31.4.2.1).

- Diffusion Models: According to popular Diffusion Models (DM) in the literature (e.g., Abrahamson & Rosenkopf, 1997; Bass, 1969; Choi, Sang-Hoon, & Jeho, 2010), the willingness of an individual to adopt a new microblogging technology at time t, U^t_u is modeled by three main elements: (i) the standalone benefit of the new technology, (ii) network effects, and (iii) the idiosyncratic reservation utility. Formally, $U^t_u = Q_u + \gamma N^{t-1}_u - R_u$, where Q_u represents the service's intrinsic value perceived by employee u, N^{t-1}_u denotes the proportion of adopters in u's neighborhood at time t −1, γ represents the relative importance against stand-alone benefits, and R_u indicates u's inherent reluctance or reservation about adopting the new service. Note that quantity Q_u is not affected by whether other people adopt it or not.

Simulation results produced by the baselines and compared to the true adoption curve are shown in Figure 31.10 Specifically, Figures 31.10(a) and 31.10(b) show simulation results produced by the SI model and the ICM model respectively, for varying infection probability values, whereas, Figure 31.10(c) shows simulation results produced by the DM model, for varying numbers of initial adopters.

Simulation results produced by either the SI model or the ICM model do not fit the real cumulative number of adoptions over time. High infection probability values result in sudden outbreaks, whereas very small probability values result in smooth cumulative distributions that do not exhibit the statistical properties of the true cumulative number of infected users. The total number of infections and the time required to infect the whole body of employees is also inconsistent with the observed adoption curve. ICM further results in sudden epidemics, which often end up being restricted to a small subset of the population (i.e., fail to cover the entire population) and eventually come to a halt. No new infections are achieved due to the fact that each exposure has a single chance of success. If the result of an exposure is no infection, that connection is not examined again. Hence, if the root of a sub-tree in the formal organizational hierarchy is not infected, the infection cannot proceed further down the sub-tree. The simulation results corroborate our conjecture that the naive conditional probability does not directly give the probability increase due to influence via multiple joining friends (Bakshy et al., 2012). In the case of DM, when the first true adopter is selected to start the infection, the epidemic progresses slowly. Instead, when five true

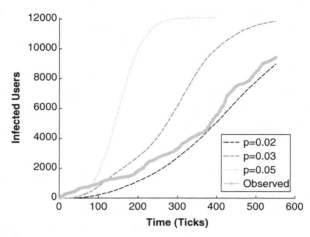

Figure 31.10 *Observed and predicted cumulative number of employees who have adopted the new technology. Time is measured in days. Solid lines show the outcome of simulations based on (a) the SI model and (b) the ICM model for various infection probabilities, and (c) the DM model based on a varying number of initial adopters.*

adopters are used, the epidemic is substantially speeded up. When the seed set contains seven of the true adopters, the simulation result adequately fits the observed adoption curve, without however exhibiting the statistical properties of the true cumulative number of infected users. Overall, this model too fails to capture the hidden dynamics of technology adoption at the workplace.

Next, we show the outcome of ten runs of our TGI model (see Section 31.5.1) in Figure 31.11. The figure also shows the average of the ten runs. Notice a very good alignment between the reality and simulated epidemics in all cases. Not all runs result in the total number of true infections by the time threshold. Further, a few runs overestimate the cumulative number of infections, resulting in rapid epidemics. Unlike the baselines, our complex contagion model fits more naturally the true cumulative number of infected users in all cases. Specifically, the simulation results remarkably follow the speedups and slowdowns of adoption over time, exhibiting nonlinear characteristics as the true adoption curve. Some runs diverge from the true curve after about 400 days. However, running the model numerous times and averaging the results seems to adequately approximate the statistical properties of the true cumulative number of infected users. We conclude that this is a direct result of the asymmetric contagion due to the hierarchical influence to adoption and the integration of peer pressure due to growing popularity of the microblogging service at the enterprise.

Finally, we present the outcome of ten runs of our LGI model (see Section 31.5.2), and their average, in Figure 31.12. In this case too, simulated epidemics match the reality very well. Similar to the epidemics produced by our model, not all runs result

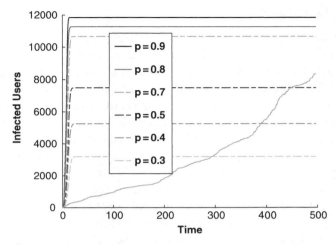

Figure 31.11 *Observed and predicted cumulative number of employees who have adopted the new technology. Time is measured in days. Solid lines show the outcome of simulations based on TGI model (Section 31.5.1).*

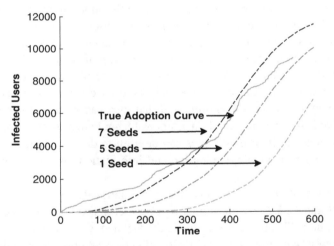

Figure 31.12 *Observed and predicted cumulative number of employees who have adopted the new technology. Time is measured in days. Solid lines show the outcome of simulations based on LGI model (Section 31.5.2).*

in the total number of true infections by the time threshold. Further, smooth regimes of adoption, speedups and slowdowns of the acceptance of the microblogging service from employees is apparent. Unlike our TGI model, our LGI model slightly overestimates the cumulative number of infections. In all cases however, we find that this model too fits rather closely to the true cumulative number of infected users, replicating the statistical properties of the empirical epidemic.

31.6 Conclusion

The underlying process that drives adoption of new technologies at the workplace is unknown and non trivial. In this Chapter, we provided an extensive analysis of an extracted network of threaded discussions in a corporate microblogging service. We argued that the "smaller" world that online social networks developed in this context exhibits a strongly connected core of highly interconnected employees with high correlation between user activities. The analysis of threaded discussions as a social network provided insights into the structure of informal communication using the microblogging service. In addition to daily microblogging activities, we further examined the effect of the formal organizational structure to the adoption mechanism of the microblogging service. We found, microscopically, that employees' tendency toward adopting the new microblogging service is influenced by their direct supervisors (dependency on the network structure). We used ι-score as a prominent indicator of influence imposed by managers on their teams, and we demonstrated that middle level managers are on average more successful in promoting the adoption of the new service. Further, we empirically measured employees' likelihood of adopting the new microblogging service with respect to the behavior of the general crowd.

In addition to discussing the patterns that capture the adoption likelihood increment as a function of the overall service popularity among the employee population, we showed how these observations were incorporated into two intuitive and simple computational models that capture the process of adoption both at the *microscopic* and the *macroscopic* levels. Simulation results showed that these models provide great improvements over widely used diffusion models in the online social network analysis literature, and that they can be used to shed light into the mechanisms driving adoption of new technologies at the workplace. In turn, the models and their predictions can be used to develop better strategies for rapid and efficient technology adoption and information dissemination at the workplace.

As a word of caution, we note that the computational models discussed in Sections 31.5.1 and 31.5.2 rely on estimating causal effects only within the formal organizational chart. This limitation is due to the fact that we are unable to observe the actual adoption "cascade" (i.e., who really influences whom). Nevertheless, the computational models discussed in Section 31.5 can be extended in numerous ways. First, in the real world, topologies other than tree structure may exist. The more general problem of influence over an arbitrary graph has been recently explored in Srivastava, Chelmis, & Prasanna, 2014, 2015a, and 2015b. Second, the computational models discussed in Section 31.5 can be extended to allow for influence scores to vary over time, as well as incorporate different roles individuals assume in the adoption process, accounting for influence variations as a function of employees' level in the organization hierarchy. Third, the effect of network evolution (e.g., layoffs or new hires) on influence can be incorporated in the computational models discussed in Section 31.5, since one's influence may intuitively increase with seniority in the company. Finally, studying adoption dynamics in the presence of competing technologies or numerous technologies being introduced at around the same time is a challenging open research direction.

We conclude by drawing a preliminary linkage between the computational analysis of the adoption and engagement patterns discussed in this Chapter to existing IOP theories of influence. Roberson & Colquitt (2005) used social network theory to explain the roles of structural equivalence and cohesion in the development of shared perceptions of team members about how the team as a whole is treated, and linked such perceptions to team effectiveness outcomes. Similar to Roberson & Colquitt (2005), our proposed computational models account for the social processes that lead to the emergence of the observed dynamics. We conjecture that combining sociological and psychological approaches with computational analysis of interaction logs can thus become a powerful tool to (i) articulate the processes that lead to observed patterns at various levels of analysis (i.e., joint analysis of the interaction network structure, formal organizational hierarchy, and underlying influence processes); (ii) benefit managers from an analysis of network patterns and interactions so as to be able to understand influence boundaries, the development of shared perceptions of new technologies benefits, and the potential linkage of such perceptions to effectiveness outcomes; and (iii) offer guidance for influencing shared perceptions in the presence of barriers including but not limited to leadership behaviors, cultural diversity, self-interest and self-motivation, and conflicting goals (e.g., self-interest as opposed to the interests of the organization as a whole).

References

Abrahamson, E. & Rosenkopf, L. (1997). Social network effects on the extent of innovation diffusion: A computer simulation. *Organization Science, 8*(3), 289–309.

Anagnostopoulos, A., Kumar, R., & Mahdian, M. (2008). Influence and correlation in social networks. *The 14th ACM SIGKDD International Conference on Knowledge Discovery and Data Mining* (pp. 7–15). New York, NY: ACM Press.

Bakshy, E., Karrer, B., & Adamic., L. A. (2009). Social influence and the diffusion of user-created content. *The 10th ACM conference on electronic commerce* (pp. 325–334). New York, NY: ACM Press.

Bakshy, E., Rosenn, I., Marlow, C., & Adamic, L. (2012). The role of social networks in information diffusion. *The 21st international conference on world wide web* (pp. 519–528). New York, NY: ACM Press.

Bass, B. M. (1990). From transactional to transformational leadership: Learning to share the vision. *Organizational dynamics, 18*(3), 19–31.

Bass, F. M. (1969). A new product growth for model consumer durables. *Management Science, 15*(5), 215–227.

Budak, C., Agrawal, D., & Abbadi, A. E. (2012). Diffusion of information in social networks: Is it all local? *The 12th international conference on data minings* (pp. 121–130). Washington, DC: IEEE Computer Society.

Burkhart, T., Werth, D., & Loos, P. (2012). Context-sensitive business process support based on emails. *The 21st international conference on world wide web* (pp. 851–856). New York, NY: ACM Press.

Cha, M., Mislove, A., & Gummadi, K. P. (2009). A measurement-driven analysis of information propagation in the flickr social network. *The 18th International Conference on World Wide Web* (pp. 721–730). New York, NY: ACM Press.

Chelmis, C. & Prasanna, V. K. (2013a). An empirical analysis of microblogging behavior in the enterprise. *Social Network Analysis and Mining*, *3*(3), 611–633.

Chelmis, C. & Prasanna, V. K. (2013b). The role of organization hierarchy in technology adoption at the workplace. *The 2013 IEEE/ACM international conference on advances in social networks analysis and mining* (pp. 8–15). New York, NY: ACM Press.

Chelmis, C., Ajitesh, S., & Prasanna, V. K. (2014). Computational models of technology adoption at the workplace. *Social Network Analysis and Mining*, *4*(1), 199.

Choi, H., Sang-Hoon, K., & Jeho, L. (2010). Role of network structure and network effects in diffusion of innovations. *Industrial Marketing Management*, *39*(1), 170–177.

Chvátal, V. (1979). The tail of the hypergeometric distribution. *Discrete Mathematics*, *25* (3), 285–287.

De Jong, J. P. & Den Hartog, D. N. (2007). How leaders influence employees' innovative behaviour. *European Journal of Innovation Management*, *10*(1), 41–64.

Ghosh, R. & Lerman, K. (2010). Predicting influential users in online social networks. The KDD Workshop on Social Network Analysis.

Gomez Rodriguez, M., Leskovec, J., & Krause, A. (2010). Inferring networks of diffusion and influence. *The 16th ACM SIGKDD international conference on knowledge discovery and data mining* (pp. 1019–1028). New York, NY: ACM Press.

Granovetter, M. (1978). Threshold models of collective behavior. *American Journal of Sociology*, *83*(6), 1420–1443.

Günther, O., Krasnova, H., Riehle, D., & Schöndienst, V. (2009). Modeling micro-blogging adoption in the enterprise. The 15th Americas Conference on Information Systems.

Guy, I., Sigalit, U., Inbal, R., Adam, P., & Michal, J. (2011). Do you want to know?: Recommending strangers in the enterprise. *The ACM 2011 conference on computer supported cooperative work* (pp. 285–294). New York, NY: ACM Press.

Hartline, M. D., III, J. G., & McKee, D. O. (2000). Corridors of influence in the dissemination of customer-oriented strategy to customer contact service employees. *Journal of Marketing*, *64*(2), 35–50.

Hethcote, H. W. (2000). The mathematics of infectious diseases. *SIAM Review*, *42*(4), 599–653.

Hua, G. & Haughton, D. (2012). A network analysis of an online expertise sharing community. *Social Network Analysis and Mining*, *2*(4), 291–303.

Huang, J., Thornton, K. M., & Efthimiadis, E. N. (2010). Conversational tagging in twitter. *The 21st ACM conference on hypertext and hypermedia* (pp. 173–178). New York, NY: ACM Press.

Jacquez, J. A. & Simon, C. P. (1993). The stochastic SI model with recruitment and deaths: I. Comparison with the closed SIS model. *Mathematical Biosciences*, *117*(1–2), 77–125.

Kamp, C. (2010). Untangling the interplay between epidemic spread and transmission network dynamics. *PLoS Computational Biology*, 6, (11).

Kempe, D., Kleinberg, J., & Tardos, É. (2003). Maximizing the spread of influence through a social network. *The ninth ACM SIGKDD international conference on knowledge discovery and data mining* (pp. 137–146). New York, NY: ACM Press.

Kraut, R. E., Fish, R. S., Root, R. W., & Chalfonte, B. L. (1990). Informal communication in organizations: Form, function, and technology. In I. S. Oskamp & S. Spacapan (Eds.), *Human reactions to technology: The Claremont Symposium on Applied Social Psychology* (pp. 145–199). Beverly Hills, CA: Sage Publications.

Krishnamurthy, B., Gill, P., & Arlitt, M. (2008). A few chirps about twitter. *The first workshop on online social networks* (pp. 19–24). New York, NY: ACM Press.

Kwak, H., Lee, C., Park, H., & Moon, S. (2010). What is Twitter, a social network or a news media? *The 19th international conference on world wide web* (pp. 591–600). New York, NY: ACM Press.

Leskovec, J., Adamic, L. A., & Huberman, B. A. (2007). The dynamics of viral marketing. *ACM Transactions on the Web*, *1*(1), 5.

Li, C. T., Kuo, T. T., Ho, C. T., Hong, S. C., Lin, W. S., & Lin, S. D. (2013). Modeling and evaluating information propagation in a microblogging social network. *Social Network Analysis and Mining*, *3*(3), 341–357.

Lin, C. Y., Wu, L., Wen, Z., Tong, H., Griffiths-Fisher, V., Shi, L., et al. (2012). Social network analysis in enterprise. *Proceedings of the IEEE*, *100*(9), 2759–2776.

McPherson, M., Smith-Lovin, L., & Cook, J. M. (2011). Birds of a feather: Homophily in social networks. *Annual Review of Sociology*, *27*(1), 415–444.

Mislove, A., Marcon, M., Gummadi, K. P., Druschel, P., & Bhattacharjee, B. (2007). Measurement and analysis of online social networks. *The 7th ACM SIGCOMM Conference on Internet Measurement* (pp. 29–42). New York, NY: ACM Press.

Newman, M. E. (2002). Spread of epidemic disease on networks. *Physical Review E*, *66*(1), 016128.

Noe, R. A. & Wilk, S. L. (1993). Investigation of the factors that influence employees' participation in development activities. *Journal of Applied Psychology*, *78*(2), 291.

Pinder, J. E., Wiener, J. G., & Smith, M. H. (1978). The Weibull distribution: A new method of summarizing survivorship data. *Ecology*, *59*(1), 175–179.

Roberson, Q. M. & Colquitt, J. A. (2005). Shared and configural justice: A social network model of justice in teams. *Academy of Management Review*, *30*(3), 595–607.

Schifanella, R., Barrat, A., Cattuto, C., Markines, B., & Menczer, F. (2010). Folks in folksonomies: social link prediction from shared metadata. *The Third ACM International Conference on Web Search and Data Mining* (pp. 271–280). New York, NY: ACM Press.

Solomon, S., Weisbuch, G., De Arcangelis, L., Jan, N., & Stauffer, D. (2000). Social percolation models. *Physica A: Statistical Mechanics and Its Applications*, *277*(1), 239–247.

Srivastava, A., Chelmis, C., & Prasanna, V. K. (2014). Influence in social networks: A unified model? *IEEE/ACM International Conference on Advances in Social Networks Analysis and Mining* (pp. 451–454).

Srivastava, A., Chelmis, C., & Prasanna, V. K. (2015a). Social influence computation and maximization in signed networks with competing cascades. *IEEE/ACM International Conference on Advances in Social Networks Analysis and Mining*, (pp. 41–48).

Srivastava, A., Chelmis, C., & Prasanna, V. K. (2015b). The unified model of social influence and its application in influence maximization. *Social Network Analysis and Mining*, *5*(1), 66.

Strang, D. & Macy, M. W. (2001). In search of excellence: Fads, success stories, and adaptive emulation. *American Journal of Sociology, 107*(1), 147–182.

Valente, T. W. (1996). Social network thresholds in the diffusion of innovations. *Social Networks, 18*(1), 69–89.

Weng, J., Lim, E. P., Jiang, J., & He, Q. (2010). *Twitterrank: finding topic-sensitive influential twitterers. The Third ACM International Conference on Web Search and Data Mining* (pp. 261–270). New York, NY: ACM Press.

Wu, A., DiMicco, J. M., & Millen, D. R. (2010). Detecting professional versus personal closeness using an enterprise social network site. *The SIGCHI Conference on Human Factors in Computing Systems* (pp. 1955–1964). New York, NY: ACM Press.

Yang, J. & Leskovec, J. (2010). Modeling information diffusion in implicit networks. *10th international conference on data mining* (pp. 599–608). Washington, DC: IEEE Computer Society.

Zangerle, E., Gassler, W., & Specht, G. (2011). Using tag recommendations to homogenize folksonomies in microblogging environments. *International conference on social informatics* (pp. 113–126). Springer.

Zhang, J., Ackerman, M. S., & Adamic, L. (2007). *Expertise networks in online communities: structure and algorithms. The 16th International Conference on World Wide Web* (pp. 221–230). New York, NY: ACM Press.

Zhang, J., Qu, Y., Cody, J., & Wu, Y. (2010). A case study of micro-blogging in the enterprise: Use, value, and related issues. *The SIGCHI Conference on Human Factors in Computing Systems* (pp. 123–132). New York, NY: ACM Press.

Zhao, D. & Rosson, M. B. (2009). How and why people Twitter: The role that micro-blogging plays in informal communication at work. *The ACM 2009 International Conference on Supporting Group Work* (pp. 243–252). New York, NY: ACM Press.

32 Advantages and Unintended Consequences of Using Electronic Human Resource Management (eHRM) Processes

Richard D. Johnson and Dianna L. Stone

32.1 Introduction

In recent years, technology has fundamentally changed the way work is accomplished, and has revolutionized the field of human resource management (HR; Society for Human Resource Management, 2002). A recent survey suggested that nearly all organizations are utilizing technology to support core HR practices (Sierra-Cedar, 2016), and this technology is transforming the way that organizations recruit, select, motivate, train, and retain employees (Gueutal & Stone, 2005; Kavanagh & Johnson, 2018; Stone et al., 2015). For instance, organizations are increasingly using electronic human resource management (eHRM), or internet-based technologies to manage HR processes including e-recruitment, e-selection, e-learning, e-performance management, and e-compensation (Stone & Dulebohn, 2013). Organizations typically use eHRM to decrease transaction times, reduce administrative costs, and streamline burdensome HR processes (Johnson et al., 2016). In addition, eHRM may enhance an organization's ability to achieve its key goals of attracting, motivating, and retaining talented employees (Stone, Stone-Romero, & Lukaszewski, 2003).

Although there are a number of advantages of using eHRM in organizations, researchers also argued that eHRM has some unintended consequences (Stone et al., 2003). For example, it has the potential to invade personal privacy, increase adverse impact against minority groups, and magnify the workload of employees and managers (Stone et al., 2003). Given that eHRM processes have a host of advantages and inadvertent consequences, we believe that Industrial and Organizational (IO) psychologists and HR professionals should understand these issues before advising organizations to adopt them.

In view of the growing importance of technology in HR, and the advantages and unintended consequences of using eHRM, the primary purposes of this chapter are to (a) identify the potential advantages and unintended consequences of using eHRM to achieve HR goals, (b) consider the existing research on the advantages and unintended consequences of using eHRM, (c) offer directions for future research on the topic, and (d) suggest strategies that IO psychologists and HR practitioners can use to enhance the overall effectiveness and acceptance of these new processes. Although there are numerous ways that organizations are using eHRM (e.g., e-mentoring, e-lancing, e-recruiting), we plan to limit our review to the use of e-recruitment, e-selection, e-learning, e-performance management, and e-compensation. The primary reason for this is that these processes are more widely supported by technology, and more widely used, in organizations than others (e.g., e-mentoring, e-lancing). Thus, in the following sections we consider the advantages of eHRM for organizations and individuals, and the potential limitations of using these systems for the same stakeholders. We also offer directions for future research and practice on the issues.

32.2 Goals of Human Resource Systems in Organizations

The primary goals of the HR system in organizations are to attract, motivate, and retain organizational members in their roles (Katz & Kahn, 1978). Further, research on HR strategy revealed that employee performance is more important than ever because today's organizations compete on the basis of the talents and skills of their workers (Huselid, 1995; Jackson & Schuler, 1995). In order to achieve these goals, HR systems must meet several important objectives (Stone et al., 2003). First, they must facilitate the attraction of highly talented applicants through effective recruiting practices (Breaugh & Starke, 2000). Second, they must improve productivity through selection systems that enhance the correspondence between job requirements and employees' knowledge, skills, and abilities (KSAs; Stone et al., 2003). Third, HR systems should ensure that employee skills are developed and upgraded as organizational and job requirements change. Fourth, HR systems should increase retention of workers through effective compensation and reward systems. Fifth, they should help organizations communicate HR policies and practices so that all members are aware of them, assist organizations with the development of HR plans, and minimize overall administrative costs. Sixth, they should be responsive to the needs of internal and external stakeholders (e.g., applicants, employees, managers, and HR professionals), ensure that organizational policies are fair, help the organization increase the inclusion of diverse group members, and facilitate equal employment opportunities (Stone et al., 2003). Several authors have noted that organizations are increasingly using eHRM to achieve these goals (Gueutal & Stone, 2005; Johnson, Lukaszewski, & Stone, 2016; Stone & Dulebohn, 2013), but they also maintain that eHRM may result in both advantages and unintended consequences (Stone et al., 2003) for these different stakeholders. In the sections that follow, we consider two of the multiple stakeholders who use eHRM, discuss advantages and limitations of these systems for each stakeholder, and consider how these new systems can meet HR goals.

32.3 eHRM and Multiple Stakeholders

There are a number of stakeholders who use eHRM, and each of these groups has different interests, values, and motives, e.g., applicants, employees, retirees, managers, HR professionals, and the organization as a whole (Stone et al., 2003). Not surprisingly, the interests of these stakeholders often conflict at different times. For instance, organizations and HR professionals typically value collecting as much data as possible from applicants in order to make valid hiring decisions, and prevent negligent hiring lawsuits (Stone, Lukaszewski, & Isenhour, 2005). In contrast, applicants want to present the most positive information possible in order to enhance their chances of being hired for the job (Stone et al., 2003). They also value privacy, (e.g., control over personal information), in order to prevent stigmatization or manage positive impressions (Stone & Stone, 1990). Thus, in the organization's quest for information, they may inadvertently violate applicants' actual or perceived rights to privacy. As a result, there may be inherent conflict between an organization's desire for information, and an applicant's desire to control information.

In addition, organizations cannot assume that eHRM will have the benefits and consequences intended by designers. A gap often exists between software designers and those using systems in terms of their perceptions of the value, meanings, and outcomes of using software (Johnson, Marakas, & Palmer, 2006; 2008). As Orlikowski (1992) notes, a software package implemented to support organizational goals, may conflict with the needs of other stakeholders. The organizational implications of new technologies often emerge unexpectedly, and employees may not use technology in the way software developers originally intended (DeSanctis & Poole, 1994; Markus & Robey, 1988). Ultimately, how eHRM is implemented and appropriated by employees is a reflection of a complex set of technology, organizational, cultural, and employee factors that may have unanticipated outcomes for organizational stakeholders. Thus, it is important for organizations to consider these unintended consequences, and for researchers to investigate the potential outcomes of these consequences.

32.4 Use of eHRM to Attract, Motivate, and Retain Employees

In the following sections, we present the advantages and unintended consequences of using eHRM for recruitment, selection, training, and compensation/reward systems for two stakeholders (e.g., organizations and individuals). Whenever possible, we provide support for our arguments about the benefits and limitations of eHRM by using the results of research on each process. We present the advantages for each stakeholder first, followed by the limitations.

32.4.1 e-Recruitment

The primary goal of recruitment is to attract highly talented applicants, and motivate them to apply for jobs (Breaugh & Starke, 2000; Rynes, 1991). If an organization has a large pool of qualified applicants then they can be very selective, and hire the best individuals for their positions. In recent years, organizations have replaced traditional recruitment methods (e.g., newspaper ads) with web-based or electronic recruiting (e-recruiting) practices. E-recruiting can be defined as the use of technology such as websites and social media to (a) find and attract potential job applicants, (b) keep them interested in the organization during the selection process, and (c) influence their job choice decisions (Chapman et al., 2005). Given the increased use of these new e-recruiting methods, research revealed that there are a number of advantages and inadvertent consequences of using them (Chapman & Godollei, 2017).

Advantages for Organizations.   The use of e-recruiting provides a number of benefits for organizations. First, e-recruitment can reduce administrative burdens through the automation of job applications, resume scans, and organizational responses to applicants (Stone et al., 2003). For example, e-recruitment typically allows applicants to complete an application online or upload a resume to the internet. Next, the software automatically parses the application or resume and formats it into a structure that is useful for automated screening. Not surprisingly, research found that the use of e-recruitment reduced cycle time by 25 percent, and decreased costs by 95 percent compared to traditional methods (Cober et al., 2000). Finally, e-recruiting gives organizations the opportunity to automatically track applicants, monitor performance and post-hire retention rates, and identify the factors that affect successful placements (Stone et al., 2003). These data can help improve the recruitment and retention process in organizations (Dulebohn & Johnson, 2013).

Second, e-recruitment allows organizations to attract a greater number of active and passive applicants, and to do so with a broader geographic reach. With e-recruitment, organizations can compete globally for talent by posting an open position on recruitment websites or job boards such as careerbuilder.com or monster.com. These practices allow organizations to target applicants globally rather than just locally through traditional recruitment sources. This process can dramatically increase the number of applicants who apply for each position, as well as attract a broader set of qualified applicants (Chapman & Godollei, 2017). For example, Kia Motors received 43,000 applications within 30 days for 2500 open positions when they opened a new plant in Georgia (Adams, 2008).

Research also indicated that e-recruiting may help organizations identify passive job applicants. For instance, some organizations use internal and external systems or social network sites (e.g., LinkedIn) to review individuals' backgrounds, and identify those who might be qualified for job openings. Then, they contact individuals and offer them the opportunity to apply for jobs. By using internal systems to identify employees for promote-from-within opportunities, it may have a positive impact on current employee satisfaction and retention rates. Research also revealed that professional social media sites liked LinkedIn were very effective in identifying and attracting passive job applicants (Nikolaou, 2014). In an interesting study, researchers found that e-recruiting attracted more highly educated and achievement-oriented people than traditional recruiting sources (McManus & Ferguson, 2003).

E-recruiting can help enhance an organization's brand identity and heighten applicant attraction (Stone et al., 2003), helping distinguish it from its competitors (Ulrich, 2001). For example, companies such as Cisco, Disney, and Google develop images that they want to convey to potential employees, and these images are often conveyed on recruiting web-sties. In particular, Disney uses the term "cast members" to refer to all employees because one of their primary goals is to be one of the world's leading producers and providers of entertainment. These brand identities become part of the organization's culture, and play a key role in attracting job applicants. E-recruiting can also extend an organization's brand by communicating the company culture and values to prospective applicants.

Further, the design of the recruitment website interface itself can affect the extent to which the benefits of e-recruitment are realized. The design can signal prospective applicants about the quality and attractiveness of the firm. Recruitment website characteristics (e.g., ease of use, navigability, quality of aesthetic appeal) can heighten applicants' attraction to the organization. In one study, researchers found that applicants reacted more positively to recruitment websites when they were efficient and easy to use than when they were not (Sinar & Reynolds, 2001). Other studies revealed that applicants preferred companies with high quality websites (e.g., high quality graphics, aesthetic appeal) (Zusman & Landis, 2002), and website design influenced applicants' impressions of the organization (Scheu, Ryan, & Nona, 1999). However, other research indicated that the attractiveness of the website had little or no influence on applicant attraction to organizations (e.g., Cober et al., 2003). Overall, the studies showed that the aesthetics associated with the website had more of an influence on inexperienced than experienced job applicants (Sinar & Reynolds, 2001). Further, research showed that recruitment websites can communicate person–organization fit, and that, in turn, can increase organizational attractiveness and intentions to apply for jobs (Dineen, Ash, & Noe, 2002; Dineen & Noe, 2009). Taken together, research suggested that an efficiently designed and aesthetically pleasing website can increase applicant perceptions of the attractiveness of working for an organization.

Advantages for Individuals. E-recruiting also provides several key advantages for applicants. First, e-recruiting can help applicants quickly gain information about internal job opportunities with organizations. This may also enhance the satisfaction and retention of current employees because they are likely to perceive that there are advancement opportunities within the organization. E-recruiting can also help individuals easily gather information about external job openings, the hiring organization, and vacancy characteristics (e.g., pay, continuing education, career opportunities) any time of the day or night. In support of this argument, Furtmuller, Wilderom, and van Dick (2010) found that some of the most important characteristics of e-recruiting for applicants were timeliness of job postings, quick access to websites, the ability to access information all of the time, and the ability to gather information about salary, continuing education, and career opportunities in the organization. Further, the results of their study indicated that the ease of finding information on websites was important. In addition, for those who have grown up with computers, e-recruiting is viewed more favorably than traditional application methods, because prospective applicants can gather a variety of information about jobs and organizations before actually applying for positions (Zusman & Landis, 2002).

Next, with the amount of information available to potential applicants online, e-recruiting allows them to more fully assess their organization–job fit, and tailor their application to organizational job requirements. For example, websites can be designed so that applicants receive timely feedback and can directly assess their fit with the organization. Research found that increasing applicants' knowledge of person-organization fit, leads to fewer applicants, but those who do apply for jobs are a better fit with the organization (Dineen et al., 2002; Dineen & Noe, 2009). In addition, specialized websites such as Dice.com (engineering & information technology), USAJobs (federal civil service), and EntertainmentCareers.net (entertainment industry) allow applicants to directly identify and target their searches to the appropriate industries. In fact, Furtmuller et al. (2010) found that websites that were customized for specialized openings or niches were positively related to applicants' satisfaction with e-recruiting. Similarly, a study by Allen, Mahto, and Otondo (2007) found that tailoring recruiting websites to the needs of individual applicants lead to higher levels of attraction to organizations. E-recruiting also makes it easier for individuals to apply for a job. With many job boards, individuals can create a profile, upload a resume, and use these to apply for many different jobs with just a click of a button. Furtmuller et al. (2010) indicated that applicants' ability to easily and quickly apply for jobs was positively related to their reactions to recruitment websites.

Unintended Consequences for Organizations.   Organizations may also experience a number of unintended consequences when using technology to attract job applicants. Although e-recruiting clearly increases the quantity of applicants who apply for jobs, studies indicated that it may not always enhance the overall quality of applicants (Galanaki, 2002). In fact, research indicated that e-recruiting methods were more likely to appeal to jobs hoppers with relatively unfavorable backgrounds than their counterparts (McManus & Ferguson, 2003). In particular, the study revealed that 35 percent of those applying for jobs on e-recruiting sites had three or more jobs in the last five years. Thus, the use of e-recruiting may have a positive impact on attraction, but may not increase employee retention rates. Although the use of e-recruiting has expanded in recent years, one of the unintended consequences of this new method is that organizations may actually attract larger numbers of poorly qualified applicants and those who are a poor fit with the organization.

E-recruiting has also been shown to reduce recruitment costs and cut cycle times, it can increase administrative burdens in other ways. Although we argued above that e-recruiting may decrease administrative burden in some ways, it may also dramatically increase the number of applicants who apply for jobs. Thus, some researchers argued that the sheer volume of applicants may increase the administrative workload for organizations (Chapman & Webster, 2003). In addition, even though organizations use software to scan resumes or applications for keywords, the criteria used for determining keyword scoring may not always be based on job analysis (Mohamed, Orife, & Wibowo, 2002). This means that keyword-scoring systems may not be job related, and may not be a valid means of predicting job performance (Stone et al., 2003), and may violate legal standards (e.g., U. S. Civil Rights Laws; Stone et al., 2005).

In addition, not all applicants may respond positively to e-recruiting. For this reason, e-recruiting may result in negative applicant reactions to the organization, and may deter talented applicants from applying for or accepting jobs. For example, research by Furtmuller et al. (2010) revealed that when applicants found that the website was difficult to use or if data were lost when applying for jobs, they did not return to the website to reapply for jobs. Likewise, the same research found that one of the potential problems with e-recruitment is that it is much too impersonal and inflexible, and does not offer applicants the opportunity to interact with a person (e.g., interviewer or current employee; Stone et al., 2003). Thus, the impersonal nature of e-recruiting may negatively influence applicants' attraction, and prevent the organization from attracting the most talented applicants (Johnson, Stone, & Navas, 2011; Kiesler, Siegel, & McGuire, 1984).

Similarly, applicants may be dissatisfied with e-recruiting because it involves a one-way communication system that reduces or eliminates the opportunity to ask questions or gain a realistic preview of working for the organization (Stone et al., 2015). In order to deal with this limitation, some organizations (e.g., Cisco) are giving applicants the opportunity to "make a contact or friend" in the organization so that they can gather more information about what it is like to work there. Research on this strategy found that applicants who were high in collectivism values were more attracted to organizations when they had an opportunity to make a contact than when they did not (Harrison & Stone, 2015). However, this strategy had no impact on attraction of applicants who were high in individualism. As result, offering applicants the opportunity to make a contact in the organization may ameliorate some of the limitations associated with the impersonal nature of e-recruiting, but it may not solve the problem for all applicants (Harrison & Stone, 2015).

Although e-recruiting generally leads to an increase in applicants (Johnson & Gueutal, 2012), poorly designed recruitment websites can actually decrease the number of applicants who apply for jobs. Although research has revealed consistently that the content of websites influences applicants' attraction to organizations, there has been relatively little research on the characteristics of the message itself (Chapman & Godollei, 2017). Research suggested that the cognitive or fact-based messages used on most websites are not as persuasive as emotion-based messages (Kraichy & Chapman, 2014). For example, a website for a hospital might provide fact-based messages on vacancy characteristics (e.g., pay, benefits), and emotionally based messages on the goals of the organization (e.g., the mission of this organization to care for and cure patients so that they live fulfilling lives). The research showed that the emotion-based messages have more of an impact on applicant attraction than fact-based messages. In addition, research indicated that recruiting websites that provide information on what an employer wants from applicants (e.g., organizational demands-based fit) were less appealing than those that included information on what an organization could provide applicants (e.g., applicants' needs-based fit; Schmidt, Chapman, & Jones, 2015).This strategy suggests that, just like traditional recruiting, two-way communication processes can be utilized with e-recruiting. In addition, it indicated that using broad-based messages to appeal to all applicants might not motivate all individuals to apply for jobs.

Further, research showed that tailoring website information to fit the profile of potential applicants had a positive impact on attraction to organizations (Dineen & Noe, 2009; Kraichy & Chapman, 2014). Other research revealed that applicants who shared an organization's values (specified on the website) were more attracted to the organization than individuals who did not share those values (Harrison & Stone, 2015). Therefore, it is important for organizations to understand how the choices they make in designing the content of websites affects potential applicants.

Finally, the use of e-recruitment may increase the risk of adverse impact for members of some protected groups. When an organization uses e-recruitment exclusively, it may not reach all applicants in the labor market (Stone et al., 2003). The primary reason for this is that there is a digital divide, or gap in access to and ability to use computers in the USA and worldwide (Stone, Krueger, & Takach, 2017). The lack of access to computers and e-recruitment websites can result in a disproportionately negative impact on members of some protected groups (e.g., racial and ethnic minorities, older applicants, those in rural areas). As might be expected, the digital divide has narrowed over time, but recent surveys indicated that 13 percent of the 324 million people in the USA still do not use the internet, and 33 percent do not have access to broadband at home (Pew Internet, 2017). The lack of internet and broadband access is correlated with age, disability status, educational level, income, community type (e.g., rural vs. urban), and to a lesser extent racial or ethnic background (Pew Internet, 2017). Thus, many individuals in our society may not have access to recruitment websites, may not learn about job openings, and may not be able to apply for jobs. Although researchers have cautioned that this may be a problem with e-recruiting (Stone et al., 2005; Stone et al., 2003), we know of no empirical research on the issue. Thus, e-recruiting may actually increase the job-related problems experienced by minority group members, and reduce diversity in organizations (Stone et al., 2003). To address this risk, organizations might use both traditional and online strategies for recruiting so that all individuals have an equal opportunity to apply for jobs.

Unintended Consequences for Individuals. Apart from the unintended consequences for organizations, e-recruiting also has some inadvertent negative consequences for individuals. For example, the design of a recruitment website can actually have a negative impact on applicants' attraction to organizations and application for jobs. For example, research revealed that applicants were deterred from applying for jobs when they lost data or had difficulty navigating the website (Furtmüller et al., 2010). Studies also found that applicants were often discouraged and prevented from applying for jobs when websites were inflexible or cumbersome to use (Cober et al., 2003; Selden & Orenstein, 2011). Further, eye-tracking studies found that when applicants spent a great deal of time searching for links to key information on websites, they were dissatisfied with the application process, and less likely to apply for jobs (Allen et al., 2013).

The use of e-recruiting may also lead applicants to view the recruiting process as too impersonal, reducing the likelihood that they will apply for or accept jobs offers. One reason for this is that e-recruiting replaces traditional relationships with interviewers or recruiters with encounters with technology (Gutek, 1995). In support of this argument, research revealed consistently that individuals are more dissatisfied when they are required to interact only with technology than when they have an opportunity to interact with people (Gutek et al., 1999). Further, research by Furtmuller et al. (2010) indicated that applicants viewed the lack of an opportunity to interact with people in the recruitment process as one of the key limitations of e-recruiting systems.

As noted above, e-recruiting can also increase the risk of adverse impact. This is not only an important issue for organizations, but also for applicants. Research has revealed repeatedly that older applicants, women, Hispanic-Americans, African-Americans, and Native Americans were less likely to use and accept e-recruiting than their counterparts (Galanaki, 2002; McManus & Ferguson, 2003; Zusman & Landis, 2002). Early research on e-recruiting found that well educated, computer literate, white male applicants were more likely to use it than women, ethnic minority applicants, or those with low levels of education or computer ability (McManus & Ferguson, 2003). Thus, e-recruiting may not give all applicants the opportunity to learn about job openings or apply for jobs, and this may create an adverse impact on some protected group members (e.g., older applicants, racial/ethnic minorities; Stone et al., 2005)

Finally, job applicants may perceive that e-recruiting has the potential to invade their privacy (Stone et al., 2003). One reason for this is that when applicants apply for jobs they relinquish control over very personal information (e.g., social security number, social media content, credit or background history), and organizations may sell information submitted on recruitment websites to others (e.g., marketers) without applicants' permission (CBS News, 2017; Stone et al., 2003). Further, individuals are concerned that current employers may gain knowledge that they have applied for other jobs, and this may negatively affect their employment prospects (Searle, 2002). Research by Furtmuller et al. (2010) found that two of the key factors affecting applicants' satisfaction with recruitment websites were the opportunities to control information and the ability to use privacy settings. This research is consistent with other eHRM research that suggests that employees perceive that their privacy has been invaded when there are unclear or no privacy policies (Eddy, Stone, & Stone-Romero, 1999; Lukaszewski et al., 2016). Although a number of researchers have argued that the use of e-recruiting has the potential to invade personal privacy (Stone et al., 2005; Stone et al., 2003), we know of no empirical research that has directly addressed this potential limitation. Thus, research is needed to identify the factors that affect applicants' perceptions that their privacy has been invaded in the e-recruiting process.

32.4.2 e-Selection

Traditional selection systems often require that applicants visit an organization to complete paper applications, take pre-employment tests (e.g., cognitive ability, work samples), and meet with HR professionals or managers for interviews (Stone et al., 2013). However, research found that 74 percent of organizations are now using various forms of technology (e.g., electronic job analyses, internet-based job applications, internet or computerized tests, videoconference or telephone interviews) to facilitate the selection process (CedarCrestone, 2010). The use of technology (e.g., e-selection) has transformed the selection process dramatically (Kehoe et al., 2005; Stone et al., 2013). From early mainframe systems that stored data on selection tests to today's proctored internet testing and videoconferenced interviews, e-selection is streamlining testing and enhancing the convenience for applicants and employers (Chapman, Uggerslev, & Webster, 2003; Kehoe et al., 2005). These new selection systems have a number of advantages and unintended consequences for organizations and individuals that are considered below. It merits noting that some of the advantages and limitations are similar to those for e-recruiting because recruiting and selection are interrelated processes.

Advantages for Organizations. There are a number of advantages for organizations that use technology to facilitate the selection process. First, e-selection can streamline the initial screening process, and reduce the administrative burden associated with reviewing numerous applications or resumes. For example, organizations can develop keyword systems based on job analysis, and use them to determine if applicants meet the minimum job standards. These systems can also automatically generate letters to applicants indicating if they are qualified or not qualified for jobs, and provide information about the next steps in the process. E-selection can deliver timely feedback to applicants, enhance applicants' impressions of the organization, and improve the standardization and efficiency of application reviews. Early research in this area found that organizations felt that the automatic scanning and screening of resumes helped them reduce administrative costs without a loss in the quality of candidates (Baker, DeTienne, & Smart, 1998). It merits noting that these findings were based on surveys of HR directors rather than objective assessments of candidates and outcomes. Standardization also enhances the fairness of the selection process because all applicants are reviewed using the same keywords and systems (Stone et al., 2003).

Second, e-selection can facilitate the employment testing process, because applicants can use the internet to complete employment tests at remote locations at their convenience. Research found that over two-thirds of companies are already using unproctored internet testing (Fallaw, Solomonson, & McClelland, 2009). Whether an applicant completes an electronic test in person or remotely, e-selection enhances the speed, timeliness, and flexibility associated with employment testing, and gives organizations the opportunity to test international applicants without high travel costs. It also decreases the need for test proctors and testing facilities, which decreases overall costs associated with testing.

Third, e-Selection can also improve the efficiency of selection by using computer adaptive testing (CAT). CAT is a form of testing where the ease or difficulty of the test is adjusted based upon the previous answers of the test-taker. Research revealed that testing time can be reduced with CAT by up to 50 percent without a reduction in the validity of the test (Alkhadher, Anderson, & Clarke, 1994; Overton et al., 1997). Fourth, e-selection can automatically score selection tests, and give applicants immediate feedback on the degree to which they are qualified for jobs. Fifth, e-selection allows organizations to interview applicants in remote locations, through telephone, videoconferencing, and other forms of technology.

Sixth, e-selection can assist organizations in the validation process by collecting and storing data used to evaluate the validity of inferences made from selection predictors (e.g., tests, interviews, training and education data) or of the overall effectiveness of the process (Stone et al., 2003). For instance, the data from e-selection can help an organization determine if cognitive ability tests or interviews predict performance, and to assess the costs and utility of various selection methods. Further, organizations can generate online surveys to examine applicants' reactions to the selection process, and the data from these surveys can be used to improve selection procedures (Stone et al., 2003). Data from the selection system can also be linked to data from the core organizational Human Resource Information System (HRIS) to assess the relation between scores on selection methods and retention, promotion, and performance patterns over time.

Advantages for Individuals. Not surprisingly, e-selection also has a number of benefits for individuals. First, e-selection can increase the convenience of selection for applicants. Instead of having to go to a testing center, potentially taking time off from work, to complete the test, candidates are now can arrange a time to take a test at a location and time of their choosing, and on a device with which they are familiar (Makransky & Glas, 2011). Second, because e-selection standardizes the selection processes and makes it easier and more convenient for applicants to apply for jobs, these systems may also enhance applicants' satisfaction and perceptions of fairness.

Although this argument appears plausible, results of research on applicants' reactions to e-selection, computerized testing, and electronic interviews have been mixed (Anderson, 2003). For instance, results of research indicated that young applicants reacted more positively to computerized or multimedia cognitive ability tests than paper-based tests (e.g., Potosky & Bobko, 2004). Research by Salgado and Moscoso (2003) indicated that examinees preferred an internet-based personality inventory over a paper version because it was viewed as less intimidating. However, other research has indicated that some individuals have reacted negatively to e-selection (Martin & Nagao, 1989).

In addition, e-selection can increase applicant perceptions of fairness in the selection process. The utilization of standardized keyword searches to screen applications or resumes and determine if applicants are qualified for jobs can communicate to applicants that the screening is based on merit and skill rather than superfluous issues. In support of this argument, research has found that applicants reported that e-selection provided fairer screening methods than traditional selection systems (Searle, 2002).

Further, advanced communications tools are being used to facilitate the interview *processes*. In particular, with videoconferencing tools supporting synchronous and asynchronous video interviewing, participants no longer have to travel to the organization to sit for interviews, nor do they always have to arrange a mutually convenient time to sit for an interview with an organization. Researchers argued that this standardization may also enhance the degree to which racial/ethnic minority applicants perceive that the screening process is fair (e.g., Silvester, et al., 2000; Stone et al., 2013). For instance, Silvester et al. (2000) argued that the decreased opportunity to be aware of an applicant's race or other physical features in telephone interviews may reduce biases inherent in this process. In addition, Anderson (2003) argued that the use of technology in the interviewing process may minimize unfair discrimination and adverse impact in selection.

However, research showed that applicants typically preferred face-to-face (FtF) interviews to electronic interviews, and viewed the company's image more favorably when the interview was conducted FtF than electronically (Stone & Dulebohn, 2013). In addition, research revealed that one problem with videoconference interviews was that it was difficult for interviewers and interviewees to discern facial expressions, body language, or other forms of nonverbal communication (Stone et al., 2013). Thus, we believe that additional research is needed to determine if electronic interviews allow organizations to conduct valid selection interviews.

Unintended Consequences for Organizations.   Even though there are clearly a number of benefits of using e-selection, there are also several unintended consequences for organizations. First, there is a risk that the use of computerized or internet-based testing may not be equivalent to previously validated tests (Stone et al., 2013). Much of the research on this topic examined whether computerized and paper-and-pencil tests generate comparable test scores (Drasgow, 1984). Some research showed that computerized timed tests were only slightly harder than paper forms of the tests, and the correlation between test forms was quite high ($r = 0.95$). In addition, a study by Buchanan and Smith (1999) found that scores for online and paper test forms were equivalent. However, other research revealed that scores for online ability tests were lower than those for paper-and-pencil tests, and there was a moderate correlation between online and paper-and-pencil test scores ($r = 0.60$; Potosky & Bobko, 2004). Still other research found that the mean scores on computerized situational judgment tests (SJTs) were lower and showed more variability than those on paper-and-pencil versions (Ployhart et al., 2003). The same study found that computerized SJTs had higher reliability estimates, and higher relations with other measures than paper test forms. The research on the equivalence of personality inventories also revealed inconsistent results. Some studies indicated that computerized and paper versions of inventories were equivalent (Chuah, Drasgow, & Roberts, 2006; Cronk & West, 2002; Oswald, Carr, & Schmidt, 2001; Salgado & Moscoso, 2003). Yet results of other research found that scores on the two types of tests were not equivalent (Coyne et al., 2005).

Second, one of the most critical issues associated with e-selection is that scores or ratings on the new selection procedures (e.g., online applications, computerized tests, electronic interviews) may not allow decision-makers to make valid inferences about applicants' job performance. One reason for this is that keyword systems used to screen applications may not be based on job analysis or job requirements (Mohamed et al., 2002). Another reason is that scores on computerized tests may not be equivalent to those on paper-and-pencil versions (Potosky & Bobko, 2004). Stone et al. (2013) argued that one possible reason that they are not equivalent is that cognitive ability tests may be much more demanding than paper tests because applicants have to attend to two cognitive tasks simultaneously. For instance, applicants must navigate the software to complete the test at the same time they are focusing on the content of the test, so it is not clear if scores on the tests are a function of applicants' cognitive abilities or their computer skills.

Similarly, electronic interviews lack the media richness of FtF communication (Kiesler et al., 1984; Stone & Lukaszewski, 2009), and provide fewer social, visual, aural, and nonverbal cues than provided by FtF interaction (Daft & Lengel, 1986). Thus, the use of electronic interviews does not always allow interviewees to clarify the meaning of messages, ask questions, or regulate the exchange of information (Kiesler et al., 1984; Stone & Lukaszewski, 2009), and this may decrease the extent to which interview ratings are accurate. Electronic interviews may also limit the degree to which the interviewer ratings can be used to make valid inferences about interviewees' job performance (Stone & Lukaszewski, 2009).

Third, e-selection has the potential to create an adverse impact for members of some protected groups (Stone et al., 2017). The primary reason for this is that many racial/ethnic minorities, older individuals, and those with low socioeconomic status (SES) may not have access to computers or the internet and often have low levels of computer skills. This can create a disadvantage for those completing online tests. Specifically, there is a risk that those with lower computer self-efficacy (CSE; Marakas, Yi, & Johnson, 1998) or higher computer anxiety (Heinssen, Glass, & Knight, 1987) may perform more poorly on online tests than they would on a paper-and-pencil test or compared to those with higher CSE or lower computer anxiety.

Given that many ethnic minorities, older applicants, and those with low SES may score lower on computerized tests because of lower CSE, the use of e-selection techniques may also reduce diversity in organizations. Today's organizations want to increase their diversity so that they can attract diverse customers, and generate innovative products or services. However, when organizations use e-selection, it may place artificial limits on the degree to which diverse applicants (e.g., racial/ethnic minorities, older individuals) are able to score highly on selection tests (Stone et al., 2013). Despite the importance of this issue, we know of no empirical research on this topic.

Unintended Consequences for Individuals. Although e-selection makes it easier for applicants to apply for jobs, there are also a number of unintended consequences for individuals who use these systems. For instance, the use of e-selection procedures may increase the perceived difficulty levels of tests or interviews. One reason for this is that the ability to use e-selection depends on the applicants' computer skills and computer self-efficacy. Therefore, lack of computer skills may have a negative impact on test scores. In addition, some studies showed that applicants reacted more negatively to computerized tests or electronic interviews than traditional methods (Anderson, 2003; Stone et al., 2013). For instance, Potosky and Bobko (2004) and Harris, Van Hoye, and Lievens (2003) found that applicants reacted more negatively to computerized tests when they felt that the tests would put them at a disadvantage in terms of technical problems (e.g., computer crashes) than when they did not. Still other research revealed that there were more negative reactions to computerized tests when applicants (a) had low levels of computer skills, (b) had test anxiety, (b) had little test-taking experience, and (d) were older rather than younger (Anderson, 2003; Potosky & Bobko, 2004; Wiechmann & Ryan, 2003).

Further, results of several studies showed that applicants reacted more negatively to electronic than FtF interviews (Bauer et al., 2004; Chapman et al., 2003). For instance, Bauer et al. (2004) found that FtF interviews were viewed as fairer than electronic ones. Similarly, Chapman et al. (2003) indicated applicants were more likely to accept job offers when organizations used FtF interviews than those conducted by telephone or videoconferencing procedures. One reason for this is that applicants may perceive that electronic interviews are more impersonal and mechanical than FtF interviews (Stone et al., 2013). Likewise, they may believe that electronic interviews give them fewer opportunities to manage positive impressions than FtF ones because it is more difficult to assess social and nonverbal cues with electronic interviews (Stone et al., 2013).

Second, applicants are more likely to perceive that e-selection may result in an invasion of privacy than traditional methods. There are several reasons for this. Individuals may perceive that e-selection allows organizations to collect and store very personal information about them (e.g., social security number, test scores, reference letters) that may be stolen and used by others. Applicants are often concerned that when they release personal information to potential employers they lose control over the information, and that it may be released to others (e.g., law enforcement, government agencies) without their permission. Further, they may also worry that the data collected through background checks and social media may be inaccurate, and have a negative impact on their job opportunities (Stone et al., 2013). Several studies have examined the degree to which e-selection is viewed as invasive of privacy (Bauer et al., 2004; Eddy et al., 1999; Lukaszewski et al., 2016), and the results of this research revealed that individuals were more likely to perceive these procedures were an invasion of privacy when (a) they were unable to control the release of data to third parties, (b) the data were disclosed to third parties without permission, (c) inaccurate or potentially stigmatizing data were collected, and (d) there was no opportunity to check the accuracy of data.

A third unintended consequence for individuals is that some individuals may perceive that the methods are unfair or potentially discriminatory. As noted above, women, older applicants, and members of racial/ethnic minority groups may perceive that e-selection is unfair because these individuals often have less personal access to computers or the internet, and may have lower computer skills than others. In addition, their low computer skills may result in higher levels of computer anxiety and stereotype threat. Stereotype threat refers to the risk of confirming a negative stereotype about one's group (e.g., women, racial minorities, older workers with poor computer skills) (Steele, Aronson, & (1995). For instance, stereotype threat theory predicts that when women are faced with the stereotype that they will underperform on a test relative to men and they will become anxious and their performance will be consistent with the stereotype.

Further, researchers argued that social context factors including differences in socialization, ability stereotypes, and stereotype threat are likely to affect applicants' reactions to e-selection (Stone et al., 2017). For instance, Cooper (2006) found that gender-role stereotypes led to stereotype threat, computer anxiety, and poor computer performance. In turn, this can negatively affect test scores. Although we know of no research on the extent to which the use of e-selection methods in organizational contexts evokes stereotype threat, a meta-analytic review of stereotype threat on cognitive ability test scores revealed that stereotyped test takers (women and racial minorities) suffered from situational stereotype threat and reduced performance (Nguyen & Ryan, 2008). Thus, when individuals perceive that they will be stereotyped as having low computer skills and low cognitive abilities, we can expect that their test performance will be lower on e-selection methods than traditional ones. Likewise, they should be more likely to view e-selection methods as less fair and more discriminatory than other types of procedures. It merits noting that research is needed to test these predictions.

32.4.3 e-Learning

There are multiple ways to define e-learning, but common across all definitions are the characteristics of time, place, technology, and control (Piccoli, Ahmad, & Ives, 2001). Time focuses on whether a training class meets synchronously or asynchronously. With many e-learning initiatives, trainees are able to log in and complete training at their convenience, rather than attending a specific class at a specific time. E-learning is also geographically distributed, with trainees able to access learning materials from any location over a computer, tablet, or mobile phone. In addition, course materials are stored in electronic repositories and all interactions (if any) between trainees and the instructor are technology mediated. Finally, a hallmark of newer e-learning initiatives is increased learner control, where trainees are able to exert more control over learning processes such as pace, content, structure, and format of training (Fisher, Wasserman, & Orvis, 2010; Johnson & Brown, 2017). Therefore, for the purpose of this paper, e-learning is defined as "training or educational initiatives which provide learning material in online repositories, where course interaction and communication and course delivery are technology mediated" (Johnson, Hornik, & Salas, 2008, p. 356). This definition gets at the heart of technology mediation of learning while allowing for time, place, and control to vary.

Advantages for Organizations.   E-learning provides three major advantages for organizations: cost savings, improved training speed, and training flexibility. One of the biggest expenses in corporate training are travel related, with estimates suggesting that as much as 40 percent of training costs are travel related (Zhang, 2003). By reducing training-related travel, e-learning can help reduce training costs. Research consistently found that that e-learning can reduce costs and improve efficiency (Salas, DeRouin, & Littrell, 2005). For example, Ernst and Young was able to cut training costs by 35 percent and training time by 52 percent through e-learning (Hall & LeCavalier, 2000). In addition, IBM was able to cut $400 million from their training budget (Mullich, 2004), and Cisco was able to reduce training costs by 40–60 percent (Gill, 2000). Finally, e-learning is becoming increasingly mobile. This "mobile learning" is argued to provide employees with more tightly focused, timely, job relevant, multimedia experiences that can be accessed on demand (Johnson & Brown, 2017). The promise behind mobile learning is that individual motivation to train will be improved through these focused multimedia experiences, and that organizations can use it to develop a more flexible, learning-centered culture.

Advantages for Individuals.   When evaluating the effectiveness of e-learning, individual outcomes should parallel those with traditional training programs: trainee reactions, learning, and on-the job performance. E-learning research has often focused on training satisfaction as an important reaction and outcome of interest (Johnson, Hornik, et al., 2008). Satisfaction may even more important in an e-learning setting due to the large dropout rates and the finding that individuals who are less satisfied with their experiences will be less likely to enroll in e-learning in the future (Carswell & Venkatesh, 2002; Lim, 2001). Some have argued that e-learning may negatively impact training satisfaction because it isolates trainees and reduces communication among them (Garrison & Arbaugh, 2007; Welsh et al., 2003). However, research consistently found that effectively designed e-learning initiatives can increase trainee satisfaction with e-learning. For example, high quality, well-designed, easy to use, reliable, and useful (e.g., helps effectively support learning processes) technology can improve satisfaction (Arbaugh, 2005; Johnson, Gueutal, & Falbe, 2009; Webster & Hackley, 1997). In addition, factors such as learner control (Fisher et al., 2010), trainee interaction (Arbaugh & Rau, 2007; Johnson, Hornik, et al., 2008), and social presence (Arbaugh, 2001; Gunawardena & Zittle, 1997) can each improve training satisfaction.

In addition to satisfaction, researchers have often focused on the value or relevance of the training to the learner. Also called utility judgments, this reaction to training reflects the extent to which the leaners believe that the training will provide them with the knowledge and skills to improve their on-the-job performance or will contribute to a skill that will help them move forward with their education. Meta-analytic research has found that trainees' utility judgments are often a better predictor of training transfer than how well a learner performed during training (Alliger et al., 1997).

Research found that a number of factors contributed to the utility judgments of trainees. These include technology design (Arbaugh, 2014), course interactivity (Arbaugh & Benbunan-Fich, 2007; Arbaugh & Rau, 2007; Sitzmann et al., 2008), self-efficacy (Johnson et al., 2009; Johnson, Hornik, et al., 2008), and social presence (Arbaugh, 2001; Johnson, Hornik, et al., 2008). It is important to note, though, with respect to interaction and utility judgments, some studies did not find a statistically significant relationship between trainee interaction and utility judgments (Arbaugh & Hornik, 2006; Johnson, Hornik, et al., 2008).

Finally, learning is a benefit for both individuals and organizations, but we consider it under the heading of individuals because improved skills should clearly be an advantage for employees (Kraiger, Ford, & Salas, 1993). Despite the richness of this construct, most of the research on e-learning has focused on declarative knowledge. As with the other learning outcomes, research consistently found that technology capabilities (Carswell & Venkatesh, 2002; Johnson et al., 2009; Johnson, Hornik, et al., 2008)), task complexity (Granger & Levine, 2010; Yanson & Johnson, 2016), interaction with trainers (Inayat et al., 2013), computer self-efficacy (Johnson, Hornik, et al., 2008), trainee interaction (Alavi, Marakas, & Yoo, 2002; Schmidt & Ford, 2003), and metacognitive and self-regulated learning strategies (Schmidt & Ford, 2003; Sitzmann & Ely, 2010) all play an important role in how trainees learn. One interesting finding is that social presence, although an important factor in employee reactions to training, is often not related to performance (Baturay, 2011; Johnson, Hornik, et al., 2008).

E-learning also provides a number of additional advantages for trainees. First, it can provide them with flexibility. That is, trainees can take the training at a time and location that is convenient to them. This means that they will not have to take time away from their daily tasks to complete the training. E-learning can also provide trainees with greater control over learning processes as well. One of the core arguments of the benefits of e-learning to trainees is that it increases learner control (Bell & Kozlowski, 2008; Brown, Howardson, & Fisher, 2016; DeRouin, Fritzsche, & Salas, 2004). Learner control reflects the degree to which the trainee has discretion or responsibility over choices within the learning environment (DeRouin et al., 2004). Environments with greater learner control are those where activities such as pace, content, and structure of the training environment are within the control of the trainee (Fisher et al., forthcoming). For example, in environments with higher learner control, trainees can choose the time and place to engage in training, how much to practice, and how to take advantage of the learning features within the e-learning environment. Some of the benefits of learner control to employees are improved knowledge and skill development (Hughes et al., 2013; Kraiger & Jerden, 2007), better training transfer (Carolan et al., 2014; Keith & Frese, 2005), and higher trainee satisfaction (Bell & Kozlowski, 2008; Karim & Behrend, 2014; Orvis, Fisher, & Wasserman, 2009).

In addition, some studies have found that increased learner control was related to lower off-task attention (Orvis et al., 2009), and meta-analytic research has found that increased learner control over learning pace can improve trainee learning (Carolan et al., 2014; Kraiger & Jerden, 2007).

Unintended Consequences for Organizations. In addition to the numerous benefits of e-learning, there are a number of unintended consequences that may arise when implementing e-learning. The first of these is that the organizations may equate return on investment (ROI) with training value. Although both are important measures of e-learning success, they are not the same. ROI is a financial metric that assesses the benefits of the e-learning programs relative to its costs. However, the value of e-learning does not come from its efficiency alone. The most efficient and "cost-effective" training programs will not provide real value to the organization if trainees do not change behaviors or bring new knowledge and skills to the organizations that improve organizational effectiveness. In fact, if ROI is the metric of choice for assessing the effectiveness of e-learning, then organizations may be tempted to create inexpensive training materials that replicate classroom content.

The problem with this is that simply replicating the traditional classroom online can be a recipe for failure. That is, what works in a traditional classroom may not directly translate to the online environment (Sitzmann et al., 2006). Instead, when moving online, organizations will have to think carefully about how to design the environment. This may mean that more expensive video capabilities, rich communication, tools, and instructor-led experiences may be necessary. Organizations should consider the investments in technology and pedagogy necessary to design effective e-learning classes. Therefore, a more effective e-learning program that leads to improved employee knowledge and organizational outcomes, may not have a high ROI through traditional metrics, but may lead to stronger employee and organizational performance in the long run.

A second unintended consequence of e-learning is that it can be isolating (Garrison & Arbaugh, 2007; Welsh et al., 2003) and less engaging than traditional classroom training (Salas et al., 2005). Trainees can feel disconnected (Flood, 2002) and less motivated in e-learning (Long, Dubois, & Faley, 2009), which can lead to decreased training satisfaction, increased dropout rates, and decreased completion rates. Research found that in corporate and educational initiatives, dropout rates can be as high as 50–80 percent (Flood, 2002; Long et al., 2009; Zielinski, 2000).

Unintended Consequences for Individuals. The first unanticipated consequence for individuals is that not everyone is ready to utilize learner control, and this can negatively impact training outcomes (Granger & Levine, 2010). Technology, mediation of content, and interaction creates additional complexity, which can make learning more difficult, especially when the training is already complex (DeRouin et al., 2004). For example, research revealed that when trainees are provided additional control over learning, it can increase off-task attention and lower performance (Karim & Behrend, 2014). In addition, meta-analytic research indicated that if trainees are allowed to select their own sequence or order of content, it can actually negatively impact learning outcomes (Carolan et al., 2014; Kraiger & Jerden, 2007).

Research also suggested that learner control may be less appropriate for short-term training, a form of training that organizations continue to pursue, than longer-term training (DeRouin et al., 2004). The major reason for this is that trainees would not have time to develop the skills necessary to most effectively leverage the control given to them. Further, research indicated that learner control may be more beneficial for skill- or procedural-based outcomes than for cognitive-based outcomes when trainees have limited to no prior experience (Kraiger & Jerden, 2007).

Finally, research also found that there are individual differences in how individuals respond to learner control. Characteristics such as age (younger), ability (higher), self-efficacy (higher), experience (more), and goal orientation (learning) can affect how much trainees may benefit from learner control (Bell & Kozlowski, 2008; Hughes et al., 2013; Orvis et al., 2010; 2009). Overall the findings are clear that many individuals desire learner control, but organizations must carefully consider when and how to apply learner control. For some, increasing control can counter-intuitively lead to lower performance and learning.

Moving to e-learning can also inadvertently reduce networking opportunities for employees that can enhance their careers and improve knowledge sharing within the organization (Johnson & Gueutal, 2012). Simply attending training at the same time as others can bring together a diverse set of employees with different backgrounds and locations, who will share information and knowledge about their jobs and the company. This informal knowledge sharing can build connections throughout the company and can pay dividends down the line. Although we consider this an unintended consequence, we also know that this is an outcome that is not easily quantified through traditional training networks.

Finally, moving to e-learning often shifts the training burden to the employee during off work hours. For example, although e-learning may provide "flexibility" for employees to complete training any place and anytime, many organizations require employees to complete training on their personal time. This means that training, which was typically conducted as part of an employee's regular duties is now being done on non-work, non-compensated time. Thus, employees may react negatively to e-learning when it bleeds into their family or personal time. This can negatively affect employee attitudes toward the organization as well.

32.4.5 e-Compensation & e-Benefits

Another area of HR that has been automated through the use of technology is compensation and benefits. Together, compensation and benefits have three major goals: to provide a fair and competitive package for employees, to align employee performance with organizational goals, and to do so in a cost effective manner (Stone et al., 2015). The use of technology to support compensation is called e-compensation, and it "uses web-enabled technology to help managers design, implement, and administer compensation systems" (Johnson & Gueutal, 2012, p. 20). With respect to employee benefits, technology is often used to help employees learn about benefits, select benefits, and manage their benefits themselves. In a recent survey, over 60 percent of organizations indicated that they currently utilize some form of e-compensation, and nearly all indicated that they utilized technology to support benefits administration (CedarCrestone, 2010).

Advantages for Organizations.   As with other areas of HR, the use of technology to support compensation and benefits increases efficiency and lowers costs. For example, one organization was able to save $850,000 per year in administrative costs by automating their compensation planning system (Brink & McDonnell, 2003). In addition, companies such as Dell, Raytheon, and Motorola found that e-compensation was able to reduce compensation planning time by over 50 percent, and in some cases reducing it to less than six weeks (Gherson & Jackson, 2000; Society for Human Resource Management, 2007; Workscape, 2010). Research also found that e-benefits can reduce the cost of some benefits transactions by over 90 percent (Cedar, 1999). These savings can be realized because HR professionals are freed from spending time on open enrollment, and many of the paper forms and materials can be moved online for employees to access at their convenience.

A second area where technology can improve organizational outcomes is by providing improved data accuracy. Both scientific (Mauldin, 2003) and industry research (Workscape, 2010) revealed that these systems can reduce errors and increase decision-making accuracy. E-compensation can also allow organizations to better integrate data from external (e.g., pay surveys) and internal (e.g., current compensation) sources. This provides them with an opportunity to identify any areas of inequity in compensation structures. Without these data, it is less likely that an organization can develop a truly effective compensation system.

One of the major goals of compensation planning is to ensure equity in compensation decisions. Given that perceptions of inequity can affect employee satisfaction and performance (Dulebohn, 2003; Smith, 1996), it is important that organizations maintain equity in compensation. The improved accuracy associated with e-compensation enables managers to develop compensation strategies that improve both internal and external equity. More complete, timely, and accurate data can help managers make better compensation decisions for their employees. In addition, rather than reacting after the fact to changing compensation patterns in their local environment, they can quickly and efficiently integrate external pay data into compensation plans, and more proactively address pay issues within the firm to reduce the risk of losing employees due to pay differentials.

Finally, e-compensation can have a positive impact on organizational citizenship behaviors (OCB). OCBs are extra-role behaviors, not required by the organization, that add value to the organization (Organ, 1988). Previous research found that a well-designed e-benefits system was positively related to employee perceptions of organizational support and OCBs. Specifically, systems that are accurate, secure, easy to use, and provide convenience to the employee lead to stronger satisfaction levels (Huang et al., 2004), higher levels of perceived organizational support, and increased levels of engagement in OCBs (Huang, Jin, & Yang, 2004). Thus, well-designed e-benefit systems can help employees develop a better understanding of the benefits available to them, and should enhance how employees perceive their organization and motivate them to engage in greater citizenship behaviors.

Advantages for Individuals.   There are two major advantages of e-compensation and e-benefits for employees. The first of these is increased fairness and equity in compensation decisions. As noted above, one of the biggest challenges in developing compensation plans is how to equitably compensate all employees while maintaining a sustainable cost structure. E-compensation systems can help organizations provide outcomes that are more equitable for all employees, because they can assist managers in developing consistent structures and standardized rules that apply to all employees. In addition, by integrating external data into compensation plans, it can help ensure that all employees are compensated fairly, and in a way that helps organizations increase employee satisfaction and retention levels.

The second advantage for employees revolves around benefits management. One of the growing fears for organizations and public pensions is that they are increasingly becoming underfunded, and there is a risk that promised financial benefits may not be provided to retirees (Mooney, 2017). Therefore, many individuals are interested in managing their own retirement funds through defined contribution plans such as 401k and 403b. With e-benefits, rather than relying on organizational representatives to manage their retirement funds, each employee is able to manage funds in a way that most closely aligns with their risk tolerances. In addition, the use of web-based tools places key benefits data in the hands of the employee, providing constant access to the information needed to make informed benefits decisions (Panepinto, 1995).

Finally, e-benefits, specifically the use of decision support systems and expert systems, can to help employees make better choices with respect to flexible, or cafeteria style, benefits. With cafeteria-style benefits, workers are offered a basic set of benefits, but then are allocated money to purchase additional benefits that fit their unique circumstances or that they value (Cascio, 2016). Given that employees in different life stages are likely to value different set of benefits (e.g., married couple with young children versus a 70-year-old single female), flexible benefits can help organizations meet the needs of all employees. Research has long argued that providing employees with the flexibility to choose their own benefits from a set of potential benefits will make them more informed consumers of benefits, as well as improving satisfaction with their benefits (Barber, Dunham, & Formisano, 1992).

The challenge is that selecting the best set of benefits from a variety of potential benefits is complex and may lead to confusion, poor decisions, and ultimately dissatisfaction with the benefits offered (Rosenbloom & Hallman, 1991). Researchers found, though, that benefits expertise can be embedded into technology to help employees make better benefits decisions (Sturman & Milkovich, 1995). In addition, research revealed that the use of computer-based decision aids can increase the quality of benefits decisions by employees, as well as the satisfaction with the benefits chosen (Sturman, Hannon, & Milkovich, 1996).

Unintended Consequences for Organizations.   Despite the potential value that e-compensation and e-benefits bring to organizations, there are a number of unintended consequences that may arise when they are implemented. First, these systems can be rigid and lack flexibility. One of the key assumptions behind the implementation of technology is that by introducing standards and rules, employee behaviors and actions can be shaped toward a common set of "best practices." In fact, many theories and approaches to system design implicitly assume this (Orlikowski, 1992). The challenge with this approach is that this technology may not meet the needs of employees or managers, and may constrain employee actions. For example, based on performance or a competing job offer, a manager may need to provide an employee with a 15 percent raise to retain him or her. Unfortunately, if the compensation system is not designed with the flexibility to allow a 15 percent raise in a timely fashion, there is a risk that the organization will lose the employee before the proper approvals are received.

In addition, there is a risk that managers will rely too much on the technology for decision-making. As noted by Johnson and Gueutal (2012), "Blind compliance with compensation software is an abdication of the responsibility of the manager and ineffective for the firm in the long run" (p. 23). In addition, because the business environment is evolving rapidly, technology may not be able to keep up with the changes in the business environment, causing the e-compensation system to become outdated (Stone et al., 2003). Decision models that work today will need to evolve over time to ensure that they continue to be appropriate in the future.

Finally, because many of the decisions associated with compensation become standardized and enforced through technology, and because managers are so busy, they may not take the time to fully understand the capabilities and limitations of e-compensation, and therefore may not fully understand how these systems were developed and should be utilized. Research indicated that the more data available in the system and the more decision-support tools are embedded into that system, the less time individuals and managers will spend in making the decision, and the more that they will rely on the software to make a decision for them (Todd & Benbasat, 1991; Zuboff, 1985).

Unintended Consequences for Individuals.   To date, we are not aware of any research that shows that e-compensation actually helps motivate and retain employees. In fact, there is an inherent risk in assuming that all employees are motivated by pay and market equity (Stone et al., 2015). Not all employees are driven by pay, and employees may consider other factors beyond pay when deciding to remain in a job (e.g., location, coworkers; Stone-Romero, Isenhour, & Stone, 2011; Stone et al., 2006). Therefore, to attract and retain a diverse workforce, organizations will have to consider factors beyond pay, such as work-life balance and flexible schedules as ways of rewarding high-performing employees (e.g., Cennamo & Gardner, 2008; Stone et al., 2006; Twenge et al., 2010).

The second unintended consequence of the use of e-compensation and e-benefits is that the systems often transfer work previously done by HR to employees (Stone et al., 2003). For example, with employee and manager self-service, work such as enrolling in benefits, and making compensation decisions are now done directly by the employee or the manager rather than the HR department. This transfers workload to employees that can negatively impact their productivity (Gueutal & Falbe, 2005; Stone et al., 2003). This increased workload can reduce their satisfaction and usage rates (Hawking, Stein, & Foster, 2004). In addition, managers may not have the knowledge or skills to make the most effective decisions because they lack the necessary HR compensation expertise.

Further, employees may lack the needed skills to manage complex health and retirement benefits, and may still need help from HR professions when making these decisions. For example in the move from defined benefit to defined contribution plans, the onus of investing and managing investments, is placed on the employee, and it is unlikely that they will have the expertise that pension managers have on the topic. Therefore, there is a risk that employees will make financial decisions that may not be in their best interest, and this is likely to have a negative impact on their satisfaction with the HR department and the organization.

32.5 HR Planning

Although eHRM supports a number of key HR processes, one of the most critical processes deals with HR planning. HR planning involves the analysis of current jobs, workers, and the organization environment in order to help support the organization's strategic goals (Stone et al., 2003). eHRM is an important tool for HR planning, and is often used to conduct workforce utilization analysis, succession planning, forecasting, and the calculation of analytics (e.g., turnover, productivity, and absenteeism analysis) that can be used to enhance the organization's effectiveness (Dulebohn & Johnson, 2013). eHRM also enables organizations to comply with laws and, regulations, and assess the organization's effectiveness in addressing these laws (e.g., adverse impact analysis, EEO-1or OSHA reports; Kavanagh & Johnson, 2018). Given the importance of eHRM for HR planning, we consider the advantages for organizations and individuals in the sections below.

Advantages for Organizations. The first advantage for organizations is that eHRM allows them to better conduct workforce utilization analysis to examine the makeup and skills of the current workforce, and forecast human resources supply and demand (Kavanagh & Johnson, 2018; Stone et al., 2003). For instance, eHRM can help managers forecast staffing needs, and develop database inventories of in-house talent and skills so that they can utilize the skills and training of current employees prior to searching externally for potential employees (Whitman & Hyde, 1978). This approach saves time and money, and provides advancement opportunities for current employees. In turn, employees should have higher satisfaction, commitment, and retention rates. Further, eHRM can help organizations adapt to changing goals or environmental demands, because it helps them identify employee capabilities and reassign employees to new jobs created for the changing demands. For instance, when an auto company's sales of compact cars declines and the demand for trucks increases, managers can quickly identify and reassign qualified workers from the compact cars assembly line to trucks. Not surprisingly, some car companies (e.g., Toyota) forecast the demand for different vehicles and train workers during slow times on these skills needed to produce these new vehicles. Surveys showed that most large organizations use eHRM to facilitate HR planning and work force utilization analysis (Sierra-Cedar, 2016).

Second, eHRM can assist the organization with succession planning (Stone et al., 2003; Zingheim & Schuster, 2004). Succession planning typically involves the identification of replacements for managerial and supervisory positions in the organization. For instance, eHRM can be used to identify "high potential" employees and track their performance over time, which enables the organization to assign them to key positions when the jobs become vacant (Kavanagh & Johnson, 2018). This is especially important today as large number of baby boomers are retiring and vacating critical positions in organizations. Organizations have long known the value of using technology for skill identification and succession planning. In fact, the US State Department implemented the earliest HR planning systems in the 1970s (Whitman & Hyde, 1978).

Third, eHRM can facilitate workforce analytics, specifically the analysis of key HR outcomes (e.g., productivity, turnover, absenteeism, employee satisfaction levels; Dulebohn & Johnson, 2013; Stone et al., 2003). For instance, in order to help managers understand the nature of problem areas and formulate solutions to them, eHRM can assist them with analyzing turnover or productivity rates by units, jobs, or workers (Kavanagh & Johnson, 2018). It can also be used to conduct periodic surveys of employee satisfaction levels to identify and preclude future problems. It merits emphasis that these surveys are extremely important because organizations need a dependable, motivated, and highly productive workforce in order to survive and be successful (Katz & Kahn, 1978). For example, Katz and Kahn (1978) argue that "the organization consists of patterned and motivated acts of human beings and it will continue to exist as long as the attitudes, beliefs, perceptions, habits and expectations of individuals evoke the required motivation and behavior" (p. 187). Throughout this chapter, we argued that eHRM enhances the efficiency of HR processes, but in this case, eHRM can be used to improve the overall effectiveness and survival rates of organizations. However, research is needed to examine these arguments.

Fourth, eHRM can assist organizations in meeting government-reporting requirements (Johnson & Gueutal, 2012). Organizations in the United States must comply with a host of federal and state laws and regulations (e.g., Equal Employment Opportunity Laws, Occupational Health and Safety Laws). One of the major advantages of eHRM is that it facilitates the completion of reports required by these laws, and decreases the time and staff needed to file them. Fifth, these reports can be used to improve key functions in organizations (e.g., enhance worker safety), which should help organizations become more effective and enhance the well-being of workers.

Advantages for Individuals.   Although HR planning is primarily beneficial for organizations, it can also have a number of key advantages for individuals. First, it can facilitate enhanced job opportunities. As noted above, eHRM can be used to facilitate workforce utilization analysis and succession planning by identifying current skills of workers and transferring them to jobs where their abilities can be utilized. This approach provides new job opportunities and advancement for current employees, which should enhance their satisfaction, commitment, and retention levels. Quite simply, when workers perceive that they have a chance for advancement or a more satisfying job in the organization, they should be more satisfied and more likely to remain with that organization.

Second, the use of eHRM in HR planning has the potential to improve employee satisfaction. For instance, online employee engagement and satisfaction surveys are now widely used in organizations to assess employees' attitudes and opinions, and they are aggregated into single indicator values that can be calculated for units or the overall organization. The primary goal of these surveys is to gauge the strengths and weaknesses of policies and procedures, and provide managers with feedback that can be used to improve organizational practices and employee attitudes. Thus, the use of online employee surveys gives managers timely information that can be used to change policies, and enhance the satisfaction levels of employees. In addition, organizations are increasingly using mobile technology to conduct short employee engagement and satisfaction surveys to assess employee engagement and satisfaction on regular basis (Boese, 2015). This can increase organizational responsiveness to employee concerns, which can improve employee satisfaction with the organization.

Unintended Consequences for Organizations.   At the same time that eHRM can provide a number of HR planning benefits, there are a number of unintended consequences that should be considered. First, there is a risk that eHRM will be viewed as a panacea, causing the organization and managers to develop unrealistic expectations that these systems can increase profits and overall organizational effectiveness. In their quest to sell HR technology to organizations, some practitioners argue that eHRM will increase organizational effectiveness, profits, and survival rates. However, we want to caution users that these systems are not a panacea, and that their ability to improve organizational profitability or survival rates depends on a number of non-technological and non-organizational factors (Brynjolfsson & Hitt, 1998; Thatcher & Oliver, 2001). Organizations cannot simply assume that improving efficiency means that these systems will improve organizational and HR effectiveness, because effectiveness depends on both internal efficiency and environmental issues (e.g., market for products or services; Katz & Kahn, 1978). Increased profits and survival rates also depend on the organization's environment and demand for products and services.

Unintended Consequences for Individuals.   The use of eHRM in HR planning can also have unintended consequences for employees. For instance, it may lead employees to perceive that they are "human capital" rather than individual human beings, and this may lead to them to perceive that the organization does not care about their individual satisfaction levels or well-being. Even though that is not the intention of HR planning, if planning is used to create policies that do not consider the well-being or fairness to individuals, it may result in dissatisfaction and turn-over rates. Thus, we caution individuals that eHRM is not a silver bullet that will solve all organizational problems and sources of discontent.

32.6 Discussion

Essentially, all large organizations have made investments in technology as a central component of their HR strategy. These new technologies have brought with them a change in HR policies, and in how HR is practiced. Traditional HR has been replaced by eHRM, where HR tasks are infused with web-based desktop and mobile technologies that bring with them the potential for HR to transform its focus, skills, and operations. The question remaining is whether technology enables organizations to meet their primary goals of attracting, selecting, motivat-ing, and retaining talented employees. For all of the areas we have reviewed, it is clear that eHRM brings both advantages, and also unintended consequences. In each of the HR areas reviewed (e.g., recruitment, selection, training, compensa-tion and benefits, & HR planning), eHRM is clearly increasing the efficiency and decreasing the costs associated with these functions. However, for eHRM to help HR meet its goals and add value to organizations, it must enable HR to become more effective in attracting, motivating, and retaining their workforces. To date, most of the research on eHRM has examined factors associated with their imple-mentation (e.g., use of websites for recruiting, computerized tests for selection, and gamification in training), and relatively little research has examined their overall effectiveness. Thus, we believe that additional research is needed to assess the degree to which they enable HR to meet their primary goals.

32.6.1 Impact of New Technologies on eHRM

We also know that technology is rapidly changing, and technologies are emerging daily that can affect eHRM. The future of eHRM will be dominated by social and mobile technologies that allow employees and employers to connect and share knowledge for mutual benefit (Kavanagh & Johnson, 2018). Several newer tech-nologies are increasing both the amount of information available on employees, and how that information is utilized. Thus, in the following paragraphs we consider several technologies (e.g., virtual reality [VR], gamification, the Internet of Things [IoT] and wearables, and artificial intelligence [AI] and big data), and discuss how they might influence the practice of HR.

32.6.1.1 Virtual Reality and Virtual Worlds

Virtual reality is a technology that allows individuals to immerse themselves in a three-dimensional space where they can view, move, and interact with objects, as if they were real (Aguinas, Henle, & Beaty Jr, 2001; Mujber, Szecsi, & Hashimi, 2004). VR can help organizations meet their goals of attracting highly qualified job applicants. VR headsets can give applicants a realistic preview of what it is like to work in the organization. For example, Deutsche Bahn utilizes these headsets at job fairs where they immerse applicants in the everyday organizational activities to show them what it is like to work there (Dixon, 2017). In addition, VR can provide higher fidelity, and stronger assessment of prospective employee's skills. Rather than taking a paper-and-pencil test, a prospective building inspector can virtually inspect a building as part of the hiring process (Johnson, Thatcher, & Burleson, 2016)

Virtual reality also has the potential to impact training and development (Johnson & Brown, 2017). For example, military and commercial airlines have used flight simulators for decades, and research has shown that these simulators can improve training outcomes (Hays et al., 1992). This finding is consistent with research from a number of domains, such as such as medicine (Larsen et al., 2012), and oil exploration (Brasil et al., 2011), that has shown the efficacy of virtual reality simulations in training.

Finally, a newer form of virtual reality, virtual worlds, is beginning to emerge that may have implications for both recruiting and training. Virtual worlds are three-dimensional digital representations of a physical space where an individual is represented by an avatar (e.g., simulated body) through which they interact with the environment (deNoyelles, Hornik, & Johnson, 2014). Virtual worlds have been argued to improve trainee interaction (Merchant et al., 2012), engagement (Mennecke et al., 2011; Stone et al., 2015), and learning outcomes (Hornik & Thornburg, 2010) compared to a traditional online course. The major reason for this is that virtual worlds provide a richer communication environment, with increased audio and visual cues. Despite the potential advantages to both virtual reality and virtual worlds, the use of these new tools can add technological and communication complexity, which can make them challenging to use (Mennecke, Hassall, & Triplett, 2008). For this reason, researchers will need to draw on work from diverse fields such as computer science, psychology, and human computer-interaction (HCI) to determine how to most effectively design and deploy this technology.

32.6.1.2 Gamification

Gamification is the application of gaming elements to non-game contexts (Robson et al., 2015). Game elements can be embedded in tasks, or game elements such as achievement levels, badges, rewards, and leaderboards, and can be used to identify the top performers and contributors. Although not a new technology per se, the evolution and ubiquity of technology has made the use of gamification more readily available to organizations. Gamification is valuable because it can increase engagement and focus on tasks as well as take advantage of the competitive nature of humans. Organizations such as the US Army, L'Oreal, and Marriott have all used games to gain applicants' attention, help them learn about the organization, and to encourage them to apply for positions within the firm (Efron, 2016). Other organizations are utilizing games as part of the selection process, where applicants are given games to play and insights and assessment are made through how the applicant plays the game (Fetzer, 2015). The premise behind the use of games in selection is that the applicant becomes so engrossed in playing the game that they cease to focus on it as an assessment tool. Thus, faking should be reduced as the applicant focuses less on the assessment and more on the game.

Finally, since Salas' early recommendations to utilize games as part of e-learning (Salas et al., 2005), the use of games in e-learning has grown steadily. The use of games in e-learning is argued to increase its attractiveness, reduce anxiety, encourage practice, and create a more engaging learning environment (Johnson & Brown, 2017). Empirical evidence suggests that some of these goals are being met. Specifically research has shown that gamification can improve course participation (Snyder & Hartig, 2013), training motivation (Dominguez et al., 2013), and learning (McDaniel, Lindgren, & Friskics, 2012).

Ultimately, we believe gamification has the potential to transform many functions of HR, in particular recruitment, selection, and training. However, there are a number of outstanding questions that researchers must address when utilizing gamification. For example, when utilizing gamified activities in selection, which aspects of the activity relate to the criterion, and what are the psychometric properties of the new gamified activity? In addition, how will employees or candidates react to gamified activities? Research suggests that not all will respond positively to gamification. For example, some individuals have responded negatively to the leaderboards (Dominguez et al., 2013). Other research suggests that poorly designed gamified activities can reduce engagement and actually turn people away from the organization (Foster et al., 2012). Before the full impact of gamification is understood, researchers need to develop theoretically driven models of the role gamified activities can play in HR.

32.6.1.3 Internet of Things and Wearables

The Internet of Things (IoT) is a "worldwide network of interconnected objects uniquely addressable based on standard communication protocols" (Gubbi et al., 2013). IoT embeds sensors, transmitters, and receivers in static objects, such as roads or bridges, clothing, watches, and thermostats, that are able to send and receive data without human intervention. Wearables are technology devices that are either standalone (e.g., smart watches) or embedded within other objects, such as clothing, that utilize the IoT to send and receive data. It has been predicted that within the next few years, over two million employees will be required to wear health and fitness devices as a condition of employment (Gartner, 2015). In addition, Three Square Market has embedded a microchip in over 60 percent of their workforce that employees can use for activities as varied as entry into the building and purchasing food (Astor, 2017). Given the growing importance of maintaining health costs, many organizations are increasingly turning to wearables to support employee health. For example, when Indiana University Health provided a fitness tracker to encourage better employee health, they found that over 35 percent of their workforce used the fitness tracker, and over 90 percent of these employees were motivated to continue the healthy changes after the trial period (Wright, 2017). In addition, new wearable devices (e.g., smartphones embedded in glasses, watches, or other wearable devices) should facilitate all types of communication with employees, including information about benefits.

However, there are some concerns that may arise with the use of IoT and wearables. First, despite the success of the IU Health program, research suggests that it is hard to keep employees engaged for more than six months. Second, given that many of these devices are capturing personal information and transmitting it across the internet, there are privacy and security concerns associated with their use (Kavanagh & Johnson, 2018).

32.6.1.4 Artificial Intelligence and Big Data

The final technological innovation that should affect the practice of HR is artificial intelligence (AI) and big data. SHRM has identified AI as one of the top technology trends of 2108, and, coupled with big data and intelligent apps, it is expected to drive spending and decision-making in human resources (Wright, 2017). Artificial intelligence is a blanket term for software applications that simulate human intelligence. AI has long been used in organizations to automate processes such as loan processing and make cognitive insights, such as predicting what a customer will purchase based upon past habits (Davenport & Ronanki, 2018). Big data refers to massive data sets that are characterized by high volume, high velocity, and high variety (Eaton et al., 2012). Essentially, for I/O psychologists and human resource managers to fully leverage AI and big data, they will need to have expertise, not only in their base field, but also in statistics, decision-making, and technology (Maurath, 2014).

Although human resources has been somewhat late to embrace big data, recent research suggests that over 30 percent of organizations are now comfortable utilizing basic analysis tools, with the goal of becoming more skilled at utilizing these more sophisticated techniques (Fleck, 2016). For instance, organizations can use AI to develop algorithms that can support more effective selection decisions, reducing potential human biases inherent in these systems, and allow organizations to hire the best person for the job. They are also using AI to expedite the initial screening process, automatically screening applications or resumes to determine which applicants should be considered for jobs.

AI can also help organizations select the most talented job applicants and increase employee motivation of employees through more effective compensation and reward systems (Stone et al., 2003). For instance, AI can be used to develop algorithms that will enable managers to combine data about applicants (e.g., training and experience data, test results, interviews, background checks), and help them make more effective selection decisions. Although organizations are using decision support systems (DSS) to develop compensation plans and model the consequences of changes in compensation rates, it is likely that AI will be used to develop sophisticated algorithms that enable compensation managers to expedite the planning process and create more effective plans. In addition, as noted earlier, it is very challenging for employees to identify the optimal benefits packages, and how to most effectively manage retirement plans (e.g., 401k, 403b). Through AI, we believe that organizations will help employees model and select the best benefits for themselves and their families. Although organizations have made great strides in improving compensation and benefit systems, we know that these new technologies will greatly improve these processes and help them meet their intended goals (e.g., motivate and retain employees).

Another goal of HR is to develop HR plans that allow organizations to forecast and develop strategies that can be used to manage their workforces. eHRM greatly facilitates HR planning and enables organizations to conduct workforce utilization analysis, succession planning, forecasting, and the development of analytics that can be used to assess the effectiveness of HR processes. Thus, even though Big Data is not actually a new technology, the use of big data in HR is relatively new, because it involves the analysis of extremely large data sets that reveal patterns, trends, and associations among HR practices and various outcomes (e.g., performance levels, turnover rates, employee satisfaction, administrative costs). Big Data allows HR to develop and examine a number of analytics that assess the extent to which HR is meeting their intended goals.

At the same time, a major risk of the use of AI and big data are that managers and employees may assume that the data produced by the system represents a decision, rather than input to a decision (Kavanagh & Johnson, 2018). As Cappelli (2015, p. 5) notes, "machine learning produces facts, rather than conclusions." More research is needed to better understand how to deploy these new technologies in a way that not only helps organizations meet their HR goals, but does so in a way that creates more motivated, and productive employees. The challenge is that with sometimes-conflicting goals, it may be challenging to best support all HR stakeholders.

32.7 Conclusion

In summary, organizations are increasingly using eHRM to conduct recruitment, selection, training, compensation, and HR planning. Although there are clearly a number of benefits associated with these new systems (e.g., lower administrative costs, decreased administrative burdens) there are also some unintended consequences associated with them (e.g., invasion of individual privacy, increased adverse impact and workload). As a result, we believe that organizations should be aware of both the advantages and disadvantages of these new systems before they are implemented in organizations. In this paper, we reviewed the research on the use of eHRM in several areas of HR, and considered their benefits and limitations. We also considered how new technologies might change the practice of HR in the future. Even though we believe that the use of technology can enable organizations meet their key HR goals, additional research is needed to assess their effectiveness. It is our hope that this paper will help organizations use technology wisely to enhance their HR systems, and ensure that individuals are treated fairly in the process.

References

Adams, T. (2008). Kia receives 43,000 applications for West Point auto plant. *Columbus Ledger-Enquirer*. Retrieved from www.ledger-enquirer.com/news/local/arti cle28988608.html.

Aguinas, H., Henle, C. A., & Beaty Jr., J. C. (2001). Virtual reality technology: A new tool for personnel selection. *International Journal of Selection and Assessment, 9* (1–2), 70–83.

Alavi, M., Marakas, G. M., & Yoo, Y. (2002). A comparative study of distributed learning environments on learning outcomes. *Information Systems Research, 13*(4), 404–415.

Alkhadher, O., Anderson, N., & Clarke, D. (1994). Computer-based testing: A review of recent developments in research and practice. *European Work and Organizational Psychologist, 4*(2), 169–189.

Allen, D. G., Biggane, J. E., Pitts, M., Otondo, R., & Van Scotter, J. (2013). Reactions to recruitment web sites: Visual and verbal attention, attraction, and intentions to pursue employment. *Journal of Business and Psychology, 28*(3), 263–285.

Allen, D. G., Mahto, R. V., & Otondo, R. F. (2007). Web-based recruitment: Effects of information, organizational brand, and attitudes towards website on applicant attraction. *Journal of Applied Psychology, 92*(6), 1696–1708.

Alliger, G. M., Tannenbaum, S. I., Bennett Jr., W., Traver, H., & Shotland, A. (1997). A meta analysis of the relations among training criteria. *Personnel Psychology, 50*, 341–358.

Anderson, N. (2003). Applicant and recruiter reactions to new technology in selection: A critical review and agenda for future research. *International Journal of Selection and Assessment, 11*(2–3), 121–136.

Arbaugh, J. B. (2001). How instructor immediacy behaviors affect student satisfaction and learning in web-based courses. *Business Communication Quarterly, 64*(4), 42–54.

Arbaugh, J. B. (2005). Is there optimal design for on-line MBA courses? *Academy of Management Learning & Education, 4*(2), 135–149.

Arbaugh, J. B. (2014). System, scholar or students? Which most influences online MBA course effectiveness? *Journal of Computer Assisted Learning*, 30(4), 351–362.

Arbaugh, J. B. & Benbunan-Fich, R. (2007). The importance of participant interaction in online environments. *Decision Support Systems, 43*(3), 853–865.

Arbaugh, J. B. & Hornik, S. (2006). Do Chickering and Gamson's seven principles also apply to online MBAs. *The Journal of Educators Online, 3*(2), 1–18.

Arbaugh, J. B. & Rau, B. L. (2007). A study of disciplinary, structural, and behavioral effects on course outcomes in online MBA courses. *Decision Sciences Journal of Innovative Education, 5*(1), 65–95.

Astor, M. (2017). Microchip implants for employees? One company says yes. New York Times. Retrieved from www.nytimes.com/2017/07/25/technology/microchips-wisconsin-company-employees.html.

Baker, W. H., DeTienne, K., & Smart, K. L. (1998). How Fortune 500 companies are using electronic resume management systems. *Business Communication Quarterly, 61* (3), 8–19.

Barber, A. E., Dunham, R. B., & Formisano, R. A. (1992). The impact of flexible benefits on employee satisfaction: A field study. *Personnel Psychology, 45*(1), 55–74.

Baturay, M. H. (2011). Relationships among sense of classroom community, perceived cognitive learning and satisfaction of students at an e-learning course. *Interactive Learning Environments*, *19*(5), 563–575.

Bauer, T. N., Truxillo, D. M., Paronto, M. E., Weekley, J. A., & Campion, M. A. (2004). Applicant reactions to different selection technology: Face-to-face, interactive voice response, and computer-assisted telephone screening interviews. *International Journal of Selection and Assessment*, *12*, 135–148.

Bell, B. S. & Kozlowski, S. W. J. (2008). Active learning: Effects of core training design elements on self-regulatory processes, learning, and adaptability. *Journal of Applied Psychology*, *93*, 296–316.

Boese, S. (May 6, 2015). The engagement solution. Human Resource Executive.

Brasil, I. S., Neto, F. M. M., Chagas, J. F. S., de Lima, R. M., Souza, D. F. L., Bonates, M. F., & Dantas, A. (2011). An intelligent agent-based virtual game for oil drilling operators training. Paper presented at the Virtual Reality (SVR), 2011 XIII Symposium on, Uberlandia.

Breaugh, J. A. & Starke, M. (2000). Research on employee recruitment: So many studies, so many remaining questions. *Journal of Management*, *26*(3), 405–434.

Brink, S. & McDonnell, S. (2003). *IHRIM Go-To-Guides: e-compensation*. The e-merging technology series. Burlington, MA: IHRIM.

Brown, K. G., Howardson, G., & Fisher, S. L. (2016). Learner control and e-learning: Taking stock and moving forward. *Annual Review of Organizational Psychology and Organizational Behavior*, *3*, 267–291.

Brynjolfsson, E. & Hitt, L. M. (1998). Beyond the productivity paradox. *Communications of the ACM*, *41*(8), 49–55.

Buchanan, T. & Smith, J. L. (1999). Research on the internet: Validation of a World-Wide Web mediated personality scale. *Behavior Research Methods, Instruments. & Computers*, *31*(4), 565–571.

Cappelli, P. (July/August 2015). Can Machines Ponder HR? Human Resource Executive, p. 5.

Carolan, T. F., Hutchins, S. D., Wickens, C. D., & Cumming, J. M. (2014). Costs and benefits of more learner freedom: Meta-analyses of exploratory and learner control training methods. *Human Factors*, *56*, 999–1014.

Carswell, A. D. & Venkatesh, V. (2002). Learner outcomes in an asynchronous distance education environment. *International Journal of Human-Computer Studies*, *56*, 475–494.

Cascio, W. F. (2016). *Managing human resources: Productivity, quality of work life, profits* (10th edn.). New York, NY: McGraw Hill.

CBS News. (2017). The Data Brokers: Selling Your Personal Information. Retrieved from www.cbsnews.com/news/the-data-brokers-selling-your-personal-information/.

Cedar. (1999). 1999 Human Resources Self-Service Survey. Baltimore, MD: Cedar.

CedarCrestone. (2010). *CedarCrestone 2009–2010 HR Systems Survey*. Retrieved from www.cedarcrestone.com/research.php.

Cennamo, L. & Gardner, D. (2008). Generational differences in work values, outcomes and person-organisation values fit. *Journal of Managerial Psychology*, *23*(8), 891–906.

Chapman, D. S. & Godollei, A. (2017). E-Recruiting: Using technology to attract job applicants. In G. Hertel, D. L. Stone, R. D. Johnson, & J. Passmore (Eds.),

The Wiley-Blackwell *handbook* of the *psychology* of the *internet* at *work* (pp. 213–230). Chichester, UK: Wiley Blackwell.

Chapman, D. S., Uggerslev, K. L., Carroll, S. A., Piasentin, K. A., & Jones, D. A. (2005). Applicant attraction to organizations and job choice: A meta-analytic review of the correlates of recruiting outcomes. *Journal of Applied Psychology, 90*, 928–944.

Chapman, D. S., Uggerslev, K. L., & Webster, J. (2003). Applicant reactions to face-to-face and technology-mediated interviews: A field of investigation. *Journal of Applied Psychology, 88*, 944–953.

Chapman, D. S. & Webster, J. (2003). The use of technologies in the recruiting, screening, and selection processes for job candidates. *International Journal of Selection and Assessment, 11*, 113–120.

Chuah, S. C., Dragsow, F., & Roberts, B. W. (2006). Personality assessment: Does the medium matter?. *Journal of Research in Personality, 40*, 359–376.

Cober, R. T., Brown, D. J., Blumental, A. J., Doverspike, D., & Levy, P. (2000). The quest for the qualified job surfer: It's time the public sector catches the wave. *Public Personnel Management, 29*(4), 479–494.

Cober, R. T., Brown, D. J., Levy, P. E., Keeping, L. M., & Cober, A. L. (2003). Organizational web sites: Web site content and style as determinants of organizational attraction. *International Journal of Selection and Assessment, 11*, 158–168.

Cooper, J. (2006). The digital divide: The special case of gender. *Journal of Computer Assisted Learning, 22*, 320–334.

Coyne, I., Warszta, T., Beadle, S., & Sheehan, N. (2005). The impact of mode of administration on the equivalence of a test battery: A quasi-experimental design. *International Journal of Selection and Assessment, 13*, 220–223.

Cronk, B. C. & West, J. L. (2002). Personality research on the internet: A comparison of web-based and traditional instruments in take-home and in-class settings. *Behavior Research Methods, Instruments, & Computers, 34*, 177–180.

Daft, R. L. & Lengel, R. H. (1986). Organizational information requirements, media richness and structural design. *Management Science, 32*, 554–571.

Davenport, T. & Ronanki, R. (2018). Artificial intelligence for the real world: Don't start with moon shots. Harvard Business Review (January-February), 108–116.

deNoyelles, A., Hornik, S. R., & Johnson, R. D. (2014). Exploring the Dimensions of Self-Efficacy in Virtual World Learning: Environment, Task, and Content. *Journal of Online Learning and Teaching, 10*, 255–271.

DeRouin, R. E., Fritzsche, B. A., & Salas, E. (2004). Optimizing e-learning: Research-based guidelines for learner-controlled training. *Human Resource Management, 43*(2–3), 147–162.

DeSanctis, G. & Poole, M. S. (1994). Capturing the complexity in advanced technology use: Adaptive structuration theory. *Organization Science, 5*(2), 121–147.

Dineen, B. R., Ash, S. R., & Noe, R. A. (2002). A web of applicant attraction: Person-organization fit in the context of web-based recruitment. *Journal of Applied Psychology, 87*(4), 723–734.

Dineen, B. R. & Noe, R. A. (2009). Effects of customization on application decisions and applicant pool characteristics in a web-based recruitment context. *Journal of Applied Psychology, 94*, 224–234.

Dixon, L. (2017). This Firm Uses Virtual Reality to Recruit. Should Others Follow? Retrieved from www.talenteconomy.io/2017/03/13/firm-uses-virtual-reality-recruit-others-follow/.

Dominguez, A., Saenz-de-Navarrete, J., De-Marcos, L., Fernandez-Sanz, L., Pages, C., & Martinez-Herraiz, J. J. (2013). Gamifying learning experiences: Practical implications and outcomes. *Computers & Education, 63*, 380–392.

Drasgow, F. (1984). Scrutinizing psychological tests: Measurement equivalence and equivalent relations with external variables are the central issues. *Psychological Bulletin, 95*, 134–135.

Dulebohn, J. H. (2003). Information technology implementation: The need for compensation system congruency. In D. L. Stone (Eds.), *Advances in human performance and cognitive engineering research* (vol. 3, pp. 153–186). Greenwich, CT: JAI Press.

Dulebohn, J. H. & Johnson, R. D. (2013). Human resource metrics and decision support: A classification framework. *Human Resource Management Review, 23*, 71–83.

Eaton, C., Deutsch, T., Deroos, D., Lapis, G., & Zikopoulos, P. (2012). *Understanding big data: Analytics for enterprise class hadoop and streaming data.* San Francisco, CA: McGraw Hill.

Eddy, E. R., Stone, D. L., & Stone-Romero, E. F. (1999). The effects of information management policies on reactions to human resource information systems: An integration of privacy and procedural justice perspectives. *Personnel Psychology, 52*(2), 335–358.

Efron, L. (2016). How gaming is helping organizations accelerate recruitment. *Forbes.* Retrieved from www.forbes.com/sites/louisefron/2016/06/12/how-gaming-is-helping-organizations-accelerate-recruitment/.

Fallaw, S. S., Solomonson, A. L., & McClelland, L. (2009). Current trends in assessment use: A multi-organizational survey. Paper presented at the 24th Annual Meeting of the Society for Industriall and Organizational Psychology, New Orleans, LA.

Fetzer, M. (2015). Serious games for talent selection and development. *TIP: The Industrial-Organizational Psychologist, 52*(3), 117–125.

Fisher, S. L., Howardson, G., Wasserman, M., & Orvis, K. (forthcoming). How do learners interact with elearning? Examining patterns of learner control behaviors. AIS Transactions on Human Computer Interaction, 9(2), 75–98.

Fisher, S. L., Wasserman, M., & Orvis, K. (2010). Trainee reactions to learner control: An important link in the e-learning equation. *International Journal of Training and Development, 14*(3), 198–210.

Fleck, C. (2016). An algorithm for success. HR Magazine (June), 130–135.

Flood, J. (2002). Read all about it: On-line learning facing 80 percent attrition rates. Turkish *Journal* Online of Distance Education, 3(2).

Foster, J. A., Sheridan, P. K., Irish, R., & Frost, G. S. (2012). Gamification as a strategy for promoting deeper investigation in a reverse engineering activity. Paper presented at the 2012 American Society for Engineering Education Conference.

Furtmüller, E., Wilderom, C., & Van Dick, R. (2010). Sustainable e-Recruiting portals: How to motivate applicants to stay connected throughout their careers? *International Journal of Technology and Human Interaction, 6*(3), 1–20.

Galanaki, E. (2002). The decision to recruit online: A descriptive study. *Career Development International, 7*, 243–251.

Garrison, D. R. & Arbaugh, J. B. (2007). Researching the community of inquiry framework: Review, issues, and future directions. *The Internet and Higher Education, 10*(3), 157–172.

Gartner. (2015). Gartner Reveals Top Predictions for IT Organizations and Users for 2016 and Beyond. Retrieved from www.gartner.com/newsroom/id/3143718.

Gherson, D. & Jackson, A. P. (2000). Web-based compensation planning. In A. J. Walker (Ed.), *Web-based human resources* (pp. 83–95). New York, NY: McGraw-Hill.

Gill, M. (2000). E-learning technology and strategy for organisations. In K. Fry (Ed.), *The Business of e-learning: Bringing your Organization in the Knowledge Economy.* Sydney, Australia University of Technology.

Granger, B. & Levine, E. (2010). The perplexing role of learner control in e-learning: Will learning and the transfer benefit suffer? *International Journal of Training and Development, 14*(3), 180–197.

Gubbi, J., Buyya, R., Marusic, S., & Palaniswami, M. (2013). Internet of Things (IoT): A vision, architectural elements, and future directions. *Future Generation Computer Systems, 29*(7), 1645–1660.

Gueutal, H. G. & Falbe, C. M. (2005). eHR: Trends in delivery methods. In H. G. Gueutal & D. L. Stone (Eds.), The brave new world of eHR: Human resources management in the digital age (pp. 190–225). San Francisco, CA: Jossey-Bass.

Gueutal, H. G. & Stone, D. L. (2005). *The brave new world of eHR:Human resources management in the digital age.* San Francisco, CA: Jossey-Bass.

Gunawardena, C. N. & Zittle, F. J. (1997). Social presence as a predictor of satisfaction within a computer-mediated conferencing environment. *The American Journal of Distance Education, 11*(3), 8–26.

Gutek, B. A. (1995). *The dynamics of service: Reflections on the changing nature of customer/provider interactions.* San Francisco, CA: Jossey-Bass.

Gutek, B. A., Bhappu, A. D., Liao-Troth, M. A., & Cherry, B. (1999). Distinguishing between service relationships and encounters. *Journal of Applied Psychology, 84*(2), 218–233baker.

Hall, B. & LeCavalier, J. (2000). E-learning across the enterprise: The benchmarking study of best practices. Retrieved from www.brandon-hall.com/elacenbenstu.html.

Harris, M. M., Van Hoye, G., & Lievens, F. (2003). Privacy and attitudes towards internet-based selection systems: A cross-cultural comparison. *International Journal of Selection and Assessment, 11*(2/3), 230–236.

Harrison, T. L. & Stone, D. L. (2015). Understanding an e-recruiting method: Aligning website features and applicants' values. Paper presented at the Academy of Management Annual Meeting, Vancouver, CA.

Hawking, P., Stein, A., & Foster, S. (2004). E-HR and employee self service: A case study of a Victorian public sector organisation. *Journal of Issues in Informing Science and Information Technology, 1*, 1019–1026.

Hays, R. T., Jacobs, J. W., Prince, C., & Salas, E. (1992). Flight simulator training effectiveness: A meta-analysis. *Military Psychology,* 4(2), 63–74.

Heinssen, R. K., Glass, C. R., & Knight, L. A. (1987). Assessing computer anxiety: Development and validation of the computer anxiety rating scale. *Computers in Human Behavior, 3*(1), 49–59.

Hornik, S. & Thornburg, S. (2010). Really engaging accounting: Second Life™ as a learning platform. *Issues in Accounting Education, 25*(3), 361–378.

Huang, J.-H., Jin, B.-H., & Yang, C. (2004). Satisfaction with business-to-employee benefit ssytems and organiational citizenship behavior. *International Journal of Manpower, 25*(2), 195–210.

Huang, J.-H., Yang, C., Jin, B.-H., & Chiu, H. (2004). Measuring satisfaction with business-to-employee systems. *Computers in Human Behavior*, *20*, 17–35.

Hughes, M. G., Day, E. A., Wang, X., Schuelke, M. J., Arsenault, M. L., Harkrider, L. N., & Cooper, O. D. (2013). Learner-controlled practice difficulty in the training of a complex task: Cognitive and motivational mechanisms. *Journal of Applied Psychology*, *98*, 80–98.

Huselid, M. A. (1995). The impact of human resource management practices on turnover, productivity, and corporate financial performance. *Academy of Management Journal*, *38*, 635–672.

Inayat, I., Amin, R., Inayat, Z., & Salim, S. S. (2013). Effects of collaborative web based vocational education and training (VET) on learning outcomes. *Computers & Education*, *68*, 153–166.

Jackson, S. E. & Schuler, R. S. (1995). Understanding human resource management in the context of organizations and their environments. *Annual review of psychology*, *46* (1), 237–264.

Johnson, R. D. & Brown, K. G. (2017). e-Learning. In G. Hertel, D. L. Stone, R. D. Johnson, & J. Passmore (Eds.), *The Wiley-Blackwell handbook of the psychology of the internet at work*. Chichester, UK: Wiley-Blackwell.

Johnson, R. D. & Gueutal, H. G. (2012). *Transforming HR through technology: The use of eHR and human resource information system in organisations*. Alexandria, VA: Society for Human Resource Management. Retrieved from www.shrm.org/about/foundation/products/Documents/HR%20Tech%20EPG-%20Final.pdf

Johnson, R. D., Gueutal, H. G., & Falbe, C. M. (2009). Technology, trainees, metacognitive activity and e-learning effectiveness. *Journal of Managerial Psychology*, *24*(6), 545–566.

Johnson, R. D., Hornik, S., & Salas, E. (2008). An empirical examination of factors contributing to the creation of successful e-learning environments. *International Journal of Human-Computer Studies*, *66*(5), 356–369.

Johnson, R. D., Lukaszewski, K. M., & Stone, D. L. (2016). The evolution of the field of human resource information systems: Co-evolution of technology and HR processes. *Communications of the Association for Information Systems*, *38*, 533–553.

Johnson, R. D., Marakas, G. M., & Palmer, J. W. (2006). Differential social attributions toward computing technology: An empirical investigation. *International Journal of Human Computer Studies*, *64*(5), 446–460.

Johnson, R. D., Marakas, G. M., & Palmer, J. W. (2008). Beliefs about the social role and capabilities of computing technology: Development of the computing technology continuum of perspective. *Behaviour & Information Technology*, *27*(2), 169–181.

Johnson, R. D., Stone, D. L., & Navas, D. S. (2011). *Factors Related to the Digital Divide and Hispanics' Use of Computers*. Paper presented at the Academy of Management Annual Meeting, San Antonio, TX.

Johnson, R. D., Thatcher, J. B., & Burleson, J. (2016). A framework and research agenda for studying eHRM: Automating and informating capabilities of HR technology. In D. L. Stone & J. H. Dulebohn (Eds.), *Research in human resource management: Human resource management theory and research on new employment relationships* (pp. 225-253). Charlotte, NC: Information Ag.

Karim, M. N. & Behrend, T. S. (2014). Reexamining the nature of learner control: Dimensionality and effects on learning and training reactions. *Journal of Business and Psychology, 29*(1), 87–99.

Katz, D., & Kahn, R. L. (1978). *The social psychology of organizations* (2nd edn.). New York, NY: Wiley.

Kavanagh, M. J. & Johnson, R. D. (2018). *Human resource information systems: Basics, applications, and future directions* (4th edn.). Thousand Oaks, CA: Sage.

Kehoe, J. F., Dickter, D. N., Russell, D. P., & Sacco, J. M. (2005). E-selection. In H. G. Gueutal & D. L. Stone (Eds.), *The brave new world of e HR: Human resource management in the digitalaAge*. San Francisco, CA: Jossey-Bass.

Keith, N. & Frese, M. (2005). Self-regulation in error management training: Emotion control and metacognition as mediators of performance effects. *Journal of Applied Psychology, 90*, 677–691.

Kiesler, S., Siegel, J., & McGuire, T. W. (1984). Social psychological aspects of computer-mediated communication. *American Psychologist, 39*, 1123–1134.

Kraichy, D. & Chapman, D. S. (2014). Tailoring web-based recruiting messages: Individual differences in the persuasiveness of affective and cognitive messages. *Journal of Business and Psychology, 29*(2), 253–268.

Kraiger, K., Ford, J. K., & Salas, E. (1993). Application of cognitive, skill-based, and affective theories of learning outcomes to new methods of training evaluation. *Journal of Applied Psychology, 78*(2), 311–328.

Kraiger, K. & Jerden, E. (2007). A meta-analytic investigation of learner control: Old findings and new directions. In S. M. Fiore & E. Salas (Eds.), *Toward a science of distributed learning* (pp. 65–90). Washington, DC: American Psychological Association.

Larsen, C. R., Oestergaard, J., Ottesen, B. S., & Soerensen, J. L. (2012). The efficacy of virtual reality simulation training in laparoscopy: a systematic review of randomized trials. *Acta obstetricia et gynecologica Scandinavica, 91*(9), 1015–1028.

Lim, C. K. (2001). Computer self-efficacy, academic self-concept, and other predictors of satisfaction and future participation of adult distance learners. *The American Journal of Distance Education, 15*(2), 41–51.

Long, L. K., Dubois, C., & Faley, R. (2009). A case study analysis of factors that influence attrition rates in voluntary online training programs. *International Journal of E-learning, 8*(3), 347–359.

Lukaszewski, K. M., Stone, D. L., & Johnson, R. D. (2016). Impact of human resource information system policies on privacy. *AIS Transactions on Human-Computer Interaction, 8*(2), 58–73.

Makransky, G. & Glas, C. A. (2011). Unproctored internet test verification: Using adaptive confirmation testing. *Organizational Research Methods, 14*(4), 608–630.

Marakas, G. M., Yi, M. Y., & Johnson, R. D. (1998). The multilevel and multifaceted character of computer self-efficacy: Toward clarification of the construct and an integrative framework for research. *Information Systems Research, 9*(2), 126–163.

Markus, M. L. & Robey, D. (1988). Information technology and organizational change: Causal structure in theory and research. *Management Science, 34*(5), 583–598.

Martin, C. L. & Nagao, D. H. (1989). Some effects of computerized interviewing on job applicant responses. *Journal of Applied Psychology, 74*(1), 72–80.

Mauldin, E. G. (2003). An experimental examination of information technology and compensation structure complementarities in an expert system context. *Journal of Information Systems Research*, *17*, 19–41.

Maurath, D. (2014). A critical incident for big data. *TIP: The Industrial-Organizational Psychologist*, *51*(3), 16–25.

McDaniel, R., Lindgren, R., & Friskics, J. (2012). Using badges for shaping interactions in online learning environments. Paper presented at the 2012 IEEE International Professional Communication Conference, Orlando, FL.

McManus, M. A. & Ferguson, M. W. (2003). Biodata, personality, and demographic differences of recruits from threes sources. International Journal of Selection and Assessment, 11, 175–183.

Mennecke, B. E., Hassall, L. M., & Triplett, J. (2008). The mean business of Second Life: Teaching entrepreneurship, technology and e-commerce in immersive environments. *MERLOT Journal of Online Learning and Teaching*, *4*(3), 339–348.

Mennecke, B. E., Triplett, J. L., Hassall, L. M., Conde, Z. J., & Heer, R. (2011). An examination of a theory of embodied social presence in virtual worlds. *Decision Sciences*, *42*(2), 413–450.

Merchant, Z., Goetz, E. T., Keeney-Kennicutt, W., Kwok, O., Cifuentes, L., & Davis, T. J. (2012). The learner characteristics, features of desktop 3D virtual reality environments, and college chemistry instruction: A structural equation modeling analysis. *Computers & Education*, *59*(2), 551–568.

Mohamed, A. A., Orife, J. N., & Wibowo, K. (2002). The legality of key word search as a personnel selection tool. *Employee Relations*, *24*, 516–522.

Mooney, A. (May 15, 2017). US faces crisis as pension funding hole hits $3.85tn. Financial Times. Retrieved from www.ft.com/content/f2891b34-3705-11e7-99bd-13beb0903fa3.

Mujber, T. S., Szecsi, T., & Hashimi, M. S. (2004). Virtual reality applications in manufacturing process simulation. *Journal of materials processing technology*, *155*, 1834–1838.

Mullich, J. (2004). A second act for e-learning. *Workforce Management*, *83*, 51–55.

Nguyen, H. H. D., & Ryan, A. M. (2008). Does stereotype threat affect test performance of minorities and women? A meta-analysis of experimental evidence. *Journal of Applied Psychology*, *24*, 645–662.

Nikolaou, I. (2014). Social networking web sites in job search and employee recruiting. *International Journal of Selection and Assessment*, *22*, 179–189.

Organ, D. (1988). *Organizational citizenship behavior: The good soldier syndrome*. Lexington, MA: Lexington Books.

Orlikowski, W. J. (1992). The duality of technology: Rethinking the concept of technology in organizations. *Organization Science*, *3*(3), 398–427.

Orvis, K. A., Brusso, R. C., Wasserman, M. E., & Fisher, S. L. (2010). E-nabled for e-learning? The moderating role of personality in determining the optimal degree of learner control in an e-learning environment. *Human Performance*, *24*(1), 60–78.

Orvis, K. A., Fisher, S. L., & Wasserman, M. E. (2009). Power to the people: Using learner control to improve trainee reactions and learning in web-based instructional environments. *Journal of Applied Psychology*, *94*, 960–971.

Oswald, F. L., Carr, J. Z., & Schmidt, A. M. (2001). The medium and the message: Dual effects of supervision and web-based testing on measurement equivalence for ability and personality measures. Paper presented at the Society for Industrial and Organizational Psychoogy Annual Meeting, San Diego, CA.

Overton, R. C., Harms, H. J., Taylor, L. R., & Zickar, M. J. (1997). Adapting to adaptive testing. *Personnel Psychology, 50,* 171–185.

Panepinto, R. (1995). Voice technology for 401(k) plans. *Benefits Quarterly, 11,* 8–11.

Pew Internet. (2017). Minorities use of the internet and broadband. Retrieved from www .pewinternet.org/fact-sheet/internet-broadband/.

Piccoli, G., Ahmad, R., & Ives, B. (2001). Web-based virtual learning environments: A research framework and a preliminary assessment of effectiveness in basic IT skills training. *MIS Quarterly, 25*(4), 401–426.

Ployhart, R. E., Weekley, J. A., Holtz, B. C., & Kemp, C. (2003). Web-based and paper-and-pencil testing of applicants in a proctored setting: Are personality, biodata, and situational judgment tests comparable? *Personnel Psychology, 56*(3), 733–752.

Potosky, D., & Bobko, P. (2004). Selection testing via the internet: Practical considerations and exploratory empirical findings. *Personnel Psychology, 57,* 1003–1034.

Robson, K., Plangger, K., Kietzman, J. H., McCarthy, I., & Pitt, L. (2015). Is it all a game? Understanding the principles of gamification. *Business Horizons, 588*(4), 411–420.

Rosenbloom, J. S., & Hallman, G. V. (1991). *Employee benefit planning.* Upper Saddle River, NJ: Prentice Hall.

Rynes, S. L. (1991). Recruitment, job choice, and post-hire consequences: A call for new research directions. In M. D. Dunnette & L. M. Hough (Eds.), *Handbook of industrial and organizational psychology* (2nd edn., vol. 2, pp. 399–444). Palo Alto, CA: Consulting Psychologists.

Salas, E., DeRouin, R., & Littrell, L. (2005). Research-based guidelines for designing distance learning: What we know so far. In H. G. Guetal & D. L. Stone (Eds.), *The brave new world of eHr* (pp. 104–137. San Francisco, CA: Jossey-Bass.

Salgado, J. F. & Moscoso, S. (2003). Internet-based personality testing: Equivalence of measures and assesses' perceptions and reactions. *International Journal of Selection and Assessment, 11,* 194–205.

Scheu, C., Ryan, A. M., & Nona, F. (1999). Company web sites as a recruiting mechanism: What influences applicant impressions. Paper presented at the Society for Industrial and Organizational Psychology Annual Conference, Atlanta, GA.

Schmidt, A. M. & Ford, J. K. (2003). Learning within a learner control training environment: The interactive effects of goal orientation and metacognitive instruction on learning outcomes. *Personnel Psychology, 56,* 405–429.

Schmidt, J. A., Chapman, D. S., & Jones, D. A. (2015). Does emphasizing different types of person–environment fit in online job ads influence application behavior and applicant quality? Evidence from a field experiment. *Journal of Business and Psychology, 30*(2), 267–282.

Searle, R. H. (2002). Organizational justice in e-recruiting: Issues and controversies. *Surveillance & society, 1*(2), 227–231.

Selden, S. & Orenstein, J. (2011). Government E-Recruiting Web Sites: The influence of e-recruitment content and usability on recruiting and hiring outcomes in US state governments. *International Journal of Selection and Assessment, 19*(1), 31–40.

Sierra-Cedar. (2016). Sierra-Cedar 2015–2016 HRSystems Survey: 18th Annual Edition. Alpharetta, GA: SierraCedar.

Silvester, J., Anderson, N., Haddleton, E., Cunningham-Snell, N., & Gibb, A. (2000). A cross-modal comparison of telephone and face-to-face selection interviews in graduate recruitment. *International Journal of Selection and Assessment*, *8*(1), 16–21.

Sinar, E. F. & Reynolds, D. H. (2001). Applicant reactions to internet-based selection techniques. Paper presented at the 16th Annual Conference of the Society for Industrial and Organizational Psychology, San Diego, CA.

Sitzmann, T., Brown, K. G., Casper, W. J., Ely, K., & Zimmerman, R. D. (2008). A review and meta-analysis of the nomological network of trainee reactions. *Journal of Applied Psychology*, *93*(2), 280–295.

Sitzmann, T. & Ely, K. (2010). Sometimes you need a reminder: The effects of self-regulation on regulatory processes, learning and attrition. *Journal of Applied Psychology*, *95*(1), 132–144.

Sitzmann, T., Kraiger, K., Stewart, D., & Wisher, R. (2006). The comparative effectiveness of web-based and classroom instruction: A meta-analysis. *Personnel Psychology*, *59*(3), 623–664.

Smith, T. L. (1996). Using computer technology to enhance learning: Compensation in the real world. *Journal of Education for Business*, *72*(2), 98–101.

Snyder, E. & Hartig, J. R. (2013). Gamification of board review: A residency curricular innovation. *Medical Education*, *47*(5), 524–525.

Society for Human Resource Management. (2002). *The future of the HR profession: Eight leading consulting firms share their visions for the future of human resources.* Retrieved from www.shrm.org/pressroom/Documents/future_of_hr.pdf.

Society for Human Resource Management. (2007). SHRM case study: Manager self-service. Retrieved from www.shrm.org/hrdisciplines/technology/Articles/Pages/CMS_006604.

Steele, C. M., & Aronson, J. (1995). Stereotype threat and the intellectual test performance of African Americans. *Journal of Personality and Social Psychology*, *69*(5), 797–811.

Stone, D. L., Deadrick, D. L., Lukaszewski, K. M., & Johnson, R. D. (2015). The influence of technology on the future of human resource management. *Human Resource Management Review*, *25*(2), 216–231.

Stone, D. L., & Dulebohn, J. H. (2013). Emerging issues in theory and research on electronic human resource management (eHRM). *Human Resource Management Review*, *23*(1), 1–5.

Stone, D. L., Johnson, R. D., Stone-Romero, E. F., & Hartman, M. (2006). A comparative study of Hispanic-American and Anglo-American cultural values and job choice preferences. *Management Research*, *4*, 7–22.

Stone, D. L., Krueger, D., & Takach, S. (2017). Social issues associated with the internet at work. In G. Hertel, D. L. Stone, R. D. Johnson, & J. Passmore (Eds.), *Handbook of the Psychology of the Internet at Work* (pp. 423–448). Chichester, UK: Wiley Blackwell.

Stone, D. L., & Lukaszewski, K. M. (2009). An expanded model of the factors affecting the acceptance and effectiveness of electronic human resource management systems. *Human Resource Management Review*, *19*(2), 134–143.

Stone, D. L., Lukaszewski, K. M., & Isenhour, L. C. (2005). E-recruiting: Online strategies for attracting talent. In H. G. Gueutal & D. L. Stone (Eds.), *The brave new world of eHR: Human resources management in the digital age* (pp. 22–53). San Francisco, CA: Jossey Bass.

Stone, D. L., Lukaszewski, K. M., Stone-Romero, E. F., & Johnson, T. L. (2013). Factors affecting the effectiveness and acceptance of electronic selection systems. *Human Resource Management Review*, 23(1), 50–70.

Stone, D. L., Stone-Romero, E. F., & Lukaszewski, K. (2003). The functional and dysfunctional consequences of human resource information technology for organizations and their employees. In D. L. Stone (Ed.), *Advances in human performance and cognitive engineering research* (pp. 37–68). Oxford, UK: JAI Press.

Stone, E. F. & Stone, D. L. (1990). Privacy in organizations: Theoretical issues, research findings, and protection mechanisms. *Research in personnel and human resources management*, 8(3), 349–411.

Stone-Romero, E. F., Isenhour, L. C., & Stone, D. L. (2011). Relations among values, ethnicity, and job choice trade off preferences. Paper presented at the Academy of Management Annual Meeting, San Antonio, TX.

Sturman, M. C., Hannon, J. M., & Milkovich, G. T. (1996). Computerized decision aids for flexible benefits decisions: The effects of an expert system and decision support system on employee intentions and satisfaction with benefits. *Personnel Psychology*, 49(4), 883–908.

Sturman, M. C. & Milkovich, G. T. (1995). Validating expert systems: a demonstration using personal choice expert, a flexible employee benefit system. *Decision Sciences*, 26(1), 105–118.

Thatcher, M. E. & Oliver, J. R. (2001). The impact of technology investments on a firm's production efficiency, product quality, and productivity. *Journal of Management Information Systems*, 18(2), 17–45.

Todd, P. & Benbasat, I. (1991). An experimental investigation of the impact of computer based decision aids on decision making strategies. *Information Systems Research*, 2(2), 87–115.

Twenge, J. M., Campbell, S. M., Hoffman, B. J., & Lance, C. E. (2010). Generational differences in work values: Leisure and extrinsic values increasing, social and intrinsic values decreasing. *Journal of Management*, 36(5), 1117–1142.

Ulrich, D. (2001). From e-Business to e-HR. IHRIM Journal, 5, 90–97.

Webster, J. & Hackley, P. (1997). Teaching effectiveness in technology-mediated distance learning. *Academy of Management Journal*, 40(6), 1282–1309.

Welsh, E. T., Wanberg, C. R., Brown, K. G., & Simmering, M. J. (2003). E-learning: emerging uses, empirical results and future directions. *International Journal of Training and Development*, 7(4), 245–258.

Whitman, T. S. & Hyde, A. C. (1978). HRIS: Systematically matching the right person to the right position. *Defense Management Journal*, 14(2), 28–34.

Wiechmann, D. & Ryan, A. M. (2003). Reactions to computerized testing in selection contexts. *International Journal of Selection and Assessment*, 11(2/3), 215–229.

Workscape. (2010). Automated compensation planning process enables more strategic decision making at Raytheon. Retrieved from www.workscape.com/~/media/Files/Client_Case_Studies/WorkscapeRaytheonCaseStudy.ashx.

Wright, A. (2017). Top HR Technology Trends for 2018. Retrieved from www.shrm.org/resourcesandtools/hr-topics/technology/pages/top-hr-technology-trends-2018.aspx.

Yanson, R. & Johnson, R. D. (2016). An empirical examination of e-learning design: The role of trainee socialization and complexity in short term training. *Computers & Education*, *101*, 43–54.

Zhang, D. (2003). Powering e-learning in the new millennium: An overview of e-learning and enabling technology. *Information Systems Frontiers*, *5*(2), 201–212.

Zielinski, D. (2000). The lie of online learning. *Training*, *37*(2), 38–40.

Zingheim, P. & Schuster, J. R. (2004). What's the next great pay and reward innovation? Business value, paying for skill, and the internet. *IHRIM Journal*, *3*(5), 47–50.

Zuboff, S. (1985). Automate/informate: The two faces of intelligent technology. *Organizational Dynamics*, *14*(2), 5–18.

Zusman, R. R. & Landis, R. S. (2002). Applicant preferences for web-based versus traditional job postings. *Computers in Human Behavior*, *18*, 285–296.

33 Technology and Social Evaluation: Implications for Individuals and Organizations

Roshni Raveendhran and Nathanael J. Fast

In recent years, an unprecedented proliferation of technological devices has led to marked changes in human behavior. This is especially evident in the modern workplace that leverages advances in numerous areas such as text analytics, natural-language processing, data science, and the Internet of Things (IoT) to create novel technological tools that can influence employee behaviors and organizational outcomes (Cain, 2016). For example, collaboration tools (e.g., Slack, Google Drive) have expanded the limits of teamwork by allowing employees from different parts of the world to work remotely with each other. Similarly, immersive technologies such as virtual reality (VR) and augmented reality (AR) enable employees to virtually interact and work with each other in a digital workplace. In addition to enabling new ways for employees to connect, novel workplace technologies are also transforming how employees are being managed. Managers now have access to a variety of technological tools such as applications on employees' phones and computers, sociometric badges equipped with microphones and sensors, and intelligent software systems that allow them to monitor employees more closely than ever before. From these examples, it is evident that technological advances have the potential to upend and transform traditional workplaces by disrupting key industries, and by altering the ways in which organizational actors engage with each other and with their work.

Although there is considerable discussion in I/O psychology scholarship and practice on the extent to which technology can influence organizational processes and outcomes, far less attention is being paid to the *psychological impact* of novel technologies on employees and managers. Novel technologies such as VR/AR and IoT devices that have the potential to dramatically influence organizations and employees (Future Workplace Study, 2016) have only recently become increasingly prevalent in our society. Thus, it is perhaps not surprising that we have paid little attention to the psychological and behavioral consequences for the individuals using these technologies. However, early findings suggest that the psychological impact of these emerging technologies will be considerable. In this chapter, we develop insights about the psychological and behavioral consequences of new technologies for organizational actors. In particular, we focus on the idea that social situations (contexts in which people interact with or behave in the presence of others) inherently allow for the possibility of evaluation by others and, as a result, may introduce a fear of negative evaluation. Building on this idea, we explore how novel technologies can influence people's psychological experiences in social settings and consequently, affect their behaviors.

To examine the psychological impact of novel technologies on individuals, we focus on two of the most influential types of new technologies that have become increasingly popular in recent years – behavior-tracking technology, and virtual/ augmented reality. These two technologies are among the top ten technological trends that are expected to have a significant strategic impact on organizations in 2018 (Gartner, 2017). Consistent with this expectation, it is also predicted that worldwide spending on behavior-tracking technologies and virtual/augmented reality will together exceed over $200 billion by 2020 (Gartner, 2016; IDC, 2017). In light of the organizational and societal impact that these two technologies are expected to have in the near future, we anticipate that examining the psychological impact of these novel technologies can offer important insights for both research and practice in industrial/organizational psychology.

In this chapter, we position our examination of the psychological impact of novel technologies in the context of monitoring and communication – two key organizational functions that have garnered considerable attention among scholars and practitioners in I/O psychology. Monitoring and communication are among the most common organizational functions that have been constantly transformed through technological advancements. In our discussion, we specifically focus on how behavior-tracking technology has changed the way monitoring occurs in organizations, and explore how virtual/augmented reality has transformed organizational communication.

The rest of the chapter is structured as follows: We begin by describing how social situations engender social evaluation and highlight the psychological consequences of experiencing social evaluation. Following this, we explain why we examine the psychological consequences of novel technologies in the context of monitoring and communication and highlight how social evaluation undergirds these organizational functions. In the subsequent section, we explore how technology influences users' concerns about social evaluation. Next, we offer an in-depth discussion of how novel technologies – behavior-tracking technology and virtual/ augmented reality – influence the psychology of organizational actors in the context of monitoring and communication. Finally, we conclude by highlighting how a better understanding of the psychological impact of novel technologies can offer important insights for both researchers and practitioners.

33.1 Social Evaluation

When people interact with others or operate in the presence of an audience they feel concerned about being negatively evaluated by others (Schlenker & Leary, 1982). These concerns result from being in an evaluative situation where one's behavior can be scrutinized by others and can possibly be rated as inadequate. In social interactions where people become the focus of others' attention, the prospect of interpersonal evaluation leads them to perceive a lower likelihood of obtaining satisfactory judgments from others (Schlenker & Leary, 1982). In this way, social situations inherently allow for possible evaluation by others and can make people focus on the possibility of being negatively evaluated by others (Leary, 1983; Van Boven, Lowenstein & Dunning, 2005). Potential negative evaluations can make people feel inadequate in evaluative situations (Muller & Butera, 2007).

The perception that one may possibly be negatively evaluated by others in a social situation is psychologically aversive to people, as it affects how others perceive and treat them (Goffman, 1959; Leary & Kowalski, 1990), and also affects how people view themselves (Leary & Baumeister, 2000). Negative social evaluation is also psychologically aversive as it leads to a range of negative feelings including feelings of embarrassment (Modigliani, 1971), social anxiety (Schlenker & Leary, 1982), and shame (Tangney, 1992). In social situations that entail performing before a competent (versus incompetent) audience where the possibility of negative evaluation is more salient, people report experiencing greater tension and nervousness (Jackson & Latane, 1981) and behave in ways indicative of embarrassment (Brown & Garland, 1971; Garland & Brown, 1972). Similarly, perceived negative evaluation of one's global self by others leads to feelings of shame. Shame, in turn, is often associated with a feeling of being exposed to others such that people think about how their defective self would appear to others (Tangney, 1999). Social situations also result in social anxiety when people are motivated to make a specific impression on others, but expect that others will react unfavorably toward them or negatively evaluate them (Schlenker & Leary, 1982).

In addition to being psychologically aversive, the possibility of being negatively evaluated by others is a physiological stressor for individuals. Cortisol is the hormone that is produced in the body as a response to threat experiences. Increases in cortisol levels in the body have been linked to receiving negative social feedback (Koslov, Mendes, Pajtas, & Pizzagalli, 2011; Jamieson & Mendes, 2016). In a meta-analysis of 208 acute stressor studies (Dickerson & Kemeny, 2004), performance tasks characterized by social evaluative threat (e.g., presence of an evaluative audience) were associated with cortisol responses more than four times larger than tasks without these evaluative elements. Taken together, these results suggest that social-evaluative contexts that may potentially result in negative evaluation by others lead to conditions that can be both psychologically and physiologically aversive.

33.2 Social Evaluation in Monitoring and Communication

Monitoring and communication are key organizational functions that have received substantial attention in the management and I/O psychology literatures. The criticality of monitoring and communication for organizations is evident from their inclusion in various taxonomies of key managerial and organizational functions (e.g., Fayol, 1949; Komaki, Zlotnick, & Jensen, 1986; Mintzberg, 1973; Yukl, 1989). In addition to their importance, monitoring and communication are among the organizational functions that have been continually influenced by technological advancements. For example, developments in information technology were accompanied by computer-aided monitoring of employees (Chalykoff & Kochan, 1989), electronic performance monitoring (Aiello & Kolb, 1995) and even close monitoring of employees' communications (Smith & Tabak, 2009). Today, a typical manager in a modern workplace can closely monitor various employee's behaviors including the time they spend at their desks, the extent to which they use instant messaging and social networks while at work, when and how they use various productive and non-productive applications, and their emails as they are being written (Bernstein, 2014). Similarly, advances in information technology have significantly transformed organizational communication. Initial technological developments enabled us to communicate with each other through telephones, facsimiles, and pagers. Further developments in information technology allowed for communicating via emails and video conferencing tools. Now, we have access to increasingly sophisticated technologies such as smartphones and virtual/augmented reality (VR/AR) that enable us to interact with others in an immersive manner. Both the importance of monitoring and communication in organizations, and the potential for technology to transform these organizational functions are factors that motivated us to examine the psychological impact of novel technologies in the context of these functions. Next, we describe how social evaluation is a critical psychological factor that influences both monitoring and communication.

33.2.1 Monitoring and Social Evaluation

Monitoring is a critical aspect of management that allows managers to obtain information about the performance of subordinates (Komaki, Zlotnick, & Jensen, 1986), use this information to differentiate between high and low performers, and appropriately administer contingent rewards (Komaki, 1986). Monitoring also allows subordinates to secure information about the importance of various tasks (Larson & Callahan, 1990). However, beyond having an informational role, monitoring influences the relationship between those who engage in monitoring and those who are monitored. Strickland (1958) found that monitoring can reduce trust between the two parties. Along these lines, Adams (1976) noted that frequent monitoring could lead to distrust and negative evaluations. Consider the example of an employee having to copy his boss on emails that he sends to other team members. Although there is no formal observation occurring in this context, the very act of copying the boss on emails falls under the purview of monitoring. In fact, studies show that copying the boss on emails makes employees feel evaluated and less trusted (De Cremer, 2017). In addition to influencing the cognitions and behaviors of employees who are being monitored, the act of *engaging* in monitoring can, itself, lead to psychological discomfort for managers. Knowing that monitoring might signal distrust, managers may feel negatively evaluated by subordinates (Raveendhran, Fast, & Carnevale, 2018). Such negative social evaluation, or even the fear of being negatively evaluated by others, can lead to psychologically aversive feelings (e.g., Schlenker & Leary, 1982) Thus, social evaluation is a critical psychological factor that underlies both the experience of monitoring and the experience of being monitored.

33.2.2 Communication and Social Evaluation

Given the importance of communication in organizations, we now turn our attention to understanding how social evaluation influences people's communication behaviors. From interpersonal communication to interacting with a group or with much larger audiences, communication inherently involves evaluation apprehension due to a fear of being negatively evaluated by one's audience. In fact, communication scholars have extensively examined the effects of evaluation (or anticipated evaluation) and the fear or anxiety associated with communication under numerous labels – stage fright (e.g., Clevenger, 1959), reticence (e.g., Phillips, 1968), and audience sensitivity (e.g., Paivo, 1964). Communication apprehension (e.g., McCroskey, 1977) pertains to an individual's level of fear/anxiety associated with communication and is rooted in the likelihood of being evaluated by others. In fact, communication apprehension is highly correlated with social anxiety, which is defined as anxiety resulting from the prospect or presence of personal evaluation in real or imagined settings (Leary, 1983; Schlenker & Leary, 1982). Thus, social evaluation plays a critical role in people's psychological experiences associated with organizational communication.

33.3 Technology and Social Evaluation

Social evaluation plays an important role in organizational contexts for a number of reasons. First, being evaluated by others (or even the likelihood of evaluation) is related to performance. An extensive body of work in social psychology including research on social loafing, creativity, goal setting and social facilitation has examined the link between social evaluation and performance (e.g., Amabile, 1983; Karau & Williams, 1993; Locke & Latham, 2002; Zajonc, 1965). A comprehensive examination of *how* social evaluation affects performance in these contexts suggests that the potential for evaluation leads people to either expend greater effort on tasks or quit trying, depending on individuals' experience of difficulty with the tasks (Harkins, 2006). Second, social evaluation (or the potential for evaluation) influences individuals' behaviors towards others in a social setting. When people are in situations that have the potential for evaluation, they may be less likely to engage in negative behaviors toward others such as physical or verbal harassment, abusive behaviors, counter-productive behaviors, stealing, or slacking. Third, social evaluation may negatively influence the probability of learning in organizations. In fact, research on social facilitation suggests that evaluation apprehension elicits the arousal of dominant responses in people and inhibits learning (Martens & Landers, 1972). Fourth, social evaluation likely reduces people's intrinsic motivation at work and enhances their attentiveness towards external factors such as rewards and punishments (Deci, Koestner & Ryan, 1999). Fifth, social evaluation affects creativity. In fact, fear of evaluation is negatively related to originality and ideation fluency, two common measures of creativity (Amabile, 1979).

Given the increasing prevalence of novel technologies in modern organizations, it is important to consider how using technology for monitoring and communication influences people's experiences of social evaluation in the workplace. Social situations allow for likely negative social evaluation by others. Therefore, in those situations, individuals focus on the possibility of negative evaluation (Leary, 1983; Van Boven, Lowenstein & Dunning, 2005). This awareness of the potential for negative evaluation in social situations imposes external pressures on people to behave in certain ways. When we know that other people may evaluate us negatively, we are constrained by the need to avoid making a negative impression on others (Nicholls, 1984; Ryan & Connell, 1989). However, technology may be able to mitigate the evaluative pressures of social situations. In our earlier work, we show that technology attenuates undesirable social cues that may otherwise be present in social interactions and mitigates social risks associated with evaluation (Raveendhran & Fast, 2018; Raveendhran, Fast & Carnevale, 2018). Thus, our work offers evidence supporting the idea that technology reduces people's experiences of social evaluation. Reduced social evaluation associated with technology is related to an increased likelihood of adopting technological products for monitoring (Raveendhran & Fast, 2018) and communication (Raveendhran, Fast & Carnevale, 2018).

In summary, social evaluation is a critical psychological factor that influences employees' behaviors and underlies key organizational functions such as monitoring and communication. When individuals are in social situations where they may likely be negatively evaluated by others, they anticipate negative social evaluation and, as a result, experience psychological aversion in the form of embarrassment and social anxiety. Technology, by attenuating social cues, reduces individuals' concerns about social evaluation in social situations. In the following sections, we examine how novel technologies such as behavior-tracking and virtual/augmented reality have transformed monitoring and communication respectively, and highlight how these technologies influence organizational actors' experiences of social evaluation in those contexts.

33.4 Behavior-Tracking Products: A Novel Technology for Monitoring and Implications for Social Evaluation

Research suggests that by the year 2020, people will be using more than 40 billion devices that are connected to the Internet, allowing them to transmit data wirelessly (ABI Research, 2014). This phenomenon, characterized by a network of physical objects that contain embedded technology to interact with their environments, is referred to as the 'Internet of Things (IoT)' (Gartner, 2018a). Some of the most commonly seen manifestations of the IoT are smart technologies in cars, home appliances and other home systems (e.g., temperature control), voice-activated assistants in our phones, technological personal assistants in our homes (e.g., Google home, Alexa), physician-recommended health monitoring devices, road sensors, and public safety and security devices. A recent survey indicated that experts anticipate the rapid spread of IoT devices between now and 2026, until humans and machines are seamlessly connected in a ubiquitous and unavoidable manner (Pew Research Center, 2017). This heightened connectivity through the IoT is expected to enable the collection of vast amounts of data about people, ultimately allowing organizations to devise effective ways to influence people's preferences and behaviors (Silva, 2017).

One of the most popular manifestations of the IoT is that of behavior-tracking products. Behavior-tracking products continuously track information about users and have the potential to offer real-time feedback based on that information. Common examples include devices such as smart watches, personal fitness and health trackers, smart glasses, and various computer/mobile applications that track users' personal information including their movements, physical location, personal health- and sleep-related behaviors, and work habits. The increasing popularity of these devices is evident in the rapid rate at which these products are being adopted. Recent reports suggest that sales from wearable devices generated $28.7 billion in revenue in 2016 and that this expected to grow to $61.7 billion by 2020 (Gartner, 2016). Importantly, organizations are beginning to integrate behavior-tracking technologies into the workplace to leverage them for motivating employees, enhancing productivity, improving health, and to monitor employees. In fact, organizations handed out over 12 million wearable behavior-tracking devices in 2016 and this number is expected to reach around 83 million by 2021 (ABI Research, 2016).

Behavior-tracking devices may benefit organizations in a number of ways. Behavior-tracking products are associated with improved employee health and wellness. Wearable devices such as smart watches and Fitbit measure the quantity and intensity of physical activity and use visual and motivational tools to track progress and keep users engaged. In 2015, Emory university expanded their health challenge that encouraged employees to become active. Over 6,300 Emory employees participated in the challenge that spanned eight weeks and 82 percent of these participants remained active throughout the 8-week period (Miller, 2017). In addition to health benefits, organizations may also expect to gain financial benefits through reduced healthcare costs when having employees who are healthier and more engaged. For example, Carewise (a wellness program provider whose members use Fitbit), found that healthcare costs increased by only 0.7 percent annually for their users who were more engaged in using behavior-tracking fitness devices compared to 24 percent for less engaged users (Wilson, 2013). Finally, behavior-tracking products are associated with increased productivity. A recent study conducted by Rackspace revealed that employees wearing wearables at work became 8.5 percent more productive (Boitnott, 2015). These examples suggest that behavior-tracking products have the potential to impact various organizational outcomes, if they are introduced and integrated appropriately. The potential for behavior-tracking products to impact various organizational outcomes suggests that these products may quickly be adopted by organizations. The possible pervasiveness of behavior-tracking products also highlight that it is important to consider the psychological costs and benefits for employees using these products.

33.4.1 Behavior-Tracking Products for Monitoring: Benefits and Downsides

Behavior-tracking products enable fine-grained, digital monitoring of employees by continuously collecting large amounts of data on employees' behaviors. Organizations can now use employees' personal networks of beacons and sensors connected to behavior-tracking products to identify people and track their behaviors based on personal information gathered through those devices. In addition to tracking personal health-related data through fitness trackers, organizations also track employees' behaviors at work through sensors added to employees' desks and behavior-tracking badges. For example, the senior management at the Daily Telegraph tracked the amount of time their journalists spent at their desks through sensors that picked up on body heat (Derousseau, 2017). Another behavior-tracking product that is becoming increasingly popular among organizations is the sociometric badge. Sociometric badges are wearable electronic badges that automatically measure micro-behaviors of employees such as the amount of face-to-face interaction they have with others, their conversational time, their physical proximity to other people, and physical activity levels using social signals from vocal features, body motion, and relative location (Kim, McFee, Olguin, Waber & Pentland, 2012). In addition to allowing organizations to closely and intensely monitor their employees, behavior-tracking products enable organizations to monitor various minute aspects of employees' physical states and behaviors. The influx of large amounts of data about employees' behaviors through these behavior-tracking products may be used by organizations to improve their work processes, communication and feedback mechanisms, and their management practices.

As organizations are increasingly integrating behavior-tracking technologies into the workplace, employees are becoming vulnerable to innumerable privacy-related risks. Behavior-tracking products are connected to the Internet and many of them transmit user-generated data, including consumers' names, email-addresses and passwords without encryption (Hunt, 2015). Moreover, gathering personal information about employees' behaviors outside work (such as in the case of company-sponsored fitness trackers) can be perceived as a breach of employees' privacy. Integrating immense amounts of employees' personal data into the organization's system could also be a huge security risk. In fact, when employees are digitally connected to the organization via behavior-tracking products, these devices can likely become an enabler for cyberattacks (Cox, 2017). In 2016 alone, there were a total of 980 security breaches across various industries including the government/military and healthcare compromising over 35 million records (Identity Theft Resource Center, 2016). People are, in general, reticent to share personal information with others (especially employers). Yet, it is interesting to note that people are quickly embracing behavior-tracking products, as evidenced by the rapid proliferation of these devices in organizations. In fact, three out of five people who responded to the State of Workplace Productivity Survey said that they would be willing to use behavior-tracking wearable devices at work if they helped them do their jobs better (Corsello, 2013).

In addition to privacy and security related risks, behavior-tracking products can also have a direct, negative psychological impact on employees. When organizations use behavior-tracking products to continuously track employees' micro-behaviors – such as the amount of time spent at desks, face-to-face interactions, tone of voice in meetings, and physical proximity to others – employees may begin experiencing their work environments as autonomy-infringing. When employees experience a lack of autonomy, it can negatively affect their job satisfaction (Hackman & Oldham, 1975), hinder creativity (Oldham & Cummings, 1996), and reduce motivation and productivity (Spector, 1986). In fact, studies show that employees are inherently opposed to monitoring (Chalykoff & Kochan, 1989) and may also experience monitoring as coercive (Sewell & Barker, 2006). Given that behavior-tracking products allow organizations to continually monitor employees' micro-behaviors, employees might experience such intensive monitoring as both denigrating and stress-inducing (Nussbaum & duRivage, 1986), hindering health and well-being. In addition to the sense that one is being constantly monitored, the access to real-time feedback that behavior-tracking products offer can negatively affect employees' motivation. This is consistent with research showing that receiving feedback that can hurt one's sense of self can be detrimental for both motivation and performance (e.g., Kluger & DeNisi, 1996). Thus, both the salience of constantly being monitored and the continuous access to feedback about one's behaviors that behavior-tracking products afford can lead to negative psychological consequences for employees.

33.4.2 Reducing Social Evaluation through Technology: Implications for Monitoring

In the context of monitoring, reducing social evaluation through technology may influence subordinates' attitudes toward monitoring. Although monitoring is a key component of organizational control, close supervision of subordinates through monitoring is known to reduce perceived autonomy and sense of self-responsibility (Deci, 1975). Studies show that monitoring discourages employees from engaging in extra-role organizational citizenship behaviors (i.e., behaviors that are above and beyond one's roles and responsibilities and have a positive effect on the organization) as they might believe that those behaviors will not be evaluated positively by their managers (Neihoff & Moorman, 1993). Technology can mitigate these negative effects of monitoring by reducing employees' concerns about social evaluation associated with monitoring. This has important implications for the extent to which employees have favorable attitudes toward technologies used for monitoring. In our earlier work, we demonstrate that participants in the role of employees show a greater preference for technology-backed monitoring compared to human-backed monitoring, and have a higher willingness to work for organizations that use behavior-tracking products (with no human involvement) to monitor them (Raveendhran & Fast, 2018). Thus, behavior-tracking products may be more positively received by subordinates when they know that these devices can reduce the experience of social evaluation that is prevalent in direct monitoring by managers.

33.5 Virtual Reality/Augmented Reality (VR/AR): Novel Technologies for Communication and Implications for Social Evaluation

Virtual reality (VR) is a computer-generated simulation of a three-dimensional (3D) environment "that surrounds a user and responds to that individual's actions in a natural way" (Gartner, 2018b). In this sense, VR allows the creation of virtual environments where people can interact with one another through avatars that represent their digital selves. An avatar is a digital representation of the user that reflects the user's behaviors, typically in real time (Bailenson & Blascovich, 2004). Virtual reality allows users to immerse themselves into their simulated environment and experience it as if it were real. Users can experience these virtual environments visually through devices such as VR headsets, in a tactile manner through devices such as VR gloves and in a fully immersive manner through virtual avatars where body language and social cues are salient.

A distinct, but related form of technology is augmented reality. Augmented reality (AR) refers to "the real-time use of information in the form of text, graphics, audio, and other virtual enhancements integrated with real-world objects" (Gartner, 2018c). In other words, augmented reality is a technology that integrates virtual information, such as digital images and objects, with the user's environment in real-time. In doing so, AR adds richness to the user's environment while allowing the user to interact with the environment in a realistic way. While VR allows for user experience in a virtual space, AR allows users to enhance their real-world experience by superimposing virtual digital objects on to the real-world environment.

Virtual reality/augmented reality technologies have the potential to transform organizational communication as increasing numbers of employees are working remotely. In fact, Gallup's recent State of the American Workplace report revealed that 43 percent of American employees spend at least some time working remotely, while 20 percent work entirely remotely (Gallup, 2017). Reiterating this idea, IDC suggests that by 2020, more than 105 million employees – nearly three quarters of the American workforce – will be mobile workers (IDC, 2015). Effective communication is both critical and challenging when employees work together remotely and VR/AR technologies can help enable it. VR offers an immersive experience where users can seamlessly interact and work with others in a virtual environment. Similarly, as AR exists at the intersection of the physical and digital worlds, it can enable users to interact with people in remote locations by projecting their digital image in real-time to the three-dimensional spaces surrounding them (Steiner, 2017).

As VR/AR are becoming both commercially viable and affordable, consumers and businesses alike are investing heavily in these technologies. Forecasts suggest that worldwide spending on VR/AR technologies will be $13.9 billion in 2017, and that this will increase to over $143 billion by 2020 (IDC, 2017a). VR and AR are currently being used in various industries such as defense, medicine, gaming, architecture, manufacturing, marketing, and education, to name a few. In fact, VR and AR are among the top technological trends that are expected to have a strategic impact on organizations in 2018 (Gartner, 2017). A recent survey of 4,000 full-time employees from small, medium and large businesses in ten countries revealed that two-thirds (66 percent) of employees were willing to use VR products at work (Future Workplace Study, 2016). Similarly, it is expected that by 2021, one-third of employees working in the information sector will leverage AR to interact with real-world objects, utilize digital information, and collaborate with others (IDC, 2017b).

The utility of VR/AR is evident in the numerous ways these technologies are being used in different organizations. In the manufacturing industry, for example, Ford uses Oculus Rift, a popular VR device, to create virtual models of cars so that designers from different teams can collaborate and work on design improvements (Gaudiosi, 2015). Raytheon, a defense organization, uses fully immersive VR technology that allows employees to manipulate virtual prototypes of warfighters, create simulations that indicate how ground battles unfold, what missiles look like in flight, and how satellites move in space (Pepitone, 2016). Similarly, NASA used virtual reality to train astronauts where they created a virtual simulation of the repair of Hubble telescope and allowed astronauts from different locations across the globe to simulate the repair as though they were in the same room (Roberts, Kossek, & Ozeki, 1998). Organizations such as Toyota, American Apparel, IBM, Reuters, Sun Microsystems, and Wells Fargo have experimented with Second Life, a VR platform, as a potential way to reach consumers (Wasko, Teigland, Leidner, & Jarvenpaa, 2011).

Not unlike VR, augmented reality is also currently used in diverse ways by organizations. ThysenKrupp, an elevator manufacturer, uses AR to visualize an elevator repair before a technician reaches a site and provides the technician with resources to effectively complete the repair (Lopez, 2016). In the retail sector, organizations like IKEA, Overstock.com, and Wayfair use AR to superimpose virtual images of furniture onto their physical environments in order to help them see exactly how a piece of furniture will look like in their own space (Armstrong, 2017). In marketing, there are numerous examples of organizations leveraging AR to enhance consumer experience. To promote their Jurassic Park franchise, Universal Studios Orlando uses AR to allow park visitors to directly engage with digital dinosaurs (Levski, 2017). From these examples, it is evident that VR and AR have numerous useful applications in various business domains.

33.5.1 Virtual Reality/Augmented Reality for Communication: Benefits and Downsides

VR and AR are promising communication tools that allow people to interact with others in highly realistic virtual or virtually augmented environments. Communicating via VR/AR affords an immersive and natural way to interact and collaborate more effectively when working remotely. The rising popularity of VR/AR tools and the increasing effectiveness of computing power are motivating numerous organizations to use virtual workplaces as a complement to the real world for communication. VR can be quite cost-effective for organizations as employees can meet and work together in a virtual environment without being physically present (Colbert et al., 2016). VR/AR may also help virtual team members feel more psychologically present by blocking out the external environment and reducing the perceived distance between users (Cummings & Bailenson, 2016). Furthermore, by creating an immersive interaction experience where people can see each other's facial expressions and gestures in real-time, these tools create a holistic communication experience that may make them more preferable than traditional video conferencing tools. Virtual or virtually augmented environments can also be more engaging for users for a number of reasons. First, such environments are objectively rich because they offer a variety of social cues by making a range of visual stimuli, objects, and environments available to the user. Second, they simultaneously offer numerous channels for communication including audio, video, and text (Wasko et al., 2011). Next, three-dimensional virtual environments enhance perceptions of telepresence and enjoyment (Nah, Eschenbrenner, & DeWester, 2011).

VR and AR also provide several advantages for collaboration by enhancing communication and enabling real-time feedback. In this sense, these tools can enable collaboration without employees having to be co-located. In the manufacturing industry, for example, AR tools such as smart glasses can deliver appropriate information and real-time feedback directly to workers' line of sight at the right moment. This allows workers to continue their jobs without needing to stop what they are doing to go through a training manual. When workers are faced with pressing issues, AR tools allow them to launch training videos or connect with experts who may be in different locations to get real-time assistance. The efficiency gains that AR affords allows employees to be more productive at work. Various studies show that, across different contexts, the use of AR increased productivity by an average of 32 percent (Abraham & Annunziata, 2017). In the context of team work, VR tools allow remote teams to be present in the same "virtual" room where teams can work together by using collaborative tools such as whiteboards that may be present in the virtual environment. AltspaceVR, a virtual reality company that creates communication platforms, enables organizations and individuals to connect in shared digital environments. In these environments, users can use VR headsets to meet with each other in a way that is more natural than possible through video conferencing, brainstorm like they are in the same room and communicate seamlessly. These examples suggest that both VR and AR enable users to more effectively collaborate with each other in virtual or virtually augmented environments.

Despite these benefits, VR and AR are not without limitations. First, given that VR technology may not be able to always accurately simulate real-world environments in the virtual world, users may find it difficult to treat virtual recreations of things with the same psychological merit. Palmer Luckey, the founder of Oculus VR, has indicated that until technological advances allow for tools that can perfectly capture the real-environment and map that to a virtual environment, it might be difficult to ensure that users treat virtual environments with the same weight (Lapowsky, 2015). Second, VR users face a significant challenge in making sense of the new virtual environments and in understanding how to interact with other avatars and objects in such environments (Wasko et al., 2011). For instance, people are inclined to mimic their behaviors from the real world in a virtual environment and do not easily let go of the physical and social constraints of the real world when interacting in a virtual environment (Brown, 2011). Moreover, navigating and interacting with others in a virtual environment can sometimes be distracting for users and can create negative affect (Nah et al., 2011).

Third, people's levels of engagement when using VR depends heavily on the extent to which they identify with their digital avatars. Studies show that people reported feeling more engaged and immersed in the virtual environment when they perceived the avatar as an extension of themselves rather than as an interaction tool (Wasko et al., 2011). A key factor that influences whether people identify with their avatars is the extent to which the avatar's facial and bodily characteristics bare resemblance to their actual selves. This is a limitation because organizations may not have the resources to create avatars that physically resemble each member of their workforce and, therefore, may run the risk of creating virtual environments where employees are not fully engaged. Thus, to improve users' identification with and cognitive connection to their digital avatars, it will be important to create VR technologies that are realistic representations of the users. Finally, various individual and situational factors influence the extent to which people perceive VR technologies as useful. The perceived usefulness of VR affects users' likelihood of using these technologies. For example, people's propensity to trust, their degree of anxiety about communicating via novel technologies, and other stable personality traits such as extraversion and openness affect people's likelihood of using VR (Jacques, Garger, Brown & Deale, 2009). Therefore, it is important to ensure that VR tools have features that can make people feel at ease, increase their levels of trust, and reduce their anxiety towards the technology.

Augmented reality also has some important limitations. First, the constant overlay on digital information on to our physical environment could lead to users experiencing cognitive overload and digital fatigue (Busel, 2017). A constant stream of incoming information through augmented reality can also be quite distracting and can take away from people's experience of their immediate physical and social environments (Eaton, 2009). Moreover, people using AR tools tend underestimate their reaction times in the real-world due to the difficulty associated with switching focus back from the augmented versions of their environments (Sabelman & Lam, 2015). This can be especially problematic as this can directly affect people's ability to react to hazards in their physical environments. Finally, augmented reality also poses serious threats to privacy and cyber security. AR tools blur the divide between the physical and the digital worlds and, in doing so, increases the severity of security threats that can permeate the physical world (Busel, 2017). For example, if the data appearing in a cockpit AR display becomes compromised, the jet may potentially veer off course. Given the limitations associated with both VR and AR, it will be important for organizations to consider how to effectively integrate these tools in the workplace.

33.5.2 Virtual Reality/Augmented Reality and Social Evaluation

In the context of communication, reducing social evaluation through technology can have important implications for both managers and subordinates. Communication research suggests that technology is quite effective in reducing communication apprehension. For example, shy individuals experience less communication apprehension when they interact via virtual reality in virtual worlds (Hammick & Lee, 2014). Compared to face-to-face interactions, virtual environments are described as quite effective in reducing people's likelihood of detecting negative or inhibitory feedback cues from others (Stritzke, Nguyen & Durkin, 2004). Reducing employees' communication apprehension and concerns about negative evaluation will be critical for ensuring they speak up and offer feedback and suggestions intended to improve organizational functioning. This is important, given that employee voice behavior is an important component of effective organizations (Detert & Burris, 2007).

For managers, novel technologies such as virtual reality reduce concerns about social evaluation when they engage in behaviors that may be perceived negatively by their subordinates. This is particularly evident in the communication context. A survey of 616 managers conducted by Interact (a communication consultancy) and Harris Poll in 2016 revealed that 69 percent of managers were uncomfortable communicating with their employees (Interact Report, 2015; Solomon, 2016). Novel technologies like VR/AR can be particularly helpful to buffer managers from their discomfort associated with communicating with employees. In our prior work, we found that managers showed a greater preference for using virtual reality to monitor subordinates and communicate with them in situations where they anticipated negative evaluation (Raveendhran, Fast & Carnevale, 2017). Moreover, communication between managers and subordinates can be improved through technology due to reduced social evaluation. Research suggests that technology can have a positive effect on subordinates similar to transformational leadership by reducing evaluation apprehension and engendering flexibility in communication between managers and subordinates (Avolio & Kahai, 2003; Kahai, Sosik, & Avolio, 2003). Furthermore, communication via technology may be less noisy as typical impression management tactics that people use in face-to-face interactions to manage or avoid negative evaluation are minimized when interacting via technology (DeRosa, Hantula, Kock, & D'Arcy, 2004). Therefore, when interacting via novel technologies like virtual reality, managers may more easily facilitate coordination of work without having to pay attention to interpersonal impression management behaviors. Thus, reduced social evaluation through technology has several important implications for communication for both managers and subordinates in organizations.

33.6 Downsides of Reducing Social Evaluation Through Technology

In this chapter, we have suggested that technology can reduce people's concerns about negative social evaluation, and highlighted the benefits of reducing social evaluation concerns in the context of monitoring and communication. Despite the numerous benefits described in the previous sections, reducing social evaluation concerns through technology can also have negative consequences for users. Reducing social evaluation concerns through technology can lead to the abandonment of novel technologies, reduced performance, and reduced sensitivity to privacy. Each of these effects can have important implications for employees and organizations. In this section, we briefly examine each of these downsides of reducing social evaluation through technology.

33.6.1 Implications for Abandonment of Technology

Technological products may be abandoned for a number of reasons. For example, if users find that the product is difficult to use, or that the product is no longer useful to them, or if they are bored of using the product, they are likely to abandon the product. A study on assistive technologies for individuals with disabilities revealed that 29.3 percent of all assistive devices were abandoned by users and the most common reasons for abandonment were a lack of consideration of user opinion in selection, easy device procurement, poor device performance, and changes in user needs or priorities (Phillips & Zhao, 1993).

Most of the common reasons cited for the abandonment of technological products pertain to objective aspects of the product itself while ignoring subjective psychological experiences of the users. We suggest that, beyond objective product-related factors, there is an important psychological factor that can help explain individuals' abandonment of technology. Specifically, we suggest that when using technological products, people do not feel negatively evaluated for discontinuing use. As a result, there is no psychological cost to quitting the technology. That is, reducing concerns about negative evaluation through technology also reduces people's commitment toward using the technology as there are no negative psychological or social effects associated with abandoning the technology in such cases.

33.6.2 Implications for Goal Pursuit

In addition to being both psychologically aversive (e.g., Schlenker & Leary, 1982) and physiologically stressful (e.g., Dickerson & Kemeny, 2004), the likelihood of negative social evaluation in a situation can also affect how we select, perceive and pursue goals. Studies show that when pursuing goals related to performance, people are motivated by a need to demonstrate competence either by seeking favorable or avoiding negative evaluations from others and that these motivations have distinct implications for how individuals choose goals and pursue them (Elliot & Harackiewicz, 1996; Middleton & Midgley, 1997). Thus, when pursuing goals related to performance (especially in the presence of others), people's goals are oriented toward avoiding negative judgments or toward obtaining positive judgments.

Beyond influencing people's motivations during goal pursuit, social situations also impact the salience of people's goals and their commitment toward attaining those goals. For example, Shah (2003) found that even mere mental representations of significant others increased the salience of the goals to which they are closely associated and motivated individuals to persist in attaining those goals. Similarly, Brockner, Rubin and Lang (1981) found that the presence of an audience during goal pursuit can make individuals feel compelled to persist and continually invest resources toward attaining the goal in order to save face and avoid negative evaluations (even when the likelihood of goal attainment is low). Thus, pursuing goals in the presence of others compels individuals to persist in attaining those goals to avoid the likelihood of being negatively evaluated in that social situation. Given that technology reduces concerns about social evaluation, employees may be more likely to slack at work or expend less effort when they know that they are monitored solely through technology (e.g., behavior-tracking products).

33.6.3 Implications for Privacy

Privacy is an important antecedent condition for individuals to maintain a positive social identity as it pertains to controlling which groups and individuals one interacts with and how one is viewed by them (Alge, 2001). One of the main benefits of privacy is anonymity, which allows people to do what they want to do without fear of social evaluation (Pedersen, 1997). In situations where people feel less concerned about social evaluation, such as when using technology, they are likely to feel more in control of their social identity and therefore, their sensitivity toward privacy concerns is likely to reduce. In fact, studies show that increased perceived control decreases people's concerns about privacy and increases their likelihood of disclosing sensitive personal information (Brandimarte, Acquisti & Loewenstein, 2013).

According to a recent survey assessing Americans' attitudes about privacy, security and surveillance, 93 percent of respondents reported that being in control of who can get information about them is very important, 90 percent of respondents reported that controlling what information is collected about them is important and 55 percent of respondents supported the idea of online anonymity for certain activities (Pew Research Center, 2015). A key underlying motivation for seeking control over both the content of information that others can access, and the audience that receives this information pertains to concerns about being evaluated (potentially negatively) by others. Similarly, desiring anonymity also pertains to avoiding negative evaluation by others. Thus, when technology reduces concerns about social evaluation, people may pay less attention towards privacy threats and may be more likely to divulge personal information through technology (compared to face-to-face interactions).

33.7 Future of Technology in the Workplace and the Role of Social Evaluation

As the modern workplace continues to be transformed by new technologies, employees will work in a digital mesh of intelligent systems that can act autonomously. Artificial intelligence and machine learning will encompass systems that learn, adapt and function autonomously. These systems will have the potential to drive digital innovation in several business areas. Virtual personal assistants may become more prevalent in the workplace and reduce employees' workloads by enabling more efficient coordination. Autonomous robots in the workplace may help make work processes more efficient by performing tasks that are difficult or dangerous without creating liabilities. Entire businesses may be created on digital technology platforms with a fully digital workforce.

Technology can reduce concerns about social evaluation. However, we know that social evaluation has both benefits and downsides in the workplace. Therefore, it will be critical for organizations to consider the implications for social evaluation when deciding to integrate novel technologies in their workplaces. Organizations must carefully consider how the characteristics of their workforce, their organizational culture and the nature of tasks influence the pertinence of social evaluation in a given situation and choose technological solutions appropriately, based on these considerations.

33.8 Conclusion

In this chapter, we discussed how technology has transformed the modern workplace with a specific focus on understanding the psychological impact of novel technologies on employees. In particular, we examined how technology influences people in social situations where there is a possibility for being negatively evaluated by others. We suggested that technology can reduce social evaluation concerns and examined the implications of this idea in the context of monitoring and communication. We contextualized our discussion even further by focusing on two novel technologies that are becoming increasingly pervasive and popular – behavior-tracking technology and virtual/augmented reality. We delved into understanding these technologies, and explored the opportunities and challenges associated with using them for monitoring and communication. Furthermore, we examined how these novel technologies influenced people's experiences of social evaluation in monitoring and communication contexts. Through this chapter, we hope to have provoked our readers to consider the importance of examining the psychological impact of novel technologies on employees and organizations while providing initial steps toward a more comprehensive understanding of the topic.

References

ABI Research. (August 20, 2014). More than 30 billion devices will drive wireless connected devices to 40.9 billion in 2020. Retrieved from www.abiresearch.com/press/the-internet-of-things-will-drive-wireless-connect/.

ABI Research. (September 29, 2016). New workplace wearables bridge communication gap between employees and systems. Retrieved from www.abiresearch.com/press/new-workplace-wearables-bridge-communication-gap-b/.

Abraham, M. & Annunziata, M. (March 13, 2017). Augmented reality is already improving worker performance. *Harvard Business Review*. Retrieved from https://hbr.org/2017/03/augmented-reality-is-already-improving-worker-performance.

Adams, J. S. (1976). The structure and dynamics of behavior in organizational boundary roles. *Handbook of Industrial and Organizational Psychology, 1175*, 1199.

Aiello, J. R. & Kolb, K. J. (1995). Electronic performance monitoring and social context: Impact on productivity and stress. *Journal of Applied Psychology, 80*(3), 339.

Amabile, T. M. (1979). Effects of external evaluation on artistic creativity. *Journal of* Personality *and Social Psychology, 37*(2), 221.

Amabile, T. M. (1983). The social psychology of creativity: A componential conceptualization. *Journal of Personality and Social Psychology, 45*(2), 357.

Alge, B. J. (2001). Effects of computer surveillance on perceptions of privacy and procedural justice. *Journal of Applied Psychology, 86*(4), 797.

Armstrong, P. (September 30, 2017). Smart companies are already using Apple's ARkit to make cash registers ring. *Forbes*. Retrieved from www.forbes.com/sites/paularmstrongtech/2017/09/30/smart-companies-are-already-using-apples-arkit-to-make-cash-registers-ring/#1aa8ae59253d.

Avolio, B. J. & Kahai, S. S. (2003). Adding the "E" to e-leadership: How it may impact your leadership. *Organizational Dynamics, 31*(4), 325–338.

Bailenson, J. N. & Blascovich, J. (2004). Avatars. In Encyclopedia of human-computer interaction. Great Barrington, MA: Berkshire Publishing Group.

Bernstein, E. (2014). The transparency trap. *Harvard Business Review, 92*(10), 58–66.

Boitnott, J. (April 28, 2015). Wearable tech is improving employee productivity and happiness. Retrieved from www.entrepreneur.com/article/245458.

Brandimarte, L., Acquisti, A., & Loewenstein, G. (2013). Misplaced confidences: Privacy and the control paradox. *Social Psychological and Personality Science, 4*(3), 340–347.

Brockner, J., Rubin, J. Z., & Lang, E. (1981). Face-saving and entrapment. *Journal of Experimental Social Psychology, 17*(1), 68–79.

Brown, R. H. (March 28, 2011). Virtual world, mobile tech finding use as innovative education tools. Retrieved from www.masshightech.com/stories/2011/03/28/weekly9-Virtual-world-mobile-tech-finding-use-as-innovative-educationtools.html.

Brown, B. R. & Garland, H. (1971). The effects of incompetency, audience acquaintanceship, and anticipated evaluative feedback on face-saving behavior. *Journal of Experimental Social Psychology*, *7*(5), 490–502.

Busel, M. (July 7, 2017). The 6 biggest challenges facing augmented reality: A look at the biggest risk factors for near-term AR adoption. Retrieved from https://medium.com/the-mission/the-6-biggest-challenges-facing-augmented-reality-8d48c470286d.

Cain, M. (November 2, 2016). Top 10 emerging technologies in the digital workplace. *Forbes*. Retrieved from www.forbes.com/sites/gartnergroup/2016/11/02/top-10-emerging-technologies-in-the-digital-workplace/#1af99ffc1e48.

Chalykoff, J. & Kochan, T. A. (1989). Computer-aided monitoring: Its influence on employee job satisfaction and turnover. *Personnel Psychology*, *42*(4), 807–834.

Clevenger Jr, T. (1959). A synthesis of experimental research in stage fright. *Quarterly Journal of Speech*, *45*(2), 134–145.

Colbert, A., Yee, N., & George, G. (2016). The digital workforce and the workplace of the future. *Academy of Management Journal*, *59*(3), 731–739.

Corsello, J. (January, 2013). What the Internet of Things will bring to the workplace. *WIRED*. Retrieved from www.wired.com/insights/2013/11/what-the-internet-of-things-will-bring-to-the-workplace/.

Cox, L. (March, 2017). Personal technology in the workplace: Wearables. Retrieved from https://disruptionhub.com/wearables-in-the-workplace/.

Cummings, J. J. & Bailenson, J. N. (2016). How immersive is enough? A meta-analysis of the effect of immersive technology on user presence. *Media Psychology*, 19(2), 272-309.

Deci, E. L. (1975). *Intrinsic motivation*. New York, NY: Plenum.

Deci, E. L., Koestner, R., & Ryan, R. M. (1999). A meta-analytic review of experiments examining the effects of extrinsic rewards on intrinsic motivation. *Psychological Bulletin, 125(6)*, 627–668.

De Cremer, D. (April, 2017). CC'ing the boss on email makes employees feel less trusted. Retrieved from https://hbr.org/2017/04/ccing-the-boss-on-email-makes-employees-feel-less-trusted.

Detert, J. R. & Burris, E. R. (2007). Leadership behavior and employee voice: Is the door really open? *Academy of Management Journal, 50*(4), 869–884.

DeRosa, D. M., Hantula, D. A., Kock, N., & D'Arcy, J. (2004). Trust and leadership in virtual teamwork: A media naturalness perspective. *Human Resource Management, 43*(2-3), 219–232.

Derousseau, R. (June 14, 2017). The tech that tracks your movements at work. Retrieved from www.bbc.com/capital/story/20170613-the-tech-that-tracks-your-movements-at-work.

Dickerson, S. S. & Kemeny, M. E. (2004). Acute stressors and cortisol responses: a theoretical integration and synthesis of laboratory research. *Psychological Bulletin, 130*(3), 355.

Eaton, K. (August 26, 2009). Three unexpected dangers of augmented reality. Retrieved from: www.fastcompany.com/1339617/three-unexpected-dangers-augmented-reality.

Elliot, A. J. & Harackiewicz, J. M. (1996). Approach and avoidance achievement goals and intrinsic motivation: A mediational analysis. *Journal of Personality and Social Psychology, 70*, 461–475.

Fayol, H. (1949). *General and Industrial Administration*. New York, NY: Pitman.

Future Workplace Study (July 18, 2016). Dell and Intel Future Workforce Study provides key insights into technology trends shaping the modern global workplace. Retrieved from: www.dell.com/learn/us/en/uscorp1/press-releases/2016–07-18-future-workforce-study-provides-key-insights.

Gallup (2017). State of the American Workplace. Retrieved from: www.gallup.com/reports/199961/state-american-workplace-report-2017.aspx.

Gartner (February 2, 2016). Gartner says worldwide wearable devices sales to grow 18.4 percent in 2016. Retrieved from: www.gartner.com/newsroom/id/3198018.

Gartner (October 4, 2017). Gartner identifies the top ten strategic technology trends for 2018. Retrieved from: www.gartner.com/newsroom/id/3812063.

Gartner (2018a). Internet of Things. Retrieved from: www.gartner.com/it-glossary/internet-of-things/.

Gartner (2018b). Virtual Reality (VR). Retrieved from: www.gartner.com/it-glossary/vr-virtual-reality/.

Gartner (2018c). Augmented Reality (AR). Retrieved from: www.gartner.com/it-glossary/augmented-reality-ar/.

Garland, H. & Brown, B. R. (1972). Face-saving as affected by subjects' sex, audiences' sex and audience expertise. Sociometry, 280–289.

Gaudiosi, J. (2015). How Ford goes further with virtual reality. Retrieved from: http://fortune.com/2015/09/23/ford-virtual-reality/. Date published: September 23, 2015.

Goffman, E. (1959). The moral career of the mental patient. *Psychiatry*, *22*(2), 123–142.

Hackman, J. R. & Oldham, G. R. (1975). Development of the job diagnostic survey. *Journal of Applied Psychology*, *60*(2), 159.

Hammick, J. K. & Lee, M. J. (2014). Do shy people feel less communication apprehension online? The effects of virtual reality on the relationship between personality characteristics and communication outcomes. *Computers in Human Behavior*, *33*, 302–310.

Harkins, S. G. (2006). Mere effort as the mediator of the evaluation-performance relationship. *Journal of Personality and Social Psychology*, *91*(3), 436.

Hunt (February 5, 2015). Experts: Wearable tech tests our privacy limits. Retrieved from: www.usatoday.com/story/tech/2015/02/05/tech-wearables-privacy/22955707/.

IDC (June 23, 2015). IDC forecasts U.S. mobile worker population to surpass 105 million by 2020. Retrieved from: www.businesswire.com/news/home/20150623005073/en#.VYmhfEZB58m.

IDC (February 27, 2017a). Worldwide spending on augmented and virtual reality forecast to reach $13.9 billion in 2017, according to IDC. Retrieved from: www.idc.com/getdoc.jsp?containerId=prUS42331217.

IDC (October, 2017b). IDC futurescape: Worldwide connected devices and augmented reality/virtual reality 2018 Predictions. Retrieved from: www.idc.com/research/viewtoc.jsp?containerId=US43145617.

Identity Theft Resource Center (December 13, 2016). 2016 Data breach category summary. Retrieved from: www.idtheftcenter.org/images/breach/ITRCBreachStatsReport Summary2016.pdf.

Interact Report (February, 2015). New Interact Report: Many leaders shrink from straight talk with employees. Retrieved from: http://interactauthentically.com/new-interact-report-many-leaders-shrink-from-straight-talk-with-employees/.

Jackson, J. M. & Latané, B. (1981). All alone in front of all those people: Stage fright as a function of number and type of co-performers and audience. *Journal of Personality and Social Psychology, 40*(1), 73.

Jacques, P. H., Garger, J., Brown, C. A., & Deale, C. S. (2009). Personality and virtual reality team candidates: The roles of personality traits, technology anxiety and trust as predictors of perceptions of virtual reality teams. *Journal of Business and Management, 15*(2), 143.

Jamieson, J. P. & Mendes, W. B. (2016). Social stress facilitates risk in youths. *Journal of Experimental Psychology: General, 145*(4), 467.

Kahai, S. S., Sosik, J. J., & Avolio, B. J. (2003). Effects of leadership style, anonymity, and rewards on creativity-relevant processes and outcomes in an electronic meeting system context. *The Leadership Quarterly, 14*(4), 499–524.

Karau, S. J. & Williams, K. D. (1993). Social loafing: A Meta-Analytic Review and Theoretical Integration. *Journal of Personality and Social Psychology, 65*(4), 681–706.

Kim, T., McFee, E., Olguin, D. O., Waber, B., & Pentland, A. (2012). Sociometric badges: Using sensor technology to capture new forms of collaboration. *Journal of Organizational Behavior, 33*(3), 412–427.

Kluger, A. N. & DeNisi, A. (1996). The Effects of Feedback Interventions on Performance: A Historical Review, a Meta-analysis, and a Preliminary Feedback Intervention Theory. *Psychological Bulletin, 119*(2), 254–284.

Komaki, J. L. (1986). Toward effective supervision: An operant analysis and comparison of managers at work. *Journal of Applied Psychology, 71*(2), 270.

Komaki, J. L., Zlotnick, S., & Jensen, M. (1986). Development of an operant-based taxonomy and observational index of supervisory behavior. *Journal of Applied Psychology, 71*(2), 260.

Koslov, K., Mendes, W. B., Pajtas, P. E., & Pizzagalli, D. A. (2011). Asymmetry in resting intracortical activity as a buffer to social threat. *Psychological Science, 22*(5), 641–649.

Lapowsky, I. (April 23, 2015). Oculus' founder on the pros and cons of VR for social good. Retrieved from: www.wired.com/2015/04/palmer-luckey-social-change/.

Larson, J. R. & Callahan, C. (1990). Performance monitoring: How it affects work productivity. *Journal of Applied Psychology, 75*(5), 530.

Leary, M. R. (1983). A brief version of the Fear of Negative Evaluation Scale. *Personality and Social Psychology Bulletin, 9*(3), 371–375.

Leary, M. R. & Baumeister, R. F. (2000). The nature and function of self-esteem: Sociometer theory. *Advances in Experimental Social Psychology, 32*, 1–62.

Leary, M. R. & Kowalski, R. M. (1990). Impression management: A literature review and two-component model. *Psychological Bulletin, 107*(1), 34.

Levski, Y. (2017). 10 Real world examples of AR marketing success. Retrieved from: https://appreal-vr.com/blog/10-augmented-reality-marketing-examples/.

Locke, E. A. & Latham, G. P. (2002). Building a Practically Useful theory of goal setting and task motivation: A 35-year odyssey. *American Psychologist, 57*(9), 705.

Lopez, M. (November 11, 2016). Augmented and virtual reality fuel the future workplace. Retrieved from: www.forbes.com/sites/maribellopez/2016/11/11/augmented-and-virtual-reality-fuel-the-future-workplace/#b19b9de185df.

Martens, R. & Landers, D. M. (1972). Evaluation potential as a determinant of coaction effects. *Journal of Experimental Social Psychology, 8*(4), 347–359.

McCroskey, J. C. (1977). Oral communication apprehension: A summary of recent theory and research. *Human Communication Research, 4*(1), 78–96.

Middleton, M. J. & Midgley, C. (1997). Avoiding the demonstration of lack of ability: An underexplored aspect of goal theory. *Journal of Educational Psychology, 89*(4), 710.

Miller, S. (May 17, 2017). Best practices for using wearable devices in wellness programs. Retrieved from: www.shrm.org/resourcesandtools/hr-topics/benefits/pages/wearable-trackers-best-practices.aspx.

Mintzberg, H. (1973). *The nature of managerial work*. New York: Harper & Row.

Modigliani, A. (1971). Embarrassment, facework, and eye contact: Testing a theory of embarrassment. *Journal of Personality and social Psychology, 17*(1), 15.

Muller, D. & Butera, F. (2007). The focusing effect of self-evaluation threat in coaction and social comparison. *Journal of Personality and Social Psychology, 93*(2), 194.

Nah, F. F. H., Eschenbrenner, B., & DeWester, D. (2011). Enhancing brand equity through flow and telepresence: A comparison of 2D and 3D virtual worlds. *MIS Quarterly*, 731–747.

Niehoff, B. P. & Moorman, R. H. (1993). Justice as a mediator of the relationship between methods of monitoring and organizational citizenship behavior. *Academy of Management Journal, 36*(3), 527–556.

Nicholls, J. G. (1984). Achievement motivation: Conceptions of ability, subjective experience, task choice, and performance. *Psychological Review, 91*(3), 328.

Nussbaum, K. & DuRivage, V. (1986). Computer monitoring: Mismanagement by remote control. *Business and Society Review*, 56, 16–20.

Oldham, G. R. & Cummings, A. (1996). Employee creativity: Personal and contextual factors at work. *Academy of Management Journal, 39*(3), 607–634.

Paivio, A. (1969). Mental imagery in associative learning and memory. *Psychological Review, 76*(3), 241.

Pedersen, D. M. (1999). Model for types of privacy by privacy functions. *Journal of Environmental Psychology, 19*(4), 397–405.

Pepitone, J. (October 27, 2016). Designing the workplace of the future: Virtual reality and 3D panoramas. Retrieved from: http://money.cnn.com/gallery/technology/2016/10/25/workplace-of-the-future/index.html.

Pew Research Center (May 20, 2015). Americans' attitudes about privacy, security and surveillance. Retrieved from: www.pewinternet.org/2015/05/20/americans-attitudes-about-privacy-security-and-surveillance/.

Pew Research Center (June 6, 2017). The Internet of Things connectivity binge: What are the implications?. Retrieved from: www.pewinternet.org/2017/06/06/the-internet-of-things-connectivity-binge-what-are-the-implications/.

Phillips, G. M. (1968). Reticence: Pathology of the normal speaker. *Communications Monographs, 35*(1), 39–49.

Phillips, B. & Zhao, H. (1993). Predictors of assistive technology abandonment. *Assistive Technology, 5*(1), 36–45.

Raveendhran, R. & Fast, N.J. (2018). Tracked by technology: Adoption of behavior-tracking products. *Unpublished manuscript*. University of Southern California.

Raveendhran, R., Fast, N.J., & Carnevale, P.J. (2018). Hiding behind technology: Managers adopt technology to avoid negative evaluations. *Unpublished manuscript*. University of Southern California.

Roberts, K., Kossek, E. E., & Ozeki, C. (1998). Managing the global workforce: Challenges and strategies. *The Academy of Management Executive, 12*(4), 93–106.

Ryan, R. M. & Connell, J. P. (1989). Perceived locus of causality and internalization: examining reasons for acting in two domains. *Journal of Personality and Social Psychology, 57*(5), 749.

Sabelman, E. & Lam, R. (June 23, 2015). The real-life dangers of augmented reality. Retrieved from: https://spectrum.ieee.org/consumer-electronics/portable-devices/the-reallife-dangers-of-augmented-reality.

Schlenker, B. R. & Leary, M. R. (1982). Social anxiety and self-presentation: A conceptualization model. *Psychological Bulletin, 92*(3), 641.

Sewell, G. & Barker, J. R. (2006). Coercion versus care: Using irony to make sense of organizational surveillance. *Academy of Management Review, 31*(4), 934–961.

Shah, J. (2003). Automatic for the people: how representations of significant others implicitly affect goal pursuit. *Journal of Personality and Social Psychology, 84*(4), 661.

Silva, C. (June 6, 2017). The Internet of Things is becoming more difficult to escape. Retrieved from: www.npr.org/sections/alltechconsidered/2017/06/06/531747037/the-internet-of-things-is-becoming-more-difficult-to-escape.

Smith, W. P. & Tabak, F. (2009). Monitoring employee e-mails: Is there any room for privacy?. *The Academy of Management Perspectives, 23*(4), 33–48.

Spector, P. E. (1986). Perceived control by employees: A meta-analysis of studies concerning autonomy and participation at work. *Human Relations, 39*(11), 1005–1016.

Steiner, F. (April 6, 2017). Future of communication with VR and AR. Retrieved from: https://medium.com/ma-communication-design/future-of-communication-with-vr-ar-aa9792f7223e.

Strickland, L. H. (1958). Surveillance and trust. *Journal of Personality, 26*(2), 200–215.

Stritzke, W. G., Nguyen, A., & Durkin, K. (2004). Shyness and computer-mediated communication: A self-presentational theory perspective. *Media Psychology, 6*(1), 1–22.

Solomon, L. (March 9, 2016). Two-thirds of managers are uncomfortable communicating with employees. Harvard Business Review. Retrieved from: https://hbr.org/2016/03/two-thirds-of-managers-are-uncomfortable-communicating-with-employees.

Tangney, J. P. (1992). Situational determinants of shame and guilt in young adulthood. *Personality and Social Psychology Bulletin, 18*(2), 199–206.

Tangney, J. P. (1999). The self-conscious emotions: Shame, guilt, embarrassment and pride. In T. Dalgleish & M. J. Power (Eds.), Handbook of cognition and emotion, 541–568.

Van Boven, L., Loewenstein, G., & Dunning, D. (2005). The illusion of courage in social predictions: Underestimating the impact of fear of embarrassment on other people. *Organizational Behavior and Human Decision Processes, 96*, 130–141.

Wasko, M., Teigland, R., Leidner, D., & Jarvenpaa, S. (2011). Stepping into the internet: New ventures in virtual worlds. *MIS Quarterly, 35*(3), 645–652.

Wilson, J. (September, 2013). Wearables in the workplace. Retrieved from: https://hbr.org/2013/09/wearables-in-the-workplace.

Yukl, G. (1989). Managerial leadership: A review of theory and research. *Journal of Management, 15*(2), 251–289.

Zajonc, R. B. (1965). Social facilitation. *Science, 149*(3681), 269–274.

Index